A DICTIONARY OF
MODERN LEGAL USAGE

A DICTIONARY OF
MODERN
LEGAL USAGE

Bryan A. Garner

OXFORD UNIVERSITY PRESS
New York • Oxford

Oxford University Press

Oxford   New York   Toronto
Delhi   Bombay   Calcutta   Madras   Karachi
Petaling Jaya   Singapore   Hong Kong   Tokyo
Nairobi   Dar es Salaam   Cape Town
Melbourne   Auckland

and associated companies in
Berlin   Ibadan

Published by Oxford University Press, Inc.
200 Madison Avenue, New York, New York 10016

First issued as an Oxford University Press paperback, 1990

Oxford is a registered trademark of Oxford University Press

Library of Congress Cataloguing-in-Publication Data
Garner, Bryan A.
A dictionary of modern legal usage.
Bibliography: p.
1. Law—United States—Terms and phrases.
2. Law—United States—Language. 3. Legal composition.
4. English language—Usage. I. Title.
KF156.G367   1987   340'.03   87-13276
ISBN 0-19-504377-4
ISBN 0-19-506578-6 (pbk)

2 4 6 8 10 9 7 5 3

Printed in the United States of America

To my wife, Teo

FOREWORD

Garner's *Modern Legal Usage* not only defines a wealth of terms and expressions but also offers an abundance of clear, concise directions for their correct and effective use in English. Although legal terms here receive special attention, the scope of these directions on usage remains as broad as the language itself, whether one's community be that of American English or British English. The dictionary clearly defines many misused or confusing words, legal and nonlegal, and contains much useful information on syntax, pronunciation, and spelling.

Here may be found up-to-date information and practical guidelines on language and style—including discussions of obstacles and pitfalls in communication—all directed toward improved legal writing, whether in judicial opinions, briefs, pleadings, or letters. The entries on generic writing problems, such as SPLIT INFINITIVES, FUSED PARTICIPLES, MISPLACED MODIFIERS, and TITULAR TOMFOOLERY, draw copious examples from legal opinions, briefs, and law review articles. Garner examines problems peculiar to legal writing, such as BIBLICAL AFFECTATION, LAW REVIEWESE, CITATION OF CASES, and the handling of CASE REFERENCES. These discussions are generally entertaining as well as informative, and many of these topics have never been treated so extensively in a book on legal writing style.

Lawyers, law students, and general readers interested in clear expression or convincing argument will all find this to be a valuable resource. What is the best noun corresponding to the verb *to recuse?* Do you say you *confected* a pleading? Do you *confront* issues before a *hairbrained* [*sic*] judge? Do you *imply* intention from someone's actions, or, as a judge, do you *imply* terms into a contract? Are you fond of using *meaningful* and *hopefully* and *mental attitude?* Are you prone to employ *as to* or to prefer *conclusional* over *conclusory?* Have you *foregone* discovery and stated the *gravamen* of your argument? What do you understand the meaning of *Lochnerize* to be? In the judgment of an appellate court, what are the correct objects of *reverse* and *remand?* Should you have questions or hesitation about the use of these or other expressions in legal writing, *Modern Legal Usage* offers clear-cut and judicious guidance.

Along with explanations of legal meanings of otherwise ordinary English words, there are law terms that have been omitted in the standard unabridged dictionaries, for example, *adversarial, conclusory, enjoinable, litigational, pretextual, quashal, recusement,* and *veniremember.* Also recorded are many words having legal meanings that are neglected in the standard dictionaries, such as *duplicitous, imply, judicial, probate, remote,* and *supersede.*

Garner pinpoints differences between any number of near-synonyms: *collateral estoppel* (or *issue preclusion*) and *res judicata; compel* and *impel; concurrent jurisdiction* and *pendent jurisdiction; fictitious, fictive,* and *fictional; incident to* and *incidental to; material* and *relevant; quantum meruit* and *quantum valebant,* and hundreds of similar sets of words. Most of us will find entries that renew explanations of terms and expressions learned in law school and long since forgotten. We may likewise encounter distinctions and nuances that are new to us.

Modern Legal Usage helps lay to rest some of the linguistic superstitions that many of us grew up with, such as blanket prohibitions against split infinitives, against beginning sentences with *and* or *but*, against using *between* with more than two objects, and so on. Language is rarely if ever governed by absolute proscriptions (see FORBIDDEN WORDS), and Garner is careful to lead the reader to discriminate and differentiate, rather than to latch on to oversimple formulas that can so easily displace true thought about what constitutes good writing. Surely one of the missions of this book is precisely to foster such thought.

The meaning that language carries, and the spirit it arouses, are the product of words and phrases, comprehensible words and phrases. Excess language misdirects. Ambiguous language confuses. Errors in grammar, in diction, in spelling, as well as in fact or logic, distract and destroy confidence. No writer can afford to underestimate the importance of precise, well-placed words. Compiled with the writer's interests in mind, *Modern Legal Usage* is not only an essential reference but also a lively, personal commentary on legal language as used today.

Thomas M. Reavley
United States Court of Appeals
for the Fifth Circuit

CONTENTS

ACKNOWLEDGMENTS

Grateful acknowledgment is made to the following publishers and journals for their permission to quote from the works listed below:

Farrar, Straus & Giroux, Inc.:

W. Follett, *Modern American Usage.* Copyright © 1966 by Hill & Wang. Reprinted by permission of Hill & Wang, a division of Farrar, Straus & Giroux, Inc.

Merriam-Webster Inc.:

Webster's Third New International Dictionary (3d ed. 1961). By permission. © 1986 by Merriam-Webster Inc., publisher of the Merriam-Webster ® dictionaries.

Little, Brown & Co.:

D. Mellinkoff, *The Language of the Law* (1963).

New York University Law Review:

Gibson, *Literary Minds and Judicial Style,* 36 N.Y.U. L. Rev. 915, 930 (1961).

Oxford University Press:

Concise Law Dictionary (1983).
H. W. Fowler, *A Dictionary of Modern English Usage* (1926 & 2d ed. 1965).
The Oxford English Dictionary (1933).
The Oxford English Dictionary Supplements (1972–86).
D. Walker, *Oxford Companion to Law* (1980).
E. S. C. Weiner, *Oxford Guide to English Usage* (1983).

Pepperdine Law Review:

Raymond, *Editing Law Reviews: Some Practical Suggestions and a Moderately Revolutionary Proposal.* Reprinted from Pepperdine Law Review, Volume 12, Number 2, 1985, Copyright © 1985 by Pepperdine University School of Law.

Texas Tech Law Review:

Calvert, *Appellate Court Judgments:* 6 Tex. Tech L. Rev. 915 (1975).

West Publishing Co.:

Black's Law Dictionary (4th ed. 1968 & 5th ed. 1979).

Yale Law Journal:

Leff, *The Leff Dictionary of Law: A Fragment.* By permission of The Yale Law Journal Company and Fred B. Rothman & Company from *The Yale Law Journal,* Vol. 94, pp. 1855–2251.

INTRODUCTION

In 1921, an article in the *American Bar Association Journal* called for a book on "writing legal English."[1] The author of that article, Urban A. Lavery, pointed out that lawyers rarely consult a book on grammar or composition even once to the hundred of times they consult lawbooks; and yet, as he observed, when convincing argument is to the fore, or clearness of expression is desired, the elements of good writing are often more important than piled up citations of cases.[2] Since Lavery proclaimed his judgment, many books on "writing legal English" have been published, but none with the broad scope or easy accessibility that might allow readers to resolve at a glance the myriad questions of grammar and style that arise in legal writing. Filling that gap is the goal of this book.

Anglo-American law has a language of its own, consisting in a vocabulary with an unusually large number of foreign phrases, archaic words and expressions, terms of art, and argot words. Its style, formal and conservative in utterance, reflects the dignity and solemnity with which the profession views its mission. These distinctive qualities of legal language—evident alike in the speech and the writing of lawyers—are well enough documented. What has remained uncollected and unscrutinized in any systematic way is the vast body of legal usage.

For a specialized language that is highly developed, the language of law remains remarkably variable, largely because it has been incompletely recorded and mapped. In this respect it is analogous to English before eighteenth-century grammarians attempted to reduce its variability and make logical its many quiddities. This is not to say, of course, that the language of the law has the malleable capacity of Elizabethan English, which, in the hands of a creative genius like Shakespeare, could be supremely expressive and evocative. Quite the opposite. Stare decisis remains at the core of our system of law, so much so that the continual search for precedents often discourages legal writers from straying beyond precisely how things have been said before. As a result, locutions (many of them Elizabethan in origin) have become fossilized in legal language over generations. And the inheritors of that language cannot always distinguish mere form from necessary substance, to the extent that form and substance are ever separable.

Legal traditionalists may be justified in not wanting to throw over too readily what has long served well. Yet tradition alone is not sufficient reason for retaining outmoded forms of language. Modern legal writers must strike a difficult balance in the quest to simplify legal English. They should not cling perversely to archaic language, which becomes less comprehensible year by year, for its own sake. Nor should they seek to jettison every word or phrase that bears the stamp of legal tradition.

As for students of law, they learn the technical language that they will need—the quirks of legal jargon, the peculiar idiomatic expressions, the grammatical idio-

---

[1] Lavery, *The Language of the Law*, 7 A.B.A. J. 277 (1921).
[2] *Id.* at 280.

syncrasies, the neologisms that cannot be found even in the most current unabridged dictionaries—largely by osmosis. These linguistic matters are, for the most part, seldom discussed by lawyers or law professors; rather, they are part of the spoken and written legal discourse that neophyte lawyers absorb every day and learn to use unconsciously. This casualness in acquiring the language frequently leads to variable and contradictory linguistic habits that need explicating, codifying, and, in some instances, taming.

Granted these basic facts of legal language—the course of its growth, the challenge of its use, the pattern of its acquisition—this book aims at serving three primary functions. First, it helps lawyers chart their way safely through the bogs of legal language. In the past, anyone wanting such a guide has had to make do with general writing manuals. Though this dictionary lays no claim to comprehensiveness, it offers the legal writer guidance on hundreds of specific points of usage. The advice it gives is generally on the conservative side of usage and grammar, for the simple reason that lawyers generally write in a relatively formal context. Lapses from what has come to be accepted as correct irritate and distract the educated reader, and thus make the writing less persuasive. Yet the conservative approach exemplified in these pages aspires to be an *informed* conservatism, one that neither battles hopelessly against linguistic faits accomplis nor remains blind to the inevitable growth and change that occur in language.

Second, the dictionary addresses a great many problems of usage that do not ordinarily arise in the writing of persons untrained in the law, and therefore that are not addressed in standard writing guides. Certainly it covers territory common to more general guides, as inevitably it must; but one of its chief uses should be in pointing out divergences between legal and lay usage, many of which have remained heretofore unrecorded. To this end, the dictionary serves lawyers and nonlawyers alike, for it can help both groups to bridge the linguistic gulf that separates them, to the degree that is possible. Nonetheless, the greater effort here needs to be made by lawyers, who in recent years have become increasingly aware of the importance of using legal language that is simple and direct. Indeed, simplicity and directness, two of the touchstones of good writing, are advocated throughout this dictionary in an effort to tag and to discard legalese and highfalutin obfuscation.

Third, this work may serve, to some extent, as an instrument of reform. Where lawyers and judges use terms imprecisely or ambiguously (or, indeed, incorrectly), this dictionary often presents standards that will enhance rather than destroy valuable nuances. If ever a prescriptive approach to language is justified, it is in law, where linguistic precision is often of paramount concern, and where ambiguity and vagueness (except when purposeful) are quite intolerable. Within its compass, the dictionary thus seeks to preserve the rich differentiation in our legal vocabulary, to set out some of the important grammatical usages and traditional idioms, and to oppose slipshod usages that blur well-developed distinctions. Of course, no work of this kind can be a panacea for the problems that occur in legal writing. But such a work can realistically seek to make legal writers sensitive to the aesthetic possibilities of their prose, to goad them into thinking more acutely about what works in a given context, and what does not.

Modern Legal Usage is arranged so that the legal writer, unsure of or puzzled by a particular word or point of grammar, can consult a specific entry addressing the problem at hand. Virtually all the sentences that are quoted to illustrate legal usage, including linguistic pitfalls, originated in judicial opinions. A few come from statutes, fewer still from lawyers' briefs and other sources. The authors of the quoted specimens generally remain anonymous, because ordinarily it is unimportant *who* made a particular mistake. Attention should be focused on the mistake itself, and how to remedy it. Where stare decisis is the ruling principle, citations are necessary; in a dictionary of usage they are not, except of course when documenting usages that are lexicographically noteworthy. Whenever specimens do receive attribution, the importance of that fact lies in documenting the source, not in giving context to the quoted matter; hence subsequent histories of cases cited are not given.

Undertaking to write a dictionary of this kind is a precarious task. For by setting oneself up as an arbiter of usage, one also sets one's prose before the magnifying glasses of readers, who are certain to find blemishes of one sort or another. Such was H. W. Fowler's fate in his *Dictionary of Modern English Usage* (1926), a work that has served me as both exemplar and caution. For whatever may be amiss or at fault in this dictionary, I readily acknowledge full responsibility in advance.

As my manuscript swelled, any number of friends and colleagues looked on with far more than a polite interest. Several have actively contributed to whatever merit the final product has. Randall K. Glover of Austin and Kelly Bowers of Seattle called problematical words to my attention almost daily during the year we worked side by side for Judge Thomas M. Reavley. The Judge himself, whose approach to life and law cannot but inspire, gave me the kind of advice and encouragement that emboldens one to persevere.

Several fellow lawyers undertook to read large portions of the manuscript and made expert comments throughout. My learned friends Dr. Betty S. Flowers, David Radunsky, Michelle D. Monse, Roy J. Grogan, Jr., Hal Roberts Ray, Joe W. Pitts III, Alfredo Estrada, Roger Arnold, Lindsay H. Lew, Kenneth S. Klein, Lisa M. Black, Laura Cale, Sim Israeloff, and Jeffrey B. Brawner have all left the work sharper than they found it. I am indebted also to the late John N. Jackson, whose comments reflected years of thought on the subject of legal writing style.

The Honorable Robert W. Calvert, formerly Chief Justice of the Supreme Court of Texas, generously read and marked up a prototypical draft of the work; he kept me on the reader's path and gave me a number of useful ideas. I am grateful to Justice Sandra Day O'Connor for corresponding with me on some of the stylistic practices of the United States Supreme Court.

Edmund S. C. Weiner, the accomplished Oxford lexicographer, and Martin S. Stanford, an extremely knowledgeable and thoughtful editor in New York, minutely read the full manuscript and made innumerable improvements. To these two scholars I am especially beholden, as I am to my father, Dr. Gary T. Garner, who spent many hours reading galleys.

Finally, I cannot adequately express my gratitude to my dear wife, to whom this book is dedicated, for her keen insights and unfaltering support in the face of what must have seemed at the outset to be a grossly overambitious task.

CLASSIFIED GUIDE

This guide lists articles that may be grouped according to (1) usage, i.e., points of diction, grammar, syntax, rhetoric, and style; (2) the formation of words, and their spelling and inflections; (3) pronunciation; and (4) punctuation and typography. In following the outline set forth in the second edition of H. W. Fowler's *Modern English Usage* (1965), the guide does not include any entries that are concerned only with the meaning or idiomatic use of title words, or their spelling, pronunciation, etymology, or inflections.

I Usage

II Word Formation, Inflection, and Spelling

A. General

B. Word Beginnings

C. Word Endings

III   Pronunciation

IV   Punctuation and Typography

PRONUNCIATION GUIDE

The pronunciation system for this work is drawn from the *Oxford American Dictionary* (1980). Pronunciations are shown within virgules. Syllables are separated by hyphens in pronunciations, and syllables spoken with the greatest stress are shown in boldface type. Following is the pronunciation key:

a	*as in*	act, bat, marry	ng	*as in*	bring, singer, thank
ă	*as in*	ago, suitable, metal	o	*as in*	odd, box, hot
ah	*as in*	father, calm	ŏ	*as in*	official, lemon, ardor
ahr	*as in*	arm, cart, bar	oh	*as in*	oat, bone, sew
air	*as in*	air, dare, scary	ohr	*as in*	board, four, hoarse, adore
aw	*as in*	all, walk, saw	oi	*as in*	oil, join, toy
ay	*as in*	age, came, say	oo	*as in*	ooze, soon, too, rule
b	*as in*	boy, habit, rib	oor	*as in*	poor, tour, sure
ch	*as in*	chin, teacher, beach	or	*as in*	bored, for, horse, adorn
d	*as in*	dog, ladder, head	ow	*as in*	out, mouse, now
e	*as in*	egg, bed, merry	p	*as in*	pin, caper, cap
ĕ	*as in*	taken, nickel, lawyer	r	*as in*	red, carry, near
ee	*as in*	eat, meat, see, key	s	*as in*	sit, lesson, nice, cellar
eer	*as in*	ear, beer, tier	sh	*as in*	she, ashen, rush
f	*as in*	fat, effort, puff	t	*as in*	top, butter, hit
g	*as in*	get, wagon, big	th	*as in*	thin, method, path
h	*as in*	hat, ahead	*th*	*as in*	this, mother, breathe
hw	*as in*	wheat, nowhere	u	*as in*	up, cut, come
i	*as in*	if, give, mirror	ŭ	*as in*	suppose, circus, feature
ĭ	*as in*	pencil, credible	ur	*as in*	her, fir, burn, hurry
ɪ	*as in*	ice, bite, fire, spy	uu	*as in*	book, full, woman
j	*as in*	jam, magic, edge	v	*as in*	van, river, give
k	*as in*	king, token, back	w	*as in*	will, awoke, quick
l	*as in*	leg, alley, tell	y	*as in*	yes, you
m	*as in*	me, common, him	z	*as in*	zebra, lazy, tease
n	*as in*	no, manner, tan	zh	*as in*	vision, pleasure

LIST OF ABBREVIATIONS

adj. = adjective
adv. = abverb
AHD = *American Heritage Dictionary* (1975)
Am. = American
AmE = American English
Aus. = Australia
Black's = *Black's Law Dictionary* (4th ed. or 5th ed.)
Br. = British
BrE = British English
c. = century
ca. = circa
CDL = *A Concise Dictionary of Law* (1983)
cf. = compare with
COD = *The Concise Oxford Dictionary* (7th ed. 1982)
colloq. = colloquial
ed. = edition; edited by
e.g. = *(exempli gratia)* for example, for instance
Eng. = England; English
esp. = especially
ex. = example
fr. = from; derived from; found in
G.B. = Great Britain (i.e., England, Scotland, and Wales)
Gk. = Greek
id. = *(idem)* in the same work; used in citations only
i.e. = *(id est)* that is
Ir. = Ireland; Irish
L. = Latin
La. = Louisiana
lit. = literally
MEU1 = H. W. Fowler's *A Dictionary of Modern English Usage* (1926)

MEU2 = H. W. Fowler's *A Dictionary of Modern English Usage* (2d ed. rev. E. Gowers 1965).
n. = noun
N.B. = *(nota bene)* note well
OAD = *Oxford American Dictionary* (1980)
OCL = *The Oxford Companion to Law* (1980)
OED = *The Oxford English Dictionary* (1888– 1933)
OED Supp. = *The Oxford English Dictionary Supplements* (1972–86)
pl. = plural
orig. = originally
Oxford Guide = *The Oxford Guide to English Usage* (1983)
q.v. = *(quod vide)* which see; (qq.v. is pl. form)
repr. = reprint; reprinted by
rev. = revision; revised by
Rhod. = Rhodesia (or Zimbabwe)
S.Afr. = South Africa
Scot. = Scotland
Sp. = Spain; Spanish
specif. = specifically
U.C.C. = Uniform Commercial Code
U.S. = United States
U.S.C. = United States Code
usu. = usually
vb. = verb
v.i. = verb intransitive
v.t. = verb transitive
W2 = *Webster's New International Dictionary* (2d ed. 1939)
W3 = *Webster's Third New International Dictionary* (3d ed. 1961)
W9 = *Webster's Ninth New Collegiate Dictionary* (9th ed. 1984)

As for symbols within the work, a virgule or solidus (/) is placed between separate illustrative quotations. A parenthetical geographic reference following such a quotation, such as (Eng.) or (Aus.), indicates the national origin of the quotation. (Illustrative quotations not having a geographic reference are American in origin.) Small capitals refer the reader to the article so indicated, for further information.

THE DICTIONARY

A

a; an. This entry treats of two common problems with the indefinite articles; for a general discussion of the use of definite as well as indefinite articles, see ARTI-CLES. **A.** Choice of *a* or *an*. The indefinite article *a* is used before words beginning with a consonant sound, including -*y*- and -*w*- sounds. The other form of the indefinite article, *an*, is used before words beginning with a vowel sound. Hence *a European country, an LL.B. degree, a* or *an historian, a uniform, an F.B.I. agent, an SEC subpoena.*

The distinction between *a* and *an* was not solidified until the nineteenth century. Before that time *an* preceded most words beginning with a vowel, regardless of the actual sound of the first syllable. The U.S. Constitution reads: "The Congress shall have Power . . . To establish an uniform Rule of Naturalization. . . ." U.S. Const. art. I, § 8.

Writers on usage dispute over whether the correct article is *a or an* with *historian, historical,* and a few other words. The traditional rule is that if the -*h*- is sounded, *a* is the proper form. If we follow that rule in the U.S. today, most of us would have to say *a historian;* one might seem to be affecting archaic British usage in using *an.* (Even Fowler advocated *a* before *historic(al)* and *humble.*)

The theory behind using *an* in such a context, however, is that the -*h*- is very weak when the accent is on the second rather than the first syllable (giving rise, by analogy, to *an habitual offender, an humanitarian, an hallucinatory image,* and *an harassed schoolteacher*). Thus no authority countenances *an history,* though several older ones prefer *an historian* and *an historical.* Cardozo wrote: "What we hand down in our judgments is *an hypothesis.* It is no longer a divine command." Holmes used the same phrase.

Today, however, *an hypothesis* and *an historical* strike most readers and listeners as affectations. If one sounds the -*h*- in such words, it is best to avoid pretense and use *a.* Thus *a hypothecation, a hereditament, a hallucinatory image, a harassed schoolteacher.* An humanitarian is,

judged even by the most tolerant standards, a pretentious humanitarian. See **humble.**

B. In Distributive Senses. *A,* in the distributive sense ⟨ten hours *a* day⟩, is preferable to *per,* which belongs to commercialese and LE-GALESE. It is wrong to think of *a* as informal or colloquial in this context. The natural English idiom is "sixty hours *a* week" and "ten dollars *a* pair," not "sixty hours *per* week" and "ten dollars *per* pair." E.g., "At oral argument, St. Genevieve suggested that nominal damages be awarded at one dollar *per* [read *an*] acre."/ "These employees were paid less than the minimum hourly wage and they regularly worked more than forty hours *per* [read *a*] week without receiving overtime pay."

Nonetheless, *per* is at least minimally acceptable, except in the phrase *as per,* q.v. And in a few contexts, *per* is the only idiomatic word; this is especially common when the word is used in attributive senses. E.g., "The case asks whether the same *per-unit* lease term amounts to a tax on imports in violation of the Import-Export Clause of the Constitution."

A.B. See **able-bodied seaman.**

abalienate. See **alien,** v.t.

abandoned property. See **lost property.**

abandonee means, not "one who is abandoned," as the suffix -EE might suggest, but "one to whom property rights [in a thing] are relinquished." Leff writes that "there are numerous circumstances in which abandonment of something by one person will have the practical or even legal effect of vesting that thing in a particular other person, who thus may usefully be called an *abandonee.*" Leff, *The Leff Dictionary of Law,* 94 Yale L.J. 1855, 1856 (1985). See -EE.

abate is a FORMAL WORD common in legal contexts, meaning either (1) "to nullify;

1

quash; demolish" ⟨to abate a legal action⟩; or (2) "to diminish" ⟨to abate a debt⟩. The *OED* records a technical legal sense that is rarely if ever used today, "to intrude or thrust oneself forcibly or tortiously into a tenement between the death of the owner and the accession of the legal heir" ⟨abatement of freehold⟩. Today *abate* is used primarily in sense (1), e.g.: "In suits for abatement of a nuisance, courts have directed an officer of the court to engage a contractor specifically to *abate* the nuisance."

The adjective is *abatable,* as in, "Appellants further contend that, where a nuisance is *abatable,* the damages assessed must be limited to the rental value of the property."

ABBREVIATIONS. See ACRONYMS AND INITIALISMS & INITIALESE.

abbuttals. See **abutment.**

abdicate may mean (1) "to disown"; (2) "to discard"; or (3) "to renounce." In legal writing it usually takes on the third meaning listed. E.g., "How can so massive a negation of democracy, so total an *abdication* of lawmaking power to judges be permitted to continue in a nation supposedly still devoted to the principles of self-government?"/ "Until these devices begin to work, I do not believe the criminal law can *abdicate* its responsibility simply because the problem is massive and complex."

abduce; abduct. These words overlap in meaning, but are not interchangeable. Both may mean "to draw away (a limb, etc.) from its natural position" (*OED*). Yet the more common meaning of *abduct* is "to lead away by force." (For a fuller definition, see **abduction.**) Although the *OED* contains a notation that *abduce* is archaic, *W3* does not label it so.

abductee. See -EE.

abduction; kidnap(p)ing; child-stealing. *Abduction* = the act of leading (someone) away by force. It constitutes a statutory offense in many states; e.g., *abduct* is statutorily defined in one state as "to restrain a person with intent to prevent his liberation by: (A) secreting or holding him in a place where he is not likely to be found; or (B) using or

threatening to use deadly force." Tex. Penal Code Ann. § 20.01 (Vernon 1974).

In G.B., *abduction* is generally given a narrower sense: "the offence of taking an unmarried girl under the age of 16 from the possession of her parents or guardian against her will" (*CDL*). The *OCL* additionally defines *abduction* in English law as taking "a girl under 18 or a defective woman of any age from the possession of her parent or guardian for the purpose of unlawful sexual intercourse, or a girl under 21 with property or expectations of property from such possession to marry or have unlawful sexual intercourse, or . . . taking away and detaining any woman with the intention that she shall marry or have unlawful sexual intercourse with a person, by force or for the sake of her property or expectations of property." Whereas in the U.S. *abduction* has virtually no connotations relating to the sex of the victim, in G.B. the victim is almost invariably a woman. *Abduction of voters* is also a criminal offense in G.B.

Kidnapping = the act or an instance of stealing, abducting, or carrying away a person by force or fraud, often with a demand for ransom (*W3*). *Kidnapping* (the *-pp-* spelling is preferred) is not restricted in application to children as victims, though the etymology suggests it. *Child-stealing* is the technical statutory term for the abduction of children.

abductor. Pl. *-tors, tores.* The English plural, *abductors,* is preferable to the Latin plural, *abductores.*

aberration; aberrance (-cy); aberrant, n. *Aberrant,* almost always used in reference to persons, means "a deviant; one deviating from an established norm." *Aberration* is not limited to persons, and means (1) "a deviation or departure from what is normal or correct," or (2) "a mental derangement." *Aberrance* and *-cy* are NEEDLESS VARIANTS of *aberration.*

aberrational; aberrant, adj.; **aberrative.** *Aberrational* = of or pertaining to an aberration (see the preceding entry). E.g., "It is our duty to allow a decision to be made by the Attorney General's delegate, as long as it is not so *aberrational* that it is arbitrary rather than the result of any perceptible rational approach." *Aberrant* = deviating from behavioral or social norms. *Aberrative* = tending to be aberrational.

abet. See **aid and abet.**

abetment (= the act of abetting) is some-times erroneously made *abettance* or *abettal,* both NEEDLESS VARIANTS.

abettor, -er. In both BrE and AmE, *abettor* is the more usual spelling; the *OED* states that it "is the constant form of the word as a legal term." *Abettator* is the defunct LAW LATIN term from old English law. Cf. **bettor.** See -ER, -OR.

abeyance has a general sense ("a state of suspension, temporary nonexistence, or in-activity" [OED]) and a technical legal sense ("expectation or contemplation of law; the position of waiting for or being without a claimant or owner" [OED]). Even in legal con-texts, however, the general lay sense is com-monly used, as in, "Texas would not consider his claim if this action were held in *abeyance.*"

abhorrent, meaning literally "shrinking from in abhorrence" or "strongly opposed to," is frequently used of things in legal con-texts to mean "so far removed from as to be repugnant or inconsistent" (*OED*). E.g., "The very nature of a partnership is such that joint tenancy between one of the partners and a stranger to the partnership would be *abhorrent* to the Act."

abide. A. General Senses. *Abide* = (1) to stay ⟨the right of entering and abiding in any state in the Union⟩; (2) to tolerate, withstand; (3) to obey; (4) to await; or (5) to perform or execute (in reference to orders or judgments). The last is the strictly legal meaning: "Since we do not doubt that the court will promptly proceed to *abide* our judgment and certify our decision before proceeding to trial, we decline to issue a peremptory order at this time."
   Abide also commonly takes on the sense "to await," as in the following legal construction: "The judgment should be reversed, and a new trial granted, with costs to *abide* the event."
   Abide by is a PHRASAL VERB meaning "to ac-quiesce in or conform to"; e.g., "Jurors must *abide by* the oath with respect to both sentenc-ing and determining guilt or innocence."/ "Eastman indicated his intention to *abide by* the plea agreement, clearly hoping that this would be a consideration in favor of leniency."
   Abiding = lasting, enduring. E.g., "The two

gifts are both of a kind that indicates an *abid-ing* and unconditioned intent—one to a church, the other to a person whom she called her adopted son."
   B. Past-Tense and Past-Participial Forms. With the meanings most probably to be found in legal texts ("await" and "execute"), *abided* is the preferred past tense and past participle. In the archaic sense "to stay, dwell," *abode* is the preferred past tense, and either *abode* or *abided* in the past participle. For most ordinary purposes, *abided* serves well without seeming stilted.

ab initio; in initio. The former means "from the beginning" ⟨an act beyond one's legal competence is void *ab initio*⟩; the latter means, as its prefix suggests, "in the begin-ning." Neither LATINISM seems quite justified in ordinary contexts, although *ab initio,* which in legal writing is used commonly in the phrase *void ab initio,* is common enough not to be particularly objectionable. "A secured from an equity court, *ab initio,* an injunction against B." Leff notes that the phrase is some-times used in the sense "thoroughly," a rough equivalent of "from first to last." Leff, *The Leff Dictionary of Law,* 94 Yale L.J. 1855, 1863 (1985). E.g., "We find respondent's ar-gument that the decision in that case is con-trolling here unpersuasive *ab initio,* because the relevant language of the two statutes dif-fers materially."

abjudge; adjudge. These words are anti-thetical in one sense. *Abjudge* is a rare term (not in most abridged dictionaries) meaning "to take away by judicial decision" (*OED*). *Ad-judge,* in contrast, means "to award, grant, or impose judicially" (*id.*). One *abjudges from* and *adjudges to.* For the other senses of the latter term, see **adjudge.**

abjudicate is synonymous with *abjudge,* q.v.

abjure; adjure. The former may mean either (1) "to renounce," or (2) "to avoid." The latter means (1) "to charge or entreat sol-emnly, as if under oath, or under the penalty of a curse" (*OED*). The nominal forms are *ab-juration* (or *abjurement*—now defunct) and *ad-juration.* The adjectival forms end in -*tory.*

abjurer, -or. The -*er* spelling is preferred. See -ER, -OR.

-ABLE. A. Choice of *-able* or *-ible*. Many adjectives have competing forms ending in *-able* and *-ible*. Some of these have undergone DIFFERENTIATION in meaning; the less commonly used forms in some pairs are merely NEEDLESS VARIANTS of the predominant forms. What follows are lists of the most frequently troublesome words of this class.

It should be noted that *-able* (in contrast with *-ible*) is a living suffix, which may be added to virtually any verb without an established suffix in either *-able* or *-ible*. These are some of the adjectives preferably spelled *-able: actionable, addable, advisable, affectable, allegeable, analyzable, annexable, arrestable, assessable, averageable, bailable, blamable, changeable, chargeable, circumscribable, commensurable, committable, condensable, conductable, connectable, contestable, contractable, conversable, convictable, correctable, definable, demurrable, detectable, diagnosable, diffusable, endorsable, enforceable, excisable, excludable, expandable, extendable, garnishable, ignitable, immovable, improvable, includable, inferable, movable, noticeable, patentable, perfectable, persuadable, ratable, redressable, retractable, salable, suspendable, tractable, transferable, willable.*

The following words, limited in number because *-ible* is not now a living combining form in English, are spelled with the *-i-: accessible, adducible, admissible, audible, avertible, collapsible, collectible, combustible, commiscible, compactible, compatible, comprehensible, compressible, concussible, contemptible, controvertible, convertible, corrodible, corruptible, credible, deducible, deductible, defeasible, defensible, descendible, destructible, digestible, discernible, divisible, edible, educible, eligible, erodible, exhaustible, expressible, fallible, feasible, flexible, forcible, fusible, horrible, impressible, incorrigible, indelible, intelligible, inventible, invincible, irascible, irresistible, legible, negligible, omissible, ostensible, perceptible, permissible, plausible, possible, producible, protectible, reducible, reprehensible, repressible, responsible, reversible, revertible, risible, seducible, sensible, submersible* (or *submergible*), *suggestible, suppressible, susceptible, terrible, transfusible, vendible, visible.*

Some adjectives with the variant suffixes have different meanings. Thus *impassable* means "closed, incapable of being traversed"; its twin, *impassible,* means "unable to feel pain," or, less distinctively, "impassive, emotionless." *Passable* and *passible* have correspondingly positive meanings. (These pairs are formed from different Latin roots, L. *pas-*

sus "having suffered" and L. *passare* "to step"). Similarly, *impartible* means "not subject to partition" and *impartable* "capable of being imparted." *Conversable* means "oral," whereas *conversible* is a NEEDLESS VARIANT of *convertible. Forcible* means either "effected by means of force" ⟨forcible entry⟩ or "characterized by force"; *forceable,* much less frequently encountered, would be the better term to describe a door that is "capable of being forced open." See **forcible.**

B. Appended to Nouns. This suffix is usually appended as a passive suffix to verbs (e.g., *forgettable, avoidable, reproachable*). Sometimes, however, it has been joined with nouns, e.g., *objectionable, actionable, dutiable, marriageable, salable.* These do not mean "able to be objectioned," "able to be actioned," and so on. *Objectable* would perhaps have been the more logical formation, though time, idiom, and usage have made many such forms as *actionable* both ineradicable and unobjectionable.

C. Converting *-ate* Verbs into *-able* Adjectives. When the suffix *-able* is added to a transitive polysyllabic word ending in *-ate,* that suffix is dropped. Hence, *accumulable, calculable, estimable,* etc. See -ATABLE. Exceptions, however, occur with the two-syllable words, e.g., *rebatable, debatable.*

able-bodied seaman; able seaman. The former, though of far more recent vintage, seems to be the usual term in admiralty law, meaning "a merchant seaman certified for all seaman's duties" (*AH*). It is abbreviated *A.B. Able seaman* is the phrase used in the United States Shipping Code, 46 U.S.C. § 672 (1982). It would be difficult and footless to categorize either as a NEEDLESS VARIANT of the other.

abode. See **abide** (B).

abolishment; admonishment. These nouns are inferior to the organically derived *abolition* and *admonition;* no longer is there any difference in meaning between the *-ment* and the *-tion* forms. The *-ment* forms waywardly persist in much legal writing. E.g., "The Securities Industry Association issued a 'legal alert' that refers to the NYSE memo and its strongly worded *admonishment* [read *admonition*] to have securities loan arrangements covered by written agreement."/ "The Legislature must be given a fair opportunity to take whatever action it should deem advisable before the *abolishment* [read *abolition*] of the long-accepted immunity."

aborigine was long considered to be correct only in the plural form, *aboriginal* being the singular noun. Today, however, *aborigine* has entered standard English as a singular noun. But in Australia, *Aboriginal* with the initial capital is the only correct form in formal usage.

abortee. See -EE.

aborticide = the act of destroying a live fetus. One might think that this is a NEEDLESS VARIANT of *abortion*. But that term, technically, refers to something rather different: "the expulsion of a nonviable fetus" (*W3*). *Aborticide* is, however, an ill-formed equivalent of *feticide*. If, as the dictionaries suggest, it is formed on the verb *abort*, then ironically it is what Fowler called an abortion, but here is termed a MORPHOLOGICAL DEFORMITY. If it were formed on the noun *abortus* (= an aborted fetus), then it would be illogical, for one does not "kill" (*-cide*) a fetus that has already been aborted. *Aborticide* is to be avoided in favor of the superior alternative, *feticide* (BrE *fœticide*).

abortion. See **aborticide**.

ABORTIONS. See MORPHOLOGICAL DEFORMITIES.

abortive; aborted. *Abortive* may mean (1) "unsuccessful," or (2) "inchoate." With the first meaning listed, it takes on the figurative sense of *aborted* (= cut short), as *an abortive trial*, i.e., one cut short before the verdict by, e.g., settlement of the dispute. (Note that *-ive*, an active suffix, here has a passive sense.) E.g., "A jury convicted appellants of various offenses arising out of an *abortive* scheme to import a large quantity of marijuana into the United States from Mexico." In the following sentence, *abortive* has the sense "unsuccessful" without the connotations of "cut short": "More cross-examinations with well-chosen objectives are rendered *abortive* by the pursuit of 'will o' the wisp' decoys than by any other single factor."

Abortive is archaic in reference to abortions of fetuses, except in the sense "causing an abortion"; and in that sense, it is a NEEDLESS VARIANT of *abortifacient*.

about; approximately. *Approximately* is a FORMAL WORD; *about* is the ordinary, perfectly good equivalent. *About* should not be used, as it often is, with other terms of approximation such as *estimate* or *guess*, because it means "roughly" or "approximately." Hence, "roughly about $10,000" is redundant.

above. A. *Above* meaning "more than" or "longer than." This usage is to be restricted to informal contexts. "*Above* [read *more than*] six-hundred lawsuits have been filed since the tragedy."/ "Should the piano remain, by mutual consent, *above* [read *longer than*] the term of four months, it is understood that the company is to pay Stieff interest at the rate of six percent per annum."
B. *Above* is an acceptable ellipsis for *above-mentioned* if clear in context. E.g., "The *above* arguments apply only to judicial disqualification under section 455(a)." After all, one rarely sees *below-mentioned* or *undermentioned*; some phrase such as *discussed below* is far more natural.

It was long thought that *above* could not properly act as an adjective; but the word has been so used in legal writing throughout this century, even by the best legal writers. E.g., "If the *above* sections were the only law bearing on the matter, they would create a civil liability to make reparation to any one whose rights were infringed." (Holmes)/ "Yet in the middle of the *above* passage from Lord Lindley's opinion there is a sudden and question-begging shift in the use of terms." (Hohfeld) The *OED* records this use from 1873 and states: "By ellipsis of a pple. as *said, written, mentioned, above* stands attributively, as 'the above explanation.'"

Some critics have suggested that *above* in this sense should refer only to something mentioned previously on the same page, but this restriction seems unduly narrow. Nevertheless, it is generally better to make the reference exact by giving a page or paragraph number, rather than the vague reference made possible by *above*. Idiom will not, however, allow *above* to modify all nouns: *above vehicle* is unidiomatic in place of *above-mentioned vehicle*. Better yet would be *the vehicle*, if we know from the context which one we are talking about.

A less than common and NEEDLESS VARIANT of *above-mentioned* is *before-mentioned*. See **afore** & **aforesaid**.

above-made is an unnecessary word, and an ugly one. E.g., "The following decisions of this court fully sustain the *above-made* statements [read *these statements* or *the above statements*]."

above-quoted, above-styled, above-mentioned, above-captioned, and other such compounds must be hyphenated; one sees the tendency nowadays to spell *above-quoted* and *above-mentioned* as single words. Actually, it is best to avoid these compounds altogether when possible by using more specific terms of reference; i.e., instead of writing *the above-mentioned court,* one should name the court (or, if it has just been named, write *the court, that court,* or some similar identifying phrase).

above-referenced. See **reference,** v.t.

abridge; violate. Constitutional and other rights are often said to be *abridged* or *violated.* A connotative distinction is possible, however. *Violate* is the stronger word: when rights are *abridged,* they are merely diminished; when rights are *violated,* they are flouted outright. Following are examples of the milder term: "The provision of a new and sanitary building does not ensure that it will be operated in a constitutional way; the first amendment can be *abridged* in the cleanest quarters."/ "A statute denying nonresidents the privilege of serving as trustees of living trusts might be unconstitutional as *abridging* the privileges and immunities of citizens of the United States."

abridg(e)able. The shorter form is preferred in the U.S. and generally in British legal writing, although the *OED* prefers the longer form.

abridg(e)ment. The British usually spell it with the *-e-,* and the Americans always without it. Armed with this knowledge, an American writer should not defend his "misspelling" on grounds that he prefers the BrE form. Cf. **acknowledg(e)ment** & **judg(e)ment.**

abrogate; obrogate; arrogate. *Abrogate,* far more common than *obrogate,* means "to abolish (a law or established usage) by authoritative or formal action; annul; repeal." *Abrogate* is occasionally confused with *arrogate* (= to usurp). The proper use of *abrogate* is illustrated here: "Texas courts will *abrogate* school dis-

trict policies only when they clearly violate statutory provisions."

Obrogate is a civil-law term meaning "to repeal (a law) by passing a new one" (*OED*).

Arrogate (= to usurp) is properly used in the following sentence: "Courts may *arrogate* the authority of deciding what the individual may say and may not say, and there may be readily brought about the very condition against which the constitutional guaranty was intended as a permanent protection." See **arrogate.**

abscond is both transitive ("to hide away, conceal (anything)" [*OED*]) and intransitive ("to depart secretly or suddenly; to hide oneself"). The latter is more common in modern contexts: "Abram *absconded* about December 20, 1928, and his whereabouts are unknown."

abscondence; abscondment; absconsion. The second and third are NEEDLESS VARIANTS rarely found; *abscondence* is the preferred nominal form corresponding to the verb *abscond,* q.v.

absent (= in the absence of; without) is commonly used as a preposition in legal writing. It can be effective if sparingly used. E.g., "The statute, in permitting a verdict of guilty *absent* a finding of a design to effect death, allows the imputation of intent from one defendant to another."/ "*Absent* a clear manifestation of a contrary intent, it is presumed that the settlor intended the trustee to take a fee simple so that in selling he could pass title as owner rather than as donee of a power."

absentee, used as an adverb, is a new and useful linguistic development. E.g., "Our inquiry as to [read *into*] why the defendants took Alaniz and her son and daughter to vote *absentee* has to begin with whether or not the request came from Alaniz herself." It would be cumbersome in that context to have to write, "to vote as absentees." *W3* records *absentee* as a noun only, but the adverbial usage is increasingly widespread. The word may function also as an adjective, as in *absentee landlord.*

ABSOLUTE CONSTRUCTIONS. Nominative absolutes, increasingly rare in modern prose, allow the writer to vary his syntax while concisely subordinating incidental matter. Such phrases do not bear an ordinary grammatical relation to the rest of the sentence, inasmuch as the noun or noun phrase does not perform any one of the functions (subject, object, apposition, etc.) that ordinarily attach nouns grammatically to other words in the sentence. Yet the whole absolute phrase acts as an adverbial modifier of some verb; e.g., *the court adjourning, we left the courtroom* = when the court adjourned, we left the courtroom.

The following sentences illustrate the nominative absolute. "In *Martin v. Texas, Harlan writing* again for a unanimous Court, the defendant's allegations of discrimination were unsupported by any evidence whatever and were denied." (If a pronoun were to be used instead of *Harlan*, the absolute phrase would read "he writing again for the court.")/ "For the purposes of this proceeding, at least, it is conceded that the collision was solely the result of Holeman's negligence, *he* apparently *having been* intoxicated at the time."/ "*The husband being* about to sail, the alleged parol agreement sued upon was made." (Eng.)/ "*This court having found* that the two types of uses under the trademark maintenance program were not sufficient uses to avoid prima facie proof of abandonment, the district court must specifically address Exxon's intent to resume use of the HUMBLE trademark."

Here the writer attempted a nominative absolute, but incorrectly used the possessive rather than the nominative case: "The trial court concluded [that] Vance was not a good candidate for non-state prison sanction, *his* [read *he*] having 'manipulated the system before.'" *Vance v. State*, 475 So. 2d 1362, 1363 (Fla. App. 1985).

absolute, decree. See **decree absolute.**

absolute liability. See **strict liability.**

absolute, rule. See **decree absolute.**

absolve, depending on the context, takes either *of* or *from*. One is absolved *of* financial liability, and absolved *from* wrongdoing—assuming the courts treat one kindly. In the following sentence, *from* appears wrongly in place of *of*: "If the mother contributed nothing to his support because she was absolved *therefrom* [read, if we must, *thereof*] under the act, no expectation of pecuniary advantage exists."

Here the opposite error appears: "Cnudde considered that Hardgrave's letter completely *absolved* her *of* [read *from*] any charges of improper behavior in her teaching methods or in the context of her course."

absorb; adsorb; sorb. *Absorb* is the common term meaning "to soak up"; *adsorb* is a scientific term used in reference to condensation of gas. *Sorb* is a relatively obscure term comprehending both of its prefixed siblings.

abstract, v.t.; **abstractify.** *Abstract* is the CHAMELEON-HUED verb meaning (1) "to separate," (2) "to summarize" ⟨to abstract a judgment⟩, (3) "to divert," (4) "to steal," or (5) "to make (something concrete) abstract." In sense (4), *abstract* more particularly means "to withdraw, deduct, remove, or take away (something)" (*OED*). The *OED* labels this word a EUPHEMISM in the sense "to take away secretly, slyly, or dishonestly; to purloin." In this sense, *abstract* is a FORMAL WORD that really beclouds the act it describes: "Universal's funds were surreptitiously *abstracted* and deposited in Richfield's account." A more common word, such as *remove* or *withdraw*, would be preferable.

Abstractify is not listed in the dictionaries, though it has appeared in legal texts. It serves as a pejorative alternative for sense (5) of *abstract*. Perhaps it is a useful invention, for there is no reason for *abstract* to undergo any further degeneration of meaning.

abstracter. Although the *OED* notes that *-or* is "analogically the more regular form," that form is now obsolete. *Abstracter* is the preferred spelling. See -ER, -OR.

abstractify. See **abstract.**

abstraction means to laymen: (1) (rarely) "the act of removing"; (2) "an abstract idea"; (3) "abstractedness"; or (4) "an example of abstract art" (*OAD*). In law, however, *abstraction* = the act of taking, usu. wrongfully or fraudulently, as in *abstraction of funds*. In the phrase *abstraction of water* (= the taking of water from a river or other source of supply [*CDL*]), the word connotes no wrongdoing, for in England one may obtain a license. See **abstract,** v.t.

ABSTRACTITIS. "How vile a thing . . . is the abstract noun! It wraps a man's thoughts round like cotton wool." A. Quiller-Couch, *On the Art of Writing* 109 (1916). *Abstractitis* is

H.W. Fowler's term for writing that is so abstract and obtuse (hence abstruse) that the writer himself does not know what he is trying to say—far be it from the reader, then, to give such writing a coherent meaning. Rigorous thought, together with careful revision, eliminates abstractitis.

One short example may suffice to illustrate this malady: "This Note, therefore, structures its analysis around a consideration of definitional methodology and proposes a constitutional definition of religion on the basis of that consideration." What? The sentence states that the note proposes a definition of religion on the basis of a consideration of methodology, which makes little sense. See OBSCURITY.

The Fowlers quote the following sentence in *The King's English* (1906): "One of the most important reforms mentioned in the rescript is the unification of the organization of judicial institutions and the guarantee for all the tribunals of the independence necessary for securing to all classes of the community equality before the law." Quiller-Couch takes this example and suggests instead this revised version: "One of the most important reforms is that of the courts, which need a uniform system and to be made independent. In this way only can men be assured that all are equal before the law." A. Quiller-Couch, *The Art of Writing* at 109–10.

The newest vogue in legal theorizing, Critical Legal Studies, is characterized by abstractitis and JARGONMONGERING, the favored words in the field being *purposivist, constitutive, coopting, demobilizing, structuralism, deconstruction, formalism,* and *praxis,* among others. See Schwartz, *With Gun and Camera through Darkest CLS-Land,* 36 Stan. L. Rev. 413, 440 (1984). Some of the work from this school of thought reads on this order: "In the reciprocity of roles that are artificial, you think people are more alienated in that bank than I think they are. I think there's more intersubjective zap and unalienated relatedness among tellers." Gabel & Kennedy, *Roll Over Beethoven,* 36 Stan. L. Rev. 1, 25 (1984).

By some accounts, abstractitis leads to far worse things. "If concepts are not clear," wrote Confucius, "words do not fit." But he did not stop there: "If words do not fit, the day's work cannot be accomplished, morals and art do not flourish. If morals and art do not flourish, punishments are not just. If punishments are not just, the people do not know

where to put hand or foot." Confucius, Analects XIII, 3. It is no frivolous assertion to say that, when we descend into abstractitis, more than just our language is afflicted.

ABSTRACT NOUNS, PLURALS OF. See PLURALS (B).

abstractor. See **abstracter.**

abutment; abuttals. An *abutment* is the place at which two or more things abut. *Abuttals*—a term used only in the plural—means "land boundaries." *Abuttals* is usually used of abstract boundaries, and *abutments* usually of physical structures (e.g., the walls of bridges adjoining land). *Abbuttals* is a variant spelling to be avoided.

abutter, -or. *Abutter* is the accepted spelling.

abysm(al); abyss(al). The nouns are synonymous in signifying "a bottomless gulf." *Abyss* is the more current form, and is therefore to be preferred. Though *abysm* is obsolescent, *abysmal* thrives (indeed, has become trite) as a figurative term for "deep" or "immeasurably great" (*W3*) ⟨abysmal benightedness⟩. *Abyssal* is a technical oceanographic term.

accede; exceed. *Accede* = (1) "to agree or consent"; (2) "to come into office or a position of stature"; or (3) "to enter a treaty or accord." It is an intransitive verb that takes the preposition *to. Exceed,* a transitive verb, means (1) "to surpass," or (2) "to go beyond the proper limits." The first syllable of *accede* should be pronounced with a short *-a-,* so as to differentiate its sound from *exceed.*

accent, v.t.; **accentuate.** These synonyms have a latent distinction that might usefully be observed. Fowler notes that *accent* is more common in literal, and *accentuate* in figurative, senses. Hence one properly *accents* the third syllable of *appellee,* and *accentuates* the weaknesses in an opponent's legal arguments. E.g., "These elements, although *accentuating* the wrong, are not the essence of it."

acceptance, -cy; acceptation. The first is used to express the active sense of the verb (to accept), and the second the passive sense (to be accepted). *Acceptance* = the act of accepting; *acceptation* = the state of being accepted ⟨widespread acceptation of the doctrine of strict liability in tort was long in coming⟩. *Acceptancy* is a NEEDLESS VARIANT of *acceptance*, just as *acception* is for *acceptation*.

Acceptance is a common word. Following are examples of *acceptation* used correctly: "In actions of slander, words are to be taken in their common *acceptation*." / "That there is no right of property in a dead body in the ordinary *acceptation* of that term [Which term: *property* or *dead body*?] is undoubtedly true when limited to a property right in the commercial sense."

acceptance for honor; acceptance supra protest. Both terms mean "a form of acceptance of a bill of exchange to save the good name of the drawer or an endorser" (*CDL*). Both are TERMS OF ART, *acceptance for honor* perhaps being the more generally comprehensible of the two. *Acceptance supra protest* ought to be avoided.

accepter, -or. "The first form is now generally used for one who accepts. The second (earlier) form is the legal term, one who accepts, or undertakes the payment of, a bill of exchange." M. Nicholson, *A Dictionary of American-English Usage* 6 (1957). *Acceptor* has also been used in law, however, of one who accepts an offer to enter into a contract. *Accepter* is preferable in that sense.

access, as a verb, has its origins in COMPUTERESE. Like a number of nouns turned into verbs (e.g., *contact*), it now seems increasingly well ensconced in the language. As Fowler notes with regard to *contact,* it is an ancient and valuable right for English-speaking peoples to turn their nouns into verbs when they are so minded. *Gain access to* or some other such equivalent is admittedly ungainly alongside *access,* though the latter still jars sensitive ears. "Other electrical units do not *access* the electric energy source through the plug."

accessory, n.; **accessary,** n. *Accessory* now predominates in AmE and BrE in meaning both "abettor" and "a thing of lesser importance." Though Fowler believed a distinction existed between *accessory* and *accessary* (the first applying primarily to things, the second to persons), the second is now merely a NEEDLESS VARIANT of the first and should be eschewed.

These words should be pronounced with the first *-c-* as a hard *-k-* sound; a common mispronunciation is /*ă-ses-ă-ree*/. The same is true of *accession,* which should have a hard *-c-* followed by a soft one. See **accomplice.**

accident; incident. "Available statistics establish that flight engineers have rarely been a contributing cause or factor in commercial aircraft *accidents* or *incidents*." Here *incident* apparently means "near-accident," and for the purposes of nonce-differentiation may be justified. *Incident* should be avoided, however, as a EUPHEMISM for *accident.*

accidentally. So spelled; *accidently* is a solecism. The confusion may arise from the form of *evidently* and *patently.* Cf. **incidentally.**

acclimate, -ation; acclimatize, -ization. The *-ize* forms are preferred by Fowler and other authorities, although the shorter forms are now more common in the U.S., especially with the verb. Nevertheless, *W9* includes the primary definitions under *acclimatize* and *acclimatization,* the better forms. In the noun, using *acclimatization* keeps our listeners from confusing the homophones *acclimation* and *acclamation.*

accommodatum. See **commodatum.**

accomplice; accessory. *Accomplice* is the broader term, meaning "one who is a party to a crime, either as a perpetrator or as an accessory" (*CDL*). Thus *accessory* is a subclass of *accomplice* meaning "one who is a party to a crime that is actually committed by someone else (the perpetrator)" (*CDL*). See **accessory.**

accomptant general. See **accountant general.**

accord; accordance. To be *in accord* is to be in agreement. E.g., "This holding was in *accord* with the overwhelming weight of authority in the state courts as reflected in Wigmore's classic treatise on the law of evidence."

This phrasing should not be used in place of a more direct statement, e.g.: "The adoption of this method was based on the premise that the order in point of time of deposits and withdrawals was essential to proof, and that the burden was upon claimant; we are not *in accord with* [read *we reject* (or *disagree with*)] that view."

To be *in accordance* is to be in conformity or compliance. *In accordance* is sometimes cumbersome, but often useful. E.g., "The search was conducted *in accordance* with FCI regulations and without excessive use of force." *Out of accordance with* = not in conformity with.

Accord is wrongly used for *accordance* in the following sentences: "The agency disbursed funds in *accord* [read *accordance*] with the plan."/ "In *accord* [read *accordance*] with the approach taken by this court in these decisions, we hold that the presentation of an administrative claim in excess of $100,000 is a sum certain under 28 C.F.R. § 14.2."

accord, v.t.; **afford,** v.t. These are CHAMELEON-HUED words that share the meaning "to furnish or grant," as commonly used in legal texts ⟨accorded (or afforded) all the rights due him under due process⟩. Yet some DIFFERENTIATION is possible: *Accord* has the nuance of granting something because it is suitable or proper ⟨accord litigants a stay of costs pending appeal⟩. E.g., "Where the challenged law operates to the peculiar disadvantage of a suspect class, the court *accords* the distinction no presumption of constitutionality."/ "The children were not *accorded* procedural due process before school officials reached the conclusion that they could not continue to attend school."

Accord in this sense should usu. take a personal object, not an inanimate one; this error most commonly occurs when *accord* is used as high-sounding substitute for *give:* "I cannot subscribe to the court's sweeping refusal to *accord* [read *give*] the equal protection clause any role in this entire area of the law."/ "Courts generally *accord* [read *give*] statutory language its commonsense meaning." The origin of the correct use of *accord* lies in the historical (and still current) sense "to grant (a thing asked) *to* (a person), to give with full consent, to award" (*OED*).

Afford, in contrast, is the more general term meaning "to furnish (something) as an essential concomitant" ⟨afford *to* the indigent defendant legal representation⟩. E.g., "The Sixth Amendment guarantees that a person brought to trial in any federal court must be *afforded* the right to assistance of counsel before he can be validly convicted."/"If we *afford* relief *to* this town, will we have to do like-

wise as each unincorporated village decides to incorporate?"

Intransitively, *accord* takes the prepositions *in, to,* or *with,* depending on the context ⟨we *accord in* our opinions⟩ ⟨we *accord to* plaintiff his due⟩ ⟨this *accords with* the prevailing view⟩.

accord, n.; **concord,** n.   Both mean "an amicable arrangement between parties, esp. between peoples or nations; compact; treaty." *Accord* is perhaps the less formal word, and the more frequently used today. See **concord**(A).

accord, used as a signal in citations, ordinarily indicates that the authority cited directly supports the proposition, but in a way slightly different from previously cited authorities. It is best to include a parenthetical explanation of what that difference is, rather than leaving the reader to search for it. Sometimes it introduces like cases from other jurisdictions. See CITATION OF CASES.

accordance.   See **accord.**

accord and satisfaction; compromise and settlement.   The former appears usually in contractual contexts. Though the two phrases may overlap to some extent, *compromise and settlement* is used in the context of a dispute more probably giving rise to litigation. It applies to all disputes, not just to those arising from contracts. The two substantive words in *compromise and settlement* are broader than those in *accord and satisfaction,* but *compromise* is roughly analogous to *accord,* and *settlement* to *satisfaction.*

An *accord* is an agreement to substitute for an existing debt or obligation some alternative form of discharging that debt; a *satisfaction* is the actual discharge of the debt by the substituted means. Stated otherwise, an *accord* is the agreement to perform (in an alternative way), and the *satisfaction* is the actual performance. Any claim (whether disputed, unliquidated, or undisputed and liquidated) may be discharged by an *accord and satisfaction.*

But only a disputed or unliquidated claim may be the basis for a *compromise and settlement.* Though the two words in this phrase have been used with a variety of meanings and even synonymously, at base *compromise* means "an agreement between two or more persons to settle matters in dispute between them"; *settlement* means "the performance of promises made in a compromise agreement."

according(ly). A. *According to.* This is a weak form of attribution ⟨according to Corbin, . . .⟩; a text sprinkled with *according to's* gives the appearance of having little originality. Legal writers should avoid it.

B. *Accordingly* is occasionally misused for *according.* "This section applies, *accordingly* to the provisions thereof, except to the extent that there is involved . . . a military or foreign affairs function of the United States." 5 U.S.C. § 553 (1982). In that sentence, *thereof* should be *hereof;* indeed the entire *according*-phrase might advantageously be excised. [Read *This section applies unless a military or foreign-affairs function of the United States is involved.*]

C. *According as* = in a manner corresponding to the way in which; just as. E.g., "The special law is either favorable or unfavorable *according as* it enlarges or restricts, in opposition to the common rule, the rights of those for whom it is established." (See the quotation from Blackstone under **misdemeanor.**)

D. For *according* as an acceptable dangling modifier, see DANGLERS (C).

accost = to approach and usu. to speak to in an abrupt or challenging manner. The word has no connotations of physical contact. Hence it is inappropriate here: "One lady leaving the shop was grabbed by the arm and in a threatening manner told that she had better not go in the place again because it was a 'scab' shop; another lady was likewise *accosted* and told that she ought to be shot for going into that 'scab' shop." *Accost* is not a strong enough word for this context; *assault* (in the layman's sense) might have served better. Cf. **altercation.**

accountable takes *for* or *to,* not *from.* "A factor or commission merchant is to be held strictly accountable *from* [read *for*] any deviation from instructions received from his principal."

accountancy. See **generally accepted accounting principles.**

accountant general; accomptant general. The latter spelling—originating in the Renaissance habit of respelling French loanwords on the Latin model—is archaic. Cf. **comptroller.**

accounting. See **generally accepted accounting principles.**

accouter(ments), -tre(ments). As with many other words having this suffix, the *-er* is the AmE, the *-re* the BrE form.

accrual; accruer. *Accruer,* like *accruement,* is an obsolete form of *accrual,* the general noun corresponding to the verb *accrue. Accruer* survives only in the phrase *clause of accruer.* Yet *accrual* has made substantial inroads even into this phrase, so that *accrual* and *accruer* now coexist needlessly. It is time to reject the archaic, and to establish firmly the modern form. Hence we should write *clause of accrual.*

accrue. A. Restriction to Financial Context. At least two critics have recommended that this word be restricted to monetary contexts, quite unaware of its most common meaning in legal contexts. Interest *accrues,* we may be certain, but so do causes of action—at least in jurisdictions in which they do not *arise.* See (B). E.g., "Plaintiff's cause of action for silicosis did not *accrue* until the plaintiff either knew of or had reason to know of the disease."

This use should not be extended further to mean "to inure to the benefit of," however, as here: "The appellate issue turns on whether the tax attributes associated with operations of certain commercial real estate properly *accrued to* [read *inured to the benefit of*] the corporation that held legal title."

B. *Accrue* and *arise.* In reference to causes of action, some courts have held that *accrue* and *arise* are synonymous, others that they can be distinguished. *Arise* may refer to the onset of the underlying wrong (e.g., exposure to asbestos), whereas *accrue* may refer to the ripeness of the claim (e.g., contraction of asbestosis or discovery of the disease). We need not set down a rule of usage so much as beware of the ambiguities of these terms in this particular context.

accruement. See **accrual.**

accruer. See **accrual.**

accumulate, -tive; cumulate, -tive. The former is far more common as the verb; the latter is current only in the adjective it yields (*cumulative*). *Accumulate* and *cumulate* both mean "to pile up; collect." *Cumulate,* however, should generally be avoided as a NEED-LESS VARIANT. *Accumulate* has the additional intransitive sense "to increase."

The adjectives demonstrate more palpable DIFFERENTIATION. In one sense they are synonymous: "increasing by successive addition," in which meaning *cumulative* is the usual and therefore the preferred term. *Cumulative* also means: (1) "relating to interest or a dividend paid to the corpus if not disbursed when due"; or (2) in law, "increasing in force as a result of additional or supporting evidence." In Scots law, *cumulative* is used also to mean "concurrent" ⟨to serve *cumulative* sentences⟩.

Accumulative = acquisitive; inclined to amass. In addition, it has the meanings ascribed to *cumulative.* Yet it would be salutary to strengthen the distinction and restrict *accumulative* to the sense "acquisitive."

accusation; accusal. The first, of course, is current; the second is obsolete. Cf. **recusal, -ation.**

accusatory; accusatorial; accusative. *Accusatory* (= accusing; of the nature of an accusation) is occasionally confused with *accusatorial*, which means "of or pertaining to an accuser," or, more specifically, "indicating the form of criminal prosecution in which the alleged criminal is publicly accused of his crime and is tried in public by a judge who is not also the prosecutor" (*W3*) ⟨accusatorial procedure⟩.

Accusatorial, denoting the common-law system of criminal procedure, may be contrasted with the civil-law term *inquisitorial* (which describes "a system of criminal justice . . . in which the truth is revealed by an inquiry into the facts conducted by the judge" [*CDL*]). Despite its neutral sense in civil law, common-law writers frequently use *inquisitorial*, as contrasted with *accusatorial*, in pejorative senses, e.g.: "The interrogation described in *Miranda* illustrated the extreme importance that American society placed on criminal prosecution, allowing tricks, cajolery, and even coercion to secure evidence from the suspect; the distinction between the *inquisitorial* and the *accusatorial* systems had become blurred." A variant term for *accusatorial procedure* is *adversary procedure*, although the latter term may suggest civil as well as criminal proceedings.

Accusative, although sometimes used in the place of *accusatory*, should be restricted to its grammatical sense relating to the objective case of nouns. E.g., "The feelings, attitudes, and relations of the parents of the five-year-old child are strained, *accusative* [read *accusatory*], and acrimonious." *Rodgers v. Hill,* 453 So. 2d 1057, 1058 (Ala. Civ. App. 1984)./ "There is no contention herein that the witness was emotional, condemnatory, *accusative* [read *accusatory*], or demanding vindication." *McQueen v. Commonwealth,* 669 S.W.2d 519, 523 (Ky. 1984).

accuse may be used transitively or, less commonly, intransitively. Here it is intransitive: "It is conceivable that the Court has overstepped its boundaries as the dissenting Justices *accuse.*" See **charge.**

Usually a word for criminal-law contexts, *accuse* has also been used to introduce allegations of noncriminal conduct (as in the preceding quotation). E.g., "The teams stand *accused*, essentially, of refusing to grant plaintiff's cablecast rights in furtherance of a conspiracy with Cablevision to monopolize cable television trade in Huntington."

accuse; charge. One is *accused of,* but *charged with,* a misfeasance.

accused, n., = the defendant in a criminal case. From a stylistic point of view, *accused* becomes awkward in the possessive case or as a plural: "The *accused's* silence may generate a reasonable inference that the accused believed the statement to be true." Usually this awkwardness can be remedied by use of the genitive: "The *silence* (or *statement*) of the accused . . ."; or, "The *accused person's silence* (or *statement*) . . . ." Cf. **deceased.**

accuser, -or. The *-er* form is standard. See -ER, -OR.

acerbic is generally inferior in AmE to *acerb;* other things being equal, choose the shorter word. E.g., "The court castigated the defense counsel's *acerbic* [read *acerb*] charges." *Acerbic* is standard in BrE, in which *acerb* is virtually unknown. The noun is *acerbity.*

acknowledg(e)ment. As with *judgment* and *abridgment*, the spelling without the *-e-* is preferable in AmE, *acknowledgement* being more common in BrE.

a consiliis. See **of counsel.**

acquaintanceship should be rejected in favor of *acquaintance;* it adds nothing to the language except another syllable, which we scarcely need. E.g., "The trial judge's *acquaintanceship* [read *acquaintance*] with the witness was not unusual in that it is to be expected that he would have contacts with other members of his bar in the normal practice of law."

acquiesce takes *in* or *to.* Some authorities have suggested that *in* is the only proper preposition. Yet the *OED* shows age-old examples with the construction *acquiesce to,* and its labeling that construction obsolete must be deemed a premature judgment, for it is fairly common in legal texts. *Acquiesce with* is not, however, in good use. The verb has three distinct syllables /ak-wi-*es*/.

acquirement; acquisition. "The former denotes the power or faculty of acquiring; the latter, the thing acquired." E. Partridge, *Usage and Abusage* 17 (1973). E.g., "His *acquirements* in law surpass his *acquisition* of wealth." Both also mean "the act of acquiring," though *acquisition* is more usual.

acquit as a past tense or participial adjective is obsolete for *acquitted.* It lives only in the LAW FRENCH phrase *autrefois acquit* (= heretofore acquitted).

acquittal; acquittance; acquitment. The first is the usual term, meaning both (1) "a release or discharge from debt or other liability" (*W3*); and (2) "a setting free or deliverance from the charge of an offense by verdict of a jury, sentence of a court, or other legal process" (*id.*). Leff writes: "One might loosely refer to a party 'acquitted' in a civil action, though one would ordinarily be tempted to use the terminology only if the cause were quasi-criminal, e.g., an action charging actual fraud, or an intentional physical tort like battery." Leff, *The Leff Dictionary of Law,* 94 Yale L.J. 1855, 1905 (1985). *Acquitment* is obsolete for *acquittal.*

Acquittance is obsolete in all senses except "a written release evidencing discharge of an obligation." Perhaps it would be advantageous to allow *acquittance* this commercial meaning, and to leave *acquittal* to the criminal law. Here *acquittance* appears in typical but mild LEGALESE: "When a deposit has been made in the names of two persons, payable to either, such deposit or any part thereof may be paid to either person whether the other is living or not; and the receipt or *acquittance* of the person so paid shall be a valid and sufficient release and discharge to the bank for any payment so made."

acquittal-prone. See **guilt-prone.**

acquittee = one acquitted of a crime. "The court examined procedures for releasing insanity *acquittees.*" This word is an ugly NEOLOGISM; *acquitted defendants* is better. See -EE.

ACRONYMS AND INITIALISMS. Three points merit our attention here. First, we should be aware of the difference between the two types of abbreviated names. An *acronym* "is composed of the initial letters or parts of a compound term. It is usually read or spoken as a single word, rather than letter by letter" (e.g., *radar* = radio detection and ranging). An *initialism* "is also composed of the initial letters or parts of a compound term but is generally verbalized letter by letter, rather than as a single 'word'" (e.g., *r.p.m.* = revolutions per minute). E. Crowley & H. Sheppard, *Acronyms, Initialisms and Abbreviations Dictionary* (9th ed. 1984).

Second, the question often arises whether to place periods after each letter in an acronym or initialism. Search for consistency on this point is futile. The trend nowadays is to omit the periods; including them is the more conservative and traditional approach. Yet surely if an acronym is spoken as a single word (e.g. ERISA, ERTA), periods are meaningless. If an initialism is made up of lowercase letters, periods are preferable: *rpm* looks odd as compared with *r.p.m.,* and *am* looks like the verb (as opposed to *a.m.*). One method of determining whether to omit or include periods is to follow the form of the organization one names (e.g., *IRS, HUD*), although inconsistencies are common.

Third, the best practice is to give the reader some forewarning of uncommon acronyms by spelling out the words and enclosing the acronym in parentheses when the term is first used. The reader may at first be confused by a reference to *CARPE Rules,* until he realizes that three or four lines above this acronym the writer has made reference to a Committee on Academic Rights, Privileges, and Ethics.

Finally, as illustrated under the entry entitled INITIALESE, the use in a single text of a number of these abbreviated forms leads to dense and frustrating prose.

act; action. These are important words in law; yet they are often used indiscriminately. To be sure, the words overlap a great deal, and it is difficult to delineate the distinctions accurately. *Act* is the more concrete, *action* the more abstract word. Generally, *act* denotes the thing done, *action* the doing of it. Crabb approaches a workable demarcation:

> When these words are taken in the sense of the thing done, they admit of a . . . distinction. An *act* is the single thing done, or what is done by a single effort, as that is your *act* or his *act*; an *action* may consist of more *acts* than one, or embrace the causes or the consequences of the action, as a bold *action*, to judge of *actions*, etc.
> Hence it is that the term *act* is more proper than *action* where it is so defined as to imply what is single and simple, as an *act* of authority, an *act* of government, an *act* of folly, and the like; but otherwise the word *action* is to be preferred where the moral conduct or character is in question. We may enumerate particular *acts* of a man's life, as illustrative of certain traits of his character, or certain circumstances of his life; but to speak at large of his *actions* would be to describe his character.
> G. Crabb, *Crabb's English Synonymes* 24–25 (1917).

As a further gloss, I might add that *action* suggests a process—the many discrete events that make up a bit of behavior—whereas *act* is unitary. As Crabb suggested, one is held responsible (or not) for one's *actions* and not, generally, for one's *acts*.

act; enactment. The former has many meanings, but, when used as a synonym for *statute*, it is usually clear from the context. Strictly, *enactment* should refer to the passing or enacting of a law (i.e., its enactment), but not to the law once enacted. E.g., "The purpose of an *enactment* [read *act*] is embedded in its words even though it is not always pedantically expressed in words." *United States v. Shirey*, 359 U.S. 255, 261 (1959) (per Frankfurter, J.)./ "Several states that have patterned their surveillance statutes on the federal model have simply incorporated this exception into their *enactments* [read *acts*; see INELEGANT VARIATION], and other states have adopted consent surveillance statutes." *Enaction* is a NEEDLESS VARIANT of *enactment*. To sum up, courts pass on the constitutionality of *acts*, not *enactments*; one witnesses the *enactment* of a bill.

actio(n). In phrases such as *actio(n) ex contractu* and *actio(n) ex delictu*, *action* is better than *actio*. Better yet is *contract action* or *tort action*.

action. See **act**.

action; suit. Originally, *action* was confined to refer to proceedings in a court of law; *suit* referred to proceedings in chancery (or equity), as well as to prosecutions at law. When the jurisdictional distinction existed, an *action* ended at judgment, but a *suit* in equity ended after judgment and execution. Today, since virtually all jurisdictions have merged law and equity, the terms *action* and *suit* are interchangeable.

actionable has two important senses: (1) "furnishing grounds for a lawsuit"; and (2) "liable to a lawsuit." Another possible meaning is suggested by this sentence: "He had an *actionable* intent—that is, he would act on it." But the dictionaries do not record any definition consistent with this usage (i.e. "giving rise to an act or action"), which is predicated upon a misunderstanding of *action* (= lawsuit) as used in the term (i.e. "giving rise to a lawsuit").

Sense (1) listed above is the most usual in legal contexts: "One of the general rules governing this action is that words are *actionable* when spoken of one in an office of profit which may probably occasion the loss of his office."/ "Plaintiff Banks states no *actionable* claim of constitutional deprivations."

action on the case, a LOAN TRANSLATION of the LAW FRENCH *action sur le case*, is the common-law term for a personal tort action. E.g., "This is an *action on the case* by husband for the alienation of affections of his wife by her parents, the defendants." *Trespass on the case* and *case* alone, qq.v., are variant forms. None of these phrases is used much in contemporary legal prose.

activate. See **actuate**.

act of God. See **vis major**.

actual; constructive. These words are opposed in a variety of legal phrases, e.g., *con-*

structive as against *actual fraud, constructive* as against *actual possession.* When *actual* is used in such a phrase, the extrinsic facts merit the legal conclusion that, e.g., fraud or possession exists. When *constructive* is used, the extrinsic facts do not fall within the strict definition of, e.g., fraud or possession, but the court finds (or is requested to find), usu. on equitable grounds, that the legal conclusion of fraud or possession should apply. See **constructive.**

actual fact, in. A redundancy: all facts are actual, just as they are all true. When one is uncertain of the truth of allegations, then there might be "alleged facts." *In actual fact* is a pomposity for *actually.* Cf. *in truth and in fact.*

actuality is frequently a turgid substitute for *reality* or *fact.* E.g., "The existence of a fiduciary relationship is to be determined from the *actualities* [read *facts*] of the relationship between the persons involved."/ "The great divide in the equal-protection decisions lies in the difference between emphasizing *actualities* [read *realities*] and the abstractions of legislation."
  In actuality is always inferior to *actually.*

actuate; activate. The Evanses wrote that *actuate* = to move (mechanical things) to action, and that *activate* = to make active. B. Evans & C. Evans, *Contemporary American Usage* 10 (1957). The distinction is a fine one not generally followed by dictionaries. Here *actuation* is correctly used: "A blade brake control device would stop the blade less than one second after *actuation.*"
  More often, however, *actuate* and *actuation* appear in legal prose as fancy substitutes for *motivate* and *motivation* in a variety of contexts. This usage should generally be avoided on stylistic grounds, although it is not strictly incorrect. "To prevent imposition of a constructive trust, the wife would have to establish by a preponderance of the evidence that the conveyance was *actuated* [read *motivated*] by fraud."/ "The wrong was *actuated* [read *motivated*] by a positive design to injure the third person to whom the duty was due."
  The temptation to use *actuate* rather than *motivate* is much greater where the noun *motive* appears. Perhaps we should allow it in such contexts, though a simple rewording obviates the need for *actuate.* E.g., "When one exercises a legal right, *the motive that actuates*

him is immaterial [read *one's motives are immaterial*]."/ "Counsel had the absolute privilege of making such deductions, even though they were false and he *was actuated by improper motives* [read *had improper motives*]."/ "The showing of invidiousness is made if a defendant demonstrates that *the government's selective prosecution is actuated by constitutionally impermissible motives* [read *the government, in its selective prosecution, was acting on constitutionally impermissible motives*]." See **animate.**

actus reus. See **mens rea.**

A.D. This abbreviation (for *Anno Domini,* not *after death*) is unnecessary after dates in legal documents. In fact, it is absurd to use it with a twentieth-century date.

ad for *advertisement* is acceptable only in very informal contexts.

adapt and *adopt* are occasionally confounded. To *adapt* something is to modify it for one's own purposes; to *adopt* something is to accept it wholesale and use it.

adapt(at)ion, -(at)ive. The longer form is preferred in the noun (*adaptation*), the shorter in the adjective (*adaptive*).

a dato; a datu. Both LEGALISMS mean "from the date," and both are anachronistic.

addable, -ible. The former is preferred. See -ABLE (A).

addicted; dependent. In the realm of human reaction to drugs, the distinction between these terms can be an important one. One who is *addicted* to a habit-forming drug has a compulsive physiological need for it. One who is *dependent* on a drug has a strong psychological reliance on it after having used it for some time. *Addiction,* then, is primarily physical, whereas *dependency* (also known as *habituation*) is primarily psychological.

additament is a NEEDLESS VARIANT of *addition.*

address = (1) to call attention to, or (2) to state (a question) (to someone). In sense (1) it is a FORMAL WORD that is sometimes inappropriately used: "That portion of the trial court's decree is not, therefore, assailed by

Maria Rosa, as clearly her discontent *addresses* [read *centers on* or *arises out of*] the denial of a jury trial on the only factual issues raised having to do with proper division of the estate." This sentence exemplifies HYPALLAGE run amuck; generally, *address* should take personal subjects, although by legitimate transference one might say that arguments or pleas *address* certain points. But *discontent* is not a proper subject for the verb. Following is a correct use of the term: "These points of error all relate to events after the making of the contract, and fail to *address* the issue of fraud in the inducement."

Address should be accented on the second syllable as both noun and verb.

addressee. See -EE.

adduce; educe; deduce. All are useful in reference to evidence. To *adduce* is to put forward for consideration something such as evidence or arguments. E.g., "In the original panel opinion we held that Rushing's live testimony at trial would have had only a cumulative effect on this issue, because Wells had access to and did *adduce* testimony concerning the town's supervision and training of Rushing."

To *educe* is to draw out or evoke or elicit. E.g., "That divorce judgment, after the filing of this suit, was reversed and remanded for retrial by a Texas intermediate court on October 27, 1983, as was *educed* on further showings made in the federal trial court before that court's judgment of dismissal now before us on appeal."

To *deduce* is to derive a conclusion or infer. E.g., "The jury could reasonably have *deduced* that defendant intended such a result." See **deduce.**

adducible; adduceable. *Adducible* is the regular form. See -ABLE (A).

adeem is the verb form of *ademption;* the pair is analogous to *redeem/redemption.*

ademption. The two types of *ademption* are usefully distinguished. *Ademption by extinction* is the forfeiture of a legacy, bequest, or devise by the beneficiary because the property specifically described in the will is not in the testator's estate at his death. *Ademption by satisfaction* occurs when the testator, while alive,

gives property to a donee named in his will, with the intention of rendering the testamentary gift inoperative.

adequate; sufficient. Though originally both words were used in reference to quantity, today there is a trend toward using *adequate* qualitatively, and *sufficient* quantitatively. Hence *adequate* means "suitable to the occasion or circumstances," and *sufficient* means "enough for a particular need or purpose."

In contracts, with respect to *consideration,* q.v., a special distinction applies. One rule of consideration is that it need not be *adequate* but it must be *sufficient.* Here, not having to be *adequate* means that the consideration need not be a realistic economic equivalent of the promise it buys, whereas being *sufficient* means that it must have some economic value, and that it must not stem from a pre-existing legal duty.

ad fin(em) = to the end. One would be hard-pressed to justify the Latin phrase in place of the English equivalent. (See LATINISMS.) The phrase is sometimes used in citations in a sense similar to *et seq.,* q.v, but the better practice is to cite to specific pages, that is, to give an ending as well as a starting point. If, however, *ad fin.* is to be used, a period should follow the abbreviated form (as just given). The period is erroneously omitted in Leff, *The Leff Dictionary of Law,* 94 Yale L.J. 1855, 1931 (1985).

adherence; adhesion. Both words derive from the verb *to adhere,* but *adhesion* is generally literal and *adherence* generally figurative. One should write of *adherence* to tenets or beliefs, and of *adhesion* of bubble gum to the sole of one's shoe. The word more frequently called upon in legal contexts is *adherence:* "There are also authorities to the contrary and we might make mention of a retreat by the Supreme Court of Nebraska from *adherence* to the rule." Both words take the preposition *to.* "This holding mandates close adherence *from* [read *to*] the letter of the law."

Yet the standard rules of usage relating to these words find exceptions in the law. One exception to the foregoing advice is the phrase *adhesion contract* or *contract of adhesion.* Said to have been introduced into legal nomenclature by Patterson in *The Delivery of a*

Life Insurance Policy, 33 Harv. L. Rev. 198, 222 (1919), the term refers to a standard printed contract prepared by one party, to be signed by the party in a weaker position, usu. a consumer, who has little choice about the terms of the contract. The metaphor suggested is that the consumer must *adhere* to the contract as presented, or reject it completely. *Adhesion,* then, has a figurative rather than a literal sense in this legal phrase.

Another exception, not so frequently encountered, involves treaties. When a government enters into some but not all of the provisions of a treaty already existing between two other governments, *adhesion* is the term to describe the third government's entrance into the treaty.

ad hoc, adv. & adj., is a widespread and useful term meaning "for this specific purpose." Though some witch-hunting Latin-haters have questioned its justification in English (see, e.g., Vigilans, *Chamber of Horrors* 26 (1952)), it is firmly established and serves legal language well when used correctly ⟨ad hoc committee⟩. E.g., "The majority opinion insufficiently considers the basic substantive rules of law invoked by plaintiff's complaint; it is an *ad hoc* opinion that grants desired relief to needy persons but its effects on established law could be serious."

The phrase should be avoided in slipshod senses such as "improvised from whatever is at hand," as here: "This procedure is carried out on a very *ad hoc* [read *haphazard?*] basis."/ "Lawyers and judges apparently devise voir dire questions in a fairly *ad hoc* [read *haphazard* or *desultory*] way; sometimes prosecutors inadvertently pose questions that work to the advantage of the defense, and vice-versa." *On an ad hoc basis* is always verbose for *ad hoc,* adv. (See **basis.**) Moreover, *ad hoc* is never properly qualified by *very* or *fairly,* for the result is meaningless. Finally, attempts to coalesce the phrase into one word have failed, and should be forgotten. Cf. **pro hac vice.**

ad idem = to the same effect; to that effect. E.g., "That being so, there was no consensus *ad idem,* and therefore no binding contract."/ "At the end of the short trial I felt constrained to find that the plaintiff and defendant *were never ad idem* [read *never had the same understanding*] on the purported sale of land by the defendant to the plaintiff." (Eng.) An English equivalent, such as *to that effect,* is generally more comprehensible than this Latin phrase, and even more elegant. See FORBIDDEN WORDS.

adjacent; contiguous. These words should be distinguished. *Adjacent* = lying near. *Contiguous* = directly abutting or bordering on. See **adjoin.**

adjective law is not a set of rules governing nominal modifiers, but rather the aggregate of rules on procedure. In law as in language, the adjectival affects the substantive. E.g., "Determined to uphold the constitutionality of a Texas statute whatever obstacles bar the way, the majority opinion tramples every procedural rule it considers; if this en banc decision is precedent, it assuredly rewrites the *adjective law.*"

ADJECTIVES. A. Uncomparable Adjectives. A number of adjectives describe absolute states or conditions, and cannot take comparative degrees in *most* or *more, less* or *least,* or intensives such as *very* or *quite* or *largely.* The illogic of such combinations is illustrated in this sentence: "It is possible that this idea too has outlived its usefulness and soon will be largely discarded." The literal meaning of *discard* impinges on the metaphor here: it is hard to imagine a single idea being halfway discarded, though certainly it could be halfway discredited.

The best-known uncomparable adjective is *unique* (= being one of a kind). Because something is either unique or not unique, there can be no degrees of uniqueness. Hence *more unique* and *very unique* are incorrect. Yet something may be *almost unique* or *not quite unique*—if, for example, there were two such things extant. Many other words belong to this class, for example *preferable:* "We think that, while perhaps the denial did not follow the *most preferable* course, it was adequate." (Omit *most.*)

Following is a short list of uncomparable adjectives: *absolute, adequate, basic, certain, chief, complete, devoid, entire, essential, false, fatal, final, first, fundamental, ideal, impossible, inevitable, irrevocable, main, major, manifest, minor, necessary, only, perpetuity, possible, preferable, principal, stationary, sufficient, true, unavoidable, unbroken, uniform, unique, universal, void, whole.*

The general prohibition against using these

words in comparative senses should be tempered with reason; it has exceptions. Good writers occasionally depart from the rule, but knowingly and purposefully. Poor writers use uncomparable adjectives indiscriminately, and in the end weaken their writing through hyperbolic qualification. See WEASEL WORDS.

B. Adjectives as Nouns. Words in the English language frequently have the ability to change parts of speech. Thus nouns may act as adjectives (*deposition testimony, court protocol*) and adjectives as nouns. Legal writers refer to *innocents* (= innocent persons) and *necessaries* (= necessary things). *Indigent* was originally an adjective (15th c.), but it came to be used as a noun (16th c.). The same process occurred with *hypothetical, postmortem, principal* (= principal investment), *ignitables, potential, explosives,* and *recitative.* More modern examples are *finals* (= final examinations) and *classifieds* (= classified advertisements). We must resist the benighted temptation to condemn such shifts in parts of speech, while observing that the more recent semantic shifts remain unsuitable for formal contexts. Cf. NOUNS AS ADJECTIVES.

C. Phrasal or Compound Adjectives. These are generally hyphenated, e.g.: *child-support payments, fourteenth-amendment rights, conspiracy-law dispute, civil-rights case, good-faith exception, two-party check, horse-and-buggy days, third-degree assault.* The value in hyphenating such phrasal adjectives is that the reader is not momentarily misled into thinking that the modifying phrase is really itself a noun. Such hyphenation cuts down on NOUN PLAGUE, q.v. For instance, *common law* is the noun phrase and *common-law* the adjectival phrase; when the phrase has no hyphen, the reader does not expect a noun to follow it. One sees the pronounced improvement in readability especially when two compound adjectives modify one noun: *common-law mirror-image rule, long-latency occupational-disease cases.* Other common phrases in legal writing are *take-nothing judgment, in-court testimony, paid-in capital,* and *agency-enabling statute.* A few phrasal adjectives such as *bona fide,* in which the words have no English meaning singly, are exceptions to the rule of hyphenation.

The following examples demonstrate the hesitation caused by a missing hyphen: "The *benefit of insurance and waiver of subrogation* clauses [read *benefit-of-insurance and waiver-of-subrogation* clauses] in the affreightment con-

tracts are invalid because they conflict with the plaintiff's marine cargo insurance policy."/ "Merely because a *court made rule* [read *court-made rule*] has been in effect for many years does not render it invulnerable to judicial attack once it becomes obsolescent."/ "The applicable *one year statute of limitations* [read *one-year statute of limitations*] started to run from December 13, 1959."

The hyphens become especially important when the compounds are compounded: "The government argues that this designation is ineffective because it reflects a *ten-* rather than a *two-year* federal sentence."/ "A court faced with enforcing a *general-* or *public-interest* law, however, should give vent to its imagination, since such a law is designed to vest discretion in the judicial branch." Here the hyphens were not supplied, to the reader's puzzlement: "The situs of this case is the small city of Apopka, Florida, located *in the fern and foliage growing region* [read *in the fern- and foliage-growing region*] north of Orlando."

Yet when one takes to toying with a snake-like compound, it is time to rework the sentence: "Each contract included *a waiver-of-all-rights-to-subrogation clause* [read *a clause waiving all rights to subrogation*]."/ "We found no merit in any other issue raised, *including an ineffective-assistance-of-counsel claim* [read *including a claim of ineffective assistance of counsel*]." Here is a particularly ugly specimen: "We are *law-of-the-case-bound* in this matter and thus cannot reconsider this contention."

With compound adjectives denoting periods of time and amounts, plurals should be dropped in the adjectival phrase. Hence, "The record is silent as to whether Annie Bell was born after a normal *nine months pregnancy* [read *nine-month pregnancy*]." Likewise, one should write *three-week hiatus, fourteen-hour-a-day schedule,* and *four-year decline.* The exception is with fractions (a two-thirds vote).

Note, however, that compound adjectives, when predicative, are not usually hyphenated: "This rule is *well worn*," but "This is a *well-worn* rule." An exception is *short-lived,* which is always hyphenated. See HYPHENS.

D. Equivalency of Adjectives Paired by Conjunctions. Where two adjectives, both modifying the same noun, are quite unrelated in sense, they should not be separated by *and* or by a comma. E.g., "An interesting contrast in judicial philosophy as to the scope of an employee's ethical duty is revealed in a *similar and Texas case* [read *similar Texas case*]." On the

punctuation of successive adjectives, see
PUNCTUATION (C)(1).

E. Modification of Adjectives Ending in
-*ed.* See **very** (B).

F. Adjectives Ending in -*ly.* See ADVERBS (B).

G. Postpositive Adjectives. See POSTPOSI-
TIVE ADJECTIVES.

H. Place-Names as Adjectives. See PLACE-
NAMES AS ADJECTIVES.

adjoin   means both "to join" and "to lie adjacent to." In the latter sense, it is transitive
and should take a direct object: "The park was
likened to a garden that traditionally (as an
appurtenance) *adjoined to a residence* [read *adjoined a residence*]." Etymologically, *adjoining*
means "directly abutting; contiguous," as opposed to *adjacent,* q.v.

adjudge; adjudicate; dijudicate; judge.
Adjudge = (1) to consider judicially; to rule
upon; (2) to deem or pronounce to be; or (3)
to award judicially. *Adjudicate,* q.v., shares all
three meanings of *adjudge,* and is more common in sense (1) than *adjudge.* In senses (2)
and (3), *adjudge* is the more usual term: "Nor
can a court of equity adjudge [sense (2)] the
decree of any other court binding or punish
the violation of any decrees but its own."/
"Costs are adjudged to appellant [sense (3)]."
(For examples of *adjudicate* in sense (2), see
adjudicate (B).)

Dijudicate (= to decide between; adjudicate)
is a rare term without justification in modern
prose.

Judge is the general term meaning "to try a
person or case as a judge does." Additionally,
it has the lay meaning "to form a critical estimate of." *Judge* should not be used in sense
(2) of *adjudge,* as here: "Plaintiff argues that
the society must declare a winner of the contest or be judged [read *adjudged*] to have
breached an implicit agreement with the
contestants."

The Evanses wrote that *adjudicate* was more
common than *judge* in reference to disputes
outside the courts. B. Evans & C. Evans, *Contemporary American Usage* 261 (1957). Lawyers,
however, restrict *adjudicate* to contexts involving courts or other resolvers of disputes,
whereas they may use *judge* in nonlegal senses. See **adjudicate.**

Adjudge is best used with the object immediately following: "The court found him
guilty of the charge and *adjudged* him in con-

tempt." There is a tendency (to be avoided)
to insert *as* after *adjudge,* e.g., "adjudge as
bankrupt" for "adjudge bankrupt." See **abjudge.**

adjudg(e)ment.   See **judg(e)ment.**

adjudicataire.   See **adjudicator.**

adjudicate.   A. Proper Object with. Disputes and controversies are adjudicated, or
"settled judicially"; *property* cannot be adjudicated, although conflicting rights in it can
be. E.g., "The supersedeas bond must be in
the amount of the judgment or the value of
property adjudicated [read *property in dispute,* or
property subject to adjudication]."/ "We reverse
the judgment of the Supreme Court of Kansas
insofar as it held that Kansas law was applicable to all the *transactions that it sought to adjudicate* [read *transactions giving rise to this controversy* (or *adjudication*)]." See **adjudication.**
Cf. **litigate.**

B. Meaning "to deem." *Adjudicate* frequently means "to deem or pronounce judicially," sense (2) of *adjudge,* q.v. "Neither do-
lomite nor granite has been *adjudicated* a
'mineral.'"/ "Once laws are validly enacted it
is not for the courts to *adjudicate* upon their
wisdom, their appropriateness, or the necessity for their existence." (Eng.)/ "Associates
continued to deteriorate financially and in
1975, it was placed in liquidation and, in separate proceedings, *adjudicated* a bankrupt."
(Most legal texts written in BrE say that an
insolvent entity is "adjudicated bankrupt,"
not "adjudicated a bankrupt," as in AmE.)
For other senses of *adjudicate,* see **adjudge.**

adjudicated   has come into use as an adjective. Thus instead of writing, "The ward *was
adjudicated* an incompetent," some legists
have begun to write, "The ward is *an adjudicated* bankrupt." The adjectival usage purports
to give the statement more authority, for it focuses on what the subject *is,* as opposed to
what someone *has done to it.*

adjudication; adjudicature.   The latter is a
NEEDLESS VARIANT. (See **judicature.**) On the
plural use of *adjudication,* see PLURALS (B).

Leff writes that, in modern usage, "*adjudication* can . . . be used as a rough synonym for
litigation, e.g., 'the matter is in *adjudication*
now.'" Leff, *The Leff Dictionary of Law* 1855,

1934 (1985). This SLIPSHOD EXTENSION should be eschewed unless, of course, the writer intends to refer to the deliberative process of judges and not to the courtroom proceedings in which lawyers take part. See **adjudicate** (A) & **litigate.**

adjudicative, -tory; judicative, -tory, -torial. As between *adjudicative* and *adjudicatory,* both meaning "having the character or attribute of adjudicating," the former is standard, easier to pronounce, and better sounding. Yet the latter, as if to cause vexation, appears with some frequency. Thus, even though we have *adjudicative facts* and *adjudicative hearings,* our legal texts reveal *adjudicatory proceedings* and *an adjudicatory action.* There is no need for the two to coexist, for no workable DIFFERENTIATION now appears to be possible. One is best advised to use *adjudicative* in all contexts.

Judicative is a NEEDLESS VARIANT of *adjudicative.* Likewise, *judicatorial* is a NEEDLESS VARIANT of *judicial.* For *judicatory,* see **judicature.** See also **judicative.**

adjudicator; adjudicataire; judicator. *Adjudicator* = one that adjudicates. If used merely for *judge,* it is a pomposity. Here it is defensible: "We find nothing in the history or constitutional treatment of military tribunals that entitles them to rank along with Article III courts as *adjudicators* of the guilt or innocence of people charged with offenses for which they can be deprived of their life, liberty, or property." *Adjudicataire,* a term from Canadian law, means "a purchaser at a judicial sale" (*W3*). *Judicator* is a NEEDLESS VARIANT of *adjudicator.*

adjudicature for *adjudication.* See **judicature** & **adjudication.**

adjure. See **abjure.**

adjurer, -or. The *-er* spelling is preferred. See -ER, -OR.

adjuster, -or. *Adjuster* is the preferred spelling. See -ER, -OR.

adminicular(y). *Adminicular* (= corroborative), seen usu. in the phrase *adminicular evidence,* is the standard adjectival form of the noun *adminicle,* meaning "supporting or corroborative evidence" (*OED*). In Scots law, *ad-*

minicle has the more specific meaning "any writing tending to establish the existence and terms of a lost document."

administer; minister. *Administer* suffices in most legal contexts. It is a transitive verb and, in its most common legal sense, means "to manage and dispose of the estate of a deceased person, either under a will or under letters of administration" (*OED*). E.g., "Generally speaking, a natural person has the same capacity to take, to hold, and to *administer* property under a trust as he has to take, to hold, and to *administer* property for his own benefit." *Administer* may also mean (1) "to dispense (as justice or as punishment); or (2) "to give (an oath)."

The verb *minister,* now primarily intransitive, shares these last two meanings, albeit only rarely. *Minister* is most commonly used in the sense of attending to others' needs, or, in religious contexts, of administering sacraments. Persons in need are *ministered to.* E.g., "A testator's favor expressed in a will may be won by devoted attachment, self-sacrificing kindness, and *ministering to* him through friendship and love."

administerial. See **administrative.**

administrable; administratable; administerable. The first form is correct; the others are near-abominations, and NEEDLESS VARIANTS to boot. See -ATABLE.

administrate is an objectionable BACKFORMATION from *administration;* it should be avoided as a NEEDLESS VARIANT of *administer.*

administrative; administerial; administrational. *Administrative* is the general, all-purpose term meaning "of or pertaining to administration or *an* administration." *Administerial* and *administrational* are NEEDLESS VARIANTS.

administrator; executor. Both terms refer to the personal representative who administers the estate of a decedent. An *executor* is named in a will, whereas an *administrator* is court-appointed. There are two kinds of the latter: an *administrator cum testamento annexo* (or *c.t.a.*) and an *administrator de bonis non* (or *d.b.n.*). The second phrase is elliptical for *administrator de bonis non administratis* (= administrator of goods not administered).

An *administrator c.t.a.* is one "with the will annexed"; in fact, the Latin abbreviation or phrase is often Englished *administrator with the will annexed,* a healthy practice eliminating the need for mnemonic devices for remembering the Latin. An *administrator d.b.n.* ("of goods not administered") is named when a previous administrator for the intestate has for some reason failed to complete his administration. When an *executor* so fails, the court appoints an *administrator cum testamento annexo, de bonis non.* Sometimes a MINGLE-MANGLE version is used: "The plaintiff was duly appointed *administrator de bonis non with the will annexed.*"

administratrix.   See SEXISM (C).

admiralty; maritime; law of the sea. *Black's* states that the first two terms are "virtually synonymous" in referring to the law of marine commerce and navigation, the transportation at sea of persons and property, and marine affairs in general. Today the words are used interchangeably.

Yet Article III, section 2 of the U.S. Constitution is not redundant in providing, "The judicial power shall extend . . . to all Cases involving admiralty and maritime Jurisdiction." One commentator notes that *admiralty* (dated from c. 1327 in the *OED*) was the better-known term when the Constitution was drafted, and that *maritime* (*OED*: 1550) was used in conjunction with *admiralty* for two reasons: "(1) to exclude that jurisdiction which the English Admiralty anciently exercised or attempted to exercise over nonmaritime cases arising ashore, and (2) to preclude a resort to those English instances in which common-law courts encroached upon the jurisdiction of admiralty." E. Jhirad, A. Sann & B. Chase, 1 *Benedict on Admiralty* § 101 (7th ed. 1983).

Law of the sea is a nontechnical term synonymous with *admiralty* or *maritime law.*

admissible, -able; admittable. The first is standard; the second and third are NEEDLESS VARIANTS to be avoided. *Admissible* = (1) allowable; or (2) worthy of admittance (i.e., gaining entry).

admission. A. And *admittance.* The distinction between these terms is old and useful, but it has a history of being ignored. The latter term is purely physical, as in signs that read "No admittance." E.g.,"Plaintiff instituted an action to enjoin defendant from refusing her *admittance* to its amusement park because of her race or color, or for any other reason not applicable alike to other citizens."

Admission is used in figurative and nonphysical senses, such as: "His *admission* to the bar in 1948 began a career that would be long and noteworthy." *Admission* is also used, however, in physical senses when rights or privileges are attached to gaining entry: "The *admission* of aliens into the United States is considerably more restricted in this century than it was in the last."

B. And *confession.* In criminal law, a distinction has traditionally existed between these words: an *admission* is a concession that an allegation or factual assertion is true without any acknowledgment of guilt with respect to the criminal charges, wheras a *confession* involves an acknowledgment of guilt as well as of the truth of predicate factual allegations.

C. In Civil Litigation. Although laymen tend to associate *admission* with criminal law (see B), it has broad uses in noncriminal evidentiary contexts: "An *admission* is a statement oral or written, suggesting any inference as to any fact in issue or relevant fact, unfavourable to the conclusion contended for by the person by whom or on whose behalf the statement is made." J.F. Stephens, *The Law of Evidence* 23 (1876).

admit of = to allow; to be susceptible of. E.g.,"This clause in the contract *admits of* two interpretations."/ "The former construction should be adopted if the language used will *admit of* such a construction."

admittance. See **admission** (A).

admitted to the bar; called to the bar. The former is the American phrase for qualifying to practice law; the latter is the British phrase for qualifying to practice as a barrister (as distinguished from a solicitor). *Called to the bar,* q.v., appears infrequently in the U.S.

admit to is much inferior to *admit.* E.g., "In 1978, appellant admitted *to* [omit *to*] killing his wife and daughter and pleaded guilty to two charges of first-degree murder."

admonish; monish.   See **admonition.**

admonishment.   See **abolishment.**

admonition; monition. In general usage, both mean "a warning; caution." *Admonition* is the more common, less technical term: "We must follow the Supreme Court's *admonition* that courts ought not to impose constitutional restraints that would inhibit the ability of the political branches to respond through immigration policy to changing world conditions." *Admonition* has the additional sense "a mild reprimand."

Monition is the more specialized legal term; it may mean (1) in admiralty and civil-law contexts, "a summons to appear and answer in court as a defendant or to contempt charges"; (2) in ecclesiastical contexts, "a formal notice from a bishop mandating that an offense within the clergy be corrected." The object of a monition is a *person monished.*

admonitory, -ial; monitory, -ial. The *-ory* forms predominate.

adopt. See **adapt.**

adoption; ratification; novation. In contractual contexts, these three words have deceptively similar meanings. *Adoption* of a contract is accepting it as one's own, or consenting to be bound by it, though it was entered into by someone else acting on one's behalf. A *ratification* is the confirmation of a contract performed or entered into on one's behalf by another who at the time assumed without authority to act as an agent. These two words are near-synonyms. *Novation* has two important meanings: (1) "the substitution of a new contract between parties in place of an existing contract"; and (2) "the substitution of a new party in an existing contract." Sense (1) predominates in American law.

In corporate law, the distinctions have relevance, and are somewhat different, when a promoter enters into a contract that purports to bind a newly formed corporation, or one soon to be formed. If a promoter contracts with a third person where it is understood that the corporation will be formed, the corporation is later properly said to *adopt* the contract. *Ratify*, in contrast, is the proper word when the corporation already existed when the contract was executed. If, after a corporation *adopts* or *ratifies* the contract, the promoter is expressly relieved from liability, the *adoption* or *ratification* becomes a *novation.*

adoptive; adopted. *Adoptive* = (1) related by adoption ⟨an adoptive son⟩; or (2) tending to adopt ⟨adoptive admissions under Fed. R. Evid. 801(d)(2)(b)⟩. The phrase *adopted father* is an example of HYPALLAGE, q.v., to be avoided in favor of *adoptive father*. The original Latin word, *adoptivus,* applied both to the adopting parent and to the adopted child.

Here the correct usages are observed: "If an *adopted* child can inherit from or through his natural or *adoptive* parents, the child of an *adopted* child can claim through him in an appropriate case."/ "The controlling statute provides that an *adopted* child inherits through his *adoptive* parent."

adpromissor (= surety, bail) has two plural forms in *adpromissors* and *adpromissores,* the latter being unEnglish and therefore inferior. (See PLURALS (A)). The dilemma between plural forms is easily remedied by writing *sureties.*

adsorb. See **absorb.**

adulter. See **adulterer.**

adulteration; adultery. *Adulteration* = (1) the act of debasing, corrupting, or making impure; (2) a corrupted or debased state; or (3) something corrupted or debased. *Adultery* = sexual intercourse engaged in voluntarily by a married person with a person of the opposite sex who is not the lawful spouse. (See **adulterine bastard.**) The Latin verb *adulterare,* from which both English words derive, encompasses all these senses.

adulterer; adulter; adulteress, -tera; adulterator. *Adulterer* is the usual form meaning "one who commits adultery." *Adulter* is an obsolete variant of *adulterer* that also had the meaning of *adulterator* (= counterfeiter).

Adulteress is the feminine form, now disfavored because of the growing awareness of SEXISM—likewise with *adultera,* the term from the civil law. *Adulterator,* as suggested above, derives from the noun *adulteration,* and not from *adultery,* like the other personal nouns discussed in this entry.

adulterine bastard. Leff defines this phrase as "the child of a married woman by a man other than her husband," and comments: "As 'adultery' has come to include sexual relations by a married man with a woman not his wife, whether she is married or not, the term *adulterine bastard* has sometimes come to include a child born to an unmarried woman by a married man. This makes no difference, as no legal consequences presently attach to adulterine bastardy that do not attach to plain old bastardy." Leff, *The Leff Dictionary of Law*, 94 Yale L.J. 1855, 1951 (1985). The form *adulterine bastard* is preferable to *adulterous bastard*, the latter suggesting an unfaithful son-of-a-bitch rather than a child produced by adultery.

The very term *bastard* is now being displaced by euphemistic terms in legal contexts. See EUPHEMISMS.

adulterous; adulterine; adulterant; adulterate, adj.; **adulterated.** *Adulterous* and *adulterate* both mean "of, characterized by, or pertaining to adultery," the former term being the more common. E.g., "We think there was evidence that his conduct and that of the defendant had a legitimate tendency to prove *adulterous* inclination, although insufficient to establish criminal conversation." *Adulterate*, adj., more common in Shakespeare's day than in ours, has been relegated to the status of a NEEDLESS VARIANT.

Adulterine = (1) spurious; (2) illegal; or (3) born of adultery ⟨adulterine bastard⟩. *Adulterant* = tending to adulterate. *Adulterated* = (1) corrupted or debased, or (2) vitiated or made spurious.

adultery; fornication. The latter implies that neither party is married; where one of the participants in the activity is married, *adultery* is the proper term. See **adulteration.**

adumbrate (= [1] to foreshadow, or [2] to outline) is a formal word that has been called an affectation. But legal writers have considered it serviceable in formal contexts. "The contours of the action for indemnity among tortfeasors were *adumbrated* by the Louisiana Supreme Court."/ "The majority's holding and reasoning in *Alvarez-Gonzalez II* tended to expand the concept of functional equivalency as *adumbrated* by the Supreme Court fourteen years earlier in *Almeida-Sanchez*."

advance; advancement. Generally, the former refers to progress, the latter to promotion. Hence, one might get an occupational *advancement*, but one speaks of the *advance* of civilization. E.g., "The advancement [i.e., promotion] of religion has ever been held to be one of the principal divisions of charitable trusts."/ "These actions, according to the complaint, violated the plaintiff's rights under the first and fourteenth amendments to associate for the *advancement* of their common interests in dealings with the college."/ "Any one of these considerations might tend toward the *advancement* of the employees."

In senses suggesting the action of moving up or bringing forth, *advancement* is the proper word. "Considering the backlog of cases in most jurisdictions and the absence of any further right to *advancement* on the court calendar, the significance of victory or defeat at this stage is readily apparent."/ "The *advancement* of a prosecutorial-vindictiveness claim brings into conflict two antithetical interests."

The distinction gets fuzzier in financial contexts. Although we speak (properly) of *cash advances* and *advances on royalties*, in law *advancement* takes on a sense similar to that which *advance* has in these phrases. Leff defines *advancement* in this sense as "a gift, i.e., an expenditure not legally required, made by a parent to or on behalf of a child, with intention that the value thereof be deducted from the amount that the child would otherwise receive if the parent died intestate." Leff, *The Leff Dictionary of Law*, 94 Yale L.J. 1855, 1952 (1985). E.g., "The father had made numerous *advancements* to the son by way of establishing him in life with a college education, by setting him up in business and by buying him an automobile and other items of personal property."

This legal usage is too well entrenched to allow a precisian's attempted "correction" of it: "This use led in turn to the 'hotchpot clause' in deeds and wills, similarly designed to ensure that an *advance* [read *advancement*] inter vivos to one of the class entitled to share in the estate should be brought to account."

advancee is an inaesthetic and unnecessary NEOLOGISM. E.g., "The Code does not state in detail what the writing must contain, although as applied to a writing by the intestate, a statement of an 'intent to advance' would seem necessary and presumably also a description of the property and the name of the *advancee* [read *recipient of the advancement*]." See -EE.

advancement. See **advance.**

adventitious, -titial. *Adventitious* means "added extrinsically" or "accidental." It was formerly a legal term meaning "befalling a person by fortune," and was opposed to *profectitious* (= deriving from a parent or ancestor). These terms are now archaic except in the civil law. *Adventitious* is used today, however, in nonlegal senses, e.g., "His single-minded pursuit of great wealth had the *adventitious* effect of getting his daughter married into the higher aristocracy" (Leff's ex.).

Adventitial is a medical term that means "of or pertaining to a membrane that covers an organ."

ADVERBS, PROBLEMS WITH. A. Placement of Adverbs. A fairly well-known manual on legal style cautions its readers to avoid splitting verb phrases with adverbs, e.g., "He had quickly gone to the scene of the crime," recommending instead, "He quickly had gone to the scene of the crime." This nonsense apparently derives from a phobia of anything resembling a SPLIT INFINITIVE. Here a phobic writer fell into the awkward phrasing: "The task of questioning veniremen and evaluating their answers is more difficult *than anything that heretofore has been attempted* [read *than anything that has heretofore been attempted*] in the process of jury selection."

In fact, as all reputable authorities agree, frequently the most proper and natural placement of an adverb is in the midst of the verb phrase. E.g., "The corporation *was virtually bankrupted* by the massive tort liability."

B. Awkward Adverbs. Adjectives ending in -ly often make slightly cumbersome adverbs, e.g., *sillily, friendlily, uglily,* and so on. One need not be timid in writing or pronouncing such adverbs when they are called for; but if they seem unnatural, one can easily rephrase the sentence, e.g. *in a silly manner.* Words such as *timely* and *stately,* however, act as both adjectives and adverbs.

In any event, unusual adverbs are to be used sparingly. Some writers display an overfondness for them. One judicial opinion, for example, contains the adverbs *corollarily, consideredly,* and the spurious *widespreadedly,* q.v. See *United Medical Laboratories v. Columbia Broadcasting System, Inc.,* 404 F.2d 706 (9th Cir. 1968).

C. Adjectives or Adverbs after Linking Verbs. English contains a number of linking verbs (or copulas) apart from *to be,* e.g. *appear,*

seem, become, look, smell, taste. These verbs connect a descriptive word with the subject; hence the descriptive word following the linking verb describes the subject and not the verb. We say *He turned professional,* not *He turned professionally.*

Legal writers frequently fall into error when they use linking verbs. One must analyze the sentence, rather than memorize a list of common linking verbs, much as this may help. Often an unexpected verb of this kind appears, e.g.: "No other testimonial privilege sweeps so *broadly* [read *sweeps so broad*]." The writer is in effect saying that the privilege *is* broad; he does not really intend to describe a manner of sweeping.

adversary, adj.**; adversarial; adversarious; adversative; adversive; adverse.** *Adversary,* which can act as both noun and adjective, is the legal term used in phrases such as *an adversary relationship.* E.g., "The need to develop all relevant facts in the *adversary* system is both fundamental and comprehensive."

Adversarial is not listed in any dictionary, though it is fairly common in place of the adjective *adversary.* E.g., "Rarely does this type of *adversarial* [read *adversary*] relationship exist between school authorities and pupils." *New Jersey v. T.L.O.,* 469 U.S. 325, 349-50 (1985) (Powell, J., concurring)./ "The evolution of this area of the law has been and will remain a product of the interaction of two *adversarial* forces—prosecutors who seek to exclude all scrupled jurors, and defense counsel eager to retain them." In some contexts, *adversarial* connotes animosity ⟨adversarial conferences⟩, whereas *adversary* is a neutral, clinical word.

Adversarious (= hostile), though listed in the *OED,* has dropped from the language. *Adversative* is a term of grammar and logic meaning "expressing an antithesis or opposition" ⟨adversative conjunction⟩. *Adversive* is an anatomical term for "opposite." For *adverse,* see the next entry. In sum, the only word here discussed that is of much use to lawyers is *adversary. Adversarial* may develop a DIFFERENTIATION in sense that will justify its existence; until that time, it is best avoided.

adversary procedure. See **accusatory.**

adverse; averse. Both may take the preposition *to; adverse* also takes *from.* To be *averse to* something is to have feelings against it. To be *adverse to* something—the phrase is usually used of things and not of people—is to be turned in opposition against it.

Adverse is used as an adjective in the phrase *adverse party* (= opposing party) in reference to persons, but seldom elsewhere. In reference to circumstances, *adverse* means "potentially afflictive or calamitous," but most great triumphs come in the face of adverse conditions.

Adverse(ly) to for *against* is a slight pomposity. E.g., "The court rendered a judgment *adverse to* [read *against*] the plaintiff."/ "Most of the questions raised by this appeal have been disposed of *adversely to* [read *against*] the appellants in the companion case decided this day."

advert; avert. To *advert to* something is to refer to it, to bring it up in speech or writing. It is a word best reserved for contexts that are especially formal, except in BrE, where it is more common. "Finally, I must *advert to* the pain suffered and to be suffered by the appellant as a result of the car accident." (Eng.) (See **allude**.) The word should not be used in its etymological sense "to turn to," as here: "*Before adverting to* [read *Before turning to*] the factual setting, we briefly outline the legal context in which the issue of fraudulent transfer arises."

To *avert* is to turn away or avoid, or to ward off. Thus a national leader might *avert* his eyes from being seen if he had failed *to avert* a political scandal. "The rule *averts* potential diplomatic embarrassment from the courts of one sovereign sitting in judgment over the public acts of another." See **avert.**

advertise; advertize. The former spelling is standard (AmE, BrE).

advisatory. See **advisory.**

advise. A. In Commercial Contexts. Here *advise* takes on a meaning with which laymen are generally unfamiliar. It means "to announce; give formal notice of." E.g., "The letter of credit was *advised* through the Bank of America in Quito, Ecuador." In such contexts, *advise* has very nearly taken on the meaning "to negotiate."

B. For *tell* or *say.* This is a pomposity to be avoided. "I was *advised* by him [read *He told me*] that the deadline had not yet elapsed."/

"The dispatcher returned their call in several minutes but *advised* [read *told*] them that the computer had broken down, and that he could not check the registration."

C. And *instruct.* In G.B., barristers are said to *advise* solicitors (or clients through solicitors), whereas solicitors *instruct* barristers. See **attorney** (A).

advisedly means, not "intentionally," but "after careful consideration."

advisement; advice. Judges frequently take matters *under advisement,* meaning that they will consider and deliberate on a particular question before the court. E.g., "Punishment for contempt is hereby taken *under advisement* by the court." *Advisement* is best not used outside the legal idiom for *advice* or *advising* ⟨the advising of entry-level officers⟩.

adviser, -or. The *-er* spelling is sanctioned over the *-or* spelling in the dictionaries. Note, however, that the adjectival form is *advisory.* See -ER, -OR.

advisory; advisatory. The latter is a NEEDLESS VARIANT of *advisory,* which commonly appears in phrases such as *advisory opinion, advisory capacity,* and *advisory council.*

advocaat is only tenuously connected with legal usage, but interestingly so. It is the Dutch term for *lawyer* that formed the compound word *advocatenborrel* (= lawyer + drink), and that has given its name to an eggnog in Holland supposed to soothe the overworked vocal cords of lawyers. Surely we could all use some from time to time.

advocacy; advocation. The first is the art or work of an advocate; the second was formerly the term in Scots law for an appellate court's review of lower-court decisions. *Advocation* should not be used, although occasionally it is, where *advocacy* will suffice.

advocate; advocator. The latter is a NEEDLESS VARIANT.

advocation. See **advocacy.**

advocatory = of or pertaining to an advocate. Hence it corresponds to *advocacy,* q.v., not *advocation.*

advocatus diaboli is the Latin term for *Devil's advocate.* It is an example of what Fowler termed "polysyllabic humor," and should be used cautiously if at all. Its opposite is *advocatus dei.*

advowson. This archaic legal term, though suggestive of a type of person, refers to a property right, transferable and inheritable in perpetuity, in an ecclesiastical office.

ae is a remnant of the Latin digraph, formerly ligatured (æ), appearing in such words as *aegis, aesthetic,* and *praetor* In most Latinate words in which this digraph once appeared, the initial vowel has been dropped. One sees this tendency still at work in *(a)esthetic, (a)eon,* and *(a)ether.* Compare the retention of the digraphs in BrE (e.g., *anaesthetic* and *foetus*) with the shortened forms *anesthetic* and *fetus,* which are prevalent in AmE. See **pr(a)edial.**

aegis was originally a mythological term meaning "protective shield" or "defensive armor." The word is now used exclusively in figurative senses. One must be careful not to confuse *aegis* with *auspices* (= sponsorship; support). E.g., "Generally, it is required that what has been done regularly under the *aegis* [correct] of the law will be considered valid and will remain so even after a change in legislation." Idiom requires *under the aegis,* not *with the aegis.*

aetiology. See **etiology.**

affect; effect. In ordinary usage, *affect* is always a verb; it means "to influence; to have an effect on." *Effect,* as suggested by its use in that definition, is a noun meaning "result" or "consequence." To *affect* something is to have an *effect* on it. (See **impact.**) As a verb, *effect* is virtually synonymous with *effectuate,* q.v. It means "to bring about; produce."

In the following sentences, *affect* is wrongly used for the noun *effect:* "This argument has been rejected since neither the enactment nor the repeal of guest statutes has had any appreciable *affect* [read *effect*] on premiums."/ "The participants must be afforded maximal protection against harmful side *affects* [read *effects*]."

Likewise, *effect* is sometimes misused for *affect.* See **effect.**

AFFECTATION, LITERARY. See PURPLE PROSE & LITERARY ALLUSION (B).

affected, adj.; **affective; affectional; affectionate.** *Affected,* as an adjective, means "assumed artificially; pretended" (*OED*); *affective* = emotional; *affectional* = pertaining to affection; and *affectionate* = loving, fond.

Just as *affect,* q.v., is sometimes misused for *effect, affective* is sometimes wrongly placed where *effective* belongs: "The parties to the contract would have had to stipulate an *affective* [read *effective*] date." We might prefer to call this a typographical error rather than an ignorant bungle.

affectable, -ible. The former spelling is preferred. See -ABLE (A).

affection; affectation. The former means "love, fondness"; the latter, "pretentious, artificial behavior." In Elizabethan English, these words were used more or less interchangeably, but now each has acquired its own distinct sense—which is good for the language.

Affectation doctrine is sometimes seen for *affects doctrine* in the context of American constitutional law, specifically of the commerce clause. E.g., "*Wickard v. Fillburn* is yet another application of the '*affectation* [read *affects*] doctrine.'" *Affects* is the correct word because the test is whether the activity "affects" commerce. *Effects doctrine* (i.e., "that has effects") would be another possibility, but it has not gained currency. Note that the noun corresponding to *affect* (= to influence) is *effect,* not *affectation.* See **affect & effect.**

affectional, -tionate. See **affected.**

affective. See **affected.**

affeer; amerce. Both words mean generally "to fine." Specifically, *affeer* = to fix the amount of [a fine] (*W3*). The variant spellings *affeere* and *affere* should be avoided. *Amerce* = to fine arbitrarily (*OED*), meaning that the amount of the fine is not prescribed by statute, but rather is lodged in the discretion of the court. Etymologically speaking, when being *amerced* one is "at the mercy" of the court.

The nominal forms are *affeerment* and *amercement*—*amerciament* having gone the way that all NEEDLESS VARIANTS should. *Amerce* has no recorded personal nominal form. *Affee-ror* and *affeerer* are competing forms, the *-or* spelling perhaps the better one because it is more distinctly pronounceable.

affianced. See **affined.**

affiant /ă-fī-ănt/ specifically means "one who gives an affidavit." Broadly, and less accurately, it refers to any deponent.

affidavit. So spelled.

affined; affianced. *Affianced* = engaged, betrothed. *Affined* = closely related; connected. Archaically, *affined* means "obligated."

affinity; consanguinity. The former refers to relationship by marriage, the latter to relationship by blood. The distinction is usually carefully observed in legal writing. E.g., "The statutes prescribe the classes of persons entitled to appointment as administrator and indicate an order of precedence based on kinship by *consanguinity* or *affinity with* the decedent."

Affinity takes the preposition *between* or *with*, not *to* or *for*.

affirm. Usually only judgments are *affirmed* by appellate courts; cases are *remanded*; and opinions or decisions are *approved* or *disapproved*. See JUDGMENTS, APPELLATE-COURT. The practice of writing, "The trial court was *affirmed*," is informally an acceptable ellipsis for "The trial court's judgment was *affirmed*," but such phrasing should not appear in formal legal writing. E.g., "Had the trial judge followed his initial decision and overruled the motion for new trial without expressing any desire for leniency, he would be affirmed [read *his judgment would be affirmed*]."

affirmance; affirmation. There is, unfortunately, some overlap of these terms. Yet a useful rule might be formulated: When an appellate court affirms a lower court's judgment, there is an *affirmance*. In all other contexts, *affirmation* is the preferable term. E.g., "Finally, we refer to the restatement and *affirmation* of the doctrine in *Hood v. Francis*." In the following sentences, *affirmance* is used where *affirmation* would be better: "The long-established recognition in Massachusets of the doctrine of independent significance makes unneces-sary statutory *affirmance* [read *affirmation*] of its application to pour-over trusts."/ "The court held that the instrument was a conveyance and a recognition, acceptance, and *affirmance* [read *affirmation*] of the devise, and not a renunciation."

Here the opposite error appears, *affirmation* for *affirmance*: "After the final decision in *Finney* and the appellate court's *affirmation* [read *affirmance*] of the judgment, the district court determined that the petitioner was not entitled to any relief other than injunctive relief already granted to class members."

Quite apart from its ordinary meaning, *affirmation* has a specialized legal sense: "a formal and solemn declaration, having the same weight and invested with the same responsibilities as an oath, by persons who conscientiously decline taking an oath" (*OED*). Today *affirmation* has the additional sense "a statement by someone who is not required to take an oath, but who nevertheless is subject to the penalties of perjury for lying"; many American jurisdictions now have statutes permitting *affirmations* under circumstances in which it would be inconvenient to obtain the acknowledgment of a notary public. The person *affirming* is termed an *affirmant*. See the next entry.

affirmant; deponent. When one gives evidence by deposition, and swears to the truth of one's testimony, one is termed a *deponent*. When, instead of swearing or taking an oath, one affirms or solemnly asseverates that the testimony is true, one is termed an *affirmant*.

affirmation. See **affirmance.**

affirmative action. As Leff notes, this term has been used in various legal contexts, including the National Labor Relations Act (in which it refers to the power or any steps taken to carry out the purposes of the Act), but its most important use in American legal writing today is in the context of civil rights. See Leff, *The Leff Dictionary of Law* 1855, 1967 (1985). *Affirmative action* today refers to attempts at reversing or mitigating past racial discrimination. The idea it denotes is a controversial one, and the term therefore has positive connotations to some, negative connotations to others.

affirmative, in the; in the negative. These phrases have been criticized as jargonistic and pompous. (See, e.g., Quiller-Couch's statement quoted under JARGONMONGERING.) They appear frequently in legal writing, and in other types of formal prose. E.g., "The sole question raised on this appeal is whether the Texas rule that a defendant must prove duress by a preponderance of the evidence violates the due process clause of the fourteenth amendment; answering *in the negative,* we affirm."/ "The Sixth Circuit, when confronted with the identical question, answered *in the affirmative* and permitted the use of this same deposition against asbestos companies not represented in *DeRocco.*"

This phrasing is probably superior to the closest alternative: "Reversing the judgment of the bankruptcy court, we answer both questions presented 'No.'" In the formal context of judicial opinions, *in the affirmative* and *in the negative* should be allowed to exist peacefully. But when these phrases are used of mundane questions in mundane situations, they look foolish.

affixture; affixation; affixion. *Affixture =* the state of being affixed; *affixation =* the act of affixing or the use of an affix. *Affixion = affixation* or *affixture,* but it adds nothing to either; it should be avoided as a NEEDLESS VARIANT.

afflatus; inflatus. For the sense "inspiration," or "supernatural impulse," *afflatus* is standard term. E.g., "The decisions under the revenue acts have little weight as against legislation under the *afflatus* of the Eighteenth Amendment." (Holmes, J.) *Inflatus* and *afflation* are secondary variants. The plural of *afflatus* is *afflatuses,* not *afflati.*

afflict. See **inflict.**

affluent and *affluence* are accented on the first rather than the second syllable.

afford. See **accord.**

affranchise. See **franchise.**

affray; fray. Both terms, though somewhat quaint, are still used in legal opinions. *Affray* has the precise legal meaning "unpremeditated fighting in a public place that tends to disturb the public peace." It was formerly used more often than it is today.

affreighter. See **charterer.**

affreightment; affretement. The former is standard in common-law countries, and in Louisiana (a civil-law jurisdiction). E.g., "Owners will be more likely to permit their charterers to enter freely into contracts of *affreightment* if owners know that no 'secret liens' will arise from obscure provisions in subagreements." (La.) *Affretement* is the spelling used in French civil law.

affront. See **effrontery.**

aficionado is often misspelled *afficionado,* as in *Butts v. National Collegiate Athletic Association,* 751 F.2d 609, 613 (3d Cir. 1984).

afore (= before) is a dead ARCHAISM except in the phrases *aforesaid* and *aforementioned,* qq.v. Words like *aforedescribed* need not be rescued from oblivion.

aforesaid; aforementioned. These LEGALISMS have little or no justification in modern writing. They are often used unnecessarily where the reference to what has already been named is clear. E.g., "Plaintiff, in the normal routine of his employment, was exposed to various toxic materials and irritants. Exposure *to the aforementioned* [read *to these*] substances and irritants caused him to contract pneumoconiosis, and finally he died of lung cancer caused by his occupational *exposure to the aforementioned* [read *to these*] toxic substances."

Worse yet, *aforesaid* is a word of imprecision. "It may refer to what is next-before, to the next-to-the-next-before, or to everything that has gone before." D. Mellinkoff, *The Language of the Law* 305 (1963). In those contexts in which the reference is intended to be vague, it would be better to use *above-stated,* or some equivalent less stilted and legalistic than *aforesaid.* See FORBIDDEN WORDS & **said.**

The word *aforesaid* is, of course, a past participial combination (*afore + said*) that is almost always used adjectivally (aforesaid land). Occasionally, however, it appears as the past participle of a verb: "The association secretly and with intent to deprive appellant of the opportunity of purchasing said property, and with the intent to profit through the information obtained as *aforesaid,* immediately began to negotiate with the owner for the purchase of said property." The literary quality of that sentence speaks for quality of the participial use of *aforesaid.*

aforethought (= thought of in advance) is now used only in the phrase *malice aforethought.* It is essentially synonymous with *premeditiated* or *prepense.* See POSTPOSITIVE ADJECTIVES, **prepense** & **willfulness.**

a fortiori is an argumentative term meaning "by even greater force of logic." It is used effectively in the following sentences: "If an act is not a civil wrong, it cannot, *a fortiori,* be criminal." (Eng.)/ "If a person who deliberately and advisedly rejects all belief in God and a future state is a competent witness, *a fortiori,* a child who has received no instructions on the subject must be competent also." (Eng.)/ "The courts of this county could not interfere before condemnation; nor, *a fortiori,* can they interfere after condemnation and sale."

Legal writers frequently use *a fortiori* as an adjective as well. Generally, such adjectival usages should be resisted. E.g., "We have set forth the other two lines of possible proof only to suggest the *a fortiori* [read *even stronger*] position presented in the instant case."/ "The *Smith-Bay* court regarded *Flanagan* as being *a fortiori* [read *even more compelling*] on that issue." The emphatic form of the term is *a multo fortiori* (= by far the stronger reason).

Afro-American. See **black.**

after-acquired = obtained after a certain (specified) time. The term is ordinarily placed before the noun it modifies: "The agreement to hold the proceeds of the sale in trust is, in effect, an agreement to hold *after-acquired* personal property in trust."

afterborn = born after (a certain event, such as the father's death or the birth of a sibling). This word is used as both noun and adjective in pretermitted child statutes. As a noun in such a statute, it means "a child born after the execution of a will." *W3* and *OED* hyphenate the word, and contain no nominal entry, but the modern trend is to make it one word capable of acting as a noun.

aftereffect should be spelled as one word.

afterward(s). See **-ward(s).**

against. See **contra, versus** & **as against.**

against conscience is a primarily BrE equivalent of *unconscionable,* q.v. "It is clear that any civilized system of law is bound to provide remedies for cases of what has been called unjust enrichment, that is, to prevent a man from retaining the money of or some benefit derived from another which it is *against conscience* that he should keep." (Eng.)

ag(e)ing. See MUTE E.

agency, as a TERM OF ART, refers to any relationship in which one person acts for another in commercial or business transactions. Laymen are largely unfamiliar with *agency* used in this way, although they understand the personal noun *agent* as meaning "representative."

agenda is (1) the plural form of *agendum,* which means "something to be done" (another, less proper plural of *agendum* being *agendums*); and, more commonly, (2) a singular noun meaning "a list of things to be done" or "a program." The plural of *agenda* in this second sense is *agendas.* Decrying *agendas* as a double plural is footless.

aggrandize; engrandize; ingrandize. The last two are NEEDLESS VARIANTS for the first.

aggravate for *annoy* or *irritate,* though documented as existing since the 1600s, has never gained the cachet of stylists and should be avoided in formal writing. Properly, *aggravate* = to make worse; exacerbate. This meaning obtains in many legal phrases, such as *aggravated assault. Aggravate* in its proper sense is opposed to *mitigate* or *extenuate.* E.g., "Here the indignity was of an *aggravated* sort; it occurred at a public place and in the presence of a large number of people."/ "It is clear that a state cannot explicitly make the murder of a white victim an *aggravating* circumstance in capital sentencing."

Even the brilliant Justice Holmes nodded once, using *aggravate* for *irritate* in one of his letters to Sir Frederick Pollock in 1895: "our two countries *aggravate* each other from time to time. . . ." 1 *Holmes-Pollock Letters* 66 (1941).

aggravated damages. See **punitive damages.**

aggregate, n.; **aggregation.** Both may mean "a mass of discrete things or individuals taken as a whole," *aggregate* being the more usual term. *Aggregate* stresses the notion "taken as a whole" (as in the phrase *in the aggregate*), and *aggregation* more "a mass of discrete things." Here the former term is used: "The price, while of trifling moment to each reader of the newspaper, is sufficient in the *aggregate* to afford compensation for the cost of gathering and distributing the news."

For "the act of aggregating," only *aggregation* will suffice. E.g., "There should not be *aggregation* of two or more obtainings of credit for the purpose of one offense."/ "It is a mass that has grown by *aggregation,* with very little intervention from legislation."

Aggregating is sometimes misused for *totaling* in reference to sums: "Before us, appellant argues that the fines imposed, *aggregating almost $15,000* [read *totaling almost $15,000* or *in the aggregate almost $15,000*] were excessive.

aggrieve (= to bring grief to; to treat unfairly) is now used almost exclusively in legal contexts, and almost always in the form of a past participle. E.g., "An *aggrieved* spouse is not compelled to seek the courts of another state for the protection of her marital status."/ "Suppression of the product of a Fourth Amendment violation can be successfully urged only by those whose rights have been violated by the search itself, not by those who are *aggrieved* solely by the introduction of damaging evidence."

a gratia. See **ex gratia.**

agreation; agrement. The first is a process, and the second is the usual result of the process. *Agreation* = a diplomatic procedure whereby a receiving state makes a prior determination whether a proposed envoy will be acceptable; *agrement* = the approval of a diplomatic representative by the receiving state.

agree. A. And *concur.* In G.B., appellate judges who join in an opinion are said to *agree,* whereas in the U.S. they *concur.*

B. *Agreed to* and *agreed upon.* These are somewhat awkward as adjectival phrases, but when used in direct modification of nouns, they should be hyphenated. E.g., "This clause refers to our previously *agreed-to* verbal contract." (See **verbal.**) / "To the extent that the nonoccurrence of a condition would cause disproportionate forfeiture, a court may excuse the nonoccurrence of that condition unless its occurrence was a material part of the *agreed-upon* exchange."

In a few phrases, *agreed* suffices as an idiomatic ellipsis for *agreed-upon,* as in *agreed verdict,* q.v., and *agreed judgment.* Generally, the entire phrase should appear: "As shown by the charge in the *agreed* [read *agreed-upon*] statement, Jan, at the time of the distribution, is the only child of an only child of a child of Hastings."/ "It cannot be said as a matter of law that their delay for an hour and a quarter was reasonable; the facts as to this are not *agreed* [read *agreed upon*]."

agreed verdict (BrE) = *consent decree* (AmE).

agreement; contract. The former may refer either to an informal arrangement with no consideration (e.g., a "gentlemen's agreement") or to a formal legal arrangement supported by consideration. *Contract* is used only in this second sense. The distinction applies also with the verbs *agree* and *contract.* The intended sense of *agree(ment)* is usually clear from the context.

AGREEMENT, GRAMMATICAL. See CONCORD.

agree with; agree to; agree on. *Agree with* means "to be in accord with (another)"; *agree to,* "to acquiesce in (usu. the performance or specifications of something)." *Agree on* refers to the subject of the agreement: One agrees *with* someone *on* a certain settlement. E.g., "Plaintiff *agreed with* defendant *on* the contractual provisions relating to time of delivery."

agrement. See **agreation.**

agricultur(al)ist. The shorter form is preferred: *agriculturist.* Actually, *farmer* is even better if it applies.

ahold and its variant *aholt* are dialectal. They might perhaps be justified in bizarre contexts such as this: "Plaintiff, driving her car, suddenly becomes convinced that God is taking *ahold* of the steering wheel."

-aholic; -aholism. Speakers and writers should avoid indiscriminately appending these newfangled "suffixes" to words to indicate various addictions. Each time this is done, a MORPHOLOGICAL DEFORMITY is created.

aid and abet. This phrase is a well-known legal DOUBLET that, like most doublets, has come down to us from the Middle Ages and Renaissance, when it was common to embellish terms with synonyms. Singly, *aid* is the more general term, *abet* generally appearing only in contexts involving criminal intent. *Aid and abet* is not a needless REDUNDANCY, as many suppose; it is a TERM OF ART meaning "to assist the perpetrator of the crime while sharing in the requisite intent." *United States v. Martinez,* 555 F.2d 1269, 1271 (5th Cir. 1977). It is still used in both the U.S. and G.B. Here it appears in the agent-noun form: "The appellant now makes the further claim that the complaint charged the defendant as an original instigator only, and that he cannot be held liable thereunder as an *aider and abettor.*"/ "The court stated that it had found no other case discussing whether a nonparty *aider and abettor* is subject to the court's jurisdiction." See **abettor.**

Sometimes it is turned into a triplet: "The further contention of the appellant is that defendant's acts are insufficient to support the trial court's conclusions that he knowingly *aided, abetted, and assisted* in the prosecution of false charges against defendant, and adopted them as his own." The phrase *aided and abetted* is quite sufficient; *assisted* is superfluous.

aid(e)-de-camp (= military aide) is borrowed from the French and should retain the Gallicized spelling—*aide*—especially considering that *aide* is itself now an English word (meaning "a staff member under one's authority"). The plural is *aides-de-camp.*

airworthy is used in reference to aircraft, and means "fit for operation in the air" (*W3*). The word, surprisingly enough first used in 1829, was analogized from *seaworthy,* q.v.

aitiology. See **etiology.**

alas; alack. *Alas* should express woe caused by a lamentable state of affairs. Here, in a quotation from a journal entitled *Ethnicity,* it is nonsensical: "There have been a number of meetings around the land about ethnicity (the phenomenon, *alas,* not this journal)." The writer would hardly bemoan the increasing attention given to ethnicity as an academic subject, even if he were editor of the journal. He means, perhaps, to include a witty parenthesis such as *to be sure.*

Alack is archaic; *alas and alack* is a tiresome CLICHÉ.

al barre. See **at (the) bar.**

albeit. This conjunction, though pronounced archaic by Eric Partridge (the British lexicographer), thrives in AmE, both legal and nonlegal; and it still appears in BrE, esp. in legal writing. The *COD* labels it "literary." *Albeit* means "though" and introduces concessive phrases and sometimes subordinate clauses. *Howbeit,* in contrast, means "nevertheless" and begins principal clauses.

A. Introducing Phrases. The predominant modern use is for *albeit* to introduce concessive phrases: "The parties addressed the issue, *albeit* in fairly leisurely fashion."/ "Petitioner located employment in 1978, *albeit* at a lower wage than he earned working for the respondents."

B. Introducing Clauses. *Albeit* may begin a clause, albeit *although* is more common in this context: "The fifty-five mile-an-hour speed limit has its benefits; it also has its costs, *albeit* they may not seem apparent because a majority is willing to pay them."/ "When the relevant credit extends to £10, that is the moment at which the offense is committed, *albeit* it may be by aggregating a series of smaller sums." (Eng.)/ "We think that we have for review a decision on a stipulated record, *albeit* the matter was styled as a determination on motions for summary judgment."

C. For *even if.* Archaically, *albeit* is sometimes used for *even if* in beginning a clause: "Separate and distinct false declarations that require different factual proof of falsity may properly be charged in separate counts, *albeit* [read *even if*] they are all related and arise out of the same transaction or subject matter." This use of the term is to be discouraged.

aleatory; stochastic; fortuitous. These words have similar but distinct meanings. *Aleatory* = depending on uncertain contingencies ⟨contingent remainders are aleatory⟩. E.g., "We will respect the *aleatory* nature of the settlement process, whether any of the parties are ultimately found to have made a favorable settlement."

Stochastic = random. *Fortuitous, q.v.,* = accidental, occurring by chance. See **fortuitous.** Cf. **adventitious.**

alias is both adverb (= otherwise [called or named]), as an elliptical form of *alias dictus,* and noun (= an assumed name), today usually the latter. *Alias* refers only to names, and should not be used synonymously with *guise* (= assumed appearance, pretense).

alibi. A. As a Noun for *excuse.* The words are not synonymous, although the confusion that has grown out of their meanings is understandable. *Alibi* is a specific legal term referring to the defense of having been at a place other than the scene of a crime. By SLIP-SHOD EXTENSION it has come to be used for any excuse or explanation for misconduct, usually that shifts blame to someone else.

The Evanses wrote of this term: "Cynicism and the common man's distrust of the law have tinged *alibi* with a suggestion of improbability and even of dishonesty. Purists insist that it should be restricted to its legal meaning, and those who wish to be formally correct will so restrict it. In so doing, however, they will lose the connotation of cunning and dishonesty which distinguishes it from *excuse.*" B. Evans & C. Evans, *Contemporary American Usage* 24 (1957). Lawyers perhaps more than others ought to "wish to be formally correct."

B. As an Adverb. In recent years *alibi* has been used as an adverb (meaning "elsewhere" ⟨he proved himself *alibi*⟩), but this usage should be eschewed. Although "elsewhere" is the original Latin meaning of *alibi* (originally a locative of L. *alius* "other"), in English it has long served only as a noun, and it is an affectation to hark back to the classical sense.

C. As a Verb. Nor should *alibi* be used as a verb, as it is in the following sentences. The first is doubly bad, for the misbegotten verb is based on the misused noun: "The party cannot *alibi* [i.e., excuse] losses in the election."/

"The defendants *alibied themselves* [i.e., exculpated themselves by proving that they were not at the scene of the crime] and accused other men."/ "The conspirators attempted to *alibi* one another." The *O.E.D. Supp.* records this usage from 1909 and labels it colloquial.

alien, adj., takes the preposition *from* or, more commonly, *to.* For purposes of DIFFERENTIATION, "there is perhaps a slight preference for *from* where mere separation is meant (*We are entangling ourselves in matters alien from our subject*), and for *to* when repugnance is suggested (*cruelty is alien to his nature*)" (*MEU2* 17).

alien, v.t.; **alienate; abalienate.** When we talk about property changing hands, the best choice of verb is *convey* or *transfer* rather than any of these legalistic words. But if some form of *alien-* must be used, the most common and therefore the best word in all senses is *alienate,* whether one writes about alienation of property or of affections. The layman may understand that in certain contexts *alienate* means "to transfer (as property)"; he has little chance of understanding *alien* in such a context—much less *abalienate* (a NEEDLESS VARIANT from the civil law). E.g., "Since property owned by tenants by the entireties is not subject to the debts of either spouse, they may *alien* [read *alienate*] it without infringing the rights of their individual creditors."/ "The rule of common law is that a man cannot attach to a grant or transfer of property, otherwise absolute, the condition that it shall not be *alienated.*" *Aliene* is an archaic variant spelling of the verb *alien.*

Alienate frequently takes on the lay sense in legal writing, as in the phrase *alienation of affections,* or as here: "This false statement was designed to *alienate* supporters of plaintiff and to affiliate them with the other candidate."

alienee (= one to whom ownership of property is transferred) is an unnecessary, and unnecessarily obscure, equivalent of *grantee.* See the quotation in the following entry.

alienor; alienist. *Alienor* (= one who transfers property) is equivalent to *grantor;* it should be avoided where *grantor* or *transferor* will serve: "Conveying lands by means of a fictitious or collusive suit, commenced by arrangement by the intended *alienee* [read *grantee* or *recipient*] against the *alienor* [read *grantor*]" (quoted in *OED*).

Alienist is an obsolescent term for *psychiatrist*. E.g., "The only witness testifying that the testator was incompetent was an *alienist* who had never seen him and the testator's divorced wife who had not seen him in two years."

alimony. See **palimony.**

alio intuitu is not a justified LATINISM, with so many more precise alternatives such as *from a different point of view* or *with respect to another case (or condition)*. E.g., "Counsel urges us to reject all observations to the contrary in the other authorities as made *alio intuitu* [read *under different circumstances*] on the strength of admissions." (Eng.).

aliquot; aliquant. *Aliquant* = being a part of a number or quantity but not dividing it without leaving a remainder ⟨4 is an *aliquant* part of 17⟩ (*W3*); *aliquot* = contained an exact number of times in something else ⟨4 is an *aliquot* part of 16⟩ (*id.*).

These are technical terms generally best left to technical contexts. *Aliquot* adds nothing to this sentence: "Compromises are contracts of settlement, and the compromise of one *aliquot* part of a single liability and payment of the balance in full is a settlement of all parts of such single liability."

One justified technical use of these terms occurs in the field of trusts, where payment of an *aliquot* or *aliquant* part of the consideration for transfer of legal title may determine whether the presumption of a resulting trust will arise. When a payor's contributions for the purchase of property in another's name are *aliquot* parts of the purchase price, some courts presume the contributions to be a gift or loan; when, however, these contributions are *aliquant* parts of the purchase price, the presumption does not arise. See *Restatement (Second) of Trusts* § 454 comment c (1959). This distinction may be obsolescent; the *Restatement* rejects it in comment b to section 454.

The term *aliquot* is also used in determining whether a gift of property in a will is a specific or a general legacy: "A gift of all, or an *aliquot* part, of the testator's estate is a general legacy."/ "In the absence of a clearly expressed intention of the testator to the contrary, a bequest of all the testator's personal property, an *aliquot* portion or the remainder thereof, or any bequest in similar general terms, is a general and not a specific legacy." See **legacy.**

aliunde (= from another source, from elsewhere) is a LATINISM peculiar to legal contexts. For example, *evidence aliunde* = evidence from outside (an instrument, e.g.), extraneous evidence. Today the word has little justification in place of an English equivalent. E.g., "It is said that the authorities cited for the plaintiff clearly establish that if the defendant, without having any lawful right, or by a right or threat *aliunde* [read *outside*] the exercise of a lawful right, had maliciously broken up the contractual relation existing between the plaintiff and Libersont, the party damaged could have maintained an action against the defendant therefor."

ALJ; A.L.J.; a.l.j. The usual abbreviation for *administrative law judge* is *ALJ* (without periods).

all. **A.** *All (of).* The more formal construction is to omit *of* and write, when possible, "*All* the arguments foundered." E.g., "Appellant was to guarantee unconditionally appellee's performance under the purchase agreement, including *all* appellee's obligations and liabilities." When the phrase is followed by a pronoun, *all of* is the only idiomatic choice ⟨*all of them*, not *all them*⟩. Before general nouns, *all of* is more common in AmE than in BrE; nevertheless, it should generally be avoided in formal writing. Rarely, *all of* reads better than *all* even where a pronoun does not follow: "All of John's property was therefore subject to the IRS lien."

B. With Negatives. *Not all* is usually the correct sequence in negative constructions. "It seems that *all* things were *not* going well in Wheeler's own unit." This expanded version of the idiomatic "All is not well" does not work. [Read either *It seems that not all things were going well* or, better, *It seems that all was not well.*]/ "*All* writers did *not* [read *Not all writers*] accept Coke's dictum; some still cling to it as historical fact without even his qualification 'most commonly.'" (D. Mellinkoff)

C. And *any. All* follows a superlative adjective; *any* follows a comparative adjective.

Constructions such as *more . . . than all* are illogical. See OVERSTATEMENT.

all and singular is a collective equivalent of *each and every.* It is almost always unnecessary.

all deliberate speed. See **with all deliberate speed.**

allegation; allegement; allegatum. The second and third forms are NEEDLESS VARIANTS to be eschewed.

allegator = one who alleges. It is not often used, even in legal writing, perhaps because of its jocular suggestiveness of *alligator.*

allegatum. See **allegation.**

allege; contend. To *allege* is formally to state a matter of fact as being true or provable, without yet having proved it. The word once denoted stating under oath, but this meaning no longer applies. To *contend,* in the advocatory sense, means "to state one's position in a polemical way, to submit." (In its popular sense, *contend* means "to strive against.")

Allege should not be used as a synonym of *assert, maintain, declare,* or *claim. Allege* has peculiarly accusatory connotations. One need not allege only the commission of crimes; but certainly the acts alleged must concern misfeasances or negligence.

allegeable; allegible. *Allegeable* is the only recognized form of the word.

allegedly does not mean "in an alleged manner," as it would if the adverb had been formed as English adverbs generally are. Follett considered adverbs like this one ugly and unjustified (esp. *reportedly*). Yet *allegedly* is a convenient space- and time-saver for *it is alleged that* or *according to the allegations.* Though not logically formed, *allegedly* is well established and unobjectionable, if used in moderation. See **reportedly.**

allegement. See **allegation.**

allegible. See **allegeable.**

aller sans jour. See LOAN TRANSACTIONS.

all fours. See **on all fours.**

allide; collide. The former is used only in a special context in reference to ships in admiralty law. When two ships *allide,* one of them is stationary; ships *collide* when both are moving before impact. *Black's* notes that the distinction is not carefully observed. See **collision.**

allision. See **collision.**

ALLITERATION, UNDUE. Repetition of sounds, especially excessive sibilance (too many *-s-* sounds, as in that very phrase) can easily distract the reader. Though alliteration is especially common with *-s-,* other unconscious repetitions of sound may occur. In the following sentence (Uniform Probate Code 2-104), three words in a five-word phrase rhyme: "This section is not to be applied where its application would result in a taking of intestate estate by the state." [Read *This section does not apply where its application would result in the escheat of an intestate estate.*] Although one can avoid use of *state, intestate estate* is well-nigh unavoidable. (The English Parliament enacted the Intestates' Estate Act, 15 & 16 Geo. VI & 1 Eliz. II, c. 64 (1952).) Sometimes one wishes that we could make use of the terms *willed* and *unwilled* rather than *testate* and *intestate:* "It is familiar law that the will is the source of the beneficiaries' title in the case of *testate estates,* while in *intestate estates* the source of title is the statute."

The best way to avoid the infelicity of undue alliteration is to read one's prose aloud when editing. See SOUND OF PROSE, THE.

allocatee. See -EE.

allocator; allocatur. *Allocator* = one who allocates. *Allocatur* (lit., "it is allowed") in former practice meant "a certificate duly given at the end of an action, allowing costs" (*OED*).

allocute (= to deliver an allocution, q.v.) is a BACK-FORMATION from the noun *allocution.* Although some years ago the verb might have been viewed as a barbarous MORPHOLOGICAL DEFORMITY, just as *electrocute* once was, we should accept *allocute* as a useful addition to legal language. E.g., "The appellants assert that the district court erroneously found that it had no cause to *allocute.*"

Because *allocution,* q.v., most properly refers to the court's and not to the criminal defendant's address, it is the court that *allocutes;* this distinction has has given way to SLIPSHOD EXTENSION, however: "The trial judge denied the defendant the opportunity *to allocute.*"

allocution; allocutus. *Allocution* is inadequately defined by the major dictionaries (usu. some variation on "a formal address"). In modern legal usage, the word refers to the requirement that the trial judge in a criminal case address the defendant asking the latter to speak in mitigation of the sentence to be imposed. By transference, the word has come to denote the accused person's speech in mitigation of the sentence, rather than the judge's address asking the accused to speak. E.g., "The contention of this federal habeas corpus petitioner that he was not accorded his right of *allocution* in state court fails to raise a federal question." *Allocutus* is a NEEDLESS VARIANT and an unnecessary LATINISM. See **elocution.**

al(l)odium, -ial. *Black's* and the *OED* list *allodium* (= land held in fee simple absolute) as standard, *alodium* as a variant; *W3's* listing is the opposite. Both forms may lay claim to etymological precedent. *Allodium* seems to be the more common and, because unanimity is desirable on this point, should be used to the exclusion of its single-elled counterpart. The plural is generally *allodia.*

Alodian is an erroneous form of *allodial,* the proper adjective.

all of. See **all** (A).

allograph; autograph. An *allograph* is an agent's writing or signature for the principal. An *autograph,* of course, is one's own signature.

allow; permit. These words have an important connotative difference. *Allow* suggests merely the absence of opposition, or refraining from an absolute proscription. *Permit,* in contrast, suggests affirmative sanction or approval.

In British texts, *allow,* when used in reference to appeals, means "to sustain (for the appellant)." E.g., "For these reasons I think the judgment of the court below was wrong and that this appeal should be *allowed.*" (Eng.)

allowable, though structurally an adjective, often functions as a noun in legal contexts. As a noun it refers to the amount of oil or gas that an operator is allowed to extract from a well or field in one day, under proration orders of a state regulatory commission. E.g., "A well bottomed in this sand had an *allowable* that would enable it to recover an amount of oil and gas in excess of the tract's fair share of production from both reservoirs." See ADJECTIVES (B).

all ready. See **already.**

all right; alright. *Alright* for *all right* has never been accepted as standard, and probably never will be. Although the phrase is considered unitary, the one-word spelling has not been recognized "perhaps because the expression remains largely an informal one" (*Oxford Guide*).

all together. See **altogether.**

allude. **A.** And *advert* & *refer.* To *allude* is to refer to (something) indirectly or by suggestion only. To *advert* or *refer* is to bring up directly, *advert,* q.v., being the more FORMAL WORD. *Allude* is commonly misused for *refer;* the indirect nature of *allusion* is an important element of the word's sense. E.g., "In a work purporting to discuss the ethical side of practice, a passing *allusion* [read *reference*] to the subject seems eminently proper if not necessary."/ "As the above notice contained an *allusion* to the plaintiff, and also statements that he considered were calculated to damage his character and the credit of his firm, a solicitor was consulted, and a letter was written by him to the defendants, protesting against the plaintiff's name being used as intended in the advertisement." (Eng.) (Here the final phrase reveals that the name was actually mentioned: that the publication contained a *reference,* not an *allusion,* to the plaintiff.) In the following sentence the writer creates an OXYMORON: "There being no words expressly *alluding* [read *referring*] to that contingency, the court is to cure the defect by implication."

B. And *illude* & *elude.* For *allude,* see (A) of this entry. To *illude* is to deceive with an illusion; to *elude* is to avoid or escape. Here *elude* is misused for *allude,* a startling blunder: "That is the reason for the problem the dean was *eluding* to [read *alluding to*]."

C. For *suggest.* This is an attenuated use of *allude* to be avoided. "Appellants attempt to *allude* [read *suggest*] that their assistance in evading Iranian currency controls and that rebating money to appellee in American money was a major service that takes the contract outside the purview of the U.C.C."

ALLUSION. See LITERARY ALLUSION.

allusive, -sory. *Allusive* is standard.

alluvio(n); alluvium. In the strictest sense, *alluvion* means "the flow or wash of water against a riverbank," and *alluvium* "a deposit of soil, clay, or the lack of such a deposit caused by an alluvion." *Alluvion* has come, however, to be used for *alluvium*—a regrettable development, for the DIFFERENTIATION is worth preserving. *Alluvio* is the Roman-law term for *alluvion*.

The plural forms of the English terms are *alluvions* and *alluviums* (or, less good, *alluvia*). See PLURALS. The adjective for *alluvium* is *alluvial, alluvious* and *alluvian* being NEEDLESS VARIANTS. *Alluvion* has no clear-cut adjective; it should act as its own adjective.

ally. As a noun, the accent is on the first syllable; as a verb, on the second.

almoi(g)n. See **frankalmoi(g)n(e).**

alodian. See **al(l)odium.**

alongside of for *alongside.* The word *alongside,* as a preposition, means "at the side of." Hence, one car is parked alongside another, logs are stacked alongside one another. It is unnecessary to write *alongside of.*

already; all ready. *Already* has to do with time ⟨finished already⟩, and *all ready* with preparation ⟨we are all ready⟩.

alright. See **all right.**

also. See **too** (A).

alterative; alterant. Both words may act as noun and adjective. As adjectives, they both mean "causing alteration." As nouns, however, the meanings diverge. An *alterant* is "anything that alters or modifies." *Alterative* is a term used in medical contexts—though rarely now by physicians—meaning "a medicine that gradually changes unhealthy bodily conditions into healthy ones."

altercation. This word refers to "a noisy brawl or dispute," not rising to the serious-ness of physical violence. Here the word is almost certainly misused for *fight* in the physical sense: "While serving a term of imprisonment in a North Carolina penitentiary, the respondent Perry became involved in an *altercation* with another inmate; a warrant issued, charging Perry with the misdemeanor of assault with a deadly weapon." Leff ill-advisedly wrote that "coming to . . . blows is not totally excluded from the ambit of this term," and used it for a physical affray in his entry on *aggressor.* Leff, *The Leff Dictionary of Law,* 94 Yale L.J. 1855, 2003, 1981 (1985). For authority limiting the term to the sense "wordy strife," see the *OED, W2, W3,* and Partridge, *Usage and Abusage* 27 (1973).

alter ego (lit., "other I") = a second self. To laymen, it means "a kindred spirit" or "a constant companion." To American lawyers it has a special meaning in the corporate context: "a corporation used by an individual in conducting his own personal business, such that a court may impose personal liability (by piercing the corporate veil, q.v.) when fraud has been perpetrated on third persons dealing with the corporation." The phrase should not be hyphenated.

alternate; alternative. A. As Nouns. An *alternative* is a choice or option—usually one of two choices, but not necessarily. It has been argued by etymological purists that the word (fr. L. *alter* "the other of two") should be confined to contexts involving but two choices; Fowler termed this contention a fetish, and it has little or no support among other stylistic experts or in actual usage. E.g., "None of the *three alternatives* pretends to show the sequence of transactions."/ "The defendant is directed to provide to the court within fourteen days in affidavit form information concerning *three alternatives.*"

Indeed, *alternative* carries with it two nuances absent from the near-synonym *choice.* First, *alternative* may suggest adequacy for some purpose ⟨ample alternative channels⟩; and second, it may suggest compulsion to choose ⟨the alternatives are liberty and death⟩.

Alternate, n., means: (1) "something that proceeds by turns with another"; and (2) "one who substitutes for another." It is helpful to understand that *alternative* is called upon for use far more frequently than *alternate.*

B. As Adjectives. *Alternative* = mutually

exclusive; available in place of another (*COD*). E.g., "Nevertheless, if he has failed to show an unlawful conspiracy and monopoly, he has under his *alternative* demand shown a cause of action to recover damages from either or both of the defendants."

Alternate = (1) coming each after one of the other kind, every second one; or (2) substitute. This sentence illustrates sense (1) of *alternate*: "The examination may be made either by one person reading both the original and the copy, or by two persons, one reading the original and the other the copy, and it is not necessary (except in peerage cases) that each should *alternately* read both." (Eng.) Here sense (2) of *alternate* applies: "Statutes providing for *alternate* jurors to sit on a case so that they can substitute for jurors ceasing to sit on the case sometimes provide for additional peremptory challenges with respect to such jurors."/ "Thereafter, the testator decided he did not wish to nominate this *alternate* executor."

In the following sentences *alternate* is misused for *alternative*, a common mistake, perhaps understandable because of the close sense (2) of *alternate*: "Nor does it appear likely that further conversations would have convinced counsel to pursue *alternate* [read *alternative*] defenses [i.e., defenses available in place of the primary defense pleaded]."/ "Appellant based his claim on *alternate* [read *alternative*] theories."/ "The court permitted a damage action there despite the existence of the *alternate* [read *alternative*] remedy."

The notion that an *alternative* is one of two choices is strongly enough rooted that *two alternatives* usually seems redundant: "Where a trust instrument contains *two alternative conditions* [read *contains alternative conditions*], of which the first might be too remote and the second, which actually occurs, is not too remote, the rule is not violated." At all events, because *alternative* suggests mutual exclusivity when referring to two objects, *either* is redundant when used in proximity: "A search of the record in this case establishes a likely absence of complete diversity between the parties *on either of two alternative theories* [read *on either of two theories* or *on alternative theories*]."

although; though. As conjunctions, the words are virtually interchangeable. The only distinction is that *although* is more formal and dignified, *though* more usual in speech and familiar writing. In certain formal contexts, however, *though* reads better. *Though* serves also as an adverb ⟨He stated as much, though⟩.

Tho and *altho* are old-fashioned truncated spellings that were at one time very common, but failed to become standard. They should be avoided.

although . . . yet was formerly a common construction; these two words were once considered CORRELATIVE CONJUNCTIONS. Today the construction is seen only in the most formal contexts: "*Although* the relation of parent and child subsists, *yet* if the child is incapable of performing any services, the foundation of the action fails." (Eng.) In most modern contexts, either conjunction will suffice to give the same meaning as if both were used.

altogether; all together. *Altogether* = completely; wholly. "Such appeals are *altogether* frivolous." *All together* = at one place or at the same time. "The defendants were tried all together."

alumni; alumnae; alumnor. The first, strictly speaking, refers to male graduates; the singular form is *alumnus*. The second refers to female graduates, the singular being *alumna*. Nowadays, however, *alumni* refers to males and females alike. The same is not true, however, of *alumnae*, which can refer only to women. "Throughout its history, the Securities and Exchange Commission has attracted lawyers of the highest quality; among its *alumnae* [read *alumni*], for example, are Mr. Justice William Douglas, Judge Gerhard Gesell, Professor Louis Loss, and Professor Homer Kripke." This statement might come as a surprise to the illustrious persons mentioned.

A more common mistake than confusing the gender of these words is confusing their NUMBER, as by using *alumni* or *alumnae* as a singular. That these are plural forms of *alumnus* and *alumna* should be apparent to anyone with even the faintest familiarity with Latin.

An *alumnor* is one employed to work with or at an ex-students' association. The word is a MORPHOLOGICAL DEFORMITY, because the *-or* suffix should generally be appended to a verb, and *alumn* is no verb.

alumnus. This term is obsolete as a LEGALISM for *foster-child*; today it means only "a graduate."

a.m., A.M.; p.m., P.M. It does not matter whether capitals or lowercase letters are used, as long as a document is consistent throughout. The lowercase letters are now more common. The phrases for which these abbreviations stand are *ante meridiem* and *post meridiem,* not *meridian.* Periods are preferred in these abbreviations.

amalgam; amalgamation. Some DIFFERENTIATION is possible. *Amalgam,* the older term, means "a combination." *Amalgamation* means primarily "the act of combining or uniting; consolidation" ⟨effecting an amalgamation of the companies⟩. *Amalgamation* is best avoided in the sense given to *amalgam.* "This decision is authority for the view that the beneficiary can assert his equitable title on any part of the *amalgam,* whether it is in the account or has been changed into an investment or in any other identifiable form." (Eng.)

ambassador; embassador. The former is the preferred spelling. See **embassy.**

ambiance. See **ambience.**

ambidexter. See LAWYER, DEROGATORY NAMES FOR.

ambience; ambiance. The first form, the English form, is preferable. The latter is a Frenchified affectation that has become a VOGUE WORD. See **ambit.**

AMBIGUITY, despite what many lawyers seem to believe, inheres in all writing. Even the most tediously detailed documents that attempt to dispel all uncertainties contain ambiguities; indeed, usually the more voluminous the writing, the more voluminous the ambiguities. See MYTH OF PRECISION. Nevertheless, we must strive to rid our writing of ambiguities that might give rise to misreadings. DRAFTING especially is a constant battle against ambiguity, "a battle that can never be entirely won." R. Goldfarb & J. Raymond, *Clear Understandings* 21 (1982).

The war against ambiguity should not be waged by overwriting and attempts at hyperprecision through exhaustive specificity. Rather, the legal writer should work on developing a concise, lean, and straightforward writing style, along with a sensitivity to words and their meanings. Once a writer has

acquired such a style, ambiguities tend to become more noticeable, and therefore easier to correct. At the same time, an increased linguistic sensitivity allows one to see ambiguities in what might previously have seemed a model of clarity.

What exactly *is* an ambiguity? William Empson, the greatest expounder of ambiguity, has defined it as "any verbal nuance, however slight, which gives room for alternative reactions to the same piece of language." W. Empson, *Seven Types of Ambiguity* 19 (1930; Penguin ed. 1977). *Ambiguity* is to be distinguished from *vagueness:*

> It is unfortunate that many lawyers persist in using the word *ambiguity* to include vagueness. To subsume both concepts under the same name tends to imply that there is no difference between them or that their differences are legally unimportant. Ambiguity is a disease of language, whereas vagueness, which is sometimes a disease, is often a positive benefit. . . . Whereas *ambiguity* in its classical sense refers to equivocation, *vagueness* refers to the degree to which, independently of equivocation, language is uncertain in its respective applications to a number of particulars. Whereas the uncertainty of ambiguity is central, with an 'either-or' challenge, the uncertainty of vagueness lies in marginal questions of degree.
>
> R. Dickerson, *The Interpretation of Statutes* 48–49 (1975).

Dickerson, of course, discusses ambiguity from the vantage of the legal drafter rather than that of the poet; for the latter, ambiguity is hardly "a disease of language." As Empson has so well demonstrated, in literature it is often "a positive benefit."

Following are some examples of the more common types of ambiguity in legal writing. Some of these are equivocal only in a technical (or stickler's) sense (i.e., are patent ambiguities); others create real dilemmas in meaning (i.e., are latent ambiguities); either way, these ambiguities detract from the context in which they appear.

A. Uncertain Stress. "Even if a merchant sells a product, if he was not engaged in selling that particular product in the normal course of business, he may not be held liable." Read the sentence once stressing *may,* the next time stressing *not* in the final clause. Rewording the sentence eliminates the ambiguity. Assuming the writer meant to say that the merchant is immune from liability (and not that he *might* or *may* be immune), he might better have written: *he cannot be held liable* (see **can**) or *he is not subject to liability.* See **may**.

B. Syntax. The ordering of sentence-parts is basic to clarity. When phrases are arranged with little reflection, ambiguities are certain to arise.

1. Verbal Correspondence. "The parties shall make every reasonable effort to agree on and have prepared as quickly as possible a contract. . . ." Should the sentence read "to have prepared"? Does *have* correspond syntactically to *shall,* to *make,* or to *agree*? The three possible meanings vary substantially.

"The artificial entity may sue or be sued as though it were a person, it pays taxes, it may apply for business licenses in its own name, it may have its own bank account, it may have its own seal, and so forth." All the *its* in this sentence have the antecedent *entity.* Yet, because of the placement of the first *it,* one is led to believe that the later ones will have a parallel structure ("as though it were a person, as though it pays taxes, as though it may apply. . . ."). Thus the reader is syntactically sidetracked for a moment until he can get his train of thought back on the writer's tracks.

2. Poorly Placed Modifiers. "No well shall be drilled within two-hundred feet of any residence or barn now on said land without lessor's consent."—No well may be drilled without the lessor's consent? (This, obviously, is the intended meaning.) Or is it that the barn must be on the lessor's land without his consent?/ "The court concluded that literacy tests had abridged the right to vote on account of race or color." The right to vote on account of race or color was abridged? No: the right to vote was abridged on account of race or color.

NOUN PLAGUE exemplifies one type of poorly placed modifiers. For example, *alimentary canal smuggling* was intended by the United States Supreme Court to mean "smuggling contraband goods by concealing them temporarily in one's gut." But the phrase suggests "the smuggling of alimentary canals." E.g., "A divided panel . . . reversed [defendant's] convictions, holding that her detention violated the Fourth Amendment . . . because the customs inspectors did not have a 'clear indication' of *alimentary canal smuggling* at the time she was detained." *United States v. Montoya de Hernandez,* 473 U.S. 531, 533 (1985).

These problems are remedied easily enough by thoughtful attention to one's prose, and by editing and revising with the realization that the legal writer harms only himself when he burdens his reader with these dilemmas in meaning. The draftsman who commits these sins does his client a disservice, unless, of course, that client enjoys litigation for the sake of litigation.

ambit; ambience. The former means "scope," the latter "the immediate environment; atmosphere." Here the former is correctly used: "Yet this very narrow *ambit* of judicial review does not release us from our responsibility to scrutinize the record in its entirety to determine whether substantial evidence does support the Secretary's findings." See **ambience.**

ambulance chaser. See LAWYERS, DEROGATORY NAMES FOR.

ambulatory (lit., "able to walk") has the special sense in the law of wills "taking effect not from when [the will] was made but from the death of the testator" (*CDL*), or "capable of being revised." A will is *ambulatory* because it is revocable until the testator's death. E.g., "The holding of the chancery court was based on the proposition that a will is *ambulatory,* speaks only at the death of the maker, and the 1955 will having been destroyed in the lifetime of the testatrix, it never had the effect of revoking the 1954 will."

ameliorate; meliorate. *Ameliorate* is the standard term meaning "to make or become better." E.g., "These anomalies appear sufficiently enmeshed in the current tangled web of jurisprudence on this subject to be beyond *amelioration* by a panel of this court."/ "Society's view of land as a commercial asset plays an important part in the law of *ameliorative* waste." *Meliorate* is a NEEDLESS VARIANT.

It is incorrect to use *ameliorate* as if it meant "to lessen": "The First, Second, and Eleventh Circuits found that any resort to Iranian courts to recover the movants' monetary losses, should the preliminary injunction be denied, would be futile and that the Iran-United States Claims Tribunal did not *ameliorate* [read *lessen*] the likelihood of irreparable injury."

amenability; amenity. These words, of unrelated origin, are occasionally confused.

Amenability = legal answerability; liability to being brought to judgment ⟨amenability to the jurisdiction of the foreign forum⟩. *Amenability* takes the preposition *to*. E.g., "Appellant makes passing reference to the tripartite test for personal jurisdiction, but chose not to address the issue of its *amenability to* suit under the Mississippi long-arm statute."

Amenity = (1) agreeableness; (2) something that is comfortable or convenient; or (3) a convenient social convention. Here the word is almost certainly misused: "Fiat moved to dismiss the action against it for lack of personal jurisdiction, arguing that it was . . . *not susceptible to the amenities of a Massachusetts forum* [read *not amenable to the Massachusetts forum*]."

amend; emend. Both derive from the Latin verb *emendare* (= to free from fault). *Amend* = (1) to put right, change; or (2) to add to, supplement. This is the general word; the other is more specialized. *Emend* = to correct (as a text).

Amend out has been used to mean "to excise." E.g., "This provision, essentially the same as that in the Senate bill, was *amended out* on the House floor." *Taken out, cut out,* or *excised* would have been more felicitous. See PARTICLES, UNNECESSARY & **out.**

The nominal forms of *amend* and *emend* are *amendment* and *emendation.*

amenity. See **amenability.**

a mensa et thoro (lit., "from board and bed") is a decree of divorce, now generally outmoded, that was the forerunner of modern judicial separation. The LATINISM seems little justified today. "This was only a divorce *a mensa et thoro,* equivalent to the modern judicial separation and infrequent at that." (Eng.)/ "In *Barber v. Barber,* the Supreme Court held that a wife could sue in federal court in Wisconsin on the basis of diversity of citizenship to enforce a New York state court decree granting her a divorce *a mensa et thoro.*"

amercement; amerciament. *Amercement* = (1) the imposition of a fine, or (2) the fine so imposed. *Amerciament* is an archaic variant. *Merciament* is an aphaeretic form generally to be avoided. See **affeer.**

AMERICANISMS AND BRITISHISMS. Throughout this book Americanisms are labeled "AmE" and Britishisms are labeled "BrE." For a guide to distinctions not covered here, see Norman W. Schur, *English English* (1980); Norman Moss, *British/American Language Dictionary* (1984); and Martin S. Allwood, *American and British* (1964). For differences in editorial style, compare *The Chicago Manual of Style* (13th ed. 1982) with Judith Butcher, *Copy-Editing: The Cambridge Handbook* (2d ed. 1981).

amicable; amiable. The former we borrowed from Latin, the latter from French—but they are at base the same word. Useful DIFFERENTIATION has occurred between these words, however. *Amiable* applies to persons ⟨an amiable judge⟩, *amicable* to relations between persons ⟨an amicable settlement⟩.

amicus curiae; friend of the court. The Latin phrase is well established, and is not likely to be replaced in legal writing by its LOAN TRANSLATION, *friend of the court.* At times lawyers have forgotten the role of the *amicus curiae;* he is "one who, not as [a party], but, just as any stranger might, for the assistance of the court, gives information of some matter of law in regard to which the court is doubtful or mistaken, rather than one who gives a highly partisan account of facts." *New England Patriots Football Club, Inc. v. University of Colorado,* 592 F.2d 1196, 1198 n.3 (1st Cir. 1979) (ellipses omitted).

Amicus curiae practice is less restricted in the U.S. than in England, where "it is customary to invite the Attorney General to attend, either in person or by counsel instructed on his behalf, to represent the public interest, [although] counsel have been permitted to act as *amicus curiae* [read *amici curiae?*] on behalf of professional bodies (e.g., the Law Society)" (*CDL*). In the U.S., virtually anyone with interests affected by the litigation, or indeed with political interest in it, may, when represented by counsel, be approved as an *amicus curiae.*

Amicus is frequently used as an elliptical form of *amicus curiae.* E.g., "This *amicus* believes in an absolute prohibition of the practice."/ "The court also rejected the state's contention that since the United States is only an *amicus,* it cannot ask for affirmative relief."

Amicus also serves as an elliptical adjective: "Texas also failed to seek intervention or file an *amicus* brief in a Second Circuit case directly reviewing the contract rates."

Amicus is sometimes even used as an ellipsis for *amicus brief*: "In its *amicus*, El Salvador explains its interest in securing the ultimate relocation of the pilot station of what it views as its national carrier." *Airline Pilots Ass'n Int'l, AFL-CIO v. TACA Int'l Airlines, S.A.*, 748 F.2d 965, 971 (5th Cir. 1984). This ellipsis is perhaps too elliptical, because *amicus* does not readily suggest itself as a shortened form of *amicus curiae brief* or *amicus brief*, either of which should have appeared in the quoted sentence.

The term *amicus curiae* is often used as a POSTPOSITIVE ADJECTIVE, although the modern trend is to place it before the noun it modifies. E.g., "The conclusion of the Administrator, as expressed in the brief *amicus curiae*, is that the general tests point to the exclusion of sleeping and eating time of these employees from the work-week and the inclusion of all other on-call time."/ "When he represents no new questions, a third party can contribute usually most effectively and always most expeditiously by a brief *amicus curiae* and not by intervention."

Friend of the court, as an equivalent of *amicus curiae*, is primarily journalistic; it appears in many newspapers and journals with a general appeal. E.g., "In a *friend-of-the-court* brief, the home builders say that permitting lawsuits for damages would show that the Supreme Court recognized 'limits on local regulatory powers that destroy private property rights.'" *Wall Street J.*, Jan. 9, 1985, § 2, p. 25, col. 3. Even this translated phrase, however, must baffle the lay reader not familiar with court practice. The translation is therefore of limited value. See LOAN TRANSLATIONS.

The plural of *amicus curiae* is *amici curiae*. Frequently the singular is wrongly used for the plural: "The practice is particularly used in the U.S. Supreme Court, where organizations deeply interested in an area of constitutional law . . . will frequently petition for and be granted permission to participate as *amicus curiae* [read *amici curiae*]." Leff, *The Leff Dictionary of Law*, 94 Yale L.J. 1855, 2012 (1985)./ "The utilities may seek to present their views as *amicus curiae* [read *amici curiae*], and leave to do so is here granted."/ "Counsel for respondents, as *amicus curiae* [read *amici*

curiae], assert that conclusion as their principal argument before this court."

The singular is pronounced /ă-*mee*-kus-kyoor-ee-I/ and the plural /ă-*mee*-kee-*kyoor*-ee-I/ or /ă-*mee*-see/.

amid(st); in the midst of; mid; 'mid. *Amid* and *amidst* are somewhat learned, to the degree that they have been branded bookish or quaint. The charge may be unjust, for *amid(st)* has its uses (see **among** (C)). AmE prefers *amid*, and BrE *amidst*; in the U.S., *amidst* is considered a literary word. *In the midst of* is an informal and wordy equivalent. The preposition *mid* is poetic in all but traditional phrases (e.g., *midnight*, *midstream*) or scientific uses; if the word is appropriate, however, *mid* is better than '*mid*.

amok. See **amuck.**

amoral. See **immoral.**

among. A. And *amongst*. Forms in -*st*, such as *whilst* and *amidst*, are generally ARCHAISMS. *Amongst* is no exception: in AmE it is best avoided. "The question posed by this case has engendered division *amongst* [read *among*] the commentators as well as a conflict *amongst* [read *among*] the courts of appeal."/ "The same rule also applied to a communication between members of a society pledged to maintain good morals *amongst* [read *among*] its adherents."

Amongst seems more common and even more tolerable in BrE, where it carries no hint of affectation: "The first count of the declaration stated that plaintiff had contracted to perform in the theatre for a certain time, with a condition, *amongst* others, that she would not sing or use her talents elsewhere during the term without plaintiff's consent in writing." (Eng.)

Dreidger writes: "To divide *amongst* seems to be a little clearer than to divide *among*; in all other cases *among* is probably to be preferred." E. A. Dreidger, *The Composition of Legislation* 78 (1957). His first statement is unfounded: *divide amongst* provides no gain in clarity, and no difference in connotation or denotation.

B. And *amid*. *Among* is used with COUNT NOUNS, and *amid* with mass nouns. Thus one is *among* people but *amid* a furor. In the following sentence, *among* is misused for *amid*:

"The DEA agents discovered large quantities of marijuana *among the shipment* [read *amid the shipment*]." See **amid(st)**.

Here *among* is used with a mass noun where *a part of* would be better: "*Among the evidence* [read *A part of the evidence*] cited in support of the theory is Brawner's denial of any concrete knowledge of plaintiff's intentions."

C. And *between.* See **between** (A).

amorous; amatory, -tive. *Amorous* = (1) strongly moved by love and sex; (2) enamored; or (3) indicative of love. *Amatory* = of, relating to, or expressing sexual love (*W9*). *Amative* is a NEEDLESS VARIANT, not of *amatory*, but of *amorous*.

amortise. See **amortize**.

amortization; amortizement. The first is the regular and preferred form.

amortize, -ise. The *-ize* form is preferred in both AmE and BrE.

amortizement. See **amortization**.

amount; number. The former is used of mass nouns, the latter of COUNT NOUNS, q.v. Thus we say "an increase in the *amount* of litigation" but "an increase in the *number* of lawsuits."

amphibious, adj., is frequently used in reference to seamen who work both ashore and on ship. E.g., "Our past decisions have enunciated several factors to be evaluated in determining whether an *amphibious* employee becomes the 'borrowed' employee of other than his payroll employer."/ "The cases all involve the delicate question whether the federal interest in an *amphibious* worker's personal injury claims is sufficiently strong to justify federal courts' supplanting state law with federal common law of admiralty." This extended sense of *amphibious* probably had its origin in the phrase of World War II vintage, *amphibious forces.*

amphibology, -ological; amphiboly, -olous. The *-ology* forms predominate. E.g., "The term 'and/or' as ordinarily used is a deliberate *amphibology* [= quibble; ambiguous wording]." The other forms are NEEDLESS VARIANTS.

amuck; amok. The former is preferable, according to the majority of authorities. *Amok* is a transliteration of the Malaysian word, but this respelling appeared too late to acquire the stamp of approval.

amuse. See **bemuse**.

an. See **a; an**.

anachronism; parachronism; prochronism; archaism. All these words indicate that, in some respect, the time is out of joint. An *anachronism* is any error in chronology, or something that is chronologically out of place. "We rejected the longstanding but *anachronistic* rule of *Lincoln.*"/ "Professor Wigmore termed the privilege against adverse spousal testimony 'the merest *anachronism* in legal theory and an indefensible obstruction to truth in practice.'" *Parachronism* is a NEEDLESS VARIANT of *anachronism.*

A *prochronism* is a reference to an event at an earlier date than the true date. An *archaism* is something archaic, outmoded, or old-fashioned. E.g., "Death statutes have their roots in dissatisfaction with the *archaisms* of the law that have been traced to their origin in the course of this opinion." See ARCHAISMS.

anachronistic; anachronous; anachronic. The last two are NEEDLESS VARIANTS.

analects, -ta. The English plural is preferred to the Latin (AmE, BrE).

analog. See **analogy**.

analogism. See **analogy**.

analogous; analogical. These words mean different things. *Analogous* = similar in certain respects. This word should be avoided where *similar* suffices; the two are not perfectly synonymous. *Analogical* = of or expressing an analogy. E.g., "At common law, reasoning in the *analogical* form becomes increasingly unwieldy as the number of common-law precedents increases." (Cf. **tautologous, -ological.**) Note that *analogous* is pronounced with a hard *-g-*, *analogical* with a soft *-g-*.

analogy; analog(ue); analogism. An *analogy* is a corresponding similarity or likeness;

in logic, *analogy* means "an inference that, if two or more things are similar in some respects, they must be alike in others." An *analogue* is a thing that is analogous to something else. E.g., "The *Esso* decision suggests that *analogues* to such traditional equity doctrines as laches, election of remedies, and estoppel may justify a finding of peculiar circumstances." (The spelling *analog* should be confined to technical contexts involving physics or computers.) *Analogism* is a term meaning "reasoning by analogy."

analyse. See **analyze.**

analysis. See **analyzation.**

analyst; analyzer; analyzist. The last two are NEEDLESS VARIANTS.

analytic(al). No DIFFERENTIATION has surfaced between the two forms. The shorter generally serves better, although occasionally the longer form may be more euphonious, as where another *-al* adjective is proximate: "In most cases, the court treats the validity of a particular allegedly charitable trust as a legal issue to be decided largely by *analytical* and historical methods."/ "But the use of civilian treatises by English and American *analytical* and historical jurists had led to attempts to force common-law institutions and doctrines into civilian molds which retarded their effective development" (R. Pound).

The longer form appears in the phrase *analytical jurisprudence* (= the study and examination of law in terms of its logical structure [*W3*]).

analyzation, a pseudo-learned variant of *analysis*, has no place in the language.

analyze, -lyse. The former is AmE, the latter BrE. *Analyse* does not merit a bracketed *sic* when quoted by an American writer, as here, in a sentence from a well-known law review: "The dust jacket tells us: 'In this book, the author brings to bear empirical evidence and legal theory in a critical comparison of English and American discovery, and analyses [*sic*] and evaluates the differences between the two systems." That *sic* demonstrates nothing but the quoter's ignorance. See **sic.**

analyzer; analyzist. See **analyst.**

ananym. See **anonym.**

anarchy, -ic(al), -ial; anarchism, -ist(ic). *Anarchism* is a political theory antithetical to any form of government; *anarchy* is a state or quality of society. Only *anarchy* (= lawlessness, disorder) has pejorative connotations. Here *anarchism* is misused for *anarchy:* "Unless we find a better way of working together, sheer *anarchism* [read *anarchy*] will result." The preferred adjectival forms are *anarchic* and *anarchist.*

ancestor (= one who precedes in lineage) is occasionally misused for *descendant* (= one who follows in lineage). E.g., "The limited partner may transfer her interest by testamentary disposition or gift to a spouse (unless legally separated), issue, or *ancestors* [read *descendants*] of the limited partner, or to a trust established for the exclusive benefit of such spouse, issue, or *ancestors* [read *descendants*]."

Only in legal writing does *ancestors* include parents as well as grandparents and others more remote. A layman does not generally think of his father or mother as an *ancestor.* See **ascendant.**

ancillarity = the quality of being ancillary or of maintaining ancillary jurisdiction (in the U.S., jurisdiction assumed by the federal courts for purposes of convenience to the parties, although the reach of the jurisdiction exercised extends beyond the constitutional or congressional grant). *Ancillarity* is not recorded in any dictionary, but is gaining ground as a legal term. E.g., "The concept of *ancillarity* may explain decisions which hold that actions to enforce an alimony or custody decree are outside the diversity jurisdiction, if the decree remains subject to modification by the court that entered it." *Lloyd v. Loeffler*, 694 F.2d 489, 492 (7th Cir. 1982) (per Posner, J.).

and. **A.** Beginning Sentences. It is rank superstition that this coordinating conjunction cannot properly begin a sentence. And for that matter, the same superstition has plagued *but*, q.v. But this transitional artifice, though quite acceptable, should be sparingly used; otherwise the prose acquires an undesirable staccato effect.

B. For *or*. Oddly, *and* is frequently misused for *or* where a singular noun, or one of two nouns, is called for. E.g., "Prisoners' cases are usually heard before federal magistrates *and* district judges." This construction wrongly implies that magistrates and district judges go together, that is, that they hear such cases at the same time. The true sense of the sentence is "magistrates *or* district judges."

C. In Enumerations. Legal writers have a tendency, especially in long enumerations, to omit *and* before the final element. To do so in legal writing is often infelicitous: the reader is jarred by the abrupt period ending the sentence, and may even wonder whether a part of the enumeration has been inadvertently omitted. One may occasionally omit *and* before the final element in an enumeration with a particular nuance in mind: without *and* the implication is that the series is incomplete— rhetoricians call this construction "asyndeton"; with *and* the implication is that the series is complete. This shade in meaning is increasingly subtle in modern prose.

Finally, on the question of punctuating enumerations, the best practice is to place a comma before the *and* introducing the final element. See PUNCTUATION (C)(2).

and etc. See **etc.**

and/or, a legal and business expression dating from the mid-nineteenth century, has been vilified for most of its life. Lawyers have been among its most ardent haters, though many continue to use it. The term has been referred to as "that befuddling, nameless thing, that Janus-faced verbal monstrosity, neither word nor phrase, the child of a brain of someone too lazy or too dull to express his precise meaning, or too dull to know what he did mean, now commonly used by lawyers in drafting legal documents, through carelessness or ignorance or as a cunning device to conceal rather than express meaning." *Employers' Mutual Liability Insurance Co. v. Tollefsen,* 219 Wis. 434, 263 N.W. 376, 377 (1935) (per Fowler, J.). Another court has stated: "To our way of thinking the abominable invention *and/or* is as devoid of meaning as it is incapable of classification by the rules of grammar and syntax." *American General Insurance Co. v. Webster,* 118 S.W.2d 1082, 1084 (Tex. Civ. App.—Beaumont 1938) (per Combs, J.).

These are rather uncharitable views, more amusing than insightful. *And/or,* though undeniably clumsy, does now have a specific meaning; moreover, it saves a few words that otherwise would have to be repeated. Still, the phrase "lends itself as much to ambiguity as to brevity . . . it cannot intelligibly be used to fix the occurrence of past events." *Ex parte Bell,* 122 P.2d 22, 29 (Cal. 1942). *And/or* "commonly mean[s] 'the one or the other or both.'" *Local Division 589 v. Massachusetts,* 666 F.2d 618, 627 (1st Cir. 1981). (See the quotation under **amphibology.**) This definition suggests the handiest rewording: a good way to avoid the term is to write *unlawful arrest or malicious prosecution, or both,* instead of *unlawful arrest and/or malicious prosecution.*

Sometimes *and/or* is inappropriate substantively as well as stylistically. Mellinkoff has assembled a number of legal documents that the indecisiveness of *and/or* has been held to ruin: an affidavit ("fraud and/or other wrongful act"); a finding ("associate and/or employ"); a pleading ("office and/or agent"); and indictment ("cards, dice, and/or dominoes"); and a judgment (in an action that described the plaintiff by the formula *A and/or B*). D. Mellinkoff, *The Language of the Law* 309 (1963). At least one court anticipated Mellinkoff:

> The highly objectionable phrase *and/or* . . . has no place in pleadings, findings of fact, conclusions of law, judgments or decrees, and least of all in instructions to a jury. Instructions are intended to assist jurors in applying the law to the facts, and trial judges should put them in as simple language as possible, and not confuse them with this linguistic abomination.
>
> *State v. Smith,* 51 N.M. 328, 184 P.2d 301, 303 (1947).

Moreover, the term gives a false sense of precision when used in enumerations.

> In an enumeration of duties or powers, either conjunction is generally adequate. If *or* is used, no one would seriously urge that if one enumerated duty or power is performed or exercised, the remainder vanish; and if *and* is used, no one would say that an enumerated duty or power cannot be exercised or performed except simultaneously with all the others.
>
> E.A. Dreidger, *The Compositon of Legislation* 79 (1957).

Or/and is a rare variant of *and/or* with none of the latter's virtues, and all its vices. Rather than hopelessly confusing readers by resorting to its pretended nuance, one should abstain from it completely.

and other good and valuable consideration. This phrase is used in consideration clauses of contracts. Sometimes it is false, as when all the legal consideration for the contract given is mentioned explicitly. The phrase should be avoided unless it serves a real function; that is, unless the rest of the items of consideration are too numerous and individually trifling to merit specific inclusion, or unless the parties to the contract do not wish to recite the true price in a publicly recorded document. The drafter of a contract should have some purpose in mind in using this phrase.

and which. See **which** (c).

anecdotal, -dotic(al). The first is standard; the other forms are NEEDLESS VARIANTS. In reference to evidence, *anecdotal* refers not to anecdotes, but to personal experiences of the witness testifying. Leff trenchantly calls *anecdotal evidence* "a term of abuse in assessing a social science argument." Leff, *The Leff Dictionary of Law*, 94 Yale L.J. 1855, 2023 (1985). E.g., "In probing discriminatory intent, the trial court may examine the history of the employer's practices, *anecdotal* evidence of class members, and the degree of opportunity to treat employees unfairly in the appraisal process."

anent. Bernstein writes, "Except in legal usage, *anent* [= about] is archaic and semiprecious." T. M. Bernstein, *More Language That Needs Watching* 24 (1962). He could have omitted *except in legal usage* and *semi*. Apparently the term is still used in Scotland; another usage critic (following Fowler) has given somewhat narrower guidelines: "[A]part from its use in Scotch law courts, [*anent*] is archaic." M. Nicholson, *A Dictionary of American-English Usage* 25 (1957). Perhaps the best statement is that *anent* "is a pompous word and nearly always entirely useless." P. Marks, *The Craft of Writing* 47 (1932).

The term was not uncommon through the first half of this century. E.g., "*Anent* [read *With regard to*] the dismissal, the bank's attorney testified that . . . the memorial company had advertised the property for sale on December 7." *Gandy v. Cameron State Bank*, 2 S.W.2d 971, 973 (Tex. Civ. App.—Austin 1927). Today it is rather rare in legal writing, but examples of it can still be found: "The district court denied Fiat's motion to dismiss . . .

and ordered the parties to resolve any dispute *anent* [read *about* or *over*] service on that basis." *Boreri v. Fiat S.P.A.*, 763 F.2d 17, 19 (1st Cir. 1985).

anesthetic, n.; anesthesia. An *anesthetic* (e.g., ether) causes *anesthesia* (= loss of sensation). AmE prefers these spellings, BrE *anaesthetic, anaesthesia*.

anesthetist; anesthesiologist. Generally, *anesthetist* will serve for "one who administers an anesthetic." The term dates from the late nineteenth century. *Anesthesiologist*, of World War II vintage, refers specifically to a physician specializing in anesthesia and anesthetics.

ANFRACTUOSITY, or syntactic twisting and turning and winding, has been one of the historical banes of legal prose. It was more common in the late nineteenth and early twentieth century than it is today. Let us trace our gradual liberation from anfractuosity, noting that the modern throwbacks are increasingly rare. The following is a classic nineteenth century example:

> Unless the code, by abolishing the distinction between actions at law and suits in equity, and the forms of such actions and suits, and of pleadings theretofore existing, intended to initiate, and has initiated new principles of law, by which a class of rights and of wrongs, not before the proper subjects of judicial investigation and remedy, can now be judicially investigated and remedied, the facts stated in the plaintiff's complaint in this action, do not constitute a cause of action, and the demurrer of the defendant to that complaint is well taken.
>
> *Cropsey v. Sweeney*, 27 Barb. 310 (N.Y. 1858).

Here, from 1919, is perhaps the quintessential example of what *not* to do syntactically:

> Upon the petition of Armour & Co. of New Jersey, Armour & Co. of Texas, a foreign and domestic corporation, respectively, and F.M. Etheridge and J.M. McCormick, of Dallas, Texas, having for its purpose the cancellation of a contract between the City of Dallas, the Texas & Pacific Railway Company, and the Wholesale District Trackage Company, on the ground that it was void, because illegal, and for temporary injunction restraining all parties

thereto from performing said contract or any portion thereof pendente lite, and alleging that the petitioners were taxpayers of the City of Dallas, and sued for themselves and all other taxpayers in said City of Dallas, Hon. Horton B. Porter, judge of the Sixty-Sixth district court in Hill County, upon the sworn allegation that the proceeding was a class suit, by fiat indorsed upon the petition in Hillsboro, directed the clerk of the district court of Dallas County to file the petition and docket the cause in the Fourteenth District Court in Dallas County, and upon the petitioners entering into a bond in the sum of $10,000, conditioned as required by law, to forthwith issue the temporary injunction.

City of Dallas v. Armour & Co., 216 S.W. 222, 223 (Tex. Civ. App—Dallas 1919).

Perish the thought of one idea to a sentence! This phenomenon frequently occurs when one tries to sum up the entire case—the facts and the law—in one sentence. From 1984: "Here, the hazard—the scaffolding which was unsafe to work on until its guardrail was installed as planned—was a temporary structure, not a part of the ship itself, its gear, or equipment, which was created and used entirely by the independent contractor, who both owned and controlled it." And here, from 1985:

Also of importance, without Ms. Stanlin's testimony that lawn mowers were actually missing from the Four Seasons store, it is doubtful that the delivery by the driver (even if he was Marshall) of two boxes, of unknown content, showed that two lawn mowers, or any, were dropped off at Frederick Street, even though one of the (perhaps previously discarded) boxes indicated that, at least at one time, a lawn mower had been contained within it.

Frequently, anfractuosity leads to grammatical and syntactic blunders. E.g., "We further hold it was reversible error to deprive the jury of the opportunity to consider the opinions of those who best knew the person whose fate *they* were to determine, and with it, the opportunity to reject, accept, and assign weight to evidence concededly relevant, *which*, as the exclusive arbiters of fact, *was* the jury's sole function." In that sentence, *which* has no clear antecedent, and therefore *was* has no clear subject; *they* should be *it* in reference to the jury.

When the syntax becomes so involuted that it is unwieldy, or when the subject has become so far removed from the verb that the reader no longer remembers the subject when he reaches the verb, it is time to break the sentence up into two or more tractable sentences. As Cardozo once wrote, "the sentence may be so overloaded with all its possible qualifications that it will tumble down of its own weight." Cardozo, *Law and Literature*, 52 Harv. L. Rev. 471, 492 (1939).

angry takes the prepositon *at* or *with*. The phrase *angry at* is used in reference to things ⟨he was *angry at* the judge's denial of the injunction⟩, and *angry with* in reference to persons ⟨he was *angry with* the opposing counsel⟩.

animadversion was once a legal term meaning "the act of taking judicial cognizance [q.v.] or notice of." Today it means "harsh criticism," as here: "One who advertises by anonymous announcements has so far lowered the dignity of his calling as to merit the severe *animadversion* of his professional colleagues."

animate (= to move to action) has been used as a substitute for *actuate*, q.v. "While the evidence may have shown that the action was *animated* by malice, in the ordinary acceptation of the term, the proof fails to show any legal malice." Like *motivate*, *animate* is a serviceable replacement for *actuate*, the ready LEGALISM.

animus is a double-edged term. At times it is neutral, meaning "intention; disposition." This is the generally accepted legal meaning in legal contexts in G.B. and occasionally in the U.S. E.g., "This doctrine was overruled by statute in England, and the jury is now permitted to judge the whole case, and to decide not merely upon the responsibility of the publication, but upon the *animus* with which it was made."

More often in the U.S. *animus* denotes ill-will, as if it were synonymous with *animosity*: "Appellant's lower salary was based on impermissible gender *animus*."/ "None of these houses were hooked up to city water and sewage lines until 1981; Campbell claims that this was due to racial *animus* on the part of city officials."

This malevolent sense stems perhaps from

the several Latin phrases denoting malicious intentions, such as "the intent to injure": "In my opinion all the circumstances prove that the words were spoken without *animus injuriandi*—even if they had the defamatory meaning ascribed to them." (S.Afr.) Similar phrases are *animus furandi* (= the intention to steal), *animo felonico* (= with felonious intent), and *animus defamandi* (= the intent to defame). These phrases are, happily, obsolescent if not obsolete.

Several neutral *animus* phrases have persisted, especially in the law of wills; yet these LATINISMS generally add nothing to analysis, and muddy the waters. We know something is amiss when lawyers begin grammatically misusing Latin terms. For example, *animo revocandi* = with the intent to revoke (a will). In Latin, it is in the ablative case (equivalent to adverbial uses in English); here it is properly used: "It was generally held in common-law courts that by the destruction, *animo re vocandi*, of a will containing a revocatory clause, a former preserved uncanceled will was thereby revived." In the following sentence, however, *animo revocandi* is wrongly used as a noun phrase: "To effect revocation of a duly executed will, by any of the methods prescribed by statute, two things are necessary: (1) the doing of one of the acts specified; and (2) the intent to revoke—the *animo revocandi* [read *animus revocandi*]." Just the opposite mistake appears here, the nominative being used where the ablative belongs: "There can be no conflict between these ambulatory instruments—these wills—until death, and as the latter were destroyed *animus revocandi* [read *animo revocandi*], they thus never constituted wills under § 64-59, and never revoked the 1938 and 1939 wills."

The same sorts of errors occur with other phrases, such as *animus testandi* (= testamentary intent) and *animo testandi* (= with testamentary intent). "The admissibility of such evidence for the purpose of establishing the *animo testandi* [read *animus testandi*] when offered for the purpose of supporting the writing as a testamentary disposition, is, in our opinion, the most serious question involved in this case." We can avoid these embarrassments by sticking to what we all know: English.

Of course, the British seem to know their Latin better, and only rarely misuse *animo* for *animus*, or vice versa. But they are apt to go off the deep end in their proclivity for LATIN-

ISMS: "The *animus vicino nocendi* may enter into or affect the conception of a personal wrong." (Eng.)

annex, n.; **annexation; annexment; annexion.** *Annex* = something annexed or attached, as an appendix or a wing of a building. *Annexation* = the act of annexing or the state of having been annexed. In the parlance of property law, *annexation* refers to the point at which a fixture becomes a part of the realty to which it is attached. *Annexment* and *annexion* are NEEDLESS VARIANTS of *annexation*.

annex (= attach) appears more frequently in BrE than in AmE, and in both far more frequently in legal than in nonlegal writing. "The facts are stated in the case, to which are *annexed* four representative contracts." (Eng.)

Annex is more physical in connotation than *attach*, and probably should not be used figuratively: "The courts do, nevertheless, at times deny validity to a condition *annexed* [read *attached*] to a testamentary gift where the condition is calculated to influence the future conduct of the beneficiary in a manner contrary to the established policy of the state."

Attach or annex is an unnecessary DOUBLET: "The officer's certificate, under official seal, *must be attached or annexed to the will* [read *must be attached to the will*] in form and content substantially as follows."

annexable. So spelled.

annihilate is rather too strong a term for *nullify* in legal contexts. "Where no execution issues within the prescribed time, the judgment is *annihilated* [read *nullified*]." See **annul.**

annotation; note; lawnote; casenote. An *annotation* is a note added for the sake of explanation or criticism. In law, *annotations* appear in the Lawyers' Edition of the United States Reports and in American Law Reports (ALR). *Annotations* usually follow the text of a reported case.

A *note* or *lawnote* is a scholarly legal essay shorter than an article and restricted in scope, usually written by a student for publication in a law review. In this sense *note* and *lawnote* are synonymous, the latter being slightly more specific. A *casenote* is so restricted in scope that it deals only with a single case;

lawnotes, in contrast, tend to treat many cases in a general area of the law.

announce; annunciate; enounce; enunciate. *Announce*, the best-known of these terms, may mean (1) "to proclaim"; (2) "to give notice of"; or (3) "to serve as announcer of." *Annunciate* is a NEEDLESS VARIANT, except in religious contexts. *Enunciate* = (1) to formulate systematically; (2) to announce, proclaim; or (3) to articulate clearly. *Enounce* is a NEEDLESS VARIANT in sense (1) of *enunciate.*

In reference to judicial opinions, *announce* means "to write for the majority." E.g., "Mr. Justice Douglas *announced* the judgment of the Court and delivered the following opinion, in which the Chief Justice, Mr. Justice Black and Mr. Justice Reed, concur." *Screws v. United States*, 325 U.S. 91, 92 (1945).

annoy. See **aggravate.**

annuitant; pensioner. *Annuitant* = a beneficiary of an annuity. *Pensioner* = a person receiving a pension. For some purposes the terms are interchangeable. Yet *annuitant* has less disparaging connotations, perhaps because the person it denotes has usually established his own annuity, whereas a *pensioner* is generally the beneficiary of a pension provided by a third party, as the government or an employer. *Pensioner* also suggests one who lives off a very limited fixed income.

annul; nullify. These words have much the same meaning ("to counteract the force, effectiveness, or existence of"). *Annul* more strongly suggests abolishing or making nonexistent by legal action ⟨to annul a marriage⟩. E.g., "If at any time the seisin happens to be without a home it immediately returns to the transferor (or to his heirs if he is dea), and all subsequent interests are *annulled* and destroyed." *Annul* frequently appears in the verbose phrase *annul and set aside;* the last three words of that phrase are unnecessary.

Nullify has the broader meaning, and generally carries no necessary implication of legal action. "The Eighth Circuit *nullified* a breach-of-contract judgment obtained against the corporation in an Iranian court." / "The senator's vote was not *nullified*, but rather cast in the absence of certain information." See **set aside.**

annunciate. See **announce.**

anoint is sometimes misspelled *annoint*, as in *Gulf States Telephone Co. v. Local 1692, AFL-CIO*, 416 F.2d 198, 201 (5th Cir. 1969).

anomalous; anomalistic. *Anomalous* is the general adjectival form of *anomaly. Anomalistic* refers only to astronomical anomalies.

anomie; anomy. The former spelling is preferred; the adjective is *anomic.*

anonym(e); ananym. An *anonym* (preferably spelled without the final -e-) is an anonymous person. (See **pseudonym.**) An *ananym* is a pseudonym arrived at by spelling the author's name backwards (as, hypothetically, *Renrag* for *Garner*).

answer. To laymen this word denotes a reply to a question or a solution to a problem. In U.S. law, it refers to the first pleading of a defendant addressing the merits of the case. In G.B., however, *answer* = (1) a reply to an interrogatory; or (2) an answer to a divorce petition.

ANTE-; ANTI- The prefix *ante-* means "before," and *anti-* "against." Thus *antecedent* (= something that goes before) and *antipathy* (= feelings against, dislike). In but one word, *anticipate* (= to consider or use *before* the due or natural time), *ante-* has been changed to *anti-*. In compound words, the prefix *anti-* may cause ambiguities. See **antimarital facts privilege** & **antinuclear protester.**

ante; supra; ubi supra; infra; post. Literally *ante* = before, and *supra* = above. Both *ante* and *supra* are used in legal texts to make reference to the preceding part of the text, as in "supra at 11." *Ubi supra* was formerly used where *supra* now appears. It means "where above," and really has no place in modern legal writing.

Because *supra* is the more usual term, and because it is desirable that we achieve uniformity on this point, the recommendation here is to use *supra* for general purposes, not *ante*. An additional advantage of *supra* is that it translates directly into English. "See note 5 above" is English; "See note 5 before" is not.

The U.S. Supreme Court is one of few courts that distinguish between the signals *supra* and *ante* in usage; it also makes a distinction between *infra* and *post*. The term *ante* is used to cite to a previous opinion published in the same volume of the United States Reports, whether or not that opinion is for the same case as that in which the citation appears. For example, *ante* is used in a dissent to cite to pages in the majority opinion. *Supra* is used to refer either to earlier pages within the same opinion or to a previously cited authority. The Supreme Court uses *post* correlatively with *ante,* and *infra* with *supra.*

The phrases *ut infra* (= as below) and *ut supra* (= as above) are not current in legal writing, although they were common up to the mid-twentieth century.

All these Latin words—*supra, ante, infra, post*—should be used only as signals; they should not replace ordinary English terms in prose. E.g., "We discuss this argument *infra* [read *below*] and remand for the appropriate findings." Even in their use as signals, these terms are often vague without some specification of the reference; they are generally best avoided in CITATION OF CASES. See **ex ante.**

antecede, v.t., has become nothing more than an inflated and NEEDLESS VARIANT of *precede,* though the adjectives *antecedent* and *precedent* have distinct uses. In exalted prose, such as the passage following, it may be justified. "Language survives everything—corruption, misuse, ignorance, ineptitude. Linking man to man in the dark, it brought man out of the dark. It is the human glory which *antecedes* all others. It merits not only our homage but our constant and intelligent study." (Anthony Burgess)

antecedent; prior. Used as adjectives, e.g. qualifying *debt,* these words are generally inferior to *earlier* or *pre-existing.* Like *previous, prior* may occasionally be justified; *antecedent* may on rare occasions be forgivable, but not here: "Until the bonds mature, a purchaser for value, without notice of their invalidity as between *antecedent parties* [read *previous parties* or *predecessors in interest*], would take them discharged from all infirmities."/ "An allegation of special damages as a matter of aggravation is a substantive allegation of fact, and not an inference of law resulting from facts *antece-*

dently [read *previously*] stated." As phrasal prepositions with *to,* they are never justified; see the next entry; see also **previous to & prior to.** Cf. **anterior to.**

antecedent to for *before* is a ludicrous pomposity. "If the D has the right, when did it accrue to him? If at all, it must have been *antecedent to* [read *before*] the finding by the plaintiff, for that finding could not give the defendant any right."/ "An alien in America, *antecedent to* [read *before*] the revolution, was entitled to all the rights and privileges of an alien in England, and many more." Cf. **anterior to, previous to & prior to.**

If the phrase is to be used, however, it should not lose the particle *to,* as here: "*Antecedent* [insert *to*] the assigned Justice['s—see FUSED PARTICIPLES] joining the Court, facets of this controversy were here in *In re Powers's Estate.*" *In re Estate of Powers,* 134 N.W.2d 148, 150 (Mich. 1965).

antecedents (= background; record) is broader in AmE than in BrE, where it means "an accused or convicted person's previous criminal record or bad character" (*CDL*). In legal writing in the U.S., this term may be used in reference to a witness as well as an accused: "Where the litigation is important the character, reputation, and *antecedents* of the main witnesses of the adverse party should be investigated thoroughly." In such contexts, however, *background* would be a better term.

ANTECEDENTS, AGREEMENT OF NOUNS WITH. See CONCORD.

ANTECEDENTS, FALSE. An antecedent is a noun or noun phrase that is referred to by a pronoun. When used correctly and effectively, antecedents are explicitly mentioned, are prominent, and are not far removed from the pronouns that substitute for them. A variety of problems can occur, however, some of which are here discussed.

A. Ghostly Antecedents. The problem of nonexistent antecedents occurs frequently when a word such as *this* or *it* (see DEICTIC TERMS) is intended to refer, not as it should to a preceding noun, but to the action accomplished in the verb phrase. E.g., "They are also told that X., a doctor employed by defendant, will vaccinate anyone who wishes to have this done." What is the noun that acts as antecedent of *this*? We may supply the antecedent *vaccination,* but the sentence itself should supply the antecedent./ "To some degree, though not quantified, defendant's sales have declined; but quantification is not required because defendant is not seeking damages therefor [for what?]." The writer intended to say that plaintiff is not seeking damages for the decline in sales; but he failed to say it./ "The foregoing sufficiently answers, *if any be necessary* [read *if any answer be* (or *is*) *necessary*], the suggestion that the statute is unconstitutional." See ANTICIPATORY REFERENCE (C).

B. False Attraction. In the context of problems with antecedents, false attraction occurs when an antecedent that would normally refer to the subject is intended, rather, to refer to a noun appearing between the subject and *this* or *it,* or some other DEICTIC TERM. E.g., "Harrelson nonetheless contends now that the admission of this testimony was reversible error because it had been hypnotically induced." What had been *hypnotically induced?* The writer intended to convey that the *testimony,* not its *admission,* had been induced by hypnosis. See SUBJECT-VERB AGREEMENT.

C. With Possessives. A noun in the possessive case is not a suitable antecedent for a pronoun, because the possessive makes the noun functionally an adjective. The parts of speech of an antecedent and its referent must match. "Indeed, the Court's reading of the plain language of the Fourth Amendment *is* incapable of explaining even *its* own holding in this case." What is the subject of *is,* the antecedent of *its?* The intended antecedent is *court,* but the possessive *court's* is merely an adjective modifying *reading,* and is incapable of acting as the antecedent of *it,* or as the subject of *is.* [Read *Indeed, the Court in its reading* . . .]/ "There may have been inimical voices raised among the jury, *such as the foreman's, who* [read *such as that of the foreman, who*] had just had an unpleasant brush with the bailiff." See APPOSITIVES (A), DEICTIC TERMS & **it.**

antedate; predate. Both words are so commonly used that it would be presumptuous to label either a NEEDLESS VARIANT. One sees a tendency to use *antedate* in reference to documentary materials, and *predate* in reference to physical things and historical facts. E.g., "The origin of the rule *predates* our dual fed-

eral-state court system." The DIFFERENTIATION is worth enhancing.

antemortem; antemortal; premortal; premortem; premortuary. *Antemortem* corresponds to *postmortem,* q.v. *Premortal* = (1) occurring before the time when human mortality was assumed (i.e., quite ancient); (2) occurring immediately before death. *Premortem* is a NEEDLESS VARIANT of *antemortem* and *premortal. Premortuary* = occurring before the funeral. The distinction between *antemortal* and *premortal* (in sense (2)) is that *antemortal* refers to any time before death, whereas *premortal* refers to the time immediately preceding death.

antenuptial; prenuptial. The latter is far more common in AmE today; *antenuptial* is the usual term in BrE, however. It is bootless, then, to label either a NEEDLESS VARIANT. "The court ordered a trial on the issue of the validity of the *antenuptial* [or *prenuptial*] agreement."

anterior to for *before* is, like its various bombastic competitors, almost risible. It would be, alas, if some lawyers did not use it with a straight face. E.g., "The authorities petitioner cites to the effect that an express contract made *anterior to* [read *before*] his entering upon his duties is essential to a claim by an officer of a corporation for compensation, are against rather than for him." Cf. **antecedent to, prior to** & **previous to.**

ANTHROPOMORPHISM, the attribution of human qualities or characteristics to things, is not uncommon in the language of the law. One common manifestation of this phenomenon occurs in phrases referring to what a statute does or does not *contemplate,* e.g.: "The very purpose of the statutory provision *contemplates* a result contrary to the statute, disproportionate as it might be." Or this, a form of HYPALLAGE: "A *concerned jurisdiction* is one that in view either of *its thinking* about the particular substantive issue raised or of its more general legal policies, can be taken to have *expressed some interest* in regulating an aspect of the multistate transaction in question."

Occasionally, anthropomorphism reflects poor style, as when a writer refers to the mindfulness of pellucidity: "Notwithstanding the fact that it is centered chiefly in construction, *pellucidity* in legal writing is not *unmindful* of discriminating diction and choice figures of speech." There are no choice figures of speech in that sentence.

antiaircraft. See VOWEL CLUSTERS.

anticipatable (= that can be expected or anticipated) is listed in the *OED*, with one citation from 1872, but appears in neither *W2* nor *W3*. "Stone's statement . . . was elicited to dispel the *anticipatable* suggestion that the government might be using threats of prosecution to induce Schbley to testify favorably." *United States v. Fusco*, 748 F.2d 996, 998 (5th Cir. 1984). The quoted sentence illustrates the loose usage of *anticipate* discussed in the following entry; *foreseeable* would have been the better word. See -ATABLE.

anticipate for *expect* or *foresee. Anticipate* = (1) to take care of beforehand; to preclude by prior action; forestall; or (2) to expect. Sense (2) has long been considered a SLIPSHOD EXTENSION; it should be avoided in formal legal writing. "Generally the measure of damages for a tort is the amount that will compensate for all the detriment proximately caused thereby, whether it could have been *anticipated* [read *foreseen*] or not."/ "It is clear that the parties and the court still *anticipated* [read *expected*] that further remedial proceedings would take place before the court approved any proposal."/ "It is not clear that the defendant might reasonably have *anticipated* [read *foreseen*] being haled into court in Louisiana."

Use of *anticipated* in the sense "eagerly awaited" constitutes still further corruption of the word. E.g., "The Supreme Court decided nearly twenty cases during its 1983-84 term relating to the Fourth Amendment; among these, the 'good-faith exception' cases were perhaps the most *anticipated* and controversial."

Here the word is used correctly: "The trailer court was not built, nor was the sewage plant, at the time the action was started, and thus the injunction was sought against an *anticipated* nuisance." (Here *anticipated* = considered before the appropriate time.)/ "A spendthrift clause restrains the power of a beneficiary to *anticipate* his right to income or perhaps to principal."

anticipatory, -tive. The former is standard in phrases such as *anticipatory breach*.

ANTICIPATORY REFERENCE is the vice of referring to something that is yet to be mentioned. Thus a sentence will be leading up to the all-important predicate, but before reaching it will refer to what is contained in the predicate. The reader is temporarily mystified. E.g., "Conflict of laws is the study of whether or not, *and if so, in what way*, the answer to a legal problem will be affected because the elements of the problem have contacts with more than one jurisdiction." This sentence would better read: "Conflict of laws is the study of whether the answer to a legal problem will be affected because the elements of the problem have contacts with more than one jurisdiction; and, if so, how the answer will be affected."

Only rarely can anticipatory reference be used in a way that does not disturb the reader, e.g.: "We think it is clear—*and no party disputes this point*—that the statutory commitment of review of FCC action to the Court of Appeals affords this court jurisdiction over claims of unreasonable delay." For innocuous examples with personal pronouns, see the second paragraph in (c) below. The vexatious examples, which are far more common, occur in a variety of forms.

A. Pro-verbs *(do*-words). "Texas, as *do* most jurisdictions, recognizes three general theories of recovery under which a manufacturer of a defective product may be held liable under strict liability principles." (One must either put *as do most jurisdictions* after the verb, or change the *as do* to *like.*)/ "Law professors, *as do* [read *like*] state court judges, produce a body of writing that can be analyzed to discern their political philosophies." See **like.**

A related error occurs with *have:* "The court, *as have* [read *like*] the parties, construes this motion as one for judgment notwithstanding the verdict."

B. Nominal References. "Kramer made, among others, the following untrue and misleading statements of material fact." [Read *Kramer made the following untrue and misleading statements of fact, among others.*]/ "In an action, *inter alia, to recover* [read *In an action to recover, inter alia,*] moneys allegedly due, plaintiff appeals."

C. Pronouns. "The defense *of itself* is without a doubt one of the foremost concerns of any nation." [Read *A nation's defense of itself is without doubt one of its foremost concerns.*]/ "The formidable difficulty involved in *its* definition and measurement is partially responsible for the lack of attention to quality." (*Its* has no clearly identifiable antecedent in the sentence just quoted; only at the end of the sentence do we realize that *quality* is the subject.)/ "Even if *he* construed the evidence most favorably to the state, *a reasonable juror* should have doubted that the left side of the safe was within the building." (Reverse the positions of *he* and *a reasonable juror*.)/ (Opening sentence of an opinion:) "After a hearing at which *he* and *his* office manager testified, appellant Reehlman, an orthopedic surgeon, was adjudged in contempt for disobeying a subpoena." (Recast the sentence so that *he* and *his* follow *Reehlmann*.)/ "Assuming *it* applies to claims based on injunctive relief, *the doctrine of res judicata* would not bar a suit based on acts of the defendant that have occurred subsequent to the final judgment asserted as a bar." (Reverse *it* and the italicized noun phrase.) See ANTECEDENTS, FALSE (A).

Occasionally an anticipatory reference by pronoun is acceptable, but only where the "antecedent" follows the reference closely: "Making *himself* understood is *the writer's* first task."/ "Independently of the scope of *his* response to the auditor's request for information, *the lawyer* may have as part of his professional responsibility an obligation to advise the client concerning the need for public disclosure."

D. Alternatives. "Of what *if any significance* [read *significance, if any,*] was the court's characterization of the gearshift knob as a safety device?"

ANTICIPATORY SUBJECTS. See EXPLETIVES.

anticlimatic is solecistic for *anticlimactic*. See **climactic**.

antilapse statute. See **lapse statute**.

antimarital facts privilege. This is an obtuse name for the evidentiary privilege allowing a spouse not to testify about "marital facts," i.e., intimate facts relating to the marriage. The phrase *antimarital facts* = facts whose disclosure tends to harm the marriage. The prefix *anti-* causes the problem, for the privilege is not "antimarital." Yet the disclosure of the facts *is* thought to be "antimarital." The ambiguity caused by the prefix disappears when an alternative name for the

privilege is used, e.g., *privilege against adverse spousal testimony, spousal privilege,* or *marital privilege.* The first of these alternative versions is used by the Supreme Court in *Trammel v. United States,* 445 U.S. 40 (1980).

antinomy; antimony. These words are not to be confused. *Antinomy* = a contradiction in law or logic; a conflict of authority. This is the word used in legal contexts: "Apparently the realization of the deep-going *antinomies* in the structure of our system of contracts is too painful an experience to be permitted to rise to the full level of consciousness."/ "We are presented in this case with an apparent conflict or *antinomy* between two rights that are equally regarded by the law." (Eng.) *Antimony* is rather arcane, meaning "a brittle silvery-white metallic element, used esp. in alloys" (*COD*).

antinuclear protester is technically ambiguous, though everyone should know what is intended. For the literally minded, however, it might refer to "a protester *denouncing* the antinuclear cause," instead of "a protester *espousing* the antinuclear position." Thus it might be preferable to write *nuclear-energy* (or *-weapon*) *protester* or *antinuclear advocate.* See **protest.**

antipathy takes *against, to, toward,* or *for.* The writer of the following sentence haplessly inserted one of the few unidiomatic prepositions: "J.W. has focused on the 'terrible plight of the American Indian' as a strategem to publicize his *antipathy of* [read *antipathy toward*] government in general and, ludicrously, socialism in particular."

antithetic(al). The longer form has become established in the phrase *antithetical to* and in most other contexts. The shorter form should be avoided as a NEEDLESS VARIANT. *Antithetical* = exhibiting direct opposition. E.g., "We believe that requiring domestic litigants to resort to the Hague Convention to compel discovery against their foreign adversaries encourages the concealment of information—a result directly *antithetical* to the express goals of the Federal Rules and of the Hague Convention." (*Directly antithetical* verges on REDUNDANCY.) The phrase should not be used as a mere synonym of *opposed,* a slightly broader word.

anxious. This word properly means "uneasy; disquieted; worrying." To use the word as a synonym for *eager* is to give in to SLIPSHOD EXTENSION. "The wife seeks the court's directions as to the validity of the decree absolute and is *anxious* [read *eager*] to know what her present status is." (Eng.)/ "Defense counsel in death cases are *anxious* [read *eager*] to retain the scrupled jurors that prosecutors seek to exclude."

any. **A.** Singular or Plural. *Any* may be either singular or plural. Here is an example of the (rarer) singular use: Consider whether any of the presidential statements is inconsistent with the modern Court's claims." In such contexts *any* is elliptical for *any one*, q.v.
   B. In Legislation. *Any* is greatly overworked in statutes ⟨if *any* person shall commit *any* action upon *any* other person which. . . .⟩. Usually, replacing *any* with the indefinite article *a* or *an* results in heightened readability.

anyhow (= in any way; in any manner) is colloquial, almost dialectal, for *anyway* or *nevertheless*. E.g., "He understood the right to remain silent, but decided to talk *anyhow* [read *anyway*]."

anymore for *nowadays* is a dialectal usage, as in "Anymore, the price of housing is outrageous." Also, *any more* should be two words, not one: "He asked to know whether he needed to do *anymore* [read *any more*] fundraising."

anyone; any one. In reference to persons, *anyone* should be spelled as one word. Formerly it was written as two words; now, however, the unification of the phrase is complete.
   Yet sometimes the phrase is wrongly made one word when, not meaning "anybody," it should be two: "A question might arise as to *anyone* [read *any one*] or all of these legitimate 'conceivables.'" *Any one* = any single person or thing (of a number).

anyplace is not in good use. The word is vastly inferior to *anywhere*. *Any place* should always be two words ⟨at any place⟩. See **someplace.**

anything; any thing. The distinction is sometimes important in legislative DRAFTING. *Any thing* implies an opposition to *any person*. *Anything* is the far more general word meaning "whatever thing."

any time should always be spelled as two words. E.g., "A recipient of such aid may not sue a participating state *anytime* [read *any time*] a previously provided benefit is deleted from a program."

apanage. See **ap(p)anage.**

apart from. See **aside from.**

apex forms the plurals *apexes* and *apices*. The English plural, *apexes*, is preferred.

apology; apolog(ue); apologia. *Apology*, in its general sense, applies to an expression of regret for a mistake, usually with the implication of guilt. It may also refer to a defense of one's position, a sense shared with *apologia*. The latter should preempt this meaning for purposes of DIFFERENTIATION. An *apologue* is an allegory that conveys a moral. (*Apolog* is not recorded in the dictionaries and should be avoided; but see **analog** & **catalog(ue).**)

apostasy, -acy. The latter spelling is inferior; the Greek etymon is *apostasia*

a posteriori. See **a priori.**

APOSTROPHES. See PUNCTUATION (A).

appal(l). The standard spelling is *appall*.

ap(p)anage. Though in today's French, the language from which the word was borrowed, *apanage* is the spelling, in the French of the sixteenth century it was spelled with two -*p*-s. We borrowed the word from the French early in the seventeenth century, and the *OED* notes that the spellings have been "equally common" in English. The *OED* favors *apanage*, whereas *W3* favors *appanage*. The latter certainly *appears* more English, and on that basis alone might be deemed preferable.
   We in America have little cause to use the term except figuratively. In its literal and historical sense, *appanage* /*ap-ă-nij*/ means "a grant (as of lands or money) made by a sovereign or a legislative body for the support of

dependent members of the royal family" (*W3*). Because we are not saddled with such burdens, we use the term figuratively to mean "a customary or rightful endowment" (*W3*).

apparatus has the plural forms *apparatus* and *apparatuses*. The former is a Latin plural and the latter an English plural. When referring to more than one apparatus in Latin, write *apparatus*. When using English, however, use *apparatuses*. See PLURALS (A).

apparent is frequently misused in the press, and sometimes in legal writing, in reference to fatal maladies. "Cardinal Cody died this morning of an *apparent heart attack*." One does not die of an *apparent heart attack*. [Read *Cardinal Cody died this morning, apparently of a heart attack*.]

For the sense of *apparent* in *heir apparent*, see **heir** (B).

appeal. A. Noun. In the U.S., cases are said to go *on appeal;* in G.B., the idiom *under appeal* is common. E.g., "Their Lordships are of opinion that the decision *under appeal* is not in accordance with that principle." (Eng.) The British phrase *appeal allowed* is equivalent to the American *reversed*. See **appeal allowed & allow.**

B. Verb. Depending on the context, *appeal* may be either intransitive or transitive in the U.S. Usually one *appeals from* a judgment. E.g., "Defendant *appeals from a verdict* and judgment against him in an action for libel."/ "We find no error in the decree *appealed from*."/ "Plaintiff *appealed from* an order sustaining separate demurrers of the defendants on the ground that the complaint does not state a cause of action."

Just as often, however, *appeal* is used transitively in the U.S. E.g., "Appellant *appeals his* conviction of possessing a firearm after having been convicted of a felony."/ "The United States *appeals* the suppression of evidence obtained during a warranted search."/ "Nolen *appeals* the award of an injunction against him."/ "The petitioners *appeal* a decision of the Tax Court upholding a deficiency in their taxes of $379,255 in 1975."

In G.B., where the transitive use is obsolete, one *appeals against* a lower court's decree. E.g., "The architect *appealed against* the master's order to Chapman J. who allowed his appeal and set aside the master's order." (Eng.)/ "The order was *unappealed against*." (Eng.)

appeal allowed; appeal dismissed. These British phrases are equivalent to the usual American judgments *reversed* and *affirmed*. See JUDGMENTS, APPELLATE-COURT.

appealer. See **appellant.**

appear. The phrase *it would appear* is invariably inferior to *it appears* or *it seems*. There is no need for the modal verb *would* in this construction, unless a hypothetical SUBJUNCTIVE is intended. "As of the middle of this century, *it would appear* [read *it appears*, or, depending on the sense, *appeared*] that the extent of present development along these lines has [or *had*] been somewhat overstated."

appellant; appealer; appellor. Perhaps few readers have seen or heard any term other than the first. *Appealer* has not gained currency and should not be introduced as a fancy variant of *appellant*, properly pronounced /ă-**pel**-ănt/.

Appellor is an archaic term from English law meaning "one who accuses of crime, demands proof of innocence by wager of battle, or informs against an accomplice [by *approvement*, q.v.]" (*OED*).

appellant, adj.; **appellate; appellative.** *W3* records *appellant* as having been used adjectivally in phrases such as *appellant jurisdiction*, perhaps mainly by laymen. In legal writing, however, the adjective corresponding to the noun *appeal* is invariably *appellate*. *Appellate* is defined by Johnson as "the person appealed against," the meaning now given *appellee*. But today the word is used only as an adjective.

Appellative, adj., is a specialized grammatical term. *Appellative interrogation* is a variant name for *rhetorical question*, q.v. As a noun, *appellative* = term, name. E.g., "It is a matter of common knowledge that the *appellative* 'revenue laws' is never applied to the statutes involved in these classes of cases."

appellor. See **appellant.**

appendixes, -dices. Both are correct plural forms for *appendix*, but *appendixes* is preferable in nontechnical contexts.

appertain; pertain. Some DIFFERENTIATION is possible. Both take the preposition *to*, but *appertain* usually means "to belong to rightfully" ⟨the privileges appertaining to this degree), whereas *pertain* usually means "to re-late to; concern" ⟨the appeal pertains to defendant's Fifth Amendment rights⟩.

Here *appertain* is correctly used: "The general principle seems to be that jurisdiction over an inchoate crime *appertains* to the state that would have had jurisdiction had the crime been consummated." (Eng.)/ "The ancient remedy of a bill of peace originated in and *appertained* to the jurisdiction of the court of chancery."

In the following sentence, however, it appears to have been used merely as a fancy variant of the more usual *pertain*: "There is a compelling reason why district courts should not be divested of jurisdiction over matters 'incident to or *appertaining* [read *pertaining*] to an estate' regarding pending probate proceedings."

appetite; appetance, -cy. In all but scientific contexts, *appetence* and *appetancy* are NEEDLESS VARIANTS of *appetite*.

applicable. A. And *appliable; applyable.* These two variants are incorrect forms. *Applicable*, the correct form, is properly accented on the first, not on the second, syllable.

B. And *applicative, -tory.* The last two forms are NEEDLESS VARIANTS of *applicable. Applicative* is also a NEEDLESS VARIANT of *applied*, as in the phrase *applicative psychology.*

applicant; applicator; applier. An *applicant* is "one who applies for something (as a position in a firm)." *Applicator* = (1) a device for applying a substance, or (2) one who applies a substance. *Applier* is a NEEDLESS VARIANT of *applicator.*

applyable. See **applicable** (A).

appointor, despite its odd appearance, is the accepted spelling of the legal correlative of *appointee.*

apposite. See **apt.**

APPOSITIVES point out the same persons or things by different names, usually in the form of explanatory phrases that narrow in on the precise meaning of a prior more general phrase. Thus, in the sentence "My brother Brad is a musician," *Brad* is the appositive of *brother.* Usually, in phrases less suc-

cinct than *my brother Brad* (in which *Brad* is restrictive), the appositive is set off by commas or parentheses: "Plaintiff's decedent, John Doe, was killed in a plane accident," or, "The appellee in this case (XYZ, Inc.) has counterclaimed against the appellant." In these hypothetical sentences, *John Doe* is the appositive of *decedent,* and *XYZ, Inc.* is an appositive of *appellee.* Two problems crop up with appositives.

A. With Possessives. An appositive should match its antecedent syntactically. Here is the correct use of an appositive with a possessive antecedent: "A cannot confer on C *his, A's,* right to possess and deal with the chattel for a partnership purpose." (The appositive is unnecessary, however; see MYTH OF PRECISION.)

Having either an antecedent or an appositive that is possessive (and therefore adjectival) matched up with a nominal mate creates awkwardness, as in the following sentences: "In this case, appellant challenges the district court's grant of T. J. Stevenson & Co.'s (*Stevenson*) *motion* [read (*Stevenson's*) *motion*] for summary judgment."/ "In his petition, Wagner misrepresented to the court that federal jurisdiction became apparent during *plaintiff's, Davis,* [read *plaintiff Davis's*] closing argument." Actually, the sentences quoted are not syntactically wrong, but merely awkward.

Here are two other examples of strictly technical appositives that are ungainly without reason: "Appellee-plaintiffs Donald and Doris Taylor's property was damaged by floods in the summer of 1975." [Read *The property of the appellee-plaintiffs, Donald and Doris Taylor, was damaged.*]/ "The scope of your brief should not be affected *by the scope of your opponent, the appellant's brief* [read *by the scope of that of your opponent, the appellant*]." See POSSESSIVES (H).

B. Punctuation. This problem has been touched on earlier in this entry. Generally, commas (or, less frequently, parentheses) must frame all but the most succinct appositives used in a possessive phrase (e.g., *my brother Blair, his wife Lynn,* etc.). When commas are omitted in nonpossessive phrases, the effect is that of a RUN-ON SENTENCE: "Plaintiffs offered the testimony of Jesus Leon an airport mechanic." (A comma should appear after the name *Jesus Leon.*)

Emphatic appositives are never set off by a comma; e.g., "He himself testified that the hiring requirement of a college degree was unrelated to performance on the job."

appraisal; appraisement. *W3* treats these as variants; the *OED* definitions suggest some divergence in meaning. Both may mean "the act of appraising, the setting of a price, valuation." But *appraisement,* when connoting the acts of an official appraiser, is the term usually used in reference to valuation of estates; it appears far more frequently in legal than in nonlegal texts. The more broadly applicable term *appraisal* is also frequent in legal texts, in figurative as well as literal senses. E.g., "The order, in my view, is too strong, too broad, and not fine-tuned enough in its *appraisal* of the statutory language, the legislative history, and the congressional purposes."/ "The court's *appraisal* of appellant's claim of prosecutorial vindictiveness must adhere to the principles established by the Supreme Court in *Blackledge v. Perry.*"

Appraisal commonly appears in the writing of both legists and laymen, but is more a part of the everyday language. Ironically, however, Fowler classified it among those words "that have failed to become really familiar and remained in the stage in which the average man cannot say with confidence off-hand that they exist" (*MEU1* 14). Since he wrote that, however, *appraisal* has become the standard term in G.B. as well as in the U.S., largely because of the American influence. *Appraisal* is now preferred in all ordinary contexts, unless the connotative distinction frequently given to *appraisement* is desired.

As with many other pairs of variant word terms, here the vice of INELEGANT VARIATION may tempt the writer. E.g., "The inventory and *appraisement* will then be filed by the attorney in the executor's name with the clerk of court, who will record them. The purpose of the inventory and *appraisal* [read *appraisement*] is to serve as the basis upon which the executor makes his accounts and furnishes information concerning the estate to interested persons; however, the *appraisal* [read *appraisement*] is conclusive upon no one."

appraisal valuation, though fairly common in corporate-law contexts in the U.S., is illogical and redundant.

appraise; apprize; apprise. The first two mean "to valuate"; the last "to inform." In these sentences *appraise* is used for *apprise:* "Doctors have an obligation to keep their patients *appraised* [read *apprised*] of their condi-

tion [*conditions* makes better sense, because not all patients' conditions will be the same]."/ "The objection nowhere *appraised* [read *apprised*] the trial court that Ford Motor was complaining that the inquiry be limited."

A rarer mistake is for *apprise* to be misused for *appraise:* "The discussion thus far should indicate the limited value of superficial observation in *apprising* [read *appraising*] the effects of appellant's mental illness." Here *apprise* is correctly used: "It does not follow that because an officer may lawfully arrest a person only when he is *apprised* of facts sufficient to warrant a belief that the person has committed or is committing a crime, the officer is equally unjustified, absent that kind of evidence, in making any intrusions short of an arrest."

Partridge comments that *apprize* is obsolescent except in Scots law. *W3* indicates, however, that *apprize* (= to make a judicial sale [of a heritable estate] for the benefit of a creditor) is now obsolete in Scots law, and that it survives only in the sense "to value or appreciate."

appraisement. See **appraisal.**

appreciate = (1) to fully understand; (2) to increase in value; or (3) to be grateful for. The last meaning began as a SLIPSHOD EXTENSION, but is now established.

apprehend; comprehend. *Apprehend* = (1) to seize in the name of the law; to arrest ⟨to apprehend a criminal⟩; or (2) to lay hold of with the intellect (*OED*). It should not be used as a supposed FORMAL WORD for *believe,* as here: "We *apprehend* [read *believe*] that it is unnecessary at this time to cite authority in support of the right in equity to maintain class suits." *Comprehend* = (1) to understand, grasp with the mind, or (2) to include, comprise, contain. See **comprehend.**

apprehension does not always mean "fear," its common lay meaning. It frequently takes on nominal senses corresponding to the verb *apprehend,* q.v. "In the law of torts, one of the necessary ingredients of an assault is apprehension by the plaintiff of the imminent contact." Here *apprehension* refers merely to perception, not to fear or anxiety. See **apprehend.**

apprise; apprize. See **appraise.**

appro is an abbreviated form of *approval*, in phrases such as *goods on appro*. It is appropriate for telegrams but not for legal prose.

approbate and reprobate (= to accept and reject), used in the context that one may not accept the benefits of a legal document while challenging some of its conditions, is an unjustified LATINISM that Leff aptly calls "insufferably fancy." Leff, *The Leff Dictionary of Law*, 94 Yale L.J. 1855, 2046 (1985). The simpler words used in the definition are preferable.

Approbate may be justified when it refers to an act expressing a legal or authoritative approval. E.g., "It must follow that all arranged or Sikh marriages are a priori void, unless the parties knew each other beforehand or *approbated* the marriage afterwards." (Eng.)

approbation; approval; approvement. There is no generally accepted distinction between the first two words, apart from the observation that the first is more unusual and dignified. Follett suggests that we restrict *approbation* to a favorable response on a particular occasion, and use *approval* for a general favorable attitude. W. Follett, *Modern American Usage* 72 (1966). E.g., "Again expressing our *approbation* of this doctrine, we conclude that the proof tendered should have been admitted." Follett's distinction would suggest that *approval* be used here: "This extreme view has never met the *approbation* [read *approval*] of the bar, either in England or in America, and is repudiated by the great majority of reputable practitioners."

Rarely does *approbate* justifiably supersede *approve;* but for a legal nuance of the verb *approbate,* see **approbate and reprobate.**

Approvement is an old term with two quite distinct meanings at common law: (1) "the practice of criminal prosecution by which a person accused of treason or felony was permitted to exonerate himself by accusing others and escaping prosecution himself" (*Black's*); and (2) "the conversion to his own profit, by the lord of the manor, of waste or common land by enclosure and appropriation" (*OED*).

approbatory, -tive. *Approbatory* is the standard form.

appropriate, v.t.; expropriate. The verb *appropriate* may mean (1) "to give to a partic-

ular person or organization for a specific purpose" ⟨government-appropriated moneys⟩; or (2) "to take from a particular person or organization for a specific purpose." The first sense is the more usual in the U.S. (and better known to the layman), perhaps because it is better to give than to receive. Following are examples of sense (2), the lawyer's sense: "Under this authorization she withdrew from the bank various sums of money, a considerable amount of which she evidently *appropriated* to her own use without any accounting to him."/ "The only matter that has been urged before us is whether defendant may lawfully be restrained from *appropriating* news taken from bulletins issued by complainant, for the purpose of selling it to defendant's client."

Expropriate means (1) "to exercise eminent domain over; to take, by legal action, private land for public use"; or (2) "to transfer title to another's property to oneself." See **misappropriate.**

In sense (2), *appropriate* is distinguished from *expropriate* inasmuch as a private or semipublic entity does the former, whereas a public governmental entity does the latter. The difference between the terms is carefully observed by the courts. E.g., "[I]t makes no difference in determining the amount to be awarded that the property was *appropriated* and not formally *expropriated.*" *Gray v. State Through Department of Highways*, 250 La. 1045, 202 So. 2d 24, 30 (1967) (emphasis added).

appropriation can mean either (1) "exercising control over property" or (2) "bringing about a transfer of title or of a nonpossessory interest in the property." Here a court has overstated the traditional significance of the term: "Implicit in the meaning of the word *appropriation,* when it comes to competing and equal possessory interests in property, is that the accused person must have exercised 'unauthorized' control over the property." *Freeman v. State*, 707 S.W.2d 597, 605 (Tex. Crim. App. 1986). See **misappropriate.**

approval. See **approbation.**

approve. A. *Approve (of). Approve* may be either transitive or intransitive, but in legal usage is usually the former (i.e., it usually takes no *of*). "In our system evidentiary rulings provide the context in which the judicial process of inclusion and exclusion *approves* some conduct as comporting with constitutional guarantees and *disapproves* other actions by state agents."

B. And *endorse.* The two should be distinguished. To *approve,* apart from the legal sense of giving official sanction, is to consider right or to have a favorable attitude toward. The verb conveys an attitude or thought. To *endorse* is to support actively and explicitly. The word connotes action as well as attitude.

approvement. See **approbation.**

approvingly cited is awkward for *cited with approval.* "Judge Rubin found that neither of two kinds of contracts met the *Howey* test for an investment contract, a finding *approvingly cited* [read *cited with approval*] in *Moody v. Bache & Co.*" Other awkward variations have appeared: "This suggestion, as illustrated by the *Rogers* decision, was *approvingly used* [omit *approvingly*] in the Commerce Clearing House Rewrite Bulletin of June 8, 1983." The implication here is that, by *using* a suggested legal theory, the user implicitly *approves* that theory.

approximate; approximal; proximate. *Approximate* = (1) closely resembling; (2) nearly accurate; or (3) close together. *Approximal* = contiguous. *Proximate* = (1) very near; or (2) directly related. See **proximate.**

approximately about is a REDUNDANCY. See **about.**

a prendre. See **profits à prendre.**

a priori; a posteriori. These terms are best left to philosophical contexts. Very simply, *a priori,* the more common term, means "deductively; reasoning from the general to the particular," and *a posteriori* means "inductively; reasoning from the particular to the general, or from known effects to their inferred causes." Here *a priori* is used correctly, although the writer might better have written *deductive:* "*Witherspoon's* teaching is not limited to that particular inference; it counsels against any *a priori* judicial assumptions about the views of veniremen."

A priori becomes vague and confusing when it is used to mean "presumably" or "without detailed consideration," as here: "But we cannot say, *a priori,* without evidence, that there is not a sufficient rational distinction between

such restaurants and other commercial establishments to warrant a study." This usage is a SLIPSHOD EXTENSION.

Laymen frequently misuse *a priori* for *prima facie* in the U.S. and in G.B.

apropos (of). The two variations of this phrase are generally inappropriate in legal writing in the place of some English equivalent; they may prove serviceable in informal letters. *Apropos of* (suggested by the French phrase, *à propos de*) is well established in English, and is correct. Yet *apropos* may be used as a preposition to mean "concerning, apropos of." Hence there is generally no reason to include *of.* The preposition *to* is always incorrect with *apropos.*

apt; apposite. Both words mean "fit; suitable"; *apposite,* common in legal writing, is a FORMAL WORD. *Apt* for *likely* is a loose usage. As Fowler explains, however, "in British usage *apt* always implies a general tendency; for a probability arising from particular circumstances *likely* is the word" (*MEU2* 34). The same distinction applies in the best American usage. In the following sentences, *apt* is correctly used of general or habitual tendencies, rather than a likelihood in a particular instance. "The restaurant is extremely popular and generally *apt* to be crowded."/ "Psychiatrists are more *apt* to see people face to face, sitting up and once a week rather than the traditional five times." (Note the MISPLACED MODIFIER and the lack of PARALLELISM in the final clause. A less awkward structure, and one easier to take in at a first reading, would be: "Psychiatrists are more apt to see people face to face, to see them sitting up, and to see them once rather than five times a week.")

a quo; a qua. *A quo* = from which. A court *a quo* is a court from which a cause has been removed (*Black's*). *A qua* was originally a solecism for *a quo.* It has gained some degree of currency in legal prose, although *a quo* remains the preferred term. Because *a quo,* the correct form, has persisted alongside the bastardized version, it is not overreaching to say that we should stick with what is correct. It is the only form given, for example, by Leff in his *Dictionary of Law,* 94 Yale L.J. 1855, 2050 (1985). "On March 30, 1984 the district court *a qua* [read *a quo*] stayed the scheduled execution, dismissed with prejudice the foregoing enumerated claims 2, 4, and 5 and docketed an evidentiary hearing on claims 1 and

3."/ "The sole question posed on appeal is whether the federal court *a qua* [read *a quo*] had personal jurisdiction over the nonresident defendant." (Cf. **terminus a quo** & **terminus ad quem.**)

arbiter. See **arbitrator.**

arbitrage; arbitration. For the sense of *arbitration,* see the entry under that word. *Arbitrage* = the simultaneous buying and selling of currencies or securities at different values in order to profit by price discrepancies.

arbitrage(u)r. The English spelling without the Frenchified *-u-* might seem preferable in English-language contexts. But the dictionaries prefer *arbitrageur,* with stress on the final syllable.

arbitral; arbitrary. *Arbitral* = relating to arbiters or arbitration; *arbitrary* usually may be equated with "capricious, randomly chosen." (See **arbitrary.**) It also has a more and more disused legal meaning: determinable by the decision of a judge or tribunal rather than defined by statute. This, take note, was the *original* meaning of *arbitrary.* Could it be that its other, more modern meanings have grown out of this first one?

Arbitral may serve either *arbitrator* or *arbiter.* In legal language, it is almost invariably the adjectival form of *arbitrator,* q.v. ⟨arbitral discretion⟩. It also sometimes corresponds to the noun *arbitration,* as in the phrase *arbitral tribunal.* See *Graphic Communications Union v. Chicago Tribune Co.,* 779 F.2d 13, 15 (7th Cir. 1985).

arbitrament; arbitrement. The first spelling is standard for this word, meaning (1) "the power to decide for others," or (2) "a decision or sentence." When first imported into English from French in the late sixteenth century, the word was spelled with *-e-* in the penultimate syllable. Thereafter the spelling was Latinized to *arbitrament,* which the *OED* notes has been the accepted spelling since about 1830. Following is an illustration of sense (1): "The court may not leave both the questions of law and of fact to the *arbitrament* of the jury."

In sense (2), the word was once common in arbitration contexts; it referred to the arbitrators' decision or award. This particular use is labeled obsolete in Seide, *A Dictionary of Arbitration* 24 (1970).

arbitrary; unreasonable. These words are extremely complex in law, their senses not readily encapsulated; but their most elemental senses are worth noting. *Arbitrary* = with no purpose or objective. (See **arbitral.**) *Unreasonable* = with a purpose that is excessively imposed.

arbitration; mediation. The results of *arbitration* are binding—that is, the parties to the arbitrator's decision are bound by it. In *mediation,* to the contrary, the mediator merely tries to help two disputing parties reach a mutually agreeable solution; however, the parties are not bound by a mediator's decisions.

arbitrator; arbiter. An *arbitrator* is a person chosen to settle differences between two parties embroiled in a controversy. *Arbiter,* in contrast, is more general, meaning "anyone with power to decide disputes, as a judge." E.g., "As long as the pleas of both employer and employee are lawful, the courts have not been constituted *arbiters* of the fairness, justice, or wisdom of the terms demanded by either the employer or the employee."

The terms do, however, overlap considerably, and they cause confusion on both sides of the Atlantic. Yet when referring to legal arbitration, one should term the resolver of disputes the *arbitrator.* "To order arbitration is not to approve in advance of all or everything that the *arbiter* [read *arbitrator*] does."

Leff rightly rejects a distinction of a different nature: "Sometimes a distinction is sought to be made between an *arbiter,* who decides according to rules, and an *arbitrator,* who is free to settle matters in his own sound discretion. But the distinction doesn't hold; *arbiters* often have huge moments of discretionary power, and more important, most *arbitrators* today proceed according to elaborate rules, both procedural and substantive." Leff, *The Leff Dictionary of Law,* 94 Yale L.J. 1855, 2050 (1985).

The phrase is always *final* or *ultimate arbiter,* not *arbitrator.* E.g., "The judicial system is regarded as the *ultimate arbitrator* [read *ultimate arbiter*] of disputes."/ "In an earlier and ruder age the appeal was to arms, and force was the final *arbiter.*" *Arbitor* is incorrect for *arbiter.* See **arbitral.**

archaism. See **anachronism.**

ARCHAISMS, outmoded words or expressions that are not yet obsolete, abound in the language of the law. This work attempts to treat them individually under specific entries. A great many are collected under the entries FORBIDDEN WORDS, LAWYERISMS & LATINISMS.

archetype; prototype. These words are close in meaning, but their DIFFERENTIATION should be encouraged. As commonly used, *archetype* means "a standard or typical example," whereas *prototype* means "the original type that has served as a model for successors." In the sentence following, *prototype* is misused for *archetype:* "The *prototype* [read *archetype*] of a personal benefit requiring heightened judicial scrutiny is cash flowing directly to the union officer from the union treasury."

archetypic, -ical; prototypic, -ical. Inconsistently enough, the preferred adjectival forms are *archetypal* and *prototypical.*

architectural; architectonic. *Architectural* is usually the literal, and *architectonic* the figurative, term. Whereas *architectural* relates to the design of physical structures, *architectonic* relates to rational organization or to the abstract structure of a thing or idea. Although *architectonic* is sometimes used like *architectural,* it should be confined to figurative or abstract senses to make the DIFFERENTIATION complete.

Arden, Enoch. See **Enoch Arden law.**

ARGOT. This term referred originally to the spoken language of street vagabonds and petty crooks in France. By extension, it has come to mean the language, spoken and written, that members of any social, occupational, or professional group use to communicate with one another. As used in this book, the term *argot* means the jargon, that is, the full range of specialized vocabulary, devised by lawyers to save themselves time and space in communicating with each other, and occasionally even to conceal meaning from those uninitiated into the law.

Argot covers a broad range of legal vocabulary from the almost slangy (*horse case*) to the almost technically precise (*res ipsa loquitur*). And although an expression that is labeled "argot" fails to rise to the level of a TERM OF ART, it remains a useful bit of shorthand for

presenting ideas that would ordinarily need explaining in other, more circumlocutory terms if persons who lack experience in the law are to understand them.

Argot thus has a strong in-group property, which is acceptable when one lawyer talks with another or addresses a judge. Argot is unacceptable when the purpose of using it is to demonstrate how much more the speaker or writer knows as a specialist than ordinary listeners or readers do. The intended audience, then, should be the primary concern of a lawyer in deciding which words to use to express himself intelligibly. In a bench trial a lawyer may be justified in referring to the *corpus delicti* (not truly a TERM OF ART), but in a jury trial, a lawyer who uses this term is likely to lead the jury into confusion, puzzlement, and even misjudgment.

As an archetypal example of argot, the phrase *case on all fours* denotes "a reported case in which the facts and law are so closely similar to the one at hand as to be indistinguishable from it." This phrase of four short words is much more economical than the definition. But the shorthand phrase, useful as it is to lawyers, remains inscrutable, unless explained, to virtually all laymen. Such jargonistic phrases (certainly justifiable in many contexts) collectively fall under the rubric of this entry.

For illustrative purposes, a list of typical argot words follows: *adhesion contract* (see **adherence**), *alter ego, Blackacre, case at bar, case-in-chief, clean hands, clog on the equity, cloud on title, conclusory, four corners of the instrument, in personam, instant case, on all fours, pierce the corporate veil, reasonable man, res integra* (or *res nova*), *res ipsa loquitur, sidebar, Whiteacre.* These phrases are treated separately in individual entries.

arguendo is unnecessary in place of *for the sake of argument.* Although brevity would commend it, its obscurity to laymen is a distinct liability. E.g., "Assuming *arguendo* that her answers establish that she actually attempted to warn appellant, the court of appeals erred in inferring that her having done so established that she was acting as a state agent." *Arguendo* is one of those LATINISMS that neophyte lawyers often adopt as pet words to advertise their lawyerliness.

argufy = to dispute, wrangle. Krapp calls this term "illiterate or, in cultivated speech, a humorous and contemptuous form of *argue.*"

G. P. Krapp, *A Comprehensive Guide to Good English* 50 (1927). Lawyers could use a good sarcastic term for *argue,* and *argufy* fills the bill. Cf. **speechify.**

argument(ation). *Argumentation* refers to the act or process of arguing, or the art of persuading. *Argument* should be reserved for all other contexts.

argument(at)ive. The longer form is preferred as an adjectival form of *argumentation.*

ARGUMENT, MODES OF. The Romans categorized and gave names to several different modes of argument, all of which are still used today. Although it might be somewhat precious to use some of the more recondite Latin phrases in ordinary contexts (e.g., *argumentum ad crumenam*), they make as good material for footnotes as most of what appears in legal footnotes. Following are some of these phrases, each of which is preceded by *argumentum:*

   ab impossibili = argument from impossibility

   ab inconvenienti = argument from inconvenience

   ad baculum = argument dependent on physical force to back it up

   ad captandum − argument appealing to the emotions of a crowd

   ad crumenam = argument appealing to the purse or self-interest

   ad hominem − argument based on disparagement or praise of another that obscures the real issue

   ad ignorantiam = argument based on one's adversary's ignorance

   ad invidium = argument that appeals to hatred or prejudice

   ad misericordiam = argument appealing to pity

   ad populum = argument appealing to the crowd

   ad rem = argument on the point at issue (what every good judge likes to hear)

   ad verecundiam = argument appealing to one's modesty

   a simili = argument by analogy or similarity

   ex silentio = argument out of silence (based on the absence of solid evidence)

arm's-length; arms-length. In phrases such as *arm's-length transaction,* the correct form is to make *arm* possessive; the phrase is usually and best hyphenated when it appears before the noun it modifies, e.g.: "The stock was sold in an *arm's-length* transaction."/ "The renewal did not result from independent, *arms-length* [read *arm's-length*] negotiations." It also frequently appears in the phrase *at arm's length* (= not having a confidential relationship), in which *arm's length* is not hyphenated.

around is informal for *about* or *approximately,* and should be avoided in favor of either of those substitutes.

around; round. In AmE *around* is preferred where in BrE *round* is.

arraignment; indictment. The meanings of these terms may vary, depending on the jurisdiction. An *indictment* is almost universally the instrument charging a person with a felony. See, e.g., Fed. R. Crim. P. 6-9. It also loosely refers to the act of charging someone with a crime. An *arraignment,* within the federal system of the U.S., is the "reading [of] the indictment or information to the defendant or stating to him the substance of the charge and calling on him to plead thereto." Fed. R. Crim. P. 10. See **indictment.**

arrant; errant. The original word was *errant,* which means "traveling, wandering" ⟨knight errant⟩. By extension it has come to mean "straying out of bounds" and "erring, fallible." (See **errant.**) *Arrant* began as an alteration of *errant,* and originally had the same sense ("wandering"), but now usually appears as a term of contempt in the phrase *arrant knave.* It means "utter; extreme" or "egregious; outstandingly bad."

array; arrayal; arrayment. The three terms differ. *Array* is the most common, meaning (1) "order or arrangement"; (2) "venire; a panel of potential jurors, or a list of impaneled jurors" ⟨after challenges for cause to the first *array* of jurors in the box⟩; (3) "clothing"; (4) "militia"; (5) "a large number" ⟨an *array* of setbacks⟩; (6) "a series of statistics or a group of elements." The specific meaning is usually apparent from the context. (See CHAMELEON-HUED WORDS.) By the definition under sense (2), *array* may refer either to a roster of jurors or to the body of jurors collectively.

   Arrayal = the act of arraying or ordering. *Arrayment* shares this meaning, but more commonly means "clothing, attire." *Arrayment* developed into another form that is now more generally used in this archaic and learned sense, *raiment.*

Array as a verb has the special legal senses (1) "to impanel a jury for trial" ⟨the jurors have been arrayed on the panel⟩, or (2) "to call out the names of the jurors one by one" ⟨the defense lawyers scrutinized the jurors as they were arrayed⟩.

arrear(s); arrearage(s). The most common use of either of the terms is the phrase *in arrear(s)* (= behind in the discharge of a debt or other obligation). Current AmE idiom calls predominantly for *in arrears,* whereas the BrE and the older AmE idiom is *in arrear. In arrearages* is obsolete.

Arrearage, a LEGALISM, legitimately remains only in the sense "the condition of being in arrears." In all other meanings *arrears* serves: (1) "unfinished duties" ⟨*arrears* of work that have accumulated⟩; and (2) "unpaid or overdue debts" ⟨the creditor has reached an agreement with the debtor on settling the *arrears*⟩. E.g., "Earned income credits constitute 'refunds of federal taxes paid' and 'overpayment to be refunded' subject to withholding to satisfy child-support *arrears.*"

Yet legal writers frequently use *arrearage* (not even listed in the *COD*) where *arrears* would be preferable: E.g., "In *Fanchier v. Gammill,* a Nevada court had awarded a wife alimony that, because of *arrearages* [read *arrears*], she was forced to reduce to a judgment in Mississippi."

In the singular, *arrearage* is common enough in legal texts to be perhaps forgivable, *arrear* being an unnatural-sounding singular. "This order recites findings that appellant paid $1000 of the $4000 *arrearage* found to exist by the 1982 order, leaving an *arrearage* of $3000 denominated in the order as 'amended *arrearage.*'" The *OED Supp.* records a catachrestic American use of *arrears* as a singular: "They constitute a large *arrears* [read *arrear* or *arrearage*], which should be dealt with speedily."

arrestable. So spelled. See -ABLE (A).

arrestee. See -EE.

arrester, -or. The former is the preferred form.

arrivee. See -EE.

arrogate, a transitive verb, should not be used reflexively, as here: "Should a justice court attempt to grant a divorce, its decision would be invalid as if the reader were to *arrogate himself to do so* [read *to arrogate to himself this power* or *to appoint himself to do so*]." See **abrogate.**

arse; ass. *Arse* is the spelling (in the anatomical sense, not in horse-sense) in formal English.

arsen(i)ous. The spelling with the *-i-* is standard; the other form is a NEEDLESS VARIANT. *Arsenious* (= of or pertaining to arsenic) should not be confused as being an adjectival form of *arson,* which acts as its own adjective. *Arsenious* has four distinct syllables.

artefact. See **artifact.**

article, as a v.t., means "to bind by articles," and is conjugated *articled, articling.* An *articled clerk,* for instance, was formerly the term for an apprentice bound to serve in a solicitor's office in return for learning the trade. The verb is invariably used in reference to apprenticeships.

ARTICLES. A. Omitted Before Party Denominations. It is a convention in legal writing to omit both definite and indefinite articles before words such as *plaintiff, defendant, petitioner, respondent, appellant,* and *appellee.* It is almost as if these designations in legal writing become names, or proper nouns, that denote the person or persons referred to. The convention is a useful one, inasmuch as excision even of such slight words can lead to leaner, more readable sentences. One need not even be consistent within a piece of writing, where euphony would be served by departing from consistency. But the convention should not spread beyond these few standard party designations, for beyond these standard party-names the convention may seem unidiomatic. E.g., "If *decedent* [read *the decedent*] disposes of his estate by will, he devises property and the takers are devisees, even though the subject is personal property."/ "*Intervenors*' [read *The intervenors*'] opposition to plaintiff's motion has two bases." (See the examples under (B) of this entry in which *taxpayer* appears without an article.)

To some, the practice of omitting these articles may seem symptomatic of LEGALESE. They are entitled to their point of view. The rest of us can enjoy not having to write, "The plaintiff, now *the appellant,* sued *the defendant,* now *the appellee.*" (In fairness, though, "*Plaintiff,* now *appellant,* sued *defendant,* now *appellee*" is not much better reading.)

B. Wrongly Omitted. There is a contagious tendency in legal writing to omit articles before nouns, perhaps on the analogy of the special legal convention for party-names (see A). E.g., "Distinction must be recognized between the review proceeding here involved and those which . . . are allowed only . . . through a 'civil action commenced . . . in a district court.'" *White v. United States,* 342 F.2d 481, 484 (8th Cir. 1965). In our quest for concision through CUTTING OUT THE CHAFF, however, our writing should not become so abbreviated that we omit necessary articles; articles are more than mere chaff: they are signposts for the reader, who may become temporarily lost without them. There is a tendency, for example, in tax cases, to refer to *taxpayer* without an article, as if it were a proper name. E.g., "Federal law also required that *taxpayer* [read *the taxpayer*] make contributions under the Federal Insurance Contributions Act."/ "*Taxpayers'* [read *The taxpayers'*] request for compensatory and punitive damages is barred by the doctrine of sovereign immunity." These usages offend a sensitive ear, whether it is the mind's ear or one's actual ear.

Here are a few similar examples: "In approaching *solution* [read *a solution*] to this problem, we must look beyond the immediate consequences of the decision of this case."/ "The award as remitted by *trial judge* [read *the trial judge*] was not so gross as to be contrary to right reason."/ "If a sale is necessary, the representative can sue to set aside a fraudulent conveyance made by decedent during *lifetime* [read *his lifetime*]." For exceptions to the general rule, see (A) above.

C. Wrongly Inserted. Writers sometimes unidiomatically insert articles where they have no business; this phenomenon is inexplicable, except insofar as we can identify the writer's failure to distinguish between COUNT AND MASS (NONCOUNT) NOUNS. E.g., "The nature of the agency relationship is such that the principal would be subject to *a* vicarious liability [omit *a*] as a defendant to another who may have been injured by the agent's

negligence."/ "The Commission has taken the position that it may by its order allow *an* overproduction [omit *an*] for a period of time to meet the market demand."

D. Repeated. When two or more nouns are connected by a conjunction, it is usually best to repeat the article before each noun. When the article is not repeated, the sense conveyed is that the nouns are identical or synonymous. "The committee elected a secretary and treasurer" (one person); "The committee elected a secretary and a treasurer" (two persons).

The article should not be repeated in a second, parallel adjectival phrase. "Appellant testified and the United States admitted that P.A.L. was a validly formed and *an* existing corporation [omit *an*]."

E. Indefinite. See **a; an.**

artifact; artefact. The former spelling is standard in AmE, the latter in BrE.

artificial person. See **juristic(al) person.**

artisan; artizan. The former spelling is standard.

as A. Causal words: *as; because; since; for.* In the causal sense *as* should generally be avoided, because (not *as!*) it may be misunderstood as having its more usual meaning "while," especially when it is placed anywhere but at the beginning of the sentence. Fowler states: "To causal or explanatory *as*-clauses, if they are placed before the main sentence . . . there is no objection." E.g., "*As* the case has been discussed here and below without much regard to the pleadings, we proceed to consider the other grounds upon which it has been thought that a recovery could be maintained." (Holmes, J.)/ "*As* I read the court's opinion to be entirely consistent with the basic principles which I believe control this case, I join in it." The reverse order is infelicitous, however, unless the reader necessarily knows what is to be introduced by the *as*-clause: "We do not explore the problem further, *as* [read *since*] the issue of damages was not litigated below."

The causal *as* becomes troublesome even at the beginning of a sentence when a temporal *as* appears in the same sentence. "*As* Nelda returned to her occupation *as* soon *as* appellant drove her from Newark to New York, and *as* he knew full well that she would do this, one might suppose that the violation of the Mann Act was clearly established." The first and last occurrences of *as* in that sentence are causal, the second and third temporal; the causal words should be changed to *since* or *because.*

Because of the syntactic restrictions on *as,* we are left with three general-purpose causal conjunctions. *Because* is the strongest and most logically oriented of these. *Since* is less demonstratively causal and frequently has temporal connotations. But using *since* without reference to time is not, despite the popular canard, incorrect. *For* is the most subjective of the three, and the least used. If *because* points out a direct cause-effect relationship, *for* signals a less direct relationship, adding independent explanation or substantiation. Moreover, *for* is a coordinating conjunction, and not, like *because* and *since,* a subordinating conjunction; hence it can properly begin sentences.

B. In ANTICIPATORY REFERENCE. When coupled with *do*-words, *as* can cause mischief of the kind outlined under ANTICIPATORY REFERENCE (A). E.g., "Texas, *as do* [read *like*] most jurisdictions, recognizes three general theories of recovery in products liability." See **like** (C).

C. And *like.* See **like** .

as . . . as. A. And *so . . . as.* In positive statements, the *as . . . as* construction is preferred. "If the guard had thrown [the packaged explosive] down knowingly and willfully, he would not have threatened the plaintiff's safety, *so far as* [read *as far as*] appearances could warn him." (Cardozo, J., in *Palsgraf.*) / "*So long as* [read *As long as*] the courts fail to come to grips with that fact, *so long as* [read *as long as*] they persist in assuming that every juror has a precise and firmly held position, the process of jury selection will be unpredictable, arbitrary, and ultimately lawless."

Twenty years ago it was commonly held that *so . . . as* is preferable to *as . . . as* in negative statements such as, "The limitations period was *not so* long *as* I had thought." But *as . . . as* generally serves equally well in such negative statements. Following is a construction in which *not so . . . as* does not read as well as *not as . . . as:* "Back at Bennie's Corners, affairs were not going so happily as they were at McGill University." On first reading this sentence, the reader may be temporarily misled into thinking that *so* means "very," in its colloquial sense, as it would if the sentence ended after *happily.* See **as long as & so as.**

B. Repetition of Verb After. Often, when the second *as* in this construction is far removed from the first *as,* the verb is repeated for clarity: "Perhaps no area of corporate law is *as* beset with conflicting judicial opinions, variations among statutes, and confusion and uncertainty concerning the likely outcome of litigation *as is* the duty of loyalty."

as against is frequently misused for *against.* The former means "towards, with respect to, in regard to" (*OED*); here it is used correctly: "Every admission is deemed to be a relevant fact *as against* the person by or on whose behalf it is made." (Eng.)/ "When two or more persons conspire together to commit any offence or actionable wrong, everything said, done, or written by any one of them in the execution or furtherance of their common purpose is deemed to be so said, done, or written by every one, and is deemed to be a relevant fact *as against* each of them." (Eng.)

But *as against* is sometimes misapprehended as meaning "against": "Defendant was allowed, however, to testify *as against* [read *against*] the plaintiff [if the defendant gave adverse testimony]."/ "In a trial for felony the prisoner can make no admissions so as to dispense with proof, though a confession may be proved *as against* [read *against*] him." (Eng.)

Because *as against* is an idiom with a more or less set meaning in English, it should not be used in unfamiliar ways, such as in an ellipsis of *as being against:* "The policy is void *as against public policy* [read *as being against public policy*] because it opens a wide door by which a constant temptation is created to commit for profit the most atrocious of crimes."

as and when. This is a redundant expression; either *as* or *when* will suffice. "The bill provides that the balances shall be met by the Exchequer *as and when* [read *as*] they mature for payment." (Eng.—ex. fr. V. H. Collins, *Right Word, Wrong Word* 19 (1956)).

The variant *when and as* is equally bad: "A court of equity acts *only when and as* [read *only when*] conscience commands."

as a whole. See **in whole.**

ascendant, -ent. The *-ant* spelling is preferred in the general sense ("dominant"). The phrase *in the ascendant* is sometimes misconstrued to mean "ascending"; actually, it means "dominating, supreme." The phrase has been handed down to us from medieval astrology.

The *-ant* spelling is preferred also in the specialized legal sense in which *ascendant* corresponds to *descendant*. E.g., "The Louisiana courts have held that a decedent must be legitimate in order for an *ascendant* or sibling to recover for his death." See the next entry.

ascendant (ancestor); collateral; descendant. In the language of decedents' estates, both *ascendant* and *ancestor* mean "a person related to an intestate or to one who claims an intestate share in the descending lineal line (e.g., parents and grandparents)." *Ancestor*, q.v., is the more universally comprehensible word. A *descendant* is one who is descended from an ancestor, or offspring in any degree, near or remote. A *collateral* is a relative who traces relationship to the intestate through an ancestor in common, but who is not in the lineal line of ascent or descent.

ascension; ascent. Both mean "the act of ascending." *Ascent*, however, has these additional senses: (1) "the act of rising in station or rank, or in natural chronological succession" 〈the ascent of man〉; (2) "a method of ascending" 〈an unorthodox ascent〉; and (3) "the degree of slope or acclivity" 〈a steep ascent〉.

as concerns. See **as regards.**

as do. See **as** (B) & ANTICIPATORY REFERENCE (A).

as follow(s). *As follows* is always the correct form, even for a long enumeration.

aside from was once considered inferior to *apart from*. It has become standard, although found primarily in AmE.

as, if, and when. This phrase, which commonly appears in real estate contracts, could almost always be made *when* with no loss in meaning. See **as and when, if and when** & DOUBLETS AND TRIPLETS.

as if; as though. Attempts to distinguish between these idioms have proved futile. Euphony should govern the choice of phrase. Partridge observes that *as if* is usually preceded by a comma, and that *as though* rarely is.

as is; as was. "He bought the company 'as is.'" Although a martinet of logic might insist on *as was* in the preceding sentence, that phrase is jarringly unidiomatic. *As is,* in the context of that sentence, is really an elliptical form of *on an "as is" basis,* and is infinitely better than that paraphrase.

as long as; so long as. These phrases are not purely temporal constructions; more often than not, they express a condition rather than a time limit 〈as long as the transferee abides by these restrictions, he may enjoy possession of the land〉. See **as . . . as.**

as much as or more. When *than* follows these words, the second *as* must appear 〈as much as or more than〉. A common error is to write *as much or more than.* Here, however, *as much or more* (not followed by *than*) is correct: "A legatee or devisee can witness a will if he takes *as much or more* as heir if the testator dies intestate." See ILLOGIC (A).

as of now, and *as of generally,* have been criticized as illiteracies and barbarisms. Lord Conesford wrote that "an illiteracy is introduced when the words *as of* precede not a date, but the adverb *now. As of now* is a barbarism which only a love of illiteracy for its own sake can explain. What is generally meant is *at present.*" Conesford, "You Americans Are Murdering the Language," in *Advanced Composition* (ed. J. E. Warriner et al.) 374, 383 (1968). But *as of* in the sense deprecated by Conesford is not a bad usage, and *as of now* does not mean "at present"—rather, it means "up to the present time." Follett also disapproved of the phrase, recommending in its stead *up to now* or *for the present,* but *as of now* is today unobjectionable in AmE.

As of should nevertheless be used with caution. The phrase frequently signifies the effective legal date of a document, as when the document is back-dated or when the parties sign at different times. When such a nuance is not intended, *as of* is the wrong phrase. E.g., it is often inferior to *on*: "The plaintiff's employment with the defendant ended *as of* [read *on*] September 30." And it is sometimes superfluous: "The merger agreement was *dated as of* [read *dated*] October 21, 1979."

as of right is acceptable legal shorthand for *as a matter of right.* "Writs of error to the state courts have never been allowed *as of right."*

as of yet. See **as yet.**

as per is commonly understood to mean "in accordance with" or "in accordance with the terms of." *In re Impel Mfg. Co.,* 108 F. Supp. 469, 473 (E.D. Mich. 1952). It should, however, be commonly eschewed. It is an unrefined locution common among lawyers and legal secretaries. Originating in commercialese, *as per* is almost always redundant for *per.* Yet even *per* is a LATINISM in place of which many everyday equivalents will suffice (e.g., *according to* or *in accordance with*). E.g., "The memorandum noted that the release between Avondale and Bean *as per* [read *in accordance with*] clause 6 thereof indicated an intent to allow third-party claims and was not a full release."/ "The secretary distributed the residual assets *as per* [read *in accordance with*] the judgment of the Louisiana court."

aspersions, to cast is a prolix CLICHÉ for *to asperse*—but the verb is little known.

asphyxia; asphyxiation. The former refers to the condition of having insufficient oxygen resulting in suffocation. The latter is the action of producing suffocation.

asportation is a TERM OF ART and LATINISM meaning "the act of carrying off." *Asportation* is a necessary element of *larceny,* q.v. (See also **burglary.**) "The writ of trespass on the case might be joined with trespass quare clausum fregit or trespass for the *asportation* of chattels." (Eng.) This old word has been adapted in modern contexts to mean "the act of driving (a vehicle) off": "Thereafter, by convoluted reasoning, it is held that under the facts of this case the *asportation* [= *the driving off*] of the automobile is a continuing process."

as regards; as respects; as concerns. *As regards* is a much maligned phrase; it is usually inferior to *regarding* or *concerning,* but it is not a solecism. E.g., "That service when finally effected was technically improper *as regards* the newspaper and two of the individual defendants."/ "It is true that Lady Dufferin's interest was a protected life interest, but she was left free *as regards* dealing with it in one particular way: surrender in favor of persons entitled in remainder." (Eng.) The phrase was a favorite of the great legal scholar W. N. Hohfeld, who used it frequently in his *Fundamental Legal Conceptions* (1919).

Though *as regards* is no more objectionable than *with regard to,* the whole lot of such phrases is suspect: "Train your suspicions to bristle up whenever you come upon *as regards, with regard to, in respect of, in connection with, according as to whether,* and the like. They are all dodges of jargon, circumlocution for evading this or that simple statement." A. Quiller-Couch, *The Art of Writing* 114 (1916; repr. 1961). Cf. **regard.**

As respects and *as concerns* are equivalent phrases not commonly found outside legal writing. E.g., "This obligation may be limited by the certificates so that the insurance applies only to an injury *as respects* [better: *to*] ASI's operations."/ "Presentments as a method of instituting prosecutions are obsolete, at least *as concerns* [better: *in*] the federal courts."

ass. See **arse** & **pompous ass.**

assail (= to attack) is usually used figuratively in both legal and nonlegal contexts. Both *attack* and *assail* are used of findings and holdings of lower courts with which an appellant is displeased: "Appellants *assail* particularly these findings by the district court."/ "The writ of habeas corpus involves a collateral attack, while in certiorari the judgment is directly *assailed."*/ "In my opinion, the county court judge's finding cannot be *assailed* and the appeal must be dismissed with costs." (Eng.)

assassin; assassinator. The latter is a NEEDLESS VARIANT. "The first amendment is not a shelter for the character *assassinator* [read *assassin*]."

assault; battery. These terms have distinct meanings in criminal and delictual contexts. Essentially, an *assault* is the use or threat of force upon another that causes that person to have a well-founded fear of physical injury or offensive touching. A *battery* is the use of force or violence on another (in the criminal sense), or any repugnant intentional contact with another (in the tortious sense).

Shooting a gun just to the side of someone, if that person reasonably fears physical injury, or shooting a blank gun directly at him, would be an *assault*. Hitting him with a bullet makes the act a *battery*, even if he never knew he was hit. In the delictual sense, an uninvited kiss by a stranger would be considered a *battery*, q.v.

Leff notes that the distinction is observed only by lawyers, and even by them not consistently. "[I]n ordinary language, and even to some extent in legal talk, the two are conflated, and one speaks of an *assault* frequently in referring to the whole incident, from the threat through its consummation. Indeed, at least in ordinary understanding, use of the word *assault* most likely requires the actual *battery*; most people would not use 'He got angry and *assaulted* her' to describe an incident in which no physical contact was made." Leff, *The Leff Dictionary of Law*, 94 Yale L.J. 1855, 2069 (1985).

assaulter. So spelled.

assaultive is the only adjective corresponding to *assault*. E.g., "The prior conviction here was for rape—an *assaultive* crime."

assay; essay. These words, related etymologically, have distinct meanings. *Assay* = to test, to analyze. E.g., "The degree of harm must be *assayed* in light of the entire charge, the state of the evidence, the arguments of counsel, and any other relevant information revealed by the record of the trial as a whole."/ "Tenuous theories of liability are better *assayed* in the light of facts than in a pleader's suppositions."

Essay, though sometimes as a verb used synonymously with *assay*, most frequently takes on the meaning "to attempt; to try to accomplish." E.g., "The supreme court of the state has decided, in a case definitely involving the point, that the legislature has not *essayed* to interfere with the constitutional liberty of citizens to organize a party and to determine the qualifications of its members."/ "Lawyers' language *essays* precision by choice of particular words and phrases, and by devices of composition such as numbering, lettering, indexing, and even symbolic logic." *Essay* thus used is quite formal and somewhat archaic; *attempt* or *try* serves better in ordinary contexts. Cf. **endeavor.**

assemblage; assembly. An *assemblage* is a disorganized group of persons or things. An

assembly is a group of persons that is organized and united for some common purpose.

assent; consent. These words are very close in meaning, yet "there is some implication that *assent* is more active and enthusiastic than *consent*, the meaning of which sometimes slides over almost to 'acquiescence.'" Leff, *The Leff Dictionary of Law*, 94 Yale L.J. 1855, 2069 (1985).

assenter, -or, For "one who assents," *assenter* is standard. *Assentor* has the specialized legal meaning in England of "one who, in addition to the proposer and seconder of a candidate's nomination in an election, signs the nomination paper of that candidate." It should not be used in other senses.

assertedly. See **reportedly, allegedly & confessedly**

assertive, -tory. The former is the word for ordinary purposes; the latter was at one time used by grammarians in reference to sentences or constructions in the form of affirmations. *Assertory* is used in but one legal phrase, *assertory oath*, which denotes a statement of facts under oath.

asseverate. See **aver.**

assign, v.t., is frequently merely an inflated synonym of *give*. E.g., "We dismiss for reasons expressed above and those *assigned* by the district court." The verb is a less inflated LEGALISM when used in the sense "to transfer," as in "He *assigned* his right in the property to his son."

assign, n.; **assignee.** Both words mean "one to whom property rights or powers are transferred by another." *Assignee* is more understandable to laymen, who know *assign* as a verb only. The DOUBLET *heirs and assigns* is unlikely to disappear, however; *assign* as a noun almost always appears, as in the phrase just adduced, in the plural.

assigner. See **assignor.**

assignment; assignation. *Assignment* = (1) the transfer of property, or the property so transferred; (2) the instrument of transfer; or (3) a task or job. *Assignation* = (1) assignment; (2) tryst; or (3) assign (meaning "one to whom property rights or powers are transferred"). *Assignation* is a NEEDLESS VARIANT in the first and third senses listed, and should be confined to the second, in which it is truly useful.

assignment of error = a specification of errors made at trial and contained in an application for writ of error directed to an appellate court. On appeal one *assigns error* to certain alleged prejudicial mistakes at trial. (See **error**.) E.g., "By proper *assignments of error* and cross-errors, the correctness of each of the trial court's conclusions of law and that part of the temporary injunction undertaking to prescribe a form of permissible picketing is challenged."

assignor, -er. In all legal senses, *assignor* is preferred; it is the correlative of *assignee*. *Assigner* has appeared in nonlegal contexts, and there it should remain. See -ER, -OR.

assise. See **assize**.

assist, n., has come into the language through basketball lingo ⟨with an assist from counsel⟩. It should be avoided as a newfangled variant of *assistance.*

assize, as a verb, means "to assess, or fix the quantity or price of something." As a noun, it refers to (1) a statute setting the measure, weight, or price of anything; (2) a trial to a jury; or (3) the finding of the jury in such a trial.

In the plural (*assizes*), the term refers to the sessions or sittings of a court, especially of a superior court in England or Wales, held twice a year, at which cases are tried by a judge and jury. The *assizes* ceased to exist in Great Britain after the Courts Act 1971. *Assise* is a variant spelling generally best avoided.

associate together is a REDUNDANCY; *associate together in groups* is even worse: "The first amendment protects the right of all persons to *associate together in groups to further* [read *to associate in furtherance of*] their lawful interests."

associational, -tive. The *OED* defines these words as virtual synonyms ("of, pertaining to, or characterized by association"). It suggests, however, that *associational* refers to particular associations ⟨his associational loyalties⟩, whereas *associative* refers to association gen-

erally. But *W3* suggests that *associative* is now largely confined to contexts involving psychology and mathematics. Certainly the usual term in legal contexts is *associational:* "Further, it is extremely doubtful that the rights to visitation asserted by the Thornes are the sorts of *associational* rights protected by the first amendment."

assoil; assoilzie. *Assoil* (= to pardon, release, acquit) is an obsolete ecclesiastical term for the reversal of an excommunication. *Assoilzie,* a Scottish dialectal variant, is still used in Scots law in the sense "to acquit by sentence of court" (*W3*).

ASSONANCE. See ALLITERATION, UNDUE.

assort(at)ive. The longer form is preferred.

assume; presume. There is no clear-cut distinction between these words, except perhaps that *presumptions* are more strongly inferential and more probably authoritative than mere *assumptions,* which are usually more hypothetical. E.g., "Defendants rely upon the ancient legal *presumption* that a woman is considered legally capable of bearing children at any age."/ "Where any document purporting to be thirty years old is produced from any custody that the judge considers proper, it is *presumed* that the signature and every other part of such document is in that person's handwriting." (Eng.)

Presumptions lead to decisions, whereas *assumptions* do not: "We *assume,* without deciding, that except for the provisions of section 18 of the Decedent Estate Law the trust would be valid." The phrase *we assume, without deciding* is a favorite of common-law courts.

Where adverbs are concerned, one should always use the common forms derived from *presume;* that is, *presumably* (= I presume, it is to be presumed) or *presumptively* (= there is a presumption at law that). Here the writer seems to have been trying to avoid the simple term in favor of a more outlandish one: "However, the life tenant is *assumedly* [read *presumably*] entitled to $5,760 per year."

Assumptive is pretentious for either *assumed* ⟨assumptive beliefs⟩ or *assuming* or *presumptuous* ⟨an assumptive character⟩. For the sense of *presumptive* in *heir presumptive,* see **heir** (B).

assumpsit, a LAW LATIN term, means literally "he undertood" or "he promised." "Of the terms used in connection with the subject of restitution, *assumpsit* is one of the oldest and also perhaps the most troublesome." Note, *Restitution: Concept and Terms*, 19 Hastings L.J. 1167, 1182 (1968). The term originally applied to an action for breach of a simple contract, then was extended (after *Slade's Case* [1602]) to cases in which no independent agreement to pay could be proved, and finally to implied contracts and quasi-contracts. This CHAMELEON-HUED WORD is no longer widely used by common-law courts; in England the cause of action was abolished by the Judicature Acts of 1873–75.

assumption, in lay writing, most commonly means "a supposition"; in legal contexts it frequently takes on the older sense "the action of taking for or upon oneself" (*OED*). E.g., "It is not clear whether ITT consented to an *assumption* of indebtedness." See **assume.**

assumption of the risk; contributory negligence. Originally these two were separate doctrines, but *assumption of the risk* has been, in most jurisdictions, subsumed by the doctrine of *contributory* (or *comparative*) *negligence. Assumption of the risk* = the principle that a party who has taken on himself the risk of loss, injury, or damage befalling him consequently cannot maintain an action against the party having caused the loss. An example of assumed risk is the man who volunteers his profile to a friend who wants to practice sword-throwing.

Perhaps because *assumption of the risk* as applied by the courts came to bar otherwise meritorious claims, legal scholars began to point out that *contributory negligence* could be applied to any case involving *assumption of the risk*. And with the rise of *comparative negligence*, q.v., the doctrine of *assumption of the risk* became especially unjust if applied to bar a claim.

assumptive; presumptive. See **assume.**

assurance; insurance; ensurance (obs.). The nouns follow from the verbs; hence the reader might first consult the next entry. Since *ensurance* is no longer with us, *insurance* is the nominal form of both *insure* and *ensure.* Usually, *insurance* refers to indemnification against loss (from the verb *insure*); in G.B., *as-* *surance* is commonly given this meaning, although Partridge notes its decline; its one surviving use in this sense is in reference to life policies. Generally, however, *assurance* = that which gives confidence.

In the U.S., *assurance* chiefly means "pledge" or "guaranty." E.g., "*To give further assurance* [better: *To further ensure*] that these rules will not be breached, the states may wish to add 'safeguard' provisions." (See SPLIT INFINITIVES.)/ "The reviewing court may inquire whether there is adequate *assurance* that the respondent will be protected against the loss of proprietary information."/ "The heirs would have no *assurance* that the question of the personal fault of the executor would be properly tried."/ "Respondents received *assurance* that the customers would be willing to give them their laundry work."

Assurance also has the specialized, rather rare legal meaning "the act of transferring real property." *Assure* formerly had the corresponding meaning "to convey by deed."

assure; ensure; insure. A. *Assure* for *ensure*. One person *assures* (makes promises to, convinces) other persons, and *ensures* (makes certain) that things occur or that events take place. Any predicate beginning with *that* should be introduced by the verb *ensure,* if the verb is in the active voice. Here *assure,* which always takes a personal object, is properly used: "If Lucy's promise to pay for the Zehmer's farm becomes enforceable merely on the Zehmers' making their promise in return, how is Lucy *assured* [correct, because passive voice] that he will not have to pay the price unless he gets the farm?"/ "Although the court's instruction did petitioner no harm, it was thought that petitioner was *assured* a new trial if counsel had complained."

In the following sentences, *assure* is misused for *ensure:* "This course will be more likely to *assure* [read *ensure*] that the police officer will not be exposed to personal liability."/ "The State's strong interests in *assuring* [read *ensuring*] the marketability of property within its borders would also support jurisdiction."/ "Filing of a solicitation letter *assures* [read *ensures*] the public's ample protection."

Ensure is properly used in the following sentences: "Changes were made to *ensure* against overexpenditures in the program."/ "The verdict *ensured* that he would spend a long time in jail."/ "The requirement of minimum contacts *ensures* that the states, through their courts, do not reach beyond the limits imposed on them by the status as coequal sovereigns in the federal system."

B. *Insure* and *ensure*. *Insure* should be restricted to financial contexts involving indemnification; it should refer to what insurance companies do; *ensure* should be used in all other senses of the word. Intransitively, *insure* is commonly followed by the preposition *against* ⟨insure against loss⟩; it may also be used transitively ⟨insure one's valuables⟩. Following is a commonplace peccadillo: "Care must be taken to *insure* [read *ensure*] that the return of the loser does not become the guideline of the judgment."

C. Nominal Forms. See **assurance.**

assured, n. See **insured.**

assurer, -or. The *-er* spelling is preferred. See -ER, -OR.

as the case may be. See **case** (A).

as though. See **as if.**

as to is a vague, all-purpose preposition that should be avoided whenever a more specific preposition will fit the context. *As to* does not clearly establish syntactic or conceptual relationships; it has been demonstrated to hamper the comprehensibility of texts in which it appears. Were it not a phrase, it might justifiably be classed among FORBIDDEN WORDS.

A. Indefensible Uses. To illustrate the slippery variability of *as to*, a list of problematic usages follows; in each example, another preposition would more directly and forcefully express the thought.

1. For *of*. "Registration in the Patent and Trademark Office creates presumptions *as to* [read *of*] ownership and the exclusive right to use."/ "A contract in a lease giving an option of purchase might be good, provided it did not infringe the law *as to* [read *of*] perpetuities."/ "The jury was also instructed that if it believed appellant was guilty of either murder or involuntary manslaughter, but was unsure *as to* [read *of*] which, it was to find him guilty of the lesser offense."

2. For *on*. "The UCC is silent *as to* [read *on* or *with regard to*] the reconciliation of different terms."/ "The will violates the common-law rule *as to* [read *on*] contingent remainders."/ "But the question really must be regarded as an open one, *as to* [read *on*] which commen-

tators disagree."/ "We find no authority for the contention that the rule *as to* [read *on*] the destruction of contingent remainders should be applied to a case in which the estate is vested in quality but contingent in quantity."/ "Because the State produced no evidence *as to* [read *on*] this essential element, it is impossible to say that a rational trier of fact could have found beyond a reasonable doubt the facts necessary to support the life sentence."

3. For *with*. "In the business of life insurance, the value of a man's life is measured in dollars and cents according to his life expectancy, the soundness of his body, and his ability to pay premiums; the same is true *as to* [read *with*] health and accident insurance."

4. For *for*. "The rule is the same *as to* [read *for*] specialists."

5. For *to*. "Offeree must wait until he gets an *answer as to* [read *answer to*] his counteroffer."/ "Was the option provision too uncertain to be enforced, so that parol evidence should not have been *admitted as to* [read *admitted to*] clarify its meaning?"/ "He was entirely *indifferent as to* [read *indifferent to*] the results."

6. For *by*. "Counsel was continually surprised at trial *as to* [read *by*] the evidence presented by his opponent."

7. For *in* or *into*. "When the petition is correct *as to* [read *in*] form, a notification shall be prepared."/ "The court submitted issues to the jury inquiring *as to* [read *into*] what was a reasonable attorney's fee."

8. For *applicable to*. "That is so fundamental a doctrine *as to* [read *applicable to*] fiduciaries of all sorts, that it is somewhat surprising to find it questioned."

9. Completely Superfluous. "The trial court failed to *specify as to what* [read *specify what*] predicate under the statute plaintiff relied upon."/ "The Court does not *say here as to how* [read *say here how*] carefully the survey was conducted."/ "The only *real issue* in the case is *as to* [read *real issue . . . is*] the question of insanity." / "The *question is as to* [read *question is*] the validity of the twenty-eighth clause of the will of Mary C. Durbow, a childless widow." See **question as to whether.**

10. Used Twice in One Sentence, with Differing Meanings. "The defense moved for a judgment of acquittal *as to* [read *on*] all counts, arguing, *as to* [read *with respect to*] the tax evasion count, that an affirmative act of concealment had to be found to convict the defendant."/ "The question *as to* [superfluous] whether information *as to* [read *about*] particular processes or other matters was 'confidential' or 'secret' is outside the scope of this annotation."/ "Petitioner's right to a salary before it was voted to him was so indefinite *as to* [read *in*] both amount and obligation *as to be* [read *that it was*] unenforceable."/ "It is the contention of the contestant that the residuary legatees under the will *so* unduly and improperly influenced the testator to make the will in their favor *as to* [read *with regard to*] the residue of this estate *as to render* [read *that they rendered*] the will of no legal effect." In each of the last two sentences quoted, the final *as to* is a part of the phrase *so . . . as to,* q.v. The suggested changes of those phrases to clauses beginning with *that* are for the purpose merely of enhancing clarity; apart from the confusion caused by using *as to* twice in different senses, the phrase *so . . . as to* is used in those sentences in a technically proper way.

B. Defensible Uses. The best use of the locution is when introducing the discussion of a matter previously mentioned only cursorily in the text: "*As to* these nine plaintiffs who failed to apply for re-appointment, the ruling in *McBee v. Jim Hogg County* requires rejection of their section 1983 claims."/ "*As to* whether the object that this bill discloses was sought to be attained [see PASSIVE VOICE (F)] by the members of the union was a lawful one, the authorities of this country are clearly in conflict." In beginning sentences in this way, *as to* is equivalent to the more colloquial *as for.*

The phrase is defensible when used for *about.* Nevertheless, it is stylistically inferior to *about* in most contexts, as in the following sentences: "The buyer was silent *as to* [better: *about*] the disclaimer."/ "Any doubt *as to* [better: *about*] the existence of a material fact is to be resolved against the moving party."/ "Complaints *as to* [better: *about*] procedural irregularities in a condemnation case must be preserved at the trial court level by motion, exception, objection, plea in abatement, or some other vehicle."

The phrase is sometimes a passable shorthand form of "with regard to" or "on the question of," a meaning it properly carries when beginning a sentence. E.g., "California has done what we think should here be done; it has made its solution *as to* life insurance proceeds consonant with its other community property laws."/ "The trial court entered

judgment of nonsuit *as to* all defendants, from which plaintiff appeals."/ "The document is silent *as to* beneficial title." (Eng.)/ "The district court erred in denying the new trial sought *as to* the dismissal." In each of these sentences the *as to* phrase can be used to start the sentence and link it more firmly with a topic mentioned previously.

as to whether. The Fowlers describe it as "seldom necessary" in *The King's English* 344. That judgment has withstood the test of time. See **question as to whether.**

as well as. See **together with** & SUBJECT-VERB AGREEMENT (H).

as yet is invariably inferior to *yet* alone, *thus far,* or some other equivalent phrase. "The judge has not decided as yet." [Read *The judge has not yet decided.*]/ "One must question whether the stipulation automatically extended to the *not-as-yet filed claim* [read *yet unfiled* or *yet-to-be filed claim*]."/ "No court has as yet [read *has yet*] held that such an injunction is entitled to full faith and credit in the sense that the action toward which the injunction is directed must be abated."/ "Plaintiff has as yet [read *thus far*] had no opportunity to testify about this matter." *As of yet* is illiterate. Cf. **as of now.**

asylee is becoming a standard word in the language of the law for "a refugee applying for asylum." It has not yet made its way into the dictionaries. Like many personal nouns in *-ee,* it is illogically formed. But illogical morphology has not presented an obstacle to many other forms in -EE, q.v. "This portion of the complaint as amended alleges . . . that plaintiffs as a class are '*asylees.*'" *Fernandez-Roque v. Smith,* 539 F.Supp. 925, 932 (N.D.Ga. 1982). / "[T]he severity of harm to the erroneously excluded *asylee* outweighs the administrative burden of providing an asylum hearing." *Chun v. Sava,* 708 F.2d 869, 877 (2d Cir. 1983).

at is incorrect when used with any locative such as *where,* e.g., "Where is it at?"

-ATABLE does not generally appear other than in *-able* adjectives derived from two-syllable verbs (e.g., *create, vacate*), because in those short words the adjective would become unrecognizable. Fowler notes some long exceptions to the general rule (*inculcatable, inculpatable, incubatable*), and states his standard: "The practice should be to use *-atable* where the shorter form is felt to be out of the question." (*MEU2* 41) Other examples with which the shorter form is impracticable are *anticipatable, translatable,* and *infiltratable* (so that *infiltrable* not be thought to be derived from *infilter* [= to sift or filter in] rather than from *infiltrate*).

The following words, which occur with some frequency in legal prose, are better formed with *-able*: *abdicable, accumulable, accommodable, activable, administrable, affiliable, aggregable, agitable, alienable, allocable, appreciable, appropriable, arbitrable, articulable, calculable, communicable, compensable, confiscable, cultivable, delegable, delineable, demonstrable, detonable, expropriable, generable, inextirpable, inextricable, infuriable, infatuable, inebriable, invalidable, investigable, litigable, navigable, obligable, obviable, operable, originable, participable, penetrable, perpetrable, perpetuable, predicable, propagable, registrable, regulable, replicable, repudiable, segregable, vindicable, violable.*

at all events; in any event. These phrases are perfectly synonymous. The former is more common in BrE, the latter in AmE. Yet *at all events* does appear infrequently in American texts as well: "*At all events,* from an early date, if not in Glanville's time, the necessity of a formal delivery of devised land to the executor was got rid of in England as Beseler says that it was on the continent." (Holmes)/ "When the option to purchase is given to Clarkson, it prima facie *at all events* means to include Clarkson's assigns."

In legal writing these phrases are preferable to *in any case* when used in the same sense, because *in any case* contains the confusingly ambiguous word *case,* q.v., which usually refers to a lawsuit in legal contexts.

at arm's length. See **arm's-length.**

at bar. See **at (the) bar.**

at common law, a LOAN TRANSLATION of the LAW FRENCH *al common ley,* is the legal idiom used to introduce statements of common-law doctrine. E.g., "*At common law,* the death of the injured person or of the tortfeasor, at any time before verdict, abated the action."/ "'*At common law,*' says Sir. W. Erle,

'every person has individually, and the public also have collectively, a right to require that the course of trade be kept free from unreasonable obstruction.'" (Eng.) The preposition *at* is not used, however, in references to the civil law.

at fault; in fault. An American critic once wrote that "hunting dogs [that] lose the scent are said to be *at fault.* Hence the phrase means perplexed, puzzled." He added that *in fault* means "in error, mistaken," with this example: "No certified public accountant should be *in fault.*" C. Stratton, *Handbook of English* 24, 158 (1940). Today, however, *at fault* is commonly used in the sense "responsible for a wrong committed; blameworthy." E.g., "Apportionment of the percentages of fault among the parties found to be *at fault* cannot be accepted." The phrase is virtually never used for *perplexed* or *puzzled.* See **in fault.**

at first blush. This phrase, common in legal writing, occurs in BrE as well as in AmE. *At first blush* is a home-grown equivalent of the LATINISM *prima facie,* q.v., but the two have distinct uses. Rather than serving as a simple adjective or adverb like *prima facie,* the phrase *at first blush* conveys the sense "upon an initial consideration or cursory examination." E.g., "*At first blush,* a reading of the rule would countenance joinder of the United States as a defendant along with another defendant in a situation such as is present here."/ "*At first blush* this punishment does not seem very severe." *At first blush* is becoming a grossly overworked CLICHÉ. The variant phrase *on first blush* is not idiomatic.

at hand; in hand. In the U.S., the former has ousted the latter in figurative senses, because *in hand* is most frequently used literally, as in "I have the contract *in hand.*" One still occasionally sees the figurative *in hand,* but this is not the current idiom: "When justice in the cause *in hand* [read *at hand*] has been attained as near as may be and has been attained on grounds and in a manner prescribed by law, the duty of the judge under the civil law has been performed."/ "In their briefs in connection with Smith's motion, counsel on both sides state that they have been unable to find any case dealing with the specific problem *in hand* [read *at hand*]."

In G.B., however, *in hand* is frequently used in the metaphorical sense: "The court might have reached the same decision on the simple ground that the rule in Clayton's case was irrelevant to the issue *in hand.*" (Eng.)

at issue. See **issue** (A).

at law. See **under law.**

at present. See **at the present time.**

attach. See **annex.**

attached hereto is a REDUNDANCY for *attached.* It is a LEGALISM to be avoided.

attain, v.; **obtain.** The two are sometimes confused. *Attain* = to achieve, accomplish. E.g., "Another's business may be attacked only to *attain* some purpose in the eye of the law." *Obtain* = to get, acquire ⟨obtain a license⟩. It is a FORMAL WORD.

Attain, in another sense, is also a FORMAL WORD for "to reach (an age)". E.g., "In *Saunders v. Vautier,* the English Chancery Court granted a petition by the sole beneficiary to terminate a trust upon his *attaining* the age of majority."

attainder; attaint, n. Both nouns derive from the (originally French) verb *attaint* (= to accuse, convict). As legal terms they are primarily of historical interest. *Attainder* usually appears in the phrase *bill of attainder* or *act of attainder,* and means "the act of extinguishing someone's civil rights by sentencing him to death or declaring him to be an outlaw, usu. in punishment for treason or a felony." *Attaint* was formerly used to mean "the conviction of a jury for giving a false verdict" (*OED*).

attaint; taint. These terms were originally unrelated, but the senses of the former came to be heavily tainted by erroneous association with the latter. *Attaint* = (1) to subject to attainder, to condemn; (2) to touch or affect; or (3) [obs.] to accuse. *Attaint* is justified today only in sense (1); *taint* is otherwise the better word. E.g., "In trials for high treason, or misprision of treason, no one can be indicted, tried, or *attainted* (unless he pleads guilty) except upon the oath of two lawful witnesses." (Eng.)

Taint = (1) to imbue with a noxious quality or principle; (2) to contaminate or corrupt; or (3) to tinge or become tinged. *Taint* is by far the more common word in modern writing: "The Court found that the initial illegal entry did not *taint* the discovery of the evidence subsequently seized under the valid warrant."/ "It is urged that if evidence is inadmissible against one defendant or conspirator, because *tainted* by electronic surveillance illegal as to him, it is also inadmissible against his codefendant or co-conspirator."

Taint is just as frequently used as a noun: "The practice is not shown to be such as to fix upon complainant the *taint* of unclean hands."

attempt. See **endeavor** & **assay**.

attestant. See **attester.**

attestation clause; testimonium clause. Both appear at the end of a will. The *testimonium clause* is signed by the testator, the *attestation clause* by the witnesses to the will. A typical *testimonium clause* reads: "This will was signed by me on the 14th day of October, 1985, at Wilmington, Virginia."

The *attestation clause* recites the formalities required by the jurisdiction in which it might be necessary to probate the will. It raises a presumption that the formalities recited have been performed, and thus aids the proponent of the will at probate. A typical *attestation clause* reads: "The foregoing instrument, consisting of four typewritten pages, was signed and declared by the testator to be his last will in the presence of us, who, at his request, and in his presence and the presence of one another, have subscribed our names as witnesses."

attest(at)ive; attestational. *Attestative* is the best adjective corresponding to *attestation;* it means "of or relating to attestation." *Attestational* is a NEEDLESS VARIANT. *Attestive* is a NEEDLESS VARIANT of *attesting.*

attester, -or; attestator; attestant. *Attester* is standard in legal contexts. The others are NEEDLESS VARIANTS.

at (the) bar (= now before the court) derives from the LAW FRENCH phrase *al barre. At* *the bar*, which appears in early decisions such as *Marbury v. Madison* and *McCulloch v. Maryland*, has gradually been displaced in the U.S. by *at bar* in phrases such as *in the case at bar*. E.g., "In the case *at bar* there was no necessity of proving spite or ill will toward the plaintiff."/ "We think that no more was covered than situations substantially similar to those then *at bar*."

The British still use *at the bar*, "Until the present argument *at the bar* it may be doubted whether shipowners or merchants were ever deemed to be bound by law to conform to some imaginary 'normal' standard of freights or prices." (Eng.)

Leff states that *at bar* is used, esp. in law school, to refer to a case already decided and at the time under discussion by professor and students. Leff, *The Leff Dictionary of Law*, 94 Yale L.J. 1855, 2088 (1985). I have never heard this use of the phrase; it smacks of the judge-manqué. Cf. **at (the) trial.** See **sub judice.**

at the present time; at this time; at present. These are inferior to *now, nowadays,* or *today.*

at the time that; at the time when. These phrases are invariably verbose for *when.*

at (the) trial. The shorter form is the more usual and the more idiomatic in the U.S. "At *the trial* [read *at trial*], a nonsuit was denied." In the U.S. *at the trial* is outmoded except as an adverbial of place ⟨he was seen at the trial⟩. Cf. **at (the) bar.**

In G.B., however, judges still write *at the trial:* "The practice has been, wherever possible, to adduce *at the trial,* before pronouncement of decree nisi, evidence of the proposed arrangements for the children." (Eng.)

Still another vanishing idiom is *on (or upon) the trial:* "On *the trial* plaintiff was nonsuited."/ "No such evidence was produced *upon the trial.*" Today both phrases would be *at trial* in American legal writing.

at this time. See **at the present time.**

attorney. A. And Its Near Synonyms: *attorney* [*at law*]; *lawyer; barrister; solicitor; counsel*[*l*]*or.* Lawyers, like those in other walks of life, have long sought to improve their descriptive titles. Boswell relates: "The Society of Procurators, or Attornies, had obtained a

royal charter, in which they had taken care to have their ancient designation *Procurators* changed into that of *Solicitors,* from a notion, as they supposed, that it was more genteel." 4 *Life of Johnson* 128 (1791).

The connotations of *attorney* and its near synonyms have historically been quite different in G.B. and the U.S. Mellinkoff writes that the eighteenth-century efforts

to deodorize the word *attorney* [were] later abandoned, and in the nineteenth century it was supplanted in England by *solicitor.* There *solicitor* lacks the offensive American connotation, as in 'No peddlers or solicitors.' In England, *attorney,* for a lawyer, survives only as *the attorney* (the attorney general), while in America the chief respectable lawyer-solicitor is the *solicitor-general.*

D. Mellinkoff, *The Language of the Law* 198 (1963).

The two most common terms, *lawyer* and *attorney,* are not generally distinguished even by members of the profession. From the American point of view, "*attorney, attorney-at-law,* and *lawyer* are synonymous terms" for all practical purposes. G. Malcolm, *Legal and Judicial Ethics* 6 (1949). Today there seems to be in the U.S. a notion that *attorney* is a more formal (and less disparaging) term than *lawyer.* Technically, *lawyer* is the more general term, referring to one who practices law. *Attorney* literally means "one who is designated by another to transact business for him." An *attorney,* technically and archaically (except in the phrase *attorney in fact* [see (B) below]), may or may not be a lawyer. Thus Samuel Johnson's statement in his *Dictionary* that *attorney* "was anciently used for those who did any business for another; now only in law."

From the fact that an *attorney* is really an agent, Bernstein deduces that "a *lawyer* is an *attorney* only when he has a client. It may be that the desire of *lawyers* to appear to be making a go of their profession has accounted for their leaning toward the designation *attorney.*" T. M. Bernstein, *The Careful Writer* 60 (1965). Yet this distinction between *lawyer* and *attorney* is rarely, if ever, observed in practice.

In the U.S., those licensed to practice law are admitted to practice as "attorneys and counselors." (The *-l-* spelling of *counselor* is preferred in AmE, the *-ll-* spelling in BrE.) This combination of names is unknown in English law, in which *attorney* = solicitor, and *counsellor* = barrister. Yet "in the United States, the term *attorney* has come to have a generic significance that embraces all branches of legal practice." G. W. Warvelle, *Essays in Legal Ethics* 53 (1902).

In G.B., a *solicitor* or *attorney* does all sorts of legal work for clients but does not appear in court; a *barrister* or *counsellor* is a trial lawyer or litigator. In the U.S., *counsel* and *counselor* are both, in one sense, general terms meaning "one who gives (legal) advice," the latter being the more formal term. *Counsel* may refer to but one lawyer or, as a plural, to more than one lawyer. See **counsel & postman.**

B. Kinds of Attorneys (*attorney in fact; attorney at law*). The former means "one with power of attorney to act for another; legal agent." E.g., "It is held in *Tynan v. Paschal* that a letter of a decedent to his *attorney in fact* directing him to destroy his will does not operate ipso facto as a revocation of it." The latter means "a licensed lawyer." The plural forms are *attorneys in fact* and *attorneys at law*. See (D).

C. As a Verb. *Attorney*, like *lawyer*, has come to be used as a verb. E.g., "Among a number of mock trials that lawyers have liked to write is a *Trial of Sir John Falstaff*, wherein the Fat Knight is permitted to answer for himself concerning the charges against him, and *to attorney* his own case." (Eng.) See **lawyering.**

D. Plural. *Attornies* is an obsolete plural of the word (see the quotation from Boswell under (A) of this article); *attorneys* is now the universally accepted plural. Cf. *monies*, which is inferior to *moneys.*

attorneying. See **attorney** (C) & **lawyer,** v.i.

attorney-client privilege should be hyphenated.

attorney's fees; attorneys' fees; attorney fees. The first of these now appears to be prevalent. See Attorney's Fee Act, 42 U.S.C. § 1988 (1982). The plural possessive *attorneys' fees* is just as good, and some may even prefer that term in contexts in which there is clearly more than one attorney referred to. *Attorney fees* is inelegant but increasingly common. It might be considered a means to avoid having to get the apostrophe right. (But cf. *expert-witness fees.*) *Counsel fees* is another, less-than-common variant.

The only form to avoid at all costs is *attor-*

neys fees, in which the first word is a genitive adjective with the apostrophe wrongly omitted. This form appears in Leff, *The Leff Dictionary of Law*, 94 Yale L.J. 1855, 1969 (1985), under "affirmative relief."

attorney general, made plural, forms *attorneys general* in the U.S., *attorney-generals* in G.B.

attornies. See **attorney** (D).

attornment has two analogous senses, the first relating to personal property and the second relating to land. It may mean either (1) "an act by a bailee in possession of goods on behalf of one person acknowledging that he will hold the goods on behalf of someone else" (*CDL*); or (2) "a person's agreement to hold land as the tenant of someone else." Both senses are used in G.B. and in the U.S.

An English court has stated that the *attornment* clause in mortgages "is entirely obsolete and *at the present time* [q.v.] performs no useful purpose." *Steyning & Littlehampton Building Society v. Wilson,* [1951] Ch. 1018, 1020.

at trial. See **at (the) trial.**

attribute, n.; **attribution.** Although these terms overlap to a great extent, a distinction might advantageously be observed: *attribution* = the act or an instance of ascribing a characteristic or quality; *attribute* = a characteristic or quality so ascribed.

attributive, -tory. The former is the standard term.

ATTRIBUTIVE NOUNS. When a proper name is used attributively as an adjective, the writer should capitalize only that portion used in attribution. In *Southmark Properties v. The Charles House Corp.,* 742 F.2d 862 (5th Cir. 1984), the opinion is scattered with references to "The Charles House property." *The,* however, should be lowercased, for the skeletal phrase is "the property," and only *Charles House* is being used attributively. The definite article, then, derives from the skeletal phrase and not from the name of the party, even though the name of the party is *The Charles House Corporation.*

at variance. See **variance.**

at which time is invariably prolix for *when.*

at will. *Employee at will* is an ellipsis for *employee at [the employer's] will. At will* is slowly changing from a POSTPOSITIVE to a prepositive modifier ⟨an at will employee⟩.

atypical; untypical. The preferred term is *atypical.*

auctorial. See **authorial.**

aught (= [1] anything; [2] all) is an ARCHA-ISM to be avoided. E.g., "*For aught that appears* [read *For all that appears*], this prohibition may have been wholly undeserved." Cf. **naught.**

auspices. *Under the auspices* is frequently misconstrued as meaning "in the form of" or "in accordance with." Actually, it means "with the sponsorship or support of." The term is properly used in this sentence: "The contest was determinable *under the auspices* of the newspaper company."

Here are examples of the all-too-frequent misusage: "The issue on appeal is the extent to which the Federal Savings and Loan Insurance Corporation, *under the auspices of* [read *in the form of*] a receivership or conservatorship, can preclude judicial review of a state claim."/ "After rendition of the circuit court's opinion and order, plaintiffs filed a motion for new trial with the court of appeals *under the auspices of* [read *under* or *in accordance with*] Fed. R.Civ. P.50(d)." See **aegis.**

autarchy; autarky. *Autarchy* = absolute rule or sovereignty, autocracy. *Autarky* = national economic self-sufficiency; isolationism.

authentification is incorrect for *authentication.*

author is becoming standard as a verb, though fastidious writers still avoid it. Generally it is a highfalutin substitute for *write, compose,* or *create.* E.g., "*Shelley v. Kraemer* stands at least for the proposition that, where parties of different races are willing to deal with one another, a state court cannot keep them from doing so by enforcing a privately *authored* [read *created*] racial restriction."/ "The orderly administration of an injunctive decree must be carried through by the court that *authored* [read *composed* or *originated*] and is administering that decree."

Nor is attribution to a collective body among the legitimate uses of this word: "Congress adopted an inclusionary approach when it *authored* [read *drafted* or *framed*] this rule." *Coauthor* has been considered more acceptable as a verb, perhaps because *co-write* seems deadpan.

With reference to *the author* (= I), see FIRST PERSON (B).

authoress. See SEXISM (C).

authorial; auctorial. The latter is a stuffy NEEDLESS VARIANT of the former.

autograph. See **allograph.**

autopsy; postmortem. These equivalents are each current in AmE and BrE. *Autopsy* is slightly more common in the U.S., and *postmortem* the same in G.B.

autopsy, v.t., was not until recently recorded in the dictionaries. It means "to perform a postmortem examination on." E.g., "Their testimony should be rejected as a matter of law because it ignored pathological studies of *autopsied* tissues of the bronchi and lungs that did not reveal the presence of chromates."

autrefois is a LAW FRENCH term, meaning "on another occasion, formerly," used in the phrases, more common in G.B. than in the U.S., *autrefois acquit* (= a plea in bar of arraignment that the defendant has been acquitted of the offense by a jury) and *autrefois convict* (= a plea in bar of arraignment that the defendant has been convicted of the offense by a jury).

auxillary is a bastard formation probably having arisen from confusion of *auxiliary* with *ancillary.*

avail, because it is most properly a reflexive verb only ⟨he availed himself of the opportunity⟩, does not work in the passive voice. E.g., "Congress meant that damages from or by floods should not afford any basis of liability against the United States regardless of *whether the sovereign immunity was availed of or not* [read *whether the government availed itself of sovereign immunity*]."

The verb is best not used as a nonreflexive transitive or intransitive verb. In each of the following examples, *help, profit,* or *benefit* should replace *avail:* "The defence of fair dealing may *avail* a defendant who cites passages from the plaintiff's work in order to criticise the underlying doctrine or philosophy." (Eng.)/ "Plaintiff has not brought this action under any of the civil-rights statutes, and it would not have *availed* him if he had."/ "Plaintiff testified that the contract of employment was for life; even if it were, however, the contract would *avail* him nothing, for an employment contract for life is prohibited under our law."

Avail is frequently used also as a noun: "The evidence in this regard, to have *avail,* should be of the most satisfactory kind."/ "We know that the admonition to the children would be wholly impotent and of no *avail.*"

availment (= the act of availing oneself of something) is omitted from most dictionaries, but is common in American legal writing. E.g., "The conditions necessary for *availment* of this provision are not present in the instant suit." *Henderson v. Prudential Insurance Corp.,* 238 F.Supp. 862, 866 (E.D. Mich. 1965)./ "If on remand the plaintiffs amend their pleadings accordingly, they will have established a case on the purposeful *availment* issue sufficient to resist dismissal on the face of the pleadings." *Thompson v. Chrysler Motors Corp.,* 755 F.2d 1162, 1173 (5th Cir. 1985).

avenge; revenge. To *avenge* is to visit fitting retribution upon; to *revenge* is to inflict suffering or harm upon another out of personal resentment. *Avenge* and *vengeance* have to do with justice and the legal process, *revenge* with getting even. *Revenge* is both intransitive and transitive; *avenge* is transitive only. Moreover, *revenge* may be a noun, whereas *avenge* may not. Both verbs take the preposition *on.*

aver; asseverate. These terms are popular with lawyers as substitutes for *say* or *state. Aver* has its place in solemn contexts—it should not be lightly used. *Asseverate,* an even weightier word, is seldom justified. Both refer to affirmations of fact, usu. with no implication that an oath has been taken.

average is a word that assumes a broad sample of subjects. The word does not mix well with *each:* "Each Houston partner *averages* ten years of Houston experience." [Read *Partners in Houston have an average of ten years' experience.*] See **each.**

averageable. So spelled.

averment; averral. *Averment* is the preferred nominal form of *aver* in both the U.S. and G.B. "One plea on which the respondents' case depends is the relevancy of *averments.*" (Eng.)/ "Upon review of a dismissal for failure to state a claim, we must accept all well-pleaded *averments* as true and view them in the light most favorable to the plaintiff." *Averral* is a NEEDLESS VARIANT.

averse. See **adverse.**

avert (= to turn away, prevent), when used for *advert,* is a MALAPROPISM. E.g., "Appellee correctly *averts* [read *adverts*] to the delineation in *Brown Shoe Co. v. United States,* in which the Supreme Court stated that 'the outer boundaries of a product market are determined by the reasonable interchangeability of use.'" See **advert.**

avertible, -able. The *-ible* form is preferable. See -ABLE (A).

aviate; avigate. No distinction was originally intended with the introduction of *avigate,* although some DIFFERENTIATION in emphasis has emerged. *Aviate,* a BACK-FORMATION of *aviation* first used in the late nineteenth century, means "to operate an aircraft." *Avigate,* a PORTMANTEAU WORD formed from *aviate* and *navigate,* means "to handle and guide (i.e., navigate) an aircraft in the air." *W3* records *avigation* but not *avigate;* the *OED* and *OED Supp.* neglect both words.

In the American law of easements, the usual phrase is *avigational* or *avigation easement.* E.g., "An *avigational* easement permits free flights over the land in question." *United States v. Brondum,* 272 F.2d 642, 645 (5th Cir. 1959)./ "We see no reason why an *avigation* easement may not be acquired by prescription in this state." *Drennen v. County of Ventura,* 112 112 Cal. Rptr. 907, 909 n. 2 (Cal. Dist. Ct. App. 1974).

avocation; vocation. These words are almost opposites, although many writers misuse *avocation* for *vocation.* The former means "hobby," whereas the latter means "a calling or profession." Here is the common mistake: "We defer to the opinions of our legal advisers, physicians, tradesmen, and artisans in all matters relating to their respective *avoca-*

tions." Did the writer of that sentence have in mind golf, gardening, and numismatics?

avoid, void, v.t.; **avoidance, voidance.** In legal writing these verb and noun pairs are perfectly synonymous. In law *avoid* often means "to make void or to cancel," although in the language of laymen it invariably means "to refrain from" or "to escape or evade." Here is an example of *avoid* in the old-fashioned legal sense: "We are next to consider, how a deed may be *avoided,* or rendered of no effect." (Blackstone)/ "Strictly, the word 'voidable' means valid until *avoided." Void* can act as noun, verb, or adjective. The noun *voidance* denotes "the act of voiding."

The legal senses of *avoid* and *avoidance* invariably confuse laymen, who are accustomed to the ordinary meanings of these words. It might therefore be advisable to prefer *void* and *voidance.* E.g., "If the wife has inchoate dower in land transferred in living trust and does not release her dower, her dower claim is not *avoided* [read *voided]."* / "The Wills Act of 1837 added a provision *avoiding* [read *voiding*] the interest of a party whose spouse was a witness, but went on to declare that no will should fail because the witnesses thereto were incompetent." The archaic sense of *avoid* is ensconced in a number of statutes, e.g.: "[T]he trustee may *avoid* any transfer of property to the debtor." 11 U.S.C. § 547(b).

Here the popular meaning of *avoid* appears in a legal context in such a way that a lawyer might at first wonder whether the legal meaning was intended: "The affidavit contains nothing more than a recital of unsupported allegations, conclusory in nature; as such, it is insufficient to *avoid* summary judgment."

In its lay sense "to evade or escape," *avoid* is sometimes misused for *prevent* or *circumvent:* "Wide public participation *avoids* [read *prevents*] the problem of unfairness."

avowal; avowry, avowtry. The noun corresponding to *avow* in its common meaning ("to declare openly") is *avowal.* Its sibling, *avowry,* serves as the nominal form corresponding to the specialized common-law meaning of *avow* ("to acknowledge, in an answer, that one has taken something, and to justify the act"). *Avowry* is the equivalent in actions of replevin to the general common-law doctrine of confession and avoidance.

E.g., "The reply of a plaintiff to an *avowry* by a defendant in a replevin action might take one of several forms." F. A. Enever, *History of the Law of Distress* 199 (1931). *Avowtry* is an obsolete synonym of *adultery.*

avulsion. Lawyers may run across the medical as well as the legal use of this word; hence it may be useful to understand the common thread in meaning. Generally, *avulsion* = the action of pulling off, plucking out, or tearing away; forcible separation (*OED*). In law, *avulsion* = the sudden removal of land, by change in a river's course or by the action of flood, to another person's estate; in which event, contrary to the rule of *alluvion* (q.v.) or gradual accretion of soil, it remains the property of the original owner (*OED*). Medically, however, the term has come to denote "a tearing away of a structure or part accidentally or surgically" (*W3*) ⟨*avulsion* of the diseased limb⟩.

await; wait. *Await* is always transitive (i.e., it takes a direct object), and *wait* is always intransitive. One *awaits* something, but one *waits for* or *on* something. If no object is supplied, *wait* is the proper term: "Then she brought the dishes in to where the family *awaited* [read *waited*], sitting at the low table."

awake(n). See **wake.**

award over is verbose for *award.* E.g., "What is at stake, as far as the charity is concerned, is the cost of reasonable protection and the amount of the insurance premium, not the *awarding over* [read *awarding*] of its entire assets in damages." See PARTICLES, UNNECESSARY & **over** (A).

aw(e)less. The spelling with the *-e-* is standard.

awful originally meant "inspiring or filled with awe." E.g., "No tribunal can approach such a question without a deep sense of importance, and of the *awful* responsibility involved in its decision." *McCulloch v. Maryland,* 17 U.S. (4 Wheat.) 316, 400 (1819) (per Marshall, C.J.). Its meaning has now degenerated to "horrible, terrible."

awhile; a while. Whenever this term is introduced by a preposition, it should be spelled as two words ⟨he rested for a while⟩. Generally, however, one should use the term adverbially without the preposition, and spell it as one word ⟨he rested awhile⟩.

axiom = an established principle that is universally accepted within a given framework of reasoning or thinking. The term should not be used of propositions argued for by advocates; if the issue is the subject of controversy, it is not an *axiom,* unless the question is the applicability of an axiom to a given situation.

B

backadation. See **backwardation.**

backberend; backberand; backbearing. This Anglo-Saxon term (meaning "having in one's possession," and used of a person carrying off stolen property [lit., "bearing it on his back"]) is now preferably spelled *backberend.* The other spellings are NEEDLESS VARIANTS. See **handhabend.**

BACK-FORMATIONS, or clippings, are words formed from what are mistakenly assumed to be derivatives. The commonest manifestations of this process occur when *-tion* nouns are erroneously foreshortened to make verbs in *-ate;* such back-formations are especially objectionable when they stand merely as NEEDLESS VARIANTS of already extant verbs: *administrate* (*administer*), *indemnificate* (*indemnify*), *cohabitate* (*cohabit*), *interpretate* (*intrepret*), *delimitate* (*delimit*), *orientate* (*orient*). *Sculpt,* arguably a NEEDLESS VARIANT of *sculpture,* v.t., is now actually the more common verb.

Many back-formations never gain real legitimacy (e.g., *enthuse*), some are aborted early in their existence (e.g., *ebullit, frivol*), and still others are of questionable vigor (e.g., *effulge, elocute, evanesce*). *Burgle,* q.v., (back-formed from *burglar*) continues to have a jocular effect (in the U.S.), as do *emote* and *laze.* Three twentieth-century back-formed words, *choate, liaise,* and *surveil* (qq.v.), have come to be used with some frequency in legal contexts.

Many examples have survived respectably, among them *donate, orate, resurrect, diagnose, aviate,* and *spectate. Enthuse* may one day be

among these respectable words, although it has not gained approval since it first appeared in the early nineteenth century. But those that have become accepted as legitimate words have filled gaps in the language, and won acceptance through their usefulness. The best rule of thumb is to avoid newborn back-formations that appear newfangled, but not, like a prig, to eschew faintly recognizable back-formations that are nonetheless useful. Only philologists today recognize as back-formations *beg* (from *beggar*), *peddle* (from *peddler*), *rove* (from *rover*), *type* (from *typewriter*), and *jell* (from *jelly*).

back of; in back of. These colloquial phrases are inferior to *behind* in both literal and figurative uses. E.g., "Before negligence can be predicated on a given act, *back of* [read *behind*] the act must be sought and found a duty to the individual complaining, the observer of which would have averted or avoided the injury."

backpay is commonly spelled as one word in American legal writing. The British tend to spell it as two words.

backwardation; backadation. Leff defines this term (having two forms) as, "in stock market parlance, a fee paid by a seller for the privilege of delaying the delivery of securities past their normal delivery date," and puts his main entry under *backadation.* See Leff, *The Leff Dictionary of Law,* 94 Yale L.J. 1855, 2113 (1985). Most dictionaries, however, spell the term *backwardation.* Fowler included the term in his "ill-favored list" of HYBRID derivatives, but it has become standard.

bade. See **bid.**

bad; badly. See ADVERBS (C).

bail is a CHAMELEON-HUED legal term. As a noun, it means (1) "the person who acts as a surety for a debt"; (2) "the security or guaranty agreed upon"; or (3) "release on bail of a person in custody." As a verb, *bail* means (1) "to set free for security on one's own recognizance for appearance on another day"; (2) "to become a surety for"; or (3) "to guarantee."

Modern idiom requires *release on bail,* although formerly *in bail* was not uncommon: "Mr. Bartletta was then taken before the recorder and released *in bail* to await the act of the grand jury."

bailable = admitting of or entitled to bail. Thus it may refer to persons or to offenses. E.g., "Furthermore, the record shows that Dovalina's attempted murder charge was not *bailable.*" (One might as naturally have written that Dovalina himself was not *bailable,* because he had been charged with attempted murder.)/ "Even if Congress is free to define *nonbailable* offenses, certainly the allowable justifications are limited and cannot include punishing a defendant before the final determination of his guilt." See -ABLE.

bail bondsman. See **bailor.**

bail de la seisine. See LOAN TRANSLATIONS.

bailee; bailie. *Bailee* = one to whom property is bailed, or delivered in trust. E.g., "*Bailees* alone could sue for a conversion and were answerable over for the chattel to their bailor" (Holmes, J.). *Bailie* is a term for a Scottish magistrate; it is also a dialectal variant of *bailiff,* q.v.

bailer. See **bailor.**

bailie. See **bailee.**

bailiery; bailiary. The former is the preferred form of this word, meaning "the jurisdiction of a bailie."

bailiff has come, perhaps only in law school mock trials and moot court, to be used as a verb meaning "to act as bailiff." If that is so, it will perforce soon infiltrate the speech of the profession. It is an acceptable colloquialism, but should not appear in serious print.

bailiwick; sheriffwick. *Bailiwick* = the office, jurisdiction, or district of a bailiff. Figuratively, it has become synonymous with *domain.* *Sheriffwick* = the office, jurisdiction, or district of a sheriff.

Because in one sense *bailiff* and *sheriff* are synonymous, the derivatives in *-wick* have become synonyms. *Bailiwick* is the more common of the two: "At common law, a sheriff has no jurisdiction beyond the borders of his county, the rule being that the acts of an officer outside of his county or *bailiwick* are un-

official and necessarily void unless expressly or impliedly authorized by statute." *Bailiffry* is a NEEDLESS VARIANT, and *bailivia* is an obsolete variant, of *bailiwick. Sheriffdom* is a variant form of *sheriffwick.* See **sheriffalty.**

bailor, -er; bailee. *Bailor* and *-er* are not at all clearly distinguished in actual legal usage, although they might easily and usefully be given clear DIFFERENTIATION. *Bailor* and *bailee* (i.e., the persons on the giving and receiving ends of a bailment) are correlative personal nouns. E.g., "No *bailee* is permitted to deny that the *bailor* by whom any goods were entrusted to him was entitled to those goods at the time when they were so entrusted." (Eng.) See **bailee.**

Bailer (or *bail bondsman*) should be reserved for the sense "one who attaches bail (the surety in criminal law)." Nevertheless, the spelling *bailor* is often used in that sense, and *bailer* appears occasionally in civil contexts. With the certain advent of objections to *bail bondsman* on grounds of SEXISM, we ought to encourage wider use of *bailer* in this sense.

banc. See **en banc.**

bandit has two plural forms, *bandits* and *banditti.* The native English form (*bandits*) is preferred.

banish, v.t., generally takes the preposition *from* ⟨he was banished from the country⟩. Krapp cites the use "The king *banishes* you his presence," with two objects, but this use is archaic.

bankrupt; bankrout. The latter is an obsolete form of the word. In the English Renaissance, scholars respelled French borrowings such as *bankrout* on the Latin model, hence *bankrupt.* Many of these respellings did not survive (e.g., *accompt* for *account*); *bankrupt* is one of the few that did. See **comptroller.**

bankruptee, n., is an unnecessary NEOLOGISM equivalent to the well-established *bankrupt,* n., = one that has declared bankruptcy. E.g., "For legal purposes, the family homestead can include up to 200 acres (100 for a single adult) of real property that aren't located within city, town, or village limits, and/or one acre of land, plus any temporary residence if the *bankruptee* [read *bankrupt*] has not acquired another home." Shropshire, *The Nouveau Broke*, D Magazine, Nov. 1986, at 89 (inset).

bar. In the U.S., all lawyers are members of a bar, whether they are litigators or office practitioners. In G.B., only barristers, as opposed to solicitors, make up the *Bar* (the word is customarily capitalized in G.B.). See **called to the bar** & **attorney** (A).

bar; debar; disbar. The first two have closely related meanings. *Bar* means "to prevent (often by legal obstacle)." E.g., "The English Statute of Westminster II *barred* dower of a wife who deserted her husband and committed adultery; and some states have statutes *barring* an elective share on a similar principle."/ "The court concluded that these warranty disclaimers did not necessarily *bar* a breach of contract claim."/ "Legislative immunity does not, of course, *bar* all judicial review of legislative acts." *Bar* serves also as a noun ⟨a bar to all claims⟩.

Debar, a somewhat archaic FORMAL WORD, means "to preclude from having or doing." E.g., "It would require very persuasive circumstances enveloping congressional silence to *debar* this Court from re-examining its own doctrines."/ "There is no reason why the plaintiff should be confined to his action on the special agreement, and be *debarred* his remedy on the assumpsit implied by law." (Eng.) *Disbar* means "to expel from the legal profession." The corresponding nouns are *debarment* and *disbarment*.

bargained-for exchange. This phrase is sometimes erroneously rendered *bargain for exchange*. Here variations of it are correctly used: "The doing of the act constitutes acceptance, the *bargained-for* consideration, and the offeree's performance."/ "If the termination of obligations were an immediate *bargained-for* right of consequence, he would presumably have taken advantage of his freedom from testamentary obligation to make a new will."

The origin of the phrase *bargained-for exchange* may be seen from this sentence: "Consideration is something bargained for and given in exchange."

bargainee (= the purchaser in a bargained-for exchange) is more obscure than *purchaser*, but the word is perhaps a necessary correlative of *bargainor*. See -EE.

bargainer, -or. The two forms are not synonymous, as one might suspect. *Bargainer* means "one who bargains." *Bargainor* has a more specific legal meaning: "the seller in a bargained-for exchange."

bargee is illogically formed with the -ee suffix, but it is established. See -EE. *Bargee* (17th c.) is a variant of *bargeman* (14th c.), without the infelicity of SEXISM. E.g., "The story of the Elmhurst's *bargee* was that off Bedloe's Island a third tug of the railroad . . . came alongside, struck the barge a heavy blow on her port quarter, nearly capsizing her, driving her forward against the barge ahead, and breaking some planks forward." *Sinram v. Pennsylvania R.R.*, 61 F.2d 767, 768 (2d Cir. 1932)(per L. Hand, J.).

barratry; simony. Why these terms are sometimes confused is not at all apparent. *Barratry* = (1) (in Scots law) the accepting of a bribe by a judge; (2) vexatious persistence in, or incitement to, litigation (*OED*). The adjective is *barratrous*, the agent noun *barrator*. *Simony* = the purchase or sale of an ecclesiastical promotion. The adjective is *simoniac(al)*, the agent noun either *simonist* or *simoniac*.

barrister. See **attorney** (A) & **solicitor**.

barristerial = of or pertaining to a barrister; lawyerly. The term is, naturally, more British than American.

basis is sometimes wrongly used for *reason*. E.g., "The court, after a full review of the authorities, concluded that there was now no sound *basis* [read *reason*] why the value of life insurance coverage, as well as the cash surrender value, might not be considered in a property division between parties to a divorce action."

This word may also do mischief in adverbial constructions (on a ---- basis), where a simple adverb would serve better. "The commission was set up *on a provisional basis* [read *provisionally*]."/ "Those issues must be *determined on a case-by-case basis* [read *determined case by case*]."/ "The attorney represented his clients *on a contingent-fee basis* [read *for a contingent fee*]." See FLOTSAM PHRASES.

The plural of *basis,* as well as *base,* is *bases;* the pronunciations differ, however: for *basis,* the plural is pronounced /*bay-seez*/, for *base* /*bays-ez*/.

bastard, a term of abuse generally, is still used with technical neutrality in the law. E.g., "Although a *bastard* cannot inherit from his parents or other ancestors at common law, statutes or judicial decisions permit a *bastard* to inherit from his mother and the mother to inherit from her *bastard.*" This technical neutrality is not, however, today without comic overtones. See EUPHEMISMS.

bastardy = (1) the condition of a bastard; illegitimate birth; or (2) the begetting of bastards; fornication (*OED*). Today in sense (1), *illegitimacy* is the more usual term, and the preferable one for avoiding unduly derogatory connotations. Sense (2) is not common.

bathos; pathos. These two words frequently cause confusion. *Bathos* means "a sudden descent from the exalted to the trite, or from the sublime to the ridiculous." *Pathos* means "sympathetic pity," and is useful, e.g., in reference to juries.

battery connotes to the layman physical violence. The legal meaning, however, is "the intentional or negligent application of physical force to, or the offensive contact with, someone without his consent." E.g., "[T]he *battery* here was a technical one, and was accompanied by neither physical injury nor violence. It was a mere touching of the person of the plaintiff, a mere incident of the restraint, the false imprisonment." *Fisher v. Rumler,* 239 Mich. 224, 214 N.W. 310, 311 (1927). See **assault.**

beak is a BrE slang term for a magistrate or justice of the peace.

because causes problems when used as a conjunction after *reason.* Here the construction is inverted: "*Because* [read *That*] the lessor accepted the first payment is no reason to conclude that the corporation existed by estoppel." See **reason is because.** On *because* generally, see **as** (A).

before for *by.* Cases come *before* courts, which then *review* those cases (i.e., *review* is by

those courts). "We note that such a determination is a matter placed within the sound discretion of the district judge, and review *before* [read *by*] us is very limited."

beg is occasionally used in dissenting opinions in the phrases *beg to differ* and *beg to advise.* These are ARCHAISMS to be eschewed.

begat; begot. See BIBLICAL AFFECTATION.

beget is today used only figuratively. E.g., "The services and gifts must have been rendered with a frequency that *begets* an anticipation of their continuance." In its literal sense, *beget* is an ARCHAISM. E.g., "When proof has been given of the non-access of the husband at any time when his wife's child could have been *begotten,* the wife may give evidence as to the person by whom it was *begotten.*" (Eng.) The more usual term today is *to conceive* or *to father.*

begging the question does not mean "evading the issue" or "inviting the obvious questions," as some mistakenly believe. The proper meaning of *begging the question* is "basing a conclusion on an assumption that is as much in need of proof or demonstration as the conclusion itself." The formal name for this logical fallacy is *petitio principii.* In the following sentence the writer mangled this SET PHRASE and misapprehended its meaning: "This explanation begs the issue."

As for an example of *begging the question,* here is a classic one: "Reasonable men are those who think and reason intelligently." *Patterson v. Nutter,* 78 Me. 509, 7 A. 273, 275 (1886). This statement begs the question, "What does it mean to think and reason intelligently?"

begin. A. *To begin.* As an introductory phrase used to enumerate reasons, the idiomatic phrase is *to begin with,* not *to begin.* In the following sentence, the lack of the preposition *with* makes *to begin* sound narrowly chronological, as if *A* actually began something and then, at some indeterminate point, stopped: "To begin, A played a substantial role in negotiating both agreements." [Read *To begin with, A played a substantial role in negotiating both agreements.*]/ "To begin [add *with*], it was clear that Dixon suffered a permanent injury and that he died of an unrelated disease."

B. And *commence & start. Begin* is the usual word, to be preferred in nine times out of 10. *Commence* is a FORMAL WORD; ceremonies and exercises are likely to *commence,* as are legal proceedings. *Start* is usually used of physical movement ⟨to start running⟩. Both *begin* and *start* may be followed by an infinitive, but not *commence.* See **commence.**

behalf. A distinction exists between *in behalf of* and *on behalf of.* The former means "in the interest or in defense of" ⟨he fought in behalf of a just man's reputation⟩; the latter, *on behalf of,* means "as the agent of, as representative of" ⟨on behalf of the corporation, I would like to thank . . . ⟩ ⟨he appeared on behalf of his client⟩.

Upon behalf of is now considered much inferior to *on behalf of.* "We conclude that the public interest involved in this dispute compels us to look beyond the immediate interests of the named litigants and to consider the situation of the natural gas consumers *upon* [read *on*] whose behalf the Mississippi Power Service Commission has intervened." See **upon.**

behavior. See COUNT AND MASS (NONCOUNT) NOUNS (B) & PLURALS (B).

behavior(al)ism. The correct name for the doctrine that human behavior provides the only significant psychological data is *behaviorism.*

behest is a stonger word than *request;* it means (1) "a command," or (2) "a strong urging." *Bequest,* q.v., is sometimes misused for *behest,* as here: "It is enough that a writing defamatory in content has been read and understood at the *bequest* [read *behest*] of the defamer."/ "At his *bequest* [read *behest*], I undertook this onerous task, but have been thankful to him for so urging me." This is a MALAPROPISM.

behoof is the noun, *behoove* (AmE) or *behove* (BrE) the verb. Both noun and verb have an archaic flavor. Historically, the verb in BrE was pronounced, as it now is in AmE, to rhyme with *move* and *prove.* In BrE today "it is generally made to rime with *rove, grove,* by those who know it only in books" (*OED*).

belabor; labor, v.t. Modern dictionaries suggest that in practice the words are interchangeable. Historically, however, in the best usage *belabor* is not to be used figuratively in phrases such as *to belabor an argument;* the preferred expression is *to labor an argument.* The popular grammarian Edwin Newman has chided a justice of the U.S. Supreme Court for writing "to say more would belabor the obvious," stating: "To *belabor* the obvious is to hit it, which hardly seems judicial conduct." E. Newman, Foreword to M. S. Freeman, *A Treasury for Word Lovers* viii (1983).

Following are still other examples: "Without *belaboring* [read *laboring*] the point, we observe that the separation agreement in this case will be at least partly performed in Texas because the payor resides in that state."/ "A will be conceded his right against B without undue *belaboring* [read *laboring*]."

belated has made its way into legal language as a synonym of *untimely.* E.g., "We must decline to entertain appellant's *belated* cross-points." Its use in this context is perfectly acceptable.

belie = (1) to disguise, give a false idea of; (2) to leave unfulfilled; or (3) to contradict or prove the falsity of. Sense (3) is by far the commonest in legal contexts. E.g., "The Court suggests that the search for valuables in the closed glove compartment might be justified as a measure to protect the police against lost property claims; again, this suggestion is *belied* [i.e., *contradicted*] by the record."/ "Appellant contends that his lawyer's failure to put on evidence at the penalty stage prejudiced his ability to avoid the death sentence; but the nature of the evidence appellant asserts his attorney should have presented *belies* [i.e., *proves the falsity of*] the argument." See **vitiate.**

below is often used by appellate courts to mean "at the trial-court stage." E.g., "As the district court noted *below,* this litigation involves only that portion of the contract relating to the actual construction of the platform."

below-mentioned; under-mentioned. The former is AmE or BrE; the latter is BrE only. *Below,* like *above,* q.v., is frequently used as an ellipsis for *below-mentioned.*

bemuse; amuse. The former is frequently taken to be a fancy variant of the latter; the meanings differ significantly, however. *Bemuse* = (1) to plunge into thought, preoccupy; or (2) to muddle (one's mind); bewilder. Here sense (2) of *bemuse* applies: "It is easy to see why an equity court, *bemused* by the expression 'Equity acts in personam and not in rem,' would be tempted to say that an equity court has no 'power' to affect directly land titles in another state." *Amuse* needs no definition here.

bench, like *court,* q.v., has come to stand, through metonymy, for judges collectively, as in the phrase *bench and bar.*

bencher, in England, means "one who sits on a bench" (*OED*), and usually refers to a member of the governing body of one of the Inns of Court. E.g., "I happen to be a *Bencher* of the Inner Temple, and whilst the former glories of the Inns of Court have in a large measure departed, some things abide throughout the centuries." (Lord Justice Birkett)/ "There was thus little occasion for controversies as to discipline to be brought before the judges, unless the *benchers* failed in the performance of their duties." *People ex rel. Karlin v. Culkin,* 162 N.E. 487, 490 (N.Y. App. 1928) (per Cardozo, C.J.). *Benchers* are known also as *Masters of the Bench.* Archaically, the term was used more generally in reference to magistrates, judges, assessors, and senators.

benchmark (= a point of reference from which to make measurements) is best spelled as one word.

bench trial has become a common equivalent of *trial to the bench* (= a nonjury trial).

benefic(ent); beneficial; benevolent. The etymological difference between *beneficent* and *benevolent* is that between deeds and sentiments. *Beneficent* = doing good, charitable (*benefic* now being merely a NEEDLESS VARIANT). *Benevolent* = well-wishing, supportive, (emotionally) charitable. The DIFFERENTIATION should be cultivated; we should reserve *beneficent* for "doing good," and *benevolent* for "inclined or disposed to do good." In the following sentences, *benevolence* is used for *beneficence:* "The beneficiary of a charity (e.g., one who uses a charitable hospital) has impliedly [q.v.] waived his right to sue in tort, by virtue of having accepted its *be-*

nevolence [read *beneficence*]."/ "The will and the entire record reveal that the decedent was a very *benevolent man* [read *beneficent man*] who was in the habit of making charitable gifts all over the world."

Beneficial has the general meaning "favorable, producing benefits," and the specialized legal meaning "consisting in a right that derives from something (as a contract or an expectancy) other than legal title" ⟨beneficial interest⟩, a sense that derives from the older legal meaning "of or pertaining to usufruct" (*OED*). E.g., "An alien may generally become trustee of property that he can own *beneficially*."/ "The supervised administration embraces a determination of the persons *beneficially* entitled to the estate after debts, expenses, and taxes are paid." See **maleficent.**

beneficiary. See **cestui que trust** & **devisee.**

benefit. Invariably the passive form of this verb can be advantageously made into an active construction: "Defendant has an adverse interest because he would *have been benefited by* [read *have benefited from*] a ruling in favor of the insurance company." See BE-VERBS (B).

benefit(t)ed; benefit(t)ing. These words should be spelled with one -*t*-, not two. See DOUBLING OF CONSONANTS.

benefittees has not yet made its way into the dictionaries, though it has appeared in American legal prose. E.g., "The final House version of the bill included no mention of existing seniority systems and the *benefittees* thereunder." The double -*tt*- is incorrect (cf. *benefited*) because the accent does not fall on the penultimate syllable. The better spelling of the word, if we are to have it at all, is *benefitee.* (See -EE.) But the word is almost certainly unnecessary for *beneficiary.*

benevolent. See **benefic(ent).**

benign; benignant. The latter is a NEEDLESS VARIANT. The antonym of *benign,* however, is *malignant.*

bequeath; devise; devolve. *Bequeath* = to give personal property by will. Laymen and lawyers alike use this term metaphorically:

"While its origins are somewhat obscure, we know that the marital privilege is *bequeathed* to us by the long evolution of the common law, not by constitutional adjudication." See **legate.**

Devise = to give real property by will. As a noun, *devise* refers to the realty so given—the analogue for personal property is *bequest.* The Uniform Probate Code uses only the term *devise* to describe giving property by will whether the property is real or personal; it would be bootless to call this well-ensconced terminological shift incorrect. See **devise.**

Devolve = to pass on (an estate, right, liability, or office) from one person to another. In the context of estates, *devolve* usually takes the preposition *upon,* and sometimes *to.* See **devolve.**

bequest; bequeathal; bequeathment. *Bequest* = (1) the act of bequeathing; or (2) personal property (usu. other than money) disposed of in a will. *Bequeathal* and *bequeathment* are NEEDLESS VARIANTS of sense (1) of *bequest.*

Bequest should not be used as a verb, as I once used it in this sentence: "And by so felicitously using the words newly *bequested* [read *bequeathed*] to English, [Shakespeare], more than any other writer of the English Renaissance, validated the efforts of earlier and contemporary neologists." B. Garner, *Shakespeare's Latinate Neologisms,* 15 Shakespeare Stud. 149, 151 (1982).

Bequest is sometimes confused with *behest,* q.v.

bereave, v.t., yields past-tense forms *bereft* or *bereaved,* and the same forms as past participles. *Bereaved* is used in reference to loss of relatives by death. *Bereft* is used in reference to loss of immaterial possessions or qualities.

As Bryson has observed, to be *bereft of* something is not merely to lack it but to have been dispossessed of it. *Dictionary of Troublesome Words* 26 (1984). Hence this use is incorrect: "The Mann Act was not designed to cover voluntary actions *bereft of* [read *lacking*] sexual commercialism."

bestowal; bestowment. The latter is a NEEDLESS VARIANT. E.g., "We held that a change in judicial interpretation or view of applicable law after final judgment has been entered does not furnish a basis for a bill of review and the *bestowal* of equitable relief."/

"The term 'endowment' has been defined as the *bestowment* [read *bestowal*] of money as a permanent fund, the income of which is to be used in the administration of a proposed work."

bet ⟩ bet ⟩ bet. *Betted* is incorrect.

betrothal; betrothment. The latter is a NEEDLESS VARIANT.

bettor is the standard spelling for "one who bets or wagers." *Better* has also been used in this sense, but is liable to confusion with the comparative form of *good.* Cf. **abettor.**

between. **A.** *Between & among. Between* is commonly said to be better with two, and *among* with more than two, things. Fowler calls this a "superstition," and quotes the *OED:* "In all senses *between* has been, from its earliest appearance, extended to more than two. . . . It is still the only word available to express the relation of a thing to many surrounding and individually; *among* expresses a relation to them collectively and vaguely: we should not say *the space lying among the three points* or *a treaty among three Powers.*" The rule as generally enunciated, then, is merely simplistic. Although it is an accurate guide for the verb *divide* (*between* with two objects, *among* with more than two), the only ironclad distinction is that stated by the *OED. Between* expresses one-to-one relations of many things, and *among* expresses collective and undefined relations.

Article VII of the U.S. Constitution uses *between* to express reciprocal relations: "The Ratification of the Conventions of nine States, shall be sufficient for the Establishment of this Constitution *between* the States so ratifying the Same." Yet even the more valid distinction is a relatively new one, not observed by the English courts in 1607: "All the Justices, viz., POPHAM, Chief Justice of England, COKE, Chief Justice of the Common Pleas, FLEMING, Chief Baron, FENNER, SEARL, YELVERTON, WILLIAMS, and TANFIELD, JJ., were assembled at Sergeants-Inn, to consult what prerogative the King had in digging and taking of saltpetre to make gunpowder by the law of the realm; and upon conference *between* them, these points were resolved by them all, una voce." *The Case of the King's Prerogative in Saltpetre,* 12 Co. 12 (1607).

In the same case in which Justice Marshall several times writes, "*among* the defendant, the forum, and the litigation," Justice Brennan, in his concurring and dissenting opinion, writes: "*between* the controversy, the parties, and the forum state." See *Shaffer v. Heitner*, 433 U.S. 186 (1977). The latter phrasing might be said to express a more specific individual relation between each of the named things, the former phrasing (perhaps consciously) expressing a vaguer relation.

B. *Between* and Numbers. This may cause problems, if the numbers at either end of the spectrum are intended to be included. E.g., "If three petitioners and one respondent advance to Round Three from a bracket, then those four teams' names will be placed in a hat, and *between one and three* [read *from one to three*] teams will be chosen to switch sides." (Two is the only whole number between one and three.)

C. *Between you and I.* A commentator has pointedly termed this locution "a grammatical error of unsurpassable grossness." One can add little to that judgment.

D. *Between; as between.* Sometimes *as between* (= comparing; in comparison of) is misused for the straightforward preposition. E.g., "The contractual *provisions as between* [read *provisions between*] the parties are as follows." Cf. **as against.**

E. Fewer Than Two Objects. This construction is a peculiar brand of ILLOGIC, as in *between each house* or *between each speech* (instead of, properly, *between every two houses* and *between speeches*). Another manifestation of this error is *between . . . or*, with two prepositional objects, rather than *between . . . and*: the misuse results from confusion between *either . . . or* and *between . . . and.*

betwixt is an ARCHAISM.

BE-VERBS. **A.** Wrongly Omitted in Non-Finite Uses. *Be*-verbs, usually in the infinitive or participial form, are often omitted from sentences in which they would add clarity. One explanation is that they are intended to be "understood." (See UNDERSTOOD WORDS.) But this explanation does not excuse the ambiguities and awkwardnesses often caused by such omissions. The bracketed verbs in the sentences following were originally omitted: "These devices can be used to intercept a wire or oral communication; specifically designated as not [*being*] such devices are telephone or telegraph equipment furnished to a user and used in the ordinary course of business, and hearing aids."/ "The annotation necessarily starts with the assumption that the process or information involved was regarded as [*being*] of a secret or confidential nature."/ "If the western film offer were found [*to be*] different [*from*] or inferior to the musical film offer, it makes no difference whether Parker reasonably or unreasonably refused the second offer."/ "Because this instruction was substantially similar to the willfulness instruction at the end of the trial, which we have previously held [*to be*] proper, the instruction was not erroneous."/ "If I thought those two cases [*to be*] in point, I should have to consider them very carefully, but I do not." (Eng.)

B. Circumlocutory Uses. Verb phrases containing *be*-verbs are often merely circumlocutory ways of saying something better said with a simple verb. Thus *be determinative of* for *determine* is verbose. But *be determinative* is all right where there is no object, as in Judge Learned Hand's statement: "All such attempts are illusory, and, if serviceable at all, are so only to center attention upon which one of the factors may *be determinative* in a given situation."

The following circumlocutory uses of *be*-verbs are common in legal writing; the simple verb is ordinarily to be preferred: *be abusive of (abuse), be amendatory of (amend), be benefited by (benefit from), be conducive to (conduce to), be decisive of (decide), be derived from (derive from), be desirous of (desire or want), be determinative of (determine), be dispositive of (dispose of), be in agreement (agree), be in attendance (attend), be indicative of (indicate), be in dispute (dispute or disagree), be in error (err), be in exercise of due care (exercise due care), be in existence (exist), be influential on (influence), be in receipt of (have received), be operative (operate), be persuasive of (persuade), be possessed of (possess), be productive of (produce), be probative of (prove), be promotive of (promote), be violative of (violate).*

Many such wordy constructions are more naturally phrased in the present tense singular: *is able to (can), is authorized to (may), is binding upon (binds), is empowered to (may), is unable to (cannot).*

C. Unidiomatically Used in Place of Action Verbs. One should always use the specific verb that conveys the idea of the action described, rather than an unspecific *be*-verb: "Some agencies adopt procedures that permit some public participation; understandable pressures from interested outsiders *are* [read *demand*] that more should (or in some cases must) do so.''

beyond cavil. See **cavil, beyond.**

bi-; semi-. One can remember the proper prefix in a given context by noting that *bi-* means ''two,'' and *semi-* ''half.'' Hence *bimonthly* = every two months (not ''twice a month'') and *semimonthly* = every half-month, or twice a month. *Biweekly* and *semiweekly* work similarly. Still, *bi-* has been used to mean ''occurring twice in a (specified span of time)'' so often (and legitimately, e.g., in *biennial*) that, for the sake of clarity, it may be better to avoid the prefix altogether when possible. See the next entry.

biannual; biennial; semiannual. *Biannual* and *semiannual* both mean ''occurring twice a year.'' *Biennial* means ''occurring once every two years.'' The distinction between these words becomes important, for example, when employment contracts provide for ''*biannual* meetings of the committee to dispose of accident and bonus questions, and any other agreements.'' It is imprudent, however, to rely on a word like *biannual* for such a contractual provision. See **bi-.**

BIBLICAL AFFECTATION. In many respects the language of the law is the language of the King James Version (1611) or of Shakespeare. It is full of the ARCHAISMS we associate either with the Bible or, less commonly, with Shakespeare. Thus the Supreme Court of Mississippi recently published a sentence containing *doth*, q.v., which many of us have encountered only in traditional versions of the Bible. Likewise, *hath* and *hast* appear occasionally in DRAFTING (of a mediocre kind). Courts still occasionally use the Elizabethan *burthen*, q.v., as a variant of *burden*, though it has not been current for several centuries. And much of the syntax of legal prose is Biblical: ''A lawyer may never give unsolicited advice to a layman that he retain a client.'' See **that** (B).

Even today one can open up law reports and read of a *bounden duty*, as in the line from the *Book of Common Prayer*, ''We beseech thee to accept this our *bounden duty* and service.'' E.g., from the law: ''It is enough for this purpose that valiant efforts were made to persuade the district to do voluntarily what the United States Supreme Court and the California Supreme Court had held was its *bounden duty*.'' *Los Angeles Branch NAACP v. Los Angeles Unified School District*, 750 F.2d 731, 752 (9th Cir. 1984)(Pregerson, J., concurring). The origins of the phrase were legal and not religious, but today ''when we say *bounden duty* we do not call in any way to mind the bond [that] tied the feudal underling to his lord or the apprentice to his master.'' Simon, *English Idioms from the Law*, 76 Law Q.Rev. 283, 285 (1960).

Though traditions die hard, these are linguistic anachronisms that do not merit perpetuation. They needlessly widen the rift between what is legal and what is lay, and unwholesomely lend the air of priestly sanctity to the legal profession. Even the terms *lay* and *legal* used as opposites, much like *lay* and *ecclesiastical*, unnecessarily conjure up this notion, though they are not easily avoided.

It is worth adding to this discussion that citation to the Bible as legal precedent is not an admirable practice. Cardozo once wrote, ''In days not far remote, judges were not unwilling to embellish their deliverances with quotations from the poets. I shall observe toward such a practice the tone of decent civility that is due those departed.'' *Law and Literature*, 52 Harv. L. Rev. 471, 484 (1939). Yet the practice of quoting from the Bible has persisted. Here is an example from a judicial opinion of an American state supreme court:

[As] far as money buried or secreted on privately owned realty is concerned, the old distinction between treasure-trove, lost property, and mislaid property seems to be of little value and not worth preserving. The principal point of distinction seems to be the intent of the true owner who necessarily is not known and not available. Therefore the evidence on his intent will usually be scant and uncontroverted. . . . I would guess his motivation often to be that of the one-talent servant in the parable in the 25th Chapter of Matthew: ''And I was afraid, and went and hid thy talent in the earth. . . .'' We should hold that the owner of the land has possession of all property secreted in, on, and under his land and continues to hold possession for the true owner, who, incidentally, may not always be the person doing any burying. Matthew 13:44—''Again, the kingdom of heaven is like unto treasure hid in a field; the which when a man hath found, he hideth, and for joy thereof goeth and selleth all that he hath, and buyeth the field." What reason is there for transferring possession to the individual who happens to dig up the property? Or for guessing about the intent or the memory of the person doing the burying? A simple solution for all of these problems is to maintain the continuity of possession of the landowner until the true owner establishes his title.

The thing speaks for itself.

bicentennial; bicentenary. See **centennial.**

bid (= to offer a bid) forms *bid* in the past tense. In the sense of *bid farewell,* the past tense is *bade,* rhyming with *glad,* and the past participle is *bidden.* "She did as she was *bid* [read *bidden*]."

bid, n.; tender, n.   In AmE, both terms are used, whereas in BrE only the latter would appear, in the sense "a submitted price at which one will perform work or supply goods."

biennial = every two years. If we scale the numerical summit, we have *triennial* (3), *quadriennial* (4), *quinquennial* (5), *sexennial* (6), *septennial* (7), *octennial* (8), *novennial* (9), *deceddial* (10), *vicennial* (20), *centennial* (100), *millenial* (1000). See **bi- & biannual.**

bigamy; polygamy; digamy; deuterogamy. *Bigamy* = going through a marriage ceremony with someone when one is already lawfully married to someone else (*CDL*). It may be committed knowingly or unknowingly; if knowing, *bigamy* is a criminal offense.

Digamy and *deuterogamy* both mean "a legal second marriage occurring after divorce from or death of the first spouse." *Deuterogamy* is the more common term (to the extent that either might be called common!) and is not, like *digamy,* liable to confusion with *bigamy.* Hence *digamy* should be considered a NEEDLESS VARIANT.

Polygamy is the generic term for "multiple marriages," and encompasses *bigamy;* it is much used by anthropologists, describing both *polygyny* (the practice of having several wives) and *polyandry* (the practice of having several husbands).

bilateral; unilateral. A *unilateral* contract is one in which a promise is given by one party in exchange for the actual performance by the other party. A *bilateral* contract is one in which each party promises a performance, so that each party is an obligator on his own promise and an obligee on the other's promise.

bill.   See **suit.**

bill in chancery; bill in equity.   See **chancery.**

billion.   In the U.S. and France, *billion* means "one thousand millions" (= 1,000,000,000); but in G.B., Canada, and Germany, it means "one million millions" (= 1,000,000,000,000). An American *trillion,* q.v., equals the British *billion.* In BrE, however, the AmE meaning is gaining ground, esp. in journalism and technical writing.

bill of indictment.   See **indictment.**

bill of lading.   See **lading.**

bimonthly; semimonthly.   See **bi-; semi-.**

birth, v.i., was used with some frequency in the Middle Ages as a verb. It fell into disuse, however, and only recently has been revived in AmE ⟨the birthing of babies⟩. Some dictionaries label it dialectal. Given its usefulness and its long standing in the language, there can be no substantial objections to it.

biweekly; semiweekly.   See **bi-; semi-.**

black; Black; Negro; Afro-American. Currently it is best to use *black* (lowercase), n. & adj. E.g., "In *Jones v. Alfred H. Mayer Co.,* the complaint charged a refusal to sell petitioner a home because he was *black.*"

Blackacre is the proverbial example of real estate in hypothetical property problems. Abutting tracts are usually called *Whiteacre, Brownacre,* or some other colorized denomination. These terms have long been a part of the common-law tradition: "Where a devise is of *blackacre* to A., and of *whiteacre* to B. in tail, and, if they both die without issue, then to C., in fee, here A. and B. have cross remainders by implication." (Blackstone)

black-letter law. *Black-letter* is a term that describes Gothic or Old English type in antiquated books ⟨black-letter type⟩. By extension it came to be applied to legal principles that are fundamental and well settled or statements of such principles in a quasi-mathematical form. Law students frequently distinguish between professors with a predilection for *black-letter law* (what the law is) and those whose interest lies more in public policy (why the law is or what it ought to be). See the next entry & **hornbook law.**

Blackstone lawyer = *black-letter lawyer.* Because Blackstone is known as the jurist who systematically laid out black-letter principles for Anglo-American law, one whose primary interest and expertise is in these black-letter principles is termed a *Blackstone lawyer.*

blamable. See **blameworthy** (B).

blame, v.t., should take a person as the direct object, as in, "I *blame him* for the fires," rather than "I *blame the fires* on him." In the best usage, one *blames* a person; one does not, properly, *blame* a thing *on* a person.

blameworthy. A. And *culpable.* Though the two words are etymologically equivalent, in twentieth-century usage the Anglo-Saxon *blameworthy* has tended to be used in noncriminal, the Latinate *culpable* in criminal contexts. Hence *blameworthy* in civil contexts: "The indemnitee's conduct is sufficiently *blameworthy* to preclude indemnity."/ "Plaintiff is not *blameworthy* in failing to bring suit earlier; thus laches does not apply."/ "We also consider whether there was trickery or *blameworthy* action by the police."

And *culpable* in criminal contexts: "The court's focus must be on the defendant's *culpability,* not on those who committed the robbery and shot the victims."/ "The defense of mistake of fact was not available as a defense to negate the *culpable* mental state of criminal negligence."/ "It is reasonable to presume that the sentencing judge who revokes probation takes a fresh look at the defendant's *culpability* and circumstances and considers at that point the amount of time the defendant should be required to serve." See **guilty.**

Occasionally, however, *culpability* creeps into civil contexts, as here in the context of punitive damages, a hybrid remedy: "Exemplary damages are awarded only in cases of extreme *culpability* and are limited to the plaintiff's demonstrable litigation expenses."

Nevertheless, the writer of that sentence was describing egregious conduct, and *blameworthiness* today hardly seems appropriate for flagrant conduct.

B. And *blameful; blamable. Blameworthy* and *blamable* both mean "deserving to be blamed." The latter is a NEEDLESS VARIANT. *Blameful* (= imputing blame; blaming) has been mistakenly used for *blameworthy.* We need not use up more words for the meaning replicated by *blameworthy* and *blamable.*

blandish; brandish. The former means "to cajole; to persuade by flattery or coaxing." The latter means "to wave or shake in a menacing or threatening way."

blatant; flagrant. There is a well-defined distinction, but each word is frequently misused for the other. What is *blatant* stands out glaringly or repugnantly; what is *flagrant* is deplorable and shocking; this latter term connotes outrage. A perjurer might tell *blatant* lies to the grand jury to cover up for his *flagrant* breach of trust. Egregious criminal acts are *flagrant* ⟨flagrant arson⟩, not *blatant.* E.g., "For any *flagrant* dereliction or disregard of professional duty on the part of the attorney, the license by which he was admitted to practice may be revoked."/ "The court could have properly determined, as it did, that Batson's conduct was so *flagrant* as to justify severe sanctions."

Blatant is correctly used in this sentence: "The question concerning the blinding of the Libyan in the Colorado shooting was *blatantly* improper." Here *flagrant* is misused for *blatant:* "The constitutional violation is *flagrantly* [read *blatantly*] apparent in a case involving the imposition of a maximum sentence after reconviction."/ "No matter how infrequently the special counsel has brought Hatch Act charges in the past, federal employees can hardly be faulted for concluding that registering voters in *flagrant* [read *blatant*] disregard of the special counsel's advice is not worth the grave risk to their livelihoods."

Black's defines *flagrant necessity* as "a case of urgency rendering lawful an otherwise illegal act," and *flagrantly against the evidence* as "so much against the weight of the evidence as to shock the conscience and clearly indicate passion and prejudice of the jury." *Flagrant* is the wrong choice of word in the first phrase, though arguably correct in the second because of the element of shock. *Blatant necessity* would be the better wording for the first phrase, *blatant* here taking on its nonpejorative meaning "completely obvious or strikingly conspicuous"; a *blatant necessity* would allow one, e.g., to commit battery upon another by shoving him out of the way of an oncoming bus.

The phrase *blatantly obvious* is a REDUNDANCY. E.g., "The reasons for the dropping pass rate on the bar exam *are blatantly obvious* [read *are obvious*]."

BLENDS. See PORTMANTEAU WORDS.

bloc; block. Political groups or alignments are *blocs. Block* serves in all other senses.

blot on title. See **cloud.**

blue sky laws. In the early twentieth century, *blue sky* meant "an unsound investment, esp. in fake securities." Hence laws designed to protect gullible investors in securities have been given the name *blue sky laws.* The phrase is used in G.B. as well as in the U.S.

blunderbuss (= an obsolete firearm that scatters shot and is intended for close-range shooting) is often used figuratively in legal contexts. E.g., "This claim—on which every serious constitutional question turns—was pleaded in *blunderbuss* fashion in each of the complaints."/ "Many of the discovery requests are specific, many are *blunderbuss,* and many seek discovery previously refused by the court."/ "Since double payments can be prevented by a letter or a telephone call, it is unreasonable to accomplish this objective by the *blunderbuss* method of denying assistance to all indigent newcomers for an entire year." The more recent sense of *blunderbuss* (= a blundering person) has nothing to do with this sense. The term is infrequently misspelled *blunderbus.*

Sometimes the equivalent *scatter-gun* is used: "'Fraud, deceit, negligence, or estoppel' is a *scatter-gun* blast that could hardly miss winging the intended quarry."

blush, at first. See **at first blush.**

bodily heirs; heirs of the body; body heirs. The first and second are the classic formulations of the phrase, both unobjectionable. *Body heirs* is much inferior to *bodily heirs* for two reasons: first, generally we should not use a noun adjectivally when we have a serv-

iceable adjective; and second, *body heirs* is so little used that it grates on the legally trained ear.

body corporate is a variant of *corporation* that emphasizes the entity and the members that make it up rather than the abstract notion (*corporation*); *body corporate* is now used more commonly in BrE than in AmE.

boilerplate (= ready-made or all-purpose language that will fit a variety of contexts) is best spelled as one word in AmE, although *W3* lists it as two. E.g, "Each complaint contained *boilerplate* pleading of damages." For BrE, the *COD* gives the word as a hyphenate, *boiler-plate.* For an example of boilerplate language, see **attestation clause.**

bombastic is sometimes misconstrued to mean "strident" or "violent." Properly, *bombastic* (lit., "full of stuffing or padding") means "pompous; highfalutin; overblown." Here is a journalistic example of the error: "'If there is any change in the mood of the kids, it is for the worse,' says the Brixton police superintendent. 'They are more bombastic, they are cocky, they threaten riot as an answer if they don't get what they want.'" (Eng.) This confusion may arise from the suggestiveness of *bomb* in *bombastic.*

bona fide(s); good faith; bonne foi. *Bona fide,* adj., is understood by educated speakers of English; as a legal term, it is unlikely to give way completely to *good-faith,* adj. *Bona fides,* n., however, has lost much of its ground in legal writing to *good faith,* n. One writes, "He executed the contract in *good faith,*" not really thinking of *bona fides* as an alternative wording, although admittedly it is sometimes used: "General creditors of legatees may have a right to question the *bona fides* by which such legatees surrender any portion of their property after the right to it becomes vested." Generally, *good faith* is to be preferred. The pronunciation of *bona fides,* /boh-nă-*fI*-deez/, unlike that of its adjectival sibling, sounds foreign and bombastic. *Bonne foi,* a Frenchified variant, sounds still more so; fortunately, it is rarely encountered.

Bona fide was originally adverbial, meaning "in good faith" ⟨the suit was brought bona fide⟩. E.g., "The landlord may distrein any [stolen] goods of his tenant . . . unless they have been *bona fide* sold for a valuable consideration." (Blackstone)/ "Every person has a privilege in the interest of public justice to put the criminal law in motion against another whom he *bona fide,* and upon reasonable and probable cause, believes to have been guilty of a crime." (Eng.)/ "They acted *bona fide* in the best interests of the society of masons."

Today it is more commonly used as an adjective ⟨it was a bona fide suit⟩. None of the forms of this term should be hyphenated or written as one word, as *bona fide* sometimes is. The opposite of *bona fide* is *mala fide,* q.v.; the opposite of *bona fides* is *mala fides.*

In legal contexts, the adjectival *bona fide* should be avoided in the lay sense arrived at through SLIPSHOD EXTENSION, namely "genuine; not fake." E.g., "Even within the 50-mile area, containers that go directly to the owner of the cargo or to *bona fide warehouses* [read *genuine warehouses*] are exempted from the rule."

bona vacantia (lit. "vacant goods") is a TERM OF ART meaning "property not disposed of by a decedent's will and to which no relative is entitled upon intestacy." E.g., "The Crown sought to interpose a claim to *bona vacantia* between creditors and former members." (Eng.) The phrase should not be used when *unclaimed property* or *ownerless goods* will suffice.

book, bring to. See **bring to book.**

bookkeeper. So spelled (the only word in the English language with three consecutive sets of doubled letters); *bookeeper* is a common error.

bootstrap(ping) derives from the expression *to pull oneself up by one's bootstraps* (a futile effort). Through attenuation in meaning *bootstrapping* has progressed from a futile effort to an extremely difficult one that ultimately succeeds; the term is now often used, esp. in law, in the sense "making a success out of one's meager resources." E.g., "The majority uses state law to *bootstrap* a federal equal protection violation."/ "Government may not *bootstrap* probable cause from an innocent act of a police officer after the instructions to arrest."

bordereau (= [1] a note of account or, more commonly, [2] a description of reinsured risks) is the singular, *-reaux* the plural.

The word has recently come to be used as a verb: "American and Southeastern Fire Insurance Co., to which the policy had been 'bordereauxed,' refused payment." *Merchants Nat'l Bank v. Southeastern Fire Ins. Co.,* 751 F.2d 771, 773 (5th Cir. 1985). The proper verb form, however, would be *bordereau* (singular), not *-reaux.* Hence, in the above quotation the word should be *bordereaued* or *bordereau'd.* See MUTE E.

born; borne. Both are past participles of *bear, borne* for general purposes (e.g. She *has borne* a child, the burden he *has borne*) and *born* only as an adjective or as a part of the fixed passive verb *to be born. Bear in mind* yields *borne in mind:* "It should be *born in mind* [read *borne in mind*] that while the *McAlester* factors will often plainly indicate that immunity is available, there are situations in which immunity must be afforded even though one or more of the factors does not obtain."

both. A. *Both . . . and.* This construction comprises a pair of CORRELATIVE CONJUNCTIONS, q.v., that must frame syntactically analogous parts of a sentence. E.g., "The Chancellor decided all questions *both of law and fact* [read *both of law and of fact* or *of both law and fact*]."

B. *Both . . . as well as.* This construction is incorrect for *both . . . and.* E.g., "Attorney's fees are expressly authorized *both under* section 1983, 42 U.S.C. § 1988, *as well as under* [read *both under . . . and under* or *under . . . as well as under*] the Rehabilitation Act, 29 U.S.C. § 794a(b)."/ "Both Norton as well as the judges [read *Norton as well as the judges* or *Both Norton and the judges*] conceded that Moses had a cause of action for special assumpsit on the agreement to indemnify him against the consequences of his agreement."

C. *Both & each other.* The construction *both . . . each other* is a redundant expression. "*Both* Signad and Sugar Land are seeking in personam, rather than in rem, judgments against *each other.*" The sentence would bear either *both* or *each other,* but it cannot take them together. *Both alike* is also a REDUNDANCY: "The statutes of these states *are both alike* [read *are alike*]."

bottleneck is accepted as standard in the dictionaries. Certainly it has legitimate figurative uses, e.g., "Our *bottleneck* in housing is particularly far-reaching and decisive."

Oddly, the word may never have been used in a literal sense (i.e., "the neck of a bottle").

bottom, v.i. & v.t., may be used literally: "The well was *bottomed* in sand A." Or it may be used figuratively, as it more frequently is in legal contexts: "The district court properly dismissed plaintiff's section 1983 claim, *bottomed* on her assertion of an illegal arrest."/ "The cause of action is *bottomed* on the duty of care owed by a vessel to all who are lawfully on board, including stevedores." This peculiar legal idiom was originally nonlegal, dating in the *OED* from 1637. From a modern stylistic point of view, *base* might be preferable to *bottom* in figurative senses.

The transference to a nominal sense of *bottom* can only provoke laughter: "Title VI on its own *bottom* [read *foundation*] reaches no further than the Constitution." *Guardians Association v. Civil Service Commission,* 463 U.S. 582, 589–90 (1983)./ "The decisions demonstrate that the due process approach considers each case on its own *bottom* [read *basis*]." The use of *bottom* in these two sentences smacks of ANTHROPOMORPHISM and suggests that the writers are callipygianists.

bottomry; bottomage. *Bottomry,* denoting a special type of contract in admiralty, may be used as both n. & v.t. *Bottomage* is a NEEDLESS VARIANT from LAW FRENCH.

bound bailiff. See **bumbailiff.**

bounden. See BIBLICAL AFFECTATION.

bounteous is poetic or literary for *bountiful,* which is preferred in legal contexts.

bounty, which is becoming an ARCHAISM, is current in the context of wills and estates, although little used elsewhere. It means "munificence; liberality in giving; gift" (*COD*). E.g., "The court will distribute the testator's *bounty* equally among all persons belonging to the class designated in the will, wherever the person."/ "Spendthrift trusts allow the donor to control his *bounty,* through the creation of the trust, so that it may be exempt from liability for the donee's debts."/ "The testator may, if he chooses, fail to make provision in his will for his children, though they are the natural objects of his *bounty.*"

b(o)urgeois. The spelling with the -*o*- is preferred.

bracery. See **embracery.**

BRACKETS, USE OF. See PUNCTUATION (K).

brainstorming is a voguish term for "thinking hard in a group." The word is generally a ludicrous affectation. E.g., "Steers and other company officials held a private *brainstorming* conference where they initiated the idea that the employees should withdraw from the union." (Omit *brainstorming.*)

brandish. See **blandish.**

breach can be a troublesome word. Its most frequent legal use is in the phrase *breach of contract. Breach* should always suggest its more common cognate, *break.* One can either *breach* or *break* a contract; and another may refer to one's *breach* or *breaking* of it. That much is simple.

In general usage, *breach* is confused with two other words, *breech,* n. (= [1] buttocks; or [2] the lower or back part of something, as a gun) and *broach,* v.t. (= [1] to make a hole in to let out liquid; or [2] to bring up for discussion). The confusion of *breach* with *breech* consists in writers' mistakenly using the latter where *breach* belongs ⟨breach of a treaty⟩. The lapse with *broach* occurs when someone writes of *breaching* (read *broaching*) a topic. The meanings of *breach* and *broach* become close only in reference to dikes or levees (*breach* = to break open; *broach* = to make a hole in).

breachee is objectionable as an obtuse word for "injured party" or some similar phrase. It is also an illogically formed word, because it does not mean "one who is breached (by another)," but rather "one whose contract has been breached." *Breachee* is not, like *refugee,* an established exception. See -EE.

breacher (= a party in breach). So spelled. See **contract-breaker.**

breakdown = (1) failure; or (2) subdivision. The former meaning is much older (ca. 1832); the latter has been considered OFFICIALESE since it first appeared in the middle of this century.

breaking and entering. See **housebreaking.**

breast (of the court), in the. See LOAN TRANSLATIONS.

breath; breathe. The first is the noun, the second the verb. How one might mistake *breath* for *breathe* is almost inexplicable: "The complainant began screaming and appellant again covered her nose and mouth with his hand; the complainant began gagging and could not *breath* [read *breathe*]."

breathable. See **breath(e)able.**

breathalyzer; intoxilyzer; drunkometer. *Breathalyzer* is a PORTMANTEAU WORD for *breath-analyzer,* the nominal form for which is *breath-analysis.* In BrE the word is *breathalyser* (standard) or *breathaliser;* in AmE it is sometimes spelled *breathalizer,* although *-lyzer* is more common: "The taking of a *breathalyzer* test with the consent of a defendant accused of driving while intoxicated violates none of his rights."

Intoxilyzer, likewise a PORTMANTEAU WORD (for *intoxication-analyzer*), is an increasingly popular term for the device that measures blood-alcohol content. See, e.g., *State ex rel. Collins v. Seidel,* 691 P.2d 678, 679 (Ariz. 1984). *Intoxilyzer* is new enough, however, that it is not included in the dictionaries. *Drunkometer,* a HYBRID, was widespread when the device was still new (in the 1930s), but has fallen into disuse, perhaps because of its jocular effect.

In referring to the test performed rather than to the device performing it, *breath test* is the most succinct phraseology, used often by the United States Supreme Court and by British courts as well. *Breathalyzer test,* a somewhat inferior variant, is also commonly used. See, e.g., *Simpson v. State,* 707 P.2d 43, 45 (Okl. Crim. App. 1985).

breath(e)able. The parenthesized *-e-* should be omitted: *breathable.* See MUTE E.

breech. See **breach.**

brethren has survived as the plural of *brother* only in religious and legal contexts. "In this case, I have the misfortune to differ in opinion from my *brethren.*" (Story, J.) Courts have considered the word generic in testamentary contexts (i.e., as referring both to males and to females). It may come to be accepted as a term for fellow judges of either sex, though SEXISM is a substantial impedi-

ment. It is too early to say. *Sistren* is the analogous archaic plural of *sister;* that plural, unlike its brother, is now chiefly dialectal. See **brother.**

Brothers is sometimes used where *brethren* would normally appear, e.g., "While I see more ambiguity than do my dissenting *brothers,* it is of no matter because we do not write on a clean slate."

brief, n. In the U.S., the word means "the written arguments of counsel for consultation by the court." In G.B., it means "a document by which a solicitor instructs a barrister to appear as an advocate in court" (*CDL*).

brief, v.t., occurs primarily in legal, military, diplomatic, and business contexts. E.g., "Both the statutory and constitutional issues have been fully *briefed* and argued here." The legal use of this term is an Americanism (see **brief,** n.). See also **debriefing.**

briefcase gets its name from the legal profession, being originally "a case in which lawyers carry their briefs." *Briefcase* and *attaché (case)* are the only terms current in AmE. In BrE, *brief-bag* (for barristers?), *deed-case* (for solicitors?), and *attaché* are used.

briefing attorney. See **clerk.**

briefly = (1) soon; or (2) not for long. Thus it may cause ambiguities in some contexts ⟨he will deliver his speech briefly⟩. Cf. **presently.**

BRIEF WRITING, except on technical points *passim,* is none of my business here. For good discussions of the subject, see Edward Re's classic *Brief Writing and Oral Argument* (1965; 6th ed. 1987); Girvan Peck's *Writing Persuasive Briefs* (1984); and Jean Appleman's *Persuasion in Brief Writing* (1968).

bright-line rule = a judicial rule of decision that is simple, straightforward, and avoids or ignores the ambiguities or difficulties of the problems at hand. E.g., "Much as a *bright-line rule* would be desirable, in evaluating whether an investigative detention is unreasonable, common sense and ordinary human experience must govern over rigid criteria." Cf. **hard and fast rule.**

brilliance, -cy. *Brilliance* is preferred in describing a quality or state. *Brilliancy,* not quite a NEEDLESS VARIANT, may be called on to mean "something brilliant" ⟨the brilliancies in Justice Holmes's writings are legion⟩.

bring; take. "*Bring* is confused with *take* only by the illiterate or the unthinking." E. Partridge, *Usage and Abusage* 61 (1957). The *OED* notes that *bring* "implies motion towards the place where the speaker or auditor is, or is supposed to be, being in sense the causal of *come;* motion in the opposite direction is expressed by *take* [being in sense the causal of *go*]." The distinction would seem to be too elementary for elaboration here, but: "One of plaintiff's duties was to pick up old tie plates from around the railroad tracks and *bring* [read *take*] them to a central location."

bring error = bring an appeal. See **error.**

bring to book = to arrest and try. E.g., "The genuinely unfortunate aspect of today's ruling is not that fewer fugitives will be *brought to book.*"

BRITISHISMS. See AMERICANISMS.

broach. See **breach.**

broad. See **wide.**

broad brush is a legal METAPHOR signifying a general or sweeping effect. E.g., "We are aware that exemption is a *broad brush*; the club that loses its exemption becomes taxable on income from all sources, including dues, assessments, and membership fees."

broadcast; forecast; telecast; cablecast; radiocast. These are the correct forms for the past as well as for the present tense. Adding *-ed*, though fairly common, is incorrect.

Broadcast sometimes acts as an illusory intransitive. "There are no doubt substantially more individuals who want to *broadcast* than there are frequencies to allocate." Though it has no object in this sentence, *broadcast* is not really used intransitively, for the object is understood. Obviously one broadcasts *programs*, and there is no need to specify what would be broadcast if it is plainly understood.

brokerage; brokage. *Brokerage* = (1) the business or office of a broker; or (2) a broker's fee. The archaic *brokage* (or, alternatively, *brocage*) = the corrupt jobbing of offices; the

bribe unlawfully paid for any office (*OED*). In this sense, *brokage* is the lay equivalent of *simony.* (See **barratry.**) *Brokage* is also an archaic NEEDLESS VARIANT of *brokerage.*

brother. This term is often used, by judges, of a male associate on the bench. E.g., "Our trial *brother* [i.e., the trial court] fell into error of law in his analysis by his implicit assumption that the appellant's 'substantial disability' provided the postal service legally sufficient grounds for rejecting appellant's bid for the clerk/carrier position." See **brethren.**

A substitute for *brother* in this context, perhaps useful in avoiding SEXISM or in referring to a fellow judge who is a woman, is *colleague:* "I disagree with my *colleagues* because I believe the stipulation signed by the two attorneys was at best ambiguous."

brother-in-law. Pl. *brothers-in-law.*

brush, broad. See **broad brush.**

brusque; brusk. The former spelling is preferred.

brutum fulmen (= an empty noise; an empty threat) is no TERM OF ART; it is the worst type of LATINISM in the law, expressing a commonplace notion for which a variety of English phrases suffice. E.g., "A court of equity cannot lawfully enjoin the world at large, no matter how broadly it words its decree; if it assumes to do so, the decree is pro tanto *brutum fulmen* [read *ineffectual*] and the persons enjoined are free to ignore it."

budget-making is best hyphenated. See **decision-making.**

buggery is a legal term usually meaning "sodomy," but sometimes also "bestiality." *Bugger* (= sodomite) was originally a respectable legal term, though now it is a dialectal term of playful abuse, not necessarily implying sodomy. Here the original meaning obtains, albeit with contemptuous overtones: "The middle age of buggers is not to be contemplated without horror" (V. Woolf).

In G.B., *buggery* is the more usual legal term than *sodomy.* It means "anal intercourse by a man with another man or a woman or bestiality by a man or a woman" (*CDL*). The active bugger is guilty as the *agent*, whereas the receiving bugger is called (and is guilty as) the *patient*. See EUPHEMISM.

bulk large is an acceptable variant of *loom large*. E.g., "Transferability of interests should not ordinarily *bulk large* in the decision whether or not to incorporate."/ "It *bulks very large*, for instance, in every census of India." Both *loom large*, q.v., and *bulk large* have become CLICHÉS.

bumbailiff is a BrE slang term for "a bailiff or sheriff's officer who collects debts." *Bum* (= buttocks) was aptly coupled with *bailiff* in this term—actually a corruption of *bound bailiff*—because of the debt-collectors' habit of catching debtors from behind. This humorous word is now obsolescent. See **bailiwick.**

buncombe; bunkum. This term (meaning "political talk that is empty or insincere") derives from Buncombe County, North Carolina, because the congressman from the district embracing that county early in the nineteenth century felt compelled, despite interruptions, to "make a speech for Buncombe." *Buncombe* has remained the standard spelling, and is to be preferred because it recalls the interesting origin of the word.

burden of proof; onus of proof. The former phrase is usual in legal writing in the U.S.; both phrases are used in G.B. Here is an example of phrase that is slightly uncommon to American lawyers: "The judge next directed the jury as to the *onus of proof* upon the issue of provocation." (Eng.) See **onus** & LOAN TRANSLATIONS.

bureau. The better plural form is *bureaus*; the Frenchified plural, *bureaux*, should be avoided as an unnecessary pretension.

burgeon literally means "to put forth buds; sprout." Although some usage experts have considered it objectionable in meaning "to flourish, grow," no good reason exists to avoid *burgeon* in these figurative senses: but it should be used of growth at its incipient stages, not of full-blown expansion. Here it seems inappropriate: "The creation of thirty-five new circuit judgeships in 1978 was not intended as a long-term solution to the problem, but was simply one response to *burgeoning* caseloads."/ "Unsanitary and unsafe, many of our overflowing prisons no longer

have the capacity to legally hold the *burgeoning* inmate populations created by our ever-increasing war on crime."

burglarious = of, relating to, or inclined to burglary. *Burglariously* (L. *burglariter*) was formerly obligatory in indictments for burglary at common law.

burglarize; burgle. *Burglarize* is an American coinage from the late nineteenth century meaning "to rob burglariously" (*OED*). It is still largely confined to AmE. *Burgle*, a BACK-FORMATION of comparable vintage, has the same meaning; in AmE, *burgle* is usually facetious or jocular, whereas in BrE it is standard and colorless.

burglary; robbery; theft; larceny. These four terms may overlap to a degree, but no two are perfectly synonymous. *Burglary* = (1) (in the classic sense) the act of breaking and entering another's house at night with intent to commit a felony (e.g., murder); (2) (in the modern AmE sense) the act of breaking and entering a building with the intent to commit a felony (dropping the requirements that it be (a) a house and (b) at night); or (3) (in the modern BrE sense) the offense either of entering a building, ship, or inhabited vehicle (e.g., a caravan) as a trespasser with the intention of committing one of four specified crimes in it (*burglary with intent*) or of entering it as a trespasser but subsequently committing one of two specified crimes in it (*burglary without intent*) (*CDL*). The specified offenses in G.B. are, for *burglary with intent:* (1) stealing; (2) inflicting grievous bodily harm; (3) causing criminal damage; and (4) rape. And for *burglary without intent:* (1) stealing or attempting to steal; and (2) inflicting or attempting to inflict grievous bodily harm.

Robbery = feloniously taking personal property by force or threat of force from the immediate presence of the victim. *Theft* is a statutory wrong that is broader than *robbery*, although laymen often consider the words synonymous; *robbery* means "the taking of personal property belonging to another without his consent, and with the intent to deprive the owner of its value." *Theft* is also broader than *larceny* (= the felonious stealing of personal property, the fraudulent taking and carrying away [*asportation*, q.v.] of a thing without claim of right), for it includes the lawful acquisition and subsequent appropriation of the personalty. In England, the common-law felony of larceny was superseded by the Theft Act of 1968.

The exact definitions of these terms may vary from jurisdiction to jurisdiction. But it is universal that *people* are the objects of *robbery; places* are the objects of *burglary;* and *things* are the objects of *larceny* and *theft.*

In American legal writing, when *of* follows *burglary,* some infelicity or other is almost certain to follow; *burglary of an automobile* would traditionally have been considered a legal blunder, though several states now have statutes that incorporate this phrase; *burglary of a building* is a REDUNDANCY, unless the reference is to a particular building, as *burglary of the Stokes Building.*

burgle. See **burglarize.**

burthen is an ARCHAISM and a NEEDLESS VARIANT of *burden* that still occasionally burdens legal writing. Shakespeare used it frequently, but it has little place in twentieth-century prose. E.g., "That the title of the land, when acquired by the community, was taken in the name of the wife, imposes no additional *burthen* [read *burden*] upon the purchaser of inquiring into the equities of the husband and wife in respect to it."

bus. Pl. *buses. Bus ⟩ bused ⟩ bused.* The present participle is *busing. (Bussed* = kissed, *bussing* = kissing.)

Leff knowingly uses *bussing* for *busing* in *The Leff Dictionary of Law,* 94 Yale L.J. 1855, 1967 (1985). In his entry under *busing,* Leff takes the position that the word is "also properly spelled *bussing.*" Acceptance of that dictum would destroy the DIFFERENTIATION that has evolved between the forms, and therefore is to be taken as unsound. *Busing* is preferred even in G.B. in nonosculatory senses. See *Oxford Guide* 9.

bush lawyer is an Australian term meaning "a person pretending to have considerable legal knowledge" (*W3*). This term might deserve universal adoption, for we *need* such a name. See LAWYER, DEROGATORY NAMES FOR.

bussing. See **bus.**

but. A. Beginning Sentences with. It is a canard that beginning a sentence with *but* is stylistically slipshod. Cf. **and.**

B. More Than One in a Sentence. Putting this subordinating conjunction twice in one sentence invariably makes the sentence unwieldy and less than easily readable. E.g., "There is authority for damages when the employment denied would have enhanced the employee's reputation, as a motion-picture credit would, *but* this has been applied only once in the United States, *but is* [read *though it is*] common in England." See the following subsection.

C. For *and.* This is not an uncommon mistake. One must understand the nature (if not the technical names) of both coordinating conjunctions (e.g., *and*) and subordinating conjunctions (e.g., *but*). E.g., "Summary judgment is a potent weapon, *but* [read *and*] courts must be mindful of its aims and targets and beware of overkill in its use." The second clause almost necessarily follows from the first; it does not state an exception to or qualification of the first. Hence *and* is the appropriate conjunction.

D. Preposition or Conjunction. The use of *but* in a negative sense after a pronoun ("No one but *she* or *her*") has long caused confusion. If we take *but* to be a preposition (meaning "except"), the objective *her* (or *him*) follows. But if we take *but* as a conjunction, the nominative *she* (or *he*) would be proper.

The correct form depends on the structure of the sentence. If the verb precedes the *but*-phrase, the objective case should be used: "None of the defendants were convicted *but him.*" If, however, the *but*-phrase precedes the verb, the nominative case is proper: "None of the defendants *but he* were convicted." This sentence is considered equivalent to "None of the defendants were convicted, *but he was convicted.*" *But* thus acts as a conjunction when it precedes the verb in a sentence such as this, from Thomas Jefferson: "You, however, can easily correct this bill to the taste of my brother lawyers, by making every other word a 'said' or 'aforesaid,' and saying everything two or three times, so that nobody *but we* of the craft *can understand* the diction, and find out what it means."

but for = if not for, except for. This phrase has become a useful LEGALISM, as in the following sentences: "The evidence also showed that, *but for* the negligence of Lee-Vac, the socket would never have failed."/ "It is therefore quite plain that *but for* the constitutional prohibition on the operation of segregated public parks, the City of Macon would continue to own and maintain Baconsfield."/ "A bad motive will render a conveyance or transfer of property void which, *but for* the bad motive, would have been valid." In American legal writing, the phrase is frequently used attributively as an adjective: "A '*but for*' relationship between the illegality and the obtaining of the challenged evidence must exist for the evidence to be suppressible under the 'poisonous fruit' doctrine."/ "If we use the tort concept of *but-for* causation to determine when a causal connection is present, it seems clear that *but for* the police officer's submission to the magistrate, the warrant would not issue and the search or arrest would not occur."/ "This circuit has adopted a *but-for* test of causation in determining whether a particular injury was the result of operations on the shelf." When the phrase is used attributively ⟨but-for relationship⟩, it is better to hyphenate the phrase (as in the second and third examples) than to use quotation marks around the phrase (as in the first example).

but rather is usually unnecessary, either word singly doing the work that both purport to do. E.g., "The court does not mean to suggest by this opinion that all former sufferers of mental illness should be permitted to own firearms; *but, rather,* [read *rather,*] if Congress has determined that there are circumstances under which former criminals can own and possess weapons and a means is provided to establish such an entitlement, former mental patients are entitled to no less."

but yet is always a REDUNDANCY for *yet*. E.g., "This report focuses on three *disparate but yet related* [read *disparate yet related*] areas of broker-dealer compliance." Cf. **as yet.**

buy; purchase. As a verb, *buy* is the ordinary word, *purchase* the more FORMAL WORD. *Purchase,* q.v., may also act as a noun; *buy* is informal and colloquial as a noun ⟨a good buy⟩.

by and with is a classic legal REDUNDANCY with but one legitimate use. "For appointments to constitutional offices the phrase *by and with the advice of the Senate* is a TERM OF ART and should not be changed." R. Dickerson, *Legislative Drafting* 75 n. 4 (1954). See DOUBLETS AND TRIPLETS OF LEGAL IDIOM.

by(e)-election. *By-election* is preferred in both AmE and BrE.

by(e)law. Not only the spelling but also the sense differs in the U.S. from that in G.B. In the U.S., *bylaws* are most commonly the administrative provisions of a corporation that are either attached to the articles of incorporation or kept privately. In G.B., *byelaws* are regulations made by a local authority or corporation, such as a town or a railway (see the quotations below).

The spelling without the -*e*- is preferred in AmE. Though etymologically inferior, *byelaw* (sometimes hyphenated) is standard in British legal texts, and is so spelled in the *CDL*. E.g., "Clause four requires the contractor to comply with Acts of Parliament and *bye-laws.*" (Eng.)/ "It would surprise me if the courts of England would hold that when the English Parliament gave the Birmingham Municipality the authority to make *bye-laws* for the good government of the city, it intended also to give the municipality the authority to segregate West Indians from Europeans in the use of public conveniences." (Rhod.) The house style of Oxford University Press in G.B., however, is *by-law*.

by its four corners. See **four corners.**

by means of is usually verbose for *by*.

by-product is usually hyphenated, though there is a tendency to make it one word.

by the court; per curiam. *By the court* is merely an English translation of *per curiam* (see LOAN TRANSLATIONS), a term that appears in opinions not attributed to any one member of the court. Contrary to the notion that some lawyers have, *per curiam* opinions usually deal with routine matters that are seen by the judges as having little precedential value; they often dispose of such cases summarily. *Per curiam* opinions should not be construed as exhibiting greater unanimity among members of the court than a signed opinion without a dissent.

Some courts variously use both *per curiam* and *by the court*, of course without differentiation. (Though the practice is now rare, some courts have used merely *the court* for *per curiam* opinions.) It might be best to stick with a single phrase, lest readers of the opinions come to think there must be a distinction. On the one hand, *per curiam* is unambiguous and can be used attributively (*per curiam opinion*), whereas *by the court* may create ambiguities in speech and in writing. Though it is a LATIN-ISM, *per curiam* is a useful and well-established one: it is not likely to be discarded any time soon. On the other hand, *by the court* is at least a comprehensible phrase to all speakers of English, even if they do not all understand its import. Certainly this is the better phrase for popular journalism.

by virtue of.   See **virtue of, in & by.**

byword (= a proverb or saying) is best spelled as one word and not hyphenated. "We are not harking back to Latin *bywords* (*Nemo debet esse judex in propria causa* [i.e. "No man ought to be a judge in his own case"]) without sanction of our highest court."

C

cab(b)ala(h). The preferred spelling in AmE is *cabala*. The standard BrE spelling is *cabbala*.

calculate out   is verbose for *calculate*. E.g., "I need her to *calculate out* [read *calculate*] her lost profits." Cf. **distribute out.** See PARTICLES, UNNECESSARY.

calculus is best confined to mean "a method of calculation," and not "calculation" itself. Here it is properly used: "One factor that weighs heavily in this *calculus* [i.e., *method of calculation*] is Louisiana's interest in providing effective means of redress for its residents."

In the following sentence, *calculus* should be replaced by *calculation*: "It is no answer to say that chance would have been of little value even if seasonably offered; such a *calculus* [read *calculation*] of probabilities is beyond the science of the chancery."

By SLIPSHOD EXTENSION of its proper use in the sense "a method of calculation," *calculus* has come to be used in the sense "a method of analysis" or even "analysis," a use that is vague and imprecise: "Many of the questions that are posed by the contemporary due process *calculus* [read *analysis*] cannot be answered with confidence."

calendar is used in G.B. for *docket* or *cause-list* in criminal cases only; in the U.S. it is used for both civil and criminal cases.

caliber, -re. The preferred spelling in the U.S. is *-er*, in G.B. *-re*.

call. See **put.**

called to the bar = admitted to practice. Though primarily a BrE locution (used only of barristers), it has come to be used infrequently by American lawyers as well. E.g., "When I was first *called to the bar*, I received a very large certificate bearing the Governor's signature evidencing my appointment as Attorney at Law and Solicitor in Chancery." Letter, S. B. Rounds, quoted in W. Safire, *I Stand Corrected* 417 (1984). See **admitted to the bar.**

callous; callus. The former is the adjective ("hardened, unfeeling"), the latter the noun ("hardened skin").

calumny is a somewhat old-fashioned equivalent of *defamation*. *Calumny* may refer to either (1) the act of falsely and maliciously misrepresenting the words or actions of others, calculated to injure their reputation (*OED*), or (2) the false charges or imputations themselves. Although this term was once used as a technical legal word in the common law, today it is more literary than legal. The phrase *breath of calumny* is an old CLICHÉ.

The verb is *calumniate*. E.g., "I suppose this woman to be completely innocent of the offence laid to her charge; but she has not been wantonly or maliciously *calumniated*." (Eng.) *Calumnize* is a NEEDLESS VARIANT. The adjective is *calumnious* (*calumniatory* being a NEEDLESS VARIANT), and the agent noun is *calumniator*.

camera (lit., "chamber") is used in the phrase *in camera*, q.v. See also **chambers.**

can; may. The distinction between these words has been much discussed. Generally, *can* expresses physical ability ⟨he can lift 500 pounds⟩; *may* expresses permission or authorization ⟨the defense may now close⟩, and sometimes possibility ⟨the trial may end on Friday⟩. Although only an insufferable precisian would insist on observing the distinction in speech or informal writing (esp. in questions such as, "Can I wait until August?"), the careful writer is best advised, nevertheless, to use these words with care in formal legal contexts.

cancel (out). See PARTICLES, UNNECESSARY.

cancel(l)ed. Because the primary accent falls on the first syllable, in AmE the -*l*- should not be doubled in the second syllable. The -*ll*- spelling often mistakenly crops up in American writing, as in this passage: "Unless *cancelled* [read *canceled*] as provided in the agreement, the option could be exercised by giving written notice thereof no later than April 1, 1968." Note, however, that in *cancellation* the ells *are* doubled. See DOUBLING OF FINAL CONSONANTS.

candidacy; candidature. The former is the regular term in the AmE, the latter in BrE.

cannot should not appear as two words, except in rare instances such as, "With the principles of good English and literary composition to guide the author, legal writing *can not* only be literature, but also be good literature of obvious excellence and enduring value," in which *not* is part of the phrase *not only . . . but also*. See **not** (B). *Cannot* is much preferable to *can't* in formal writing. See CONTRACTIONS.

cannot help but; cannot help ———ing; cannot but. In formal contexts, the last two phrases are preferred: "*I cannot help but think* [read *I cannot but think* or *I cannot help thinking*] that the immediate recording of the claim is entitled to equal effect from a constitutional point of view."

canon; cannon. *Canon* = (1) a corpus of writings; (2) an accepted notion or principle; or (3) a law or regulation. *Cannon* = (1) a big gun; or (2) the ear of a bell, by which the bell hangs.

canon law = the codified law governing a church. The adjectival form of *canons* (= the laws or rules of the church) is *canonical*, which has long been a secularized synonym of *axiomatic*: "This court has so repeatedly held that complete dominion and authority over the property imports a fee simple title in the devisee that the rule is *canonical*." See **axiom**.

canonist = a specialist in ecclesiastical law. Cf. **civilian**.

canvass; canvas. *Canvass,* n. & v.t., means, in its verb senses, (1) "to examine (usu. votes) in detail"; (2) "to discuss or debate"; (3) "to solicit orders or political support"; or (4) "to take stock of public opinion." Here sense (4) applies: "An alderman stated that he had *canvassed* the board of aldermen, and that 23 would oppose the measure." Sense (1) is also common in legal contexts: "It was contended for the husband that there must be some evidence called or some substantial opening of the case or some *canvassing* of the issues." (Eng.)/ "Having determined that our rules on prosecutorial vindictiveness govern the instant case, we must *canvass* the competing policies, beginning with the defendant's interest in minimizing the apprehension of prosecutorial vindictiveness." The noun *canvass* means "the act of canvassing."

Canvas, almost always a noun, is the heavy cloth. In its rare verbal sense, it means "to cover with such a cloth."

capable of = (1) able to be affected by; of a nature, or in a condition, to allow or admit of; admitting; susceptible (*OED*); (2) having the needful capacity, power, or fitness for (some specified purpose or activity) (*id.*); or (3) having capacity, ability, or intelligence. Sense (1) is far more common today in legal than in lay writing: "Allegations of perjured testimony must be supported by substantial factual assertions *capable of* resolution by an evidentiary hearing."/ "'Submission to arbitration' is *capable of* more than one meaning." (Eng.)

Sense (2) appears widely in lay and legal writing, but is not used in quite the same way; whereas laymen usually connect a participial phrase to *capable of,* lawyers frequently follow it with a simple noun. E.g., "Appellees argue that the purchase of automobiles in New York would not occur but for the fact that the automobiles are *capable of use* in distant states like Oklahoma." The layman of today would write *capable of being used.*

capacitas rationalis is a LATINISM whose perpetration in non-Roman contexts is unforgivable, what with English phrases like *rational capacity, rational faculties,* and *reason* and *rationality* to do the work. In the following sentence the phrase arguably refers to the Roman-law doctrine: "The principle of *capacitas rationalis* embodies the free-will retributive idea that man is a rational being with the capacity to understand his actions intelligently and control them accordingly." (Eng.)

capacitate = to qualify; to make legally competent. This term is a fancy LEGALISM, in place of which *qualify* or *make competent* is more comprehensible not just to laymen, but to most lawyers.

capacity; capability. These words overlap, but there are nuances. *Capacity* = the power to receive, hold, or contain. Figuratively, it refers to mental faculties in the sense "the power to take in knowledge." In law, it is frequently used in the sense "legal competency or qualification." *Capability* = (1) power or ability in general, whether physical or mental; or (2) the quality of being susceptible of.

capias (lit., "that you take," used of writs of attachment or arrest) is a singular noun with the plural form *capiases*. Yet *capias* is occasionally misapprehended as being plural as well as singular. E.g., "On behalf of himself and others similarly situated, Stephen Crane brought an action complaining that Dallas County regularly issued *capias* [read *capiases*] without a finding of probable cause by a neutral and detached magistrate."

capital; capitol. The former is a city, the seat of government; the latter is a building in which the state or national legislature meets (fr. L. *capitoleum*, the Roman temple of Jupiter). *Capital*, whether as noun or as adjective, is called on far more frequently.

capitalist(ic). *Capitalist* is the general adjective; the *-istic* form, a favorite of Marxists, is pejorative.

CAPITALIZATION. There are a number of conventions of capitalization in legal writing, a few of which are here discussed. These conventions are variable, to be sure, inasmuch as practices in capitalizing are generally governed more by personal taste than by a code of rules. Section (A) below prescribes a rule of capitalization, but sections (B), (C), and (D) are included more for purposes of explaining and describing conventions than for stating rules.

   A. Rules of Law. These are variously written with initial letters either capitalized (as if they were titles) or lowercased. Even when we capitalize, however, the extent of capitalization is not settled; thus we have *the rule in*

Shelley's case, the Rule in Shelley's case, the Rule in Shelley's Case, and *The Rule in Shelley's Case.* The first of these is a mere description; the second is not quite logical, for it looks descriptive with *case* but titular or nominal with *Rule*; the third is the best form, and the most usual; and the fourth makes *the* a part of the name or title, which makes sense for a book or article bearing that name, but not for general references to the rule.

   Other rules of law have just as many variations. See, e.g., **Rule against Perpetuities.** In questionable instances, the best policy is to determine to what extent general legal usage has sanctioned a certain phrase as being a rule of law, and then to capitalize those words essential to the name of the doctrine or rule of law. Hence *the doctrine of the Destructibility of Contingent Remainders* but *the Rule in Shelley's Case; Destructibility of Contingent Remainders* frequently appears without *the doctrine* or *the rule,* which is not really a part of the name of the rule, but *Shelley's Case* almost never occurs without *the Rule in* preceding it. Likewise *the Rule Forbidding a Remainder to the Grantor's Heirs* and *the Doctrine of Worthier Title.*

   B. Vessel Names. These are now more commonly capitalized than not. But the habit of using all capitals is apparently of fairly recent origin. In a typical nineteenth-century case, *The Harrisburg,* 119 U.S. 199 (1886), the name of the ship had only the first letter capitalized; yet modern cases often write *THE HARRISBURG* when referring to the ship in that case. The older, more conservative convention might seem preferable, since words in all capitals are often distracting on the printed page. Cf. INITIALESE.

   C. Judges' Names. It has long been a tradition, both in English and in American courts, to spell judges' names in all capitals when the names are referred to in opinions— though not elsewhere. (For an older English example, see the quotation under **between** (A).) The U.S. Supreme Court regularly follows this practice. E.g., "This view garnered three votes in *Arnett,* but was specifically rejected by the other six Justices. See [*Arnett v. Kennedy,* 416 U.S. 134, 166-67 (1974)] (POWELL, J., joined by BLACKMUN, J.); *id.* at 177–78, 185 (WHITE, J.); *id.* at 211(MARSHALL, J., joined by DOUGLAS and BRENNAN, JJ.)." *Cleveland Board of Education v. Loudermill,* 470 U.S. 532, 540 (1985).

   D. Trademarks. Some judges prefer to use all capitals in spelling out trademarks. See, e.g., *Conan Properties, Inc. v. Conans Pizza, Inc.,* 752 F.2d 145 (5th Cir. 1985). This convention has the advantage of distinguishing between the mark and the party, as here: "In addition, starting from the time of the changeover to *EXXON* as its primary mark, *Exxon* developed plans for extended use of the *HUMBLE* mark, as reflected in numerous internal memoranda."

capital punishment, whether one is for or against what it denotes, is a legal EUPHEMISM for state-imposed death.

capitol. See **capital.**

capitulatory, not *capitulative,* is the adjective corresponding to *capitulation.* E.g., "A defendant might moot the suit by taking unilateral *capitulatory* action."

captor; capturer. The latter is a NEEDLESS VARIANT.

Cardozo is not only widely mispronounced /kahr-**doh**-za/ instead of /kahr-**doh**-zoh/; it is misspelled *Cardoza* in *State v. Saia,* 302 So. 2d 869, 879 (La. 1974) (Summers, J., dissenting).

carte blanche; carta blanca. The former is the usual phrase in English contexts; it does not take an article. "Codefendants conspired with the securities swindler and gave him a *carte blanche* to conceive and carry out a securities fraud." (Omit *a* before *carte blanche.*)/ "It is almost meaningless to contemplate a 'regulatory' policy that gives every regulated entity *carte blanche* to excuse itself from the consequences of the regulation."

cartelize = to organize into a cartel. See -IZE. Yet *cartel* has three quite different meanings: (1) "an agreement between hostile nations"; (2) "an anticompetitive combination usu. that fixes commercial prices"; and (3) "a combination of political groups that work toward common goals." Modern usage favors sense (2).

case. **A.** Generally. "*In the case of John Doe deceased, etc.,* is the sort of jargon which disfigures almost all legal writing." P. Marks, *The Craft of Writing* 52 (1932). "It is permissible, of course, to write of a law case, a medical

case, or a case of linen, but it certainly is not advisable to use *case* in any other way." (*Id.* at 53) Quiller-Couch condemned this word as "Jargon's dearest child," esp. in the phrase *in the case of,* in his essay "Jargon," in *On the Art of Writing* (1916; repr. 1961). *In the case of* is, to be sure, generally an obnoxious phrase; it has its legitimate uses, but not generally in legal writing, in which *case* so frequently refers to lawsuits, not instances. Even in the sense synonymous with *cause, in the case of Monroe v. Pape* is always inferior to *in Monroe v. Pape.* E.g., "The case of Blair v. Commissioner* [read *Blair v. Commissioner*] is to be distinguished from the present case in that there the corpus of the trust was in existence."

The worst offenders are the phrases *in any case* [read *in any event*], *in the case of* [usu. best deleted or reduced to *in*], *in every case* [read *always* or *in every instance*], and *as the case may be* [not easily circumvented]. "There is perhaps no single word so freely resorted to as a trouble-saver, and consequently responsible for so much flabby writing." (Fowler, *MEU2* 76.) Especially does *case* conduce to flabbiness when it is used twice in a sentence with different meanings: "I shall read in extenso the passage of general importance in *case* the instant *case* (or part of it) is reported." (Eng.)

B. As Ellipsis for *trespass on the case & action on the case.* See the entries under those phrases.

C. And *cause.* See **cause** (A).

case at bar. This is the most usual expression in which *at bar* is used, but legal and evidentiary issues may be *at bar,* as well as cases. E.g., "*National Union* involved a termination clause similar to the one *at bar.*" See **at (the) bar.**

case-in-chief. This term is useful legal ARGOT. It means "that part of a trial in which the party with the initial burden of proof presents his evidence, after which he rests" (*Black's*). E.g., "In numerous cases this court has held that mention of the fact of defendant's silence following arrest by the prosecutor in his *case-in-chief* is a violation of constitutional dimensions."/ "The issue was raised by the offer of the gun as a part of the state's *case-in-chief.*" The phrase should be hyphenated. See **in chief.**

case(-)law. This term appears in modern texts as two words, as hyphenated words, and as a single word. Although all three forms can be found in abundance, the phrase predominantly appears as two words. But there may be an evolutionary trend to make the phrase solid. E.g., "That kind of surveillance does not, under the *caselaw*, constitute an actionable invasion of privacy." *Pemberton v. Bethlehem Steel Corp.*, 502 A.2d 1101, 1107 (Md. App. 1986). See **decision(al) law.** Cf. **organic law.**

caseload. Listed as two words in *W3*, this term is usually spelled as one word in American legal writing. Cf. **case(-)law.**

casenote. See **annotation.**

CASE REFERENCES. A. Short Form References. The usual practice is to use, for shorthand reference to a case already mentioned, the first name in the style of the case, or the more distinctive name if the first is fairly common or is a place-name (e.g., state names, *United States, Board of Education*, etc.). Hence *Erie R.R. v. Tompkins*, when shortened, is *Erie*, not *Tompkins*; but *Marshall v. Mulrenin* usually becomes *Mulrenin*, and *National Mutual Insurance Co. v. Tidewater Transfer Co.* is shortened to *Tidewater*. Case names are not usually abbreviated when the parties' names are short; e.g., *Roe v. Wade* is never shortened.

It is a good idea to avoid using shortened names attributively when the name might seem to ridicule the court. Thus, one would not want to write *the Seven Elves court* or *the Wolfish court* when referring to the courts that decided *Seven Elves v. Eskenazi*, 635 F.2d 396 (5th Cir. 1981), and *Bell v. Wolfish*, 441 U.S. 520 (1979). See (c) below.

B. Locatives with. *In which*, not *where*, is the better way of referring to what the facts were or the court said in a given case. E.g., "Second, we rely . . . on this Court's decision in *Lewis. There* [read *In that case*], Lewis, an employee of Timco, sued Atwood Oceanics, the vessel owner." See **where** (A).

C. As Attributive Adjectives. A number of cases have become so well known by the courts that routinely apply them as precedents that these courts have come to use the shortened case names as adjectives. There is no harm in this habit, although a citation to the case may be helpful to the less well-informed reader. Rarely, for example, is *Erie R.R. v. Tompkins* cited with the phrase *Erie-*

bound, q.v. Other adjectivally used case names appear in phrases such as *a Terry frisk* or *Terry stop* (fr. *Terry v. Ohio*, 392 U.S. 1 (1968)), *Miranda warning* (fr. *Miranda v. Arizona*, 384 U.S. 436 (1966)), and *Allen charge* (fr. *Allen v. United States*, 164 U.S. 492 (1896)).

Citation to the full case is especially important when lesser-known cases are used as adjectival phrases, a practice not to be engaged in without restraint. E.g., "Langa contends that his counsel failed to move for a mistrial when the government elicited co-conspirator hearsay testimony without first securing a *James* ruling." The adjective *James*, which will draw a blank for most readers, refers to *United States v. James*, 590 F.2d 575 (5th Cir.) (en banc), *cert. denied*, 442 U.S. 917 (1979).

In some instances, the precedent itself is unimportant to the phrase, and the case name has merely been adopted to denote certain types of factual situations, as with *Totten trust* (fr. *In re Totten*, 179 N.Y. 112, 71 N.E. 748 (1904)) and *Mary Carter agreement* (fr. *Booth v. Mary Carter Paint Co.*, 202 So. 2d 8 (Fla. Dist. Ct. App. 1967)). When, as in these phrases, the case name is used not to refer to precedent but to describe certain facts or denote types of transactions, citing the case is virtually always unnecessary. See CITATION OF CASES.

D. Hypallage with. It is unobjectionable to write that a certain case *held* something, rather than to say that the court, in that case, held. . . . This practice is an innocuous form of HYPALLAGE. E.g., "*National Carbide* held that the Tax Court had improperly failed to distinguish between 'agency' and 'practical identity' when it ruled the subsidiaries were true agents."

case-specific = patterned after or adjusted to the facts of a given case ⟨case-specific instructions⟩.

case, trespass on the. See **trespass on the case.**

case where is much inferior to *case in which*. See **where** (A) & CASE REFERENCES (B).

cast is the correct past tense and past participle, *casted* being an incorrect variant. See **broadcast.**

casual. Because it is occasionally mistaken

for *causal* (and vice versa), *casual* may at first seem wrong in certain contexts even when it is properly intended: "It was precisely this sort of *casual* evidentiary inference that *Witherspoon* expressly condemned: 'It cannot be assumed that a juror who describes himself as having conscientious or religious scruples against the infliction of the death penalty . . . thereby affirms that he could never vote in favor of it.'" The meaning apparently intended in that sentence is "offhand, cursory." But inferences are often *causal* in nature, hence the reader's initial expectation that *causal* would have been the right word; if the writer had chosen *careless* or *desultory* (or some other word) rather than *casual,* the careful reader's expectations would not be undercut. See SOUND OF PROSE, THE.

casualty; casuality. *Casuality* is an obsolete NEEDLESS VARIANT of *casualty,* the usual word.

casus omissus = a case omitted or not provided for, as by a statute (and therefore governed by the common law) (*W2*). This LATINISM has such a specific meaning not readily conveyed by a simpler phrase that one might be tempted to hail it as a useful addition to the legal vocabulary. E.g., "The appellant, however, contends that the section does not apply because it provides that the disponer (i.e., the wife) shall be liable to be taxed': the wife, it is said, is not a taxable person and so this provision does not operate; there is a *casus omissus.*" (Eng.) But few American lawyers, even learned ones, know it.

CATACHRESES are words improperly used. This dictionary treats throughout of catachreses in legal writing.

cataclysm; cataclasm. The meanings of these words are fairly close, esp. in figurative senses. A *cataclysm* is a tremendous flood or violent disaster. A *cataclasm* is a tearing down or disruption.

catalog(ue). Though librarians have come to use *catalog* with regularity, *catalogue* is still the better form. *Cataloging* makes about as much sense as *plaging.* "If the professionals decline to restore the *-u-* to the inflected forms," wrote Follett, "let them simply double the *-g-.*" W. Follett, *Modern American Usage*

97 (1966). The U.S. Supreme Court has used the more conservative form: "The cases we have reviewed show . . . the impossibility of resolution by any semantic *cataloguing.*" *Baker v. Carr,* 369 U.S. 186, 217 (1962).

catapult, in keeping with the metaphor, is best a transitive, and not an intransitive verb. The correct use of this verb in the active voice demands an agent and an object, as in "The men *catapulted* stones over the wall." Where agents are omitted, the verb must appear in the passive voice: "He was *catapulted* to fame." With such a construction, the means is implied. Yet a common blunder today is: "He *catapulted* to fame." This verb, even when used figuratively, so inevitably calls to mind its literal sense that, used intransitively, it is illogical. See METAPHORS.

categorical question. See **leading question.**

categorically = without qualification. E.g., "Testimony of appellant and of appellant's witnesses of the agreement was by the respondent *categorically* denied."

causa causans. See CAUSATION (B).

causal; causative. These words have, unfortunately, been muddled by legal writers. The meanings should be kept distinct. *Causal* is the more common word, meaning "of or relating to causes; involving causation; arising from a cause." *Causative* = operating as a cause; effective as a cause. These two words share the sense "expressing or indicating cause," although *causal* is preferred for that sense.

In the following sentences, the words are correctly used: "A plaintiff may still recover attorneys' fees if he can show both a *causal* connection between the filing of the suit and the defendant's actions and that the defendant's conduct was required by law." (*Causal link* and *causal connection* are SET PHRASES.)/ "Plaintiffs are unable to show how any additional discovery could supply an inference of conspiratorial or *causative* conduct any stronger than that provided by the contracts themselves."/ "In *Sohyde* we found relevant to the jurisdictional analysis that all the *causative* factors could have as easily occurred on land and that the injury and damages were indistinguishable from those arising from land-based blowouts.''

Here, *causal* is misused for *causative:* ''Appellant's argument is that appellee was asked to pay only for those damages resulting from its defective product and thus was not charged with any injury attributable to other *causal* [read *causative*] faults [i.e., faults that would tend to cause the injury].''

In the following sentences, the opposite mistake appears: ''The court's use of the words 'produced by' clearly reflects the *causative* [read *causal*] element of the *Christie* test.''/ ''The final type of cancer and mesothelioma evidence—Comstock's expert testimony on the *causative* [read *causal*] relationship between asbestos exposure and those diseases—is relevant to the issue of liability.'' See **casual.**

causality; causation. These words have a fine distinction. *Causality* = the principle of causal relationship; the relation of cause and effect. *Causation* = the causing or producing of an effect. In law, *causation* has long been given the additional sense ''the relation of cause and effect,'' a sense best reserved to *causality* in nonlegal contexts.

Causation should not be used for *cause,* as here: ''Under the facts of *Kubrick,* the plaintiff had actual knowledge of his injury and its *causation* [read *cause*].''

causa mortis . (= in contemplation of one's death) is a LATINISM and TERM OF ART used primarily in the phrase *gift causa mortis* (or the thoroughly Latinate phrase *donatio causa mortis*). E.g., ''The power of a donor, in a gift *causa mortis,* to revoke the gift and divest title of the donee is another clear example of the legal quantities now being considered.''/ ''A gift *causa mortis* must be made when the donor is in imminent peril of death and under such circumstances that the gift would not be made were it not for the peril.'' In G.B., the phrase is often written *mortis causa.*

causation. See **causality.**

CAUSATION is one of the subjects that have inspired legal writers to don their philosophers' caps and to work out any number of systems of analysis. The general principles of analysis have proved to be more or less universal in Anglo-American jurisdictions, but the terminology of that analysis does vary; hence the following explanations.

A. *Proximate cause, legal cause,* and *direct cause.* The terms are used interchangeably. The term *proximate cause* has become an indispensable term in American tort law, meaning simply ''a cause that directly produces an effect; that which in natural and continuous sequence, unbroken by any new independent cause, produces an event, and without which the injury would not have occurred.'' (See **but for.**) The Latin equivalent is *causa proxima.*

The *CDL* does not include an entry on *proximate cause,* since the term *legal cause* is more usual in G.B. *Direct cause* is now increasingly rare.

B. *Immediate cause, effective cause,* and the LATINISM *causa causans.* These terms are used to denote the last link in the chain of causation (as, e.g., a *supervening cause*). *Causa causans* is little used outside G.B.

C. *Producing cause.* This term is virtually synonymous with *proximate cause,* but is used in particular contexts such as workers' compensation in some jurisdictions. The choice of term is usually statutorily prescribed.

D. *Intervening cause* and *supervening cause.* These denote a cause that comes into active operation *after* a defendant's negligence, even if that cause does not break the chain of causation; *intervening* and *supervening* are used in a temporal sense in reference to the chain of causation. *Intervening* is the better choice of term, for *supervening cause* is sometimes confused with *superseding cause.* See (E).

In G.B., the LATINISMS *novus actus interveniens* and *nova causa interveniens* are commonly used. See LATINISMS.

E. *Superseding cause.* This denotes an *intervening cause* that breaks the chain of causation. Thus if X shoots Y, who is then stabilized and recovering nicely but soon dies after poor medical treatment, that medical negligence will be held to be a *superseding cause.* The phrase *supervening cause* is also sometimes used in this sense, but it should be avoided because of its use also for *intervening cause.* See (D).

causative. See **causal.**

cause. A. And *case.* Both terms are used to describe litigated actions. *Case* is more commonly used, although *cause* remains current in the speech and writing of lawyers. The peaceful coexistence of these terms need not be threatened by branding either one a NEED-

LESS VARIANT. When writing or speaking for laymen, however, *case* is the term that will not confuse.

Black's notes that DIFFERENTIATION is possible between these terms, although if it does exist at all it is little heeded: "*case* not infrequently has a more limited signification, importing a collection of facts, with the conclusion of law thereon," whereas "*cause* imports a judicial proceeding entire, and is nearly synonymous with *lis* in Latin, or *suit* in English."

B. And *action.* Although *cause* and *action* are nearly synonymous, the legal idioms in which the phrases are used differ. Thus an *action* or *suit* is said to be 'commenced,' but a *cause* is not. Similarly, a *cause* but not an *action* is said to be 'tried.' Any substantive distinction between the words is subtle: broadly, *action* connotes legal procedure and *cause* denotes the merits of the dispute.

C. Disposition by Courts. *Causes* (or *cases*) are *on dockets*; they may be *remanded* (by an appellate court) or *disposed of* (by any court). But they may not be *reversed* or *affirmed.* E.g., "This is the keystone of the opinion below: If it is in error, the *cause must be reversed* [read *judgment must be reversed*]." See JUDGMENTS, APPELLATE-COURT.

cause-list is the BrE term corresponding to *docket* or *calendar,* qq.v., in AmE.

cause of action; right of action. These terms should be distinguished. *Cause of action* has been interpreted by the courts in two distinct ways: to refer to *the facts,* and to refer to *rights.* Generally, it refers to facts, "the grounds that entitle a person to sue" (*CDL*). Sometimes *cause of action* is misused for *prima facie case,* q.v., as here: "Plaintiff failed to make out his *cause of action* [read *prima facie case*], and therefore his claim must fail."

Right of action has two senses: (1) "the right to take a particular case to court" (*CDL*); and (2) "a chose in action." Here sense (1) obtains: "The foundation of the *right of action* was a family relationship with the deceased."

cautionary; cautious. *Cautionary* = encouraging or advising caution. E.g., "This time we do not award damages but sound a *cautionary* note to those who would persistently raise arguments against the income tax that have been put to rest for years." *Cautious* = exercising caution.

caveat (lit., "let him beware") means, in lay speech and writing, merely "a warning," from the common phrase *caveat emptor* (= let the buyer beware). In legal prose, however, *caveat* often signifies "a notice, usually in the form of an entry in a register, to the effect that no action of a certain kind [e.g., probate of a will] may be taken without first informing the person who gave the notice (the *caveator*)" (*CDL*). E.g., "In the probate practice of many states, a will contest commences with the filing of a *caveat* or written objection setting forth the facts upon which the contest is based."/ "The question on this appeal is whether a judgment creditor of an heir may file and prosecute a *caveat* to a will of the ancestor of that heir, by which real property is devised to other persons."

caveat, v.t., is an extension of the nominal use described in the preceding entry. E.g., "The petition has no right or interest in the property or estate of the testator necessary to maintain a suit to *caveat* the last will and testament of the testator."/ "In all jurisdictions, either by statute or by general principles, the right to *caveat* is limited, as it is in Maryland, to persons who have an interest in the property." The verb is inflected *caveated, caveating.*

caveator; contestant. A *caveator* is not one who warns, but one who challenges the validity of a will. The person whose interest is challenged is termed the *caveatee.* See **caveat.** *Contestant* is used in jurisdictions in which the procedure of filing a *caveat* is not used. E.g., "We now return to the statute that the *contestant* says was disregarded when George and the Gillises subscribed their signatures to the questioned instrument."

cavil, beyond (= beyond even the most trivial objection) is a favorite expression of judges. E.g.,"The fact of damage was established *beyond cavil.*"

cease is a FORMAL WORD for *stop* or *end.* E.g., "In a jurisdiction that bases the imposition of exemplary damages on general deterrence, the fact that the defendant has *ceased* the offending conduct is irrelevant, as the exemplary damages may be used as a future deterrent to others."

cease-and-desist order should be hyphenated thus. See ADJECTIVES (C). Usually used of administrative orders, this DOUBLET performs a useful function. (The simpler expression *stop order* is confined to securities law.)

cede; secede; concede. The distinctions are as follows. *Cede* = to give up, grant, admit, or surrender. "By the Treaty of October 4, 1864, the Klamath Indian Tribe *ceded* approximately twenty million acres of aboriginal land to the government of the United States." *Secede* = to withdraw formally from membership or participation in. *Concede* = (1) to admit to be true; (2) to grant (as a right or a privilege); or (3) to admit defeat in (as an election).

ceiling, used in the sense of "maximum," is in itself unobjectionable, but can sometimes lead to unfortunate mixed metaphors. E.g., "The task force recommended a general *increase* in the *ceilings.*" One *raises* a ceiling rather than *increases* it. An English writer on usage quotes a preposterous example about "a ceiling price on carpets." In using words figuratively, one must keep in mind their literal meanings. See METAPHORS. Cf. **catapult.**

censor, v.t.**; censure,** v.t. To *censor* is to oversee and revise, to selectively suppress or edit. E.g., "The right of the superintendent in the exercise of a reasonable discretion to *censor* the ordinary mail written by a patient who has been adjudged insane is not challenged."

To *censure* is to criticize severely, to castigate. E.g., "In 1978, the Alabama Court of the Judiciary *censured* a judge for merely associating with a former convict."/ "The SEC may remove from office or *censure* any officer or director of a self-regulatory organization if it finds that he has willfully violated the rules or abused his position."

censorious (= severely critical) is the adjective corresponding to the verb *censure,* not *censor.*

censure. See **censor.**

centennial; centenary. In all the anniversary designations (*bi-, sesqui-,* etc.), whether as adjective or as noun, the *-ial* forms are preferred in AmE, the *-ary* forms in BrE.

center around for *center on* or *in.* Something can *center on* (avoid *upon*) or *revolve around* something else, but it cannot *center*

around, as the center is technically a single point. The error is common, e.g.: "Policy considerations usually center first *around* [read *on*] registration in the U.S. Patent and Trademark Office."/ "The controversy centered *around* [read *on*] a case pending before the court."/ "Even in this context a federal court may well decline jurisdiction if the tortious conduct is part of an ongoing series of disputes centering *around* [read *on*] the marital relationship."/ "The controversy here centers *around* [read *on*] the regulations promulgated by the Commissioner and their proper construction and application." The PHRASAL VERB is frequently used when a straightforward BE-VERB would be preferable: "Perhaps the greatest concern to issuers considering junior stock *centers around* [read *is*] the accounting treatment of junior stock."

Center has been used of late as a transitive verb, perhaps to avoid the prepositional problem: "Computation of pecuniary damages recoverable for a barge's injury in a maritime collision *centers* [i.e., *is at the center of*] this cause." This phrasing is unidiomatic, however.

CENTURY-DESCRIPTIONS. Some of us, apparently, forget from time to time that *twentieth century* describes the 1900s, that *nineteenth century* describes the 1800s, and so on. Thus R. B. Collins's article entitled *Can An Indian Tribe Recover Land Illegally Taken in the Seventeenth Century?,* 1984-85 Preview of United States Supreme Court Cases no. 8, p. 179 (Jan. 18, 1985), which discusses land acquired by New York from the Oneida Indians in 1795. The title should refer to the *eighteenth century,* not the *seventeenth.*

What particular years make up the course of a century has also caused confusion. The *Oxford Guide to English Usage* points out that

strictly, since the first century ran from the year 1 to the year 100, the first year of a given century should be that ending in the digits 01, and the last year of the preceding century should be the year before, ending in two noughts. In popular usage, understandably, the reference of these terms has been moved back one year, so that one will expect the twenty-first century to run from 2000 to 2099.

Oxford Guide 95 (1983).

One other point merits our attention. As compound adjectives, the phrases denoting centuries are hyphenated; but they are not hyphenated as nouns. Hence, "The twelfth-century records were discovered in the nineteenth century." See ADJECTIVES (C).

ceremonial, -ious. The DIFFERENTIATION between these words lies more in application than in meaning; both suggest a punctilio in following the customs and trappings of ceremony. *Ceremonial* is the general word; it relates to all manner of ceremonies, and is used only of things. E.g., "Doubtless many divorced men disinherit their wives, some even with *ceremonial* bonfires and whoops of joy; what we are considering, however, is the probable intent of those divorced men who do not destroy their wills." *Ceremonious*, lightly disparaging, suggests an overdone formality, and is used of both persons and things.

certain can cloy as readily as almost any other word; *said*, q.v., surpasses it, but not by much: "[The plaintiff] was lawfully possessed of a *certain* donkey, which said donkey of the plaintiff was then lawfully in a *certain* highway, and the defendant was then possessed of a *certain* waggon and *certain* horses drawing the same." *Davies v. Mann*, (1842) 10 M. & W. 546, 546, 152 Eng. Rep. 588, 588. The *OED* labels this use of *certain*, as well as the phrase *certain of* ⟨certain of his possessions⟩ "somewhat archaic." The latter phrase is here used: "She brought suit under section 1983 in the United States District Court against Rotramel and the city, alleging that their actions had deprived Tuttle of *certain of* his constitutional rights."

certainty; certitude. *Certainty* = (1) an undoubted fact; or (2) absolute conviction. Sense (2) is very close to that reserved for *certitude*, which means "the quality of feeling certain or convinced." E.g., "The only thing that gives us slight pause is the question how much *certitude* the agents must have that the premises they are entering, though not listed on the dealer's license as his place of business, really are such." Holmes stated, rather memorably, "*Certitude* is not the test of *certainty*. We have been cock-sure of many things that were not so." O. W. Holmes, *Natural Law*, in *Collected Legal Papers* 311 (1920).

certiorari (L. "to be informed") refers to a writ or remedy by which appellate review is gained. The most troublesome aspect of the

word is its pronunciation: /sursh-ee-ŏ-*rar*-ee/ or /sursh-ee-ŏ-**rahr**-ee/.

certitude. See **certainty.**

certworthy, -worthiness. These legal NEOLOGISMS are used as ARGOT by those who practice before or closely follow the U.S. Supreme Court. *Certworthy* = meriting consideration on appeal by grant of a writ of certiorari. E.g., "From these circumstances emerge the '*certworthy*' question whether the Fourth Circuit's *Erie* duty obliged it to certify the false imprisonment issue to the Florida Supreme Court." Stern, Gressman & Shapiro, *Supreme Court Practice* 843 (6th ed. 1986). / "The substantiality and *certworthiness* of the certification question are further augmented. . . . " *Id.* at 844. Cf. **enbancworthy.**

cesser is a LEGALISM meaning "the premature termination of some right or interest" (*CDL*). It usually appears in the phrase *cesser clause* or *cesser provision*. E.g., "The oldest method of protecting the beneficiary from his own indiscretions is the *cesser* provision or forfeiture clause, which provides that the interest of the beneficiary ceases if he assigns or his creditors attempt to reach his interest by legal process."

cession; session. *Cession* = a giving up, granting; the act of ceding. E.g., Powell, *Professional Divestiture: The Cession of Responsibility for Lawyer Discipline*, 1986 Am. B. Found. Res. J. 31. It is used often of nations or peoples who *cede* land. *Session* = a meeting or gathering, and is used of deliberative bodies ⟨court is in session⟩.

cestui /*sed-ee*/ (= beneficiary) commonly appears as an elliptical form of *cestui que trust*, q.v. For example, "The only person who can object to the disposition of the trust property is the one having some definite interest in the property—he must be a trustee, or a *cestui*, or have some reversionary interest in the trust property."/ "If the *cestui* has the transaction with the trustee set aside, of course he must return any consideration paid by the trustee to him." As with the full phrase, *beneficiary* is a preferable term.

cestui que trust /*sed-ee-kee-trust*/ (originally, in LAW FRENCH, *cestui à que trust*, lit., "that person for whose benefit") is a legal AR-

CHAISM that persists in the U.S., but is obsolescent in G.B. The phrase is inferior to the simple word *beneficiary*, which is far more widely understood. E.g., "No trustee can be compelled to produce (except for the purpose of identification) documents in his possession as such, which his client, *the cestui que trust* [read *the beneficiary*], would be entitled to refuse to produce if they were in his possession." (Eng.)

The plural has been variously formed *cestuis que trust*, *cestuis que trusts*, and *cestuis que trustent*. The first of these forms is preferred, and is most common. E.g., "The trusts cannot be terminated, nor can the share of either one of the *cestuis que trust* be paid over to him." On elliptical use of the phrase, see **cestui.**

cestui que use (originally, in LAW FRENCH, *cestui à que use*, lit., "that person for whose use") refers to the beneficiary of a use, q.v. Today the term appears primarily in historical contexts, inasmuch as uses have been abolished in England. E.g., "The *cestui que use* of a freehold estate had no action at common law to enforce his claim against the feoffee." / "The person who enjoyed a use was known as the *cestui que use;* the feoffor to use and the *cestui que use* might be the same person or different persons." Some American jurisdictions retain the term, however; as with *cestui que trust, beneficiary* is a preferable term in modern contexts.

ceteris paribus (= other things being equal or the same) is an unnecessary LATINISM, since we have the common English phrase. Cf. **mutatis mutandis.**

chairman; chairwoman; chairperson; chair. Sensitivity to SEXISM has impelled some writers to use *chair* rather than *chairman*, on the theory that doing so avoids gender-bias. E.g., "Governor James Thompson, *co-chair* of the task force, urged that most of the recommendations to combat violent crime would be of no avail for a nation left with no place to put violent offenders because of a lack of safe, humane prison facilities." Certainly *chair* is better than *chairperson*, an ugly and trendy word.

For many of us, however, there is nothing incongruous in having a female *chairman*, inasmuch as *-man* has historically been sexually colorless. Our numbers are declining, however, and if we are to be driven to a substitute

wording, we ought to ensure that *chair* (which goes back to the mid-17th c.) and not *chairperson* becomes the standard term. See SEXISM (B).

chambers. This word refers to the private office of a judge or magistrate. In G.B., it additionally has the sense "the offices occupied by a barrister or group of barristers" (*CDL*). The word is always plural in form, regardless of the number of rooms denoted. Laymen sometimes wrongly make the word singular, as in *judge's chamber*. See, e.g., M. Nicholson, *A Dictionary of American-English Usage* (1957), under *camera*.

The one use in which the singular *chamber* is correct is as an adjective: "During this period, however, other events not formally reflected in the record took place; these include *chambers conferences* [read *chamber conferences* or *conferences in chambers*], which were, of course, known to the district court."

CHAMELEON-HUED WORDS. "In any closely reasoned problem, whether legal or nonlegal, chameleon-hued words are a peril both to clear thought and to lucid expression." W.N. Hohfeld, *Fundamental Legal Conceptions* 35 (1919; repr. 1966). More than one great legal mind has made this observation: "When things are called by the same name, it is easy for the mind to slide into an assumption that the verbal identity is accompanied in all its sequence by identity of meaning." *Lowden v. Northwestern Bank & Trust Co.*, 298 U.S. 160, 165 (1936) (per Cardozo, J.). "A word is not a crystal, transparent and unchanged, it is the skin of a living thought and may vary greatly in color and content according to the circumstances and the time in which it is used." *Towne v. Eisner*, 245 U.S. 418, 425 (1918) (per Holmes, J.).

The English language, and therefore the language of the law, is full of multivalent words that have a number of different, sometimes quite different, meanings. There are at least two types of chameleon-hued words. The first type consists in words like *temporal*, which has a number of distinct meanings: (1) of or relating to time ⟨temporal relations of events⟩; (2) secular, not spiritual ⟨temporal pastimes⟩; (3) chronological ⟨temporal sequence⟩; or (4) of or relating to the temples on the side of one's skull ⟨temporal lobes⟩. As another example, Frankfurter wrote, "I do not use the term *jurisdiction* because it is a verbal coat of too many colors." *United States v. L.A. Tucker Truck Lines, Inc.*, 344 U.S. 33, 39 (1952) (Frankfurter, J., dissenting).

The second type consists essentially in words, usually adjectives, that are empty vessels, to be filled with meaning by the reader. Lawyers are fond of such terms as *reasonable, substantial, meaningful,* and *satisfactory.* These terms are often usefully vague, and allow draftsmen to provide a standard for performance in unforeseen circumstances. It is worth the warning, however, to note that "a competent draftsman would not deliberately pick a word which instead of controlling the context is easily colored by it." *In re Estate of Coe,* 42 N.J. 485, 201 A.2d 571, 577 (1964).

champerty; maintenance. "It would seem that in England contingent fees are held to be within the inhibition of the statutes of *champerty* and *maintenance.*" These words denote related but distinct offenses. *Champerty* is "the illegal proceeding, whereby a party [often a lawyer] not naturally concerned in a suit engages to help the plaintiff or defendant to prosecute it, on condition that, if it be brought to a successful issue, he is to receive a share of the property in dispute" (*OED*). *Maintenance* is "the action of wrongfully aiding and abetting litigation; sustentation of a suit or suitor at law by a party who has no interest in the proceedings or who acts from any improper motive" (*OED*).

The element of pecuniary return is absent from the notion of *maintenance.* Pollock noted at the turn of this century that "[a]ctions for maintenance are in modern times rare though possible." Pollock, *The Law of Torts* 211 (1887). The same might now be said of *champerty,* although *contingent fees,* q.v., which might be said to fit within the traditional definition of *champerty,* are common in the U.S.; they have been excepted from the prohibition of *champerty* and in most cases are proper under the canons of ethics.

The adjectival form of *champerty* is *champertous,* and the agent noun is *champertor* (labeled obsolete by the *OED,* but with no such notation in *W3*). Following is an example of the adjective: "For an agreement to be *champertous,* the financier must have no interest in the litigation to be financed." *United States ex rel. Balboa Ins. Co. v. Algernon Blair, Inc.,* 795 F.2d 404, 409 (5th Cir. 1986).

chancellor = (1) in England (before 1875),

the nominal head of the Court of Chancery and of the whole judiciary, and also Speaker of the House of Lords and a member of the Cabinet; (2) in the U.S., a judge in equity, or on any court denominated "chancery." In short, the title is not nearly as exalted in the U.S. as it is in G.B. Here are some examples of the term's use: "Plaintiff finally invokes the rule that findings of the *chancellor* on conflicting evidence will not be disturbed unless clearly and palpably against the weight of the evidence."/ "There is no claim of fraud or overreaching and the *chancellor* found that the agreement was not unfair or inequitable under the circumstances." See **chancery.**

chancellor's foot. John Selden, the seventeenth-century barrister, said, "Equity is a roguish thing, for law we have a measure to know what to trust to. Equity is according to the conscience of him who is Chancellor as it is larger or narrower so is equity. Tis all one as if they should make the standard for the measure we call a foot to be the *Chancellor's foot.*"

The phrase has continued to stand for inequitable variability in court rulings. E.g., "[T]he defense of entrapment enunciated in these opinions was not intended to give the federal judiciary a *chancellor's foot* veto over law enforcement practices of which it did not approve." *United States v. Russell,* 411 U.S. 423, 435 (1973). American courts, alas, have sometimes got the reference wrong: "Hundreds of years ago, likewise, equity ceased to be the measure of the '*King's foot.*'" *United States v. Parkinson,* 240 F.2d 918, 921 (9th Cir. 1956).

chancery; equity. *Chancery* = (1) the office of the Chancellor; (2) a court of equity; or (3) equity. Sense (1) is most usual in England, primarily as a historical usage: "The *Chancery,* in fact, readily abandoned any legal topic as soon as the common law mended its ways and provided a more adequate treatment." (Eng.) Sense (3) is today almost purely an American extension of the word ⟨principles of chancery⟩. E.g., "The general rule in Virginia is that a cestui que trust is not bound by a decree rendered against his trustees in a *chancery* suit to which he is not a party."/ "Before probating the second will it was not necessary to file a bill in *chancery* under the statute to set aside the probate of the former will." Formerly, American legists used *bill in* *equity* and *bill in chancery* interchangeably. Today in Delaware, the *Court of Chancery* has jurisdiction over insolvency and receiverships of corporations.

Equity has three basic senses that are relevant in comparing it with *chancery:* (1) evenness, fairness, justice; (2) the application to particular circumstances of the standard of what seems naturally just and right, as contrasted with the application to those circumstances of a rule of law; and (3) the body of principles and rules developed since medieval times and applied by the Chancellors of England and the Courts of Chancery. Sense (1) is the general sense used by laymen and lawyers alike; sense (2) is the commonest meaning in legal contexts; and sense (3), in the narrow definition given, is historical and generally British. Senses (2) and (3) are the senses in which *chancery* is sometimes used for *equity,* q.v.

chancy is colloquial and undignified for *uncertain* or *risky.* E.g., "Each party recognizes that it must make some response to the demands of the other party, for issues left unresolved will be submitted to the court, a recourse *that is always chancy* [read *that always has risks*] and may result in a solution less acceptable than might be reached by horse-trading."

channelize; channel, v.t. The *COD* suggests some DIFFERENTIATION between these terms. *Channel* = (1) to form channels in, to groove; or (2) to guide. *Channelize* = to convey (as if) in a channel; to guide. *Channel* is the common term, to be used unless the connotations suggested by the definition of *channelize* are peculiarly appropriate.

channel(l)ed; channel(l)ing. These words take one *-l-* in the U.S., two in G.B. See DOUBLING OF FINAL CONSONANTS.

character; reputation. These words are frequently used in the law of defamation and of evidence. Very simply, the semantic distinction is that *character* is what one is, whereas *reputation* is what one is thought by others to be.

charge, n. & v.t. **A.** In the Sense "accusation." To write that someone has been *accused* of a *charge* is a REDUNDANCY. E.g., "In announcing Mr. X's suspension, the [newspaper] management pointed out that 'Mr. X

had neither been accused nor convicted of any charge (read *had neither been charged nor convicted*)." (Follett, *Modern American Usage* 47 (1966).) See **accuse.**

B. Active & Passive Use. *In charge of,* Nicholson writes, may be used both actively and passively, e.g.: "The livestock were left *in charge of* the foreman; the foreman was left *in charge of* the livestock." The usual way of wording the passive construction is *in the charge of,* which prevents any possible ambiguities. E.g., "The truck was *in charge of* [read *in the charge of*] Mack Free, who was instructed not to permit any person to ride upon or drive it." To one not accustomed to *in charge of* in the passive construction, subject and object appear to have been confused, i.e., the sentence seems to say that the truck had control of or authority over Mack Free. One more example: "It had been the practice in Texas to assign a Pullman conductor to trains with two or more sleeping cars, while in trains with only one sleeping car that car was *in charge of* [read *in the charge of*] a porter."

C. *That*-phrase Objects. It is permissible to write, "He charged that the prosecutorial misconduct was of constitutional dimensions," although in G.B. *charge* generally takes a direct object, either a person or a thing. E.g., "Count one *charged* the defendant that on or about October 27, 1969, being an undischarged bankrupt he had obtained credit to the extent of £451 13s. 9d. from Lloyds Bank Ltd without informing the said bank that he was then an undischarged bankrupt." *Regina v. Hartley,* [1972] 2 Q.B. 1.

Both direct objects and *that*-phrase objects are common in the U.S. Here is another example of the latter type: "The complainant further *charged* that the above-mentioned book was printed by defendant."

D. *Charge the jury.* When the trial judge *charges* the jury, or gives the jury its *charge,* he instructs the jurors on the standards to be applied in their decision. "The trial judge, in *charging the jury,* required no less than this." The nominal phrase is *jury charge* (= the judge's instructions).

E. And *accuse.* See **accuse.**

chargé d'affaires. Pl. *chargés d'affaires.*

chargee = the holder of a charge upon property, or of a security over a contract (*OED*). E.g., "I see no difficulty in holding that the *chargee,* though not actually clothed with any legal estate himself, is notionally so clothed." (Eng.) The term is a British LEGALISM, unrecorded in American dictionaries (apart from *W2*).

Charta, Magna. See **Magna C(h)arta.**

charterer; affreighter. Both mean "a person to whom a vessel is chartered in a charterparty." *Charterer* is more usual. See the quotation under **affreightment.**

charterparty. American dictionaries spell the phrase as two words (the *CDL* spells it as one), but the courts on both sides of the Atlantic increasingly make it one. See, e.g., the English work *Scrutton on Charterparties and Bills of Lading* (18th ed. A. Mocatta, M. Mustill & S. Boyd 1974). Of course, "[d]ictionaries lag behind linguistic realities," *Security Center, Ltd. v. First National Security Centers*, 750 F.2d 1295, 1298 n.4 (5th Cir. 1985); perhaps the dictionaries will soon list *charterparty* as a single word.

Charter is not to be encouraged as an elliptical form of *charterparty*, because it has so many other meanings that using it in this way may give rise to uncertainties, even if in many admiralty contexts it may well be unambiguous. The tendency to use *charter* is understandable if we view *charterparty* as two words; the solution is to spell it as one.

chary (= cautious) is a FORMAL WORD close in meaning to *wary*. It is a favorite word of some judges. "We have been extremely *chary* about extending the 'commercial speech' doctrine beyond this narrowly circumscribed category." The word sometimes implies "sparing, ungenerous" ⟨chary of praise⟩.

chasm is pronounced /kaz-ĕm/.

chasten; chastise. These words are close in meaning, but distinct. *Chasten* = to discipline, punish, or subdue. *Chastise* = to punish, thrash. In the U.S., *chastise* has also the dialectal sense "to castigate, criticize."

Chastise is so spelled; *chastize*, an incorrect spelling, is not uncommon. See -IZE.

chattel mortgage. See **mortgage.**

chattels is commonly defined as "personal property," but this definition misleads. The proper definition is "any property other than freehold land"; a leasehold interest in land, having characteristics of both real and personal property, is termed a *chattel real*. E.g., "American courts have been much more liberal than the courts of England in recognizing future interests in *chattels real*."

Tangible or intangible personal property is termed *chattels personal*. E.g., "Chattels personal may be consumable or nonconsumable, tangible or intangible." The distinction is best observed fastidiously; nevertheless, this terminology is falling into disuse. *Chattel personal = chose*, q.v.

cheatee. See -EE.

chicane(ry). In contexts other than those involving horse racing and card games, *chicane* is a NEEDLESS VARIANT of *chicanery* (= trickery). "The lack of business ethics displayed by defendant invites and receives the condemnation of all who love fair play and scorn *chicane* [read *chicanery*] and deceit."/ "Ancient complaint about the attorney's *chicane* [read *chicanery*] was reinforced in the sixteenth century with the addition to the English language of the opprobrious 'pettifogger.'"

chide ⟩ chid ⟩ chid are the preferred inflections in the U.S., *chide ⟩ chided ⟩ chided* in G.B. Wherever one is, the variant past participle *chidden* should be avoided.

chief judge; presiding judge. On U.S. Circuit Courts of Appeals, the *chief judge* is the active judge (i.e., not having taken senior status, that is, gone into semiretirement) with the longest service on a particular court. A *presiding judge* is the senior active judge on one of the three-member panels that routinely hear and decide cases.

chief justice. Copperud writes that "the correct federal title is *chief justice of the United States*, not *of the Supreme Court*." R. Copperud, *American Usage and Style* 69 (1980).

childlike; childish. The former has positive connotations of simplicity, innocence, and truthfulness. The latter has negative connotations of puerility, peevishness, and silliness.

child-stealing. See **abduction.**

chill (= to inhibit, discourage ⟨to chill a person's rights⟩) is now a common term in American legal ARGOT. The standard phrase is *chilling effect*, e.g.: "The majority held that the waiting-period requirement is unconstitutional because it has a *chilling effect* on the right to travel."

The origin of this use of the word lies in the figurative sense, recorded by both the *OED* and *W3*, "to affect as with cold; to check, depress, or lower (warmth, ardour, etc.); to damp, deject, dispirit" (*OED*). All the examples quoted in the *OED* to illustrate this sense involve the chilling of something, usually an emotion, that is figuratively warm (enthusiasm, courage, admiration, zeal, etc.).

American lawyers have extended this use of the word and applied it to rights and freedoms, to the exercise of those rights and freedoms, and even to the persons exercising them. E.g., "Courts have said that the danger that the mere pendency of the action will *chill* the exercise of First Amendment rights requires more specific allegations than would otherwise be required."/ "If a law has no other purpose than to *chill* the assertion of constitutional rights by penalizing those who choose to exercise them, then it is patently unconstitutional."/ "Liberal notions of notice pleading must ultimately give way to immunity doctrines that protect us from having the work of our public officials *chilled* or disrupted by participation in the trial or the pretrial development of civil lawsuits."

The basic phrase *chilling effect* is sometimes jargonistically elaborated: "The purpose of this limitation is to prevent juries from giving excessive awards, and thereby imposing a pecuniary *chill factor* on the media." See SET PHRASES. Because of its indiscriminate use, *chill(ing)* is quickly becoming a legal CLICHÉ.

choate. Holmes wrote in 1878 that he had read in a legal text from California that "the wife on marriage acquires an *inchoate* right of dower which by the death of her husband becomes *choate*." *Holmes-Pollock Letters* 11 (2d ed. Howe 1961). *Choate*, a BACK-FORMATION from *inchoate*, is a malformed word, for the prefix in *inchoate* is intensive and not negative. (See **in-.**) The word derives from the Latin verb *inchoare* "to hitch with; to begin." Yet, because it was misunderstood as being a negative (meaning "incomplete"), someone invented a positive form for it, namely *choate* (meaning "complete").

The word has become more or less standard in the phrase *choate lien*, corresponding to *inchoate lien*. Justice Minton used the word in *United States v. City of New Britain*, 347 U.S. 81, 84 (1954): "The liens may also be perfected in the sense that there is nothing more to be done to have a *choate* lien—when the identity of the lienor, the property subject to the lien, and the amount of the lien are established." The three requirements mentioned in that quotation make up what has come to be known in the U.S. as the *choateness doctrine*, which means that "where a security interest arising under state law . . . comes into conflict with a federal tax lien, the state law security interest 'attaches' only when it becomes *choate*." *J.D. Court, Inc. v. United States*, 712 F.2d 258, 261 (7th Cir. 1983).

Although the word is the product of incorrect etymology, is ugly and illogical, it would be futile to call for its obliteration from the legal vocabulary. It has supplied a name for a fairly arcane legal doctrine, which is unlikely to be renamed. *Choate* is recognized in legal literature as "an illegitimate back formation" (Plumb, *Federal Liens and Priorities*, 77 Yale L.J. 228, 230 [1967]), but it is used even by those who deprecate its origins. See **inchoate.**

choreograph and *orchestrate*, q.v., have become CLICHÉS when used figuratively. In the most jejune language of the day, careers are *choreographed* and events are *orchestrated*. See VOGUE WORDS.

chose, n., is a LAW FRENCH word meaning literally "a thing." In modern legal writing, *chose* = chattel personal, q.v. E.g., "In other words, the plaintiff seeks to get at a particular *chose* or res that the defendant has and to deprive defendant of it."

Traditionally *choses* are of two kinds. *Choses in possession* are tangible goods capable of being actually possessed and enjoyed (e.g., books and clothes); *choses in action* are rights that can be enforced by legal action (e.g., debts or causes of action in tort). E.g., "If the *chose in action* is not embodied in a writing or evidenced thereby, delivery must be by a written assignment."/ "No particular formalities are required for a gift of a *chose in action* not represented by a so-called indispensable account." The phrase *chose in action* is sometimes anglicized *thing in action*. Cf. **chattels.**

chose jugée = a matter already settled, and

therefore not open to further consideration. This phrase is an unnecessary French equivalent of *res judicata,* q.v.

chrysalis. Pl. *chrysalides.*

chuse, an archaic spelling of *choose,* is used in Article I, Section 2 of the U.S. Constitution, and indeed throughout the document. The archaic spelling also occurred in British opinions of the period: "[S]he did not *chuse* to expose herself to contempt again. The action then is to depend entirely on the nerves of the actress; if she *chuses* to appear on the stage again, no action can be maintained. . . ." *Ashley v. Harrison,* (1793) Peake 256, 258 (K.B.) (spelling modernized at 170 Eng. Rep. 148, 149).

C.I.F. See **F.O.B.**

circumlocution is roundabout speech or language, or using many words where one or two would suffice. It is not the nominal form of *circuitous,* which means "winding, tortuous, anfractuous"—the noun for *circuitous* being *circuity,* and the adjective corresponding to *circumlocution* being *circumlocutory.*

CIRCUMLOCUTION. See *BE*-VERBS (B) & PERIPHRASIS.

circumscribable; circumscriptable, -tible. The first form listed is preferred. See -ABLE (A).

circumspection = cautiousness; watchfulness; prudence ⟨the judge exercised circumspection in disbelieving the interested witnesses⟩. This word is sometimes misunderstood as meaning "examination." E.g., "The circumstances surrounding the removal are far from typical and present what the court ascertains as a novel question, requiring almost a complete *circumspection* [read *examination*] of the removal provisions for its resolution."

circumstances. Some writers prefer *in the circumstances* to *under the circumstances.* The latter is unobjectionable, however, and is much more common. E.g., "*Under the circumstances,* we are of the opinion that the sole purpose for which the trust was created has become impossible of accomplishment and has been terminated." Fowler wrote that the insistence on *in the circumstances* as the only right form is "puerile."

circumstantial evidence; indirect evidence. The former is the more common phrase in both the U.S. and G.B. for evidence from which the fact-finder may infer the existence of a fact in issue, but which does not directly prove the existence of the fact. See **direct evidence.**

circumvent; undermine. *Circumvent* may mean "to undermine," e.g.: "Resort to judicial injunction to *circumvent* the decision of Board 2901 would subvert the purpose of the Railway Labor Act." But *circumvent* is connotatively a somewhat more neutral word than *undermine.* See **obviate.**

CITATION OF CASES. The standard work in the field is *A Uniform System of Citation* (14th ed. 1986). For British form, see *Manual of Legal Citations,* in two parts (1959). Also valuable are C.E. Good's *Citing and Typing the Law: A Course on Legal Citation and Style* (2d ed. 1987); D.M. Bieber's *Current American Legal Citations* (1983); and M.O. Price's *Practical Manual of Standard Legal Citations* (2d ed. 1958). For Canadian legal writers, the *Canadian Guide to Uniform Legal Citation* (2d ed. 1988) and C.S. Tang's *Guide to Legal Citation: A Canadian Perspective in Common Law Provinces* (1984) are serviceable guides. For identification of obscure citations, esp. in historical materials, Marion D. Powers's *Legal Citation Directory* (1971) is useful. A few points not within the purview of those works merit our attention here.

A. Beginning Sentences with Citations. It is a poor stylistic practice to begin a sentence with a citation, e.g.: "26 U.S.C. § 7213 provides that it is unlawful for any officer or employee of the United States to willfully disclose to any person . . . tax returns or return information." A better method is to state the proposition and to place the citation at the end of the sentence.

B. Mid-Sentence Citations. The legal writer's general preference should be not to cite cases in mid-sentence, for it is distracting to the reader, especially if that citation is longer than fifteen or so characters (as an appeals court case that was denied certiorari). Only occasionally does it seem appropriate, e.g.: "Our holding in *Harrington v. Bush,* 553 F.2d 190 (D.C. Cir. 1977), requires us to reject Senator Helms's arguments and to deny him standing."

Courts formerly tried setting off these mid-sentence citations in parentheses, but the results are little better than any other mid-sentence citations, and doing so does not conform to the general rules of legal citation. Here is an egregious example:

> The doctrine of incorporation by reference, even if applicable at all where an intent to incorporate in the usual sense is negatived (*In re Estate of York*, 95 N.H. 435, 437, 65 A.2d 282, 8 A.L.R.2d 611; Lauritzen, *Can a Revocable Trust Be Incorporated by Reference*, 45 Ill. L. Rev. 583, 600; Polasky, *"Pourover" Wills and the Statutory Blessing*, 98 Trusts & Estates 949, 954-955; compare *Old Colony Trust Co. v. Cleveland*, 291 Mass. 380, 196 N.E. 920; *Bolles v. Toledo Trust Co.*, 144 Ohio St. 195, 58 N.E.2d 381, 157 A.L.R. 1164; Restatement [2d]: Trusts, § 54, comments e–j, 1), could not import the nonexistent amendment.
> *Second Bank-State Street Trust Co. v. Pinion*, 341 Mass. 366, 170 N.E.2d 350, 352 (1960).

C. Incidental Use of Case Names. See CASE REFERENCES.

cite, n. Use of *cite* as a noun is poor in place of *citation*. Cf. *quote* for *quotation*.

cite, v.t. **A.** General Senses and Use. *Cite,* v.t. = (1) to commend ⟨the mayor cited him for his commendable pro bono work⟩; (2) to adduce as precedent or as binding law ⟨counsel then cited the appropriate statutory provision⟩; or (3) to summon before a court of law ⟨he was cited for contempt⟩.

In sense (2), the object of *cite* should be the precedent or statute cited, not the person to whom it is cited. The following loose usage is not uncommon in the U.S.: "In support of their claim *they cite us to section 5238 of the code* [read *they cite section 5238 of the code (to us)*]." The dative phrase *to us* is unnecessary.

B. And *quote*. Lawyers commonly differentiate between these words. To *cite* an authority is to give its substance and to indicate where it can be found. To *quote* is to repeat someone else's exact words and to enclose them in quotation marks. In legal writing, citations routinely follow quotations.

citizen. **A.** And *resident*. With U.S. citizens, the terms *citizen* and *resident* are interchangeable in reference to state residency or citizenship. The words are not interchangeable when other political entities (e.g., cities) are the frame of reference, for *citizen* implies po-

litical allegiance and a corresponding protection by the state, whereas *resident* denotes merely that one lives in a certain place. E.g., "Plaintiff, a *citizen* of the State of Washington, seeks a declaratory judgment pursuant to 28 U.S.C. § 400." (He is a *citizen* of Washington merely by virtue of being a U.S. citizen and residing in that state; yet he is able to avail himself of the protections of state law; hence *citizen* is appropriate.)

With foreign citizens, the distinction between *resident* and *citizen* becomes acute, inasmuch as an alien remains a *citizen* of a foreign country but may be a *resident* of a state. For purposes of American diversity jurisdiction in federal courts, the alien's *citizenship*, rather than his *residency*, controls, under the principle first laid down in *Breedlove v. Nicolet*, 32 U.S. (7 Pet.) 413, 431-32 (1833). See **citizenship.**

B. And *subject*. *Subject* (= a person subject to political rule, any member of a State except the Sovereign [*COD*]) is not merely the British equivalent of the American *citizen*. A *citizen* is a person from a country in which sovereignty is believed or supposed to belong to the collective body of the people, whereas a *subject* is one who owes his allegiance to a sovereign monarch.

citizenry; citizens. Both are acceptable plurals of *citizen, -ns* being the more general. Two aspects of *citizenry* distinguish it: first, it is a COLLECTIVE NOUN (although it frequently takes a plural verb), emphasizing the mass or body of citizens; and second, *citizenry* is, as *W2* notes, frequently used by way of contrast to soldiery, officialdom, or the intelligentsia. Here it is opposed to one part of officialdom (some might say *intelligentsia*): "The written Constitution lies at the core of the American 'civil religion'; not only judges but also the *citizenry* at large habitually invoke the Constitution."

citizen's arrest; private arrest. The former phrase is current in both the U.S. and G.B. The latter phrase is a primarily British variant.

citizenship; domicile; residence, -cy. "For purposes of federal diversity jurisdiction, *citizenship* and *domicile* are synonymous." *Hendry v. Masonite Corp.*, 455 F.2d 955 (5th Cir. 1972). For other purposes, however, the words are quite different. *Citizenship* denotes the status of being a citizen, with its attendant rights and privileges. *Domicile* = residency at a particular place accompanied with positive or presumptive proof of an intention to remain there for an unlimited time. *Mitchell v. United States,* 88 U.S. (21 Wall.) 350, 352 (1875) (quoting *Guier v. O'Daniel,* 1 Binn. 349 n.1). See **citizen** (A). *Residence* is, for legal purposes, usable in place of *domicile,* but is broader, inasmuch as in one sense it is a FORMAL WORD for "house, home." See **domicil(e)** & **residence, -cy.**

civil death, a LOAN TRANSLATION of *mors civilis,* was formerly opposed to *natural death.* At common law, a person banished or outlawed, or one having entered a monastery, was said to have suffered a *civil death.* This LEGAL FICTION is still applied in some American states in reference to prisoners. Mellinkoff considers the fiction unnecessary and confusing in the modern world:

> For the sake of preserving the fiction of *civil death,* which satisfied the logic and rules of an earlier day, words are robbed of all ordinary meaning, yet nothing of technical sharpness results. As it is now, the rules that govern the civil rights of prisoners must still be spelled out in statute and case law. In the confusion over the metaphysics of *civil death* even earnest men find themselves wandering. Much simpler to drop the whole *civil death* business.
> D. Mellinkoff, *The Language of the Law* 328 (1963).

The opposite of this phrase, *natural life,* q.v., is a legal ARCHAISM that lives with us still, although its usefulness too is largely gone.

civilian, n., = a lawyer in a civil-law, as opposed to common-law, jurisdiction. As an adj., *civilian* = *civil-law.* In the three sentences that follow, the first two uses of the word exemplify the noun, the last two the adjective. "'Jura realia' and 'personalia' are expressions occasionally used by modern *civilians* as adjectival forms of 'jura in rem' and 'in personam.'"/ "Kent and Story, who were the leaders in the development of our law in the formative era and along with Blackstone and Coke were its oracles, were learned *civilians,* and the exigencies of commercial law, for which Blackstone and Kent furnished no useful material, led to increasing use of *civilian*

materials by text writers and courts." (R. Pound)/ "Albert Tate, Jr., a *civilian* scholar, then an intermediate appellate court judge, later a justice of the Louisiana Supreme Court, and now a member of this court, expressed the view that the 1912 Legislature amended 456, vastly expanding the items specifically covered."

Civilian, n. & adj., appears also in its lay sense (= [of or relating to] a nonmilitary person) in legal contexts, e.g.: "A *civilian* trial, in other words, is held in an atmosphere conducive to the protection of individual rights, while the military trial is marked by the age-old manifest destiny of retributive justice."/ "The Articles of War were revised to provide for military trial, even in peacetime, of certain specific *civilian* crimes committed by persons 'subject to military law.'"

civil law.   A. As Noun. The term *civil law* is ambiguous; the legal writer should be careful to specify which meaning he attributes to the term. *Civil law* − (1) [to a common-law practitioner] private law, as opposed to criminal law, administrative law, military law, or ecclesiastical law ⟨civil litigation⟩; (2) [to a comparative law specialist within the common-law system] the civil-law tradition in civil-code countries, the entire legal system in nations falling within the civil-law tradition; and (3) [to a civil-law practitioner] the fundamental content of the legal system (as opposed to public and commercial law)—of persons, of things, of obligations.

Yet another, rather archaic sense of *civil law* is "the law imposed by the state," as opposed to *moral law.* E.g., "A favorite theory with many of the philosophers is that ethics is an exposition of the moral law as distinguished from the *civil law;* the former being imposed by the conscience, the latter by the power of the state." G. W. Warvelle, *Essays in Legal Ethics* 4 (1902).

B. As Adjective. Like its sibling *common law,* q.v., this term should be hyphenated when it is used adjectivally ⟨civil-law jurisdiction⟩, and written as two words when used as a noun ⟨the civil law of Louisiana⟩.

claim.   A. Transitive Verb. *Claim* = (1) to take or demand as one's right; (2) to assert emphatically (something of questionable or questioned credibility). Sense (1) of *claim* often appears without an explicit object (i.e., with the object as an UNDERSTOOD WORD). E.g., "Plaintiffs are sisters of Mrs. Girard and claim as her heirs [i.e., *claim her estate as her heirs*]."

Sense (2), primarily an Americanism, is subject to SLIPSHOD EXTENSION when writers use *claim* to mean merely "to say," as in, "He *claims* [read *states* or *says*] the Supreme Court has never ruled on the point." But it is a groundless hobbyhorse to insist that this verb can properly mean only "lay claim to" or "demand as one's due," and not "assert, allege." *Claim* has long been used in the latter as well as in the former sense. E.g., "The police officer *claimed* that he had heard a rumor months earlier that the defendant would meet a drug buyer at some restaurant."/ "The defendant also *claimed* that there could be no rescission as restitutio in integrum was not possible, the plaintiffs having at a clearing sale disposed of the plant, machinery, and stock." (Aus.)

B. Noun. Out of sense (2) of the verb has grown the nominal sense "assertion, contention" ⟨her claim that the immunity applies here⟩, in addition to the older sense "a right to something." To be avoided at all costs is the use of the term in different senses in a single context: "The government *claims* [read *argues*] that Sherlock's *claim* [read *assertion*] of fifth amendment privilege is moot." Either substitution eliminates the problem.

claim quit. See **quitclaim.**

claim(s) agent (or **adjuster**). *Claims* is the standard form.

class is not interchangeable with *kind* or *type*. We may have a type or kind of *thing*, but a class of *things*. E.g., "In this *class of case* [read *type of case* or *class of cases*], the contract is executed by the promoter and the third-party when both are aware that the corporation has not been formed."

classic(al). *Classical* is used of anything relating to "the classics" (whether in Greek or Latin literature, English literature, or music); *classic* may also serve in this sense, although not in phrases such as *classical education* or *classical allusions*. *Classic,* an easily overworked word, has the additional sense "outstandingly authoritative or important."

clause of accrual (or **accruer**). See **accrual.**

clean, v.t.; **cleanse.** *Clean* is literal, *cleanse* figurative. Hence *cleanse* is often used in religious or moral contexts, or, as here, in law: "[T]he court can take ex post facto measures to *cleanse* the error." *Marine Coatings of Alabama, Inc. v. United States,* 792 F.2d 1565, 1568 (11th Cir. 1986).

clean hands is a metaphor from equity, derived from the maxim *He who comes to equity must come with clean hands,* i.e. must be free from taint of fraud. E.g., "The maxim that he who comes into equity must come with *clean hands* is far more than a mere banality."/ "The nature of the *unclean-hands* defense in patent and unfair competition litigation has not been clearly established." A memorable statement of the principle is: "He that hath committed Iniquity, shall not have equity." R. Francis, *Maxims of Equity* 5 (1727).

cleanliness; cleanness. *Cleanliness* is used of persons and their habits, *cleanness* of things and places.

cleanse. See **clean.**

clear(-)cut, adj., should be hyphenated. "The testator, thus indicating a *clearcut* [read *clear-cut*] intention to postpone vesting until the termination of each trust, created a remainder contingent upon survival of the life beneficiary."

clearly. "[I]t seems to be a familiar joke among some ironic observers that when a judge (some other judge) begins a sentence with a term of utter conviction (*Clearly, Undeniably, It is plain that . . .*), the sentence that follows is likely to be dubious, unreasonable, and fraught with difficulties." Gibson, *Literary Minds and Judicial Style,* 36 N.Y.U. L. Rev. 915, 925 (1961). This skepticism has grown from an abuse of these terms to express certainty. Where they are used merely to buttress arguments, they become WEASEL WORDS and weaken those arguments. They should be used only where one's bitterest opponent could not object.

cleave, v.t., has the opposite meanings (1) "to divide or separate" and (2) "to adhere to firmly." In sense (1), *cleave* yields the past tense *cleft* (or, less good, *clove*) and the past participle *cleft* (or *cleaved*, again not preferred). The past participial adjective is *cloven*. Hence, "He cleft the Devil's cloven hoof with a cleaver."

In sense (2), the verb is inflected *cleave* 〉 *cleaved* 〉 *cleaved*. The *COD* sanctions, for BrE usage, *cleave* 〉 *clove* 〉 *cloven* for all senses, though *cleft* is used adjectivally in set phrases such as *cleft palate* or *stick*. Luckily, the term is a literary one, so that generally only literary scholars must trouble themselves with these inflections.

clench. See **clinch.**

clerk; law clerk; summer associate; extern; briefing attorney. The rather undignified term *clerk* is used of American law students who work for law firms before receiving their law degrees and passing the bar exam. In response to the meniality connoted by this term, some lawyers have borrowed *extern* from the medical profession, but its use is not widespread. For clerks who work with a firm during the summer months, lawyers have hit upon *summer associate,* which has gained currency throughout the U.S. among firms that recruit heavily.

Law clerk is used also to describe those select graduates who spend a year or two as judges' apprentices. These young lawyers have usually already passed the bar exam and accepted a permanent position for the following year. Hence, although they are already *lawyers,* the apparent meniality of *law clerk* is especially ironic. Some courts therefore call their clerks *briefing attorneys,* but to one accustomed to the unpretentiousness of *law clerk* this term seems inflated. The best advice is to follow the practice of a particular firm or judge: at a firm that hires *law clerks,* no one should call himself a *summer associate* (though the reverse practice is unobjectionable); if a judge hires *law clerks,* none of them should call himself a *briefing attorney.* The understated title *law clerk* is to be worn as a badge of honor.

clew. See **clue.**

CLICHÉS. Why is it that, in legal prose, common sense always *dictates* certain actions? That precedents are never to be *lightly overruled*? That lower federal court decisions are never correct (but merely *not clearly erroneous*)? Why are trial judges whom appellate courts agree with always *learned,* but never wise or perspicacious or erudite? Why is an evidentiary hearing of any significance always termed *full-blown*? Too often in legal writing, parties *strenuously object*; judges write *vigorous dissents*; principles of law are never settled but that they are *well-settled*; trial judges always have *sound discretion* rather than mere discretion; bad statutes are inevitably *constitutionally infirm* rather than invalid or, better yet, unconstitutional; opinions we agree with are invariably *well-reasoned,* but almost never cogent or compelling.

Clichés should generally be used sparingly in any sort of writing, but especially in legal writing. Yet we are beset with hackneyed phrases inappositely employed in legal briefs and judicial opinions. To begin with, a good writer must have sensitized himself to what a cliché is. Acquiring this sensitivity requires some degree of literary taste, but mostly a background of having read widely. One need not read very many American judicial opinions to find, e.g., that *We do not write on a clean slate* (or *on a tabula rasa*) is a commonplace often repeated.

Some legal clichés, of course, such as *not clearly erroneous,* merely track the language of statutes or of precedents. Yet if a lower court's holding is right or correct, is it not also *not clearly erroneous*? Sometimes there is little or no need to use the exact language of the statute; if the lower court's holding is seen to be correct, then there is little chance that the appellate court in so stating its views has misapplied the standard of review, regardless of whether that is the clearly erroneous standard or the abuse-of-discretion standard.

General English clichés are also common in the language of the law. E.g., "*It all started* on a *fatal day* [*fateful day?*] in December of 1981, when the Equity Shipping Corporation chartered its vessel to the GHR Energy Corporation."/ "In the *hallowed days of yore,* parties seeking to stay their proceedings in an action at law had to *cross the street* into a court of equity for an injunction." (The main clause of this sentence manages to *sound* like a cliché without actually being one.) It would be easy to list hundreds of English-language clichés such as *time is of the essence, crystal clear, proverbial snowball in hell, dire need,* and *flatly refused*; but no purpose would be served. If one finds oneself writing or talking in ready-made phrases, it is time to draw back and frame the thought anew; the occasional cliché may be justifiable, to be sure; it is the habitual use of clichés that is stylistically objectionable. For a full discussion of clichés, see Eric Partridge's *Dictionary of Clichés* (1963) and James Rogers's *Dictionary of Clichés* (1985).

Finally, if one must use a cliché, do it straightforwardly. Slight variations on clichés are neither clever nor cute. E.g., "He wore his heresy on his sleeve." (Figuratively, only one's feelings can be worn on one's sleeves.) Likewise, one should not change *madding crowd* to *maddening crowd.* See SET PHRASES.

One lawyer has written wittily of the dissolution of his partnership, citing in part "an occupational nervous affliction" that causes lawyers to spout clichés. The culminating altercation, this lawyer recalled, sounded like this:

"You're being arbitrary and capricious!"

"Well you're being willful and wanton!"

"Are you suggesting that in futuro we do business separate and apart?"

"I'm telling you that you have been guilty of cruel treatment of me and have inflicted personal indignities upon me, rendering my life burdensome so that it is no longer possible for me to remain your partner!"

"Does this mean that our agreement is null and void?"

"It means that it's of no further force and effect."

"In that event I will no longer be responsible for your debt, default or misdoings," he rejoined. "And I'll want the library for myself, free and clear of any encumbrances."

McKinlay, *Legal Cliché Experts,* 49 Fla. B.J. 444 (1975).

cliental = of or relating to a client. The *OED* labels this word "rare," but the Merriam-Webster dictionaries contain no such notation. Still, lawyers have little occasion to use it.

clientele; clientelage; clientage; clientry; clients. The last is the best: the least pretentious and most common. *Clientele* has degenerated somewhat in meaning, having been widely used in nonprofessional contexts. E.g., "The complaint alleges that the plaintiffs are engaged in business as high-grade dressmakers under the name 'Boue Soeurs,' with the most exclusive *clientele.*" Often when *clientele*

appears in professional contexts, it is used in reference to the oldest profession.

Clientage, clientelage, and *clientry* are NEEDLESS VARIANTS of *clientele.*

climactic; climacteric; climatic. *Climactic* is now established as the adjective of *climax,* though formerly it was thought to be inferior to *climacteric,* which, having lost the battle, is now to be avoided as a NEEDLESS VARIANT. *Climatic* is the adjective of *climate;* occasionally it becomes a MALAPROPISM for *climactic.*

clinch; clench. Similar in meaning, these words are used differently. *Clench* is applied to physical matters, and *clinch* is used figuratively. Hence one *clenches* one's jaw or one's fist, but *clinches* an argument or debate. The exceptions to this rule are in boxing, carpentry, and metalworking: clutching one's opponent in boxing is *clinching,* and fastening with a screw or a rivet is likewise *clinching.* Apart from these specialized meanings, *clinch* should be reserved for nonphysical contexts.

CLIPPING. See BACK-FORMATIONS.

clog. See **cloud.**

closely held corporation. Because *closely* is an adverb, it is unnecessary to hyphenate the phrase *closely held.*

close of the evidence is the legal idiom denoting the end of the presentation of testimony in a trial. E.g., "At the *close of all the evidence,* the district court granted an instructed verdict in favor of appellee on nearly all the issues."

closure; cloture. The general noun corresponding to the verb *to close* is *closure.* E.g., "The court held that *closure* of a trial must be necessitated by a compelling governmental interest." *Cloture* is preferred in the U.S. in but one narrow sense: "the procedure of ending debate in a legislative body and calling for an immediate vote." *Closure* is usual in G.B. in this parliamentary sense.

clothe. In law, persons are frequently described metaphorically as being *clothed* with certain powers or privileges. E.g., "He was *clothed* with the apparent authority to enter into contracts for the corporation."/ "The will imposed no duties upon the trustee; it *clothed* her with no discretionary powers."/ "Mrs. Sterdahl, her innocence of wrongdoing established, stands before us *clothed* with the protection equity provides in favor of all bona fide purchasers of interests in property."/ "The Supreme Court under the Constitution and statutes of this state is *clothed* with the power to exercise both appellate and original jurisdiction." If sparingly used, this legal CLICHÉ might be tolerable; but it is sufficient to say merely that a person *has* the powers or privileges in question.

cloture. See **closure.**

cloud; clog. A *cloud on title* is a defect in the owner's title to a piece of land arising, e.g., from a lien, an easement, or a court order. The phrase is generally an American one. E.g., "An action to remove a *cloud* on the title to property is a remedy or form of proceeding originating in equity jurisprudence."/ "Flint and others brought a bill to restrain appellee from proceeding further and for a declaration freeing their title from the *cloud* cast upon it by appellee's judgment."/ "The historical equity suit to remove a *cloud* on title suffered from some self-imposed handicaps; it could not be used to cancel an instrument constituting a *cloud* that was void on its face."

A *clog on the equity* (often written *clog on the equity of redemption*) is a provision in a mortgage deed that prevents a mortgagor from getting back his property free from encumbrance upon payment of the debt or performance of the obligation for which the security was given. The phrase is more usually BrE than AmE. E.g., "The mortgage had a *clog on the equity*." (Eng.) The metaphor is an old one in law: R.W. Turner, in *The Equity of Redemption* 29 (1931), quotes a court that wrote, in 1639: "[I]n some cases . . . the mortgagee will suddenly bestow unnecessary costs upon the mortgaged lands, of purpose to *clogg* the lands, to prevent the mortgager's redemption" (quoting *Bacon v. Bacon,* Tot. 133). See METAPHORS, LEGAL.

clue; clew. *Clue* is the only current spelling for the sense "a hint; a bit of evidence." The spelling *clew* survives as a nautical term ("the lower corner of a sail") and as a sewing term ("a ball of thread").

CO-. Generally, a hyphen should not be used with this prefix. Only when the hyphen-

ated form is established (e.g., *co-respondent, co-relation*), when the unhyphenated form may lead the reader to mistake the syllables (e.g., *co-citation, co-heir*), or when the writer believes he is creating a new form (e.g., *co-plaintiff, co-secretary*) should the hyphen appear.

co-appellant; co-appellee. These terms are used to denote the relation of joint parties on appeal. E.g., "The appellant was a policeman in the City of Newport, and had executed a bond as required by law, with his codefendant and *co-appellant,* National Surety Co., as surety thereon."

co-citation is best hyphenated. This word, not uncommon in legal writing, is not listed in the *OED* or in *W3.* See **co-.**

co(-)conspirator. Hyphenating the word indicates immediately to the reader what the primary word (*conspirator*) is. See **co-.**

C.O.D. = (1) cash on delivery (*COD & W3*); (2) collect on delivery (*COD & W3*); (3) cash on demand (*Black's*); or (4) costs on delivery (*OED Supp.*). Whatever the abbreviation stands for, its effect is the same.

codal (= of or relating to a code) is an adjective used in some civil-law jurisdictions to refer to the civil code. E.g., "Although C.C. 3467-72 express a *codal* disfavor toward suspension of prescription, the jurisprudence has nevertheless recognized the doctrine of 'contra non valentem'." (La.)/ "Professor Malone suggested that enterprise liability should be founded directly upon the basic *codal* language, 'Every act whatever of a man that causes damage to another obliges him by whose fault it happened to repair it.' La. Civ. Code art. 2315(A) (West Supp. 1985)."

The only adjectival form of *code* recognized by the dictionaries, however, is *codical* (= pertaining to, or of the nature of, a codex or code). It is not used by civilians in Louisiana.

codefendant. This word, meaning "a joint defendant," is common; oddly, however, *co-plaintiff* is rare (the *OED* suggests it is a nonce-word).

codicil; will. *Codicil* = a testamentary instrument ancillary to a will that adds to, varies, or revokes provisions in the will. *Will* = a written or oral expression of one's intention regarding the disposition of one's property at death. See **last will and testament & will.**

co-employee is a NEEDLESS VARIANT of *co-worker.*

coequal, n. & adj., often means nothing that *equal* does not also mean; it should be rejected in such contexts. E.g., "All constitutional rights are *co-equal* [read *equal*] and must be harmonized with each other, no one such right being permitted to override or submerge another."

The word is useful only in implying the standard of comparison; for example, in a snippet quoted in the *OED,* "the co-eternal and co-equal Son," if only *equal* had been used, the reader would wonder, Equal with what? *Co-equal* implies the second and third things with which the Son is said to be equal. This nuance is rare, however; for most purposes, *equal* suffices. Cf. **copartner.**

coercible. So spelled. See -ABLE (A).

coercion, though originally applicable only to physical force, is now commonly used of moral and economic pressures. E.g., "It has never been held by this court that a labor union is without justification in fairly setting forth its claims by newspaper advertisements as a legitimate means of economic *coercion.*" Such uses are a natural extension of the original sense ("the control by force of a voluntary agent or action").

cofiduciary = joint fiduciary. The word is best not hyphenated. See **co-.**

cognation; cognition. *Cognition* = thinking; use of the intellect. *Cognation* = a cognate relationship. In Roman law, *cognation* (specif., natural relationship by descent from a common ancestor, whether through males or females) was opposed to *agnation* (relationship through males only).

cognitive; cognitional. The latter is a NEEDLESS VARIANT. *Cognitive* = of or pertaining to cognition, or to the action or process of knowing. It should be avoided in its use as a jargonistic filler, as here: "The totality of the relevant facts supports the finding that the City of Apopka has engaged in a systematic pattern of *cognitive* acts and omissions, selecting and reaffirming a particular course of mu-

nicipal services that inescapably evidences discriminatory intent." What the word means in that sentence is a minor mystery.

cognitor is an archaic word for *attorney* that derives from Roman law and existed in English only briefly.

cognizable; cognoscible. *Cognizable* /*kog-ni-ză-běl*/ = (1) capable of being known; perceptible; (2) capable of being, or liable to be, judicially examined or tried; within the jurisdiction of a court of law (*OED*). Sense (2) is common in the phrase *cognizable claims:* "Nor do I believe that a criminal suspect who is shot while trying to avoid apprehension has a *cognizable claim* of a deprivation of his sixth amendment right to trial by jury." *Cognoscible* is a NEEDLESS VARIANT.

cognizance; recognizance. Though superficially similar, these words have unrelated meanings. *Cognizance* = (1) knowledge, esp. as attained by observation or information; or (2) the action of taking judicial notice. Sense (2) is rarer now than it once was. *Recognizance* = (1) the bond by which a person engages before a court or magistrate to observe some condition, e.g., to keep the peace, pay a debt, or appear when summoned (*COD*); or (2) the sum pledged as a surety of this bond. See **recognizance.**

cognizant; cognisant. The -*z*- spelling is preferred in AmE and in BrE.

cognoscente, -ti. This word, almost always used in the plural (-*ti*), is misspelled only a little less frequently than it is used. E.g., "The criminal *cogniscenti* [read *cognoscenti*] will quickly learn that, when this judge's proffer is rejected, the defendant, if convicted, will pay a higher price; it is a denial of due process for the judge thus to stain his robes." That example illustrates an ironic use of the term; generally, *experts* or *authorities* will suffice, either one being easier to spell.

cognoscible. See **cognizable.**

cohabit, the verb for *cohabitation,* is analogous to *inhabit. Cohabitate* is a misbegotten BACK-FORMATION: "As more couples adopt this lifestyle, our courts will be called upon with increasing frequency to settle disputes over the legal rights of *cohabitating* [read *cohabiting*] couples."

cohabit(at)ive. The general rule is that, in Latinate nouns of this type, the adjectival form derives from the nominal form. Thus *cohabitative* is the correct form, following from the noun *cohabitation.*

co-heir. See **co-**.

cohort(s). Even legal usage, traditional and formal as it is, has given in to the modern sense (some would say corruption) of this word, e.g.: "Respondent and two *cohorts* were indicted for robbing a savings and loan." Traditionally, *cohort* has been a mass noun denoting "a band of warriors." "The extension of *cohort* to nonmilitary uses is natural enough," Follett writes,

> but if the word is to retain its force it should observe two requirements: (1) it should designate members, too numerous to be conveniently counted, of some sort of united group, and (2) it should imply some sort of struggle or contest. *No one of the candidates succeeded in completely marshaling his cohorts before the first ballot / To the legion of the lost ones, to the cohort of the damned*—in such uses the sense of the word is preserved.
> W. Follett, *Modern American Usage* 99 (1966).

This is a very conservative view of the word, especially given the fact that the sense "colleague, associate, companion" has been by far the most common in the last quarter century. Nevertheless, this newer meaning has remained a rather informal one for this respectable word, which in formal writing should retain its older sense.

coin a phrase. To *coin* is to mint afresh or to invent; it does not mean "to employ," as persons who commit the following error apparently think: "*To coin an old phrase*, we are guardedly optimistic." One cannot coin an old phrase.

collapsible. So spelled. See -ABLE (A).

collate. See **collocate**.

collateral, n., = (1) a person collaterally related to a decedent; or (2) security for a loan. See **ascendant** (sense 1) & **collateralize** (sense 2).

collateral estoppel; issue preclusion; res judicata. The lines of demarcation in meaning are distinct; yet these terms have long caused confusion among judges and advocates. *Collateral estoppel* and *issue preclusion* are synonymous; the latter phrase has sprung perhaps from a desire to be more descriptive in naming this legal doctrine. *Collateral estoppel* is the doctrine that prevents the relitigation of an issue that was actually litigated and was a critical and necessary part of the earlier judgment. The judgment on the issues litigated in the first action, then, is binding upon the parties in all later litigation in which those issues arise.

Res judicata is the same principle, but broader: it is "the principle that when a matter has been finally adjudicated upon by a court of competent jurisdiction it may not be reopened or challenged by the original parties or their successors in interest" (*CDL*). *Res judicata* implies, then, that no further issues exist relating to the dispute, whereas with *collateral estoppel* there may be other adjudicable issues. The best way of remembering these doctrines clearly is to view *collateral estoppel* as a miniature of *res judicata:* the former applies to issues, the latter to entire lawsuits.

One might cite any number of instances in which judges have written *collateral estoppel* when they meant *res judicata* and vice versa. E.g., "Although the court of appeals in our present case speaks in terms of *res judicata* . . . , the court actually applies principles of *collateral estoppel* in affirming the award of indemnity. . . . *Collateral estoppel* is narrower than *res judicata*. It is frequently [termed] *issue preclusion* because it bars relitigation of any ultimate issue of fact actually litigated and essential to the judgment in a prior suit." *Bonniwell v. Beech Aircraft Corp.*, 663 S.W.2d 816, 818 (Tex. 1984).

collateralize = (1) to serve as collateral for; (2) to make (a loan) secure with collateral. This word looks newfangled, and it is, having been recorded only as far back as 1941. For real estate lawyers (conveyancers) and bankers, however, it is a useful word for summing up what otherwise would take several words. Both senses are common, as: (Sense [1]) "The property purchased *collateralized* the notes."/ (Sense [2]) "It is significant that the bank realized that the loan was *collateralized*."

collectible, -able. The *-ible* spelling is preferred. See -ABLE (A).

COLLECTIVE NOUNS. Consistency in the use of singular or plural is the main consideration in the skillful handling of collective nouns. If, in the beginning of an opinion, the judge writes *the jury was,* he should to refer to *jury* as a singular noun throughout; if he wishes to emphasize the individual persons more than the body of persons, he may decide to write *the jury were.*

There is little "right" and "wrong" on this subject: collective nouns take sometimes a singular and sometimes a plural verb. The trend in the U.S. is to regard the collective noun as expressing a unit; hence, the singular is the usual form. When the individuals in the collection or group receive the emphasis, the plural verb is acceptable. But generally in AmE writing collective nouns take singular verbs, as in *the jury finds, the panel is, the faculty demands, the board has decided,* etc.

Just the opposite habit generally obtains in G.B., where collective nouns tend to take plural verbs. A text in BrE on statute-drafting has even attempted to enshrine this habit, albeit without giving reasons: "Though the practice varies, in legislative DRAFTING it is advisable to treat collective nouns as plural: that is, such nouns as *authority* or *Board* should be followed by a verb in the plural." A. Russell, *Legislative Drafting and Forms* 86 (1938). The British tend to write, e.g., "The *board have* considered the views of the judges of the appellate division." (Eng.)

In the days soon after the American Revolution, not surprisingly, the American practice was closer to the prevailing British practice. E.g., "The House of Representatives shall chuse *their* [modernly, *its*] Speaker and other Officers; and shall have the sole Power of Impeachment." U.S. Const. art. I, § 2./ "The Senate shall chuse *their* other Officers. . . ." U.S. Const. art. I, § 3.

The reversal in practice has become so firmly established in the U.S. that it is hardly wrong to say that, with certain collective nouns, singular verbs are *preferred.* One cannot be doctrinaire on this point of usage, however. The dilemma frequently occurs with nouns such as *majority* and *press* and *faculty.* E.g., "The press *have* [read (in U.S.) *has*] the same rights that the rest of the community *have* [read (in U.S.) *has*]."/ "Constitutionalizing basic welfare benefits for the poor will not happen as long as the middle class *remain* [read (in U.S.) *remains*] so conservative, so numerous, and so prosperous." For examples with *jury,* see the entry under that word.

These are questions more of local idiom than of correct or incorrect grammar. *Majority* can be especially troublesome for those seeking consistency. "The majority in *their* [read (in U.S.) *its*] footnote 6 *allude* [read *alludes*] to the testimony of Hinojosa." This preference for singular verbs with *majority* leads us down unidiomatic paths in sentences such as this, however, in which the noun best takes the plural verb: "A majority of the members of the committee *are* [rather than *is*] satisfied that the applicant is qualified for membership. See COUNT & MASS (NONCOUNT) NOUNS.

collegial; collegiate. It would serve the purposes of DIFFERENTIATION, and would not run counter to educated usage, to reserve *collegial* as the adjective corresponding to *colleague,* and *collegiate* as the adjective for *college.* E.g., "The argument that the parole commission, because it is a small *collegial* body, is able to render more consistent decisions than federal judges, is debatable."

collide. See **allide.**

collision; allision. Both are used, in the law of admiralty, in reference to vessels that meet each other unexpectedly. In an *allision,* one of the vessels is stationary. In a *collision,* usually both are moving, although *collision* does not necessarily imply force from each of the clashing objects.

Since we have this DIFFERENTIATION in the terminology of admiralty, however, we should observe the distinction, if only in this limited context. E.g., "The litigation before us arises out of a series of four *collisions* by ships over a two-month period." In the following sentence, *allision* would have been the better word: "This case arises out of a *collision* [read *allision*] that allegedly occurred between a tug owned by Dow and a boat docked alongside the plaintiff's shrimp boat." (The docked boat was stationary, presumably.) Even specialized authorities have used *collision* in this way, however: "The anchored vessel is almost, and usually quite, helpless to avoid *collision,* and moving vessels must keep clear of her." J. W. Griffin, *The American Law of Collision* § 145 at 348 (1949). See **allide.**

Allision is most properly used only of two ships, and not, e.g., of a ship and a bridge or dock: "This case arises out of an *allision* [read *collision* or *accident*] that occurred after midnight in early 1982, when the Tug Beth, with two barges in tow, struck the closed lift span of the Galveston Railway Causeway Bridge."/ "The dock, on the bank of the Calcasieu River near Lake Charles, was struck by the barge on July 4; at some point before the *allision* [read *collision* or *mishap*], a socket had failed."

collocate; collate. *Collocate* = (v.t.) to arrange in place; to set side by side; (v.i.) to occur in conjunction with something (*W9*). *Collate* = (1) to compare minutely and critically; (2) to collect and compare for the purpose of arranging accurately; or (3) to assemble in proper order ⟨he collated the appendixes to the brief⟩.

Both terms are useful in legal analysis, *collocate* being perhaps more common, especially in the form of the noun *collocation* (= a distinct arrangement, esp. of words). E.g., "The element in intellectual productions that secures copyright protection is not the knowledge, truths, ideas, or emotions that the composition expresses, but the *collocation* of visible or audible points—of lines, colors, sounds, or words."/ "In considering the general question of property in news matter, it is necessary to distinguish between the substance of the information and the particular form or *collocation* of words in which the writer has communicated it."

collogue, v.i., is an informal word meaning "to confer in private." Krapp labeled it "colloquial for *talk confidentially.*" G. P. Krapp, *A Comprehensive Guide to Good English* 152 (1927). Yet it is useful as a verb corresponding to the noun *colloquy*, q.v., which is frequently found in legal prose.

COLLOQUIALITY, within the bounds of modesty and naturalness, is to be encouraged in legal writing as a counterbalance to the frequently rigid and pompous formalities. Many people misunderstand the meaning of colloquiality, however. The term is not a label for substandard usages; rather, it means "a conversational style." The writer of this sentence demonstrates an understanding of the term's meaning: "The Federal Securities Act of 1933 and state statutes *colloquially* called 'blue sky laws' require corporations to register issues of securities with the SEC or state security commissions before they are sold publicly."

The best legal minds look kindly upon colloquiality: "[A]lthough there are no certain guides [in the interpretation of a statute], the *colloquial* meaning of the words of the statute is one of the best tests of purpose." *Brooklyn*

National Corp. v. C.I.R., 157 F.2d 450, 451 (2d Cir. 1946) (per L. Hand, J.). "The courts will not be astute to discover fine distinctions in words, nor scholastic differentiations in phrases, so long as they are sufficiently in touch with affairs to understand the meaning which the man on the street attributes to ordinary English." *Vitagraph Co. v. Ford*, 241 F. 681, 686 (S.D.N.Y. 1917).

All this is to say that colloquiality is fine in its place. In formal legal writing, occasional colloquialisms may serve to give the prose more variety and texture; they may even be appropriate in judicial opinions in moderation. Still, the colloquial tone should not overshadow the generally serious tone of legal writing, and should never descend into slang.

colloquy; colloquium. The plural form of *colloquy* (= a formal discussion, as between a judge and counsel) is *colloquies.* Following is a typical use of the word: "The record from the state court contains no *colloquy* between appellant and the court with respect to this issue." (The old word in this sense was *interview*, common in the 19th c.) The verb corresponding to *colloquy* is *collogue*, q.v.

Colloquium (= an academic conference or seminar) is frequently misspelled *colloquim.* *W9* prefers the plural *-quiums*, the (British) *COD -quia.* Many academicians seem to use *colloquia* (and even *auditoria*) merely to avoid possible criticism by colleagues, however unwarranted.

collude. Occasionally this word is misunderstood, primarily by laymen, to mean "to collaborate," rather than (properly) "to collaborate in wrongdoing." The mistake is especially common with the noun, *collusion.* Fowler cites the example, "The two authors, both professors at Innsbruck, appear to be working in *collusion* [read *collaboration*]." (*MEU2* 95.)

collusive, -ory. *Collusive* is preferred; *collusory* is a NEEDLESS VARIANT.

color. In the phrase *under color of state law*, the word *color* = appearance, semblance, guise. The development of this bit of legal ARGOT is instructive:

Sometimes a party put in a plea designed to make what was really a point of fact appear to be a point of law, so as to transfer the decision from the jury to the judge: this was called *colour.* The expression was in due course applied to the title [that] was in question. 'If the defendant,' wrote Blackstone, 'in assise or action of trespass, be desirous to refer the validity of his title to the court rather than to the jury, he may state his title specially, and at the same time *give colour* to the plaintiff, bad indeed in point of law, but of which the jury are not competent judges.' Blackstone, *Commentaries* 309 (emphasis in original).

> Simon, *English Idioms from the Law,* 76 Law Q.Rev. 429, 440 (1960).

Alongside this sense of an apparent or prima facie title or right there has developed the modern expressions *no color of title, no color of right,* and *no color of law,* meaning without any sort of title or right.

colorable is used in law in the sense "having at least a prima facie aspect of justice or validity" (*OED*) ⟨a colorable claim to property⟩. See **color.**

colore officii (= by color of office) is a LATINISM without redeeming value. "As a general rule, the corporation is not responsible for the unauthorized and unlawful acts of its officers, though done *colore officii.*" The English translation serves far better, and is not passed over uncomprehendingly, as the Latinism probably will be by most readers.

combination; confederacy; conspiracy. The first two are somewhat more neutral than the third. E.g., "Appellants announce their willingness to accept this definition of the boycott, substituting the word *confederacy* or *combination* for *conspiracy.*" *Combination* = the banding together or union of persons for the pursuance of some common goal. The *OED* notes that it was formerly used synonymously with *conspiracy,* but it has appreciated in meaning. E.g., "A strike is one of the legal means to which parties have a right to resort to enforce a legal *combination.*" Today *combination* is often used in antitrust contexts. *Confederacy* = a union by league or contract between persons, bodies of men, or states, for mutual support or joint action; a league, alliance, compact (*OED*). The *OED* states that in law this word has traditionally been given a bad sense, as if synonymous with *conspiracy;* no longer is such a meaning predominantly given to the word.

Both *confederacy* and *combination* may refer to an agreement by two or more persons to do an illegal act, but this sense is best reserved for a third word. *Conspiracy* = an agreement between two or more people to behave in a manner that will automatically constitute an offense by at least one of them (e.g., two people agree that one of them shall steal while the other waits in a getaway car) (*CDL*).

combine, n., is an American business colloquialism synonymous with *combination,* usually implying fraudulent or anticompetitive ends. Krapp disapproved of this use of the word in 1927, and Bernstein approved of it in 1965, but only as a casualism. So it remains. See **combination.**

come down is the intransitive PHRASAL VERB used of judicial decisions. E.g.,"When the decision finally *came down* in October it was based upon more study than a case ordinarily receives in our court or in any other with an equally heavy docket." Cf. its counterparts in the active voice, **hand down** & **hand out.**

come(s) now has traditionally been the standard commencement in a pleading. It is falling into well-deserved desuetude. The phrasing *comes now* is an example of archaic INVERSION. *Comes now* is the form for a singular, *come now* for a plural subject. It is not uncommon for modern pleaders to bungle subject-verb agreement with inverted phrases of this kind, as in "*Comes now the plaintiffs, Russ and Leslie Blanchard,* [read *Come now the plaintiffs* . . .]. The wording in a judicial order analogous to this phrase is "*Came on* for consideration the defendant's motion."

Comes now the plaintiff is occasionally mispunctuated, e.g., "Comes, now, the plaintiff. . . ." The first comma in the phrase should follow *plaintiffs,* after which the person's name acts as an APPOSITIVE. Placing a comma after the verb demonstrates the writer's misunderstanding of the inversion of subject and verb. This antiquated wording is sometimes modernized *now comes.*

comic(al); comedic. These words are confusingly similar. *Comic* and *comical* both mean "funny" or "humorous." *Comic* is generally used, however, of what is intentionally funny, and *comical* of what is unintentionally funny. Hence the latter term may mean "laughable" in a derisive sense. *Comedic* = of or pertaining to the form or nature of a dramatic comedy (as the opposite of *tragic*).

comity = courtesy among political entities (as nations or courts of different jurisdictions). The word is sometimes mistaken as meaning "league" or "federation," esp. in the phrase *comity of nations*.

commander-in-chief.   Pl. *commanders-in-chief*.

COMMAS. See PUNCTUATION (C).

commemorative, -tory. The usual form is *-tive; -tory* is a NEEDLESS VARIANT.

commence; begin; start. Except in describing formal ceremonies or exercises, or legal actions, *commence* is usually unnecessarily stilted for *begin*, with which it is denotatively equivalent. The *OED* notes that *"begin* is preferred in ordinary use; *commence* has more formal associations with law and procedure, combat, divine service, and ceremon[y]." *Commence* is justified in these sentences: "This action was *commenced* against the defendants under these circumstances, the father having died before the *commencement* of the action."/ "It is settled that a prevailing party may recover fees for time spent before the formal *commencement* of the litigation on such matters as attorney-client interviews."

Following are examples of the stilted *commence*: "Early in the year 1922 some newcomers *commenced* [read *began*] selling papers in a London area which, in the opinion of the London district council of the retail federation, was already sufficiently equipped with retail newsagents." (Eng.)/ "When the plane failed to return, a search was *commenced* [read *started* or *begun*]."/ "Ilsa then *commenced* [read *began*] living in California with her mother during the school year and spending vacations with her father." (One does not, idiomatically, *commence* to live somewhere.) See **begin** (B).

Commence has long been criticized by stylists when introducing an infinitive; *begin* is here preferable: "In most cases, the Mississippi statute *commences* [read *begins*] to run on the date of the wrongful act."

Definite nuances exist with *start* as opposed to *begin* or *commence*. Usually used of physical movement, *start* suggests an abruptness not present in *begin*; one *starts* to do something or engage in some activity (e.g., to run).

commendable; commendatory. The former means "praiseworthy, laudable," and the latter means "expressing commendation; laudatory."

commensurate, -able. In all but mathematical contexts, *commensurable* is a NEEDLESS VARIANT of *commensurate*. *Commensurable* legitimately means "having, or reducible to, a common measure; divisible without remainder by the same quantity" (*OED*). *Commensurate* means: (1) "coextensive"; or (2) "proportionate." Here the rarer term, *commensurable*, is used where its sibling should appear: "The policy initially issued must be read to cover all the expenses arising from Gina's mental disability, *commensurably* [read *commensurately* (i.e., coextensively)] with coverage from other illnesses."

comment(ate). The longer form is a BACK-FORMATION from *commentator*, but an established one dating from the late eighteenth century. If *commentate* were only a NEEDLESS VARIANT of *comment*, its existence would be unjustified. But it enjoys the DIFFERENTIATION of meaning "to give a commentary on" or "to expound persuasively or interpretatively." Hence legal commentators *commentate* rather than *comment* when expounding the law. The word is, of course, grandiose when used of television journalists who cover sporting events, though it is too late to object to their being called *commentators*.

commerce. Formerly, *commerce* was usable in all the senses of *intercourse;* hence the phrase *sexual commerce* (= sexual intercourse) in many older legal writings (not necessarily involving prostitution). See **intercourse.**

commercial paper. See **negotiable instruments.**

comminate; comminute. The former means "to denounce," the latter "to pulverize."

com(m)ingle. *Commingle* (= to mingle together) is now the accepted spelling. *Comingle*, though slightly older, has failed to become standard. "There has been a tendency to *co-mingle* [read *commingle*] the Full Faith and Credit Clause of the Constitution with the doctrine of comity by cross-citing various cases between the two principles." *Mingle* has also been used in reference to combining funds, but *commingle* is the more usual term. "The situation is analogous to one where a wrongdoer *mingles* his own funds with other funds he has misappropriated." *Commingles* would ordinarily appear in such a context.

comminute. See **comminate.**

commission. See **commitment.**

commissionee. See -EE.

commissioner, -or. The former spelling is standard.

commitment; committal; commission. *Commitment* and *commission* are common words that will here be discussed only to the extent that they are confusable with *commit-tal*, which is in all but two specific senses a NEEDLESS VARIANT. In England, a *committal* in civil proceedings is a method of enforcing judgment by obtaining an order that a person be committed to prison (*CDL*). E.g., "The mode of enforcing decrees in the time of Henry VI down to the end of the reign of Charles I., where the party was taken, appears to have been by *committal* to the Fleet prison; for the Chancellor could not bind the right, he could only coerce the person." 1 Spence, *Equitable Jurisprudence* 390 (1846)./ "The judge had inherent jurisdiction to make a *committal* order ex parte [committing a delinquent party to jail]." (Eng.) See **committer.**

Committal also has the sense "the action of committing the body to the grave at burial" (*OED Supp.*). E.g., "A decent *committal* of the body to the deep in accordance with the custom in such matters ordinarily discharges the duty which the law imposes."

In the sense "the action of committing an insane or mentally retarded person to the charge of another," *commitment* is the usual and the preferred term: "The appointment of a guardian or committee for the person and property of another is not conclusive evidence as to the mental capacity of such person to execute a deed; nor is *commitment* to the insane asylum."/ "The broad rule generally

prevails that a valid proceeding to commit a person to an insane asylum requires an opportunity for the incompetent to be heard before the order of *commitment* is issued."/ "At a proceeding before the Circuit Court of Albemarle County it was adjudged that the infirmities of Mary Thomas did not require the *committal* [read *commitment*] of her person to a guardian." *Commitment* is also the preferred term in the broad sense of "the action of entrusting, giving in charge": "Few men retain their money in their own custody but commit its care to others, both for the feeling of security that such *committal* [read *commitment*] engenders and the facility with which it may be transferred and paid out by means of checks."

Commission is preferred in the sense "the action of doing or perpetrating (as a crime)." The *OED* records examples of *committal* and even of *commitment* in this sense, but these are anomalous.

committable, -ible. The first is preferred. See -ABLE (A).

committal. See **commitment.**

committer, -or. These words constitute one of the few pairs in -er / -or with a clear-cut DIFFERENTIATION. *Committer* is the general word meaning "one who commits (e.g., a crime)." *Committor* is an uncommon legal term for "a judge who commits an insane or mentally retarded person to the charge of another." See -ER, -OR.

commodatum; accommodatum. The usual spelling of this term from Roman law, meaning "a gratuitous loan (of something) for use," is *commodatum.*

common. See **mutual.**

commonality; commonness; common-alty; commonage; commonty. The common character of these words may cause confusion. The ordinary words are *commonality* and *commonness;* although historically these words have overlapped, they are best kept separate, in accordance with the following definitions. *Commonness,* the general noun corresponding to *common,* may mean: (1) "the state or quality of being common"; (2) "the quality of being public or generally used" ⟨the commonness of the thoroughfare⟩; (3) "the having of run-of-the-mill qualities" ⟨the commonness of his writing⟩; or (4) "vulgarity" ⟨the commonness of a sot⟩. *Commonality* = the possession of an attribute in common with another. The term is usual in class-action suits. E.g., "The district court denied class certification because it found that the petitioner had not satisfied the *commonality* and typicality prerequisite of Federal Rule of Civil Procedure 23 [i.e., the class members having claims with factual and legal issues *in common* with one another]."

The remaining words are more easily distinguished. *Commonalty* = (1) commoners; the general body of the community (excluding nobility); (2) a municipal corporation (a sense to be avoided with this word, as *corporation* is the ordinary word); or (3) a general group or body. *Commonage* = (1) the right of pasturing animals on common land; (2) the condition of land held in common; or (3) an estate or property held in common (*OED*). *Commonty*, in its existing uses, is a NEEDLESS VARIANT of *commonage*.

common law. A. As Noun. In modern usage, *common law* is contrasted with a number of other terms. First, in denoting the body of judge-made law based on that developed originally in England, *common law* is contrasted by comparative jurists to *civil law*, q.v. Second, "with the development of equity and equitable rights and remedies, *common law* and equitable courts, procedure, rights, remedies, etc., are frequently contrasted, and in this sense *common law* is distinguished from *equity*" (*OCL*). Third, the term is similarly distinguished from ecclesiastical law. Finally, and perhaps most commonly within Anglo-American jurisdictions, *common law* is contrasted with *statutory law* ⟨statutes in derogation of the common law are to be strictly construed⟩. See **at common law.**

B. As Adjective. The phrase is hyphenated when used adjectivally, and has no hyphen when it serves as a noun. Both uses are illustrated in this sentence: "But these are all *common-law* cases, and the *common law* has its peculiar rules in relation to this subject." Cf. **civil(-)law** (B).

common-law marriage has one meaning in the U.S., another in Scotland, and still an-

other in England. In the U.S., it generally denotes an agreement to marry, followed by cohabitation and a public recognition of the marriage. In Scotland, the phrase denotes cohabitation for a substantial period with the acquisition of the reputation of being married (an agreement to marry not being necessary). And in England, *common-law marriage* is now used only of a marriage celebrated according to a common-law form in a place where the local forms of marriage cannot be utilized, e.g., a desert island, or are morally unacceptable to the parties, e.g., a Mohammedan country, or where no clergyman is available (*OCL*). Additionally, the phrase has in G.B. the meaning "an illicit union of some duration" (see the next entry). In none of these jurisdictions is the phrase to be confused with its near-homophone *common-law mortgage*.

common-law wife is a misnomer of sorts; "[n]o such woman was known to the common law, but [the phrase] means a woman who is living with a man in the same household as if she were his wife. She is to be distinguished from a *mistress*, where the relationship may be casual, impermanent, and secret." *Davis v. Johnson*, [1979] A.C. 264, 270 (per Lord Denning, M.R.). The *OCL* states that "the term *common-law wife* is sometimes applied [no doubt as a EUPHEMISM] to a concubine or mistress where the relationship is of some duration or stability." In the U.S., this use of the term is properly considered a corrupt one. See **common-law marriage.**

common lawyer is incorrect for *common-law lawyer*. The repetition of *law* in the latter phrase is no cause for anxieties about REDUNDANCY. E.g., "But there the court of appeal, the Privy Council, has been largely composed of *common-law lawyers*." O.W. Holmes, *The Common Law* 27–28 (1881; repr. 1946).

commonness. See **commonality.**

commonsense, adj., should be preferred over *commonsensical* or *commonsensible*. The noun is *common sense*.

commonty. See **commonality.**

commonweal; commonwealth. The first is the general welfare or common good. E.g.,

"Testamentary conditions in general restraint of marriage are regarded as contrary to public policy and to the *commonweal.*" *Commonwealth* = a nation, state, or other political unit ⟨the British Commonwealth⟩.

commorientes = persons who die at the same time (*CDL*). Although this LATINISM would seem to be useful in the context of simultaneous-death statutes, it is little used in the U.S. Presumably the term is more common in G.B., for it is included in the compendious *CDL*.

communication is often used as a COUNT NOUN in the law of evidence. It refers to any writing or conversation from one person to another or between persons. Partridge states, in reference to *communicate* and *communication,* that if all you mean by *communicate* is *write* or *tell,* or by *communication* a *note* or a *letter,* then say so. E. Partridge, *Usage and Abusage* 77 (1973). As a general rule, his advice is well taken; but if the lawyer particularly wishes to emphasize the applicability of a rule of evidence relating to *communications,* use of the longer, broader word is certainly justified.

communicative, -tory. The latter is a NEEDLESS VARIANT.

communitize, -ization; unitize, -ization. These two sets of terms, from the American law of oil and gas, are sometimes used interchangeably, but it is useful to distinguish between them. The following definitions are based on those contained in Williams & Meyers, *Oil and Gas Terms* 652, 938 (6th ed. 1984). *Unitization* = the joint operation of all or some portion of a producing reservoir. Use of the verb *to unitize* has been traced back to the mid-nineteenth century, albeit then in a different context.

Communitize and *communitization* are legal NEOLOGISMS dating from the mid-twentieth century and recorded in no standard nonlegal dictionary. *Communitization* (known also as *pooling*) = the bringing together of small tracts sufficient for the granting of a well permit under applicable rules for the spacing of wells. E.g., "The court treated the situation as if all had signed a single instrument and held that a *communitization* of royalty interests resulted, since there was no proof of a contrary intention." / "The tract was *communitized,* and.

identical leases covering the entire tract were signed by each partial owner."

commute. A. And *commutate.* The latter is a technical term relating to electricity. *Commute* is the legal term meaning (1) "to exchange (a punishment or penalty) for one of less severity"; or (2) "to change (one kind of payment) into or for another; esp. to substitute a single payment for a number of payments, a fixed payment for an irregular or uncertain one, or a payment in money for one in kind (e.g. a tithe)" (*OED*). Today sense (1) of *commute* is more common ⟨the governor commuted his prison sentence to sixty days of community service⟩.

B. And *pardon.* To *commute* a punishment or penalty is to reduce it, or to substitute in its place a milder punishment or penalty. To *pardon* one who has been convicted or punished is to excuse him without exacting any penalty.

compact, n., adj. & v.t. The noun is accented on the first syllable, the verb on the second. The adjective is rendered both ways, preferably /kŏm-**pakt**/ except in reference to midsize cars.

compactible, -able. The former is preferred. See -ABLE (A).

company law is the British equivalent of the American phrase *corporate law,* q.v. E.g., "My Lords, this appeal raises a question of some importance to those concerned with the niceties of *company law.*" (Eng.)

COMPANY NAMES are commonly given abbreviated forms in legal prose. Often writers go to absurd lengths to specify what the short form of the company name is in parentheses, e.g., *Morgan Data Processing and Filming Co., Inc. (hereinafter "Morgan").* This habit becomes ridiculous after we have seen three or four parties with distinctive names treated in this way. The better practice in most legal writing is to give the full name when the party is first identified, and then to use the short form thereafter without parenthetical explanation. When companies named, in short form, *Morgan* and *Stevens* and *Broadmoor* and *Datapoint* are involved in litigation or are parties to a contract, nobody will confuse one with another if only these abbreviated names are used. Omitting the cumbersome *herein-after* phrases also minimizes the somnifacient effects of LEGALESE.

The exception to this advice, of course, occurs when a man named *Morgan* is sued in conjunction with his company *Morgan, Inc.* When names are confusingly similar, it is best to spell out exactly which abbreviation is used with which name, and then to use those forms consistently. This practice does not require *hereinafter*. E.g., "Plaintiff has sued both John Morgan ('Morgan') and Morgan Inc. ('the Company')."

comparable; comparative. The former is stressed on the first syllable, the latter on the second. *Comparable* = capable of being compared; worthy of comparison ⟨comparable salaries⟩. *Comparative* = (1) of or pertaining to comparison ⟨a comparative discourse of the laws⟩; (2) involving comparison ⟨the field of comparative law⟩; or (3) estimated by comparison ⟨comparative distances⟩.

comparative negligence; contributory negligence. In the U.S., a plaintiff's *contributory negligence* (= his own carelessness for his own safety or interests, which contributes materially to damage suffered by him as a result partly of his own fault and partly of the fault of another person or persons [*CDL*]) has traditionally, in accordance with the common-law rule, acted as a complete bar to recovery. But most states have now adopted statutes providing for *comparative negligence,* which acts to reduce the plaintiff's recovery proportionally to his fault in the damage rather than to bar recovery completely. The terms *contributory negligence* and *comparative negligence* have remained quite distinct.

In G.B. however, the separate term *comparative negligence* is not used. The common-law rule of *contributory negligence* was altered by the Law Reform (Contributory Negligence) Act of 1945, which provides that "if the plaintiff is partly in fault, his claim is not defeated, but the damages recoverable are to be reduced to such extent as the court or jury thinks just and equitable having regard to the claimant's share in the responsibility for the damage" (*OCL*). Thus *contributory negligence* in G.B. means roughly what *comparative negligence* means in the U.S.; rather than devising a new term, the English have continued using

the old term, but with a new meaning. See **assumption of the risk.**

COMPARATIVES AND SUPERLATIVES. A. Choice Between Comparative & Superlative. When two items are being compared, a comparative adjective should be used ⟨the greater of the two⟩; when more than two are being compared, the superlative should be used ⟨the greatest of the three⟩. The blunder of using the superlative adjective when only two items are compared is not at all uncommon: "That is only half the story, and not the *most* [read *more*] important half."/ "The table reveals that, as between closely held and public corporations, the closely held corporation is by far the *most* [read *more*] numerous."

B. Terminational as Opposed to Analytic Comparatives and Superlatives. Apart from anomalies like *good* ⟩ *better* ⟩ *best,* comparatives and superlatives are formed either internally by the addition of the suffixes *-er* and *-est* (e.g., *broader, broadest*) or externally with the words *more* and *most* (e.g., *more critical, most critical*). A number of words have a choice of forms (e.g., *commoner, -est* or *more, most common; tranquil(l)er, -est* or *more, most tranquil; stupider, -est* or *more, most stupid; naiver, -est* or *more, most naive*). The terminational forms are usually older, and some of them are obsolescent; the choice of form in any given context will depend on which form sounds better. The variation in forms here is not to be stifled by absolute rules.

C. Swapping Horses. The form of a comparison cannot change once the construction has begun. One writes *more . . . than,* or *as . . . as;* but the two do not mix: "Nowhere else is there a *greater* need to substitute a panel of three experienced judges for a jury *as* [read *than*] in medical malpractice."

D. *Be*-Verbs Repeated after Comparatives. It is almost always unnecessary to repeat the verb *to be* before the second element of the comparison. The prolix and infelicitous construction seems to thrive more in legal than in other writing. E.g., "Such a law *is less likely than is* [omit the second *is*] the Texas education statute to qualify as the least onerous alternative."

compare (with) (to). The usual phrase is *compare with;* this phrase means "to place side by side, noting differences and similarities between" ⟨let us compare his goals with his actual accomplishments). *Compare to* = to observe or point only to likenesses between ⟨the psychologist compared this action to Hinckley's assassination attempt⟩. Cf. **contrast** (B).

Compare and contrast is an English teacher's tautology, for in comparing two things (one thing *with* another) one notes both similarities and differences.

COMPARISONS, FALSE. Writers must beware of attempting to compare incomparables. "The unwritten intent of the parties of a lignite and coal lease will probably differ *from those of an oil and gas lease* [read *from that of,* i.e., the intent of those who are] parties to an oil and gas lease." The writer of that sentence mistakenly compared a singular *intent* to plural *parties.*

Follett adduces the following example, "International Harvester says that storage space is reduced by 40 percent when compared with baled hay," and observes: "Two storage spaces lend themselves to comparison; so do two methods of concentration; but to compare storage space with baled hay is to scatter ideas at random." W. Follett, *Modern American Usage* 101 (1966). See ILLOGIC (A).

compartment(al)ize. The longer form is standard in both the U.S. and G.B. E.g., "Assuming that it makes sense to *compartmentalize* in this manner the diagnosis of such a formless 'disease,' tremendous gaps in our knowledge remain, which the record in this case does nothing to fill." *Powell v. Texas,* 392 U.S. 514, 524 (1968).

compel; impel. *Compel* is the stronger word, connoting force or coercion, with little or no volition on the part of the one compelled. *Impel* connotes persuasive urging, with some degree of volition on the part of the one impelled. *Compel* is properly used when the legal process is brought to bear on people's actions: "The pleas are no more improperly *compelled* than is the decision by a defendant at the close of the state's evidence at trial that he must take the stand or face certain conviction." / "He has not yet reached the age of 25 years, and he brings this bill to *compel* the trustees to pay to him the remainder of the trust fund."

Here *impel* is properly used: "Applying these notions to the present case *impels* the conclusion that appellant's motion at the close of all the evidence should be read as a motion for a directed verdict."/ "Does a procedural merger of law and equity automatically *impel* a modification of principles of equitable jurisdiction?"/ "With these principles in mind, we are *impelled* to agree with the probate court's decision that appellants violated the in terrorem clause of decedent's will." In the first two examples just quoted, the object of *impel* (i.e., the court) is understood.

But the courts have been less than punctilious about the distinction between *compel* and *impel;* sentences like the following are common: "Our analysis *compels* the conclusion that FERC lacks the authority to suspend initial rate filings." Perhaps this use of *compel* stems from a desire for the court (again, the understood object) to suggest that it simply had no choice in its holding. The device is largely rhetorical, and so clichéd as to be ineffective. See **impel.**

compellable, primarily a legal term, was formerly used in the broad sense "that may be compelled (to do something)." Today it is generally used (though not necessarily) in the sense "subject to being compelled (to give evidence)." The term is far more common in G.B. than in the U.S. E.g., "A bank or officer of a bank is not, in any legal proceeding to which the bank is not a party, *compellable* to produce any banker's books." (Eng.)/ "No husband is *compellable* to disclose any communication made to him by his wife during the marriage, and no wife is *compellable* to disclose any communication made to her by her husband during the marriage." (Eng.)

compensable, -sible. *Compensable* is the preferred form. The *-ible* spelling is incorrect; the frequency of its use is explained perhaps by a mistaken analogy to *comprehensible.* See -ABLE. A nuance exists between these terms. *Compensable damages* = those damages capable of being recovered; damages for which compensation is available. *Compensatory damages* = those damages intended to make the plaintiff whole again; actual damages. *Compensable damages* are hypothetical; *compensatory damages* are those actually awarded or to be awarded to a party.

compensate. A. Transitive or Intransitive. *Compensate* may or may not take *for,* and either way means "to make up for, to counterbalance." E.g., "When it is conceded that mental suffering may be *compensated (for)* in actions of tort, the right of the plaintiff to recover in this case is established." The modern tendency is to omit *for*, but the sound of a sentence may outweigh the interests of concision.

B. And *recompense.* These verbs are almost precisely synonymous ⟨to recompense the victim for his injuries⟩, but *recompense, q.v.,* is a FORMAL WORD less commonly used.

compensatory, -tive. The latter is a NEEDLESS VARIANT.

competence, -cy. A. Of Persons. Though Fowler considered *competency* a NEEDLESS VARIANT, these terms have come to exhibit some DIFFERENTIATION, which should be further encouraged. *Competence* usually has the lay sense "a basic or minimal ability to do something." E.g., "An exhaustive study of the deficiencies of applying a mechanism originally developed to decide who owns title to Blackacre to the management of general disasters is beyond the *competence* and available time of its writer."/ "*Incompetence* of counsel is not necessarily established by omission of a claim."

Today *competency* is a NEEDLESS VARIANT in all but one sense. It is increasingly confined to the legal sense of "the ability to understand problems and make decisions; ability to stand trial." A severely mentally retarded person, an incompetent, is said to suffer from legal *incompetency. Competency to stand trial* is the usual phrase.

In referring to qualifications in general, as to witness a will or to testify in court, *-ce* is the usual form. E.g., "The common-law rules concerning the competence [i.e., the qualification to testify in court] of attesters were derived from the rules concerning the *competence* of witnesses in litigation."/ "Statutes in the United States tend to correlate the standard of *competence* to attest a will with the ability of the witness to comprehend and relate the facts." Only when the reference is clearly and solely to mental disability is *-cy* the preferred form.

Sometimes *competency* is confused with *competence:* "Where the station agent incidentally acts as the telegraph agent in many sparsely settled communities where the business will not permit the employment of a full-time telegraph agent, it is apparent that such *compe-*

tency [read *competence*] cannot be secured." And vice versa: "Appellants contend that their son lacks the mental *competence* [read *competency*] to waive his legal rights, and they maintain that he lacks the *competence* [read *competency*] to decide whether to pursue or to waive the benefits of 28 U.S.C. § 2254."

Writers should avoid the INELEGANT VARIATION of alternating between the two terms in a single writing: "Enriquez's *competency* challenge is twofold. First, he contends that he was denied due process because the state trial court did not hold a hearing to determine his *competence* [read *competency*] to stand trial. . . . [T]he Supreme Court [has] held that a defendant has a procedural due process right to a *competency* hearing." *Enriquez v. Procunier,* 752 F.2d 111, 113 (5th Cir. 1984).

B. Used of Adjudicative or Rule-Making Bodies. *Competence* is frequently used for qualification or capacity of an official body to do something. E.g., "Before any court can enter a valid judgment or decree, it must have *competence* to do so."/ "Hardly anyone has ever doubted the *competence* of a legislature to enact a comparative negligence statute."/ "With respect to most crimes, the credibility of a witness is peculiarly within the *competence* of the jury, whose common experience affords sufficient basis for the assessment of credibility."

C. Of Evidence. In older legal writing, *competence* = admissibility. Thus references to the *competence of evidence* were fairly common. Again, *-cy* is a NEEDLESS VARIANT in this context. Following is an example in the adjectival form: "Evidence of a conviction is only prima facie, and may be rebutted by *competent* evidence that impeaches the validity of the judgment." See **incompetence** & **competent.**

competent is used in archaic senses in the law. Generally the word is used only of persons, whereas in law it is used of courts, of evidence, and of cases. It is even used indefinitely: "It seems *competent*, if war exists, for the military authorities to use special military court machinery, and to impose any sentence, even death, without being disabled, in another case, from applying procedure of a more limited character." (Eng.) This use of the word, in the sense "proper, appropriate," was labeled obsolete by the *OED.* Yet it still appears in legal writing, albeit less and less frequently. E.g., "The general rule is that recital of a written instrument as to consideration is not conclusive, and it is *competent* to inquire into consideration and to show by parol evidence the real nature of the consideration."/ "In the present case it was *competent* for the plaintiff to recover for the intestate's pain, suffering, and disability during his period of life following the assault."

More frequently, *competent* = (1) (of a judge or court) having jurisdiction or authority to act ⟨When a court of *competent* jurisdiction has obtained control of property, that control may not be disturbed by any other court⟩; (2) (of witnesses) having capacity; qualified to testify in court concerning the material facts ⟨A will is void unless attested by the number of *competent* witnesses required by statute⟩; (3) (of a case) within the jurisdiction of the court; or (4) (of evidence) admissible. See **competence & incompetent**.

This word is still further complicated in legal contexts by its frequent appearance in its lay sense (= professionally adequate; properly qualified): "Omission of the testimony may have been so material as to deprive the proceeding of fundamental fairness, despite appellant's otherwise *competent* representation."/ "A jury could conclude that appellee failed to fulfill its dual obligation to provide a *competent* service engineer to supervise installation of the purchased equipment."

complacency, -ce. The latter is a NEEDLESS VARIANT. "The law should not regard with *complacence* [read *complacency*] any man who repudiates or ignores the obligation to provide necessaries to his family."

complacent; complaisant. The former means "self-satisfied; smug." The latter means "obliging; tending to go along with others."

complainant; complainer. *Complainant* is, both in the U.S. and in G.B. (except Scotland), the technical term for one who enters a legal complaint against another. *Complainer* is the Scottish equivalent of *complainant.* E.g., "Seven months later there were served upon the *complainer,* not one, but five separate complaints." (Scot.)/ "In the heart of the Island of Lewis near the head of Loch Erisort there is a clachan called Balallan, in which the *complainer* keeps the local store, selling articles of clothing, provisions, and general merchandise." (Scot.) In the U.S., *complainer* is gener-

ally understood as meaning "one who habitually complains." Cf. **pursuer.**

complaisant. See **complacent.**

compleat is an archaic variant of *complete* with no place in modern contexts, unless facetiousness is intended. Even so, it is a one-word CLICHÉ.

compliment; complement. These words are often confounded. The first means "to praise," the second "to supplement appropriately or adequately."

comply takes *with,* not *to.* E.g., "You have also asked whether the budget for Cameron County *complies* in form *to* [read *with*] the requirements of the county budget statutes."

compose; comprise. Correct use of these words is simple, but increasingly rare. The parts *compose* the whole; the whole *comprises* the parts; the whole is *composed* of the parts; the parts are *comprised* in the whole. *Comprise,* the more troublesome word in this pair, means "to contain; to consist of." E.g., "The evidence clearly showed that the committee *comprised* members from inside as well as outside the Bank."/ "Every act causing an obstruction to another in the exercise of the right *comprised* within this description would, if damage should be caused thereby to the party obstructed, be a violation of this prohibition." (Eng.) A number of mistakes occur with *comprise:*

A. Erroneous Use of *is comprised of.* The phrase *is comprised of* is always wrong and should be replaced by either *is composed of* or *comprises.* E.g., "We also judicially notice that the 123d Judicial District Court of Shelby County *is comprised of* [read *comprises*] two counties, Panola and Shelby." Sometimes the simplest of verb phrases is what is needed: "In the course of the search, the agents noticed that the ceiling of the barracks was *comprised* [read *made up*] of removable acoustical tiles." Following is the correct use of *is composed of* where the careless writer would put *is comprised of:* "The organization *is composed of* certain employees of the Chicago Railway Co."

B. *Comprise* for *are comprised in.* "Discriminatory tests are impermissible unless shown by professionally acceptable methods to be predictive or significantly correlated with important elements of work behavior that *comprise* [read *are comprised in*] the job for which the candidates are being evaluated."

C. *Comprise* for *constitute*. *Comprise* is more and more commonly used in a sense opposite its true meaning ("to contain, include, embrace"). It should not be used for *compose* or *constitute*. E.g., "To the extent that pension rights derive from employment during coverture, they *comprise* [read *constitute*] a community asset subject to division in a dissolution proceeding."/ "Cotenants *comprise* [read *constitute*] not a number of individuals, each owning an undivided interest, but a corporate entity."/ "With a joint tenancy, cotenants *comprise* [read *constitute*] a corporate unity."/ "The front and back of this Order *comprise* [read *constitute*] the entire agreement affecting this purchase."

D. *Comprise* for *are*. This is an odd error based on a misunderstanding of the meaning of *comprise*. E.g., "The appellants *comprise* [read *are*] nine of sixteen defendants convicted in the federal district court on one or more counts of an eleven-count indictment."

composition means, at common law, "the adjustment of a debt, or avoidance of an obligation or liability, by some form of compensation agreed on between the parties" (*W2*). This noun corresponds to the verb *to compound*, q.v., and often means merely "a compounding." E.g., "If a slave killed a freeman, he was to be surrendered for one half of the *composition* to the relatives of the slain man, and the master was to pay the other half." O.W. Holmes, *The Common Law* 17 (1881; repr. 1946).

compos mentis. See **non compos mentis.**

compound, v.t., has been the victim of a SLIPSHOD EXTENSION arising from its primarily legal sense. The word has three basic meanings: (1) "to put together, combine, construct, compose" ⟨to compound sand and gravel⟩; (2) "to settle (any matter) by a money payment, in lieu of other liability" ⟨to compound a debt⟩; and (3) "to forbear from prosecuting for consideration" ⟨to compound a felony⟩. The noun corresponding to this verb is *composition*, q.v. Following is an example of the legal use (sense (3)): "The plaintiff offered to prove that the money mentioned in the

agreement was not in fact paid to *compound* a felony, but to settle the plaintiff's claim against Dygert."

The word has been sloppily extended because "nonlawyers have misapprehended the meaning of *to compound* a felony. . . . [The word] is now widely abused to mean: to make worse, aggravate, multiply, increase." P. Howard, *New Words for Old* 19 (1977). Examples of this looseness of diction abound now even in legal writing. E.g., "This deliberate perpetuation of the unconstitutional dual system can only have *compounded* the harm of such a system." *Green v. County School Board,* 391 U.S. 430, 438 (1968)./ "The elective share is further reduced in jurisdictions that compute the share on the basis of the net estate after taxes, thus *compounding* the loss of protection for the spouse."/ "With the expansion of equity jurisdiction, such problems have been enormously *compounded*."/ "The situation for the prosecution was *compounded* by the star witness's evasion of subpoenas by hiding in Ireland."

It is not quite true, then, at least in the U.S., that "to write 'he *compounded* the offence' (when what is meant is that he did something to aggravate the offence) is to vex every lawyer who reads the sentence, and to provoke numbers of them to litigious correspondence in defence of their jargon." P. Howard, *New Words for Old* 20 (1977). Nevertheless, we may justifiably lament the fact that generations of young lawyers will not understand the phrase *to compound a felony* when they see it in the older lawbooks.

Notably, *compound* has also been used in civil cases to refer to a settlement (sense (2)): "The parties *compounded* the case after completing discovery."/ "He *compounded* the case with the defendant for a cash payment." Whereas *compounding a felony* is a criminal offense, *compounding a civil case* is perfectly proper. In civil contexts, *settle* is by far the more common term, however.

comprehend. In lay contexts, this word means, almost exclusively, "to grasp mentally"; in legal contexts, it frequently means "to include, encompass." E.g., "These instructions would *comprehend* damages for any disfigurement of the plaintiff's nose."/ "No judicial opinion can *comprehend* the protean variety of the street encounter, and we can only judge the facts of the case before us."/ "By confining herself to the use of the generic term, the present testatrix *comprehended* all the various religious, educational, benevolent, and humanitarian objects that the single word 'charity' connotes." See **apprehend**. Cf. **embrace**.

comprehensible; comprehendible. The latter is a NEEDLESS VARIANT.

comprise. See **compose**.

compromise = (1) to agree to settle a matter ⟨the parties agreed to compromise and to drop their claims against each other⟩; or (2) to endanger ⟨the disclosure of the information might *compromise* intelligence sources⟩. See **accord and satisfaction**.

compromise; settlement. Though the words have been used with a variety of meanings and even synonymously, at base *compromise* means "an agreement between two or more persons to settle matters in dispute between them"; *settlement* means "the performance of promises made in a compromise agreement." See **accord and satisfaction**.

comptroller is pronounced identically with *controller*. To pronounce the -p- is semiliterate. *Comptroller* is used especially of public offices; *controller*, however, means the same thing and is not deceptively spelled. *Comptroller* is more common in the U.S. than in G.B., where it is archaic.

The strange spelling of *comptroller* originated in the zeal of fifteenth-century Latinists who sought to respell medieval French loan-words on the "purer" Latin model. Thus *account* became *accompt*, and *count* became *compt*. *Comptroller* is one of the few survivals among such respellings, and it is also one of the bungles perpetrated by those ardent Latinists: the *con-* in *controller* was mistakenly associated with the word *count*, when in fact it is merely the Latin prefix. Thus the respelling should never have been. But we are several centuries too late in correcting it.

compulsory purchase is the BrE term for *eminent domain* or *expropriation*. Here the phrase appears in verb form: "Tophams also contended that, since the racecourse would in any event be closed down and left derelict, when it would be *compulsorily purchased* by the local authority for housing purposes, an injunction would be of no benefit to Lord Sef-

ton." (Eng.) See **eminent domain** & **condemn**.

COMPUTERESE, the jargon of computer wizards, is making inroads into standard English. Thus *access* and *format* and *sequence* have become verbs, *input* has enjoyed widespread use as both noun and verb, and *on-line* has begun to be used as a model for NEOLOGISMS (e.g., *on-stream* used of an oil well). No one can rightly object, of course, to the use of computerese in computing contexts, where it is undeniably useful. But many computer terms have come to have figurative senses, thereby invading the general language rather than remaining denizens of a restricted jargon. Careful users of language are wary of adopting any of these trendy locutions. Though some of them may remain and become standard, just as many may well become defunct or may never lose the jargonistic stigma attaching to them.

computerize. See -IZE.

concede. See **cede**.

concededly. See **reportedly, confessedly** & -EDLY.

concensus. See **consensus**.

concept; conception. Both *concept* and *conception* may mean "an abstract idea." *Conception* also means "the act of forming abstract ideas." Fowler writes that *conception* is the ordinary term, *concept* the philosophical term. Often the latter is used as a high-flown equivalent of simpler words such as *design, program, thought*, or *idea*. The more appropriate word was used by Hohfeld in the title of his *Fundamental Legal Conceptions* (1919); the better ordinary use is illustrated here: "Such a holding would directly contradict fair-market-value standards and our *conceptions* of justice."

conceptual(istic); conceptive; conceptional. These words are very close. *Conceptual* and *conceptional* both mean "of or pertaining to a conception or idea." *Conceptual* is the usual term, *conceptional* a NEEDLESS VARIANT. *Conceptive* = of or relating to the process of mental conception (i.e., conceiving).

Conceptualistic = (1) of or relating to the philosophical or psychological doctrine of conceptualism (a nonlegal technical sense); or (2) employing or based on conceptions. In sense (2), *conceptualistic* is more than slightly pejorative: "Appellants put forth the *conceptualistic* argument that the promoter cannot be the corporation's agent when the corporation has not yet been formed."

conceptualize is usually a bloated word that is not to be favored over *conceive* or *visualize.*

concerned with, be. This verb phrase is weak; usually *concern* can be put into the active voice with a gain in directness. E.g., "The *Green* case *was concerned with* [read *concerned*] whether a violation that continued after a freedom-of-choice plan was initiated required affirmative action."/ "This appeal is primarily *concerned with* [read *This appeal concerns primarily*] orders of the district court directing that two public institutions of higher education be merged into a single institution." Cf. **deal with.**

concert = agreement of two or more persons or parties in a plan, design, or enterprise. E.g., "There was *concert* of action." This sense thrives in legal language but is all but defunct in lay language, apart from the adjective *concerted*, q.v., and the phrase *in concert.*

In concert = working collectively toward the same end. It does not mean merely "together," as here: "Individual symptoms of intoxication, when manifesting themselves alone *instead of in concert* [read *instead of simultaneously or together*], bear little relation to ascertainable criminal conduct." Here the phrase is correctly used: "The amended complaint alleges that defendant worked *in concert* with Cooke in illegally breaching the franchise agreement."

concerted means "unified, accomplished with the aid of others," not "strong" or "strenuous." Thus "He did not make a *concerted* effort to get to work on time" is an anacoluthon, inasmuch as one person cannot make a concerted effort. See **concert.**

concessionaire; concessioner. The former is standard, the latter a NEEDLESS VARIANT.

conciliatrix, -tress. See SEXISM (C).

concision; conciseness. Drawing a fine distinction, Fowler wrote that "*concision* means the process of cutting down, and *conciseness* the cut-down state" (*MEU2* 304).

conclusive, conclusory, conclusionary, -al. *Conclusive* is the common word, meaning authoritative; decisive." E.g., "The statements of individual legislators, even sponsors, are much less *conclusive* on the issue of congressional intent than are official committee reports."/ "Admissions are rarely *conclusive* of the facts stated."

No English dictionary lists *conclusory* as a main entry. The *OED*, listing it as a variant of *conclusive*, calls it "rare." Yet the word is now quite common in American legal writing, and it does not coincide in meaning with *conclusive.* The DIFFERENTIATION is worth encouraging. *Conclusory* = expressing a mere conclusion of fact without stating the specific facts upon which the conclusion is based. For example, the statement "She is an illegal alien" is conclusory, whereas "She admitted to me that she is an illegal alien" is not. The term has been used in this way in American legal writing since the mid-twentieth century: "Facts in detail supporting *conclusory* statements herein are available in the record." *People v. Hines*, 29 N.E.2d 483, 487 (N.Y. App. 1940)./ "[A] *conclusory* statement by a layman on such a question is not entitled to substantial weight as an admission." *Mietlinski v. Hickman*, 136 N.Y.S.2d 321, 325 (App. Div. 1954).

Following are examples of typical uses of *conclusory:* "Ultimately, this [plain-meaning approach to nineteenth-century boilerplate] produces a largely insensitive and *conclusory* historical inquiry that ignores how events almost certainly appeared to the tribe." *Oregon Department of Fish and Wildlife v. Klamath Indian Tribe*, 473 U.S. 753, 787 (1985) (Marshall, J., dissenting)./ "The attachment here does not suffer the flaw of being based on an affidavit containing only *conclusory* allegations."/ "An administrative law judge's *conclusory* opinion, which does not encompass a discussion of the evidence contrary to his findings, does not warrant an affirmance."/ "Because these arguments are not fully briefed, but are merely stated in *conclusory* fashion, we need not and do not address their merit." The adverbial form of *conclusory* is *conclusorily:* "She *conclusorily* asserts that her positions in the district court and on appeal were 'substantially justified.'"

Some legal writers, apparently loath to use *conclusory*, have resorted to *conclusional* in the sense previously given: "[T]he allegations are vague, *conclusional* [read *conclusory*], or inartistically expressed." *United States v. Sanders*, 373 U.S. 1, 22 (1963)./ "[T]he stricken portions of

[the] affidavits contained *conclusional* [read *conclusory*] statements which neither the trial court nor this court may consider in passing upon motions for summary judgment." *Public Utility District v. Washington Public Power Supply System*, 705 P.2d 1195, 1202 (Wash. 1985) (en banc)./ "While the moving papers contend [that] the employment of new counsel will entail additional expense, the application on this point is *conclusional* [read *conclusory*] and does not establish [that] the hiring would work a substantial hardship." *In re Adler*, 494 N.Y.S.2d 828, 830 (N.Y. Surr. Ct. 1985). The *OED* defines *conclusional* as "of or pertaining to the conclusion; final," and calls it not only "rare" but "obsolete" as well. *W3* lists *conclusional*, however, and attributes to it the sense "constituting a conclusion," very nearly the sense here given to *conclusory*. Yet, in American law at least, *conclusory* has become so widespread that *conclusional* should be considered nothing better than a NEEDLESS VARIANT.

Still another such variant is *conclusionary*, which was experimented with for a time and still occasionally appears; but it has lost the battle for supremacy and should be rejected in favor of *conclusory*: "We are moreover impelled to the opinion, derived from our experience . . . , that *conclusionary* [read *conclusory*] evidence of this nature is immaterial to the issues." *National Labor Relations Board v. Donnelly Garment Co.*, 330 U.S. 219, 230 (1947)./ "The defendant's second numbered contention makes a broad *conclusionary* [read *conclusory*] statement. . . ." *United States v. Boykin*, 275 F. Supp. 16, 17 (M.D. Pa. 1967).

concord. A. And *concordat. Concord* is the FORMAL WORD meaning "an amicable arrangement between parties, esp. between peoples or nations; compact; treaty." In law the word has sometimes been used as a NEEDLESS VARIANT of *accord* or *compromise* in the senses outlined under **accord and satisfaction.**

Concordat = an agreement between church and state. It has been used additionally as a variant of *concord*, but is to be avoided in that sense.

B. And *accord*, n. See **accord.**

CONCORD = grammatical agreement of one word with another to which it relates. Concord embraces number, person, case, and gender. It applies to (1) a subject and its verb;

(2) an adjective and its noun; (3) a pronoun and its noun; and (4) a relative and its antecedent.

Errors in concord are not at all uncommon. One of the most frequent blunders is the lack of agreement between a pronoun and its noun. E.g., "The *prosecution* contends that *it* has a right pursuant to Federal Rule of Evidence 607 to impeach its own witnesses; in addition, *they assert* [read *it asserts*] that a prior inconsistent statement of the witness may be admitted to attack his credibility."/ "Neither party has waived *their* [read *his* or *its*] right to a jury trial."/ "The issue on this appeal is whether the district court abused its discretion in ordering *each party* to bear *their* [read *his* or *its*] own costs and expenses in this litigation." See **each** (A). See also SUBJECT-VERB AGREEMENT.

Another common mistake is to attribute one result to two separate subjects, when logically a separate result necessarily occurred with each subject. E.g., "Barry Kendall Hogan and Mark Bradford Hogan appeal their *conviction* [read *convictions*] of importing marijuana and conspiracy to import and possession with the intent to distribute the drug."/ "The result is that the plaintiffs, with an order *in their pocket* [better: *in their possession*] that they say is too wide, have let that order be served on the defendants in those wide terms." (Eng.) (The image *in their pocket* becomes unwieldy and ineffective when there is more than one actor.) The following sentence is a close one: "The government argues that the *stop of appellees' cars* need be justified only by reasonable suspicion." Or should it be *stops of appellees' cars*? Not if government officers stopped several cars with one action.

concur, to a layman, means "to agree." To American judges it has two senses: (1) "to join in a judicial opinion, adopting the reasoning and result as one's own"; (2) "to agree with a judicial decision, but not necessarily on the grounds given in the majority opinion supporting the decision." *Concur* takes *in* ⟨concur in the opinion⟩ or *with* ⟨I concur with you⟩. See **agree.**

Sense (2) is really a form of *to concur specially* (= to *write specially*, q.v.), that is, to express one's concurrence in a separate opinion. E.g., "Justice Holmes, who *concurred specially*, regarded the Washington decree as a personal obligation binding upon the husband and entitled to full faith and credit in Nebraska."

concurrent; consecutive; cumulative. Used in reference to more than one penal sentence assessed against a person, these terms mean, respectively, (1) "running simultaneously," i.e., the time served in prison is credited against two or more sentences; (2) "running one after the other," i.e., the prisoner begins serving the second sentence only after completing service of the first; and (3) "to be carried into effect after the convict has suffered a punishment to which he has already been sentenced" (*W3*), i.e., the second sentence has been imposed in a separate, later proceeding. (For the sense of *cumulative* in corporate contexts, see the entry under that word.)

concurrent jurisdiction; pendent jurisdiction. These terms may confuse even experienced lawyers. *Concurrent jurisdiction* = overlapping jursidiction; jurisdiction exercised by more than one court at the same time over the same subject matter and within the same territory, the litigant having the initial discretion of choosing the court that will adjudicate the matter. *Pendent jurisdiction* = (in U.S.) exercise by federal courts of jurisdiction over matters falling under the purview of state law, on grounds that the state-law claims are so intertwined with the federal claims that they are best adjudicated in tandem.

concussion; contusion. *Concussion* = (1) violent shaking; shock; or (2) injury to the head caused by a heavy blow. *Contusion* = a bruise; an injury resulting from a blow that does not break the skin.

condemn; contemn. To *condemn*, in one sense, is to render judgment against a person or thing ⟨the court condemned the prisoner to life in prison⟩. The word has mostly passed from legal usage into general usage in figurative senses ⟨his looks condemn him⟩. E.g., "We would have serious doubts about this case if the encouragement of guilty pleas by offers of leniency substantially increased the likelihood that defendants, advised by competent counsel, would falsely *condemn* themselves."

In the U.S., *condemn* has the additional legal sense "to pronounce judicially (land, etc.) as converted or convertible to public use (*OED Supp.*). E.g., "To *condemn* land is to set it apart or expropriate it for public use." *San Joaquin* *Land & Water Co. v. Belding*, 35 P. 353, 356 (Cal. 1894)./ "A leasehold interest, of course, is a property interest and consequently may not be *condemned* for a public use without just compensation." *In re Commonwealth of Pennsylvania*, 447 A.2d 342, 344 (Pa. Commw. 1982).

To *contemn* is to hold in contempt, to despise. By far the rarer word, *contemn* is occasionally used in contexts of the legal sanction of *contempt*, q.v. More commonly, however, *contemn* is a literary word. In legal contexts, the related agent noun *contemnor*, q.v., is common. See **contemn.**

condemnation. See **eminent domain & compulsory purchase.**

condemned, n., becomes awkward when used in the possessive. "I also believe that a ruling on a *condemned's* competency to waive federal collateral relief should not be cloaked by the hands-off deference of Fed. R. Civ. P. 52(a)." The periphrastic possessive (*of the condemned*) is to be preferred where it is possible. Cf. **accused, deceased & insured.** See PLURALS (D).

condemnee is an American legal NEOLOGISM meaning "one whose property is expropriated for public use or damaged by a public works project." E.g., "The *condemnee* whose lands were flooded by the works was permitted to abandon in the appellate court the charge of negligence." *State v. Dart*, 202 P. 237, 239 (Ariz. 1921)./ "A tenant, therefore, is a *condemnee* . . . when its leasehold interest is taken, injured or destroyed." *In re Commonwealth of Pennsylvania*, 447 A.2d 342, 344 (Pa. Commw. 1982). See -EE.

condemner, -or. The *-er* spelling is preferred in the general sense of "one that disapproves." But in the U.S., *-or* predominates in the sense "a public or semipublic entity that expropriates private property for public use."

condensable, -ible. The former spelling is preferred. See -ABLE (A).

condign = well-deserved. Today the word is generally restricted to forms of punishment, not of praise. To write of *condign awards* or *laurels* is to betray a deafness to modern idiom.

condition of repair is wordy for *condition*. E.g., "When the Texas Flag is in such a *condition of repair* [read *condition*] that it is no longer a suitable Emblem for display, it should be totally destroyed, preferably by burning, and that privately."

condition subsequent. See **subsequent** & POSTPOSITIVE ADJECTIVES.

condole, v.i.; **console,** v.t. To *condole* is to express sympathy; one *condoles with* another *on* a loss. To *console* is to comfort (another), esp. in grief or depression.

condonation; condonement; condonance. *Condonation* = the complete forgiveness and blotting out of a conjugal offense (even to the extent of surrendering all claim for damages against the adulterer), followed by cohabitation (*Stroud's Judicial Dictionary* 4th ed.). E.g., "On any view, if the wife be right in her evidence, the intercourse which she had with her husband in the van in February 1966 amounted to *condonation* of the cruelty which she alleged." (Eng.) To a layman, the quoted sentence sounds rather fantastic (as if one *condones* cruelty by later giving in to sexual advances).

The original sense of the word was much broader: "the pardoning or remission of an offense or fault; action toward the offender that implies his offense is passed over" (*OED*). E.g., "The ultimate consent of the woman does not have a retroactive effect by relation, and operate as a *condonation* of a crime which has become complete, for the rules of criminal law are not founded upon legal fictions." Today, in both the U.S. and G.B., the word is almost always confined to matrimonial offenses. *Condonance* is a NEEDLESS VARIANT. *Condonement* is a technical term in certain card games.

conduce is often a better and shorter way of saying *be conducive:* "The people have an original right to establish such principles as shall most *conduce to* their own happiness."/ "Nothing *conduces to* brevity like the caving in of the knees" (Holmes, J., explaining his habit of writing opinions while standing). See *BE*-VERBS (B).

conduit, a favorite legal metaphor, is pronounced /*kon-doo-it*/ in the U.S., /*kon-dit*/ or /*kun-dit*/ in G.B.

confect = to prepare (something), usually from varied materials. It is a FORMAL WORD, unbefitting a mundane context in which it means merely "to draft": "The issue is whether summary judgment was appropriate where the language of the release in question was arguably ambiguous and there had been no discovery as to the intent of the parties in *confecting* [read *drafting*] the release."

confederacy. See **combination.**

confer. In Latin, *confer* meant "to compare," whence the present meaning of the abbreviated form of *compare*, namely *cf.* The unabbreviated form *confer* no longer has this meaning; today it means (intransitively) "to come together to take counsel and exchange views" or (transitively) "to bestow, usually from a position of authority." In this latter sense, one *confers* something *on*, not *in*, another. E.g., "We cannot accept the proposition that appellant's acquiescence to Ilsa's desire to live with her mother *conferred* jurisdiction over appellant *in* [read *on*] the California courts in this action." See **convey.**

conferencing. The *OED* records *conference* as a (rare) verb from 1846. The *OED Supp.* and *W3* omit it. Though increasingly common among American lawyers, *conferencing* is a bloated NEEDLESS VARIANT of *conferring.* The word has also become rather widespread in the U.S. in the form *teleconferencing,* a favorite activity of some lawyers; it may survive in that MORPHOLOGICAL DEFORMITY.

conferment; conferral. The latter is a NEEDLESS VARIANT. *Conferment* formerly meant "something conferred," but now is restricted to the sense "the act of conferring or bestowing." E.g., "Nor can it be said that defendant acquiesced in the *conferment* of a benefit upon him."

confer(r)able. This word is spelled -*rr*- and is stressed on the second syllable.

conferral. See **conferment.**

confessedly = (1) by general admission or acknowledgment; (2) by personal confession (*OED*). Follett rather too narrowly ruled that "the test of legitimacy for an adverb made from an adjective is that it fit the formula *in* [*x*] *manner*" (*Modern American Usage* 279

[1966]), a formula that *confessedly* does not fit. Follett's primary objection was to *reportedly*, q.v., the earliest recorded use of which was 1901. *Confessedly* has been used since at least 1640, however, and undeniably (or perhaps confessedly) is useful, especially in legal writing. Adverbs in -EDLY are not, however, to be overdone.

Following are several unobjectionable uses of *confessedly*. Sense (1): "As far as equitable rules differ from those of the law, they are *confessedly* more just and righteous, and their disappearance would be a long step backward in the progress of civilization." (Pomeroy)/ "The doctrine is *confessedly* derived from the unwillingness of a court to give its peculiar relief to a suitor who in the very controversy has so conducted himself as to shock the moral sensibilities of the judge."/ "No poll, no majority vote of the affected, no rule of expediency, and certainly no *confessedly* subjective or idiosyncratic view justifies a judicial determination."

Sense (2): "*Confessedly* this is not an action ex contractu upon a promise of marriage, in which the seduction might be pleaded and proved as an aggravation of damages; but it is clearly an attempt to recover ex delicto." See -EDLY & **reportedly**.

confide in; confide to. The former phrase (= to trust or have faith) is more common in general usage ⟨to confide in one's friends⟩. *Confide to* (= to entrust [an object of care or a task], to communicate [something] in confidence) still commonly appears in legal prose. E.g., "Discretion was *confided to* the governing board."/ "The courts will not interfere with the exercise of discretion by school directors in matters *confided* by laws *to* their judgment."

confidence = (1) assured expectation; firm trust; or (2) the entrusting of private matters. Sense (2) has limited currency in general usage, as in the phrase *to take another into one's confidence* (i.e., to tell another private matters in trust). It is more generally used in law, as in this sentence from the Statute of Frauds, 29 Chas. II, c. 3 (1677), which illustrates a use of the word not uncommon today in legal prose: "And . . . from and after the said four and twentieth day of June all declarations or creations of trusts or *confidences* of any lands, tenements, or hereditaments shall be manifested and proved by some writing signed by the party."

configuration. See **constellation.**

confirmatory, -tive. The latter is a NEEDLESS VARIANT. In the law of evidence, *confirmatory* is sometimes used as an equivalent of *corroborative*, q.v.

confirmer, -or. The general word for "one who confirms" is *confirmer*. The obsolescent legal term (meaning "one who confirms a voidable estate; the grantor in a deed of confirmation") is spelled *-or*.

confiscable; confiscatable. The latter is a malformed NEEDLESS VARIANT. See -ATABLE.

confiscatory is the adjectival form corresponding to the verb *confiscate*. It means "of the nature of, or tending to, confiscation" (*OED*). E.g., "The rate of return prescribed by the commission would have to be clearly *confiscatory* or outside the purview of the statute to permit judicial interference with the determination." Colloquially, it has been used in the sense "robbing under legal authority" ⟨confiscatory landlords⟩ (*OED*).

conflicts (referring to the law of choice of law) is often used as a shortened form of *conflict of laws*. E.g., "The late Brainerd Currie spearheaded the drive to focus attention on the often overlooked key to intelligent *conflicts* analysis—the policies underlying the laws of different states in putative conflict."

confluence; conflux. The latter is a NEEDLESS VARIANT.

conform takes the preposition *to* or *with*. Fowler objected to *conform with*, but most authorities find it quite acceptable.

conformable, -ly. These terms are today used almost exclusively in legal contexts. *Conformable* = according in form or character to. E.g., "The Court of Appeal altered its own order as not being *conformable* to the order pronounced." (Eng.)

Conformably to = in conformity with; in a manner conformable to. E.g., "*Conformably* to what has been said above, we are of opinion that the testatrix did not contemplate that the words 'contracts or debts' should apply to those natural obligations which a husband owes to his wife."/ "If both the law and the Constitution apply to a particular case, so that the court must decide that case *conformably* to the law, disregarding the Constitution, or *conformably* to the Constitution, disregarding the law—the court must determine which of these conflicting rules governs the case." (Marshall, C.J.) The rarer phrase *conformably with* = in accordance with.

conformity; conformance. *Conformity* is the standard term, *conformance* being a NEEDLESS VARIANT that is not uncommon in legal prose. E.g., "I consider the disclosure not to be in *conformance* [read *conformity*] with section 171."/ "The trial court was right in holding the United States savings bonds to be the property of the survivors; this is in *conformance* [read *conformity*] with the statute as well as with the federal regulations." In the sentences that follow, *conformity* is used correctly: "Evidence of other crimes, wrongs, or acts is not admissible to prove the character of a person in order to show that he acted in *conformity* therewith."/ "The jurisdiction in civil actions shall be exercised and enforced in *conformity* with the laws of the United States."

confront for *present* is now almost a VOGUE WORD among American judges. It is essentially hyperbolic, suggesting that the court comes "face to face with" the issues it decides. E.g., "This case *confronts us with the question whether* [read *presents the question whether*] a nonresident plaintiff asserting a cause of action based on a tort that occurred outside the state is exempt from these qualification requirements."/ "The court here *confronts* [read *addresses* or *decides*] issues no less difficult than those discussed in the court's recent opinion concerning the layoffs of firefighters."/ "When *confronted* [read *presented*] with a statute that is plain and unambiguous on its face, we ordinarily do not look to the legislative history as a guide to its meaning." In this last example *confront* is especially inappropriate because it connotes grappling or resistance, and an unambiguous statute gives no trouble to the interpreter.

confusable, -ible. The former spelling is preferred. See -ABLE (A).

congeries is a singular noun. *Congery* and *congerie* are false singular nouns recorded by the *OED Supp.* and *W3*, formed on the mistaken assumption that *congeries* (Fr. "a collection, aggregation") is the plural of such a

noun. All forms but *congeries*, sing. & pl., should be avoided. The word is pronounced /kon-jĕ-**reez**/ in the U.S., and /kŏn-**jeer**-eez/ or /kŏn-**jeer**-y-eez/ in G.B.

congratulatory, -tive; congratulant. *Congratulatory* is the usual word. The other forms are NEEDLESS VARIANTS.

Congress does not require an article. "*The Congress* [read *Congress*] has said that interest shall be calculated from the date of the entry of the judgment." *Affiliated Capital Corp. v. City of Houston*, 793 F.2d 706, 713 (5th Cir. 1986) (Higginbotham, J., concurring). *The Congress* is a quirk to be avoided.

congressional, like *constitutional,* should be written with the lowercase -c-, even though the noun corresponding to the adjective is capitalized.

Congressperson is unnecessary for either *Congressman* or *Congresswoman*. See SEXISM (B).

congruent; congruous. These words are largely synonymous in meaning "in agreement or harmony; appropriate." Distinctions in use are possible, however. *Congruous* is the more widely used term, meaning "appropriate, fitting; marked by harmonious agreement." The negative form *incongruous* appears even more frequently than the positive form.

Congruent has legitimate uses in math and physics, and is also prevalent in the sense "coincident throughout; in accordance with." E.g., "The court has established procedures and standards for the admissibility of co-conspirator statements *congruent* with the Federal Rules of Evidence."

The corresponding nouns are *congruence* and *congruity*. *Congruency* is a NEEDLESS VARIANT.

conjoin generally provides no nuance not included in *join* or *combine*. E.g., "The lower court rejected appellant's contention that the terms of the will and the circumstances surrounding testatrix when it was executed *conjoined* [read *joined* or *combined*] to reflect an intention to exercise the power of appointment."

W9 defines *conjoin* as "to join together for a common purpose." *Join together* is, of course, a venial REDUNDANCY, just as *conjoin* is something of a one-word redundancy. But these phrases do slightly shade *join*. Perhaps on rare occasions when the precise nuance suggested by the *W9* definition is desired, *conjoin* is the proper word.

conjurator. See **conjurer.**

conjure. In the sense "to supplicate, beseech," this verb is accented on the second syllable /kŏn-*joor*/; in the sense "to play the sorcerer," the first syllable is stressed /*kon*-jŭr/.

conjurer, -or; conjurator. *Conjurator* is an obsolete LEGALISM meaning "one joined with others by an oath; a co-conspirator." *Conjurer* is the preferred spelling for the word meaning "a magician; juggler."

connectible, -able. The former is preferred. See -ABLE (A).

connection; connexion; connexity. The spelling *-tion* is preferred in the U.S.; *-xion* is an almost obsolete spelling formerly preferred in G.B. The word means basically (1) "the act of connecting" ⟨the connection of these loose ends⟩; (2) "the state of being connected" ⟨the connection of these events⟩; or (3) "a connecting part" ⟨the bridge's connection with the land⟩.

Lawyers use *connexity* in a distinct way, as a synonym of *connectedness* (= the quality of being connected). E.g., "The more likely the public is to make an assumption of *connexity* between the providers of related services, the less similarity in the trademarks is needed for a finding of likelihood of confusion." Cf. **nexus.**

connect together is a common REDUNDANCY. If the sense "to connect with one another" is called for, *interconnect* is the word: E.g.,"A transaction is a group of facts so *connected together* [read *interconnected*] as to be referred to as a legal name, as a crime, as a contract, a wrong, or any other subject of inquiry that may be in issue." (Eng.) See **together.**

connexity. See **connection.**

connivance is not, as is popularly supposed, "conspiracy to act together for an illegal end," although it is a form of collusion.

Connivance is the passive allowing of another to act illegally or immorally. It is silence and neglect when one should be vocal and monitory.

In England, *connivance* is usually confined to marital settings; the *CDL* defines it as "behaviour of a person designed to cause his or her spouse to commit a matrimonial offence." Cf. *Stroud's Judicial Dictionary* (4th ed.) ("the willing consent to a conjugal offence [in the sense of being an accessory before the fact], or a culpable acquiescence in a course of conduct reasonably likely to lead to the offence being committed").

connotate. See **connote.**

connotation does not mean "ramification" or "suggestion," as in these two statements by President Carter: "The political *connotations* [of the release of the American hostages in Iran] do not concern me."/ "Secretary of State Vance did not want any action with any *connotation* of military action." In the latter sentence, the word is used in the sense of "suggestion," which is close to a correct usage. But words *connote*; actions do not.

Connotations are the emotive nuances of words, including tone, flavor, and associational senses. Here the term is correctly used: "If, therefore, the title of this article suggests a merely philosophical inquiry into the nature of law and legal relations, the writer may be pardoned for repudiating such a *connotation* in advance."/ "Some authorities suggest that 'issue,' unlike 'children,' has a biological *connotation*."

Sometimes *connotation* appears to have been confused with *denotation* (= the literal meaning of a term). E.g., "'Contest of a will' is a term of art, the *connotation* [read *meaning*] of which is made clear in the context of the appropriate Probate Code sections." See the two entries following.

CONNOTATION & DENOTATION. Those with a sensitivity to language understand not just the dictionary definitions of words and sentences (*denotation*), but the undercurrent of suggestions and implications that inheres in all language (*connotation*). This sensitivity is no less important to the judge interpreting a statute than it is to the literary critic. In a will, for example, connotations may be the real clues to the testator's intent where the literal meanings of words provide no clues.

But connotative sensitivity is also what informs great writing. Cardozo well understood the effect of connotative associations: "What a cobweb of fine-spun casuistry is dissipated in a breath by the simple statement of Lord Esher in *Ex parte Simonds,* that the court will not suffer its own officer 'to do a shabby thing.' If the word *shabby* had been left out, and *unworthy* or *dishonorable* substituted, I suppose the sense would have been much the same. But what a drop in emotional value would have followed. As it is, we feel the tingle of the hot blood of resentment mounting to our cheeks." Cardozo, *Law and Literature,* 52 Harv. L. Rev. 471, 480 (1939).

connote; denote. *Connote* = to imply in addition to the literal meaning; *denote* = to signify the literal meaning, to indicate. *Denote* is rarely if ever misused; *connote,* however, is becoming increasingly rare in its correct senses. Here the word is correctly used: "The essential characteristics of an estate, then, are three in number: first, an estate is always an interest in land; second, an estate is always an interest that is, will, or may become possessory; and third, the term always *connotes* ownership measured in terms of duration."

Yet *connote* is frequently misused for *denote,* just as *literally* is often misused for *figuratively.* E.g., "The tendency of judges to adhere to concepts and doctrines familiar to past ages is hardly anywhere more evident than it is in the law relating to the relationships *connoted* [read *denoted*] by such terms as 'leasehold,' 'landlord,' and 'tenant.'"/ "'Cannot' *connotes* [read *denotes*], not unwillingness, but inability."/ "A plea is invalid if the defendant has not a full understanding of what the plea *connotes* [read *means*]."

Moreover, words connote; acts do not: "The mere act of sending a child to California to live with her mother is not a commercial act and *connotes* [read *suggests*] no intent to obtain a corresponding benefit in the State." Nor do readers connote: "While we are accustomed to *connote* [read *think of*] the same ideas in morals and ethics, and while to a considerable extent the two words involve the same general notion, yet they are distinct in that morality represents existing facts, while ethics is the scientific hypothesis for the explanation of existing facts." See **connotation.**

In the following sentence, *connote* is used in the sense "to suggest; to lead to the conclu-

sion of." With this example one can see just how mushy this word has become: "If such testimony must necessarily *connote* [read *lead to the conclusion of*] adultery on her part, then it cannot be said that the common law has otherwise closed its eyes to this fact of life." (The ANTHROPOMORPHISM in this sentence is unobtrusive and even effective.)

Connotate is a NEEDLESS VARIANT of *connote.*

consanguineous, -guine, -guineal, -guinean. The preferred legal adjective corresponding to *consanguinity* is *consanguineous* (= descended from the same parent or ancestor). *Consanguineous* is opposed to *affinal* (see **affinity**).

Consanguinean is the Roman law term meaning "having the same father." It is opposed to *uterine* (= having the same mother).

Consanguine and *consanguineal* have been taken up by anthropologists and linguists and given DIFFERENTIATION. Thus *consanguine* = based on an extended group of blood relations esp. of unilinear descent and constituting the functional familial unit in a society (*W3*). *Consanguineal,* which shares this sense, is a NEEDLESS VARIANT of *consanguine.*

consanguinity (= relationship by blood) is a lay as well as a legal term. Here is a classical legal use: "Neither of these two women was related to the testator either by marriage [i.e., by affinity] or by *consanguinity,* while the contestant was his nephew and his only heir at law." Degrees of consanguinity are determined differently by the various legal systems of the world.

Often *consanguinity* is used figuratively: "There is apparently no intimate *consanguinity* between the case sub judice and the proceeding that pends in an alien jurisdiction." *Relation* might be better than such bombastic uses of *consanguinity,* however. See **affinity &
kindred.**

conscience has not been recorded in the dictionaries as a verb. The writer of the following sentence apparently thought *conscience* is equivalent to *contemplate:* "The rule does not *conscience* [read *contemplate*] joinder." The only related use recorded in the *OED* is *conscienced* (= having a conscience) ⟨a loose-conscienced person⟩.

conscionable is not a mere NEEDLESS VARIANT of *conscientious,* though some dictionaries suggest it. As a positive correlative of *unconscionable*, it means "conforming with good conscience; just and reasonable" and is used of things as opposed to persons ⟨a conscionable bargain⟩. See **unconscionable**.

consecutive. See **concurrent**.

consensual; consentaneous; consentient. *Consensual,* the most common of these terms, means "having or expressing or made with consent." *Consentaneous* and *consentient* both mean (1) "unanimous," or (2) "agreeing." Neither is common enough for the other to be labeled a NEEDLESS VARIANT.

consensus = a widely held opinion or generally accepted view. Hence two common phrases, *consensus of opinion* and *general consensus,* are prolix. E.g., "There was a *general consensus* [omit *general*] that to drink whisky is wrong and that to be a nurse is discreditable." In the following sentence, we are accosted by a double REDUNDANCY: "The *general consensus of opinion* [omit *general* and *of opinion*] seems to be that the gist and foundation of the right in all cases is the wrongful act."

The *OED* defines *consensus* as "the collective unanimous opinion of a number of persons"; hence a consensus of two is impossible: "An acceptance of an offer made ought to be notified to the person who makes the offer, in order that the two minds may come together; unless this is done, the two minds may be apart, and there is not that consensus [read *agreement*] which is necessary to the English law to make a contract."

Consensus is unrelated to *census;* confusion between the two causes some writers to lapse into the misspelling *concensus.*

consent. See **assent**.

consentaneous. See **consensual**.

consent decree (U.S.) = *agreed verdict* (G.B.).

consentient. See **consensual**.

consequent(ial); subsequent. *Consequent* = following as a result. *Consequential,* a rarer and usually legal term, means "following as an indirect or secondary result" ⟨consequential damages⟩. In its other proper sense, *consequential* may serve as an opposite of *inconse-*quential, and hence mean "important," and occasionally "self-important." In the following sentence it means "important; of consequence," a sense prematurely labeled obsolete by the *OED:* "A few months' further delay pending determination on the governing issue in the District of Columbia litigation cannot be seriously *consequential.*"

In all other senses, *consequent* is the correct term where the choice is between the shorter and longer forms. E.g., "The evidence tended to show that the plaintiff was very much excited, and that the happening of the accident and the *consequent* injury to the casket and the body occasioned her serious mental pain and suffering."/ "The registrar transferred the application to the Divorce Registry so that it might be heard in London; *consequent upon* that direction, the application came before Mr. Registrar Kenworthy." (Eng.)

Frequently, *consequent* is misused for *subsequent,* perhaps partly because of the logical fallacy post hoc ergo propter hoc (= after this, therefore because of this), which snares persons who equate sequence with causation, thinking that if one event occurred after another, the second event must have been caused by the first.

consequentials, n., = consequential damages. E.g., "Had the parties excluded *consequentials* by contract, the court would have had to identify the value differential [q.v.] component of the buyer's total loss." This lawyers' colloquialism should be discouraged in formal legal writing. Cf. **incidentals**.

conserva(n)cy. The preferred spelling of this essentially BrE word is *conservancy* (= a commission or court having jurisdiction over a port or river, to regulate the fisheries, navigation, etc. [*OED*]). In all other senses, *conservancy* is a NEEDLESS VARIANT of *conservation.*

conservational; conservative; conservatory. These words are to be distinguished. *Conservational* = of or pertaining to conservation. *Conservative* = characterized by a tendency to preserve or keep intact or unchanged; believing in the maintenance of existing political and social institutions. *Conservatory* = preservative.

conservator; curator. Both are general as well as specific legal terms. *Conservator* is often used in the sense "a court-appointed guardian of an incompetent" (the conservator shall have the charge of the incapable person). Primarily a civil-law term (used, e.g., in Scotland), *curator* has an identical meaning; this term has been adopted in a number of common-law jurisdictions, however, as in several American states.

conservatory, adj. See **conservational.**

consider (as) (to be). When followed by a noun or noun phrase, *consider as* is never justified stylistically, and many authorities consider it an error. "Such conduct has long been *considered as solicitation* [read *considered solicitation*]." *Consider* may, however, properly be followed by the infinitive *to be,* especially if the noun phrase after *consider* is at all long. "Ignoring our many precedents to the contrary, he *considers* the tax code, and especially that portion implementing the personal income tax, *to be* unconstitutional."/ "Prescott drove in his own car from Chelsea to Boston by way of the Mystic River Bridge, which he considered was [read *to be;* or delete *was* and omit *to be*] the most direct route."

The collocation of *consider* and *as* is acceptable when the phrase is followed by a participial phrase: "He is not *considered as* abandoning his objection because he does not submit to further proceedings without contest."

considerable used adverbially is a dialectal usage. "Bylaws usually may be amended with *considerable* [read *considerably*] more facility than the articles of incorporation."

consideration. A. Legal Sense. The law uses *consideration* in a technical sense generally unknown to laymen: "the act, forbearance, or promise by one party to a contract that constitutes the price for which he buys the promise of the other" (*CDL*). This word is one of the lawyer's basic TERMS OF ART.

B. As a COUNT NOUN. In law, by virtue of the technical meaning explained under (A), *consideration* may be a count noun, whereas in general English usage it is not so used. E.g., "A basic principle of contract law is that one *consideration* will support multiple promises by the other contracting party." Nevertheless, the phrase *other valuable consideration* is used rather than *other valuable considerations.*

C. Idiomatic Constructions. Legal idiom requires *in consideration of* but *as consideration for,* in the sense of the word given under (A).

D. *Valuable consideration* and *good consideration.* The former phrase refers to an act, forbearance, or promise having some economic value; the latter refers to natural love or affection, or moral duty. To create an enforceable contract, *valuable consideration* is required. *Good consideration* is no good.

considered opinion, when used of oneself ("It is my considered opinion that . . ."), is an indefensible CLICHÉ, *opinion* being a sufficiently strong word. No one thinks his opinions are ill-considered. But one may think another's opinions to be ill-considered: "Was that X's *considered opinion?*" "No, it was just a crude prejudice he had picked up."

consignatary, -tory. For this civil-law term equivalent to *consignee, Black's* gives *-tory,* and *W3* and *OED* give *-tary.* The *OED* lists *consignatory* only as a variant of *cosignatory* (= a joint signatory). Historical civilian usage seems to recommend *consignatary.*

consignee (= one to whom goods are consigned) is pronounced /kon-sǐ-*nee*/ or /kon-sI-*nee*/. Cf. **consignor.**

consigner. See **consignor.**

consignment; consignation. These words denote quite different things, though the root concept is the same. *Consignment* is the more usual term in common-law jurisdictions, meaning "the act of delivering goods to a carrier to be transmitted to a designated agent." *Consignation,* primarily a term from Scots and French law, means "the act of formally paying over money, as into a bank, or to a person legally appointed to receive it, often because it is the subject of a dispute."

consignor, -er. *Consignor* is the technical correlative of *consignee,* q.v. A *consignor* dispatches goods to another in *consignment.* In Scots law, a *consigner* is one who makes a *consignation* of money in dispute. The two words are often pronounced differently: *consignor* /kon-si-*nohr*/ or /kŏn-sI-nŏr/; *consigner* /kŏn-sI-něr/.

consistent with. A common illiteracy in American law is to use this phrase adverbially rather than adjectivally. For adverbial uses, *consistently with* (= in a manner consistent with) should be used. E.g., "Thereafter, all medical facilities will be equipped *consistent with* [read *consistently with*] these standards and all new construction of health care facilities will be *consistent with* [adj.] the standards."

consist in; consist of. American writers too often ignore the distinction. *Consist of* is used in reference to materials; it precedes the physical elements that compose a tangible thing; the well-worn example is that cement *consists of* sand, gravel, and mortar. "The document admitted to probate *consists of* a single sheet of legal cap paper, folded in the middle in the usual way along the short dimension, making four pages of equal size."

Consist in (= has as its essence) precedes abstract elements or qualities, or intangible things; e.g., a good moral character *consists in* integrity, decency, fairness, and compassion. The proper use of *consist in* is illustrated in the following sentences: "When the subjection of one person to another is not slavery, it *consists* simply *in* the right of requiring of another what he is bound to do or not to do."/ "The second cause of action *consists in* the effort of all the plaintiffs to be protected from being discharged because the defendants struck work."/ "The equitable relief prayed for *consists in* enjoining the officers from making use of the property as evidence, and in ordering the property restored to its owner."

In the sentences that follow, *consist of* is wrongly used for *consist in;* the mistake is especially common in the U.S.: "The alleged negligence consisted *of* [read *in*] the act of a hospital nurse in injecting a foreign substance into plaintiff's left arm, causing pain and permanent injury."/ "In understanding any major political move, it is a mistake to focus only on the move itself. Understanding depends upon seeing all of the interrelations; the art of politics consists *of* [read *in*] using those interrelations."/ "Where the plaintiff's contributory negligence consists *of* [read *in*] being inattentive, and not discovering a risk he should have discovered, he will not be barred from strict liability recovery."/ "His wrong, if wrong there be, would consist *of* [read *in*] some threat, of something beyond the mere termination of his contract with his employer."/ "By statute in some states the crime of statutory rape consists *of* [read *in*] sexual intercourse with a female below a certain age."

console. See **condole.**

consolidation. See **joinder** (B) & **merger.**

consols = funded government securities with no maturity date (in G.B.). The word is invariably in the plural form, because it originated as an abbreviation for *consolidated annuities.* E.g., "In *Standing v. Bouring, consols* were transferred from the plaintiff's name into the joint names of herself and her godson, a person to whom, it was held, she was not in loco parentis." (Eng.) See **consul.**

consortium; society. In the phrases *loss of consortium* and *loss of society,* the two words are synonymous in the context of husband and wife. *Society,* however, is a broader term, describing other than marital relationships, such as father-child and brother-sister. Thus generally only a spouse may sue for *loss of consortium* (L. "partnership"—related to *consort*), whereas any close relation may sue for *loss of society.* Both terms refer to the nonpecuniary interests a person may have in the company, cooperation, affection, and aid of another. See **society.**

In England, where only a husband could sue for loss of consortium, the cause of action was abolished as a cause of action by the Administration of Justice Act of 1982. *Consortium* is pronounced /kŏn-*sor*-shi-ŭm/ or, more usually, in G.B., /kŏn-*sor*-di-ŭm/. The plural is *-tia.*

conspectus; prospectus. These terms are not synonymous. A *conspectus* is a comprehensive survey, summary, or synopsis. A *prospectus* is a document describing the chief features of something that is forthcoming.

conspiracy. See **combination.**

conspiratorial; conspirative, -ory; conspirational. The first is standard; the others are NEEDLESS VARIANTS.

conspire together is a REDUNDANCY. "The defendants *conspired together* [omit *together*] with persons unknown to import cannabis resin." (Eng.)/"The defendants have *conspired together* [omit *together*] to conceal their tortious and fraudulent conduct." See **together.**

constellation, like *configuration,* is often used figuratively to describe a specific group of facts in a case. E.g., "The contrary is likely to be true if both parties have moved for summary judgment on different legal theories dependent on different *constellations* of material facts."

constitute   is often an overblown substitute for *make.* And it is an ARCHAISM to give *constitute,* like *make,* a direct object followed by an objective complement. E.g., "No particular words, technical or otherwise, or form of expression in an instrument are necessary to *constitute* [read *make*] it a lease."/ "I deem it unnecessary to consider whether such an interest would *constitute* [read *make*] her a legal representative of J.P. Robertson after his death, as I do not believe she ever acquired such an interest."

To use *constitute* in the sense "to make up, compose" is more in accord with modern English usage. E.g., "This system of classification is employed for convenience in describing the effect upon the operation of provisions in the will caused by changes in property *constituting* the estate after the will is executed." See **compose** (C).

constitutional   should not generally be capitalized, though *Constitution* (in reference to the United States Constitution or any particular constitution) should be. The adjective has two meanings: (1) "of or relating to the Constitution" ⟨constitutional rights⟩; and (2) "proper under the Constitution" ⟨constitutional actions⟩. Here is an illustration of sense (1): "The diversion of a job to a competitor is not an invasion of a *constitutional* right." And here of sense (2): "The Wisconsin statute, which is similar to the Norris-LaGuardia Act, has also been held *constitutional.*" The opposite of *constitutional* in sense (1) is *nonconstitutional,* and in sense (2) *unconstitutional.* See **nonconstitutional.**

constitution(al)ist.   The standard form of the term is *constitutionalist* (= [1] one who studies or writes on the Constitution; or [2] a supporter of constitutional principles).

constitutionalize   = (1) to provide with a constitution ⟨to constitutionalize the new government⟩; (2) to make constitutional; to bring into line with the Constitution ⟨plans to constitutionalize the currently segregated school district⟩; or (3) to import the Constitution into ⟨the dissenter accused the majority of unnecessarily constitutionalizing its decision⟩. Senses (2) and (3) are relatively new

and are unrecorded in the *OED* and *W3.* Here is an example of sense (3): "*New York Times v. Sullivan* was the first major step in what proved to be a seemingly irreversible process of *constitutionalizing* the entire law of libel and slander."

constitutionally   has at least four senses in legal contexts: (1) "in a constitutional manner; in a way that comports with the Constitution" ⟨constitutionally assembled⟩ ⟨constitutionally enacted⟩; (2) "under the provisions of the Constitution" ⟨constitutionally deficient⟩ ⟨constitutionally impermissible⟩; (3) "so as to bear on the Constitution" ⟨constitutionally speaking⟩; (4) "by the Constitution" ⟨constitutionally prohibited⟩. Sense (1) is the only legal sense given by the *OED* and *W3.*

constrain   = (1) to force; or (2) to confine forcibly. Sense (1) is the more common of the two. It is a favorite word of dissenting judges: "It is for such reasons that I am *constrained* to dissent."/ "I regret that I am *constrained* to dissent from the holding of the court in this case." Sense (2) is primarily literary.

construction   is the nominal form of both *construct* and *construe,* in law usually the latter. A layman might think that *construction of statutes* is the business of legislatures, since they *construct* statutes; but *construction* in that phrase means "the process of construing," which falls within the purview of the courts. See **interpretation.**

constructive; constructional.   These terms are not to be confused. *Constructive* is given a meaning in law that is unknown elsewhere; it "denotes that an act, statement, or other fact has an effect in law though it may not have had that effect in fact" (*OCL*). Thus we have the phrases *constructive fraud* and *constructive trust* and other phrases describing legal FICTIONS, q.v. See **actual.**

Constructional = of or pertaining to the act or process of construing. E.g., "When the taker of a prior interest is one of several heirs of the designated ancestor at the ancestor's death, no *constructional* tendency is sufficiently definite to be capable of statement."

constructive fraud; legal fraud.   The former is the more common phrase denoting forms of unintentional deception or misrepresentation that are held to be fraudulent. It is also clearer: *legal fraud* might suggest to the unwary that the fraud is, e.g., presumed or sanctioned by law, rather than that it is considered in law to be fraud. For the difference between *fraud in law* and *legal fraud*, see **fraud** (B).

consul; counsel; council. *Consul* = a governmental representative living in a foreign country to oversee commercial matters. *Counsel* = a legal adviser or legal advisers. See **counsel & attorney** (A). *Council* = a body of representatives. See **council.**

consulate; consulship. *Consulate* = the office, term of office, jurisdiction, or residence of a consul. *Consulship* = the office or term of office of a consul. *Consulate* is the more common and (therefore) the broader term. *Consulship* may be useful in conveying precisely one's meaning.

consult takes the prepositions *with* (documents or other persons), *on* or *upon*, or *about* (a matter). The verb may be used transitively ⟨to consult the will itself⟩ as well as intransitively, in combination with any of the propositions previously named.

consultation. The English writer Philip Howard has stated that *consultation*

> can mean a conference at which the parties, for example, lawyers or doctors, *consult* or deliberate. Modern legal usage confines this sense to meetings with more than one counsel present. You can have a *consultation* with your doctor on your own. But you must be able to afford the fees of at least two lawyers simultaneously before you can properly describe your meeting with them as a *consultation*.
> P. Howard, *Weasel Words* 57 (1979).

The *OCL* defines *consultation* as "a meeting of two or more counsel and the solicitor instructing them for discussion and advice."

No such restrictive meaning is given the term in the U.S. If you consult with your lawyer on a certain matter, then that act is *consultation*.

consult(at)ive; consult(at)ory. The forms in *-ory* are NEEDLESS VARIANTS. Both *consultative* and *consultive* are old, the former recorded from 1583, the latter from 1616. Because the adjectival form of Latinate words in *-tion* follows from the nominal form, *consultative* is the preferable form. "Purely *consultive* [read *consultative*] experts are those not relied upon in whole or in part by testifying experts." See **consultation.**

consummate has one pronunciation as adjective /kŏn-**sum**-it/ and another as verb /kon-sŭ-**mayt**/.

contact, v.t. *Contact* is now firmly ensconced as a verb, though this use of the word was vehemently objected to a generation ago. Brevity recommends it over "to get in touch with," and it should not be considered stylistically infelicitous even in formal contexts. E.g., "These witnesses were recently *contacted* by petitioner's counsel and agreed to make new affidavits."

contagious; infectious. These words are misused even by educated writers and speakers. A *contagious* disease is communicable by contact with those suffering from it. An *infectious* disease spreads by contact with the germs, e.g. in the air or in water. Some *contagious* diseases are not *infectious*, and vice versa.

contemn = to treat (as laws or court orders) with contemptuous disregard. E.g., "We find that jurisdiction exists based on both the inherent power of a court to reach those who knowingly *contemn* its orders and the minimum contacts analysis set out below." The *OED* notes that this word is "chiefly a literary word," but it is used just as frequently in legal as in literary contexts. See **condemn.**

contemner, -or. The *OED, W3,* and *Black's* list the spelling in *-er* as the predominant one; nineteenth-century British and American usage overwhelmingly preferred that spelling, which is still the better one: "In *Dustman,* the Texas Supreme Court ordered the *contemner* discharged in view of his established inability to make the child-support payments ordered in his divorce judgment." The *-or* spelling, now common in the U.S., remains inferior to *contemner.* "In reaching our decision, we do not reach the issue whether such nationwide jurisdictional provisions would of themselves establish jurisdiction over alleged nonparty *contemnors* [read *contemners*]." See **-ER, -OR.**

contemplative is accented on the second syllable: /kŏn-***tem***-plă-tiv/.

contemporary; contemporaneous. Both refer to simultaneity. *Contemporaneous* is usually used of actions and things, *contemporary* of persons. *Contemporary* has the additional informal meaning "modern." This sense of the word should be avoided in contexts referring to past times, as in this example quoted by Bernstein: "An anti-Jeffersonian charge by Justice Chase in 1803, reprinted in this collection, was one count in his impeachment by a Jeffersonian Congress; more *contemporary* items in the collection include papers by Justices Hugo Black and Robert H. Jackson." When no other time-frame is mentioned, then we may infer "contemporary with us" (= modern), but not in historical contexts. *Cotemporaneous* is a NEEDLESS VARIANT of *contemporaneous;* likewise, *cotemporary* is a NEEDLESS VARIANT of *contemporary.*

Here *contemporary* is misused for *contemporaneous,* unless the writer means to personify the statute mentioned: "As the court acknowledges, the 1924 statute must be examined in light of its *contemporary* [read *contemporaneous*] legal context." Clearly, no personification is intended.

Contemporaneous does not precisely mean "simultaneous"; rather, it means "belonging to the same time or period; occurring at about the same time." Thus the following sentences are correct, although *simultaneous* does not properly fit in each slot filled by *contemporaneous:* "Courts regard with particular respect the *contemporaneous* construction of a statute by those initially charged with its enforcement."/ "Where a conveyance in trust is made voluntarily, without solicitation or undue influence, and no fraud is shown prior to, or *contemporaneous* with, the execution of the deed, but consists in repudiating the agreement to reconvey, the case is not removed from the operation of the Statute of Frauds."/ "These uncertainties in proof by parol evidence are at least partially eliminated in the Uniform Probate Code by the requirement that the advancement be 'declared in a *contemporaneous* writing by the decedent or acknowledged in writing by the heir.'"

contempt; contemptibility; contemptuousness. These words are quite distinct. *Contempt* = (1) (generally) the act of despising; the condition of being despised; (2) (in law) action interfering with the administration of justice. *Contemptibility* = the quality or fact of being worthy of scorn. *Contemptuous* = the quality of being scornful or disdainful. See **contumac(it)y.**

contempt of court = action of any kind that interferes with the administration of justice by the various courts of law. There are several different types of contempt. *Direct contempt* is that which occurs in open court (e.g., foul language spoken to a judge), whereas *constructive contempt* (sometimes called *indirect* or *consequential contempt*) results from actions outside court, such as failing to comply with orders. Another dichotomy is that between *civil* and *criminal contempt;* the former consists in failing to do something ordered by the court for the benefit of another litigant, whereas the latter consists in acts that obstruct justice.

contemptuous. A. And *contemptible.* The former means "expressing contempt," the latter "worthy of contempt or scorn." Both are terms of disparagement, *contemptible* being the stronger of the two. See **contempt.**

B. And *contumacious.* See **contumacious.**

contemptuousness. See **contempt.**

contend. See **allege & contest.**

content(s). When referring to written matter or oral presentation, *content* = the ideas or thoughts contained in [the words] as opposed to the method of presentation. Follett disapproved of the modern tendency to use *content* as well as *contents* for "what is contained," but the usage is old and is now common. E.g., "Since Justice Black did not define the *content* and scope of this exception, that critical task has fallen to the lower courts."

Contents is used of material and nonmaterial ingredients alike. E.g., "The bottles were securely and completely wrapped in paper and tied with a string so that the *contents* of the package could not be seen or observed."/ "The declarations of a deceased testator as to his testamentary intentions, and as to the *contents* of his will, are deemed to be relevant when his will has been lost, and when there is a question about what were its *contents.*" (Eng.)/ "The testator who has revoked a previous will should not be fettered by the *contents* of that previous will when he sets about his new testamentary work." Still, *content* is now more common for the nonmaterial things contained in something (as in documents).

The word *contents* should never be used of human beings, as the callous sentence that follows demonstrates: "The impact and disintegration of the aircraft extended over several seconds *before the aircraft and its human contents came to rest* [read *before the aircraft and those aboard came to rest*]."

conterminous. See **coterminous.**

contest, n.; contestation; litiscontestation. These terms are to be differentiated. *Contest* = (1) debate; controversy; dispute ⟨without contest⟩; or (2) a friendly competition. *Contestation* = disputation or controversy, as between parties at law; verbal contention; keen argument (*OED*); (2) the contesting or disputing (of a point or claim) ⟨assertions not open to contestation⟩; or (3) an assertion contended for ⟨the appellant's contestation is untenable⟩. *Litiscontestation*, a legal term used primarily in Scots and civil law, means (1) "the formal entry of a suit in a court of law" (*OED*); or (2) "a legal process by which controverted issues are established and a joinder of issues arrived at" (*W3*).

contest, v.t.; contend. In the sense "to fight (for)," *contest* is almost always transitive ⟨to contest a will⟩ ⟨to contest an election⟩, and *contend* is intransitive ⟨to contend against an opponent⟩. *Contend* may be transitive when it means "to maintain, assert," and is followed by *that* ⟨appellants contend that the notice was not timely filed⟩.

contestant is one of two terms used for a person who contests a will, the other being *caveator*. E.g., "If the will has been probated informally, a *contestant* may initiate the formal probate within three years from the decedent's death to set aside the informal probate and either probate another will or have the decedent adjudicated intestate." Additionally, *contestant* = a participant in a competition. The word has been common only since the mid-nineteenth century. See **caveator.**

contestation. See **contest,** n.

contested election, in the U.S., means "an

election the validity of whose results has been challenged"; in G.B., it means "a political race with more than one candidate." See **candidacy.**

context of, in the; in a . . . context. This phrase is often used superfluously. E.g., "The Commission's rationale for the mosaic that finally emerges [see METAPHORS, MIXED & MANGLED] with respect to principal transactions not only is interesting, *but also may be helpful in the context of understanding* [read *but also may be helpful in understanding*] the related issue of a dealer's obligation in principal transactions to charge prices reasonably related to the market price."/ "During the seventh century B.C., Egypt was repeatedly though always briefly occupied by Assyrian armies and later *infiltrated by Greek and other Aegean elements in a military and subsequently a commercial context* [read *infiltrated militarily and later commercially by Greek and other Aegean elements*]."

contiguous means, not merely "close to" or "near," but "adjacent." It is commonly misused in the phrase *the forty-eight contiguous states,* which is illogical, inasmuch as only a few states can be *contiguous* to one another. *Contiguous to* for *next to* is sometimes a pomposity. (See **adjacent.** Cf. **adjoin.**) This adjective should always be construed with *to.* E.g., "In this appeal, Mirador argues that it has a valid easement over Booker's lot, which is *contiguous* on the southern side *to* Mirador's landlocked parcel."

contingency, -ce. The latter is a NEEDLESS VARIANT.

contingent fee; contingency fee. The former is the preferred form of this term. It denotes an agreement that no fee will be charged for the lawyer's services unless the lawsuit is successful or is settled out of court. Usually, a contingent fee calls for larger compensation to be paid than the lawyer would normally charge, often a percentage of the money recovered or the money saved, to compensate for the risk involved. Cf. **champerty.**

contingent remainder; contingent interest. Each phrase is used on both sides of the Atlantic, but the former is more common in both the U.S. and G.B. See **remainder.**

15

continual; continuous. *Continual* = frequently recurring. E.g., "Many stock certificates have been and are being issued daily in the names of two or more persons as joint tenants with rights of survivorship and issuing corporations and their transfer agents are *continually* acting in reliance upon the effectiveness of the survivorship provisions."

Continuous = occurring without interruption. E.g., *continuous use*, in reference to a roadway, etc., is wrong for *continual use.* Here *continuous* correctly appears: "*Continuously* since May 28, 1906, J. S. K. and M. E. K. have been husband and wife."/ "Although the witnesses sign first, by the weight of authority the attestation is effective if the testator and witness sign in one *continuous* transaction."

continuance; continuation; continuity. *Continuance* has virtually opposite senses in lay and legal usage. Generally, it means (1) "keeping up, going on with, maintaining, or prolonging"; or (2) "duration; time of continuing." E.g., "Plaintiff is entitled to this higher salary during his *continuance* in defendant's employ."/ "The fact that any person was born during the *continuance* of a valid marriage between his mother and any man is generally conclusive proof that he is the legitimate child of his mother's husband." (Eng.)

But in American law, it means "postponement; the adjournment or deferring of a trial or other proceeding until a future date" ⟨motion for continuance⟩. E.g., "There is no support in the record for the complaint that the district court failed to grant a *continuance* to the defense." See **continue.**

Continuation = continued maintenance; carrying on or resumption of (an action, etc.); that by which a thing is continued (*COD*). E.g., "The question whether a corporation is a *continuation* of a predecessor has been fermenting in the past decade."/ "During the *continuation* of the relation, the attorney, for most purposes, stands in the place of the client, who will be bound by whatever the attorney may do or say, in the regular course of practice, in the conduct of the cause."/ "*Continuation* of the use of the property as a municipal park carries out a larger share of Bacon's purpose than the complete destruction of such use by the decree we today affirm."

Continuity = connectedness; unbrokenness; uninterruptedness ⟨the continuity of the litigation process was broken up by a number of continuances⟩.

continue; stay, v.t. "We are accustomed to *continue* an action in the sense of plodding on. But it was possible in Scotland and was once possible in England (and still is in legal language) to *continue* in the sense of knocking off or adjourning." I. Brown, *I Give You My Word* 112 (1964). It is this transitive use of *continue* (= to postpone) in legal contexts that yields the legal use of *continuance,* q.v.

Only in legal parlance is *stay* current as a transitive verb. Stranger than *continue, stay* means "to stop, arrest, delay, prevent (an action or proceeding)" ⟨to stay the proceedings⟩. E.g., "I do order that until such indemnity be given all further proceedings be *stayed.*" (Eng.) See **stay.**

continue on is a minor but bothersome prolixity. E.g., "The pleader's standoffish 'one' *continued on* as meaningless rote." *Continue* or *persist* is always better than *continue on.*

continuity. See **continuance.**

continuous. See **continual.**

continuum. Pl. *continuums* or *continua.* The foreign plural should be eschewed.

contours is such a popular metaphor that it has become a VOGUE WORD among lawyers and judges. E.g., "The EEOC administrative regulations provide some basis for outlining the *contours* of the accommodation duty."

contra, n., adj., adv., & prep., is a LEGALISM for *against, contrary,* etc. Except as a signal in citations, it should be avoided in favor of its more common equivalents. E.g., "Partitions in kind as well as partitions by sale and division of the proceeds were sustained, although there was some *contra* [read *contrary*] authority invalidating a partition in kind."/ "These provisions of the Code are, of course, *contra* [read *contrary*] to the common-law rules that have discouraged use of powers of attorney."/ "That case is, on its surface, *contra* [read *to the contrary*], but the use of a questionnaire and its relationship to Rule 4(a) were not considered by the court."

contracept, v.i., is a BACK-FORMATION that is not included in the dictionaries. It is a jargonistic word popular among social workers. E.g., "Rather than become pregnant, our adolescents should learn about sex and, if they are to be active, *contracept* [read *use contraception*]."

contract, n. & v. **A.** General Slipperiness. "One moment the word [*contract*] may be *the agreement* of the parties; and then, with a rapid and unexpected shift, the writer or speaker may use the term to indicate the *contractual obligation* created by law as a result of the agreement." W. N. Hohfeld, *Fundamental Legal Conceptions* 31 (1919; repr. 1946). Legal writers should be sensitive to any such semantic change within a given context.

B. Pronunciation. As a noun, *contract* is accented on the first syllable /*kon-trakt*/; as a verb, on the second /*kŏn-trakt*/. Cf. **contrast** & **compact.**

C. And *covenant. Contract* is the general term. *Covenant* now applies (1) to agreements under seal, and (2) to undertakings contained in deeds or implied by law in deeds, as in the phrase *covenant running with the land.*

D. And *agreement.* See **agreement.**

contract breach is inferior to *breach of contract.* E.g., "It is true, as plaintiffs contend, that the victim of the *contract breach* [read *breach of contract*] may recover damages that would place him in the same position he would have occupied if the defaulting party had performed." (Use of *victim* in reference to one disadvantaged by breach of contract borders on OVERSTATEMENT.)

contract-breaker = breacher. E.g., "A *contract-breaker* can be charged with the amount of an expected gain that his breach has prevented, if, when the contract was made, he had reason to foresee that his breach would prevent it from occurring." See **breacher.**

contract implied in law. See **quasi contract** & **implied contract.**

CONTRACTIONS should be avoided in all but the most informal writing. The one exception is that they are permissible when one quotes, in a formal context, the spoken or written words of another. See **cannot.**

contract quasi. See **implied contract** & **quasi contract.**

contradictory, -tive, -tional; contradictious. *Contradictory* = opposite, contrary. *Contradictious* = inclined to contradict or quarrel; the word is applied to persons. *Contradictive* and *contradictional* are NEEDLESS VARIANTS of *contradictory.*

contradistinction; contrast. These words may be distinguished, if not contradistinguished. *Contradistinction* = distinction by opposition; *contrast* = dissimilarity (but not necessarily opposition). E.g., "The Seventh Amendment preserves the right to a jury trial not only for suits in which the right existed at common law, but also for suits in which legal rights were to be ascertained and determined, in *contradistinction* to those in which equitable rights alone were recognized, and equitable remedies were administered."/ "The word 'children' in its primary and natural sense is always a word of purchase and not of limitation; it is employed in *contradistinction* to the term 'issue.'"/ "[T]hese differences in phraseology . . . must not be too literally *contradistinguished* [i.e., be too literally made to seem opposites]." *Brush v. Commissioner,* 300 U.S. 352, 362 (1937).

Contradistinction should not be used where *contrast* suffices. E.g., "The term 'constitution' is ordinarily employed to designate organic law in *contradistinction* [read *contrast*] to the term 'laws,' which is generally used to designate statutes or legislative acts."

contraindicate began as a medical term meaning "to make (as a treatment) inadvisable." It has made its way into legal parlance, despite the contraindication of use of such jargon. E.g., "The plan shall include provision for a system to ensure that no prisoner is assigned to do work that is *contraindicated* [read *inadvisable*] given his medical condition."

contra proferentem is a TERM OF ART, the name of the doctrine that, in interpreting documents, ambiguities are to be construed against (unfavorably to) the drafter. E.g., "On appeal, AHP argues principally that we should reverse the judgment of the district court and enter judgment in its favor on the ground that the language of the policies is ambiguous and that one of the two interpretations of the policies advocated by AHP should thus be adopted under the doctrine of *contra proferentem.*"

contrary takes the preposition *to; from* is no longer standard.

contrast. A. Prepositions with. One *contrasts* something *with* something else, not *to;* but it is permissible to write either *in contrast to* or *in contrast with.*

C. *Compare and contrast* is an English teacher's REDUNDANCY. See **compare.**

D. Pronunciation. As a noun, *contrast* is accented on the first syllable /**kon**-trast/; as a verb, on the second /kŏn-**trast**/.

contravene; controvert. These words, occasionally confused, should be distinguished. *Contravene* = (1) (of persons) to transgress, infringe (as a law); to defy; (2) (of things) to be contrary to, come in conflict with. E.g., "It is argued that the regulation, in limiting the amount of money any single household may receive, *contravenes* a basic purpose of federal law."/ "The court ruled that the statutory provision was a penalty and that allowing a wrongdoer to insure himself against it would *contravene* public policy."

Controvert = to dispute or contest; to debate; to contend against or oppose in argument. E.g., "Under the pleadings, when the issues were joined in fraud, undue influence, failure of consideration, and mistake, the court had jurisdiction to hear and determine the *controverted* facts."/ "The appellant's counsel does not very seriously *controvert* the correctness of the answer finding the minor guilty of contributory negligence."

contribute for *attribute* is nothing less than a MALAPROPISM. But it is suprisingly common in the U.S.: "The great majority of these deaths can be *contributed* [read *attributed*] to misuse of smoking materials."/ "To what may we *contribute* [read *attribute*] the company's success on appeal?"

contribution; indemnity. These words frequently appear in tandem in the legal phrase *contribution and indemnity,* but many users of the phrase forget the individual significations of the words. *Contribution* is (1) the right to demand that another who is jointly responsible for injury to another contribute to the one required to compensate the victim, or (2) the actual payment by a joint tortfeasor of his share of what is due. It may entail an equal sharing of the loss, but in some jurisdictions entails a payment proportional to one's fault. *Indemnity* is (1) a duty to make good any loss, damage, or liability another has incurred, or (2) the right of an injured person to claim reimbursement for his loss. Whereas *contribution* involves a partial shifting of the economic loss, *indemnity* involves a complete

shifting of the economic loss. See **indemnity.**

Rather than use the phrase *contribution and indemnity* imprecisely and indiscriminately, the party seeking recompense should decide whether he is entitled only to one or the other, and then use that term only.

contributory, -tive, -torial, -tional. Each of these word forms has a different meaning. *Contributory* = (1) making contribution; that contributes to a common fund; or (2) bearing a share toward a purpose or result ⟨contributory negligence⟩. *Contributive* = having the power of contributing; conducive ⟨exercise is contributive to health⟩. *Contributorial* = of or relating to a contributor. *Contributional* = of or relating to (a) contribution. *Contributary* is a NEEDLESS VARIANT of *contributory.*

contributory negligence. See **comparative negligence & assumption of the risk.**

controller. See **comptroller.**

controvert. See **contravene.**

contumacious; contemptuous. Both terms mean roughly "scornful," but the former is more frequently used as a legal term meaning "willfully disobedient of a court order." E.g., "Although certain money decrees are enforceable by contempt because they are not debts, imprisonment is nevertheless permissible only for *contumacious* behavior."/ "Finding that the record does not support a finding of *contumacious* conduct or a clear record of unexplained delay, we reverse the dismissal for plaintiff's failure to prosecute."

Here *contumacious* is used in the lay sense ("recalcitrant"), in which it is chiefly a literary word: "We should not encourage litigants to act *contumaciously* out of fear that otherwise their constitutional rights will evaporate."/ "Despite respondent's adamant—even *contumacious*—refusal to cooperate with Hotchkiss or to take the stand as Hotchkiss advised, Hotchkiss succeeded in getting a 'hung jury' [q.v.] on the two most serious charges at the first trial."

Contemptuous is the more usual term among laymen as the adjective for *contempt,* but it is used also in legal contexts, which usually favor *contumacious:* "Ordinarily purpose or intent is irrelevant in determining whether an offensive act is *contemptuous;* the nature of the act itself is determinative." *Ex parte Krupps,* 712 S.W.2d 144, 154 (Tex. Crim. App. 1986) (citing 13 Tex. Jur. 3d 182, Contempt § 1)./ "The NLRB petitioned this court for an adjudication of civil contempt against the company for violating an order of this court; the company's allegedly *contemptuous* conduct consists in maintaining an overbroad rule prohibiting employee solicitation and distribution of materials, including union campaign materials." See **contemptuous.**

contumac(it)y; contumely. *Contumacity* is a long NEEDLESS VARIANT for *contumacy* (= willful contempt of court). *Contumacy,* then, is a particular kind of *contempt of court,* q.v. E.g., "In case of *contumacy,* the Chancellor would order the arrest of the defendant, and his imprisonment for contempt." (Eng.) The adjectival form is *contumacious,* q.v.

Contumaciousness should be reserved for the sense "the quality of being contumacious," and should not be used as a longer variant of the preferred noun: "While we do not wish to understate the significance of this omission, we find it to be more a matter of negligence than of purposeful delay or *contumaciousness* [read *contumacy*]."

Contumely, easily confused with *contumacy,* is a literary word meaning "rude and haughty language." Thus Shakespeare wrote, in *Hamlet,* of "the proud man's contumely."

contusion. See **concussion.**

convener, -or. The first is the preferred form. See -ER, -OR.

conventione(e)r. Today the usual term for one attending a convention is *conventioneer.*

conversable. See **conversible.**

conversation(al)ist. The standard term is *conversationalist.* Older authorities preferred *conversationist,* but the word is little used.

converse; reverse; obverse; inverse. These words denote various types of opposition. *Converse* = a statement derived from another statement by transposing important antithetical members (equitable support without legal foundation, legal foundation without equitable support). *Obverse* = the inference of another proposition with a contra-

dictory predicate by changing the quality of the original proposition (no men are immortal, all men are mortal) (*COD*). *Inverse* = the inference of another proposition in which the subject term is the negative of the subject of the original proposition and the predicate is unchanged (no colorable challenge of this trial could be entirely frivolous, some non-colorable challenge of this appeal could be frivolous). *Reverse,* the broadest of these terms, means simply "the contrary."

Conversely = in the converse manner or order; by conversion. E.g., "Words that are libelous per se do not need an innuendo, and, *conversely,* words that need an innuendo are not libelous per se." Here the word is nonsensically used: "Subadditivity means that it is always cheaper to have a single firm produce whatever combination of outputs is supplied to the market, *and conversely* [read *and it is more expensive to have several firms produce whatever output is supplied to the market*]."

conversible, -able; convertible. *Conversible* is a NEEDLESS VARIANT of *convertible. Conversable* = oral. See -ABLE (A).

conversion means, in tort law, "the act of wrongfully converting (something) to one's own use." This sense is virtually unknown to laymen. The adjectival form of the word is *conversionary.*

convertible. See **conversible.**

convey. A. And *conveyance,* v.t. The latter, hypothetically "to accomplish the conveyance of," does not exist except as implied in the form of the agent noun *conveyancer,* q.v., and the gerund *conveyancing,* q.v. This verb denotes what the lawyer does. *Convey* denotes what the seller does (usu. through a lawyer). See **conveyancer.**

In the phrase *convey away, away* is unnecessary. See PARTICLES, UNNECESSARY.

B. For *confer.* This is an inexplicable lapse. E.g., "Appellee's and appellant's respective citizenships of France and Georgia therefore *conveyed* [read *conferred*] diversity jurisdiction on the federal courts." See **confer.**

conveyance, n. **A. Legal Senses.** In law, the noun *conveyance* refers not only to the actual transfer of an interest in land, but also to the document (usually a deed) by which the transfer occurs.

B. For *car* or *automobile*. *Conveyance* is sometimes used as a FORMAL WORD for *car*. It should be avoided when possible. E.g., "The negligence of a driver of a private *conveyance* [read *car*] was not imputed to the guest." The only context in which it might be justified is that in which the writer intends to be so broad as to cover any vehicle, vessel, or aircraft.

C. And *conveyal*. *Conveyance* is the better noun corresponding to the verb *to convey; conveyal* is a NEEDLESS VARIANT.

conveyance, v.t. See **convey** (A).

conveyancer; conveyor, -er. The two terms are distinct. A *conveyor* (the *-or* spelling predominates in legal contexts) must usually have a *conveyancer*, a lawyer specializing in real estate transactions. Hence the English law journal entitled *The Conveyancer*. A *conveyor* is the person who transfers or delivers title to another. E.g., "The conveyance shall be given effect according to the intention of the *conveyor*."/ "After the English Chancellor began to enforce uses it was contended that a use for the *conveyor* or the person furnishing the consideration for the conveyance was presumed if no consideration was furnished by the conveyee and no use was expressed for the conveyee." See -ER, -OR & **convey.**

Outside law, *conveyer* is the general spelling for "one that conveys." In mechanical uses, however, as in *conveyor belt*, the *-or* spelling is standard.

conveyancing, a term more common in G.B. than in the U.S., is often understood in a sense analogous to that of *conveyance* (= the document by which land is purchased). E.g., "Lawyers have been doing basically the same things—*conveyancing* property, drawing up wills, and so on—for a long time." (Eng.) Actually, however, it has a much wider import. *Conveyancing* comprises the drafting and completion of all kinds of legal instruments, not just those having to do with the transfer of land. E.g., "Even in those statutes, the same objectives in administering trusts can be obtained by proper *conveyancing* techniques."

conveyee (= one to whom property is conveyed) is a legal NEOLOGISM not recorded in dictionaries. For an example of its use, see the second quotation under **conveyancer.** See also -EE.

convict, v.t. In the legal idiom, one is convicted *of* crimes but *on* counts.

convictable, -ible. The former is preferred. See -ABLE (A).

conviction, it may surprise some readers to know, is used in reference to misdemeanors as well as to felonies.

conviction-prone. See **guilt-prone.**

convince; persuade. Generally, *convince* is properly followed by an *of*-phrase or a *that*-clause ⟨he convinced the jury of his client's innocence⟩ ⟨he convinced the jury that his client was innocent⟩. *Persuade* is usually followed by an infinitive. It is a fall from stylistic grace to write "He *convinced her to go through with the crime* [read *persuaded her to go through with the crime*; or better: *persuaded her to commit the crime*]." See **persuade.**

co-opt = (1) to select as a member; or (2) to assimilate; absorb. The preferred nominal form is *co-optation,* not *co-option;* the preferred adjectival form is *co-optative,* not *co-optive.*

copacetic; copesetic. The former spelling is preferred for this tongue-in-cheek term meaning "okay; satisfactory." The word is informal and jocular.

coparcener. A. And *parcener.* The latter has become a NEEDLESS VARIANT, though dating from the thirteenth century, whereas *coparcener* dates from the fifteenth century. The prefix *co-* emphasizes the jointness in the term's meaning "a joint heir." Cf. **copartner.**

B. And *copartner.* These were originally the same word, *partner* having been a corrupt spelling of *parcener* in the thirteenth century. Now, however, the DIFFERENTIATION between the words is so complete that few know of their common origin. See the following entry.

copartner need not exist alongside *partner.* The joint relationship (i.e., that the existence of one partner implies the existence of one or more other partners) is clear to all native speakers of English. (That jointness is not clear in *parcener* — see **coparcener.**) Because *copartner* adds nothing to the language of the law, it should be avoided.

copesetic. See **copacetic.**

coplaintiff. See **codefendant.**

copulable derives from *couple,* v.t., not from *copulate.*

COPULAS, ADVERBS OR ADJECTIVES AFTER. See ADVERBS (C).

copulate. See **fornicate.**

copy, v.t., in the sense "to send a copy to" ⟨He copied me with the letter⟩, is a voguish casualism to be avoided. It is fast becoming standard American lawyer's ARGOT.

copyright has existed as a verb since the early nineteenth century. Hence the adjective *copyrightable.*

copywrite is a not infrequent mistake for *copyright.* Cf. *playwriting* for *playwrighting.*

coram (lit., "in the presence of") begins many of the LATINISMS known to the law. *Coram nobis* (= before us; the court of King's Bench, originally) was the name of a writ of error directed to a court for review of its own judgments and predicated on alleged errors of fact. E.g., "This is an appeal from a judgment denying this appellant's petition for writ of error *coram nobis.*" *Coram vobis* (= before you) gave its name to the writ of error by an appellate court to a trial court for correction of the latter's error of fact. These phrases are obsolescent if not obsolete in most jurisdictions.

Two other phrases in which *coram* appears are *coram judice* (= in the presence of a judge) and *coram populo* (= in public). Both are unjustifiable LATINISMS. See **coram non judice.**

coram non judice = (1) outside the presence of a judge; or (2) before a judge but not the proper one, or one who cannot take legal cognizance of the matter. This is the one LATINISM beginning with *coram* that is still fairly frequently used. E.g., "When a judge acts in the clear absence of all jurisdiction, the proceeding is *coram non judice.*"/ "If a judge issues a pretended process, one unknown to the law, the proceeding is *coram non judice* and the judge is liable in trespass to the party injured." See LATINISMS.

corespondent; correspondent. There is an important difference between these terms. In jurisdictions in which appellees are called *respondents, corespondent* = co-appellee. This word has a more specific legal meaning, however; in divorce suits, when adultery was commonly a ground for divorce, the *corespondent* was the man charged with the adultery and proceeded against together with the wife, or *respondent.* E.g., "The judge clearly disbelieved the *corespondent,* who was the key witness on the issue of adultery." (Eng.)/ "The *corespondent* cited in the supplemental petition was called and gave evidence of adultery which was completely denied by the wife." (Eng.)

A *correspondent,* of course, is a letter-writer, an on-location news-gatherer, or a business representative.

corollarily is a failed lexical experiment. "*Corollarily* [read *As a corollary*], it would follow that such an extent of actual application may occur as to provide substantial probativeness of the reasonableness of the understanding and belief engaged in." *United Medical Laboratories, Inc. v. Columbia Broadcasting System, Inc.,* 404 F.2d 706, 707 (9th Cir. 1968). The *OED* notes that the adjectival use of *corollary* is "rare"; the adverbial use is not mentioned, and would not have been here but for an ill-advised fancy on the part of a judge.

coroner; coronator. The latter is a NEEDLESS VARIANT.

corporal; corporeal. These terms have undergone DIFFERENTIATION. *Corporal* = of or affecting the body ⟨corporal punishment⟩. The meaning is unclear here: "He participated in four *corporal* lineups." *Corporeal* = having a physical material body, substantial ⟨corporeal beings, as opposed to spiritual ones⟩. E.g., "Ancient German law, like ancient Roman law, sees great difficulties in the way of an assignment of a debt or other benefit of a contract; men do not see how there can be a transfer of a right unless that right is embodied in some *corporeal* thing."

In the following sentence, *corporeal* is misused for *corporal:* "The court may punish *corporeally* [read *corporally*] by imprisonment."

corporate law; corporation law; company law. The usual term in the U.S. for the law of corporations.is *corporate law.* The equivalent in G.B. is *company law.,* q.v. *Corporation law* is a variant phrase occasionally used.

corporateness now has only the sense "the quality of being a body corporate [i.e. a corporation]." E.g., "The name of a corporation must contain a word indicating *corporateness.*" Formerly it meant "corpulence" and "bodiliness" as well.

corporation, in the U.S., refers to "an entity (usu. a business) with authority under law to act as a single person, with rights to issue stock and exist indefinitely." In England, *corporation* (or *body corporate,* q.v.) is defined more broadly as "an entity that has legal personality, i.e. that is capable of enjoying and being subject to legal rights and duties" (*CDL*). Often, in G.B., where *company* is the more usual term, *corporation* is used elliptically to mean a *municipal corporation* (= the authorities of a municipality that carry on civic business). See **juristic person.**

corporational is a NEEDLESS VARIANT of *corporate.*

corporation law. See **corporate law.**

corporeal. See **corporal.**

corporeal hereditaments = land and fixtures. The defining words are preferable to this highfalutin LEGALISM, the precise meaning of which is unclear even to some seasoned lawyers. See **hereditament(s).**

corporeality; corporeity. A distinction is possible. *Corporeality* = corporeal existence; *corporeity* = materiality, substantiality, the quality of having substance.

corpus; principal; res; trust property; subject matter of the trust. These are the various terms used in reference to the property held by a trustee. *Principal,* q.v., *trust property,* and *subject matter of the trust* are perhaps most comprehensible to laymen, and might be preferred on that account. The five terms are widely used in legal writing, however, and it is unlikely that any of them will disappear. See **res.**

Corpus is the Latin word meaning "body." It usually denotes an abstract collection or body ⟨a substantial corpus of legal commen-

tary in this field⟩. In the following sentences, *corpus* is used in its most usual legal context, involving trusts: "The *corpus* of the trust was composed of securities."/ "The trustee was authorized to distribute trust income or *corpus* to the beneficiaries."/ "The power to pay out trust *corpus* necessarily involves a power to terminate the trust in whole or in part." The plural form is *corpora.*

corpus delicti (lit., "the body of a crime") is generally outmoded as a variant of *actus reus,* q.v. The general sense of *corpus delicti* is "the nature of the transgression." E.g., "The confession in evidence was an extrajudicial confession—voluntary and without pressure, after caution and after the *corpus delicti* had been established." *McDaniel v. Commonwealth,* 183 Va. 481, 32 S.E.2d 667, 670 (1945). The one (lay) sense in which it is not likely to disappear is "the body of a murdered person." The phrase is sometimes misspelled *corpus delecti,* a sort of macabre etymological double entendre. E.g., "The confession may be used to establish the *corpus delecti* [read *corpus delicti*]." *Wooldridge v. State,* 653 S.W.2d 811, 816 (Tex. Crim. App. 1983).

corpus juris = the body of law; the law as the sum of laws. E.g., "We must then determine what *corpus juris* governs the third-party defendant's liability to Marathon for the extra repair expenses caused by the hydrocouple failure." The term is well known because of the treatise entitled *Corpus Juris Secundum;* in normal contexts, however, it is best to write *body of law.* See LATINISMS.

correctable, -ible. The former is preferred. See -ABLE (A).

correctitude; correctness. *Correctitude* is a PORTMANTEAU WORD or blend of *correct* and *rectitude.* It refers to what is proper in conduct or behavior, and has moralistic overtones. *Correctness* serves as the noun of *correct,* adj., in all its other senses. E.g., "The *correctness* of the decision is maintained, with an able and elaborate discussion of reasons and authorities, in *Langdell on Contracts.*"

correctional; corrective. *Correctional* = of or pertaining to correction, usu. penal correction ⟨correctional institution⟩. E.g., "He demonstrated by his plea that he is ready and willing to admit his crime and to enter the *correctional* system in a frame of mind that affords hope for success in rehabilitation." *Corrective* = tending to correct ⟨corrective measures⟩.

correctness. See **correctitude.**

CORRELATIVE CONJUNCTIONS, or conjunctions used in pairs, should frame structurally identical sentence-parts, sometimes called "matching parts." Simple nouns never cause problems: *both lions and wolves.* When we use constructions with noun phrases and even clauses, however, PARALLELISM may become a problem. Following are examples with some of the more common correlative conjunctions.

A. *Neither . . . nor.* "The jury may have concluded that the entranceway was neither negligently constructed *nor maintained* [read *nor negligently maintained*] by the Investment Company."/ "Finding *neither error of law or fact* [read *neither error of law nor error of fact,* or *error neither of fact nor of law*], we affirm."

B. *Either . . . or.* "Easements can be of either *an affirmative or negative nature* [read *can be either affirmative or negative in nature*]." See **either** (A).

C. *Both . . . and.* "*Both* teachers *and* students have pressed their first amendment rights of free speech to *both* assign and read materials *and* to discuss topics of their choice." Using *both . . . and* twice in one sentence should be avoided. In this sentence note also that students have not *pressed to assign materials*—only *teachers* have. One must be certain that all that follows modifies both subjects, not just one. Further, the splitting of the infinitive here adds to the reader's burden; "to both assign" should read "both to assign . . . and to discuss topics of their choice."

D. *Although . . . yet.* "*Although* the rule is apparently otherwise in a majority of the other American jurisdictions, *yet* we hold that statutes of limitation run as well between spouses as between strangers." This constuction, like the one illustrated in the next example, occurs in formal prose; it has become less and less common to use both *although* and *yet.*

E. *Notwithstanding . . . yet.* "*Notwithstanding* that the interests may be adverse, *yet* if they are to be amicably adjusted there may be no impropriety in having each side represented by the same counsel." See (D).

F. Other Correlatives. Some of the other common correlatives in English are: *although . . . nevertheless; as . . . as; if . . . then; just as . . . so; not only . . . but also; since . . . therefore; when . . . then; where . . . there; whether . . . or.*

correspondent. See **Corespondent**

corrigendum; erratum. These words are used synonymously to note errors made in printing discovered only after the work has gone to press. *Corrigendum* (lit., "correction") is perhaps technically more accurate (inasmuch as a correction is being made). But *erratum* (lit., "error") is older in English and more common. The plurals are *corrigenda* and *errata.*

corroborate should be used transitively ⟨the last witness corroborated the testimony of other witnesses⟩. The intransitive sense ("to give confirmation," in contrast with "to give confirmation *to*") should be avoided. Thus one writes, "The circumstances *corroborate* his presence in the city when the crime was committed," not, "The circumstances *corroborate* with his presence in the city when the crime was committed." In other words, *corroborate with* is inferior to *corroborate.*

corroboration = the confirmation of (a statement) by additional evidence. E.g., "Because the testimony of a settlor seeking to revoke a trust is likely to be unreliable, and because solemn written instruments are not to be lightly overturned, strong *corroboration* of the settlor's testimony is required in order to warrant the granting of relief."

corroborative, -tory. The former is standard, *-tory* being a NEEDLESS VARIANT. "The witness's status as an accomplice, in the absence of *corroborative* evidence, was solely a question of state law."

corrodible, -sible. The former is preferred, because with it the verb from which the adjective derives is more readily apparent. See -ABLE (A).

corrupter, -or. The *-er* spelling is preferred. See -ER, -OR.

cost-effective and *cost-efficient* are the current jargonistic adjectival phrases for *economical.* See VOGUE WORDS.

cotemporaneous; cotemporary. See **contemporary.**

coterminous; coterminant; coterminate; coterminal; conterminous. *Conterminous* is the oldest and the basic term meaning "having or enclosed within a common boundary." *Coterminous,* an altered form of the original term, shares the meaning of *conterminous,* but also means "coextensive in extent or duration." For the sake of DIFFERENTIATION, *coterminous* should be confined to this figurative or metaphorical sense, and *conterminous* reserved for physical and tangible senses. E.g., "A proprietor whose full rights of ownership extend up to a common terminal with those of the petitioner is an immediately *conterminous* [read *coterminous*] proprietor." (Eng.)/ "It cannot be seriously argued as a general matter that the constitutional limits of congressional power are *coterminous* with the extent of its exercise in the late eighteenth and early nineteenth centuries."

Coterminant, coterminate, and *coterminal* are NEEDLESS VARIANTS.

cotortfeasor is inferior to *co-tortfeasor,* because the length of the word deceives the eye, *cotort* (suggesting *cohort*) wrongly seeming at first to be the primary word rather than *tortfeasor.*

could not help but. See **cannot help but.**

council; counsel. *Council* (= a deliberative assembly) is primarily a noun. *Counsel* (= to advise) is primarily a verb, but in legal writing is used commonly in the sense "a legal adviser or legal advisers." See **counsel & consul.**

councillor; counselor. The former is a member of a council, the latter one who gives advice (usu. legal advice). See **attorney** (A).

councilmanic is an unfortunate adjectival form of *councilman.*

counsel.   A. Scope of Term. In G.B., *counsel* is used only of barristers (litigators), whereas in the U.S. it is frequently used of office practitioners (e.g., *general counsel*) as well as of litigators.
   B. Number. *Counsel* may be either singular or plural; in practice it is usually plural. Here is an example of *counsel* as a singular noun: "Counsel *is* reminded that allegations sufficient for this showing must be included within the complaint."

Following are the more typical examples of its use as a plural; in 1819, the court reporter in *McCulloch v. Maryland* wrote: "The Court dispensed with its general rule, permitting only *two counsel* to argue for each party."

Counsels has mistakenly appeared as a plural of *counsel:* "Some of the argument, by agreement between the *counsels* [read *counsel*], does not appear in the record." See **attorney** (A), **consul & council.**

counsel fees.   See **attorney's fees.**

counsel(l)or; counsel(l)ing, -el(l)able. The preferred spellings are *counselor, counseling,* and *counselable* in the U.S., and *counsellor, counselling,* and *counsellable* in G.B. See DOUBLING OF FINAL CONSONANTS & **attorney** (A).

COUNT & MASS (NONCOUNT) NOUNS. Count nouns are those that denote enumerable things, and that are capable of forming plurals (e.g., *cases, parties, settlements, offers*); mass (noncount) nouns are often abstract nouns—they cannot be enumerated (e.g., *mitigation, courage, mud*). Many nouns can be both count ("He gave several *talks*") and mass ("*Talk* is cheap"), depending on the sense. These are few, however, in comparison to the nouns that are exclusively either count or mass. Use of these two types of nouns may implicate problems with NUMBER, especially when the use of count nouns strays into a use of mass nouns or vice versa. See PLURALS (B).
   A. *Fewer* and *less.* A good rule of thumb is to use *fewer* with plural nouns (*calories, soldiers*) and *less* with singular nouns (*unemployment, discrimination*). A beer may have fewer, but not less, calories. See **less** (A).
   B. Treating a Mass Noun as a Count Noun. One may have a "congeries of negligent acts," but not a "congeries of negligence." Here are some other examples of mistakenly treating mass nouns as if they were countable: "For *every violence* [read *every act of violence*], there is a victim."/ "*A compliance with* [read *Compliance with*] the demand would have exposed defendant to danger of bodily harm." See PLURALS (B). On a related point, see COLLECTIVE NOUNS.

countenance, give . . . to is usually an unnecessary PERIPHRASIS for *countenance, v.t.* E.g., "Courts have indeed used language that *seems to give countenance to* [read *seems to countenance*] the notion that, if a plot is worked out, it cannot be copyrighted."

counterclaim is one word, unhyphenated. See **cross-claim.**

countersignature = a second signature on an instrument attesting to its authenticity. The verb is *to countersign.*

countervail = to counterbalance; to compensate for. This word is probably used one-hundred times in legal writing for every time it appears in nonlegal writing. E.g., "The interests of nonminorities in not taking another test do not sufficiently *countervail* these needs."

The word most often appears as a participial adjective. E.g., "Vidrine filed no *countervailing* affidavits."/ "Nevertheless, *countervailing* policy considerations have been evident ever since the Statutes of Mortmain, restricting the amounts of wealth that may be transferred out of the normal channels of social organization." There is nothing inherently wrong with the word, but *countervailing considerations* is on the verge of becoming a legal CLICHÉ.

countless applies only to COUNT NOUNS. E.g., "Porters recently have been carrying *countless* baggage to and from passengers' cars." One may have *countless bags* but not *countless baggage.* See COUNT & MASS NOUNS.

coupled with. See **together with.**

coupon should be pronounced /koo-pon/. The first syllable is distressingly often sounded as /kyu/. This pronunciation betrays an ignorance of French and of the finer points of English. One bristles to imagine *coup d'etat* pronounced with /kyu/ as the first syllable.

court. A. Metonymy. *Court* is frequently used as a metonymous substitute for *judge.* E.g., "The *court himself,* possessed of a countenance and bearing elsewhere commanding, appeared little more than a pygmy here, in spite of *his* elevation on the bench." (Ex. fr. Horwill, *Modern American Usage* (2d ed. 1944)

s.v. *court.*)/ "The district *court* again stated the opinion that *he* disagreed with the circuit court and its conclusion bearing on the sufficiency of evidence."/ "In our opinion, it would seriously restrict the trial *court's* ability to partition the community estate fairly if *he* had no power to direct the named insured of title to life insurance policies that are an integral part of the community estate."

B. As a Collective Noun. Today *court* is used in the U.S. as a COLLECTIVE NOUN taking a singular verb. In G.B., the plural verb usually appears with this noun, when more than one judge sits on the court: "The *court* of appeal *have* concurred." (Eng.) Long ago, this construction was common even in the U.S.: "The *Court were* unanimously of opinion, that writs of error to remove causes to this court from inferior courts, can regularly issue only from the clerk's office of this court." *West v. Barnes,* 2 U.S. (2 Dall.) 401 (1791) (mem.).

courthouse. One word.

court-martial is hyphenated both as noun and as verb. The *OED* lists the verb as colloquial, an observation now antiquated. As to spelling, in the U.S., the final *-l* is not doubled in *court-martialed* and *court-martialing,* although in G.B. it is. See DOUBLING OF FINAL CONSONANTS. The plural of the noun is *courts-martial.*

court of appeal(s). Both forms appear, but *appeals* is more common in the U.S., whereas *appeal* is the only form in G.B. The correct form is the statutorily prescribed or the customary form of a given jurisdiction. Following is an example of the less usual American form: "In 93 Cal. App. 2d 43, the Court of *Appeal* affirmed the judgment."

court of first instance = (1) a court in which any proceedings are initiated; or (2) the trial court as opposed to an appellate court. The *CDL* marks sense (2) as a loose usage.

court of law is a formal phrase for *court,* which suffices in ordinary legal contexts. E.g., "The word 'say' is important in this context, because when a document is under scrutiny in a *court of law,* attention will be paid only to what, as a piece of natural language, it appears actually to declare." (Eng.) Today *court of law* often merely emphasizes the dignity of the judicial institution referred to; but in a few jurisdictions, and certainly in historical contexts, it may usefully distinguish a lawcourt from a court of equity or from some other type of court. See **lawcourt.**

cousinhood; cousinage. *Cousinage* has the disadvantage of possible confusion with *cozenage* (= fraud); thus *cousinhood* might be considered preferable.

couth, a BACK-FORMATION from *uncouth,* has never been accepted by authorities as a proper word.

covenant, v.i. & v.t. To *covenant* is to enter into a covenant or formal agreement, to agree or subscribe to by covenant. E.g., "A father *covenants* to transfer an estate to his daughter and her husband-to-be."/ "Other claims made by the appellant in respect of dispositions made by himself were allowed but the claim to deduct Mrs. Reynolds's *covenanted* payments was disallowed." (Eng.) Nonlawyers are unaccustomed to the verbal uses of the word. See **contract** (C).

covenantor, -er. The *-or* form is preferred. See -ER, -OR.

coverages. "Mr. P. is being paid a salary of approximately $61,000 per year including certain insurance *coverages.*" This plural of what has traditionally been a mass noun is now common. See PLURALS (B) and COUNT & MASS NOUNS.

covert; overt. *Covert* is best pronounced like *covered,* except with a *-t-* at the end /kuv-ert/. Still, /koh-vert/, nearly rhyming with *overt* (but for the accent), is the more common pronunciation in AmE nowadays. See **discovert.**

coverture = the condition or position of a woman during her married life, when she is by law under the authority and protection of her husband (*OED*). The word reeks of SEXISM, although it is unobjectionable in historical contexts. Traditionally used only in reference to wives, this word has recently been applied to husbands as well: "In community-property jurisdictions, with some exceptions, the spouse has an interest during *coverture* in the community fund."/ "At common law, dower

attached only to an estate of inheritance of which the husband was seised at some time during *coverture.*"

Usually, in contemporary contexts, some phrase such as *during marriage* will suffice in place of the legalistic *during coverture.* E.g., "Community property is a system of regulating rights and obligations of husband and wife *during coverture* [read *during marriage*]."

coworker. See **co-employee.**

cozen is a literary and archaic word meaning "to cheat." The word has never been used as a specific legal term, and is generally to be avoided in legal writing. See **cousinhood.**

cozenage. See **cousinhood.**

creator is a somewhat exalted name for one who establishes a trust. E.g., "The second type of statute provides that where the *creator* of such trust reserves to himself for his own benefit a power of revocation, a court, at the suit of any creditor of the *creator,* may compel the exercise of such power of revocation so reserved, to the same extent and under the same conditions that such *creator* could have exercised them." See **settlor.**

creature. Legal idiom has developed a peculiar kind of taxonomy, in which legal doctrines or principles are described as *creatures.* E.g.,"Adoption, in this country, is entirely a *creature of statute* and is unknown at common law."/ "The cause of action is wholly a *creature of equity.*" The *OED* quotes the following English example from 1855: "The railway and the rights of the railway are the *creatures* of the Act of Parliament." A useful phrase, *creature of* etc. should not be so overworked as to become another tiresome legal CLICHÉ.

credal. See **cre(e)dal.**

credible; credulous; creditable. *Credible* = believable; *credulous* = gullible, tending to believe; and *creditable* = worthy of credit, laudable. See **incredible.**

credit (= to give credence to) for *believe* is now almost peculiar to legal writing, but is an acceptable legal idiom: "Black and Danley contradicted each other in their testimony, and the court *credited* Danley."/ "It may be that the court below did not consider such evidence substantial or did not *credit* its validity, but we are unable to determine from a silent record the thought processes of the court below."/ "The trial judge was entitled to *credit* her testimony."

creditable; credulous. See **credible.**

cre(e)dal. The preferred spelling is *creedal;* the spelling *credal* is a nonstandard variant.

crevice; crevasse. These two words are often confused. A *crevice* is a narrow crack or break, as in a sidewalk or a wall. A *crevasse* is a large split or rupture, as in a levee, glacier, or embankment. E.g., "It is a fundamental principle that no damages lie against federal or state government, or local agencies, on account of an accidental *crevasse* in the levees."

crier (= a court officer who calls the court to order) has the variant spelling *cryer,* which is to be eschewed. Today the bailiff usually acts as crier; hence *bailiff* has almost supplanted the term *crier.* See **hear ye & oyez.**

criminality = the quality or fact of being criminal. "Underlying this specific issue are more fundamental principles regarding the creation of criminal liability and the extent to which a defendant's belief in the *criminality* of his acts affects such liability." This term has the variants *criminalness* and *criminalty,* neither of which should appear in modern legal writing.

criminalize, an Americanism of 1950s vintage, means "to make illegal; to outlaw." E.g., "Relying on . . . Iowa Code § 721.2 . . . , which *criminalizes* subornation of perjury, the Iowa court concluded that . . . Robinson's actions . . . were required." *Nix v. Whiteside,* 475 U.S. 157, 162 (1986)./ "With great force, Judge Newman argues in dissent that the entire indictment should be dismissed because Congress did not intend to *criminalize* the activities of commercial photo processors such as Petrov."

criminal law. See **civil law.**

criminalness; criminalty. See **criminality.**

criminate; incriminate. *Incriminate* is now the more usual form in both the U.S. and G.B., although 100 years ago *criminate* was the more common of the two. Today it is a NEEDLESS VARIANT. E.g., "The constable told the prisoner that he need not say anything to *criminate* [read *incriminate*] himself, but that what he did say would be taken down and used as evidence against him." (Eng.)/ "This Act qualifies the rule that a witness is not bound to answer questions that *criminate* [read *incriminate*] himself by declaring that he is not excused from answering questions that fix him with a civil liability." (Eng.)/ "In the law of evidence, the privilege against *self-crimination* [read (today) *self-incrimination*] signifies the mere negation of a duty to testify." (Hohfeld) See **incriminate.**

criminative, -tory. These are NEEDLESS VARIANTS of *incriminatory,* q.v. See **criminate.**

crisis forms the plural *crises,* not *crisises.*

criterion, -ria. *Criteria* is the plural, *criterion* the (originally Greek) singular. A Ph.D. in linguistics once defended *criteria* as a singular because "not everyone knows that the singular is *criterium*"! (Infrequently one even sees, though not infrequently enough, *criterias.*) The plural *criterions* was tried for a time, but failed to become standard. Here the correct forms are used: "The test is whether a handicapped individual who meets all employment *criteria* except for the challenged discriminatory *criterion* can perform the essential functions of the position in question without endangering the health and safety of others."

Following are examples of *criteria* wrongly made singular: "The determining *criteria* [read *criterion*] is the function of the attorneys' fees in the litigation process."/ "Appellant contends that the trial court used an improper *criteria* [read *criterion*] and denied appellant due process by basing its decision on its prior belief."

It has even happened that *criterion* has been mistaken as a plural, perhaps because *criteria* is so frequently misused as a singular: "In *Johnson,* a panel of this court noted that it was appropriate to carefully review the basis upon which the district court made its award, upon finding that improper *criterion* [read *criteria*] were utilized." See PLURALS (A).

cross-claim; counterclaim. In most American jurisdictions, *counterclaim* refers to a claim by a defendant against the plaintiff used as an offset against the original claim; and a *cross-claim* is a claim by one coparty against another, as by one defendant against a co-defendant. Each word has been used for the other, but this DIFFERENTIATION should be encouraged and fastidiously followed in practice. *Cross-claim* is now often spelled in the U.S. as one unhyphenated word.

In England, *counterclaim* is defined as "a cross-claim brought by a defendant in civil proceedings that asserts an independent cause of action but is not also a defense to the claim made in the action by the plaintiff" (*CDL*). *Cross-action* is frequently used in Great Britain for *cross-claim.* These terms are somewhat less restricted in G.B. than in the U.S., for *cross-claim* may refer either to (1) an action brought by the defendant against the plaintiff, or (2) an action brought by a defendant against a co-defendant in the same suit.

cross-complain is a variant of *cross-claim,* v.i. "The defendant *cross-complained* under the same contract."

cross-examination is hyphenated; *direct examination,* q.v., is not.

cross-national should always be hyphenated, just as *cross-cultural* should be. Many social scientists drop the hyphens to form single words. Cf. **transnational.**

c.t.a. See **administrator.**

cubiclize. See -IZE.

culpa is a civil-law term meaning "negligence." The English words *fault* and *negligence* are far preferable in English contexts. Pl. *-ae.*

culpable; inculpable; culpatory; culpose. *Culpable* = guilty, blameworthy. (See **blameworthy.**) *Inculpable* is a troublesome word to be avoided, for it may be interpreted as meaning either "able to be inculpated [i.e. guilty]," or "not culpable [i.e. innocent]." The latter sense has historically been attributed to the word.

Culpatory and *culpose* are rare terms, the former meaning "expressing blame," the latter "characterized by criminal negligence." Nei-ther has anything to recommend it; one who uses either term, or *inculpable* for that matter, is culpable of a stylistic infelicity.

cultiv(at)able. The shorter form is preferred. See -ATABLE.

cultured; cultivated. Correctly, the former is used of the person, the latter of the mind. A *cultured* person has refined tastes; a *cultivated* mind is well trained and highly developed.

cumbrance is a NEEDLESS VARIANT of *encumbrance,* q.v.

cum testamento annexo. See **administrator.**

cumulate. See **accumulate.**

cumulative, in its general lay sense, means "composed of accumulated parts; acquiring or increasing in force or cogency in successive additions" ⟨cumulative effect or argument⟩. The term has various specific legal senses. The most complex of these, used now chiefly in the corporate field, relates to a system of voting developed originally in nineteenth-century British school-board elections. *Cumulative voting* = a system of voting by which each voter has a number of votes equal to the number of representatives (usu. corporate officers) to be elected, so that a voter may concentrate all his votes on one person or distribute them as he wishes among the candidates.

Cumulative is used of evidence in the sense "tending to prove the same point that other evidence has already been offered to prove." In the context of wills, *cumulative* is sometimes used of legacies in the sense "given by the same testator to the same legatee." For the criminal-law sense of *cumulative,* see **concurrent.**

curable. In general English usage this word is used only of diseases; in legal usage, it is used in reference to any defects or deficiencies. Here *curable* = remediable, correctable: "We are confident that the deficiencies in the affidavits are readily *curable.*" / "Whatever harmful inferences might have been drawn from these questions were of the *curable* type and were removed by the court's instructions." See **cure.**

cur. adv. vult is the abbreviation of *curia advisari vult* (= the court wishes to consider the matter). It appears at the end of the written arguments reproduced in British law reports, and indicates that the judgment of the court was delivered (as Americans might always expect) on a date later than the hearing, rather than extemporaneously at the conclusion of the hearing, as is common in England. An alternative abbreviation is *c.a.v.* or *C.A.V.*

curative, -tory; curatorial. For the meaning "of or relating to the cure of diseases," *curative* is preferred. *Curative* is also used in the legal sense "corrective" ⟨curative instructions to the jury⟩. See **cure** & **curable.** *Curatory* is a NEEDLESS VARIANT. *Curatorial* = of or relating to a curator.

curator. See **conservator.**

curatory, -torial. See **curative.**

cure = to correct. In general usage, *cure* is used only in reference to diseases, literal or metaphorical; but in law it is used, as legal ARGOT, in reference to any defect or deficiency. Thus *incurable error* means "error at trial that cannot be corrected by the judge." E.g., "The plan proposed to *cure* a pre-petition default and acceleration on a debt on Grubb's principal residence." See **curable.**

curia advisari vult. See **cur. adv. vult.**

cursory; cursorial. *Cursory* = perfunctory; superficial. *Cursorial* = of or pertaining to running.

curtail means "to cut back," not "to stop completely." Therefore, it is difficult to ascertain what distinction the writer of this sentence intended: "Irrigation has cut down on, if not *curtailed,* water production of springs that once fed it."

Here *curtail* is correctly used: "Although a testator has broad power to dispose of his property by will, his power is *curtailed* to a limited degree by the operation of certain statutes and collateral common-law rules."

CURTAILED WORDS. See BACK-FORMATIONS.

curtesy; dower. These medieval common-law terms, which are defunct in England (the rights they represent having been abolished in 1925), live on in several American jurisdictions. The words denote correlative rights. *Curtesy* = the tenure, usu. a life estate, of a husband in the lands of his deceased wife. The word began as a variant spelling of *courtesy* (= courteous behavior). "The widower of the beneficiary of a trust of land is entitled to *curtesy* in the beneficiary's interest under the same circumstances under which he would be entitled to *curtesy* in a corresponding legal interest in land."

Dower = the right of a wife, on her husband's death, to a third of the land of which he was seised for her life, of which, with few exceptions, she cannot be deprived by any alienation made by him. "Today in most states an elective share, supplanting or supplementing *dower* and *curtesy,* has evolved." See **dower.**

Inchoate dower and *curtesy intitiate* are the terms denoting the spouse's interest in the other spouse's estate while both are living and after the birth of issue capable of inheriting. "*Inchoate dower* once prevented the husband from transferring realty during his life to defeat his wife's *dower;* the common-law marital right together with his *curtesy initiate* ensured his interest in the wife's realty."/ "Such a scheme to defraud the spouse was impossible when wealth consisted of realty, and either *inchoate dower* or *curtesy initiate* operated to bar conveyance without consent." See **initiate tenant by curtesy.**

curtilage is sometimes misspelled *curtilege,* perhaps on the mistaken analogy of *privilege.* The word means "the land around a house and within an enclosure." Thus: "An airplane used in drug smuggling was located within the *curtilage* of his residence."/ "It is also apparent that their continued progress toward the large barn was not proscribed by the Constitution as long as they remained in open fields, outside the *curtilage.*" The term is used in the U.S. and in England, but not in Scotland.

custodian. In the legal sense, this word means "guardian" or "protector." It is used euphemistically in lay contexts to mean "janitor."

custody; possession. Whereas one may have *custody* of both persons and things, one may have *possession* of things only.

cut against; cut in favor of. These idioms are favorites of the legal profession; they should be used sparingly, lest they become full-fledged CLICHÉS. "Although we do not find *Murdoch* particularly relevant here, it *cuts, if at all, against* RSR's position."

cutting edge is a legal CLICHÉ and a VOGUE WORD. E.g., "By and large, the gains made in the safe and efficient administration of our prisons may be attributed to the anonymous professionals who daily toil at the *cutting edge* of our efforts to improve, while at the same time securing, our penal institutions." In the cant of our day, every law review seeks to be *on the cutting edge* of the law.

CUTTING OUT THE CHAFF refers to getting rid of unnecessary verbiage. It is not an easy task; indeed, verbosity and obscurity are usually the result of facile and slapdash writing. Many recurrent phrases are mere deadwood. For example, *Speaking for myself, I think* . . . , aside from being redundant, adds nothing to the sentence when we know who is speaking and have intelligence enough to deduce that the speaker is stating an opinion. Some courts have written of *reasonable-minded defendants,* as if there might be *reasonable-footed* or *reasonable-chested* defendants; reason is only in the mind.

The following are wordy sentences with more concise alternatives supplied: "*In a large part* [*in large part* is idiomatic], it was our anticipation of this type of claim *which* [read *that*] cautioned us for so long against abrogation of the immunity rule." [Better: *Our foresight of such claims long cautioned us against abrogating the immunity rule.*] / "It was a package of *small size* . . . [read *It was a small package. . .*]." / "The economist's goal in formulating normative rules is *that of* [delete *that of*] 'efficiency' [note that *efficiency* needs no quotation marks]."/ "A will is ambulatory in character and subject to change at any time." [Read *A will is ambulatory.*]

The traditional legal predilection for nouns over verbs, of gerunds over verbal participles, is the cause of much deadweight. E.g., "The defendants had the duty to take reasonable care to protect her, *including probably the giving of a warning to her or to the plaintiff* [read *including, probably, warning her or the plaintiff*]." See VERBOSITY, REDUNDANCY & SUPERFLUITIES.

cy(-)pres. This LAW FRENCH term is predominantly spelled as two words. The British put an accent grave on *pres*. Meaning "as near as," *cy pres* (originally *sì près, ici-près* or *aussi-près*) is used in the context of charitable gifts.

This phrase carries different senses modernly and at common law.

> At common law . . . , the Crown exercised its prerogative power to apply funds given for a charitable purpose without regard for the settlor's intention. Property otherwise given for a particular charitable purpose which became incapable of fulfillment was directed by the chancellor under the doctrine of *cy pres* to another charitable purpose which fell within the general charitable intention of the settlor.
>
> The prerogative power, of course, does not exist in this country. The *cy pres* doctrine applied in the United States is a rule of judicial construction designed to approximate as closely as possible the desires of the settlor.
>
> *La Fond v. City of Detroit,* 357 Mich. 362, 98 N.W.2d 530, 534 n. 1 (1959).

Today in Great Britain, however, the sense is the same as in the U.S., the court being bound by this doctrine to make a scheme for the funds to be applied to a charitable purpose as close as possible to the original one.

The State of Georgia has a statute with the following explanation: "When a valid charitable bequest is incapable for some reason of execution in the exact manner provided by the testator, donor, or founder, a court of equity will carry it into effect in such a way as will [as] nearly as possible effectuate his intention." Ga. Code Ann. § 108-202 (1959).

D

damage; injury. There is a modern tendency to refer to *damage to property,* but *injury to the person.* It is not an established distinction. Blackstone did not observe it, having titled one section of his great treatise *Injury to Property,* and neither the English nor the American courts have consistently observed it. One could not be faulted for restricting one's usage in this way, but neither could one be faulted for writing *damage to persons* or *injury to property.*

damage(s). "[T]he word *damage*, meaning 'Loss, injury, or deterioration,' is to be distinguished from its plural,—*damages*—which means 'a compensation in money for a loss or damage.'" *American Stevedores, Inc. v. Porello,* 330 U.S. 446, 450 n.6 (1947) (quoting *Black's*). In the following sentence, the two terms are correctly used: "After actual *damage* is shown it is unnecessary to show its money extent to sustain a judgment for exemplary *damages.*"

Often, however, the words are misused: "In Massachusetts exemplary damages are not recoverable in an action for libel; only actual *damage* [read *damages*] may be recovered."/ "The tornado caused an estimated $20,000,000 in *damages* [read *damage*]."/ "Most commercial flights arrive at their destinations safely; unfortunately, when an accident does occur, the physical, emotional, and economic *damages* [read *damage*, for this is a mass noun in this context] may be enormous." (*Economic damages*, in any event, would be a REDUNDANCY.)

Damage is used adjectivally to correspond with *damages*, n. E.g., "Alternative safeguards . . . reduce the need for a private *damage action* [= *action for damages*]." *Forrester v. White,* 792 F.2d 647, 658 (7th Cir. 1986).

damages, punitive (or exemplary). See **punitive damages.**

damnatory. Though this word might appear to be related to *damnum* and *damnify*, qq.v., the relation is etymological only. This is not a legal term per se, but a general word equivalent to *condemnatory*, which is more comprehensible. E.g., "If the person sued is proved to have allowed his view to be distorted by malice, it is quite immaterial that somebody else might without malice have written an equally *damnatory* criticism." (Eng.)

damnify (= to inflict injury upon) is generally an unnecessary LEGALISM for *injure*. The *OED* notes that this word was common in the seventeenth century, but is now rare. One might excuse the word's use in the second example below, but not in the first: "I am satisfied that the injured person is *damnified* by

having cut short the period during which he had a normal expectation of enjoying life." (Eng.) (The writer did not want to repeat *injure*—this use smacks of INELEGANT VARIATION.)/ "Where the principle of damnum sine injuria applies, the person *damnified* has no right of action against the person responsible for causing the loss because the latter has not, in causing or allowing the harm to befall, been in breach of legal duty to him." (Eng.) (It would make no sense to say the person had been *injured* when we have just stated that he was *sine injuria* [= without injury].)

damnosa h(a)ereditas = an inheritance more onerous (e.g., because burdened with debts) than profitable. Generally the term is spelled *haereditas*. Originally a Roman-law term, *damnosa haereditas* has been extended by modern legal writers to refer to anything one acquires that turns out to be disadvantageous.

damnous = of the nature of a *damnum* (q.v.), i.e. causing loss or damage. The word is obsolescent legal ARGOT, not a TERM OF ART. "They have injuriously, as distinguished from *damnously*, affected the plaintiff's rights." See **damnum absque injuria.**

damnum = loss. "The loss, *damnum*, is capable of being estimated in terms of money." (Eng.) This term is hardly justified in any context not involving analysis by the doctrine of *damnum absque injuria* (q.v.). In the sentence quoted it adds nothing. See **damnum infectum.**

damnum absque injuria; damnum sine injuria. Either phrase may be Englished *damage without injury.* The phrases denote damage for which there is no remedy at law. Still used with some frequency in G.B., the phrases are comparatively rare in American legal prose. "If disturbances or loss come as a result of competition or the exercise of like results by others, it is *damnum absque injuria* unless some superior right by contract or otherwise is interfered with." (Eng.)/ "He says that it is *damnum absque injuria*, intimating that the acts of the defendant, who justifies a libelous publication, do not constitute a wrong in its legal sense, and then proceeds to observe that this is agreeable to the reasoning of the civil law." Cf. **injuria absque damno.**

damnum infectum = loss not yet suffered but only apprehended. This LATINISM is more a hindrance than an aid to analysis, for most readers must look it up.

damnum sine injuria. See **damnum absque injuria.**

DANGLERS are ordinarily unattached participles, either present participles in -*ing* or past participles, that do not relate syntactically to the nouns they are supposed to modify. In effect, the participle tries to sever its relationship with its noun or pronoun and thus to become functionally a preposition. Gerunds may also dangle precariously (see (B)). Usually, recasting the sentence will remedy the AMBIGUITY, ILLOGIC, or incoherence.

Danglers are of two types, the majority being unacceptable and a few being acceptable because of long-standing usage. In the normal word order, a participial phrase beginning a sentence (*Running by the lake,*) should be followed directly by the noun acting as subject in the main clause (*I saw the two defendants*). When that word-order is changed, as by changing the verb in the main clause to the passive voice, the sentence becomes illogical or misleading: *Running by the lake, the two defendants were seen.* It was not the two defendants that were running, but the witness. This is the unacceptable type of dangling modifier.

Examples of acceptable danglers are easy to come by. We all know that there is nothing wrong with *Considering the current atmosphere in the legislature, it is unlikely that the legislation will pass.* Several other examples are discussed in (c) below.

A. Unacceptable Dangling Participles. In the sentences that follow, mispositioned words have caused grammatical blunders. Perhaps the most common legal sentence containing a dangling participle is this: "Finding no error, the judgment of the district court is affirmed." Literally, this sentence states that the judgment found no error; the subject, namely *the court,* remains unmentioned. [Read *Finding no error, we affirm the judgment of the district court.*]

This is the type of problematic dangler cited at the outset, in which an active participle is followed by a main clause in the passive voice. Here is another typical example: "*View-ing the record* [read *If we view the record*] in the light most favorable to appellants, the most that can be said is that Yellow Cab secured from the city an exclusive concession whose anticompetitive effects stem primarily from a valid municipal policy."

The classic example occurs, however, when the wrong noun begins the main clause, that is, a noun other than the one expected by the reader when he has digested the introductory participial phrase. E.g., "*Accepting* for present purposes the showing made, *the facts of the claim were* [read *we find the facts to be*] as follows." (It is not the *facts* that *accept*; it is *we,* the writer and his readers. The error in the sentence just quoted seems to have been brought about by fear of the FIRST PERSON.)/ "*Having reached that conclusion,* [read, e.g., *Inasmuch as we have reached that conclusion,*] all that remains is to choose an appropriate remedy and to frame the appropriate relief."

Another manifestation of this error is to begin the main clause with an EXPLETIVE (e.g., *it* or *there*) after an introductory participial phrase: "Applying those principles to the facts in the case at bar, it is clear that plaintiffs cannot recover." [Read *If we apply these principles to the case at bar, it becomes clear that....*]/ "Applying the foregoing standards, it is our opinion that the case under consideration is the type of case in which federal jurisdiction should be exercised." [Read *Applying the foregoing standards, we believe that the case....*]

We should not forget midsentence danglers, which are harder for the untrained eye to spot. E.g., "It is the purpose of this note to re-examine the existing law, *placing emphasis upon* [read *to emphasize*] the interests to be protected, and to draw some conclusions as to its adequacy in protecting them." (Note that this is very poor writing, because it could be included as boilerplate in almost any lawnote imaginable; the writer should craft his language specifically for the case at hand, generalizing, to be sure, but not making it so general that it is well-nigh universal. Further, the writer should have been aware of the natural triad lurking in his sentence, i.e., the infinitive phrases.)

B. Dangling Gerunds. These are close allies to dangling participles, but here the participle acts as a noun rather than as an adjective. E.g., "In arguing this case before the appeals court it became clear that the appellant had not clearly stated his position in his brief."

[Read *It became clear, in argument of this case before the appeals court, that appellant had not clearly stated his position in his brief.*]

C. Acceptable Danglers, or Disguised Conjunctions. Any number of present participles have been used as conjunctions or prepositions for so long that they have lost the participial duty to modify specific nouns. In effect, the clauses they introduce are adverbial, standing apart from and commenting on the content of the sentence. Among the commonest of these are *according, barring, concerning, considering, judging, owing, regarding, respecting, speaking, taking* (usu. *account of, into account*). Thus, "Generally *speaking,* an alien may become trustee of property that he can own beneficially."/ "*Conceding* for the purposes of the discussion that the happening of the accident was an invasion of her legal rights, it does not follow that damages for such suffering are necessarily recoverable."/ "*Admitting* the facts with reference to the purchase of the merchandise to be claimed by appellees, then is it not community property and subject to levy?"/ "*Taking* this one step further, perhaps the FASP would be more willing to consider an approach that would focus only on the 'giveaway' plans and permit the 'real' plans that have all the attributes of high-risk investments to continue to be accounted for as securities."

data, the plural of *datum,* is frequently misused as a singular; *datum* is the singular noun. "There is no *data* [read *There are no data*] available on the number of pesticide containers recycled in the state."/ "Therefore, the *data* upon which this report is based are more detailed than *that* [read *those*] of the individual departments." (See CONCORD.)/ "While I regard the opinion of plaintiff's expert as greatly exaggerated and plaintiff's statistical analysis as materially flawed, the *data* concerning reports of rapes and attempted rapes in the prison *raises* [read *raise*] a significant question regarding the staff attitude toward homosexual rape before 1980."/ "I believe plaintiff's *data raises* [read *raise*] a rational basis for evaluating the response of the prison." The *Oxford Guide* allows the singular use of *data* in computing and allied disciplines (see COMPUTERESE); whether lawyers own computers or not, they should use *data* as a plural.

Datum is still used when a single piece of information is referred to: "The crucial *datum* in this case is the nature of Borg-Warner's claim to the Seneca."/ "The Corps had the burden of proving either that the *datum* has already been considered or that it is insignificant."

Data is a COUNT NOUN; thus *many data* is correct and *much data* is not.

database. One word.

DATES. A. Order. One may unimpeachably write either *May 26, 1984* or *26 May 1984.* The latter is often better in prose, for it takes no commas.

B. Month and Year. *February 1985* is better than *February of 1985.* There is no need for a comma between the month and the year.

C. As Adjectives. Our generation has taken to making adjectives out of dates, just as it has out of PLACE-NAMES, q.v. E.g., "This matter arises out of a *September 1980* divorce decree." Today this occurs in the U.S. even in formal legal prose. The better rendering of the sentence just quoted would be, "This matter arises out of a divorce decree of September 1980." Although occasionally using dates adjectively is a space-saver, the device should not be overworked: it gives prose a breezy, journalistic look.

D. Written Out. Although the validity of a legal document almost never depends on its being dated, lawyers often go to extreme lengths to express the date in words; *1 January 1988* becomes *the first day of January, One thousand nine hundred and eighty-eight.*" A waste.

E. In Contracts. To avoid litigation on the question whether *until December 31, 1986* includes all of that day, the drafter should state explicitly that an option, e.g., will expire at 12:00 noon Central Standard Time on a certain day.

datum. See **data.**

d.b.n. See **administrator.**

deadline is one word; formerly it was hyphenated.

deadly; deathly. The former means "able to cause death." (See **lethal.**) The latter means "like death."

deal with; deal in. People in business *deal*

in what they buy and sell ⟨he deals in stocks and bonds⟩, but they *deal with* other persons. *Deal* should not be used transitively where *deal in* is intended. Although one *deals* cards, one does not *deal drugs;* one *deals in drugs* (if one is utterly reprobate). "The principal witness for the government was S., an undercover detective who had been assigned to investigate allegations that C. was *dealing* [read *dealing in*] drugs."

Deal with is a vague PHRASAL VERB for which there is almost always a better, more specific substitute. E.g., "This commentary will *deal with* [read *discuss*] a variety of matters, including problems of judicial jurisdiction and constitutional limitations on choice of law."/ "We do not *deal with* [read *discuss*] various objections to the plan of merger filed after this appeal was taken." (Cf. **concerned with, be.**) Where, however, *deal with* is roughly equivalent to *handle,* it is unobjectionable: "The court held that state courts dividing community property in divorce proceedings could not *deal with* nondisability military retirement benefits."

dearth = scarcity. It is commonly misunderstood, however, as meaning "lack." E.g., "There is a complete *dearth of* [read *lack of,* or *There is no*] authority on the application of the words 'cause or permit' consequent upon the absolute conveyance of the freehold." (Eng.)

death; demise; decease, n.; **surcease.** Here we have the common word, followed by three FORMAL WORDS (in order of increasing formality) that act almost as EUPHEMISMS. There is nothing wrong with *death,* although the word inherently has unpleasant connotations. But that is the nature of the subject, and writing *decease* or *surcease* in legal contexts is only a little less ridiculous than writing *going to meet his Maker. Deceased,* adj., is quite acceptable, having been established by usage and not striking most readers as circumlocutory. See **demise, deceased & surcease.**

death case, as used by the federal courts, commonly means "a case involving capital punishment." It has nothing to do with *wrongful death.* E.g., "The measure of an individual's competency under *Rees* to waive federal habeas review in a *death case* is informed by considerations very different from those underlying the standard for competency to stand trial."

deathly. See **deadly.**

death-qualified jurors are jurors who cannot be disqualified under *Witherspoon v. Illinois,* 391 U.S. 510 (1968); in other words, *death-qualified jurors* have been selected because they have no absolute ideological bias against the death penalty. A *death-qualified jury,* then, is held fit to decide cases involving the death penalty. E.g., "Appellant argues that more recent studies provide stronger empirical evidence that *death-qualified jurors* are biased in favor of conviction and tend to belong to certain discrete groups."

debar. See **bar.**

debark. See **disembark.**

debarkation; debarcation. The former is the preferred spelling.

debate, v.t. & n. (Eng.)**; argue, argument** (U.S.). British lawyers sometimes use *debate* where American lawyers would write *oral argument* or *argue.* E.g., "Since the matter has been *debated,* it may be desirable for me to say that I accept counsel's view that the test of practicability is that of workability." (Eng.)/ "I would refer first to contracts for the sale of goods which were touched on in the course of the *debate.*" (Eng.) Here is an example of the ordinary American usage: "It became clear, in *argument* of this case before the appeals court, that appellant had not clearly stated his position in his brief."

debauch; debouch. These words are liable to confusion. The former means "to defile; to seduce away from virtue; to corrupt"; the latter means "to emerge or cause to emerge; to come out into open ground." The nouns are *debauchery* and *debouchment. Debauch* is pronounced /di-**bawch**/, and *debouch* /di-**boosh**/.

de bene esse (lit. "of well-being") denotes a course of action that is the best that can be done under the circumstances, or in anticipation of the future. The *CDL* gives the example of obtaining a witness's deposition when he will likely be unable to attend the court hearing. Sometimes *appearance de bene esse* is used as a variant of *special appearance,* though this substitution is not recommended.

This LAW LATIN term is of unknown origin, and does not appear in Classical Latin. It serves no purpose today in ordinary legal writing. Cf. **esse** & **in esse**.

debenture; bond. "In general the term *debenture* in British usage designates any security issued by companies other than their shares, including, therefore, what are in the United States commonly called *bonds*. When used in the United States, *debenture* generally designates an instrument secured by a floating charge junior to other charges secured by fixed mortgages, or, specif., one of a series of securities secured by a group of securities held in trust for the benefit of the debenture holders. In some cases the debenture is no more than an unsecured promissory note of the corporation bearing a fixed rate of interest" (*W2*).

debility; debilitation. *Debility* = weakness; feebleness. *Debilitation* = the action of making weak or feeble.

debitum is an ARCHAISM and a NEEDLESS VARIANT of *debt* that is still sometimes used in Scotland.

de bonis asportatis. See **trespass**.

de bonis non. See **administrator**.

debouch. See **debauch**.

debriefing for *briefing*. *Debrief,* used chiefly in military or espionage operations, means (1) "to interrogate (e.g., a spy) to obtain valuable information"; (2) "to instruct someone not to reveal any classified information after he leaves a sensitive position"; or (3) "(colloquially) to obtain information from (a person) on the completion of a mission or after a journey" (*OED Supp.*). Here sense (1) applies: "Driver asserts that the government knew from its '*debriefing*' of the coconspirators pursuant to their plea agreements which of the hundreds of calls were made by Benton to other drug sources." *United States v. Driver*, 798 F.2d 248, 251 (7th Cir. 1986).

Some law firms apparently fancy themselves involved in the espionage business. One, in its firm résumé, states: "Feedback is an important part of a summer associate's experience at the firm; in addition to regular in-

formal contact, we have periodic *debriefings* for each summer associate throughout the summer, and one at the conclusion of the summer associate's stay." Even in a figurative sense, this use of *debrief* fails, for the associate is no doubt primarily the recipient, not the source, of the transfer of information; hence, *brief* (= to give important information to) is the correct verb.

debut. This word, when used as a verb, is disapproved by 97 percent of the usage panel for the *AHD*, for what that is worth. The forms *debuted* and *debuting* are certainly ugly to the philologist. The *OED*, surprisingly, records examples as far back as 1830. For the moment, however, the verb *debut* has taken on the character of a VOGUE WORD and should be avoided on that account.

decease. See **death**.

decease, v.i. = to die. "He *deceased* without issue." This verbal use of *decease* is even more pompous than the nominal use. The straightforward *die* is almost always better. Cf. **death**.

deceased, n.; **decedent.** When these terms are used in the possessive case, no one would argue that *deceased's* is more euphonious than *decedent's*. Yet the term *deceased's* appears frequently in legal prose, esp. in that of British writers, for *decedent* is obsolete in G.B. The awkwardness of *-ed's* can be overcome either by resort to *decedent's* or by writing *of the deceased* (which is, unfortunately, not possible in all contexts). Cf. **accused** & **insured**.

We may find no solace in our unhappy dilemma between these words, for even *decedent* sounds especially legalistic; it is common, however, in American legal writing. E.g., "Appellant was under no duty to speak or inquire concerning detail of *decedent's* wealth."

deceptive, -tious. The latter is a NEEDLESS VARIANT.

decide on is usually prolix for *decide*. E.g., "The meaning of 'defect' is for the courts to *decide on* [read *decide*]." See PARTICLES, UNNECESSARY.

decimate. Originally this word meant "to kill one in every ten," but this etymological sense, because so uncommon, has been abandoned except in historical contexts. Now *decimate* generally means "to cause great loss of life; to destroy a large part of." The word should not be used of a complete obliteration or defeat. Nor should it be used lightly of just any defeat.

decision; opinion; judgment. Technically, in the U.S. judges are said to write *opinions* to justify their *decisions* or *judgments;* they do not write *decisions* or *judgments.* E.g., "Last July, Judge Scalia wrote a majority *decision* [read *opinion*] that subjects defendants who claim insanity to examination, without requiring that their lawyers be present, by government psychiatrists, who may testify against them." See JUDGMENTS, APPELLATE-COURT.

decisional. See **decisive.**

decision(al) law. The preferred form of this American equivalent of *case law* is *decisional law.* E.g., "The rule of our *decision law* [read *decisional law*] puts upon the bailee the burden of proving that the loss did not result from his negligence."/ "Present *decisional law* would seemingly entitle plaintiff to relief under section 1983."/ "The weight of *decisional law* is now to the effect that when a married man makes provision in his will for his wife, and is thereafter divorced, with a property settlement between them, such change in condition and circumstances of the parties impliedly [q.v.] revokes the previously executed will in favor of the wife."/ "The statutes have produced a respectable body of decisional law."/ "Apart from the statute, the plaintiff is entitled to interest as a matter of *decisional law.*" See **case(-)law** & **jurisprudence** (B). Cf. **organic law.** See also **decisive.**

decisioning for *deciding* or *decision-making* is an example of abhorrent social science cant.

decision-making, n., is a generic term for *deciding* and, though useful in some contexts, is much overworked in current legal writing. The word smacks of sociological cant, and is often merely a grandiloquent way of saying *deciding:* after all, when one makes decisions, one decides.

It is now frequently spelled as one word,

even by the U.S. Supreme Court. And the word is so spelled in Paul Brest's book *Processes of Constitutional Decisionmaking* (1975). One sees the same one-wordism tendency at work in the term *budgetmaking,* q.v. These compounds are too bulky to look like anything but jargonistic English; a simple hyphen does a lot.

decisive; decisional. *Decisive* is frequently used in the sense "determinative" in legal writing, and is used of things as opposed to persons. In lay contexts, of course, *decisive* almost always refers to persons and means "resolute." Following are examples of the legal usage. "It is this last-mentioned omission in our statute that is *decisive* against the contention of the defendants that the law of this Commonwealth has been changed in their favor."/ "The determinative facts presented in the case at bar are, however, few, and the *decisive* principles are established."/ "The fact that the contractors are forced to do what they do not want to do is not *decisive* of the legality of the labor union's acts."/ "Although the facts in that case are wholly dissimilar from the facts in the case at bar, the principle thus broadly and tersely stated is one that should be *decisive* of this case."

Decisional = of, or of the nature of, deciding or a decision. The *OED* notes that *decisional* is "rare," and the *OED Supp.* does not modify that notation. It may have been rare one-hundred years ago, but today it is common in American legal writing. E.g., "This court's *decisional* process would not be significantly aided by oral argument."/ "Moreover, the employees had, as part of their *decisional* process, examined copies of the work-rules agreement in effect in Texaco's Louisiana plant." See **decisional law.**

declaim; disclaim. The former is what lawyers do in court, the latter what manufacturers do in warranties. To *declaim* is to speak formally in public (whence the adjective *declamatory*); this word is frequently misused for *disclaim,* meaning "to make a disclaimer, disavow, repudiate."

declaration of trust; trust deed; trust agreement. These terms are variously used to name the instrument creating a trust.

declarative, -tory; declamatory. In grammar we have *declarative* sentences, but in law we have *declaratory* judgments, statutes, and acts. Both words mean "having the function of declaring, setting forth, or explaining"; their DIFFERENTIATION lies in established uses, not in meaning. For virtually all legal contexts, *declaratory* is the word. E.g., "In the seventeenth and eighteenth centuries, Roman law was taken to be *declaratory* of the law of nature" (R. Pound).

Declamatory, which is sometimes confused with *declaratory,* means "haranguing; of or pertaining to declaiming oratorically."

decline, v.i. & v.t. This verb has two distinct senses, and yields two nominal forms. *Declination* derives from *decline* in the sense "to refuse," and *decline,* n., derives from *decline* in the sense "to go downhill."

decorous is pronounced with the primary accent on the first syllable, /*dek-ŏ-rus*/.

decree; judgment. Traditionally, judicial decisions are termed *decrees* in courts of equity, and *judgments* in courts of law. E.g., "Such a testamentary trust may be terminated only by a *decree of a court of equity,* regardless of any stipulation by all parties in interest." Nevertheless, in modern usage *decree* is broad enough to refer to any court order, whether or not the relief granted or denied is equitable in nature.

decree, v.t. = (1) to command by decree; or (2) to award judicially; to assign authoritatively. Here sense (2), undifferentiated in most dictionaries, applies because it is construed with a direct object and a *to*-phrase: "But the probate court did not *decree* the estate to the widow, and then make her a constructive trustee of such estate for the benefit of the parents."

decree absolute; decree nisi. These phrases, far more common in G.B. than in the U.S., are very similar. *Decree nisi* = a conditional decree of divorce, nullity, or presumption of death (*CDL*). "In March she commenced proceedings for restitution of conjugal rights, and on July 30 she obtained a *decree nisi.*" (Eng.)/ "A child had been born to the wife petitioner between petition and the *decree nisi* and the court was not informed of its birth." (Eng.)

Decree absolute = a decree of divorce, nullity, or presumption of death that ends a legal marriage and enables the parties to remarry. A *decree nisi,* conditional in nature, becomes a *decree absolute* after a time if there is no contrary reason. *Rule absolute* and *rule nisi* are often used as equivalents of *decree absolute* and *decree nisi.*

decretal = (1) of or relating to a degree; or (2) of or relating to a decree. Sense (2) is usual in legal writing. E.g., "The *Ruiz* court is the court that should adjudicate Johnson's equitable claims that actions by prison officials have violated the *Ruiz* decree; since Johnson's damage allegations are based on the same actions, they implicate the same *decretal* values."/ "The decree is modified on the law by striking from the first *decretal* paragraph the following words." *Decretorial, decretory,* and *decretive* are NEEDLESS VARIANTS.

Decretal may also be a noun: "The precedents of compulsion to accomplish governmental *decretals* are found rather in the Court of the Star Chamber, of unhappy memory." *Decrees* would actually be the better word in that sentence, for *decretals* specifically are "letters containing a papal ruling, particularly one relating to matters of canonical discipline, and most precisely a papal rescript in response to an appeal" (*OCL*).

decry; descry. *Decry* = to disapprove of; to disparage. E.g., "In 1908 Roscoe Pound *decried* decision-making from first principles—a process described in Germany as *Begriffsjurisprudenz*—and warned against the law becoming too scientific."

Descry = to see in the distance, to discern with the eye. Here it is used figuratively: "In the foregoing paragraphs we have endeavored, by the relations and facts that may be gathered and by the words used by the testator, to *descry* the testator's intention."

dedicatory, -tive, -torial. The first form is preferred; the other two are NEEDLESS VARIANTS.

deduce; deduct. The former means "to infer"; the latter "to subtract." *Deduct* is sometimes misused in place of *deduce.* Here *deduce* is wrongly used: "We *deduce* [read *glean*?] from approved authorities the following principles as pertinent to this case." See **adduce & deducible.**

deducible; deductible. The former means

"inferable." E.g., "The government agents relied on evidence not otherwise known or *deducible* by them."/ "I believe the governing principles to be *deducible* from the terms of the pertinent statutes." *Deductible,* a favorite word of tax specialists, means "capable of being (usu. lawfully) subtracted." See **deduce.**

deed. A. As Noun. At common law, *deed* referred to any sealed instrument that was signed and delivered. In G.B., this broad sense still applies. In the U.S., however, the narrower sense of a writing by which land is conveyed is almost uniformly applicable.
 B. As Verb. *Deed,* v.t., is an Americanism dating from the early nineteenth century. E.g., "The agreement also contains a section under which the trustor was authorized to deposit with the trustee securities, personal property, and sums of money, and to *deed* to the trustee real property." English solicitors *convey* or *transfer by deed.*

deed of trust; trust deed. The classical form of this term, meaning "a deed conveying property in trust, and usu. evidencing a mortgage," is *deed of trust.* But either form suffices.

de-emphasize. This word should always be hyphenated, for the reader may at first see *deem.* See HYPHENS.

deem is a FORMAL WORD often used in legislation to create LEGAL FICTIONS; that is, a statute may provide that something is or is not to be *deemed* something else, or, with a significant difference, that this something is to be *deemed* not something else. In general usage, *deem* is somewhat archaic for *judge* or *esteem.*

deemster. See **dempster.**

de facto; in fact. Although the terms convey the same notion, their uses are well distinguished. *De facto* is always two words, not one, and is used prepositively, whereas *in fact* is used after the noun it modifies ⟨de facto segregation, attorney in fact⟩.

defalcate; peculate; embezzle. These three words are broadly synonymous, all three meaning "to misappropriate money in one's charge." *Defalcate* and *peculate,* the latter being slightly more common and referring

to public moneys, are FORMAL WORDS that are neutral in color. *Embezzle* is the popular word that is charged with negative CONNOTATIONS. See **defalcation & peculation.**

defalcation may refer either to the act of embezzling or to the money embezzled. E.g., "No one would venture to expose corporate *defalcation* [i.e., the act] if every word and sentence, and every fact and every inference, had to be justified by unquestionable legal evidence."/ "Evidence was adduced tending to show that the *defalcation* [i.e., the money embezzled] was wasted on horse racing and other forms of gambling." See **defalcate & peculation.**

defamation; libel; slander. *Defamation* = an attack upon the reputation of another. It encompasses both *libel* (written defamation) and *slander* (spoken defamation). See **libel.**

defamatory, -tive. *Defamatory* is the usual word; *defamative* is a NEEDLESS VARIANT.

defeasance is a legal word meaning (1) "the rendering null and void (of a previous condition)"; (2) "a condition upon the performance of which a deed or other instrument is defeated or made void" (*OED*). Sense (1) is more usual: "The provision in the will that the interest was to be divided among 'them' every year necessitates the construction that the testatrix intended the gift of income also to be subject to *defeasance* by not surviving until the respective dates of distribution." But sense (2) is not uncommon: "In absence of a clause of *defeasance,* or one providing for a change of beneficiaries, the beneficiary in an ordinary policy of life insurance has a vested interest, which the insured cannot divest at his mere volition."

defeasible is a learned lay word in its negative form (*indefeasible*), but in itself is a legal word only. It means "capable of being made void." E.g., "The title to the gift causa mortis passed by the delivery, *defeasible* only in the lifetime of the donor, and his death perfects the title in the donee by terminating the donor's right or power of defeasance."

defective, -ible; deficient. The primary difference to be noted is between *defective* (= faulty; imperfect; subnormal) and *deficient* (= insufficient; lacking in quantity). *Defectible,* the least common of the three terms, means "likely to fail or become defective."

In the following sentence, *deficiency* is misused for *defect:* "The trial court failed to submit to the jury an issue inquiring *whether the multipiece wheel was defective due to a design deficiency* [read *whether the multipiece wheel had a design defect*] that would cause the wheel to separate explosively during foreseeable uses." The blunder may have been caused by an attempt at INELEGANT VARIATION.

defence. See **defense.**

defendant. A. Pronunciation. *Defendant* is sometimes pronounced, esp. it seems by law school professors, with a strong accent on the last syllable, rhyming with *ant.* Presumably, this pronunciation helps legal neophytes remember how to spell the word. Apart from this pedagogically affected pronunciation, the correct way to pronounce the word is /di-**fen**-dånt/.

B. As a POSTPOSITIVE ADJECTIVE. The adjective *defendant* is commonly placed after the noun it modifies when that noun is *party.* E.g., "The plaintiff chose both the forum and the *parties defendant. . ."* (Harlan, J.).

defendant in error = respondent, appellee. See **error** & **plaintiff in error.**

defender is used in Scotland for *defendant,* as the name of the party opposite a *pursuer,* q.v.

defense; defence. *Defence* is the British, *defense* the American spelling. Yet the British spelling was used by American courts through the early twentieth century; Judge Learned Hand, for example, used the *-ce* spelling in *Sinram v. Pennsylvania R.R.,* 61 F.2d 767 (2d Cir. 1932). The British spelling is best avoided in America, lest one's writing seem affected.

defer; defer to. The former, meaning "to postpone," yields the nouns *deferment,* q.v., and its NEEDLESS VARIANT *deferral.* The latter, meaning "to give way to," yields the noun *deference.*

deferential. See **differential.**

deferment; deferral. *Deferral* is less good than *deferment* as the noun corresponding to

the verb *to defer.* "The filing of the state action mandates *deferral* [read *deferment*] of our decision." See **defer.**

defer(r)able. The preferred form is *deferrable.* See DOUBLING OF FINAL CONSONANTS.

deficient. See **defective.**

definite; definitive. These words are increasingly confused. *Definite* = fixed, exact, explicit. *Definitive* = authoritative; conclusive; exhaustive; providing a final solution. E.g., "Usually the standard of 'certainty' is applied *definitively* by the trial judge in passing upon the admissibility of evidence and in deciding whether the case is to be submitted to the jury at all."/ "The trial court raised, but did not rule *definitively* on, the timeliness question."

The most frequent error is misuse of *definitive* for *definite* E g , "The ALJ erred in not setting forth, in *definitive* [read *definite*] language, his assessment of the relative credibility of the evidence."

deforce = (1) to keep lands from the true owner by means of force; or (2) to oust another from possession by force. Here, the writer apparently mistook *deforce* as a correlative of *enforce,* which it is not: "One may maintain an action to enforce a lien against another who has *deforced* it."

degenerative, -tory. The latter is a NEEDLESS VARIANT.

degradation (= a lowering in character or quality) is a MALAPROPISM when used for *derogation* (= an abrogation or violation), as here: "The rebate and veto provisions deprived the third parties, in *degradation* [read *derogation*] of the strong policy favoring settlements, of a chance themselves to compromise these claims." But the words do share the sense "detraction from the honor or reputation of; lowering or lessening in value or estimation" (*OED*).

degree is the word used in law for various classifications and specifications, as for classifications in *consanguinity,* q.v., and grades based on the seriousness of crimes. Today most American jurisdictions differentiate first-degree from second-degree murder on the basis of the gravity of the offense (gauged, e.g., by premeditation and purpose), whereas at common law first- and second-degree felons were principals and accessories, respectively.

dehors is a pompous little LAW FRENCH word (meaning "outside of; beyond the scope of") that should generally be avoided. The plethora of examples, selected from writings of the 1980s, indicates the prevalence of this nasty-sounding term /di-*hohr*/. It serves absolutely no purpose but to sound legalistic. E.g., "Adopting the controlling state-law rule in this diversity case, we find that the court erred in excluding all evidence *dehors* the contract."/ "Defendant's responsibility is based on statutorily imposed legal fault, *dehors* any requirement of negligence."/ "The fact that the persons who are in the class intended to be the ultimate beneficiary are required, as a condition for inclusion in the class, by prescription *dehors* the bequest itself, to contribute certain sums of money periodically to the fund that is nominally the beneficiary of the bequest does not in itself prevent the bequest from being charitable and benevolent."/ "But if this were not apparent and she had made the will under a mistake as to the supposed death of her son, this [see the next entry] could not be shown *dehors* the will."

DEICTIC TERMS (e.g., *this, that, it, he*) are those that point definitely at something, usu. an antecedent, or at least they do when used properly. (Etymologically, *deictic* means "capable of proof," and conjures up the notion of pointing to conclusive evidence.) In the following sentence, the deictic term *these* points to no explicit referent. "Officials at checkpoints that are judicially deemed the functional equivalent of a border have been granted increasingly intrusive power in connection with the search of vehicles at these checkpoints, without any requirement of probable cause or reasonable suspicion. *These* include the power to stop and question occupants about aliens and to search in automobile cavities that could conceal aliens." We can deduce, of course, that the writer meant *powers*, though he used the singular noun in the first sentence.

Likewise, *this* should always have a clear, single-phrase antecedent; a sentence-long antecedent will not do. Here this has none: "Although statutes in derogation of the common

law are to be strictly construed, *this* does not mean that the statute should be given the narrowest possible meaning."

de jure has three senses: (1) "of right; lawful"; (2) "as a matter of right"; and (3) "by law." In sense (1) it is contrasted with *de facto* (= in fact, but usually unlawfully so) ⟨de facto as opposed to de jure segregation⟩. In sense (2), it is contrasted with *de gratia* (= as a favor gratuitously bestowed). And in sense (3) it is opposed to *de aequitate* (= by equity).

Sense (1), illustrated in the following sentence, is the most usual: "That issue will have to be determined in light of the fact that the United States recognizes the West German Government as the *de jure* government over the territory it controls but does not recognize the East German Government."

delapidation. See **dilapidation.**

delegatee (= one to whom a debtor is delegated) is not, despite its appearances to the contrary, a NEEDLESS VARIANT of *delegate* (= one who represents or acts for another or a group of others). See -EE.

deliberate; deliberative. These words have clear DIFFERENTIATION. *Deliberate* = (1) intentional, fully considered; or (2) unimpulsive, slow in deciding. *Deliberative* = of, or appointed for the purpose of, deliberation or debate (*COD*).

Deliberative is misused for *deliberate* in both sense (1) and sense (2). Here is an example of the former: "The express revocation of a will is a *deliberative* [read *deliberate*] act and operates as an immediate revocation of the will to which it refers."

deliberate speed. See **with all deliberate speed.**

deliberative. See **deliberate.**

delict; delictum. The preferred term is *tort*. *Delict* (= an offense against the law) is the more common of the two variants here to be discussed, but both are inferior in modern contexts to the usual word (*tort*). "Although *a child of tender years* [read *a young child*] may be incapable of committing a *legal delict* [read *tort*] because of his lack of capacity to discern the consequences of his act, nevertheless, if the act of a child would be *delictual* [read *tortious*] except for this disability, the parent with whom he resides is legally at fault and, therefore, liable for the damage occasioned by the child's act."

Delictum is a Latinate variant to be eschewed, because it is no more learned or impressive than *delict.* Additionally, *deliction* is a NEEDLESS VARIANT of *delict* not countenanced by the dictionaries.

delict(u)al. The preferred form is *delictual,* assuming this word is to be used advisedly in place of its near-equivalent, *tortious.* E.g., "The Louisiana Supreme Court held that Article 2971 limited only the innkeeper's contractual, not his *delictual,* responsibility."

Delictual may be more useful than its nominal brother *delict,* for it signifies "of or relating to a tort," whereas *tortious* signifies either "relating to" or "constituting a tort" ⟨tortious conduct⟩. (See **tortious** (A).) *Delictal,* recorded in the *OED Supp.* as appearing in only one source (in 1913), is a NEEDLESS VARIANT of *delictual.*

delictum. See **delict.**

delimit(ate). *Delimit,* the preferred form, is not merely a fancy variation of *limit,* as many seem to believe. E.g., "The manufacturer may possibly *delimit* [read *limit*] the scope of his potential liability by use of a disclaimer in compliance with the statute."/ "The court held on several occasions that certain congressional attempts to *delimit* [read *limit*] its jurisdiction were unconstitutional attempts to invade the judicial province."

Properly, *delimit* means "to define; delineate," as here: "If the challenged conduct of respondents constitutes state action as *delimited* by our prior decisions, then that conduct was also action under color of state law and will support a suit under section 1983."

delineate, (lit. "to draw or sketch") means figuratively "to represent in words; to describe." It is sometimes misused for *differentiate.* E.g., "A corporate seal is probably desirable since it helps to *delineate* [read *differentiate*] corporate transactions from individual transactions."

delinquent, in the U.S., is applied to both things and people ⟨delinquent taxes⟩ ⟨juvenile delinquents⟩. In England it applies only to people.

deliverance, when used for *opinion,* is somewhat grandiose; it is an extension of the Scots law sense "a judicial or administrative order." E.g., "In days not far remote, judges were not unwilling to embellish their *deliverances* with quotations from the poets." (Cardozo)/ "Fully aware of Mississippi's imprimatur on section 6 we might—by piecing together some of our own *deliverances* and the District Court opinions dutifully following them—come up with a fair prediction of what Mississippi would hold in this case, but we do not think this would be a wise course." See **delivery** (A).

delivery. A. And *deliverance. Delivery* is the more usual word, used of a transfer or conveyance (of something), utterance ⟨a stammering delivery of the speech⟩, or giving birth. *Deliverance* is a legal and religious term usu. meaning "rescue, release," although at one time it overlapped with *delivery* in almost every sense. In law, *deliverance* has meant (1) "the jury's verdict"; (2) "in an action of replevin, delivery of goods unlawfully taken"; or (3) (in Scots law) "judgment delivered." See **deliverance.**

B. And *livery.* The word *livery* has a number of obsolete and archaic senses, but in law has been used in the sense "the legal delivery of property into a persons's possession," as in the phrases *livery of seisin* and *to take or have livery of.* The student can better understand *livery* if he reads it mentally as "delivery." See **livery of seisin.**

C. Cant Uses. It has become voguish in some circles to use *delivery of* where *providing* or *provision for* would normally appear, esp. in reference to services. Like any other trendy expression, it ought to be avoided. E.g., "It is irrational to equate the cost of total confinement with the alleged harm resulting from a change in method of *the delivery of* [read *providing*] dental services." See VOGUE WORDS.

delusive, -sory; delusional. *Delusive* = (1) tending to delude, deceptive; or (2) of the nature of a delusion. Usually sense (1) applies. *Delusional* is the more usual term for sense (2). E.g., "Defendant acted under a completely *delusional* perception of reality." *Delusory* is a NEEDLESS VARIANT.

demagogue may be an intransitive, but not a transitive, verb; that is, one may demagogue (= play the demagogue), but one may not demagogue *something.* In this sentence, the verb incorrectly has an object: "The fate of the complicated immigration bill could be influenced by what happens at the convention, whose participants may be tempted to *demagogue* the issue."

demarcation; demarkation. The former is the preferred spelling.

demean; bemean. Formerly, authorities on usage disapproved of *demean* in the sense "to lower, degrade," holding that instead it properly should be used reflexively in the sense "to conduct (oneself)." For example, Vizitelly wrote that *"demean* signifies 'to behave' and does not mean *debase* or *degrade."* F. Vizitelly, *A Desk-Book of Errors in English* 62 (1909). The meaning "to behave," now somewhat archaic, is used infrequently in legal contexts, e.g.: "The oath of office now generally administered in all the states requires the lawyer to uphold the law; to *demean* himself, as an officer of the court, uprightly; to be faithful to his trust."

Yet the more common lay sense is now widespread even in legal prose, and has been with us since at least 1601. E.g., "We do not *demean* the role of pattern instructions by reminding that they cannot substitute for case-specific thought and adjustment."/ "Nowhere in the common-law world—indeed in any modern society—is a woman regarded as a chattel or *demeaned* by denial of a separate legal identity and the dignity associated with recognition as a whole human being."

Meanwhile, the word with which *demean* was confused in arriving at its popular meaning, *bemean* (= to debase), has become virtually obsolete.

de minimis is a shortened form of the Latin maxim *de minimis non curat lex* (= the law does not concern itself with trifles). It is used in law in the sense "so insignificant that a court may overlook (it or them) in deciding the issue or case." E.g., "Winter maintains that his unauthorized sales of non-Carvel products were *de minimis* and cannot possibly be deemed to have a sufficient effect on interstate commerce." *Franchised Stores of New York, Inc. v. Winter,* 394 F.2d 664, 670 (2d Cir. 1968). *De minimis* sometimes appears, as here, to act merely as a fancy substitute for *minimal*: "The amount of advertising by plaintiff was *de minimis,* as it had been in business only a matter of months."

De minimis non curat lex is a sentence in itself. When invoking the maxim by declaring something to be a mere trifle, one writes that it is *de minimis.* The entire maxim should not be inserted when only the "trifling" portion is called for: "The testimony regarding the landscaping in the common areas was unsatisfactory, but this insufficiency is considered to be *de minimis non curat lex."* The sentence is an anacoluthon. If an entire maxim is used, it should fit into the sentence syntactically. But here we have, in translation, "this insufficiency is considered to be [*the law does not concern itself with trifles*]." The writer should have ended the sentence with *de minimis.*

Usually *de minimis* precedes the noun it modifies: "There is a *de minimis* level of imposition with which the Constitution is not concerned."/ "Failure to elect the required number of directors is a *de minimis* deviation from the corporate formalities."/ "To avoid costly, vexatious, *de minimis* litigation, to eliminate conflict and confusion, and to comply with the requests of bench and bar to make clear and definite the rules with respect to situations that frequently arise, I would add the following."

Sometimes the phrase is used as an attributive noun (meaning "something that is de minimis"): "CPI may be barred from asserting its trademark rights nationwide because of its failure to challenge what it may have considered a *de minimis."*

demise, v. & n. The meanings of the verb *demise* are (1) "to convey by will or lease"; (2) "to pass by descent or bequest"; or (3) "to die." The corresponding definitions of *demise* as a noun are (1) "the conveyance of an estate by will or lease, or the lease itself"; (2) "the passing of property by descent or bequest"; and (3) "death." The popular meaning of *demise,* of course, is "death"; laymen are sure to be bewildered by the legal senses. The popular meaning is an extension of the legal meanings, for historically the transference of property usually resulted from a sovereign's death. Hence the change of focus from conveyance to death. Sometimes even in legal contexts *demise* carries its nominal lay meaning: "Equating isolated instances of lawyer misconduct with the *demise* of legal ethics would be as foolhardy as ignoring the problem."/ "Mrs. Byrd's will was drawn by a Virginia practitioner two months after her husband's *demise."* See **death.**

Sense (1) of the verb and noun are illustrated in these sentences. Because even sense (1) contains two quite distinct meanings, a more specific word might be better: "If land is *demised* [read *leased*] for the term of one-hundred years or more, the term shall, as long as fifty years thereof remain unexpired, be regarded as an estate in fee simple."/ "A chargee by way of legal mortgage is to be deemed to have a charge by way of *sub-demise* [read *sublease*], and therefore a legal estate in the property charged." (Eng.)

The adjective is *demisable:* "Because this tenure derived its whole force from custom, the lands must have been *demisable* by copy of court roll from time immemorial" (Jowitt).

dempster; deemster. These are variant forms of the same word, which for most purposes has only historical significance. Both mean basically "a judge." *Dempster* was formerly used in Scotland, and *deemster* is still used on the Isle of Man. The *OED* notes that *deemster* "has been used in the general sense as a historical ARCHAISM by some modern writers"; the temptation to do so should be resisted.

demur; demure. *Demur* is the verb meaning "to file a demurrer, which denies that the complainant is legally entitled to relief." E.g., "Defendant *demurred* to each count." *Demure* is the adjective meaning (1) "sober, grave, serious"; or (2) "coy in an affected way."

demurrer; demurral; demur, n.; demurrage. A *demurrer* was a common-law pleading that stated that even if the other party's allegations were proved, that other party would not be entitled to succeed, and therefore that the demurring party was entitled in law to succeed on the facts alleged and admitted by the other. E.g., "The court was right in sustaining the *demurrer.*" Today, *demurrers* are obsolete in England and in most if not all American jurisdictions.

Idiomatically speaking, *demurrers* were *interposed:* "The circuit court of Cook County sustained a *demurrer interposed* by appellants to a bill for injunction filed by appellees and entered a decree dismissing the bill for want of equity."

Demur, n., is the archaic nonlegal word for "the act of demurring; an objection raised or exception taken to a proposed course of ac-

tion" (*OED*). The word is now chiefly literary. *Demurral* is a NEEDLESS VARIANT of *demur.*

Demurrage is a maritime-law word meaning "a [liquidated] penalty imposed on a charterer of a vessel, or in some instances the consignee of the vessel's goods, for delays in loading or unloading the ship's cargo." *Trans-Asiatic Oil, Ltd. v. Apex Oil Co.,* 804 F.2d 773, 774 n. 1 (1st Cir. 1986). It is usually used in the plural, *demurrages.*

denote for *denominate.* This error is not uncommon. "The issue can reasonably be *denoted as* [read *denominated,* or better, *called*] one of procedure."/ "M.Y.J. promised to pay $5,000 to Allegheny College by a writing *denoted* [read *denominated*] an Estate Pledge." See **connote.**

de novo, adv. & adj. This LATINISM, usually an adjective ⟨de novo review⟩, as an adverb means "anew." E.g., "We review a summary judgment *de novo.*"

deny (= to declare untrue; repudiate; to refuse to recognize or acknowledge) is frequently misused for other words.

A. For *refuse.* These words are synonymous in certain constructions, such as *He was denied* (or *refused*) this. But in modern usage *refuse* properly precedes an infinitive, whereas with *deny* this construction is an ARCHAISM: "The Federal Judge ordered the Governor to testify, but he *denied* [read *refused*] to do so."

B. For *deprive:* "The cumulative effect of the errors *denied them of a fair trial* [read either *denied them a fair trial* or *deprived them of a fair trial*]."

depart, a FORMAL WORD meaning "to go" or "to leave," may be a transitive verb, and often is in legal prose, although in lay usage it is almost always intransitive. Hence legal writers state that someone *departed the premises,* whereas the lay writer would probably state that someone *departed from the premises.*

dependence, -cy. These variants have undergone DIFFERENTIATION. *Dependence* is the general word meaning (1) "the quality or state of being dependent"; or (2) "reliance." *Dependency* is a geopolitical term meaning "a territory under the jursidiction of, but not formally annexed by, a nation." (See **territory.**) These words are commonly misspelled *-ance,* *-ancy.*

dependent, n.; **dependant.** The older spelling is *-ant.* The *OED* notes that "from the 18th c. (like the adj.) spelt *dependent,* after L.; but the spelling *-ant* still predominates in the [noun]." *W9* countenances *-ent* over *-ant.* The *COD* continues the Oxonian preference for *-ant,* noting that *-ent* is chiefly American. Certainly the British DIFFERENTIATION in spelling between the adjective and the noun is a useful one; but American writers cannot be faulted for using the *-ent* spelling for the noun.

dependent relative revocation. "The doctrine of *dependent relative revocation* is basically an application of the rule that a testator's intention governs; it is not a doctrine of defeating that intent." This phrase, common in the American and British law of wills, confuses all but lawyers specializing in wills and estates. It has nothing to do with revoking one's dependent relatives; rather, it means "revocation of a will by a testator who intends to replace it by another, effective will" (*CDL*). The law regards as mutually dependent the acts of destroying one will and of substituting another in its place, when both acts are parts of one plan. The two acts are thus "related," or *relative.* We might wish for a less monstrous phrase.

deplane. This word, like *inplane* and *reinplane,* is characteristic of airlinese, a relatively new brand of jargon. Careful writers and speakers stick to time-honored expressions like *get off, get on,* and *get on again.* See **inplane.**

depone; depose. In legal contexts, to *depone* (a relatively rare word) is to testify, and to *depose* is (v.i.) to bear witness or testify, or (v.t.) to take a deposition of someone. *Depose* also has the historical meaning "to dethrone or kill (a king)." Krapp recorded *depose* as being used in legal contexts for "to state," e.g., "The witness *deposes* that he has seen." G. P. Krapp, *A Comprehensive Guide to Good English* 188 (1927). Actually, today that sense survives only in the DOUBLET *deposes and states,* a common phrase in affidavits. Following are illustrations of the usual legal usages: "The attesting witness *deposed* to the circumstances of the will's execution."/ "The defendant's attorney then *deposed* the plaintiff."

deponent. See **affirmant.**

deport; disport. The latter word is sometimes confused with the former, which means (1) "to behave (oneself)"; or (2) "to banish, remove." The latter is a reflexive verb meaning "to display oneself sportively."

deportation; deportment. Both derive ultimately from L. *deportare* (= to carry off, convey away), but to say that these words have undergone DIFFERENTIATION is a great understatement. *Deportation* = the act of removing (a person) to another country; the expulsion of an alien from a country. *Deportment* = the bearing, demeanor, or manners of a person.

depose. See **depone.**

depositary, -tory; depositee. Most authorities on usage have agreed through the years that *depositary* is the better term in reference to persons with whom one leaves valuables or money for safekeeping, and that *depository* is preferred in reference to places. The Uniform Commercial Code, however, contains the term *depositary bank,* and this phrase has therefore become common. E.g., "*Depositary banks* rely on a strict set of rules to know when a check has been accepted or dishonored." Following is an example of the traditional use of *depositary*: "The *depositary* in escrow . . . has the absolute duty to carry out the terms of the agreement." *In re Missionary Baptist Foundation of America, Inc.,* 792 F.2d 502, 504 (5th Cir. 1986).

Depository has continued to be used consistently of places. E.g., "The Nuclear Waste Policy Act of 1982, 42 U.S.C. § 10101 *et seq.,* is a comprehensive statute providing for the establishment by the Department of Energy of a geologic *depository* for the disposal of high-level radioactive waste." *Depositee* is a NEEDLESS VARIANT of *depositary.*

deposition. A. As Verb. *Deposition* should not be used as a verb for *depose.* E.g.,"After they were *depositioned* [read *deposed*], they were asked to come forward with the relevant discoverable documents." See **depone.**

B. As Noun. *Deposition* serves as the noun for both *depose* and *deposit.* "The landfill sites were physically unsuitable for hazardous-waste *deposition* [= the act of depositing]." In the legal sense, as the noun for *depose, deposition* = (1) a declaration or statement of facts made by a witness under oath and reduced to writing for subsequent use in court proceedings (*OCL*); or (2) (in ecclesiastical law) a penalty by which a clergyman's patronage or other dignity is taken from him.

depository. See **depositary.**

depravity; depravation. The former is the condition of being depraved or corrupt; the latter is the act or process of depraving or corrupting. See **deprivation.**

deprecate; depreciate. The former is increasingly misused for the figurative senses of the latter, whereas the latter is too often confined to its literal meaning. *Deprecate* = to disapprove regretfully. The phrase *self-deprecating* is a virtual impossibility, except perhaps for those suffering from extreme neuroses. *Depreciate*, transitively, means "to belittle, disparage"; and intransitively, "to fall in value" (used of securities or investments). Thus *self-depreciating*, with *depreciate* in its transitive sense, is the correct phrase.

Here the U.S. Supreme Court nodded: "We do not *deprecate* [read *depreciate*] Fourth Amendment rights. The security of persons and property remains a fundamental value which law enforcement officers must respect." *Alderman v. United States*, 394 U.S. 165, 175 (1969).

The intransitive use of *depreciate* (= to decline in value), primarily financial and legal, has evolved into the transitive sense "to claim tax deductions (for) on the basis of depreciation" (he depreciated his house). This use of the word is colloquial, and should be avoided in formal legal contexts.

depreciatory, -tive. Both mean "disparaging." In G.B., *depreciatory* is the predominant term; in the U.S., the two forms are almost equally frequently used. Still, *depreciative* might reasonably be labeled a NEEDLESS VARIANT.

deprivation; privation. Both mean "the action of depriving or taking away." The words share that general sense as well as specific senses relating to the depriving of an office, position, or benefice. *Deprivation* is the ordinary word; *privation* is more literary.

depute, v.t.; **deputize.** To *depute* is to delegate ⟨these responsibilities he deputed to his

attorney-in-fact⟩, and to *deputize* is to make (another) one's deputy or to act as deputy.

deraign, v.t., is the legal ARCHAISM still often referred to, meaning "to settle (a dispute or claim) by combat or wager." A right-minded folk etymologist might conclude that the word was arrived at by metathesis of *derange*.

dereliction = abandonment, esp. through neglect or moral wrong, as in *dereliction of duty*. E.g., "By hypothesis he has committed the gravest *dereliction* possible—a complete repudiation of the trust he expressly assumed." The *OED* notes that in legal prose *dereliction* is still used in the neutral sense of physical abandonment; if this sense persists at all in current legal usage, it is obsolescent.

derisive, -sory; derisible. *Derisive* = scoffing; expressing derision. *Derisory* = worthy of derision or of being scoffed at. Though *derisive* and *derisory* at one time overlapped and were frequently synonymous, the DIFFERENTIATION is now complete, and using the two as synonyms is erroneous. *Derisible* is a NEEDLESS VARIANT of *derisory*.

derogate is regularly used in two quite distinct senses in legal prose: (1) transitively, it means "to disparage"—"We do not *derogate* these values, however, if we are unable to find them to be protected by the Constitution"; and (2) intransitively, it means "to detract" (with the prep. *from*)—"The court's position *derogates from* the highly sensitive discretion that is inherent in the parole function."

derogation of, in. This phrase is used 99 times in legal contexts for every one use in nonlegal contexts. It means "in abrogation or repeal of (a law, contract, or right)." Hence the maxim: *Statutes in derogation of the common law are to be strictly construed.* E.g., "The district court found that the intervenor's position would effectively give the employer control of the settlement process *in derogation of* the policy that settlements are favored in the law."

Derogation from is another idiom, meaning "prejudice, destruction (e.g., of a right or grant)." E.g., "It is an established rule that a grantor cannot be permitted to *derogate from* his grant."/ "If the perpetrator of this fraud is the counsel in the case, then, as an officer of the court he has offended and may be punished for a *derogation from* professional integrity." See **degradation.**

descendant. See **ascendant.**

descendible, not *descendable,* is the preferred form. See -ABLE (A).

descent. A. And *purchase.* These words are distinguished in the law of property. *Descent* refers to the acquisition of property by act of law (as by inheritance), whereas *purchase* is acquisition of property by the act of oneself or another (as by will or gift). In legal contexts, then, *purchase* is much broader than the general lay sense "buying." E.g., "These incidents did not accrue if the property was acquired through *purchase,* and, in order to obviate this means of curtailing the payment of incidents, title by *descent* was declared to be more worthy than title by *purchase;* if a gift over might pass to an heir by *descent* rather than by *gift* [i.e., *purchase*], he took his title through inheritance." See **purchase.**

B. And *distribution & inheritance.* At common law, intestate real property passes by *descent* and intestate personal property passes by *distribution.* Both *heirs* (who take by descent) and *distributees* (who take by distribution) may properly be said to *inherit* or *take by inheritance.* In the U.S., the Uniform Probate Code has simplified the historical terminology, supplanting all these specific terms with the general phrase *intestate succession.* See **succession.**

descry. See **decry.**

desegregation; integration. No distinction between a legal requirement of *integration* and a legal requirement of *desegregation* is ordinarily observed in legal usage, but the distinction may be important in understanding the constitutional law of race and the schools. Certainly it would be useful, in reference to schools in the U.S., if we distinguished between court-ordered *desegregation* (= the abrogation of policies that segregate races into different institutions and facilities) and court-ordered *integration* (= the incorporation of different races into existing institutions for the purpose of achieving a racial balance).

deserts. See **just deserts.**

deshabille. See **dishabille.**

designee is a MORPHOLOGICAL DEFORMITY for *designate,* n. See -EE.

desirable; desirous. *Desirable* is used in reference to things (or members of the opposite sex), *desirous* in reference to people's emotions. What is *desirable* is attractive and worth seeking; the word applies to anything that arouses a desire. *Desirous* = impelled by desire.

The phrase *be desirous of* is usually a circumlocution for the verb *desire* or *want.* E.g., "The appellant was desirous of securing the property immediately." [Read *The appellant desired* [or *wanted*] *to secure the property immediately.*]/ "Plaintiff's brother and sister, his cobeneficiaries under the trust, *were not desirous of terminating it* [read *did not want to terminate it*]."/ "In these cases, the plaintiffs ask equity to enjoin white property owners *who are desirous of selling* [read *who want to sell*] their houses to Negro buyers simply because the houses were subject to an original agreement not to have them pass to Negro ownership." See BE-VERBS (B).

desist is a FORMAL WORD for *stop* or *leave off.* E.g., "If he *desists* from the act of signing because of weakness or for some other reason, the partial signature may not be the signature that the statute requires." See **cease-and-desist order.** Cf. **cease.**

de son tort is a TERM OF ART used in the two phrases *executor de son tort* and *trustee de son tort. De son tort* is a LAW FRENCH phrase (meaning "by his own wrongdoing") that denotes the breach of a fiduciary duty. An *executor de son tort* is a person who, without legal authority, takes it on himself to act as executor or administrator as by acting or dealing with any of the decedent's property, apart from acts necessitated by humanity or necessity (OCL). Usually an *executor de son tort* acts to the detriment of beneficiaries or creditors of the estate. A *trustee de son tort* acts similarly in respect of a living person's property. E.g., "Plaintiff contended that when the first trust was consolidated with the Union Trust Co., the office of trustee, under the terms of the will, thereby automatically became vacant and that the successor, from that time on, acted as trustee *de son tort.*" See **ex maleficio.**

despatch. See **dispatch.**

despite; in spite of. The two are interchangeable. The compactness of *despite* recommends it.

despiteous; dispiteous. *Despiteous* = with despite; despiteful; scornful. *Dispiteous* = pitiless.

despoilation for *despoliation* (= pillaging, plundering) is a not uncommon blunder that surprises primarily because it occurs in otherwise highly literate writing.

destination. See **ultimate destination.**

destructible; destroyable. The latter is a NEEDLESS VARIANT. *Destructible* and *-bility* are frequently used in the law: "There is ample justification for a search of the arrestee's person and the area within his immediate control—construing that phrase to mean the area from within which he might gain possession of a weapon or *destructible* evidence."/ "This rule is known as the Doctrine of the *Destructibility* of Contingent Remainders."

detainal. See **detention.**

detainee (= a person held in custody) is a twentieth-century NEOLOGISM that has proved useful in legal contexts. E.g., "The *detainee* must be promptly brought before a magistrate for a probable cause determination." See -EE.

detainment; detainer. See **detention.**

detectable, -ible. The former spelling is preferred. See -ABLE (A).

detector, -er. The former spelling is preferred. See -ER, -OR.

detention; detainment; detainal; detainer. *Detention* = holding in custody; confinement; compulsory delay. *Detainment* and *detainal* are NEEDLESS VARIANTS. *Detainer* is a specialized legal term meaning (1) "the action of detaining, withholding, or keeping in one's possession"; (2) "the confinement of a person in custody"; or (3) "a writ authorizing prison officials to continue holding a prisoner in custody."

determent. See **deterrence.**

determinable = (1) terminable; or (2) able to be determined or ascertained. Sense (1) is common in the law (determinable fee), but generally ought to be avoided in deference to the more universally understandable *terminable.* In a few SET PHRASES, it should be allowed to remain. E.g., "A possibility of reverter is the future interest left in one who creates a fee simple conditional or a *fee simple determinable.*" But in other contexts, it ought be be simplified, for it is merely an unnecessary LEGALISM: "The award constituted the employment as one that was *determinable* [read *terminable*] on a day's notice." (Aus.)

In these sentences, sense (2) is intended: "The applicant has a *determinable* physical impairment that can be expected to result in death."/ "To have standing under the Clayton Act, an antitrust plaintiff must demonstrate that the extent of his injury is *determinable* and not speculative."/ "This court affirmed the dismissal of the federal claims, but held that the validity of the state-law claims was a matter of state law best *determinable* by the state courts."/ "Such damages would be *determinable* in terms of the fee that would have been charged appellant by a competent and properly prepared service engineer less the market value of the services that Reindl provided."

determinacy, the correct form, is sometimes incorrectly rendered *determinancy.* E.g., "A number of jurisdictions have increased markedly the *determinancy* [read *determinacy*] with which sentences are set."

determinant. See **determiner.**

determinate, adj. *Determinate sentencing* came in response to the phrase *indeterminate sentencing,* which denotes a practice that was common in the U.S. up until the early 1970s (no specific time being set for prison sentences, e.g., "10 to 20 years"). E.g., "A *determinate* jail sentence for disobedience of a negative injunction is usually considered to be improper in civil contempt actions." The adverb *determinately* is sometimes confused with *determinedly* (= with determination).

determination of whether. The preposition *of* is unnecessary. See **whether.**

determine. A. Archaic Sense. Used without a direct object, *determine* in legal prose is an ARCHAISM in the sense "to terminate; bring or come to an end." E.g., "He had a determinable [q.v.] estate; it was never *determined;* he died owning it, and now after the *determination* of the trust it is part of the intestate estate, to be distributed as such."/ "If no issue of her body then survive, then all the principle of said estate then remaining shall be divided among my heirs-at-law in proportion to their heirship and upon the principal of said fund being distributed in accordance with the directions of this clause, then said trust shall cease and *determine*." Laymen are likely to be confused by this legalistic usage; hence a simpler wording might often be called for, e.g., "The trust shall *terminate*."

B. *Determine (whether)(if)*. *Determine if* is now regarded as inferior to *determine whether* in formal writing, although historically *if* has occurred at least as often in reputable writers. "This court has on four previous occasions been called upon to *determine if* [read *determine whether*] allegedly unconstitutional actions taken by legislators or legislative employees are insulated from judicial review by the Speech or Debate Clause."

determiner; determinant. Both mean "that which determines." Preference might be given to the Anglo-Saxon suffix *-er*, but one could not be faulted for using either term: euphony should be the determiner. "Much has been written about the *determinants* of foreign policy in the new states of Africa." Only *determiner* suffices when a person ("one who determines") is denoted.

deterrent, n.; deterrence; determent. A *deterrent* is that which deters. *Deterrence* is preventing by fear. *Determent* is the act or fact of deterring.

detinet. See **detinuit.**

detinue; replevin; trover. *Detinue* and *replevin* are common-law remedies for the specific recovery of personal property. *Detinue* developed from the writ of debt to provide for the return of wrongfully detained goods. The losing defendant had the option, at common law, of returning the property or paying the plaintiff an amount equal to its value, as determined at trial. *Detinue* has been abolished by statute in England, but exists in many American jurisdictions.

Replevin originated as an action to test the legality of another's seizure of goods (*distraint*, q.v.). In G.B., it has been restricted to this particular situation, whereas in the U.S. *replevin* has become an available remedy for any case of wrongful taking of chattels.

Trover is a common-law remedy for compensatory damages for conversion of personal property.

detinuit; detinet. These common-law actions have deceptively similar names. *Detinuit* (lit., "he has detained") = an action of replevin in which the plaintiff already possesses the goods for which he sues. *Detinet* (lit., "he detains") = an action alleging simply that the defendant is wrongfully withholding money or chattels.

detoxicate; detoxify. *Detoxify* is prevalent in the U.S., *detoxicate* in G.B.

detractive, -tory. The latter is a NEEDLESS VARIANT of *detractive* (= tending to detract; defamatory).

deuterogamy. See **bigamy.**

devastavit; devisavit. These terms are easily confusable; they call for explanation in modern contexts. *Devastavit* (L. "he has wasted") = the failure of a personal representative to administer a decedent's estate promptly and properly. E.g., "The writ may be used to enforce the personal liability of an executor or administrator, where a *devastavit* has been committed." See **waste.**

Devisavit is invariably used in the phrase *devisavit vel non* (L. "he devises or not"), which in former practice was an issue sent from an equity or probate court to a court of law to determine the validity of a purported will. E.g., "One may, upon an issue of *devisavit vel non*, prove that a part of the executed instrument was not the testator's will." See **vel non.**

deviance, -cy; deviation. The general term for "an act or instance of deviating" is *deviation* ⟨deviation from orthodox religion⟩. E.g., "Pioneer contends that, in proceedings under section 10207, a charitable corporation must be given an opportunity to correct its *deviation* from its articles, as it would if the proceedings were quo warranto." *Deviation* is more neutral in connotation than *deviance*, which means "the quality or state of deviating from established norms, esp. in social customs." *Deviancy* is a NEEDLESS VARIANT.

deviant; deviate. A. As Adjectives. *Deviant*

is normal. The *OED* labels both of these adjectives "obsolete" and "rare." The *OED Supp.* (1972) deletes the tag on *deviant* and cites numerous examples in the sense "deviating from normal social standards or behavior." The word is common in legal writing: "The government failed to present the expert testimony necessary to establish that the photographs would appeal to the prurient interest of a clearly defined *deviant* group."

W3 records *deviate* as an adjective, and it is not uncommon in American legal prose: "The hospital and morgue staff all testified that no *deviate* sexual intercourse was performed on complainant while she was under their care and control." Still, *deviant* is the preferred adjective.

Deviant is often used in figurative senses; for example: "*Deviant* rulings by circuit courts of appeals, particularly in apparent dicta, cannot generally provide the justified reliance necessary to warrant withholding retroactive application of a decision construing a statute as Congress intended it."

B. As Nouns. Both *deviate* and *deviant* are used as (generally pejorative) nouns meaning "a person who, or thing which, deviates, esp. from normal social standards or behavior; spec., a sexual pervert" (*OED Supp.*). *Deviate* seems to be slightly more common.

deviation. See **deviance.**

devisavit. See **devastavit.**

devise, n.; bequest; legacy. These words denote types of clauses in wills, each having acquired through DIFFERENTIATION a more or less generally accepted sense among lawyers. A *devise* traditionally disposes of real property (only in legal usage is this word a noun). In the U.S. this tradition has been changed by statutes (see the next entry), but the traditional wording is strongly rooted, and most legal writers confine *devise* to contexts involving real property: "The court, to conform to the testator's true intent, included part of lot 16 in this *devise*."/ "In *Matter of Champion*, the testator executed a will containing a *devise* of land 'now in my occupation.'"

A *bequest* disposes of personal property other than money, although the modern tendency is to include testamentary gifts of money as well as gifts of other personalty. *Legacy* is the more proper term for a clause disposing of money. Each of the terms may refer

not only to the clause in the will, but to the gift itself. See **will** & **bequest.**

devise, v.t.; bequeath. In the traditional legal idiom, one *bequeaths* personal property and *devises* real property. E.g., "Apple's intention to *devise* him a mere life estate in the property would have severely hindered his real estate development scheme." The restriction to real property has not always obtained, however; the *OED* quotes an Englishman who in 1347 *devised* his gold ring to a lady companion. Similar usages appeared up to the eighteenth century.

Under both the Restatement of Property and the Uniform Probate Code (in the U.S.), neither of which distinguishes in terminology between real and personal property, to dispose of any property by will is to *devise* it, the recipients being *devisees* even if the subject of the disposition is personal property. In England, however, *devise* is said to refer properly only to dispositions of real property (*OCL* & *CDL*).

It should not escape our attention that the simple verb *give* almost always suffices as well as, and with less confusion than, *bequeath* or *devise.*

The general nonlegal sense of *devise* (= to plan or invent) is also used in legal contexts: "The Rule in Shelley's Case was *devised* in feudal times."/ "The old real actions such as writs of right and writs of entry, dating back to the Norman Conquest, were *devised* to provide for the specific recovery of real property." See **bequeath.**

devisee; legatee; heir. These words have traditionally been distinguished, although in practice *devisee* and *legatee* are often used interchangeably. A *devisee* is the recipient of a *devise*, q.v. *Devisee of land* would once have been considered redundant, but arguably is not redundant in light of the changed meaning in the U.S. of *devise*. E.g., "A *devisee of land* is usually regarded as receiving his title at the instant of the testator's death."/ "We are of the opinion that this case falls within the general rule, and that the property in question passes to the residuary *devisees*."

A *legatee* is one who receives a legacy. It is sometimes opposed to *devisee*. E.g., "Where partial revocation by physical act is permitted, there can be no partial revocation of the words of a will if the effect is to change the construction of the remainder clause or to increase a provision made for someone other than the residuary *legatee* or *devisee.*"/ "Neither a *legatee* nor, in most states, a *devisee*, can establish his rights against third parties until the will under which he takes is probated."

An *heir* takes by inheritance (or *descent*, q.v.) rather than through a will or gift (by purchase); thus *heir* is not properly used of a *devisee* or *legatee*.

deviser, -or; divisor. A *deviser* is one who invents or contrives. A *devisor* is one who disposes of property by will. E.g., "The will must be subscribed and attested in the presence of the *devisor* by three or four credible witnesses, or else it will be utterly void and of no effect." *Divisor* is a mathematical term referring to the number by which another number is divided.

devisibility; divisibility. The former means "the capability of being devised or bequeathed"; the latter means "the capability of being divided."

devoid, a variant of *void,* adj., is current only in the idiom *devoid of:* "The case was totally *devoid* of evidence that any such crime had been committed." This phrase is a favorite of hyperbolists, and should be used cautiously.

devolution; devolvement. The latter is a NEEDLESS VARIANT. In the first two specimens that follow, *devolution* means "the passing of the power or authority of one person or body to another" (*OED*); in the third, it means "the causing of anything to descend or fall upon (anyone)" (*id.*). "It may be convenient to deal first with the *devolution* of that appointive property."/ "The circumstance that the settlor specifically reserved a power to appoint a taker means, if it means anything, that she wanted to affirm and emphasize that she desired to retain control of her property up to the time of her death and to direct its *devolution* thereafter."/ "The reasoning for so deciding is that *devolution* of property of a decedent is controlled entirely by the statutes of descent and distribution."

devolutive; devolutionary. The former is the preferred adjective corresponding to the noun *devolution*, q.v. "The Viators took a *devolutive* appeal from the judgments against them in the trial court." (La.) *Devolutionary* is a NEEDLESS VARIANT.

devolve takes *on* or *upon*. E.g., "Where a person has been held to answer a criminal charge it *devolves upon* the state's attorney to duly prosecute the charge regardless of his personal views." See **bequeath**.

devolvement. See **devolution**.

devotee. See -EE.

dext(e)rous, -tral. *Dexterous* (the preferred spelling in AmE is with the *-e-*) means "clever, adept, skillful, artful." In BrE the term is spelled *dextrous*. *Dextral* = on the right; right-handed.

diagnosis; prognosis. Courts recognize the important distinction between these words. A *diagnosis* is an analysis of one's present bodily condition with reference to disease or disorder. A *prognosis* is the projected future of a present disease or disorder. E.g., "As to the *diagnoses* and *prognoses* of the physicians, they are not so clear and consistent as to validate removing the issue of arbitrary and capricious denial of the maintenance and cure from the jury." See **prognosis**.

diagram(m)ing. See **program(m)ing** & DOUBLING OF FINAL CONSONANTS.

dialectal; dialectic(al). These words are frequently confused. The adjective for *dialect* (= a regional variety of language) is *dialectal*. Here the wrong word is used: "The court stated that the word 'opry' is a *dialectical* [read *dialectal*] variation of 'opera,' which has been in common use from the eighteenth century to the present, and that 'opry' has been and is now used to describe a show consisting of country music, dancing, and comedy routines."

Dialectical = of or relating to logical argument, historical development, or the resolution of contradictory ideas. The term is usually confined to philosophical contexts. As an adjective, *dialectic* is a NEEDLESS VARIANT of *dialectical*.

dialog(ue); duologue. *Dialogue* = (1) a conversation between two or more persons; or (2) the exchange of ideas. The longer spelling is preferred. (Cf. **catalog(ue).**) *Duologue,* a rather uncommon term, means "a conversation between two persons only."

dicta. See **dictum.**

dictatrix. See SEXISM (C).

diction = (1) enunciation, distinctness of pronunciation; or (2) word-choice. Often sense (2) is overlooked. This book addresses in large measure problems of legal diction.

dictum. A. Full Phrase. *Dictum* is a shortened form of *obiter dictum* (= a nonbinding, incidental opinion on a point of law given by a judge in the course of a written opinion delivered in support of a judgment). The full phrase still occasionally appears: "The principle of stare decisis impliedly imposes upon the writer of the opinion the obligation to refrain from *obiter dicta* and to confine himself to the precise questions involved." Judge Posner has aptly defined *dictum* as "a statement in a judicial opinion that could have been deleted without seriously impairing the analytical foundations of the holding—that, being peripheral, may not have received the full and careful consideration of the court that uttered it." *Sarnoff v. American Home Products Corp.*, 798 F.2d 1075, 1084 (7th Cir. 1986).

British legal texts use *dictum* as well as *obiter* as the shortened form of *obiter dictum*. E.g., "In considering the *dicta* cited to us from the cases to which we referred we bore in mind the importance of interpreting judicial pronouncements in the context of the questions which the court had to decide." (Eng.)/ "The view of Lord Tenterden C.J. in *Collier v. Hicks*, although *obiter*, has always been accepted as authoritative on this aspect of the law." (Eng.) See **obiter.**

Obiter dictum is not, however, the only type of dictum. *Black's* notes also *simplex dictum* (= *ipse dixit*, q.v.) and *gratis dictum* (= a statement made by a party, but not obligatorily). One can safely assert that *dictum* as used in modern legal writing almost never stands for either of these highly specialized terms.

B. Number. *Dictum* is the singular form of *dicta*, which in law are "remarks made in a judicial opinion that are not binding law." *Dicta* is frequently misused as a singular noun. E.g., "I do agree with the court's observation that dicta *is* [read *are*] not binding in future cases."/ "Even if the Fourth Circuit's doctrine is sound, the rationale of its holding is not applicable here and its dicta *approves* [read *approve*] our holding."/ "We are not bound by *dicta* of a minority of the en banc court, and we decline to follow *it* [read *them*; or make it *dictum . . . it*]."/ "Language in *Stack v. Boyle* tying the availability of bail to the presumption of innocence is mere *dicta* [read *dictum*]."

Here the number is correct: "I care not for the supposed *dicta* of judges, however eminent, if they be contrary to all principle. The *dicta* cited *were* probably misunderstood, and at all events they are to be disregarded." (Mansfield, J.)/ "Pioneer contends that the Constitution of the United States compels us to follow here the *dictum* in the College of California case; it is settled, however, that judicial decisions may be overruled and *dicta* disapproved without violating either the due process clause or the contract clause of the Constitution." (Traynor, J.)/ "The *dictum* in *Gifford v. Dyer* that relief will be given if the mistake and what would have been done in the absence of the mistake appears upon the face of the will has been approved in *dicta* in a number of decisions."

C. Articles with. In the legal idiom, *dictum* generally does not take an article unless the article is acting as a DEICTIC TERM. E.g., "The *dictum* in the principal case is derived from the treatment of mistakes in revocation." Usually, however, the article is unnecessary: "The court of appeals correctly identified *a dictum* [read *dictum*] in *Brown v. United States* as the source of what has become known as the 'substitute facilities doctrine.'" / "Counsel inform us that this court has never answered the question, and that they are confident in asserting that the point has not been directly passed upon in the United States and that any reference to this question of law in any case is pure *dictum*."

D. Lay Sense. In general nonlegal contexts, *dictum* often means (1) "a statement of opinion or belief held to be authoritative because of the dignity of the person making it"; or (2) "a familiar rule." In these lay senses, *dictum* takes an article. E.g., in sense (2): "It is a familiar *dictum* that the law will scrutinize with jealous care all transactions between parties who stand in confidential relations."

dietitian; dietician. The former spelling is preferred.

differ (from) (with). To *differ from* is to be unlike, whereas to *differ with* is to express a divergent opinion. E.g., "With respect to legacies out of the personal estate, the civil law, which in this respect has been adopted by courts of equity, *differs* in some respects *from* the common law in its treatment of conditions precedent.''

difference. See **differential.**

different (from) (than). *Different than* is often considered inferior to *different from*. The problem is that *than* should follow a comparative adjective (e.g., *larger than, sooner than,* etc.), and *different* is not comparative—though, to be sure, it is a word of contrast. Writers should generally prefer *different from*. *Than* implies a comparison, i.e., a matter of degree; but *differences* are ordinarily qualitative, not quantitative, and the adj. *different* is not strictly comparative. E.g., ''Minors are treated differently *than* [read *from*] adults in the criminal justice system.''

Still, it is indisputable that *different than* is sometimes idiomatic, and even useful insofar as *different from* frequently is not interchangeable with it, as here: ''Corporate residency is *different* for venue *than* for diversity purposes.'' Also, *different than* may properly begin clauses, where attempting to use *different from* would be so awkward as to require another construction: ''The record establishes that Wakefield is a *different* person mentally and emotionally *than* he was before his loss of hearing.''

Where, however, *from* nicely fills the slot of *than*, it is to be preferred: ''The fact that the injury occurred in a *different* manner *than* [read *from*] that which might have been expected does not prevent the chauffeur's negligence from being in law the cause of the injury.'' (Andrews, J., in *Palsgraf*.)/ ''If the testator makes a gift of property that is of a different nature *than* [read *from*] that of the property bequeathed, an application of the doctrine of ejusdem generis gives rise to a presumption that he did not intend to adeem.'' The *Oxford Guide* (p. 102) notes that when the adverb *differently* is used, *than* is ''especially common . . . and has been employed by good writers since the seventeenth century.'' E.g., ''A civil-rights suit is to be treated no differently *than* any other civil action.''

Different to is a common British construction, unobjectionable when used by British writers: ''He may say that the other has wholly failed in performance and given him a thing *different* in kind *to* that which was bargained for, or of no substantial value.'' (Eng.)

Not infrequently writers will use *different*

superfluously with *other than*: ''The right of the district court to require the commissioners' court, by mandamus, to place a *different* [delete] valuation on the property of the railway company *other than* the value theretofore placed on said property by the commissioners' court is discussed in the case of *Dillon v. Bave*.''

differentia (= a distinguishing mark or characteristic) is a technical biological term that was long ago appropriated by legal writers, although often it is used merely to mean ''a distinction.'' The term is more common in G.B. than in the U.S. E.g., ''The only *differentia* that can exist must arise, if at all, out of the fact that the acts done are the joint acts of several capitalists, and not of one capitalist only.'' (Eng.)/ ''The question in every case is whether the tribunal in question has similar attributes to a court of justice or acts in a manner similar to that in which such courts act. This is of necessity a *differentia* that is not capable of precise limitation.'' (Eng.) The plural is *differentiae*.

differential. A. For *difference*. The *OED* records the noun *differential* only in specialized mathematical and biological senses. As a popularized technicality, it was extended to mean ''a difference in wage or salary.'' E.g., ''[P]ayment [may be] made pursuant to . . . a *differential* based on any other factor other [sic] than sex.'' Equal Pay Act, 29 U.S.C. § 206(d) (1) (1982) (emphasis added).

The intrusion of this word into the domain of *difference* should stop there, however. The following use of *differential* was ill advised: ''Most of the foreign news reaches this country at the City of New York, and because of this, and of time *differentials* [read *differences*] due to the earth's rotation, the distribution of news matter throughout the country is principally from east to west.''

B. And *different*. *Differential*, adj. = (1) of, exhibiting, depending on, a difference; or (2) constituting a specific difference. The adjective is not nearly as often misused as the noun (see (A) above): ''*Differential* treatment of parties who are similarly situated raises questions about whether the agency is administering its program in a fair, impartial, and competent manner.''/ ''I am unhappily aware that this ruling will create anomalies through *differential* recognition of the acts of judges appointed respectively before and after U.D.I.''

(Eng.)/ "This tactic enables the court to characterize state goals that have been legitimated by Congress itself as improper solely because it disagrees with the concededly rational means of *differential* taxation selected by the legislature."

C. And *deferential.* These near-homophones sometimes trip up semiconscious writers and speakers. *Deferential* = showing deference; respectful.

differentiate. See **delineate.**

DIFFERENTIATION is the linguistic process by which words of common etymology gradually diverge in meaning, each taking on a distinct sense. Examples of this process, which, as the opposite of SLIPSHOD EXTENSION, continually enriches the language, are referred to throughout this work.

difficult of, an archaic construction, is common still in legal prose. E.g., "The complications that can arise when divorces are invalid are *difficult of solution.*" Formerly this phrasing was seen in literary as well as in legal writing. See **of** (B).

digamy. See **bigamy.**

digital is commonly used as the adjective corresponding to *finger* in contexts such as the following: "[T]he issue of *digital* rape was raised at trial." *State v. Roden,* 380 N.W.2d 669, 670 (S.D. 1986)./ "He argues that officials subjected him to a *digital* rectal search that violated his fourth, fifth, and eighth amendment rights."

dignitas is a preposterous LATINISM in place of the ordinary word *dignity.* E.g., "I accept the fact, therefore, that the applicant has suffered an injury to his *dignitas* [read *dignity*] by the respondent's actions." (Rhod.)

dignity exists in law in a sense obsolete in nonlegal contexts. It is used to mean "rank; magnitude," esp. in the phrase *of constitutional dignity.* E.g., "A statute and a constitution, although of unequal *dignity,* are both laws, and rest on the will of the people."/ "The constitutional requirement of substantial equality and fair process can be attained only where counsel acts in the role of an active advocate in behalf of his client, as opposed to that of amicus curiae; the no-merit letter and the procedure it triggers do not reach that *dignity.*"/ "The duty that Botkin owed defendant, in making those payments, was of a *dignity* with, if not superior to, any that he owed to plaintiff."

dijudicate. See **adjudge.**

dilapidation. So spelled; *delapidation* is a common misspelling.

dilat(at)ion. The better nominal form of the verb *to dilate,* from an etymological point of view, is *dilatation.* But *dilation* is common in AmE medical contexts. In other senses, *dilatation* (= [1] speaking or writing at length; or [2] expansion) should be used.

dilation of the eyes. Strangely, there is a misconception afoot that *dilation* means "constriction or narrowing of the pupils," when in fact just the opposite is meant. To *dilate* on a subject is to expand on it, and for one's pupils to *dilate* (e.g., from being in the dark or from the use of certain drugs) is likewise for them to enlarge. See **dilat(at)ion.**

dilatory = tending to cause delay (dilatory pleas or exceptions). This word is little known to laymen.

dilemma = a choice between two unpleasant or difficult alternatives. This word should not be used by SLIPSHOD EXTENSION for *plight* or *predicament.* The adjective is *dilemmatic.*

dilutee = an unskilled worker added to a staff of skilled workers. See -EE.

diminution; diminishment. The latter is a NEEDLESS VARIANT. "But there are procedural safeguards against *diminishment* [read *diminution*] of the infant's award." *Diminution* /dim-i-**nyoo**-shŏn/ or /**noo**-shŏn/ is often mispronounced /dim-yoo-**nish**-ŏn/, by metathesis, and sometimes is erroneously spelled *dimunition.*

diminutive, meaning "small" is not pronounced /di-**min**-ŭ-tiv/, but rather /di-**min**-yŭ tiv/, with a liquid -u-.

direct is often used as an ellipsis for *direct examination.* E.g., "His testimony on *direct* did not relate to any inculpatory or exculpatory comments by Mr. P." Cf. **cross** & **redirect.**

direct cause. See CAUSATION (A).

directed verdict; instructed verdict. The phrases are synonymous. The (U.S.) Federal Rules of Civil Procedure use *directed verdict.* Both phrases exemplify HYPALLAGE, inasmuch as the jury, and not the verdict, is what is directed or instructed.

direct evidence; original evidence. Both of these phrases are used as antonyms of *hearsay evidence* and *circumstantial evidence* (or *indirect evidence*). *Direct evidence* is more common. As an opposite of *hearsay,* it means "a statement in reference to another's previous words, made by a witness in court to prove the truth of the matter asserted." As an antonym of *circumstantial evidence, direct evidence* = a statement of a witness that he perceived a fact in issue with one of his five senses or that he was in a particular physical or mental state (*CDL*).

It would be helpful by way of DIFFERENTIATION to use *original evidence* as an antonym of *hearsay evidence,* and *direct evidence* as an antonym of *circumstantial evidence.*

direct examination; examination-in-chief. The latter is a chiefly British variant of the former. See **direct & cross-examination.**

direction. See **jury instruction.**

directional. See **directory.**

DIRECTIONAL WORDS. A. In *-ward(s).* BrE has an affinity for *-wards* words. "There was a taxicab proceeding *westwards* whose driver was called as a witness." (Eng.) In AmE *-ward* is the preferred form across the board. Hence *toward* is preferred in the U.S., *towards* in G.B.
B. Verbose Constructions. Use of such words as *easterly* and *northerly* in phrases like *in an easterly direction* is prolix. In fact, the simple word for the direction (*east*) usually suffices in place of the words ending in either *-erly* or *-wardly.* "The appellee was riding his bicycle *northwardly* [read *north*] on 29th Street just before the accident; appellant was driving his car *in a southerly direction* [read *south*] on Jackson Street." The one useful distinctive sense that *southwardly* and *southerly* convey is "in a direction more or less south."
C. Capitalization. The words *north, south,*

east, and *west* should not be capitalized when used to express directions; they are properly capitalized when they denote regions of the world or of a country (e.g., Midwest, Far East, the South).

directory; imperative. These words have been used distinctively for purposes of statutory interpretation. "Mandatory provisions [in a statute] have . . . frequently been classified as either *imperative* (when failure to comply renders all subsequent proceedings void) or *directory* (when the subsequent proceedings are valid, though the persons failing to carry out the action enjoined [i.e., mandated] by Parliament may sometimes be punishable)." *F. v. F.,* [1971] P. 1, 11. E.g., "It has been held that a violation is a substantial and not a mere technical error, since such a statute is *imperative* and not *directory.*"

In the U.S., frequently, the distinction is rather different: *directory* is opposed to *mandatory,* and is only a little stronger than *precatory,* q.v.: "Statutes that regulate and prescribe the time in which public officers shall perform specified duties are generally regarded as *directory* only."

In the following sentence, *directional* (= of or relating to, or indicating, spatial direction) is wrongly used for *directory:* "The sentence is a *directional* [read *directory*] provision indicating when and how she is to receive the payments." *Coker v. Coker,* 650 S.W.2d 391, 395 (Tex. 1983) (Spears, J., dissenting).

directress, -trix. See SEXISM (C).

disability. A. And *liability; inability.* These words, which overlap only slightly but are infrequently confounded, are best keenly distinguished. *Disability* = (1) the lack of ability to perform some function; or (2) incapacity in the eyes of the law. *Liability* = (1) probability; (2) a pecuniary obligation; or (3) a drawback. *Inability* = the lack of power or means.

B. And *disablement. Disablement* = (1) the action of disabling; or (2) the imposition of a legal disability. Here sense (1) applies: "Under a credit insurance policy the beneficiary is the creditor and, upon the death or *disablement* of the insured, the benefits or proceeds of the policy automatically accrue to the creditor for the purpose of discharging the debtor's financial obligations." See (A) for the senses of *disability.*

disadvantage, v.t., appears regularly in legal writing, but generally only the past participial form *disadvantaged* appears in lay writing, usu. functioning as an adjective ⟨disadvantaged student⟩. Following are examples of typical legal usage: "The statute *disadvantages* those who would benefit from laws barring racial, religious, or ancestral discrimination."/ "The state may no more *disadvantage* any particular group by making it more difficult to enact legislation in its behalf than it may dilute a person's vote."/ "The district court judge held that the EEOC could not show sex discrimination violating section 703(d)(1) of Title VII because females had not been *disadvantaged* with respect to males."

disaffirmation; disaffirmance. For the word meaning "repudiation," the distinction drawn at *affirmance,* q.v., would recommend the form *disaffirmation.* The *COD* recommends *-tion,* but *W9* records only *-ance,* a common form in AmE. Try as we might for consistency, we are unlikely to achieve it here. *Disaffirmation* is better, but *disaffirmance* cannot be strongly criticized. E.g., "The common-law method for reaching this remedial goal is through an out-of-court *disaffirmance* of the contract followed by a legal restitutionary action."/ "The tentative trust becomes absolute and irrevocable on the death of the depositor before the beneficiary without revocation or some decisive act or declaration of *disaffirmance,* entitling the beneficiary to the balance remaining at the time of the depositor's death, but not to anything more than such balance."

disappoint (of) (in). *Disappoint* is used in legal contexts in a sense rare in lay contexts, namely, "to deprive; to frustrate in one's expectations." E.g., "A court of equity will then sequester the benefits intended for the electing beneficiary, to secure compensation to those persons whom his election *disappoints.*"/ "The courts will not *disappoint* the interest of those for whose benefit the party is called upon to exercise the power."

Usually the term *disappointed* refers to heirs who take neither an intestate share of an estate nor a share by will. E.g., "Under such circumstances, the gift to the class is implied, and the testator could not have intended the objects of the power to be *disappointed* of his bounty by the failure of the donee to exercise

such power in their favor." To be *disappointed in* a thing, as opposed to *of* it, is to have received or attained it but to consider it as not measuring up to one's expectations.

Often *disappointed* is used as a past participial adjective: "He is known in the law as a *disappointed* legatee, and the doctrine of acceleration of remainders should be adopted at the expense of *disappointed* legatees."

disapprobation is an especially FORMAL WORD meaning "disapproval." It is perhaps allowable in weighty contexts: "On the opening of the cause, Lord Kenyon expressed his *disapprobation* of the action; but his lordship permitted the cause to proceed." (Eng.) But in ordinary prose it leads to topheaviness: "Employees may feel the need to sign the petition in order to curry favor with or avoid *disapprobation* [read *disapproval*] by company officials." See **approbation.**

disapprove, like *approve,* q.v., may be transitive as well as intransitive. "We *disapprove* the dicta in that case." This use of the word is far more common in legal than in nonlegal writing.

disassemble. See **dissemble.**

disassociate; dissociate. Though common, *disassociate* is inferior to *dissociate,* q.v., of which it is a NEEDLESS VARIANT.

disasterous is a fairly common misspelling of *disastrous.* See, e.g., Leff, *The Leff Dictionary of Law,* 94 Yale L.J. 1855, 2038 (1985), s.v. *aphrodisiac.*

disbar. See **bar.**

disbark. See **disembark.**

disbarment; disbarring. Both mean "the action of expelling a lawyer from the bar." *Disbarment* is the more common noun in the U.S. E.g., "A threat of personal chastisement made by an attorney to a judge out of court for his conduct or rulings during the trial of a cause pending is strictly unprofessional and furnishes grounds for *disbarment.*"/ "The effect of a *disbarment* is the utter extinction of professional character."

In G.B., the gerund in *-ing* is common: "*Disbarring* may be imposed by the benchers as the ultimate punishment on a barrister guilty of conduct unbecoming the profession." (Eng.) See **bar.**

disbelief; unbelief; nonbelief; misbelief. *Disbelief* is the mental rejection of something after considering its plausibility; it results from active, conscious decision. *Unbelief* denotes the state of doubt, but of not having made up one's mind. *Nonbelief* is a NEEDLESS VARIANT of *unbelief.* "*Nonbelief* [read *Unbelief*] of the prosecutor in the guilt of the person charged with crime is evidence of want of probable cause for the prosecution." A *misbelief* is an erroneous or false belief.

disburse; disperse. *Disburse* is used only in reference to distribution of money ⟨the directors disbursed dividends to the stockholders⟩. *Disperse* is used in reference to distribution of all other things, such as crowds or diseases.

disc. See **disk.**

discernible, -able. The former spelling is preferred. See -ABLE (B).

discharge was formerly common as a variant of *dismiss* in mandates. E.g., "Case *discharged.*"

disciplinary; disciplinatory. The latter is a NEEDLESS VARIANT. *Disciplinary* = (1) related to discipline; or (2) carrying out punishment. Here sense (2) applies: "The special master considered the company's disparate enforcement of its no-solicitation policy to be mitigated by the legality of the warning, apology, mistake, or failure to result in *disciplinary* action."

disclaim. See **declaim.**

disclose; expose. There are important differences. *Disclose* = to reveal any factual matter. *Expose* = (1) to lay bare or unmask something bad; or (2) to place in a perilous condition.

discomfit(ure). *Discomfit* (= to frustrate, disconcert) is best used only as a verb. The preferred noun is *discomfiture.* Ill-trained writers use phrases such as *much to his discomfit,* in

which either *discomfort* or *discomfiture* is intended.

discommend is the opposite of *recommend,* not of *commend.*

disconcertion; disconcertment. The preferred noun corresponding to the verb *to disconcert* is *disconcertion.*

discontinuation; discontinuance; discontinuity. See **continuance.**

discover is, except in legal ARGOT, obsolete in the sense "to uncover, reveal." (See **discovery.**) The verb now generally means "to find, detect."

discoverable, in American law, means "subject to pretrial discovery" ⟨discoverable documents of the corporation⟩. This sense goes beyond the general meaning of "ascertainable."

discovert is not an opposite of *covert* as ordinarily used—*overt* is. *Discovert* means "unmarried, whether widowed, divorced, or never having married," or, more technically, "not subject to the disabilities of coverture." E.g., "She united with her husband in making a sale to her brother of the land put into their possession by her father's executor, and she subsequently acknowledged it when *discovert.*" See **covert.**

discovery, as a term of legal ARGOT, means "disclosure by a party to an action, at the instance of the other party, of facts or documents relevant to the lawsuit." See **discover.**

discrete; discreet. The former means "separate, distinct," the latter "cautious, judicious." *Discreet* is most commonly used of speaking or writing. The usual error is to misuse *discreet,* the more common term in non-legal language, for *discrete.* Here, in this quotation from a casebook, the opposite blunder is committed: "Consider again Pound, ante, p. 64, Hierarchy of Sources and Forms in Law. *Compare* Keeton's discussion of overruling precedents—rules vis-a-vis principles—ante, pp. 839–40, *with* Pound. Is the average opinion writer this *discrete* [read *discreet*]?"

Discrete is sometimes used meaninglessly: "The prosecution apparently made the strikes simply in an effort to procure, from among those summonsed and not disqualified, a jury that, under the *discrete* [read *peculiar?*] facts of this particular case, would be least likely to be partial to Leslie." Here *discrete* is correctly used: "The petitioner made no suggestion below that any *discrete* portion of the work product from the administrative proceedings was work that was both useful and of a type ordinarily necessary to advance the civil-rights litigation to the stage it reached before settlement."

discriminant. See **discriminatory.**

discriminate is an intransitive verb; it cannot properly be used transitively, as here: "Blacks are *discriminated* [read *discriminated against*] in that city." The correct use is here exemplified: "Appellant doubtless suspected that she had been *discriminated against* even before that time."

discriminatee = a person unlawfully discriminated against. None of the dictionaries record this term, but it is increasingly common in American legal writing. E.g., "The *discriminatee* is the innocent party in these circumstances." *Baxter v. Savannah Sugar Refining Corp.,* 495 F.2d 437, 445 (5th Cir. 1974)./ "In the instant case, back seniority . . . is just as necessary to make *discriminatees* 'whole' under Title VI." *Guardians Association v. Civil Service Commission,* 466 F. Supp. 1273, 1287 (S.D.N.Y. 1979)./ "The NLRB routinely awards backpay to restore *discriminatees* to the economic position they would have enjoyed absent the unfair labor practice." *Warehouse and Office Workers' Union v. N.L.R.B.,* 795 F.2d 705, 718 (9th Cir. 1986). See -EE.

discriminating. See **discriminatory.**

discrimination is not a COUNT NOUN. Thus one should not write *discriminations* for *discriminatory practices* or *instances of discrimination.* See PLURALS (B).

discriminatory, -tive; discriminating; discriminant. Of these, only *discriminative* is ambiguous, it being a NEEDLESS VARIANT of both *discriminatory* (= applying discrimination in treatment, esp. on ethnic grounds) and *discriminating* (= keen, discerning, judicious).

Discriminant is a NEEDLESS VARIANT of *discriminating.*

Because *discriminatory* has extremely negative connotations, and *discriminating* quite positive connotations, the noun *discrimination* suffers from a split personality, sometimes brought to the surface in judicial writing: "The majority's fallacy lies in using the word *discrimination* as a synonym for *discrimination on the basis of race.* Such usage may suffice in common parlance, but for purposes of analyzing the proof in a [42 U.S.C.] § 1981 suit it is, if I may not be misunderstood in so expressing it, too *undiscriminating.*" *Carter v. Duncan-Huggins, Ltd.,* 727 F.2d 1225, 1247 (D.C. Cir. 1984) (Scalia, J., dissenting).

discussible is poor when used as a pseudo-softener for *debatable,* as here: "It is *discussible* [read *debatable*] whether such a policy was wise."

disembark is generally considered preferable to *debark* or *disbark. Disembark* is the usual term in G.B., appearing, for example, in the Immigration Act § 11 (1971). Following is an American specimen: "The carrier shall be liable for damage sustained in the event of death or bodily injury if the accident that caused the damage took place in the course of any of the operations of the embarking or *disembarking.*"

disenable is a NEEDLESS VARIANT of *disable.*

disenact, which the *OED* notes as being "rare," is an unnecessary word, inasmuch as we have *repeal, revoke, set aside, abolish,* and various other more specific words.

disenfranchise. See **disfranchise.**

disentail = to bar the entail (on an estate) and convert into a fee simple. See **entail.**

disentitle takes the preposition *to,* not *from.* E.g., "At this third intermediate stage, the delay will not be a repudiation but will *disentitle* the responsible person *from* [read *to*] specific performance." (Eng.)/ "Although the husband and the wife agreed that their financial position was such that only a nominal order could be made against the husband, they wished to have determined the issue whether the wife's conduct *disentitled* her *to* an order for maintenance." (Eng.)

disfranchise; disenfranchise. The former is the preferred form of this word, meaning "to deprive of the right to vote." E.g., "In *Toney,* the registrar of the same parish misapplied Louisiana election statutes in purging voter lists, resulting in the *disenfranchisement* [read *disfranchisement*] of many more blacks than whites."/ "In a memorandum opinion, the district court found that *disenfranchisement* [read *disfranchisement*] of blacks was a major purpose for the convention at which the Alabama Constitution of 1901 was adopted, but that there had not been a showing that provisions *disenfranchising* [read *disfranchising*] those convicted of crimes were based upon the racism present at the constitutional convention."

disfunctional. See **dysfunctional.**

dishabille /dis-ă-*beel*/ is so spelled.

disherison (= [1] the act of disinheriting, [2] the state of being disinherited), labeled obsolete in *Black's,* still enjoys limited currency. E.g., "*Disherison* of a child invites contest of the will. When a child is disinherited a trial judge is likely to submit the will to a jury on an issue of mental capacity, fraud, or undue influence." J. Ritchie, N. Alford, & R. Effland, *Decedents' Estates and Trusts* 142 (1971)./ "Posthumous avarice leading to *disherison* is bad; living greediness is bad too." *Disinheritance* is a simpler word that far more readers and listeners will understand. *Disinherison* is the term generally used in civil law.

disincentive; nonincentive. The former provides an incentive not to do something; the latter is no incentive at all.

disinformation; misinformation. These words are not synonyms. *Disinformation* = deliberately false information ⟨Soviet disinformation⟩. *Misinformation* = incorrect information.

disinherison. See **disherison.**

disintegrative, -tory. The latter is a NEEDLESS VARIANT.

disinterest(ed); uninterest(ed). *Disinterest* is impartiality or freedom from bias; hence *disinterested* means "impartial." *Uninterest* (recorded fr. 1952) means "lack of interest," and *uninterested* "having no interest." Traditionally, *disinterest* has denoted "impartiality" as well as "lack of interest." Hence, it has been difficult to keep the past participial adjectives entirely separate, and many linguists have given up the fight to preserve the distinction between them.

Nevertheless, the distinction is still best recognized and followed, especially in the law, where the sense of *interest* that gives rise to *disinterested* (as in "interested party") still commonly appears. E.g., "Any other rule would make important questions of the title to real estate largely dependent upon the uncertain recollection and testimony of *interested* parties."/ "In each case 'due process of law' requires an evaluation based on a *disinterested* inquiry pursued in the spirit of science." (Frankfurter, J.) Because it is virtuous for judges to remain *disinterested,* we had better not forget what that word means: "The district court thus rejected the not totally *disinterested* testimony of the family members on the issue of fraudulent transfer."/ "No *disinterested* person reading the article can come to the conclusion that it was printed in a spirit of fair criticism or designed for the public good."

Following are sentences in which *disinterested* is misused: "Many people are *disinterested* [read *uninterested*] in politics and do not vote." Wright, Miller, & Cooper, *Federal Practice and Procedure* § 3611 at 511 (West 1984)./ "The son of a lawyer who practiced here, he grew up removed from politics, and today he remains totally *disinterested* [read *uninterested*] in politics—to the point of never voting."

disinvestment. Defined in *W9* as "consumption of capital," *disinvestment* has come to mean "the withdrawal of investments for political reasons." E.g., "The arguments opposing *disinvestment* [from South Africa] fall into two categories." *Divestment* is also used in this sense. See **divest(it)ure.**

disk; disc. *Disk* is the more usual spelling in all but three specific meanings. *Disc* is the spelling used for the senses (1) "a phonograph record"; (2) "a videodisc"; and (3) "a tool making up part of a plow." Otherwise, *disk* is the preferred spelling for general reference to thin circular objects, intervertebral disks, celestial bodies, and computer disks.

dismissal; dismission. The much older word *dismission* (1547) has given way almost completely to the upstart *dismissal* (1806), considered a mere variant less than a century ago. E.g., "The school board initially sought *dismissal* of this suit on the ground that petitioners had failed to apply to the state board for assignment to New Kent School." Today, *dismission* is, except in some highly specialized contexts, an obsolete and NEEDLESS VARIANT.

disorganized; unorganized. The former means "in confusion or disarray; broken up"; the latter means "not organized" merely in the negative, but not in the pejorative, sense.

disparaging for *disconcerting* or *discouraging* is a MALAPROPISM. E.g., "The plight of the Mexican national in the United States has been *disparaging* [read *discouraging*]." See MALAPROPISMS.

dispatch; despatch. The former spelling is preferred in both AmE and BrE.

disperse. See **disburse.**

dispiteous. See **despiteous.**

dispone is a term from Scots law meaning "to make over, convey, assign, grant, officially or in legal form." From the verb are derived the terms *disponee* (= grantee), *disponer* (= conveyer), and *disponible* (= capable of being assigned). E.g., "Such *disponer* shall, nevertheless, during the period of the minority of such minor, be liable to be taxed in respect of the sums so payable as if such disposition had not been made." (Eng.)/ "It is implicit in the ordinance that the husband and no one else may dispose of the wife's income; the husband therefore is the only possible *disponer*." (Eng.)

disport. See **deport.**

disposal; disposition. Both mean generally "a getting rid of," but *disposal* has more often to do with trash or inconsequential items, whereas *disposition* is used of assets given to relatives and friends by will. *Disposition* connotes a preconceived plan and an orderly arrangement.

dispose for *dispose of*. "In the past, pesticide wastes *disposed* [read *disposed of*] in the ground have contaminated groundwater used for drinking and irrigation."

disposition. See **disposal.**

dispositive, -tory. The latter is a NEEDLESS VARIANT. *Dispositive* is the usual word used in reference to testamentary plans. E.g., "It is simply what it appears to be, that is, an ambulatory, *dispository* [read *dispositive*], reciprocal testamentary undertaking between two people to pass, upon the death of the maker first to die, his or her property to the survivor."/ "Not only are written words awkward means for communicating ideas; but also descriptions in *dispositive* instruments have an inherent vice of almost immediate obsolescence."/ "In an era when several transfers are often made as part of an integrated estate plan, it will be desirable to merge control of administration under a single trust with a single *dispositive* plan."

disproportionate, -al. See **proportionate.**

dispute; disputation. These words should be differentiated. *Dispute* = controversy ⟨goods in dispute⟩, whereas *disputation* = formal argument or debate.

disqualified; unqualified. These words have quite different senses. *Unqualified* = not meeting the requirements. *Disqualified* = disabled; debarred. An *unqualified* judge should not be a judge. A *disqualified* judge must recuse himself from hearing a certain case, for example because a close relative is one of the parties.

disquiet is used in law in the sense of disturbing a person's possession of property. E.g., "If the buyer is *disquieted* in his possession, he may suspend the payment of his price until the seller has restored him to quiet possession." See **quiet.**

dissatisfied; unsatisfied. Some DIFFERENTIATION exists between these words. To be *unsatisfied* is to be less than completely satisfied, whereas to be *dissatisfied* is to be positively bothered by the lack of satisfaction. In law, when one is in arrears, one's debts remain *unsatisfied*.

disseise; disseize. The preferred form of this legal word is *disseise.* See **seise.**

disseisor, -ee. These are the correlative terms for the parties involved in disseisin (= dispossession of a person of his estates). E.g., "The *disseisee* of goods, as well as the *disseisee* of land, has a right in rem."/ "The dispossessed owner of land, as we have seen, could always recover possession by an action; though deprived of the res, he still had a right in rem. The *disseisor* acquired only a defeasible estate."/ "The equitable beneficiary of a restrictive covenant has rights even against wrongful possessors, or *disseisors,* of the servient land that they shall not act contrary to the terms of the restrictive agreement."

disseize. See **disseise.**

dissemble; disassemble. The former means "to present a false appearance," the latter "to take apart."

dissent, n.; **dissension, -tion.** *Dissent* refers to a difference of opinion, whether among judges or others. *A dissent,* as opposed to *dissent* as an uncountable noun, refers to a dissenting judicial opinion. E.g., "The *dissent* regards the interest in maintaining our nation's adherence to long-standing principles of international law as not compelling." *Finzer v. Barry,* 798 F.2d 1450, 1464 (D.C. Cir. 1986).

Dissension (the *-sion* spelling is preferred) refers to contentious or partisan arguing. E.g., "The contract terms had already been substantially executed when the *dissension* arose among those jointly interested in the venture."

dissent, v.i., takes *from,* not *to.* E.g., "I must dissent *to* [read *from*] the majority's holding that appellant's detention and ensuing search and seizure were lawful."/ "Because of the waste of time, resources, and effort of the criminal justice system that will ensue, I must dissent *to* [read *from*] what the majority does in this cause."

dissenter; dissentient, n. *Dissenter* is the standard term in AmE for "one who withholds assent, or does not approve or agree"; *dissentient* is the more usual form in BrE, because the term *dissenter* (usu. with an initial cap.) has a special religious and social meaning in British history ("i.e., one who dissents or refuses to conform—specif., from the 17th c. on—to the tenets and practices of the Church of England").

dissenting; dissentient, adj.; **dissentious.** *Dissentient* is sometimes used in G.B. where *dissenting* would ordinarily appear in the U.S. E.g., "The agent was appointed to execute an instrument of transfer on a *dissentient* shareholder's behalf." (Eng.)/ "In the court of appeals the judge delivered a *dissentient* judgment in favor of the appellants." (Eng.) The word is not unknown in American legal writing: "Without retracting or in any way departing from our former *dissentient* views, I concur in the action taken by the majority on the instant appeal. . . ." *In re King's Estate,* 66 A.2d 68, 72 (Pa. 1949) (Jones, J., concurring). One ambiguity that may be caused by use of *dissentient* is that readers might interpret it as a derogatory word opposite to *sentient;* the true opposite of *sentient* (= feeling), however, is *insentient. Dissentious* = given to dissension; quarrelsome.

dissimilar takes the preposition *to* rather than *from.* E.g., "The facts in that case are wholly dissimilar *from* [read *to*] the facts in the case at bar." Here the preferable collocation is illustrated: "Those cases were decided under facts *dissimilar to* those existing in the present case." Cf. **dissentitle.**

dissiminate is a fairly common misspelling of *disseminate.*

dissociate; disassociate. *Dissociate* is the preferred term; *disassociate* is a NEEDLESS VARIANT. *Dissociate* takes the preposition *from.* E.g., "Disassociated *with* [read *from*] the subject thereof, whatever it may be, a title or a name composed of ordinary words cannot acquire the status of property, as all who speak or write have the inherent right to use any and all words in the English language."

dissolution. See **marriage dissolution.**

distil(l). The spelling *distill* is preferred in AmE, *distil* in BrE.

distinct; distinctive. The first means "well defined, discernibly separate" ⟨distinct speech⟩, and the second means "serving to distinguish, set off by appearance" ⟨a distinctive red bow tie). *Distinct* speech is well enunciated, whereas *distinctive* speech is idiosyncratically accented, different from that of surrounding speakers. *Distinctive* is sometimes misused for *distinguished* (= notable; famous).

distinguish, v.t., = to note a difference. Used intransitively, the verb becomes *distinguish between* = to make a distinction (the court distinguished between premeditated and spontaneous acts). In legal contexts, the transitive *distinguish* is frequently used in the phrase *to distinguish a case* = to provide reasons for deciding a case under consideration differently from a similar case that may or may not be a precedent. Cf. **differentia.**

distrain = to seize goods by way of distress (*CDL*); to constrain or force (a person) by the seizure and detention of a chattel or thing, to perform some obligation (*OED*). See **distraint.**

distrainor, -er. The *OED* states that *-or* is "a more technical form than *distrainer*, and correlative to *distrainee*." Of course, *distrain* itself is a technical word; it may as well have a technical Latinate agent-noun suffix (*-or*).

distraint; distress. In legal contexts, both mean "the seizure of goods as security for the performance of an obligation" (*CDL*). *Distraint* would seem to be the better term, for it looks like the verb from which it derives and does not, like *distress*, have an ordinary English meaning. But *distress* is the prevalent term for this sense.

distribute out is prolix for *distribute*. E.g., "No income is *distributed out* [omit *out*] (or is deemed to be *distributed out* [omit *out*] under the DNI rules) to the residuary beneficiaries." See **out** & PARTICLES, UNNECESSARY.

distribution. See **descent** (B).

divers; diverse. These words have distinct meanings. Very simply, *divers* implies severalty, and *diverse* implies difference. *Divers* (= various, sundry) remains a part of the language in the U.S. only as a curiosity. Formerly it meant not only "various," but "several" as well: "[T]he rent was behind for *divers* years." *Sir Anthony Sturlyn v. Albany*, Cro. Eliz. 67, 78 Eng. Repr. 327 (Q.B. 1587). Today it is an ARCHAISM, and its only accepted meaning is "various," as in Frankfurter's phrase "di-

vers judicially inappropriate and elusive determinants." *Baker v. Carr*, 369 U.S. 265, 268 (1962) (Frankfurter, J., dissenting). Other modern examples follow: "Defendant is possessed of large means and is engaged in the business of a banker in said village of Howard Lake, at Dassel, Minnesota, and at *divers* other places."/ "Defendants inserted the said notice as an advertisement in *divers* local and other newspapers." (Eng.)/ "Two months later he was indicted in Florida for conspiring there and in *divers* other districts."

Diverse means "markedly different; unlike." It takes the preposition *from*. E.g., "Each case incorporated state-law tort claims against manufacturers of protective respiratory equipment, all of whose citizenship was *diverse* from that of the plaintiff."

Frequently it is used in the U.S. without a preposition to denote a difference in citizenship that gives rise to federal jurisdiction: "We granted the motion because the record otherwise evidences a substantial likelihood of *diverse* citizenship." See **diversity.**

diversity. As an adjective, *diversity* is frequently used in American legal writing as a shortened form of *diversity jurisdiction*. E.g., "In a *diversity* case in this circuit, federal courts apply a federal rather than a state standard."

divest(it)ure; divestment. The standard noun corresponding to the verb *to divest* is *divestiture*. E.g., "It is agreed that the history and language of the laws for control of monopolization properly permit the application by the courts of orders requiring *divestiture* of properties of an existing monopolist in order to prevent the continuance of the evil." *Divesture* is an obsolete variant.

The other variant, *divestment*, not at all uncommon, might seem to be a NEEDLESS VARIANT; yet it appears in a number of SET PHRASES in property law, such as *vested interest subject to divestment*. E.g., "Many courts hold that the beneficiary takes a vested interest subject to *divestment* upon change of beneficiary in accordance with the provisions of the policy."/ "The registration of stock ownership on the books of the corporation in appropriate statutory language is sufficient to vest legal title, subject to *divestment* if the circumstances surrounding the transaction warrant it."/ "This view may be justified on the theory that title passes to the grantee immediately, subject to a life estate reserved in the grantor and subject to a further condition of *divestment* upon nonperformance by the grantee." See **disinvestment.**

dividable. See **divisible.**

divide up. See PARTICLES, UNNECESSARY.

divisible; dividable. The latter is a NEEDLESS VARIANT.

divisor. See **deviser.**

divorcement is now obsolete for *divorce* in the sense "the dissolution of the marriage tie," although it has (oddly) persisted in this sense up to this century. E.g., "[I]n the event of the death or *divorcement* of the wife before the decease of the husband, he shall have the right to designate another beneficiary." Mo. Rev. St. § 7895 (1906). *Divorcement* survives in the general figurative sense "the severance or complete separation of any close relation" ⟨the divorcement of church and state in the U.S.⟩.

divulgence; divulgation; divulgement. Though the latter two date from the early seventeenth century, *divulgence*, which dates from the mid-nineteenth century, is now the preferred noun corresponding to the verb *to divulge.*

docket, in the U.S., means "a schedule of cases pending." In G.B., it means "a register of judgments issued by the court." *Docket* may be used as a verb in both BrE and AmE. E.g., "The case was *docketed* and tried shortly thereafter." See **calendar** & **cause-list.**

doctrinal; doctrinaire; doctrinary. The first is the neutral term, meaning "of or relating to a doctrine." E.g., "The *doctrinal* commentary upon *Taddeo* thus far has been unanimously favorable." *Doctrinaire* = dogmatic; impractically adhering to dogma. *Doctrinary* is a NEEDLESS VARIANT of *doctrinaire.*

document; instrument. These terms are quite similar in import, but *document* is slightly broader. *Document* refers to any written thing, whereas *instrument* (q.v.) usually refers to a legal document with a specific legal import.

DOG FRENCH. See LAW FRENCH.

DOG LATIN. See LAW LATIN.

dogma. Pl. *dogmas, -mata.* The English plural is preferred.

Domesday Book; Doomsday Book. The former is the accepted spelling in modern texts of the name for the great census or survey of England's landholdings, buildings, people, and livestock that was ordered by William the Conqueror and completed (except for several districts in the North) in 1086.

domesticate; domesticize. See **domiciliate.**

domicil(e); residence. "*Residence* comprehends no more than a fixed abode where one actually lives for the time being. It is distinguished from *domicile* in that *domicile* is the place where a person intends eventually to return and remain." *Catalanotto v. Palazzolo,* 46 Misc. 2d 381, 259 N.Y.S.2d 473, 475 (1965). *Domicile* is spelled both with and without the final *-e,* but the better and more common spelling is with it.
  In England, *domicile* means "the country that a person treats as his permanent home and to which he has the closest legal attachment." See **citizenship.**

domiciliary is both adjective ("of or pertaining to domicile") and noun ("one belonging to a domicile").

domiciliate; domesticate; domesticize. *Domiciliate* = to establish a domicile or home. *Domesticate* = (1) to make domestic; or (2) to make a member of the household. Sense (1) here applies: "Before the jury retired, Colonial intimated that it intended to request the court to take judicial notice of the *domesticated* Oregon judgment." *Domesticize* is a NEEDLESS VARIANT of *domesticate.*

dominance; domination. *Dominance* = the fact or position of being dominant. *Domination* = the act of dominating; the exercise of ruling power.

dominant; servient. These terms are usually used in reference to *estates* or *tenements* in the law of easements. A *dominant* estate has the benefit of a servitude or easement over the *servient* estate.

domination. See **dominance.**

dominion is a FORMAL WORD used in legal contexts, esp. in the U.S., to mean "control, possession." E.g., "Alford argues that the evidence presented as to that count failed to demonstrate that she had any *dominion* over any marijuana in the Western District of Texas."

donate, a BACK-FORMATION from *donation,* was formerly considered a vulgar equivalent of *give.* Today, however, it is a more FORMAL WORD than *give* that is frequently used of charitable bequests.

donatio mortis causa is an unjustified LATINISM for the slightly less Latinate *gift causa mortis.* See **causa mortis.**

donative, -tory. As an adjective, the latter is a NEEDLESS VARIANT. "This evidence is far short of the clear and convincing proof necessary to rebut the presumption of *donative* intent." For the nominal sense of *donatory,* see the next entry.

donee = one to whom something is given. E.g., "After the final accounting is approved, the probate judge will issue an order directing the executor to distribute the decedent's personal estate to the testamentary *donees.*" *Donatory* is a little-used equivalent. See the next entry. See also -EE.

donor; donator. The latter is a problematic word, meaning either (1) "donor" or (2) "donee." It should be avoided in favor of *donor* or *donee, q.v.* See **settlor.**

Doomsday Book. See **Domesday Book.**

doomster; doomsman. These are both variants of *deemster* or *dempster, q.v.*

doth for *does,* though archaic and obsolete, still occasionally appears in judicial pronouncements, such as this, by the Mississippi Supreme Court in 1981: "[T]his Court having sufficiently examined and considered the same and being of the opinion that the same should be denied *doth* order that said motion be and the same is hereby denied." Quoted in *Jones v. Thigpen,* 741 F.2d 805, 809 (5th Cir. 1984). Methinks, forsooth, that we should throw over this term, as well as the rest of the

LEGALESE verily immortalized in that sentence.

The word is also used in orders of the English courts. E.g., "This court *doth* declare that there was a valid and binding contract." (Eng.)

double entendre originally referred to any ambiguity giving rise to more than one meaning, but now connotes that one of those meanings is indecent or risqué.

double jeopardy; former jeopardy. These terms are not precisely the same. *Double jeopardy* is the fact of being prosecuted twice for substantially the same offense. A plea of *former jeopardy* informs the court that one has previously been prosecuted for the same offense. E.g., "This precise point was addressed in a case in which, the defendant having been indicted for perjury and having filed a plea of *former jeopardy*, it was held that subsequent falsehoods on the same trial under the same oath did not make new perjuries, but only exhibited additional ways in which the perjury was committed."/ "Conditioning an appeal of one offense on a coerced surrender of a valid plea of *former jeopardy* for another offense exacts a forfeiture in plain conflict with the constitutional bar against *double jeopardy.*"

DOUBLE NEGATIVES. See NEGATIVES (A).

DOUBLETS AND TRIPLETS OF LEGAL IDIOM. Amplification by synonym has long been a part of the English language, and especially a part of the language of the law. In the English Renaissance, this habit was a common figure of speech called *synonymia.* It is often supposed that the purpose of these paired or strung-along synonyms was etymological, that is, that writers in the Middle Ages and Renaissance would pair a French or Latinate term with an Anglo-Saxon approximation as a gloss on the foreign word. Thus we have, as survivals in legal language, *acknowledge and confess* (Old English and Old French), *act and deed* (Latin and Old English), and *goods and chattels* (Old English and Old French).

The philologist George Philip Krapp argued against this explanation. He saw the purpose of this mannerism as "rhetorical or oratorical rather than etymological." G. P. Krapp, *Modern English: Its Growth and Present Use* 251 (1909). He pointed out that such doubling occurred abundantly in Old English, when no substantial foreign element existed in the language, and that it often occurs in later writings without regard for etymology. Although Krapp was undoubtedly correct to emphasize the rhetorical importance of doubling, he was wrong to assume that the figure did not take on a utilitarian significance as well in Middle and early Modern English. The purpose of doubling was dual: to give rhetorical weight and balance to the phrase, and to maximize the understanding of readers or listeners.

Still another explanation has emerged for the particular fondness that lawyers have for this stylistic quirk. It is a cynical one: "This multiplication of useless expressions probably owed its origin to the want of knowledge of the true meaning and due application of each word, and a consequent apprehension, that if one word alone were used, a wrong one might be adopted and the right one omitted; and to this something must be added for carelessness and the general disposition of the profession to seek safety in verbosity rather than in discrimination of language." 1 Davidson, *Precedents and Forms in Conveyancing* 67 (3d ed. 1860).

The most obviously rhetorically inspired phrases are alliterative. Rhetoricians call these reduplicative phrases: e.g., *aid and abet; have and hold; part and parcel; trials and tribulations; rest, residue, and remainder; laid and levied; mind and memory.* Many others, in addition to conveying no nuance in meaning, have no aesthetically redeeming qualities, but even informed opinions on a point of this kind are likely to diverge. Following are two lists, the first containing common doublets in legal writing, the second containing some of the common triplets. Any number of variations, as by inversion (or, with triplets, by reordering), are possible.

Doublets

able and willing
act and deed
agree and covenant
agreed and declared
aid and abet (q.v.)
aid and comfort
all and sundry
all and singular
amount or quantum
annoy or molest
annulled and set aside
answerable and accountable
any and all

attached and annexed
authorize and direct
betting or wagering
bills and notes
bind and obligate
by and under
by and with
canceled and set aside
cease and come to an end
cease and determine
chargeable and accountable
covenant and agree
custom and usage
deed and assurance
deem and consider
deposes and says
desire and require
do and perform
dominion and authority
due and owing
each and all
each and every
escape and evade
exact and specific
execute and perform
false and untrue
final and conclusive
finish and complete
fit and proper (q.v.)
for and in behalf of
fraud and deceit
free and clear
from and after
full and complete
full faith and credit
full force and effect
good and effectual
good and tenantable
goods and chattels
have and hold
keep and maintain
kind and character
kind and nature
known and described as
laid and levied
leave and license
legal and valid
liens and encumbrances
made and signed
maintenance and upkeep
make and enter into (a contract)
means and includes
mind and memory (q.v.)
name and style
new and novel
null and of no effect
null and void
object and purpose
order and direct

other and further (relief)
over and above
pardon and forgive
part and parcel (q.v.)
peace and quiet
perform and discharge
power and authority
premeditation and malice aforethought
repair and make good
restrain and enjoin
reverts to and falls back upon
save and except
separate and apart
separate and distinct
set aside and vacate
shall and will
shun and avoid
similar and like
sole and exclusive
son and heir
successors and assigns
supersede and displace
surmise and conjecture
terms and conditions
then and in that event
title and interest
total and entire
true and correct
type and kind
uncontroverted and uncontradicted
understood and agreed
unless and until
uphold and support
various and sundry
will and testament

Triplets

cancel, annul, and set aside
form, manner, and method
general, vague, and indefinite
give, devise, and bequeath
hold, possess, and enjoy
lands, tenements, and hereditaments
ordered, adjudged, and decreed
pay, satisfy, and discharge
possession, custody, and control
ready, willing, and able
remise, release, and forever quitclaim
repair, uphold, and maintain
rest, residue, and remainder (q.v.)
right, title, and interest
vague, nonspecific, and indefinite
way, shape, or form

Mellinkoff recommends avoiding virtually all coupled synonyms. See D. Mellinkoff, *Legal Writing: Sense and Nonsense* 189-90 (1982); *The Language of the Law* 349-62 (1963). At least one writer has taken issue with this recommendation on grounds that doublets are a prosodic feature of English and many other languages. He argues: "Since coupled synonyms are by definition redundant, they do not increase the density of ideas contained within a sentence; therefore, they rarely endanger its clarity. Since coupled synonyms add beauty to writing without sacrificing clarity, I see nothing sinful in their moderate use." Charrow, Review, *Legal Writing: Sense and Nonsense,* 30 U.C.L.A. L. Rev. 1094, 1102 (1983).

The primary problem with such arguments, on either side of the issue, is that they fail to identify the types of writing in which doublets may appear or should not appear. In DRAFTING documents to be interpreted, for example, the legal effects of this stylistic mannerism must be considered. *Stroud's Judicial Dictionary* (4th ed. 1971), under *contiguous,* q.v., states that *contiguous* is "as nearly as possible" synonymous with *adjoining,* but points to a case in which the phrase *adjoining or contiguous* was read by the court as if it were *adjoining or near to,* "so as to give *contiguous* a cognate, but not identical, meaning with *adjoining.*" If the drafter of that phrase meant contiguous when he wrote *contiguous,* then his habit of coupling it with *adjoining* got him into trouble. (Cf. **adjacent.**) The problem stems, of course, from the fundamental canon of construing legal documents that states that every word is to be given meaning and nothing is to be read as mere surplusage. In drafting, then, doublets may be given unforeseen meanings by clever interpreters. This danger, however, is more likely to appear with less common doublets and triplets: no judge would interpret *rest, residue, and remainder* as referring to three discrete things.

A second context to be considered is ritual language, as in *the truth, the whole truth, and nothing but the truth,* a resounding phrase that conveys the gravity and majesty of the oath being taken. *Last will and testament,* q.v., may also properly be placed under the heading of ritual language, which is always directed to a lay rather than to a legal audience, the purpose being as much emotive as it is informational.

A third context in which doubling occurs is that of legal commentary and judicial opinions. Here the coupling of synonyms can rarely be said to "add beauty," as the writer quoted above suggested; rather, it is almost always a blemish. For in this context, legal style most nearly approximates literary style, and amplification by synonym has been out of rhetorical fashion for hundreds of years. Although one might well title a client's will *Last Will and Testament,* if one were to write an opinion construing that document, it would be better to begin, "In this appeal we are called upon to construe the disposition of realty in *John Doe's will*" rather than *John Doe's last will and testament.*

Yet one might well write *terms and conditions,* if by the inclusion of both words an added nuance is intended. That is the test in ordinary legal prose: Is a shade of meaning supplied by the second or third synonym, or is it just so much deadwood?

DOUBLING OF FINAL CONSONANTS. Unaccented syllables in inflected words are sometimes spelled differently in AmE and in BrE. Americans generally do not double a final *-l-* before the inflectional suffix, whereas the British generally do. Thus *initialed* and *initialing* (AmE) but *initialled* and *initialling* (BrE). A number of other words follow this paradigm, e.g., *cancel, label, marshal, parcel, signal, total, travel,* and *unravel.*

The British always double the final consonant after a full vowel in words such as *kidnapped, -ing* and *worshipped, -ing.* In the U.S., *kidnapping* is preferred over *kidnaping* (see **abduction**) as an exceptional form (cf. *formatted, formatting*), though *worshiped, -ing* follows the general American rule. *Programmed* and *programming* are the preferred spellings on both sides of the Atlantic, the single *-m-* spellings being secondary variants in AmE; for the probable reason underlying this American inconsistency, see **program(m)er.**

The British-American split is seen also in words like *jewel(l)er, pupil(l)age,* and *travel(l)er,* the British preferring two *-l-*s rather than the one used by Americans. Writers and editors should make themselves aware of these minor differences in spelling, and be wary of inserting *sic* (q.v.) when quoting a foreign text.

Apart from words ending in *-l-* and exceptions noted *(kidnapping, programming,* and *worship(p)ed),* all English-speaking countries follow the same rules on doubling. When a suffix beginning with a vowel is added, the final consonant of the word is repeated only if (1) the vowel sound preceding the consonant is represented by a single letter (hence *bed, bedding* but *head, heading*); or (2) the final

syllable bears the main stress (hence *occúr, occúrred* but *óffer, óffered*). Some of the more commonly misspelled words not already mentioned are these: *biased, busing* (q.v.), *combated, focused, benefited, transferred.*

doubt. A. *Doubt that & doubt whether.* The former is used primarily in negative sentences and in questions. E.g., "We do not *doubt that,* had the time spent in federal prison not been credited to any sentence, appellant would be entitled to have that prison time credited against his state sentence." *Doubt whether* is used in positive assertions. E.g., "We *doubt whether* such conduct falls within the ambit of appellant's duties as supervisor."

B. Followed by a Negative. *Doubt* can be a confusing word when followed by a negative, as in: "I *doubt* whether the court will not take the further step when necessary." This sentence merely states that the writer thinks courts *will* take the further step of which he speaks.

C. And *misdoubt.* See **misdoubt.**

doubtless(ly). *Doubtlessly* is incorrect for *doubtless* (a mild expression of certainty), *no doubt* (a stronger expression of certainty), or *undoubtedly* (the strongest of these three expressions of certainty). The word *doubtless* is itself an adverb ⟨the Framers doubtless feared the executive's assertion of an independent military authority unchecked by the people⟩; therefore, *doubtlessly* is unnecessary. E.g., "Had Zellars been driving in the wrong lane he would *doubtlessly* [read *doubtless*] have had a little more time and a better chance to avoid striking the child."/ "While it is not impossible to say precisely when men first arrived in North America, *doubtlessly* [read *doubtless*] the original Americans emigrated from Asia at least fifteen thousand years ago and entered the continent during the Pleistocene epoch, or Ice Age, by way of the Bering Land Bridge." See **clearly.**

doubt of for *doubt about.* E.g., "The language of the statute leaves no doubt *of* [read *about*] its intent." See HYPALLAGE.

dowable = entitled to dower, q.v. E.g., "A wife is *dowable* in equity of all lands in which her husband possessed a beneficial interest at the time of his death."/ "According to the early English common law, the widow of a trust beneficiary was not *dowable* in the trust property because one could not be seised of an equitable interest in land and dower attached only to an estate of inheritance of which the husband was seised at some time during coverture.''

dower; dowry. The terms are related etymologically (fr. L. *dot-, dos* "gift, marriage portion"), but are quite distinct in modern usage. *Dower* = the widow's legal share during her lifetime of the real estate owned by her deceased husband—at common law dower was only a life estate, but in many American jurisdictions dower (or the elective share) has been expanded into a fee. E.g., "In a few states the widow has *dower* only when the husband was trust beneficiary at his death." (See **curtesy**.) *Dowry* = the money, goods, or real estate that a woman brings to her husband in marriage. Both terms are waning in use.

down payment. Two words.

downplay, v.t., is not in good use; *play down* is preferred. Both expressions are colloquial.

dowry. See **dower**.

draconian, -ic. *Draconian,* the usual form, should generally be spelled in lower case. The word is derived from the name *Draco,* a Greek legislator of the seventh century B.C. who drafted a code of severe laws. For a judicial analogue, see **rhadamanthine**.

draft; draught. See **draftsman**.

DRAFTING is a specific type of legal writing dealing with instruments or legal documents that are to be construed by others. Statutes, wills, regulations, and contracts are drafted. The style of drafting is considerably different from that of other legal writing, as in judicial opinions and legal commentary. Many of the worst mannerisms of LEGALESE pervade legal drafting, for the MYTH OF PRECISION has traditionally been one of the drafter's tenets.

A century ago an English practitioner delineated the specific characteristics of drafting. The style of good drafting, wrote J. G. Mackay,

> is free from all colour, from all emotion, from all rhetoric. It is impersonal, as if the voice, not of any man, but of the law, dealing

with the necessary facts. It disdains emphasis and all other artifices. It uses no metaphors or figures of speech. It is always consistent and never contradicts itself. It never hesitates or doubts. It says in the plainest language, with the simplest, fewest, and fittest words, precisely what it means. These are qualities which might be used to advantage more frequently than is common in literature, and unfortunately they are not to be found in many legal compositions, but they are essential to good legal composition, and are not essential to literary composition.

> Mackay, *Introduction to an Essay on the Art of Legal Composition Commonly Called Drafting,* 11 Law Q. Rev. 326, 326 (1887).

For suggested guides on drafting, see LEGAL WRITING STYLE (C).

draftsman; draughtsman. *Draughtsman* is the BrE spelling of *draftsman*. E.g., "The ingenuity of equity *draughtsmen* was under that system greatly exercised in drawing answers in such a form that it was impossible to read part of them without reading the whole." (Eng.) *Draughtsmanship* should not be used in AmE, as it is in K. York & J. Bauman, *Remedies* 182 (1973). *Drafter* is a neutral, nonsexist equivalent preferred by those wary of terms in *-man*. *Draftsperson* is a wholly unnecessary NEOLOGISM. See SEXISM (B).

drag ⟩ dragged ⟩ dragged. See **drug**.

dramshop = a business selling alcoholic drinks; a bar. Of eighteenth-century origin, the term appears today only in the phrases *dramshop suits, dramshop claims,* and *dramshop statutes. Dramshop claims* involve allegations that liquor establishments serving underage or obviously intoxicated patrons should be held liable for consequent drunk-driving accidents.

draughtsman. See **draftsman**.

draw. Only in the legal idiom does *draw* retain the sense "to frame (a writing or document) in due form" (*OED*), as a synonym of *draft* ⟨to draw a will⟩. E.g., "While the petition has been *drawn*, with obvious meticulous care, to avoid the semblance of seeking mandatory relief, in essence and effect it presents no other objective." *American National Bank v. Sheppard,* 175 S.W.2d 626, 628 (Tex. Civ. App.—Austin 1943).

drawee = payor ⟨drawee bank⟩. Inasmuch as lawyers understand *drawee* and *payor* to be synonymous, *drawee/payor* makes little sense. "A payee or other true owner of an instrument that is cashed under a forged endorsement may sue directly *the drawee/payer* [read either *the drawee* or *the payor*] bank."

drouth; drought. The former is archaic in BrE, but still frequently appears in AmE texts. Nevertheless, *drought* is the preferred form in both linguistic communities.

drug for *dragged* is a nonstandard dialectal form common in the South (U.S.): "He then *drug* [read *dragged*] the body into the house."

drunk; drunken. "In older and literary usage," the *Oxford Guide* notes, *drunk* and *drunken* were "the predicative and attributive forms respectively; now usually allocated to distinct senses, namely 'intoxicated' and 'given to drink.'"

We do, however, have the fixed idiom *drunken driving,* defined by the *CDL* as "driving while affected by alcohol." *Drunken* here means "exhibiting or evidencing intoxication." E.g., "This was the year the courts joined the legislatures in earnest in the five-year-old crackdown on *drunken* driving."/ "Smith, a *drunken* driver, traveling at eighty miles an hour or faster, weaving from side to side of the road, tried to pass the plaintiff's automobile."

drunkometer. See **breathalyzer.**

dubious distinction has the dubious distinction of being one of our most overworked CLICHÉS.

dubitante = doubting. The term is used in law reports of a judge who is doubtful about a legal proposition but is loath to declare it wrong. E.g., "Mr Justice Rutledge acquiesces in the Court's opinion and judgment *dubitante* on the question of equal protection of the laws."

Some judges use this term after their names in separate opinions, as if it were analogous to *concurring* or *dissenting*. Apparently the purpose of doing so is to signal that the judge has grave doubts about the soundness of the majority opinion, but not so grave as to cause him to dissent.

due process of law. When applied to judicial proceedings, this phrase traditionally "mean[s] a course of legal proceedings according to those rules and principles which have been established in our system of jurisprudence for the protection and enforcement of private rights." *Pennoyer v. Neff,* 95 U.S. 714, 733 (1877).

due to should be used to mean "attributable to," and often follows the verb *to be* (sometimes understood in context). The phrase is commonly misused as a conjunctive adverb for *because of, owing to, caused by,* or *on grounds of.* E.g., "The trial was lost *due to* [read *because of*] his damaging admissions."/ "*Due to* [read *Because of*] the close interrelation between these two rights, we believe that Wiggins's petition fairly raised the issue of his right to counsel."/ "Because the state court did not specify whether it denied habeas relief on the merits or *due to* [read *on grounds of*] procedural default, we must interpret the state court's silence."/ "*Due in part to* [read *In part because of*] the widespread enactment of pretermitted heir statutes, the majority of the courts have been unwilling to hold that birth of issue alone revokes a will."

Here the phrase is correctly used: "We conclude that since the defendant knew of his right to a speedy trial, the failure of the government *due to* clerical error or oversight to request the Indiana prison authorities to advise the defendant of his right does not violate the statute."/ "A distinction must be drawn between cases in which the difficulties are *due to* uncertainty as to the causation of the damage, in which questions of remoteness arise, and those which are *due to* the fact that the assessment of damages cannot be made with any mathematical accuracy." (Eng.)

Due followed by an infinitive is not a form of the phrase *due to,* although it looks deceptively similar. E.g., "Because 'security center' is a generic term not entitled to service mark protection, the district court decision is *due to be* reversed."

dul(l)ness. *Dullness* is correct.

duologue. See **dialogue.**

duplicitous; duplicative, -ory. *Duplicitous* (= marked by duplicity) is a twentieth-century coinage generally understood to mean "deceitful." The American courts have latched onto the word in the sense of doubleness, from the old legal meaning of *duplicity* (= double pleading). Hence, "A *duplicitous* indictment is one charging two separate crimes in the same count." *United States v. Ellis,* 595 F.2d 154, 163 (3d Cir. 1979). Following are other typical examples: "The grounds of the motion insisted on here are that the indictment is *duplicitous,* and that the weapon is not so described." *Davis v. State,* 46 Fla. 137, 35 So. 76, 76 (1903). (The specimen just quoted antedates the earliest known use [1928] given in *W9.*)/ "The allegation in a single count of a conspiracy to commit several crimes is not *duplicitous.*" *Braverman v. United States,* 317 U.S. 49, 54 (1942)./ "Acosta argues further that the indictment was *duplicitous* because it joined separate conspiracies into one count." *United States v. Acosta,* 763 F.2d 671, 696 (5th Cir. 1985)./ "An indictment charging rape in one count in having intercourse with a female under the statutory age of consent and in another count in having intercourse with a female whose mind was so weak as to render her incapable of consenting, both referring to the same transaction, is not *duplicitous.*" A literate laymen would be utterly confused by this use of the word.

Duplicitous should not be extended beyond its sense of doubleness in pleading, indictments, etc., as it is here: "There is a suggestion that some of the work performed by counsel for Baxter was *duplicitous* [read *duplicative*] because of a change in counsel during the preparation stages of the litigation." *Baxter v. Savannah Sugar Refining Corp.,* 495 F.2d 437, 447 (5th Cir. 1974).

Duplicative, which one might have preferred in the sense given to *duplicitous,* has been adopted for other uses in the law. "As between federal district courts, . . . the general principle is to avoid *duplicative* litigation." *Colorado River Water Conservation Dist. v. United States,* 424 U.S. 800, 817 (1976)./ "Recent Supreme Court decisions have emphasized the risk of *duplicative* recoveries and other factors without mentioning antitrust standing as a distinct inquiry."/ "The policy of minimization of *duplicative* enforcement might well prevail over concerns of centralization."/ "We realized at the time of the decision that unifying school systems often would cause elimination of *duplicative* jobs." *Duplicatory* is a NEEDLESS VARIANT. See **multiplici(t)ous** (B).

duplicity is frequently used in law for *duplication.* E.g., "The defendant suggested that the 340 billable hours resulted from a *duplicity*

of time spent by the plaintiff's attorney and his five associates."/ "The county prosecutor was even heard boasting to a member of the press that he had a '*duplicity*' of evidence!" These uses of the word are poor; they derive from the true legal meaning "the pleading of two (or more) matters in one plea; double pleading" (*OED.*) The word should not, by SLIPSHOD EXTENSION, be used of other types of doubleness. See **duplicitous.**

The nonlegal sense of *duplicity* (= deceitfulness, double-dealing) is also quite common in legal contexts: "When a lawyer's falsehood and *duplicity* is established he becomes a professional outcast."/ "The trial judge stated that he doubted the plaintiff's veracity; but the right of a party to have his own statement is not diminished when the district court suspects *duplicity.*"

duress; durance. *Duress* = (1) the infliction of hardship; (2) forcible restraint; or (3) compulsion illegally exercised to force a person to perform some act. *Durance* is an archaic LEGALISM sharing sense (2) of *duress.* Neither word is needed in that sense, however.

during such time as is verbose for *while.*

during the course of is almost always verbose for *during.*

duteous. See **dutiful.**

dutiable = subject to the levy of a duty. E.g., "The dual purpose of the search is to ascertain whether an illegal alien is seeking to cross the border and whether contraband or *dutiable* property is being smuggled."

dutiful; duteous. The usual term is *dutiful.* Although formerly in good use, *duteous* is an archaic NEEDLESS VARIANT.

duty(-)bound. This term of American legal ARGOT, an adjectival rendering of the phrase *bounden duty,* should be hyphenated. E.g., "Seamen, of course, are wards of admiralty whose rights federal courts are *duty-bound* to jealously protect." / "As long as the Supreme Court of the United States adheres to its longstanding construction of the Second Amendment, this court and all other Texas courts are *dutybound* [read *duty-bound*] to follow and apply that construction."/ "The appellant advances a rule to the effect that because of the engagement of the parties a confidential relationship resulted whereby decedent was *duty bound* [read *duty-bound*] to make a full disclosure to appellant of the extent, nature, and value of his property." Usually a simple *bound* suffices.

dynamic, n., is a VOGUE WORD generally best avoided. E.g., "In the first case, a negotiation is stipulated. In the second, the *dynamic* leads almost inevitably in that direction." [Read *In the second, a negotiation is almost inevitable.*]

dysfunctional (= functioning abnormally) is so spelled; *disfunctional* is a not uncommon misspelling.

E

each. **A.** Number. *Each* takes a singular verb, and pronouns having *each* as an antecedent must be in the singular. E.g., "*Each is* entitled to benefits under this program."/ "A high-water mark was reached in *Morris Trusts v. Commissioner,* in which *each* of ten trusts *were* [read *was*] held to create two separate trusts."/ "Persuasive arguments exist that *each* of the first two criteria *is* satisfied."

Sometimes *each* is mistaken as the subject in a sentence in which it acts in apposition, as in "A and B each *withdraw* [not *withdraws*]." Here the mistake is made: "Smith and Jones *each has his reason* [read *each have their reasons*] for not complying with the request for production."

B. Delimiting the Application of *each.* Especially in contexts in which *all* appears before *each,* it may be important to use defining words after *each.* Thus "suppose a statute required *all directors* to take an oath of secrecy, and imposed a penalty on *each director* in the event of a violation. If half the directors took the oath and half failed, could they all be prosecuted or only those who failed?" E. A. Dreidger, *The Composition of Legislation* 78 (1957). The remedy lies, of course, in writing that the penalty is imposed on *each director who fails to take the oath,* assuming that is the intended meaning.

each and every. This trite phrase should generally be eschewed, but especially it should not be plugged in where only one of the adjectives properly modifies what follows. E.g., "Plaintiff has performed *each and every* of his obligations under the contract." *Each* works fine here, but not *every,* for one cannot say, "He has performed *every* of his obligations." One who insists on being bromidic should write: "Plaintiff has performed *each and every one* of his obligations under the contract." Cf. **and/or** & **if, as, and when.**

each other; one another. The former phrase is used of two persons or entities; the latter is best confined to contexts involving more than two. E.g., "One of us would turn to the foregoing comment and find that the two terms cancel *one another* [read *each other*]."

In using these phrases, it is important to know precisely what is being compared. In the following sentence, *elements constituting the basis of damages* are being compared, although the writer mistook *causes of action* as the units of comparison: "Having examined the jury instructions and the special verdict in this case, we find that the elements constituting the basis of damages of *each* of the two causes of action were not sufficiently distinguished *from one another* [read *from those of the other*] to ensure that there was no double compensation." The use of *each* before *one another* is what caused the problem; the writer was guilty of SWAPPING HORSES from *each other* to *one another.* See COMPARISONS, FALSE.

early on is not the odious locution that some people think. Slightly informal, it is perfectly idiomatic in both AmE and BrE.

easement; right of way. The former term is now obsolete in all but the legal sense, whereas the latter is common among laymen. An *easement* is either a legal or an equitable right enjoyed by a landowner to benefit from nearby land. Often *easements* take the form of *rights of way* (= rights to pass over another person's land). But a *right of way* may be granted by license (to the person) as well as by easement (inuring to the land). See **right of way.**

eastwardly, -erly. See DIRECTIONAL WORDS.

ebullit. See BACK-FORMATIONS.

ecclesiastical law; canon law. Although these generic terms overlap a great deal, *ecclesiastical law* broadly covers all laws relating to a church, whether from state law, divine law, natural law, or societal rules; *canon law* is more restricted, referring only to the the body of law constituted by ecclesiastical authority for the organization and governance of a Christian Church. See **canon law.**

economic; economical. *Economical* means "thrifty," or, in the current jargon, "cost-effective." *Economic* should be used for every other meaning possible for the words, almost always in reference to the study of economics. Hence we have *economic studies* and *economic interest* but *economical shopping.*

EDITORIAL "WE." See FIRST PERSON (A).

-EDLY. Words ending in this way are more pervasive in law than elsewhere. Often the classic adverbial formula *in a . . . manner* does not work with these words; thus *allegedly* does not mean "in an alleged manner," *purportedly* does not mean "in a purported manner," and *admittedly* does not mean "in an admitted manner." Rather, the unorthodox formula for these words is *it is . . . -ed that,* i.e. *allegedly* (= it is alleged that) and so on. Instead of bewailing the unorthodoxy of these words in *-edly,* we should be thankful for their promotion of conciseness and continue to use them (if only sparingly). We have many of them, such as *supposedly, allegedly, assertedly, reportedly, admittedly, confessedly,* and *concededly.* See **allegedly, confessedly & reportedly.**

Nonetheless, forms in *-edly* ought to be avoided if a ready substitute exists: "[A] bank may indeed be *liable for unauthorizedly revealing* [read *liable for revealing without authorization*] the state of a depositor's accounts to his creditors." *Schuster v. Banco de Iberoamerica,* 476 So. 2d 253, 255 (Fla. App. 1985) (Schwartz, J., dissenting). See **qualifiedly.**

educ(at)able. The shorter form is correct. See -ATABLE & **educible.**

education(al)ist; educator. *Educationist* (the preferred form) = an educational theorist. In the U.S., the term has acquired negative connotations. In G.B., it has come to be used in the sense of *educator,* which in the U.S. means "a teacher; one engaged in educational work."

educational; educative, -tory; educable. *Educational* = (1) having to do with education

⟨educational issues⟩; (2) serving to further education ⟨educational films⟩. *Educative* = tending to educate; instructive ⟨educative lectures⟩. *Educatory* is a NEEDLESS VARIANT of *educative. Educable* = capable of being educated ⟨educable pupils⟩.

educe, v., (= to elicit; evoke) should be distinguished from *adduce* (= to bring forward for analysis) and from *educt,* n. (= something educed). E.g., "In the present case, the factual showing thus *educed* [i.e. *developed, brought out*] does not so unequivocally point to a borrowed employee relationship as to permit a summary judgment." Here the sense is correct, but the word is matched with the wrong subject: "We need not reach this issue, because *no factual showing was educed* [read either *no showing was made* or *no facts were educed*] by the defendant to negate the allegations of her complaint that the failure to reemploy her resulted from gender-based discrimination." See **adduce.**

educible; educable. The former means "capable of being educed, or drawn out." The latter means "capable of being educated." See **educational.**

-EE. A. General Principles. This suffix (fr. French past participial *-é*) originally denoted "one who is acted upon"; the sense is inherently passive. Thus we have *acquittee* (= one who is acquitted); *arrestee* (= one who is arrested); *conscriptee* (= one who is conscripted); *detainee* (= one who is detained); *educatee* (= one who is educated [by an *educator*]); *expellee* (= one who is expelled); *inauguree* (= one who is inaugurated); *indictee* (= one who is indicted); *invitee* (= one who is invited); *liberee* (= one who is liberated); *permittee* (= one who is permitted); *returnee* (= one who is returned); *selectee* (= one who is selected); *separatee* (= one who is separated); *shelteree* (= one who is sheltered); *smugglee* (= one who is smuggled); *telephonee* (= one who is telephoned).

The suffix has also a dative sense, in which it acts as the passive agent noun for the indirect object; this is the sense in which the suffix is most commonly used in law: *abandonee* (= one to whom property rights are relinquished); *advancee* (= one to whom money is advanced); *allocatee* (= one to whom something is allocated); *allottee* (= one to whom something is allotted); *consignee* (= a person to whom something is consigned); *covenantee* (= one to whom something is covenanted); *disclosee* (= one to whom something is disclosed); *grantee* (= one to whom property is granted); *indorsee* (= one to whom a negotiable instrument is indorsed); *lessee* (= one to whom property is leased); *patentee* (= one to whom a patent has been issued); *payee* (= one to whom money is paid); *pledgee* (= one to whom something is pledged); *referee* (= one to whom something is referred); *remittee* (= one to whom something is remitted); *trustee* (= one to whom something is entrusted); *vendee* (= one to whom something is sold). At least one word in *-ee* has both a normal passive sense and a dative sense. *Appointee* = (1) one who is appointed; or (2) one to whom an estate is appointed. Sense (2), of course, is primarily legal.

The suffix *-ee*, then, is correlative in sense to *-or*, the active agent-noun suffix: some words in *-ee* are formed as passive analogues to *-or* agent nouns, and not from any verb stem: *indemnitee* (= one who is indemnified; analogue to *indemnitor*); *preceptee* (= student; analogue to *preceptor*).

These are the traditional uses of the suffix. There is a tendency today, however, to make *-ee* a general agent-noun suffix without regard to its passive sense or the limitations within which it may take on passive senses. Hence the suffix has been extended to PHRASAL VERBS, even though only the first word in the phrase appears in the *-ee* word: e.g., *discriminatee* (= one who is discriminated against); *tippee* (= one who is tipped off). Then other prepositional phrases have gradually come into the wide embrace of *-ee*: *abortee* (= a woman upon whom an abortion is performed); *confiscatee* (= one from whom goods have been confiscated); *optionee* (= one against whose interests another has an option).

Some *-ee* words contain implicit possessives: *amputee* (= one whose limb has been removed); *breachee* (= one whose contract is breached); *condemnee* (= one whose property has been condemned). In still other words, *-ee* does not even have its primary passive sense: e.g., *arrivee* (= one who arrives); *asylee* (= one who seeks asylum); *benefitee* (= one who benefits [or "is benefited"]); *escapee* (= one who escapes); *standee* (= one who stands). *Adjudicatee*, oddly, has no direct relation to its verb; in civil law, it means "a purchaser at a judicial sale." Finally, the suffix is sometimes

used to coin jocular words such as *cheatee* (= one who is cheated).

The upshot of this discussion is that *-ee* has been much abused, and that writers must be careful of the forms they use. For active senses we have *-er*, *-or*, and *-ist* at our service; we should be wary of adopting any new active forms in *-ee*, and do our best to see that *standee* and *escapee* and similar forms come to an eternal rest. Otherwise we risk wasting any sense to be found in this suffix. For example, "the unskilled workers used to 'dilute' skilled workers in time of war should have been called *diluters* instead of *dilutees*; the skilled were the *dilutees*" (*MEU2* 146).

B. Word-Formation. The principles applying to words in -ATABLE apply also to agent nouns in *-ee*. Thus we have *inauguree*, not *inauguratee*; *subrogee*, not *subrogatee* (though the latter is infrequently used mistakenly for the former).

C. Stylistic Use of. Stylists know that *-ee* agent nouns are often inferior to more descriptive terms: they sometimes objectify the persons they describe, though the writer may intend no callousness: E.g., "On October 19, 1966, a jury convicted Enriquez of capital murder of Kay Foss, the *abductee* [read *the woman abducted*], and imposed the death penalty."

effect, v.t.; **effectuate.** Most dictionaries define these words in the same way, but an emerging DIFFERENTIATION exists that should be encouraged. Although both mean "to accomplish, bring about, or cause to happen," stylists have generally considered *effect* the preferable word, *effectuate* a NEEDLESS VARIANT. No longer need this be so.

Here *effect* is used in the preferred sense: "This classification process *effected* by the maximum grant regulation produces a basic denial of equal treatment."/ "This is an appeal from a decree of the probate court dismissing a petition brought by appellant, administrator of the estate of Sallie Storrs Tate, for the purpose of *effecting* a final settlement, of the estate of the late Zophar M. Mansur."

Ordinarily in legal contexts, *effectuate* means "to give effect to," and not "to bring about." Thus it is not here synonymous with *effect*: "The board also ordered the following affirmative action which it was found would *effectuate* ["give effect to," not "bring about"] the policies of the administration."/ "The rule has been read by courts in a manner that *ef-*

fectuates its function of timely notice without creating technical traps for the unwary."/ "Any harshness that may have resulted from the state court's decision can be attributed solely to its intention to *effectuate* as nearly as possible the explicit terms of Senator Bacon's will."/ "We have emphasized the need to consider the law enforcement purposes to be served by the stop as well as the time reasonably needed to *effectuate* those purposes."/ "We extend our efforts, as we ought to, toward *effectuating* the testator's intentions."/ "Where one makes an imperfect gift to a natural object of his bounty and dies believing that he has an effective gift, a court of equity will *effectuate* the gift by declaring his heir to be a constructive trustee."

Here *effect* is misused for *effectuate*: "We properly must inquire beyond those minimal historical safeguards for securing trial by reason to ensure that the commands of justice are *effected* [read *effectuated* (i.e. 'given effect')]."

The opposite error here appears: "The auditing judge awarded $2,629 to appellee for the purpose of preserving the unproductive real estate until a sale thereof could be *effectuated* [read *effected*]."/ "The extent of this equity, whether *effectuated* [read *effected*] by specific performance or by restitution, will be dealt with in detail later."

Effect (= to bring about) is sometimes misused for *affect*, v.t. (= to influence, have an effect on): "The fact that findings and conclusions under Rule 296 are not titled separately from the judgment does not *effect* [read *affect*] their validity." / "The persons *effected* [read *affected*] by the fraud on the corporation, if the fraud were permitted, would be the subsequent stockholders and creditors." See **affect.**

Affectuate has appeared as an error for *effectuate*: "Notice of release by appellant in and of itself certainly is sufficient notice to *affectuate* [read *effectuate*] a valid release." See **affect.**

effective. See **effectual.**

effective cause. See CAUSATION (B).

effectively = (1) in an effective manner; well ⟨to speak effectively⟩; (2) in effect, actually; or (3) completely. Sense (2), common in legal writing, appears here: "The United States Courts of Appeals are *effectively* [i.e. 'in effect'] courts of last resort."

Effectually is incorrect for sense (3) of *effectively*: "Such property is withdrawn from the jurisdiction of the courts of the other authority as *effectually* [read *effectively*] as if the property had been entirely removed to the territory of another sovereignty."/ "He was damaged by appellant's willful trespass just as *effectually* [read *effectively*] as if he were the real owner of the bridge." The same is true of sense (2): "*Effectually* [read *Effectively*], since this carpet measures only 54 inches in width, there are many more seams than would be necessary in a standard 12-foot carpet." See **effectual.**

effectual; effective; efficacious; efficient. All these words mean generally "having effect," but they have distinctive applications. *Effective* = having a high degree of effect (used of a thing done or of the doer) ⟨effective administration of justice⟩ ⟨the court's power to fashion an *effective* equitable remedy⟩. *Efficacious* = certain to have the desired effect (used of things) ⟨efficacious drugs⟩. *Efficient* = competent to perform a task; capable of bringing about a desired effect (used of agents or their actions or instruments) ⟨an efficient organization⟩. *Efficient* increasingly has economic connotations in law that are evident, e.g., in the phrase *cost-efficient*, q.v.

Effectual, perhaps the most troublesome of these words in practice, means "achieving the complete effect aimed at"; it is used apart from the agent. E.g., "I think that unity of organization is necessary to make the contest of labor *effectual*." (Holmes)/ "The wrongful taking of chattels was, therefore, a more *effectual* disseisin than the ouster from land."/ "The court held that the transaction constituted an *effectual* trust for the benefit of those named."/ "The testatrix adopted the suggestion of her attorney to revoke her will by written memoranda, admittedly *ineffectual* as revocations by subsequent writings."/ "If that were so, every imperfect security, however invalid as a real right, would be *effectual* as a trust." (Eng.) On the use of *effectually* for *effectively*, see **effectively.**

effectuate. See **effect,** v.t.

effete does not mean "effeminate" or "sophisticated and snobbish." Rather, it means "worn out, barren, exhausted."

efficacious; efficient. See **effectual.**

effrontery (= shameless insolence) for *affront* (= an open insult) is a MALAPROPISM.

E.g., "To overturn the judge's denial of the motion to recuse would be an *effrontery* [read *affront*] to his character."

effulge. See BACK-FORMATIONS.

e.g. (= for example) is used to introduce representative examples. Using the abbreviation *etc.* after an enumeration following *e.g.* creates a superfluity, since one expects nothing more than a representative sample of possibilities. But *etc.* might be required after *i.e.* (= that is) to show the incompleteness of the list.

Black's (5th ed.) misuses *i.e.* for *e.g.* in its entry for *layman*: "One who is not of a particular profession (i.e. nonlawyer)." The abbreviation should be *e.g.*, not *i.e.*, because under the definition a nondoctor as well as a nonlawyer would be a *layman*; *nonlawyer* is intended only to provide an example.

One should be certain that it is clear what the signal refers to: "Out-of-pocket losses include medical expenses, lost earnings, and the cost of any labor required to do things that the plaintiff can no longer do himself (*e.g.*, a housekeeper)." But "things the plaintiff can no longer do himself" are not exemplified by *a housekeeper*. (Or does the writer mean *be a housekeeper*?) In any event, wherever the reader encounters an *e.g.* he rightly expects a sampling of appropriate items—not an ambiguous or an all-inclusive listing. Here it might be, *e.g.*, *keep house, drive a car, tend the garden.* See **i.e.**

egoism; egotism; egocentrism; egocentricity; egomania. *Egoism* is a legitimate philosophical term meaning "a doctrine that self-betterment is the guiding method of existence, or that self-interest is the primary motive in all one's actions." The use of *egoism* in the sense "selfishness" is a SLIPSHOD EXTENSION. *Egotism* = arrogance; an exaggerated sense of self-importance; self-praise. *Egocentrism* and *egocentricity* are synonymous, with perhaps a slight nuance. *Egocentrism* = the quality of being self-centered and selfish; looking only to one's own feelings and needs. *Egocentricity* = the quality of being egocentric, individualistic, or self-centered. *Egomania* is extreme *egocentrism.*

egregious /i-**gree**-jŭs/ formerly meant merely "outstanding," but has been specialized in sense so that it now means "outstandingly bad." It is a pejorative adjective.

egress; ingress. *Egress* = the right or liberty of going out. *Ingress* = the right or liberty of going in. The legal phrase *ingress, egress, and regress* = the right to enter, leave, and re-enter.

Courts and lawyers have sometimes mistaken the import of these terms. *Black's* (4th & 5th eds.) erroneously defines *ingress, egress, and regress* as "the right (as of a lessee) to enter, *go upon* [read *leave*], and *return from* [read *return to*] the lands in question." The same dictionary states that *egress* is "often used interchangeably with the word *access*," apparently confusing *egress* with *ingress.* See **ingress.**

either. A. Number of Elements. Most properly, *either . . . or* can frame only two alternatives, and no more: "He testified that in the last few years terraza had been used more extensively in entranceways than *either* marble, tile, cement, *or* asphalt [omit *either*]." See CORRELATIVE CONJUNCTIONS.

B. Constructions in *not . . . either*. These should be made into *neither . . . nor* constructions. E.g., "*Other states do not require either a notice or registration* [read *Other states require neither notice nor registration*], although they may require filing of a report of sale."

C. Singular or Plural. Nouns framed by *either . . . or* take a singular verb when they are both singular, or where only the latter is singular. E.g., "There was no evidence that either DeGraft or his corporation *were* [read *was*] under the control of defendants."

The same principle applies to nouns that should agree in number with the subject: "The situation should not be viewed in terms of whether the Constitution somehow makes a teacher or librarian the proper *selectors* [read *selector*] of a curriculum or books."/ "If *either* had been a male *they* [read *the couple*, or, depending on the sense, *he*] would have been prohibited from intermarrying." See CONCORD & SUBJECT-VERB AGREEMENT (F).

D. *Either or both.* "One must plead either or both that the state has established a procedure that itself is constitutionally deficient or that it has provided no adequate remedy for aberrational [q.v.] departures by its servants from proper procedures." [Read *One must plead either that . . . or that . . . , or both.*]/ "Judicial sanctions in civil contempt proceedings may, in a proper case, be employed *for either or both of two purposes* [read *for either of two purposes*]." (If *both* rationales exist, then no one would seriously argue that the sanctions are unavailable.)

ejaculate can really no longer be used in sober writing as a synonym for "exclaim."

ejectment; ejection; ouster. These terms are deceptively similar, but have important differences. *Ejectment* and *ejection* are names of actions at law, whereas *ouster* is a legal wrong. *Ejectment* = trespass to try title; a legal action brought by one claiming a right to possess real property against another in possession. This action was abolished in G.B. in 1875, but persists in some American jurisdictions. E.g., "We think it is clear in this case that the complainants in this bill might have brought *ejectment* for the land against the tenants in possession." *Ejection* is the term for a similar action in Scots law.

Ouster is something different: "the act of wrongfully dispossessing someone of any kind of hereditament, such as freehold property" (*CDL*).

ejusdem generis is a canon of construction providing that when general words follow the enumeration of persons or things of a specific meaning, the general words will be construed as applying only to persons or things of the same general class as those enumerated. C. Sands, 2A *Sutherland's Statutes and Statutory Construction* § 47.17 (4th ed. 1973). E.g., "The assembly of machinery is not *ejusdem generis* with 'cleaning, lubricating, and painting.'" The term is pronounced /ee-**yoos**-dĕm-**jen**-ĕ-ris/ or (BrE) /ee-**jus**-dĕm/.

eke out. Journalists often misuse this verb phrase by writing, e.g., that Smith *eked out* a victory over Jones in the election (as if the phrase meant, in colloquial terms, "squeaked by Jones"). *Eke out* properly means "to supplement, add to, or make go farther or last longer." Here the phrase is correctly used: "It was considered possible to solve all legal problems by deduction from the actual rules of English law, *eked out* [i.e. supplemented] perhaps by careful borrowing from the Roman jurists." One may *eke out* one's income by working nights as well as days. But one does not, properly, *eke out* an existence: "Appellant claimed to have brought more than $70,000 with him from Vermont, when his testimony showed that during his period there he was *barely able to eke out an existence* [read *barely able to make ends meet*, or some other CLICHÉ]." The phrase does not mean "to acquire by difficulty or drudgery."

elaborate, v.i. & v.t., is commonly intransitive in nonlegal contexts ⟨to elaborate on a point⟩, and transitive in legal contexts ⟨to elaborate a point⟩. E.g., "A well-known passage in Blackstone's Commentaries *elaborates* the so-called fourfold unity of a joint tenancy." Although both *to elaborate* and *to elaborate on* may mean "to work out in detail," the former suggests "to produce by labor," and the latter suggests "to explain at greater length." Awareness of this nuance allows one to choose the apter phrasing.

elder, eldest. These are variants of *older* and *oldest*, with restricted uses: one refers to an *elder* brother or sister, or to the *eldest* son or daughter, but elsewhere the form is out of place. *Older* and *oldest* may always substitute for *elder* and *eldest*.

elect is a LEGALISM meaning "to choose deliberately." This FORMAL WORD, generally followed by an infinitive in legal prose, should not be used where a simple *choose* will suffice. E.g., "The petitioner *elected* [read *chose*] to declare the entire indebtedness to be immediately due and payable."/ "It is suggested that he does not have the mental capability to *elect* [read *choose*] to continue further judicial examination of his conviction."/ "With the consent of the trustees, he may *elect* [read *choose*] to take his benefits in a lump sum, or part lump sum and part annuity." The changes here suggested are stylistic merely; *elect* cannot be said to be wrong—it is merely symptomatic of LEGALESE.

electee (= one chosen or elected) is recorded in the *OED* and supported by a single quotation, from 1593. One might suppose that, because *electee* appears in neither the *OED Supp.* nor *W3*, it was a sixteenth-century nonce word that is long since defunct. So prudent writers would suppose; yet revival of *electee* has been attempted: "Any other conclusion would make the beginning of a term of office depend on the will of the *electee* rather than the will of electors as the latter has been unequivocally expressed." *Ex parte Sanders*, 215 S.W.2d 325, 326 (Tex. 1948). Whether the word will gain limited currency as a correlative of *elector* it is too early to say. For now it remains a mere curiosity. See -EE.

elective. This term is used primarily in relation to political elections. *Elective* = appointed by election; subject to election. In legal writing, however, *elective* is used more broadly of legal choices: "The widow took her *elective share* of the estate."

electorial is a common error for *electoral* (= of or relating to electors) in the phrase *electoral college.*

eleemosynary /el-ĕ-*mos*-ĭ-*ner*-ee/, related etymologically to the word *alms*, is a FORMAL WORD for *charitable*. It is more common in legal than in nonlegal prose. E.g., "The church seeks and obtains the *eleemosynary* contributions of the laity, not for private gain, but for the aid of pious institutions and objects of every nature."/ "The court held the cy pres statutes inapplicable because the trust was not for a charitable, benevolent, or *eleemosynary* purpose."

ELEGANT VARIATION. See INELEGANT VARIATION.

elemental, -tary. *Elemental* is the more specific term, meaning "of or relating to the elements of something; essential." E.g., "We do what *elemental* justice and fundamental fairness demand under the necessitous circumstances." *Elementary* means "introductory; simple; fundamental." E.g., "It is *elementary* that an executory contract, in order to be enforceable, must be based upon a valuable consideration."

eligible may equally well be construed with either *for* or *to* (an office). *Eligible for* is more common today than *eligible to*, but the latter has unimpeachable credentials: "No person except a natural born citizen . . . shall be *eligible to* the office of president." U.S. Const. art. II, § 1./ "No judge of any court . . . shall during the term for which he is elected or appointed, be *eligible to* the legislature." Tex. Const. art. III, § 19.

elisor /ĕ-*ll*-zĕr/, omitted from *W3* but generally included in unabridged dictionaries, means "a person appointed by a court to return a jury, serve a writ, or perform other duties of the sheriff or a coroner in case of his disqualification" (*W2*). Though comparatively rare, the term is still used in some American jurisdictions. E.g., "In view of our holding that the *elisor* was an interested person, we do not reach a determination as to the validity of the service of process under Ba-

hamian law." *Wakeman v. Farish,* 356 So. 2d 1323, 1325 (Fla. App. 1978).

elocution; locution; allocution. *Elocution* = style in speaking; the art of speaking persuasively. *Locution* = a word or phrase. For *allocution,* see the entry under that word.

eloi(g)n is a an archaic legal term meaning "to convey or remove out of the jurisdiction of the court or of the sheriff" (*OED*). Generally the word is spelled *eloign* rather than *eloin.*

else's. Such possessive constructions as *anyone else's* and *everybody else's* are preferred to the obsolete constructions *anyone's else* and *everybody's else.*

elude. See **allude.**

elusive, -sory; illusive, -sory. *Elusive* (rather than *elusory*) is the usual adjective related to *elude; illusory* (rather than *illusive*) is the usual adjective related to *illusion.* Here *illusive* has almost certainly been misused for *elusive:* "The discussion almost inevitably returns to the *illusive* [read *elusive*] subject of what the Supreme Court really held. . . ." *In re Baldwin-United Corp.,* 52 Bankr. 541, 544 (Bankr. S.D. Ohio 1985). See **illusory.**

EM-; IM-. See EN-; IN-.

emanate = (1) to flow forth, issue, originate *from* a person or thing as a source; or (2) to proceed from a material source (*OED*). Sense (2) applies to physical senses. E.g., "The use of a human investigator was a factor involved in *State v. Groves,* where an airplane pilot's detection of an odor *emanating* from luggage he was unloading led to a sniff of that luggage by a trained police dog."

The word is coming to be overworked in sense (1), rising almost to the level of a VOGUE WORD. Its use in the law is old: "In discussing this question, the counsel for the state of Maryland have deemed it of some importance, in the construction of the constitution, to consider that instrument not as *emanating* from the people, but as the act of sovereign and independent states." *McCulloch v. Maryland,* 17 U.S. (4 Wheat.) 316, 402 (1819) (per Marshall, C.J.).

Judges today seemed enamored of the word, which is fast becoming another legal CLICHÉ: "Moreover, there are other suggestions such as that *emanating* from Dean Wigmore at a time when the question whether the parol evidence rule was proper subject-matter for evidence or contracts had not been decided."/ "It appears that the first advancement statute was based on the custom of London and York, and that the custom must have *emanated* from the Roman (or civil) law principle of collatio bonorum, requiring a bringing into hotchpot."/ "Defendant pleaded guilty to two counts of bank robbery charged in an indictment *emanating* from the District of Minnesota."

emancipation; mancipation. The former means "the act of freeing from slavery," the latter "the act of enslaving."

emasculate means literally "to castrate," but has come figuratively to mean "to deprive of strength and vigor, to weaken." The word is a favorite of judges in dissent. E.g., "More important in the long run than this misreading of the federal statute, however, is the court's *emasculation* of the equal protection clause as a constitutional principle applicable to the area of social welfare administration."/ "Under the majority's *emasculation* of the Act, no determination need be made whether the substantial question is likely to be determined favorably on appeal." Cf. **eviscerate.**

embarrass is today used in the sense "to encumber, hamper, impede" almost exclusively in legal contexts. E.g., "Even in Tucker Act cases the problem of joinder should not be *embarrassed* by any doctrine of sovereign immunity." (The Tucker Act allows certain persons to sue the government.)/ "We think that the arguments of the parties are considerably *embarrassed* by factors not touched upon by the parties." Most laymen would find puzzling these uses of *embarrass.*

embassador. See **ambassador.**

embassy; legation. Often assumed to be synonymous, these words should be distinguished. An *embassy* is under an ambassador, and a *legation* is under a minister, envoy, chargé d'affaires, or some other diplomatic agent.

embezzle; misappropriate; steal. *Embez-*

zle is always used in reference to fiduciaries who take for their own use money entrusted to them. *Misappropriate* means "to take for oneself wrongfully," and may or may not be used of a fiduciary. *Steal,* like *misappropriate,* is a broader term than *embezzle;* it has the same meaning as *misappropriate,* but much stronger negative connotations. See **defalcate, misappropriate,** & **peculation.**

embrace, in figurative senses, may mean (1) "to include," or (2) "to adopt." Here sense (1), largely a legal sense, applies: "Personal liberty or the right of property *embraces* the right to make contracts for the sale of one's own labor and the employment of one's individual and industrial sources."/ "There is no support in the record for the proposition that Bombay's business and goodwill could be protected only by a restrictive covenant *embracing* almost all of the North American continent."/ "The general article was interpreted to *embrace* only crimes the commission of which had some direct impact on military discipline."

Sense (2), used in legal and nonlegal contexts alike, is exemplified in this sentence: "While appellants try to argue that dilution cases involve a mixed question of law and fact not governed by the clearly erroneous standard, we cannot *embrace* this argument."

embrace(o)r. This term, meaning "one guilty of embracery [= the offense of influencing a jury illegally and corruptly]," is best spelled *embracer,* preferred by the *OED* and the *AHD.* *W3* includes its main entry under *embraceor,* with the ill-formed suffix.

embracery; imbracery; bracery. The first form is standard for this word, which denotes the offense of attempting to corrupt or instruct a jury to reach a particular conclusion by means other than evidence or argument in court, as by bribing or threatening jurors. *Imbracery* and *bracery* are NEEDLESS VARIANTS.

emend. See **amend.**

emigrant; émigré. There is a latent DIFFERENTIATION between these words. An *emigrant* is one who leaves a country to settle in another. *Émigré* has the same sense, but applies especially to one in political exile. The first acute accent is often omitted (*emigré*) in AmE.

emigrate. See **immigrate.**

émigré. See **emigrant.**

eminent. See **imminent.**

eminent domain; condemnation; expropriation. The seventeenth-century civilian Grotius coined the term *eminens dominium*, from which our phrase derives. In G.B., *eminent domain* is primarily a term of international law. In the U.S., it refers to the power of federal and state governments to pronounce judicially (land, etc.) as converted to public use. The usual BrE term for this sense is *expropriation. Condemnation*, an Americanism, has virtually the same sense: "judicial assignation (of property) to public purposes, subject to reasonable compensation." E.g., "This is a *condemnation* proceeding brought by the County of Matagorda to condemn four parcels of land." See **compulsory purchase.**

emote. See BACK-FORMATIONS.

empanel; impanel. *Empanel* (= to swear a jury to try an issue [*CDL*]) is now the preferred spelling in both the U.S. and G.B. E.g., "The cause came on for trial with a jury duly *empaneled*." *Impanel* was formerly a common spelling, used, e.g., in *Franklin v. South Carolina*, 218 U.S. 161, 166 (1910).

empathy; sympathy. *Empathy* is the ability to imagine oneself in another person's position and to experience all the sensations connected with it. *Sympathy* is compassion for or commiseration with another.

emphasis added; emphasis supplied. These citation signals are both used to indicate that the writer quoting another's words has italicized some of them. There is no distinction in meaning between the phrases, as some writers occasionally assume. *Emphasis in original* is used to indicate that the italics appeared in the original quoted material.

empiricize, not in the dictionaries, has made an appearance in an American law report: "Just as experienced physicians render diagnoses on the basis of symptoms they sense, but often cannot *empiricize* [= confirm or verify by testing] or articulate, so too, we are told, can those who work among prisoners develop 'senses' concerning the potential

for impending disobedience or unrest." *Abdul Wali v. Coughlin*, 754 F.2d 1015, 1018 (2d Cir. 1985).

empirics is not in good use for *empiricism*. Cf. **esoterics.**

employe(e). Although *employé*, the French form, might logically be thought to be better as a generic term, *employée* (which in French denotes the feminine gender) is so widespread (without the accent mark) that it is not likely to be uprooted. *The Wall Street Journal* and a few other publications remain staunch adherents to the form *employe* (minus the acute accent on the final -*e*); but *employee* is standard.

It did not always have such a stronghold, however. *Employe* was once common in English. E.g., "We need hardly repeat the statement . . . that in the Employers' Liability Act Congress used the words 'employé' and 'employed' in their natural sense, and intended to describe the conventional relation of employer and *employé*." *Hull v. Philadelphia & Ry.*, 40 S.Ct. 358, 359 (1920) (spelled *employee* at 252 U.S. 475, 479).

employer and employee; master and servant. The former phrase seems to be supplanting the latter, which at best sounds antiquarian.

emulate; immolate. The former is to strive to equal or rival, to copy or imitate with the object of equaling. The latter is to kill as a sacrifice.

Emulate is frequently misused, as, e.g., here for *adopt*: "I cannot believe that a company trying to estimate the effect of a marketing tool would *emulate* [read *adopt*] the methods that lawyers use in taking depositions."

EN-; IN-. No consistent rules exist for determining which form of the prefix to use before a given word. In the U.S. at present, the spellings *entrust, enclose, inquire* (= to ask), and *increase* are standard. The spellings in G.B. for those words are *entrust, enclose, enquire* (= to ask), and *increase*, but the variants *intrust* and *inclose* still appear with some frequency. Especially troublesome to writers are word-pairs with varying prefixes according to inflection: *encrust* but *incrustation; engrain* (= to dye in the raw state) but *ingrained* (= deeply rooted). For a discussion of *in-* as both privative and intensive, see NEGATIVES (B.)

enable. The phrase *enabling statute* was perhaps first used specifically in reference to the act (32 Hen. VIII. c.28) by which tenants-in-fee and certain others were "enabled" to make leases (*OED*). Now the phrase is used in reference to any statute conferring powers, and in the U.S. usually to a congressional statute conferring powers on executive agencies to carry out various tasks delegated to them. E.g., "Procedural uniformity seems to be weakening, as the Congress has become increasingly willing to prescribe detailed codes of procedure in *enabling* legislation." See **disenable.**

enact. The platitude is that courts adjudicate, rather than legislate. Some judicial decisions seem to belie this principle; still, it is unidiomatic to refer to a court as enacting doctrines: "The Supreme Court has *enacted* [read *enunciated* or some other word] a 'public safety' exception to *Miranda*."

enactment = (1) the action or process of enacting ⟨enactment of the bill⟩; or (2) a statute. The word is best not used by legal writers in sense (2), although it has been so used almost from its beginning. Still, to use *enactment* in sense (2) is to add an unneeded synonym and to muddle a useful distinction. The plural almost always manifests this stylistically poor use: "*Congressional enactments* [read *Congressional acts* or *Federal statutes*] come to this court with an extremely heavy presumption of validity."

Nevertheless, sense (2) is so pervasive that we can do little else but avoid it in our own writing; criticism of its users (as opposed to its *use*) is unfair, given its pervasiveness. The *OCL* and *CDL* define *enactment* only in sense (2): "a statute or Act of Parliament, statutory instrument, by-law or other statement of law made by a person or body with legislative powers" (*OCL*). Likewise, it is used in sense (2) in the Assimilative Crimes Act, 18 U.S.C. § 13 (1982), which states that certain acts or omissions are "not made punishable by any enactment of Congress." Perhaps the use of the term in the last-quoted example arose from the mistaken notion that *act* in *acts and omissions* might be confused with *act of Congress*. Even were that true, *federal statute* would suffice in place of *act of Congress*.

en banc; in banc; in banco; in bank. *W3* lists only *en banc* (= in full court; F. lit. "on the bench"), which is certainly the predominant form in English-speaking countries. *In banc* and *in bank* also appear in a few jurisdictions, but these are not widespread. The Supreme Court of Arizona uses *in banc*, as in *Spur Industries, Inc. v. Del E. Webb Development Co.*, 494 P.2d 700 (Ariz. 1972) (*in banc*), whereas the Supreme Court of California uses *in bank*. See, e.g., *In re Los Angeles County Pioneer Society*, 40 Cal. 2d 852, 257 P.2d 1 (1953) (*in bank*); *People v. Collins*, 219 Cal. Rptr. 1, 706 P.2d 1135 (Cal. 1985) (*in bank*). *In banco* is listed in *Black's* (5th ed.), but is rarely if ever used.

En banc being now the usual spelling, the burden falls on English-speaking lawyers to pronounce the word correctly. Certainly the anglicized pronunciation /in-**bank**/ is unexceptionable; the French approximation /on-**bonk**/ is also common, although in some regions it is considered precious.

enbancworthy (= worthy of being considered en banc) is a term concocted by, and still generally confined to, the judges of the United States Court of Appeals for the Fifth Circuit. As legal ARGOT formed on the model of words like *seaworthy* and *airworthy*, it is useful shorthand, though odd-sounding. E.g., "This opens up a whole array of influences which for nearly all cases [affect] . . . whether the case is *enbancworthy*." *Allen v. Johnson*, 391 F.2d 527, 532 (5th Cir. 1968) (per Brown, C.J.)./ "As one who shares his misgivings, I feel obligated to state concisely my reasons for believing that the present case is *enbancworthy*." *Becker v. Thompson*, 463 F.2d 1338, 1339 (5th Cir. 1972) (Brown, C. J., dissenting)./ "Briefs and oral arguments on rehearing en banc led the Court to conclude that this case is not *enbancworthy*." *McLaurin v. Columbia Municipal Separate School District*, 486 F.2d 1049, 1050 (5th Cir. 1973)./ "Although standing alone, this problem would hardly be *enbancworthy*, we conclude that action by us is appropriate rather than letting stand the panel's analysis of third-party beneficiary." *Hercules, Inc. v. Stevens Shipping Co.*, 698 F.2d 726, 736 (5th Cir. 1983). Cf. **certworthy.**

enclose; inclose. The former spelling is now preferred in all senses. E.g., "The complaint alleged that certain statements in the publication (those *inclosed* [read *enclosed*] in brackets) were false." See EN-.

enclosed herewith and *enclosed herein* are unnecessary for *enclosed*; in both phrases, the first word conveys the idea redundantly expressed by the second. See the following entry.

enclosed please find is archaic deadwood in lawyers' correspondence for *enclosed is* or *I have enclosed.* Whether the phrase was originally commercialese or LEGALESE, it has been cant since its creation.

enclosure; inclosure. The former spelling is preferred in all senses. See EN-.

encomium. Pl. *-iums, -ia.* The English plural is preferred. See PLURALS (A).

encrease is an obsolete spelling of *increase* used, e.g., in the U.S. Const., art. I, § 6. See EN-.

encrust; incrust. See EN-.

encumbrance; incumbrance; cumbrance. The preferred spelling is *encumbrance* in both the U.S. and G.B. E.g., "The court erred in holding that the shares of stock to Lillian Conway Fine is free and clear of liens and *encumbrances.*" Yet *incumbrance* is the spelling used in the British Finance Act of 1975. *Cumbrance* is a NEEDLESS VARIANT.

encumbrancer is a slightly archaic equivalent of *lienholder.* (See **lienor.**) A variant spelling to be avoided is *incumbrancer.*

endeavor is a FORMAL WORD for *attempt* or *try.* E.g., "No such clemency can be extended to an attorney who deliberately and persistently *endeavors* to submit evidence that is clearly incompetent and that, as a lawyer, he is presumed to know is incompetent."
   The same is true of *endeavor* as a noun: "To attempt to limit English competition in this way would be as hopeless an *endeavour* as the experiment of King Canute."

endemic. See **epidemic.**

end(ing). *End,* not *ending,* is the proper correlative of *beginning.* E.g., "The turnover of the Sinai is a beginning, not an *ending* [read *end*]." Obviously, the writer was trying for parallel *-ing*s.

endnote. See **footnote.**

endorse; indorse. The usual spelling in

nonlegal contexts is *endorse;* that is the only acceptable spelling of the word when used figuratively to mean "to express approval of." In legal senses relating to negotiable instruments, *indorse* predominates in the U.S.; the word is so spelled thoughout the Uniform Commercial Code. This latent DIFFERENTIATION ought to be encouraged. In Great Britain, however, *endorse* is the more frequent spelling even in the context of commercial paper.
   Indorse on the back is a REDUNDANCY; the root *dors-* means "back."

endorsee. See -EE.

end product is usually unnecessary for *product.*

ends and objects. See DOUBLETS AND TRIPLETS OF LEGAL IDIOM.

energy-saving should be hyphenated, although some writers are beginning to treat it as a newfangled one-word compound. E.g., "Tax credits are available for *energysaving* [read *energy-saving*] measures—up to $300 for insulation and up to $4,000 for installing a solar-heated unit." (Cf. **decision-making** & **policy-making.**)

enervate; innervate. The former means "to drain the vigor out of," the latter "to supply with energy."

enfeoff; infeoff. See **feoff.**

enforce; inforce. The latter is an archaic spelling that makes a vestigial appearance in *reinforce.* See EN-.

enforceable; enforcible. *Enforceable* is the preferred, standard spelling in both the U.S. and G.B. "Thus a condition annexed to a bequest designed to prevent the marriage of the testator's daughter with a particular individual is valid and *enforcible* [read *enforceable*]."

enfranchise. See **franchise.**

engraft; ingraft. The word is best spelled *engraft.* See EN-.

engrandize. See **aggrandize.**

engross, ingross; enrol(l), inrol(l). The preferred spellings are *engross* and *enroll*

(AmE), *enrol* (BrE). Both words have to do with the preparation of legal documents. To *engross* a legal document (as a deed) is to prepare a fair copy ready for execution. To *enroll* it is to enter it into an official record upon execution. See **enrol(l)ment.**

enjoin from; enjoin upon. *Enjoin* generally has exactly opposite meanings in the U.S. and G.B. Still, the diametrical meanings are possible in both places; the difference lies in the relative frequency of the two uses. The British ordinarily use *enjoin* to mean "to prescribe, mandate" ⟨enjoin *upon* or *to*⟩, a sense found occasionally in AmE. E.g., "While a becoming respect for all who 'sit in judgment' is strictly *enjoined,* both as a moral and a professional duty, a healthy respect only is intended, not a servile obsequiousness."/ "Courts are ill-suited to resolve hypothetical issues and are constitutionally *enjoined* to decide only concrete cases."/ "Secrecy of counsel is *enjoined upon* the jurors by an oath of ancient lineage." (Cardozo) Although this sense exists in the U.S., its occurrence is rare in comparison with the other sense of *enjoin.*

Americans generally use it to mean "to prohibit" ⟨enjoin *from*⟩. E.g., "The court *enjoined* the company from selling any further cargoes of Nigerian oil to buyers other than the plaintiff."

In the sense "to prohibit by injunction," *enjoin* is preferable to the BACK-FORMATION *injunct,* dated in the *OED Supp.* from 1872. See **enjoinder.**

enjoinable (= capable of being enjoined) is contained in no major English dictionary, but has been useful to American judges. Note that *enjoin* as contained in this word has its negative sense "to prohibit." E.g., "[A]ll such activity would be properly *enjoinable* insofar as it advocated a strike by public employees." *In re Berry,* 436 P.2d 273, 285 (Cal. 1968)./ "Spur's operation was an *enjoinable* public nuisance." *Spur Industries, Inc. v. Del E. Webb Development Co.,* 494 P.2d 700, 706 (Ariz. 1972)./ "[W]e find that appellees' use of the house and adjoining premises as a church constitutes a clear and *enjoinable* violation of the restriction in issue here." *Kessler v. Stough,* 361 So. 2d 1048, 1050 (Ala. 1978)./ "That secondary picketing is unlawful and *enjoinable* today in almost every other industry is none of our business." *Burlington Northern R.R. v. Brotherhood of Maintenance of Way Employees,* 793 F.2d 795, 802 (7th Cir. 1986).

enjoinder; enjoinment; injunction. The words of the Fowler brothers are as apt today as they were eighty years ago:

> As *rejoin rejoinder,* so *enjoin enjoinder.* The word is not given in the [*OED*], from which it seems likely that Dickens ["Merely nodding his head as an *enjoinder* to be careful."] invented it, consciously or unconsciously. The only objection to such a word is that its having had to wait so long, in spite of its obviousness, before being made is a strong argument against the necessity of it. We may regret that *injunction* holds the field, having a much less English appearance; but it does; and in language the old-established that can still do the work is not to be turned out for the new-fangled that might do it a shade better, but must first get itself known and accepted.
>
> H. W. Fowler & F. G. Fowler, *The King's English* 53 (1906, O.U.P. ed. 1978).

The *OED Supp.* contains two illustrative examples of *enjoinder,* but *injunction* still generally "holds the field" in both positive and negative senses of *enjoin,* q.v.

Yet *enjoinder* has become more common than it was in Fowler's day in the sense of "a command, esp. one that prohibits." E.g., "But the constitutional *enjoinder* against waste does not mean that the riparian owner must . . . clear all water-consuming native growth. . . ." *Allen v. California Water & Telephone Co.,* 176 P.2d 8, 18 (Cal. 1946). Through SLIPSHOD EXTENSION it has been used as an equivalent of *admonition,* as here: "[Bishop] is also reputed to have written that classical *enjoinder,* 'Hard cases make bad law.'" *Horsley v. State,* 374 So. 2d 375, 377 (Ala. 1979) (Beatty, J., dissenting).

Enjoinment, labeled archaic in *W3* and missing from *W2,* is recorded in the *OED* from the seventeenth century in the sense "the action of enjoining." Today this word might almost be considered common in law; certainly, in denoting the action itself rather than the result of the action (an *injunction*), it is useful. E.g., "[Rights] are vested when the right to *enjoinment,* present or prospective, has become the property of some particular person or persons as a present interest." *Steinfeld v. Nielsen,* 15 Ariz. 424, 465, 139 P. 879, 896 (1913)./ "[I]t in and of itself constitutes a sufficient basis for the *enjoinment* of defendant's continued picketing." *Baldwin v. Arizona Flame Restaurant,* 313 P.2d 759, 765 (Ariz. 1957).

In the following sentence, *enjoinder* is used where *enjoinment* would be more apt: "The trial court's restraint and *enjoinder* [read *enjoinment*] of defendants from interfering in the liquidation is mooted and reversed by virtue of our ruling." *Heard v. Carter,* 285 S.E.2d 246, 249 (Ga. App. 1981).

enjoy is frequently used in legal writing in the sense "to have, possess." E.g., "This covenant ensures that the tenant shall *enjoy* the possession of the premises in peace and without disturbance by hostile claimants." The word fails, however, in reference to having or possessing something undesirable, as in "He *enjoys* failing health," labeled a catachrestic use by the *OED.* (That sentence actually looks more jocular than catachrestic.)

enjoyment (= the exercise of a right) occurs now only in legal contexts. E.g., "Although she had the full power and authority to withdraw the whole or any part of the capital of the trust in question, she never reduced it to possession or converted it to her *enjoyment.*"

enlarge has figurative senses (*extend* or *broaden*) in legal writing that it lacks in other contexts. Thus it is used of abstractions like time and powers. E.g., "We hold that the *enlarged* visitation time would be in the best interest of the child."/ "The *enlarged* property right that the legislature intended to confer is only an expectant interest dependent upon the contingency that the property to which the interest attaches becomes part of a decedent's estate."/ "An agent cannot *enlarge* or qualify the testator's express instructions even when acting bona fide." (Eng.)

enlargement, in the legal idiom, often means "extension." E.g., "The company had filed a request with this Court for a thirty-day *enlargement* of time in which to file an appellate brief." See **enlarge.**

Enoc(h) Arden law. This phrase contains one of the few LITERARY ALLUSIONS that have given names to legal doctrines. *Enoch Arden,* a poem by Tennyson, tells the story of a man who, lost at sea for many years, returns home to find his wife married happily to his former rival for her affections; broken-hearted, he resolves that they shall not know of his return until after his death. Thus *Enoch Arden law* = a statute providing for divorce or exempting from liability for remarriage on the ground of

unexplained absence of husband or wife for a specified number of years, usu. seven (*W3*). E.g., "*Enoch Arden statutes* protect bona fide purchasers from devisees, legatees, heirs, or distributees and the personal representative when the supposed 'decedent' whose estate has been distributed is found to be alive."

enormity; enormousness. The historical DIFFERENTIATION between these words should not be muddled. The former means "outrageousness, hideousness"; the latter means "hugeness." Misuse of *enormity* is all too frequent: "Third, if by chance the jury had discovered the penalty sections of appellant's pleadings, these too were relevant to offset appellant's argument about the *enormity* of the excess charge." (In this sentence the writer no doubt intended to refer to the magnitude (*enormousness*) of the excess, not its wickedness (*enormity*).)/ "The *enormity* [read *enormousness*] of the problem was indicated by Congress's extended hearings." (The correction assumes that the writer intended to refer to the *extent* of the problem, rather than to its moral implications, an assumption borne out by the context from which the quotation was pulled.)

enounce. See **announce.**

enquiry is the regular British form for the word equivalent to *question; inquiry,* in G.B., means "an official investigation." In the U.S., *inquiry* serves in both senses. See EN-.

en re is downright wrong for *in re,* but it has occurred in otherwise good prose.

enrichment. See **impoverishment & unjust enrichment.**

enroll. See **engross.**

enrol(l)ment (= the official registration of a document) is spelled -*ll*- in the U.S. and -*l*- in G.B. See **engross.**

en route. Two words. The *en* is best pronounced like "on," an approximation of the French pronunciation; /*en*/ is acceptable, but /*in*/ should be avoided.

This term is now voguish in figurative senses: "*En route* to its conclusion, the court rejected the defendant's argument that under the now-repealed Youth Corrections Act, any probation imposed upon a defendant eligible for YCA treatment had to be imposed under the Act rather than under the adult probation provision."

In route is a solecism: "Since the truck was departing from Florida *in route* [read *en route*] to New Orleans on November 12, appellant required that appellee's products be in Miami in time to be loaded on appellant's truck."

ensample is an ARCHAISM for *example.*

ensue; insue. The former spelling is standard. E.g., "This was an assault, although no harm *ensued* to the plaintiff."/ "If the persuasion be used for the indirect purpose of injuring the plaintiff or of benefiting the defendant at the expense of the plaintiff, it is a malicious act that is actionable if injury *ensues* from it."

ensurance. See **assurance.**

ensure; insure. See **assure.**

entail, n. & v.t. The transitive verb *entail* = (1) (in general usage) to make necessary, to involve; or (2) (in legal usage) to leave (land) to a line of heirs so that none of them can give it away or sell it (*OAD*). Specifically, an *entailed* interest is an equitable interest in land under which ownership is limited to a person and the heirs of his body (either generally or those of a specified class) (*CDL*). E.g., "A devise followed by a direction that the property should be 'closely *entailed*' was cut down to a tenancy for life, remainder to the issue." (Eng.) See **disentail.**

In addition to sense (2) of the verb, the general nonlegal sense often appears in legal writing: "An unprivileged falsehood need not *entail* universal hatred to constitute a cause of action."/ "The district court's analysis did not *entail* sufficient scrutiny of the particular negligent acts that were found to have been committed."

The noun *entail* (= a fee limited to the grantee's issue or a class of his issue) corresponds only to sense (2) of the verb. E.g., "Johnson spoke well of *entails,* to preserve lines of men whom mankind are accustomed to reverence." (Eng.) The noun *entailment* corresponds to sense (1) of the verb.

enter for *enter into.* Idiomatically speaking, one *enters into a contract with another;* one does not merely *enter a contract.* E.g., "It was the in-

tent of appellant and appellee at the time the contract was *entered* [read *entered into*] that appellant was obligated to provide insurance necessary to cover its indemnity obligations."/ "At the time the contract is *entered* [read *entered into*], the agreed-upon payment must be a reasonable forecast of just compensation for the harm that would be caused by a breach." Even so, *to enter into a contract with* is usually prolix for *to contract with.* See the next entry.

enter in is a REDUNDANCY for *enter.* E.g., "With his presently appealed claims to tens of millions of dollars in punitive damages against defendants enjoying immunity to all such claims, to attorneys' fees when he at all times acted *pro se,* and the like, we stand at the gate of the realms of fantasy; we decline to *enter in* [read *enter*]."/ "Defendant's agents *entered into Texas* [read *entered Texas*] on several occasions for the purpose of financing the constitution." On an idiomatic use of *enter into* in law, see **enter.**

entering judgment. See **rendition of judgment.**

entertain = to give judicial consideration to. E.g., "Under *Pennhurst II,* the court below had no power to *entertain* Kitchens's contract claim regardless of the existence or fate of her other causes of action."/ "The court held that since Hanzl's payments were voluntary and received innocently by the defendants, there was no jurisdiction to *entertain* the suit."

enthral(l); inthral(l). The spelling *enthrall* is standard in the U.S., *enthral* in G.B. The *in-* spellings are to be avoided.

enthuse is a substandard BACK-FORMATION avoided by writers and speakers who care about their language. "He *enthused* [read *stated enthusiastically,* or perhaps *gushed*] that she was remarkable shortly after meeting her." See BACK-FORMATIONS. *Enthused,* adj., is always inferior to *enthusiastic.*

entirety, -ties. See **tenancy by the entireties.**

entrance; entry. Both *entrance* and *entry* may refer to the act of entering. In reference to structures, *entrance* connotes a single opening, such as a door, whereas *entranceway* and *entry* suggest a longer means of access, as a corridor or vestibule.

entrust, not *intrust,* is now the usual and preferred spelling. The latter is often seen in legal opinions of the late nineteenth and early twentieth centuries. E.g., "This protection reaches all alike, whether accused of a crime or not, and the duty of giving it force and effect is obligatory upon all *intrusted* under our Federal system with the enforcement of laws." *Weeks v. United States,* 232 U.S. 383, 392 (1914). See EN-.

entry. See **entrance.**

entry of judgment. See **rendition of judgment.**

enumerable; innumerable. Though close in pronunciation, these words have opposite meanings. *Innumerable* = unable to be counted. *Enumerable* = countable. The words should be pronounced distinctly, lest those listening misunderstand.

ENUMERATIONS. A. *First(ly), second(ly), third(ly); one, two, three.* The best method of enumerating items is the straightforward *first, second,* and *third.* The forms *firstly, secondly,* and *thirdly* have an unnecessary syllable, and *one, two,* and *three* seem especially informal. E.g., "This leaves but two possible effects of the service mark's continued use: *One* [read *First*], no one will know what CONAN means. *Two* [read *Second*], those who are familiar with the plaintiff's property will continue to associate CONAN with THE BARBARIAN." See **firstly.**

B. Comma Before the Last Member. "How to punctuate . . . enumerations," wrote Follett, "is argued with more heat than is called forth by any other rhetorical problem except the split infinitive." W. Follett, *Modern American Usage* 397–98 (1966). Fashions in public-school textbooks and journalists' manuals come and go, but only one method is ironclad in avoiding unnecessary ambiguities: inserting a comma before the final member. Thus *a, b,* and *c* rather than *a, b* and *c.* The problems arise with members containing two or more items, as *a and b, c and d, e and f, and g and h.* The last two members are muddled if the comma is omitted. See PUNCTUATION (C)(2).

enunciate (= to state publicly) is often used of judicial pronouncements, especially where legal doctrines are concerned. E.g.,

"The validity of petitioner's larceny conviction must be judged not by the watered-down standard *enunciated* in *Palko,* but under this court's interpretations of the Fifth Amendment double-jeopardy provision."/ "We approve of the majority rule as *enunciated* in the cases appearing in the note quoted above." See **announce.**

enure. See **inure.**

envelop is the verb ("to wrap or cover"), *envelope* the noun ("wrapper, covering").

enviable; envious. That which is *enviable* is worthy of envy or arouses envy. A person who is *envious* suffers from envy. *Envious* usually takes the preposition *of* 〈her envy of her sister's success〉, but may take also *against* or *at.* See **jealousy.**

envisage; envision. The former has been used since the early nineteenth century, whereas the latter was born early in this century. Today *envision* is more common in the U.S., *envisage* being somewhat literary. Both mean "to visualize," but there is perhaps an incipient DIFFERENTIATION under way. As suggested by *W9, envision* = to picture to oneself, whereas *envisage* = to contemplate or view in a certain way. Thus: "We conclude that orders denying appointment of counsel to litigants who cannot afford counsel fall into the class of order *envisaged* by *Cohen.*"/ "Who is it that is *envisaged* by the instrument as an object of the possible bounty of the bank?" (Eng.)/ "The constructive trust as *envisaged* by the court in *Elliott* is a hybrid remedy."/ "In some of the older authorities it seems to have been *envisaged* that there were only two possible outcomes—either the transaction was void or it was valid." (Eng.)

Envisage seems more appropriate when inanimate objects are the subject; hence *envision,* which denotes a more human process, seems inapposite in this sentence: "The UCC clearly *envisions* [read *envisages*] that a contract came into being under the facts of this case." Yet it seems quite defensible here: "But there is no doubt that the Senate *envisioned* no role for the states on Indian lands."

envy. See **jealousy** & **enviable.**

eo instante, -ti. The dilemma in spelling is best resolved by writing *at the very instant, instantly,* or *immediately.* "To avoid the rule that a dead man could not be a felon, a suicide was to be counted a felon *eo instante* [read *at the instant*] he killed himself."/ "When the contract is made, the existing, binding law, whatever it may be, being the obligation on promisor to perform his undertaking, *eo instanti, attaches* [read *attaches immediately*]."/ "The judgment of the appellee attached *eo instante* [read *instantly*] on the intestate's death."

epic. See **epochal.**

epidemic; endemic. A disease is *epidemic* that breaks out and rages in a community, only to subside some time afterward. A disease is *endemic* that is constantly with a certain population or region.

epilog(ue). The longer spelling is customary and preferred.

epithet = (1) an especially apt adjective, whether the quality described is favorable or unfavorable; or (2) an abusive term. Sense (2) is slowly driving out sense (1), a trend to be fought against.

epoch = (1) a date of an occurrence that starts things going under new conditions; or (2) "a period of history." Some stylists object to sense (2) as an example of SLIPSHOD EXTENSION, but that extension occurred in the seventeenth century, and the best writers today use the word in that sense: "Some historians have said that a meaningful history of humankind could be written around *epochs*, with each *epoch* having its own pervasive characteristics, and that the pervasive characteristic of the age in which we live is technological change." (P. Keeton)

epochal; epic(al). The former means "marking an epoch, or a new period in chronology." The word should not be used lightly. "Five devastating *epochal* floods have visited the valley since the establishment of the commission." (Only if the writer intended to convey that five epochs had passed since the establishment of the commission—an unlikely meaning—would *epochal* have been correct.)

Epical is a NEEDLESS VARIANT of the adjective *epic*, meaning (1) "of or relating to an epic [= a long heroic narrative]," or (2) "surpassing what is ordinary or usual."

equable. See **equitable.**

equally. This word should not be used with *both*, as it is here: "Both magistracies are *equally* independent in the sphere of action assigned to handing down sentences of fine and imprisonment." [Read *The two magistracies are equally independent*. . . .] *Both . . . equally* is redundant. See **equally as** (C).

equally as is almost always incorrect. The exceptions are noted under (E). **A.** *Equally as . . . as* is incorrect for *as much . . . as* or *as . . . as*. E.g., "The evidence is insufficient where it merely establishes that it is *equally as* [omit *equally*] probable that the requisite connection between the injury and the employment exists *as* that such connection does not exist."

B. *As equally as* is a variant of the usual blunder illustrated under (A). "To hold otherwise would be to succumb to a nominalism and a rigid trial scenario *as equally* [omit *equally*] at variance *as* ambush with the spirit of our rules."

C. *Both . . . equally as* is a double REDUNDANCY. "*Both* appeals are *equally as* frivolous." [Read *The appeals are equally frivolous*.] See **equally.**

D. Inversion. The phrase is sometimes inverted and rendered *as equally* after NEGATIVES; still it is wrong. "No valid reason is apparent why the aforesaid categories are *not as equally* [read *not equally*] applicable to convictions for crimes in other states."

E. Permissible Uses. E.g., "If the deceased, in his lifetime, has done anything that would operate as a bar to recovery by him of damages for the personal injury, this will operate *equally as* a bar in an action by his personal representatives after his death."

equate takes the preposition *with*, not *to.*

equitable; equable. *Equitable* derives from *equity*, and has associations of justice and fairness, or that which can be sustained in a court of equity. To laymen it generally means "fair," whereas to lawyers it may mean "fair," but just as often means "in equity" ⟨equitable jurisdiction⟩⟨equitable remedies⟩. *Equable* = even; tranquil; level.

equity is used in both G.B. and the U.S. to refer to a principle of justice or system of law. In the U.S., however, it often refers to "the interest that a borrower has in mortgaged property; the amount of the principal debt that has been paid." *Equity* does properly convey this meaning, despite Horwill's assertion to the contrary in *Modern American Usage* (1935) (s.v. *equity*).

Speaking more broadly, *equity* is a CHAMELEON-HUED WORD; hence it is advisable to pin down the particular meaning one attributes to it in a given context. One commentator has identified seven different senses for the noun *equity*, excluding the sense relating to mortgaged property: (1) what is fair and just; (2) natural law [itself rather chameleon-hued]; (3) a system of law that corrects failures of justice in the main body of the law; (4) a theory of justice in which the operation of legal precepts is adjusted to the exigencies of special circumstances; (5) a body of law that was administered in the English Court of Chancery when it was a separate court; (6) (in civil law) a method of interpretation of Code provisions in accordance with the spirit and general purpose of the statute; and (7) (in Anglo-American law) a body of legal precepts that introduces into law, in suits for specific relief, criteria of justice that are based on higher ethical values than those ordinarily required in actions for damages. See Newman, *The Place and Function of Pure Equity in the Structure of Law*, 16 Hastings L.J. 401, 403–04 (1965). See **chancery.**

-ER, -OR. These agent-noun suffixes can be especially vexatious to the legal writer. The historical tendency in the law has been to make the Latinate *-or* the correlative of *-ee* (q.v.), hence *indemnitee/indemnitor, obligee/obligor, transferee/transferor, offeree/offeror, donee/donor*. Often, however, the choice of suffix seems based on caprice. In the famous contracts case *Household Fire & Carriage Acc. Ins. Co. v. Grant*, [1879] 4 Ex.D. 216 (C.A.), Lord Justice Thesiger used the spellings *acceptor* and *offerer*, whereas the modern trend is to write *accepter* and *offeror* in legal contexts.

Attempts to confine *-er* to words of Anglo-Saxon origin and *-or* to those of Latin origin are fruitless, because so many exceptions exist on both sides of the aisle. Nevertheless, it may be said that Latinate words usually take *-or*, though there are exceptions, the following (in the *-er* column) being only a few:

	-er
adapter	dispenser
conjurer	eraser
corrupter	idolater
digester	promoter

	-or
abductor	ejector
collector	impostor
corrector	purveyor
distributor	surveyor

Sometimes there is a distinction in meaning between variant forms of the same word with these two suffixes, as with *bargainer* and *bargainor*, q.v., or latent distinctions, as with *bailer* and *bailor*, q.v.

-ER, -RE. Words borrowed from French generally arrived in English with the *-re* spelling. Most such words have gradually made the transition to *-er*. A few words may be spelled only *-re*, such as *acre, chancre, massacre,* and *mediocre*, because of the preceding *-c-*. Still others—the great majority—have variant spellings, the *-er* ending usually being more common in AmE and the *-re* ending normal in BrE. The following words have variants subject to this distinction: *accouter, -re; caliber, -re; center, -re; goiter, -re; liter, -re; louver, -re; luster, -re; maneuver, -re; meager, -re; meter, -re* (in BrE, *meter* = the measuring device as well as the measure); *miter, -re; niter, -re; reconnoiter, -re; scepter, -re; sepulcher, -re; somber, -re; specter, -re; theater, -re.*

ergo is a slightly archaic equivalent of *therefore* that is occasionally useful for its succinctness. E.g., "The United States Supreme Court does not recognize the vicarious exclusionary rule; *ergo*, Daan cannot assert the illegality of Bryan's intention and the seizure of the marijuana cigarettes."

Erie-bound = (of a federal court in the U.S.) required to apply the holding in *Erie R. Co. v. Tompkins*, 304 U.S. 64 (1937). This term is frequently used by federal courts in their opinions, because *Erie v. Tompkins* teaches that, where federal laws are not involved, a federal court exercising diversity jurisdiction (and therefore applying state law) must follow the common law of the state in which it sits. *Erie-bound* is fast becoming a CLICHÉ, because the proposition is so well established that ordinarily there need be no invocation of *Erie v. Tompkins* every time a federal court applies state law. Following are two typical examples of use of the phrase: "In this diversity case, we are *Erie-bound* to follow the substantive law of Mississippi."/ "The result we think a Louisiana court would reach, and the one we are *Erie-bound* to follow in this diversity case, was reached by the district court." See CASE REFERENCES (C).

eristic(al), meaning "of or pertaining to controversy or disputation," is best spelled *eristic.*

ermine (the fur of a weasel-like animal) has come to be used figuratively with reference to the ermine in the official robes of judges in England. The word evokes rather grand notions of a judgeship. This use of the word occurs even in the U.S., where ermine is not used in judges' robes. E.g., "A judge loses none of his social instincts by assuming the *ermine,* and while his position is changed he is still a lawyer."/ "From such liability, the justice cannot hide behind his judicial *ermine.*" Cf. **woolsack.**

erodible, -able; erosible. The best form is *erodible.* See -ABLE (A).

err, one of the most commonly mispronounced words in legal contexts, should properly rhyme with *purr.* It is incorrect, from a strict point of view, to mouth it like *air.* See **error** (C).

errant = (1) traveling ⟨knight errant⟩; (2) fallible, straying from what is proper. Sense (2) overwhelmingly predominates: "The February 14 order neither granted nor denied an order of any such character or effect; at best the court *errantly* issued an 'advisory opinion' over which it retained the power of revision."/ "Instead, the Supreme Court instructs, the proper recourse is an objection to the trial judge and prompt action from the bench in the form of corrective instructions to the jury, and when necessary, an admonition to the *errant* advocate."

Errant is properly used of persons or their actions; it is not synonymous with *erroneous,* as one writer apparently thought: "Appellant argues that the district court failed to consider the evidence urged as being 'newly discovered'; this *errant* [read *erroneous*] conclusion is based on a misinterpretation of the district court's opinion." See **arrant.**

errata is the pl. form of *erratum.* The English plural *erratums* is not used. See **corrigendum.**

erronious is an erroneous spelling of *erroneous.*

error, n. **A.** General Senses. *Error* = (1) a mistake of law in a judgment or order of a court in some procedural step in legal proceedings (*CDL*); (2) an appeal.

As illustrating sense (2), the official name of the highest court in Connecticut is the Supreme Court of Errors. The report in *McCulloch v. Maryland,* 17 U.S. (4 Wheat.) 316, 317 (1819), contains the heading "*Error* to the Court of Appeals of the state of Maryland." This sense developed as an elliptical form of *writ of error.* E.g., "There was a judgment of the Court of Civil Appeals affirming a judgment for plaintiff, and defendant brings *error.*" See **plaintiff in error.**

B. For *in error* or *erroneous.* This use, though increasingly common in the U.S., should be avoided, for it wrongly makes *error* adjectival. E.g., "The subsequent final order overruling respondent's motion for new trial, based on his failure to pay the attorneys' fees, was *error* [read *erroneous*]."/ "Defendants argue that this instruction was *error* [read *erroneous*] because it allowed the jury to determine the admissibility of the hearsay statements of co-conspirators."/ "Hauser contends that this holding *is error* [read *is in error*], asserting that the defendant was not entitled to a reasonable time in which to place flares when the emergency was created by the defendant's negligence."

C. For *err,* v.i. This mistake commonly appears in appellate briefs. If we were inclined to be generous to the lawyers who err in this way, we might attribute the mistake to secretaries who misunderstand dictation. Yet the fault cannot rightly be laid on the secretaries. The court in *Stolte v. Mack Financial Corp.,* 457 S.W.2d 172, 174 (Tex. Civ. App.—Texarkana 1970), subtly highlighted this error in an advocate's brief in three successive points of error. Here is a typical misuse: "The district court *errored* [read *erred*] in approving appellee's plan where there was no prior determination of the nature and extent of the constitutional wrong." Correctly pronouncing *err,* q.v., would reduce the frequency of this blunder.

escalate (= to increase in seriousness or intensity) is a voguish use of the word. E.g., "The encounter with the suspect did not *escalate* into an arrest."

escapee (= one who escapes) should more logically be *escaper* or *escapist.* See -EE. The *OED Supp.* suggests that *escapee* is waning in use and that *escapist* is emerging as the standard agent noun. That development is to be encouraged.

escheat may be both noun and verb. As the former, it means "the lapsing of land to the state (in G.B., to the Crown) upon the death of the intestate owner without heirs." A LAW FRENCH word originally meaning "inheritance," it came to apply at common law to the lord's succession to a tenant's fief when the tenant died seised without heir. From the perceived unfairness of the system—once the lords had begun to abuse it—evolved the aphaeretic form *cheat*.

Escheat is used more commonly as a verb than as a noun in legal writing. Here is a typical example of the verbal use of *escheat*: "The property in case of intestacy should *escheat* to the state." The following sentence is illustrative of the nominal use: "The court would be less concerned with the influencer's motive in a contest between him and the state claiming an *escheat* than it would be in a contest between him and the donor's surviving spouse." *Escheatment*, which appears in the *OED Supp.*, is a NEEDLESS VARIANT.

eschew; eschewal, n. The second syllable of both words is pronounced just as the word *chew* is pronounced, /*es-choo*/. For some reason, many seem to believe that the *esch-* sequence in this term is pronounced *esh-*. It is not. The pronunciation with an *esh-* sound sounds like a sneeze.

escrow has two nominal senses: (1) "a deed delivered but not to become operative until a future date or until some condition has been fulfilled"; (2) "a deposit held in trust or as security" ⟨in escrow⟩. Sense (2), labeled "a perversion" by *Black's* (4th ed.), was a nineteenth-century American coinage that is now current in both AmE and BrE.

Escrow, used as a verb since 1916, is now common in American legal writing in the sense "to put into *escrow* [sense (2)]." E.g., "The cognizant officials of FDIC consented to the sale and to the *escrowing* of proceeds of sale with the rights of all claimants to follow those proceeds." *In re Jeter*, 48 Bankr. 404, 409 (Bankr. N.D. Tex. 1985)./ "By *escrowing* the funds for the purpose of improving municipal services in the black community, the court took the first step toward ensuring that the unconstitutional disparities would be cor-

rected rather than perpetuated." Today it is common in American real-estate law to speak of *escrowing* all types of documents—that is, holding them with the understanding that they will not be released until some condition is met. This use corresponds to sense (1) of the noun.

escrowee (= the depositary of an escrow) is a curious term, there being no correlative agent noun in *-er* or *-or*. Recorded in *W3* but ignored in the *OED* and its *Supplement*, the term is not uncommon in modern American legal prose. E.g., "[T]he assignment from Avon to the *escrowees* was recorded in the Patent and Trademark Office." *Haymaker Sports, Inc. v. Turian*, 581 F.2d 257, 262 (C.C.P.A. 1978) (Baldwin, J., dissenting).

esoterics is incorrect for *esoterica*. E.g., "Though we are asked to engage in the *esoterics* [read *esoterica*] of constitutional and statutory construction, we find it unnecessary because our decision here can rest on more mundane grounds."

especial; special. *Especial* (= distinctive, significant, peculiar) is the opposite of *ordinary*. E.g., "The public press is entitled to peculiar indulgence and has *especial* rights and privileges." *Special* (= specific, particular) is the opposite of *general*.

Especial is too rarely used in the U.S. today, even in learned and legal prose. "A disregard of the command of the statute is a wrongful act and, where it results in damage to one of the class for whose *especial* benefit the statute was enacted, the right to recover the damages from the party in default is implied." In the following sentence it is wrongly used for *special*, used in contrast to *general*: "Positive laws either contain general principles embodied in the rules of law or for *especial* [read *special*] reasons they establish something that differs from those general principles."

espouse = (1) to marry or give in marriage; or (2) to adopt or support (as a doctrine or cause). Sense (1), the literal sense, is rarely seen today even in legal writing, but it does occur: "She was accused afterward of being depressed because she had discovered that there were thirty other persons whom she could not legally *espouse* even if they did ask her."

Espouse in sense (2) is often misused. In the following sentence, it is used as if it were synonymous with *endorse* (applied to persons as well as things): "In defeating plaintiff, we do not decry him, nor do we *espouse* [read *endorse*] his adversary." And here it is incorrectly used for *expound* or *set forth*: "Having *espoused* [read *expounded*] our view of the intent of Congress, we are nonetheless bound by the prior decisions of this circuit." (The court obviously did not *espouse* a view if it could not follow it.)

The proper use of the word in sense (2) appears here: "Some people see in the conduct of lawsuits something more than mere forensic battles waged by paid champions ready to *espouse* either side of an argument."

Esq. is commonly used with lawyers' names in written addresses in the U.S., nowadays with the names of men and women alike. It is incorrect to use this title with any other title, such as *Mr.* or *Ms.* In G.B., of course, *esquire* is used of any man thought to have the social status of a gentleman.

One law review has devoted several pages to an article on whether women attorneys should use *esquire*. See Eaton, *An Historical View of the Term Esquire as Used by Modern Women Attorneys*, 80 W.Va. L.Rev. 209 (1978). As to the title and purpose of that article, however, it is worth noting that "*Esq.* is . . . not used on oneself, e.g. neither on a card (which bears *Mr.*) nor on a stamped-and-addressed envelope enclosed for a reply (which has merely A.B.X—or A.B.X.—without prefix)." Ross, *U and Non-U: An Essay in Sociological Linguistics*, in *Noblesse Oblige* (ed. Nancy Mitford 1956). The question, then, is whether others should append *Esq.* to women attorneys' names in mailing addresses. The answer is that this practice is perfectly acceptable, and indeed common today. If precisionists are bothered by this practice, they should pretend that *Esq.* when used of women stands for *esquiress* (recorded in the *OED* from 1596).

essay, v.t. See **assay.**

esse (= essence, essential nature) is a pedantic LATINISM. E.g., "This appeal forces us to acknowledge a lumbering, antedeluvian concept that remains embedded in the judicial *esse*." *Coastal (Bermuda) Ltd. v. E. W. Saybolt & Co.*, 761 F.2d 198, 200 (5th Cir. 1985). See **in esse & de bene esse.**

essoi(g)n, n. & v. *Essoign* is a variant spelling of the noun only; *essoin* is the preferred spelling for both noun and verb. The word (meaning "an excuse for not appearing in court at the appointed time") is used only in G.B.

estate-tail. See **tail & entail.**

estimate, n.; **estimation.** A distinction should be observed. *Estimate* = an approximate calculation or judgment. *Estimation* = the process of approximately calculating or judging.

estop (= to stop, bar, hinder, or preclude) is now a legal term only. It may be construed either with an infinitive or with *from* + *-ing*. Thus: "The licensee of a trademark is *estopped* to deny the mark's validity."/ "The trust company is *estopped* from disputing the effect of the decree."

This verb may also be reflexive, in the sense "to be precluded by one's own previous act or declaration from doing or alleging something" (*OED*). E.g., "While the case ostensibly presents the question whether a common carrier by water may ever *estop itself* by inequitable conduct from exacting the full measure of the shipper's obligation to pay tariff charges, the true nature shows it to be something quite different."

estoppel. So spelled; the word is sometimes misspelled *estoppal*, as in Leff, *The Leff Dictionary of Law*, 94 Yale L.J. 1855, 1974, 2104 (1985), under *agency by estoppal* and *authority by estoppal*.

estray is an ARCHAISM used in law for "stray animal." See **waifs and (e)strays.**

et al. is the abbreviated form of the Latin phrase *et alii* (= and others). It is used only of persons, whereas *etc.*, q.v., is used of things.

etc. A French proverb states, "God save us from a lawyer's *et cetera*." The point is well taken. More than four-hundred years ago, John Florio wrote: "The heaviest thing that is, is one *Etcetera*." It is heaviest because it implies a quantity of things too numerous to mention. These are some of the most sensible words ever written on *etc.*:

Every writer should be on his guard against the excessive use of *etc*. Instead of finishing a thought completely, it is easy to end with an *etc.*, throwing the burden of finishing the thought upon the reader. If the thought is adequately expressed, *etc.* is not needed. If the thought is not adequately expressed, *etc.* will not take the place of that which has not been said. The use of *etc.* tends to become a slovenly habit, the corrective for which is to refrain from using *etc.* except in the dryest and most documentary kind of writing.

> G. P. Krapp, *A Comprehensive Guide to Good English* 229 (1927).

Lawyers should generally—in pleadings, for example—attempt to be as specific as possible rather than make use of this term. Still, it would be foolish to lay down an absolute proscription against using *etc.*, for often one simply *cannot* practicably list all that should be listed in a given context. Hence, rather than convey to the reader that a list is seemingly complete when it is not, the writer might justifiably use *etc.* (always the abbreviation).

And etc. is an ignorant error, *et* being the Latin *and*. *Etc.* differs from *et al.* in that it refers to things and not to people. (See **et al.**) The *-t-* in the first syllable of *etc.* should never be pronounced as a *-k-*. On the use of *etc.* with *e.g.* and *i.e.*, see **e.g.**

ethician, ethicist. The former is the correct term, although the latter sometimes incorrectly appears in its place. E.g., "Families of imperiled infants, together with their advisers (physicians, religious leaders, individual and institutional *ethicists* [read *ethicians*]) should be permitted to retain their decision-making autonomy."

ethics; ethos. The distinction escapes many writers, but it is plain. *Ethics* = the field of moral science. (The singular form *ethic* = a set of moral principles.) *Ethos* = the characteristic spirit and beliefs of a community, people, system, or person. Here the nicety keenly appears: "We introduce here no new or radical *ethic* since our *ethos* has never given moral sanction to piracy." *E.I. Dupont deNemours & Co. v. Christopher,* 431 F.2d 1012, 1016–17 (5th Cir. 1970).

etiology for *cause* is unnecessary and pompous. "What was the *etiology* [read *cause*] for his withdrawal from the position?" This use apparently stems from the medical use: "There are several diagnostic tests a physician may perform to determine the *etiology* of a painful back condition." *Aetiology* is the BrE spelling whereas *aitiology* is a secondary spelling to be avoided.

ETIOLOGY. See CAUSATION.

et seq. When citing a statute, it is better to give the reader an end point as well as a beginning one. Otherwise, the reader is left to conjecture just how many sections are encompassed in 29 U.S.C. §§ 621 *et seq.* Hence the phrase *et seq.* (short for *et sequentes* = the following ones) should be used sparingly if at all. The problem is exacerbated by the fact that *et seq.* serves also as the abbreviation for the singular *et sequens* (= and the following one), though presumably few users of the phrase know that.

et ux. See **ux.**

ETYMOLOGICAL AWARENESS is developed only by increased reading and a conscious sensitivity to words and their origins. Ignorance of etymologies can easily lead writers astray, as when a journalist gave the label *holocaust* (Gk. "burnt whole") to a flood. Following are sentences in which writers wandered into etymological bogs: "The right to exclude or to expel aliens in war or in peace is an inherent and *inalienable* right of every independent nation." (Here the root *alien-* causes problems, when we say a country has an *inalienable* right to exclude *aliens.*)/ "What we are concerned with here is the automobile and its *peripatetic* [= able to walk up and down, not just *itinerant*] character." (Automobiles can hardly be said to walk.)/ "This is a result which, if at all possible *consonant* [lit., "sounding together"] with *sound* judicial policy, should be avoided." In the first and third specimens, a senseless repetition of the root sense occurs; in the second, the writer has insensitively abstracted and broadened a word still ineluctably tied to its root sense. Cf. VERBAL AWARENESS.

Euclidean; Euclidian. The *-ean* spelling is standard.

EUPHEMISMS are supposedly soft or unobjectionable terms substituted in place of harsh or objectionable ones. (To discerning readers, of course, some euphemisms are objectionable because unnecessarily mealymouthed.) For example, the keynote system of indexing legal topics used by West Publishing Co. has gone from *Bastards* in the Eighth Decennial Digest (1966–76) to *Illegitimate Children* in the Ninth Decennial Digest (1976–81), and, more recently, in Federal Digest 3d (1985), to *Children Out-of-Wedlock*. Often, as just illustrated, euphemisms are roundabout and clumsy rather than direct. To take a common example, we read of a *rodent operative* or an *extermination engineer* rather than a *rat-catcher*; more up-to-date, we see *pregnancy termination* rather than *abortion*. In law, *unnatural offense* (or *crime*) *against nature* is not uncommon in place of *homosexuality* or *sodomy*. Indeed, Leff gives *abominable and detestable crime against nature* as a "rather enthusiastic euphemism . . . found in many nineteenth-century (and some current) statutes, referring to a not fully specified range of sexual crimes." Leff, *The Leff Dictionary of Law*, 94 Yale L.J. 1855, 1866 (1985).

Euphemisms are often subtler than the examples just given. Thus *incident* appears in place of *accident* in a U.S. statute limiting total liability for a single "nuclear incident" to $200,000,000, perhaps because *incident* is vaguer and less alarmist. Today *revenue enhancement* is commonly used in the U.S. by those who favor a *tax increase*, but who are reluctant to call it by its understandable name.

In the mock-heroic style that was popular in the nineteenth century, and even up to a few decades ago, euphemisms were quite common. For example, here a judge uses an elaborate euphemism for the hymen: "[The statute] further says to the libertine, who would rob a virtuous maiden, under the age of 18 years, of *the priceless and crowning jewel of maidenhood*, that he does so at his peril." *Bishop v. Liston*, 112 Neb. 559, 199 N.W. 825, 827 (1924).

We should not forget that some subjects call out for euphemisms or circumlocutions. Explicitness or directness would be undesirable to almost everyone here: "Due process concerns were not offended when a prison inmate was subjected to an attempted *digital* rectal search, based upon a reliable informer's tip." Still, the final phrase might advantageously be changed, because *tip* verges on losing its metaphorical quality in that particular context. See **digital.**

EUPHONY. See SOUND OF PROSE, THE.

EUPHUISM. See PURPLE PROSE.

euthanasia; mercy killing. Both are widespread, the former perhaps being more connotatively neutral.

euthan(at)ize = to subject to euthanasia. If we must have such a word, the longer is better formed and older, dating in the *OED* from 1873. See -IZE.

evacuee. See -EE.

evanescence is sometimes used incorrectly to mean "departure" or "disappearance." E.g., "Upon his aunt's *evanescence* [read *departure*], he continued to drive the mower, still in first gear."

Here the adjective *evanescent* is correctly used in the sense "tending to vanish away": "The evidence in *Cupp*, to be sure, was highly *evanescent*; but no less so is any evidence that an alerted suspect can dispose of if the police should wait to act until they have obtained a warrant."/ "Interests of beneficiaries of private express trusts run the gamut from valuable substantialities to *evanescent* hopes."

evangelical; evangelistic. Today the older term *evangelical* (fr. ca. 1531) is so closely tied with fundamentalist, proselytizing Christians that it should not be applied more generally. *Evangelistic* (fr. ca. 1845), though also redolent with Christian associations, may be used more broadly to mean "militantly zealous."

even date for *the same date* originated in commercialese, but has infected lawyers' writing as well. The best practice is to name the date a second time or to write *the same date*. E.g., "The court did not rule on either the request for preliminary injunction or the motion to dismiss until January 30, 1984, *at which time* [read *when*] the court dismissed the case with prejudice for the reasons set forth in the court's memorandum and order *of even date* [read *of the same date*]."

event, in the. The phrase in the U.S. is *in the event that* + clause; the British generally write *in the event of* + noun phrase. Both are ordinarily inferior to *if*. The phrase *in the eventuality* is especially pretentious. E.g., "The statutes provide that, *in that eventuality* [read *in that event*], the named person shall be deemed to have died immediately after the testator.

eventuality is a needless pomposity for

event. E.g., "Bobbitt would be amply protected from this *eventuality* [read *event*]." *Hospital Consultants, Inc. v. Potyka,* 531 S.W.2d 657, 665 (Tex. Civ. App.—San Antonio 1975). See the preceding entry.

eventuate is "an elaborate journalistic word that can usually be replaced by a simpler word to advantage." G. P. Krapp, *A Comprehensive Guide to Good English* 231 (1927). E.g., "It is quite plain that the Fourth Amendment governs 'seizures' of the person that do not *eventuate* [read *result*] in a trip to the station house and prosecution for the crime."/ "Their final argument is that their Fifth Amendment rights were not adequately protected by the grant of use immunity by the state court, since it would not protect them from use of their compelled testimony in a federal prosecution, should one *eventuate* [read *ensue* or *occur*]."/ "As a general proposition, one who executes a will believes that the testament covers all contingencies that might *eventuate* [read *occur* or *happen*]." (Note the INELEGANT VARIATION of *will* and *testament* in the final specimen.)

everybody. See **everyone.**

everybody else's. See **else's.**

everyone; everybody. These are singular nouns. See SEXISM (A).

everyone else's. See **else's.**

everyplace should be avoided as a vulgarism; *everywhere* is the proper word.

evidence. **A.** As a Count Noun. *Evidence* is not generally taken to be a count noun; hence the plural form is unusual at best. E.g., "'Creation science' means the scientific *evidences* [read *evidence*] for creation and inferences from *those* scientific *evidences* [read *that . . . evidence*]." See COUNT & MASS NOUNS.
   B. And *testimony.* These words overlap but are not always interchangeable. *Testimony* is a subspecies of *evidence*; it refers only to evidence received through the medium of witnesses. *Evidence*, on the contrary, includes all means by which an alleged fact in issue is established or disproved; thus *evidence* may include documents and tangible objects.

evidence, v.t.; **evince.** These words, which are lawyers' favorites, are often inferior to *show* or *express* or *indicate.* Properly, to *evidence* something is to be the proof, or to serve as evidence, of its existence or truth or occurrence (*MEU2* s.v. *evidence*). Here it is correctly used: "If the owner of an interest in land declares himself trustee of the interest for the benefit of another, the writing *evidencing* the trust may be signed by the declarant before, at the time of, or after the declaration."/ "Admittedly the distinction between acts *evidencing* a continuing conspiracy and acts constituting further agreements or fresh conspiracies is a fine one." (Eng.)
   More often than not, however, it is used loosely for *show, demonstrate,* or *express:* "Texas asserts, without support, that the Bus Act *evidences* [read *shows*] an intent not to grant the ICC jurisdiction over intrastate charter operations and charges that the legislative history of the statute further *evidences* [read *demonstrates*] Congress's intent to provide for the preemption of intrastate regular-route transportation and not of intrastate charter transportation."/ "Even the majority opinion *evidenced* [read *showed*] a subtle but potentially powerful shift in the law."
   Evince properly means "to show, exhibit, make manifest," but has been objected to as "a bad word and unnecessary . . . a favourite with callow journalists." Partridge, *Usage and Abusage* 113 (1973). It is greatly overworked in legal writing, as the cornucopia of specimens evinces: "The court in that opinion *evinced* even more reluctance to compare the worth of unequal jobs."/ "Although the testator may not have intended that Charles share as legatee or devisee under his will, he *evinced* no intention that he was to be excluded as next of kin, through operation of the laws of intestacy."/ "Had the petitioners challenged the underlying convictions and requested an opportunity to replead, the court stated, the cases would not have been moot; the court thus *evinced* a tendency to favor specific requests for relief in habeas petitions."/ "As in the 93d and 94th Congresses, at no time did the 95th Congress *evince* an intent to afford states reclamation authority on nonreservation Indian lands."

evidenciary is wrong for *evidentiary.*

evidentiarily is the adverb corresponding to *evidentiary,* adj. It is often used as a SENTENCE ADVERB in the sense "in terms of evidence." E.g., "It turns out, however, that *evi-*

dentiarily we do not now have such a case before us." *McLaurin v. Columbia Municipal Separate School District*, 486 F.2d 1049, 1050 (5th Cir. 1973) (Coleman, J., concurring).

evidentiary; evidential. It would be nice to pronounce *evidential* a NEEDLESS VARIANT and be done with it, but that (older) form seems to predominate in G.B. (see *OED & COD*), though *-ary* also appears in BrE. We might even brand it a needless variant in the U.S., where in legal writing *evidentiary* far outstrips *evidential* in frequency of use. E.g., "There is a kind of *evidential* [read *evidentiary*] estoppel." *Holly Hill Citrus Growers' Association v. Holly Hill Fruit Products, Inc.*, 75 F.2d 13, 17 (5th Cir. 1935)./ "If, therefore, the unaltered document is produced for inspection, the facts thus ascertained must, as regards the alleged contractual agreement, be purely *evidential* [read *evidentiary*] in character."

But *evidential* has been useful to some legal theorists, like Hohfeld, in meaning "furnishing evidence" as opposed to "of or relating to evidence" (the sense in which *evidentiary* predominates). If we could enhance this latent DIFFERENTIATION, the language of the law of evidence would be richer for it. Following are examples from Hohfeld's *Fundamental Legal Conceptions* (1919): "An *evidential* fact is one which, on being ascertained, affords some logical basis—not conclusive—for inferring some other fact."/ "The facts important in relation to a given jural transaction may be either operative facts or *evidential* facts."

evince. See **evidence,** v.t.

eviscerate (= to disembowel) has become a VOGUE WORD among legal writers in its metaphorical applications. Because of its strong meaning, it is not to be used lightly. "Clearly *eviscerating* the Tenth Amendment's restrictions on the accretion of power by the United States Government, *Garcia* offered the conservative wing of the court an opportunity to express its displeasure at the majority's rejection of 'almost 200 years of the understanding of the constitutional status of federalism.'"

Here *eviscerate* approaches meaninglessness: "To permit any complainant to restart the limitations period by petitioning for review of a rule would *eviscerate* the congressional concern for finality embodied in time limitations on review." An intent may be *undermined*; but the metaphor of *eviscerating* does not work

with a gossamer object like *concern*, even if it is said to be "embodied." Cf. **emasculate.**

evoke for *invoke* is almost a MALAPROPISM. E.g., "If Rumbaugh is incompetent to waive his right to federal habeas review, his parents have standing to *evoke* [read *invoke*] a next-friend proceeding."

exalt; exult. To *exult* is to rejoice exceedingly. To *exalt* is to raise in rank, place in a high position, or extol. *Exalt* is rather frequently misspelled *exhalt* or *exhault*, as in *Committee on Professional Ethics and Conduct v. Munger*, 375 N.W.2d 248, 251 (Iowa 1985): "It would be *exhalting* [read *exalting*] form over substance to require the Committee . . . to amend its complaint. . . ."

examination-in-chief. See **direct examination.**

example; exemplar; exemplum; exemplification. *Example* is the general term. *Exemplar* = an ideal or typical example. E.g., "The Court of Appeals found critical significance in the fact that the grand jury had summoned approximately twenty witnesses to furnish voice *exemplars* [i.e. typical specimens]." *U.S. v. Dionisio*, 410 U.S. 1, 12 (1973) (per Stewart, J.)./ "A testator of sound mind may prefer a prodigal son or even an unrepentant sinner to a son who has been an *exemplar* [i.e. an ideal example] and pattern of virtue." *Exemplum*, except in specialized literary senses, is a NEEDLESS VARIANT of *example*. *Exemplification* = (1) (in law) an attested copy of a document ⟨an *exemplification* is a copy of a record set out either under the Great Seal or under the Seal of the Court⟩; (2) the act or process of serving as an example ⟨by way of exemplification⟩; or (3) a case in point.

example where is always inferior to *example in which*. See **where** (A). Cf. **case where.**

ex ante; ex post. These adverbial LATINISMS are likely to confuse most readers. *Ex ante* = based on assumption and prediction; subjective. *Ex post* = based on knowledge and facts; objective. In the following sentences, *prospectively* and *retrospectively* would lead to greater comprehensibility with no loss in the sense: "Judges should be aware that their decisions create incentives influencing conduct *ex ante* [read *prospectively*] and that attempts to divide the stakes fairly *ex post* [read *retrospectively*] will alter or reverse the signals that are desirable from *an ex ante* [read *a prospective*] point of view."/ "Attorneys general were generally effective *in determining ex ante* [read *in predicting*] the policy orientation of future judges." See **ex post facto.**

ex cathedra; ex officio. *Ex cathedra* = (1) (adv.) from the chair; with authority; (2) (adj.) authoritative. Following is a literal adverbial use: "In expressing this view, both in legal literature and *ex cathedra*, he was, in effect, reverting to the standpoint of Lord Mansfield, who regarded quasi-contract as being essentially an equitable institution." (Eng.) *Ex officio* (= by virtue of one's office) may likewise be both adj. and adv. ⟨the chairman is an *ex officio* member of all standing committees⟩ ⟨the chairman became a member *ex officio*⟩. *Ex officiis* is a NEEDLESS VARIANT. *Ex officio* should be neither hyphenated nor spelled as one word.

exceed. See **accede.**

exceedingly is hyperbolic when used for *quite* or *very.* E.g., "Newspaper prices seldom change; the prices of chewing gum, flashlight batteries, and chloroform are *exceedingly* [read *quite*] stable."

excel. So spelled; *excell* is an infrequent misspelling.

except. A. As Verb. *Except* = (1) to exclude, omit; (2) = to object, take exception. The latter is the more frequent legal meaning: "The court overruled the objection, and the defendants *excepted*." Sense (2) has given rise to the special legal sense of the word, "to appeal." E.g., "Verdict was for plaintiff in each action, and defendant *excepts*."
B. As Preposition and Conjunction. When *except* begins a noun phrase rather than a clause (i.e., a phrase with a verb), it is a simple preposition not followed by the relative pronoun *that* ⟨all persons *except* farmers owning fewer than 500 acres⟩. But when, as a conjunction, *except* introduces a clause, it should be followed by *that*, which is here incorrectly omitted: "The corporate existence shall be deemed to have continued without interruption from the date of dissolution, *except* [read *except that*] the reinstatement shall have no effect upon any issue of personal liability of the directors."

C. As Conjunction. *Except* for *unless* is an ARCHAISM that persists only as a vulgarism. Here is the archaic use: "I devise this land to A and her heirs forever, *except* she should die without heir born of her own body." Quoted in *Roach v. Martin's Lessee,* 1 Har. 548, 28 Am. Dec. 746 (1835). And here is the modern vulgarism: "Wheat produced on excess acreage may be neither disposed of nor used except upon payment of the penalty, or *except* [read *unless*] it is stored as required by the Act or delivered to the Secretary of Agriculture."
D. *Excepting.* This word should not be used as a substitute for *except*, except in the phrase *not excepting.* E.g., "The majority of the cases dealing with the problem, *excepting* [read *except*] two, have applied the ruling to the case which resulted in the abolition of the doctrine of sovereign immunity."/ "He further provided that the property should under no circumstances be sold or alienated or at any time devoted to any *other purpose or use excepting as far as herein specifically authorized* [read *other purpose or use than is herein authorized*]."

exception takes the preposition *to*, not *from.* E.g., "Application of foreign law must be analytically understood as an exception *from* [read *to*] the basic rule calling for the application of the lex fori."

exceptionable; exceptional. The first is sometimes misused for the second. *Exceptionable* = open to exception; objectionable. *Exceptional* = out of the ordinary; uncommon; rare; superior.

exception proves the rule, the. This phrase is the popular rendering of what was originally a legal maxim, "The exception proves (or confirms) the rule in the cases not excepted" (*exceptio probat regulam in casibus non exceptis*). Originally *exception* in this maxim meant "the action of excepting"—not, as is commonly supposed, "that which is excepted"—so that the true sense of the maxim was that by specifying the cases excepted, one strengthens the hold of the rule over all cases not excepted.

At least two spurious explanations of *the exception proves the rule* exist. One is that because a rule does not hold in all instances (i.e., has exceptions), the rule must be valid. This misunderstanding of the phrase commonly manifests itself in the discourse of those who wish to argue that every rule must have exceptions. A more sophisticated, but equally false, explanation of the phrase is that *prove* here retains its Elizabethan sense (derived from the Latin) "to test," so that the sense of the phrase is that an exception to a rule "tests" the validity of the rule. This erroneous explanation appears, of all places, in Tom Burnam's *Dictionary of Misinformation* 79 (1975).

exceptor (= one who excepts or objects) was formerly used in some jurisdictions as an equivalent of *appellant.* E.g., "*Exceptors* place considerable stress on the case of *Marshall v. Frazier.*" See **except** (A).

excess of, in (= beyond the confines of) is a LEGALISM used in the context of actions *ultra vires,* q.v. The phrase is unobjectionable per se. E.g., "The district court ruled that the regulations had been promulgated *in excess of* the EPA s authority under the Clean Air Act."/ "It is contended that the minister acted *in excess of* his jurisdiction." (Eng.)

excise. There are two unrelated words *excise:* one means "to remove"; the other means "to impose an excise tax on." Here the first sense applies: "The jury had been selected at the time the sealing was entered; therefore, *excising* the documents and releasing them to the public was an alternative to sealing that should have been considered." For the second sense, the *OED* quotes Blackstone as follows: "Brandies and other spirits are now *excised* at the distillery." The *OED* labels this sense obsolete, but *W3* and *W9* suggest that it lives on.

exciseman; excisor. In view of the modern trend of avoiding needless SEXISM in language, *excisor* is to be preferred.

excludable, -dible, -sible. The preferred form is *excludable.* See -ABLE (A).

exclusionary = tending to exclude, or characterized by exclusion ⟨exclusionary rule⟩. This word, recorded first (fr. 1817) in the works of Bentham, began as a peculiarly legal word and has remained so.

exclusive means "with no exceptions" and should be used carefully. An ill-advised use appears in 28 U.S.C. § 1346: "The district court . . . shall have *exclusive* jurisdiction of civil actions on claims against the United States." This is not so, since circuit courts and the Supreme Court may also properly have jurisdiction on appeal. What was meant is "exclusive original jurisdiction." See OVERSTATEMENT.

exclusive federal jurisdiction. See **preemption, federal.**

ex contractu; ex delicto. The phrases *in contract* and *in tort* are much preferable to these LATINISMS. E.g., "Doubtless this is the rule of law today in all ordinary actions, either *ex contractu or ex delicto* [read *in contract or in tort*]."/ "Appellee maintains that it is entitled to attorneys' fees and costs incurred in the successful defense against appellant's *ex delicto claim* [read *tort claim*]."/ "Precise classification of rights *as ex contractu or ex delicto* [read *as being in contract or in tort*] was no more characteristic of fifteenth-century English legal thought than it is today."/ "Any one of various possible groups of specific operative facts would suffice, as far as the defendant's obligation *ex delicto* [read *in tort*] is concerned." See **delictual.**

exculpate; exonerate. Whereas the former has the primary sense "to free from blame or accusation," the latter means literally "to free from a burden," and only by extension is synonymous with the former. See **exonerate & inculpate.**

exculpatory, -tive. The latter is a NEEDLESS VARIANT.

excusal; excusation. In reference to prospective jurors, the correct phraseology is, e.g., *excusal for cause from the venire panel. Excusation* is an obsolete word meaning "the action of offering an excuse" (*OED*).

ex delicto. See **ex contractu.**

execute (= to sign and deliver; to make valid by observing certain required formalities) is useful lawyers' ARGOT in reference to completing legal documents ⟨she executed her will⟩. In this sense the word means "to go through the formalities necessary to the validity of (a legal act)—hence, to complete and give validity to (the instrument by which such an act is effected) by performing what the law requires to be done" (adapted fr. *OED*). *Execute* also has several other senses in law: (1) "to carry into effect ministerially (a law, a judicial sentence, etc.)"; (2) "to perform or carry out the provisions of a will" (i.e., what the executor does—this use of the term is now somewhat rare); (3) "to perform acts of (justice, e.g.) or give effect to a court's judgment"; or (4) "to levy execution *on* (property of a judgment debtor)" ⟨when the judgment became final, the prevailing plaintiff's attorney had the marshal execute on defendant's nonexempt property⟩. Sense (4) appears to be peculiar to the U.S., and is given in none of the standard unabridged dictionaries. But it falls logically under the second broad sense listed in the *OED*: "to do execution upon."

executor, -er. The *-er* spelling is obsolete. An *executor* is either (1) "one who does or performs some act"; or (2) "one who, appointed in a testator's will, administers the estate." In sense (2), the accent falls (familiarly) on the second syllable /ig-*zek*-yŭ-tŏr/; in sense (1), the accent is on the first syllable /*ek*-sĕ-kyoot-ĕr/. See **administrator.**

executory, -torial. *Executory* = designed to take or capable of taking full effect only at a future time (*OED*) ⟨an executory judgment⟩ ⟨executory contract⟩. *Executorial* = of or pertaining to an executor.

executrix, -tress. The former is the usual feminine form of *executor*, which may itself serve as a neuter form covering both sexes. Legal writers usually distinguish between the sexes with this term, however. See SEXISM (C).

exegesis; epexegesis; eisegesis. Knowledge of these terms is useful to anyone having to interpret writings. *Exegesis* = explanation or exposition (as of a word or sentence). E.g., "[I]n interpretation of federal statutes and congressional intent . . . semantic *exegesis* is not conclusive." *International Union v. Marshall*, 584 F.2d 390, 397 (D.C. Cir. 1978). *Epexegesis* = the addition of a word or words to convey more clearly the meaning implied, or the specific sense intended, in a preceding word or sentence (*OED*). *Eisegesis* = the interpretation of a word or passage by reading into it one's own ideas (*OED Supp.*).

exemplar. See **example.**

exemplary has two almost contradictory connotations: *exemplary damages* make an example out of a wrongdoer, whereas *exemplary behavior* is model behavior. *Exemplary* is some-

times misunderstood as meaning "severe" in phrases such as *exemplary punishment*.

exemplary damages. See **punitive damages.**

exemplification. See **example.**

exemplum. See **example.**

exempt appears not uncommonly in the U.S. as an ellipsis for *tax-exempt*. Usually this usage occurs in contexts in which the reader has already learned that the subject at hand is tax exemptions, and not other types of exemptions. Following is a typical specimen: "An *exempt* organization has the privilege of preferred second- or third-class mailing rates." Weinlein, *Federal Taxation of Not-for-Profit Arts Organizations*, 12 J. Arts, Mgmt., & Law 33 (Summer 1982).

exercise for *existence* is a puzzling error. E.g., "A presumption of undue influence arises from proof of the *exercise* [read *existence?*] of a confidential relation between the testator and such a beneficiary, coupled with activity on the part of the latter in the preparation of the will." (A *confidential relation* is not *exercised*.)

exertive, -tional. *Exertive* = tending to exert or rouse to action (*OED*) ⟨resolve is an exertive emotion⟩. *Exertional*, though recorded in none of the Oxford or Merriam-Webster dictionaries, has appeared (usu. in the negative form) in American law cases in the field of social security disabilities. *Exertional* = of or pertaining to exertion. E.g., "[H]e is unable to return to his past relevant work and suffers from a *non-exertional* impairment." *Warmoth v. Bowen*, 798 F.2d 1109, 1110 (7th Cir. 1986)./ "[W]henever a *nonexertional* impairment is presented the Secretary must introduce a vocational expert to testify that jobs in the workplace exist for a person with that particular disability." *Bapp v. Bowen*, 802 F.2d 601, 604 (2d Cir. 1986).

ex facie (= in view of what is apparent, lit., "from the face") is not justified as a legal LATINISM, inasmuch as so many ordinary English words, such as *evidently*, *apparently*, or *on its face*, suffice in its stead. "*Ex facie* [read *Patently*] those transfers would be the same in form and in effect precisely as the instrument of transfer now before us." (Eng.) Here the phrase is wrongly made adjectival: "The Companies Act of 1948 brought into being that which was *ex facie* [read *evident*] in all its essential characteristics." (Eng.)

ex gratia; a gratia. *Ex gratia* means "as a favor, not by legal necessity" ⟨ex gratia payment⟩. *A gratia* is a NEEDLESS VARIANT.

exha(u)lt is a misspelling of *exalt*, q.v.

exhorbitant is a misspelling of *exorbitant*, q.v.

exigency, -ce. The form in *-cy* is standard; the other is a NEEDLESS VARIANT.

exige(a)nt. *Exigeant* is a NEEDLESS VARIANT of the standard form, *exigent*.

existing. Legal drafters should beware of the AMBIGUITY of this word. It may mean "existing at the time of the writing" or "existing at some time after the writing," if not specifically put within a time frame.

exit has been an acceptable verb since the early seventeenth century. Those who object to it on grounds that one does not "entrance" a building have a misplaced prejudice.

exlex; ex lege. Good legal writers have little or no use for these terms; nevertheless, it is well to know their meanings. *Exlex* is an adjective meaning "outside the law; without legal authority" ⟨an exlex government⟩, whereas *ex lege* is an adverb meaning "as a matter of law" ⟨property forfeited ex lege⟩.

ex maleficio = (adv.) by malfeasance; (adj.) tortious. There is no reason why this phrase should not be Englished. E.g., "We do not find these allegations sufficient, either on authority or on principle, to establish a constructive trust *ex maleficio* [read *resulting from malfeasance*]."/ "In the character of a trustee *ex maleficio* [read *by virtue of malfeasance*], he shall be held to make good the things to the person who would have the property." See **de son tort.**

ex necessitate (= of necessity) is a Latinistic pollutant. E.g., "They argue that adoption of the doctrine would be a nullification of the rule that executory limitations are void unless they take effect *ex necessitate* [read *of necessity*] and in all possible contingencies within the prescribed period."

exodus, a much abused word, refers to the simultaneous departure of many people. It is not the term to describe one lawyer's leaving a firm: "Likewise, negotiations failed on whether Poindexter's ex-firm was entitled to reimbursement of several thousand dollars in costs expended on the Nicol case upon Poindexter's *exodus* [read *exit*] or upon the conclusion of the case." Occasionally *exodus* is mistakenly thought to be the equivalent of *influx*, which is actually an antonym.

Exodus should be avoided as a verb: "Poor people have no ability to *exodus from* [read *leave en masse*] an impoverished state for richer ones."

ex officio. See **ex cathedra.**

exonerate, in the sense "to free from responsibility," should be used only in reference to people. Hence the following use is erroneous: "Held, affirmed for DuPont since there was no evidence that the booster [a component in an explosive device] was responsible for the explosion, and the evidence offered by plaintiff tended to *exonerate* [read *rule out*] the booster." Cf. **exculpate.**

In its sense "to free from encumbrances," of course, *exonerate* is used of liens. E.g., "We find that the decedent did not expressly signify any intention not to *exonerate* the property here from the mortgage lien." Whereas *acquit* takes *of*, *exonerate* takes the preposition *from*: "We affirm the lower court's holding that it was the intention of the testator that this legacy be *exonerated from* all liens."

ex'or is an archaic abbreviation of *executor*.

exorbitant (lit., "having departed or deviated from one's track [*orbita*] or rut") is sometimes mistakenly spelled *exhorbitant*, perhaps out of confusion with *exhort*. E.g., "Daon's own appraiser agreed that this price was *exhorbitant* [read *exorbitant*]." *Foster v. Daon Corp.*, 713 F.2d 148, 149 (5th Cir. 1983).

expandable, -dible, -sible. The first is the preferred form. See **-ABLE (A).**

ex parte; inter partes. These correlative terms of legal ARGOT are familiar enough to all lawyers to be useful; they should be simplified for the lay audience, however. Neither phrase should be hyphenated. Only one party is involved in an *ex parte* proceeding (e.g., an action to obtain a temporary restraining order against an adversary that has not yet appeared in the suit), whereas more than one party is involved in an *inter partes* proceeding (e.g., the minitrial between adversaries in which the successful applicant for a temporary restraining order seeks to extend injunctive relief by obtaining a preliminary injunction).

Ex parte = from one side only. E.g., "Because appellee declined to participate in the proceeding, the arbitration was conducted *ex parte.*"/ "The incongruous result follows that a newspaper may freely, if without actual malice, publish the contents of a complaint if it has been filed on an *ex parte* application for injunction."/ "Petitioner maintains that the judge was unduly and falsely influenced during an allegedly *ex parte* conversation with the prosecution."

Ex parte is sometimes ignorantly misused for *sua sponte*, q.v.: "The court was not free to deny plaintiff's motion to vacate judgment under Rule 60(b)(2) based upon its *ex parte* [read *sua sponte*] determination that to do otherwise would be somehow contrary to the public policy of bringing disputes to a conclusion."

Inter partes = from both sides; between parties. This term is not as often used as *ex parte.* E.g., "In other states these courts may conduct *inter partes* proceedings if the contestant files a caveat after the *ex parte* proceeding has begun." See **inter partes.**

expatiate; expatriate. *Expatiate* means (1) "to wander"; or (2) "to discourse on (a subject) at length." *Expatriate* means (1) "to leave one's home country to live elsewhere"; or (2) "to banish; exile."

expect is informal or colloquial for *think* or *suppose*, as here: "I *expect* that it will take three weeks," instead of, "I think it will take three weeks." Most properly, *expect* means "to look forward to and rely on." See **anticipate.**

expectancy, -ce; expectation. We have the idioms *life expectancy* and *meet one's expectations*, but aside from distinguishing uses in these phrases, most lawyers would be hard-put to set out the distinction. Despite an overlap in actual use, there is a clear-cut DIFFERENTIATION that ought to be observed with care. An *expectancy* is the position of being entitled to a possession at some future time, either as a remainder or reversion, or on the death of someone (*OED*). E.g., "Being thus conditioned on his surviving, the interest of Williams until the death of Farkas was a mere *expectancy.*"/ "It is also agreed that at common law the transfer of a mere possibility or *expectancy*, coupled with an interest, is void."

Expectation = the action of mentally looking for someone to come, forecasting something to happen, or anticipating something to be received (*OED*). E.g., "The statute creates a presumption that parole release will be granted, which in turn creates a legitimate *expectation* of release absent the requisite finding that one of the justifications for deferral exists."/ "Perhaps the most common recovery sought in contract cases is a reimbursement for damage to what is known as the plaintiff's *expectation* interest."

Here idiom is violated by *life expectation:* "By the wrongful injury his normal life *expectation* [read *expectancy*] had been shortened." The opposite error here occurs, *expectancy* for *expectation:* "Punishment of the contract-breaker is so subordinated to the main goal of fulfilling the injured party's *expectancy* [read *expectation*] of gain that it has received practically no recognition as a remedial consideration."

Writers who favor INELEGANT VARIATION are especially fond of these terms. E.g., "The district court considered the balance due on Todd's repair contract in computing Auto's damages solely in order to ensure that Auto received no more than its *expectation.* Because the repairers were obligated in solido to *pay this expectancy* [read *pay the amount of this expectation*], the district court correctly subtracted the balance due under the contract from the amount of their total liability."

expectant heir. See **heir** (B).

expectation. See **expectancy.**

expediency, -ce. The former is usual. E.g., "While *expediency* can furnish no reason or basis upon which to determine the constitutionality of the retroactive operation of the act, we cannot refrain from noting the unworkability of the rule under present-day economic conditions."

expedient(ial); expeditious. *Expedient* = advantageous; desirable. *Expeditious* = quickly accomplished; prompt. *Expediential* is a NEEDLESS VARIANT of *expedient*.

expend is a FORMAL WORD for *spend* that is not always appropriate in ordinary contexts. E.g., "Generally speaking, students have no constitutional right to *expend* [read *spend*] classroom time on a subject unrelated to what they are supposed to be learning."

experimentalize is a NEEDLESS VARIANT of *experiment*.

expiration; expiry. The word *end* is best where it will suffice. *Expiry* is the usual word for "termination" in BrE, whereas in AmE *expiration* is far more common. Thus: "There could be no difficulty here about the date of performance; it was on the *expiry* of the two years." (Eng.)/ "The district court denied reinstatement to Marchelos, reasoning that Marchelos had no security interest in his job because he had no reasonable expectation of continued employment beyond the *expiration* of his contract on August 31, 1979."

expire. See **run** (A).

explain. See **explicate**.

EXPLETIVES. In general usage, *expletives* are understood to be curse words or exclamations. This sense was fortified in AmE during the Watergate hearings, when coarse language was omitted from the White House tapes with the phrase *expletive deleted*. In grammar, however, expletives are words that have no special meaning, but stand (usually at the beginning of a clause) for a delayed subject. The two most common expletives are *it* and *there* when beginning clauses or sentences.

   A. With Passives. When used after verbs in the passive voice, expletives often wrongly give the impression that they have antecedents. E.g., "The burial was to take place at Highgate, and *it* was intended to take the body by train from Winooski to Cambridge Junction over the defendant's road and thence over the connecting road to Highgate." (The full passive is *it was intended (by someone) to take the body*; yet, on first reading, *it* appears to refer to *burial*.)

   B. Number. The INVERSION occasioned by expletives sometimes leads writers astray

with regard to the number of the subject. "*There remains* for trial *these issues* [read *There remain . . . these issues*] raised in respondent's counterclaim." See SUBJECT-VERB AGREEMENT (K).

   C. Expletive *it* Alongside Pronoun *it*. The expletive *it* should not be used in the same immediate context as the pronoun *it*. "*It* is concluded that *it* [i.e., the plaintiff corporation] is entitled to interest." [Read *We conclude that it is entitled to interest.*] See **it**.

explicate; explain. The terms are synonymous, but are used in different contexts. *Explain* is the ordinary term. *Explicate* (lit., "to open up pleats; to unfold") is more learned and connotes formal, orderly presentation or justification. Oddly, the adjectives *explicable* and *inexplicable* are more frequently used than the verb *to explicate*.

explodable; explosible. The former is preferred.

exploitative, -atory; exploitive. The second and third forms are NEEDLESS VARIANTS.

explosible. See **explodable**.

exportize is an abomination for *export*, v.t. See -IZE.

expose. See **disclose**.

exposé should have the acute accent on the final letter (-*é*) to prevent confusion with the verb *to expose*. E.g., "Investigative reports, following in the tradition of the muckrackers, are always looking for an *expose* [read *exposé*]."

ex post. See **ex ante**.

ex post facto is slightly pompous but fairly common when used for *after the fact*. The phrase does have legitimate uses in the sense "retroactive," as in *ex post facto laws*. E.g., "Application of the newly enacted burden to this defendant runs afoul of the *ex post facto* prohibition [i.e., the prohibition against enacting laws that punish retroactively]." An English writer once called this use, which appears in the U.S. Constitution and in Blackstone, "a grotesque misuse of the expression." Note, 133 Law Q. Rev. 8, 9 (1918). His was the grotesque error. The phrase was formerly sometimes spelled *ex postfacto*.

Ex post for *ex post facto* is an odd ellipsis without literary legitimacy. "As a rule, therefore, courts will not engage in *ex post inquiries* [read *ex post facto inquiries*] regarding the substantive fairness of contract terms." Note, *Post-Employment Restraint Agreements*, 52 U. Chi. L. Rev. 703, 704 (1985). (On the technically correct sense of *ex post*, see **ex ante**.) Yet another strange shortening of the phrase is *post facto* for *ex post facto*: "[C]hanges may not be instituted now in the expectation of *post facto* [read *ex post facto*] ratification at some indeterminate future time." *Henderson v. Graddick*, 641 F. Supp. 1192, 1203 (M.D.Ala. 1986).

expound; propound. The former means "to explain," the latter "to set forth; put forward for consideration." *Expound* is often misused. E.g., "Perhaps a sixteen-year-old boy would choose to refrain from sex in fear of the druggist's calling his father; then males as well as females would be virgins when they are married, as traditional views would *expound* [read *encourage* or *favor*]."/ "The board considered the wearing of the black arm band in class a political act *expounding* [read *conveying?*] to the students only one side of a controversial issue and, as such, constituting an unethical practice by a member of the teaching profession."

Expound is best used transitively: one *expounds* an idea or doctrine; one does not need to expound *on* it. Likewise, one *propounds* evidence. See **propound** & **proponent**.

express(ed). Sometimes within the same writing will be found references to "*express* and implied contracts" and to "*expressed* and implied contracts." The preferred adjective in the sense "specific, definite, clear" is *express*. E.g., "The decision depends in no way on an agreement, *expressed* [read *express*] or implied." (Eng.) See **implied**.

expressible, -able. The former is preferred. See -ABLE (A).

expropriate. See **appropriate**.

expropriation. See **eminent domain**.

exquisite is best pronounced with the first syllable accented /*eks-kwiz-it*/; it is acceptable in AmE, however, to stress the second /*ik-skwiz-it*/.

Although there is historical justification for

using *exquisite* (= acute) in reference to pain, modern readers are likely to find this use macabre at best, for they generally understand the word as meaning "keenly discriminating" ⟨exquisite taste⟩ or "especially beautiful" ⟨an exquisite vase⟩. Following is an example of the obsolescent sense: "From this we cannot say that it was unreasonable for the jury to infer that the decedent was conscious after impact and before her death, suffering during that period from both impact injuries and the *exquisite* [read *excruciating*] pain of massive burns." In the sentence that follows, the word is loosely used in the sense "acute, intense"; this use is likely to befuddle many readers: "Claimant's counsel might be faced with the *exquisite* [omit *exquisite*] dilemma of whether to forgo any fee application and thereby preserve his client's meager judgment, or jeopardize the client's judgment by applying for fees and thereby giving the government an incentive to appeal."

ex rel., the abbreviation for L. *ex relatione* (= upon relation or information), is now used almost exclusively in styles of cases. E.g., *United States ex rel. Carter v. Jennings*, 333 F. Supp. 1392 (E.D. Pa. 1971).

extemporaneous; extempore, adj.; **extemporary; extemporal.** In AmE, the first is the usual form. The others might be considered NEEDLESS VARIANTS, but *extempore* is most common in BrE.

extemporaneously; ex tempore, adv. In the U.S. the latter is the Latin-lover's (or Anglophile's) NEEDLESS VARIANT of the former. *Ex tempore*, like the adjective *extempore*, is what one usually encounters in G.B.

extendable, -dible, -sible. The preferred form is *extendable*. See -ABLE (A).

extended opinion = a separate opinion. "Mr. Justice Brennan, concurring in part and dissenting in part, filed an *extended opinion*." See **write specially**.

extenuate (= to lessen the seriousness of [a fault or a crime] by partial excuse) should be used only of the fault that is minimized, not of the person. The *OED* cites improper uses (so labeled) such as, "The pursuer's steward . . . *extenuated* himself calmly enough," in which the word is used as if it meant "to extenuate the guilt of; to plead partial excuses for" (*OED*).

extern. See **clerk.**

extinguishment; extinction. Both words are nouns corresponding to the verb *to extinguish.* If there is a DIFFERENTIATION, it is that *extinguishment* refers to the process, and *extinction* to the resultant state. *Extinguishment* means in law "the cessation or cancellation of some right or interest" (*CDL*). E.g., "Both the Senate Bill and the House amendments provided for recordation of mining claims and for *extinguishment* of abandoned claims."

extortionate, -tionary, -tive; extorsive. *Extortionate* (= [1] given to or characterized by extortion; [2] [of prices] exorbitant) is the standard term, the others being NEEDLESS VARIANTS. E.g., "The vice arises only when he employs *extortive* [read *extortionate*] measures, or when, lacking good faith, he makes improper demands." *State National Bank v. Farah Manufacturing* Co., 678 S.W.2d 661, 684 (Tex. App.—El Paso 1984)./ "Wright and Armstrong urge, among other things, that the court erred in finding a nexus between the *extortionate* conduct and interstate commerce." *United States v. Wright*, 804 F.2d 843, 844 (5th Cir. 1986).

extortioner, -ist; extorter. The first is most usual, the others being NEEDLESS VARIANTS.

EXTRA- (= lying outside the province or scope of) is a prefix that in modern English has been used to form hundreds of new adjectives, mostly for learned or literary purposes. The prefix has been adopted by many legal writers to form NEOLOGISMS not yet found in unabridged dictionaries. These writers usually do no harm, and in fact occasionally coin useful words. *Extralegal* and *extrajudicial* both date from the early seventeenth century; following are three representative examples of twentieth-century legal neologisms using this prefix: a note entitled *Intercircuit Conflicts and the Enforcement of Extracircuit Judgments*, 95 Yale L.J. 1500 (1986)./ "[T]he business judgment rule would shield the directors' decision to terminate a derivative suit against an *extracorporate* party." Note, *Derivative Suits and the Special Litigation Committee*, 29 Wayne L. Rev. 149, 167 (1982)./ "The decision to withhold enforcement of the immigration laws is *extrastatutory*; it constitutes one of the Execu-

tive's inherent prerogatives." *Hotel & Restaurant Employees Union v. Attorney General*, 804 F.2d 1256, 1279 (D.C. Cir. 1986) (Silberman, J., concurring in part and dissenting in part).

extrajudicial; out-of-court. These terms are precisely equivalent. The latter is more readily comprehensible to readers and listeners, but it can be awkward. Euphony should govern the choice of term. E.g., "The constitutional privilege has no application to an *extrajudicial* confession, whether or not it is under oath."/ "The mere fact that sworn testimony may differ from *extrajudicial* statements does not constitute perjury, particularly where the discrepancy is extremely slight."/ "The due process clause should not be treated as a uniform command that courts throughout the nation abandon their age-old practice of seeking information from *out-of-court* sources to guide their judgment toward a more enlightened and just sentence."

exult. See **exalt.**

ex vi termini = by the force of the term; by the very meaning of the expression used. This LATINISM has no place in modern legal writing. "It is said that words not actionable *ex vi termini* [read *in themselves*] cannot be made so by innuendo."/ "In the second will there are no words that *ex vi termini* [omit *ex vi termini*] import a disposition of real property."

eyeing. So spelled; *eying* is a blunder.

eyewitness is spelled as one word, not two.

F

face of, in the = in front of; directly opposite; when confronted with. This idiomatic expression has become a part of legal ARGOT. E.g., "Commenting upon the recent disarmament of the Highlanders, which had been so drastic that they were defenseless *in the face of* a gang of robbers or pirates, he remarked that 'Laws that place the subjects in such a state of insecurity contravene the first principles of the compact of authority: they exact obedience, and yield not protection.'" (Eng.)/ "Nor will equity engraft the doctrine of subrogation on a transaction *in the face of* an agree-

ment that negatives the idea of subrogation."
See **fly in the face of.**

face, on its. In this expression *face* refers to
the inscribed side of a document. It means "in
the words of, in the plain sense of" ⟨the document on its face indicates testamentary in-
tent⟩. The phrase is sometimes used figuratively of things other than documents. E.g.,
"A libel is harmful *on its face.*"

One must be careful of context with this
shopworn phrase. When the subject is plural,
and the phrase becomes *on their face,* there is
a technical failure of CONCORD that can sometimes be risible: "Most laws, however, discriminate or mete out different treatment *on
their face.*" (No one wants to see treatment
meted out on anyone's face; though the sentence refers *to the face of* the statute, nonetheless the imagery suggests something different.)/ "*On their face,* the municipal historic
preservation ordinances satisfy requisite due
process criteria."/ "Some of these statutes
were held to be unconstitutional *on their face*
or as applied." (Note that in these last two
sentences the plural form *on their faces* would
be even worse.) See METAPHORS.

The *face* idiom is an old one in the law. "In
our opinion the writ ought not to be allowed
by the court if it appears from the *face* of the
record that the decision of the federal question which is complained of was so plainly
right as not to require argument." *The Anar-
chists' Case,* 123 U.S. 131, 164 (1887). See **ex
facie.**

facial = complete; on its face; as a whole.
E.g., "The cases before us are governed by the
normal rule that partial, rather than *facial,* in-
validation is the required course for such statutes." The adverbial use is almost as common
as the adjectival use; *facially* does not mean
"in a facial manner," but "on its face": "The
court of appeals erred by *facially invalidating
the statute in its entirety* [i.e., *invalidating the statute on its face*]."/ "We hold that the plaintiff
has standing to challenge the constitutionality of the ordinance, and that the section in
its present form is *facially overbroad and unconstitutional* [i.e., *overbroad and unconstitutional on
its face*]."

facilitate (= to aid, help) is a FORMAL WORD
to be used sparingly, for it often is jargonistic,
as is the agent noun *facilitator* (= helper).
"The commission's improved decision un-

doubtedly *facilitates* this court's review by clarifying the issues involved." As Fowler and
others have noted, it is better to write that an
action (e.g., the *court's review,* in the sentence
just quoted) is facilitated rather than that the
actor (e.g. *the court*) is facilitated.

fact, adj.; **factual.** In phrases such as
fact(ual) question, the longer form is preferable. Notwithstanding that *fact question* is jarring, it is potentially misleading to the reader.
In the following sentence, for instance, the
use of *factual* would have circumvented the
reader's thinking that *existence of fact* is an unhyphenated phrasal adjective: "If the proceedings are characterized as a trial on a stipulated record, the existence of *fact questions*
[read *factual questions*] will not undermine the
result." The sentences that follow illustrate
the better usage: "We are directed by statute
and Supreme Court precedent to accord a presumption of correctness to such state court
factual findings."/ "Petitioners contend that
the ICC impermissibly substituted its judgment for the *factual findings* of the state
commission."

Notably, *factual* has two meanings: (1) "of
or involving facts" ⟨factual issue⟩; (2) "true"
⟨a factual depiction⟩. Here sense (2) is illustrated in a sentence in which *fact* would be
not just inferior, but wrong: "If this were a
factual account of what happened, the plaintiff would not have a cause of action." See
fact-finding & fact situation.

Sense (1) of *factual,* the more usual meaning, appears in the following sentences: "The
ICC's section 11501(c) jurisdiction is not of a
limited nature, but in a proper case is plenary,
and may allow the ICC to delve into the *factual* record before the state agency."/ "The
rule contemplates that only *factual* questions
will be submitted to the jury to which the
judge will apply the law, supplementing, if
necessary, any *factual* determinations not submitted to the jury."

fact, n.; **factum.** *Fact* (lit., "a thing done")
means "an action performed, an event, an occurrence, or a circumstance." In legal writing, *fact* has the additional particularized
sense "an evil deed; a crime." Thus we have
the expressions *before the fact, after the fact,* and
confess the fact.

Factum, the Latinate form of the word, has
several meanings: (1) [regarding change in
domicile] "a person's physical presence in a

new domicile"; (2) "due execution of a will"; (3) "a fact or statement of facts"; and (4) "an act or deed." In senses (3) and (4), the only ones contained in the *OED,* the word has no merit in modern contexts (except in the phrase *fraud in the factum* [senses 2 & 4], for which see **fraud** (A)); few lawyers would understand *factum* when so used. In sense (1), *factum* is perhaps a TERM OF ART; nevertheless, the term calls for elucidation.

Sense (2) occurs frequently in the context of wills, where it is generally no more useful or specific than *execution:* "It might be argued that logically the only question upon the probate was the *factum* [read *execution*] of the instrument." In the SET PHRASE *fraud* or *mistake in the factum,* however, the use of *factum* is well ensconced: "There is a close analogy, however, to the situation in which a provision in a will by mistake in the *factum* is denied effect."/ "When there has been a fraudulent representation concerning the nature of the instrument or its contents, usually described as a fraud in the *factum,* it is well settled that the will or a fraudulently induced part of a will should be denied probate."

fact(-)finder should be hyphenated, not spelled as two words. Likewise, *fact-finding* is best hyphenated rather than spelled out in two words. The trend is to make both terms solid, but that trend is at best incipient.

fact-finding = the finding of facts; *factual finding* = a finding of fact. E.g., "The agency's decision that an impact statement was not required pretermitted the *fact-finding* process designed by Congress."/ "The court's *factual finding* on that issue precluded recovery by the plaintiff."

Fact-finding is often mistakenly used not in reference to the process, but to mean "a finding of fact," e.g.: "The earlier ruling was a *fact-finding* [read *factual finding*]."/ "On the basis of the above *fact-findings* [read *factual findings*], plaintiff has failed to make out a prima facie case."/ "The magistrate declined to enter any meaningful [q.v.] *factfindings* [read *factual findings*] on the incidents surrounding the workover crew's hotel room arrangement, which appellant contended had precipitated the discharge." See **finding.**

factional; factious; fractious. These words are confusingly similar. *Factional* = of or relating to a faction. *Factious* = given to faction;

acting for partisan purposes. *Fractious* = refractory, unruly, fretful, peevish. See **factitious.**

factitious; fictitious. Both have the basic sense "artificial." *Factitious* = (1) man-made and not natural; (2) sham; produced by contrivance. *Fictitious* = imaginary, not real. This latter term is often used of testimony, accounts of facts, or stories. See **fictitious.**

fact of the matter, the. This phrase is trite FUSTIAN that may serve as a filler in speech, but that generally has no justification in writing. Infrequently it gives the needed rhythm.

factor properly means "an agent or cause that contributes to a particular result." It should not be used, by SLIPSHOD EXTENSION, in the sense "a thing to be considered; event; occurrence." In law *factor* is used also in the sense "consignee" or "commission agent."

factotum = a general servant with myriad duties. The preferred plural is *-tums* rather than *-ta.* "The agents suspected that the appellees were driving stolen vehicles, not that they served as *factota* [read *factotums*] of illegal aliens." *United States v. Miranda-Perez,* 764 F.2d 285, 289 (5th Cir. 1985). See PLURALS (A).

facts cannot literally be false; if something is a fact, then it is by its very nature true. Yet in law one often reads and hears of the "truth" or "falsity" of certain facts. E.g., "Presumably there were good reasons in the interest of justice nearly 100 years ago which impelled the court to fetter its own power to get at the *true facts.*" (Eng.)/ "No order shall recite *untrue facts.*" This is an acceptable practice, for *facts* in such a context is really an elliptical form of *alleged facts.* Hence: "Subject to later case development, the Texas measure of probative value, 'tending to establish the presence or absence, *truth or falsity of a fact,*' does not seem functionally distinct from the federal definition, 'to make the existence of the *fact* more probable or less probable.'" See **actual fact.**

fact situation; factual situation. What is implied by these terms is that a *fact situation* = a situation with a given set of facts (hypothetical or actual); and that *factual situation* = a situation that exists or existed in fact. When coupled with the noun *situation, factual* tends to take on sense (1) listed in the entry under *fact, adj.* Cf. *fact(ual) determinations*, in which *factual* assumes sense (1).

facts, under the is an acceptable legal idiom. E.g., *"Under the facts* of the case at bar, we cannot say that the district court erred in allowing the inclusion of this testimony." Cf. **circumstances, under the.**

fact that, the. It is imprudent to say, as some have, that this phrase ought never to be used. At times it cannot reasonably be avoided. One writer has suggested that *because* will usually suffice for *the fact that.* See Vigilans, *Chamber of Horrors* 63 (1952). Yet rarely, if ever, is *because* a good substitute.

Where *the fact that* can be easily avoided, however, it should be. E.g., *"The fact that* [read *That*] the right to protection was founded upon the doctrine of secondary meaning rather than, for example, upon common-law technical trademark law or statutory trademark law, generally has not been regarded as controlling a determination of the proper geographic scope of protection."

The pluralized form, as in *"The facts that* . . ."* is usually unnecessary and awkward for the singular, where the discrete facts discussed are easily considered part of an overall structure or pattern. *"The facts that* [read *The fact that* or *that*] the records in this case were made by the proprietor and were in his possession *were* [read *was*] irrelevant to the determination whether their creation was compelled, the majority said." See FLOTSAM PHRASES.

fact-trier. See **trier of fact.**

factual. See **fact,** adj.

factual finding. See **fact-finding.**

factum. See **fact,** n.

fair use; fair dealing. The defense of *fair use,* in actions for copyright infringement, is known also as *fair dealing* in G.B. The term *fair use* (not *fair usage*) is the one applied in 17 U.S.C. § 107 to describe the kinds of limitations the law places on the exclusive rights of copyright.

fall due is the idiomatic legal phrase meaning "to become due" and used of negotiable instruments. E.g., "He paid the notes as they *fell due."*

false plea; sham plea. Both terms mean "an obviously frivolous or absurd pleading that is made only for purposes of vexation or delay." *Sham plea* (or *pleading*) has been the more common of the two in the U.S.; the *CDL* (British) contains the main entry under *false plea.*

false swearing. See **perjury.**

fantasy; phantasy. The former is now the preferred spelling in both AmE and BrE.

far-reaching is one of our most overburdened adjectival phrases. This otiose metaphor should be used cautiously; the phrase should always be hyphenated. E.g., "This argument, which is of *far-reaching* significance, was designed to show that the union was not in breach of the court's orders." (Eng.)/ "They had no notification that any complaint was being made under section 6(k), which is a different and, in this case, more *far-reaching* matter." (Eng.)

farther; further. Both are comparative degrees of *far,* but they have undergone DIFFERENTIATION. In the best usage, the former refers to physical distances, the latter to figurative distances. "The Supreme Court looks no *farther* [read *further*] than whether the distinctions have some 'rational basis.'"/ "But the immunity goes *farther* [read *further*]." In BrE, *further* is used both physically and figuratively, whereas *farther* is physical only.

The superlatives are *farthest* and *furthest. Furthermost* is rare for *farthest* (not *furthest*).

fastly is an obsolete form that now exists only as a barbarism, inasmuch as *fast* is an adverb as well as an adjective.

fatal. In legal ARGOT, this word means "providing grounds for legal invalidity." This sense is common: "The court pointed out that uncertainty as to the fact of damage is *fatal."*/ "While the parties have extensively argued and briefed a number of questions, one basic proposition is dispositive of, and *fatal* to, the position taken by the plaintiffs."/ "The fundamental, and in the end *fatal,* deficiency in Montana's reading of the statute is its failure to acknowledge, much less account for, language that equally plainly compels the conclusion that Congress did not intend that funds derived from Indian lands be distributed to the states.''

father-in-law. Pl. *fathers-in-law.*

fault, at or *in.* See **at fault** & **in fault.**

fealty was an old English law term meaning ''the fidelity on the part of a feudal tenant or vassal to his lord'' (*OED*). Today it is used figuratively as an ARCHAISM for *fidelity*: ''If I begin to quote from the opinions of Mr. Justice Holmes, I hardly know where I shall end, yet *fealty* to a master makes me reluctant to hold back.'' (Cardozo)

feasance = the doing or execution of a condition or obligation. This term is not nearly as common as the negatives *malfeasance* and *misfeasance.* See **malfeasance.**

federal jurisdiction, exclusive. See **preemption, federal.**

fee. Plurals formed from compounds with this word can be problematic. One textbook, for example, has *fee tails* but *fees simple.* The better practice is to make *fees* plural, whether the phrase is *fees simple absolute, fees simple determinable,* or *fees tail.* See POSTPOSITIVE ADJECTIVES.

　　Fee often acts as an elliptical form of *fee simple.* E.g., ''Our society acknowledges that the *fee* owner of a piece of land has the right to decide present and, to some extent, future use of the land.'' See **fee simple.**

feel is a weak and informal substitute for *think* or *believe* or *maintain* or *submit.* E.g., ''In order for this opinion to have any real meaning, we *feel* [read *believe*] the stipulation of facts should be summarized in considerable detail.''/ ''I *feel* [read *think* or *believe*] that to deprive the parties who were responsible for the abolition of the antiquated and anachronistic doctrine of sovereign immunity of their day in court is unjustified.''

fee simple. The fee simple estates are: (1) fee simple absolute; (2) fee simple conditional; (3) fee simple determinable; and (4) fee simple subject to a condition subsequent. When *fee simple* is used alone, *fee simple absolute* is almost invariably the intended meaning:

''Their contention is that the will vested a life estate only in Fred Sybert, while respondent contends that the Rule in Shelley's Case operated to vest a *fee simple* estate in him.'' The plural is *fees simple.* See **fee.**

fee tail (F. *tailler* = to cut to some chosen shape) = an estate of inheritance entailed or limited to some particular class of heirs of the person to whom it is granted (*OED*). The estate is largely defunct in American jurisdictions, and was abolished in England in 1925, but survives there as an equitable interest. See **entail, fee,** & **tail.**

felonious is used rarely of persons, almost always of acts. E.g., ''Over the last twenty-five years five judges have been disciplined for associating with criminals; in most of the cases, the judges performed specific favors for their *felonious friends* [better: *felon-friends*].'' The *OED* cites but one (nineteenth-century) sentence in which *felonious* is used of a person in the sense of someone who ''has committed felony.''

feme covert. See **fem(m)e co(u)vert(e).**

feme sole = (1) an unmarried woman; (2) a married woman handling the affairs of her separate estate. This LAW FRENCH term is now obsolescent since the distinctions that it denotes are falling into disuse. Here are typical traditional uses: ''During their natural lives, they were to use and enjoy the house, subject to their own control, and to be managed by them as *femes sole.*''/ ''The court relied upon the analogy of a *feme sole* who makes a bequest to her surviving husband, saying that the subsequent exercise of volition could not be deemed testamentary in a legal sense.'' See SEXISM (C).

FEMININE ENDINGS. See SEXISM (C).

FEMININE PRONOUNS USED GENERICALLY. See SEXISM (A).

fem(m)e co(u)vert(e). Though it would be spelled differently in modern French, the accepted spelling in Anglo-American jurisprudence of this LAW FRENCH term is *feme covert* (omitting all the optional letters). This spelling has been preferred since Blackstone's time. The plural is *femes covert.* See **coverture,** LAW FRENCH & SEXISM (C).

feoff; enfeoff; infeoff. The usual form of the verb meaning "to put in legal possession (of a freehold interest)" is *enfeoff. Feoff* and *infeoff* are NEEDLESS VARIANTS.

feoff; fief. Both are common-law terms. *Feoff* (= to put in legal possession) is not properly a noun. "The Rule in Shelley's Case was devised in feudal times to assure feudal landlords the receipt of their rents from their *feoffs* [read *feoffees,* q.v.], or tenants." A *fief* is a fee, or an estate in land held on condition of homage and service to a superior lord, by whom it is granted and in whom the ownership remains.

Feoffment (fr. L. *feoffare* "to give one a fief") is an ancient form of conveyance, defined by Blackstone as "the gift of any corporeal hereditament to another." 3 Blackstone, *Commentaries* 310 (Tucker ed. 1803). E.g., "The English common law, influenced by the notion that a life tenant could make a tortious *feoffment* that barred subsequent exercise of the power, permitted release of all except a power simply collateral."/ "No collateral of the half-blood inherited in any event; when collaterals did inherit, the land remained within the family into which it had been brought by *feoffment.*"

feoffee = the person to whom a freehold estate in land is conveyed by feoffment, or a trustee invested with a freehold estate in land. E.g., "The doctrine of worthier title had its origins in the feudal custom of awarding certain valuable incidents to the overlord upon the descent of property held by a *feoffee.*"/ "The Statute of Uses converted the equitable interest of the cestui que use into a legal interest and extinguished the legal interest of the *feoffee* to use."/ "A collateral relation who inherited had to be of the blood of the first purchaser (or *feoffee*) of the land." See -EE.

feoffor, -er. The former spelling predominates. E.g., "On the creation of any estate of freehold, whether in possession or remainder, the seisin must pass out of the transferor (the *feoffor*), i.e. there must be a livery of seisin."/ "Since the value of the use depended upon the ability of the cestui que use to enforce his claim, the transfer of freeholds to the use of the *feoffor* or a third-party became common when the Chancellor enforced the feoffee's duties as a routine matter."

feticide. See **aborticide.**

fetus. Pl. *fetuses.*

feudal, -atory, -atary, -atorial. The only important words are *feudal* and *feudatory,* the others being NEEDLESS VARIANTS. *Feudal* = of a feud or fief. *Feudatory* = feudally subject to, under overlordship (*COD*).

fewer; less. *Fewer* emphasizes number, and *less* emphasizes degree or quantity. *Fewer number* and *fewest number* are illogical tautologies, inasmuch as *fewer* means "of smaller number." E.g., "The *fewest number* [read *smallest number*] of people use the library between 4:30 and 7:00 p.m." [Or, better, read *The fewest people use the library between 4:30 and 7:00 p.m.*] See **less.**

fiat (= a judge's decree) means "let it be done" in Latin. The word in its broad, popular sense has come to connote arbitrariness: "I cannot pretend to the power by judicial *fiat* to affect property located in the Bahamas."/ "We agree with the Seventh Circuit that a ruling that the marketing of handguns constitutes an ultrahazardous activity would in practice drive manufacturers out of the business and would produce a handgun ban by judicial *fiat.*"

More technically, *fiat* also denotes in many Anglo-American jurisdictions any one of a number of decrees rendered by a court in pursuance of its jurisdiction. For example, in Texas practice, most motions must contain a *fiat* (to be filled in by the court) fixing the time for a hearing on the motion.

fiber is the AmE, *fibre* the BrE spelling. Frequently in asbestosis cases in the U.S., *fibre* appears instead of *fiber.* But the latter spelling is preferred in any context in the U.S.

fictional. See **fictitious.**

FICTIONS, LEGAL. These are assumptions that conceal, or presume to conceal, the fact that a rule of law has undergone alteration, its letter remaining unchanged, its operation being modified. Maine, *Ancient Law* 26 (5th ed. 1888). Colloquially, *legal fiction* = an untruth.

In jurisprudence a legal fiction denotes an uncontrovertible averment in an action. In the history of English law legal fictions have had three main functions. The first was to extend the jurisdiction of a court: such was the averment, used to give the Court of Exchequer jurisdiction, that the plaintiff was indebted to the Crown but was the less capable of discharging his debt by reason of the defendant's default to him (which was the true cause of action); or the averment that a contract in fact made abroad was made at the Royal Exchange in Cheapside—a decisive step towards the embodiment into the common law of the whole body of the law merchant. Secondly, legal fictions were designed to avoid cumbersome and archaic forms of action: thus, the fictitious lease, entry and ouster made the action of ejectment applicable to freeholds to the exclusion of the old real actions. Thirdly, fictions were used to extend the scope of a remedy: for example, the allegation that the defendant had found the plaintiff's chattel but refused to deliver it up made the superior remedy in trover not only supersede the action of detinue [q.v.] but also available for most claims in relation to chattels.

Simon, *English Idioms from the Law*, 76 Law Q.Rev. 283, 304 (1960).

To understand legal fictions we must understand the difference between what is said and what is actually meant: "The best way to talk clearly and precisely and to talk sense is to understand as fully as possible the relation between predication and suggestion, between 'saying' and 'meaning.'" Barfield, *Poetic Diction and Legal Fictions*, in *The Importance of Language* 51, 71 (M. Black ed. 1962).

fictitious; fictive; fictional. These forms are distinguishable. *Fictional* = of, pertaining to, or having the characteristics of fiction. This is the adjective to be used of LEGAL FICTIONS. E.g., "There are many instances in which equity has protected purely personal rights, though in some instances the courts have reached that result by finding *fictional* property rights—declaring things property rights that were in truth not of that character."/ "The use of these words in connection with legal relations is, strictly speaking, figurative or *fictional*."

Fictitious = (1) sham; or (2) imaginary. Here sense (1) is illustrated: "Government officials should be free to make decisions without fear or threat of vexatious or *fictitious* suits and alleged personal liability."/ "The ques-

tion is whether A, the acceptor of a bill of exchange, knew that the name of the payee was *fictitious*." (Eng.)/ "The aspect of the Abscam investigation leading to this bribe began in 1979 when an FBI agent took on the undercover role of one Tony DeVito, president of the *fictitious* Abdul Enterprises."

Sense (2) here obtains: "After describing a *fictitious* vehicle on each certificate, he then obtained titles and registrations from the state."/ "The ejectment action involved a *fictitious* party plaintiff."

In the following sentences, *fictitious* is used where *fictional* would be better: "That some rule of evidence or law could have been evolved by the court to require the court to hold by some *fictitious* [read *fictional*] or artificial reasoning that the testatrix did not know the contents of the will is repugnant, to say the least." (Eng.)/ "The decision of Sachs J. in the *Crerar* case will help the probate court to give effect to the wishes of other testators, and to avoid imputing to them a *fictitious* [read *fictional*] knowledge and approval of testamentary documents whose meaning they did not know and would not have approved." (Eng.)

Fictive = having the capacity of imaginative creation ⟨fictive talent⟩. Apart from this narrow sense, rarely of use in legal writing, *fictive* is used as a NEEDLESS VARIANT of both *fictional* and *fictitious*. E.g., "There has been some *fictive* [read *fictional*] talk to the effect that the reason why a nonresident can be subjected to a state's jurisdiction is that the nonresident has impliedly consented to be sued there." (Beginning and ending a sentence with the word *there* is to be avoided.)

fiduciary; fiducial. *Fiduciary*, as both noun and adjective, is the unvarying legal form of the word. *Fiducial*, used by historians and philosophers in certain contexts, has not found a home in the law.

fief. See **feoff.**

fieri facias (lit. "cause to be done") is a LATINISM that has given its name to a writ of execution of judgment. It is commonly abbreviated *fi.fa.*

Fifteen, the. This phrase refers to the Court of Session, in Scotland. E.g., "'The Fifteen' decided against the minister and awarded damages against him." A. McNair, *Dr Johnson and the Law* 54 (1948).

filt(e)rable. The preferred spelling is *filterable.*

final analysis, in the. See **in the final analysis.**

final destination. See **ultimate destination.**

finalize = (1) (v.t.) to complete; bring to an end; put in final form; or (2) (v.i.) to conclude. Originally an Australianism, *finalize* is a favorite word of jargonmongers. For that reason alone, and also because it is a NEOLOGISM that does not fill a gap in the language, it is to be avoided. E.g., "No decision of this court has squarely held that we have a capricious residual power to *finalize* [read *make final* or *bring to an end*] otherwise nonfinal appeals."/ "Westinghouse responded to the solicitation with a series of bids that were *finalized* [read *made final*] in a full proposal to Reynolds offering to manufacture the desired equipment for about $250,000." See -IZE.

final outcome; final result. These are common REDUNDANCIES, inasmuch as an *outcome* or *result*, as generally understood, is final. E.g., "We do not intimate what the *final result* [better: omit *final*] should be, but as for an alleged violation of the Voting Rights Act, we should not write until the court below shows that it considered all the evidence." Cf. **ultimate destination.**

FINAL PREPOSITION. See PREPOSITIONS (C).

final result. See **final outcome.**

financ(i)er. *Financer* = one who finances a particular undertaking or on a particular occasion. E.g., "Prior to 1972, commentators debated inconclusively over whether a 'true' consigner was required to notify a secured *financer* of the consignee's inventory whose agreement included an after-acquired property clause." *Financier* = one whose business it is to lend money.

finding; holding. A court properly has *findings of fact* and *holdings* or *conclusions of law.* The writer of the following sentence observed the distinction meticulously: "Because we

find that the jury's finding of concurrent fault is amply supported by the evidence, we *hold* that appellee is entitled to full indemnity."

In appellate courts, properly, only *holdings* are affirmed, whereas *factual findings* are disturbed only when clearly erroneous, against the great weight of the evidence, etc., depending on the standard of review. Generally, it is not correct for an appellate court to say that it *affirms* a finding of fact.

Nor should the verb *find* be used when the court rules on a point of law. E.g., "We *find* [read *hold*] that the trial court properly instructed the jury on the Louisiana law of strict liability of the custodian of a defective thing under La. Civil Code art. 2317." See JUDGMENTS, APPELLATE-COURT & **fact-finding.**

fin(e)able. See MUTE E.

finis = end; conclusion. This term should be used just as if one of the defining words were in its place: "But sometimes it denotes the judgment that writes *finis* [read *a finis*] to the entire litigation, after all appellate remedies have been either exhausted or, as here, abandoned." Sometimes *finis* is used to signal the end of a book; using it in this way has the sanction of long tradition.

finnicky is an inferior spelling of *finicky,* which is an inferior form of *finical.*

first and foremost is a CLICHÉ that should not be used merely for *first.* The *OED* describes it as a "strengthened" phrase and dates it from the sixteenth century.

first blush, at. See **at first blush** & **face, on its.**

first-come-first-served is correct; *first-come-first-serve* is the mistaken rendition that is commonly encountered.

first impression, case (or question) of is an English equivalent of the LATINISMS *res nova* and *res integra.* E.g., "With that principle in mind, we shall proceed to consider the appropriate scope of Section 501, a *question of first impression* in this circuit." See **res integra.**

first instance, in the, a CHAMELEON-HUED and often a FLOTSAM PHRASE, is "now used alternatively to *first, at first,* or *in the first place.* It comes from the sense of *instance* as a suit or process in a court of justice. . . . We still speak of a *court of first instance* [i.e., a trial court]." Simon, *English Idioms from the Law*, 76 Law Q.Rev. 429, 433 (1960). E.g., "It seemed to him undesirable that there should be conflicting decisions by judges of *first instance* [i.e., trial judges] on such a point."

Here the phrase is used for *in the first place:* "The purpose of that legal maxim *in the first instance* is the protection of minor children." We might classify *in the first instance* as a SET PHRASE, ruling out the variation here in evidence: "The trial court should have considered this overlooked but timely factual opposition in the *original instance* [read *first instance*]." See **instance.**

firstly, secondly, thirdly,   etc. are today considered inferior to *first, second, third*, etc. Many stylists prefer using *first* over *firstly* even where the remaining signposts are *secondly* and *thirdly*. See ENUMERATIONS (A).

first party.   See **party of the first part.**

FIRST PERSON.   As a general matter, it has been said that "the first person (*I, we, us*) is not usually used in legal writing because in an analysis of fact and law it seems best to have the emphasis on the facts and the law, and not on the analyzer." N. Brand & J. O. White, *Legal Writing: The Strategy of Persuasion* 123 (1976). This statement is true of DRAFTING and of BRIEF WRITING, but not always of OPINION WRITING. It is difficult to state in one fell swoop a rule applicable to all legal writing, being diverse as it is. Instead, a few specific topics are here addressed in turn.

   A. The Collegial *we* of Judges. The collegial *we* in which judges write their opinions is a useful stylistic device; but it sometimes traverses time with mind-boggling ease: "The court of appeals holding conflicts with *our* holdings in *Hendon v. Pugh*, 46 Tex. 211, 212 (1876) and *Faver v. Robinson*, 46 Tex. 204 (1876). In *Hendon, we* remanded a default judgment." *Uvalde Country Club v. Martin Linen Supply Co.*, 690 S.W.2d 884, 884 (Tex. 1985). It is questionable whether *we* really works when used by a modern court to overleap such a stretch of time; some less strained expression like *this court* might have been better in that sentence.

   B. Awkward Avoidance of First Person. *"The writer of this opinion* had supposed that this was to be at least inferred from what was

said in the opinion of *Lamb v. S. Cheney & Son.*" Such artifices as *this writer,* or the graceless variation just adduced, serve no real stylistic purposes, and in fact are inferior to the straightforward pronouns *I* and *me*, assuming the writing permits of an authorial injection of personality. Legal writing rarely allows such minor personal indulgences, except in correspondence or in judicial opinions in which a judge writes for himself alone. When the writer refers to himself, he may as well use the appropriate personal pronoun rather than some stilted periphrasis. But often a simple rewording makes use of the first person unnecessary.

   C. Approaching Autobiography. For a highly autobiographical and first-personish opinion, see *Paine & Williams v. Baldwin Rubber Co.*, 23 F. Supp. 485 (E.D. Mich. 1938) (per Tuttle, J.). This opinion on a patent question is larded with language such as, "I hold that . . . ," "I take the case as I would an ordinary patent case," and "It seems to me that. . . ." The capstone, however, is this passage, which I quote at length to convey the full flavor of the autobiographical style at its most personal and anecdotal.

> My experience began in the country and on the farm. I never laid the carpet directly in contact with the floor. The floor was a pretty rough one. Our loosely compacted base was straw or the old weekly newspapers. The usual thing was to put straw or paper under that carpet to protect it. The purposes were just the same as the purposes that this patent had in mind. It was yielding and would come back with a certain resilience, it made it warmer when the wind got under the house, it protected against the cold, made the temperature more uniform, was nicer to walk over, didn't wear out so quickly. I can't think of any of the things that would be in the Turner patent that were not right in that old carpet with the papers under it, unless it be the fabric, and I say that is not a material part of the claim. That, however, was in a way present. It was not uncommon to cover the floor with straw, place papers over the straw, and then stretch the carpet over the paper. The paper served as a fabric to hold the loose straw in place.
>
> *   *   *
>
> The carpets of our boyhood were not only flexible but they extended out beyond the margin of the fibrous substance which was underneath the carpet. No one ever carried the straw out to the edge of the carpet. We

always kept it back. We didn't want it sticking out with the whiskery effect described. No woman would want straw sticking out around her carpet.

Id. at 486–87.

fisc = the public treasury. The *OED* notes that the word is "now rare," but it is not uncommon in American legal writing. E.g., "[C]ases like this . . . cumulatively pose a negligible threat to the *national fisc.*" *Swietlik v. United States,* 779 F.2d 1306, 1313 (7th Cir. 1985) (Cudahy, J., dissenting)./ "But protection of the *fisc* does not motivate all 'impoundments'; the executive can also use that power to obstruct programs and policies with which he disagrees."/ "Any profits obtained by Ginnie Mae inure solely to the benefit of the federal *fisc.*" (N.B.: *Public fisc,* unlike *federal fisc,* is a REDUNDANCY.)

In Scots law, the word is spelled *fisk,* and it means specifically "the public treasury or 'Crown,' to which estates lapse by escheat" (*OED*).

fit ⟩ fitted ⟩ fitted. *Fit* is not correctly a past tense, though AmE wants to make it one. In the following examples it is used incorrectly: "The sections mentioned are really law review articles *fit* [read *fitted*] into a textbook."/ "An arrest on the basis of a stale description that could plainly have *fit* [read *fitted*] many people has been held invalid."/ "Justice O'Connor asked why the publisher did not ask the court to rule that his newsletter *fit* [read *fitted*] within the bona fide newspaper exemption to the act."/ "*Parratt v. Taylor fit* [read *fitted*] particularly well into this fourth situation." One sees the tendency to commit this error even in what is generally considered well-edited journalism: "Gordon Getty had never quite *fit* [read *fitted*] in at his father's oil company." Wall Street J., Dec. 20, 1985, at 1, col. 6.

Here the past tense is correctly used: "At the present time a barber so employed and paid by the defendant is occupying and nominally conducting the shop thus *fitted* and furnished by the defendant."/ "Consequently, unless there was a formal writ that exactly or nearly *fitted* the applicant's case, he generally had to take such inadequate relief as the inferior local courts offered, or go remediless."

fit and proper is a tiresome legalistic DOUBLET with no claim to being either a TERM OF ART or a melodious phrase. One should write either *fit* or *proper,* without yoking them together so predictably.

flagrancy, -ce. The latter is a NEEDLESS VARIANT.

flagrant. See **blatant.**

flagrante delicto. See **in flagrante delicto.**

flagrant necessity. See **blatant.**

flak (= criticism) is sometimes misspelled *flack,* which is the proper spelling of the term meaning "a press agent."

flammable; inflammable. The former is now accepted as standard. Though examples of its use date back to 1813, in recent years it has become widespread as a substitute for *inflammable,* in which some persons mistook the prefix *in-* to be negative rather than intensive. Traditionally, the forms were *inflammable* and *noninflammable*; today they are *flammable* and *nonflammable.* Purists have lost the fight to retain the older forms. See NEGATIVES (B) & NON-.

flaunt; flout. Confusion of these terms is distressingly common. *Flout* means "to contravene or disregard; to treat with contempt." *Flaunt* means "to show off or parade (something) in an ostentatious manner," but is often incorrectly used for *flout,* perhaps because it is misunderstood as a telescoped version of *flout* and *taunt.* E.g., "Significantly, that trip tends to show that some of these defendants have continued to *flaunt* [read *flout*] the law by their employment practices." Even the highest court in the United States has erred on this point: "Nor should those who *flaunt* [read *flout*] the rules escape unscathed." *Alderman v. United States,* 394 U.S. 165, 175 (1969).

Here *flaunt* is correctly used: "In February 1978, Bryant urged the Oklahoma legislature to pass the anti-advocacy statute to stop 'the *flaunting* of homosexuality' and to protect schoolchildren."/ "Words like 'reasonable,' 'substantial,' and 'satisfactory' *flaunt* their lack of precision." *Flout* correctly appears in these sentences: "The offenses did not involve any question of the *flouting* of military authority, the security of a military post, or the integrity of military property."/ "A man may not *flout* with impunity his obligation to provide necessaries to his dependent children."

One federal appellate judge who misused *flaunt* for *flout* in a published opinion, only to be *sic*'d and corrected by judges who later quoted him, appealed to *W3* and its editors, who, of course, accept as standard any usage that can be documented with any frequency at all. The judge then attempted to justify his error and pledged to persist in it. See W. Safire, *I Stand Corrected* 158–59 (1984). Seeking refuge in a nonprescriptive dictionary, however, merely ignores the all-important distinction between formal contexts, on the one hand, in which the strictest standards of usage must apply, and informal contexts, on the other, in which venial faults of grammar or usage may, if we are lucky, go unnoticed (or unmentioned). Judges' written opinions fall into the former category.

floes (= sheets of ice [fr. Norweg. *flo*, meaning "flat layer"]) should not be confused with *flows*: "Hovering over the ice *flows* [read *floes*], they looked for survivors amid the wreckage and debris."

flotsam; jetsam; lagan. Blackstone called these "the barbarous and uncouth appellations" for goods abandoned at sea. 2 Blackstone, *Commentaries* 292-93 (Tucker ed. 1803). *Flotsam* is goods that are cast into the sea and float on the surface of the water. *Jetsam* is goods thrown overboard that sink in the sea and remain under water. *Lagan* is goods sunk in the sea but attached to a buoy so that they may be found again. *Flotsan* and *ligan* are obsolete spellings of *flotsam* and *lagan*.

These terms have largely outlived their usefulness, except in metaphorical senses. *Flotsam and jetsam* is the CLICHÉ used figuratively to mean "miscellaneous unimportant materials; dispensable articles."

FLOTSAM PHRASES just take up space without adding to the meaning of a sentence. Thus there is usually no reason, where it is clear whose opinion is being expressed, to write *In my opinion* or *It seems to me that*. Other examples are *hereby, in terms of, on a . . . basis, my sense is that, in the first instance*, and *the fact that*. (Admittedly, some of these phrases may be useful in speech.) A favorite flotsam phrase of lawyers in their pleadings is *at all relevant times*: "At all relevant times, Burndy and Teledyne were competitors in the manufacture

and sale of split bolt connectors." We have enough written words without these mere space-fillers.

flounder; founder. Both verbs signal failure, but the literal senses, and therefore the images conveyed metaphorically, differ. To *flounder* is to struggle and plunge as if into mud. To *founder* is (of a ship) to fill with water and sink, (of a building) to fall down or give way, (of a horseback rider) to fall to the ground.

flout. See **flaunt.**

flowchart, v.t. The verbal use of this word is not recorded in the dictionaries, although it was perhaps inevitable, what with the verbal use of *chart*. W9 does record the gerund *flowcharting*. Following is an example of the verb: "To the extent that actual, historical vacancies in the employer's workforce can be *flowcharted* with reasonable accuracy, the court should award back pay to the minority employees who . . . would have occupied those vacancies but for discrimination." *United States v. U.S. Steel Corp.*, 520 F.2d 1043, 1055 (5th Cir. 1975).

flowed; flown. These words, surprisingly, are frequently confused. *Flowed* is the past tense and past participle of *flow*. *Flown* is the past participle of *fly*. See **overfly.**

flow from. In legal writing, few things *derive from, result from*, or are *caused by* other things; effects always seem to *flow from* causes. This is one of our most overworked legal CLICHÉS. E.g., "Our analysis necessarily *flows from Strickland v. Washington*."/ "To show antitrust injury, the plaintiff must establish that the injury to his business *flowed from* defendant's alleged monopolization of the retail truck market."/ "There is no injury in law resulting in damages except that which *flows from* an unlawful act."/ "We conclude that any fraud conferred on Borg-Warner no rights in addition to those *flowing from* its status as a holder of an unperfected security interest."

A related locution is *follow from*: "The complaint also states that Swift was substantially certain the Trupiano's injuries would *follow from* its intentional acts."/ "The trust doctrine purportedly *follows from* normative principles."

flown. See **flowed.**

fly in the face of is a legal CLICHÉ. E.g., "In the present case it *flies in the face of* common sense to say that there was a true consent to the marriage when the parties knew each other by sight for no more than minutes and when they have not even spent one whole day together as man and wife." (Eng.)

Fly in the teeth of is an inexcusable rending of the cliché. "[N]either court is required to accept, as credible, unsupported self-serving testimony that *flies in the teeth of* unimpeachable contradictory evidence and universal experience." *New England Merchants National Bank v. Rosenfield,* 679 F.2d 467, 473 (5th Cir. 1982). Cf. **face of, in the.**

F.O.B.; C.I.F. These abbreviations, which are short for *free on board* and *cost, insurance, and freight,* denote types of contracts for the international sale of goods, and now also sales involving domestic transportation. With a *C.I.F.* contract, the seller agrees not only to supply the goods but also to make a contract of carriage with a sea carrier, under which the goods will be delivered at the contract port of destination, and a contract of insurance with an insurer, to cover them while they are in transit (*CDL*). With an *F.O.B.* contract, the seller's duty is fulfilled by placing the goods aboard the carrier.

Domestically, the use of *F.O.B.* [*destination*] indicates that freight charges have been paid to transport the goods as far as the named destination, whatever it may be (e.g., seller's plant or buyer's dock).

focus, n. Pl. *foci.*

foist takes the preposition *on.* E.g., "It does not in fact impute moral turpitude to plaintiff in *foisting* an article of the characteristics described by defendant *upon* [read *on*] the public." *Foist off on* is awkward and prolix: "Defendant has been shown to have *foisted* bogus companies *off on* [read *on*] the public." The *OED* quotes Charlotte Brontë as having written *foist off on,* but calls the phrase "rare."

follow from. See **flow from.**

following (= after), when used to begin a sentence or clause, often results in a MISPLACED MODIFIER. "*Following* [read *After*] a bench trial, the district court voided portions of the plaintiff's settlement agreement."/ "*Following* [read *After*] a bench trial on the issue of liability, the district court held that the lessees and operators of the Galveston Bridge were 80% at fault." The problem, of course, is that the reader might expect something like "Following these precedents, we affirm."

foment is incorrect as a noun for *fomentation.* "There is a lot of *foment* [read *fomentation*] going on around the Israeli border." (It seems likely, however, that the writer confused *ferment* [= agitation] with *foment* [= to incite or rouse]).

footnote; endnote. Technically, *footnotes* appear at the foot of the page, and *endnotes* at the end of an article or chapter or at the end of a book. But *endnotes* are often called *footnotes.*

FOR-, FORE-. These prefixes, it will be observed in many of the entries following, have caused a great deal of confusion. One can usually arrive at the correct prefix for any given word by remembering that *for-* means either "completely" or "against," and that *fore-* means "before."

fora. See **forum.**

for. See **as** (A).

for all intents and purposes; to all intents and purposes. Both forms are used. E.g., "The legacy should pass to the heirs, devisees, distributees, etc. of such devisee or legatee, in like manner, *to all intents and purposes,* in law and in equity, as if such devisee or legatee had survived the testator and had then died intestate."/ "On these facts the Seventh Circuit held that the district court erred in referring the case to a magistrate without the consent of the parties because the hearing before the magistrate was, *for all intents and purposes,* a civil trial." Often this collocation qualifies as a FLOTSAM PHRASE.

forbade. See **forbid.**

forbear and *forebear* are not cognate, though they are confused in every conceivable way. *Forbear* is the verb meaning "to refrain from objecting to; to tolerate." The verb is inflected *forbear* ⟩ *forbore* ⟩ *forborne.* E.g.,

"The plaintiff alleged that she *forbore* to sing for him, though engaged, whereby she lost great profits." (Eng.)

Forebear, the noun, means "ancestor" (usually used in the plural). *Forebearer* is an incorrect form of this noun. *Forbear* is occasionally misused for *forebear:* "We approach the study of history not merely in a spirit of piety to our *forbears* [read *forebears*] but our purpose will be to scan the panorama with a certain discernment."

Forebearance is not a word; the term is *forbearance.* "The actual amount of money of which the borrower has use, detention, or *forebearance* [read *forbearance*] is held to be the true principal of the loan in testing for usury."

forbid ⟩ forbade ⟩ forbidden. *Forbid* takes the preposition *to* or, informally, *from.* Fowler stated that *forbid from doing* is unidiomatic, and strict standards of usage do not allow it.

The preterite *forbade* (rhyming with *glad*) is illustrated here: "The plaintiff neither *forbade* nor encouraged its employees to join the union." *Forbid* is sometimes wrongly used as a past-tense form: "The Texas statute, in the teeth of the prohibitions referred to, *forbid* [read *forbade*] Negroes to take part in a primary election."

FORBIDDEN WORDS. Blanket prohibitions are rarely valid, but they are useful in establishing rules to be flouted only in the rarest instances. It would hardly be an exaggeration to say that no sentence, and no document, would suffer from the absence of these terms. Herewith, then, a short index expurgatorius:

A. Generally Useless Words: *ad idem; aforementioned; aforesaid; beforementioned; hopefully; instanter; interface; inter se; irregardless; ore tenus; parameters; quoad; said* (for *the,* etc.)*; same,* n. (for *it,* etc.)*; simpliciter; ss.; such* (for *the, that,* etc.)*; to wit; vel non; whatsoever; whensoever; wheresoever; whosoever; -wise* (*taxwise,* etc.).

B. Ignorant Malformations: *ideialogy* for *ideology; miniscule* for *minuscule.*

force and arms, with, is a LOAN TRANSLATION of *vi et armis,* q.v.

force and effect is a DOUBLET that has become part of the legal idiom in the phrases *in full force and effect* and *of no force or effect,* neither of which is a TERM OF ART. Either synonym would suffice just as well as the doublet; but the emphasis gained by *force and effect* may justify use of the phrase, more likely in DRAFTING (contracts and statutes) than in OPINION WRITING.

force majeure; force majesture. Literally "a superior force," *force majeure* is the usual form of this LEGALISM denoting an event or effect that can be neither anticipated nor controlled. *Force majeure* is the LAW FRENCH equivalent of the Latin *vis major,* q.v. *Force majesture* is a NEEDLESS VARIANT.

forcible; forceable; forceful. Oddly, we have *forcible* but *enforceable,* q.v. *Forcible* is the usual and preferred form; the word means "effected by force against resistance." E.g., "Piracy is defined as robbery or *forcible* depredation on the high seas."/ "In an action for *forcible* abduction of children, the father is entitled to damages for the injury done to his feelings."

The spelling *forceable* at one point seemed entrenched in the phrase *forceable entry and detainer* in Texas, although the Texas Rules have now changed to the spelling *forcible. Forceable* frequently appears where *forcible* should: "The jury found that Flynn *forceably* [read *forcibly*] dispossessed plaintiff of his dinner plate." See -ABLE (A).

Forcible, which properly refers only to physical force, has frequently been misused for *forceful,* which may be used figuratively as well as literally: "The intention of the parties is *forcibly* [read *forcefully*] expressed in the agreement."/ "Counsel may state the facts as *forcibly* [read *forcefully*] as possible, but he must not enlarge them."/ "This case *forcibly* [read *forcefully*] points out the anomaly brought about by the Rule in Shelley's Case."

FORE-. See FOR-, FORE-.

forebear. See **forbear.**

forecast. See **broadcast.**

foreclose (a person) *from* (an action) is an archaic construction still used in the law: "The rule against double recovery *forecloses* the wife *from* recovering for the loss of her husband's financial support." Today *foreclose* most commonly takes as an object one or more possibilities or choices ⟨his failure of the exam forecloses the possibility of a promotion).

Forclose is an erroneous form of *foreclose.* "If there is only one beneficiary, against whom there is a defense, this [*sic*] obviously *forcloses* [read *forecloses*] the action."

foregather. See **forgather.**

forego; forgo. The former, as suggested by the prefix, means "to go before." The latter is the term meaning "to do without; to pass up voluntarily; waive; renounce." One of the most persistent errors in legal and other writing is the use of *forego* where *forgo* is intended. One court has actually construed *forego* as meaning "voluntarily relinquishing," misspelling the very word it was interpreting! See *O'Neill v. Keegan,* 376 Pa. 606, 103 A.2d 909, 911 (1954).

Examples of the misuse, which are legion, follow: "Several observations with reference to the foregoing case are noteworthy. First, in the original transaction the plaintiffs were willing to *forego* [read *forgo*] the profit-making opportunity which the rock asphalt in place presented."/ "The burden that the defendant would incur to avoid the risk is itself a function of not only the cost to him, but also the broader social utility of the conduct that he would have to *forego* [read *forgo*]."/ "Unless a state permits an interlocutory appeal, a defendant faces *foregoing* [read *forgoing*] his appeal as to jurisdiction and defending on the merits."

The mistake is all around us. In the early 1980s, the President's Commission for the Study of Ethical Problems in Medicine and Biomedical and Behavioral Research issued a report entitled *Deciding to Forego* [*sic*] *Life-Sustaining Treatment.*

Forwent and *forewent* are the preterite forms, and *forgone* and *foregone* (q.v.) the past participial forms. The past participle *forgone* is more frequent in practice than *forwent*; yet, because legal writing is usually formal in tone, *forwent* is not as uncommon as in general practice. E.g., "Defendants admitted at trial that vestiges of de jure segregation still exist; hence the trial court *forwent* development of liability at trial, and concentrated solely on remedies."/ "If a university promised its faculty that it would provide professors two opportunities to challenge decisions to terminate their employment and a professor who relied on that promise *forwent* the first opportunity to raise his challenge, the university could not deprive him of the second opportunity

without violating due process." See **foregone.**

foregoing is occasionally mistaken for *following.* "Although the *foregoing quote* [read *following quotation*] is a long one, it succinctly states the entire problem with this regulation: [a long quotation follows, and none precedes this statement]." (Note also the unconscious irony in a *long* quotation that *succinctly* states a proposition!)

foregone is correct in *foregone conclusion,* but not here: "A guilty plea is the supreme instance of waiver known to our system of justice, one by which all of its trial rights and safeguards are voluntarily *foregone* [read *forgone*] and the defendant deliberately submits to conviction." See **forego.**

forehead rhymes with *horrid.*

foreign. In law, this word means "of another jurisdiction," not necessarily "of another country." Thus it is not uncommon for a court in Florida, say, to refer to a judgment of a New Mexico court as a *foreign judgment.* Exceptions occur, however, so one must read carefully. Here *foreign* in the layman's sense: "Courts of equity have, as between the parties, reviewed the judgments of *foreign* courts; a specific performance of a contract of sale of land situated in a *foreign* country will be decreed in equity."

forejudge is an equivalent of *prejudge* for which the *OED* includes only one citation more recent than the eighteenth century, and that from 1860. This twentieth-century example indicates that the writer was striving for a novel turn of phrase: "No man may be *forejudged* of life or limb, or subjected to any kind of punishment by martial law, or in any other manner than by the judgment of his peers according to the known and established laws."

foreman, -person. See SEXISM (B).

forensic = used in or suitable to courts of law or public debate. E.g., "It is the duty of the king, as parens patriae, to protect property devoted to charitable uses; and that duty is executed by the officer who represents the crown for all *forensic* purposes." (Eng.)/ "Where Parliament has used in nontechnical legislation words that, in their ordinary meaning, cover the situation before the court, it is a reasonable presumption that Parliament or its draftsmen envisaged the actual *forensic* situation." (Eng.)

Other senses have grown out of the primary one. For example, the adj. *forensic* has come to mean "rhetorical" or "argumentative" in certain contexts, the language or manner to which it refers being analogized to courtroom talk. Traditionally *forensics* = the art of argumentative discourse. Today *forensics*, as a shortening of *forensic ballistics*, is used by police officers to refer to the section of law enforcement dealing with legal evidence relating to firearms.

foreperson. See SEXISM (B).

foresake. See **forsake.**

foreseeable is occasionally misspelled *forseeable.*

forfeiture is naturally pronounced /**for**-*fi*-chūr/; pompous speakers are fond of pronouncing the final syllable /*tyoor*/.

forgather; foregather. The former is preferable, inasmuch as either might be said to be "preferable." *Gather* usually suffices.

forgo. See **forego.**

formalism; formality. These words are quite distinct. *Formality* = conformity to rules; propriety; precision of manners. *Formalism* = excessive adherence to prescribed forms; use of forms without regard to inner significance (*COD*). E.g., "To read the Sixth Amendment as forever codifying a feature so incidental to the real purpose of the amendment is to ascribe a blind *formalism* to the Framers that would require considerably more evidence than we have been able to discover in the history and language of the Constitution."/ "Many of these differentiations of the various types of future interests are historical hangovers from the rigid, inflexible *formalism* of the medieval land law."

FORMAL WORDS are those constituting an elevated level of diction. The English language has a number of levels of diction, and even synonyms that exist on different levels. Thus *his honor* is formal, *the judge* is the ordi-

nary phrase, and *the beak* (BrE slang) is vulgar. The language of the law is perhaps topheavy with formal words, as the courts are one of the institutions in Western societies that are most fully bedecked with pomp and regalia. The language used in law reflects that formality, often quite appropriately; but many lawyers (and especially laymen talking to lawyers, it seems) go overboard, resorting to unnatural pomposities (e.g., *this honorable court* used repeatedly) where ordinary words (*the court*) are called for. Following is a list of formal words that occur frequently in legal contexts, with their ordinary equivalents in a parallel list.

Formal Word	Ordinary Word
annex	attach
announce	give out
append	attach
approximately	about
assign	give
cease	stop
commence	begin
complete	finish
conceal	hide
deem	consider
demise	death
desist	stop, leave off
detain	hold
determine	end
donate	give
effectuate	carry out
emoluments	pay
employ	use
endeavor	try
evince	show
expedite	hasten
expend	spend
expiration, expiry	end
extend	give
forthwith	immediately, soon
imbibe	drink
inaugurate	begin
indicate	state, show, say
initiate	begin
inquire	ask
institute	begin
interrogate	question
intimate	suggest
necessitate	require
occasion, v.t.	cause
peruse	read
portion	part
possess	have
present	give
preserve	keep

prior	earlier
proceed	go (ahead)
purchase	buy
remainder	rest
request	ask
retain	keep
remove	take away
suborn	bribe (a juror or witness)
summon	send for, call
terminate, v.i. & v.t.	end
utilize	use
within or without	inside or outside

forma pauperis. See **in forma pauperis.**

former and *latter* can apply only to a series of two. The *former* is the first of two, the *latter* the second of two. In contexts in which more than two elements occur, *first* should be used rather than *former*, *last* or *last-mentioned* rather than *latter*. E.g., "Cities Service sued Lee-Vac and American Hoist. The *latter* [read *last two*] cross-claimed against each other."

These latter is not an impossibility if the second of the two elements is plural, e.g.: "This case was brought at the instance of the F.D.A. in the name of the United States against the individuals named as defendants, praying that *these latter* be restrained from introducing into interstate commerce certain misbranded drugs."

Confusion between the two terms is common. It may perhaps result from the Latin or Romance terminology, which is precisely opposite to ours. Here the wrong term of reference is used: "To the foregoing must be added certain constructional biases developed in a hierarchical fashion and predicated upon the proposition that the law abhors a forfeiture. Thus, if the choice is between a condition subsequent and a restrictive covenant, the *former* [read *latter*] is preferred." (The well known rule that the law abhors a forfeiture leads one to prefer a restrictive covenant over a condition subsequent. Hence the writer of the sentence just quoted stated the opposite of what he intended by confusing *former* and *latter*.)

Former and *latter* can bewilder the reader when the elements referred to are numbers. E.g., "The second rationale is distinguished from the first because with the *latter*, both parties are aware of the special circumstances under which the contract was made." The latter here syntactically is "the first," but the context in which this sentence appeared made it clear that the writer meant to say the second rationale; that is, he used *latter* in a temporal rather than in a syntactic sense.

May one have a *latter* without a *former*? Strictly speaking, not any more than one can have an *other hand* without a *one hand*, even if only implicitly. Formerly, it was not uncommon to use *latter* without a correlative. E.g., "In view of what has already been said, very little may suffice concerning a liability as such. The *latter*, as we have seen, is the correlative of power, and the opposite of immunity (or exemption)." (Hohfeld) Latterly, however, this use of the term is uncommon.

former jeopardy. See **double jeopardy.**

formula. Pl. *-as, -ae.* The English plural, ending in *-s*, is preferred in all but technical writing. Legal writers are somehow fond of the Latinate ending. E.g., "Such duality of purpose was represented by a valuation according to statutory *formulae* [read *formulas*]." (Eng.)/ "The early chancellors developed the habit of expressing legal principles in the manner and form of their ecclesiastical background—short and concise *formulae* [read *formulas*]." See PLURALS (A).

fornicate; copulate. Virginia Code § 18.2-344 provides that "[a]ny person, not being married, who voluntarily shall have sexual intercourse with any other person, shall be guilty of *fornication,* punishable as a Class 4 misdemeanor." *Copulate* is a more neutral verb referring to the sexual act without regard to legality or the legal status of the parties.

fornication. See **adultery.**

forsake 〉 forsook 〉 forsaken. *Forsake* is sometimes corrupted into *foresake.*

forseeable. See **foreseeable.**

for sure is colloquial for *certain* or *certainly.*

forswear; foreswear. The latter does not properly exist. If it did, it might mean "to swear before," since previousness is the signification of its prefix. *Forswear* is the proper synonym of *renounce* or *abrogate.* Cf. **forego; forgo.**

forswearing. See **perjury.**

forte (= a person's strong point) is best pronounced with one syllable, like *fort.* But many English-speaking people persist in the two-syllable version, /*for-tay*/, which can hardly be strongly condemned.

for the duration of is verbose for *during.*

for the reason that is prolix for *because.*

forthwith, adv., is a usefully vague term, although it may strike some as slightly antiquarian. The writer who intends a precise meaning must beware. "Three centuries ago, a distinction was made between an order to plead *instanter* ('the same day') and an order to plead *forthwith* ('such convenient time after as the court shall judge reasonable; . . . without delay')." D. Mellinkoff, *The Language of the Law* 311 (1963). In fact, *forthwith* has been attributed every shade of meaning from that just recited to "instantly." It is a fuzzy word with no pretense of precision.
     Forthwith makes no sense as an adjective, as in the phrase *a forthwith subpoena.*

fortuitous (= occurring by chance) is commonly misused for *fortunate.* Here the correct use of the term is illustrated: "Contrary to defendants' argument, the occasional *fortuitous* inclusion of a tenant in the resolution of a claim between the housing authority and the landlord affords no protection to a tenant."/ "Whether that result would follow in any other case is entirely *fortuitous,* and it may be that such a result was not intended." See **aleatory & gratuitous.**
     Fortuity is the seldom-seen nominal form of *fortuitous.* E.g., "An open venire of this last type has, or may not have, the same element of *fortuity,* of course, as a closed venire." *Fortuitousness,* which emphasizes the *quality* as opposed to the *state* of being fortuitous, is also used.

forum. The preferred plural is *forums,* not *fora.* E.g., "Public *fora* [read *forums*] generally are those places which by long tradition or by government fiat have been devoted to assembly and debate." *ACORN v. City of Phoenix,* 798 F.2d 1260, 1264 (9th Cir. 1986)./ "Without the funds obtained from solicitation in various *fora* [read *forums*], the soliciting organization's continuing ability to communicate ideas and goals may be jeopardized." See PLURALS (A).

forum non conveniens = the doctrine that an inconvenient forum, even though proper under the law, may be divested of jurisdiction if, for the convenience of the litigants and the witnesses, it appears that the action should be instituted in another forum in which the action might originally have been brought. This LATINISM has become a TERM OF ART. E.g., "The common-law *forum non conveniens,* with its stress on contacts and fairness, unhampered by a mythology of power and sovereignty, may yet create a new American law of jurisdiction based on the *forum conveniens.*"

forward(s). See **-ward(s).**

forwent. See **forego.**

founder. See **flounder.**

four corners of the instrument = the face of a legal document. The phrase is common in legal ARGOT, esp. when it is argued that the court should not consider evidence extraneous to the legal document in question. E.g., "The district judge construed the lease within its *four corners.*"/ "Viewing the testimonial record from its *four corners,* we find ourselves unable to say that the invested equity of the one tenant adds up to a greater amount than that of the other."
     Sometimes the phrase is used figuratively of things other than single documents: "In the resulting amalgam it is not possible to distinguish which notes and coins belong to the trust fund and which do not; all that can be said is that the trust fund is somewhere within the *four corners* of the account." (Eng.) (An *account* does not have four corners, although perhaps *account records* was intended.)

fours, on all. See **on all fours.**

fractious. See **factional.**

fram(e)able. The *-e-* is best omitted. See MUTE E.

framers in AmE is capitalized only in reference to the drafters of the U.S. Constitution. In all other contexts in which this word refers to legislative drafters, the word is lowercased.

franchise, n., has two quite distinct senses: (1) "the right to vote"; (2) "the sole right of engaging in a certain business or in a business with a particular trademark in a certain area."

franchise, v.t.; enfranchise; affranchise. *Enfranchise* = (1) to set free, release from bondage; (2) to give to a person or class of persons the right to vote; (3) to give to an area or class of persons the right to be represented in an elected body (*CDL*); or (4) to endow with a franchise. *Affranchise* is a NEEDLESS VARIANT. See **disfranchise.**

  Franchise = to grant (to another) the sole right of engaging in a certain business or in a business with a particular trademark in a certain area. See **franchise, n.**

franchiser, -or. *Franchiser* is preferred. The *OED* and *W3* contain only the *-er* form; the *OED Supp.* lists *-or* as a variant.

frankalmoi(g)n(e); almoi(g)n. This obsolete form of English land tenure is generally spelled *frankalmoign* in modern texts.

fraud. **A.** *Fraud in fact & fraud in the factum.* These terms refer to two very different principles. *Fraud in fact* is what is also known as *actual* or *positive fraud*, that is, a concealment or false representation by means of a statement or conduct that causes injury to another. Scienter (q.v.) is usu. required. *Fraud in the factum* occurs when a legal instrument (a "factum" at common law) as actually executed differs from the one intended for execution by the person who executes it, or when the instrument may have had no legal existence (as, e.g., because the substance of the document was misrepresented to a blind signator). See **fact; factum.**

  B. *Fraud in law & legal fraud.* These phrases are deceptively similar. *Fraud in law* is fraud that is presumed under the circumstances, as, for example, when a debtor transfers his assets and thereby impairs the efforts of his creditors to collect sums due. *Legal fraud* is another term for *constructive fraud,* q.v., or unintentional deception that causes injury to another. Because *legal fraud* is potentially ambiguous, *constructive fraud* is the better phrase. See **actual fraud & constructive fraud.**

fray. See **affray.**

freedom. See **liberty.**

freehold has been defined in two quite different ways. Most recently, the *CDL* has defined it as "the most complete form of ownership in land: a legal estate held in fee simple absolute in possession." The *OED*, and other modern authorities, define *freehold* as "a tenure by which an estate is held in fee simple, fee-tail, or for term of life." The *CDL*'s definition is unduly restrictive, for a life estate is held in freehold.

free from; free of. Both are correct, the former being preferred by most writers on style. E.g., "He is *free from* contributory negligence, but he must be content to take what the law gives him."/ "The right to be *free of* [read *free from*] state-occasioned damage to a person's bodily integrity is protected by the fourteenth amendment guaranty of due process."/ "The deed is *free of* [read *free from*] ambiguity."/ "Not only has the Supreme Court never said the press could lie about public figures and be *free of* [read *free from*] legal responsibility, it has said just the opposite."/ "We are satisfied that, when considered contextually, the court's instruction on reasonable doubt was *free of* [read *free from*] constitutional error."

  Note the shift in nominal forms: *freedom of speech* but *freedom from oppression, pestilence, coercion,* etc.

freight refers to goods transported by water as well as by land, although until recently in BrE it referred only to goods shipped by water.

fresh pursuit; hot pursuit. The former is the traditional legal phrase, dated from 1626 in the *OED*, meaning "the common-law right of a police officer chasing a felon to cross state lines to arrest him." It is often used, however, in extended senses: "There is no doubt that during continuance of war a rebel guilty of treason may be slain in actual conflict or *fresh pursuit.*" (Ir.) *Hot pursuit,* first used in the 1920s, is an equivalent term that is better known among laymen.

friend of the court. See **amicus curiae.**

from hence; from thence. The words *hence* and *thence* (as well as *whence*) are sufficient without the preposition *from*, and are preferred singly; yet grammarians have not considered *from hence*, etc., incorrect. *Hence* includes the idea of "from," inasmuch as it means "from this time, from this place." Boswell, not best known for his achievements in law, used *from thence*: "Mr. Scott of University College, Oxford ... accompanied [Johnson] *from thence* to Edinburgh." 5 *Life of Johnson* 16 (1791). See **thence** & **whence**.

from henceforth is redundant for *henceforth*, as in: "The will of the giver, according to the form in the deed of gift manifestly expressed *shall be from henceforth observed* [read *shall be observed henceforth*]." See **from hence**.

from whence. See **from hence, thence** & **whence**.

frontal attack. This late nineteenth-century expression has become common in legal ARGOT to denote a direct attack on a judgment, statute, etc. "This appeal makes the *frontal attack* that the court erred in not instructing a verdict in the bailor's favor for the total loss of the airplane."/ "Our statute does not make a *frontal attack* on the pre-existing law."

fruit(s). One writes of the *fruits of one's labor* and *fruits of a crime*, but of the *fruit of the poisonous tree* (from criminal investigation). Occasionally the entire catchword appears: "Because the illegally seized evidence provided the sole basis for the homicide arrest warrant and led directly to incriminating statements on that day, the warrant and statements are also inadmissible as *fruit of the poisonous tree*."

More often, however, the idiom is paraphrased or foreshortened, and *fruit* is generally plural: "The district court committed no error when it refused to suppress the *fruits* of the recorded conversations."/ "Because the amendment now affords protection against the uninvited ear, oral statements, if illegally overheard, and their *fruits* are also subject to suppression."

FUDGE-WORDS are common in mediocre and poor legal writing; they occur seldom in clean, precise prose. The typical phrases are *it would seem to appear that, it is suggested that*, and *it is submitted that*. E.g., "*It would appear to be clear that the Pioneer Society was* [read either *The Pioneer Society was* or *It is clear that the Pioneer Society was*] organized by a group of people who were brought together by their common

interest in the history and historical relics of Los Angeles County and the State." Cf. WEASEL WORDS.

fugitive. Only in formal writing does this word mean, in its adjectival sense, "evanescent, fleeting." E.g., "It is no answer to say that complainant spends its money for that which is too *fugitive* or evanescent to be the subject of property."/ "It is further argued that that for which the Associated Press spends its money is too *fugitive* to be recognized as property." An even more learned equivalent is *fugacious*.

fulfil(l)ment is spelled -*ll*- in AmE, -*l*- in BrE.

full-blown is often used unnecessarily. "The collective knowledge of the investigating officers amounted to probable cause for a *full-blown* arrest of appellant." An officer can either arrest or not arrest someone. *Full-blown* adds nothing.

This phrase is fast becoming a CLICHÉ in legal writing. E.g., "All final orders in *full-blown* commission licensing proceedings would be reviewed initially by the court of appeals."/ "The officers stopped short of a technical arrest or a *full-blown* search."

full-scale should be hyphenated. "A *full scale* [read *full-scale*] criminal investigation was initiated in September 1970 and indictments against eight alleged co-conspirators were returned in January 1971."

fulsome (= abundant to excess; offensive to normal tastes or sensibilities) is often incorrectly taken to mean "very full." Here, for example, *fulsomely* is used for *fully*: "The expectation that one who enters the 'public, political arena' must be prepared to take a certain amount of 'political bumping' is already *fulsomely* [read *fully*] assured by the *New York Times Co. v. Sullivan* requirement of actual malice in the defamation of public figures." Surely the state appellate judge who wrote that sentence did not mean to impugn the U.S. Supreme Court.

functus officio is a LATINISM meaning literally "a task performed," and meaning in practice "having fulfilled its purpose or discharged its duties, an officer or body is of no further use or authority." It serves the purposes of conciseness but not of lucidity. E.g., "If the laws passed are seen to have a reasonable relation to a proper legislative purpose, and are neither arbitrary nor discriminatory, the requirements of due process are satisfied, and judicial determination to that effect renders a court *functus officio.*"/ "An offer, considered as a series of physical and mental operative facts, has spent its force and become *functus officio* as soon as such series has been completed by the offeree's receipt."

fundament = (1) basis; or (2) anus or buttocks. This word can hardly be used without creating a double-entendre. "That policy has remained the *fundament* [read *foundation*] of federal appellate jurisdiction."

funeral; funereal; funerary; funebrial. *Funeral,* commonly a noun, serves as its own adjective ⟨funeral expenses⟩. *Funereal,* which is frequently confused with *funeral,* adj., means "solemn, mournful, somber." *Funerary* = of, used for, or connected with burial. *Funebrial* is a NEEDLESS VARIANT of *funereal.* Fowler wrote that "no one uses [*funerary* or *funebrial*] if he can help it" (*MEU1* 205).

further. See **farther.**

FUSED PARTICIPLES. A. The General Rule. Fowler gave the name "fused participle" to a participle used as a noun (i.e., a gerund) that is preceded by a noun or pronoun not in the possessive case. Thus *Me going home made her sad* rather than the preferred *My going home made her sad.* The fused participle is said to lack a proper grammatical relationship to the preceding noun or pronoun. No one today doubts that Fowler overstated his case in calling fused participles "grammatically indefensible" and in never admitting an exception. The grammarians Jespersen and Curme have cited any number of historical examples, and have illustrated the absolute necessity of the fused participle 'in some sentences, barring some recasting' of the sentence. E.g., *The chance of that ever happening is slight.*

But Fowler had a stylistic if not a grammatical point. Especially in formal prose, the possessive ought to be used whenever it is not unidiomatic or unnatural. In the following sentences, then, possessives would have been better used than the nouns in the objective case: "Abolition of the distinction would result in *manufacturers being* [read *manufacturers'*

being] liable for damages of unknown and unlimited scope."/ "In the second place, the danger of the *courts reaching* [read *courts' reaching*] an inequitable conclusion by refusing to modify the results of applying the legal incidents of joint tenancy to the partnership relation is done away with."/ "This is a divorce case in which the only remaining question concerns the propriety of the *trial court granting* [read *trial court's granting*] the wife a fractional interest in future military retirement benefits if and when [q.v.] received by the husband."/ "He told the jury that the really important issue was whether the plaintiff had consented to the *journalist publishing* [read *journalist's publishing*] the information about her and her former husband."/ "The plaintiffs are the freeholders of the locus in quo, and as such they have the right to forbid *anybody coming* [read *anybody's coming*] on their land or in any way interfering with it."/ "Arrest in retaliation to civil proceedings is privileged only by *one having* [read *one's having*] a warrant."/ "The extensive civil-service structure Congress had constructed militated against the *court extending* [read *court's extending*] constitutional tort liability to federal employees."/ "A question arose as to *appellant being* [read *appellant's being*] entitled to a longer notice of discontinuance." (Eng)/ "The district court accepted the prosecutor's representation that it did not believe the additional charge would result in *Krezdorn receiving* [read *Krezdorn's receiving*] a sentence greater than the one initially imposed."/ "When an uncopyrighted combination of words is published, there is no general right to forbid other *people repeating* [read *people's repeating*] them." (Eng.)/ "There is a difference in probability between *one* [read *one's*] intentionally depositing and unintentionally forgetting and the hole-in-the-pocket man."/ "The problem of *lawyers saying* [read *lawyers' saying*] too much is discussed in Chapter XIV."/ "In consideration of *appellant having* [read *appellant's having*] prevented him from sustaining death, McGowin agreed with him to care for and maintain him."/ "It is elementary that the propriety of a *court instructing* [read *court's instructing*] a verdict in favor of a party must depend on the evidence introduced before the jury."/ "The jury could find that through constant wear the terrazzo slab had over a period of time become smooth, resulting in *it being* [read *its being*] very slippery when wet."

There are many exceptions to this rule of style, however. The *Oxford Guide* states: "When using most non-personal nouns (e.g. *luggage, meaning, permission*), groups of nouns (e.g. *father and mother, surface area*), non-personal pronouns (e.g. *anything, something*), and groups of pronouns (e.g. *some of them*), there is no choice of construction: the possessive would not sound idiomatic at all." *Oxford Guide* 156 (1983). Examples follow: "An attempt to create a passive trust in this country usually results in the legal *title passing* to the trust beneficiary."/ "The judgment does not result in the *property being* attached to the locus."/ "Upon the proper *facts being shown,* the attachment may be sued out against lands, tenements, goods, and credits of the debtor."/ "There can therefore be no question about the claim here being ripe for presentation to the United States Courts."/ "The remainder is subject to being divested on the contingency of *one of the children of Ross Kost dying* before the life tenant and leaving lawful children."/ "In 1908 Roscoe Pound decried decision-making from first principles and warned against the *law becoming* too scientific."/ "The ability to watch a *decision being* made on the most elemental level is of some significance."/ "The undisputed evidence precludes the possibility of *speed being* a proximate cause of this collision."

B. Unnecessary Participles. Even when there is no choice in the idiom, there is the choice of reconstructing the sentence to avoid the questionable usage. Sometimes it is even possible merely to omit the participle, as here: "Often such an accident results from something *being* [delete *being*] in the road ahead of the preceding car."

C. No Fused Participle. Adjectival participles sometimes appear on first sight to be fused participles, but they are not. E.g., "A donee beneficiary's rights vest automatically upon the working of the contract, *knowledge* of the beneficiary *being* unnecessary."/ "This appeal arises from an *order* of the Santa Fe County District Court *granting* the motion of defendant State of New Mexico to dismiss on the ground that the action was barred by the doctrine of sovereign immunity."

FUSTIAN (lit. a kind of cotton cloth) has given its name to pompous, empty speech and writing, or highfalutin words for ordinary ideas. The following sentence, for example, might be placed in virtually any judicial opinion on any subject: "The case presents questions of far-reaching importance which demand and have received mature and deliberate consideration by the court." We should take all that for granted. See FLOTSAM PHRASES.

future, in (the). See **in future.**

G

GAAP. See **generally accepted accounting principles.**

gainsay; contradict. Originally *gainsay* was the popular word, and *contradict* the learned one; today just the opposite is true. *Gainsay* may now appropriately be labeled a FORMAL WORD. E.g., "Judge Cire was in the unique position of being able to judge the credibility of what he saw and heard firsthand, and he should not be *gainsaid* [i.e., contradicted]."/ "The eminent position of the familial right to privacy in our jurisprudence cannot now be *gainsaid* [i.e., denied]."

GALLICISMS appear frequently in English prose, and no less frequently in legal than in nonlegal writing. By Gallicisms is not generally meant the LAW FRENCH terminology that is so prevalent in law (e.g., *voir dire, de son tort*), but French terms and phrases of a nonlegal character. E.g., "It was not an abuse of the district judge's discretion and, under the circumstances, it was a proper exercise of his duty to conduct the trial process economically and efficiently and to administer the *coup de grace* to what he found to be a hopeless case." We have in general use such Gallicisms as *tour de force, succès d'estime, cul-de-sac, blasé, tête-à-tête,* and *joie de vivre.* None of these is unduly recherché, to use yet another. But foreignisms of any kind become affectations when used in place of a perfectly good English term, e.g., *peu à peu* for *little by little,* or *sans,* q.v., for *without.*

gaming; gambling. The former is the law's genteel variant of the latter. "[S]tate officialdom, when hoping to sound professional and clinical, uses the term *gaming* as having an ameliorative sense. By contrast, . . . *gambling* has a pejorative connotation." Clark, *Gaming and/or Gambling: You Pays Your Money,* 10 Verbatim 20 (Spring 1984).

gantlet; gauntlet. Although the latter is more common in most senses, the former is still preferred in one of them. One runs the *gantlet* (= a kind of ordeal or punishment) but throws down the *gauntlet* (= a glove). The trend is to use *gauntlet* for *gantlet*; like many trends, it is worth resisting. *Gauntlet* is correctly used here: "Jurists are free to state their personal views in a variety of forums, but the opinions of this court are not proper occasions to throw down *gauntlets* to the Supreme Court."

gaol; gaoler. These are variant BrE spellings of *jail* and *jailer*. The terms are pronounced the same regardless of spelling.

garden-variety, adj., = of the ordinary or familiar kind. This phrase is becoming a garden-variety CLICHÉ in legal prose. E.g., "Because *Eichelberger* was nothing more, nor less, than a *garden-variety* divorce case, one would normally have thought that the litigation had ended when the court of civil appeals overruled Mr. Eichelberger's motion for rehearing."

garnish; garnishee, v.t. In American legal writing, the usual verb form is *garnish* (= to take property, usu. a portion of someone's salary, by legal authority). *Garnishee* is usually reserved for the nominal sense ("a person or institution, such as a bank, that is indebted to or is bailee for another whose property has been subjected to garnishment"). The noun corresponding to *garnish* is *garnishment*.

In G.B., however, and in a few American jurisdictions, *garnishee* as well as *garnish* is used as a verb: "As it was composed entirely of money that did not belong to Smith, it could not be *garnisheed* by his creditor and this was sufficient to dispose of the case." (Eng.) The *OED* gives passing notice to *garnishee* as a verb and its corresponding noun *garnisheement*; the main entries are under *garnish* and *garnishment*.

garnisher, -or. *Garnisher* is preferred; it is the only spelling listed in *W3* and the prevalent spelling in legal texts.

gases, not *gasses*, is the plural form of the noun *gas*; nevertheless, for the verb *to gas*, *gassed* is the accepted past tense and *gasses* is the third-person singular form. Cf. **bus.**

gauntlet. See **gantlet.**

gender has long been used as a grammatical distinction of a word according to the sex referred to. It has newly been established in the language of the law in phrases such as *gender-based discrimination*, a use disapproved as jargonistic by some authorities. What this adds to *sex discrimination*, aside from eight letters and one hyphen, we can only guess.

Here, the better usage is illustrated: "In the court's view, the ordinance creates a conflict between first-amendment free speech guaranties and the fourteenth-amendment right to be free from *sex-based* discrimination." See **sex.**

general consensus. See **consensus.**

generalized (= made general) for *general*. "Some courts, refusing to find in the rather *generalized* [read *general*] language of the usual statute a legislative intent to abolish the concept of marital unity, have sought to adapt the incidents of ownership by the entirety to the principle that neither spouse has rights or powers superior to those of the other." The sentence does not intend to convey that the language was *made general* (by the legislature, presumably), but that it *is general*. Cf. **particularized.**

generally has three basic meanings: (1) "disregarding insignificant exceptions" ⟨the level of advocacy in this court is generally very high⟩; (2) "in many ways" ⟨he was the most generally qualified applicant⟩; (3) "usually" ⟨he generally left the office at five o'clock⟩. Sense (3) is least good in formal writing, although at times it merges with sense (1).

generally accepted accounting principles; generally accepted accountancy principles. The former is the usual phrase in the U.S., the latter in G.B. *Accountancy* is, however, used in the U.S. in other phrases and contexts. The phrases are often abbreviated *GAAP*.

generative; generational. The distinction is clear: *generative* = procreative; *generational* = pertaining to generations. "The degree of kinship between a decedent and a claimant was reckoned by taking the number of *generative* [read *generational*] steps between them or by adding the numbers of such steps between both of them and their nearest common ancestor."

generic(al)ness; genericism. *Genericness*, though odd-looking, is now the most widely used noun corresponding to *generic*, adj. It is recorded from 1939 in the *OED Supp.*, and appears most commonly in reference to trademarks. E.g., "Rovira's affirmative defense of *genericness* was not barred by the federal rules." *Keebler Co. v. Rovira Biscuit Corp.*, 624 F.2d 366, 374 n.7 (1st Cir. 1980)./ "Foreign words are translated into English and then tested for descriptiveness or *genericness*, by seeing whether that foreign word would be descriptive of the product to that segment of the purchasing public which is familiar with that language." Despite its specialized currency, *genericness* retains an unEnglish appearance. Cf. **prolificness.**

Genericalness is listed in the the *OED* and *W2*; it does not, like *genericness*, flout principles of English word formation, and might be preferred on that ground. It is omitted from *W3*, which labels the adj. *generical* archaic.

Genericism has also appeared. E.g., "There remain two defenses that licensees might make: descriptiveness and *genericism.*" Treece, *Licensee Estoppel in Trademark Cases*, 58 Trademark Rep. 728, 738 (1968). Labeled rare in the *OED*, *genericism* is perhaps the most realistic alternative to oust *genericness*.

GENITIVES. See POSSESSIVES.

genius (= the prevailing character or spirit; characteristic method or procedure) is often used in reference to law. E.g., "A federal cause of action 'brought at any distance of time' would be 'utterly repugnant to the *genius* of our laws.'" *Wilson v. Garcia*, 471 U.S. 261, 271 (1985) (quoting *Adams v. Woods*, 6 U.S. (2 Cranch) 336, 342 (1805)). The pl. *geniuses* is preferred over *genii*.

gentleman should not be used indiscriminately as a genteelism for *man*, the generic term. *Gentleman* should be reserved for reference to a cultured, refined man.

GERUNDS. The legal writer's prejudice against nouns in *-ing* is unfounded. When it comes to CUTTING OUT THE CHAFF, one effective way of reducing prolixity is to use gerunds directly; thus *adjudicating that case was difficult* rather than *the adjudication of that case was difficult*; *presenting the arguments* rather than *the presentation of the arguments*, etc.

Gestalt (= a shape, configuration, or structure that, as an object of perception, forms a specific whole or unity incapable of expression simply in terms of its parts), a VOGUE WORD, is usually capitalized. E.g., "Virtually all fact-finding was subjectively based, depending ultimately on intuition and emotion, 'hunching' in *Gestalt*-like response to the situation."

get > got > got, gotten. In formal writing, *got* is the better past participle; *gotten* is by far the more frequent form in AmE, however.

gibe; jibe. *Gibe* is both noun and verb. Nominally, it means "a caustic remark or taunt." *Jibe* is a verb only, meaning "to make things fit, uniform, or consistent."

gift, it may be surprising to learn, has acted as a verb since the sixteenth century. E.g., "All the property was *gifted* property [i.e., it took the form of gifts]." Though this usage is old, it is not now standard. English has the uncanny ability, however, to transform nouns into verbs, and to revive moribund usages. Twenty years ago *contact* was objected to as a verb, though it had been used that way since the early nineteenth century; few writers now feel uncomfortable using the word as a verb. See NOUNS AS VERBS.

Gift may soon be in the same class—still, cautious writers may prefer to use it only as a noun if the verb causes discomfort, as it well may: "The stock may not be *gifted*, pledged, or hypothecated without the board's approval." One is accustomed to thinking of *gifted children*, but not of *gifted stock*.

gift over. See **over.**

gipsy. See **gypsy.**

gist began as a legal term meaning "the real ground or point (of an action, indictment, etc.)" (*OED*), and has since passed into non-legal parlance. Yet it is still (perhaps unwittingly) used in the legal sense: "The *gist* of the libel is that certain articles called lubricators are not good articles." See POPULARIZED LEGAL TECHNICALITIES. Cf. **gravamen.**

give evidence = to testify. "The defendant *gave evidence* that he was elsewhere at the time of the alleged sale and did not make it." *Dunn v. United States*, 284 U.S. 390, 392 (1932) (per Holmes, J.).

global (= embracing a number of items or categories) is used commonly in American and British legal writing. E.g., "The wife's net income has to be calculated so as to ascertain the sum that is deemed to be the husband's by section 18 and must be added to his income similarly quantified; from this *global* sum must be deducted all that is allowable as allowances personal to him." (Eng.)/ "Plaintiff made *global* objections to the jury charge."

gloss, originally "a word inserted between the lines or in the margin as an explanatory equivalent of a foreign or otherwise difficult word in the text" (*OED*), is used in extended senses in legal contexts. E.g., "The function of chancery was to supply the deficiencies of the common law; thus equity was, in the words of Maitland, 'a *gloss* on the common law.'" (Eng.)

In its most extended sense, *gloss* is used as a COLLECTIVE NOUN equivalent to "pronouncements (usu. by a court)." E.g., "The act and its judicial *gloss* also provide the manner for distributing the recovery, if any, obtained from a third party [several cases interpreting the act are mentioned]." This sense is analogous to the nonlegal sense "a collection of explanations, glossary," and is not really exceptionable.

GOBBLEDYGOOK is the obscurantist language characteristic of jargon-mongering bureaucrats. Thus *iterative naturalistic inquiry methodology* = a series of interviews. Much legal writing is open to the criticism of being gobbledygook. One of the goals of this book is to wage a battle against it. See LEGALESE, LATINISMS, JARGON & OBSCURITY.

"The besetting sin of jurists," writes a well-known English authority, "is to conceal threadbare thoughts in elaborate and difficult language. In spite of the difficulties inherent in the subject, the problems of jurisprudence can be expressed in fairly simple language." G. W. Paton, *A Textbook of Jurisprudence* 1–2 (4th ed. 1972).

goes without saying, it, is not suitable for formal contexts, although it may be appropriate in speech or in informal prose. If it goes without saying, then it need not be said.

good, n. See **goods**.

good cause shown is one of the few standard legal expressions that are neither prolix nor inaccessible to laymen. E.g., "A writ of sequestration may be quashed or dissolved for *good cause shown.*"

good(-)faith. *Good faith* is the noun phrase ⟨in good faith⟩, *good-faith* the adjectival phrase ⟨good-faith efforts⟩. See **bona fide(s).**

goods has a variety of senses, two of which are here relevant. In the legal sense, *goods* refers to chattels or personalty. In the economic sense, however, it often refers to things that have value, whether tangible or not. For example: "The meaning and value of all *goods* (money, power, love, and so forth) are socially created and vary from one society to the next. Social *goods* do not include privately valued goods, such as sunsets or mountain air." (From a review of M. Walzer's *Spheres of Justice* (1983).)

In the sense "tangible or movable pieces of property," *goods* has traditionally appeared only in the plural form. In recent years, however, *good* has developed the sense "a tangible or movable piece of property." Though still considered unidiomatic by those with sensitive ears, this usage has made such inroads that it is unlikely to be stopped: "The buyer-seller relationship between the shipowner and *the supplier of a good* [better usage requires *a supplier of goods*, even if there is only one kind of goods] simply does not give rise to a duty on the shipowner's part not to act in such a manner as to cause an injured third party to sue the supplier as a possible defendant liable for the injuries."

goodwill. Formerly two words, then hyphenated, the term has now become one word.

goose case is legal slang for what in legal ARGOT is termed *a case on all fours*. E.g., "While there is no *goose case* in this circuit, Instruction 31 of the Fifth Circuit Pattern Jury Instructions informs our judgment." See **white-horse case.**

got, p.pl.; **gotten.** See **get.**

go to the issue of. This legal idiom is frequently shortened to *go to*, as here: "Cooper's argument that Gordon was unable to identify him in court at a distance of a few feet *goes to* her credibility concerning the extent of his involvement in the marijuana transaction."

governance. Fowler pronounced *governance* an ARCHAISM for which either *government* or *control* suffices, allowing it only in "rhetorical or solemn contexts." Yet this noun is frequently used in law to refer to running or governing a corporation. E.g., "The court emphasized that a proceeding in bankruptcy court does not address the same issues of corporate *governance* that the Delaware statute was intended to cover."

Governance does not mean "the quality of a jurisdiction's law that governs in a particular case." E.g., "While California has a significant interest *in the governance of* [read *in having its law govern*] these relationships, Texas has few, if any."

governmental; government, adj. When we have an adjective (*governmental*) to do the job, we need not resort to a noun (*government*) to do the work of the adjective. Though the trend today is to write *government agency*, the stylist writes *governmental agency*. These are the niceties of writing that make the reader's task a little easier, and that distinguish between formal and ordinary prose. Following are a few examples of the better usage: "If a *governmental* institution is to be fair, one group cannot always be expected to win."/ "The City of Akron has not attempted to allocate *governmental* power on the basis of any general principle."/ "The decision whether a public facility shall be operated in compliance with the Constitution is an essential *governmental* decision."

GOVERNMENTAL FORMS. The English language abounds in words to denote almost every conceivable form of government, usually ending in either of the suffixes *-cracy* and *-archy*, e.g., *clerisocracy* (= government by priests or scholars), *democracy* (= government by the people), *dyarchy* (= government by two rulers), *gerontocracy* (= rule by elders), *gynecocracy* (= rule by women), *monocracy* (= rule by a single person), *polyarchy* (= government by many persons), *plutocracy* (= government by the wealthy), *technocracy* (= government by technicians). We have hundreds of similar terms, some very arcane and others

more familiar, too numerous for inclusion here. See **jurocracy.**

gownsman (= one who wears a gown as an indication of his office or profession) was formerly used in G.B. of judges and barristers, but is now more likely to be used in reference to academics.

GRAMMAR. The very word is considered anathema by many persons, even those with an advanced education, not so much because it is boring (which it can be) as because it seems intimidating. Often this intimidation causes scoffers to dismiss grammar as an unimportant, trifling pursuit. To be sure, there are more important things in life, but the significance of good grammar should not be underestimated, especially by those engaged in a learned profession.

The courts have frequently addressed the subject with good sense. For example, the Supreme Court of Florida has stated: "The legislature is presumed to know the meaning of words and rules of grammar, and the only way that a court is advised of the legislature's intention is by giving the generally accepted construction, not only to phraseology of an act, but to the manner in which it is punctuated." *Florida State Racing Commission v. Bourquardez,* 42 So. 2d 87, 88 (Fla. 1949).

Courts give more leeway to laymen, but still take a commonsense approach. In examining wills, e.g., courts will forgive every error this book is designed to prevent: "When it becomes necessary to do so in order to effectuate the testator's intention as ascertained from the context of the will, the court may disregard clerical mistakes in writing, improper use of capital letters, paragraphing, abbreviation of words, punctuation, misspelling and grammatical inaccuracies, especially where the will is written by a layman who is unlearned, illiterate, or unskilled. In order to ascertain and give effect to the testator's intent, the court may disregard rules of grammar and verbal niceties, but unless a different construction is required, the ordinary rules of punctuation, capitalization, and grammar should be adhered to in construing a will." 95 C.J.S. *Wills* § 612 (1957).

Likewise with contracts: "[T]he use of inapt words or bad English . . . will not affect the validity of the agreement, although it may affect its construction." 17 C.J.S. *Contracts* § 57 (1963). And affidavits: "Where the meaning substantially appears, ordinarily errors or mistakes on the part of the draftsman in the body of [an] affidavit will be overlooked, and mere grammatical errors . . . will not vitiate the effectiveness of the instrument." 2A C.J.S. *Affidavits* § 43 (1972).

The same is true even in pleading: "Bad grammar does not vitiate a declaration, nor do other faults of style have that effect, unless they produce such a degree of obscurity as to give rise to the belief that the tribunal before whom the cause is heard might be misled as to the true issue." 41 Am. Jur. *Pleading* § 28 (1942).

Nevertheless, this book seeks to guide legal writers around these pitfalls in the belief that, even if a document's enforceability will not be marred by such lapses, the court's confidence in its reliability may well be adversely affected. Grammar is not, however, to be followed slavishly without regard for what is effective and what is idiomatic. "Wherever by small grammatical negligences the energy of an idea can be condensed, or a word stands for a sentence, I hold grammatical rigor in contempt." Thomas Jefferson, Letter to Madison, 12 Nov. 1801, in 8 *Writings of Thomas Jefferson* 108–09 (1897).

GRAMMATICAL AMBIGUITY. See AMBIGUITY.

grammaticality is to *grammar* as *constitutionality* is to *constitution.*

grandfather clause = a clause in the constitutions of some Southern American states that exempted from suffrage restrictions the descendants of men who voted before the Civil War. The *OED Supp.* wrongly labels this phrase colloquial; it is the only available name for these statutes, and it appears in dignified contexts. E.g., "The framers of Alabama's new constitution in 1901 went about the task of establishing white supremacy by adopting several constitutional provisions limiting the people who could qualify to vote. For example, a man could register if he or his ancestors had served honorably in the United States or Confederate armed forces (the *grandfather clause*)." Moreover, it has extended senses, referring to any statutory or regulatory clause exempting a class of persons or transactions because of circumstances existing before the clause takes effect.

This phrase has given rise to the verb *to grandfather* = to cover (a person) with the benefits of a grandfather clause. E.g., "Beginning in 1972, several States passed statutes permitting such acquisitions in limited circumstances or for specialized purposes. For example, Iowa passed a *grandfathering* statute which had the effect of permitting the only out-of-state bank holding company owning an Iowa bank to maintain and expand its in-state banking activities. . . ." *Northeast Bancorp, Inc. v. Federal Reserve System,* 472 U.S. 159, 163 (1985). To be *grandfathered* is to have the advantage of a grandfather clause ⟨get yourself grandfathered by establishing priority in an interest⟩.

gratify has been used in legal writing synonymously with *satisfy* in reference to rules or requirements. Neither the *OED* nor *W3* records this use. E.g., "This averment does not *gratify* the rule requiring certainty in pleading."/ "Not only the language of the statute but also the fundamental purposes can be *gratified* only by a definite decree of the court that adjudicates the illegality of the practice in the past and enjoins the defendant from repetition thereof in the future."

gratuitous; fortuitous. These two words are occasionally confounded. *Gratuitous* = done or performed without obligation to do so ⟨gratuitous promises⟩; done unnecessarily ⟨gratuitous criticisms⟩. *Fortuitous* = occurring by chance ⟨fortuitous circumstances⟩. See **fortuitous.**

gravamen = the point of a grievance or complaint. E.g., "Under the fourth and fifth complaints, the *gravamen* of the charge was that he had failed to preserve for a period of twelve months from the date of delivery the invoices relating to those and certain other goods." (Eng.)/ "The *gravamen* of plaintiffs' claim is that Apopka has intentionally maintained a racially and geographically segregated system of municipal services."/ "The *gravamen* of the complaint in this case, to quote exactly, is as follows."/ "Here, of course, there is no final order—indeed, the lack of a final order is the very *gravamen* of the petitioner's complaint."

Gravamen is used also of criminal accusations ⟨gravamen of the charge⟩, but not, properly, of crimes: "The gravamen of the crime [read *The gist of the crime*] is that the accused has used a fictitious credit card." See **gist.**

Today, nine out of ten times when this

word appears, it is in the phrase *gravamen of the complaint*; inasmuch as *gravamen* in itself means "the material part of a complaint," the phrase seems redundant. The *OED* quotes no sentences containing *the gravamen of the complaint*, although it quotes several containing *the gravamen of the charge*. Perhaps it is felt in modern prose that the phrase *of the complaint* elucidates the meaning of *gravamen*; if so, the word is recondite on its own and infelicitously redundant in the common phrase.

Gravamen is frequently misused for *crux* or *gist*, which are broader terms: "The *gravamen* [read *crux*] of appellant's argument is that he is entitled to have this 'dead time' credited against his federal sentence."/ "The *gravamen* [read *gist*] of the relief sought is the reformation or cancellation of records."/ "The *gravamen* [read *gist*] of the medical opinion in support of petitioners' position is that Rumbaugh is not able to countenance the delay inherent in the continuation of legal proceedings and the possible conversion of his death sentence to life imprisonment."

Gravaman is a common misspelling of *gravamen*. The plural forms are *gravamens* and *gravamina*, the former being preferred. The word is properly pronounced /grǎ-**vay**-měn/.

gray; grey. The former spelling is more common in AmE, the latter in BrE; both are old, and neither is incorrect.

gray mule case. See **whitehorse case.**

grievant; grievancer. The former term is commonly used in AmE in the context of arbitration. *W3* defines *grievant* as "one who submits a grievance for arbitration." E.g., "[An arbitrator's] job is to define the relief that will compensate the *grievant* if his claim is upheld." *Hotel and Restaurant Employees v. Michelson's Food Services, Inc.*, 545 F.2d 1248, 1254 (9th Cir. 1976). In practice, *grievant* often refers more narrowly to an employee who registers a complaint with an employer. Seide, *A Dictionary of Arbitration* 106 (1970). E.g., "Thomas Rogers and Robert Wilson, Jr. (*grievants*) were employed by General Services Administration. . . ." *Cornelius v. Nutt*, 472 U.S. 648, 652 (1985).

The *OED* lists *grievancer* (= one who occasions a grievance or gives ground for complaint) but not *grievant*, which is omitted also from the *OED Supp.* Thus *grievant*, a relative NEOLOGISM that *W9* traces back only to 1958,

has not yet spread beyond American legal writing. It is indisputably a useful term even if one might originally have objected to its formation.

grievous is frequently misspelled *grievious*, just as *mischievous* is frequently misspelled *mischievious*. These are grievous and mischievous malformations.

gross. See **in gross.**

ground of action is an infrequent variant of *cause of action*, q.v. "As *a child of such tender age* [read *a child so young*] was incapable of performing acts of service, the *ground of action* failed."

ground(s). Although one does not count as one ground or two grounds every argument one can muster, it is acceptable to speak of a party's relying on a certain *ground* (= reason). Yet even if he has only one reason for his position, he can take that position *on grounds of* whatever that reason is. The singular often appears in legal writing: "Filburn refused to pay *on the ground* that the Act was unconstitutional in that it attempted to regulate purely local production and consumption."

grounds for appeal; grounds of appeal. Either is correct: "The only *grounds of appeal* are (1) that the judge erred in law in not withdrawing the claim under section 43 from the jury; and (2) that he misdirected the jury as to the defendants' plea of justification." *Grounds for appeal* is perhaps more common.

ground(s) that, on (the). See **ground(s).**

groundwater. One word.

guarantee. A. And *warranty*. Originally the same word, *warranty* and *guarantee* (or *-ty*) arrived in the language through different medieval French dialects. *Guarantee* is the broader term, ordinarily meaning either (1) "the act of giving a security; the undertaking with respect to (a contract, performance of a legal act, etc.) that it shall be duly carried out," or (2) "something given or existing as security, e.g., for fulfillment of an engagement or condition" (*OED*). *Warranty*, as a legal term, has slightly more specific and elaborate senses: (1) "a covenant (either express or implied) annexed to a conveyance of realty by which the seller warrants the security of the title conveyed"; (2) "an assurance, express or implied, given by the seller of goods, that he will be answerable for their possession of some quality attributed to them" ⟨the seller hereby disclaims all warranties⟩; or (3) "in a contract for insurance, an engagement by the insured that certain statements are true or that certain conditions shall be fulfilled" (*OED*).

B. And *guaranty*. The distinction in BrE once was that the former is the verb, the latter the noun. Yet *guarantee* is now commonly used as both n. & v.t. in both AmE and BrE. Following are examples of the nominal use: "Negro citizens, North and South, who saw in the Thirteenth Amendment a promise of freedom would be left with a mere paper *guarantee* if Congress were powerless to ensure that a dollar in the hands of a Negro will purchase the same thing as a dollar in the hands of a white man."/ "Without the exclusionary rule the constitutional *guarantee* against unreasonable searches and seizures would be a mere 'form of words.' "

In practice, *guarantee*, n., is the usual term, seen often, for example, in the context of consumer warranties or other assurances of quality or performance. *Guaranty*, in contrast, is now used primarily in financial and banking contexts in the sense "a promise to answer for the debt of another." *Guaranty* is now rarely seen in nonlegal writing, whether in G.B. or in the U.S. Some legal writers prefer *guaranty* in all nominal senses.

Guaranty was formerly used as a verb, but is now obsolete as a variant of *guarantee*, v.t. E.g., "[C]ertain rights are . . . *guarantied* by the constitutional provision protecting persons against being deprived of life, liberty, or property, without due process of law." *Mugler v. Kansas*, 123 U.S. 623, 660 (1887). Here it appears in its more modern legal use as a noun: "Footnote 10 indicates that Congress is without power to undercut the equal-protection *guaranty* of racial equality in the guise of implementing the Fourteenth Amendment."

C. And *guarantor*. Both *guarantee* (fr. 1679) and *guarantor* (fr. 1853) have filled the role of agent noun for the verb *to guarantee*. These words have shared the sense "one who makes a guaranty or gives a security," but today *guarantor* has taken the field, rendering *guarantee* in this sense but a NEEDLESS VARIANT. Oddly, *guarantee* has been used not only as an equivalent of *guarantor*, but also as a passive

correlative of it consistently with other forms in -EE. Thus the *OED* quotes the following specimen of *guarantee* (= a person to whom a guarantee is given): "Guarantors are relieved by the *guarantee* being compelled, if one is ready to pay the whole, to sell him the debt of the others." This use of *guarantee* may be useful in tandem with -*or*, but the actual occurrences of it in legal prose are rare.

guardian ad litem. See **next friend.**

guilt; culpability. The latter is a matter of fact regardless of whether it ever becomes known; the former what is determined by the jury. See **guilty.**

guilt-prone (opposed to *acquittal-prone*) is coming to be used of juries in the sense "likely to convict." E.g., "Appellant contends that the process of excluding from the guilt phase of the trial prospective jurors who are unwilling to consider imposing capital punishment resulted in a jury that was impermissibly *guilt-prone* and unrepresentative of the community."

A variant is *conviction-prone:* "The argument assumes that if the prosecution strikes minority-group members on the basis of their group affiliation, then majority-group members inevitably must be likely to be as *conviction-prone* as the minority-group members are *acquittal-prone.*" Cf. **death-qualified jurors.**

guilty is almost always confined to criminal contexts, although occasionally it surfaces in civil ones. E.g., "The plaintiff was *guilty* of contributory negligence." [Better: *The plaintiff was contributorily negligent.*] See **blameworthy.**

gypsy; gipsy. The former spelling is preferred in AmE, the latter in BrE.

H

habeas is often used in AmE as an abbreviated form of *habeas corpus*, as in the common phrase *habeas relief.* E.g., "This pro se appeal concerns Timothy Rudolph's second federal *habeas* petition."/ "In 1982, we affirmed the dismissal of a prior petition for federal *habeas* relief." See the following entry.

habeas corpus (lit., "you may have the body") is the quintessential justified LATINISM that has taken on a peculiar meaning that no homegrown English term could now supply.

habendum (L. "to be possessed") denotes the part of a deed that defines the estate or interest being transferred. E.g., "The clause beginning 'to have and to hold' is the habendum and tenendum combined, and is generally called the *habendum*" (quoted in *OED*).

habitability; inhabitability. Because of confusion over the prefix *in-*, which is intensive and not negative in *inhabitability* (as in *inflammable*), today the positive form is *habitability*, the negative form *uninhabitability*. *Inhabitable* is little used today, and it is unfortunately ambiguous now when it *is* used.

had and received. This DOUBLET has historically been a TERM OF ART in the phrase *money had and received*; in pleading in assumpsit, the plaintiff declares that the defendant *had and received* certain money. In most Anglo-American jurisdictions the phrase is no longer required in pleadings.

haec verba, in. See **in haec verba.**

hairbrained. See **harebrained.**

hale into court; haul into court. The former phrase is now standard in the legal idiom. E.g., "As in the district court, Perry directs two independent constitutional attacks upon the conduct of the state in *haling him into court* on the felony charge after he took an appeal from the misdemeanor conviction."

halt. *Halting* = limping. "Progress is slow and halting." The writer of this sentence probably meant "limping along," but the sentence gives the impression of "coming to a halt."

halve (= to separate into two equal portions) is pronounced like *have.*

hand down a decision; hand out a decision. The former is the American, the latter the traditional British legal idiom, as H. L. Mencken observed in *The American Language* 246 (4th ed. 1960). Following is an example of the American phrase: "It is not extravagant to argue that *Ex parte Young* is one of the three most important decisions the Supreme Court of the United States has ever *handed down*." The BrE idiom *hand out* is seldom if ever used today.

handful. Pl. *handfuls.*

hanged; hung. Coats and pictures are *hung,* and sometimes even juries. But criminals found guilty of capital offenses are *hanged*— at least in some jurisdictions. See **hung jury.**

happily means "fortunately," not "in a happy manner," when used as in the sentence following: "*Happily,* in this appeal we find ourselves comfortably in the core of the categories where the damages are most remote." See SENTENCE ADVERBS.

harass may be pronounced in either of two ways: /*har*-iss/ or /huh-*ras*/. The former is often thought to be preferable, as with *harassment* /*har*-is-měnt/, but the latter is more common. The verb is often misspelled *harrass*. See, e.g., *Suss v. Schammel,* 375 N.W.2d 252, 256 (Iowa 1985).

hard and fast rule. This CLICHÉ is common, and sometimes useful, in legal prose. E.g., "There is no *hard and fast rule* by which it can be determined when the court will interfere by injunction to prevent what is practically a fraud upon a person engaged in business by the unfair methods of competition."/ "We have expressly rejected the suggestion that we adopt a *hard and fast* time limit for a permissible *Terry* stop." Cf. the cousin of this phrase, **bright-line rule.**

harebrained is the correct form; *hairbrained* is the common blunder. The misspelling falls just short of being what it attempts to denote. A prosecutor is quoted in *People v. Jolly,* 214 N.W.2d 849, 851 (Mich. App. 1974), as having stated to the jury: "This was no *hairbrained* young kid." The court reporter should have written *harebrained.*

hark back is now preferred over *harken back* or *hearken back*. E.g., "We do not *hark back* to Latin bywords without sanction of our highest court."

haul. See **hale.**

havoc, v.i., forms *havocking* and *havocked.*

he/she. See **he or she** & SEXISM (A).

healthful; healthy. *Healthy* is used of a person in good health, *healthful* of whatever promotes good health.

hearken back. See **hark back.**

hearsay evidence; secondhand evidence. The former is the preferred, universally understood term for evidence of the oral statements of someone other than the witness testifying and statements in documents offered to prove the truth of the matter asserted.

Hearsay is sometimes made *heresay,* an appalling error committed infrequently by inexperienced legal secretaries. Heaven forbid that lawyers should perpetrate it. To do so would be heresy. See **direct evidence.**

heart-rending is sometimes malapropistically rendered *heart-rendering.* E.g., "The true ground of action is the outrage and deprivation; the injury the father sustains in the loss of his child; the *heart-rendering* [read *heart-rending*] agony he must suffer in the destruction of his dearest hopes." The verb *rend* (= to split, tear) has nothing to do with the verb *render.* See MALAPROPISMS.

hear ye, hear ye, hear ye; oyez, oyez, oyez. Both forms of the cry are used today in American courts. The first is archaic English, the second vestigial LAW FRENCH with the same meaning. See **oyez.**

hedonic damages measure the taking away of the pleasure of being alive. Such damages are not allowed in most jurisdictions. "An Illinois jury has awarded *hedonic damages.*" National Law Journal, Nov. 26, 1984 at 3, col. 1.

hegemony /hi-*jem*-ŏ-nee/ is a fundamentally political term ("political dominance; the leadership or predominant authority of one state of a confederacy or union over the others") that has been imported into nonpolitical contexts. E.g.,"The court's duty is to protect the public from the activities of those who, because of the lack of professional skills, may cause injury; this does not mean, however, that attorneys' *hegemony* over the practice of law must be absolute."/ "With the passing of

the *hegemony* of historical jurisprudence at the close of the last century there came a revival of comparative law." (R. Pound)

height has a distinct -t- sound at the end; to pronounce this word as if it were *heighth* is semiliterate.

heinous rhymes with "pain us." This is one of the most commonly mispronounced words in legal contexts.

heir. A. *Heir (at law); (in)heritor.* These terms denote "the person entitled by statute to the land of an intestate." *Heir* is the most common term; *inheritor,* often used in extended senses ⟨inheritors of the Western tradition⟩, predominates over *heritor.* Following are specimens of the use of *heir*: "A person's *heirs,* within the primary meaning of that term, cannot be ascertained until his death."/ "The rule operates to defeat intent, but there is frequently a preliminary construction problem to determine whether the language of the creating instrument uses the term *heirs* in a restricted meaning (children, issue, etc.)."/ "In *Cahill v. Cahill,* the devise was to the testator's nephew and upon the death of the nephew 'said described property to become the property of his heirs of blood'; by Illinois law the widow, under certain conditions, and adopted children are *heirs.*"

Legal heir (= the heir of an intestate by operation of law) is another way of rendering *heir at law*: "There is nothing in the will or in the record that sustains a conclusion that she made the bequest because she wanted to make certain her *legal heirs* would not share in the estate." Still another variant synonymous with *heir at law* is *heir general.* Usually, *heir* alone is sufficient.

B. Types of Heirs: *expectant heir; prospective heir; heir apparent; heir presumptive.* A living person has no heirs, but various terms have been devised to describe potential heirs. An *expectant heir* is one who has a reversionary or remainder interest in property, or a chance of succeeding to it. E.g., "Even the *expectant heir,* who has no interest at all, may make a valid and specifically enforceable contract to convey for an adequate consideration."

A *prospective heir* is one who may inherit but may be excluded; this term embraces the two other types of heirs, *presumptive* and *apparent.* An *heir presumptive* is a person who will inherit if the potential intestate dies immediately, but who may be excluded if other more closely related heirs are born. An *heir apparent* is certain to inherit unless he is excluded by a valid will.

On the placement of the adjectives in these phrases, see POSTPOSITIVE ADJECTIVES. Sometimes the adjectives are used prepositively: "With the exception of the trustee, all the parties as thus represented—including contingent remaindermen and the *presumptive heirs*—joined in a petition to the court to consider and approve the proposed compromise of the litigation."

C. *Heir, distributee, & next of kin.* Technically, *heir* should refer only to the person entitled to the land of an intestate; either *distributee* or *next of kin* should be used of one entitled to an intestate's personal property. "Where a remainder is limited to the *heirs* or *distributees* of the creator of an estate in property, such *heirs* or *distributees* take as purchasers." See **devisee.**

heirs of the body. See **bodily heirs.**

helix yields either of the plurals *helixes* or *helices.* The unpretentious plural in *-xes* is better. Cf. **appendixes.**

help but. See **cannot help but.**

helpmate; helpmeet. *Helpmeet,* now archaic, was the original form, yet folk etymology changed the spelling to *-mate,* which is now the prevalent form. Though *helpmate* means "a companion or helper," it is generally restricted in use to one's spouse.

henceforth; henceforward. The latter is a NEEDLESS VARIANT.

he or she. Though the doctrine has been assailed as embodying SEXISM, the traditional view, still to be observed in the most formal contexts, is that the masculine pronouns are generic, comprehending both male and female. Thus cumbersome pairs such as *he or she* and *his or her* are usually unnecessary. E.g., "If a juror could be challenged for cause merely because *he or she* [read *he*] was against the death penalty in the circumstances at issue, a prosecutor could describe the particular facts of the case and demand to know how each venireman would vote at the penalty phase." If use of the masculine is objectionable to the writer, he (or she) should

make the antecedent of the pronoun plural if possible. E.g., "If *jurors* could be challenged for cause merely because *they* were against the death penalty in the circumstances at issue, a prosecutor could describe the particular facts of the case and demand to know how each venireman would vote at the penalty phase." The disadvantage of such a wording is that it too strongly suggests a singleness of mind in the group, as opposed to the uniqueness of an individual mind.

Interestingly, the forms *he or she* and *his or her* have long found acceptance in our typically verbose legal writing. Weseen wrote, "Outside of legal writing, it is not considered good form to use double pronouns, as *he or she, his or her.*" M. Weseen, *Crowell's Dictionary of English Grammar* 198 (1928). The phrase is by no means a newfangled concession to feminism. In 1837, the English Wills Act stated: "And be it further enacted, That every Will made by a Man or Woman shall be revoked by *his or her* Marriage (except a Will made in exercise of Appointment . . .)." 7 Wm. IV & 1 Vict., c. 26 (1837). Although it would have been rhetorically poor, the drafter might have subsumed into *his* the preceding noun *Woman.* See SEXISM (A).

HERE- AND THERE- WORDS abound in legal writing (unfortunately they do *not* occur just here and there), usually thrown in gratuitously to give legal documents that musty legal smell. Following are typical examples: "The exclusive right to enter upon the land, drill wells *thereon,* and remove *therefrom* the oil to exhaustion, paying *therefor* a portion of the oil extracted or the equivalent of such portion, is a property right that the law protects."/ "Humble Oil & Refining Co. entered upon this 50 acres of land and began drilling an oil well *thereon,* claiming the exclusive right to the leasehold interest *therein.*" These words are generally to be used only as a last resort to avoid awkward phrasing; certainly using one after another is stylistically abhorrent.

hereabout(s). This term, meaning "in this vicinity," is preferably spelled with the final *-s.*

hereafter; hereinafter. Perhaps because *hereinafter* sounds especially legalistic, some plain-language advocates have misguidedly recommended *hereafter* in its place. The two words have distinct meanings, however; and in any event, *hereafter* could hardly be cheered as a plain-language triumph over *hereinafter*.

Hereafter = (1) henceforth; (2) at some future time. The existence of these two meanings may make the word ambiguous, for example in legislation that is said to be *effective hereafter*. A more precise rendering of the intended meaning is *effective with the passage of this Act* or *after the day this Act takes effect*. Sense (1) is the more usual meaning of *hereafter*. A similar ambiguity plagues *heretofore*. See **hitherto**.

Hereinafter = in a part of this document that follows. E.g., "The parties have stipulated that an interchange of telegrams *hereinafter* referred to constitutes the contract." Mellinkoff warns: "While ordinarily *hereinafter* should point to the right instead of the left, below rather than above, it is a loose word, loosely used; and in at least two recorded instances judges have saved a cause if not the draftsman's reputation for alertness by interpreting *hereinafter* to mean *hereinbefore*." D. Mellinkoff, *The Language of the Law* 316 (1963).

As with *herein*, the legal writer is best advised to make the reference exact, by stating, e.g., *in this will* or *this paragraph* rather than *hereinafter*. Moreover, in introducing abbreviated names, *hereinafter* is redundant: rather than *Gulf Oil Corporation (hereinafter "Gulf")*, one should write *Gulf Oil Corporation ("Gulf")*. See **hereinabove**.

hereby is often a FLOTSAM PHRASE that can be excised with no loss of meaning; *I hereby declare* has no advantages over *I declare*.

hereditable = subject to inheritance. "'Children' is not a word of limitation; it does not point to *hereditable* succession." Apart from its use in the phrase *hereditable succession*, *hereditable* is a NEEDLESS VARIANT of *inheritable*. See **heritable**.

hereditament(s). This term suggests a relation in meaning to *inheritance*, which is misleading even though originally it did mean "things capable of being inherited." Today it means merely "land, real property," and should be avoided as an obscurantist LEGALISM. Here it is utterly redundant: "No tenant and no person claiming through any tenant of any land or *hereditament* of which he has been let into possession is, till he has given up

possession, permitted to deny that the landlord had, at the time when the tenant was let into possession, a title to such land or *hereditament*." (Eng.) The word is best accented on the second rather than the third syllable /hĕ-red-i-tă-mĕnt/.

Traditionally, the law distinguished between *corporeal hereditaments* (= tangible items of property, such as land or buildings) and *incorporeal hereditaments* (= intangible rights in land, such as easements). In England, *hereditament* has the additional sense "a unit of land that has been separately assessed for rating purposes" (*CDL*). See **corporeal hereditaments**.

hereditary. See **heritable**.

heredity for *inheritance* or *inheritability*, though once possible, is today confusingly legalistic. *Heredity* has now been confined largely to biological senses in nonlegal writing; hence legal writing need not perpetuate an archaic sense of the word. "The decedent's many prolonged affairs make the problems of *heredity* [read *inheritability*] quite complex." The nonlegal reader would interpret the quoted sentence as addressing bastardy rather than inheritance.

herein (= in this) is a vague word in legal documents, for the reader can rarely be certain whether it means *in this subsection*, *in this section* (or *paragraph*), or *in this document*. A more precise phrase, such as any of the three just listed, is preferable. See **herewith**.

hereinabove is almost always unnecessary for *above*. E.g., "I am of the opinion that defendant is liable by virtue of the express provisions of Act 34 of 1926, as I have related elsewhere *hereinabove* [read *above*]."/ "For lack of the essential findings *hereinabove discussed* [read *discussed above*], the judgment is reversed." See **above** (B), **hereafter**, & **hereinbefore**.

hereinafter. See **hereafter**.

hereinbefore; hereinafter. In legislative DRAFTING, these words should be avoided, because amendments and repeals may effect a reordering of the statute, and make either of these words inaccurate or misleading. The better practice is to be specific and write *in this act* or *in this section*. See **hereafter** & **hereinabove**.

hereto (= to this) is sometimes misused for *heretofore* (= up to this time). E.g., "Hedonic damages have not *hereto* [read *heretofore*] been recoverable in this state." See **hereafter.**

heretofore. See **hitherto.**

herewith. See **enclosed herewith.**

heritable; inheritable; hereditary. As between the first two, the second is the more common; it means "capable of being inherited": "The issue presented by this case is whether a husband's community interest in his surviving wife's civil service retirement benefits is *inheritable* upon his death by adult children of his former wife."/ "The grantee even in a deed deposited in escrow has an *inheritable* right." *Heritable* is infrequent enough today to be classed a NEEDLESS VARIANT for most purposes, although it persists in Scotland and in civil-law jurisdictions.

The negative form of the adjective has been rendered both *uninheritable* (*OED*) and *nonheritable* (*W3*). The latter is more common in the U.S. E.g., "[I]t would create an estate in fee simple which ... would be *nonheritable*." Frather, *Bequests of Orts*, 48 Mo. L.Rev. 476, 478 (1983).

Hereditary has a more restricted sense: "descending by inheritance from generation to generation" (*OED*): "In the American States it is a fundamental principle that no man can be a magistrate, a legislator, or a judge by *hereditary* right." (Eng.) See **hereditable** & **heredity.**

heritor. See **heir** (A).

heritrix, -tress. See SEXISM (C).

hesitancy, -ce; hesitation. *Hesitancy* is a quality ("the state of being hesitant; reluctance"), whereas *hesitation* is an act ("the act of hesitating"). Thus: "The courts had no *hesitancy* in holding the defamatory matter libelous."/ "We have no *hesitation* [read *hesitancy*, i.e., reluctance] in declaring that public policy requires that the interest of the beneficiary of a trust should be subject to the claims for support of his children." *Hesitance* is a NEEDLESS VARIANT.

hew = (1) to chop, cut; or (2) to adhere or conform (to). Sense (1) is illustrated in this sentence: "The appellants contend that the wife took title to the estate of her husband in fee simple absolute, which is not *hewed* down to a lesser estate by words of weaker import."

Sense (2), which is more common in modern legal prose, occurs in the following sentence: "In any event, we *hew* to the Supreme Court's broad language; if that is to be trimmed, it is for the court to do, not for us."

The preferred past participle is *hewn* in BrE and *hewed* in AmE. E.g., "The substantive distinction between admonitions and instructions is not always clear or closely *hewn to* [read, in AmE, *hewed to*]."

hiatus. Pl. *-tus, -tuses.*

higher court; upper court. Both phrases are used to denote an appellate court that reviews the judgment of a *lower court*, q.v. Following is a specimen of the less common form: "The *upper court*, on appeal, held that it was not error to admit parol evidence of extraneous facts." See **inferior court.**

hijack. Vehicles and planes are *hijacked,* not people. E.g., "Lipsig spent two years trying to get political asylum for Tshombe, who was mysteriously *hijacked* [read *abducted*?] to Algiers in the mid-sixties and detained in prison." See **skyjack.**

hindering impediment. See **impedient impediment.**

his or her. See **he or she** & SEXISM (A).

historical; historic. The former, meaning "of or relating to or occurring in history," is called upon for use far more frequently. The latter means "historically significant" ⟨the Alamo is a historic building⟩. An event that makes history is *historic*; an event of no great importance that occurred in history is *historical.* Momentous happenings or developments are *historic*; merely documented happenings or developments are *historical.* Here *historic* is correctly used: "Chief Justice Cardozo's *historic* and oft-quoted dissent in *Graf v. Hope Bldg. Corp.* has become equity's modern fount in cases in which the tyrant demands his dollars and cents on legal time whatever the impact of sickening hardship his victim suffers on account thereof."/ "In *Brown II* the Court referred to its *historic* opinion in *Brown I* as declaring the fundamental principle that racial discrimination in public education is unconstitutional."

Following are examples of *historic* used incorrectly for *historical*, the most common error with these words. The court having given a sketch of the history of different courts' holdings, it states: "We do not rest the power of the State to resort to constructive service in this proceeding upon how its courts or this court may regard this *historic* [read *historical*] antithesis." Examples are so numerous as to be tiresome; more such examples are presented here so that the point might be made forever in the reader's mind: "The *historic* [read *historical*] option of a maritime suitor pursuing a common-law remedy to select his forum, state or federal, would be taken away by an expanded view of section 1331." *Romero v. International Terminal Operating Co.*, 358 U.S. 354, 371 (1959) (per Frankfurter, J.)./ "In utilizing the Uniform Probate Code provisions, it is important to remember that the terms are used in the statutory definitions and not with their *historic* [read *historical*] connotations."/ "None of these critics sharply turned the *historic* [read *historical*] flow of law language." (D. Mellinkoff)/ "In the matter of form also, legal punctuation has followed generally the *historic* [read *historical*] pattern of all punctuation."/ "The willful acquisition or maintenance of that power is distinct from growth or development as a consequence of a superior product, business acumen, or *historic* [read *historical*] accident."/ "A law creating an open season on illegitimates in the area of automobile accidents gives a windfall to tortfeasors; but it hardly has a causal connection with the 'sin,' which is, we are told, the *historic* [read *historical*] reason for the creation of the disability."

On the question whether to write *a* or *an historic(al)*, see **a** (A).

HISTORICAL PRESENT TENSE IN OPINIONS. See OPINION WRITING (A).

hitherto; thitherto. *Hitherto* = heretofore; *thitherto* = theretofore. Obviously these ARCHAISMS are not worth using if we have defining terms—*heretofore* and *theretofore*—that are less archaic and perfectly equivalent. E.g., here, a legal writer mistook the import of *hitherto*, which does not properly appear with the pluperfect tense: "The Superior Court, conceding that it *hitherto* [read *thitherto*, or, better: *theretofore*] had refused to enjoin such conduct, recognized the growing tendency in courts to grant equitable relief under such circumstances."

hodgepodge. See **hotchpot.**

hoi polloi (= the common people, the masses). Inasmuch as *hoi* in Greek means "the," *the hoi polloi* is a technical REDUNDANCY. Nevertheless, *the hoi polloi* predominates.

hold, v.t. When used properly in the legal sense, this verb describes *what* judges do and is thus transitive. It should not be used intransitively to describe *how* judges do. In the following two sentences, the intransitive use is wrong. "Without the scarcity rationale, it seems unlikely that the *Red Lion* Court would have held *as it did*, even more unlikely that the present Court would do so."/ "This court's task, then, is to decide *how* [read *what*] the Oregon courts would hold when faced with the issue." (Courts hold *something*, they do not hold *in a certain manner*. Thus, in the second example, the noun *what*, not the adverb *how*, is the proper word.) In general English usage, of course, the intransitive use of *hold* is quite acceptable in such clauses as *The argument does not hold*.

Hold need not be followed by *to be* or *as*, although *to be* may sometimes add clarity. E.g., "We *hold permissible* [better: *hold to be permissible*] an award of extraordinary damages for frivolous appeal."/ In *Bryan v. Bigelow*, the unincorporated letter was *held testamentary* [better: *held to be testamentary*] and not admissible in evidence to rebut a resulting trust in favor of the residuary estate." But here the shorter form works better. "The defendant was *held to be liable* [read *held liable*] for breach of contract and conversion." *Held as* ⟨the award was held as permissible⟩ is idiomatically inferior.

As a noun, *holding* involves a determination of a matter of law that is pivotal to a judicial decision. Here it is loosely used in a lay sense: "Justice Jacobs quoted an 1859 New Jersey *holding* that 'Few statutes would stand if tried by standards of logic, grammar, or rhetoric.'" The opinion may have made this *statement*; but, inasmuch as it is not a statement of law, it cannot be a *holding*. See JUDGMENTS, APPELLATE-COURT & **finding.**

hold a brief for (= to defend or support) is a lawyers' idiom that has passed into general usage.

holden is an archaic past participle of *hold*, used as recently as 1850 in *Brown v. Kendall*,

60 Mass. (6 Cush.) 292 (1850): "There certainly are cases in the books, where, the injury being direct and immediate, trespass has been *holden* to lie, though the jury was not intentional." This ARCHAISM has even found its way into twentieth-century texts: "Perjury committed in a state court *holden* by permission of state law and of federal officials in a federal building, is not outside the jurisdiction of the state to punish."

holding. See **hold** & **finding.**

holding over is legal ARGOT denoting "the action of a tenant continuing in occupation of premises after his lease has expired" (*CDL*). E.g., "The tenant, *holding over* despite efforts to evict him, planted a crop that eventually the landlord harvested."

holocaust (lit., "burnt whole," fr. Gk.) is one of our most hyperbolical words, beloved of jargonmongers and second-rate journalists. The historical sense from World War II, of course, is beyond question. Figurative applications of the term, however, are often questionable. Here it is used to no avail in reference to a scandal: "C.R. would soon be engulfed in a *holocaust of controversy and pain* [read *painful controversy*] that would maim several lives, including his own, wound hundreds of other people, and jostle the foundations of the world's most glamorous industry." Inherent in the sense of the word, whether literal or figurative, is burning; thus, it may be used appropriately of fires, but not, for example, of floods. See ETYMOLOGICAL AWARENESS.

holograph. In the law of wills, a *holograph* is a will that is entirely written, dated, and signed in the hand of the testator. E.g., "Unfortunately, much litigation is stimulated by other requirements for the execution of *holographs*, and the difficulty in integrating *holographs* at probate is particularly acute."

This word is not to be confused with *hologram* (= a three-dimensional picture).

homage is best pronounced /**hom**-ij/. It is a pretension to omit the -*h*- sound. See **humble.**

homestead, v.t. The past tense of this verb is *homesteaded*. E.g., "The Chancellor adjudged the subject property *to be homestead* [read *to be*

homesteaded or *to be a homestead*] under Article X of the Florida Constitution." One who homesteads is *homesteader*. Congress enacted the Homestead Act in 1862.

homicide. See **murder.**

homogen(e)ous. *Homogeneous* (five syllables) is the usual and the etymologically preferable form. *Homogeneal, homogenetic, homogenetical* are rare forms to be avoided; they have failed to become standard and should be laid to rest.

Honorable is a title of respect given to judges, members of the U.S. Congress, ambassadors, and the like. It should be used not with surnames only, but with complete names (e.g. *The Honorable Antonin Scalia*) or with a title of courtesy (e.g. *The Honorable Mr. Scalia*). The abbreviation *Hon.* should be used only in mailing addresses.

honorable court, this, is a phrase commonly sprinkled throughout briefs. It should be sparingly used, for it tends to nauseate even those judges most susceptible to flattery. E.g., "Review by *this Honorable Court* of the granting by the district court of the motion for preliminary injunction is a routine matter in which *this Honorable Court* need determine only whether the district court abused its broad discretion in granting the preliminary injunction." The references should be to *the Court* or *this Court*, apart from the first reference in, e.g., the commencement of a pleading. (The capitalization of *court* is compliment enough.)

hopefully. So much has been written of this word that little can be added here, except to advise the reader to strike this word from his vocabulary. (See FORBIDDEN WORDS.) Briefly, the objections are that: (1) *hopefully* properly means "in a hopeful manner," and should not be used merely to mean *I hope* or *it is to be hoped*; (2) in constructions such as, "Hopefully, it will rain today," the writer illogically attributes an emotion (*hopefulness*) to an inanimate object (*it*).

In 1932, the sense "it is to be hoped" would have been inconceivable; here, in an example from that year, the word is used in the sense "in a hopeful manner": "[D]efendant would be placed in a state of servitude, for which she might *hopefully* expect to realize only her room and board in return for carrying a full share of her load." *Botkin v. Pyle*, 14 P.2d 187, 192 (Colo. 1932). By 1949, the SLIPSHOD EXTENSION of *hopefully* was well on its way: "This is the third, *hopefully* the last, stage in the adjudication of the rights of the parties in this controversy." *In re King's Estate*, 66 A.2d 68, 69 (Pa. 1949).

Sad to say, this misused word has become common in legal print. E.g., "[T]he protection of the American investing public against depredations by foreign nationals must be implemented by whatever tools are available, *hopefully* with more rather than less effectiveness." *Securities and Exchange Commission v. Myers*, 285 F.Supp. 743, 750 (D.Md. 1968)./ "*Hopefully*, everyone ought to share the view that we are our 'brother's keeper,' and that no social host worthy of another's visit to his home or to his party should be permitted to ignore his duty to exercise reasonable care for the sobriety of his guest." *Ross v. Ross*, 294 Minn. 115, 200 N.W.2d 149 (1972)./ "*Hopefully* in time the Louisiana Supreme Court will address what at least two of its justices recognize as irreconcilable decisions in this area."/ "This case is *hopefully* the final chapter in the litigation commenced in April 1978 by International Woodworkers of America alleging racial discrimination." Careful writers and speakers avoid the word, for they are likely to be misunderstood today if they use it correctly! See SENTENCE ADVERBS.

hornbook law = *black-letter law*, q.v. *Hornbooks* were originally leaves of paper with the alphabet depicted on them; these were covered by a thin plate of translucent horn and mounted on a tablet of wood for use by schoolchildren. By extension, *hornbook* came to be applied to lawbooks containing the rudiments of law. E.g., "It is *hornbook* tort *law* that one who undertakes to warn the public of danger and thereby induces reliance must perform his 'good samaritan' task in a careful manner."/ "It is *hornbook law* everywhere that silence of itself does not constitute assent."/ "The *hornbook* statement is made that a valid foreign judgment that the defendant do or refrain from doing an act other than the payment of money will not be enforced by an action on the judgment."/ "It is equally well settled, however, indeed it is *hornbook law*, that the reasonable expenses incurred by an indemnitee in defending a claim against him may be recovered of his indemnitor."

horse case. See **whitehorse case.**

hotchpot; hotchpotch; hodgepodge. The original form, still the preferred legal term, is *hotchpot.* This word was corrupted into *hotchpotch* (used by some courts), then into *hodgepodge*, which is now the usual nonlegal term meaning "an unorganized mixture." E.g., "The Bankruptcy Act of 1898 proved deficient because of its erratic and uncertain application resulting from a *hodgepodge* of state and federal statutory provisions." All of these words are spelled without hyphens. *Hotchpotch* is similarly used in the sense "a mixed stew" or "a muddle in general."

Hotchpot originally was "the blending or gathering together of properties for the purpose of securing equality of division, esp. as practised in certain cases in the distribution of the property of an intestate parent" (*OED*). E.g., "Ademption by satisfaction is related to the doctrine of advancements in intestacy, except that there is no opportunity on the part of the testamentary donee to come into *hotchpot*." In community-property states in the U.S., the term is also used in reference to the property that falls within the community estate.

hot pursuit. See **fresh pursuit.**

housebreaking is a little-used variant of *burglary*, q.v., in its classical sense. E.g., "Petitioner was charged with attempted *housebreaking*, and assault with attempt to rape in violation of articles 80, 130, and 134 of the Uniform Code of Military Justice." *Breaking and entering*, however, is a frequently used DOUBLET in that sense.

howbeit. See **albeit.**

how come is very informal, almost slang, for *why*. It should be avoided in writing.

however. It seems everyone has heard that sentences should not begin with this word. However, it is not an error to begin with *however*: it is merely not usually the best placement for stylistic purposes. E.g., "However, we regard the statutory history of section 702c as being less than univocal on this point, and for that reason cannot assent to the view propounded by appellants." [Read *We regard the statutory history of section 702c as being less than univocal on this point, however, and for that* *reason cannot assent to the view propounded by appellants.*]

Yet used in the sense "in whatever way," *however* is unimpeachable at the beginning of a sentence. E.g., "*However* the third-party actions are viewed, they necessarily are part of the claims that were included in the 'Mutual Release and Compromise.'" Following is a similar use in a different syntactic position: "But not all past error, *however* egregious, exacts a new trial and our failure to reverse is not likely to encourage future error." See RUN-ON SENTENCES.

howsoever is always inferior to *however.*

hue and cry is an archaic LEGALISM that has passed into the vernacular. At common law it referred to the public uproar that a citizen was expected to initiate after discovering a crime. See 4 W. Blackstone, *Commentaries* 292-94. See POPULARIZED LEGAL TECHNICALITIES.

human, n., for *human being* was long held objectionable by a few purists, but is so pervasive today even in formal writing that it should be accepted as standard.

humankind; mankind. The former, a seventeenth-century creation, is unexceptionable although it has its detractors; the latter is, to many people, exceptionable on grounds of SEXISM. The prudent writer will resort to *humankind,* regardless of what he may think of the virtues of *mankind.* E.g., "This inability to confront and examine the individuality of the defendant would be particularly devastating to any argument for consideration of what this court has termed 'those compassionate or mitigating factors stemming from the diverse frailties of *humankind.*'" See SEXISM (B).

humble is preferably pronounced with the -h- sounded /**hum-bĕl**/. (Cf. **homage.**) Inexplicably, the precious pronunciation without sounding the initial -h- is common in AmE. One judge went so far as to use *an* before the Humble Oil trademark: "To the contrary, purchasers were informed that the selected shipments would bear the HUMBLE name or be accompanied *by an* HUMBLE *invoice* [read *by a* HUMBLE *invoice*] but were the desired Exxon products." *Exxon Corp. v. Humble Exploration Co.,* 695 F.2d 96, 100 (5th Cir. 1983).

hung jury does not require apologetic quotation marks, as if signaling that it is colloquial or even slang. It is neither; it is a useful legal term. See the quotation in par. 2 under **contumacious.** See also **hanged.**

hurt (= a legal injury) surprises the nonlegal reader, for whom *hurt* connotes physical or emotional pain only. E.g., "The *hurts* to relations fall in numerous patterns, some simple and some complex."

HYBRIDS, or words made up of morphemes from different languages, have become even more common in the last fifty years than they were in Fowler's day. Perhaps it is our increasing ignorance of Classical tongues, or our disregard for the morphological integrity of the words we coin. Virtually all the hybrids condemned by Fowler (e.g. *amoral, bureaucracy, cablegram, climactic, coastal, coloration, gullible, pacifist, racial, speedometer*) are now passed over without mention even by those who consider themselves purists. We have our own fringe hybrids, however: *raticide, scatteration,* and *monokini* (the last being a MORPHOLOGICAL DEFORMITY as well). In law, *breathalyzer* (formerly *drunkometer*) has become standard, although in 1965 Gowers wrote that this term was "stillborn, it may be hoped" (*MEU2* 253). *Creedal,* q.v., is a commonplace. And Fowler may not be resting in peace.

hygiene used to have something to do with cleanliness and healthfulness, esp. with regard to the body. Then the bureaucrats and psychologists sullied this word with figurative senses, giving us, for example, the *State of California Department of Mental Hygiene* (see 163 Tex. 314, 354 S.W.2d 576 (1962)). And this: "What she offers in the place of a system of punishment is in fact a system of purely forward-looking *social hygiene* in which our only concern when we have an offender to deal with is with the future and the rational aim of prevention of future crime." Careful writers shun this, as they shun all bureaucratic JARGONMONGERING.

HYPALLAGE, known also as the transferred epithet, is a figure of speech in which the proper subject is displaced by what rightfully would be the object. Usually hypallage is a mere idiomatic curiosity. It has a distinguished lineage—a famous example being

Shakespeare's line from *Julius Caesar:* "This was the most unkindest cut of all." It was not the *cut* that was unkind, but rather the *cutter.* Hence the object has become the subject.

An example from legal language is the phrase "negligent tort." It is the tortfeasor, not the tort, that is negligent. Likewise in these sentences: "The mere fact that another may act to his prejudice if the true state of things is not disclosed does not render *silence culpable* or make it operate as an estoppel against one who owes no duty of active diligence to protect the other party from injury." (The silence is not arguably culpable; the person who is silent is.)/ "In *Jenkins v. Delaware,* the court held that *Miranda*'s standards for determining the admissibility of *in-custody statements* do not apply to post-*Miranda* retrials of cases originally tried before that decision." (The *statements* were not *in custody*; the person making them was.)

But this figure of speech can sometimes be used inartfully, or cause problems if the writer is not himself aware of the true subject. E.g., "The final *subclass* of originalism, what Brest calls 'moderate originalism,' *views* the text of the Constitution as. . . ." [A subclass does not view.]/ "State *courts* generally *mirrored* this theistic viewpoint." [State courts did not mirror the point of view discussed; rather, their *decisions* or *opinions* did.]/ "The authorities sustain the validity of the direction of the testator, and equity will afford protection to the donor to a charitable corporation in that the attorney general may maintain a suit to *compel the property to be held* for the charitable purpose for which it was given to the corporation." [The *property* is not being *compelled to be held*; someone is *being compelled to hold the property*.]/ "*The arguments* of the parties have *addressed themselves* in considerable part to the propriety of the district court's exercising its equitable jurisdiction to enjoin the strike in question once the findings set forth above have been made." [*The arguments themselves* haven't done the *addressing;* rather, in their arguments, *the parties have addressed themselves.*]

Hypallage can also lead to faulty metaphors: "The defendants in this case have reduced the husband to a physical wreck. The *wife is the victim of that wreck.*" [The writer does not mean to say that the *wife is a victim of her husband,* a paraplegic. Rather, she is *a victim of the defendants' actions.*]

HYPHENS. See PUNCTUATION (D) & ADJECTIVES (C).

hypnotism and *hypnosis* are not the same. One might use either term to name the art of mesmerism, but one would never say, "He is under *hypnotism.*" *Hypnotism* names only the practice or art; *hypnosis* refers either to the practice or to the state of consciousness itself.

hypo. See **hypo(thet).**

hypostatize; hypostasize. The standard form is *hypostatize* (= to make an idea into, or to regard it, as a self-existent substance or person).

hypothecate for *hypothesize.* Properly, *hypothecate* is an admiralty term meaning "to pledge without delivery of title or possession." *Hypothesize* means "to make a hypothesis." Though the former is sometimes used for the latter, and has some authority in dictionaries, the two words are best kept separate. "After the transfer is made, *A* might have another child (*Z*). Then all of *A*'s children and grandchildren who are lives in being might die; 21 years after their deaths *Z* might give birth to a child (*GC-4*); although *GC-4*'s interest would vest at birth, under the *hypothecated* [read *hypothesized*] facts it would vest remotely." *Hypotheticate* is a mistaken form of *hypothecate.*

Hypothecation is best preceded by *a* rather than by *an.* E.g., "In my opinion, the definition given by Pothier of *an hypothecation* [read *a hypothecation*] is an accurate description of a maritime lien under our law." See **a** (A).

hypo(thet). *Hypothetical* was originally used adjectivally, but has come to be an attributive noun as well. *Hypothet* is an old-fashioned American shortening of *hypothetical* in legal contexts. *Hypo* is now the more widespread legal colloquialism, and it undoubtedly sounds better.

hypothetic(al), adj. The longer form is now usual. E.g., "In the supplemental charge, the court expressly indicated that its prior remarks had been made in *hypothetic* [read *hypothetical*] form for illustrative purposes." See the preceding entry.

I

idealogical. See **ideological.**

idem (= the same), in its abbreviated form *id.*, is used in citations to refer to the cited authority immediately preceding. For example, if footnote 2 reads "Mauet, *Fundamentals of Trial Techniques* 380 (1980)," footnote 3 might read "*Id.* at 381."

The full word appears in the LATINISM *idem sonans* (lit., "having the same sound"), a rule of law that a variant spelling of a name in a document will not render the document void if the misspelling is pronounced in the same way as the true spelling (as *Growgan* for *Grogan* on a traffic ticket).

identical preferably takes *with*, not *to*. One has *identity with* something or someone, not *to* it. *Identical to* was not widely used until recently; the *OED* quotes illustrative examples only with the phrase *identical with.* Here the better phrasing is used: "Under a constitutional provision *identical with* our own, the Missouri courts have held consistently that the question of libel or no libel is for the jury."/ "The evidence is that the two prior wills contained residuary devises *identical with* those in the latest will."

Just as frequently, however, and esp. in American writing, *to* appears. It has come to be the predominant nonliterary idiom in the U.S. E.g., "The code may then provide a term substantially identical *to* [read *with*] one of those rejected."/ "Section 35031 is virtually identical *to* [read *with*] section 72411."/ "Petitioner then filed his first federal habeas petition, raising issues identical *to* [read *with*] those raised and ruled on in his state appeal."

Recently, *identify with*, used without a direct object following *identify*, has become a cant phrase, associated especially with the 1960s and 1970s. Here it is inappropriately used in reference to a nineteenth-century historical figure. "Randolph *identified with* the books he read, and took upon himself the roles suggested by his favorite authors."

ideological. So spelled, though many misapprehend its etymology, believing the word is somehow derived from our modern word *idea*, and thus misspell it *idealogical*. The blun-

der has become common enough that it appears in *W3* and *W9* (cf. **miniscule**), but inclusion in those dictionaries is not a persuasive defense of its use. Like several other, more learned words in *ideo-* (e.g., *ideograph*), *ideology* passed into English through French (F. *idéologie*), and has been spelled *ideo-* in English since the eighteenth century.

id est. See **i.e.**

idiosyncrasy. So spelled, though often erroneously rendered *-cracy.*

idyllic (= of, belonging to, or of the nature of an idyll [a short picturesque poem usu. describing rustic life]; full of charm or picturesqueness) is often misused as if it meant *ideal.* Here the two words are used side by side: "Race relations in the south today are *idyllic*, that is, *ideal*, compared to what they were thirty years ago." Clearly the writer misunderstood the import of *idyllic*, and should have used merely *ideal.*

i.e., the abbreviation for *id est* (L. "that is"), introduces explanatory phrases or clauses, and is perfectly appropriate in legal writing. Formerly it was said that, in speaking or reading, the abbreviation should be rendered *id est.* But this is never heard today, whereas the abbreviated letters *i.e.* are frequently heard in lawyers' speech. See **e.g.**

if. **A.** *And* whether. It is best to distinguish between the ways in which these words are used. *Whether* is generally preferable where one intends, not to express a conditional idea, but an alternative or possibility. *If* is often used where, in formal writing at least, *whether* is the better word. E.g., "One person inquired *if* [read *whether*] the money was lost."

In some contexts, however, use of the different words may actually shade the meaning. E.g., "Please let me know *if* you need any advice" means to get in touch only if you need advice. "Please let me know *whether* you need any advice" means to advise in any event, whether the answer is yes or no. Where no condition is intended, *whether* is the better term in formal or editorial English.

B. *If, and only if.* This is inferior and adds nothing but unnecessary emphasis to *only if.* The variation *if, but only if*, which sometimes occurs in legal writing, is unnecessary and even nonsensical for *only if*.

if and when is a legalistic phrase of questionable validity. *"If and when the Patent and Trademark Office decides the trademark is registrable, it will be published in a weekly bulletin called the Official Gazette."* (What is the antecedent of *it*? Will the *trademark* be published, or the *decision* of registrability?)

Fowler enumerated a number of suspicions that keen readers are likely to have about users of this phrase: "There is the suspicion that he is a mere parrot, who cannot say part of what he has often heard without saying the rest also; there is the suspicion that he likes verbiage for its own sake; there is the suspicion that he is a timid swordsman who thinks he will be safer with a second sword in his left hand; there is the suspicion that he has merely been too lazy to make up his mind between *if* and *when"* (*MEU1* 254). In short, one is ill-advised to use the phrase, which almost invariably is improved when simplified: "Appellant has not specifically requested backpay; *if and when* [read *if*] he does, that issue might be judged by a different standard."

An even worse manifestation of the phrase is *if, as, and when*: "Decisions in other community property states have disagreed on whether future contingent payments may be apportioned *if, as, and when* [read *as* or *when*] they mature and are received by the retired spouse."/ "We shall offer these bonds at this price, *if, as, and when* [read *if* or *when*] they are issued by the trust company." One of the three words is suitable virtually wherever this phrase appears.

iffy for *uncertain* is a colloquialism unfit for formal legal prose. E.g., "We conclude that this court should not undertake the *iffy* [read *uncertain*] task of determining whether each appellant is entitled to immunity."

if it be. See SUBJUNCTIVES.

if not is an ambiguous phrase best avoided. It may mean either (1) lit., "(even) if it is (we are, etc.) not; though not," or (2) "and even." Sense (2) is exemplified in the following sentences: "Justices of the peace who handle petty criminal cases and small claims are close to the general public and are an important, *if not* [i.e., and even an] essential, ele-

ment in any state's system of justice."/ "Many, *if not* [i.e., even] most, courts are now willing to allow a substantial award for loss of the 'companionship' of the child." Sense (1) is confusing if, as is quite likely, the reader first thinks of the phrase in terms of the more common sense (2): "We are apt *if not* vigilant to overlook the true status of the defendant husband and the defendant wife when they undertook acquisition by the entirety of the home lot." The sentence means *We are apt, if we are not vigilant, to overlook*; but the reader more familiar with sense (2) will misperceive the sentence as meaning *We are apt, and even vigilant, to overlook*. See AMBIGUITY.

ignis fatuus (= will o' the wisp; a delusive hope or desire) forms the plural *ignes fatui.*

ignitable. So spelled. See -ABLE (A).

ignominy is accented on the first, not the second, syllable /*ig-nŏ-min-ee*/.

ignoramus. Until 1934 in England, if a grand jury considered the evidence of an alleged crime insufficient, it would endorse the bill *ignoramus*, meaning literally "we do not know" or "we know nothing of this." This use of the term was a survival of the medieval practice of having juries act on personal knowledge. By extension, and as early as the seventeenth century, *ignoramus* came to mean "an ignorant person." See POPULARIZED LEGAL TECHNICALITIES.

The modern nonlegal meaning appears more frequently in modern legal writing than the historical legal meaning: "Thus, to accuse a lawyer of being an *ignoramus*, when spoken of him in his calling, is actionable per se, without proof of special damages." Pl. *ignoramuses*; the form *ignorami* is a pseudo-learned blunder (*ignoramus* not being one of the Latin nouns in *-us*). See PLURALS (A).

ignorant; stupid. Fastidious users of language distinguish between these terms. *Stupid* refers to innate ability, whereas *ignorant* refers merely to the state of one's knowledge on a particular subject. Geniuses are *ignorant* of certain facts; *stupid* people are *ignorant* of most facts.

ignorantia legis is a moderately useful LATINISM denoting the legal doctrine that ignorance of the law is no excuse (rendered in Latin *ignorantia juris neminem excusat* [lit., "ignorance of law excuses no one"]). E.g., "The effect of this provision is to continue the *ignorantia legis* principle as part of the Model Code culpability structure." The full maxim itself, however, is best rendered in English.

ilk correctly means "the same"; hence *of that ilk* means "of that same kind." Yet the word is commonly misapprehended as relating to race or family—it is not that specific.

ill. The comparative form of this adjective is *worse*, the superlative *worst*. The adverb is *ill*, *illy* being an illiterate form. Yet illiteracies have been known to creep into legal writing and even into judicial opinions: see **illy.**

illation (= the act of inferring or something inferred) is a learned term little used today, though a few modern judges are quite fond of it. *Inference* serves just as well, and more understandably.

illegal alien. See **undocumented alien.**

illegal; illicit; unlawful. These three terms are fundamentally synonymous, although *illicit* (illicit love affairs) carries moral overtones in addition to the basic sense "not in accordance with or sanctioned by law."

illegible; unreadable. *Illegible* = not plain or clear enough to be read (used of handwriting or defaced printing). *Unreadable* = too dull or obfuscatory to be read (used of bad writing).

illicit for *elicit*. One might have thought this mistake impossible, but it does occur. *Illicit* = illegal; *elicit* = to bring out, to call forth. E.g., "No testimony was *illicited* [read *elicited*] that justified this breach." See **illegal.**

illiterate = (1) unable to read or write; or (2) unlettered. Justice Holmes was wont to use this word in sense (2), the heightened sense of the word: "In the case at bar we have an *illiterate* woman writing her own will. Obviously the first sentence, 'I am going on a journey and may not ever return,' expresses the fact that was on her mind as the occasion and

inducement for writing it." *Eaton v. Brown,* 193 U.S. 411, 414 (1904) (per Holmes, J.).

ILLOGIC is really a catchall category for writing that suffers from some sort of error in thinking or some logical fallacy. Often it results from failing to be mindful of what the subject of the verb is, and to make certain that the sentence properly expresses what it is that acts upon something else, or who kicked whom.

A. Illogical Comparison. This lapse occurs commonly in locutions like *as large if not larger than,* which, when telescoped, becomes *as large than*; properly, one writes *as large as if not larger than.* Similar problems occur with classes: when members of a class are being compared, a word such as *other* must be used to restrict the class. E.g., "Our system of justice is better than any [*other*] in the world." See COMPARATIVES AND SUPERLATIVES & **as much as or more.**

Still another problem of comparison occurs when the writer forgets exactly what he is comparing. E.g., "The case involved facts virtually identical with *Ragan* [read *those in Ragan*]. See COMPARISONS, FALSE.

Here is an example of inappropriate comparison of the subject with another noun: "May a defendant who has settled with the plaintiff recover contribution from other potential defendants?" The phrase *other potential defendants* is wrong because anyone who has settled is no longer a *potential* defendant.

B. Illogical Subject of a Participle. "Any definition is likely to distinguish between religion and mere conscientious belief, *construing* the first amendment to govern the former but not the latter." (Note that a definition does not construe: see HYPALLAGE). See also DANGLERS.

C. Mistaken Subject of a Prepositional Phrase. "*Wallin was the school bus driver in which* [read *Wallin was driving the bus in which*] Hillman and Ellington and Kleven were passengers."

D. Insensitivity to Metaphor. "In my opinion that foundation is not weakened by the fact that *it is buttressed by other provisions that are also* [read *other provisions are also*] designed to avoid the insidious evils of government propaganda favoring particular points of view." (*Buttresses* can serve only to strengthen, not to weaken.)/ "The *Erie* doctrine was bastardized by its progeny." (This makes no sense, because parents, not children, create bastards.)/ "The nineteenth century has provided new impetus to literary studies, putting them on untraveled roads." (Travel creates roads: they do not exist in vacuo.) See METAPHORS, MIXED AND MANGLED.

E. Poor Use of Temporal Sequence. "Indeed, the condition of the plane after the crash *was such as to eliminate an air collision* [read *was such as to eliminate further speculation about an air collision*]."/ "The obligation of the deceased to transfer certain property, as a minimum, during his life does not negative a desire to leave other property after death, and more than the minimum, at least in the absence of new responsibilities." (A deceased person cannot have obligations to transfer property during his life.)

F. Vexatious Little Words with Plain Literal Meanings. "Acceptances must be communicated to offeror *after* [read *in*] a reasonable amount of time." (If *after* a reasonable amount of time, then the period has become *unreasonable!*)/ "Appellee argues forcefully, *as did the district court below* [read *and the district court below held*], that because IBM and the third-party firms provide identical services, the third-party firms do not constitute a separate market." (The appellee may *argue* this on appeal; but the district court *held* in its opinion. Courts do not *argue.*)

G. Complete Obliviousness in the Task of Writing. "The courts are more reluctant in considering extrinsic evidence to construe a will than to construe an inter vivos transfer." [Read *Courts are more reluctant to consider extrinsic evidence in construing a will than in construing an inter vivos transfer.*] (The original sentence suggests that courts have a choice of what to construe, as if a judge might say: "Well, here I am considering some extrinsic evidence. Why, I think I'll construe an inter vivos transfer—that would be more fun than a will!")

illude. See **allude** (B).

illusion; delusion. These words are used differently despite their similar meanings. An *illusion* exists in one's fancy or imagination. A *delusion* is an idea or thing that deceives or misleads a person.

illusory, -sive. The former is preferred. E.g., "Some courts, following the lead of New York, invoked a test whether the arrangement was *illusory*, measured in terms of the substance of the arrangement." See **elusive.**

illustrate, in modern usage, means "to provide a good example of (something); to exemplify." In the following sentence it is used ambiguously: "Hohfeld's analysis *illustrates* the fallacy of accepting too literally the 'artificial entity' theory." The writer here is not claiming—as his sentence seems to do—that Hohfeld's analysis is itself a good example of "the fallacy of accepting too literally the 'artificial entity' theory." Rather he is pointing to Hohfeld's analysis as one that elucidates well the nature of this fallacy.

Illustrate is usually accented on the first syllable, /*il-ŭ-strayt*/.

illustrative. The second syllable is accented: /*ĭ-lus-tră-tiv*/.

illy is not an acceptable adverb in formal writing, perhaps not even in nondialectal informal writing. *Ill* itself acts as an adverb. E.g., "It is freely conceded that there are many decisions contrary to this view; but, when carried to the extent contended for by the appellant, we think they are unsafe, unsound, and *illy* [read *ill*] adapted to modern conditions." See **ill.**

imbecile, adj.; **imbecilic.** The preferred adjectival form of *imbecile*, n., is *imbecile*, adj. The form in -*ic* should be avoided.

imbibe is a FORMAL WORD meaning "to drink." It occurs more frequently in legal than in nonlegal contexts. E.g., "In *Kelly v. Gwinnell,* the New Jersey Supreme Court took a major step in holding social hosts liable for the torts of their guests whom they have allowed to over*imbibe.*"

imbracery. See **embracery.**

immanent. See **imminent.**

immaterial; nonmaterial. The former term is called for in most legal contexts. "Should even a *nonmaterial* [read *immaterial*] error, if made with the intent to deceive the magistrate, invalidate a warrant?"/ "A testator is not induced by the misrepresentation if he knows the facts, or if the facts misrepresented are *immaterial.*" Although both may mean "not consisting of a material substance," *immaterial* tends to mean "of no substantial importance; inconsequential"; *nonmaterial*, in contrast, generally means "cultural, aesthetic" ⟨the nonmaterial rewards of a career in law are sometimes debated⟩.

immediate cause. See CAUSATION (B).

immigrate; emigrate. *Immigrate* = to migrate into or enter (a country). *Emigrate* = to migrate away from or exit (a country). Perhaps it is indicative of the relative worth of the two forms of government that the United States is plagued by illegal *immigration*, whereas the Soviet Union is plagued by attempts at illegal *emigration.*

Both verbs are intransitive and hence do not take objects. In the following sentence, *immigrate* is wrongly made transitive: "*Because you cannot immigrate your grandmother* [Read *Because your grandmother cannot immigrate*], she and her husband and her six children will remain undocumented."

imminent; eminent; immanent. *Imminent* means "certain and very near, impending," as in the legal phrases *imminent bodily harm* and *imminent death.* E.g., "Obviously there should be some bar to letting the owner transfer solely for the purpose of cutting down his estate tax at a time when that tax becomes *imminent.*"

Imminent does not mean merely "probable," as here incorrectly used: "We cannot assume reasonably that the Legislature intended that a statute enacted for the preservation of life and limb of pedestrians must be observed when observance would subject them to more *imminent* [read *probable*] danger."

Eminent = distinguished, of excellent repute ⟨Judge Friendly of the Second Circuit was long considered an eminent jurist⟩. The adverb *eminently* is frequently used to mean "very," as in "He is *eminently* deserving of this award," or, "The court's decision was *eminently* fair."

Immanent, primarily a theological term, means "inherent; pervading the material world" ⟨the immanent goodness of the divine will⟩.

immolate. See **emulate.**

immoral; unmoral; amoral. These three words have distinct meanings. *Immoral*, the opposite of *moral*, means "evil, depraved." The word is highly judgmental. *Unmoral* means merely "without moral sense, not moral," and is used, for example, of animals and inanimate objects. *Amoral*, perhaps the most commonly misused of these terms, means "not moral, outside the sphere of morality; being neither moral nor immoral." It is loosely applied to people in the sense "not having morals or scruples."

immovable has become in law a noun as well as an adjective, and is used almost always in the plural form. E.g., "All the cases before *Langlois* that imposed absolute liability involved dangerous activities relating to land or other *immovables* that were within the terms of those articles." See ADJECTIVES (B). The term *immovables* encompasses all immovable property, such as land, trees, buildings, and servitudes.

immune best takes *from*, not *to.* "Executive officers and other fellow employees of the injured employee are similarly immune *to* [read *from*] third-party demands." But *to* is acceptable, and so is *against.*

immunize = to render immune from or insusceptible to poison or infection (*OED*). By extension it means "to protect (from something bad)." The sense of some contagion or danger is an important element of the word in figurative as well as literal senses: "The Court concluded that the proprietary position of the state did not *immunize* it from the fourteenth amendment." (The Fourteenth Amendment to the U.S. Constitution is generally seen as a good thing, not a bad one.)

impact is not generally understood to be a count noun. "It is apparent that the ICC found Steere's 'melodramatic' list of *adverse impacts upon* [better: *adverse effects on*] the motor carrier industry unpersuasive." This use of the noun *impact* is an extension of the verbal use disapproved in the following entry.

impact, v.i. & v.t. *Impact* has traditionally been only a noun. In recent years, however, it has undergone a semantic shift that has allowed it to act as a verb. Thus uses such as, "Five states have adopted plain English laws, but only New Jersey's law severely *impacts upon* lawyers in their private practice," have become widespread (and also widely condemned by stylists). E.g., "The termination of a tenured public schoolteacher adversely *im-*

pacts on the teacher's personal and professional standing in both the educational community and the greater societal community."/ "The recently filed pro se application of Rumbaugh dramatically *impacts on* the issue before us."/ "The city argues that any step in the process that *impacts* adversely *on* black applicants is job-related and essential to the operation of the police department."

These uses of the word would be applauded if *impact* were performing any function not as ably performed by *affect* or *influence*. If *affect* as a verb is not sufficiently straightforward in context, then the careful writer might have recourse to *have an impact on*, which, though longer, to many is unquestionably preferable to the jarring impact of *impacts upon*. *Impact* is best reserved as a nominal form.

Impact has also been used as a transitive verb, but the direct object does not make the verb any more acceptable. E.g., "There was no evidence that, had he joined the medical staff, patient care would have been negatively *impacted* [better: *affected*]."/ "Petitioner maintains that the commission must adhere to the rulemaking requirements of the APA when it conclusively affects and substantially *impacts* [better: *redefines*] pre-existing rights with a retroactive rule that has the force of law." See NOUNS AS VERBS.

impanel. See **empanel.**

impartable; impartible. These are two different words. *Impartable* = capable of being imparted. *Impartible* = indivisible. The latter word is chiefly legal, used primarily in describing estates ⟨the question is whether the estate is partible or impartible⟩. See -ABLE (A).

impassible; impassable. *Impassible* = incapable of feeling or suffering. *Impassable* = not capable of being passed. See -ABLE (A).

impeach means, not "to remove from office," but "to bring a charge or accusation against." *Impeachment* may, of course, result in removal from office.

impedient impediment; hindering impediment. *Impedient* = that impedes; obstructive. Thus *impedient impediment* is the most elementary type of REDUNDANCY. Yet it has acquired a specific legal meaning, "a bar to marriage that is an obstacle to the marriage if known but that does not make the marriage

void after it has been solemnized" (*W3*). It is also called *hindering impediment*, which is just as redundant, albeit in a less obtrusive way.

impel. For the difference between this word and *compel*, see the entry under that word. *Impel to* + noun phrase is a construction not available with *compel*. E.g., "In the interest of the public good this is a hardness to be endured courageously if not cheerfully by the man whose ideals *impel* him *to* such a course."

impeller, -or. The former spelling is preferred.

imperative. See **directory.**

imperial; imperious. Deriving from the same root (L. *imper-* = power over a family, region, or state), these words have been differentiated by their suffixes. *Imperial* = of or belonging to an emperor or empire. *Imperious* = overbearing, supercilious, tyrannical.

Additionally, *imperious* = urgent, absolute, imperative. E.g., "Can we adopt that construction (unless the words *imperiously* require it) which would impute to the framers of that instrument . . . the intention of impeding their exercise by withholding a choice of means?" (Marshall, C. J.)/ "Because taxes are the life-blood of government, and their prompt and certain availability an *imperious* need, Congress has created a formidable arsenal of collection tools."

imperium (= supreme authority) forms the pl. *imperia.*

IMPERSONAL IT. See EXPLETIVES.

impersuadable; impersuasible. See **persuadable.**

impertinence in nonlegal contexts is taken to mean "presumptuous or forward rudeness of behavior or speech, esp. to a superior; insolence" (*OED*). This sense originated as a colloquialism. In legal contexts, the original sense of the term is retained: "the fact or character of not pertaining to the matter at hand; lack of pertinence; irrelevance." See **impertinent & pertinence.**

impertinent does not, in most legal contexts, have its ordinary meaning, "saucy, impudent." Rather, it means "not pertinent or relevant." E.g., "[T]he court may order stricken from any pleading any insufficient defense or any redundant, immaterial, *impertinent*, or scandalous matter." Fed. R. Civ. P. 12(f). Lawyers should beware in their pleadings of making impertinent statements of either kind. See **impertinence**.

impervious; imperviable. *Impervious* = not allowing something to pass through; not open to ⟨some people are impervious to reason⟩. The word should be avoided in the sense "not affected by" ⟨he was impervious to her screams for help⟩ ⟨expert-witnesses impervious to harsh cross-examination⟩. *Imperviable* is a NEEDLESS VARIANT.

impetus. See **impotence**.

impignorate = to mortgage, pledge, or pawn. Any of these more specific, simpler terms should be used rather than this rare, pedantic LATINISM. *Pignorate* is another form of the same word.

impinge; infringe. *Impinge* is used intransitively only; it is followed by *on* or *upon*. *Infringe*, contrariwise, may be either transitive or intransitive; hence either *to infringe someone's rights* or *to infringe on someone's rights*; but only *to impinge on someone's rights*. Though *impinge* and *infringe* are often used as if they were interchangeable, we might keep in mind these connotations: *impinge* = (lit.) to strike or dash *upon* something else, whereas *infringe* = to break in (damage, violate, or weaken).

Impinge should not be used without an object to impinge *upon*, as here: "These policies also *impinge* when we consider the potential for abuse." The writer of that sentence should have supplied the object. See **infringe**.

implead; emplead. The former spelling is standard. E.g., "We shall *implead* the Major General into the lawsuit." See **plead** & EN-.

implement is a VOGUE WORD beloved by jargonmongers, in whose language *policies are implemented. Carry out* is usually better, and certainly less vague.

implementer, -or. The former spelling is preferred.

implicate = (1) to bring into play; to involve in its nature or meaning, or as a consequence ⟨Forcible injection of a pretrial detainee with an antipsychotic drug *implicates* a constitutionally protected interest.⟩; (2) to involve (a person) *in* a charge or crime ⟨Each party strove to *implicate* the other *in* this heinous deed.⟩.

implication is the noun corresponding to both *implicate* and *imply*. Thus it means (1) "the action of implicating, or involving, entangling, or entwining" ⟨Smith's implication of Jones in the crime⟩; (2) "the action of implying; the fact of being implied or involved" ⟨by necessary implication⟩; or (3) "that which is implied or involved" ⟨implications of wrongdoing⟩.

implication of law. See **imply**.

implied; express. These adjectives are correlative. *Expressed* is sometimes incorrectly contrasted with *implied*. See **express(ed)**.

implied contract; quasi contract. "[I]f a lawyer writes: 'The proper meaning of *implied contract* is contract implied in fact, not *quasi-contract*,' he does not express what is now the invariable usage of lawyers. . . ." Glanville Williams, *Language and the Law*, 61 Law Q. Rev. 384, 385 (1945). These terms are now generally considered synonymous in denoting a contract not created by express words but inferred by the courts from the conduct of the parties, from some special relationship between them, or because of unjust enrichment of one of them.

Formerly, *implied contract* was limited in use to a contract inferred by the courts by reason of the conduct of the parties or of a special relationship between them (implied in fact), and *quasi contract* was used of an equitable remedy (also termed *indebitatis assumpsit*) imposed by courts when one party was unjustly enriched to the detriment of the other (implied in law). Some writers continue to observe this distinction. See **implied in fact & quasi contract**.

implied in fact; implied in law. The DIFFERENTIATION between these terms is sometimes muddled. *Implied in fact* = inferable from the facts of a case. *Implied in law* = imposed by operation of law, and not because of any inferences that can be drawn about the facts of a case. E.g., "Numerous decisions have held that this waiver of sovereign immunity is limited to express contracts and contracts *implied in fact* and does not extend to contracts *implied in law* or founded upon equitable principles." See **implied contract.**

impliedly; implicitly. Though neither form is strictly incorrect, *impliedly* is awkward and characteristic of LEGALESE. Fowler wrote merely that "*impliedly* is a bad form" (*MEU1* 260). Though almost unknown to laymen, it is a favorite of lawyers. *Impliedly* is old, dating in the *OED* from ca. 1400. Nevertheless, *implicitly* is almost always an improvement: "Because the quantity of court work influences quality, judicial administrators have at least *impliedly* [read *implicitly*] focused on the quality of judicial output."/ "When a person adopts the profession of law, and assumes to exercise its duties in behalf of another, for hire and reward, he *impliedly* [read *implicitly*] represents that he possesses the requisite knowledge and skill to properly conduct the matter for which he is engaged."/ "An effective argument might be made that the federal government *impliedly* [read *implicitly*] licenses an enemy alien to succeed to land by intestate succession or by will."/ "These decisions *impliedly* [read *implicitly*] hold that searches for contraband at checkpoints that are the functional equivalent of a border need not be preceded by any form of cause or suspicion."

Used on both sides of the Atlantic, *impliedly* is a graceless LEGALISM with virtually no advantages over *implicitly*, which is much to be preferred. Still, *implied* might be thought to be more concise and direct than *implicit.* Some authorities strain to differentiate the two, but such attempts are futile.

imply. **A.** Uses and Misuses of Legal Senses. *Imply* is not adequately treated in our dictionaries, for it has uses to lawyers and judges that have remained unrecorded. Specifically, it may mean: (1) "to impute or impose on equitable or legal grounds"; (2) "to read into (a legal instrument)"; or (3) "to infer." An *implied contract* (sense (1)) is often not just one implied from the facts of the case, but *implied* by the court, i.e. imposed by the court through its natural inferences. See **implied contract.**

Only sense (3) can rightly be characterized as an erroneous usage: Whereas laymen fre-

quently misuse *infer* for *imply*, lawyers and judges seem to misuse *imply* for *infer.* Thus judges will *imply* missing terms into a contract, though surely they must be *inferring* those terms from the underlying circumstances of the contract. In the layman's thinking, if the terms are *implied*, they are implied by the words or circumstances of the contract and not by the judges.

In the following sentences, *infer* should appear where we see *imply* in sense (3). These are the clear misuses: "When a possessory interest in property is conveyed, a court may *imply* [read *infer*] from the circumstances that the parties also intended to grant or reserve an easement as well despite their failure to say so in the deed."/ "In this case the defendant made an application for shares in the plaintiff's company under circumstances from which we must *imply* [read *infer*] that he authorized the company, in the event of their allotting to him the shares applied for, to send the notice of allotment by post." (Eng.)/ "The requirements of the rule are met if such an intention may be clearly *implied* [read *inferred*] from the language."

Now we come to the heretofore unrecorded sense (1) of *imply*, "to impute or impose on equitable or legal grounds," which is too well established in legal prose to call incorrect. The volume of specimens is justified in demonstrating this additional sense of the word, which is old in the law: "Is there any basis for the court's *implying* restrictions on the first lot, from its reading of the deed?"/ "The difficulty with the arguments seeking to *imply* Mary Silva's survival of Joseph as a condition is that they would result in holding that, because it is express that Joseph must survive until the period of distribution to take an inheritable interest, a similar contingency should be *implied* as to Mary."/ "Judicial willingness to *imply* new remedies in areas governed by federal law has been expressed in a number of ways."/ "Whether the execution of mutual or joint and mutual wills may satisfy the memorandum requirement without an express reference to the oral agreement depends upon the willingness of the court concerned to *imply* a contract from the transaction; most of the courts have refused to make this *implication*."/ "A killer forfeits his interest by common-law rule or by statute in a great majority of states, but in the absence of a statute dealing with homicide as a ground for forfeiture, most of the courts have been willing to *imply* such a condition to the intestate laws or the wills acts."

When put in the passive voice, this use of *imply* may be especially confusing, because the person who does the implying is left unclear. For one using any unabridged English dictionary, it would be almost impossible to divine exactly what *imply* is intended to mean: "A private right of action would probably be *implied* in favor of owners of interests in a reservoir against a fellow owner who wasted gas in violation of a Railroad Commission order." Here the passive voice masks the subject. But quite plainly the writer means to say that a court would allow such a cause of action; thus the writer is saying that the court would *imply* [i.e., "impute or impose on equitable or legal grounds"] such a cause of action.

This special legal sense is most keenly demonstrated when *imply* is coupled with *impute,* as here: "When deciding the shares, we look to the husband's and the wife's respective contributions and we see what trust is to be *implied* or *imputed* to them." (Eng.) Sometimes one could actually read *impute* in place of *imply* and have the same sense: "Malice, either actual or *imputed* [or *implied*], becomes the gist of every actionable libel; without malice, either express or *implied* [or *imputed*] by law, no tort could result from the publication of a defamatory statement concerning another."

Some legal writers have recoiled from this special legal usage, reverting instead to *infer:* "Once having discovered the ease with which a promise could be *implied* in Slade's Case, the common-law courts experienced little difficulty in extending assumpsit to these situations of implied-in-fact contracts by *inferring* a promise to pay reasonable value."/ "Apart from the difficulty of *inferring* a contract where none has been made, no agreement between husband and wife for future separation can be recognized." (Eng.) In the following sentence, in which the court writes *imply or infer from,* the word *imply* adds nothing, unless *by the circumstances* (i.e., *implicit in the circumstances*) is to be understood: "Rather, the crucial question is when can a waiver be *implied or inferred from* the actions and words of the person interrogated."

In the following sentence, *imply* is used in sense (2), "to read into (a document)": "One has merely to look at what is clearly said. There is no room for any intendment. . . .

Nothing is to be read in; nothing is to be *implied.* One can only look fairly at the language used." *Canadian Eagle Oil Co. v. The King,* [1946] A.C. 119 (H.L.).

Complicating still further the variety of meanings that *imply* can carry in legal contexts is the ordinary nonlegal sense: "We do not mean to *imply* that where joint ownership is set up in conformity with the statutory provisions, a court of equity is foreclosed from looking behind the form of the transaction and determining questions of real and beneficial interest."/ "There is nothing in the former decision that would *imply* that the sole discretion vested in and exercised by the trustees in this case is beyond court review." The following sentence is redundant: "By remanding, we *neither make nor imply the slightest intimation* [read *neither imply nor intimate anything*] about the character of the notes, or the need for extrinsic proof."

B. The Nonlegal Blunder. Courts are not immune from the layman's misusage of *infer* for *imply:* "The mere fact that Avondale's activities and conduct may have occurred ashore does not *infer* [read *imply,* or *suggest*] that Louisiana law would automatically apply."/ "The circuit court's remanding the case *inferred* [read *implied*], in the district court's view, that plaintiff's motion for new trial should be favorably considered."/ "We find no order, ruling, or stipulation stating or *inferring* [read *implying*] that the magistrate was bound by any prior evidentiary rulings of the district judge." See **infer.**

importunacy. See **importunity.**

importune is a verb meaning "to beg or beseech; entreat." It is also a NEEDLESS VARIANT for the adjective *importunate* (= troublesomely urgent), and an obsolete variant of inopportune. The intended meaning in the following sentence is not clear, but perhaps *inopportune* would have been the right word: "Although sanctions against judges may be leveled *importunely* [*inopportunely?*], the interests of the administration of justice demand that the error be on that side rather than on the side of retaining without forfeiture a judge whose effectiveness is damaged in the public view."

importunity; importunacy. The latter is a NEEDLESS VARIANT of the former, meaning "troublesome pertinacity in solicitation."

impostor, -er. In most states, the word in the heading of U.C.C. § 3-405 is spelled *impostor*, in others *imposter*. The *-or* spelling is preferred. See -ER, -OR.

impotence, -cy. The latter is a NEEDLESS VARIANT. *Impotence* in the modern literal sense should be used only in reference to *men*, a fact not recognized by the writer of this sentence: "The statute authorizes suit to annul a marriage if, at the time of the marriage, either party was permanently *impotent* for physical or mental reasons." *Black's* notes that *impotence* is "properly used of the male; but it has also been used synonymously with *sterility*." Any such use in modern contexts is an abuse of the term. The corresponding affliction for women, sometimes alleged to be a spurious affliction, is *frigidity*.

Impotence for *impetus* is a MALAPROPISM worthy of Mrs. Malaprop, Mistress Quickly, or Archie Bunker. E.g., "The main *impotence* [read *impetus*] for recruiting someone who has published is to ensure that he is used to long hours." *Impetus* means "force, impulse."

impoverishment. Only theoretically—not idiomatically—is *impoverishment* an antonym of *enrichment*. Whereas *enrich* means "to make rich *or richer*," *impoverish* means "to make poor; to reduce to indigency." E.g., "Like many a testator, who with specific devise and bequest has unwittingly *impoverished* the members of his family after his death, the settlor *impoverished* himself when he conveyed all his property in trust, and divested himself of the only means of livelihood he had." Finding a ten-dollar bill *enriches* one to some extent; but, for most, losing a ten-dollar bill would not constitute *impoverishment*.

In the following sentence, *impoverishment* is incorrectly made the correlative of the legal phrase *unjust enrichment*: "Under Louisiana law, recovery may be had for unjust enrichment only if the plaintiff proves the amount of his *impoverishment* [read *damages*?] and that the defendant was *enriched* to that extent."

impower is an obsolete spelling of *empower*.

impracticability (= practical impossibility) is sometimes wrongly spelled *impractibility*.

impractical; unpractical. Fowler had a point in believing that "the constant confusion between *practicable* and *practical* is a special reason for making use of *im-* and *un-* to add to the difference in the negatives" (*MEU1* 260), but *unpractical* has not been idiomatically accepted in the U.S. It is not included in *W9*, and even in the (British) *COD* the entry under *impractical* is longer than under *unpractical*. To a few British stalwarts, it may be worth keeping up the fight. See **practical.**

imprescriptible; imprescribable. The former is the preferred form for this word, meaning "not subject to prescription; that cannot in any circumstances be legally taken away or abandoned" (*OED*). E.g., "One of the most sacred *imprescriptable* rights of man is violated" (Field, J., in *The Slaughter-House Cases*). It is worth warning that "*imprescriptible* is one of the words that are often used without a clear conception of their meaning" (*MEU1* 261). It may be overstating the case, however, to say that the word is *often* used.

impress, n.; impressment; impression; impressure. In the legal idiom, constructive trusts are *impressed* by courts upon questionable transactions, or questionable transactions are *impressed* with constructive trusts. (See **impress,** v.t.) The question remains what to call the act of impressing a constructive trust. The answer is *impressment*: "In this instance it is doubtful that any property would have become available for trust *impressment*."

Impress, n., = a characteristic mark or quality. E.g., "A fixed contract right acquired before marriage was properly the character of which takes its *impress* from the date of the contract." *Impression* = (1) the impressing (of a mark); (2) the mark impressed; (3) an effect produced on the mind or feelings; (4) a notion (*COD*). *Impressure* is an archaic NEEDLESS VARIANT of *impression*.

impress, v.t. This verb is used of a court's imposition of a constructive trust on equitable grounds. For an explanation of characteristic phraseology, see the preceding entry. Following are examples of each of the two legal idioms with this verb: "Plaintiff's right and ability to recover depend upon removing the contract to will from the operation of the statute of frauds by part performance, and upon *impressing* a trust upon the distributed property in the hands of the defendant devisee."/ "To determine whether its assets were *impressed* with a trust, Pioneer filed an action for declaratory relief against a member of the society."

impressible, -able. The former spelling is preferred. See -ABLE (A).

impression; impressment. See **impress,** n.

imprimatur(a). The preferred form for ordinary purposes is *imprimatur;* literally, it means "let it be printed." This term (now meaning "commendatory license or sanction") is construed with the preposition *on.* E.g., "The trial judge placed his *imprimatur on* a defendant's theory."/ "It is the cause element that confers the *imprimatur* of constitutionality *on* the right."/ "A ruling admitting evidence in a criminal trial has the necessary effect of legitimizing the conduct that produced the evidence, while an application of the exclusionary rule withholds the constitutional *imprimatur.*"

improve (= to develop, as land) is a LEGAL-ISM understandable to most laymen. E.g., "The appellant negotiated for the purchase of an *improved* parcel of land in Baltimore."

improvident is a FORMAL WORD meaning "heedless, unwary, not circumspect." Judges use the word far more than other writers. E.g., "The chancellor ruled that Gilden's contract was a mere offer until approved by him, and that the trustee acted hastily, with inexperience, and *improvidently.*"/ "It is not unreasonable to expect a state's highest legal officer to know the state's law and to bring to this Court's attention the rules of state law that might demonstrate that we granted the writ of certiorari *improvidently.*"

improviser, -or; improvisator(e). The usual term for "one who improvises" is *improviser.* The *-or* spelling is not preferred. *Improvisator* is a formal equivalent, and *improvisatore* is an Italianate literary word meaning "one who composes verse or drama extemporaneously."

imprudent; impudent. *Imprudent* = rash, indiscreet. *Impudent* = insolently disrespectful; shamelessly presumptuous.

impugn; oppugn; repugn. *Impugn* = to challenge, call into question. E.g., "A most unfortunate result is that, to support its holding, the court, despite its disclaimers, *impugns* the integrity of public school teachers."/ "It is right that I should emphasize at this stage that the ethical standards of the wife's solicitors have never been *impugned.*" (Eng.) The noun is *impugnment,* q.v.

Impugn does not mean merely "to affect adversely." E.g., "The agreement's economic realignment of the parties did not *impugn* [read *impair*] the fact-finding process." In a footnote to this sentence, the court stated that the agreement "did not *affect* the ability of the court to make accurate findings of fact."

Oppugn and *repugn* are less frequently encountered than *impugn. Oppugn* = to controvert or call into question; to fight against. *Repugn* is an ARCHAISM meaning "to offer opposition or strive against; to affect disagreeably or be repugnant to."

impugnment; impugnation. The latter is an obsolete variant. Here is an example of the standard term: "Appellant contends that the district judge made many errors in his rulings concerning the conduct of the trial and the admissibility of evidence; the *impugnment* is more than a challenge to specific rulings, however."

impute (= to ascribe; to regard [usu. something undesirable] as being done, caused, or possessed by [*COD*]) takes *to.* E.g., "We are reluctant to *impute* a different meaning *to* the term where it has been used without modification, absent a compelling and certain impetus."/ "Appellee also failed to establish at trial that Agnes assigned the claim against Aetna to it, and indeed no attempt to show an assignment was made at trial; accordingly, we will not *impute* [to Agnes] such an assignment."

We see over and over again the growing idiomatic bias in favor of *imputing* undesirable things or qualities: "If the malice essential to support an action for libel can be found under such circumstances, it must be *imputed.* Malice in law is such as the law infers to exist without just or lawful excuse. The law will *impute* malice where a defamatory publication is made without sufficient cause or excuse." (See **imply.**)/ "We ought not to *impute to* others instincts contrary to our own."/ "Lafourche would be negligent only by virtue of an *imputation* of the negligence of another, in this case of its employee Savoie."

in-. See EN- & NEGATIVES (B).

in for *into.* "But to conclude that the motorist has actually agreed to be sued and has thus waived his federal venue rights is surely to move *in* [read *into*] the world of Alice in Wonderland." (Frankfurter, J.)

inability. See **disability** (A).

in accord; in accordance. See **accord.**

in actual fact. See **actual fact.**

inadmissible, -able. The former spelling is correct. See -ABLE (A).

inadvertence, -cy. The DIFFERENTIATION between these terms should be carefully observed. *Inadvertence* = an inadvertent act; a fault of inattention. E.g., "We cannot conclude that the district court abused its discretion in taking into account the lulling of Judge Bagley even though there is no suggestion that it was other than the product of oversight or *inadvertence.*" *Inadvertency* = the quality or state of being inadvertent ⟨The inadvertency of the act is not disputed.⟩. *Inadvertancy* is a common misspelling.

inalienable; unalienable. The former, used by Jefferson in the Declaration of Independence, is slightly better formed (with a Latinate prefix as well as suffix). E.g., "The New York statutes make the interest of the beneficiary of a trust to receive the income from realty or personalty *inalienable;* most trusts thus become indestructible." Some writers have recently revived *unalienable.* See NEGATIVES (B).

in any event. See **at all events.**

inapt is a NEEDLESS VARIANT of two quite different words, *unapt* and *inept.* Usually in legal contexts it is used for *unapt* or *inapposite,* either of which should be preferred to it. "The characterization of these contacts as 'fortuitous' is *inapt* [read *unapt* or *inapposite*] in the case at bar."

inasmuch as, in as much as; insofar as, in so far as. In modern AmE usage, the standard spelling of each group is *inasmuch as* and

insofar as, both single words except for the final element. In modern BrE, usage is split: *inasmuch as* is standard and the expression *in so far as* is preferred as four separate words. See **insofar as.**

inaugural, n.; **inauguration.** The ceremony for a president entering office is his *inauguration;* the speech he makes on this occasion is the *inaugural address,* sometimes shortened to *inaugural.*

inaugurate is a FORMAL WORD, some might say pompous, for *begin,* being more formal even than *commence,* q.v. "Thirteen years after *Brown II,* the only step that the Tennessee defendants had taken toward dismantling the dual system of public higher education was *inauguration* of an open admissions policy."

in back of. See **back of.**

in banc(o). See **en banc.**

in behalf of; on behalf of. See **behalf.**

in being; in esse. Professor Gray's classic formulation of the Rule against Perpetuities states: "No interest is good unless it must vest, if at all, not later than twenty-one years after some life *in being* at the creation of the trust." Through this formulation, *in being* has become a TERM OF ART, used commonly in discussions of wills and trusts. "On the date of Tilley's death, Lathan and Barrett and one great-grandchild were *in being.*"/ "At the time of executing the will, the testator had several grandchildren *in being.*"

In esse is a LATINISM that is equivalent to *in being;* except as a correlative of *in posse,* q.v., it has no justification in place of the Anglo-Saxon phrase: "These words were not used in reference to children who possibly may—but possibly may not—ever be *in esse* [read *in being*], and certainly not to those of whose existence, of course, the testator would have no knowledge." See **esse.**

in brief is understood by most readers as meaning "briefly." In American judicial opinions, however, it sometimes means "in the briefs," as here: "Before considering the evidentiary matters raised by appellants, we must address a threshold issue raised *in brief* and in oral argument."

in camera = in the chamber; privately. Usually this phrase refers to a judge's chambers (the documents were examined by the judge in camera). But the phrase is not restricted in legal contexts to refer only to judges' chambers; it may refer also to a courtroom from which all spectators are excluded.

The phrase may be either an adverb ("This court has reviewed *in camera* the portions of the memorandum that the IRS seeks to withhold.") or a prepositive adjective, as here: "The government invoked a 'deliberative processes' privilege for documents that it had turned over to the district court for *in camera* review."/ "Defense counsel conceded that he would be bound by the judge's decision after an *in camera* examination of the prosecution's reasons for refusal of the charge."

The phrase should be used of inspections, but not, through HYPALLAGE, of documents inspected. E.g., "Plaintiff then filed a motion seeking the right to inspection *of the in camera documents* [read *in camera of the documents*]."

In chambers is sometimes used rather than *in camera* in citations to opinions by single judges. For example, *Lenhard v. Wolff*, 444 U.S. 1301 (1979) (*in-chambers* opinion of Rehnquist, J.).

incapable is usu. applied to persons in modern nonlegal contexts, in the sense "unable, unfit." In law it retains its broader use in reference to things as well as to persons. E.g., "When a valid charitable bequest is *incapable* for some reason of execution in the exact manner provided by the testator, donor, or founder, a court of equity will carry it into effect in such a way as will as nearly as possible effectuate his intention." In such a context, *incapable* = not allowing or admitting of. See **capable.**

incapacitate = to deprive of legal capacity. E.g., "The Uniform Probate Code is applied to all subject matter relating to the estates of decedents, including protection of minors and *incapacitated* persons." *Incapacify* is a NEEDLESS VARIANT. See **capacitate.**

incapacitation; incapacity. These words should be distinguished in this way: *incapacitation* = the action of incapacitating or rendering incapable; *incapacity* = lack of ability in some legal respect. See **capacity.**

in case for *if.* See **case** (A).

in cases in which is usually verbose for *when* or *wherever.* See **case** (A).

inception; incipiency. Both words mean "beginning, commencement, initiation." The difference is that *inception* refers to the action or process of beginning, whereas *incipiency* refers to the fact or state of having begun. Here the two words are used merely for the sake of INELEGANT VARIATION: "That pattern fixes the character of title at the time of its *inception* or acquisition. It depends on the existence or nonexistence of the marriage at the time of the *incipiency* [read *inception*] of the right in virtue of which the title is finally extended." *Inception* is far more commonly the appropriate word.

in chambers. See **in camera.**

in chief is the phrase in legal ARGOT denoting the part of a trial, or of a witness's testimony, in which the main body of evidence is presented. "Witnesses examined in open court must be first examined *in chief*, then cross-examined, and then re-examined." Cf. **case-in-chief.**

inchoate, pronounced /in-*koh*-it/ in the U.S. and /in-*koh*-āt/ in G.B., means "just begun, not yet fully developed." The prefix is an intensive *in-*, not a negative or privative *in-*. (See **choate.**) The law has found many uses for this word: "One action was for the benefit of the survivors by reason of the death *inchoate*, so to speak, from the time of the injury to the consequent death, but ripening then and upon that event into a separate cause of action."/ "Nor would common-law dower, giving her an *inchoate* right during the husband's lifetime, help her, for dower applies only to real estate."/ "In determining whether the officer acted reasonably in such circumstances, due weight must be given, not to his *inchoate* and unparticularized suspicion or 'hunch,' but to the specific reasonable inferences that he is entitled to draw from the facts in light of his experience." See **curtesy.**

The word is sometimes a pomposity that usurps the place of an ordinary word. E.g., "Given the summary disposition of these issues, we cannot say at this *inchoate* [read *early*] stage that a fact-finder would be precluded from reasonably inferring the existence of a relevant submarket of third-party firms."

incidence (= occurrence or rate of occurrence) for *instance* (= case or example) is a CATACHRESIS: "As subsequent cases will establish, the rationale herein *has been rejected in* *most incidences* [read *has usually* (or *almost always*) *been rejected*]." See **incidents & instance.**

incident, n. **A.** And *instance.* An *incident* is an occurrence or happening; an *instance* is an example. See **instance.**
   B. Meaning "a concomitant." This sense is common in legal contexts. E.g., "The congressional dominion to expand and to contract federal-court jurisdiction always has been correctly considered to be a plenary *incident* of the Article III power to 'from time to time ordain and establish' the 'inferior courts' of the United States." (See SPLIT INFINITIVES.)/ "Courts of justice as an *incident* of their jurisdiction have inherent power to appoint guardians ad litem."/ "By such a condition, the grantor undertakes to deprive the property in the hands of the grantee of one of its legal *incidents* and attributes, namely, its alienability, which deprivation is deemed to be against public policy."/ "The decedent had the *incidents* of ownership to the life insurance."
   C. And *accident.* See **accident &** EUPHE-MISMS.

incident to; incidental to. Though to some extent interchangeable historically, these phrases have undergone a plain DIFFERENTIATION that has gained acceptance among stylists. The former means "closely related to; naturally appearing with"; the latter, "happening by chance and subordinate to some other thing; peripheral." In the following sentence, *incident* is properly used: "In an action for fraud, exemplary damages are *incident to* and dependent on the recovery of actual damages." Here *incidental* is correctly used: "It is clear that testator's plan of accumulation was merely *incidental to* his primary charitable intention to create a source that would provide continuing income over the 400-year term for the maintenance of Masonic homes."
   In the following quotations, *incidental* is misused for *incident,* a common blunder: "A half century ago, in that case, we denied damages for wrongful libel of a vessel save when the seizure resulted from bad faith, malice, or gross negligence. *Incidental thereto, on the same grounds we denied* [read *Incident to that denial, we denied on the same grounds*] recovery for attorney's fees incurred in obtaining the release of the vessel seized, without differentiating be-

tween attorney's fees and other damages."/ "The court held that the search was not *incidental to* [read *incident to*] the arrest because it was conducted six hours after the arrest and at a place other than the arrest scene." *Incidental to* has even had to be construed as meaning *incident to,* primarily because of slipshod drafting of statutes. See, e.g., *United States v. Shursen,* 649 F.2d 1250, 1257 (8th Cir. 1981).
   Sometimes courts are inconsistent in their use of these terms in a single opinion: "Closer in point . . . are cases holding that . . . [a club's] outside profits must be . . . strictly *incidental to* [read *incident to*] club activities. . . . Here the rental income was not *incident to* the operation of the club." *United States v. Fort Worth Club,* 345 F.2d 52, 57 (5th Cir. 1965). See INELEGANT VARIATION.
   Incidental is sometimes wrongly used as a prepositive *incident,* adj.: "Their primary objective is not to require the defendant to perform a contract, to carry out a trust, or to undo the effects of a fraud, but to determine the title and *incidental* [read *incident*] right to possession of the land."

incidentally; incidently. The former means "loosely, casually" or "by the way," and the latter means "so as to be incident; so as to depend on or appertain to something else." See **incident to.**

incidentals is elliptical for *incidental damages.* Cf. **consequentials.**

incidents and *incidence,* q.v., are homophones that may give listeners trouble. See **incident.**

incipiency. See **inception.**

incipient; insipient. The former means "beginning, in an initial stage"; the latter is an obsolete word meaning "unwise, foolish." Chapter C of J. Gillis Wetler's *Style of Judicial Opinions* (1960) is titled "Arkansas: American Style, and *Insipient* Transformation." A reading of the first paragraph of that chapter shows that *incipient,* not *insipient,* was the intended word. The misuse, especially for its being in such a prominent place, might be characterized as insipient.

incitement; incitation. The latter is a NEEDLESS VARIANT.

inciter (= one who incites) is so spelled. E.g., "Indeed, the alleged *inciter* or organiser is named, and the accused also says that it was this person who showed them the house and that he, the *inciter*, wanted to set it on fire." (Eng.)

inclose. See **enclose.**

inclosure is an archaic form of *enclosure*, q.v.

included. See **including.**

includable, -ible; inclusible. *Includible* is usual in estate-planning texts, and is a main entry in the *OED*; *includable*, however, is given primary sanction in *W3* and *W9*, and is now the more prevalent of the two in more general legal contexts. See -ABLE (A).

including for *namely*. *Including* should not be used to introduce an exhaustive list, for it implies that the list is only partial. In the words of one federal court, "It is hornbook law that the use of the word *including* indicates that the specified list . . . is illustrative, not exclusive." *Puerto Rico Maritime Shipping Authority v. I.C.C.*, 645 F.2d 1102, 1112 n.26 (D.C.Cir. 1981). E.g., "Several business law courses will be offered next year, *including* [read *namely*] one this summer and four next year."

Included for *including* must be a rare error: "The agreement provides that it is an Arizona agreement and that it shall be governed by the laws of the State of Arizona in all matters, *included* [read *including*] but not limited to validity, obligation, interpretation, construction, and termination."

income-average, v.i., is an unEnglish verb, but it is now common in AmE ⟨One need not income-average if one's income has been constant for the past three years⟩. The better phrasing is to say, not that one *income-averages*, but that one *averages income*.

incommensurate; incommensurable. See **commensurate.**

incomparable. The primary accent falls on the second syllable /in-**kom**-pă-ră-bĕl/. See **comparable.**

incompetence, -cy. Some lay authorities have stated that *incompetence* is the preferred form, but in legal writing a growing distinction exists between the forms. The best advice is to reserve the *-cy* form to contexts involving sanity or ability to stand trial or to testify, and to use *-ce* form when referring to less than acceptable levels of ability. E.g., "The various newspaper stories commenting on both appellant's alleged *incompetence* [read *incompetency*] to stand trial and a grand jury investigation of the district's operations also fall short of the requirements set forth in *Bollow*." These two word-forms are favorites of writers who engage in INELEGANT VARIATION; one must be consistent when the sense does not vary. See **competence, -cy** (A).

incompetent is the adjective serving both *incompetence* and *incompetency*, q.v. Here it is the adjective for *incompetency*: "Their testimony, if accepted, clearly shows that Mary was not totally *incompetent* and at times she was normal and in possession of her mental and physical faculties." And here for *incompetence*: "The evidence shows that her discharge stemmed from her being generally *incompetent* at her job: she was unable to type satisfactorily, to add and subtract, and to file in alphabetical order." See **competent.**

in concert. See **concert.**

incongruent; incongruous. Both are preferably accented on the second rather than the third syllable. For the distinction, see **congruent.**

in connection with is always a vague, loose connective. E.g., "Plaintiff sued defendant *in connection with* the lease of an irrigation system." For breach of the lease agreement? Who was the lessee, who the lessor?

inconsistency, -ce. Writers on usage formerly tried to distinguish between the forms, reserving *inconsistency* for the sense "the general quality of being inconsistent," and making *inconsistence* mean "an act of an inconsistent nature or an instance of being inconsistent." Today, however, *inconsistency* has ousted *-ce* in all senses. *Inconsistence* should be eschewed as a NEEDLESS VARIANT.

in contrast with; in contrast to. These are equally good. See **contrast** (A).

incorporeal; incorporal. See **corporal.**

incorporeality; incorporeity. See **corporeality.**

incredible; incredulous. *Incredible* = not believable. (*Noncredible* is a NEEDLESS VARIANT.) E.g., "We find *incredible* the testimony that the lawn mower slid laterally five to six feet across the grass on flat ground."/ "Sources of information are sometimes given because naming the source gives authority to an otherwise *incredible* statement."

Incredulous (= skeptical) is sometimes misused for *incredible*, as here: "The statute of limitations runs against the predecessors of the individual plaintiffs and in favor of the defendants; to argue otherwise is to border on being *incredulous* [read *incredible*]." See **credible.**

incriminate has two important senses: (1) "to charge with a crime"; (2) "to indicate involvement in the commission of a crime." The latter sense is more frequent; it applies in the phrase *self-incrimination*, and, e.g., here: "When he presents his witnesses, he must reveal their identity and submit them to cross-examination, which in itself may prove *incriminating*, or which may furnish the state with leads to *incriminating* rebuttal evidence."/ "The fingerprints were not the only evidence linking Walborn to the *incriminating* documents."

The equivalent verb *criminate*, q.v., was formerly common in AmE and BrE, but it seldom appears in modern prose. E.g., "It has also been held that the fact that a witness voluntarily testifies to matters concerning which he might refuse to answer on the ground that the answer might tend to *criminate* him does not constitute any defense to a charge of perjury." It is rightly to be considered a NEEDLESS VARIANT of *incriminate*.

incriminatory; criminatory. The former is more common, just as *incriminate* is now more common than *criminate*, q.v. "The communication may contain *criminatory* [read *incriminatory*] matter which, without this privilege, would be slanderous and actionable."

inculcatable. So spelled; see -ATABLE.

inculcate (into) for *indoctrinate*. Although these are both transitive verbs (i.e., they take direct objects), the nature of the objects is different. One *inculcates* values into people; and one *indoctrinates* people with certain values.

One does not *inculcate* people, but rather values or beliefs or ideas. The title of a law review article contains this infelicity: van Greel, *The Search for Constitutional Limits on Governmental Authority to Inculcate Youth*, 62 Texas L. Rev. 197 (1983). Fowler noted this aberration and called it "a curious mistake" (*MEU1* 266); no longer is it curious, but it is still a mistake. See OBJECT-SHUFFLING.

inculpatable, not *inculpable*, is the correct form of the word meaning "capable of being inculpated." See -ATABLE. *Inculpable* is, however, a negative form of *culpable* that means "blameless, free from guilt." Use of the term may cause ambiguities. See **culpable.**

inculpate = to accuse or incriminate. Although its antonym (*exculpate*, q.v.) can be found in nonlegal writing, *inculpate* rarely appears in nonlegal prose. But it is common in criminal-law contexts: "The prosecution asserts that a prior inconsistent statement of the witness may be admitted to attack his credibility even if the statement tends to directly *inculpate* the defendant."/ "The right to confront a witness arises only when that witness *inculpates* a defendant." The adjective is *inculpatory*: "Jardina claims that the *inculpatory* statements he made to the Secret Service should have been excluded from evidence."/ "Since the number of *inculpatory* statements cannot be said to have significantly declined in the wake of *Miranda*, consent searches would not decline in the face of a universal requirement to inform of the right to refuse." See -ATABLE.

incumbent upon or *on* has become a CLICHÉ as a way of expressing a duty or obligation. E.g., "If, however, a valid reason exists for the retention of a fund by the executor, it is *incumbent upon* him not to permit such fund to remain idle, but to invest it."

incumber; encumber. The latter is the preferred spelling. See EN-.

incumbrance. See **encumbrance.**

incumbrancer. See **encumbrancer.**

incurrence; incurment. The latter is a NEEDLESS VARIANT of the noun corresponding to the verb *to incur*. E.g., "The fault in the *incurrence* of the danger does not free the defendant from liability."/ "When a 'loss contingency' exists, the likelihood that the future event will confirm the loss or impairment of an asset or the *incurrence* of a liability can range from probable to remote." *Incurrence* is sometimes misspelled *incurrance.*

indebitatus assumpsit. See **assumpsit, implied contract & quasi contract.**

indebtedness = the state or fact of being indebted. E.g., "For purposes of 12 U.S.C. § 82, a national bank's *indebtedness* or liability does not include Federal Funds Purchased or obligations to repurchase securities sold."

Indebtedness is frequently used where the simpler word *debt* would be preferable: "The petitioner elected to declare the entire *indebtedness* [better: *debt*] to be immediately due and payable."/ "The *indebtedness* [better: *debt*] has not been paid." In this sense, *indebtedness* is a NEEDLESS VARIANT of *debt,* although in some contexts it is difficult to discern whether it is the state of being indebted or the actual debt that is being referred to.

INDEFINITE ANTECEDENT. See ANTECEDENTS, FALSE.

indemnifiable; indemnitable. The former is better.

indemnificatory; indemnitory. The latter is a NEEDLESS VARIANT not recorded in the major unabridged dictionaries, but occurring occasionally in American legal writing. *Indemnificatory* is standard. "Among these problems are those arising from the possibility of multiple subrogation claims [and] determining what types of lines of insurance are *indemnitory* [read *indemnificatory*]." *Shelby Mutual Insurance Co. v. Birch*, 196 So. 2d 482, 485 (Fla. App. 1967) (Andrews, J., dissenting)./ "[N]o decision is necessary at this time on whether the *indemnitory* [read *indemnificatory*] theory should be limited only to owners of premises." *Waller v. J. E. Brenneman Co.*, 307 A.2d 550, 553 (Del. Super. Ct. 1973).

indemnifier. See **indemnitor.**

indemnify takes the preposition *from, against,* or *for.* E.g., "Based on this finding, the district court ordered Lee-Vac to pay Cities Service's damages and to *indemnify* American Hoist *for* the expenses of its successful defense."

Usually one *indemnifies from* or *against*

losses; the *OED* records the transitive sense "to compensate, make up for" ⟨indemnify this defect⟩, and calls this sense "Obs. rare," but it has been revived: "The agreement did not require Atlas to *indemnify* losses caused by its own negligence." This sense arose apparently through HYPALLAGE, by transference of object from the person compensated to the thing for which he is compensated.

indemnitable. See **indemnifiable.**

indemnitee and *indemnitor* are MORPHOLOGICAL DEFORMITIES, since personal suffixes such as *-or* and *-ee* should be applied to verbs, and not to nouns. Yet the words are established beyond cavil in the U.S., where they originated. See -EE.

indemnitor; indemnifier. The two words are absolutely synonymous, the former being the usual form in American legal writing. *Indemnifier* is doubtless more comprehensible to most educated laymen.

indemnitory. See **indemnificatory.**

indemnity; indemnification. There is a distinction. *Indemnity* = (1) security or protection against contingent hurt, damage, or loss; or (2) a legal exemption from the penalties or liabilities incurred by any course of action (*OED*). *Indemnification* = the action of compensating for actual loss or damage sustained; the payment made with this object (*OED*). Here *indemnity* is used where *indemnification* is the intended word: "If an injury is caused by defendant's tort, a sum of money may be awarded as compensation or *indemnity* [read *indemnification*] for the loss." For the distinction between *indemnity* and *contribution,* see **contribution.**

independent(ly). **A.** Preposition with. *Independent* should take the preposition *of,* not *from.*

B. Adverb or Adjective. The proper adverbial phrase is *independently of.* E.g., "The respondent may be liable, *independently of* his tort against the owner."/ "The former class of rights exists *independently of* contract; the latter frequently arises out of contract." The phrase *independent of* is sometimes wrongly made to act as an adverbial phrase. E.g., "When a new remedy is given by statute for a right of action existing *independent of* [read *independently of*] it, without excluding other remedies already known to the law, the statutory remedy is a cumulative remedy."/ "That it differs from what is called by the same name in the common law is clear; for it exists *independent of* [read *independently of*] possession."

INDETERMINATE SUBJECTS. See EX-PLETIVES.

indexes; indices. For ordinary purposes, *indexes* is the preferable plural. *Indices*, though less pretentious than *fora* or *dogmata*, is pretentious nevertheless. Some writers prefer it in technical contexts, as in mathematics and the sciences. Though not the best plural for *index*, *indices* is permissible in the sense "indicators." Thus: "The existence of one or more of these *indices* does not necessarily preclude a summary determination that certain products or services either are reasonably interchangeable or demonstrate a high cross-elasticity of demand." Cf. **appendixes.**

indicant. See **indicative.**

indicate should not appear where *say, state,* or *show* will suffice.

indicative, -tory; indicant; indicial. *Indicative* is the usual adjective corresponding to the noun *indication* and meaning "that indicates." *Indicant* and *indicatory* are NEEDLESS VARIANTS except in archaic medical contexts. *Indicial* is the adjective corresponding to both *indicia,* q.v., and *index*; it means (1) "of the nature of an indicia, indicative"; or (2) "of the nature or form of an index."

indices. See **indexes.**

indicia, the plural of *indicium* (= an indication, sign, token), is itself a singular noun forming the plurals *indicia* and *indicias,* the former being preferred: "In *Evans v. Newton,* we held that the park had acquired such unalterable *indicia* of a public facility that for the purposes of the equal protection clause it remained public even after the city officials were replaced as trustees by a board of private citizens."

The singular *indicium* is still sometimes used: "The most reliable *indicium* of common interests among employees is similarity of their work, skills, qualifications, duties, and working conditions." *N.L.R.B. v. DMR Corp.,* 795 F.2d 472, 475 (5th Cir. 1986)./ "The challenged information is 'false' or 'unreliable' if it lacks some minimal *indicium* of reliability beyond mere allegation."/ "The word 'trademark' B used here in its broadest sense to include any *indicium* that indicates origin." (Cf. *data* and *datum.*) In the civil law, *indicium* is a species of proof similar to common-law circumstantial evidence.

indicial. See **indicative.**

indicium. See **indicia.**

indict; indite. Both words are pronounced /in-dIt/. The former means "to formally charge with a crime"; the latter, "to write, compose, dictate." A literary term, *indite* is rarely used today.

indictee (= a person charged with a crime) is not a newfangled passive noun in *-ee*; it has been used in English since the sixteenth century. See -EE.

indicter. See **indictor.**

indictment; information; presentment. In the federal courts of the U.S., a distinction exists between these charging instruments. Any offense punishable by death, or for imprisonment for more than one year or by hard labor, must be prosecuted by *indictment*; any other offense may be prosecuted by either an *indictment* or an *information*. Rule 7(a) of Fed. R. Crim. P. An *information* may be filed without leave of court. *Presentments* are not used in American federal procedure; formerly, a *presentment* was "the notice taken, or statement made, by a grand jury of any offense or unlawful state of affairs from their own knowledge or observation, without any bill of indictment laid before them" (*W2*).

Through a historical transference of meaning, *indictment*, which originally referred to the accusation of the grand jury, came to signify in the sixteenth century the document containing the accusation. See HYPALLAGE. In both the U.S. and G.B., *indictment* may refer to the proceeding or to the charging instrument known more particularly as a *bill of indictment.* See **arraignment.**

To a layman it is strange to see *information* (the charging instrument) used as a COUNT

NOUN: "Appellant was prosecuted under two *informations*, in two courts, which charged that he personally sold a sixteen-year-old boy two 'girlie' magazines on each of two dates in October 1965."

indictor, -er. The *-or* spelling is preferred.

indifference, -cy. The latter is archaic.

indigence, -cy. *Indigency* is a NEEDLESS VARIANT of *indigence*, the standard form. It still clutters some legal writing. E.g., "It is clear that the sentence was not imposed upon appellant because of his *indigency* [read *indigence*], but because he had committed a crime."

indirect evidence. See **circumstantial evidence** & **direct evidence.**

indiscernible, -able. The former spelling is preferred. See -ABLE (A).

indiscrete; indiscreet. See **discrete.**

indispensable; necessary. Justice Harlan wrote, in *Provident Tradesmens Bank & Trust Co. v. Patterson*, 390 U.S. 102, 118 (1968): "To use the familiar but confusing terminology, the decision to proceed is a decision that the absent person is merely *necessary*, while the decision to dismiss is a decision that he is *indispensable*." With regard to possible parties to a lawsuit, *necessary* refers to those who should be included but need not be, *indispensable* to those without whom the action must be dismissed. In other words, in American legal English *indispensable* means "more necessary than *necessary*."

The two words should not be redundantly coupled when no nuance is intended: "The rule has no doubt been considerably relaxed since *Peirce* [sic] *v. Corf* was decided in 1874, but I think it is still *indispensably necessary* [read either *indispensable* or *necessary*] that there should be a document signed by the party to be charged." (Eng.)

indisputable should receive its primary accent on the second, not the third, syllable /in-**dis**-pyĕt-ă-bĕl/. A common and acceptable pronunciation on both sides of the Atlantic is /in-di-**spyoo**-tă-bĕl/.

indite. See **indict.**

individual was formerly thought to be a newfangled barbarism as a noun substituting for *man, woman,* or *person.* Certainly, those more specific terms are generally to be preferred over *individual,* but this word should no longer be stigmatized. Still, *individual* is best confined to contexts in which the writer intends to distinguish the single (noncorporate) person from the group or crowd.

individualize; individuate. Both are commonly used, and they have basically the same sense ("to make individual in character, to give individuality to"); both are also so common to that it would be inappropriate to call either a NEEDLESS VARIANT, and subtle writers may in fact intend nuances. *Individualize* is much more common in legal writing. E.g., "This approach injects hypothetical extraneous considerations into the sentencing process and contradicts the judicially approved policy of *individualizing* sentences that are tailored to fit the offender." Indeed, in the U.S., *individualize* has become almost a VOGUE WORD in meaning "to humanize; to portray as an individual human being." Hence: "If the jury had been presented *individualized* evidence that he was a human being and that he had no extended record of violent crime, nevertheless, under the *Strickland* test, apparently we cannot say that counsel was ineffective unless it is shown affirmatively that the death penalty would not have been imposed had the sentencing jury been afforded this testimony."

Individuate is often used in scientific contexts and in Jungian psychology in highly technical senses, and ought generally to be confined to these uses.

indorse. See **endorse.**

indorsee. See -EE.

indubitable (= perfectly certain or evident) was destined to become a favorite word of lawyers. E.g., "The trial court was fully within its discretion in barring Nolen from selling cable assemblies to Tandy, *indubitably* a customer of Nolen's former employer." See **clearly.**

inducement; inductance; induction. *Inducement* ordinarily means "that which induces or persuades." E.g., "The interests of representative and represented must, however, be so identical that the motive and *inducement* to protect and preserve may be assumed in each." In pleading, it has in G.B. an additional sense: "Matters of *inducement* are introductory averments stating who the parties are, how connected and other surrounding circumstances leading up to the matter in dispute, but not stating such matter" (quoted in *OED*). Thus: "The first count of the declaration, after the usual *inducement* of the plaintiff's good conduct, stated that, before the [defendant's] speaking and publishing [various] defamatory words . . . the plaintiff was . . . a clerk." *Lumby v. Allday*, (1831) 1 Cr. & J. 301, 148 Eng. Rep. 1434 (Ex.).

Induction, in the context of reasoning, means "the bringing forward, adducing, or enumerating of a number of separate facts for the purpose of proving a general statement." *Inductance* is a technical electrical term.

inductee. See -EE.

indue; endue. The preferred spelling is *endue* (= to put on or clothe) ⟨endued with the mantle of apparent authority⟩.

ineffective; ineffectual; inefficacious; inefficient. See **effectual.**

INELEGANT VARIATION. "A draftsman should never be afraid of repeating a word as often as may be necessary in order to avoid ambiguity." A. Russell, *Legislative Drafting and Forms* 103 (1938). Fowler referred to as "elegant variation" the ludicrous practice of never using the same word twice in the same sentence. Over half a century ago when Fowler named this vice of language, *elegant* was almost a pejorative word, commonly associated with precious overrefinement. Today, however, the word has positive connotations. E.g., "The book is exceedingly well edited, and several essays are *elegantly* written." Lest the reader misapprehend that the subject of this article is a virtue rather than a vice in writing, I have renamed it unambiguously: *in*elegant variation. The rule of thumb with regard to undue repetition is that one should not repeat a word in the same sentence if it can be felicitously avoided; this is hardly an absolute proscription, however.

The problem is that if one uses terms that vary slightly in form, the reader is likely to deduce that some differentiation is intended.

Thus one does not write *punitive damages, punitory damages*, and *punishment damages* all in the same opinion or brief, lest the reader infer that one intends to convey a distinction. Yet one judge did just that in a single dissent. See *Jones v. Fisher*, 42 Wis. 2d 209, 166 N.W.2d 175 (1969) (Hansen, J., dissenting) (using *punitive damages* and *punitory damages*). Other judges have used both forms in a single sentence: "There is an argument for regarding the *punitory* theory of *punitive* damages as anachronistic." See **punitive.**

One frequently encounters writing on criminal law in which *informer* and *informant* (q.v.) are used alternatively, but with no purpose. "Can the *informant's* general reliability be established by an officer's interview with the *informer?*" The second use could have been easily avoided by using *him.* The following example of inelegant variation occurred within the space of two paragraphs: "A counter-letter such as we have now before us does not affect *marketability.* . . . The lots were not rendered *unmerchantable.*" See **marketable.**

The basic type of variation found objectionable by Fowler is the simple change from the straightforward term to some slightly more fanciful synonym, as here: "Several Southwestern states have established elaborate procedures for allocation of *water* and adjudication of conflicting claims to *that resource* [read *water*]." / "Such a judgment of probate cannot be collaterally *attacked* and can be *assailed* [read *attacked*] only in the manner provided by statute." / "The court held merely that a *protestant* who could have sought, but did not seek, review may not create the basis for a reviewable order by unilaterally petitioning for repeal or amendment of a regulation; to permit any *complainant* [read *protestant*, or *complainant* in each slot] to restart the limitations period by petitioning for review of a rule would eviscerate the congressional concern for finality embodied in time limitations on review." / "*Lawyers* generally have a bad reputation; today the American public holds a grudge against the half-million *counselors* [read *lawyers*] who handle its legal affairs." / "State law makes no provisions for mandatory *autopsies*, which means that justices of the peace follow different policies for seeking *postmortems* [read *autopsies* or *them*]." / "One who executes a *will* believes that the *testament* [read *it*] covers all contingencies."

Equally common in modern legal writing is

the switch from one form of a word to another: "The district court's conclusions, therefore, represent an *implicit* finding, one we can readily discern. . . . *The implied* [read *This implicit*] finding of fact was [read *is*] far from clearly erroneous."/ "Some courts have held that the gift passes by intestacy on the theory that there can be no *residue* of a *residuum* [read *residue*]."/ "The *in rem theory* would permit enforcement of the injunction by the contempt power even against persons who had no notice of the decree, since the *res theory* [read *in rem theory*] is that the whole world is bound by the court's control of the property."/ "And unlike Blackstone's blurred account, Coke made clear that his *fictional death* would not create new property rights or destroy old ones. . . . Without resort to *fictitious death* [read *fictional death*] the law stripped the felon of his property as a part of his punishment." Certain pairs may lend themselves to this snare: *arbiter & arbitrator, adjudicative & adjudicatory, investigative & investigatory, exigency & exigence.* In fact, it sometimes seems that amateurish writers believe that NEEDLESS VARIANTS were made for this specific stylistic purpose.

"The point to be observed," wrote Fowler, "is that, even if the words meant exactly the same, it would be better to keep the first selected on duty than to change guard" (*MEU2* 150).

inept. See **inapt.**

in esse; in posse. *In esse* = in actual existence; in being. *In posse* = potential; not realized. E.g., "There is no legal objection to constituting such a trustee in favor of one who was not *in esse* when the fraud was perpetrated."/ "A court would not intervene to deprive the children—*in esse* or *in posse*—of their property rights under such a provision." There is no good reason why the phrases *in being* and *potential* should not be substituted in place of these LATINISMS. See **in being & esse.**

inexpense is not, by the normal measures, a legitimate English word; it is listed in no major unabridged dictionary, and does not fill a need in the language. E.g., "[E]ven an absentee landlord could *with relative inexpense* [read *rather inexpensively*] employ someone regularly to remove these hazards." Note, *Liability for Failure to Remove or Render Safe Ice and Snow on Common Passageways and Approaches,* 41 Colum. L. Rev. 349, 352 (1941)./ "We

have yet to figure out how the relative *inexpense* [read *inexpensiveness*] of attending this university relates in any way to the fact that the administration is illegitimately spending interest generated from student money." See NEOLOGISMS & BACK-FORMATIONS.

inexpert, adj.*;* **nonexpert,** adj. An important distinction exists. *Inexpert* = unskilled ⟨the novice's inexpert cross-examination⟩. *Nonexpert* = not of or by an expert, but not necessarily unskilled. E.g., "This rule permits proof by *nonexpert* testimony."

inexplicable (= unexplainable) is best accented on the second syllable /in-**ek**-spli-kă-bĕl/, although stressing the third syllable is so widespread and venial as to be irreproachable.

inexpressible, -able. The former spelling is correct. See -ABLE (A).

in extenso (= unabridged) is a pompous LEGALISM for the simple English phrase *in full.* E.g., "Convinced beyond peradventure that *Oliver* has no impact on those parts of our opinion, we reinstate those paragraphs as if set forth here *in extenso* [read *in full*] and verbatim."/ "I asked for a full transcript of the judgment in that case and I shall read *in extenso* [read *in full*] the passage of general importance in case the instant case is reported." (Eng.) See LATINISMS.

in extremis (= at the point of death; at the last gasp) is better known than most LATINISMS, and may be used purposefully as a EUPHEMISM. E.g., "The test for imminence of death, which is required for an effective gift *causa mortis,* is equally indefinite: the donor must anticipate more than the general mortality of man, yet he need not be *in extremis.*"

infant (= a minor) is peculiar to legal language; in nonlegal contexts, *infant* means "a small child, a baby." But in law it is quite possible to write of, say, a *twelve-year-old infant.* E.g., "An exception was made for the time of filing for *infants,* incompetents, and nonresidents."

infanticide = (1) the killing of an infant; or (2) one who kills an infant. Sense (2) invariably takes an article ⟨a merciless infanticide⟩, whereas sense (1) only sometimes takes an article ⟨the infanticide committed by a deranged father⟩.

in fault is less and less frequently used for *at fault*, though formerly it was common. E.g., "In such cases the question whether the defendant was *in fault* in what he did or failed to do is ordinarily one of fact to be determined by the jury unless the jury is waived." The distinction was formerly made that *in fault* means "in error," whereas *at fault* means "perplexed, puzzled." Today, however, *at fault* or *in fault* (more common in BrE than in AmE) indicates blameworthiness. See **at fault.**

infeasible; unfeasible. The former is better.

infectious is sometimes erroneously rendered *infectuous.* See **contagious.**

infeft is an archaic Scottish variant of *enfeoff.* See **feoff.**

infeoff. See **feoff.**

infer is generally correctly used in legal writing. Properly, it means "to deduce; to reason from premises to a conclusion." E.g., "The court *inferred* that Congress must have intended to extend the suspension power to embrace initial as well as changed rates, and it relied on this *inference* to buttress its reading of the statute's literal language."

A common mistake among laymen is to use *infer* when *imply* (= to hint at; suggest) is the correct word. Yet this layman's CATACHRESIS has occasionally insinuated itself into legal writing. E.g., "Exclusion from venires focuses on the inherent attributes of the excluded group and *infers* [read *implies*] its inferiority. . . ." *United States v. Leslie,* 759 F.2d 381, 392 (5th Cir. 1985). See **imply** (B).

inference. One *draws,* not *makes,* inferences. If one says "to make an inference" (like "to make a deduction"), then many listeners will confuse *inference* with *implication.* The verb *to draw* is therefore clearer. See **infer.**

infer(r)able; infer(r)ible. The preferred form is *inferable,* accented on the second syllable /in-fur-ă-bĕl/. Fifty years ago *inferrible* was considered the best spelling, because of

the rule that a consonant should be doubled after a stressed syllable. *Inferable,* which has now ousted the other spelling, is anomalous. See DOUBLING OF FINAL CONSONANTS.

inferentially for *we can infer that.* The *OED* states that *inferentially* = in an inferential manner, but allows that it is used "sometimes qualifying the whole clause or statement: = as an inference, as may be inferred." This use defies explication, but is common in legal writing: "Judge Lumbard pointed out that even though defendant destroyed its records, the evidence *inferentially* established profits of over $1000."/ "*Inferentially,* at least, the accused is entitled to counsel and to compulsory process for bringing in his witnesses."/ "The second paragraph of the statute, by providing that an adopted child may not take by representation property coming from collateral kindred of the adopting parent, *inferentially* contemplates the child may so take from lineal kin." See SENTENCE ADVERBS. Cf. **hopefully** & **thankfully.**

inferior; superior. These comparative adjectives cannot act as adverbs. E.g., "The statute is unconstitutional not only because it *treats* former mental patients differently from *and inferior to* [read *and as inferior to*] convicts, but also because it presumptively denies former mental patients the opportunity to establish that they no longer present the danger against which the statute was intended to guard."

Only etymologically are these words comparatives; they take *to,* not *than.* They are qualified by *much* or *far,* not *more* (not an uncommon error).

inferior court = lower court. The phrase *inferior courts* is used in the Constitution to mean "all federal courts apart from the Supreme Court." It is not a term of condescension when used by a court on high. See **higher court.**

in fine, a legalistic phrase for *in conclusion,* even if literally correct, would be turgid; but using the phrase in that sense is incorrect. Properly, *in fine* = at the end; it is also used "in references to indicate that the passage cited is at the end of a book, chapter, or section" (*Black's*). This sentence, occurring at the conclusion of an opinion, exemplifies the erroneous usage: "*In fine,* [read *In conclusion,*] we reject the appellant's claim that the district court's treatment of the summaries unduly prejudiced his trial."/ "*In fine*, [read *In conclusion*,] the jury would be warranted in finding that the defendant's conduct was a high-handed and unlawful means of collecting a debt."

infirm is frequently used in reference to fatal weaknesses, whether constitutional or statutory. In fact, *constitutionally infirm* might accurately be labeled a legal CLICHÉ. E.g., "The state argues further that the statute is not constitutionally *infirm* simply because the legislature could have achieved the same result by other means."/ "Our review of the record indicates no *infirmities* in the jury's findings." See **fatal.**

in flagrante delicto (= red-handed; in the act of committing an offense) is a term now more commonly used for polysyllabic humor in nonlegal contexts than as a serious word in law. See LATINISMS.

inflammable. See **flammable.**

inflatus. See **afflatus.**

inflict; afflict. These terms are infrequently confused. *Afflict* takes *with*; *inflict* takes *on*. Living things, esp. humans, are *afflicted with* diseases; inanimate objects, esp. scourges or punishments, are *inflicted on* people.

inflicter, -or. The former spelling is better.

influence. The first syllable, not the second, receives the primary accent /*in-floo-ĕns*/, whether the part of speech is noun or verb.

inforce is an obsolete spelling of *enforce*, except in the prefixed *reinforce*. See EN-.

inform, in the sense "to determine, give form to, permeate" is somewhat archaic, but it is common in scholarly legal writing. E.g., "Whether vocational education produces salutary outcomes is *informed* in part by the nature of the dependent variable under consideration."/ "To the extent that economic analysis *informs* our decision here, we think that it favors retention of the present rule."

informant; informer. Both terms are used in reference to those who confidentially supply police with information about crimes. *In-*formant is perhaps slightly more usual in American legal contexts, *informer* in British ones. The Evanses write that *informant* is neutral, whereas *informer*, which acquired strong connotations of detestation in the seventeenth and eighteenth centuries, remains a connotatively charged term. B. Evans & C. Evans, *A Dictionary of Contemporary American Usage* 245 (1957). If that is true in lay contexts, it certainly is not true in legal writing. See INELEGANT VARIATION.

in forma pauperis (= in the form of a poor person; not liable for costs of court) is a TERM OF ART. E.g., "Under well-settled principles, a timely motion to proceed *in forma pauperis* on appeal is the substantial equivalent of a notice of appeal and is effective to invoke appellate jurisdiction." Judges frequently use the abbreviation *IFP* ⟨an IFP motion⟩.

Where the entire phrase is not used, *pauper* should appear rather than *forma pauperis*. E.g., "This packet includes four copies of a complaint form and two copies of *a forma pauperis* [read *a pauper*] petition."/ "In sum, assuming *forma pauperis status* [read *pauper status*], the prisoner complaints must be filed."/ "We grant the motion for *pauper* status but deny the application for stay of execution." See **pauper.**

information. See **indictment.**

informative, -tory. The latter is a NEEDLESS VARIANT, except in bridge, the card game.

informer. See **informant.**

in foro conscientiae (lit., "in the forum of conscience") is used in the sense "privately or morally rather than legally" (*W3*). E.g., "The moral obligation exerts just as much force the day after the limit expired as it did the day before, and, *in foro conscientiae*, the debtor should discharge the debt." (For an Englished version of this phrase, see the quotation under **infract.**)

infra; post. See **ante.**

infract (= to break in; violate; infringe) is chiefly an Americanism. Even so, it is little used outside legal writing. "This is distinctly an abuse of process, a rank perversion of the machinery of the law, and a degradation of judicial functions, but while it violates the canons of ethics, it *infracts* no legal rule, and the remedy therefor lies only in the forum of conscience." See **infringe.**

infraction (= violation, infringement) is used in legal and in sports ARGOT. E.g., "Appellants urge several other evidentiary *infractions.*"

infrequent; unfrequent. The latter is a NEEDLESS VARIANT.

infringe, v.t. & v.i. Fowler held (just as a highest court *holds*) that *infringe* is best used transitively, as here: "The association *infringed* no legal right of the appellant by its nondisclosure of this fact." The transitive is especially useful where the passive voice is called for: "An association of college faculty members and five individual educators seek vindication of their first amendment rights, which they contend *were infringed* by the action of a state college in attempting to destroy the association, in discharging one faculty member, and in discriminating against others."

Rather than *infringe upon* or *on,* some other verb such as *impinge,* q.v., *encroach,* or *trespass* is better when an intransitive verb is desired: "The plaintiff was free to make any legal contract with defendant that did not wrongfully *infringe upon* [read *impinge on*] the legal rights of others or offend against public rights." (Eng.)/ "The production of evidence demanded here does not *infringe on* [read *encroach* or *impinge on*] British sovereignty, as it calls merely for documents and not for personal appearance." See **infract** & **impinge.**

infringer. So spelled.

in future. This phrase is BrE, perhaps a direct translation of the Latin phrase *in futuro,* q.v. AmE uses the definite article: *in the future.*

in futuro is a legalistic LATINISM conveying (or failing to convey) an elementary notion for which the English language has adequate words. E.g., "It is an elementary rule that such a gift cannot be made to take effect in possession *in futuro* [read *in the future*]."/ "The point of distinction between a vested gift to be paid *in futuro* [read *in the future*] and a contingent gift to be paid to a person only upon reaching a certain age is made by Chief Justice Booth in *Carey v. Pettyjohn.*" See **in future** & **in praesenti.**

ingenious; ingenuous. These words, virtual antonyms, are frequently confused. *Ingenious,* means "crafty, skillful, inventive." *Ingenuous* means "artless, innocent, simple."

ingenuity was once the nominal form of *ingenuous,* and *ingeniosity* (last used in 1608) the noun for *ingenious.* Through a curious historical reversal of the role of *ingenuity,* it came to mean "ingeniousness." *Ingenuousness* was the only term left to do the work of the noun corresponding to the adjective *ingenuous.* Thus, although *ingenuity* appears to be the correlative of *ingenuous,* it no longer is.

ingress; egress. The correct prepositions are illustrated by this sentence: "The company breached its duty to furnish Rivers with a safe means of *ingress to* and *egress from* the vessel." See **egress.**

in gross, when used of servitudes, means "personal as distinguished from appurtenant to land." The phrase may be placed either before or after the noun it modifies. E.g., "A *servitude in gross* threatens the servient owner's autonomy, and thus deserves scrutiny."/ "This reasoning does not adequately address whether the burden should run if, as in the case of *in gross* conservation *servitudes,* there is never a benefited parcel." Cf. **run** (B).

inhabitable. See **habitability.**

in haec verba (= in these words) is the worst sort of puffed-up LATINISM for an ordinary idea. Often it is used as a phrasal adjective. E.g., "Nevertheless, the use of *in haec verba* pleadings on defamation charges is favored." *Asay v. Hallmark Cards, Inc.,* 594 F.2d 692, 699 (8th Cir. 1979). The sentence would be far more comprehensible without the LATINISM, and with a few more words: *The use of pleadings that give the defamatory words verbatim is favored.* See **verbatim.**

in hand. See **at hand.**

inhere takes the preposition *in;* it will not tolerate *within.* "Since a number of violations inhered *within* [read *in*] the same transaction, the defendant was not prosecuted more than once for the same statutory offense."

inherent takes *in* and not *to.* "We are dealing with a complexity *inherent to* [read *inherent in*] dual organizations."

The use of *inherent* in the following sentence (from a judicial opinion) obviously resulted from what we might charitably call imperfect knowledge of the word's meaning: "Nothing in the letters is of such an *inherent* nature that it inflames the passions of the jury or invokes its sympathies." In this sentence, *inherent* was apparently intended to mean "prejudicial."

inheritable. See **heritable.**

inheritance. See **descent** (B).

inheritor; heritor. See **heir** (A).

inheritrix, -tress. See SEXISM (C).

inhibitory, -tive. The latter is a NEEDLESS VARIANT. "Such taxes have a substantial *inhibitory* effect on commerce that is essentially interstate."

inimical (= hostile, injurious, adverse), a common word in legal writing, is almost a CLICHÉ in place of *adverse*, esp. in collocation with the word *interests*. "A settlor cannot force the courts to sanction his scheme of disposition if it is *inimical* to the interests of the state."

Inimicable for *inimical* is a fairly common error. The *OED* records *inimicable* as a "rare" adjective; it is not rare enough in the U.S. "For anything believed to be *inimicable* [read *inimical*] to his best interests can be thwarted or prevented by simply revoking the trust or amending it in such a way as to conform to his wishes." *Farkas v. Williams*, 5 Ill. 2d 417, 125 N.E.2d 600, 607 (1955)./ "They argue that Tullos was on board the rig for purposes *inimicable* [read *inimical*] to the legitimate interests of the rig owner."

in initio. See **ab initio.**

in issue. See **issue** (A).

INITIALESE. Justice Rehnquist once wrote, after stating the facts of a case in which seven different groups of initials were used for identification: "the terminology required to describe the present controversy suggests that the 'alphabet soup' of the New Deal era was, by comparison, a clear broth." *Chrysler Corp. v. Brown*, 441 U.S. 281, 284, 286–87 (1979). He was alluding, of course, to one of the most irritating types of pedantry that have gained a foothold in legal writing:

the overuse of abbreviated names. Originally, to be sure, abbreviations were intended to serve the convenience of the reader by shortening names; with their use, cumbersome phrases would not have to be repeated in their entirety. The purported simplifications actually simplified. E.g., "For the sake of brevity and to avoid confusion, since all persons involved in this litigation, except Mrs. Robinson, have the same surname, we will refer to Mrs. Annie S. Harlan as Annie; to Mrs. Sue Robinson as Sue; to Messrs. Jay W. Harlan and George L. Harlan as Jay and George." *Harlan v. Citizens National Bank*, 251 S.W.2d 284, 284 (Ky. 1952).

Now, however, many writers seem to have lost sight of this goal: they allow abbreviated names to proliferate in their writing, which quickly becomes a system of heiroglyphs requiring the reader constantly to refer to the original use of the term so that he will understand the significance of the heiroglyphs. It may be thought that this kind of writing is more scholarly than ordinary, straightforward prose. It is not. Rather, it is tiresome and inconsiderate writing; it betrays the writer's thoughtlessness toward the reader, and his fascination with the insubstantial trappings of scholarship.

A typical, and by no means exaggerated, example of this vice recently appeared in *Ryder Energy Distribution Corp. v. Merrill Lynch Commodities, Inc.*, 748 F.2d 774 (2d Cir. 1984). In this opinion seven hieroglyphs appear, often clumped together. We learn throughout the first few pages of the opinion that REDCO = Ryder Energy Distribution Corporation (why not call it Ryder?); NYME = New York Mercantile Exchange; FCM = futures commission merchant; CFTC = Commodity Futures Trading Commission; EFP = exchange of futures for physical; and TOI = Two Oil, Inc. Braced with this knowledge, if we can hold it, we encounter the following:

[U]nlike Hutton's, Merrill's duty sprang from two sources. Like Hutton, Merrill had the duty of an FCM representing the buyer—REDCO. In addition, however, Merrill had the duty of an FCM representing the seller—TOI. It was in its capacity as TOI's FCM that Merrill was required, under Form EFP-1, to certify that TOI owned and had possession of enough oil to cover its EFP obligations.

And this:

The following facts cannot be found in the complaint: REDCO's previous dealings with

TOI, REDCO's reasons for conducting an EFP, Merrill's inability to find REDCO an EFP partner, REDCO's introduction of TOI to Merrill, Hutton and NYME's lack of knowledge of TOI's default until June 11, and NYME's instigation of a rules compliance investigation after June 11.

And so it goes throughout the opinion, which would have reached the summit of initialese if only Merrill Lynch Commodities, Inc. had been termed MLCI, and E.F. Hutton & Co. Inc. termed EFHCO.

Almost as bad is *Kierstead v. City of San Antonio*, 643 S.W.2d 118, 120 (Tex. 1982), in which *EMT* = emergency medical technician, *FY* = fiscal year, and *FPERA* = Fire and Police Employee Relations Act: "Both parties presented their interpretations of the application of art. 1269p, § 6 vis-a-vis the override provision of FPERA, § 20 during the bench trial of the EMTs' claim in November 1979. The trial court awarded the EMTs overtime on the early contracts but denied awards for the FY 1978 and FY 1979 agreements that had specifically mentioned a 56-hour work week obligation for the EMTs." Why not *technician*, a statement that all references to years mean fiscal years, and *the Act*?

The simple solution, of course, is to adopt simplified names for parties and frequently repeated phrases, rather than initials in all capitals that depersonalize and obscure. The legal writer should never forget that effective communication takes *two*—the writer and the reader. In the words of Quiller-Couch,

> the obligation of courtesy rests first with the author, who invites the seance, and commonly charges for it. What follows, but that in speaking or writing we have an obligation to put ourselves into the hearer's or reader's place? It is *his* comfort, *his* convenience, we have to consult. To *express* ourselves is a very small part of the business: very small and unimportant as compares with *impressing* ourselves: the aim of the whole process being to persuade.
>
> Quiller-Couch, *The Art of Writing* 291–92 (1916; Capricorn Books ed. 1961).

See ACRONYMS AND INITIALISMS.

initiate   is a FORMAL WORD for *begin, open,* or *introduce.*

initiate tenant by curtesy; tenant by the curtesy initiate. These phrases are both used, but are falling into disuse. See **curtesy.**

initio. See **ab initio.**

injoin is an obsolete spelling of *enjoin,* q.v. See EN-.

injudicious; injudicial. The latter is a NEEDLESS VARIANT. The antonym of *judicial* is *nonjudicial.* See **judicial.**

injunct is colloquial for *enjoin.* E.g., "'There are no more copies left to be *injuncted,*' said the editor after the ruling." The word generally, and quite appropriately, does not appear in legal prose. See **enjoin.**

injunction. See **enjoinder.**

injunction enjoining is a common REDUNDANCY. E.g., "On the basis of these allegations, plaintiff moved for a temporary *injunction enjoining* [better: *injunction prohibiting*] the enforcement of the Michigan order."

injunctive, -tional. *Injunctive* is the standard word. E.g., "Monetary awards, like *injunctive* decrees, should be measured by the trade secrets' probable life." *Injunctional,* though not unusual early in this century, is now a NEEDLESS VARIANT. Not recorded in the major unabridged dictionaries, it has now been almost wholly displaced by *injunctive.* "[T]he *injunctional* [read *injunctive*] prohibition against picketing was supported by evidence of the unlawful purpose." *International Brotherhood of Carpenters and Joiners v. Todd L. Storms Construction Co.,* 324 P.2d 1002, 1004 (Ariz. 1958)./ "[T]here is a noticeable absence of judicial attempts so to enumerate the subjects of the remedy or delimit its field as to hamper the power of equity to grant *injunctional* [read *injunctive*] relief. . . ." *Funk Jewelry Co. v. State ex rel. La Prade,* 50 P.2d 945, 947 (Ariz. 1935)./ "It may be stated as a general rule that one not a party to the injunction suit cannot be charged with contempt in violating the injunction in the absence of service upon him of the *injunctional* [read *injunctive*] order or a showing that he had actual notice thereof." *State v. Terry,* 99 Wash. 1, 168 P. 513, 514 (1917).

injuria. See **injury.**

injuria absque damno; injuria sine damno. The English equivalent of each phrase is *injury without damage,* which denotes a legal wrong that causes no actual damage.

E.g., "It is a well established principle that an *injury without damage* creates no right to compensation." Cf. **damnum absque injuria.**

injury; injuria. The latter is a LATINISM, a NEEDLESS VARIANT, and a civil-law term to boot. How it makes its way into English-speaking common-law contexts is hard to fathom. See **damage.**

in-law is generally hyphenated or spelled as one word, and not, as in *Black's* (4th ed. and 5th ed.), spelled as two words.

in law. See **under law.**

in lieu of is now English. *Instead of* will not always suffice in its stead. E.g., "The defendant was released *in lieu of* $10,000 bond."/ "It has been held that a testamentary gift *in lieu of* dower has priority over all other testamentary gifts."

In view of for *in lieu of* is a startling solecism, and not a once-off error, found here in the least expected place: "An accord is the substitution of an agreement between the party injuring and the party injured, *in view of* [read *in lieu of*] the original obligation" (*Black's*, 4th ed.).

in limine (= at the threshold or outset; preliminarily) is a LATINISM not likely to be displaced in lawyers' ARGOT ⟨motion in limine⟩. E.g., "Let it be observed, *in limine*, that we choose to rest the decision of the question presented upon the premise that the trial judge erroneously concluded that the allegations of the complaint did not set forth a tort."/ "To prevent a consequence like this, a court of equity steps in and arrests the proceedings *in limine*."/ "In this appeal, we are faced *in limine* with a jurisdictional question."

in loco parentis (= in the place of a parent) is a justified LATINISM. Generally, the term applies to guardians and not to trustees, but much depends upon context: "The trustee is requested to remember that, the child's guardians having gone away, he is expected to act *in loco parentis*." (Eng.)/ "In a majority of states, if the testator stands *in loco parentis* to the donee, the inter vivos gift is presumed to be intended in satisfaction of the testamentary provision." The *in* is a part of the Latin phrase, and should be italicized if the rest of the phrase is in italics.

innervate. See **enervate.**

innocence, -cy. The latter is an obsolete variant.

innoculation is a misspelling of *inoculation,* q.v.

innumerable. See **enumerable.**

innundate is a misspelling of *inundate,* q.v.

inoculation. So spelled. This word is often misspelled *innoculation* or *inocculation.*

inoperative is a LEGALISM meaning "invalid." E.g., "I do not find that part of the will would be *inoperative* unless applied to the power." In recent years it has become a VOGUE WORD among government bureaucrats.

inopposite is a surprising, and happily infrequent, solecism for *inapposite.*

in order (to) (for) (that). The first phrase takes an infinitive, and is often wordy for the simple infinitive: "We granted the writ of error *in order to resolve* [read *to resolve*] the conflicting decisions among courts of appeals." The second takes a noun, and is often wordy for *for*: "The transformers had been *energized in order for use by Jones* [read *energized for use by Jones*] in the building operations." And the third, which needs no reduction, begins a noun phrase: "We remand on the sentencing issue *in order that* the district court might conduct an evidentiary hearing on that issue." See LEGALISMS AND LAWYERISMS.

in pais (= outside court or legal proceedings) is legal ARGOT deriving from LAW FRENCH, meaning literally "in the country (as opposed to in court)." "Where the terms of the trust permit a trustee to resign *in pais*, it is customary for the provisions of the trust to condition such resignation upon the resigning trustee's transferring title to the trust property to a successor trustee named in the trust instrument."

Matter in pais = matter of fact that is not in writing. *Estoppel in pais* = an estoppel not arising from a deed or contract, but, e.g., from an express statement implied by conduct or negligence. "These articles embody the principal cases of *estoppels in pais,* as distinguished from estoppels by deed or by record." (Eng.) See **estop.**

in pari delicto is legal ARGOT meaning "in equal fault; equally culpable." E.g., "Plaintiffs who are truly *in pari delicto* are those who have themselves violated the law in cooperation with the defendant."/ "The district court dismissed the complaint, concluding that the investors were *in pari delicto* with the defendants and thus barred from recovery."

in pari materia (= upon the same matter or subject) is legal ARGOT used in the context of interpreting statutes. The common maxim is that statutes *in pari materia* are to be construed together. E.g., "As is usually the case in civilian interpretative methodology, several articles are to be considered *in pari materia*."/ "*In pari materia* finds its greatest force when the statutes are enacted by the same legislative body at the same time."

in part. See **in whole** & **in pertinent part.**

in-patient should be hyphenated. Otherwise it is easily mistaken for *impatient*. E.g., "A limitation on *in-patient* hospital service to twenty-one days does not violate federal regulations."

in pectore. See LOAN TRANSLATIONS.

in personam. **A.** And *personal*. *In personam* is inferior to *personal* when used in the phrase *in personam jurisdiction* (= jurisdiction over a legal person). In many contexts, however, *personal* cannot substitute for *in personam*: "Plaintiff asserted an *in personam* admiralty claim against defendant for breach of the charter agreement." A claim *in personam* is one that is vested in a person availing against a specific person only, and imposing on him a personal liability (such as a claim for payment of money) (*OCL*).

In personam is sometimes a POSTPOSITIVE, sometimes a prepositive adjectival phrase. Traditionally it is the former: "The vast majority of federal cases are actions *in personam*." Likewise one refers to a *judgment in personam* (= a judgment rendered against a legal person) and to a *right in personam* (= a right availing against a specific legal person for liability).

B. And *in rem* (= availing against other persons generally and imposing on everyone a legal liability to respect the claimant's right). Professor Walter Wheeler Cook classified several very different ways in which these phrases are used.

There seem to be at least four different uses which need to be distinguished: 1. These phrases are used in the classification of the so-called 'primary' rights which legal and equitable actions are supposed to protect and enforce. The classification here is, of course, *rights in rem* and *rights in personam*. 2. The next use has to do with the equally well-known classification of actions as *actions in rem* and *actions in personam*. 3. A third use is in the classification of judgments and decrees as *in rem* or *in personam*. 4. The fourth use refers to the procedure used by a court in the enforcement of its judgment or decree. Here the court is said to *act in rem* or *act in personam*, as the case may be, the usual statement being that the law does the former and equity the latter.

Cook, *The Powers of Courts of Equity*, 15 Colum. L.Rev. 37, 39 (1915).

in pertinent part; in relevant part; in part. The last is best; the second, a variant of the first, is as verbose and jejune as the first.

inplane. If this word were properly formed, the *in-* prefix would be assimilated to *im-*, as it is in *improve* and *implant*. Fastidious users of language do not use the word, because it is airline cant. See **deplane.**

in point; on point. Both terms, applied to prior judicial decisions, mean "apposite; discussing the precise issue now at hand." *On point* is now the more common phrase, but both are well established in the legal idiom. E.g., "Those cases fall into two classes, only one of which, in fact, is *on point*."/ "These cases are not *in point* as authority in our case."/ "More *in point*, the duties owed by a landowner depend on the role of the person injured in his premises." *Case in point* is a popular idiom that originated in the law.

in point of fact is verbose for *in fact* or *actually*. E.g., "It was early held that 'parents' and 'children' were words used to show an intention of indicating *a family relation in point of fact* [*in fact a family relation*] as the foundation of the right of action."

in posse. See **in esse.**

in praesenti, which means merely "in the present," is a LATINISM wholly without merit. E.g., "The question here determined is whether there was a valid declaration of trust operating *in praesenti* [omit *in praesenti*] between January 28 and May 3, 1929."/ "An irrevocable *gift in praesenti* [read *present gift*] of money or property, real or personal, to a child by a parent to enable the donee to anticipate his inheritance to the extent of the gift is known as an advancement." See **in futuro.**

in propria persona = pro se, q.v. "He filed a claim of appeal and a brief *in propria persona* in the Court of Appeals." *In re Sanchez*, 375 N.W.2d 353, 355 (Mich. 1985). See **pro persona.**

input, n. & v.t. This jargonmonger's word is generally eschewed by careful writers. "Each decision-maker [q.v.] has a different optimal point of *informational input* [read *advice* or *comment*]."/ "Analysis is not restricted to studying *the influence of precareer inputs* [read *the effect of precareer influences*]." The English have the phrase *input tax*, statutorily defined in the Finance Act of 1977.

inquire; enquire. *Inquire* is a FORMAL WORD for *ask*. In the U.S., *in-* is the preferred spelling. At least one sophisticated newspaper, however, uses the *en-* spelling in its name. See EN- & **enquiry.**

inquirer; inquisitor. *Inquirer* is the more general of the two terms, meaning "one who asks questions or investigates." *Inquisitor*, not to be used where *inquirer* is called for, means "one who examines others to obtain information," and carries with it historical connotations of the Spanish Inquisition or trial by inquisition.

inquiry. See **enquiry** & EN-.

inquisitive, -torial; inquisitional. *Inquisitive* = given to inquiry, questioning, or research (*OED*). *Inquisitorial* has quite different connotations: "of the character of an inquisitor; offensively or impertinently inquiring, prying" (*OED*). E.g., "Strictly speaking, garnishment is not an action for the recovery of a debt but is *inquisitorial* in nature." (See **accusatory** for the sense of *inquisitorial procedure.*) *Inquisitional* is a NEEDLESS VARIANT of *inquisitorial*. E.g., "A defendant may assert her own Fifth Amendment right to a fair trial as a valid objection to the introduction of statements extracted from a nondefendant by coercion or other *inquisitional* [read *inquisitorial*] tactics."

inquisitor. See **inquirer.**

in re; en re; re. The preferred spelling of the two-word version is *in re* (= regarding, in the matter of). Known to laymen as a legalistic term, *in re* was once commonly used at the outset of legal documents, and now is often used before case names, e.g., *In re Wolfson's Estate*, which is frequently Englished *In the Matter of Wolfson's Estate. The Uniform System of Citation* (14th ed.) recommends (pp. 37–38), in citing cases beginning *In the Matter of,* changing that phrase to *In re.*

Sometimes, in the driest of commercial correspondence, *in re* is shortened to *re,* the ablative inflection of the noun *res*; the ellipsis carries the same meaning as *in re.* Although some authorities object to this use of the term, its conciseness makes it well-nigh irreplaceable. The best practice is to restrict it to use as a signal or introductory title announcing the subject of correspondence, and to avoid using it in sentences as part of one's syntax.

in regards to is semiliterate. The idiomatic phrases are *in regard to, in respect to* (or *of*), and *with respect to.* E.g., "This phone call to Howard on behalf of Servotech was *in regards to* [read *in regard to*] purchasing weapons in the United States for delivery in the Republic of South Africa." See **as regards.**

in rem; in rebus. The former is singular ("in or against the thing"), the latter plural ("in or against things"). Both are common in more lengthy LATINISMS. See **in personam.**

in respect of is a useful prepositional phrase, but should not appear where a simpler substitute will suffice. E.g., "He then told them that whether or not they gave *damages in respect of* [read *damages on*] the claim for libel, they still had to consider separately the claim under section 43 of the Act of 1956."

in route. See **en route.**

insert takes *in,* preferably not *into.*

insidious; invidious. A distinction exists between these words. *Insidious* = (of persons and things) lying in wait or seeking to entrap or ensnare; operating subtly or secretly so as not to excite suspicion. E.g., "The officers of a trust company owe allegiance to the shareholders as well as to the beneficiaries, and the temptation to favor the shareholders may well be more *insidious* than the temptation of an individual trustee to favor himself."

Invidious = offensive; entailing odium or ill will upon the person performing, discharging, or discussing; giving offense to others (*OED*). This term is often used of discrimination, and has been for more than two centuries. E.g., "He failed to allege motivations of class-based *invidious* discrimination." The two words ought not to be used in the same sentence, as here: "Ugly in its practice and *insidious* in its effects, *invidious* racial discrimination deserves protection in no area of society, least of all in the administration of justice in federal courts." A workable revision might be to drop *insidious* altogether and write "*invidious* in its effects, racial discrimination" etc.

insignia; insigne. The Latin singular *insigne* is rarely used. Today *insignia* (technically plural) is regarded as the singular, *insignias* as its plural. Cf. **indicia.**

insipient. See **incipient.**

insist takes the preposition *on*, not *in*. E.g., "In a society that *persists and insists in* [read *persists in and insists on*, if the ALLITERATION is really necessary] permitting its citizens to own and possess weapons, it becomes necessary to determine who may and who may not acquire them."

insistence. See **instance.**

in situ (= in its original place; back in place) is a LATINISM used in property law. It is almost always unnecessary.

insofar as (= in such degree as), spelled thus in AmE and *in so far as* in BrE, is sometimes misused because its meaning is misunderstood. One does not know exactly what this writer, for instance, had in mind: "*Insofar as* important to this appeal, Greyhound defended this suit on the grounds that, when plaintiff's cause of action arose, O was not its employee, but was B's employee or an independent contractor." A better—and grammatical—way of beginning this sentence would be, *What is important in this appeal is that Greyhound defended.* . . . See **inasmuch as.**

insoluble; insolvable; unsolvable. *Insoluble* is used both of substances that will not dis-

solve in liquids and of problems that cannot be solved. E.g., "In that form it relieves the legislature of a problem *insoluble* in bulk, by shifting the problem to judge and lawyer, who are able to cope with it in the common lay way—piecemeal."/ "A defendant's silence after he has been given *Miranda* warnings is *insolubly* ambiguous." *Insolvable* is used only of problems that cannot be solved; some stylists prefer it to *insoluble*. *Unsolvable* should be avoided as a NEEDLESS VARIANT.

in specie. See **specie.**

in spite of. See **despite.**

inst. (short for *instant*). Wood writes that this was "once a quite respectable legal term, now a piece of commercial jargon for 'the present month' (e.g., 'We beg to recognise the receipt of your letter of the 25th inst.'). Use the name of the month instead." F.T. Wood, *Current English Usage* 123 (1962). The advice is well taken. Cf. **ult.**

instal(l)ment. *Instalment* is the BrE spelling, *installment* the spelling preferred in AmE.

instance, -cy. *Instance* "in the sense of urgent solicitation or insistence [always in the phrase *at the instance of*] is a useful word; in any other sense it is useless." P. Marks, *The Craft of Writing* 53 (1932). Another legitimate meaning of the word is "an illustrative example." Here the word is useless: "It seems plain that in at least the vast majority of *instances* such a purported conveyance of lifetime services would be unenforceable and essentially nugatory under applicable state law." [Read *It seems plain that such a purported conveyance of lifetime services would usually* (or almost always) *be unenforceable and essentially nugatory under applicable state law.*]

Following are examples of the use, largely legal, that has substantive value: "Thousands of government employees would object to being forced to take polygraph tests at the *instance* of their supervisors."/ "In 1804, the court of sessions of Scotland interdicted, at the *instance* of the children, the publication of the manuscript letters of the poet Burns."/ "Apart from a limited class of expectations, a minor's contracts are not void but only voidable at his *instance*."

Instancy, a rare term, means "urgency; pressing nature; imminence" (the instancy of the danger was apparent to all).

303   **Instil(l)**

instance, v.t., = to cite as an instance, to adduce as an example in illustration or proof (*OED*). E.g., "Nowhere in the record is to be found any remark by the trial judge smacking of impropriety in the faintest degree, let alone any such as those *instanced* above."/ "'Uno' is better analogized to a term such as 'Del Monte,' *instanced* in *Pick 'N' Fly, Inc. v. Park & Fly, Inc.*"

instantaneously; instantly. "*Instantly* is virtually a synonym of at once, directly, and immediately, though perhaps the strongest of the four. *Instantaneously* is applied to something that takes an inappreciable time to occur, like the taking of an instantaneous photograph, especially to two events that occur so nearly simultaneously that the difference is imperceptible" (*MEU2* 288). E.g., "He was killed *instantaneously* [read *instantly*] in the collision of that car with the truck driven by the defendant."

instant case; instant cause; present case; case at bar. These equivalent phrases, though sometimes useful, can often be avoided by *here*, if not used vaguely. Some variation of these terms is desirable to avoid verbal tedium, but one should not be so obvious as to lapse into INELEGANT VARIATION.

Instant case is sometimes used where *this case* would be preferable. E.g., "Appellant and her husband brought *the instant* [read *this*] products liability *action* against the manufacturer of the chair."

Instant (= presently under consideration), labeled an ARCHAISM by the *OED*, is alive in the law, and has been extended beyond the basic phrase *instant case*: "Since the *instant* will has been previously construed as permitting newborn grandnieces and grandnephews to enter the class, the composition of the class has not yet been determined."/ "According to the parties' stipulation in this case, it is expected with respect to the *instant* bonds that more than half of the debt service requirements will be satisfied not from real property taxes but from revenues from other local taxes."/ "The district court dismissed the *instant* petition for abuse of the writ." This bit of legal ARGOT ought to be used sparingly if at all. See **case at bar.**

instanter easily makes our list of FORBIDDEN WORDS. There is absolutely no reason for preferring *instanter* to *instantly* or *at once*, apart from facetious reasons. There are several rea-

sons, however, for preferring *instantly*. First, it is universally comprehensible among speakers of English. Second, it conveys the nuances available to either term. Third, it is not, like its cousin the LATINISM, pompous. E.g., "Study of, and, if study warrants, changes in land use control cannot be completed *instanter* [read *instantly*]."

As further evidence of the utter dispensability of *instanter*, we should note that some legal writers have failed to understand that the term is adverbial, and have misused it as if it were an adjective: "It was an excessive statement made in the heat of the closing argument of a hard-fought case, one which was objected to and subjected to [see ALLITERATION, UNDUE] an *instanter* cautionary instruction." The writer should have used *immediate.*

instantiate (= to represent by an instance), a vintage World War II NEOLOGISM of questionable value. E.g., "The reference to defendant's silence constitutes harmless error; Chapman's fate is to *instantiate* [read *exemplify*] this third rule."

instantly. See **instantaneously.**

in statu quo is a LATINISM properly equivalent to *in statu quo ante* (= in the same condition as previously). Some writers have quite understandably assumed that there was a distinction between *in statu quo* and *in statu quo ante*, and have used the former merely to mean "in the status quo; in the same condition as now exists." Here the phrase is correctly used: "The fact that the parties cannot be put *in statu quo* precisely as to the subject-matter of the contract will not preclude a decree for rescission."/ "Depriving one of the benefit of a contract that he supposes he has made leaves everything *in statu quo*, rather than imposing a liability to which no limit can be placed."

The foregoing discussion is largely beside the point, however, inasmuch as the English renditions of the phrase are preferable to the Latinate. One should write *in the status quo* (present condition) or *in the status quo ante* (previous condition). See **status quo.**

instil(l). The preferred spelling in AmE is *instill. Instil* is preferred in BrE. This word takes the preposition *(in)to*, not *with* (he instilled character as well as knowledge into his students). Use of the latter preposition occurs

as a result of confusion of *inspire* with *instill.*
See OBJECT-SHUFFLING.

In the following sentence, *instill in* is misused for *confer on*: "Presence within a state, even temporary or transitory presence, is still a common-law basis *instilling competence in* [read *conferring competence on*] the courts of that state to adjudicate claims against a person."

instillation; instillment. The latter is a NEEDLESS VARIANT.

instinct (= imbued or charged *with*) is a recherché usage that has given the law a memorable phrase: "The whole contract is *instinct* with such an obligation."/ "There are times when reciprocal engagements do not fit each other like the parts of an indented deed, and yet the whole contract . . . may be '*instinct* with an obligation,' imperfectly expressed." (Cardozo, J.)

instinctive, -tual. The latter is a NEEDLESS VARIANT.

institute is a FORMAL WORD for *begin* or *start.* Cf. **commence.** See **begin** (B).

instruct = to give information to (as a solicitor to a barrister). E.g., "This cause has been carefully *instructed* with evidence by the practisers, who have had the conduct of it." (Eng.) See **advise** (C).

instructed verdict. See **directed verdict.**

instrument = a legal document. E.g., "A will and codicil are separate *instruments* for the purpose of execution; it would seem better to require separate physical acts of revocation." Often the word can be supplanted to advantage by *writing* or *document*, terms understandable to laymen. In any event, the phrase *written instrument* and *instrument in writing* are REDUNDANCIES when a legal instrument is clearly contemplated, inasmuch as there is no such thing as an *oral instrument.* See **document.**

insue is an archaic spelling on *ensue*, q.v.

in suit = in dispute, or (engaged) in a lawsuit. E.g., "No further incentive is needed to produce the information *in suit.*" The notation in the *OED* that this phrase from legal

ARGOT is obsolete proved to be premature. Yet the phrase is hardly common.

insurance is pronounced with the primary accent on the second syllable /in-*shoor*-ăns/. See **assurance.**

insurance adjuster (AmE) = *insurance assessor* (BrE).

insure; ensure. See **assure.**

insured, n., like *deceased* and *accused*, forms an awkward plural and possessive. Its equivalent *insurant* solves these infelicities, but it is little used. Here is a typical sentence: "This type of policy is often used to provide for the education of children or for the *insured's* retirement." An older variant of *insured* is *assured.* See PLURALS (D).

insurer, -or. The *-or* form should be avoided.

insurgence, -cy. These words have undergone DIFFERENTIATION. *Insurgence* = a revolt; the action of rising against authority. *Insurgency* = the quality or state of being in revolt; the tendency to rise in revolt (*OED*).

insurrectionary, -al. The latter is a NEEDLESS VARIANT.

integral; integrant. The latter is a NEEDLESS VARIANT as an adjective; but it exists legimately as a noun (meaning "component"): "A res is a necessary *integrant* of the concept of 'constructive trust.'"

integr(at)able. The correct form is *integrable.* See -ATABLE.

integration. See **desegregation.**

intelligent. In lay usage this word is usually confined to descriptions of persons; in legal writing it is used just as frequently of acts as it is of persons. An *intelligent* act is one that is carried out comprehendingly. E.g., "When a defendant admits his guilt in open court, he may attack only the voluntary and *intelligent* character of the act." See HYPALLAGE.

intelligent; intelligible. The former means

(of persons) "having mental power or grasp," the latter (of statements) "understandable."

intendment (= the true meaning or intention of a legal instrument) is a specialized legal term that should never be used as a fancy variant of *intention* or *intent; common intendment* = the natural meaning in legal construction; *intention* = purpose, aim, design, meaning; *intent* = *intention.* (See **intent.**) *Intendiment* is an obsolete form of *intendment.*

The general legal sense of *intendment* is "the construction put upon anything by the common law; the sense in which the law understands a thing" (*OED*). E.g., "The evidence produced upon the trial, with all its legal *intendments*, failed to fairly tend to prove that plaintiff's discharge was accomplished by the illegal acts of defendant."/ "We must take the language of the section as we find it; there is no reason for any *intendment*."/ "Should not every *intendment* be allowed that he would not elect to stand by the contract when he came of age?"

intense; intensive. The best advice, which is conventional, is to shun *intensive* wherever *intense* will fit the context. *Intensive* is really a philosophical and scientific term best left to philosophers and scientists; lawyers can make do rather nicely with *intense*: "A first-hand familiarity with the type of participation required of a defendant would not be meaningfully supplemented by *intensive* [read *intense*] scrutiny on appeal."/ "The striking divergence of opinion conspicuously exemplifies the need for dealing somewhat more *intensively* [read *intensely*] and systematically than is usual with the nature and analysis of all types of jural interests."

intent; intention. If any distinction may be drawn between *intent* and *intention*, it must be connotative: one has evil intent, but good intentions; one has the intent to murder, and the intention to do something either morally neutral or laudable. This distinction has not been fossilized in the language, however; often *intent* is used of neutral and even good motives, and arguably one may have bad as well as good *intentions*. Euphony usually governs the choice of word.

The usual phrase is *testamentary intent*, although *testamentary intention* has appeared. Following are sentences in which *intent* appears in reference to gifts or transfers of property: "We discovered the *intent* of the grantor from other factors, as shown by the instru-

ment, to give full effect to the words of limitation."/ "The charity has no large discretionary power in carrying out the general *intent* of the donor."/ "The analogy of the 'fraudulent conveyance' from the creditors' rights field has appealed to some courts, but others consider the issue of *intent* too difficult to administer."

Intention is also sometimes used: "The next question is whether it is a valid defence to an action for passing off that the defendant had no *intention* to deceive." (Eng.)/ "As long as the purposes to which the property is to be applied are limited to charitable purposes, there is no reason why the trust should not be carried out in accordance with the *intention* of the testator." *Intention* takes the infinitive form of the verb, not the present participle. E.g., "He then announced his *intention of running* [read *intention to run*] for governor."

Intent and *intention* are liable to INELEGANT VARIATION. E.g., "Such a construction results in a rule that the grantor must expressly indicate his *intention* [read *intent*, for the sake of consistency] to create a remainder in his heirs, or a presumption in favor of reversions that may be rebutted by indication of the grantor's contrary *intent*."/ "Her *intent* in executing the paper, at least as far as such *intent* is now before us, must be determined by the court as a matter of law. The paper writing does not declare an *intention* [read *intent*] to revoke the will except through its destruction, either wholly or as far as Hart is concerned by O'Kennedy."

INTER-; INTRA-. These prefixes have quite different meanings. *Inter-* means "between, among." *Intra-* means "within, in." Thus *interstate* means "between states" and *intrastate* means "within a state."

inter alia; inter alios. *Inter alia* (= among others) is used of things. *Inter alios* (= among others) is used of persons. *Inter alia* is much more common than *inter alios*. E.g., "When the balance of the purchase price was not paid on the due date, the vendor resold the house and brought this action for damages for, *inter alia*, the deficiency on the resale." (Aus.) Though not common, *inter alios* occurs far more frequently in legal than in nonlegal writing: "The Senate report stated that the residual section was intended to reach, *inter alios*, 'a person who induces another to remain silent or to give misleading information to a federal law enforcement officer.'"

Here the phrase is not only wrong, but also misplaced: "A contract *between, inter alia* [properly *inter alios*], *the manufacturer and one of its former employees* [read *between the manufacturer and, inter alios, one of its former employees*], wherein the former employee expressly agreed not to disclose any of the processes and methods of the manufacturer, was an admission of a positive character that such processes and methods were secret."

interceptor, -er. The former spelling is preferred.

intercourse. Even *lawful intercourse* has sexual overtones in modern usage that are not to be ignored. The term is best avoided in its traditional sense "mutual dealings and communication." E.g., "Notwithstanding that lawyers are often arrayed against each other as champions of opposing forces, their *intercourse* [read *dealings with one another*] should be friendly."/ "The means commonly used is the inducing of others to withdraw from such companies their patronage and business *intercourse* by threats."/ "The libel in this case deprived plaintiff of the benefits of public confidence and social *intercourse.*" To most modern readers this use of the term is an ARCHAISM.

Commerce was formerly used in virtually all senses of *intercourse*, including in the phrase *sexual commerce* (= sexual intercourse): "*Sexual commerce* or *intercourse* and *carnal knowledge* are synonymous terms." 44 Am. Jur. *Rape* § 2 (1942). See **commerce.**

interdict (= to forbid, restrain) is a FORMAL WORD often occurring in legal writing. E.g., "A supersedeas bond is a privilege extended to the judgment debtor as a price of *interdicting* the validity of an order to pay money."/ "Both cases followed and applied the due process test set out in *Ferguson* and construed its bias prohibition to *interdict* only actual bias, not the mere appearance of bias."/ "The defendants argue that all the interests in Bernard's estate will necessarily vest before the expiration of the period *interdicted* by the Rule against Perpetuities." The noun is *interdiction.* E.g., "In November 1981, the United States entered into an arrangement with Great Britain respecting the *interdiction* of vessels suspected of carrying illicit drugs."/ "On May 27, after a three-day hearing, the court granted a preliminary injunction that continued the *interdictions* of the restraining order."

Interdict is also a civil-law term used as a noun in Scotland and South Africa in a sense close to "injunction." E.g., "This is an application on notice of motion in which the applicant asks for a declaration of rights and for an *interdict.*" (Rhod.)

interface, v.i., is jargonmongers' talk. E.g., "This man possesses the ability to *interface* and relate with people from all social and economic levels." *Interface* should be left to COMPUTERESE.

interfering with a subsisting contract. See **tortious interference with contractual relations.**

interlocutor = (1) a person who takes part in a dialogue (U.S. and G.B.); or (2) a pronouncement of any order of a court (Scots law).

interlocutory relief; interim relief. *Interlocutory relief* is the phrase used in the U.S. and G.B. to mean "a temporary judicial remedy, such as a preliminary injunction." *Interim relief* is an equivalent term sometimes used in Great Britain.

intermarriage. One word.

intermarry should not be used for *marry*, which itself necessarily implies mutuality. E.g., "Before that time, his daughter, Martha Florence, *had intermarried with* [read *had married*] R.P. Watson, and five children were born unto them." This LEGALISM should be laid to rest, except when one conveys the nuance of marrying across racial or cultural lines (itself a démodé notion), or, quite the opposite, marrying only within a specified group.

intermeddle is always spelled with two *d*'s. One might not have thought *intermedling* to be anything but a typographical error, but it consistently appears that way in a popular primer on torts.

interment; internment. *Interment* = burial; *internment* = detention.

Internal Revenue Service (U.S.) = *Inland Revenue Service* (G.B.).

international law; jus gentium; law of nations. These phrases are synonymous in meaning "the system of law regulating the interrelationship of sovereign states and their rights and duties with regard to one another" (*CDL*). *International law* is the predominant term nowadays.

internecine = mutually deadly; destructive of both parties. The word is often misused. E.g., "If the case is instead based on a state-created right, with service under Rule 4(d), should federal or state law govern amenability? On this point there was an *internecine* [better: *rancorous?*] struggle in the Second Circuit, with Judge Clark and Friendly as the *protagonists* [read *antagonists*]." (See **protagonist**.)

internment. See **interment.**

interoffice. One word.

inter partes is the antonym of *ex parte*, q.v. It means "between parties; involving all parties to a lawsuit," and is perhaps a useful LATINISM in legal ARGOT, though not a TERM OF ART. E.g., "On its face it is an instrument *inter partes*." (Eng.)/ "In an *inter partes* proceeding notice on the petition is given to all interested persons by publication."/ "Sir Elwyn Jones, who appeared for the wife, placed some reliance on these documents, but since they both depended upon ex parte statements of the wife, without any argument or *inter partes* judicial investigation, I do not derive any help from them." (Eng.)/ "In the *inter-partes* [read *inter partes*] proceeding, based upon the English 'solemn' form, notice to interested parties is required and the contestant submits evidence against the will."

If the phrase were to be Englished, *inter-party*, which already has limited currency, would serve well.

interpellate. See **interpolate.**

interplead, v.t. In an *interpleader*, q.v., it is the adverse parties claiming a right to the property held by the stakeholder that are said to *interplead* their claims. Some modern writers erroneously assume that the stakeholder *interpleads*; he does not. *W3* quotes a use of *interplead* attributed to W.H. Atwell that exemplifies the mistaken assumption that it is the stakeholder that interpleads, rather than the claimants: "The insurance company, not knowing where the payment should go *between the three, interpleaded the claimants* [read, with a comma preceding, *initiated an interpleader among the three claimants*]."

Interplead forms the preterite *interpleaded.* "The adverse claims of the *interpled* [read *interpleaded*] parties must, of course, concern the same property or the same debt." (The phrase should probably be *interpleading parties*.) See **plead.**

interpleader = a suit pleaded between two parties to determine a matter of claim or right to property held by a usu. disinterested third party (called a *stakeholder*, q.v.) who is in doubt about which claimant should have the property, the purpose of the suit being to determine to which claimant delivery or payment ought to be made. Despite its appearance, then, *interpleader* generally denotes a type of lawsuit and not a person, that is, the word is not ordinarily an agent noun. The *OED* contains a subentry for *interpleader* with the definition "one who interpleads," citing a few dictionaries, but states that "it is doubtful whether the word is more than a dictionary assumption due to a misunderstanding of [the word]." Yet *W2* and *W3* contain the agentnoun sense, and it may well currently be a secondary meaning of the word.

interpolate; interpellate. The former means "to insert into a text or writing"; the latter, used in legislative reports, means "to question formally; to seek information."

interpose for *submit* ⟨to interpose a demurrer⟩ is the term traditionally used for motions made by the defense. E.g., "The counterclaimant has failed to advance a justifiable reason for its failure to timely *interpose* a claim."/ "The defense of forum non conveniens could be *interposed*, and, if meritorious, the Illinois court would dismiss the case."

interpretate is obsolete for *interpret.* "The legislative history of section 5851 strongly supports *interpretating* [read *interpreting*] an 'action' as similar to formal proceedings under the Act."

interpretation; construction. With regard to contracts and other legal instruments, although "*interpretation* and *construction* are generally regarded as synonymous and used interchangeably, it is not only possible, but desirable as well, to draw a distinction. The word *interpretation* is used with respect to language itself; it is the process of applying the legal standard to expressions found in the agreement in order to determine their meaning. *Construction*, on the other hand, is used to determine, not the sense of the words or symbols, but the legal meaning of the entire contract; the word is rightly used wherever the import of the writing is made to depend upon a special sense imposed by law." 4 W. H. Williston, *Treatise on the Law of Contracts* § 602 at 320 (3d ed. 1961). See **construction.**

interpretative; interpretive, -tional. Generally, one forms the adjective on the model of the nominal form of a word. Hence *prevention* yields *preventive*, not *preventative*. But with *interpretation*, the correct adjectival form is *interpretative* (= having the character or function of interpreting; explanatory), which should be used consistently. *Interpretive*, although it has gained ground in the last fifty years, should be laid to rest. E.g., "Appellant filed for rehearing of the new *interpretive* [read *interpretative*] rule under the FPA."/ "The question here is whether due process authorizes the Court to resort to *noninterpretive* [read *noninterpretative*] modes of constitutional adjudication." Given, though, the fact that *interpretivism* (q.v.) is a linguistic fait accompli, one would be hard put to argue very strenuously against *interpretive*. Though it may not be condemned, it should be avoided by those who know better. *Interpretational* is a NEEDLESS VARIANT. E.g., "Should the court overrule its earlier *interpretational* [read *interpretative*] decision?"

interpretivism; noninterpretivism. Among American constitutional lawyers, the terms *interpretivism* and *noninterpretivism* have become standard words for certain doctrines of constitutional interpretation. Although they have been called "misleading labels," they are unlikely to disappear. No matter how ill-formed or bastardized these forms may be (see **interpretative**), they are probably too well entrenched to be easily uprooted. E.g., "The debate is now couched as a battle between *interpretivism* and *noninterpretivism*—between the view that judges can enforce only norms stated or clearly implicit in the Consti-

tution and the position that courts can legitimately go beyond those sources."/ "The controversy has been characterized as a debate between the *interpretivists*, who believe that the Court must confine itself to norms clearly stated or implied in the language of the Constitution, and the *noninterpretivists*, who believe that the Court may protect norms not mentioned in the Constitution's text or in its preratification history." E. Chemerinsky, *The Price of Asking the Wrong Question*, 62 Texas L. Rev. 1207, 1208–09 (1984). One might prefer that the words had been *interpretationism* and *noninterpretationism.*

interregnum. Pl. *-nums, -na.* The English plural is preferred.

interrogate is a FORMAL WORD for *question*; it suggests formal or rigorous questioning.

interrogatee; interrogee. *W3* lists *interrogee* (= someone interrogated), not *interrogatee*, but the *OED* and the *OED Supp.* list *interrogatee*, not *interrogee*. Since the agent noun is *interrogator*, it makes more sense to prefer the corresponding passive form, *interrogatee.*

interrogative, -tory, adj., **-tional.** *Interrogative* (= of, pertaining to, or of the nature of, questioning; having the form or force of a question [*OED*]). The other forms are NEEDLESS VARIANTS.

interrogatory, n.; **interrogation.** *Interrogatory* = a legal questionnaire of an opposing party. *Interrogation* = (1) the act or process of questioning in depth; or (2) questioning as a form of discourse.

interrogee. See **interrogatee.**

in terrorem (= as a warning; intimidating) is used in legal ARGOT primarily of clauses in wills that threaten to dispossess any beneficiaries who challenge the terms of the will. E.g., "The *in terrorem* clause provides the penalty of forfeiture against anyone who shall contest in any court any of the provisions of this instrument."/ "Whatever else may be said, it is clear that when equity contempt decrees rely upon *in terrorem* fines, or the prospect of compensatory damages for effectiveness, the contention that equity acts in personam is further modified." Justice Frankfurter made literary use of the LATINISM: "[T]here is nothing judicially more unseemly nor more self-defeating than for this court to make *in terrorem* pronouncements. . . ." *Baker v. Carr*, 369 U.S. 186, 270 (1962) (Frankfurter, J., dissenting).

No-contest clause is often used as an anglicized equivalent of *in terrorem clause* in the context of wills. E.g., "While we find that the appellant cannot take under the provisions of the will by virtue of the *no-contest* clause, the testator cannot rewrite sections 41 and 43 of the Probate Code to prevent appellant from exercising her right to take as an heir."

interrupter, -or. The former spelling is preferred. See -ER, -OR.

inter se (= between or among themselves) is an unjustified LATINISM. "The parties are supposed to have agreed *inter se* [read *among themselves*] that the deed shall not be given in evidence without the attesting witness's being called to depose to the circumstances attending its execution."/ "Not only did the rights of the two claimants against the solicitor fail to be decided, but also their rights *inter se* [read *between themselves*] in respect of the bank account." (Eng.)/ "'Consortium' has come to mean the reciprocal rights and duties of both husband and wife *inter se* [omit *inter se*: it is redundant after *reciprocal* and *both*] resulting from marriage."/ "The Uniform Commercial Code reaffirms from the first the general freedom of the parties to determine their obligations *inter se* [read *between themselves*]." See FORBIDDEN WORDS & LATINISMS.

Inter sese is a variant form of the phrase. "Many arrangements for economy of expense and for convenience of administration may be made between carriers without subjecting them to liability as partners or as coadventurers either *inter sese* or as to third parties." (Cardozo, J.)

interspousal (= between spouses) is a relatively recent legal NEOLOGISM, included in neither the *OED Supp.* nor *W3*. It probably originated in and is largely confined to AmE. E.g., "The hospitality rationale is also indefensible when contrasted with the judicial abrogation of *interspousal*, charitable, and governmental immunities in order to provide a remedy for negligently injured persons."/

"The tax-free *interspousal* transfers may reduce the use of the so-called 'family trust' in marital deduction planning."/ "The circuit court dismissed the complaint, ruling that the defense of *interspousal* immunity barred the action." See **spousal.**

interstate; intrastate. These adjectives should not be used adverbially, as here: "Organized crime operates *interstate.* [read *in interstate commerce* or *across state lines* or *throughout the states*]." See INTER-.

interstitial, -sticial. The former is preferred.

intervener, -or. The former is the better spelling, although -*or* is common in AmE. See -ER, -OR.

intervenience. See **intervention.**

intervenor. See **intervener.**

intervention; intervenience. The latter is a NEEDLESS VARIANT.

inter vivos, meaning "between living persons," should be spelled as two words. The phrase may be either a prepositive or POSTPOSITIVE ADJECTIVE. Traditionally it has occurred after the noun: "The rule of law is well settled that in transactions *inter vivos*, where a party stands in confidential relations to another, if the dominant party receives the benefit during the existence of such relation, the party reposing the confidence may obtain relief."/ "A gift *inter vivos* may be made of land or personal property."

Here it appears as an adjective preceding the noun: "Employment contracts and employment retirement programs have proved popular for *inter vivos* dispositions."/ "It does not relate to the *inter vivos* gifts to the children, of which Ruth received the greater share; consequently the truth or falsity of the statement stands independently of the history of *inter vivos* donations."

inter vivos trust; living trust. These are the terms used to describe trusts created by the settlor during his lifetime. *Inter vivos*, though a LATINISM, is so commonly used as the general adjective (see the preceding entry) as to be unobjectionable in legal writing. *Inter* *vivos trust* is perhaps a little more common that *living trust*.

intestate (= a person who dies without a will) is an attributive noun, the adjective *intestate* having appeared several centuries before the noun. *Intestate*, n., frequently follows a possessive proper noun, although literally the usage seems curious. E.g., "David Kling, the present *plaintiff's intestate*, brought this action in his lifetime, claiming damages for an alleged malicious and willful assault."/ "*Plaintiff's intestate* made with the government two contracts in relation to the monitor." See **testate**.

   Intestate, adj., is usually used of persons, but sometimes, through HYPALLAGE, of property: "The court's conclusion that under the Hubinger case the surplus income is *intestate* is correct."

in that is commonly used for *because* or *since* in legal prose. E.g., "*In that* [read *Because*] we have overruled appellant's fourth ground of error, we also overrule ground of error number five."/ "It might be argued that the present case is distinguishable from both *White* and *Knighton in that* those cases involved final judgments that did not deal at all with the question of attorney's fees."

in the circumstances. See **circumstances.**

in the event that is usu. unnecessarily prolix for *if*.

in the final analysis; in the last analysis. Both are CLICHÉS: "*In the last analysis,* the testator had an absolute right to divert his property from this contestant; he was under no obligation to assign any reason for so doing." These trite expressions only detract from one's prose. One might better simply state the proposition without this tepid lead-in.

in the first instance. See **first instance, in the.**

in the future. See **in futuro.**

in the midst of. See **amid(st).**

inthral(l). See **enthral(l).**

in the light of is inferior to *in light of*, itself a CLICHÉ.

in toto (= completely, entirely, wholly) is a LATINISM expressing such a fundamental notion, and having so many ready English synonyms, that it is seldom if ever justified. E.g., "That material omission *negates the authorization in toto* [read *completely negates the authorization*]."/ "Neither do all the plaintiff's policies, taken *in toto* [read *as a whole*], allow, in this court's opinion, the application of that doctrine to the use of the National YWCA."

intoxilyzer. See **breathalyzer.**

in transitu is an unjustified LATINISM; the English phrase *in transit* suffices. E.g., "The right of stoppage *in transitu* [read *in transit*] was first recognized and enforced in England in the year 1690."/ "The creditors are entitled to share ratably in the assets of the defendant (except in the coke stopped *in transitu* [read *in transit*])."

intrastate. See **interstate.**

intraversion. See **introversion.**

intra vires (= within the powers) is the antonym of *ultra vires*, q.v. "Courts interfere seldom to control such discretion *intra vires* the corporation." *United Copper Securities Co. v. Amalgamated Copper Co.*, 244 U.S. 261, 263–64 (1917)./ "If express authority to differentiate on racial grounds is given, regulations made under it will be *intra vires* regardless of whether they amount to 'intangible discrimination.'" (Rhod.) *Intra vires* is not nearly as common as *ultra vires*.

intrigue, v.i., = to carry on a plot or secret love affair. It should not be used in formal prose for *interest* or *fascinate*, although this sense has long been usual in informal speech. E.g., "The question presented in appellant's first point of error is an *intriguing* [read *interesting* or *fascinating*] one."

introductory should never be used in the phrase *be introductory of* (something); one should instead write *introduce*. E.g., "This first section *is introductory of* [read *introduces*] some of the constitutional provisions that constitute part of that framework." See BE-VERBS (B).

   As a noun, *introductory* sometimes serves as a chapter title, but it is inferior to *introduction*.

INTRODUCTORY IT & THERE. See EXPLETIVES.

introversion; intraversion. The former is the preferred spelling.

intrust is an obsolete form of *entrust,* q.v.

inure; enure. The former is the standard spelling in both legal and nonlegal texts. *Inure* = (1) to take effect, come into use; or (2) to make accustomed to something unpleasant; habituate. Sense (1) is the sense that usually appears in legal contexts: "The rule is well established that whenever a contract between attorney and client *inures* to the benefit or advantage of the attorney the court will not only closely scrutinize but will actually change the ordinary rules of evidence to arrive at a determination."/ "The damages must *inure* to the exclusive benefit of the widow and children." The noun is *inurement.*

Although in sense (2) persons are *inured* to unpleasant things ⟨many battered women, tragically, become inured to violence⟩, in sense (1) *inure* is used only of positive effects: *inure to the detriment of* is an idiomatic impossibility. The author of the following sentence lacked idiomatic sensibility: "No prejudice has *inured* to the defendant because of any procedural default leading to the suspensions." Sense (2) occasionally appears in legal writing: "The steady parade of human savagery that is presented to us has an *inuring* effect."

invade is the metaphor used in the law of trusts to denote withdrawals from an initial or principal investment. E.g., "She had unlimited power to *invade* the corpus of the trust if she so desired."/ "The settlor can authorize the trustee to *invade* the principal or corpus of the trust for the benefit of the wife." See **corpus.**

invalidate; invalid, v.t. The latter is a NEEDLESS VARIANT seen only in legal writing.

inventable, -ible. The former spelling is preferred. See -ABLE (A).

inventory is commonly a verb as well as a noun in legal and business contexts. This use of the word, dating back to the sixteenth century, is perfectly acceptable. E.g., "The officer *inventories* the contents of the car."/ "Local police departments generally follow a routine practice of securing and *inventorying* the automobile's contents."/ "While the husband was creating joint tenancies for the benefit of his daughters, he was building up the value of the farm chattels, which were *inventoried* at $22,850.29."

inverse. See **converse.**

INVERSIONS, AWKWARD. Awkward are most, though not all, inversions. We have the common legalistic phrase, used routinely in court orders, that is not particularly exceptionable: "Came on for consideration the above-referenced civil action." Similarly, both *Comes now the plaintiff* and the variant *Now comes the plaintiff* are inversions. These are standard fare, however. (See **come(s) now.**)

The inversions especially to be avoided are those whose existence is attributable to amateurish literary striving. The problem with these is that, "like the atmospheric inversion that is blamed for smog, the inversion of sentences creates a kind of linguistic smog that puts the reader to work sorting out the disarranged elements, causes his eyes to smart, and perhaps makes him wish he were reading something else. . . . Straining for variety in sentence structure is usually the cause. Tired of starting with the subject and adding the predicate, some writers make a mighty effort and jump out of the frying pan into the smog." R. Copperud, *American Usage and Style* 210 (1980).

These sentences are typical: "*Unaffected would be the current status* of the defense in which the risk is expressly assumed."/ "Therefore, *concludes defendant,* there being no privity of relationship between it and plaintiff, and no fraud or deceit alleged, defendant has the right to the property." Some legislative draftsmen are addicted to minor inversions, such as *notwithstanding anything in this Act contained.* They may be minor inversions, but they cloy on the first reading of the first one. In this example, because the word *contained* is superfluous, an acceptable phrasing is *notwithstanding anything in this Act.*

Often the users of inversion are no better at grammar than they are at style; thus they have problems with number, being unable to distinguish the inverted predicate from the subject: "To the judicial bravery and congressional impetus *belong* the credit of large-scale rectification of racial injustices." Here the verb should be singular (*belongs*) because, without the inversion, the clause reads *The credit belongs to the judicial bravery and congressional impetus.*/ "By the term literature *is* [read *are*] meant those written or printed compositions which preserve the thought and experience of a race recorded in artistic form."

Occasionally inversion is called for idiomatically, but is wrongly omitted: "It is much easier to answer this at the end rather than at the beginning, for only after prolonged study *one may* [read *may one*] look back and appreciate the significance of the hornbook definition of equitable jurisprudence."

invest; vest. These words are synonymous in meaning "to establish (a person) in the possession of any office, position, or property; to endow or furnish (a person or institution) with power, authority, or privilege." *Vest* is more usual in general English usage; the use of *invest* in this sense is chiefly confined to legal writing and evangelical preaching ⟨By the power invested in me by the Holy Spirit, I declare that you shall be instantly healed!⟩. E.g., from law: "By the constitution of the United States, the President is *invested* with certain important political powers . . ." (Marshall, C.J., in *Marbury v. Madison*)./ "In a proper legal sense, the holder of the legal title is not seised until he is fully *invested* with the possession, actual or constructive."/ "His status as a cabinet officer is not itself sufficient to *invest* him with absolute immunity."/ "Article V, section 5 of the Texas Constitution has *invested* the court of criminal appeals with a mandamus power comparable to that granted the supreme court." See **vest.**

investigatory, -tive. W3 notes that *investigatory* is "chiefly British," but it occurs almost as commonly as *investigative* in American legal contexts. E.g., "It is not unreasonably intrusive, courts have often held, for a police officer to aid his own *investigatory* senses with devices that serve only to enhance those senses, such as flashlights and binoculars."/ "These statements involved alleged incompetence and *investigatory* grand jury proceedings."/ "The frisk, it was held, was essential to the proper performance of the officer's *investigatory* duties."

The *COD* lists *investigative* before *-tory*; it ap-

pears more commonly than the other, despite what the fewer examples here quoted might suggest: "The particular interests involved here were the neutralization of danger to the policeman in the *investigative* circumstance and the sanctity of the individual."/ "It was this legitimate *investigative* function that Officer McFadden was discharging when he decided to approach petitioner and his companions."

There is certainly no need for the two variants to coexist. We might be well advised to throw over *investigatory* and stick with *investigative*, or to develop some heretofore unhinted-at DIFFERENTIATION. In any event, the two terms should not be used interchangeably in a single piece of writing, as they are in *Terry v. Ohio*, 392 U.S. 1 (1968). See INELEGANT VARIATION.

invidious. See **insidious.**

in view of. See **in lieu of.**

in view of the fact that is a weak equivalent of *because*.

inviolate; inviolable. The latter suggests that something is incapable of being violated, whereas the former suggests merely that the thing has not been violated. In practice, however, the words are often used interchangeably. *Inviolate* sometimes appears as a POSTPOSITIVE ADJECTIVE. E.g., "The Court weakens, if indeed it does not in fact submerge, this basic principle by finding, in effect, a grant of substantive legislative power in the constitutional provision for a federal court system, and through it, setting up the Federal Rules as a body of law *inviolate.*"

invite is a verb; it should be avoided as a noun for *invitation*.

inviter, -or. The former is preferred. See **-ER, -OR.**

in whole; in part. Follett wrote that *in whole* is unidiomatic for *as a whole*, the former phrase having been created as a needed parallel of *in part*. He was wrong, unless we want to trace what is idiomatic back before the sixteenth century and ignore steady uses up till the present time. Both *in whole* and *as a whole* are acceptable idioms; indeed, they are not even used in quite the same way. Both mean "as a complete thing," but, whereas *as a whole* is the general phrase, *in whole* is always used as a correlative of *in part*. E.g., "In one form a statute may create a new right, while neglecting *in whole* or *in part* the matter of the remedy."

in witness whereof (= signed) is one of the quintessential LEGALISMS.

I personally is prolix for a simple *I.* Occasionally it is legitimately used to contrast one's personal opinions with an official stance that one takes for reasons of a position one holds. See FIRST PERSON.

ipse dixit (lit., "he himself said it") = something said but not proved; a dogmatic statement. E.g., "In my view, it is quite impossible to tell which phrases the terms 'knowingly and willfully' modify, and the magic want of *ipse dixit* does nothing to resolve that ambiguity."/ "The majority goes on to assert that, in this case, the question is one of law, a sheer *ipse dixit*, for the three cases cited for this proposition provide no support for it whatever." Cf. **probatum.**

ipsissima verba = the very words. Another form of the phrase, *ipsissima verbis*, means "*in* the very words." The phrases do not mean "(in) the very same words," but "(in) the very words." Here the phrase is misused: "To constitute copyright infringement, copying need not be in *ipsissima verba*."/ "Now Texas has hastened to fall into line, and has enacted this North Dakota resolve *ipsissima verbis*" (ex. fr. G. Krapp, *A Comprehensive Guide to Good English* 334 (1927)). Here both writers intended to say *in the very same words;* they might have avoided error by sticking to English. See **verbatim** & LATINISMS.

ipso facto = by the fact (or act) itself. E.g., "She urges us to overrule our previous cases holding that a general residuary clause is not presumed, *ipso facto*, to exercise a general testamentary power of appointment."/ "His conclusion that the existence of the conflict of interest *ipso facto* disqualified him from acting cannot be allowed to set aside the intention of the testator manifested in his will."/ "The English courts have taken the position that directions to destroy wills such as that contained in the principal case are *ipso facto* expressions of present intention."/ "Enrichment, *ipso facto*, does not give rise to restitutionary recovery; it must be 'unjust.'"

IRONY, an undercutting of the readers' expectations, can be effective in legal writing, but only if subtle. E.g., "Thus, we hold that the first amendment does not clothe these plaintiffs with a constitutional right to sunbathe in the nude . . . . They remain able to advocate the benefits of nude sunbathing, albeit while fully dressed." The irony occurs in the first sentence, the second containing mere tongue-in-cheek playfulness.

One of the most common types of irony is the Swiftian modest proposal, here carried out with some success: "Of course, a simple mechanism for deterring violations such as [police brutality] would be to amend section 1983 to provide that violators will be drawn and quartered. This seems like a very powerful deterrent and might substantially reduce violations of federal rights under color of state law. Aside from problems relating to fairness, however, this solution also poses problems in the deterrence framework. A powerful deterrent such as drawing and quartering might also deter worthwhile conduct [by the police]. . . . So, the deterrence rationale calls for neither too much nor too little deterrence; we need to find the right amount." *Dobson v. Camden,* 705 F.2d 759, 765 (5th Cir. 1983) (per Goldberg, J.).

irrebuttable; irrefutable. See **rebut.**

irrefragable (= unanswerable; not to be controverted), a useful term in the law, is underused.

irrefutable. See **rebut.**

irregardless is a semiliterate PORTMANTEAU WORD from *irrespective* and *regardless* that should long ago have been stamped out. *Irregardless* is common enough in speech in the U.S. that it has found its way into judicial opinions. See, e.g., *State ex rel. Fisher v. Fisher,* 85 N.E.2d 562, 563 (Ohio App. 1949). On the second day of the U.S. Supreme Court's 1986–1987 term, Chief Justice Rehnquist upbraided a lawyer who used *irregardless*, saying: "I feel bound to inform you there is no word *irregardless* in the English language. The word is *regardless."* Linguistic fastidiousness is no less important in oral than in written argument.

irrelevance, -cy. The former is generally preferred. The only plural form, however, is *irrelevancies.* See **relevancy, -ce.**

irreparable is pronounced /i-*rep*-ă-ră-bĕl/.

irreplevisable. See **repleviable.**

irrespective of = regardless of. Confusion of the two phrases has given rise to the semi-literate *irregardless of,* q.v.

irresponsive. See **unresponsive.**

irrevocable; unrevokable. The former is preferred. It is pronounced /i-*rev*-ŏ-kă-bĕl/.

issuable. In nonlegal contexts this word means "capable of being issued"; the special legal sense of the word is "that admits of an issue being taken; in regard to which or during which issue may be joined" (*OED*). E.g., "No *issuable* fact or condition existed that would authorize the governing board to exercise the discretion confided to it in the passage of that part of the zoning ordinance under attack."

issuance. See **issue** (C).

issue. A. *At issue & in issue. At issue* = (1) (of people) in controversy; taking opposite sides of a case or contrary views of a matter; at variance ⟨His views are at issue with mine.⟩; (2) (of matters or questions) in dispute; under discussion; in question ⟨the allegations at issue⟩ (*OED*). The *OED* notes that *in issue* shares sense (2) of *at issue,* but calls it rare. Having originated in mid-nineteenth-century legal contexts, *in issue* is not at all rare today. See the sentence immediately following for the modern sense of *in issue:* "In the law of evidence, facts *in issue* are either: (1) facts that, in the pleadings, are affirmed on one side and denied on the other; or (2) in actions without pleadings, all facts from the establishment of which would follow the existence, nonexistence, nature, or extent of any right, liability, disability, or immunity asserted or denied in the case." (Eng.)/ "Roman law confined to the judge, when questions of law were *in issue,* the purely mechanical task of counting

and of determining the numerical preponderance of authority."/ "The test to be applied in passing on the validity of a gift such as the one *in issue* is that of reasonableness." *At issue* is the common idiomatic phrase, whereas *in issue* is purely a specialized legal phrase.

B. *Issue as to whether* is prolix for *issue whether.* Cf. **question (as to) whether.** See **as to.**

C. *Issue & issuance. Issuance* was not used until the mid-nineteenth century, up until which time *issue* was the noun corresponding to the verb *to issue.* E.g., "These lawyers reported that not only was there a strong current of precedent during the last century for the *issue* of such injunctions, but the common-law judges had themselves advised parties to apply to the Chancery." (Eng.) A layman in the U.S. today would think *issuance* to have been an apter term in the sentence quoted.

D. *Join issue* = (1) to submit an issue jointly for decision; (2) to accept or adopt a disputed point as the basis of argument in a controversy; (3) to take up the opposite side of a case, or a contrary view *on* a question (*OED*). This idiom is more common in G.B. than in the U.S. The nominal phrase is *joinder of issue.* E.g., "After *joinder of issue,* defendant moved for summary judgment." *Bradley v. Burroughs Wellcome Co.,* 497 N.Y.S.2d 401, 402 (N.Y. App. Div. 1986).

is when; is where. These locutions are improper means of introducing a definition. Instead of writing, "'Livery of seisin' *is where* the grantor delivers possession," one should write, "'Livery of seisin' is the grantor's delivery of possession." Here is an example of the ill-phrased definition: "A bill of exchange *is when* a person takes money in one country or city upon exchange, and draws a bill whereby he directs another person in another country or city to pay so much to A or order for value received of B and subscribes it." (Eng.) The idea of defining here is misplaced; read *With a bill of exchange, one takes money. . . .*

it is often used too many times in one sentence, which leads to problems with ANTECE-DENTS. E.g., "Within such a unitary jurisdictional framework, the appellate court will, of course, require the trial court to conform to constitutional mandates, but *it* [read *the appellate court*] may likewise require *it* [read *the trial court*] to follow procedures deemed desirable from the viewpoint of sound judicial practice."/ "Applying the test of an apportionable or apportioned consideration to the contract in question, *it will be seen* [read *one will see*] at once that *it* [read *such consideration*] is severable." (See EXPLETIVES (c) & DANGLERS.)

Sometimes a single *it* may be problematic in having no identifiable antecedent: "Paraphrasing the opinion of Judge Vann in *Tabor v. Hoffman*, because an inspection of plaintiff's models may be by fair means, *it* [?] does not justify obtaining the same by unfair means." See ANTECEDENTS, FALSE (A).

ITALICS. Only a few choice words need to be written here: "To those who, however competent on their special subject, have not had enough experience of writing to have learnt [the] rudiments, it comes as natural to italicize every tenth sentence or so as it comes to the letter-writing schoolgirl to underline whatever she enjoys recording" (*MEU1* 304).

itemization is often unnecessary for *list*, q.v.

iterate. See **reiterate.**

it is I; it is me. In formal English, *it is I* is the preferred expression, *it is me* being passable in the speech of most persons (rarely if ever in writing). The latter form has been debated by grammarians for more than a century, with little result. See NOMINATIVE & OBJECTIVE CASES.

its; it's. The possessive form of *it* is *its*; the contraction for *it is* is *it's*. *Its* should never be used as a personal pronoun; in the singular *his* is preferred. "*X* conveys to the lawful children or child of any deceased lawful child of *A* to have and receive *its* [read *his*] or their deceased parent's share."

ius. See **jus.**

-IZE & -ISE. Adding the suffix *-ize* to an adjective or noun is one of the most frequently used means of forming new verbs. Many verbs so formed are objectionable. In AmE, *-ize* is more usual than in BrE, in which *-ise* is more common. But even in BrE, *-ize* is preferred to *-ise* in words in which either form of the suffix may appear. The choice arises only with words ending with the pronunciation

eyes, not with *ice*, *iss*, or *eez*. So: *precise*, *promise*, *expertise*, *remise*. Nouns in *-ise* are precluded from the choice of *-ize*; these include:

compromise	enterprise	merchandise
demise	exercise	surmise
disguise	franchise	surprise

Verbs corresponding to nouns that have *-is-* as a part of the stem (e.g., in the syllables *-vis-*, *-cis-*, *-mis-*), or identical with a noun in *-ise*, similarly take *-ise* rather than *-ize*. Some of the common verbs in *-ise* are:

advertise	despise	incise
advise	devise	merchandise
apprise	disfranchise	premise
arise	disguise	prise (open)
chastise	enfranchise	revise
circumcise	enterprise	supervise
comprise	excise	surmise
compromise	exercise	surprise
demise	improvise	televise

Generally, *-ize* verbs are formed on familiar English words or stems, e.g. *authorize*, *familiarize*, *symbolize*; or with a slight alteration to the stem, e.g. *agonize*, *dogmatize*, *sterilize*. A few words have no such immediate stem: *aggrandize* (cf. *aggrandizement*), *appetize* (cf. *appetite*), *baptize* (cf. *baptism*), *catechize* (cf. *catechism*), *recognize* (cf. *recognition*), and *capsize*.

NEOLOGISMS in *-ize* are generally to be discouraged, for they are invariably ungainly, and often superfluous. Thus we have no use for *accessorize*, *artificialize*, *cubiclize*, *fenderize* (= to fix a dented fender), *funeralize*, *ghettoize*, *Mirandize* (q.v.), *nakedize*, and so on. The law has a few of its own curiosities in *-ize* (e.g. *privatize*, *collateralize*, q.v., *communitize*), and probably needs no more. Careful writers are wary of new words formed with this suffix.

J

jackleg lawyer. See LAWYERS, DEROGATORY NAMES FOR.

jactation, jactitation. *Jactation*, lit. "a tossing or swinging of the body to and fro" (*OED*), came figuratively to mean (in both Latin and English) "boasting, bragging, ostentatious display" (*OED*). It is a learned word. Its sibling *jactitation* derives from the same Latin verb and also has the sense "a boastful declaration." In law the term has been applied specifically to boasts of marriage. Today *jactitation of marriage* = a false assertion that one is married to someone to whom one is not in fact married (*CDL*). E.g., "A decree in a suit of *jactitation* of marriage, forbidding C to claim to be the husband of A, on the ground that he was not her husband, is deemed to be irrelevant." (Eng.)

jail delivery, in the AmE, means "an escape by several prisoners from a jail"; in BrE, it means "the bringing of prisoners to trial."

jailhouse lawyer. See LAWYER, DEROGATORY NAMES FOR.

JANUS-FACED TERMS are, because of syntactic construction, overburdened in being asked to look backward and forward simultaneously. (They sometimes look forward at two different objects, or backward.) As here defined, a word so called upon can properly look one way, but not both.

Commonly known as ZEUGMA, this fault of writing occurs when a verb is incorrectly associated with two subjects or objects, an adjective with two nouns, or a noun with an antecedent and a "postcedent" (for lack of a better word) that are different. Some specimens follow, with short explanations of the problems.

A. Referring to the Case Name and the Name of the Person Simultaneously: "It is now doubtful whether McCardle (the defendant) would now be sustained," in which the writer means the opinion with the short-title form *McCardle*, though the parenthesis refers to the person. Another such example would be: "Shakespeare's powers were perhaps greatest in *Hamlet*, the most famous of tragic protagonists," in which the writer is unconsciously referring to the character and the play at the same time. Following is a sentence that avoids the problem just illustrated: "The *Roskos* court found that the plaintiff, Roskos, was coerced into resignation."

B. Pronoun Used Also as an Expletive: "When Mr. Crick writes about the nature and origin of life, it is always prudent and often a delight to pay attention." In this sentence, *it* first appears to refer to Crick's writing (though it has no clear antecedent), and then

is used as an introductory filler or expletive. [Read *It is always prudent and often delightful to pay attention to Mr. Crick's writing about the nature and origin of life.*]

C. Two Different Senses of the Same Word: "Why ought Louisiana [the state government] to have power over one who has had an auto accident there [the place]?"

D. Word Referred to as a Word, While Purporting to Have Substantive Meaning as Well: "Derived from *Slav*, of which people many were enslaved by the conquering Romans, the word [*slave*] has acquired connotations of servility, timidity, and cowardice." (Bergen Evans) The reference to *Slav* is to the word, not the people; hence the phrase that follows is illogical.

E. Preposition Given Two Meanings: "The shareholders will transact such other business as may properly come before the meeting or any adjournment thereof." Here *before* is asked to mean both "in front of" (before the convocation or meeting) and "prior to" (before adjournment). See ZEUGMA.

JARGONMONGERING. Some would say that to be a lawyer (or at least a good one) is necessarily to be a jargonmonger, that word-shuffling is the nature of the business. That view is the most pessimistic possible, and is not borne out by the evidence of the many successful straight-talking and straight-writing practitioners. If such a jaded view has any validity, the best one can do is to prove its falsity by one's own example.

It is difficult to improve on Sir Arthur Quiller-Couch's seminal analysis of jargon in his *Art of Writing* (1916; repr. 1961). He sets out its two primary vices: "The first is that it uses circumlocution rather than short straight speech. It says: '*In the case of* John Jenkins deceased, the coffin' when it means 'John Jenkins's coffin'; and its yea is not yea, neither is its nay nay; but its answer is *in the affirmative* or *in the negative*, as the foolish and superfluous *case* may be. The second vice is that it habitually chooses vague wooly abstract nouns rather than concrete ones" (*id.* at 105). "To write jargon is to be perpetually shuffling around in a fog and cotton-wool of abstract terms" (*id.* at 117). See ABSTRACTITIS.

Nothing nauseates like the real thing: "A supplement to the draft or final EIS on file will be prepared whenever significant impacts resulting from changes in the proposed plan or new significant impact information, criteria or circumstances relevant to environmental considerations impact on the recommended plan or proposed action." 33 C.F.R. § 2502.9(c)(1) (1984).

jealousy; envy. The careful writer distinguishes between these terms. *Jealousy* is properly restricted to contexts involving love and affairs of the heart, whereas *envy* is used more broadly of resentful contemplation of a more fortunate person.

Jeddart justice; Jedburgh justice; Jedwood justice. The first is now the usual form of this term, meaning "execution first, trial afterwards." The name derives from Jedburgh in Roxburghshire, Scotland (near the English border), where people along the border frequently skirmished. Probably of sixteenth-century origin, *Jeddart justice* "differs from *lynch law* in that it was done by a kind of summary court, not by persons wholly unauthorized" (*OCL*).

jemmy. See **jimmy**.

jeopardize; (en)jeopard. Horwill wrote that in AmE "*jeopard* is preferred to *jeopardize*, the common term in England." *Modern American Usage* 178 (1935) (s.v. *jeopardize*). This was not true in 1935, and it is not true today. E.g., "Fanciful rights of accused persons cannot be allowed to prevent the functioning of the police and so to *jeopardize* the safety of the public."/ "The government's suit in *Nolder*, like that of plaintiff's in *Goff*, *jeopardizes* two of the primary purposes underlying Rule 23: avoidance of duplicative litigation and inconsistent standards." *Enjeopard* and *jeopard* are NEEDLESS VARIANTS.

jeopardy. See **double jeopardy**.

jetsam. See **flotsam**.

jibe. See **gibe**.

jimmy; jemmy. A burglar's crowbar is spelled *jimmy* in the U.S., *jemmy* in G.B.

jj. is the abbreviation for *judges* or *justices*.

j.n.o.v. (= judgment non obstante veredicto) is usually abbreviated thus in lower case. Some courts write *JNOV*, but the capital letters and dropping of periods are not justified, and serve only to draw attention to themselves. The abbreviation is sometimes shortened to *n.o.v.*: "Appellee may bring his grounds for new trial to the trial court's attention when defendant first makes *an n.o.v.* [better: *a j.n.o.v.*] motion." See **judgment non obstante veredicto**.

job site should be spelled as two words. Cf. **worksite**.

joinder. A. And *jointure*. *Joinder*, the noun corresponding to the verb *to join*, is the usual term in law for the uniting of several causes of action or of parties in a single suit. E.g., "The proceeding was one that by statute binds such future interest without either *joinder* or representation of the person in favor of whom it was limited." (See **issue** (D).) *Jointure*, a much less common term, means "the holding of property to the joint use of a husband and wife for life or in tail, as a provision for the latter, in the event of her widowhood" (*OED*). E.g., "The trend is toward upholding postnuptial agreements even where obsolete statutes codify the common-law rules on *jointure*."

B. And *consolidation*. Whereas *joinder* has come to be used usually in the sense of uniting parties in a suit, *consolidation* has become in the U.S. the more usual word for uniting lawsuits into a single suit.

join issue. See **issue** (D).

joint and several = together and in separation. "Appellants *jointly and severally* covenanted and agreed that they would pay the principal sum of $280,000 on February 1."/ "The district court predicated its judgment of *joint and several liability* against the two appellants upon its findings of causal negligence of the tortfeasor and unseaworthiness of the vessel." With *joint and several liability*, the liability of two or more obligors may be enforced against them all by a joint action or against any of them by an individual action. *Solidary liability* is used in this sense in Louisiana, Puerto Rico, and civil-law countries. See **several**.

joint cooperation is a REDUNDANCY.

joint tenancy; tenancy in common. The distinction between these two terms is basic to the law of property. *Joint tenancy* = ownership of property by two or more persons who have identical interests in the whole of the property, with a right of survivorship. *Tenancy in common* = equitable ownership of property by two or more persons in equal or unequal undivided shares, with no right of survivorship. The property for each of these tenancies may be either real (land) or personal (e.g., a bank account), although the *CDL*, which reflects British legal practices, confines its definitions to real property.

join together is a REDUNDANCY that should be allowed to survive only in the marriage service, and there only because it is a bona fide remnant of Elizabethan English.

joint wills. See **mutual wills.**

joker = an ambiguous clause in a legislative bill inserted to render it inoperative or uncertain in some respect without arousing opposition at time of passage. *Bennett v. Commercial Advertiser Ass'n*, 230 N.Y. 125, 129 N.E. 343, 345 (1920). The term, as well as the practice it represents, is generally unknown to just and responsible legislators.

journal, v.t.; **journalize.** Both terms are used in the sense "to record in a journal." *Journalize* is more usual in legal contexts, e.g.: "He filed an appeal after the district judge officially *journalized* the judgment." The verb *to journal* has additional, nonlegal senses.

JOURNALESE. See TITULAR TOMFOOLERY.

judex, except in historical contexts (e.g., "English Chancery Courts, heavy borrowers from the civil law, may have derived the system of special masters from the civilian *judex* of the Roman Republic and Early Empire."), is an unnecessary equivalent of *judge.*

judge; justice. Judges often look unkindly on mistakes in their titles: "By two identical motions filed January 3, 1985 in these related actions, defendant moves for an order 'disqualifying the Honorable Mr. Justice [*sic*] Charles L. Brieant from hearing this matter on the ground that said Honorable Charles L. Brieant was the presiding justice [*sic*] in the trial of *Lany Optic Industries, Inc. v. Passport International Ltd.*'" *Tenzer v. Lewitinn,* 599 F. Supp. 973, 974 (S.D.N.Y. 1985) (per Brieant,

J.). As a general rule, judges sitting on the highest appellate level of a jurisdiction are known as *justices.* Trial judges and appellate judges on intermediate levels are generally called *judges,* not *justices.* (New York and Texas depart from these rules of thumb: in New York, *justices* sit on the trial court [the Supreme Court, oddly], and in Texas, *justices* sit on the courts of appeals [between the trial court and the Supreme Court—the latter being the highest court of appeal—which is also composed of *justices*].)

Horwill wrote that *"judge* carries with it in America by no means such dignified associations as it possesses in England. It may mean [in the U.S.] no more than a *magistrate* of a police court." Horwill, *Modern American Usage* 180 (1935). *Justice* may also denote in the U.S. a low-ranking judge, as in the phrases *justice of the peace* and *police justice.*

judge advocate. Pl. *judge advocates.*

judge, v.t. See **adjudge.**

judge-made, adj., is used generally as an antonym of *statutory.* E.g., "Some time should also be devoted to discussion of legislative as opposed to *judge-made* tort law."/ "With limited exceptions these sections of the Restatement reflect no statutes or statutory developments; they purport to be precise statements of the prevailing or better *judge-made* law, and the Reporter suggests that they may be implemented by judicial action or by statute."

judg(e)ment. *Judgment* is the preferred form in the U.S., and seems to be preferred in British legal texts, even as far back as the nineteenth century; *judgement* is prevalent in British nonlegal texts, and was thought by Fowler to be the better form.

Judgment is commonly used in G.B. in the sense in which *opinion* is used in the U.S.: "The facts of this case, which are fully stated in the *judgment* of Lord Hanworth M.R., were briefly as follows." (Eng.) See JUDGMENTS, APPELLATE-COURT & **decision.**

judgmental; judgmatic. *Judgmental* = (1) of or relating to judgment, or (2) judging when uncalled for. Sense (2) is now more common ⟨a judgmental critic⟩, but sense (1) still appears. E.g., "The qualification is generally undertaken only in an effort to make meaningful [q.v.] a whole host of *judgmental* factors applicable at a particular time." *Judgmatic*, called by Fowler a "facetious formation" because of its irregular formation on the analogy of *dogmatic*, is a NEEDLESS VARIANT of *judicious*. See **judicial.**

judgment-book; judgment-roll. A *judgment-book* is kept by the clerk of court for the entry or recordation of judgments. (See **rendition of judgment.**) A *judgment-roll* is virtually the same in American practice, although some jurisdictions such as New York call for *entry* of judgments in the *judgment-roll* and mere recordation of judgments in the *judgment-book.* The usual term in G.B. is *judgment-roll.*

judgment non obstante veredicto; judgment notwithstanding the verdict; j.n.o.v.; judgment n.o.v. Of these forms, perhaps the best unabbreviated one is *judgment notwithstanding the verdict.* Its Latin equivalent is as often as not in the U.S. erroneously rendered *verdicto* rather than *veredicto.* We must not forget the Latin phrase, however, lest young lawyers come not to understand the import of *j.n.o.v.,* q.v.

JUDGMENTS, APPELLATE-COURT. By *judgment* in this article is meant the final decree of an appellate court that acts upon a lower-court judgment, whether affirming, reversing, vacating, or whatever. The British ordinarily use *judgment* synonymously with *opinion,* whereas in the U.S. we distinguish between the *opinion* (which sets out the reasons for the disposition) and the judgment (the pronouncement of the disposition itself). This article, then, reflects primarily American practices.

A cardinal principle of judgment-drafting is that appellate opinions should make explicit how the court is disposing of the judgment or order below. Appellate courts have sometimes left the parties and the trial court uncertain about the status of a case by using vague terms such as *so ordered* and *ordered accordingly,* without a clear statement of the disposition preceding these phrases. This practice is, happily, obsolescent.

A second important point is that judges should almost make a fetish of the following distinctions: an appeals court affirms, reverses, or modifies *judgments* or *orders;* it

agrees with, approves, or disapproves *opinions* or *decisions;* and it remands *cases* (or *causes*) and *actions.* When the court lacks jurisdiction to hear the appeal, the proper disposition is usually *appeal dismissed.* Although an appellate court in its opinions may approve or disapprove the trial court's statement or use of legal propositions, the judgment proper operates only on the judgment or order appealed from—that is, appellate courts do not affirm or reverse opinions, only orders or judgments. (The appellate court may, for example, affirm the judgment below but substitute a rationale leading to that judgment.)

The terms *vacate* and *reverse* can be problematic. Practices vary: some courts *reverse* the judgment below when the trial court should have disposed of the case differently, and *vacate* when the trial court may not have been incorrect, but needs to be unconstrained by its former judgment as it carries out the further directions of the appellate court. E.g., "We *vacate* the judgment of the district court and remand the case for proceedings consistent with this opinion." Still other courts *vacate* only injunctions or administrative orders, *reversing* all other erroneous dispositions below. Courts ought to encourage consistency among their particular judges in these matters of usage.

With these guidelines in mind, it may be useful to consider a number of appellate-court judgments, as well as statements about judgments, that are illustrative of the pitfalls awaiting the unwary. The first seven examples of poor drafting that follow have been adapted, with some additions, from the excellent discussion of the former Chief Justice of the Supreme Court of Texas, Robert W. Calvert, in his *Appellate Court Judgments,* 6 Texas Tech L. Rev. 915 (1975).

1. Mistaking the Lower Court for Its Judgment. "We deny the petitions and *affirm* [read *affirm the order of*] the Interstate Commerce Commission."/ "In an opinion by Justice Brennan, the Supreme Court *affirmed* [read *affirmed the judgment of*] the Fourth Circuit."/ "For these reasons, I am of the opinion that the evidence was sufficient to warrant revocation in this case and would *affirm* [read *affirm the judgment of*] the lower court." (The tribunal appealed from is not before the higher court for approval or disapproval, affirmance or reversal; rather, its *judgment* or *order* is.)

2. Mistaking the Case for the Judgment

Below. *"The case* (or *cause*) [read *The judgment*] is affirmed." (The case or cause remains the same; an appellate-court judgment acts directly upon a previous judgment in the case, but not upon the case itself.)

3. Mistaking the Lower Court's Opinion for Its Judgment. "The *opinion* [read *judgment*] of the trial court is affirmed."/ "The *decision* [read *judgment*] of the district court is reversed."/ "For reasons stated below, we affirm the *decision* [read *judgment*] of the trial court." (The appellate court may agree or disagree with the trial court's opinion or decision; again, however, it affirms or reverses the *judgment.*)

4. Mistaking the Appellate Court's Judgment for the Trial Court's. "The judgment of the trial court is reversed and rendered." (Appellate courts ordinarily have no power or jurisdiction to render a trial court's judgment; yet appellate courts are often authorized to render judgments that should have been rendered by the trial court. Read *The judgment of the trial court is reversed; on appeal, we render judgment for. . . .*)

5. Mistaking the Judgment for the Case. "The judgment of the trial court is reversed *and remanded* [read *and the case is remanded*]." (The judgment of the trial court may be reversed, but only the *case* may be remanded.)/ "We vacate and remand the case for consideration of whether these errors were harmless." (Understood, perhaps, are the words *the judgment of the trial court* after the word *vacate;* it is generally best not to rely on UNDERSTOOD WORDS in drafting judgments, however; yet see the final paragraph of this article.)/ "The trial court's judgment is *affirmed in part, and reversed and remanded in part* [read *affirmed in part, reversed in part, and the case is remanded*]." (A case may not be remanded in part. If the judgment is not stated in sentence form, it is quite proper to write *Affirmed in part, reversed in part, and remanded.*)

6. Superfluously Granting Judgment After Reversal of a Plaintiff's Judgment. "The judgment for the plaintiff is reversed *and the judgment is here rendered for the defendant* [omit the italicized words]." (If the defendant has not filed a counterclaim, the judgment should end after the word *reversed;* the judgment is favorable to the defendant merely in denying the plaintiff recovery.)

7. Wrongly Omitting a Remand. "The judgment that the plaintiff take nothing is reversed and is here rendered for the plaintiff."

(This judgment is incomplete, unless there is only one possible form and measure of relief; if the plaintiff sought damages, the case would have to be remanded to the trial court for a determination of the measure of damages.)

8. Mistaking the Judgment for the Court Below or Its Judgment. "The district court's *judgment held* [read *opinion held*, or, better, *The district court held*] that the oral contract was dissolved by virtue of appellee's breach for failure to provide or secure the promised financing."

Finally, it is worth noting that the terms *affirm, reverse, remand,* etc. may have "understood" objects, as here: "We affirm on all issues with regard to Jack Ballard, but *reverse* insofar as the court held Mary Ballard liable for the 1969 and 1970 deficiencies."/ "We hold that Ohio's law of trade secrets is not preempted by the patent laws of the United States, and, accordingly, we *reverse.*"/ "We *reverse* and *remand.*" These elliptical phrases are unexceptionable; when, however, one of these verbs of disposition is given an object, then all such verbs in the immediate context should have explicit objects. (See item 5 above.)

judicable; justiciable. The former is a NEEDLESS VARIANT of the latter, q.v.

judicative, -tory, -torial. *Judicative* is a NEEDLESS VARIANT of *adjudicative,* q.v. *Judicatorial* is a NEEDLESS VARIANT of *judicial,* q.v. *Judicatory,* adj., = (1) of or relating to judgment; (2) by which a judgment may be made; giving a decisive indication; critical. For the nominal senses of *judicatory,* see **judicature.**

judicator. See **adjudicator.**

judicature; judicatory. *Judicature* = (1) a judge's term of office; or (2) a body of judges. It is sometimes used in G.B. where *judiciary,* q.v., usually appears in the U.S.; hence the U.S. statute is the Judiciary Act of 1789, whereas Britain has the Judicature Acts of 1873-75 and the Supreme Court of Judicature (Consolidation) Act of 1925. *Judicature* is used in the U.S. in names such as the American Judicature Society, which publishes the journal *Judicature,* by its own terms "a forum for fact and opinion relating to all aspects of the administration of justice and its improvement."

On the whole, however, *judicature* is far

more common in G.B. than in the U.S. E.g., "The chancery division placed stress upon certain provisions of the *judicature* act." (Eng.)/ "This paragraph applies to all courts of *judicature*, criminal or civil, and to all persons having by law, or by consent of parties, authority to hear, receive, and examine evidence." (Eng.)/ "It is a basic rule of English *judicature* that our courts do justice in public." (Eng.)

Judicatory = judiciary; judicature. Except in specialized senses in Scotland and in the Presbyterian Church, this term should be avoided as a NEEDLESS VARIANT. For its adjectival sense, see **judicative.**

judicial; judicious. *Judicial* = (1) of, relating to, or by the court ⟨judicial officers⟩; (2) in court ⟨judicial admissions⟩; (3) legal; (4) of or relating to a judgment. Here sense (1) is illustrated: "The requirements of this section had been *judicially* interpreted [i.e., interpreted by the court] well before defendants' actions."/ "Far more imposing is the edifice of private remedies *judicially* extracted from the Securities and Exchange Act of 1934."

Following are examples of sense (2) of *judicial*: "The record further revealed that the trial court erroneously apprised the defendant of the effect of his plea (i.e., by failing to inform him that his *judicial* stipulation had foreclosed a merit consideration of his appeal from the adverse ruling on the motion to suppress)."/ "Appellant then took the witness stand and *judicially* confessed that she had committed the offense alleged against her in the indictment."

And here sense (3): "It is now well established by *judicial* precedent that, where an attorney has taken a retainer to defend a prisoner, he is not at liberty to withdraw during the trial because he discovers that his client is guilty."

Sense (4), not recorded in unabridged or legal dictionaries, is not uncommon in legal contexts, especially in the U.S.:

Todd's liability for Auto's attorneys' fees, therefore, is fundamentally different from, for example, liability for interest on a judgment, which we held was not covered by the red-letter clause in *Alcoa Steamship Co. v. Charles Ferran & Co.*, relied on by the district court. Whereas an award of *judicial* interest is collateral to and independent of the action itself, attorneys' fees awarded as a result of breach of an implied warranty of workman-

like performance are an integral part of the merits of the case and the scope of relief.

> *Todd Shipyards Corp. v. Auto Transportation, S.A.*, 763 F.2d 745, 756 (5th Cir. 1985).

Though hardly unusual, this use of the word is certainly suspect.

Judicious has a quite different meaning: "well considered, discreet, wisely circumspect." E.g., "The court *judiciously* exercised its inherent equitable power to fashion a remedy appropriate to the wrongs committed."/ "By *judicious* application of Rule 403, a trial judge can afford the defendant in an obscenity case a fair opportunity to prove that the community displays a reasonable degree of acceptance of comparable material." / "My theory was expressed too widely in certain parts, and not widely enough in others; and Mr. Whitworth's pamphlet appeared to me to have corrected and completed it in a *judicious* manner." (Eng.) *Judgmatic* is a NEEDLESS VARIANT of *judicious.* See **judgmental.**

judicialize = to treat judicially, arrive at a judgment or decision upon (*OED*). More modernly it has evolved to mean "to take into the province of the courts." E.g., "Rulemaking proceedings have become more *judicialized.*" See -IZE.

judicial notice; judicial cognizance. The former phrase (referring to the means by which a court may take as proved certain facts without hearing evidence) is now the more common of the two in both AmE and BrE.

The verb phrase is *to notice judicially*: "While there are few absolutes in this area, we can *notice judicially*, if we need, that contemporary wills more often than not use the residuary clause to carry out the most important provisions."

judiciary, adj. Ordinarily a noun, *judiciary* is used in *W3* adjectively in the phrase *with full judiciary authority* (in definition of *en banc*). *W3* records *judiciary* as an adjective equivalent to *judicial.* It is rarely so used in legal contexts, and should be avoided in that sense as a NEEDLESS VARIANT. See **judicative.**

But in the sense "of or relating to the judiciary," which means something different from *judicial* (= of or relating to the court), q.v., the adjective *judiciary* is quite useful. E.g., "If the history of the interpretation of *judiciary* legislation teaches anything, it teaches the duty to reject treating such statutes as a wooden set of self-sufficient words." *Romero v. International Terminal Operating Co.*, 358 U.S. 354, 379 (1959).

judiciary, n., (= the judicial branch of government) is used in G.B. as well as in the U.S. (See **judicature**.) E.g., "Appellant has questioned the validity of the sections of the act relating to the last-mentioned objective, upon the theory that they are unconstitutional encroachments by the legislative branch of the government upon the powers of the *judiciary*."/ "In *Crouch v. Crouch*, we gave reasons for the federal *judiciary*'s traditional refusal to exercise diversity jurisdiction in domestic-relations cases."

judicious. See **judicial**.

jump bail (= to leave [a place] illegally while free on bail) began as slang, but has now become a respectable expression used even by judges in written opinions.

juncture. The phrase *at this juncture* should be used in reference to a crisis or a critically important time; it is not equivalent merely to "at this time" or "now." When used with these latter meanings, it is a pomposity. Here it is appropriate: "There can be no question that respondent was 'in custody' at least as of the moment he was placed under arrest; because he was not informed of his constitutional rights at this *juncture*, respondent's subsequent admissions should not have been used against him." And here it is inappropriate: "The controversy *at this juncture merely points up* [read *at this point merely illustrates*] the indefiniteness and uncertainty of the controversial portion of the decree."/ "Texas argues that delay of review is not all that it seeks to avoid by petitioning *at this juncture* [read *at this point* or *now*]."

jura. See **jus**.

jural; juridic, -idical; juratory, -atorial. *Jural* = (1) of or relating to law or its administration; legal; juristic; or (2) of or pertaining to rights and obligations. Today, *jural* is more common in sense (2): "The categories were cast in terms of *jural* relations, with a particular suit falling into one group or another depending on the character of the right sought to be enforced."/ "The same points and the

same examples seem valid in relation to all possible kinds of *jural* interests, legal as well as equitable."

Sense (1), in which *jural* is really only a NEEDLESS VARIANT of simpler terms, still sometimes appears: "Witnesses are often required to describe in meticulous detail a happening that occurred months and years before the *jural* finding of facts."/ "One legacy of the Enlightment is the belief that law is something separate from the state, a set of longstanding *jural* rules or immutable principles resting on God or 'nature' that the state supposedly enforces."

Juridical = relating to judicial proceedings or to the law; the form in *-idical* is standard. E.g., "The line of departure will be set by that unfinished classic of *juridical* righteousness, the statement that for every wrong there is a remedy."/ "The intent that must be manifested by the settlor is an intent to create the *juridical* relationship known to the law as a trust."/ "I cannot believe that the court ever meant, in listing the criteria that usually attend the creation of a remainder, to express an inflexible rule or an inexorable *juridical* formula by the use of which we would be able to derive an automatic answer in all cases." *Juridical* is sometimes mispronounced as if it were spelled *juridicial*, with a soft *-c-*.

Juratory, a rare term today, means "of or pertaining to an oath or oaths; expressed or contained in an oath" (*OED*). *Juratorial*, also rare, means "of or belonging to a jury" (*OED*).

jurat; jurant. Both mean "one who has taken an oath"; except in Scottish history, *jurant* is a NEEDLESS VARIANT that is little used. *Jurat* usually refers to a public official, although historically it could refer to a juror: "On his left was a group of twelve sworn *jurats*, selected not for their ignorance of or impartiality for the matters at hand, but precisely because they were more likely to know the truth in advance." (Eng.)

Jurat has an additional, and perhaps more common, sense: "a clause placed at the end of an affidavit stating the time, place, and officer before whom the affidavit was made." E.g., "It further appears that the *jurat* to the loyalty affidavit has been properly executed."

juratory, -atorial. See **jural**.

juridic, -idical. See **jural**.

jurisconsult = one learned in law, esp. in civil or international law; a jurist; a master of jurisprudence (*OED*). The term seems to be little used today, although it certainly merits service.

jurisdiction = the *power* of a court to decide a case or enter a decree. E.g., "There is no *jurisdiction* to insert words in order to correct a mistake even though it is proved that the testator did not know and approve of the sense carried by deficient words actually appearing in the instrument." (Eng.) By transference of sense, *jurisdiction* has come to mean additionally "the territory within which an authority may exercise its power" ⟨the accused then fled the jurisdiction⟩.

   A. And *venue*. *Venue* refers to the possible or proper *places* for the trial of a lawsuit, as distinguished from the proper forums in which *jurisdiction* (the *power* to hear the case) might be established.

   B. Prepositions with. *Jurisdiction* takes *of* or *over*. "This court does not have *jurisdiction over* the appeal."/ "How such a magistrate can be said to have had no *jurisdiction over* the charge at all, it is hard to see." (Eng.)/ "This court has *jurisdiction of* the subject matter of the claims asserted in plaintiff's first amended complaint."

jurisdictional, -dictive. The latter means "having jurisdiction" ⟨the court that is jurisdictive of this suit⟩, the former "of or relating to jurisdiction." E.g., "The time limit fixed by Rule 59(e) is *jurisdictional*: it may not be extended by waiver of the parties or by rule of the district court." This DIFFERENTIATION has only recently emerged, *jurisdictive* being, in its other senses, a NEEDLESS VARIANT of *jurisdictional*. *Jurisdictive* is rare in American legal prose.

jurisprude, recorded in neither the *OED* nor the *OED Supp.*, is listed in *W3* as a BACK-FORMATION from *jurisprudence* with the meaning "a person who makes ostentatious show of learning in jurisprudence and the philosophy of law or who regards legal doctrine with undue solemnity or veneration." The word deserves wider currency, but not without recognition of its pejorative connotations. (For the neutral personal noun corresponding to *jurisprudence*, see **jurisprudent.**) In the following sentence, *jurisprude* is wrongly used as

if it were a neutral noun: "Yet all these scientific theories of law still leave contemporary *jurisprudes* [read *jurisprudents*] unsatisfied, and for good reason." Forte, *Natural Law and Natural Laws,* 26 Univ. Bookman 75, 75–76 (1986).

jurisprudence. A. Practical or Theoretical Sense. This uncertain term has evolved curiously. The *OED* assigns to it three senses: (1) "knowledge of or skill in law"; (2) "the science that treats of human laws (written or unwritten) in general"; and (3) "a system or body of law." The original sense (1) of practical skill in the law shifted to create the meanings (2 & 3) that emphasize the body of knowledge with which skilled practitioners work.

   Though derivatives of *jurisprudence* exist in a number of Western languages, this shift in meaning from the practical to the theoretical has apparently occurred only in English. Although both senses remain alive, the theoretical one, equivalent now roughly to "philosophy of the law," predominates at present. The result, one writer has argued, is that "a word of distinguished pedigree and a well-established English meaning not essentially different from that which it bears in other languages has been made to colour like a chameleon and finally emerge as a self-contradictory chimera." Note, *A Note on the Word Jurisprudence,* 58 Law Q. Rev. 334, 339 (1942).

   Well, not exactly. We might wish for less confusion, but it looks today as if the theoretical *jurisprudence* will oust its practical competitor, labeled archaic by *W3*, and at this point there is little we can do but take note.

   B. For *case law*. In AmE *jurisprudence* has been extended even further, from "body of law" to "court decisions; case law." E.g., "The seaman's cause of action against a shipowner for unseaworthiness of the vessel is largely a child of twentieth-century *jurisprudence*." Note, *The Doctrine of Unseaworthiness in the Lower Federal Courts,* 76 Harv. L. Rev. 819, 819 (1963)./ "This holding recognized and applied as part of the general maritime law a principle previously applied by either statute or *jurisprudence* in other contexts." The French use their term *la jurisprudence* in precisely this sense. *Case law* and *decisional law* are less grandiose terms in English.

C. As a COUNT NOUN. *Jurisprudence* is not properly a count noun. E.g., "The courts for many years refused to acknowledge the existence of 'administrative law' as *a jurisprudence* [read *a branch of jurisprudence*]."

jurisprudent; jurisprudential. *Jurisprudent,* though appearing to be an adjective, is a noun meaning "a jurist, or learned lawyer." (Cf. **jurisprude.**) *Jurisprudential* = of or relating to jurisprudence. E.g., "In a real and practical sense, when such an opportunity arises, the remedial considerations (not theoretical or *jurisprudential* concepts) totally dictate the course of action the plaintiff should pursue."

jurist. In England, this word is reserved for those having made outstanding contributions to legal thought and legal literature. In the U.S., it is rather loosely applied to every judge of whatever level, and sometimes even to nonscholarly practitioners who are well respected.

Here the term is used correctly: "These topics would lead us into a very enlarged inquiry, incompatible with the object of this summary sketch; but they deserve the attention of all students of the law of prize, and it is to be hoped that some eminent *jurist* will, hereafter, examine them." Appendix on Prize Causes, 15 U.S. (2 Wheat.) 37 (1817)./ "For *jurist,* law teacher, and judge, comparative law is becoming more than a part of his general culture." (R. Pound)/ "The apportionment picture in Pennsylvania has, indeed, degenerated into a sorry state, in spite of the lofty ideals of the many sincere and scholarly *jurists* who contributed to its development over the years."

The most common error in the U.S. is to suppose that *jurist* is merely an equivalent of *judge:* "We find no constitutional question concerning the validity of Charles Milton's conviction and sentence of death about which reasonable *jurists* [read *judges*] could differ."

juristic, -istical. The form in *-istical* is a NEEDLESS VARIANT. "We can all profit by the advice this legal disciplinarian gave his students on effective *juristic* style."

juristic person; artificial person. These phrases mean "a corporate entity," and are esp. common in G.B. *Juristic person* is the usual phrase. E.g., "Countries ordinarily accept the existence of *juristic persons* brought into being in their country of origin." (Eng.)/ "A, as trustee, is not a *juristic person* separate from A, as an individual." Other names for *juristic person* are *conventional person* and *fictitious person,* which should be avoided as confusing variants.

jurocracy = government by the courts. See, e.g., D.L. Horowitz, *The Jurocracy: Government Lawyers, Agency Programs, and Judicial Decisions* (1977). The term is recorded in none of the major dictionaries, although certainly it is a useful addition to the language. See GOVERNMENTAL FORMS.

juror; juryman, -woman; jurator. *Juror* is the word to be used in all modern contexts. *Juryman* and *jurywoman* should be avoided on grounds of SEXISM, although occasionally they appear. E.g., "A petty juror may not, and it is doubtful whether a grand juror may, give evidence as to what passed between the *jurymen* [read *jurors*] in the discharge of their duties." (Eng.) *Jurator* is an obsolete equivalent.

jury is a COLLECTIVE NOUN in the U.S.; hence it is governed, in most contexts, by a singular verb. To emphasize the individual members of the jury, we have the word *jurors. The jury was* is generally preferable in AmE to *The jury were.* E.g., "The jury *are* [read *is*] to decide according to the preponderance of the evidence."/ "Judges do not decide questions of fact; the jury *do* [read *does*] not decide questions of law."/ "The jury *have* [read *has*] little use for a smart-aleck cross-examiner."/ "The jury *are* [read *is*] instructed that the words contained in the publication sued on by the plaintiff imply that the crime of murder had been committed by the plaintiff and are actionable per se."/ "The jury *are* [read *is*] bound by the instructions of the court."

In G.B., however, where using plural verbs with collective nouns is common, *jury* usually takes a plural verb.

Jury is both adjective and noun. Here it acts as an adjective: "*Dunn* still has a sound rationale, Justice Rehnquist declares: the possibility that the inconsistency was a product of *jury* lenity." The legal writer should be aware that, as a general English adjective, *jury* has, in addition to the ordinary legal meaning "of or relating to a jury," the meaning "make-shift" ⟨a jury rig⟩.

jury instruction (U.S.) = *jury direction* (G.B.).

juryman. See **juror** & SEXISM (B).

jury room is beginning to be written as one word; the *OED* lists it in hyphenated form, and *W3* lists it as two words.

jury venire. See **venire.**

jurywoman. See **juror** & SEXISM (B).

jus (= a legal right, rule, or principle of law) forms the plural *jura*. E.g., "Such a lien secures the creditor neither *jus in rem* nor *jus ad rem.*"/ "Rights to things, *jura in rem*, have for their subject some material thing, as land or goods, which the owner may use or dispose of in any manner he pleases within the limits prescribed by the terms of his right." The term is spelled also *ius*. See **jus in re(m).**

jus disponendi (= the right to dispose of property) is an unnecessary LATINISM that masks as a TERM OF ART. E.g., "He has the entire *jus disponendi* [read *right to dispose of the property*], which imports that he may give it absolutely, or may impose any restriction or fetters not repugnant to the nature of the estate that he gives."/ "Here, undoubtedly, the devisee is given an estate in fee simple by clear, unambiguous, and explicit words; this carries the *jus disponendi* [read *right to dispose of the property*]."

jus gentium. See **international law.**

jus in re(m); jus ad rem. The distinction is a simple one, although of decreasing importance: "A *jus in re* is a right, or property in a thing, valid as against all mankind. A *jus ad rem* is a valid claim on one or more persons to do something, by force of which a *jus in re* will be acquired." *The Young Mechanic*, 30 F. Cas. 873, 876 (C.C.D. Me. 1855) (No 18,180). The usual phrase is *jus in rem*, not *jus in re*.

jus sanguinis = a legal rule whereby a child's citizenship is that of his parents. We have no other name for it.

just deserts is occasionally misrendered *just desserts*, as here: "Nor can Horizon avoid its just *desserts* [read *deserts*] by its pleonastic harping on the fact that its conduct . . . has been impeccable since at least mid-June of 1983." *N.L.R.B. v. Horizon Air Services, Inc.*, 761 F.2d 22, 32 (1st Cir. 1985).

jus tertii (= the right of a third party) generally is not a useful enough LATINISM to justify its presence in legal prose. "Recovery in trover by a mere possessor against the defense of title in a third party (*jus tertii*) [omit parenthetical phrase] is apparently allowed in most states in which the question has been raised."/ "Respondents may be correct that petitioner does not possess standing *jus tertii* [read *as a third party*], but that is not the issue."

justice. See **judge.**

justiciable; judicable. The former is preferred in the sense "liable to be determined in a court of justice; subject to jurisdiction" ⟨justiciable cases and controversies⟩. Here, however, it is used nonsensically; the U.S. Supreme Court, in quoting this sentence, appropriately *sic*'d it: "There has not been enough time in which *justiciably* [sic] to decide the case." *Judicable* is a NEEDLESS VARIANT.

justiciar, n.; **justiciary.** These terms are obsolete in all but historical senses relating to medieval England.

justificatory, justificative. The latter is a NEEDLESS VARIANT of the former: "The plaintiff should have *marshaled justificatory reasons for* [better: *justified*] allowance of the amount sought."

justify, like *warrant*, q.v., generally takes as its object an action or belief, not a person. E.g., "The instant cases furnish sufficient additional indications of the settlor's intent to *justify* our giving effect to the language of the instrument limiting an estate to the grantor's heirs."

In legal prose, however, this verb frequently takes personal objects. E.g., "M. told the officer nothing that would *justify the officer in concluding* that T. was about to escape." / "The decision relied upon as *justifying* the sheriff in the levy of execution and sale of the property is *James v. Western North Carolina Ry. Co.*"/ "The interchange of opprobrious epithets and mutual vituperation and abuse will *justify* a judge in approving a verdict for the defendant, although the slanderous words were proved."/ "It could scarcely be said that the defendant would be *justified* in casting the body into the water whence it could not be reclaimed."/ "The defendant below appeals to this court on the ground that there was no evidence before the vice chancellor that *justified* him in decreeing that the defendant should pay the guardian of the infant $25 a week."

This usage is old, and perhaps only today could be considered a LEGALISM: "If, therefore, the process could be commenced in rem, the authority of *Bynkershoek* would *justify* us." *Chisholm v. Georgia,* 2 U.S. (2 Dall.) 419, 425-26 (1793). Nevertheless, it strikes the modern ear as unidiomatic and illogical.

juxtaposition cannot be a verb; although one may *position* a thing, one may not *juxtaposition* two things. *Juxtapose* is the correct verb form.

K

kangaroo court (= a court in which the principles of law and justice are disregarded and perverted) began as American slang, but is now an acceptable phrase even in formal writing if responsibly applied. *W2* records three particular types of kangaroo courts: (1) "a mock court held by vagabonds or by prisoners in a jail"; (2) "an irregularly conducted minor court in a frontier or unsettled district"; (3) "formerly, one of a number of courts in Ohio with county-wide jurisdiction, whose judge was paid by fines imposed by him upon conviction of accused persons."

kidnap(p)ed, -p(p)ing. The spellings in *-pp-* are preferred. The inferior spelling *kidnaping* is used throughout *People v. Norris,* 219 Cal. Rptr. 7, 706 P.2d 1141 (Cal. 1985). See DOUBLING OF FINAL CONSONANTS *&* **abduction.**

kill . . . dead is redundant.

kind of is a poor substitute for *somewhat, rather, somehow,* and other adverbs. It properly

functions as a noun, however, in phrases such as *this kind of writ.* See **these kind of.**

kindred, n., = consanguinity. E.g., "The policy of our laws is that heirs or next of kin who are in equal degree of *kindred* to the intestate, inherit per capita in equal shares, while those in a more remote degree, take per stirpes, or such portion as their immediate ancestor would inherit if living." See **consanguinity** *&* **affinity.**

king's foot. See **chancellor's foot.**

kinsman (= a relative) is less and less used, perhaps because of the desire to avoid SEXISM. "In *Labine v. Vincent,* the United States Supreme Court sustained a Louisiana statute permitting an 'acknowledged illegitimate to inherit from the father if the father was unsurvived by legitimate *kinsmen* or a spouse.'"

KITCHEN FRENCH. See LAW FRENCH.

knit has the past-tense forms *knit* and *knitted,* the former being preferred. Cf. **fit.**

know all men by these presents = take notice. This phrase frequently begins legal documents; following is the typical beginning of a bond: "*Know all men by these presents,* that we, X Corp., as principal, and Y Insurance Co., as surety, are held and firmly bound unto the Clerk of the United States District Court for the Eastern District of Texas, in the sum of $100.00."

know-how = the information, practical knowledge, techniques, and skill required for the achievement of some practical end, particularly in industry or technology (*OCL*). *Know-how* is considered incorporeal property, in which rights may be bought and sold. E.g., "Gates seeks to recover the damages that it allegedly incurred as a result of defendant Yuasa's alleged breach of an agreement with Gates regarding the nondisclosure of trade-secret technical *know-how.*" The phrase is best hyphenated.

kudos (fr. Gk. *kydos* "glory") is a singular noun meaning "praise, glory." It is often mistakenly thought to be a plural. *Kudo,* a false singular, has therefore come to plague many texts.

L

labor, v.t. See **belabor.**

laches. A. Singular Noun. *Laches* (LAW FRENCH meaning "idleness, slackness"), though plural in appearance, is a singular noun that is sometimes incorrectly coupled with a plural verb. E.g., "Laches *are* [read *is*] pleaded as a defense, but the claim here is essentially at law, not in equity." *Laches* = unreasonable delay or negligence in pursuing a right or claim, esp. an equitable one, that may disentitle a claimant to relief.

B. And *limitation.* The guiding principle in distinguishing these two is that "*laches* is not, like *limitation,* a mere matter of time; but principally a question of the inequity of permitting the claim to be enforced." *Galliher v. Cadwell,* 145 U.S. 368, 373 (1892). An old legal saw states that laches is a penalty for sleeping on one's rights.

From an idiomatic point of view, although we say that the statute of limitations has *run,* it is not proper to use that verb with *laches. Run,* in this context, means "(of a period of time) to come to an end, be complete, expire." Because *laches* does not refer to any specific period of time but is determined after the fact by courts, it cannot be said to have *run,* but merely to *apply* in a given case. E.g., "Because the indemnity action had not yet vested, *laches on the action had not begun to run* [read *the period to which laches might later apply had not begun*]."

lacuna is a FORMAL WORD for *gap:* "If there is such a *lacuna* in the legislative scheme, the proper remedy is not for the courts to distort the plain language of section 1512, but for Congress to enact legislation to close the gap." (Note the INELEGANT VARIATION, which is remedied by changing *lacuna* to *gap.*) The plural *lacunae* is preferable to *lacunas.*

lade (= to load) is an ARCHAISM in all senses, although it frequently appears in shipping contexts. See **laden.**

laden. A. As a Past Participle Equivalent to *loaded.* To the extent that *laden* lives, it lives primarily as a participial adjective ⟨a laden barge⟩ and not as a past participle. To use *laden* as a part of the verb phrase is to be guilty of ARCHAISM, although it is still used in shipping contexts. E.g., "The holder of the bill of lading had actual notice at the time of receiving the bill of lading that the goods had not in fact been *laden* on board." (Eng.) See **lade.**

B. For *ridden. Ridden* is the more general term, meaning "infested with" or "full of." *Laden* has not shed its strong connotation of "loaded down." Hence a place might be *laden* with things if they had been stacked there; or, more plausibly, a truck or barge might be *laden* with goods. But figuratively, *laden* fails as an effective adjective if the original suggestion of loading is ignored. E.g., "A seaman who removed his life jacket before diving into the *eddy-laden* [read *eddy-ridden*] Mississippi River to rescue another seaman was held to be contributorily negligent."

lading, bill of. *Lading* is the Old English equivalent of *loading.* Dating from the sixteenth century, *bill of lading* = a document acknowledging the shipment of a consignor's goods for carriage by sea (*CDL*). See **laden.**

lagan. See **flotsam.**

laic; lay. Whereas *laic* = nonclerical, nonecclesiastical, *lay,* which shares this sense, is broader, and encompasses the sense "nonprofessional, not expert, esp. with reference to law and medicine" (*OED*). Lawyers referred to jurors as *lay* ("unlearned, illiterate") in the LAW FRENCH of the Middle Ages. See **laity** & **layman.**

lain. See **lie** & **lay.**

laissez-faire; laisser-faire. The former spelling has long been standard.

laity is the noun corresponding to the adjective *lay;* it seems, however, to be used more commonly in religious than in legal contexts. Still, the *OED* includes the sense "unprofessional people, as opposed to those who follow some learned profession." E.g., "Fortunately for the bar and for the public, there are no rules of morality for the lawyers which do not apply with equal force to the *laity* and it is well that there should not be." See **laic** & **layman.**

lament, v.t., should not be made intransitive by the addition of a preposition. E.g., "In this space we have often *lamented over* [omit *over*] the recent rise of ultraconservatism."

lamentable is preferably accented on the first, not the second, syllable /*lăm-ĕn-tă-bĕl*/.

landlocked (= shut in or enclosed by land; almost entirely surrounded by land) is usually used in literal senses in the law. But it has its figurative uses as well: "The Chancellor is no longer fixed to the woolsack: he may stride the quarter-deck of maritime jurisprudence and, in the role of admiralty judge, dispense as would his *landlocked* brother, that which equity and good conscience impel."

landmark of the law is, as the following quotation suggests, a CLICHÉ to be sparingly bestowed on cases. E.g., "The critical decision is that of Lord Mansfield in *Moses v. MacFerlan* that truly merits the cliché, a *landmark of the law.*" See WORD-PATRONAGE.

landowner is written as one word in AmE and BrE.

language in the sense "wording (of a document)" is peculiar to the law. E.g., "Defendant points out that both sections 2223 and 2224 employ the *language* 'one who gains a thin 8,' and argues that the sense of the word 'gain' as thus used is to acquire a tangible benefit or an unconscionable thing."

lapse statute; antilapse statute; nonlapse statute. All three phrases denote (in the U.S.) the same type of statute, the meaning of which is illuminated in the quotations: "Nearly all states have enacted *lapse statutes* designed to provide a substitute beneficiary for the deceased legatee in certain situations."/ "A majority of the states have held that a *nonlapse statute* does not apply to a member of a class who was dead at the time of the execution of the will."/ "If an *antilapse statute* applies to save gifts of persons living when the will is executed but not the gifts of persons who die before the will is executed, republication of the will by codicil after the death of a legatee should not prevent an application of the statute to save the gift."

Today *lapse statute* is the most common phrase, even though it is the least logical (inasmuch as the effect of the statute is to *prevent*

the lapse of testamentary gifts). The best phrase, in terms of lucidity, is *antilapse statute.* There are judicial opinions in which both *nonlapse* and *antilapse* appear in reference to the selfsame statute; yet the terms should not be varied in a single writing. See INELEGANT VARIATION.

lapsus calami = a slip of the pen. A very good example, although it may merely be a misprint, occurs in a judicial opinion that looks as if it represents a backslide in first amendment rights. A judge writes: "The First Amendment is not a fetish. *Reversed* it must be, but this *reverence* must be tempered with a realistic approach to such problems as that now at bar." Without *reverence* to prompt the reader to understand that the judge means *Revered* and not *Reversed*, we might be quite confused about his purpose.

larcenist; larcener. *Larcenist* (= one who commits larceny) is the ordinary term; *larcener* is a primarily BrE variant.

larceny. A. *Petty larceny & simple larceny.* Two dichotomies exist in the legal analysis of larceny in various English-speaking jurisdictions. *Petty larceny* (or *petit larceny*) was at common law, and is today in many U.S. states, contrasted with *grand larceny,* the difference lying in the value of the goods stolen. *Simple larceny* is distinguished from *aggravated larceny,* the difference lying in the presence or absence of aggravating circumstances.

B. And *robbery & burglary.* See **burglary.**

largess(e). The Englished spelling *largess* is preferred, but the Frenchified pronunciation /*lahr-zhes*/ is standard.

last analysis. See **in the final analysis.**

last but not least is a CLICHÉ to be avoided.

last will and testament. Much ink has been spilled by at least one well-known writer in opposition to this phrase. See D. Mellinkoff, *The Language of the Law* 77–79, 331–33 (1963). The argument against it is that coupling *testament* with *will* is redundant, and that *last* is usually inaccurate. "When a testator has been made will-conscious, and likes the habit, *last will* adds spice to a will contest. For example [an actual case]: will No. 1 revoked by will No. 2; a later 'codicil to my last will' held to refer to No. 1, reviving it and revoking No. 2. The testator was talking about his first, not his second, when he said his *last will*" (*id.* 333).

A curious case, to be sure, and one that might lead some to conclude that *last will and testament* "is redundant, confusing, and usually inaccurate" (*id*). Yet laymen know the phrase well and understand it as a ceremonious equivalent of *will*. The DOUBLET *will and testament* is no more disturbing than many others that exist undisturbed in our language, and that even enrich it. See DOUBLETS, **testament,** & **will.**

The only recommendation to be made here is that the phrase be confined to use as a title to the document it refers to, and that general references to the document be couched in the single word *will*. If our goal is to clean up legal writing, there are worthier objects of our reforms than *last will and testament.*

latent ambiguity; patent ambiguity. See AMBIGUITY.

later. A. Without Temporal Context. *Later* should not be used unless a proper temporal context has first been established. E.g., "As Charles Evans Hughes, *later a chief justice of the Supreme Court,* [read *who was to become a chief justice,*] stated in 1907, ..." Cf. **then-.**

B. *Later on.* This collocation is venially verbose for *later*. E.g., "That deed and the description therein contained will be considered more particularly *later on* [read *later*] in this opinion."

LATINATE PLURALS. See PLURALS (A).

LATINISMS. "I think the cases are comparatively few in which much light is obtained by the liberal use of Latin phrases. . . . Nobody can derive any assistance from the phrase *novus actus interveniens* until it is translated into English." *Ingram v. United Automobile Services, Ltd.,* [1943] 2 All E.R. 71 (per du Parcq, L.J.) (quoted in 59 Law Q. Rev. 293 (1943)). In legal writing we must distinguish between TERMS OF ART, for which there are no ordinary English equivalents, and those terms that are merely vestigial Latinisms with simple English substitutes. The former category comprises useful Latinisms such as *prima facie, ex parte, de minimis, habeas corpus, alibi,* and *quorum.* Some words that do have ordinary English equivalents have nevertheless become such standard terms that they are unobjectionable, e.g., *bona fide* (= good faith), *amicus curiae* (= friend of the court), and *versus* (= against). These words have become a part of the English language, or at least necessary parts of the language of the law, and one would be misdirected to rail against them.

The rightful objects of our condemnation are the bombastic, vestigial Latinisms that serve no purpose but to give the writer a false sense of erudition. These terms convey no special legal meanings, no delicate nuances apprehended only by lawyers. They are pompous, turgid deadwood. Just as a mathematician would seem ludicrous to write 386/1544 rather than 1/4 for purposes of thereby seeming more scholarly, so the lawyer who writes *sub suo periculo* instead of *at his own risk,* strikes his reader as a laughable, if vexatious, figure.

Other phrases in this category are illustrated in the following sentences, in which the simple English equivalents are bracketed: "There is a *contradictio in adjecto* [read *contradiction in terms*] when we speak of the general damages appropriate to an indeterminate transaction." *Kerr S.S. Co. v. Radio Corp. of America,* 245 N.Y. 284, 157 N.E. 140, 142 (N.Y. App. Div. 1927) (per Cardozo, J.)./ "The author did not look upon section 44 as a section inserted *ex abundanti cautela* [read *out of abundant caution*] but as a very important protection." (Eng.)/ "An ancillary administration in this state, without assets presently here for administration, would be *mere brutum fulmen* [read *mere empty noise* (lit.), or *ineffective*]."/ "But a legacy to one to be paid when he attains the age of twenty-one years is a vested legacy; an interest which commences *in praesenti* [read *in the present*], although it be *solvendum in futuro* [read *paid in the future*], and if the legatee dies before that age, his representative shall receive it out of the testator's personal estate." (Blackstone)

Reasonableness dictates that legal writers simplify where possible, allowing the more complicated locutions to stand only if they are legally or linguistically irreducible. Otherwise, our language is easily beclouded (the Latinist would say *obnubilated*) and becomes, before we know it, a fog of words in which our readers or listeners become hopelessly lost. This is no less true in STATUTE DRAFTING than in expository writing: "In the selection of words, Latin words and, where possible without a sacrifice of accuracy, technical phraseology should be avoided; the word best adapted to express a thought in ordinary composition will generally be found to be the best that can be used." Thring, *Practical Legislation* 81 (1902).

Words are the primary tools of lawyers. Can we afford, then, to be undiscriminating in our use of those tools? Can we engage in unchecked ABSTRACTITIS with impunity? As Justice Holmes, who was doubtless aware of his oversimplification, wrote toward the end of the last century, "We must think things not words, or at least we must constantly translate our words into the facts for which they stand, if we are to keep to the real and the true." Such internal translation is most easily achieved if we use ordinary language when possible. Lawyers must learn the language of the law but wield it carefully, never losing the idiomatic flavor of the vernacular.

Particular Latinisms, their legitimacy or their turgidity, are discussed throughout this work under particular entries. For a good general work on avoiding unnecessary Latinisms, see Richard C. Wydick's *Plain English for Lawyers* (1979). See LAW LATIN & MINGLE-MANGLE.

latrine lawyer. See LAWYER, DEROGATORY NAMES FOR.

latter. See **former.**

latterly is an ARCHAISM for *later* or *lately*. E.g., "But there is a notion that *latterly* [read *lately*] has been insisted on a good deal, that a combination of persons to do what any one of them might lawfully do by himself will make the otherwise lawful conduct unlawful."

laudatory, -tive; laudable. The synonymous adjectives *laudatory* and *laudative* mean "expressing praise." The latter is a NEEDLESS VARIANT of the former. *Laudable*, in contrast, means "deserving praise." The distinction is the same as that between *praiseworthy* (= *laudable*) and the active *praiseful* (= *laudatory*).

The misuse of *laudatory* for *laudable* is all too common: "That the decision may achieve a *laudatory* [read *laudable*] result is not a valid consideration."/ "The more stringent provisions of the new act, while *laudatory* [read *laudable*] in purpose, cannot be used to enhance the punishment of individuals who committed crimes in possible reliance on the previous standards."/ "A subsequently adopted program, no matter how *laudatory* [read *laudable*], is wholly irrelevant to the issue of racial discrimination at an earlier date."

launch has become trite as used in these sentences: "Most of the miscellaneous matters relating to the *launching* [read *beginning*] of a new corporation are accomplished at a meeting of the initial directors."/ "Those injured in their rights of property are not required to suffer successive inflictions of pecuniary injury until a criminal prosecution is *launched* [read *begun*]."

laundry list is the slang phrase American lawyers commonly use to denote any sort of statutory roster of covered items.

law; the law. A distinction can be drawn between *a law* and its plural *laws*, on the one hand, words that point to one or more particular and concrete instances of legal precepts, and, on the other hand, *the law*, a phrase that signifies something more general and abstract. Thus particular precepts, such as those of the Sherman Antitrust Act (U.S.), the Theft Act (G.B.), and the like can each be called *a law*. *The law*, by contrast, is used for something much wider and more general, sometimes in conjunction with words descriptive of a recognized branch of legal science, e.g., the law of torts, or with words descriptive of a particular system of law, e.g., the law of England. Sometimes too *the law* means or includes the institutions and persons who represent and administer the law, the complex of courts and prisons, judges, lawyers, clerks, and police (*OCL* 717).

law, adj. *Law* acts in conjunction with *legal* as the adjective for *law*, n. No strict DIFFERENTIATION is possible, for we have *law studies* beside *legal studies*, *lawbooks* beside *legal books*; but *legal firm* is unEnglish in place of *law firm*, just as *law doctrine* is not used for *legal doctrine*. The *OED* and *OED Supp.* contain hundreds of examples of the attributive adjective *law*.

Law shares with *legal* the sense "pertaining to the law as a body of rules, or as a field of study." E.g., "The principal *law* question on the cross-appeals is whether the Supreme Court committed reversible error in awarding exemplary damages as incidental to injunctive relief." *Legal* has the additional sense "permitted under law; not forbidden" ⟨legal acts⟩, as the antonym of *illegal*.

law-abiding = abiding by, maintaining, or submitting to the law. E.g., "Courts do not depart from the rule that equity may not interfere, except to protect property rights of a pecuniary nature, in enjoining criminal acts exercised by one dealer to enhance his sales to the calculated pecuniary injury of a *law-abiding* competitor." See **abide.**

law clerk. See **clerk.**

lawcourt, one word, is another form of *court of law,* q.v.

LAW FRENCH refers to the Norman-French dialect used in all legal documents and judicial proceedings from the time of William the Conqueror to the reign of Edward III, and used with frequency in legal literature up to the seventeenth century. Though Law French may sound obscure to the English-speaking lawyer, its remnants abound in the language of the law, in common words such as *appeal, assault, arrest, counsel, demand, disclaimer, escheat, escrow, heir, indictment, laches, lay, lien, merger, ouster, party, process, proof, suit, tort,* and *verdict.* There are also remnants more arcane, such as *a quo* and *en ventre sa mere.* We are fortunate to have thrown over most Law-French terminology: "Law French was always a highly technical language and preserved many old Anglo-Normanisms, but with the introduction of English forms, inflections, word-order, and construction, as in the notorious 'fuit assault per prisoner la condemne pur felony que puis son condemnation ject un brickbat a le dit justice que narrowly mist'" (*OCL*). A noted legal scholar has referred to Law French as "something very like a Sid Caesar version of a foreign language." C. Rembar, *The Law of the Land* 178 n. (1980). See J. H. Baker, *Manual of Law French* (1979). Cf. LAW LATIN. See MINGLE-MANGLE.

lawgiver; lawmaker. Both are equivalents of *legislator,* but *lawgiver* connotes the promulgator of an entire code of laws, and is therefore more magisterial in tone: "To the Middle Ages the academic ideal of all Europe as the empire for which Justinian had been the *lawgiver* made Roman law a universal law." (R. Pound) / "Alfred [was] two hundred years

later than the first English *lawgivers* quoted." (Holmes) Both *lawgiver* and *lawmaker* are now preferably written as single, unhyphenated words.

lawful. See **legal.**

LAW LATIN, or dog Latin, is the bastardized or debased Latin formerly used in law and legal documents, from which we have for the most part escaped. Brewer's *Dictionary of Phrase and Fable* quotes the following jocular example: "As the law classically expresses it, a kitchen is 'camera necessaria pro usus cookare; cum sauce-pannis, stewpannis, scullero, dressero, coalholo, stovis, smoak-jacko; pro roastandum, boilandum, fryandum, et plum-pudding-mixandum.'" Stevens, *A Law Report* (Daniel v. Dishclout) (quoted in Brewer, *Dictionary of Phrase and Fable* (1894), s.v. "Dog-Latin"). See E. H. Jackson, *Law Latin* (1897). Cf. LAW FRENCH. See MINGLE-MANGLE & LATINISMS.

law merchant (= commercial law) forms the plural *laws merchant.*

lawmonger. See LAWYER, DEROGATORY NAMES FOR.

lawnote. See **annotation.**

law of nations. See **international law.**

law of the case = the decision rendered in a former appeal of a case, which under this doctrine is held to be binding. Thus, if a case is appealed a second time to a panel of a U.S. Court of Appeals, and a panel with a different makeup from the first panel hears the case the second time, it is bound by the writings of the first panel regardless of whether its members agree with those earlier writings. *Law of the case* is to be distinguished from *res judicata* and *stare decisis,* qq.v.

law of the land, first used in Magna Carta, generally means "the law in effect in a country and applicable to all members of the community, whether as a result of pronouncement of the highest court or of statutory enactment." E.g., "*Gertz* is now the *law of the land,* and until it is overruled, it must, under the principle of stare decisis, be applied by this court." In AmE, this phrase also sometimes signifies "due process of law."

law of the sea. See **admiralty.**

LAW REVIEWESE is the stilted, often jargonistic style of writing characteristically found in law reviews. Judge Posner, himself an accomplished stylist, has written of "the drab, Latinate, plethoric, euphemistic style of law reviews." Posner, *Goodbye to the Bluebook*, 53 U. Chi. L. Rev. 1343, 1349 (1987). Unless the author is a famous one whose prose the editors dare not tamper with, the edited and published writing usually takes on an "official" law-review style that is devoid of personality or individual idiom, overburdened with abstract phraseology, bottom-heavy with footnotes, humorless, and generally unobservant of strictures of grammar and diction. This last fault is perhaps ineradicable, at least in the U.S., inasmuch as legally trained young men and women are called upon to be professional editors when not one in fifty has a background suitable to the task. Nevertheless, the industry and thought that go into publishing a law review are good training, however inconsequential the product often is.

"The ideal law review," writes James C. Raymond in an iconoclastic essay,

is one that is designed not only to be referred to, but actually (and here comes the revolutionary proposal) to be read. Its articles are selected not on the basis of the number of footnotes they contain, but on the basis of the timeliness of the topic and the soundness of the scholarship. They may have no footnotes or dozens of them—all that are necessary to satisfy the curiosity of intelligent readers who are particularly interested in the topic, but no more.

In the ideal review, articles are also selected, or even solicited, at least partly on the basis of how well their authors can write. Ideal editors are prepared to instruct their assistants and even their contributors on the elements of good writing. They refuse to publish anything that they consider dull, and they have the courage to demand a revision of anything they cannot understand. They know from their own reading that the best legal writers are always more than crabbed logicians of the law. They are capable of clarity without any compromise in precision, and, when the occasion warrants, of eloquence no less memorable than Cicero's.

> Raymond, *Editing Law Reviews: Some Practical Suggestions and a Moderately Revolutionary Proposal,* 12 Pepperdine L.Rev. 371, 378-79 (1985).

No such law review yet exists, or is likely to. Still, there is a move afoot toward the establishment of faculty-edited law reviews; let us hope that these bring much-needed reform.

law's delay. The possessive is necessary in this phrase, which derives from Shakespeare: "For who would bear . . . the law's delay . . . when he might his quietus make with a bare bodkin [i.e. dagger]." *Hamlet* III.i.69-75.

lawsuit is written as one word in AmE and BrE.

lawyer, n. See **attorney** (A).

lawyer, v.i. & v.t.; **lawyering.** The *OED* lists *lawyering* ("colloquial") but not the verb *lawyer*, omitted as well in the *OED Supp.* W2 contains the verb *lawyer*, defining it as (1) "to conduct a lawsuit against"; (2) "to practice as a lawyer," noting that the term is "rare" in both senses. W3 omits *lawyer* as a verb, and appends the note "often used disparagingly" to *lawyering.*

None of these descriptions is adequate for these Americanisms. *Lawyer* is no longer rare as a verb, and it has even taken on additional senses, e.g., "to supply with lawyers": "China has never been a *lawyered* country and it is only beginning to understand and accept that for a foreign investor to come with an attorney for negotiation is not an unduly aggressive or untrusting act." Moreover, although *lawyering* may be used disparagingly in some quarters, many lawyers use it as a neutral term to describe what they do, and even as a term of praise in the collocation *creative lawyering.* See **attorney** (C).

LAWYER, DEROGATORY NAMES FOR. The English language has a formidable stock of disparaging names for lawyers. Of course, every language has its proverbs that reflect poorly in one way or another on lawyers (maybe uncomprehendingly), but probably no other has the richness in depreciative vocabulary.

1. *ambidexter* = an unscrupulous lawyer who takes compensation (or sometimes bribes) "with both hands," that is, from both sides of a controversy.
2. *ambulance chaser* = a lawyer who solicits business from accident victims at the scene of an accident or shortly thereafter; by extension, an unscrupulous plaintiffs' lawyer.

3. *jackleg lawyer* = an amateurish and dishonest lawyer.
4. *jailhouse lawyer* = an inmate who acquires some degree of legal learning and counsels his fellow inmates on drafting complaints and briefs.
5. *latrine lawyer* = a lawyer who gets his business from the rumors he hears spread in the latrine.
6. *lawmonger* = a low practitioner of law; a pettifogger.
7. *pettifogger* = a petty and disreputable lawyer who niggles over inconsequential details. See **pettifogger.**
8. *Philadelphia lawyer* = an extremely competent lawyer who knows the ins and outs of all the legal technicalities and jargon (not wholly derogatory).
9. *shyster* = a professionally unscrupulous lawyer. For the distinction between a *pettifogger* and a *shyster,* see **pettifogger.**

lawyer's lawyer. This CLICHÉ is perhaps the highest form of praise that one lawyer can bestow upon another. It is coming to be used with little discrimination, however.

LAWYERISMS. See LEGALISMS & LAWYERISMS.

lay, adj. See **laic** & **laity.**

lay; lie. These verbs are misused even by members of our learned profession; witness these specimens, from American judicial opinions: "After *laying* [read *lying*] on the ground for a few minutes, she climbed a fence and walked to the highway."/ "He said he played with guns all the time, and that he picked up a pistol *laying* [read *lying*] on the bedside table and began *waiving* [read *waving*] it around." *Still v. State,* 709 S.W.2d 672, 674 (Tex. App.—Tyler 1983).

Very simply, *lie* (= to recline, be situated) is intransitive ⟨he lies on his bed⟩, whereas *lay* (= to put down, arrange) is transitive only ⟨he laid his hand on her shoulder⟩ ⟨they laid the body in its grave⟩. The verbs are declined *lie* ⟩ *lay* ⟩ *lain* and *lay* ⟩ *laid* ⟩ *laid.* "To use *lay* intransitively, to mean 'lie,' e.g. *She wants to lay down; She was laying on the bed,* is nonstandard, even though fairly common in spoken English" (*Oxford Guide* 113). See **lie.**

layman; layperson; lay person. *Layman* is the most common of these terms, and is generally regarded as unexceptionable, although some writers avoid it on grounds of SEXISM.

W9 records *layperson* as a single word from 1972; the one-word form appears to be an Americanism. "The average *layperson* would no doubt disagree with A if he said, 'I didn't intend to injure C.'" *Layperson* is now used even by the U.S. Supreme Court. Here it appears in plural form *lay people,* an alternative of *laypersons:* "If they continue in their druidic isolation, the only course *lay people* might have is what Dick the butcher, in *Henry IV, Part Two,* suggested: 'The first thing we do, let's kill all the lawyers.'" See **lay** & **people.** See also SEXISM (B) & BIBLICAL AFFECTATION.

lead is sometimes wrongly used for *led,* perhaps on the mistaken analogy of *read/read,* and perhaps also because of confusion with the metal. E.g., "The urge to protect the Statute of Wills has *lead* [read *led*] this court to treat intent and delivery as separate requirements and to require a strict compliance with each."

leader (at the bar) is a Britishism meaning "the senior counsel for a party in a case" (*OCL*). In the U.S., *lead counsel* is the usual phrase.

leading case = an important, often the most important, judicial precedent on a particular point of law. E.g., "In *Phillips v. Phillips,* a *leading case,* the testator, after providing that the whole of his property should go to his wife, added that she might give the testator's sister and brother some periodic sums 'if she find it always convenient.'"

leading question; categorical question. Laymen frequently misapprehend *leading question* as referring to a question showing hostility or posed for the purpose of embarrassing or taking unfair advantage. Actually, as litigators well know, a *leading question* is one that suggests the answer to the person being interrogated. In Anglo-American law such questions are generally permissible only on cross-examination. *Categorical question,* another name for the same practice, is today little used.

learned; learnt. As an adjective, *learned* has two syllables, and as a past tense one. *Learnt* is a BrE variant of the past tense *learned.*

learned counsel; learned court. These are tiresome CLICHÉS in the law. E.g., "The *learned counsel,* who, in the court below, represented the appellant from the decree of the register, admitted with characteristic candor, that the testatrix, after writing the first page, proceeded to the third, then wrote last what appears at the top of the second page, and, after the completed expression of her testamentary intention, signed her name."/ "The *learned court* at special term has found that the instrument relied upon by the defendant was of a testamentary character, and did not comply with the statutory requirements of a will, and that it was therefore void."

learnt. See **learned.**

lease, v.t.; **let.** *Let* (10th c.) is three hundred years older than *lease* (13th c.) in the sense "to grant the temporary possession and use of (land, buildings, rooms, movable property) to another in consideration of rent or hire" (*OED*). But both are well established, and they are equally good. As used by (real) estate agents in G.B., the term "To Let" is more common than the phrase "For Rent," the usual term in the U.S.

lease from; lease to. To say that one *leases* property nowadays does not tell the reader or listener whether one is lessor or lessee. From its first verbal use in the thirteenth century, *lease* meant "to grant the possession of," but in the mid-nineteenth century took on the additional sense "to take a lease of; to hold by a lease." This ambiguity has made the preposition with which the verb is construed very important to clarity: the lessor *leases to* and the lessee *leases from.*

leasor; leasee. These are laymen's blunders for *lessor* and *lessee.* See **lessor.**

legacy = a gift by will, esp. of personal property and often of a sum of money. A number of types of legacies are distinguishable. A *specific legacy* or *bequest* is a testamentary gift of property that can be distinguished with reasonable accuracy from other property that is part of the testator's estate. A *general legacy* or *bequest* is a gift of personal property that the testator intends to come from the general assets of the estate.

A *residuary legacy* or *bequest* is a gift of the estate remaining after all claims against the estate have been satisfied, and all specific, general, and demonstrative legacies have been paid out. A *demonstrative legacy* is paid

from a particular source; but if the source is insufficient to satisfy the legacy, then the legacy is paid out of the general assets of the estate to the extent that the specific source is lacking. See **devise.**

legacy, v.t. See **legate.**

legal; lawful; licit. *Legal* is the broadest of these terms, meaning either (1) "of or pertaining to law, falling within the province of law," or (2) "permitted, or not forbidden, by law." These two senses are used with about the same frequency. *Lawful* and *licit* share with *legal* sense (2), "according or not contrary to law, permitted by law." The least frequently used of these terms is *licit. Lawful* is quite common: "In March 1977, the company posted a notice on the bulletin board that contained a *lawful* statement on the solicitation and distribution of materials." *Lawful* should not be used in sense (1) of *legal*, however, as here: "The judgment must be affirmed if there is sufficient evidence to support it on any *lawful* [read *legal*] theory, and every fact issue sufficiently raised by the evidence must be resolved in support of the judgment." See **illegal.**

legal cause. See CAUSATION (A).

LEGALESE has, throughout the history of Anglo-American law, been a scourge of the legal profession. Thomas Jefferson railed against statutes "which, from their verbosity, their endless tautologies, their involutions of case within case, and parenthesis within parenthesis, and their multiplied efforts at certainty, by *saids* and *aforesaids*, by *ors* and *ands*, to make them more plain, are really rendered more perplexed and incomprehensible, not only to common readers, but to the lawyers themselves." 1 T. Jefferson, *The Writings of Thomas Jefferson* 65 (Lipscomb ed. 1903).

The same is true, of course, of all types of legal writing, not just statutes or even just DRAFTING. For a humorous epitome of legalese, the following nineteenth-century example is nonpareil:

The declaration stated, that the plaintiff theretofore, and at the time of the committing of the grievance thereinafter mentioned, to wit, on, etc., was lawfully possessed of a certain donkey, which said donkey of the plaintiff was then lawfully in a certain highway, and the defendant was then possessed

of a certain waggon and certain horses drawing the same, which said wagon and horses
of the defendant were then under the care,
government, and direction of a certain then
servant of the defendant, in and along the
said highway; nevertheless the defendant, by
his said servant, so carelessly, negligently,
unskilfully, and improperly governed and directed his said wagon and horses, that by and
through the carelessness, negligence, unskil-
fulness, and improper conduct of the defendant, by his said servant, the said wagon and
horses of the defendant then ran and struck
with great violence against the said donkey
of the plaintiff, and thereby then wounded,
crushed, and killed the same, etc.

Davies v. Mann, (1842) 10 M. & W. 546,
152 Eng. Rep. 588.

Other manifestations of legalese commonly
appear. One aspect of it is its compressedness:
"The question here is whether service of citation was proper in the face of a writ of error
attack on a default judgment." Another is cer-
emoniousness, which arguably has a place in
some legal instruments: "In testimony
whereof, I have hereunto subscribed my
name and affixed my seal, this 24th day of
June, in the year of our Lord, one thousand
nine hundred and eighty five."

We have enough examples, however, of
what not to do. The nauseous (q.v.) effect of
the passage just quoted, and other passages
throughout this work, should purge readers
of any affection for or attraction to legalese.
See DOUBLETS & LEGALISMS.

LEGAL FICTIONS. See FICTIONS, LEGAL.

legal fraud. See **constructive fraud &
fraud** (B).

legalism; legality. *Legality* = strict adherence to law, prescription, or doctrine; the
quality of being legal. E.g., "A genuine dispute exists as to the *legality* of any ownership
claim made by the codepositors." *Legalism* =
(1) formalism carried almost to the point of
meaninglessness; a disposition to exalt the
importance of law or formulated rule in any
department of action, (2) a mode of expression characteristic of lawyers. See **legalistic.**

LEGALISMS AND LAWYERISMS are the
circumlocutions, FORMAL WORDS, and ARCHA-
ISMS that characterize lawyers' speech and
writing, esp. in DRAFTING. Little can be said by
way of advice except that generally lawyers

and legislators are best advised to avoid them.
It must be granted, however, that there may
be those rare contexts in which the legalistic
is preferable to the ordinary term.

Legalistic	*Ordinary*
abutting	next to
adequate number of	enough
adjacent to	next to
anterior to	before
at the time when	when
be able to	can
be authorized	may
be binding upon	bind
be empowered to	may
be unable to	cannot
by means of	by
cause to be done	have done; effect (v.t.)
contiguous to	next to
during such time as	during
enter into a contract with	contract with
enter into an agree-ment with	agree with
excessive number of	too many
for the duration of	during
for the reason that	because
in case	if
in order to	to
in the event that	if
in the interest of	for
it is directed	shall
it is the duty	shall
it shall be lawful	may
it shall be legal	may
it shall be the duty of	shall
it shall not be lawful to	may not
on or about	about
or in the alternative	or
per annum	a year
per diem	a day
period of time	period, time
point in time	point, time
previous to	before
prior to	before
prosecute (a business)	carry on
pursuant to	under, in accordance with
subsequent to	after
sufficient number of	enough
the reason being that	because

under the provisions of	under
until such time as	until

legalistic is a rather contemptuous term meaning "formalistic; exalting the importance of formulated rules in any department of action." E.g., "We are told that this is a model case for bold action on the part of a court, that we should free ourselves from the stinted *legalistic* reasoning of the eighteenth century." See **legalism.**

LEGAL MAXIMS. One judge, in a very recent opinion, wrote: "*Nulla poena sine lege* [= no punishment except in accordance with the law] is not only an ancient maxim; it is a requisite of due process." Yet nowhere in the opinion is a translation of the phrase to be found; and most law dictionaries are unavailing. Gone are the days when we can assume that lawyers are versed in Latin.

LEGAL WRITING STYLE. Throughout this book I have referred to Sir Arthur Quiller-Couch's little book *On the Art of Writing* (1916), which contains one gem after another. Of particular interest is his concluding chapter, "On Style," and a one-paragraph statement that appears somewhat earlier in the book:

> We have agreed that our writing should be *appropriate*: that it should fit the occasion; that it should rise and fall with the subject, be grave where it is serious, where it is light not afraid of what Stevenson in *The Wrong Box* calls 'a little judicious levity.' If your writing observes these precepts, it will be well-mannered writing.
>
> *Id.* at 160.

Of course, in law, seriousness almost always greatly outweighs levity; and even when levity is called for, as it rarely is, it must be "little" and "judicious." See OPINION WRITING (B).

On legal writing per se, no one has written better on stylistic excellence than Walker Gibson, whom I unapologetically quote at length.

> There is no reason at all why almost any piece of legal writing—and certainly judicial writing—may not move us with its sensitive and wise and gracious handling of language. It is true that the legal writer operates within limiting situations, and he must attend painstakingly to the minutiae of facts that confront him. Yet it is also true that he is engaged in expressing in words the chaos of life, and no poet can say more. Judicial opinions and poetry are obviously not identical forms of expression; yet, in Frost's memorable phrase about poets, the legal writer too is attempting "a momentary stay against confusion." It is hard to think of a finer thing for a man to do.
>
> A curious humility, or an equally curious arrogance, is apparent in the attitude that legal writers sometimes express toward their performances in language. One hears a lawyer or a judge remark, "Oh, I'm no stylist—I just write down the facts in plain words." This is both humble and arrogant—humble in surrendering elegance to the "creative artists," arrogant in suggesting that only "the facts" really matter. But the situation is surely quite otherwise. The poet or novelist, the historian, the physicist, the appellate judge are all deeply involved in one essential responsibility: the expression of life's complexities in mere man-made words. Wherever he starts, whatever trivial item of human experience he initially confronts, the legal writer can make a stab at eloquence. If Holmes was right, that "a man may live greatly in the law as well as elsewhere," then the consequence is that he must *write* greatly, for in law as well as in literature there is no other meaning of greatness.
>
> Gibson, *Literary Minds and Judicial Style,* 36 N.Y.U. L. Rev. 915, 930 (1961).

Following are works to which the reader is referred for further study. These represent the best references available in some of the specific niches of legal writing.

A. General Legal Writing: B. Garner, *The Elements of Legal Style* (1991); R. Goldfarb & J. Raymond, *Clear Understandings* (1982); D. Mellinkoff, *Legal Writing: Sense and Nonsense* (1982); H. Weihofen, *Legal Writing Style,* (2d ed. 1981).

B. Brief Writing. "It should never be forgotten that in a law office you will find three English styles: (1) the style of a contract, a mortgage, a conveyance, etc. [see (C) below]; (2) the style of a pleading; and (3) the style which should characterize briefs. A brief written in the other two styles is a monstrosity." P. Blair, *Appellate Briefs and Advocacy,* in *Advocacy and the King's English* 788, 791 (1960). The following works will forestall all such monstrosities: E. Re, *Brief Writing and Oral Argument* (6th ed. 1987); G. Peck, *Writing Persuasive Briefs* (1984); N. Brand & J. O. White, *Legal Writing: The Strategy of Persuasion* (1976).

C. Drafting. It is worth noting that "legal

literary writing must, of course, be distinguished from the drafting of legal documents. In statutes, conveyances, contracts, etc., certainty is the paramount aim of the draftsman rather than attractive legal style." E. C. Gerhart, *Improving Our Legal Writing: Maxims from the Masters,* in *Advocacy and the King's English* 765, 767 n.10 (1960). Yet "attractive legal style" has never detracted from certainty. These works are not just useful, but essential, for the legislative or legal draftsman: R. Dickerson, *The Fundamentals of Legal Drafting* (1965); E. L. Piesse, *The Elements of Drafting* (5th ed. rev. J. K. Aitken 1976); Dreidger, *The Composition of Legislation* (1957); Coode, *On Legislative Expression* (1842); Thring, *Practical Legislation* (1902); Robinson, *Drafting* (1973). See DRAFTING & STATUTE DRAFTING.

   D. Judicial Opinions: Unfortunately, there is a dearth of good writing on this subject. B. E. Witkin's *Manual on Appellate Court Opinions* (1977) contains much useful information, but is not widely available. Two articles worth consulting are Gibson, *Literary Minds and Judicial Style,* 36 N.Y.U. L. Rev. 915, 930 (1961), and Smith, *A Primer of Opinion Writing for Four New Judges,* 21 Ark. L. Rev. 197 (1967). See OPINION WRITING.

legate, v.t.**; legacy,** v.t.   Both may mean "to give or leave as a legacy; to bequeath a legacy to." *Legacy* is an ARCHAISM in this verbal sense, and *legate* is rather rare. *Bequeath,* q.v., is the usual word.

legatee = one who is named in a will to take personal property of any kind; one who has received a legacy or bequest. In strict common-law terminology, a distinction was drawn between a *legatee* and a *devisee,* the former receiving personal property and the latter real property. E.g.,"A devise or bequest to a child does not lapse by death, but the property so devised or bequeathed shall vest in the surviving child or other descendant of the *legatee* or devisee, as if such *legatee* or devisee had survived the testator and had died intestate." But *legatee* is often loosely used for one to whom a devise is given. See **devisee.**

legation.   See **embassy.**

legator is a NEEDLESS VARIANT of *testator* that is not frequently used, although occasionally it may be employed to mean specifically "one who bequeaths a legacy," as opposed to one devising real property. See **devise** & **bequeath.**

legible.   See **illegible.**

legislative, -torial.   The first corresponds to *legislation,* the second to *legislator.*

legist   = one learned or skilled in the law; a lawyer; a jurist. This word is underused.

legitimacy; legitimation; legitimization; legitimatization.   *Legitimacy* = the fact of being legitimate. *Legitimation* is the best word for the sense (1) "the action or process of rendering or authoritatively declaring (a person) legitimate" (*OED*); or (2) "the action of making lawful; authorization" (*id.*). E.g., "An illegitimate child may be *legitimated* by the marriage of his parents, although several states require, in addition, an acknowledgment by the father. A few states have judicial procedures for *legitimation.*" *Legitimization* and *legitimatization* are NEEDLESS VARIANTS.

legitimate; legitimize; legitimatize.   The first is the preferred form in all senses. The others are NEEDLESS VARIANTS. E.g., "This end is undoubtedly better answered by *legitimating* all issue born after wedlock than by *legitimating* issue of the same parties, even born before wedlock, so as wedlock afterwards ensues." (Blackstone)/ "If the decree absolute should be declared to be invalid, with the result that his remarriage was void, he proposes, after a valid decree absolute, to go through a further ceremony of marriage with the woman named, so that their children are *legitimated.*" (Eng.)/ "This fact suggests implicit recognition of the value of the larger body as a means of *legitimating* society's decision to impose the death penalty."

legitimation; legitimization.   See **legitimacy.**

lend.   See **loan.**

lese majesty; lèse majesté; leze majesty. The preferred form of this term, meaning "treason," is the anglicized *lese majesty.* The variant spellings should be avoided.

less.   A. And *fewer.* The former applies to mass nouns, or amounts; the latter to COUNT NOUNS, or numbers of things. The only exception is where count nouns are so great as to render the idea of individual increments meaningless. For example, "A District Court has concurrent jurisdiction under the Tucker

Act over suits for *fewer* [read *less*] than $10,000." Here, because the dollars are taken not individually but collectively as an amount, *less* is appropriate.

Less is used correctly with time: "More than three but *less* than six years after the completion of the cleanup operations, the United States instituted civil actions to recover its cleanup costs." Here *fewer* is incorrectly used with a period of time (and also with the number two, which is illogical): "The Supreme Court denied certiorari, and Milton's execution was scheduled again, for June 25, 1985, *fewer* [read *less*] than two hours from this writing." (One hesitates to fault a judge's style when he works under such exigencies.)

Less for *fewer* is an all-too-frequent error: "From 1970 to 1975, the number of pending criminal cases increased from 20,910 to 22,411, a caseload difference of *less* [read *fewer*] than four cases per authorized judgeship."/ "Further, this rule also provides that if three or *less* [read *fewer*] jurors become disabled or otherwise unable to serve, the remaining jurors may render a verdict."/ "The principal felt that this particular pupil might create *less* [read *fewer*] problems if he remained in the main school building."/ "What the juvenile court system needs is not more but *less* [read *fewer*] of the trappings of legal procedure and formalism."/ "Over the years, membership in the organization decreased until in 1941 there were *less* [read *fewer*] than 100 members; at the time of this action there were approximately 58 members still living."

Less power but *fewer powers*: hence the adjective should be *fewer* in: "The move from the Articles of Confederation to the Constitution was a shift from a central government with *less* [read *fewer*] powers to one with more powers." See **fewer.**

B. And *lesser*. *Lesser* is an exact synonym of *less*, but is confined to use as an adjective before a noun and following an article ⟨the lesser crime⟩, thus performing a function no longer idiomatically possible with *less*. Dating from the thirteenth century, this formal usage allows *lesser* to act as an antonym of *greater*, as here: "The *lesser* punishments are just as fit for the *lesser* crimes as the greater for the greater." Holmes, *The Common Law* 46 (1881; repr. 1916)./ "His thought and his memories pervade the whole with greater or *lesser* distinction."/ "We decline to hold that a guilty plea is compelled and invalid under the Fifth Amendment whenever motivated by the

defendant's desire to accept the certainty or probability of a *lesser* penalty rather than face a wider range of possibilities from acquittal to conviction and a higher penalty." / "The extent of the burden that will be tolerated will of course depend on the nature of the local interest involved, and on whether it could be promoted as well with a *lesser* impact on interstate activities."

Perhaps because of its decreasing use, *lesser* has been mistakenly supplanted by *less*, which is awkward when used attributively: "One may reduce the percentage to be taken during the summer months when a *much less* [read *lesser*] quantity of gas is needed."/ "Since Flint and his wife could have conveyed to their daughters the complete title to the property notwithstanding defendant's judgment, they could, of course, grant them a *less* [read *lesser*] estate."

The opposite offense against idiom also occurs: "The constitutional rights of minors do not receive *lesser* [read *less*] protection than the rights of adults." The *OED* states that the construction *lesser than* is obsolete.

Should *lesser* (when properly used) seem stilted, one might use *smaller* or, depending on the context, *lower*. Often *smaller* seems more natural. E.g., "The defendant in such a case would have to pay a much *lesser* [read *smaller*] amount."/ "A lease is a conveyance, usually in consideration of rent or other recompense, for life, years, or at will, but always for a *less* [read *lesser*, or—because *lessor* appears later in the sentence—*shorter*] time than lessor has in the premises."

Less is sometimes used in the sense "of lesser seriousness." E.g., "He was convicted of three felonies *less* than capital." *Lesser* is commonly used in the phrase from American criminal law, *lesser included offense*: "We also have serious doubts about whether the offense to which Garrett pleaded guilty in Washington was a *lesser included offense* within the continuing criminal enterprise charge."/ "The unavailability of the option of convicting defendant on a *lesser included offense* may encourage the jury to convict the defendant of a capital crime because it believes that the defendant is guilty of some serious crime and should be punished." This phrase is often rendered *lesser-included offense*, but it is best not hyphenated.

lessor; lessee. *Landlord* and *tenant* are simpler equivalents that are more comprehensible to most laymen.

lest is best followed by a SUBJUNCTIVE. E.g., "Strict scrutiny of the classification which a State makes in a sterilization law is essential, *lest* unwittingly or otherwise invidious discriminations *are* [read *be*] made against groups or types of individuals in violation of the constitutional guaranty of just and equal laws." *Skinner v. Oklahoma*, 316 U.S. 535, 541 (1942) (per Douglas, J.)./ "The court should not instruct the jury to weigh carefully the evidence of insanity, *lest* an ingenious counterfeit of the disease *furnish* protection to guilt."

let (= hindrance or obstacle) is used in the legal phrase *without let or hindrance.* This meaning of *let* is archaic except in law, poetry, and tennis (*let ball* = net ball). The word is not of the same derivation as the verb *let* (= to permit, allow, rent).

let, v.t. See **lease.**

lethal (= deadly, mortal) is generally used of poisons and medicines in nonlegal usage, but in legal usage still appears in the older sense relating to weapons and wounds as well: "We cannot condone *lethal* use of force as a first measure taken by police." Unlike *fatal,* q.v., *lethal* is used only in literal senses.

letters rogatory; letter(s) of request. Both terms are used in the sense "a request issued to a foreign court requesting a judge to take evidence from a specific person within that court's jurisdiction." *Letters rogatory* is the usual term in the U.S.; either *letter of request* or *rogatory letter* is used in G.B. Americans use the plural *letters* for the single request, whereas the British use the singular *letter.*

Historically, *letters of request* had a completely different meaning: "a documentary request sent by the judge of one ecclesiastical court to another, esp. to desire that a case may be withdrawn from his own jurisdiction to that of a superior court" (*OED*).

levee; levy. The former is the noun meaning "a river embankment; dike; pier." In G.B., primarily, it also has the sense "a formal reception." Occasionally *levee* is used as a verb, meaning "to provide with a levee (dike)."

Levy is usually a verb meaning (1) "to impose (as a fine) by legal sanction"; (2) "to conscript for service in the military"; (3) "to wage (a war)"; or (4) "to seize (property)" ⟨the sheriff levied on the judgment debtor's goods⟩. E.g., in sense (1): "In a civil contempt action occasioned by willful disobedience of a court order, an award of attorneys' fees may be authorized as a part of the fine to be *levied* on the defendant."/ "Alabama *levies* a tax upon photograph galleries engaged in photography."

Levy may act also as a noun, however, in two senses: (1) "the imposition of a fine, or the fine so imposed"; and (2) "the conscription of men for military service, or the troops so conscripted."

leverage, v.t. & v.i., is a twentieth-century Americanism ⟨a leveraged portfolio = one with a high amount of debt⟩. The term has definite meaning, but nevertheless may be characterized as a term used primarily by financial JARGONMONGERS.

leviable = (1) that may be levied; (2) that may be levied upon, capable of being seized in execution. Sense (2) is an American legalism. E.g., "The sheriff stated that it was impossible to find any *leviable* assets."

levy. See **levee.**

lex fori = the law of the forum. E.g., "*Lex fori* is the basic rule for choice of law." *Lex fori* is sometimes Englished *forum law*: "In conflicts cases concerning the validity of contracts, Professor Ehrenzweig would displace the basic rule pointing to *forum law* [i.e., the law of a particular forum] with the *lex validitatis.*"

leze majesty. See **lese majesty.**

liability. See **disability** (A).

liability without fault. See **strict liability.**

liable (= subject to or exposed to) should not be used merely for *likely. Liable* best refers to something the occurrence of which risks being permanent or recurrent. E.g., "If the act is one that the party ought, in the exercise of ordinary care, to have *anticipated* [read *foreseen*] was *liable* [read *likely*] to result in injury to others, then he is liable for any injury proximately resulting from it."/ "The parties are competitors in this field; and when the rights or privileges of the one are *liable* to conflict with those of the other, each party is under a duty so to conduct its own business as not unnecessarily or unfairly to injure that of the other." (The idea of recurrence is far more salient in the second than in the first sentence just quoted.)

Liable (= subject to liability) is usually confined to civil contexts in AmE, but in BrE is used in criminal as well as civil contexts: "On this evidence the trial court concluded that the appellant's conduct made him a *socius criminis* in the commission of the crime and, as such, that he was *liable* as a principal." (Eng.) *Liable* has three syllables, not two, and is thus pronounced differently from *libel*, q.v.

liaise, v.i., is a BACK-FORMATION from *liaison*, meaning "to establish liaison" or "to act as a liaison officer" ⟨diplomats who liaise with Soviet officials⟩. First used in the 1920s, this word is still stigmatized as being cant or jargon. It is pronounced /lee-**ayz**/.

liaison is best pronounced /**lee**-uh-zŏn/ in the U.S.; in Great Britain the pronunciation /**lee**-ay-zon/, taken sometimes as being semi-literate in the U.S., predominates. The non-technical senses of the word are (1) (n.) "an illicit love affair"; (2) (n.) "communication established for the promotion of mutual understanding; one who establishes such communication"; and (3) (adj.) "acting as an intermediary" ⟨liaison officer⟩.

libel; slander. The former is written defamation, the latter oral defamation. The distinction emerged in the seventeenth century, before which time both words applied to what was either written or spoken. As Gowers points out, the modern distinction is not well fixed in lay minds.

> In popular usage [the terms] are synonymous, meaning a deliberate, untrue, derogatory statement, usually about a person, whether made in writing or orally. In legal usage there are important differences. Each is an untrue and defamatory imputation made by one person about another which, if 'published' (i.e. communicated to a third person), can be a ground for a civil action in damages. Such an imputation is a *libel* if made in permanent form (writing, pictures, etc.) or by broadcasting. It is a *slander* if made in fugitive form (e.g. by speaking or gestures). A further distinction is that an action for *slander* cannot ordinarily succeed without proof that actual damage has been caused; in an action for *libel* this is unnecessary. In both cases proof that the allegation was true is a good defence.
> (*MEU2* 333.)

Here *libel* is misused for *slander*: "According to the complaint, the *libel* [read *slander*] was uttered in the presence of only one person." (See **defamation.**) *Verbal slander* is a common REDUNDANCY. See **verbal.**

Libel has the additional sense in admiralty "the complaint or initiatory pleading in an admiralty or ecclesiastical case." Hence *libelant,* for which see the following entry.

libel(l)ant = an injured seaman. "The *libelants* recovered in both Courts below." *Robins Dry Rock & Repair Co. v. Flint,* 275 U.S. 303, 307 (1927). One *-l-* is preferred in AmE, two in BrE. See DOUBLING OF FINAL CONSONANTS. The accent of *libelant* is on the first syllable.

Historically *libelant* has been an admiralty term as just defined, but the word has come to mean additionally "one who publishes a libel, a libeler." *Libeler* (in BrE *libeller*) is the older and better term for this sense; for it forestalls confusion about what the cause of action is.

libel(l)ee (= one against whom a libel has been filed) is correlative not with *libeler,* but with *libelant.* See -EE.

libeller. See **libel(l)ant.**

libel(l)ous (= defamatory, constituting libel) is spelled *-l-* in AmE, *-ll-* in BrE. E.g., "The question is whether a writing published by A of B is *libellous* or not." (Eng.) See DOUBLING OF FINAL CONSONANTS.

liberty; freedom. These synonyms have connotative distinctions. *Freedom* is the broader, all-encompassing term that carries strong positive connotations. *Liberty* suggests the past removal of restraints on specific freedoms.

license; licence. The former is the AmE spelling of noun and verb; it is the BrE spelling of the verb, whereas the latter is the BrE spelling of the noun.

licenser, -or. The former spelling is preferred.

licentiate (= one who has obtained a license or authoritative permission to exercise some function) is sometimes used of lawyers. E.g., "In the U.S. a *licentiate* in law is admitted to practice as an 'attorney and counselor,' a combination of names and functions unknown to the English law."/ "When the conduct of the *licentiate* clearly shows, either that the court was deceived at the time of his admission, or that there has been a moral degeneracy since that time, a proper case for discipline may be presented."

licit. See **legal.**

lie (= to have foundation in the law; to be legally supportable, sustainable, or proper) is a peculiar legal idiom. E.g., "A writ of certiorari does not *lie* to review the proceedings of a board the function of which is to ascertain the competency of militia officers."/ "An action will *lie* for interference with enforceable contractual rights if there is no sufficient justification for the interference."/ "If review is available by appeal, mandamus will not *lie*."/ "As a general rule, replevin will not *lie* for an undivided share in a larger mass."

Lie is used additionally in law in the figurative sense "to reside, exist." E.g., "Final appeal *lay* to the House of Lords." (Eng.)

lie forms *lay* in the past tense and *lain* as past participle, except when *lie* means "to proffer a falsity." The preterite in the following sentence is incorrect: "The issue was expressly confined to the inquiry into whether the land in dispute actually *lied* [read *lay*] within the boundaries of the original grants." See **lay.**

lien (= a legal right or interest in another's property that exists until a debt due in respect of it is satisfied) is pronounced, most properly, /*lee-ĕn*/ or /*lin*/; and commonly, but less properly, /*leen*/. In G.B., it is customary for the lienholder to retain possession of the property on which the lien has been obtained, whereas in the U.S. it is more usual that a lien does not entail retention by the lienholder. In the U.S., when the creditor possesses the collateral, *pledge* is the more usual term.

lienable. Though *lien* is not a verb, *lienable* has come to mean "capable of being subjected to a lien." Ordinarily -*able* is appended only to verb stems, although several exceptions exist (see -ABLE (B)). This Americanism is listed in neither the *OED* nor its *Supplement*; it appears in *W3*, but not in its predecessor, *W2*.

lienee means, in the U.S., "one whose property is subject to a lien," but in Australia is synonymous with *lienholder*. The Australian usage mangles any sense left in the suffix -EE, q.v.

lienor; lienholder. The former, an Americanism, is best left unused; it is hardly known in G.B. *Lienholder* is also more likely to be understood by laymen. E.g., "The debtor listed the purported *lienholder's* claim as unsecured and the *lienholder* did not object to confirmation of the plan."/ "It is also clear that the *lienor* [read *lienholder*] has, by virtue of his possession per se, rights in rem against all others that they shall not disturb that possession or harm the object possessed."

lifting the veil. See **piercing the corporate veil.**

ligan. See **flotsam.**

lighted; lit. Both are standard preterites.

like; as. A. *Like* as a Conjunction. In standard usage, *like* is a preposition that governs nouns and noun phrases, not a conjunction that governs verbs or clauses. Hence one does not write, properly, "He argued this case *like* he argued the previous one," but, "He argued this case *as* he argued the previous one." If we change *argue* to *argument*, *like* is possible: "His argument in this case was *like* his argument in the previous one." Here is another example of *like* misused as a conjunction: "*Like* [read *As*] when one says 'I do' to get married, a complaint in a lawsuit repeats certain formulas to make something happen, namely, to start the litigation in the usual way."

This relatively simple precept is generally observed in writing, but has been increasingly flouted in American speech. Examples of *like* used conjunctively can be found throughout the Middle English period; but the usage has been considered nonstandard at least since the seventeenth century. For the opposite error (*as* for *like*), see **as** (B).

B. Faulty Comparison: *like* for *as in*. "*Like Bush* [read *As in Bush*], administrative procedures are available to plaintiff to redress her grievance."/ "The State may, *like in* [read *as in*] cases where the offense charged includes lesser offenses, reduce the offense charged to the lesser included offense." See COMPARISONS, FALSE.

Like for *as with.* "*Like other* [read *As with other*] judicial rules, however, exceptions to the warrantless search-and-seizure rule have been recognized by the courts."

limitation over. See **over.**

limitation(s) period. See **statute(s) of limitation(s).**

lines and corners. See **metes and bounds.**

liquefy. So spelled. *Liquify* is a common misspelling.

liquidated damages, originally a EUPHEMISM for *forfeiture* or *penalty*, has, in many jurisdictions, become a TERM OF ART distinguishable from those other terms. *Liquidated damages* applies when the parties to a contract have agreed in advance on the measure of damages to be assessed in the event of default. It should be distinguished from *forfeiture* or *penalty*, which involves a provision imposed as a threat of punishment rather than as a genuine estimate of damages upon default.

liquify. See **liquefy.**

lis pendens; lite pendente; pendente lite. *Lis pendens* (L. "a pending lawsuit"), pronounced /lis-*pen*-dĕnz/, is a useful LATINISM that has given its name to a notice required in some jurisdictions to warn all persons that certain property is the subject matter of litigation, and that any interests acquired during the pendency of the suit must be subject to the outcome of the litigation. E.g., "The defendant says that the plaintiff's harsh conduct in holding up a whole subdivision by the *lis pendens* in this action disentitles him to such relief."

Pendente lite /pen-*den*-tee-li-tee/, less usually written *lite pendente*, is the same phrase in the present participial form, meaning "pending the lawsuit; during litigation." In G.B., administrators *pendente lite* are appointed to handle estates in dispute; in the U.S., matters are said to be *pendente lite* when they are contingent on the outcome of litigation.

Sometimes the phrase is used unnecessarily in place of an English phrase, e.g.: "The funds were deposited with the clerk of court, *pendente lite* [read *pending the outcome of the suit*]."

The extra words provide extra comprehensibility.

list. There cannot be a list of one. E.g., "The name of the winner is *listed* below." [Read *The winner is named below.*]

literally = with truth to the letter; exactly. The use of this word in the sense "truly, completely," is an example of SLIPSHOD EXTENSION. E.g., "Behavioralists and postbehavioralists alike, literally or figuratively, learn what they know of science from the natural sciences, from the outside." [Read *Behavioralists and post-behavioralists alike learn what they know of science from the natural sciences, from the outside.*]

When used for *figuratively*, where *figuratively* would not ordinarily be used, *literally* is distorted beyond recognition: "Mr. Gladstone had sat *literally* glued to the Treasury Bench." Because we know it is a metaphor, simply say: "Mr. Gladstone had sat glued to the Treasury Bench."

LITERARY ALLUSION, if not too arcane, can add substantially to the subtlety and effectiveness of writing. Allusiveness assumes a common body of literature with which all cultured persons are familiar. The effective writer is wary on the one hand of allusions that are hackneyed, and on the other hand of allusions so learned that they are inaccessible to the average educated reader. It is perhaps easier for judges than for practicing lawyers to use literary allusions, for judges have a guaranteed readership and do not suffer directly if anyone (or everyone) fails to appreciate their allusions. A lawyer submitting a brief to a judge, on the contrary, is likely to be less adventurous in literary flights of fancy. A few specimens follow, with short explanations.

A. *Effective Use of Allusion.*

1. Proverbs. A good example of effective allusiveness appears in the dissent of Justice Robert W. Hansen of the Wisconsin Supreme Court, in *Jones v. Fisher*, 42 Wis. 2d 209, 166 N.W.2d 175 (1969). He plays with an old proverb: "The *road* that has brought us to the present state of affairs in regard to punitive damages in Wisconsin courts *is* a long one, *paved with good intentions.*" Justice Hansen here subtly suggests that this is the road to hell, conjuring up the saying that "The road to hell is paved with good intentions." He might have ruined the effect by quoting the aphorism directly.

2. Biblical. "One of the prime concerns addressed in the [Magnason-Moss Warranty] Act was the warranty wherein the large print *giveth* but the small print *taketh away.*" *Gorman v. Saf-T-Mate, Inc.,* 513 F. Supp. 1028, 1035 (N.D. Ind. 1981). This alludes to Job 1:21: "Naked came I out of my mother's womb, and naked shall I return thither: the Lord gave, and the Lord hath taken away." See BIBLICAL AFFECTATION.

3. Shakespeare. "La. Rev. Stat. 14:27(A) requires specific intent to commit a crime, and in Stewart's eyes *there is the rub.*" *Stewart v. Blackburn,* 746 F.2d 262, 264 (5th Cir. 1984). This allusion may confuse the reader because of the proximity of *rub* and *eyes;* the phrase *there's the rub* (orig. fr. *Hamlet* 3.1.64) has passed into common parlance.

4. Mythology and Ancient History. "This appeal requires this court to make another trek through that *Serbonian bog* of damages in maritime cases." *Delta S.S. Lines, Inc. v. Avondale Shipyards, Inc.,* 747 F.2d 995, 997 (5th Cir. 1984). *Serbonian bog* (= a quagmire or predicament from which there is no way of extricating oneself) has become a judges' CLICHÉ, though it may have been fresh when Cardozo wrote: "The attempted distinction between accidental results and accidental means will plunge this branch of law into a *Serbonian bog.*" *Landress v. Phoenix Mutual Life Insurance Co.,* 291 U.S. 491, 499 (1934) (Cardozo, J., dissenting). The Serbonian bog is said to have been between Egypt and Palestine. Milton wrote: "A gulf profound as that *Serbonian Bog,* / Betwixt Damiata and Mount Casius old, / Where armies whole have sunk." *Paradise Lost,* ii, 592.

Here is another typical allusion to ancient history: "Most of the arguments and points made by the en banc opinion have been addressed by our panel opinion, and I will let the matter rest upon what has been said; for me to write more on the subject, which now appears settled by virtue of the majority here and the Second Circuit in *In re Taddeo,* would be largely repetitious and amount to no more than a *Parthian shot.*" *Grubbs v. Houston First American Savings Ass'n,* 730 F.2d 236, 247–48 (5th Cir. 1984) (en banc) (Jolly, J., dissenting). A *Parthian shot* is a parting shot, an allusion to the people of ancient Parthia, noted for their method of fighting on horseback

with the bow as their only weapon; after each discharge of an arrow the horse turned as if in flight—hence the modern meaning.

5. Other Literature. "We will not oblige the state to *joust windmills* by requiring that it prove what is not wrong with that which is not there to be seen." (In Cervantes' *Don Quixote,* the protagonist Don Quixote tilts at windmills under the delusion that they are giants.)/ "This old but little used section is *a kind of legal Lohengrin;* although it has been with us since the first Judiciary Act, § 9, 1 Stat. 73, 77 (1789), no one seems to know whence it came." *IIT v. Vencap, Ltd.,* 519 F.2d 1001, 1015 (2d Cir. 1975). (Lohengrin, hero of R. Wagner's opera of the same name and a knight of the Holy Grail, refuses to reveal, even to his wife, the mystery of his origins.)

B. *Poor Use of Allusion.*

1. Hackneyed Allusions. "What *is and what is not* a sham is the Hamlet-like question that has perplexed the lower courts in the two decades since the Supreme Court, in a 'new and unusual application of the Sherman Act,' enunciated the *Noerr* doctrine." *To be or not to be* (to live or not to live) is rather a different kind of question from what is and is not a sham. Moreover, *To be or not to be* (*Hamlet* 3.1.55) is a greatly overworked phrase.

Hyperbolic allusion, especially if it smacks of BIBLICAL AFFECTATION, is also ineffective. E.g., "The words, both singly and conjunctively, have been in common use and generally understood since Moses delivered the commandments and the law to his people, and up to the present time." The judge who wrote that, in the process of construing a legal document written in English, merely detracted from his persuasiveness. See OVERSTATEMENT.

2. Contrived Uses of Literature. Some judges and advocates, in their quest for originality, go off the deep end. Perhaps the worst manifestation of this phenomenon is what we might term "literary foppery," consisting in the legal writer's going to absurd lengths to display the breadth of his literary knowledge. For example, Sterne's *Tristram Shandy* is quite irrelevantly dragged into *Farr v. Nordman,* 346 Mich. 266, 78 N.W.2d 186, 193 (1956) (Black, J., dissenting). Contrived allusions and references invariably detract from the message to be conveyed.

In a striking example of artificially engrafted literariness, an American judge recently peppered one of his opinions with wholly impertinent allusions and references to William Faulkner. The opinion itself treats of the constitutionality under the Fourth Amendment of a lessor's inspection of his land to determine whether the lessee has wrongfully diverted oil production. The first sentence of the statement of facts reads: "The events underlying Auster's claims could have arisen in Yoknapatawpha County, Mississippi, but most of them happened in Calcasieu Parish, Louisiana, where Stream owned the surface and mineral rights in oil-producing property." A footnote, of course, explains that Yoknapatawpha County is the fictional setting of many of Faulkner's novels (and cites works on Faulkner by the renowned critics Cleanth Brooks and Irving Howe). The contrivance has neither purpose nor subtlety.

Worse yet, however, are the headings and subheadings throughout the opinion. We begin with "The Sound and the Fury," which is followed by "Lease in August" (*Light in August*), "The Reivers," "Intruders in the Dust" (*Intruder in the Dust*), "Auster's Gambit" (*Knight's Gambit*), "Go Down, Auster" (*Go Down, Moses*), "Requiem for a Plaintiff" (*Requiem for a Nun*), "Sanctuary," "Microchip! Microchip!" (*Absolom! Absolom!*?), "Trooper's Pay" (*Soldiers' Pay*), "As the Wells Lay Pumping" (*As I Lay Dying*), and "The Unvanquished." In short, the references and allusions to Faulkner are entirely factitious.

To some, such contrivances may be appealing. For them, one can only point to the advantages of developing a more discerning literary sensibility.

literatim. See **verbatim.**

litig(at)able. The correct form is *litigable.* See -ATABLE.

litigate = (1) to be a party to, or carry on, a lawsuit; (2) to make the subject of a lawsuit, to contest at law; (3) to dispute, contest (e.g., a point). Thus in sense (1), one *litigates* cases and causes, but in sense (2) one may *litigate* property or consequences, etc. E.g., "Qualified immunity is in part an entitlement not to be forced to *litigate* the consequences of official conduct." Cf. **adjudicate** (A).

litigation. Though it may seem unidiomatic to make *litigation* a COUNT NOUN (hence a plural), the usage is old and is today common. E.g., "[The] first and second parties now have certain *litigations* pending in the Mercer Circuit Court." *Reed v. Carter*, 268 Ky. 1, 103 S.W.2d 663, 664 (Ky. Ct. App. 1937)./ "In the realm of common-law products liability, it will suffice to cite *a* single automobile *litigation* that consumed sixty-three trial days, produced testimony from forty-one witnesses and was swamped with 240 exhibits."/ "The firm engages in general civil practice with emphasis on business *litigations.*" / "No court in which *a* *litigation* to that end might be brought has any power to pass on the existence and validity of an alleged will."

This word is best not used, however, as an equivalent of *action* or *suit*: "Whether such claims are just need not be decided to determine the rights of the parties to this *litigation* [read *suit*]." Properly, *litigation* = the action or process of carrying on a suit in law or equity (*OED*); thus it does not refer to the suit itself, but to the maintenance of it.

Here it seems to be used for *trial*: "As the rules became more numerous and more nicely distinguished, they became also less easily understood and applied by the great mass of people, until finally no one who had not given the subject particular attention could safely assume to conduct a *litigation* [read *trial*]."

litigatory; litigational. There is no single widely accepted neutral adjective corresponding to *litigation* and meaning "of, pertaining to, or involving litigation." *Litigious* is close structurally, but its strong associations with disputatiousness and contentiousness impair its candidacy. *Litigable* ⟨litigable claims⟩ and *litigant* ⟨parties litigant⟩ have other specific senses. *Litigation* sometimes functions as an adjective, as in the title of Leon Green's collection of essays *The Litigation Process in Tort Law* (1965). It works in some phrases, but not in others.

Both *litigatory* and *litigational* have been called on for service in the desired neutral sense. *Litigatory* is listed in *W2*, but is omitted from *W3* and has appeared in neither the *OED* nor its *Supplement.* Yet it is no stranger to American legal prose. E.g., "The controlling declaration . . . is that equity can and should intervene whenever it is made to appear that one party, public or private, seeks unjustly to enrich himself at the expense of another on account of his own mistake and the other's want of immediate vigilance—*litigatory* or otherwise." *Spoon-Shacket Co. v. County of Oakland*, 97 N.W.2d 25, 28 (Mich. 1959). / "Certain Florida cases, though having *litigatory* objectives different from the one at bar, employ the principle." *Brown v. Hutch*, 156 So. 2d 683, 686 (Fla. Dist. Ct. App. 1963). / "Considering the overall strength of the factual and legal bases of the surety's rejection of the claim and the *litigatory* posture of the surety, we believe that its rejection . . . was not preponderately [q.v.] reasonable." *United States Fidelity & Guaranty Co. v. Clover Creek Cattle Co.*, 452 P.2d 993, 1005 (Idaho 1969). / "Not only do the decided cases lead us to this decision but such ruling accords with modern jurisprudence which seeks to eliminate the hidden *litigatory* pitfall." *Federal Insurance Co. v. Oakwood Steel Co.*, 191 S.E.2d 298, 300 (Ga. App. 1972). / "[O]ur affirmance in the present case is predicated upon the purposes and objectives underlying declaratory judgment actions and the *litigatory* posture of the dispute involving the parties herein." *Volkswagenwerk, A.G. v. Watson*, 390 N.E.2d 1082, 1084 (Ind. App. 1979).

Litigational, a NEEDLESS VARIANT of *litigatory*, has been similarly neglected in general English-language dictionaries, though it is not uncommon. E.g., "*Litigational background of both appeals was* [read *In the litigatory background of both appeals was*] a suit instituted by plaintiff." *Morton v. Indemnity Insurance Co.*, 137 So. 2d 618, 619 (Fla. Dist. Ct. App. 1962)./ "[W]e now consider briefly a second form of specific jurisdiction . . . relating not only to the plaintiff but also to the taking of evidence and other *litigational* [read *litigatory*] considerations." von Mehren & Trautman, *Jurisdiction to Adjudicate*, 79 Harv. L. Rev. 1121, 1173 (1966). / "[T]he *Finney* court recognize[d] that the binding nature of a stipulation of dispositiveness supported the parties in their exercise of *litigational* [read *litigatory*] strategy." *Zeigler v. State*, 471 So. 2d 172, 176 (Fla. App. 1985).

litigiosity; litigiousness. If there is a nuance between these words, it is that *litigiosity* denotes the *fact* or *state* of being litigious, whereas *litigiousness* denotes the *quality* of being litigious. The fussiness of this distinction suggests that euphony is a better ground for choice between the two. In Scots law, however, *litigiosity* has a special sense: "a legal prohibition on a debtor's alienating heritable property to the effect of defeating an action . . . commenced or inchoate" (*OCL*).

litiscontestation. See **contest.**

liv(e)able. The spelling *livable* is preferred in AmE, *liveable* in BrE. "Only a willingness on the part of the courts to construe limitations as valid and to separate invalid provisions without condemning the remaining provisions has made the statutory rule *livable*." See MUTE E.

livery of seisin (= the ceremonial procedure at common law by which a grantor conveyed land to a grantee) is LAW FRENCH (orig. *bail de la seisine*) for *delivery of seisin*. It is sanctioned by centuries of legal usage, and today ordinarily appears only in historical contexts. E.g., "A transferor, A, having an estate in fee simple, could provide, upon making *livery of seisin* to B, that he should have occupancy of the land for his lifetime."/ "*Livery of seisin* was accomplished by the transferor and the transferee going on the land where the transferor symbolically delivered possession of the land to the transferee by handing him twig or clod or turf. Alternatively, *livery of seisin* could be accomplished by a statement of the transferor made in view of the land to the effect that possession was given to the transferee, followed by entry of the transferee on the land."/ "A corollary of this doctrine was the rule that *livery of seisin* was essential to the creation of a present freehold estate."

The *OED* notes that *livery and seisin* is a common error for *livery of seisin*. See **delivery** (B) & **seisin.**

living trust. See **inter vivos trust.**

loadstar. See **lodestar.**

loadstone; lodestone. This term, meaning "something that strongly attracts," is spelled *loadstone* in BrE and *lodestone* in AmE. E.g., "The intention of the testator is the guide, or in the phrase of Lord Coke, the *lodestone* of the court." Cf. **lodestar.**

loan; lend. In formal usage, it is best to use *lend* as the verb and *loan* as the noun. *Loan* is considered permissible, however, when used as a verb denoting the lending of money (as distinguished from the lending of articles).

LOAN TRANSLATIONS are English terms arrived at by translating foreign terms into English equivalents. Thus we arrive at the unEnglish-sounding *next friend* as a loan translation (or calque) of *prochein ami*. The language of the law has many such terms, usually translated from Latin or LAW FRENCH, q.v. Following is a list of some of them:

English Term	Foreign-Language Term
action on the case	action sur le case (Law French)
against the form of the statute	contra formam statuti (L.)
against the peace	contra pacem (L.)
burden of proof	onus probandi (L.)
civil death	mors civilis (L.)
damage without injury	damnum absque injuria (L.)
dead-hand	mortmain (F.)
friend of the court	amicus curiae (L.)
go hence without day	aller sans jour (Law French), ire sine die (L.)
goods and chattels	bona et catalla (Law Latin)
have and hold	habendum et tenendum (L.), aver et tener (Law French)
injury without damage	injuria absque damno (L.)
in the breast	in pectore (L.)
last will	ultima voluntas (L.)
law merchant	lex mercatoria (L.)
next friend	prochein ami (Law French)
notwithstanding the verdict	non obstante veredicto (Law Latin)
on pain of	sur peine de (F.)
plead not guilty	plaider de rien culpable (Law French)
true bill	billa vera (Law Latin)
under pain of	sous pein de (F.), sub poena (L.)
with force and arms	vi et armis (L.)

Sometimes the Englished versions require skillful inference to arrive at the meaning. E.g., "An acceptance that remains *in the breast* of the accepter without being actually and by legal implication communicated to the offeror is not a binding acceptance." (Eng.) Others have no literal significance, but have been adopted as legal names (as TERMS OF ART or legal ARGOT) for doctrines and causes of action, such as *trespass with force and arms:*"This is an action in trespass that the defendant, with *force and arms*, wilfully and maliciously assaulted, debauched, and carnally knew the daughter and servant of the plaintiff." (Eng.)

The tendency toward translating unassimilated foreign terms that are used in law into English is salutary on the whole. *Dead-hand* may never displace *mortmain*, nor *friend of the court amicus curiae*, but most of the foreign-language law terms have fallen into disuse. And most of the loan translations listed above have become familiar. Now there is little call for more loan translations, because legal English increasingly approximates general-purpose English.

loathe; lo(a)th. *Loathe* is the verb meaning "to abhor, detest." *Loath*, with its NEEDLESS VARIANT *loth*, is an adjective meaning "reluctant." Here the verb spelling is used wrongly for the adjective, a frequent error: "To require masking the provisions stating the penalties would be akin to mandating a nonjury trial of punitive damages in every case, on the ground that jurors are *loathe* [read *loath*] to award them."/ "Courts have generally been *loathe* [read *loath*] to refuse the offer of an aid to difficult problems of interpretation."/ "Yellow Cab has proved *loathe* [read *loath*] to loosen its grip on the airport market."

locale; locality. Both terms are frequently used; for the most part they are equivalent, but only *locale* has the sense "the setting or scene of action or of a story."

locate for *set up shop* or *establish residence* is an Americanism that, despite its having been criticized by several grammarians, has become standard ⟨after several years in the Plaza, the firm located in the Crescent⟩. *Locate* is transitive in BrE and means "to place" or "to ascertain the whereabouts of." In AmE, the word is used in these senses, but also in the colloquial intransitive sense of "to settle, begin residing." The sense "to fix or establish in a place" is also distinctively AmE: "Subsection (b) of the statute would seem generally to *locate* review of licensing proceedings in the courts of appeals." This usage is by no means new: "[The 1869 law] is aptly framed to remove from the more densely populated part of the city, the noxious slaughter-houses, and large and offensive collections of animals necessarily incident to [them], and to *locate* them where the convenience, health, and comfort of the people require they shall be located." *The Slaughter-House Cases*, 83 U.S. (16 Wall.) 36, 64 (1873) (per Miller, J.).

LOCATIVES. See CASE REFERENCES (B).

Lochnerize, -ization. These terms derive from the case name *Lochner v. New York*, 198 U.S. 45 (1905). *Lochnerize* = to scrutinize and invalidate economic regulations under the guise of enforcing the due process clause. The term carries no small degree of opprobrium. "*Lochnerizing* has become so much an epithet that the very use of the label may obscure attempts at understanding." L. Tribe, *American Constitutional Law* 435 (1978). E.g., "*Lochner v. New York* (invalidating New York's maximum-hours law for bakers) has come to typify the period of 'substantive due process' review, during which the Supreme Court over a strong dissent invalidated state economic and social legislation for interfering with the liberty of contract." *Town of Ball v. Rapides Parish Police Jury*, 746 F.2d 1049, 1056 n.21 (5th Cir. 1984). / "[E]qual protection was so disfavored that, during the heyday of '*Lochnerizing*,' it was called 'the usual last resort of constitutional arguments.'" (*Id.*)/ "Of course we are *Lochnerizing* and intruding into the affairs of a state." *Dunagin v. City of Oxford*, 718 F.2d 738, 755 (5th Cir. 1983) (en banc) (Higginbotham, J., dissenting).

locus; situs. Both terms are used in law to mean "a place in which something is situated or is done." *Locus* is the more concrete, specific term: "We hold that at the death of John Girdler's widow, his three daughters and granddaughter held undivided equal estates tail in the *locus.*" *Situs*, to the contrary, is more abstract, with a usu. broader, territorial sense of "place": "Such a decree ought to be entitled to full faith and credit at the *situs* of the land."/ "Holding that Mexico rather than Texas was the *situs* of the bank deposits furthers the general policies of the act of state doctrine." See **situs.**

locus in quo (= the place where something is alleged to have been done) is common in property law, but is often unnecessary in place of *locus* or *location*. Here it is perhaps justifiable, because its use implicitly incorporates the notion of allegations in a lawsuit: "It

is proper to admit photographs of the *locus in quo* even though taken 15½ months after the accident. . . ." *Hamilton v. Fean*, 221 A.2d 309, 314 (Pa. 1966).

locus standi (= the right to bring an action or challenge some decision [*CDL*]) seems to be an unnecessary LATINISM, in view of the more common American legal term *standing. Locus standi* is common in G.B., however. E.g., "First, it may be asked what, if any, *locus standi* the Law Society has in a matter of this kind." (Eng.)/ "In my view, it would be most unfortunate if the intervenor did not have a *locus standi* in appropriate cases." (Eng.)/ "The Italian standpoint is that at the present juncture the League has no *locus standi* in the dispute." (Eng.) Formerly it was used in the sense "credentials, established position of high standing." See **standing.**

locution. See **elocution.**

lodestar; loadstar. The former spelling is preferred in both AmE and BrE for this term meaning "a guiding star." (The word derives fr. O.E. *lād* [= way, course] + *star*.) The term has jargonistic uses in setting fees and damages, and these lead to METAPHORS, MIXED AND MANGLED: "In awarding attorneys' fees, the district court *increased* the *lodestar*—the product of the number of hours reasonably expended multiplied by a reasonable hourly rate—to compensate counsel for the delay in actual payment for the legal services rendered." (The figurative does not impinge on the literal sense if we write of *raising* a lodestar, but it does so impinge if we write of *increasing* a lodestar.)

lodestone. See **loadstone.**

LOGIC. See ILLOGIC.

logomachy = a contention about words. E.g., "The student of jurisprudence is at times troubled by the thought that he is dealing not with things, but with words, that he is busy with the shape and size of counters in a game of *logomachy*, but when he fully realizes how these words have been passed and are still being passed as money, not only by fools and on fools, but by and on some of the acutest minds, he feels that there is work worthy of being done, if only it can be done worthily."

J. C. Gray, *Nature and Sources of the Law* viii (1909).

logorrhea (= diarrhea of the mouth) is an affliction of which lawyers must beware.

long, adv., can stand alone, without *for.* E.g., "We have *now for long* [read *now long*] been accustomed, with some archaic survivals, to the doctrine that imposed liability depends in part upon the conscious attitude which a supposititious normal person would take towards the damage resulting from his acts." (L. Hand, J.)

long-arm statute (= a statute providing for the maintenance of jurisdiction over nonresident defendants) derives from the catchphrase *the (long) arm of the law.*

longshoreman. See SEXISM (B).

long-standing, adj. So spelled.

look over. See **overlook.**

loom large. See **bulk large.**

loose; loosen. Both words mean "to unbind; release." The DIFFERENTIATION between the two is that *loose* is generally literal, *loosen* generally figurative. See **lose.**

lord justice, the title of a judge on the (English) Court of Appeal, is pluralized *lords justices.*

lose; loose. *Lose,* v.t., = to suffer the deprivation of; to part with. *Loose* is both adj. & v.t., meaning in the latter use "to release; unfasten." See **loose.**

loser; winner. Courts sometimes use *loser* and *winner* as substitutes for *appellant* and *appellee,* respectively. E.g., "We may affirm a summary judgment only if the record, read in the light most favorable to the *loser* [i.e., appellant] reveals no genuine issues of material fact and shows that the *winners* [i.e., appellees] were entitled to judgment as a matter of law."

lost property; mislaid property; abandoned property. At common law, these descriptions of property found by someone other than its original owner operated to govern its disposition. The distinctions are still valid in many English-speaking jurisdictions. Property is said to be *lost* when the owner has involuntarily relinquished possession of it, usually by accident or forgetfulness, and cannot or is highly unlikely to recover it by diligent search. Property is *mislaid* when the owner has purposefully put it in a place and then forgotten it, but may find it by diligent searching. It is *abandoned* if the owner has knowingly forsaken his interest in the property.

loth. See **loathe.**

lower court. See **higher court** & **inferior court.**

L.S. = *locus sigilli,* meaning "place of the seal." The abbreviation was formerly used on contracts and deeds in place of an actual seal.

lunatic, formerly a clinical medical description, was likewise formerly used frequently in legal writing. E.g., "A *lunatic* has the capacity to take and hold title to property and therefore may become a trustee." Today, however, the term is one of opprobrium because of its figurative abuses; it should be used cautiously if at all.

luxuriant; luxurious. *Luxuriant,* a favorite word of metaphrasts, means "growing abundantly, lush." E.g., "The states have decided that it is better to leave a few of its noxious branches to their *luxuriant* growth, than by pruning them away to injure the vigor of those yielding the proper fruits." *Luxurious* = characteristic of luxury.

M

MACARONISM. See MINGLE-MANGLE.

magisterial; magistral. Although *magisterial* carries connotations of nobility, command, and even dictatorialness, it is also the preferred adjective corresponding to the noun *magistrate.* E.g., "While we may review *magistral* [read *magisterial*] findings of fact, subject only to the 'clearly erroneous' standard, we may overturn any conclusions of law that contradict or ignore applicable precepts of law as found in the Constitution, statutes, or case precedent." *Magistratic* and *magistratical* are NEEDLESS VARIANTS. *Magistral* = (1) of a master or masters ⟨an absolutely magistral work⟩; (2) formulated by a physician ⟨a magistral ointment⟩.

magistracy; magistrature; magistrateship. The first of these is the standard term for the office, district, or power of a magistrate, or body of magistrates. *Magistrature* and *magistrateship* are NEEDLESS VARIANTS.

magistral. See **magisterial.**

magistrate, in both G.B. and the U.S., is now generally understood as referring to a judicial officer with strictly limited jurisdiction and authority, often on the local level. Formerly, however, it retained a meaning closer to its etymological sense. The word derives from L. *magistratus* or *magister* "master," and once referred to the official first in rank in a branch of government. Hence an emperor, or a monarch, or a president might have been termed a *magistrate*. Thus it is that Cardozo referred to Chief Justice Marshall, with the greatest respect, as the *magistrate* who wrote *Marbury v. Madison*. See Cardozo, *Law and Literature*, 52 Harv. L. Rev. 471, 476 (1939). See **magisterial.**

magistrateship; magistrature. See **magistracy.**

Magna C(h)arta. The usual form is *Magna Carta*; this name should not take the article *the*. E.g., "Habeas corpus is shown by ample evidence to have been in use before the memorable occasion when royal recognition was given it in the great document of *Magna Carta*."

maihem. See **mayhem.**

maintenance, used as a verb in place of *maintain*, v.t. ⟨to maintenance a certain line of inquiry⟩, is poor. For the legal term *maintenance*, see **champerty.**

majority. A. And *plurality*. These terms are frequently used in reference to judicial opinions. *Majority* = a group of more than 50 percent (e.g., five of nine judges). *Plurality* = the group with the largest percentage where none of the percentages is 50 percent or more

(e.g., four of nine judges, when three have adopted a different position, and two others still another position). See **plurality opinion.**

Majority is almost always used in the U.S. as a COLLECTIVE NOUN, so that it takes a singular verb. E.g., "The majority *deem* [read *deems*] negotiations leading to execution of contracts admissible."/ "The majority *reach* [read *reaches*] *their* [read *its*] conclusion regarding the 50% stock dividend and the proceeds of sale by expressly overruling *Crawford Estate*." In G.B., *majority* is more frequently plural.

B. For *full age*. This LEGALISM ⟨age of majority⟩ is common in both the U.S. and G.B.

make good (= to compensate for, restore, or effect) is a legal as well as a lay idiom; its primary use in law is in the field of contracts. "By inducing Deacon to violate his duty to the respondent company, he has occasioned to them a loss which their Lordships consider that he was rightly ordered to *make good*." (Eng.)/ "The person who had brought about the mixing was entitled to claim his proper quantity, but subject to the other proprietor's being first *made good* out of the whole mass."

make a mockery of is a CLICHÉ to be avoided.

make-whole, adj. "The market value of the property deviated significantly from the *make-whole* remedy intended by the just compensation clause." To be *made whole* is to be returned to the *status quo ante* (q.v.); the verb phrase *to make whole* has been transformed into the adjectival phrase *make-whole*.

MALADROIT PROSE lumbers along without direction or focus. E.g., "The basis for, and the need of such encouragement is no longer existent" (13 words). [Read *The need for such encouragement no longer exists* (8 words).] See CUTTING OUT THE CHAFF & PHRASING.

mala fide(s). *Mala fide* (= in bad faith) is the adverb or adjective, *mala fides* (= bad faith) the noun. Unlike its sibling *bona fide*, *mala fide* is understandable to most laymen neither as adjective nor as noun, and only infrequently is it encountered in modern legal texts. The best advice is to avoid it and use the well-known Anglo-Saxon equivalent. See **bona fide(s)** & **good(-)faith.**

Two specimens of the phrase follow, both of them from late in the nineteenth century: "If advice given *mala fide*, and loss sustained, entitle me to damages, why, though the advice be given honestly [i.e., *bona fide*], but under wrong information, with a loss sustained, am I not entitled to them [i.e., damages]?"/ "Therefore, we are all of opinion that the defendant ought in justice to refund this money thus *mala fide* recovered."

mala in se; mala prohibita. See **malum in se.**

MALAPROPISMS are words used incorrectly that produce a humorous effect. The term derives from the character Mrs. Malaprop in Sheridan's play *The Rivals*; Mrs. Malaprop loves big words, but uses them ignorantly to create hilarious solecisms and occasionally embarrassing double entendres. One of Mrs. Malaprop's famous similes is *as headstrong as an allegory on the banks of the Nile*.

Following are examples of legal malapropisms. One lawyer apparently mistook *meretricious* (= marked by falsity; superficially attractive but fake nevertheless) for *meritorious* with embarrassing consequences: a plaintiff's lawyer, he asked a judge to rule favorably on his client's "meretricious claim." Other illustrations are *nefarious* (= evil) for *multifarious* ("Ties, shirts, shoes, belts, socks, and all the other *nefarious* parts of one's wardrobe") and *voracity* (= greediness with food) for *veracity* ("There would have been nothing to be gained by trying to impeach the truthfulness or *voracity* of those witnesses."). For other examples, see **avert, contribute, degradation, disparaging, effrontery, evoke, illicit, impotence, panacea, prodigious, prospectus, solicit, & surcease.**

malefaction. See **malfeasance.**

malefactor = criminal; felon. Although the term is now primarily literary, the *OED* contains the following quotation of Herbert Spencer from 1862: "By a *malefactor*, we now understand a convicted criminal, which is far from being the acceptation of 'evil-doer'."

malefeasance. See **malfeasance.**

malevolent; maleficent. Whereas the former means "desirous of evil to others," the latter means positively "hurtful or criminal to others." Hence *malevolent* has to do with malicious desires, and *maleficent* with malicious actions.

malfeasance, -zance; malefeasance; misfeasance; malefaction. Use of the words *malfeasance* and *misfeasance* is imprecise in AmE. Perhaps it is best to begin this entry with the clear-cut BrE distinctions. In BrE, the distinction between *malfeasance* and *misfeasance* is sharper than in the U.S., and somewhat different. *Malfeasance* = an unlawful act; *misfeasance* = the negligent or otherwise improper performance of a lawful act (*CDL*). *Misfeasance* also has the more specialized legal sense common in G.B.: "a legal act done in an improper or illegal way." *Malefeasance* and *malfeazance* are obsolete spellings of *malfeasance*.

In AmE, *malfeasance* is often confined to the sense "misprision; misconduct or wrongdoing by a public official." *Misfeasance* is a more general word meaning "transgression, trespass."

In the U.S., the notion in the word *malfeasance* of public office is sometimes important; but the word is often used of corporate as well as of public officials, and sometimes of other persons: "Defendants have not cited any persuasive authorities to support their view that Washington, the successor, is tainted in equity by the *malfeasance* of Oaks, its predecessor."/ "The contract shall not cover any loss of production due to the neglect or *malfeasance* of the insured."

The legislative drafter of the following statutory provision was not unorthodox in using both *malfeasance* and *misfeasance*: "Respondents were classified civil service employees, entitled under Ohio Rev. Code Ann. § 124.34 (1984) to retain their positions 'during good behavior and efficient service,' who could not be dismissed 'except for *misfeasance, malfeasance,* or *nonfeasance* in office.'" See **feasance.**

Malefaction = crime, offense. It is a FORMAL WORD that has become an ARCHAISM.

MALFORMATIONS. See MORPHOLOGICAL DEFORMITIES.

malice is often an ambiguous term, because it has been diluted in legal writing. Early in this century the dilution was noted and objected to: "when all that is meant by *malice* is an intention to commit an unlawful act without reference to spite or ill-feeling, it is better to drop the word *malice* and so avoid all misunderstanding." *South Wales Miners Federation v. Glamorgan Coal Co.*, [1905] A.C. 239, 255. Even in the nineteenth century, however, the attenuated legal meaning had taken hold: "*Malice*, in the definition of murder, has not the same meaning as in common speech ["strong ill will"], and . . . has been thought to mean criminal intention." Holmes, *The Common Law* 53 (1881; repr. 1946).

The legal and nonlegal senses can be pointedly in contrast: "Although when used in its nonlegal sense the word clearly denotes an evil or wicked state of mind, at law it does not necessarily have such a connotation; at law it simply means that the actor intentionally did something unlawful. Thus, the legal meaning of *malice* is confusing to a nonlawyer because an individual may act with good reason or from humanitarian motives but, as a matter of legal terminology, he has acted with *malice* if his act is against the law." Purver, *The Language of Murder*, 14 U.C.L.A. L. Rev. 1306, 1306 (1967). As a noncriminal example, the *malice* requirement in proving libel of a public figure does not involve spite or ill-will, only knowing falsity or a reckless disregard for the truth.

malice aforethought does not "mean a state of the defendant's mind, as is often thought, except in the sense that he knew circumstances which did in fact make his conduct dangerous. It is, in truth, an allegation like that of negligence, which asserts that the party did not come up to the legal standard of action under the circumstances in which he found himself, and also that there was no exceptional fact or excuse present which took the case out of the general rule." Holmes, *The Common Law* 62-63 (1881; repr. 1946). A more modern writer has explained: "At the present time, *malice aforethought* is used to express the idea that the accused killed his victim intentionally; no ill-will is required. The phrase is also employed to indicate simply that the killing was under such circumstances that the accused will be punished as severely as if the killing were intentional." Purver, *The Language of Murder*, 14 U.C.L.A. L. Rev. 1306, 1308 (1967). See **aforethought, prepense, & wil(l)fulness.**

malignancy; malignity. *Malignancy* should be confined to denoting any cancerous disease. *Malignity* = wicked or deep-rooted ill will or hatred; malignant feelings or actions.

malodorous. See **odorous.**

malpractice is confined in AmE to negligence or incompetence on the part of professionals (e.g., lawyers and doctors); in BrE, however, it has this meaning as well as a sense similar to *misfeasance*: "The mortgagees are not parties to the *malpractices* of the Waites, and the tenants, who were the victims of those *malpractices.*" (Eng.) The *OED* records two senses not current in the U.S.: (1) "illegal action by which a person seeks to benefit himself at the cost of others, while in a position of trust"; and (2) "a criminal or overtly mischievous action; wrongdoing; misconduct." Cf. **malfeasance.**

maltreat. See **mistreat.**

malum in se; malum prohibitum. These LATINISMS are frequently used by common-law writers. The distinction between the terms is helpful in understanding of the relation of morality to the law. *Malum in se* = evil in itself; something inherently and universally considered evil. *Malum prohibitum* = wrong merely because it is proscribed; made unlawful by statute. Thus murder is the usual example of a crime *malum in se*, but running traffic lights is said to be *malum prohibitum*. E.g., "The rule is that where a condition precedent is impossible or is illegal as involving *malum prohibitum*, the bequest is absolute, just as if the condition had been subsequent; when, however, the illegality of the condition does not concern anything *malum in se*, but is merely against a rule or the policy of law, the condition only is void."/ "A *malum prohibitum* is just as much a crime as a *malum in se.*" Holmes, *The Common Law* 46 (1881; repr. 1946). / "In other words, I propose it shall no longer be *malum in se* for a citizen to pummel, cow-hide, kick, gouge, cut, wound, bruise, maim, burn, club, bastinado, flay, or even lynch a job-holder, and that it shall be *malum prohibitum* only to the extent that the punishment exceeds the job-holder's deserts." (Mencken)

The plurals are *mala in se* and *mala prohibita*.

-man; -person. See SEXISM (B).

mancipation. See **emancipation.**

mandamus, v.t. ⟨They *mandamused* the judge.⟩, began as a colloquialism in the early nineteenth century, is labeled colloquial in *W2* (1934), but has no such notation in *W3* (1961). It has come to appear even in published opinions. E.g., "Walker urges this Court to issue a Writ of Mandamus to the Court of Appeals ordering that court to *mandamus* Johnson to produce the statement of facts." *Pat Walker & Co. v. Johnson*, 623 S.W.2d 306, 308 (Tex. 1981). Actually, the use of *mandamus* as a verb is closer to the etymological sense (L. "we charge or command") than the nominal use. The brevity of *to mandamus* recommends its more widespread adoption; no valid reasons exist to oppose it.

mandatary, n., (= one to whom a mandate is entrusted) should be distinguished both from *mandatory*, adj., and from *mandator*, n., (= one who gives a mandate).

mandate, v.t., for *prescribe* is merely verbal sloppiness. "The Federal Rules of Appellate Procedure *mandate* [read *prescribe*] the time for filing a notice of appeal."

mandatory. Horwill wrote in the 1930s that *mandatory* is little used in England, and that *obligatory* and *compulsory* are more common. The latter two terms may still be predominant, but *mandatory injunction* is now a common phrase in English law reports. See **directory.**

mandatory injunction; prohibitory injunction. The former court order requires a positive action; the latter requires restraint from action.

man-killing is still occasionally used in law to refer to the action of one man against another, but rarely in nonlegal writing. "Homicidal mania is the morbid and uncontrollable appetite for *man-killing.*" See **murder** & SEXISM (B).

mankind. See **humankind** & SEXISM (B).

manner in which is almost always unnecessarily verbose for *how.*

man-of-law = a man skilled in law; a lawyer. This word, which has decidedly positive connotations, is little used today, perhaps because the hegemony of pejorative terms. See

LAWYER, DEROGATORY NAMES FOR. See also SEXISM (B).

manservant pluralizes both words in the compound; thus *menservants.*

manslaughter. See **murder.**

mantle; mantel. *Mantle* means, among other things, "a loose robe," and is frequently used by legal writers in figurative senses. E.g., "The *mantle* of immunity should be withdrawn."/ "The court has not felt constrained by stare decisis in its expansion of the protective *mantle* of sovereign immunity." See **clothe.**
   Mantel is a different and more common word, meaning "a structure of wood or marble above or around a fireplace; a shelf."

manufacturer. So spelled. Some legal writers mistakenly write *-or.* See -ER, -OR.

many; much. *Many* is used with COUNT NOUNS (i.e., those that comprise a number of discrete or separable entities). *Much* is used with mass nouns (i.e., those that refer to amounts as distinguished from numbers). Hence, *many persons* but *much salt.* Here *much* is used incorrectly: "We do not have *much* [read *many*] facts here." (Cf. *less* for *fewer*, noting that *less* is the correlative of *much*, whereas *fewer* is the correlative of *many.*)

mare clausum = a sea under one country's jurisdiction; a closed sea. *Mare liberum* = a sea open to all. If usefulness may be judged in large measure by frequency of use, these terms are not very useful.

margin (= footnotes) occurs today primarily in legal writing, although scholars in all disciplines once commonly used it. "The order and decree dismissing the bill is set out in the *margin.*" This usage harks back to a bygone era when notes were set out in the right and left margins rather than at the foot of the page.

mariage de convenance. See **marriage of convenience.**

marijuana; marihuana. The former now predominates in judicial opinions and should be preferred. Justice Lewis F. Powell of the U.S. Supreme Court, speaking in 1986 at a luncheon, stated: "The big problem we had in the Court this past Term was how to spell *marijuana*. We were about equally divided between a 'j' and an 'h' and since I was supposed to be the swing vote on the court, and just to show my impartiality, I added a footnote in a case . . . in which I spelled *marijuana* with a 'j' once and an 'h' in the same sentence." Quoted in A.B.A. J., 1 Oct. 1986, at 34.

mariner's will. See **oral will.**

marital. See **matrimonial law** & **marriage.**

maritime. See **admiralty.**

marked is pronounced /*markt*/, as one syllable. The pronunciation /*mar-kĕd*/, in two syllables, is a vestige of the correct adverbial pronunciation /*mark-ĕd-lee*/.

marketable; merchantable. The latter is a legal ARCHAISM with no nuance not conveyed by the former. E.g., "Delivery was made subject to the condition that appellant furnish *merchantable* [read *marketable*] title."

market overt means something rather more specific than *open market*. *Market overt* = an open public market authorized and regulated by law at which purchasers of goods, with certain exceptions, acquire good title regardless of any defects in the seller's title (*W3*). *Open market* = a market with no competitive restrictions on price or availability of products.

Market overt is the less common term: "Conceivably the common-law judges might have refused to allow the bailor to recover in detinue against a bona fide purchaser, as they did refuse it against a purchaser in *market overt*; but this would have involved a weighing of ethical considerations altogether foreign to the medieval mode of thought."

marriage, adj., for *marital*. The adjectival form is better used in adjectival senses. E.g., "An aggrieved spouse is not compelled to seek the courts of another state for the protection of her *marriage* [read *marital*] status." See NOUNS AS ADJECTIVES.

marriageable; marriable. The latter is an ARCHAISM to be avoided.

marriage dissolution is a EUPHEMISM for *divorce* or *annulment*. E.g., "The Family Law Act, a response to general dissatisfaction with the social and legal procedures affecting divorce actions in California, effected substantial changes in the substantive law and procedure in proceedings for *dissolution of marriage*." Note the INELEGANT VARIATION in that sentence (*divorce . . . dissolution of marriage*)./ "The State Bar of Texas sponsored the *Marriage Dissolution* Institute in Fort Worth in February 1985." That *marriage dissolution* may technically encompass annulments as well as divorces does not redeem it.

marriage of convenience; mariage de convenance. The anglicized version is to be preferred over the Gallicism. But it should be understood rightly: *marriage of convenience* is not "a marriage that is not well thought out but is convenient to the parties involved," but "a marriage contracted for social or financial advantages rather than out of mutual love."

marshal (= to arrange in order), in its past-tense and participial forms, is frequently misspelled in AmE with a doubled -*l*-. E.g., "The strongest support *marshalled* [read, in AmE, *marshaled*] by the majority opinion is the statement by Dean Page Keeton." See DOUBLING OF FINAL CONSONANTS.

Mary Carter agreement, which owes its name to *Booth v. Mary Carter Paint Co.*, 202 So. 2d 8 (Fla. Dist. Ct. App. 1967), means "a release of the plaintiff's cause of action in return for a settlement payment, along with a provision providing that the settling defendant will be reimbursed to some specified degree from any recovery the plaintiff may receive in a suit against another non-settling defendant." *Wilkins v. P.M.B. Systems Engineering, Inc.*, 741 F.2d 795, 798 n.2 (5th Cir. 1984). See CASE REFERENCES (C).

MASCULINE AND FEMININE PRONOUNS. See SEXISM (A).

master was once regularly used to mean "principal" in legal language, and *servant* to mean "agent." This terminology is obsolescent, however. See **employer and employee.**

masterful; masterly. The *master* in *masterful* is opposed to *servant* or *slave*; in *masterly* the sense is opposite to *an unskilled worker*. A master craftsman is *masterly*; a boorish tyrant is *masterful*. Which is the correct term in the following sentence, from a nonlegal text? "Though Britain's Derek Jacobi looks about as much like Adolph Hitler as Archie Bunker, he evokes the Führer with *masterful* verve." (The actor is *masterly*; Hitler was *masterful*.)

Perhaps one reason the two words are so frequently confounded is that when an adverb for *masterly* is needed, *masterfully* seems more natural than *masterlily*. See ADVERBS (B). Indeed, "He writes *masterfully*" strikes one as much less stilted than "He writes *masterlily*." This problem with the adverbial form threatens to destroy a useful distinction between the two adjectival forms. Perhaps *masterlily* would seem less pedantic if we were to use it more often. Barring that, *in a masterly way* is always available.

master of the bench. See **bencher.**

MATCHING PARTS. See PARALLELISM.

material, adj.; **relevant.** The distinction between these terms is fundamental to the law of evidence; and it is often forgotten. *Relevant* = tending to prove or disprove a matter in issue. *Material* = having some logical connection with the facts of consequence.

Material has been the victim of lawyers' SLIPSHOD EXTENSION, and used in the sense "significant." E.g., "An immediate appeal would *materially* [i.e., significantly] advance the ultimate termination of the litigation." This sense is now commonplace in American securities law, where it is too pervasive to be considered exceptionable. It is also common in other legal contexts.

materialman. See SEXISM (B).

matrimonial law. We might question why *matrimonial* rather than *marital* came to be used in this and related phrases. *Matrimonial* is a FORMAL WORD rarely used outside the law except in reference to wedding services. Yet the law on both sides of the Atlantic has embraced this word in phrases such as *matrimonial home*, *matrimonial offense*, and *matrimonial cohabitation*. E.g., "Strangely, however, the changes in the method of quantifying rights in the *matrimonial* home have gone unnoticed." (Eng.)/ "In *matrimonial* causes because the state has an interest, special duties are laid

on solicitors and the bar." (Eng.) The American Academy of Matrimonial Lawyers is unlikely to approve of a change in terminology.

Still, in some contexts *matrimonial* seems unnecessarily turgid in the place of *marital*: "This language frequently has been applied as a general rule and the federal courts consistently have refused to entertain actions involving *matrimonial* [read *marital*] status." See **marriage,** adj.

matter has become the American lawyer's puffed-up equivalent of *case*. E.g., "I handled a fascinating *matter* [read *case*] the other day."/ "How many *matters* [read *case*] are there on the docket?"

maximum, n. & adj.; **maximal,** adj. More and more frequently, *maximum* (like *minimum*) has come to act as its own adjective. E.g., "In bidding, the contractor shall expose to the bidders the *maximum* quantities required by the work."

Maximal usually means "the greatest possible," rather than merely "of, relating to, or constituting a maximum." E.g., "The state's interest in swift and efficient punishment need not eviscerate its interest in *maximal* certainty of application." See **minimal.**

The plural of the noun *maximum* is *maxima*. "Moreover, a majority of the states pay less than their determined standard of need, and twenty of these states impose *maximums* [read *maxima*] on family grants of the kind here in issue."

may = (1) is permitted to ⟨suit may be brought in any district court⟩; (2) possibly will ⟨the court may apply this doctrine⟩; or (3) shall. Sense (3), though a lexical perversion, has come about because "courts not infrequently construe *may* as *shall* or *must* to the end that justice may not be the slave of grammar" (*Black's* 4th ed.). No drafter of a document should consciously use *may*, however, when he means *must*; the liberties taken by the courts in construing drafters' oversights should not be allowed to change the essential meanings of basic words like *may*. See **can.**

mayhem; maihem. The former is the standard spelling.

may it please the court is the standard introductory phrase that lawyers use when addressing an appellate court.

mean = (1) small; (2) obstreperous; or (3) median, average. Readers today often misunderstand sense (1). A *mean-spirited* person is not malevolent or evil; rather, the person has a small spirit, a petty mind.

Writers should distinguish between *mean* as a noun in sense (3) and *median*. The *mean* is the average. The *median* is the point in a series of numbers above which is half the series and below which is the other half.

meaningful (= full of meaning or expression) has, with some irony, rightly been criticized as a meaningless buzzword, esp. when used for *reasonable*. Here its meaning is stretched to the breaking point: "Options should be used carefully and sparingly; any options issued must expire a *meaningful* [read *reasonable*] time before the earliest possible conversion date."/ "Due process requires an opportunity for a hearing to be granted at a *meaningful* [read *reasonable*] time and in a *meaningful* [read *reasonable*] manner." *Meaningful* has also been used to mean "significant, important," as here: "We find no *meaningful* constitutional infraction." These uses have made *meaningful* a VOGUE WORD that careful writers avoid.

meantime; meanwhile. *In the meantime* is idiomatic; *in the meanwhile* is not. Both *meanwhile* and *meantime* can be used alone, though the former more naturally so.

media; medium. The former is the plural of the latter. It cannot properly be used as a singular. *Medias*, which has recently raised its ugly head, can only be described as illiterate. *Mediums* is the correct plural when the sense of *medium* is "a clairvoyant; spiritualist."

Media is often used as a shortened form of *communications media*. E.g., "If one viewpoint monopolizes the *media*, however, the discussion that flows from it will not be full and unrestricted."

median. See **mean.**

mediate (= occupying a middle position; acting through an intermediate person or thing) is opposed to *immediate*. The Rule in Shelley's Case is often stated thus: "Where the ancestor takes an estate of freehold, and in the same gift or conveyance an estate is limited, either *mediately* or immediately, to his heirs in fee or in tail, 'the heirs' are words of limitation of the estate, and not words of purchase." *Peacock v. McCluskey*, 296 Ill. 87, 129 N.E. 561, 562 (1920).

mediation. See **arbitration.**

medical; medicinal. The former applies to all aspects of a physician's practice, the latter only to what is associated with medicines.

medicalize is an -IZE neologism that is unrecorded in the dictionaries, and that serves no useful purpose. E.g., "The past two or three years have seen a flurry of attempts by doctors to invoke judicial authority for the enforced *medicalization* of pregnancy and childbirth." What does that mean?

MEDICAL TERMINOLOGY. For an admirably comprehensive treatment, see J. E. Schmidt, *Attorneys' Dictionary of Medicine and Word Finder* (1984).

medicinal. See **medical.**

medicine; medication; medicament. The second term has traditionally meant "the action of treating medically," but recently has come to have the sense "a medicinal substance, medicament." *Medicament* (= a substance taken internally or used externally in curative treatment) and *medicine* (= a substance taken internally in curative treatment) are synonymous in the sense today given to *medication* through SLIPSHOD EXTENSION. Careful writers avoid *medication* in this new use.

medium. See **media.**

meld together is a common REDUNDANCY.

meliorate. See **ameliorate.**

memento. So spelled.

memoranda, -dums. *Memorandum* is always the singular noun; either *-dums* or *-da* is correct as a plural, though the latter is so entrenched as a foreign plural that one might deem it preferable. Here the plural form is incorrectly used as a singular: "Once a valid agreement is evidenced by such a *memoranda* [read *memorandum*], the statute comes into play to prevent contradiction of the terms included in the *memoranda* [read *memorandum*] by evidence of any prior agreement."

memorialize (= to preserve the memory of; to supply the memorial of) is a word of great seriousness in lay contexts ⟨to *memorialize* the plight of European Jews in World War II⟩. In legal writing, by contrast, it is used in far more mundane contexts: "A plea agreement letter *memorialized* the respective promises of the witness and the government."/ "According to the district court, the parties intended the paragraph *memorializing* their agreed right to cease option payments only to establish a right of succession to partnership interests."

mendacity; mendicity. The former is deceptiveness, the latter beggarliness.

mens rea; actus reus. These dovetailing TERMS OF ART are basic to criminal law. *Actus reus* = the element of conduct in a crime that must be proved to secure a conviction, as opposed to the mental state of the accused (i.e., the *mens rea*) (*CDL*). Specifically, *mens rea* = the state of mind that the prosecution must prove a defendant to have had at the time of committing a crime in order to secure a conviction (*CDL*).

mental attitude is a common REDUNDANCY. E.g., "What lifts ordinary negligence into gross negligence is the *mental attitude* [read *mental state*] of the defendant."

mercantile is a FORMAL WORD that is equivalent to *commercial.*

merchantable. See **marketable.**

merciament. See **amercement.**

mercy killing. See **euthanasia.**

meretricious (= alluring by false show) has not lost its strong etymological connection with the Latin word for "prostitute" (*meretrix*). A *meretricious marriage* is one that involves either unlawful sexual connection or lack of capacity on the part of one party. E.g., "If he is right in his contention that the respondent is a man, the ceremony of marriage in this case was in fact, if not in intention, a mere sham and the resulting 'marriage' not merely a void but a *meretricious* marriage, which could not in any circumstances give rise to anything remotely matrimonial in

character." (Eng.) For a humorous misuse of the word, see MALAPROPISMS.

merger; consolidation. These terms are distinct in denoting types of corporate restructuring. In a *merger*, one company is absorbed by another, the latter retaining its own name, identity, articles of incorporation, and bylaws, and acquiring all the assets, liabilities, and powers of the absorbed company, which ceases its separate existence. In a *consolidation*, the corporations that are absorbed into a new entity lose their previous identities to form a new corporation.

merge together is a REDUNDANCY. See **together.**

merit takes the preposition *in* or *to*, not *of*. "There is no *merit of* [read *merit to*] this contention."

meritorious is usually used of parties' claims in the U.S., and not of the parties themselves. This restriction does not hold in G.B.: "There are no doubt a considerable number of cases in which an *unmeritorious* defendant escapes and a *meritorious* plaintiff suffers hardship because of his actions being statute-barred owing to bad advice on the law from his trade union or solicitor." (Eng.)

merits is often used as an ellipsis for *merits of the case* (= the substantive considerations to be taken into account in making a decision, in contrast to extraneous or technical points, esp. of procedure), as in the phrase *trial on the merits.*

mesalliance; misalliance. The French word *mesalliance* = a marriage with a social inferior; a morganatic marriage. *Misalliance* is best kept distinct in the senses (1) "an improper alliance" or (2) "a marriage in which the partners are ill-suited for each other." A *mesalliance* /*may-zahl-yahns*/ may be a happy marriage, but a *misalliance* /*mis-ă-lI-ăns*/ never is.

mesne /*meen*/ has two important senses in the law. Usually the word is used in historical contexts. In feudal contexts, a *mesne lord* is one who holds an estate of a superior lord. The estate of a mesne lord was termed the *mesnalty.* The *OED* notes that *mesne tenant* is "inaccurately used to denote one who holds of a mesne lord."

Mesne may also signify "occurring or performed at a time intermediate between two dates" (*OED*). Thus *mesne profits* are the profits of an estate received by a tenant in wrongful possession between two dates. E.g., "The court has the power of allowing the verdict to be given for *mesne profits.*" *Mesne process* = all process issued between the commencement of a lawsuit by the initial writ or pleading and the termination of the suit. E.g., "The writ upon which the plaintiff was arrested on *mesne process* was of no effect."

Messrs. is the abbreviation for *messieurs*, the plural of the French *monsieur.* In English it acts as the plural of *Mr.*

messuage = a house and its associated garden, outbuildings, and orchard (*CDL*). If the term is used with the degree of particularity specified in its definition, then it may be justified in legal contexts. Often, however, one senses that it is a highfalutin LEGALISM for *house.* E.g., "The curtilage is a garden, yard, field, or piece of void ground lying near and belonging to the *messuage.*" (Eng.)

metalaw is a twentieth-century NEOLOGISM meaning "a hypothetical legal code based on the principles underlying existing legal codes and designed to provide a framework of agreement between diverse legal systems (orig. conceived as between terrestrial and possible extraterrestrial beings)" (*OED Supp.*). The word, then, has a specific sense; it should not be used in vague, half-sensical ways.

METAPHORS. *Metaphor* is a figure of speech in which one thing is called by the name of something else, or is said to be that other thing. Unlike with *similes*, which use *like* or *as*, metaphorical comparison is implicit rather than explicit. Skillful use of metaphor is one of the highest attainments of writing; graceless and even aesthetically offensive use of metaphors is one of the commonest scourges of writing, and especially of legal writing. Those who use metaphors unrestrainedly and ineffectively almost always fancy themselves supreme stylists; hence the problem of educating readers on the uses and abuses of metaphor is a delicate one, for the worst offenders are likely to believe they know more than the would-be educator. Herewith an attempt nevertheless to educate.

A. Mixed and Mangled Metaphors. Lord Keith of Avonholm has shrewdly addressed the use of metaphors in legal writing: "A graphic phrase, or expression, has its uses even in a law report and can give force to a legal principle, but it must be related to the circumstances in which it is used." *White and Carter Councils, Ltd. v. McGregor,* [1962] A.C. 413, 438 (H.L.). The Lord Justice displayed a great deal of insight in that passage, for the *vehicle* of the metaphor (i.e., the literal sense of the metaphorical language) must be consonant with the *tenor* of the metaphor (i.e., the ultimate, metaphorical sense), which is to say the means must fit the end. To illustrate the distinction between the vehicle and the tenor of a metaphor, in the statement *That lawyer's brief is a patchwork quilt without discernible design,* the composition of the brief is the tenor, and the quilt is the vehicle. It is the comparison of the tenor with the vehicle that makes or breaks a metaphor.

A writer would be ill-advised, for example, to use rustic metaphors in a discussion of the problems of air pollution, which is essentially a problem of the bigger cities and outlying areas. Following are two characteristic specimens in which the vehicle of the metaphor is mismatched with the tenor: "By their very nature, the assumptions on which we proceed today cannot be cast in stone." (Things can be *cast* in iron or clay, but not in stone, though one may cast stones and things may be etched in stone.) / "If money drives the program, paperwork provides the tinder." (*Tinder* must start something, inflame it—paperwork is an ongoing and usu. a dull process.)

Yet the greater problem in use of metaphors is that one metaphor should not crowd another. The purpose of an image is to fix the idea in the reader's or hearer's mind; if disparate images appear in abundance, the audience is left confused or sometimes, at the writer's expense, knee-slapping. E.g., "*On the one hand,* the contract between the two is a *bipartite umbilical cord fed* by Medicare and Medicaid funds such that Lifetron can be properly termed a recipient of federal financial assistance. . . . *On the other hand,* the *parameters limned* by the Supreme Court *constrain* us to hold that the actions of this private defendant cannot be fairly attributed to the state." *Frazier v. Board of Trustees,* 765 F.2d 1278, 1295 (5th Cir. 1985). This cascade of metaphors bothers the intelligent reader far more than it helps him. In fact, they make no sense: umbilical cords feed, they are not fed;

and exactly what shape a bipartite umbilical cord would assume we have no idea, esp. if it is (rather grotesquely) resting on a hand.

Badly used metaphors are more forgivable in oratory than in writing, for with the latter the perpetrator can be charged with malice aforethought. Oratorical falls from grace are legion. Some time ago a newspaper article collected some of the oratorical gems of Michigan legislators. E.g., "This bill goes to the very heart of the moral fiber of the human anatomy."/ "From now on, I am watching everything you do with a fine-toothed comb." The following classic example comes from a speech by Boyle Roche in the Irish Parliament, delivered in about 1790: "Mr. Speaker, I smell a rat. I see him floating in the air. But mark me, sir, I will nip him in the bud." (Quoted by Simon, *English Idioms from the Law*, 76 Law Q. Rev. 283, 287 (1960).) Perhaps the supreme example of the comic misuse of metaphor occurred in the speech of a scientist who referred to "a virgin field pregnant with possibilities."

Legal *writers* must not play fast and loose with their images; they are not, like their speaking counterparts, to be forgiven so easily. To use metaphors badly in prose is amateurish and ultimately embarrassing. Writers should use metaphors sparingly, should wait for the aptest moments, elsewhere using a more straightforward style. The disadvantages in not doing so are easily enough demonstrated. The reader who finishes this paragraph, and occasionally rereads it, is likely never to acquire the bad habit himself, although he may become increasingly dyspeptic: "There are but two *conduits* or *cables*, the statutes of wills, and of descents and distributions, by which the *Grim Reaper* may at the moment of and *by the stroke of his scythe flash* the transfer and transmission of property and estate to the quick from the dead." (The Grim Reaper flashes his scythe by means of a conduit or cable?)/ "Although Sutter has *clothed* her complaint in the *garb* of a civil-rights action, we agree with the district court that her claim *boils down* to a demand for custody of the child." (A complaint clothed in a certain garb is boiled down?)/ "We need not explore the *full depths* of those issues, however. Our case may be resolved on two *narrower grounds.*" (One might, presumably, avoid full depths by standing on narrow grounds, but not on narrower grounds. Narrower than

what?)/ "The court has a *voracious appetite* for judicial activism in its fourth amendment jurisprudence, at least when it comes to restricting the constitutional rights of citizens." (Do judges who restrict constitutional rights of citizens feed on judicial activism? The metaphor makes no sense.)/ "Equal protection has become a *stout shield* to protect against the discriminatory *bite* of governmental classification." (What does a stout shield look like? Short and fat? And are shields ordinarily, or ever, used against biting attackers?)/ "To assume competency is to let the *enigmas* of psychology *breathe* our *miasmic* decree." (How do *enigmas* breathe miasmas?)/ "The rules of offer and acceptance have a *grip on the vision* and indeed on the affections held by no other rules of law, real or pseudo." (One cannot *grip* a *vision*.)/ "There is a long leap between a public right under the first amendment to attend trials and a public right under the first amendment to see a given trial televised. It is a leap that is not supported by history." (What leaps are supported by history?)/ "The legal foundation upon which *Schneckloth* rides is fiction." (A case does not "ride upon" a foundation, esp. a fictional one.)

Some dormant metaphors come alive in contexts in which the user had no intention of revivifying them. The writer must sensitize himself to these dormant metaphors. Yet another pitfall for the unwary is the cliché-metaphor that the writer renders incorrectly. E.g., things may be *stretched to the breaking point,* but not: "Cases that take years to prepare, involve reams of documents and hundreds of hours of depositions, and require weeks or months to try have *taxed* the resources of our judicial system to the *breaking point.*" See SET PHRASES & ILLOGIC (D).

B. Legal Metaphors. The legal idiom abounds in special metaphors not used elsewhere. For example, statutes of limitation are said to *run*, plaintiffs *shoulder* the burden of proof, plaintiffs have *clean* or *unclean hands*, defendants are sometimes *insulated* from liability, agents may be *clothed* with the *mantle* of apparent authority, we have suits to *quiet* title, government action may have a *chilling effect* on first amendment rights, and we may sue to remove a *cloud* on title. (See CLICHÉS.) These are dormant rather than active metaphors; originally they were creatively expressive, whereas now they are merely expressive. When used with other metaphors, however, they may clash; hence writers must try to be sensitive to the compatibility of dormant with active metaphors.

C. The Overwrought Metaphor. Extended metaphors have been out of fashion for more than a century. The most we can tolerate nowadays is the two-part metaphor: "We are faced with the further problem of *fitting the foot* of modern-day usage and understanding of gifts of intangible personal property through survivorship arrangements *into the rigid shoe* of common-law principles." Even that type of sustained metaphor strikes most readers as facile. Here are more examples of metaphorical surfeit: "Notwithstanding Golemis's alarming *diagnosis* of the *maladies* . . . the ordinance has caused, he has come to the wrong place for an immediate *antidote.* The plaintiff's present effort to use a federal venue as an *emetic* against the municipal action which (in his view) has tainted the *eupepsia* of his property rights cannot be *swallowed.* . . . [H]e must look to the Rhode Island courts for a *cure.*" *Golemis v. Kirby*, 632 F.Supp. 159, 164-65 (D.R.I. 1985)./ "Summary judgment is a *potent weapon*, and courts must be mindful of its *aims* and *targets* and beware of *overkill* in its use."/ "We find no such *hybrid* instrument, with its *dual personality*, self-executing and shifting gears, *chameleon characteristics* and *Phoenix-like qualities* as yet unknown to the law."/ "It is an error in one of these findings that *tars* the finding of likelihood of confusion with the *brush* of clear error."

metes and bounds; lines and corners. Both terms are used in deeds and surveys to describe the territorial limits of property; the method of measurement is by distances and angles from designated landmarks and in relation to adjoining properties. The more familiar phrase is *metes and bounds.*

methodology is frequently misused for *method.* Correctly used, *methodology* means "the science or study of method." Here are examples of the misuse. "Because this case involves the role of depreciation rates and *methodologies* [read *methods*] in determining the revenue requirements of a regulated utility, we begin by briefly reviewing certain basic principles of regulatory ratemaking."/ "The recent decision in *Chevron* elaborates on these principles and sets out the appropriate *methodology* [read *method*] for ascertaining whether

to afford deference to an agency's construction of its governing statute."/ "The passage enumerating the factors was meant to be an expression of the *methodology* [read *method*] to be used in deciding whether an activity should be held to be within the reach of that statute's imposition of liability."

Methodology is correctly used in the following example; the sentence was hard to come by: "Writing in a time in which *methodology in the social sciences* [i.e., the study of method in the social sciences] has become the prevailing approach, Professor von Mehren speaks of comparative study of law rather than of comparative law." (R. Pound)

mid; midst.   See **amidst.**

midwife, v.t.; **midwive.** The first is the preferred form. E.g., "This may happen when a writing judge believes with heart and soul that his position is right, but he knows that his majority is shaky; here persuasiveness must *midwive* [read *midwife*] the opinion if it is to come into existence at all."

mien (= demeanor, appearance, bearing) usually carries connotations of formidableness ⟨his forbidding mien⟩. The word is pronounced /**meen**/.

milieu is sometimes misspelled *mileau.* See, e.g., *New England Patriots Football Club, Inc. v. University of Colorado*, 592 F.2d 1196, 1198 (1st Cir. 1979). The plural *milieus* is preferable to *milieux.*

military testament.   See **oral will.**

militate.   See **mitigate.**

millenium, -ia, -iums.   The preferred plural is *-ia* in the AmE, and *-iums* in BrE; but either is acceptable on both sides of the Atlantic. See PLURALS (A).

mimic,   v.t., makes *mimicking* and *mimicked.*

mind and memory is a common DOUBLET ⟨of sound mind and memory⟩ in the context of judging testamentary capacity. Mellinkoff calls it "a snatch of confusing nonsense. . . . As in England, American lawyers have long recognized that they were using *memory* here in a special way, in the sense of understanding or mind, and that *mind and memory* did no more for testamentary capacity than *mind* alone." D. Mellinkoff, *The Language of the Law* 333, 335 (1963).

The snare lies in failing to recognize the phrase as an archaic doublet, and in misunderstanding it as setting forth independent criteria for judging testamentary capacity, since historically *mind = memory*. Especially in writing to be read by laymen (as in jury instructions), the second half of this doublet should be avoided. As the law is currently understood, one may be very forgetful and still be "of sound mind and memory." *Sound mind* is quite sufficient, and far less confusing.

MINGLE-MANGLE, known in erudite circles as *macaronism, soraismus,* or *cacozelia,* was a common vice of language in early English opinions. It consists in English larded with Latin or French, as in the following example from *Weaver v. Ward,* decided by the King's Bench in 1616: "The defendant pleaded . . . that he was . . . a trained soldier in London, of the band of one Andrews captain; and so was plaintiff, and that they were skirmishing with their musquets charged with powder for their exercise in re militari, against another captain and his band; and as they were so skirmishing, the defendant casualiter et per infortunium et contra voluntatem suam, in discharging his piece, did hurt and wound the plaintiff, which is the same, etc. absque hoc, that he was guilty aliter sive alio modo." Hob. 134, 80 Eng. Rep. 284.

For modern legal readers, mingle-mangle makes for fascinating, if not entirely comprehensible reading; following is another Latin-English example, this also from a well-known torts case: "Trespass quare vi & armis clausum fregit, & herbam suam pedibus conculcando consumpsit in six acres. The defendant pleads, that he hath an acre lying next the said six acres, and upon it a hedge of thorns, and he cut the thorns, and they ipso invito fell upon the plaintiff's land." *The Case of the Thorns,* 6 Ed. 4, Mich. 7a, pl. 18 (1466) (summarized thus in *Bessey v. Olliot & Lambert,* T.Raym. 467 (1681)).

English-French was another mongrel dialect of the law: One early report referred to a prisoner being sentenced who "ject un Brickbat a le dit Justice que narrowly mist, & pur ceo immediately fuit Indictment drawn per Noy envers le prisoner, & son dexter manus ampute & fix al Gibbet sur que luy mesme im-mediatement hange in presence de Court." (Quoted in Pollock, *A First Book of Jurisprudence* 301 (4th ed. 1918), from Dyer's Reports 188b (1688).) See LAW LATIN & LAW FRENCH.

minify. See **minimize**.

minim (= something minute) is sometimes used in the context of the maxim *de minimis non curat lex.* E.g., "The *minim* of the injury here obscures and tempts neglect of the importance of the issue." See **de minimis**.

minima. See **minimum**.

minimal; minimum, adj. Both words are used adjectivally, *minimum* as an attributive adjective in phrases such as *minimum wage.* If there is a valid nuance distinguishing these two adjectival forms, it is that *minimal* = few, little, smallest ⟨with minimal disturbance⟩ ⟨minimal support⟩ ⟨minimal objections⟩, whereas *minimum,* adj., = consisting in the fewest necessary things, or the least acceptable or lawful amount ⟨minimum contact as a basis for jurisdiction⟩ ⟨minimum wage⟩. E.g., "Most statutes set up *minimum* requirements with respect to the corporate name."/ "Congress accommodated state fears by allowing the states to retain *minimal* residency requirements." See **maximum**.

minimize; minify. These words have distinct meanings, and the latter is too much neglected. Properly, *minimize* = to keep to a minimum, and *minify* = to belittle, degrade; to represent something as smaller than it really is. *Minimalize* is not a word.

minimum, n. Pl. *minima.* E.g., "The deprivation of his protected property interest was accomplished without adherence to due process *minimums* [read *minima*]."/ "The courts must recognize broad administrative discretion whether to implement procedures above the *minima* required by Congress." See **maximum**.

minions of the law is a CLICHÉ referring to policemen or other law enforcement officers.

miniscule is one of the commonest misspellings in legal texts. The correct spelling is *minuscule.* E.g., "The selling shares owned a *miniscule* [read *minuscule*] proportion of the outstanding shares." The word derives from the word *minus,* and has nothing to do with the prefix *mini-.*

minister. See **administer.**

minuscule. So spelled. See **miniscule.**

minutia is the rare singular of the plural *minutiae,* which should always take a plural verb.

mirandize (= to read an arrestee his rights under *Miranda v. Arizona*) has become common as police-officer slang in the U.S.; it is therefore coming to be adopted by some criminal lawyers, and even judges. E.g., "First, defendant claims that the trial court erred in ruling inadmissible his exculpatory statements made to the officer after defendant was arrested and *Mirandized.*" *People v. Barrick,* 654 P.2d 1243, 1253 (Cal. 1982) (in bank). Surely, though, it is a blemish in place of some acceptable periphrasis, such as *to read* (an arrestee) *his Miranda rights.*

misalliance. See **mesalliance.**

misappropriate; appropriate, v.t. The former means "to apply (as another's money) dishonestly to one's own use." E.g., "It was held to be gross negligence for an administratrix to permit an attorney in fact to handle an estate for nine years without an accounting and settlement, during which time he *misappropriated* funds."/ "If he took title in his own name in bad faith, intending to *misappropriate* the property, he is liable for the full amount of the mortgage and interest thereon."

Appropriate has a more neutral connotation, although, in meaning "to take from a particular person or organization for a particular purpose," it is tinged with some of the negative connotations made explicit in *misappropriate. Appropriate* is the nonaccusatory term. See **appropriate** & **embezzle.**

misbelief. See **disbelief.**

mischievious is a common misspelling and mispronunciation of *mischievous.* Cf. **grievous.**

misdemeanant (= one who has been convicted of a misdemeanor) is the analogue of a *felon.* But unlike *felon,* it is little known outside the law. E.g., "Unlike with the *misde-*

meanant only once convicted, we are not prepared to summarily conclude that the offender who repeats such conduct after initial prosecution and conviction does not represent a substantial danger to society." Whether *convicted misdemeanant* is a REDUNDANCY is a close question; surely most legal readers would not think that it is: "A prosecutor clearly has a considerable stake in discouraging convicted *misdemeanants* from appealing and thus obtaining a trial de novo in the Superior Court."

Nevertheless, the senses given in the *OED* and *W3* suggest that *misdemeanant* is not properly used of one suspected of or charged with a misdemeanor, as opposed to one who has been convicted: "The better rule seems to be that an officer is not justified in killing a mere *misdemeanant* [read *suspected misdemeanant*] to effectuate his arrests."

The *OED* includes also the lay sense "a person guilty of misconduct," but legal writers should avoid using this technical term in this ambiguously broad sense.

misdemeano(u)r. The *-our* is the British spelling, *-or* the American. (See -OR, -OUR.) The word is archaically spelled *misdemesnors,* as in Blackstone: "These become either right or wrong, just or unjust, duties or *misdemesnors,* according as the municipal legislator sees proper, for promoting the welfare of the society, and more effectually carrying on the purposes of civil life."

misdoubt, equivalent to *doubt,* is an unnecessary and confusing ARCHAISM.

misfeasance. See **malfeasance.**

misfeasor (= one who commits a misfeasance) is the correct agent noun, but it is little used.

misinformation. See **disinformation.**

mislaid property. See **lost property.**

mislead. See **lead.**

misnomer (= the use of a wrong name) in law may mean "a mistake in naming a person or place," whereas in nonlegal contexts it usually refers to a misdescription of a thing. E.g., "A *misnomer* of the plaintiff in the petition does not ordinarily affect the rule that the running of the statute of limitations is interrupted by the filing of a suit."

MISPLACED MODIFIERS. When using participial forms (and especially when beginning a sentence with an *-ing* phrase), one must be sure that the noun introducing the clause that follows is what the participle modifies. Hence the preceding sentence would be incorrect if it read: "When using participial forms . . . , the noun in the main clause must be modified by the participle"—because this construction suggests that a *noun* (as opposed to a writer) can "use" a *participle*. Here is another example: "*After reading* that case, *the initial impulse* of the reader might well be to nominate it for the most arbitrary equal protection decision in recent times." Note the problem that remains here if we change the main clause to "the reader's initial impulse," where *impulse*, not *reader*, is still improperly the subject of the clause. Some of the pitfalls in this area are treated under DANGLERS.

The problem often crops up where the writer inserts a passive verb phrase after an introductory participial phrase. E.g., "In applying the intermediate standard of review, *the challenged statute must be analyzed* [read *the court must analyze the challenged statute*] to determine whether it furthers a substantial state interest."/ "In determining whether a foreign corporation should be required to defend itself in a suit in Texas arising out of a contract between it and a Texas corporation, *each case must be decided* [read *the courts must decide each case*] on its own facts." The problem is easily remedied by making certain that an *actor* or *agent* appears in the main clause, and that this actor or agent is the one *doing* something in the participial phrase.

Following is a spate of examples of some misuses to which English sentences are susceptible. Brief comments (in parentheses) are appended before each sentence is recast in an improved form: "Of the three persons involved, the entire loss fell upon the only one who was himself free from all negligence." (What is the relationship between *the three persons involved*, the *loss* incurred, and the degree of *negligence*?) [Read *Of the three persons involved, the only one to incur loss was the one free from all negligence.*]

"Without alleging fraud, accident, or mistake, the writing must be the entire contract and parol evidence must be excluded." (It is not the *writing* that alleges, but the person who seeks to have parol evidence admitted.) [Read *Unless one alleges fraud, accident, or mistake, the writing must be the entire contract and parol evidence must be excluded.*]

"Awaiting the uncertainties as to quantum of damages, the delay in recovery may increase them." (The *delay* awaits *uncertainties*?) [Read *By awaiting (the resolution of all?) uncertainties as to quantum of damages, one may increase, by the delay, the damages incurred.*]

"No discussion of the subject would be complete without an analysis of *Dalcan v. Dalcan*; read literally, the Texas Supreme Court addresses only two issues in that case." (What is read *literally*? *Dalcan v. Dalcan*, or *the Texas Supreme Court*?) [Read *No discussion of the subject would be complete without an analysis of* Dalcan v. Dalcan; *read literally, that Texas Supreme Court case addresses only two issues.*]

"Having determined that none of the appellants' complaints presents any reversible error, the judgment of the district court is affirmed." (The *judgment* has determined that there is no *reversible error*?) [Read *Having determined that none of the appellants' complaints presents any reversible error, we affirm the judgment of the district court.*]

"Kast argues that, having found CPL 2.25B to be a procedural rule, we should nevertheless not give effect to the APA's procedural-rules exception from the informal rulemaking requirements." (*Having* can here look either way: to *Kast* or to *we*. See JANUS-FACED TERMS.) [Read *Kast argues that, even though we have found CPL 2.25B to be a procedural rule, we should not give effect to the APA's procedural-rules exception to the informal rulemaking requirements.*]

"Treating the papers whereon the appeal was taken as a petition for writ of certiorari, certiorari is denied." (Is it the *certiorari* that does the *treating*?) [Read *Treating the papers whereon the appeal was taken as a petition for writ of certiorari, we deny certiorari.*]

"Having held that the commission had the power and authority to pass the order, and that such action was not arbitrary or an abuse of discretion, it must follow that this is a suit against the state that should be dismissed." (What *it* was it that *held*?) [Read *Having held that the commission had the power and authority to pass the order, and that such action was not arbitrary or an abuse of discretion, the court must dismiss this suit against the state.*]

"Applying the rule to this case, plaintiff was arrested on a facially valid warrant and she has therefore alleged no deprivation of a right secured by the Constitution and laws of the United States." (The court, not the *plaintiff*, applies *the rule to this case*.) [Read *In applying the rule to this case, we hold that the plaintiff was arrested on a facially valid warrant and therefore had no ground to allege deprivation of a right secured by the Constitution and laws of the United States*.]

"The record contains ample evidence to support the jury's verdict; synopsizing, plaintiffs offered evidence that attributed price increases to price-fixing." (The court does the *synopsizing*, not the *plaintiffs*.) Actually, this sentence needs no participle—see the rewrite. [Read *The record contains ample evidence to support the jury's verdict. In short, the plaintiffs offered evidence that attributed price increases to price-fixing*.]

"Paraphrasing the opinion of Judge Vann in *Tabor v. Hoffman*, the fact that an inspection of plaintiff's models may be by fair means does not justify obtaining the same by unfair means." (The *fact* does not do the *paraphrasing*.) [Read *To paraphrase the opinion of Judge Vann in* Tabor v. Hoffman, *the fact that an inspection of the plaintiff's models may be by fair means does not justify obtaining the same information by unfair means*.]

"Reasoning that 4,000 acres were, as both parties agreed, cleared by July 1970 as required, and that the lease also required a minimum of 700 acres to be cleared 'each year thereafter,' the contractual obligation mathematically had to be completely performed by July 1975." (The *contractual obligation* does not engage in *reasoning*.) [Read *Reasoning that 4,000 acres were, as both parties agreed, cleared by July 1970 as required, and that the lease also required a minimum of 700 acres to be cleared 'each year thereafter,' we have calculated that the contractual obligation mathematically had to be completely performed by July 1975*.]

misprision. In legal usage, this word usually means "concealment of treason or of felony by one not participating in the treason or felony." The phrase in which it most commonly occurs is *misprision of a felony*. The word may also refer, however, to seditious conduct itself or to an official's failure to perform duties of public office. More popularly, *misprision* = misunderstanding, mistake.

misremember means "to remember incorrectly," not "to forget."

Mr. See **Messrs.**

mistreat; maltreat. Most writers on usage have held that there is a difference between these terms. "To *mistreat*," write the Evanses, "is to treat badly or wrongly. The word suggests a deviation from some accepted norm of treatment and a deviation always towards the bad. To *maltreat*, to abuse, to handle roughly or cruelly, is to mistreat in a special way. The words are often used interchangeably (Horwill believes that Americans prefer *mistreat* and English *maltreat*), but *maltreat* is usually restricted to the rougher forms of mistreating." B. Evans & C. Evans, *A Dictionary of Contemporary American Usage* 302 (1957).

mistress. See **common-law wife.**

mitigatable is incorrect for *mitigable*. See -ATABLE.

mitigate; militate. *Mitigate* = to make less severe or intense; *militate* = to exert a strong influence. Here *mitigate* is correctly used: "In England, the power to *mitigate* the severity of the strict law was originally vested in the king."

Mitigate against is incorrect for *militate against*. It is a surprisingly common error: "[T]his factor *mitigates* [read *militates*] against immediate review." *Midway Manufacturing Co. v. Omni Video Games, Inc.*, 668 F.2d 70, 72 (1st Cir. 1981)./ "The reasons that *mitigate* [read *militate*] against giving the sender of a letter the type of blanket protection afforded to the author of a literary manuscript are even stronger when applied to his heirs."/ "By putting this gloss on a particularly restrictive statute, a court may contrive to retain the ancient ability of equity to *mitigate* [read *militate*] against a grossly unfair application of the statute itself." *Militate against* is perfectly acceptable: "If the obvious facts *militate against* such an intention as expressed in the document, the court can act upon the real intention as found by the court." (Eng.)

In law, *militate* (= to have force) often takes *for* or *in favor of* as well as *against*. The *OED* states that this use is rare, but today it is common in legal writing: "He argues that the same values that do not require exhaustion of state remedies *militate in favor of* his contention that the Board's denial of his fitness be regarded as an administrative determination."/ "Factors are listed which *militate for* and *against* construing such a provision as creating a determinable fee."/ "These considerations *militate in favor of* academic freedom at colleges and universities." *Militate toward* is unidiomatic: "Every incentive deriving from this decision would militate *toward* [read *in favor of*] the physicians' giving these tests."

mitigatory, -tive, -tional. The first is the preferred form.

mobocracy; ochlocracy. The latter is the better word in formal prose for "mob rule"; the former is a MORPHOLOGICAL DEFORMITY. *Ochlocracy* has four centuries of use behind it, *mobocracy* but two. *Mobocracy* retains a jocular overtone.

mockery. See **make a mockery.**

modernly (= in modern times) is accurately described by the *OED* as being "now rare"; more precisely, it might have stated "now rare, except in law." E.g., "*Modernly*, it is doubtful that *McCardle* would be sustained."/ "*Modernly*, the potential numerosity and severity of actions involving drinking drivers has become too serious to be ignored."/ "Chancery has ceased for long ages to issue new writs whereby supposed wrongs could be cured; such objectives are *modernly* to be accomplished by legislation."

MODIFIERS, MISPLACED. See MISPLACED MODIFIERS.

modus operandi (= a method of operating; a manner of procedure) is often a high-falutin substitute for *method.* Yet it is well established. Pl. *modi operandi.*

moiety. *Moiety,* a legal and literary ARCHAISM, does not mean "a small segment or portion," as some writers assume. Properly, it means "half." This word should be part of the lawyer's recognition vocabulary, but not of one's working vocabulary, for *half* is the preferable and ordinary word. E.g., "We believe that in contributing the use of his *moiety* [read *half*] in the automobile, he was in fact furnishing the automobile to Clarice, a member of his family."/ "The testator devised lands to his wife for life, and at her death one to his

heirs and the other *moiety* [read *half*] to his wife's heirs, as she might appoint."

moment in time, at this, is pomposity for *now,* or sometimes *today* and *nowadays.*

momentarily = for a moment. It does not, correctly, mean "in a moment." Cf. **presently.**

momento is a misspelling of *memento,* q.v.

monarchi(c)al. *Monarchial* is a NEEDLESS VARIANT of *monarchical,* the usual form.

monet(ar)ize. The longer form is incorrect for *monetize* (= [1] to put (a metal) into circulation as money; or [2] to give fixed value as currency [*COD*]).

monetary damages or *money damages* is a common REDUNDANCY. See **damage(s).**

moneyed; monied. The former is the correct spelling. See **monies.**

monies is an illogical and misconceived plural that, because it is so common, cannot be oppugned as a gross error. *Moneys* remains, however, the preferred form, used, e.g., in the heading of 18 U.S.C. § 2314 (1982). Likewise, the adjective is *moneyed,* not *monied. Monies* is only as logical as the obsolete plural *attornies.*

monopoly takes *of, on,* or *over.*

monthlong, an invention of the 1960s, is properly one word. E.g., "Onshore, an estimated 8,000 well-wishers braved the bad weather—the first encountered by the entourage since beginning the *monthlong* tour."

moot. A. Adjective. The *OED* lists only the sense "that can be argued; debatable; not decided, doubtful." Hence a *moot point* was classically seen as one that is arguable. A *moot case* was a hypothetical case proposed for discussion in a 'moot' of law students (see (c) below). In the U.S., law students practice arguing hypothetical cases before appellate courts in *moot court.* From that sense of *moot* derived the extended sense "of no practical importance; hypothetical; academic." Hence, "A justiciable controversy is thus distinguished from a difference or dispute of a hypothetical or abstract character, one that is academic or *moot.*"

Today, in the U.S., the predominant sense of *moot* is "having no practical significance," in both legal and nonlegal writing. Bernstein and other writers have called this sense of the word incorrect, but it is now a *fait accompli.* To use *moot* in the sense "open to argument" in AmE today is to create an ambiguity, and to confuse most of one's readers. In England, the transformation in sense has been slower, and *moot* in its older sense retains vitality.

B. Verb. Historically, *moot,* v.t., meant "to raise or bring forward (a point or question) for discussion." That sense is still current in BrE, and in American literary usage. In American legal usage, however, a new sense has taken hold: "to render moot or of no practical significance." Thus, "The settlement did not *moot* the jurisdictional question."/ "These actions presented the *mooted* question of the coverage of the policy."

C. Noun. In England, *moot,* n., has the sense "the discussion of a hypothetical case by students at the Inns of Court for practice; also a hypothetical doubtful case that may be used for discussion" (OED). E.g., "The maxim was never forgotten in the training of the English bar in the *moots* of the Inns of Court, nor in the long wrangling years of oral pleading." This use is unknown in the U.S., although its scent is apparent in *moot court.*

more important(ly). As an introductory phrase, *more important* has historically been considered an elliptical form of "What is more important . . . ," and hence the *-ly* form is thought to be the less desirable. E.g., "This provision, of course, directly conflicts with section 1235(k); *more importantly* [read *more important*], section 1273(a) defeats Montana's right to the funds collected on the ceded strip as much as it defeats that of the tribe."/ "Perhaps *most importantly* [read *most important*], the argument that *Gertz* should be limited to the media misapprehends our cases." Yet arguably, if we may begin a sentence, "Importantly, jurisdiction in the Supreme Court . . . ," we ought to be able to begin it, "*More importantly,* jurisdiction in the Supreme Court. . . ." See SENTENCE ADVERBS.

The ellipsis does not work with less idiomatic phrases. E.g., one would not say: "*More notable,* Holmes wrote this opinion. . . ." *More notably* (as opposed to *More notable*) is called

for in order that the sentence not sound anacoluthic. The same is true of "*More interestingly,* . . . ." Furthermore, if the position of the phrase is changed from the beginning of the sentence in any significant way, the usual ellipsis becomes unidiomatic and *-ly* is quite acceptable: "But neither, and *more importantly* under the *Bradley* analysis, does the statute or the legislative history direct that the statute be applied prospectively only."/ "Second, and *more importantly,* this evidence improperly emphasized a 'reasonable man' standard of knowledge."

more interestingly; more interesting. See SENTENCE ADVERBS & **more important(ly).**

more or less (= somewhat) is often used imprecisely in the sense "some degree of," as here: "Keep in mind also that the phraseology used in an instrument quite commonly is not constructed by the grantor himself; the instrument is drafted by someone with *more or less* legal learning." Less legal learning than the grantor?

more preferable. See ADJECTIVES (A) & **preferable.**

more . . . than. A. Parallel constructions. To create parallel phrasing in the use of this construction, it is often important to repeat the preposition. E.g., "Most civil audits are *more* favorably settled by an open, honest discussion about what the agent wants *than having* [read *than by having*] the attorney treat the agent as the taxpayer's mortal enemy." See PARALLELISM.

B. *More . . . than all.* See OVERSTATEMENT.

more unique. See ADJECTIVES (A).

MORPHOLOGICAL DEFORMITIES are words derived from other languages, usually Latin or Greek, whose morphemes are so put together as to outrage the lending or borrowing language's principles of word formation. Thus one does not combine the inseparable particle *dis-* with nouns to form English verbs (e.g., *dismember*) because it is impermissible by Latin morphology. In Latin, *dis-* was joined only with verbs to form privative verbs (e.g., *disentitle, disregard.*)

Any number of examples of ill-formed words made up of classical morphemes exist in modern English: *breathalyzer, drunkometer, workaholic, urinalysis, abortuary* [a PORTMAN-TEAU WORD for *abortion mortuary*], *prosumerism* [a PORTMANTEAU WORD from *pro-consumerism*], *aborticide,* and on and on. The importance of knowing something about morphology, or how word elements properly compose whole words, is that we can then create and then use NEOLOGISMS that are inoffensive to those who know the English language and other languages. And we can likewise avoid their inescapable opposition to morphological deformities, which refined writers avoid as much as possible. Cf. HYBRIDS.

mors civilis. See **civil death.**

mortgage, n., at common law, was used only of real property. The term *chattel mortgage* originated in AmE in the mid-nineteenth century, after the word *mortgage* had been extended to apply to personalty as well as realty. Even so, in actual usage *mortgage* still preponderantly applies to real rather than to personal property.

The etymology of *mortgage* is uncertain: "Glanvil's explanation of the terminology was that the mortgagee in possession had not merely the land but its profits, and the pledged land was thus dead because its profits were not reducing the debt. Littleton said it was *mort gage* ['dead pledge'] because the pledged land was dead to the borrower if the debt was not paid, and dead to the lender if it was." D. Mellinkoff, *The Language of the Law* 246 (1963).

mortgag(e)or, -er. Coke and Blackstone used the *-or* spelling; the lexicographers Johnson and Webster preferred *-er*, the latter terming *-or* "an orthography that should have no countenance." N. Webster, *An American Dictionary of the English Language* (1828). The *Law Review Quarterly* and many other British publications use *-er*; *-or* predominates in the U.S. The *-eor* spelling is nowhere used today.

mortis causa. See **causa mortis.**

mortmain (lit., "dead-hand") = the condition of lands or tenements held inalienably by an ecclesiastical or other corporation. The term suggests control from the grave, as here in a LOAN TRANSLATION: "The effect of the rule is to invalidate ab initio certain future interests that might otherwise remain in existence for a period of time considered inimical to so-ciety's interest in having reasonable limits to *dead-hand* control and in facilitating the marketability of property."

The *OED* remarks: "It seems probable that 'dead hand' in English legal use is a metaphorical expression for impersonal ownership, and is unconnected with the older feudal use of *manus mortua* to denote the custom by which serfs (and other classes included under the term *homines manus mortuae*) had no power of testamentary disposition, their possessions, if they died without legitimate offspring, reverting to the lord."

most for *very* is a poor use of the term. E.g., "The power of judicial review had a *most* inauspicious beginning." (The adjective *inauspicious* is actually stronger without a modifier; see WEASEL WORDS.) See **very** (A).

most important(ly). See **more important(ly).**

motion in the sense *to move* (as a court) is obsolete. See **move.**

motion in limine should not be hyphenated. See **in limine.**

motive is, as Wigmore has observed, a word with an unfortunate ambiguity. "That which has value to show the doing or not doing of the act is the inward emotion, passion, feeling, of the appropriate sort; but that which shows the probable existence of this emotion is termed—when it is . . . some outer fact—the 'motive.' For example, the prior prosecution of A by B in a suit at law is said to have been a 'motive' for A's subsequent burning of B's house. But in strictness the external fact of B's suit cannot be A's 'motive'; for the motive is a state of mind of A; the external fact does tend to show the excitement of the hostile and vindictive emotion, but it is not identical with that emotion." J. H. Wigmore, *The Science of Judicial Proof* 117 (3d ed. 1937).

movable is the preferred spelling in both AmE and BrE. E.g., "We conclude that a lamp plugged into a socket is a *movable* and may be removed from a residence without violating the mortgage." *Moveable* is chiefly a legal variant, but it should be avoided: "Any words which in a settlement of *moveables* [read *movables*] would be recognized by the law of Scotland as sufficient to create a right or claim in favor of an executor must receive effect if used with reference to lands in Scotland." (Sc.) See **immovable** & ADJECTIVES (B).

movant; mover. *Movant* (= one who makes a motion to the court) is the term most commonly used, appearing throughout the Federal Rules and predominantly in reported cases. E.g., "While the *movant* need not always show a probability of success on the merits, he must present a substantial case on the merits."/ "The court has determined upon undisputed facts that the nonmoving party, rather than the *movant,* is entitled to judgment as a matter of law." *Movent* is an incorrect variant spelling.

Mover, when used in the sense of *movant,* is a NEEDLESS VARIANT. E.g., "We must consider all the evidence—not just that evidence which supports the *nonmover's* [read *nonmovant's*] case—but in the light and with all reasonable inferences most favorable to the nonmoving party."

moveable. See **movable.**

move (that) the court. "I *move the court* to grant a new trial." This construction appears from a logical point of view to be incorrect. Idiom would seem to require: "I *move that the court* grant a new trial." By analogy, one might say: "I hereby *move that we* adjourn," but not "I hereby *move us* to adjourn." Yet the phrase *moving the court* is of long standing in legal language, including this from Chief Justice John Marshall in *Marbury v. Madison*: "At the last term, . . . William Marbury [et al.] severally *moved the court* for a rule to James Madison . . . ." It is incorrect to write *motion the court* in place of *move the court*: "Appellant then *motioned* [read *moved*] *the court* for a new trial." See **motion.**

much. See **many.**

muchly is nowadays considered an illiterate form, though several centuries ago it was not so stigmatized. *Much* is the preferred form in all adverbial contexts. Surprisingly, *muchly* has appeared in reported American opinions.

mulct (= to punish by a fine) is a term rarely encountered outside the law, and very infrequently within it. *Mulct* has the additional sense "to deprive or divest of," and carries pejorative connotations of unmercifulness or deceit. E.g., "The panel opinion also permits a jury to *mulct* the defendant in a def-

amation action of more than compensatory damages."

multifarious. Justice Story defined this term as meaning "improperly joining in one bill distinct matters, and thereby confounding them" (quoted in *OED*). E.g., "Because this ground of error complains of more than one act or incident, it is *multifarious* and preserves nothing for review."/ "No objection has been taken to the bill on the ground of *multifariousness.*" Outside the law, the word means merely "diversified; many and various."

multiparty is defined by the *OED Supp.* as a political term meaning "comprising several parties or members of parties; of an electoral or political system which results in the formation of three or more influential parties." Yet in law, the *party* in this word has come in the U.S. to refer to a party to a lawsuit. E.g., "When the intervention was allowed, the suit became a *multiparty* action within the meaning of Fed. R. Civ. P. 54(b)."

multiplici(t)ous. **A.** Form of the Word. Although both forms (*multiplicitous* and *multiplicious*) have existed in the English language, *W3* states (rather prematurely) that *multiplicious* is now obsolete. (It is the only form listed in the *OED*.) Certainly it is the rarer term, and does not immediately reveal its relationship with the noun *multiplicity.* Nonetheless, *multiplicious* appears in the law reports. See, e.g., *United States v. Wesley,* 748 F.2d 962, 963 (5th Cir. 1984) ("Wesley argues that his convictions . . . are *multiplicious* and violative of the double jeopardy clause of the fifth amendment."); *United States v. Stanfa,* 685 F.2d 85, 88 (3d Cir. 1982) (*multiplicious* used four times in two paragraphs). This word should not be resurrected. We should avoid multiplicitous forms of this word, and hold steady with *multiplicitous.* (When used (as in the previous sentence) for *multiple, multiplicitous* is a pomposity.)

The two forms of the word are susceptible to INELEGANT VARIATION. In a recent opinion both forms are used in consecutive paragraphs: "Even if a single fact pattern were present, the 'different evidence test' . . . would show that the counts in question were not *multiplicitous.* . . . The chief danger raised by a *multiplicious* [read *multiplicitous*] indictment is the possibility that the defendant will receive more than one sentence for a single offense." *United States v. Swaim,* 757 F.2d 1530, 1536–37 (5th Cir. 1985).

B. And *duplicitous*. The distinction is not what one might infer: "An indictment is *multiplicitous* when it charges one offense in several counts. An indictment is *duplicitous* when it charges numerous crimes in a single count." *United States v. Jones*, 648 F. Supp. 241, 242 (S.D.N.Y. 1986) (citations omitted). E.g., "If Lartey has any complaint, it is not that the indictment is *multiplicious* [read *multiplicitous*], but rather that it is *duplicitous*, charging numerous crimes in a single count." *United States v. Lartey*, 716 F.2d 955, 968 (2d Cir. 1983). See **duplicitous**.

multiply is an adverb as well as a verb: "Theresa is a *multiply* handicapped child with severe behavioral problems."

multital. See **paucital**.

muniment = a document (as a deed or charter) preserved as evidence in defense of rights or privileges belonging to a person, family, or corporation. Today this word is most commonly used in the phrase *muniment of title*. E.g., "A trust may not under those circumstances be engrafted upon a deed absolute in its terms because if that were the rule, deeds would no longer be valuable as *muniments of title*."

murder; homicide; manslaughter; man-killing. *Homicide* is the action of unlawfully killing another human being; it is the general legal term. *Murder* is the unlawful killing of a human being with malice aforethought. It is the most heinous kind of criminal homicide. At common law, *murder* was not subdivided; but in most American jurisdictions statutes have created *first-degree murder* and *second-degree murder*, the former referring to the more reprehensible forms of murder. *Manslaughter* is homicide without malice aforethought; it has a lower degree than *murder*. *Man-killing*, q.v., is a nonlegal synonym for *homicide*, used sometimes of nonhuman killers ⟨a man-killing tiger⟩.

muster. The phrase *to pass muster* began as a military term meaning "to undergo review without censure." Lawyers have picked it up especially in the sense of constitutional review. E.g., "*To pass muster*, the classifications must serve important governmental objectives and be substantially related to the achievement of those objectives."/ "The admission of evidence in this case readily *passes muster*."

This SET PHRASE is occasionally mangled: "Such political undertakings cannot *withstand constitutional muster* [read *pass constitutional muster*]." *Past muster* is an ignorant blunder for *pass muster*: "We assume that this explanation would *past muster* [read *pass muster*]."

must needs. See **needs must**.

mutatis mutandis = the necessary changes having been made; taking into consideration or allowing for the changes that must be made. This LATINISM is a useful one in formal prose, for the only English equivalents are far wordier. "What we have said in connection with the counterclaim applies *mutatis mutandis* to his defense to the complaint."/ "More usually and aptly, 'power' is used to mean 'legal power,' the connotation of which latter term is fundamentally different; the same observations apply, *mutatis mutandis*, to the term 'liberty.'"/ "What has thus far been said concerning contracts completed by mail would seem to apply, *mutatis mutandis*, to every type of contract." Cf. **ceteris paribus**.

mute. In nonlegal contexts this word has come to signify "dumb; destitute of the faculty of speech." In law, however, it retains its older use as a synonym of *silent*. E.g., "The petitioners' decision to remain *mute* during the deportability phase of the hearing was an appropriate exercise of their fifth amendment privilege."

MUTE E. In English, an unsounded final *-e-* is ordinarily dropped before the *-ing* and *-ed* inflections, e.g., *create, creating, created; rate, rating, rated; share, sharing, shared*. Exceptions to this rule are verbs with bases ending in *-ee*, *-ye*, and *-oe*: these do not drop the *-e-* before *-ing*, but they do drop it before *-ed*: *agree, agreeing, agreed; dye, dyeing, dyed; shoe, shoeing, shoed*; likewise *singe, singeing, singed*.

The suffix *-able* often causes doubt when it is appended to a base ending in a mute *-e-*. Generally, the *-e-* is dropped when *-able* is added, but a number of exceptions exist in BrE (e.g., *hireable, liveable, nameable, ropeable, saleable, sizeable, unshakeable*). But in BrE, forms such as *blamable, excercisable*, and *finable*, which follow the American rule of dropping the *-e-*, are preferred.

The almost universal exception to the AmE rule of dropping the *-e-* before a vowel is that it should be kept if it is needed to indicate the soft sound of a preceding -g- or -c-, or to distinguish a word from another with a like spelling. E.g., *changeable; hinge, hingeing; trace, traceable.* But even this exception to the rule is not uniform: *lunge* yields *lunging.* Because the given form of a word when inflected is easily forgotten and often the subject of disagreement even among lexicographers, the best course is to keep an up-to-date and reliable dictionary at one's side.

One other difference between AmE and BrE is of interest to legal writers: in AmE, the mute -e- is dropped after -dg- in words such as *acknowledgment, fledgling,* and *judgment,* whereas the -e- is retained in BrE (*acknowledgement, fledgeling,* and *judgement*). British legal writers, however, usually prefer the spelling *judgment.* See **judg(e)ment & pledg(e)or.**

mutual; common. *Mutual* = reciprocal; joint; directed by each toward the other(s). E.g., "This court has held that a contract made *by mutual letters* [read *by the mutual exchange of letters*] was not complete until the letter accepting the offer had been received by the person making the offer." *Common* = shared by two or more. *Friend in common* is preferable to *mutual friend,* although the latter has stuck because of Dickens's novel (the title to which, everyone forgets, came from a sentence mouthed by an illiterate character).

Like *together,* q.v., *mutual* creates any number of redundant expressions. E.g., "We have repeatedly held that a party may not assume successive positions in the course of a suit, or series of suits, with reference to the same fact or state of facts, which are inconsistent with each other, or *mutually contradictory* [read merely *contradictory*]." Some of the more common prolixities with this word are *mutual agreement* and *mutual cooperation.* Redundancies are especially common when *mutual* is used in conjunction with *both;* for instance, *mutually binding on both parties,* or: "An invitee has been described as one who enters on another's land with the owner's knowledge and *for the mutual benefit of both* [read either *for their mutual benefit* or *for the benefit of both*]."

mutually agree is a REDUNDANCY. See **mutual.**

mutually exclusive = each excluding the other. E.g., "It has always been hard to classify all government activity into three, and only three, neat and *mutually exclusive* categories." The phrase must be carefully used.

mutual will; joint will. Both phrases are used of reciprocal wills. A joint will is one document executed by two persons; mutual wills are separate documents.

my considered opinion. See **considered opinion.**

myriad is best used adjectivally, and not as a noun, for the adjectival use is more concise. E.g., "The Constitution does not empower this Court to second-guess state officials charged with the difficult responsibility of allocating limited public welfare funds *among the myriad of* [read *among the myriad*] potential recipients."

myself is best used reflexively, as in "I have harmed *myself* in untold ways," or "I have perjured *myself.*" It may also serve as an intensive: "I *myself* will sue the corporation on behalf of the class of persons harmed." But *myself* should not appear as a substitute for *I* or *me.* Using it thus is thought somehow to be modest, as if the reference to oneself were less direct. But it is no less direct, and the user may unconsciously cause the reader or listener to believe that he intended jocularity; or that he is somewhat doltish. E.g., "After reconsideration, upon appellee's motion for rehearing, Mr. Justice B. and *myself* [read *I*] have reached the conclusion that this court has rendered an improper judgment, and that the motion for rehearing should be granted, and the judgment of the trial court affirmed." (Is it so difficult to say simply, "We have rendered an improper judgment"?) See FIRST PERSON.

MYTH OF PRECISION, THE. "Delusive exactness is a source of fallacy throughout the law." *Lochner v. New York,* 198 U.S. 45, 75-76 (1905) (Holmes, J., dissenting). When attacked for their inscrutable use of language, lawyers have traditionally sought refuge in precision, and often silenced their critics by the invocation of precision. Not everyone has been satisfied, however, by the explanation or excuse that legal language, despite its WOOLLINESS and frequent ugliness, is more precise than the general language. "For this redundancy," wrote Jeremy Bentham early in the nineteenth century in words that still ring true,

for the accumulation of excrementitious matter [i.e. legalese] in all its various shapes . . . [and] for all the pestilential effects that cannot be produced by this so enormous a load of literary garbage,—the plea commonly pleaded . . . is, that it is necessary to *precision*—or, to use the word which on similar occasions they themselves are in the habit of using, certainty.

But a more absolutely sham plea never was countenanced, or so much as pleaded, in either the King's Bench or Common Pleas.

> 3 J. Bentham, *Works* 260 (Bowring ed. 1843) (quoted in D. Mellinkoff, *The Language of the Law* 292 (1963)).

A late nineteenth-century legist wrote, with somewhat less vitriol:

There is an abundance of affected accuracy in the addition of descriptions to distinguish persons and things needing no distinction, and in the expression of immaterial matters; but real accuracy and precision are attained quite as much by the omission of superfluous phrases, by the avoidance of tautology, by correct references and by a strict adherence to the rules of grammar, as by the use of apt words.

> 1 Davidson, *Precedents and Forms of Conveyancing* 23 (4th ed. 1874).

David Mellinkoff has done much in recent years to expose the fallacy of the argument that LEGALESE is precise. He writes:

Lawyers spend more time talking about being precise than others similarly addicted to words—politicians and the clergy, for example. Listening to these discussions about precision, and contrasting their own concern with the indifference of the street, law students and lawyers come to the effortless conclusion that with so much interest in precision, there must be a lot of it around.

> D. Mellinkoff, *The Language of the Law* 293 (1963).

In fact, there is all too little around, as Mellinkoff has so well illustrated, and as a number of entries in this work should demonstrate.

N

naked   is frequently used metaphorically in legal writing in the sense "having nothing that confirms or validates (a thing)." E.g., "The exceptions on this point present a *naked* proposition of law."/ "The plaintiff, having received only the *naked* ownership, never received any income from the property." *Naked trespasser* describes, not one who trespasses unclothed, but a trespasser with absolutely no

claim to be present on the land. "Had A.S. entered upon this land as a *naked trespasser*, without any property right therein, he would have had no basis for a claim of title until the full period of limitation had run." In trademark law, a *naked* license is a license without provision for quality control. For the correlative metaphor, see **clothe.**

nam(e)able.   See MUTE E.

namely   is generally preferable to *viz.* or *to wit,* qq.v.

natural law.   Historically a number of senses have been attributed to this term; today the preponderant sense, esp. in legal contexts, is "a law that determines what is right and wrong and that has power or is valid by nature, inherently, hence everywhere and always." L. Strauss, *Natural Law,* 11 Int'l Encycl. Soc. Sci. 80, 80 (1968). Twentieth-century legal scholars have mostly rejected the notion of natural law on positivist grounds, because genuine scientific knowledge cannot validate value judgments, and natural law is composed entirely of value judgments. The modern user of this term should be aware of the debate surrounding the concept it denotes, and of the generally low regard in which the concept is now held.

natural life.   The common conveyancing phrase *during his natural life* is better rendered *for life* or *as long as he lives.* See **civil death.**

natural person   (= a human being) is unnecessary in place of the defining phrase, except when contrast is made to *juristic person,* q.v.

naught; nought.   These are different spellings of the same word, meaning "nothing." By convention *nought* has come to signify the number zero (0), and *naught* to be used in all nonmathematical contexts in which "nothing" is meant. E.g., "The insurer may be put to the labor and expense of investigation that may, several years later, be found to have been for *naught.*"/ "The appointees in the case at bar have not appealed from the decree under consideration, and thus have evidenced their acceptance of what we have just said, although it sets at *naught* the intent of the donees."

nauseous (= inducing nausea) for *nauseated* is a common error. E.g., "According to his deposition, he was thinking of what he characterized as the 'endless chain of happenings, of mistakes' and 'ugly things' in connection with the funeral when he became *nauseous* [read *nauseated*] and experienced a heavy pressure-type pain in the chest and difficulty in breathing."/ "You won't love me any more, she gasped, *nauseous* [read *nauseated*] above the porcelain bowl."

N.B. is the abbreviation for *nota bene* (= note well; take notice).

near should not be used adverbially in place of *nearly*; that use of the word is dialectal. E.g., "A catastrophe does not seem *near* [read *nearly*] as catastrophic when it is read on the air by a female news broadcaster."

necessaries; necessities. In legal senses, *necessaries* is the usual term for "things that are indispensable (to life)." E.g., "Claims for *necessaries* furnished to the beneficiary of a spendthrift or support trust may be enforced against his trust interest." *Necessities* has the broader sense of "indispensable things," whatever the subject at hand may be.

necessary; necessitous. *Necessary*, the more common word, means "essential." (See **indispensable**.) Almost always used correctly, *necessary* is ill-used when it introduces an infinitive without a *be*-verb preceding it, e.g.: "The only Massachusetts case *necessary to analyze* [read *that it is necessary to analyze* or *that must be analyzed here*] is *Balch v. Stone*, since all other cases from that state followed the *Balch* case without further discussion of its soundness."
  Necessitous = placed or living in a condition of necessity or poverty; hard-up. E.g., "It will be found that where a gift results in mere financial enrichment, a trust has been sustained only when the court found and concluded from the entire context of the will that the ultimate intended recipients were poor or in *necessitous* circumstances."

necessitate (= to make necessary) is often inferior to *require*. Yet *require* cannot always substitute for it: "The ALJ's failure to explain his reason for crediting certain testimony while ignoring more substantial evidence could normally *necessitate* a remand."/ "Appellant knew that his insistence on his right

to represent himself would, perforce, *necessitate* his giving up his right to counsel."

necessities. See **necessaries**.

necessitous. See **necessary**.

NEEDLESS VARIANTS, two or more forms of the same word without nuance or DIFFERENTIATION, and seemingly without even hope for either, teem in the language of the law. They teem in the English language for that matter, especially in the outer reaches of the language that involve technical vocabulary. Unfortunately, the unnecessary coexistence of variant forms, adjectives in *-tive* and *-tory* for example, lead not to precision in technical writing but to uncertainties about authorial intention. (The trusting reader thinks to himself, "The writer used *punitive* on the last page but now has pressed into service *punitory*—does he intend a distinction?")
  "It is a source not of strength," wrote Fowler, "but of weakness, that there should be two names for the same thing [by-forms differing merely in suffix or in some such minor point], because the reasonable assumption is that two words mean two things, and confusion results when they do not" (*MEU1* 373). The confusion is perhaps greatest when the writer who is fond of INELEGANT VARIATION discovers the boundless mutations of form that exist in law: he will write *res judicata* in one paragraph, *res adjudicata* in the next; *a quo* in one sentence, *a qua* in the next; *recusal, recusement*, then *recusation*; and so on.
  "On the other hand," we are advised to take note, "it may be much too hastily assumed that two words do mean the same thing; they may, for instance, denote the same object without meaning the same thing if they imply that the aspect from which it is regarded is different, or are appropriate in different mouths, or differ in rhythmic value or in some other matter that may escape a cursory examination" (*MEU1* 373). Hence the layman or law student should not jump to assume that *necessaries* is uncalled for in place of *necessities*; that *acquittance* = *acquittal*; that *recusancy* is yet another needless variant of the three similar words cited above; that *burglarize* is as good for a British audience as it is for an American one; and so forth. Any number of entries throughout this work attempt to ferret out and discriminate between cognate words that have established or emerging distinctions

and those that seem, at present, to have neither. To the extent possible, words and phrases rightly classifiable as NEEDLESS VARIANTS ought to drop from the language.

need not necessarily is a REDUNDANCY. E.g., "One's misconduct *need not necessarily have* [read *need not have*] been of such a nature as to be punishable as a crime or as to justify legal proceedings of any character."/ "Those injured in accidents would come to understand that matters *need not necessarily* [read *need not*] end with a simple bow and a flourish of the checkbook."

needs must is an idiomatic phrase deriving from Elizabethan English. Its inverted sibling is *must needs*, which is slightly older. In both phrases, *needs* = necessarily. E.g., "White is not satisfied, as bolder activists are, to assert that Justices are not bound by the Constitution; he *needs must* attribute his 'eccentric' view to the Framers."

ne exeat is a LATINISM that has given its name to the writ, no longer widely used, ordering the person to whom it is addressed not to leave the country or the jurisdiction of the court. E.g., "The wife then prayed that a writ of *ne exeat* be issued forthwith to prevent the defendant from leaving the state until he had paid the support arrearages and attorneys' fees."

The name of the writ derives from the Roman-law writ of *ne exeat republica* (= let him not go out from the republic). See *Foote v. Foote*, 140 A. 312, 313 (N.J. Err. & App. 1928). The medieval writ was *ne exeat regno*.

negative, v.t. Today this usage is an ARCHAISM, *negate* having taken over the work formerly handled by the verb *to negative* (= to deny, nullify, or render ineffective). Yet *negative* persists as a verb in the law. E.g., "The defense in each instance is the same: defendant contends that the sales contract *negatived* any warranties."/ "This contention is quite plainly *negatived* by the latter part of the provision." (Eng.)/ "The affirmative action taken by Congress in 1942 *negatives* any inference that otherwise might be drawn from its silence when it reenacted the oath in 1940."/ "Such an interference with a rival trader's right to a free course of trade leads to an almost irresistible inference of an indirect motive, and is therefore—unless the motive is

negatived—a wrongful act as against his right." (Eng.)

For purposes of greater comprehensibility to nonlawyers, *negate* should be adopted as the preferred term. E.g., "His properly filing the tax returns, coupled with his obvious intelligence, *negated* the argument that he had a reasonable belief in the validity of his fifth amendment assertion."/ "The complaint *negates* the existence of a substantial justiciable controversy."

negative, in the. See **affirmative, in the.**

NEGATIVES. A. Double & Triple Negatives. Lawyers have become notorious for their proclivity to pile negative upon negative. The result is sentences that most fellow lawyers have a hard time decoding. E.g., "The order enjoined required the five railroad companies to abstain from refusing to deliver interstate shipments of livestock." (Quoted in F. E. Cooper, *Effective Legal Writing* 29 (1954).)/ "The trial court temporarily enjoined defendant from refusing to supply water service to petitioners' house on account of their not having paid a deposit, without notice and without bond."/ "Notwithstanding anything in subsection (3) of section two of the principal Act, a disablement allowance need not be considered at intervals of not less than three years in any case where the Treasury so directs." (Eng.)/ "Courts should not, by self-imposed impotence, not required by the precedents, be less efficacious."

B. Negative Prefixes. The primary negative prefixes in English are *un-*, *in-* (assimilated in many words to *il-*, *im-*, *ir-*), *non-*, and *anti-*. For purposes of simple negation, *in-* is the most particularized of these prefixes, since it generally goes only with certain Latin nouns, and *non-* is the broadest of them, for it may precede virtually any word. As a general rule, it is best to find the most suitable particularized prefix, and if none is really suitable, then to have recourse to *non-*. (*Anti-*, of course, has the special sense "against.") *Un-* usually precedes those Latin verbs ending in the Anglo-Saxon *-ed* (*unexhausted, undiluted, unsaturated*).

Consistency is often difficult to find with particular roots. For example, *unexhausted remedies* yields *nonexhaustion*, not *unexhaustion*. Likewise, we have *indubitable* but *undoubted*, *irresolute* but *unresolved*, *irrespective* but *unrespected*. From a typographical standpoint, negative prefixes cause trouble with phrasal adjectives, as in *uncross-examined civil deposition.* Roundabout wordings are usually preferable to such telescoping; hence, *a civil deposition in which the witness was not cross-examined.* See **non-.**

C. Periphrastic Negatives. Generally, "We disagree" is preferable to "We do not agree," unless some emphatic form such as the latter is called for in context to rebut an assertion to the contrary. Directness is better than indirectness.

neglectful; neglective. The latter is a NEEDLESS VARIANT that is rare or obsolete.

negligible, -geable. The latter spelling should be avoided.

negligence, -cy. The latter is a NEEDLESS VARIANT. In general usage, *negligence* = carelessness. In legal usage, *negligence* = the failure to exercise the standard of care that the doer as a reasonable man should, by law, have exercised in the circumstances (*OCL*).

negotiable instruments; commercial paper. These terms are not interchangeable. *Commercial paper* is now the more widely used term in the U.S. because of its use in article three of the Uniform Commercial Code. As to the precise distinction, *commercial paper* is the broader term: it may include nonnegotiable as well as negotiable paper, whereas *negotiable instruments* are by definition negotiable ones only.

Generally, a writing is *negotiable* when it is signed by the maker or drawer; contains an unconditional promise or order to pay a sum certain in money, and no other promise, obligation, or power given by the maker or drawer; is payable on demand or at a definite time; and is payable to order or to bearer. The absence of any one of these elements makes commercial paper nonnegotiable.

Negro. See **black.**

neither ... nor. A. Singular or Plural Verb. This construction takes a singular verb where the alternatives are singular or where the second alternative is singular. E.g., "*Neither the speed at which the car was traveling* [read *Neither the car's speed*] nor its operation through a red light *are* [read *is*] enough to make out a case against appellants provided

there was no reckless disregard for the safety of others."/ "At the time of the sale, neither defendant Warren nor Dick *were* [read *was*] aware that the sale was in violation . . . ."/ "Neither the majority nor appellant *cite* [read *cites*] any substantial evidence to the contrary."

B. Number of Elements. These CORRELATIVE CONJUNCTIONS should frame only two elements, not more; though it is possible to find modern and historical examples of *neither . . . nor* with more than two members, such constructions are, in Wilson Follett's words, "short of punctilious." E.g., "The October contract was *neither surrendered, abrogated, nor annulled* [read *was not surrendered, abrogated, or annulled*]."/ "We believe that the California Supreme Court's application of the minimum-contacts test in this case would, if sustained, sanction a result that is *neither fair, just, nor reasonable* [read *not fair, just, or reasonable* or *unfair, unjust, and unreasonable*]."/ "Finding the decision by the ICC to be supported by substantial evidence and *neither arbitrary, capricious, nor an abuse of discretion* [read *not arbitrary, capricious, or an abuse of discretion*], we deny the petitions./ "Because Rummel *neither signed, read, nor heard* [read *Because Rummel did not sign, read, or hear*] the entire document, these notes fail to qualify as a statement under this subsection."

It is, however, possible to use a second *nor* emphatically in framing three elements: "Neither inadvertent failure to provide medical care, *nor* carelessness, *nor* even deliberate failure to conform to the standards suggested by the experts is cruel and unusual punishment."Cf. **either.**

C. *Neither. . . or.* This phraseology is a gross perversion. "What if the intervention is *neither* foreseeable *or* [read *nor*] normal, but it leads to the same type of harm?"/"It appears that the admission was *neither* fraudulent *or* [read *nor*] willful and was due to oversight."/ "That it is not identical with equitable liens is equally clear; for the latter arise out of constructive trusts, and are *neither* a jus ad rem *or* [read *nor.*]"

D. Beginning Sentences with. It is permissible to begin a sentence with *neither* or *nor,* when embarking on yet another negative subject. See **nor.**

nemine contradicente; nemine dissentiente. Both of these LATINISMS mean "without opposition or dissent." The definition itself serves better than either of the recherché main entries.

NEOLOGISMS, or invented words, are to be used carefully and self-consciously. Usually they demand an explanation or justification, for the English language is quite well-stocked as it is. The most obvious neologisms in -IZE, for example, are to be eschewed. New words must fill demonstrable voids, as *conclusory*, a relatively new word, does. If a word is invented merely for the sake of novelty, then it is vexatious.

nepotism is best reserved for the sense "bestowal of official favors upon members of one's family," and not attenuated to refer to any friends or political connections. The root sense of *nepot-* in Latin is "nephew, grandson."

NEUTER FORMS. See SEXISM.

news is a singular noun. "The *news* also *has* an exchange value to one who can misappropriate it."

newsagent. One word.

next friend; guardian ad litem; prochein ami. Technically, an incompetent plaintiff sues by a *next friend*, whereas an incompetent defendant defends by a *guardian ad litem*; but the duties and powers of the representative are identical regardless of the title. *Dacanay v. Mendoza*, 573 F.2d 1075, 1076 n.1 (9th Cir. 1978).

Next friend is to be preferred to the LAW FRENCH *prochein ami*, of which it is a LOAN TRANSLATION. E.g., "By this standard an individual is deemed competent or incompetent to assert his rights for purposes of conferring standing on *next-friend* petitioners."/ "The district court sought merely to clarify that the amount awarded to the minor children would be paid to their parents as their *next friends*." See **prochein ami**.

next of kin. See **heir** (C).

next preceding is an awkward phrase, arguably illogical, that commonly appears in DRAFTING. E.g., "All assurances mentioned herein must be satisfactorily tendered on the day *next preceding* [read *before*] the closing date."/ "Anything *in the next preceding paragraph of this contract* [read *in the paragraph im-*

mediately preceding this one] notwithstanding . . . ."

nexus is the law's learned word for *connection* or *multiple connections*. There is nothing wrong, however, with using it. E.g., "The defendant's *nexus* with this country and with this district is not accidental."

nice question = a close question. In this phrase, as in other similar ones, *nice* takes on the sense "not obvious or readily apprehended; difficult to decide or settle; demanding close consideration or thought" (*OED*). E.g., "The duration of a continuing guaranty presents a *nice question*."/ "It is this nuance, this *nice* distinction, that the lawyer is looking for and that sometimes makes the precedent worth the search."/ "On motion for rehearing, appellant advances one contention requiring comment; it is a *nice* one and fairly debatable."/ "Courts-martial as an institution are singularly inept in dealing with the *nice* subtleties of constitutional law." The usage is not legal so much as learned, but it is common in the law.

nihil ad rem (= irrelevant) serves no useful purpose in the language.

nisi (= not final or absolute) is commonly used in the phrases *rule nisi, judgment nisi,* and *nisi prius*. The last of these refers to the trial court, in which issues are tried before the jury, as opposed to an appellate court. E.g., "Abuse of the opposite side was practiced not alone *at nisi prius* [i.e. at trial], but in the more dignified forum of the appellate court as well, and so widespread and deep-seated did this pernicious practice become that rarely if ever did it call forth a rebuke from the court."/ "A bold attempt is made, by seizing upon an inconsiderate recent utterance of a *justice at nisi prius* [i.e. trial judge], to make out either a case of conflict between the instant case and that of the state courts, or to show that the city's power to pass the tax law in question is shrouded in doubt." Today, *trial court* is undoubtedly more comprehensible to lawyers and laymen alike. See **decree absolute.**

no bill, v.t. See NOUNS AS VERBS.

nocent (= guilty) is obsolete. *Innocent*, the opposite form, is common.

no-compete covenant is an illogical form of *covenant* [or *agreement*] *not to compete* or *non-*

competition covenant [or *agreement*]. It should be avoided in favor of either of these longer phrases. E.g., "It seems reasonably clear that some allocation of the price to a covenant is necessary if a purchaser wants to deduct any amount for a *no-compete covenant* [read *covenant not to compete*]." See **noncompete clause.**

no doubt.   See **doubtless(ly).**

noisome is often misconstrued as meaning "noisy; loud; clamorous." In fact, it means "noxious; malodorous." (Cf. **fulsome.**) The word is related etymologically to *annoy.* Here is a correct use of it: "If the house is to be cleaned, it is for those who occupy and govern it, rather than for strangers, to do the *noisome* work." (Cardozo)

no later than   (= on or before) conveys an important nuance in the language of contracts. It is not equivalent to *before,* which does not include the date specified.

nolens volens   (= willingly or unwillingly) is not a justifiable LATINISM in modern legal prose. E.g., "Correlative to all such legal powers are the legal liabilities in other persons— this meaning that the latter are subject *nolens volens* [read *willingly or unwillingly*] to the changes of jural relations involved in the exercise of A's powers." (Hohfeld) See **willy-nilly.**

nolle prosequi(tur); non prosequitur.
A.   As Noun. The phrase *nolle prosequi* denotes the legal notice of abandonment of suit. *Nolle* is frequently used as an ellipsis for *nolle prosequi.* E.g., "We conclude that the nine-month period between the *nolle* and the defendant's rearrest is not properly chargeable as a pretrial delay for purposes of speedy trial analysis." *State v. Gaston,* 503 A.2d 594, 597 (Conn. 1986).

Nolle prosequitur is an error deriving from confusion with *non prosequitur,* which is the judgment rendered against a plaintiff who does not appear in court to prosecute his case. *Non pros* is the shortened nominal form, here functioning adjectivally: "[A]ppellants contest on appeal the trial court's opening of a *non pros* judgment entered in their favor." *Geyer v. Steinbronn,* 506 A.2d 901, 905 (Pa. Super. 1986).

B.   As Verb. *Nolle prosequi* is only a noun in England, but has two verb forms in the U.S., *nol-pros* and *nolle pros.* The term means "to

abandon a suit or have it dismissed by a nolle prosequi." E.g., "That plaintiff was arrested but never tried, and the charges against him were *nolle prossed.*" The earliest known use occurred in 1878.

Occasionally the phrase *nolle prosequi* is used as a verb in the U.S., although the shorter forms *nol-pros,* or *nolle pros* is more usual. E.g., "Gruskin's decision to permit defendant to admit responsibility for careless driving and to *nolle prosequi* the OUIL [operating a motor vehicle under the influence of intoxicating liquor] charge was an executive function." *People v. Stackpoole,* 375 N.W.2d 419, 424 (Mich. App. 1985).

Nonpros = to enter a non prosequitur against. The past tense form is *nonprossed.* Blackstone wrote *nonpros'd.* This word dates from about 1755.

nolo contendere.   So spelled.

NOMINATIVE ABSOLUTES.   See ABSOLUTE CONSTRUCTIONS.

NOMINATIVE AND OBJECTIVE CASES. One might think that a work of this kind, catering as it does to members of a learned profession, could pass over the differences between subjects and objects in pronouns. The two sentences that follow, however, belie that thought: the first was written by a lawyer, the second by a law professor. "We will need to confer with *whomever* works on this project and then have *he* or *she* draft a motion for summary judgment."/ "Third, the fault is said to lie in part with *we* 'eccentric professors.'" In the first example *whoever* should be the subject of *works* and the pronouns should be *him* and *her* as objects of *have;* in the second, *us* should be the object of the preposition *with.* See **whom** (A).

NON-   (= not) is the general-purpose negative prefix that has gained a great deal of ground since the nineteenth century. *Non-* often contrasts with *in-* or *un-* in expressing a nongradable contrast, rather than the opposite end of a scale, e.g., *nonlegal* as compared to *illegal,* or *nonscientific* as compared to *unscientific.* (See **nonconstitutional.**) Ordinarily, esp. in AmE, the prefix is not hyphenated. A number of pitfalls lie in the way of its use, as categorized below. See generally NEGATIVES (B).

A.   With Nouns. Before adding *non-* to a noun, one should determine whether the noun being negated has an antonym that would suffice. For example, if *nonpretextual* means merely "valid" or "legitimate," it makes little sense to write: "The company showed that the reason for discharging the employee was *nonpretextual* [read, if appropriate, *legitimate*]." This infelicity may sometimes derive from tracking too closely statutory language, without searching for the most appropriate word. See SOUND OF PROSE, THE.

Another disadvantage in the use of *non-* is that it is beginning to displace the simplest negative, *not.* For example, "The cases relied upon in the opinion are *non-§ 1983 cases* [read *not § 1983 cases*]." *Grandstaff v. City of Borger,* 779 F.2d 1129, 1133 (5th Cir. 1986) (Hill, J., dissenting). As this example suggests, the use of this prefix to construct phrasal nouns can be especially awkward. "The critical issue before us concerns the order and allocation of proof in a *private, non-class action* [read *private suit, not a class action,*] challenging employment discrimination."

B. With Adjectives. When adding *non-* to a compound adjective, the meaning can become especially murky: "*noncivil* rights suit"; "*nonper stirpes* distribution." E.g., "In *non-community property states* [read *common-law states*] the most troublesome issue confronting the courts and legislatures arises out of the rapid expansion of a variety of devices for bypassing probate." *Noncriminal* can usually be rendered more straightforwardly *civil*; hence *civil trial* rather than *noncriminal trial*, *private school* (in AmE) rather than *nonpublic school.*

Non- adjectives should be avoided wherever possible, even if the avoidance means using more words. "In *nonautomobile cases* [read *cases not involving automobile accidents*] there may be a homeowner's policy that triggers the lawsuit and protects the parent in a direct suit or in an apportionment."/ "Chapman transferred *his only other non-cash asset,* [read *his only remaining asset other than cash*], a used car lot, to his two minor sons."/"A Tennessee statute that allows police officers to employ deadly force to prevent fleeing felons from escaping is unconstitutional insofar as it authorizes the use of such force to stop an apparently *unarmed and nondangerous suspect* [*unarmed* probably suffices; if not, then read *unarmed suspect who does not appear dangerous*]."/ "A *nonnegligent plaintiff* [read *A plaintiff who is not contributorily negligent*] may recover her total damages regardless of allocated damages."/ "We must therefore affirm the district court's declaratory judgment that the challenged provi-

sions of the Arizona Constitution and statutes as *applied to exclude nonproperty owners from elections* [read *applied to exclude those who do not own property from elections*] for the approval of the issuance of general obligation bonds, violated the Equal Protection Clause of the United States Constitution."

As with phrasal nouns, use of *non-* with phrasal adjectives produces awkward results, e.g., *nonincome-producing*, *noninterest-bearing*, *nonpar-value*, *nontaxpaid*. E.g., "It is undisputed that soybean production is a *non-water dependent activity* [read *is an activity not dependent on water*]."/ "A couple *in a non-community property jurisdiction* [read *living in a common-law jurisdiction*], one spouse being poorer than the other, will be subject to no gift taxation in interspousal transfers of property and will thus have the same tax advantages."

C. As a Separable Prefix. *Non-* is properly an inseparable prefix only, although some writers have tried to make it separable. E.g., "The Code seems to reflect a congressional perception that the taxation of the exercise of *non qualified* [read *nonqualified,* if not *unqualified*] stock options should be tightened up."/ "Rather, proof must be presented that the *non parties* [read *nonparties*] actively participated with the named party in violating the decree." See NEGATIVES (B).

nonact. See **nonfeasance.**

nonage (= legal infancy; the condition of being under age) is rare today except in legal contexts. E.g., "The two major grounds for testamentary incapacity are *nonage* and mental disability." Cf. *minority.*

nonbailable. See **bailable.**

nonbelief. See **disbelief.**

noncompete clause or *agreement* is inferior to *noncompetition clause* (or *agreement*). The prefix *non-* may be joined to adjectives (as with *nonexistent, nonfatal, nonresponsive*), to nouns (as with *nonoccurrence, nonissue, nonacceptance*), or to present participles (as with *nonpaying, nonsmoking, nonvoting*). It is not at its best, however, when joined to a verb to make an adjective, as in *noncompete*. E.g., "The plaintiffs rely on four cases that they claim support their position that the amounts received pursuant to the *non-compete* [read *noncompetition*] agreements are 'personal service income.'" *Furman v. United States,* 602 F. Supp. 444, 451

(D.S.C. 1984). *Noncompete* is not in the dictionaries, and we may justifiably hope that it never gains their approval. The better phrase is *agreement not to compete* or *noncompetition covenant.* See **non-** & **no-compete covenant.**

non compos mentis; compos mentis. These LATINISMS are now little used, although as long as words such as *insane* and similar words are used figuratively as terms of disparagement, these learned terms (meaning "not in one's right mind" and "in one's right mind") may be useful. The phrase *non compos mentis* once gave rise to the now disused slang expression *non compos.*

nonconstitutional; unconstitutional. As used by American practitioners, these terms have distinct meanings. *Nonconstitutional* = of or relating to some legal basis or principle other than those of the U.S. Constitution. E.g., "*Miranda* established a *nonconstitutional* prophylactic rule, the violation of which creates an irrebuttable presumption of coercion that is applicable in only a limited number of circumstances."/ "*Kent v. Dulles* did invalidate a burden on the right to travel; however, the restriction was voided on the *nonconstitutional* basis that Congress did not intend to give the Secretary of State power to create the restriction at issue."

The more familiar word, *unconstitutional* = in violation of, or not in accordance with, principles found in the U.S. Constitution. E.g., "The three-judge district court held that the Act and regulations in question were *unconstitutional* both under the equal protection clause of the Fourteenth Amendment [of the U.S. Constitution] and under the Constitution of Alaska."

none = (1) not one; or (2) not any. Hence it may correctly take either a singular or a plural verb. Here is an example of the singular: "No judgment could be entered for such refunds, if found in favor of the purchasers themselves, because *none was* a party to the proceeding." *None were* would also be correct, but *none was* is more emphatic.

non est factum is legal ARGOT denoting the plea denying the execution of an instrument sued on. E.g., "The plea of *non est factum* was not available, but the case fell within the statute." (Eng.)/ "The exception is that if the defendant thought that the document he signed belonged to an entirely different legal category from that to which it in fact belonged, he can plead *non est factum* and escape liability although he did not trouble to read the document and although he misled the plaintiff into supposing that he was agreeing." (Eng.) Pl. *non est factums.* See **fact,** n. & **fraud** (A).

nonexpert. See **inexpert.**

nonfeasance; nonact. The two are distinguishable. Whereas *nonact* means merely the failure to act, *nonfeasance* implies the failure to act where a duty to act existed. E.g., "There is a presumption of adequate representation, which may be overcome by the intervenor only upon a showing of adversity of interest, the representative's collusion with the opposing party, or *nonfeasance* by the representative." See **feasance.**

nonforeseeable is a NEEDLESS VARIANT of *unforeseeable.*

nonheritable. See **heritable.**

nonincentive. See **disincentive.**

noninterpretative. See **interpretative.**

nonjudicial. See **injudicious** & **judicial.**

nonjury trial is generally inferior to *bench trial* or *trial to the bench,* for the better practice is to name something for what it is rather than for what it is not. E.g., "After a *nonjury trial* [read *bench trial* or *trial to the bench*], the district court dismissed the remaining civil-rights claims at the conclusion of the plaintiff's case."

nonlapse statute. See **lapse statute.**

nonlawyer. It is a curious practice that lawyers (and others who write about law) divide the universe into *lawyers* and *nonlawyers*; but speakers of English do it of other professions and occupations as well. E.g., "The Supreme Court later expressly limited the vessel owner's duty to *nonseamen* to situations where the workers were doing 'ship's work.'" *Layman* is usually unambiguous, although it has the potential disadvantage of SEXISM, q.v.; *nonlawyer* is clearly better than *layperson.*

nonliability is an unnecessary equivalent of *no liability* or *lack of liability.*

nonmaterial. See **immaterial.**

nonnegotiable. See **negotiable instruments.**

nonobject. See **object.**

nonobjectionable is a NEEDLESS VARIANT of *unobjectionable.* E.g., "Their attack concentrated upon provisions that permitted modification of a secured claim by reducing the amount of the periodic installments due thereon, as contrasted with the *nonobjectionable* [read *unobjectionable*] curing of a default and maintaining those payments."

non obstante veredicto (= notwithstanding the verdict) is sometimes used in the shortened form *non obstante.* E.g., "This appeal requires us to determine whether the trial judge's action in granting judgment *non obstante* for the defendant was correct." See **judgment non obstante veredicto.**

nonparticipating royalty, used often in oil and gas law, is a venial REDUNDANCY: all mineral royalties are nonparticipating.

nonplus(s)ed. The form *-ss-* is preferred.

nonpretextual. "Appellant's lawful dismissal was found by the jury to be *nonpretextual.*" Actually, the jury found that the dismissal was not pretextual—thus the finding was a negative one. To say that it "found the dismissal to be *nonpretextual*" wrongly suggests that the jury answered a question asking whether the dismissal was *nonpretextual*; instead, the jury was asked whether the dismissal was *pretextual*, and it answered "no." See **pretextual.**

nonprobate = other than by will; of or relating to some method of disposition apart from wills. E.g., "Today the proportion of property passing under probate is decreasing and the proportion of property passing by *nonprobate* methods is increasing."

nonprofit; not-for-profit. The former is more common, but the latter is increasingly used in the U.S. for greater accuracy: *nonprofit corporation* misleadingly suggests that the corporation makes no profits; but such a corporation actually *does* earn profits and then applies them to charitable purposes. *Not-for-profit* is thought to reveal more accurately that the purpose is not for private gain, though indeed the organization may profit. E.g., "*Not-for-profit* corporations and public interest groups petitioned for writ of mandamus to compel the Federal Communications Commission to decide certain unresolved matters pending before a state agency."

nonpros. See **nolle prosequi.**

nonrebuttable is a NEEDLESS VARIANT of *irrebuttable.* E.g., "In actual operation, therefore, the three statutes enact what in effect are *nonrebuttable* [read *irrebuttable*] presumptions that every applicant for assistance in his first year of residency came to the jurisdiction solely to obtain higher benefits."

nonrefoulement. See **refoulement.**

NONRESTRICTIVE CLAUSES. See RESTRICTIVE & NONRESTRICTIVE CLAUSES.

non sequitur should be spelled as two words, not hyphenated or spelled as one word.

nonstatutory. This word is sometimes replaceable by *judicial, administrative,* or some other descriptive word, as in *judicial policy-making* rather than *nonstatutory policy-making.* If it fits, the more specific word should oust *nonstatutory.*

nonsuit, v.t. (= to subject to a nonsuit) has been part of lawyers' language since the sixteenth century. "Eyre, C.J., *nonsuited* the plaintiff." (Eng.)/ "It is submitted that the appellants should be *nonsuited* on the ground that the publication was privileged." (Eng.)/ "The court *nonsuited* him and rendered judgment dismissing the action."

nonsuitability. The preferred antonyms of *suitable* and *suitability* are *unsuitable* and *unsuitableness. Nonsuitability,* a NEEDLESS VARIANT of *unsuitableness,* unsuitably suggests a relationship with *nonsuit,* q.v. Yet it is perversely used in AmE legal contexts. E.g., "The Secretary of Agriculture shall, within ten years after September 3, 1964, review, as to its suitability or *nonsuitability* [read *unsuitableness*], each area." Wilderness Act, 16 U.S.C. § 1132(b) (1982).

nontaxpaid is an opaque, ugly word to avoid. E.g., "Defendant has had a reputation with me for over four years as being a trafficker of *nontaxpaid* distilled spirits." A less concise wording should be used, e.g., *trafficker of distilled spirits upon which no taxes had been paid.*

nontriggerman = a murder defendant who did not actually kill the decedent, but who intended to do so. E.g., "The conduct of a *nontriggerman* during the planning and aftermath of a prison break, which eventually resulted in a quadruple murder, was sufficient for the imposition of a death penalty." The word is odd-looking but perhaps necessary; often *accomplice* suffices.

no one is a singular noun, and therefore acts as a singular ANTECEDENT. E.g., "This means that *no one* should be punished for speaking unless *their* [read *his*] speech will immediately lead to a definite dangerous act." See SEXISM (A) & CONCORD.

noplace is a barbarism for *nowhere*.

no question but that. The *but* in this phrase is unnecessary; the better phrase is *no question that*. E.g., "There can be *no question but that* [read *no question that*] jurisdiction to review and to affirm or set aside the Secretary's order became fully vested in the court upon the filing of the partnership's petition."

nor. See **neither . . . nor** & **not** (C).

nor for *or*. Where the negative of a clause has already appeared and a disjunctive conjunction is needed, *or* is generally better than *nor*. The initial negative carries through to all the elements in an enumeration. E.g., "Religiosity insists that there is something called religion wholly apart from any specific religion, something that has no creed *nor* [read *or*] dogma, no theology or scriptures, something that may be felt and need not be understood."/ "Her symptoms were all subjective and not supported by any medical *nor* [read *or*] other corroborating evidence."/ "When on the witness stand on the trial of this case, however, he could not see the trial judge *nor* [read *or*] the examiner who was five feet away." See **not** (C).

normalcy is inferior to *normality*. E.g., "The *normalcy* [read *normality*] of these operations changed when Press was told by his delegate that Montana-Austria requested a stop-off in Johannesburg." Born in the mid-nineteenth century and later used by President Harding, *normalcy* has never been accepted as standard by the best writing authorities.

nostrum (= panacea) forms the plural *nostrums*. E.g., "But advertisements of *nostrums* for restoration of 'lost manhood' have appeared in the daily newspapers for at least fifty years."

not. A. Placement of. When used in constructions with *all* and *every, not* is usually best placed just before those words. E.g., "*Every disclosure of a trade secret does not result* [read *Not every disclosure of a trade secret results*] in an abandonment of its element of secrecy."/"*All writers did not accept* [read *Not all writers accepted*] Coke's dictum." (D. Mellinkoff)/ "*Justice Holmes reminded us that every moral question can not* [read *Justice Holmes reminded us that not every moral question can*] be submitted to the law, and that although morality might impose restraints on legal actions, there is a vast difference between the two concepts." See **all** (B).

B. *Not only . . . but also . . . .* These CORRELATIVE CONJUNCTIONS must frame syntactic parts that match. E.g., "The offer *had to not only be made in good faith but it had to also be* [read *had not only to be made in good faith but also to be*] in such a form that it could, by an acceptance of the offeree, ripen into a valid and binding contract that could be enforced by any party to it."/ "These disclosures *led not only to new calls for greater social responsibility of corporations but also focused on* [read *not only led to . . . but also focused on*] the role of the board of directors and the need for better control mechanisms to ensure that corporate management conform with legal and moral principles of conduct." See PARALLELISM.

Not only . . . but also and *not only . . . but . . . as well* are correct. *Not only . . . but also . . . as well* is redundant. E.g., "But we cannot quarrel with a conclusion of a school administrator that treating a particular student with such care might be to the advantage *not only* of the pupil *but also* [read *but*] of the other students in the school *as well*."

C. *Not . . . nor* should usually (where short clauses are involved) be *not . . . or*. E.g., "Finding the lessee culpable is *not inherently inconsistent nor contrary to* [read *not inherently inconsistent with or contrary to*] the 'instructions.'" See **nor** & NEGATIVES.

notable; noteworthy; noticeable. *Noticeable* = easily seen or noticed (as, e.g., scars); it is generally confined to physical senses. *Notable*, having basically the same meaning, is applied to qualities as well as to material things. E.g., "The most *notable* thing about these observations is that quite obviously the word 'res', describing a thing, has a quite different connotation from 'subject matter'."/ "Some jurisdictions, *notably* New York, have attempted to solve this problem by applying more flexible and equitable standards."

Noteworthy = worthy of notice or observation; remarkable. E.g., "It is *noteworthy* that the decree and codicil attached express conditions of survivorship to the interests of Joseph and to any wife or child of Joseph but do not add any words of that character to the limitation describing Mary Silva's interest."

not all. See **not** (A) & **all** (B).

notarial is the adjectival form of *notary*.

notary; notary public. *Notary* is a common ellipsis of *notary public* in both AmE and BrE. Pl. *notaries public.* In this phase, *public* is a POSTPOSITIVE ADJECTIVE.

note; draft. A *note* is a simple promise by one party to pay money to another party or to bearer. A *draft* is an order by one person (the drawer) to pay another person (the drawee), demanding that the drawee pay money to a third person (the payee) or to bearer.

note (= lawnote). See **annotation.**

note up is the approximate British equivalent of the American term *Shepardize,* q.v. The British call their citators *noter-ups,* or, in some Commonwealth countries, *noter-uppers.*

noteworthy. See **notable.**

not-for-profit. See **nonprofit.**

notice, v.t. (= to give legal notice to or of) is a LEGALISM. E.g., "Under the present practice, however, the objecting party has no duty to *notice* a hearing, the initiative being shifted to the party seeking discovery." Or, "We have not been *noticed* [i.e., received notice] to bring the records."/ "The magistrate heard the motions to set aside the default judgment apparently by virtue of the fact that they were *noticed* for a hearing before the magistrate rather than before the district court."/ "Unless you have already done so, *notice* the depositions of all expert witnesses being offered by your opponent."

Notice should be reserved for the giving of

legal notice; legal writers should not use the word nonlegally, as here: "TACA International Airlines, in the midst of collective bargaining negotiations, *noticed* [read *let be known*] its intent to relocate its pilot base." (To the layman this usage confusingly suggests *notice* in the sense "to observe.")/ "It has been *noticed* [read *noted,* i.e., previously in a book] that some lawyers and judges were of the opinion that . . . ."

noticeable. See **notable.**

notice to quit (BrE) = *notice to vacate* (AmE). See **quit.**

notorious may mean either "famous" or "infamous," though it usually carries connotations of the latter, i.e. unfavorably known. *Notoriety* is generally more neutral, although it is coming to be tinged with the connotations of its adjectival form.

not proven. See **proved.**

notwithstanding, when introducing a clause, should usually be followed by *that.* E.g., "The law is in accord in favoring free competition, since ordinarily it is essential to the general welfare of society, *notwithstanding* [insert *that*] competition is not altruistic but is fundamentally the play of interest against interest."/ "The instrument is likely to be upheld *notwithstanding* [insert *that*] it includes additionally the reservation of power to amend the trust in whole or in part."

When introducing a verbless phrase, *notwithstanding* need not be followed by *that.* E.g., "Section 1322(b)(5) was amended to provide that its provisions were unchanged, *notwithstanding* section 1322 (b)(2)."

notwithstanding anything to the contrary contained herein, an ungainly phrase often placed in complex contracts to introduce the most important provisions, can be fairly said to mean "the true agreement is as follows." It is best used when the contract needs to spell out explicitly that a certain provision is to override another, arguably inconsistent provision.

nought. See **naught.**

NOUN PLAGUE is Wilson Follett's term for the piling up of nouns to modify other nouns. See W. Follett, *Modern American Usage*

229 (1966). When a sentence has more than three nouns in a row, it becomes much less readable. The following sentence is badly constructed because of the noun-upon-noun syndrome, which unfortunately is more common now than in Follett's day: "Consumers complained to their congressman about *the National Highway Traffic Safety Administration's automobile seat belt 'interlock' rule.*" One can hardly get to the end of the sentence to find out that we are talking about a rule. (Actually, many writers today would leave off the possessive after *Administration.*) In the interest of plague control, the following rewrite seems advisable: "*. . . the 'interlock' rule for automobile seat belts applied by the National Highway Traffic Safety Administration.*"

Readability often drops when three words that are structurally nouns follow in succession, although exceptions such as *fidelity life insurance* certainly exist. Less readable examples such as the following are the rule rather than the exception, however: "Inasmuch as incentives are inevitably tied to immeasurable subjective evaluations, it is reassuring that the *information generation stimuli* of the adversary model rest in part on other foundations."/ "The *interpretation process* provides a reminder of the *federalism aspects* of *individual right concerns.*" The plague is virtually never endurable when four nouns appear consecutively. E.g., "The direct *participation programs principal category* of registration is the minimum qualification requirement for persons whose supervisory functions are limited to direct participation programs."/ "The recent decisions compel little change in the current *state attorney solicitation rules.*"

Frequently, noun plague is a cause of ambiguity. E.g., "My brother Harlan's objections to my *Adamson dissent history*, like that of most of the objectors, relies most heavily on a criticism written by Professor Charles Fairman." Here Justice Black means "the history [of the incorporation doctrine] I recited in my dissent in *Adamson*," but the reader could just as easily arrive at "my history of the *Adamson* dissent," or "the history of opinions that dissent from *Adamson.*" A few prepositions would have remedied the problem.

One aspect of noun plague in legal writing is the traditional—and misguided—preference for nouns over verbs. Jeremy Bentham's so-called "substantive-preferring principle" was developed as a result of his bias in favor of nouns, which could be modified and multiplied, whereas "[a] verb slips through your

fingers like an eel. . . ." 10 J. Bentham, *Works* 569 (Bowring ed. 1843). Thus Bentham, like his fellow lawyers, preferred *to give motion to* rather than *to move* and *to give extension to* rather than *to extend.* Even today, lawyers frequently use such circumlocutions. See BE-VERBS (B).

Yet another root of the problem is the tendency in modern writing to make adjectives out of nouns and noun phrases, often postponing the true subject until long after the reader has left off hoping for one: "This is a breach of contract / Deceptive Trade Practices Act, Tex. Bus. & Comm. Code Ann. (Vernon Supp. 1982–83)(hereinafter referred to as 'the Act') case." *Wolfe Masonry, Inc. v. Stewart,* 664 S.W.2d 102, 102–03 (Tex. App.—Corpus Christi 1983)./ "The Public Utilities Commission made a *question of law, not fact, determination* when it allowed the LCRA to intervene."

Finally, it is worth sounding a caution against loading a single statement with too many abstract nouns ending in *-tion.* The effect is not a pleasing one: "This case involves *protection* against a second *prosecution* for the *importation conviction.*"/ "The *regulation* of *solicitation* involves the *consideration* of whether there are 'ample alternative channels for *communication* of the *information.*'" See SOUND OF PROSE (A).

NOUNS AS ADJECTIVES. English has long been noted for its ability to allow words to change parts of speech. The transmutation of nouns into adjectives is one of the most frequently seen shifts of this kind. Usually the change is unobjectionable, as in the first word in each of the following phrases: *lawbook, state action, telephone wires, home repairs, litigation problems.* A common example appears in this sentence: "In order to pose a *jury question* on the issue of *seaman status,* the plaintiff must present evidence of the following kind."

Occasionally, however, semantic shifts of this kind give rise to ambiguities or play tricks on the reader. For example, it would be unwise for one writing about a statute concerning invalids to call it an *invalid statute.* To make a somewhat different point, the reader's expectations are subverted when a noun is used adjectivally in place of the more usual adjectival form. E.g., "The subdivision was planned strictly for *residence* [read *residential*] purposes."

Often, of course, the sense conveyed is different when one uses the noun adjectivally as opposed to the adjectival form. For example, *negligence defendant* is something different from *negligent defendant*, the latter being judgmental; *negligence action* means something quite different from *negligent action*; *pornography litigation* seems to mean something different from *pornographic litigation* (which is somehow difficult to visualize).

Finally, relations often become vague when nouns that would normally follow prepositions are used as prepositive adjectives, and the relation-bearing prepositions omitted. E.g., *victim awareness* is a vague phrase; does it mean *on the part of, of, by*? E.g., *"Victim awareness* gained momentum in the early 1980s, with the passage of the Victim and Witness Protection Act." We can deduce that the intended sense is *awareness (on the part of the public) of victims and their rights*, but perhaps we should not ask our readers to have to make such deductions. The same sort of uncertainty infects *victim restitution* (= full restitution to the victim of a crime).

NOUNS AS VERBS. A type of semantic shift less common than that discussed in the preceding entry is for nouns to act as verbs. Often these usages are considered slangy, e.g.: "The movie would have *box-officed* $3 million."/ "She has been *mayoring* in Austin for six years."/ "Every youngster can *summer* in Europe."/ "If a man is not in the same city, his semen can be frozen and *air-expressed* to the doctor."

Yet nouns used as verbs often make their way into legal parlance and finally into legal print: "The grand jury had not focused on specific individuals and was playing a broader role than the typical grand jury asked simply to *true bill* or *no bill* a suspect." *Morrison v. City of Baton Rouge*, 761 F.2d 242, 247 (5th Cir. 1985). English is less than openly hospitable to this sort of innovation, at least initially; legal writers should be wary of adopting usages of this kind.

n.o.v. See **j.n.o.v.**

novation. See **adoption.**

novelty does not mean "an extreme rarity." Rather, it denotes something both rare *and new.* "Mother-son incest is so rare as to be regarded as a *novelty.*" The writer of this sentence could have better written, "Mother-son incest is an extreme rarity." *Oedipus Rex* belies any claim that incest might have to novelty.

novus actus interveniens is the primarily British legal phrase meaning literally "a new intervening act." (See CAUSATION (D) & LATINISMS.) *Novus actus* is sometimes used as an ellipsis for the full phrase. E.g., "On the assumed facts there would be in my view no *novus actus* when the trainees damaged the respondent's property." (Eng.)

now is sometimes mistakenly used for *present* or *current* as an opposite of *then*, as in *then-owner.* (See **then** (A).) "The defendants are purchasing two of the adjoining lots from the *now owners* [read *present owners*] thereof."

noway(s). See **nowise.**

now comes. See **come(s) now.**

nowhere near is colloquial for *not nearly.*

nowise (= in no way; not at all) is an adverb that should not be introduced by *in*, although legal writers seem to commit this error more often than not when using the word. *In no way* might even generally be preferable to *nowise.* Formerly spelled as two words, *nowise* should now be consistently treated as a single word. The correct use of the word is here illustrated: "The exemption of the Crown is *nowise* dependent upon the local or imperial character of the rate." (Eng.)/ "Defendant is a banker who is *nowise* in the occupation of a barber."

The mistaken uses of the word, esp. in AmE, are legion: "If any part or provision of this agreement or covenant shall be declared invalid, by judgment or court order, the same *shall in nowise* [read either *shall nowise* or *shall in no way*] affect any of the other provisions of this agreement, and the remaining portion of this agreement shall remain in full force and effect."/ "If the only purpose of the union employees was to quit the service and permanently sever their connections with their employer, appellees *would in nowise be damaged* [read *would nowise be damaged*] and could have no grounds for injunctive relief."

Noways, in legal writing at least, is a NEEDLESS VARIANT of *nowise*, although the Evanses state that it is more common in the U.S. than *nowise.* See B. Evans & C. Evans, *A Dictionary of Contemporary American Usage* 326 (1957).

NSF (= not sufficient funds) acts as an adjective where the full phrase is cumbersome and even ungrammatical ⟨an NSF check⟩.

nuclear is pronounced /*noo-klee-ăr*/, though often it is mispronounced /*noo-kyŭ-lăr*/. Though presidents and other educated persons have had difficulty pronouncing the word correctly, if one can one should.

nudum pactum (= an unenforceable agreement) has taken on different particularized senses within different legal traditions. At common law, of course, a *nudum pactum* was an agreement that failed for lack of consideration. E.g., "The contract between a maker or indorser of a promissory note and the payee forms no exception to the general rule that a promise, not supported by consideration, is *nudum pactum*." (Eng.)/ "The trial court, without hearing the counsel for the defendant, said that it was an engagement all on one side, and was therefore *nudum pactum*."/ "A mere offer to sell property, which can be withdrawn at any time, and which is made dependent on the acceptance of the person to whom it is made, is a mere *nudum pactum*."

In Roman law and civil law, in which consideration is not a necessary element of a contract, the term denoted unenforceability for some other reason, such as lack of a lawful "cause." The anglicized phrase *nude pact* has not been widely used, perhaps because each of those terms carries its own connotative baggage that may mislead.

nugatory is not a legal word per se, but it is a learned word favored by lawyers, meaning "of no force; useless; invalid." E.g., "These statutes were as effective when the Allen case was decided as now; they did not then serve to render the bequest involved *nugatory* under the circumstances."/ "But a person's liberty or right to deal with others is *nugatory* unless they are at liberty to deal with him if they choose to do so." (Eng.) Cf. **otiose.**

null (= void) is perfectly capable of standing alone. E.g., "The cancellation of the first will ought to be looked upon as *null* also, and therefore the first will is still subsisting and unrevoked." See **null and void.**

nulla bona (= no goods) is a LATINISM that has given its name to the sheriff's return on a writ of execution when he has found no property of the defendant on which to levy.

null and void. "If the powers of the legislature have not been exercised in conformity with the Constitution, the laws enacted are *null and void*." This DOUBLET is old in the law, is readily understandable to laymen, and is at worst a minor prolixity and a CLICHÉ. Though emphatic, *null and void* is susceptible to the frequent weakness of *void* alone, namely that of being interpreted to mean *voidable*. (See **void.**) *Null and void* is fundamentally innocuous, however; our plain-English jihad has far worse legalistic demons to get rid of.

nullify. See **annul.**

nullity = (1) the fact of being legally void ⟨petition for nullity of marriage⟩; or (2) something that is legally void. Sense (2) is now more common: "The government reasons that the panel's determination on the first appeal rendered the original district court judgment a *nullity*."/ "The appellate court affirmed the decree on the ground that the court was justified in exercising its inherent power to protect itself and the defendants against a multiplicity of actions, and harassing and vexatious litigation, by persisting in treating decisions of the courts as a mere *nullity*."

NUMBER. See CONCORD & SUBJECT-VERB AGREEMENT.

number of, there are a; there is a number of. The former is correct, because of the linguistic principle known as SYNESIS, q.v. "*There are a number of people* living here."/ "*There have been a number of cases* in which error or inadvertence has led to failure to comply with the provisions of section 33 or its forerunner." But, "*There is a growing number of litigated cases* on this point."

NUMERALS are best kept to a minimum in formal writing, as by spelling out all numbers less than one hundred. "During 1974 and 1975, 92 trials in the federal courts consumed 20 days or more." [Read *During 1974 and 1975, ninety-two trials in the federal courts consumed twenty days or more.*] The only exceptions to this general principle occur when the numbers are being used for calculations, appear before units of measure, or are frequent throughout the text.

nunc pro tunc (lit., "now for then") is used of judgments to indicate that they have been entered so as to have legal effect from an earlier date. E.g., "The Commission of Appeals refused to treat the lower court decision as a judgment *nunc pro tunc.*" The LATINISM is useful legal ARGOT, not a TERM OF ART, usu. appearing when a court has exercised its "inherent power . . . to make its records speak the truth by correcting the record at a later date to reflect what actually occurred [in earlier court proceedings]." *Ex parte Dickerson,* 702 S.W.2d 657, 658 (Tex. Crim. App. 1986).

nuncupative will. See **oral will.**

nuptial(s). Although *nuptial* is in good use as an adjective, the noun *nuptials* (= wedding) is generally a pomposity to be avoided. It should be left to its ineradicable place in newspaper reports of weddings, in which it allows ambitious young journalists to practice INELEGANT VARIATION.

nurturance is incorrect for *nurture,* n.

O

obit sine prole. See OSP.

obiter is primarily a British shortened form of *obiter dictum.* At times the entire phrase appears: "The language is purely *obiter dictum,* but we cite it for what it is worth." But *obiter* can be confusing when standing for *obiter dictum,* for *obiter* alone means "by the way." If the phrase must be shortened, *dictum* is the usual form in the U.S. and in G. B. E.g., "The appellees and the trial court cite *Defreese v. Lake,* which, *by obiter* [read *in dictum*], quotes the passage above from *Washburn.*"/ "What Megaw, J. said in *Yeoman Credit Ltd. v. Gregory* was *obiter* [read *dictum*]." (Eng.)/ "This was certainly the intention in that case and therefore it is submitted that the statement within the parenthesis was *obiter* [read *dictum*]." See **dictum** (A).

The plural of *obiter dictum* is *obiter dicta.* E.g., "Any comment in *Pegues I* regarding the merits of Pegues' *Singleton* claim was obiter *dicta* [read *dictum*]." A tangential comment is *dictum*; tangential comments are *dicta.* See **dictum** (B).

object, n. Only in legal writing may persons be *objects* (= probable beneficiaries). E.g., "If B is not a natural *object* of A's bounty, a pre-

sumption arises that A did not intend to make a gift of the property to B, but had some other reason for causing B to be named as grantee."/ "The rule that admits *objects* born after the testator's death and before the period of distribution, to share in the bequest, applies only where the total amount of the gift is independent of the number of *objects* among whom it is to be divided." (Eng.) Moreover, in the legal idiom, some persons may be *objects* while others are *nonobjects*: "If a donee of a special power makes an appointment to an *object* of the power in consideration of a benefit conferred upon or promised to a *nonobject,* the appointment is ineffective to whatever extent it was motivated by the purpose to benefit the *nonobject.*"

objectant; objector. Both words mean "one who contests a will." For purposes of DIFFERENTIATION, *objectant* is perhaps preferable in this sense, inasmuch as *objector* has other uses in the language of the law, such as "one who objects to the admission of certain evidence at trial," or in the phrase *conscientious objector.* Following are examples drawn from contexts involving wills: "*Objectants,* who are the decedent's next of kin, appeal from a decree of the Surrogate's Court of King's County, which adjudged the bequest in that paragraph to be a valid charitable trust and directed that letters of trusteeship issue."/ "The language of the will and the actions of the *objectors* [read *objectants*] compel the conclusions that the *objectors* [read *objectants*] are entitled to $1.00 each and are not entitled to share in the residue of the estate because of the in terrorem clause." See **caveator & contestant.** Cf. **protestant.**

objectify; objectivize. *Objectify,* dating from the mid-nineteenth century, means either (1) "to make into an object," or (2) "to render objective." *Objectivize,* a creation of the late nineteenth century, means "to render objective." It is a NEEDLESS VARIANT of *objectify,* the preferred term. E.g., "From what has been said it is apparent that the feudal law *objectified* the concept of seisin and thought of it as a tangible thing like a ball." See **reify.**

objector. See **objectant.**

OBJECT-SHUFFLING. This term, in the words of its inventor, "describes what unwary writers are apt to do with some of the many verbs that require, besides a direct object, another noun bearing to them a some-what similar relation, but attached to them by a preposition" (Fowler, *MEU1* 393). Unfortunately, there is no simple rule for determining which verbs are reversible and which are not; one must rely on a sensitivity to idiom and a knowledge of what type of subject acts upon what type of object with certain verbs. It is perfectly legitimate, for example, either to *inspire* a person *with* courage or to *inspire* courage *in* a person; but the switch does not work with similar words such as *instill* or *inculcate*. Good teachers *instill* or *inculcate values into* students, but cannot properly be said to *instill* or *inculcate students with* values. (See **inculcate**.)

Here the wrong object is used with the verb: "He continued the medicine a few days longer, and then *substituted the penicillin with tetracycline* [read *substituted tetracycline for the penicillin* or *replaced the penicillin with tetracycline*]." This use of *substitute* for *replace*, resulting from a confusion over the types of object each verb may take, is labeled "incorrect" in the *OED*.

Impress is a word that, like *inspire*, is reversible. A court may *impress* a constructive trust *on* property, or *impress* property *with* a constructive trust. E.g., "Where state law *impresses property* that a debtor holds *with a constructive trust* in favor of another, and the trust attaches, the trust beneficiary normally may recover its equitable interest in the property in bankruptcy court." Cf. **oust** & **serve**.

object to —ing. The modern idiom uses a present participle, not an infinitive. E.g., "If any person called to give evidence *objects to take* [now read *objects to taking*] an oath, such person must make the following promise and declaration."

obligable. So spelled. See -ATABLE.

obligate. See **oblige**.

obligatio. This Roman-law term carries no meaning that is not equally well conveyed by the English word *obligation*. "Being valid, the state law created an *obligatio*, a personal liability of the owner of the Hamilton, to the claimants." (Holmes, J.) Rarely did Justice Holmes so indulge himself in unnecessarily recherché terms.

obligative. See **obligatory**.

obligator. See **obligor**.

obligatory, -tive. The general term is *obligatory* (= required; mandatory). *Obligative* is a grammatical term for the mood of verbs expressing obligation or necessity.

oblige; obligate. The differences between these terms lie more in their uses than in their senses. Both words may mean "to bind by law or by moral duty." In legal contexts, the sense of either word is usually "to bind by law," whereas in lay contexts the sense of moral duty predominates. *Oblige* is used in the sense "to bind by legal tie" only in legal writing. E.g., "While one, by making an entry to the other's debit, lays him under an obligation, it is only the latter that is *obliged*."

Oblige has the additional sense "to do a favor for; to bind (someone else) by doing a favor for him." *Obligate* does not share this meaning. *Obliged* = bound by law, duty, or moral tie. The word often functions adjectivally in a way that *obligated* ordinarily does not. E.g., "The California Court of Appeals felt *obliged* to yield to the supremacy of a federal treaty over state law."

Oblige is colloquial in the sense "to favor, bestow, or entertain." E.g., "Appellant wrote the clerk of the court of appeals and requested that all motions filed by his counsel be withdrawn and that a mandate of affirmance issue forthwith; the court *obliged* and the mandate issued."/ "The court requested the government to summarize the evidence that would be offered at trial, and the government *obliged* with a description of the surveillance."

obligee has a soft -*g*-, /ob-li-**jee**/. Cf. **subrogee**.

obligor, -er; obligator. *Obligor* /**ob**-li-gohr/ is the usual and therefore the preferable form in legal writing. "Joint *obligators* [read *obligors*] may be joined, or sued, separately." *Obliger* /ō-**blī**-jĕr/ is the nonlegal form.

oblivious takes the preposition *of* in its strictest sense of "forgetful." *Oblivion* = forgetfulness or forgottenness, not momentary distraction. The more popular significance of *oblivious* today is "unmindful; unaware; unobservant." This semantic shift represents a grave attenuation in meaning. Today *to* is the more common mate of *oblivious*, though fastidious speakers and writers continue to use *of*.

Oblivious is here used correctly with regard

to the preposition, and less correctly from an etymological point of view: "The law does not discriminate between the rescuer *oblivious of* peril and the one who counts the cost." (Cardozo)

obnoxious today generally means "offensive, objectionable." In legal writing, however, it often carries the sense "contrary," as here: "To give effect to the limitation in favor of C's heir, when he is ascertained, would be *obnoxious* to the cardinal principle that a man cannot create a springing interest." An even rarer sense of the word, used only in legal and literary contexts, is "exposed to harm or liable to something undesirable." E.g., "This is a similar case, and it is *obnoxious* to similar criticism" (Eng.) (adapted from *OED* quotation).

obrogate. See **abrogate.**

OBSCURITY, it goes without saying, should be rigorously eschewed. It has myriad causes, usually rooted in imprecise thought or lack of consideration for the reader. Here is an example of the kind of obscurity typically found in the worst of legal writing: "Upon the other hand, if the defendant in error could not possibly, by the use of reasonable means and due diligence, have procured the information necessary for her to have, in order to make due proof of the death of Archie Hicks, the law did not impose upon her, as a duty, the attempted doing of an impossible thing." This obtuseness is due perhaps partly to the metaphysical notion involved, but certainly also to the pompous phraseology. See WOOLLINESS.

    A. Overelaboration. One cannot improve upon what Cardozo wrote about the MYTH OF PRECISION:

> There is an accuracy that defeats itself by the overemphasis of details. I often say that one must permit oneself, and that quite advisedly and deliberately, a certain margin of mis-statement. . . . [T]he sentence may be so overloaded with all its possible qualifications that it will tumble down of its own weight.
>
> Cardozo, *Law and Literature,* 52 Harv. L. Rev. 471, 474 (1939).

    B. Initialese. Another kind of obscurity results from the overuse of acronyms, with which the reader must constantly refamiliarize himself. E.g,. "This memorandum examines the effect of a P.U.C. determination of

L.C.R.A. standing to be an intervenor contestant as it affects plaintiff's claim that L.C.R.A. lacked sufficient interest to justify its opposition to the Texland application for C.C.N." One's writing should be more accessible to readers, containing no more than a couple of acronyms—and preferably one at a time. See INITIALESE & ACRONYMS AND INITIALISMS.

    C. Abstractness. See ABSTRACTITIS.

obsequies; obsequious. These words are unrelated in meaning. *Obsequies,* the noun, is a FORMAL WORD for *funeral. Obsequious,* the adjective, means "toadying, servilely attentive."

observance; observation. The DIFFERENTIATION between these two words is complete. *Observance* = heeding, obeying; the act of following a custom or rule. "The defendant had a right to insist upon an *observance* of the terms of the contract." *Observation* = scrutiny; study; a judgment or inference from what one has seen. One whose *observance* of the distinction is slipshod will be thought to lack *observation* of good writers.

obtain is a FORMAL WORD for *get.*

obverse. See **converse.**

obviate. Modern dictionaries such as the *OAD* that define *obviate* as meaning "to make unnecessary" are unduly restrictive. The *OED* does not even list this sense. Although *obviate* may well carry this meaning, it means more usually "to meet and dispose of or do away with (a thing); to prevent by anticipatory measures" (*OED*). E.g., "The trial court can *obviate* the problem by approving appeals only regarding issues that have an adequate record."/ "The semblance of vindictiveness that arises from the imposition of a harsher sentence the second time around must be *obviated* so that the proceedings do not leave the impression of unfairness to the defendant."/ "Defendant cites the equitable maxim, 'equity acts in personam,' invoked since the days of Coke and Bacon to *obviate* open conflicts between law and equity courts."

    In the sense "to make unnecessary," *obviate* often appears correctly in the phrase *obviate the necessity of* or *need for.* These phrases are not REDUNDANCIES, for the true sense of *obviate the necessity* is "to prevent the necessity (from arising)," hence to make unnecessary: "This posture of the case *obviates the necessity of* our attempting to articulate a generally applicable principle of 'finality' or 'ripeness' beyond what has already been said in the cited cases."/ "Professor Easterbrook would move us away from this core of first principles toward the periphery populated by managerial techniques—a realm in which the bureaucratic task of punching figures into a supposedly passive and neutral machine *obviates the need for* judges to make and defend hard choices."

Obviate is sometimes misunderstood as meaning "to make obvious" or "to remedy"; the latter error occurs here: "If the company realized that the slipperiness constituted an unreasonable risk to business visitors, it should have either taken steps to *obviate* [read *remedy*] the condition or given visitors warning thereof."

occupant; occupier. These synonyms are both old, and both have historically been used in legal writing to denote "one who takes possession of property." If any distinction in use exists, it is that *occupier* is more common in BrE than in the AmE. E.g., "The scheme of the Act at least allows, if it does not encourage, agreement between the land *occupier* and the local planning authority." (Eng.) Nevertheless, *occupant* is also used with great frequency in BrE.

occurrence. So spelled; *-ance* is a fairly common misspelling.

ochlocracy. See **mobocracy.**

ocular is turgid for *with one's eyes*; labeling it a FORMAL WORD is too tepid a description. E.g., "The testator must have the opportunity, through the evidence of *ocular* observation, to see the attestation." The word is sometimes misspelled *occular*. Cf. the misspelling *inocculation*.

odiferous. See **odorous.**

odious; odorous. *Odious* = detestable; disgusting. *Odorous* = smelly. See **odorous.**

odorous; odoriferous; malodorous. *Odorous* = smelly. *Malodorous* carries even stronger negative connotations. *Odoriferous*, a frequently misused term, has historically almost always had positive connotations in the

sense "fragrant." It should not be used in reference to foul odors. *Odiferous* is an inferior, shortened rendering of *odoriferous*. See **odious.**

-O(E)S. See PLURALS (C).

of. **A.** *Superfluous in Dates. December of 1987* should be *December 1987.* See DATES (B).

B. *Difficult of,* etc. This construction, illustrated in the examples that follow, is now peculiar to the legal idiom. It is also easily improved by making the wording more direct: "We cannot say that this effort was so *improbable of success* [read *unlikely to succeed*] that all discovery ought to have been denied."/ "To attempt to catalogue the ways and means would be undesirable, and *impossible of attainment* [read *impossible to attain*]." (Eng.)/ "He has been guilty of inability to do that which in the case of such a store in such a place must be *far from easy of performance* [read *far from easy to perform*] in the absence of skilled clerical aid." (Eng.)/ "The question posed at first blush would appear to be *one easy of answer* [read *easy to answer*]."/ "The legislature does not intend a result that is absurd, *impossible of execution* [read *impossible to execute*], or unreasonable." Cf. NOUN PLAGUE. See **difficult of.**

C. *Of a . . . nature* is almost always unnecessary, for the adjective may always be used alone—and with greater force; e.g., *act of a tortious nature* reads better *tortious act.*

D. For *from.* This usage, an ARCHAISM, is still used with some frequency by legal writers: "If I order mutton *of* [read *from*] X, and he supplies me with beef, or decomposed mutton, the failure of performance is as complete as if X had supplied nothing." It is commonly seen in the DOUBLET *to recover of and against.* See par. 2 under **purchase.**

of counsel. This anglicization of the LAW LATIN *a consiliis* is still sometimes applied to "the counsel employed by a party in a cause, and particularly to one employed to assist in the preparation or management of a cause, or in its presentation on appeal, but . . . not the principal attorney of record" (*Black's*). This term is now commonly used in the U.S. of lawyers (usu. in semiretirement) who are affiliated with private law firms as senior consultants.

of course. See **clearly.**

offer; promise. "There is surely a difference," wrote an English lawyer almost a century ago, "a profound difference in legal significance, between an *offer* and a *promise*. An *offer* is an expression of willingness to be bound by contract to the person to whom the offer is made, if he accepts the offer unconditionally and within a reasonable time. The offer then becomes a *promise*. A contract is made, and not till then, the parties are bound. Therefore an *offer* is revocable, a *promise* is not." Anson, *Some Notes on Terminology in Contract*, 28 Law Q.Rev. 337, 337 (1891). In modern usage, a promise differs from an obligation arising from a binding contract in that a mere promise need not be supported by consideration.

offeror, -er. The former is now standard in legal texts, although the latter was much used in the nineteenth century. See -ER, -OR.

office, v.t., has become a commonplace expression among American lawyers, but not among those who are fastidious in their use of language. E.g., "*Although the defendant was officed there* [read *Although the defendant had an office there*] for a while, the business address of the company is the office on 51st Street." This is a classic example of the NOUN AS VERB syndrome.

OFFICIALESE = the language of officialdom, characterized by bureaucratic turgidity and insubstantial fustian. See E. Gowers, *The Complete Plain Words* (2d ed. 1973); J.R. Masterson & W.B. Phillips, *Federal Prose: How to Write in And/or for Washington* (1948).

officious. In Dr. Johnson's day, *officious* had positive connotations ("eager to please"). Today, however, it means "meddlesome; interfering with what is not one's concern." E.g., "When the necessary goods or services are furnished without the knowledge of the trustee, who is supporting the beneficiary, recovery should be denied on the ground that the person supplying the goods or services is acting *officiously*." In legal contexts, the word frequently appears in the phrase *officious intermeddler*: "It is a correct generalization to say that the defendant is at least obligated to abstain from *officious intermeddling* calculated to induce a breach."

Fowler notes that the word "has a meaning in diplomacy oddly different from its ordinary use" (*MEU2* 412). In the context of diplomacy, the word means "having an extraneous relation to official matters or duties; having the character of a friendly communication, or informal action, on the part of a government or its official representatives" (*OED*) ⟨an officious communication⟩.

The term is often misused, however. In the following sentence it is difficult to discern what meaning the writer intended it to have, but it is impossible for a policy to be *officiously applicable*: "It is upon this assumption, that the case will be tried in a convenient forum so that the forum's policies are properly and not *officiously applicable* [read *arbitrarily applied*?] to the case, that Professor Ehrenzweig advances his central suggestion for solution of choice-of-law problems."

Here the writer apparently mistook its meaning as being "official-looking": "He still lived in the same old dormitory, in a bigger and more *officious* room." The same error is plain in one court's reference to an *officious translation* of a Belgian statute; presumably *official translation* would have been the appropriate phrase.

offing, on the is incorrect and undiomatic for *in the offing*.

offload, v.t., of South African origin; is a NEEDLESS VARIANT of *unload* or for *dump*. E.g., "The court finds that orders given to *offload* [read *dump*] garbage cannot possibly constitute unseaworthiness of the vessel."

off of is generally considered illiterate. *Off* needs no preposition after it.

offset, n., is perfectly acceptable in American legal writing. This usage is first recorded in the *OED* as an Americanism from 1769. Nearly fifty years later, John Pickering wrote: "This is much used by lawyers of America instead of the English term *set-off*; and it is also very common, in popular language, in the sense of equivalent. . . . It is not in the dictionaries." J. Pickering, *A Vocabulary* 142 (1816) (emphasis omitted).

offset, v.t., is generally inferior to *set off*, q.v., although it cannot rightly be condemned as an error.

offspring   is itself plural, and has no plural form *offsprings.* "Use of marijuana endangers one's *offsprings* [read *offspring*]." It would not be ill-considered to label this misuse illiterate.

of opinion.   See **opinion, of (the).**

oftentimes   is, in all cases, unnecessary for *often.* "Both of these statutory schemes were in harmony with the common-law doctrine of sovereign immunity, but had the effect of lessening the *oftentimes* [read *often*] harsh results *achieved in applying that doctrine.*"/ "The plaintiff gave no evidence of an intent that *oftentimes* [read *often*] appears to establish an enterprise independent of profits or losses."

of (the) opinion.   See **opinion, of (the).**

olfaction, detect by   is a laughable pomposity for *to smell.* E.g., "The marijuana was discovered in plain view during the course of a subsequent maritime search of the vessel, and, in any event, the distinctive odor of the contraband weed apparently was ubiquitous and easily *detected by olfaction* on board and well beyond the LADY MAR." Here we also have INELEGANT VARIATION (*marijuana . . . the contraband weed*) and misuse of *ubiquitous* (= universal). Cf. **ocular.**

omissible; omittable.   The latter is incorrect.

omission; omittance.   The latter is a NEEDLESS VARIANT. Once current, it has been obsolete for most of this century.

omit (+ infinitive).   This construction, in which *omit* = to neglect, appears today primarily in legal prose. E.g., "A person who wrongfully *omits to perform* a particular act required of him is liable in damages for all the consequences that may ordinarily ensue therefrom." It is a lawyers' expression that is neither ARGOT nor LEGALESE, but an obsolescent grammatical construction.

omittance.   See **omission.**

omnibus, adj. (= relating to or serving for numerous distinct objects at once; comprising a large number of items or particulars [*OED*]) is a LEGALISM most often used in the legislative phrase *omnibus bill.* But *omnibus* also has

other uses in legal writing, e.g.: "The appeal brings up for review the denial, after a hearing of . . . defendant's *omnibus* motion." *People v. Lopez,* 497 N.Y.S.2d 452, 452 (N.Y.App. Div. 1986).

on; upon.   These synonymous words are used in virtually the same ways. The distinctions are in tone and connotation. *Upon* is a FORMAL WORD that strikes the average reader or listener as legal or literary. It should be reserved for contexts in which the tone is elevated. *On* is the more usual word that is generally to be preferred. E.g., "As this case centers *upon* [read *on*] the strength of local Mississippi policies, this course is mandated by the principles of federalism."/ "The burden is *upon* [read *on*] the petitioner to show that this is true."/ "Plaintiff alleged that in reliance *upon* [read *on*] an inaccurate FHA inspection made in approving FHA mortgage insurance, he was induced to buy a house for an excessive price."
     One should never mess with idioms in which *on* appears by making it *upon,* as here: "The plaintiff received an assignment of a mortgage which *upon its face* [read *on its face*] provided it was secured by a note described in the mortgage." See **face, on its** & SET PHRASES.

on all fours   (= squarely on point with regard to both facts and law) is used of legal precedents. E.g., "*Causey v. Civiletti* is *on all fours* with Dovalina's case."/ "Despite the majority's efforts, no tinkering with the facts can put this case *on all fours* with *Mosley.*"/ "Except for the fact that *Hubinger* involved a trust to provide payment of an annuity instead of one to provide support as here, the two cases are practically *on all fours.*" See ARGOT. Cf. **whitehorse case.**

on and after   (a date) is usually unnecessary for *after* (a date), unless it is important to convey the nuance that the date mentioned is included within the scope of applicability. See **on or about.**

on appeal; on the appeal.   The former phrase is today considered more idiomatic in AmE. E.g., "*On the appeal* [read *On appeal*], the counterclaimants petitioned and were granted leave to intervene, argue, and file a brief." See **appeal** (A).

on behalf of. See **behalf.**

one. **A.** The Overdone *one*, n.: "[O]*ne* has an affirmative responsibility toward others when *one* has taken an active part in directing the manner in which these others perform their tasks or when *one* creates or is generally responsible for a dangerous situation that causes harm. . . . *One* is not liable, however, simply because *one* uses the services of an independent contractor. Nor is *one* liable because of the mere fact that the contractor performs his work on *one's* land or, as in this case, on *one's* ship." *Futo v. Lykes Bros. Steamship Co.,* 742 F.2d 209, 215 (5th Cir. 1984). Enough said.

B. *One . . . his* is inferior to *one . . . one's.* Yet this infelicity is common. E.g., "A constructive trust, on the other hand, arises when *one* obtains the legal title to property in violation of a duty *he* [better: *one*] owes to another."/ "If *one* were thoughtless, *he* [better: *one*] would be apt to say that this is a case in which part of the operative facts creating the original obligation are directly presented to the senses of the tribunal."

Even worse are constructions on the order of *one . . . such person,* as here: "The United States Supreme Court has held that *one* may be in custody for habeas corpus purposes despite the fact that *such person* [read *one*] has been released from jail or on personal bond."

C. *One,* adj., as in *"one Howard James,"* is almost always superfluous. This usage is a pretentious LEGALISM with a valid pedigree in English, but without justification in modern prose. It might even hint at BIBLICAL AFFECTATION, for the *OED* quotes from the Bible: "and of *one* Jesus, which was dead, whom Paul affirmed to be alive." Today, however, this adjectival *one* looks askance at the name following it.

one . . . his. See **one** (B).

on his own application is LEGALESE for *at his request.*

one of those (+ plural noun) who (that) takes a plural, not a singular, verb. E.g., "This is one of the legal-writing texts that *is* [read *are*] worth reading." The reason for this construction becomes apparent when we reword the sentence: "Of the legal-writing texts that *are* worth reading, this is one."

one's self is an ARCHAISM for *oneself.* "One should learn to pace *one's self* [read *oneself*]."

on its face. See **face, on its.**

only is perhaps the most frequently misplaced of all English words. Its best placement is precisely before the words intended to be limited by it. The more words separating *only* from its correct position, the more awkward the sentence; and such separation can lead to ambiguities. E.g., "A *pro se* complaint can *only* be dismissed for failure to state a claim [delete *only* after *can* and insert here] if it appears beyond doubt that the plaintiff can prove no set of facts in support of his claim which would entitle him to relief."/ "These public rights can *only* be destroyed [delete *only* after *can* and insert here] by proper municipal action."/ "*Erie* is *only* applicable [delete *only* after *is* and insert here] where there is no controlling federal statue."/ "If the intestate were a married woman and her husband became administrator, *he succeeded to the only personalty* [read *he succeeded only to the personalty*] that was not already his by the marital right."/ "Suffice it to say that I am quite satisfied that the court in that case was saying that an interrogatory may *only* be administered as to the contents of a written document [delete *only* after *may* and insert here] if secondary evidence of that document would be admissible at the trial or hearing." (Eng.)/ "A conditional promise is one which the promisor *need only perform if* [read *need perform only if*] a specified condition occurs." See **solely.**

on or about is the lawyer's hedge-phrase for dates, used esp. in pleadings. E.g., "*On or about* August 31, 1981, plaintiff and defendant entered into an assignment and assumption agreement." If the date is known with reasonable certainty, *on* is sufficient. See FUDGE-WORDS & **on and after.**

on point. See **in point.**

onus, lit. "a burden" (L.), usually carries the extended meaning "a disagreeable responsibility; obligation." In law, it also acts as an elliptical form of *onus probandi,* meaning *burden of proof.* E.g., "The mode of suing for and receiving penalties and forfeitures does not necessarily include any rules . . . as to *onus probandi.*" 1 F. Cas. 36, 37 (C.C.D. Mass. 1824)

(No. 18). *Onus of proof* is a compromise between the two more usual phrases: "The *onus of proof* should be put the other way round where a question of status of this nature arises." (Eng.) See **burden of proof** & LOAN TRANSLATIONS.

op. cit. is the abbreviation for *opere citato* (= in the work cited). It is no longer used in legal citations, and is obsolescent in other scholarly writing.

open-ended(ness) should be hyphenated, in order that it not look too monstrous. E.g., "Much more than desirable *open-endedness* seems to be involved."

operable; operative, -tional. *Operable* is now commonly used in the sense "practicable; capable of being operated." *Operative* = (1) having effect; in operation; efficacious; (2) having principal relevance ⟨*may* is the operative word of the statute⟩; or (3) (in legal BrE) expressing intent to perform a transaction (*COD*). *Operational* = engaged in operation; able to function; used in operation. E.g., "While a rate of slightly under ten violent incidents per month may seem shocking at first even for a large correctional institution, this figure must be evaluated in light of the fact that no *operational* definition of 'violence' has been established."

ophthalmology is sometimes misspelled *ophthamology* or *opthamology.*

ophthalmologist; oculist; optometrist; optician. The first two designate an M.D. whose specialty is the eye, although *ophthalmologist* is now more usual. An *optometrist* (with the degree of O.D.) is licensed to prescribe glasses and contact lenses. An *optician* makes the glasses in accordance with the prescription.

opine today usually connotes the forming of a judgment on insufficient grounds. It suggests the giving of an idle opinion, and thereby cheapens the opinion given. Formerly, however, the word was used in the sense "to express or pronounce a formal or authoritative opinion" (*OED*). The *OED* calls this sense rare; yet, in American law at least, this usage could hardly be accurately described as rare. Examples abound in which the verb is used of courts' pronouncements, without any suggestion of insufficiency of evidence. E.g., "None of the justices appear to have *opined* that the equal protection clause does not apply to illegal aliens."/ "The Supreme Court of New Jersey *opined*, in *Santor v. A. & M. Karaghensian*, that a cause of action under strict liability could be utilized to recover economic losses." We should not restrict *opine* because of its negative lay connotations; the term is a useful one in law.

It is unclear whether cheapening was here intended: "A plaintiff who does not have asbestos-related cancer may find a medical witness who will *opine* that there is a reasonable probability that he may later develop the disease." One cannot really *opine* about one's own thoughts: "I merely *opine* that I am hard-pressed to imagine a more appropriate case for the use of legislative history than the present one." [Read *I would be hard-pressed to imagine* . . . .]

opinion, v.t., is a NEEDLESS VARIANT of *opine,* q.v. "An F.B.I. document *opinioned* [read *opined*] that some of the writing on the government's exhibit was the same as handwriting exemplars taken from the defendant." (Note that to say a *document opines* is to engage in HYPALLAGE.)

opinion, of (the). Modern idiom requires *of the opinion;* to omit the definite article is to use an ARCHAISM that survives only in the law. In each of the following specimens, *the* should be inserted in the italicized phrase: "We are *of opinion* that the findings of fact by the district court entitled the appellee to the equitable relief sought."/ "If the court is *of opinion* that any evidence was improperly admitted or rejected, it must set aside the conviction." (Eng.)

Today, *of the opinion* seems to outnumber *of opinion* in legal opinions by three or four occurrences to one, in both BrE and AmE, despite what the examples just quoted might suggest. E.g., "We are *of the opinion* that plaintiff does not have a cause of action against this defendant."/ "For reasons to be stated, we are *of the opinion* that the judgment of the Supreme Court of Georgia should be affirmed."

opinions, rule against. This rule of evidence carries different senses in G.B. and in the U.S., primarily because of the different understandings of the word *opinion*.

> The opinion rule, though it developed from practices and expressions of the English courts, seems to be emphasized more generally and enforced more inflexibly here [in the U.S.] than in the mother country. In the first place a rule against 'opinions' may have had a different meaning for the English judge. We are told that in English usage of the 1700's and earlier *opinion* had the primary meaning of "notion" or "persuasion of the mind without proof or certain knowledge." It carried an implication of lack of grounds, which is absent from our present-day term *opinion* in this country. We use the word as denoting a belief, inference, or conclusion, without suggesting it is well- or ill-founded.
>
> McCormick's *Handbook of the Law of Evidence* 22 (E. Cleary 2d ed. 1972).

OPINION WRITING is a peculiar task, different from ordinary discursive or persuasive prose. The primary difficulty lies in giving either a "yes" or a "no" answer to what is often an extremely complicated problem. The decision generally must be consistent with previous judicial decisions, and must at the same time conform to the judge's notions of what justice dictates. Often, and especially in difficult cases, the doctrine of stare decisis plays tug-of-war with concientious fairness. The dilemma is especially acute inasmuch as some of the most complex problems of society and of individual human lives must be reduced to the simplest of dichotomies: yea or nay. Not all the uncertainties can be plumbed by the judge writing an opinion; his task is to justify his determination, crude as the framework may be for minimizing the possibly substantial merits of the losing side.

Dean Wigmore identified six shortcomings of judicial opinions: (1) undiscriminating citation of authority; (2) unfamiliarity with controlling precedents; (3) mechanical treatment of judicial questions; (4) misconception of the doctrine of precedents; (5) overconsideration of points of law; and (6) certain deficiencies peculiar to one-man opinions. 1 Wigmore, *Evidence* § 8 (3d ed. 1940). There are so many aspects of writing effective judicial opinions that no short treatment could pretend to cover even the primary ones. A few short observations may be helpful, however. The reader who needs more detailed guidance may read any number of articles, or

the one serviceable book on the subject. See LEGAL WRITING STYLE (D). But, all in all, we must await production of a first-rate treatise on this subject.

A. Tense. It is generally best in judicial opinions to write in the present tense when referring to the parties or facts before the court that have continuing validity, or seem to from all that appears in the record. Thus, if a judge writes, "The defendants *were* citizens of Clarksville, Tennessee," the reader must wonder whether they have moved or died. What the judge here doubtless meant is that these persons *were* defendants, but now that the trial is over they are no longer. Use of the past tense in this way needlessly puzzles the reader, even though the author knows that the opinion is being written some time after the trial or sitting.

Less troublesome, but also to be avoided, is the mannerism of using the future tense, as in "The judgment *will be* affirmed." Such statements often appear toward the beginning of an opinion, so that at the end, the court may conclude, "The judgment *will be, and hereby is,* affirmed." This messing about with tenses is unnecessary. The writing judge should be direct: "We affirm the judgment below."

B. Judicial Humor. Drollery and judicial opinions almost invariably make an unhappy combination. "[T]he form of opinion which aims at humor from beginning to end is a perilous adventure, which can be justified only by success, and even then is likely to find its critics almost as many as its eulogists." Cardozo, *Law and Literature*, 52 Harv. L. Rev. 472, 483 (1939). One of those critics of judicial humor was Justice George Rose Smith, formerly of the Arkansas Supreme Court, who observed, "Judicial humor is neither judicial nor humorous. A lawsuit is a serious matter to those concerned in it. For a judge to take advantage of his criticism-insulated, retaliation-proof position to display his wit is contemptible, like hitting a man when he's down." Smith, *A Primer of Opinion Writing, for Four New Judges*, 21 Ark. L. Rev. 197, 210 (1967). Justice Smith cited an egregious example of attempted stream-of-consciousness humor: *Hampton v. North Carolina Pulp Co.*, 49 F. Supp. 625 (E.D.N.C. 1943); it is one of the worst opinions that has come to my attention. For an example of failed poeticism and wasteful drivel, see *United States v. Sproed*, 628 F. Supp. 1234 (D. Ore. 1986).

Lest we assume, however, that judicial writing should be cheerless and sober-sided, it is worth noting Cardozo's tempered judgment: "In all this I would not convey the thought that an opinion is the worse for being lightened by a smile. I am merely preaching caution." *Law and Literature*, 52 Harv. L. Rev. 472, 484 (1939).

C. Concurrences. A judge, and especially an appellate judge, writes not just for himself, but for the entire court. In concurring opinions, of course, the writing usually becomes more individualistic:

> If a judge is occasionally possessed of an uncontrollable desire to express his personal views instead of having them continually absorbed in the compromise pronouncements of the court, he may gratify that urge by the writing of concurring or, if so disposed, even dissenting opinions. But a concurring opinion must justify itself by furnishing a different reason for the court's decision, and even then should not be resorted to unless the writer of the majority opinion refuses to accept and incorporate the suggested additions or amendments. A concurring opinion which merely says the same thing in other language is not only valueless as a contribution to the science of the law but is somewhat of a reflection on the colleague to whom was assigned the duty of explaining the views of the court.
>
> Stern, *The Writing of Judicial Opinions*, 18 Pa. Bar Ass'n Q. 40, 44 (1946).

See **dubitante** & **write specially.**

D. Drafting Mandates. See JUDGMENTS, APPELLATE-COURT.

oppugn. See **impugn.**

opt (in) (out) (for). *Opt* = to choose or decide. It is usually followed by *for* or *to*, e.g.: "If Mr. P. had refuted the statements or failed to recall them, his prior testimony and the testimony of the agents could have been introduced; Chanya *opted* not to offer the challenged testimony in an acceptable manner." In the language of class actions, however, plaintiffs are said to have the choice of *opting in* or *out* of the class. E.g., "Some states instead provide *opt-in* provisions for these rights; for example, a corporation's shareholders will not have preemptive rights unless the articles of incorporation specifically provide for them." In fact, the phrase has been extended to the persons who *opt in* or

out; in modern American legal ARGOT, they are known as *opt-ins* or *opt-outs.*

optimacy is not a variant of *optimality*; it means "aristocracy."

optimum is the noun, *optimal* the adjective. The adjective should be used in adjectival senses where it idiomatically fits. E.g., "The *optimum solution* [read *optimal solution*] is an adjudication of the permission question."

opt in. See **opt.**

option, v.i. (= to grant or take an option on), dates from ca. 1926, but remains a VOGUE WORD. E.g., "Her first screenplay was *optioned* for a mere $300,000." It may be useful legal slang or ARGOT, but is best restricted to speech.

optionee. See **optionor.**

option-giver is a more comprehensible term than *optionor*, q.v. "There seems no difficulty in recognizing a unilateral option agreement supported by consideration or embodied in a sealed instrument as creating in the optionee an irrevocable power to create, at any time within the period specified, a bilateral obligation as between himself and the *giver of the option*; correlatively to that power, there would, of course, be a liability against the *option-giver* which he himself would have no power to extinguish."

optionor, -er. Only *-or* is included in *W3*. It is useful as a correlative of the lawyers' term *optionee* (= the grantee in an option contract), although *option-giver*, q.v., is clearer.

optometrist. See **ophthalmologist.**

opt out. See **opt.**

-OR, -OUR. All agent nouns but *saviour* (BrE) take *-or* in both the AmE and BrE (e.g., *actor, relator*). The distinction between AmE (*-or*) and BrE (*-our*) usage occurs in abstract nouns. Hence the British write *colour, flavour,* and *humour,* whereas Americans write *color, flavor,* and *humor.* The following words, however, end in *-or* on both sides of the Atlantic: *error, horror, languor, liquor, pallor, squalor, stupor, terror, torpor,* and *tremor. Glamour* is the primary exception to the rule of *-or* in the AmE.

In BrE, nouns ending in *-our* change to *-or* before the suffixes *-ation, -iferous, -ific, -ize,* and *-ous* (e.g., *coloration, honorific*). But *-our* keeps the *-u-* before *-able, -er, -ful, -ism, -ist, -ite,* and *-less* (e.g., *honourable, labourer, colourful*).

or. A. For *and.* "The life tenant may be forced to choose between giving up the life estate *or* [read *and*] making a contribution to the principal payments." See **between.**

   B. *Or/and.* See **and/or.**

oral. See **verbal** & **parol.**

oral argument (U.S.) = *oral debate* (G.B.). See **debate.**

oral will; nuncupative will; sailor's will; soldier's will. The broadest term is *oral will,* of which there are two types, both obsolescent: *nuncupative wills* and *soldiers' and sailors' wills.*

Nuncupative will is an English adaptation of the LAW LATIN phrase *testamentum nuncupativum* (= an oral will). If *nuncupative wills* are valid in a given jurisdiction, the amount that may be conveyed in them is usually limited by statute. Customarily, the will must be made in the testator's last illness, and sometimes in his own house, unless he falls ill elsewhere. Two competent witnesses are usually required.

Soldiers' and sailors' wills derive from ancient military and maritime custom; in England the privilege derives from statute. The soldier must be in military service, or the sailor at sea, and, in some jurisdictions, a single witness must be present. In Great Britain, the phrases *soldier's will, mariner's will,* and *military testament* are used.

Nuncupative is often used as broadly as *oral,* i.e., to encompass soldiers' and sailors' wills. E.g.,

A *nuncupative* will is not required to be in writing. It may be made by one who, at the time, is in actual military service in the field or doing duty on shipboard at sea, and in either case in actual contemplation, fear, or peril of death, or by one who, at the time, is in expectation of immediate death from an injury received the same day. It must be proved by two witnesses who were present at the making thereof, one of whom was asked by the testator, at the time, to bear witness that such was his will, or to that effect.
   Cal. Prob. Code § 54 (repealed).

The usual practice, however, is to call only the latter kind of will *nuncupative,* distinguishing it from *soldiers' and sailors' wills. Oral* encompasses every one of these types.

orate. See **perorate** & BACK-FORMATIONS.

orchestrate, in nonmusical contexts, is a CLICHÉ and a VOGUE WORD. It is, however, arguably useful in indicating that an (apparently spontaneous) event was clandestinely arranged beforehand. This sense is included in neither *W9* nor the *COD.* Cf. **choreograph.**

ordain (= to establish by law; enact) has an archaic flavor in other than religious contexts ⟨an ordained minister⟩. The word does not mean "to provide," as the author of the following sentence mistakenly thought: *"Article 2106 ordains that* [read *Article 2106 provides that*], if the affair for which the debt has been contracted in solido concerns only one of the co-obligors in solido, that one is liable for the whole debt." (La.)

order of leave. See **parole.**

ordinance; ordnance; ordonnance. *Ordinance* (= a municipal law) is common in the AmE but rare in BrE, where *by-law* serves this purpose. In AmE, *bylaw* is generally used to mean "a corporate rule or regulation not included in the articles of incorporation." See **by(e) law.**
   Ordnance = military supplies; cannon; artillery. *Ordonnance* = the ordering of parts in a whole; arrangement.

ordinar(il)y prudent man. With compound modifiers, either two adjectives before a noun or an adverb and an adjective before a noun, one must look closely at the sense to determine whether the first word is properly an adjective or an adverb. The most common problematic phrase in the law is *ordinar(il)y prudent man,* familiar in tort law. One sees both *ordinary* and *ordinarily* in the cases, but the latter is more logical, because *ordinary* modifies *man,* whereas *ordinarily* modifies the adjective *prudent.*

   The intended meaning, of course, is *man of ordinary prudence.* We do not mean *an ordinary man;* we mean *a man who is prudent to an ordinary degree.* One problem is that *ordinarily* in one sense means "often, usually." And if we (incorrectly) give it that sense, we end up with a man who is *ordinarily* (but not always) prudent—i.e., one who sometimes may be given to imprudence. It is difficult to be dogmatic in preferring *ordinarily prudent man* over *ordinary prudent man*, because of that ambiguity. But it is preferable nevertheless. E.g., "The jury shall be instructed that the minor is charged with the duty to exercise care for his own safety, commensurate with that degree of care usually exercised by an *ordinarily prudent minor* of the same age, intelligence, and experience of the plaintiff." See SEXISM (B).

ordnance; ordonnance. See **ordinance.**

ore tenus. Either *oral* or *orally* is preferred to this FORBIDDEN WORD. E.g., "The information contained in the above exhibits to the *ore tenus testimony* [read *oral testimony*] of the officers was delivered to the prosecuting attorney on May 15."

organic law = (in a civil law jurisdiction such as Louisiana) decisional law. E.g., "Louisiana *organic law* allows an individual to contract concerning liability for negligence in all cases where such a contract is not contrary to public policy."

Bouvier defines *organic law* as "the fundamental law or constitution of a state or nation," and uses the phrase in this way. E.g., In defining the "United States of America," Bouvier states, "the republic whose *organic law* is the constitution adopted by the people of the thirteen states which declared their independence of the Government of Great Britain on the fourth day of July, 1776." The phrase is still used in this sense: "[A]t the time when our *organic laws* were adopted, criminal trials both here and in England had long been presumptively open." *Richmond Newspapers, Inc. v. Virginia*, 448 U.S. 555, 569 (1980).

The phrase *organic statute* is used of a legislative act establishing an administrative agency.

orient; orientate. The latter is a NEEDLESS VARIANT of *orient*, which means "to get one's bearings or sense of direction."

original evidence. See **direct evidence.**

original instance. See **first instance.**

original jurisdiction; primary jurisdiction. The first phrase, meaning "jurisdiction to take cognizance of a case at its commencement, to try it, and to decide the issues," is usually contrasted with *appellate jurisdiction*. In the U.S., *primary jurisdiction* is original jurisdiction that lies in an administrative agency.

orse. is the abbreviated form of *otherwise*, q.v. "In his judgment, Sir Jocelyn Simon P. referred to some of the earlier decisions, including *H. v. H.* and the more recent decision of Scarman J. in *Buckland v. Buckland (orse. Camilleri)*." (Eng.)

OSP; obit sine prole. The Latin phrase means "he died without issue"; the translation suffices if we are to write out a phrase. The abbreviation may sometimes be justified, if the targeted readers are certain to understand its import.

ostensively for *ostensibly* is a solecism. E.g., "Although deposit insurance coverage is a function that *ostensively* [read *ostensibly*] could be handled by private enterprise, the United States also wanted to and did direct the F.D.I.C. to protect the public interest." *Rauscher Pierce Refsnes, Inc. v. F.D.I.C.*, 789 F.2d 313, 315 (5th Cir. 1986).

other good and valuable consideration. See **and other good and valuable consideration.**

otherwise. A. And *other*. Properly, *other* is the adjective, *otherwise* the adverb. "CPL 2.25B has no cognizable impact, substantial or *otherwise* [read *or other*; better: *or not*], on any right or interest of Kast." / "An interested person may appear before an agency in a proceeding, whether interlocutory, summary, or *otherwise* [read *or other*; better: *or of some other kind*], or in connection with an agency function." Follett believed that "to pronounce this *otherwise* inadmissible would be to fly in the face of a strongly established usage. But usage, which can allow on sufferance, cannot prevent it from being rejected by more exact writers." W. Follett, *Modern American Usage* 242–43 (1966).

B. *Otherwise than.* This phrase is often misused for *other than*. Dreidger is wrong to characterize *otherwise than* generally as "useful to specify one predicate modifier and expressly exclude all others." E. A. Dreidger, *The Composition of Legislation* 86 (1957). Its legitimate uses are few.

In the sentences that follow, *other* is called for. "Transactions by dealers subject to Section 16 are exempted if the transactions are part of ordinary trading activities in the company's securities and incident to the dealer's establishment and maintenance of a primary or secondary market, *otherwise than* [read *other than*] on a national securities exchange or an exempt exchange."/ "What we must ensure in the welfare state, *otherwise than* [read *other than*] the welfare of almost half the nation, is the virtual certainty that only the members of the government, and those who implement their orders, shall be reputed intelligent." (Eng.)

C. *Other . . . other than.* A fairly common mistake is to repeat *other* in the phrase *other than.* E.g., "Payment may be made pursuant to a differential based on any *other* factor *other than* sex." Either one of the *others* should be dropped.

D. *Otherwise expressed.* This is cumbersome and jarring for "in other words." E.g., "*Otherwise expressed,* the law is that . . . ." See **to put it another way.**

E. As a Conjunction. For elucidation of this common error, see RUN-ON SENTENCES.

otiose (= unneeded; not useful) is a word made use of more by lawyers than by other writers. E.g., "The question whether the assignees of the reversion were bound would have been wholly *otiose.*"/ "The words of the application for appointment are not to be struck out as being merely *otiose*; they are specific words." (Eng.)/ "If Mr Wiggins's argument is correct, the words 'as though the driver were in the hirer's direct employ' are *otiose,* since there is no need to import the notion of a vicarious responsibility in a matter in which the hirer has by his own direction caused the damage." (Eng.) Cf. **nugatory.**

-OUR. See -OR.

ought should always be followed by an infinitive, although there is a tendency in the U.S. to omit the particle *to* when the expression is in the negative or interrogative. Here the correct use is illustrated: "It was argued that theaters that patronized the union *ought not to* be patronized by the public."/ "It *ought* not to lie in the licensor's mouth to say at once that he has withdrawn his permission and that he has not withdrawn it." (Eng.)

Following are examples of the incorrect use, which, oddly enough, appears in the speech and writing of persons normally considered highly literate: "What *ought* the lawyers *do to* [read *to do to*] preclude litigation?"/ "We extend our efforts, as we *ought* [read *ought to*], toward effectuating the testator's intentions." The disfavored use is especially common after *not*: "A judge *ought not cease* [read *ought not to cease*] to be a citizen merely because he becomes a judge."/ "We *ought not* [read *ought not to*] impute to others instincts contrary to our own."

ought to; should. *Ought* should be reserved for expressions of necessity, duty, or obligation; *should,* the weaker word, expresses mere appropriateness, suitability, or fittingness.

ourself; theirself. *Ourself* is technically ill-formed, inasmuch as *our* is plural and *self* is singular. But it is established in the editorial or royal style. *Theirself* is indefensible, however.

oust = (1) to eject, dispossess, or disseise (constr. with *of*); (2) to exclude, bar, or take away (constr. with *from* or *of*). Hence, idiomatically speaking, one may either *oust a court of jurisdiction* or *oust jurisdiction from a court.* Today the former expression is more common, e.g.: "A contract that makes a certain person a final arbiter of all disputes that may arise under it cannot *oust* the court *of* jurisdiction." But the alternative wording has persisted: "The section obviously envisages action in a court on a cause of action and does not *oust* the court's jurisdiction of the action." *Barge "Anaconda" v. American Sugar Refining Co.,* 322 U.S. 42, 44 (1944). See OBJECT-SHUFFLING.

ouster. See **ejectment.**

out. A. As an Unnecessary Particle in Phrasal Verbs. *Out* commonly appears superfluously in phrases such as *distribute out, cancel out,* and *calculate out.* (Colloquially, it occurs in *lose out, test out,* and *try out.*) E.g., "Judge Critz with his energy to *study out* [read *study* or *study thoroughly*] a legal question did much to promote the orderly development of law in this state." See PARTICLES, UNNECESSARY.

Out is not a needless particle here: "Generally speaking, a manufacturer can *design out* danger only on the basis of the technology reasonably available to him at the time the design was made." The phrase *design out* (= to rid of [an undesirable characteristic]) is common in patent and products-liability contexts.

B. As a Noun. This usage ⟨counsel was looking for an out⟩ is colloquial.

outcomes has all the flavor of voguish GOB-BLEDYGOOK. E.g., "The central issue, which began in discipline research but has direct corollaries for policy research, concerns the effects of variations in school programs on schooling *outcomes*." Cf. PLURALS (B).

outer bar; utter bar. The former is the more usual form of this English phrase meaning "junior barristers, collectively, who sit outside the bar of the court, as opposed to Queen's Counsel, who sit within it" (*CDL*).

outlawry is a term specifically referring to persons. It means "the action of putting a person out of the protection of the law" (*OED*), or, secondarily, "defiance of the law." It is not synonymous with *proscription* as the noun corresponding to the verb *to outlaw*, though here it is erroneously used in that sense: "Wright came to believe that the proponents of the *outlawry* [read *proscription*] of war did not expect immediate effects from the Pact but rather were thinking in terms of generations." The context makes it clear that renunciation of war is the subject of discussion (hence *the outlawing of war*); *outlawry* does not work, although one might feebly argue that war here is being personified. See ANTHROPOMORPHISM.

out-of-court. See **extrajudicial.**

outside of is always inferior to *outside*. E.g., "The district court would have no jurisdiction to render judgment against appellee, who was served with process *outside of* [read *outside*] the territorial jurisdiction of the district court."/ "*Law Latin* is intended to differentiate Latin used in the law from other languages used in the law and also from Latin words used *outside of* [read *outside*] the law." Cf. **off of.**

over. A. Special Legal Uses. In the law of property, particularly of vested and contingent interests, *over* when used after a noun denotes that the interest named, whether vested or contingent, is preceded by some other possessory interest. For example, a *limitation over* includes a second estate in the same property to be enjoyed after the first estate granted expires. E.g., "There is the same danger of the creditors' being misled by false appearances, and induced to give credit to the equitable life tenant when the will or deed of trust provides for a cesser or *limitation over*, in case of an attempted alienation, or of bankruptcy or attachment, and the argument would lead to the conclusion that the English rule is equally in violation of public policy."/ "A conveyance by a grantor with a *limitation over* to his heirs was said to be governed by the doctrine of worthier title, under which a *limitation over* to a grantor's heirs resulted in an automatic reversion in the grantor and nullified the *limitation over*."

A *gift over* is one that follows another's life estate or fee simple determinable. E.g., "A few courts have taken the position that a provision for the forfeiture of a bequest upon contest is in terrorem and will not be enforced unless there is a provision for a *gift over* in case forfeiture occurs."/ "Since the sisters all predeceased George, the defendants assert that the alternative *gifts over* failed."

Remainder over is one type of *gift over*. Although *remainder* itself connotes a preceding estate, the phrase *remainder over* is a common one. E.g., "When a life estate with the *remainder over* is created in property, especially personal property of the nature that may be transferred or appropriated, a risk exists that the remainderman might not receive the property the testator intended he should have."/ "The chancellor found the effect of the deed was to convey a life estate to the husband's daughter, with a *contingent remainder over* to the wife's children." The plural form is *remainders over*: "She gave her husband a life estate in the family plate belonging to her, with *remainders over* after his decease."

B. For *more than*. This casualism is to be avoided in formal writing. E.g., "In *Coburn*, a class action was certified on behalf of the *over* [read *more than*] 200 victims of the Beverly Hills Supper Club fire."/ "The burden of proof is on the party claiming trademark abandonment, but when a prima facie case of abandonment exists because of nonuse of the mark for *over* [read *more than*] two consecutive years, the owner of the mark has the burden to demonstrate that circumstances do not justify the inference of intent not to resume use."/ "The auditorium was filled to capacity with *over* [read *more than*] eight hundred persons present." Cf. **above** (A).

overall is a VOGUE TERM. "Conclusory [q.v.] findings as to each of the *Zimmer* criteria are no more helpful than an *overall* conclusory finding of dilution."/ "The *overall* effect of the *Gibbs* decision has been to broaden pendent jurisdiction."

overarching. The *-ch-* is not pronounced like a *-k-*.

overflown is the correct preterit for *overfly*, q.v., but not for *overflow*, which properly makes *overflowed*.

overfly (= to fly over in an airplane) is uncommon except in legal usage and pilots' argot. Following are examples from legal writing: "No prescriptive easement to *overfly* plaintiff's land was acquired."/ "During these five years plaintiffs did not actually use the *overflown* land; thus the airplanes harmed no one." See **aviate.**

overlook; oversee. The first is sometimes misused for the second. To *overlook* is to neglect or disregard. To *oversee* is to supervise or superintend. *Look over* is also differentiated from *overlook*; it means "to examine."

overly is old, dating from about the twelfth century, but is best avoided. *Overly* is almost always unnecessary, because *over-* may be prefixed at will: *overbroad, overrefined, overoptimistic, overripe*, etc.; when it is not unnecessary, it is merely ugly. Some usage authorities consider *overly* semiliterate, although the editors of *W9* have used it in a number of definitions. Certainly this adverb should be avoided whenever possible, though admittedly *over-* as a prefix is sometimes ill-sounding. Yet it usually serves well, e.g.: "It assists the legislature to avoid cumbersome and *overelaborate* wording." (Eng.) When *over-* is awkward or ugly-sounding, one might have recourse to *too*.

Another possible substitute is *unduly*. "An *overly lax* [read *unduly lax*] standard would provide antitrust plaintiffs with a windfall and would violate the established principle that

an injury without damage creates no right to compensation."

In any event, one should always be consistent within a piece of writing: In one U.S. Supreme Court opinion, we find, in successive paragraphs: "The Supreme Court affirmed, rejecting the contention that the statute violated the First and Fourteenth Amendments as being vague and *overbroad*. . . . It was held that a person could attack a statute as being *overly broad*." (*Overbroad* is always preferable to *overly broad*.)

Other specimens follow, with suggested improvements: "The old 'legal memorandum rule' is now generally regarded as an *overly technical doctrine* [read *as an overtechnical doctrine* or *as too technical a doctrine*]."/ "The loss must be foreseeable when the contract is entered into; it cannot be *overly* [read *unduly*] speculative."/ "Courts have been eager to prevent direct interference without forcing one tribunal to be *overly cautious* [read *overcautious*] about the possibility that a prior suit in another forum may involve the property."

overreach = (1) to circumvent, outwit, or get the better of by cunning or artifice; (2) to defeat one's object by going too far. Sense (1) often obtains in legal contexts. "If, from a consideration of all the facts concerning the situation of the parties at the time the contract was made, the trial court concludes that the intended wife was not *overreached*, the contract should be sustained."

overrule; overturn; reverse; set aside; vacate. *Overrule* is usually employed in reference to procedural points throughout a trial, as in evidence ⟨"Objection!" "Overruled."⟩. *Overrule* is also used to describe what a superior court does to a precedent that it decides should no longer be controlling law, whether that precedent is a lower court's or its own. *Overturn* and *reverse* are terms to describe an appellate court's change to the opposite result from that by the lower court in a given case.

Set aside and *vacate* are synonymously used to denote an appellate court's wiping clean the judgment-slate. The effect is to nullify the previous decision, usually of a lower court, but not necessarily to dictate a contrary result in further proceedings. See JUDGMENTS, APPELLATE-COURT & **set aside.**

oversee. See **overlook.**

oversight = (1) an unintentional error; or (2) intentional and watchful supervision. See **overlook.**

OVERSTATEMENT. Such words as *clearly, patently, obviously,* and *indisputably* are generally rightly seen as weakening rather than strengthening the statements they preface. They have been debased. Some legal scholars have noted that when a writer begins a sentence with one of these words, he is likely to be leading up to something very questionable. See **clearly.**

Unconscious overstatement is also a problem in legal discourse. It is never good to overstate one's case, even in minor unconscious ways, for the writing will thereby lose credibility. Good writers are very wary of injudicious exaggeration. A common pitfall is the *more . . . than all* construction: "More black students are presently enrolled at the University of Texas Law School *than have attended the school in all its history* [read *than have attended the school in previous years cumulatively,* or *than have, all told, been heretofore admitted,* or *in all its history up to three years ago*]."/ "The approach used *in the United States* [read *in the judicial system of the United States*] to achieve information input [q.v.] and accurate output is mainly adversarial in nature."

"In 1971, Congress enacted two important statutes—the Federal Election Campaign Fund Act and the Federal Election Campaign Act—both designed to reduce the corrupting influence of money on the political process." No doubt the writer intended to say that 1971 saw the enactment of two major statutes designed to reduce financial corruption in campaigns; what he has said, however, is that 1971 saw the enactment of two major statutes, which, incidentally, had to do with reducing . . . . The problem is most easily identifiable if one reads the sentence without the names of the statutes set off by long dashes. The root of the problem is *both*, which makes the clause it introduces nonrestrictive rather than restrictive. The unconscious misstatement is eliminated when we omit *both*.

Shoddy overstatement occurs frequently in popular journalism: "Perhaps Senator Kennedy is at his best with those who count most in the world—his family." Though one might get the impression from various catchpenny tabloids that the Kennedy family *does* comprise "those who count most in the world," this is not what the writer intended to con-

vey. [Read *who for him count most in the world* or *who count most in the world to him.*] See ILLOGIC.

overturn. See **overrule.**

OVERWRITING. See PURPLE PROSE.

owing; owed. Although *owing* in the sense of *owed* is an old and established usage, the more logical course is simply to write *owed* where one means *owed.* The active participle may sometimes cause ambiguities, or mislead the reader if only for a second. E.g., "In the present case, we must consider whether to recognize a new liability *owing from* [read *owed by*] parents to their children for negligent supervision."/ "This was a claim for the sum of £1108 alleged to be *owing* [read *owed*] by the defendant to the plaintiff under a contract alleged to have been made between the plaintiff and the defendant for the construction of concrete foundation work." (Aus.)/ "No claim was filed in the estate by the mortgagee of the real property, although a balance of approximately $5,000 was still *owing* [read *owed*]."/ "A promise will normally be implied from an unqualified acknowledgment that the debt is *owing* [read *owed*], or from a part payment of the debt." See PASSIVE VOICE.

OXYMORONS are immediate contradictions in terms, as in the word *bittersweet.* Any number of relative oxymorons exist in legal parlance, e.g.: *ordered liberty, equitable servitude* (servitude in equity), *all deliberate speed* (from the U.S. desegregation cases), and *substantive due process* (substantive process?). Lay examples are more ostensibly contradictory, e.g.: "The Government is *advancing backwards* toward the regulation of share dealing." See **suicide victim.**

oyez, oyez, oyez is the cry heard in court to call the courtroom to order when a session begins. The word *oyez* was the LAW FRENCH equivalent of *hear ye*, q.v., in the Middle Ages. The pronunciation was first /oh-*yets*/, later /oh-*yes*/ or /oh-*yez*/. Hence in Anglo-American courts the word has traditionally been pronounced "oh yes"; that is the pronunciation given in the *OED.* Sometimes today *oyez* is given the Frenchified pronunciation /oh-*yay*/. *Oyes,* a variant spelling, is not now widely current.

P

pace /*pay-say*/ = with all due respect to; with the approval of. The expression is used in expressing a contrary position.

pacifist; pacificist. *Pacifist* is the established form. Etymologists formerly argued that *pacificist* is the better-formed word, but it is never seen.

paction = (1) the act of making a bargain or pact; or (2) the pact so made. In sense (2), the word is merely a NEEDLESS VARIANT of *pact* or *agreement* or *bargain*. In sense (1) the word is useful, but rare.

pain of, on. The phrase *on pain of death* was once common in law to express prohibitions the violation of which would result in punishment by execution. The phrase has passed into lay contexts, in which it is used facetiously. But it remains as a shortened phrase *on pain of* in legal usage. E.g., "Is it reasonable to require prison employees to have foreseen, *on pain of* section 1983 damage liability, the future of prisoners' rights to the degree evolved under *Ruiz*?" See LOAN TRANSLATIONS.

pair is incorrect as a plural form in, "He bought two pair of shoes." *Pairs* is the plural.

pale, beyond the. This phrase, which has passed into lay parlance in the sense "bizarre; outside the bounds of civilized behavior," derives from the legal sense of *pale* from English history ("a district or territory within determined bounds, or subject to a particular jurisdiction"). In legal writing the phrase is best used with awareness of its derivation, as here: "The jurisdiction of the Court of Appeals below turned on its determination that an interpretation of Rule 68 to include attorneys' fees is *beyond the pale* of the judiciary's rulemaking authority." See POPULARIZED LEGAL TECHNICALITIES.

palimony (= a court-ordered allowance paid by one member of a couple formerly living together out of wedlock to the other [*W9*]) is a PORTMANTEAU WORD first recorded in 1979. It has become rather common, and may justify its existence by its usefulness. It is unlikely to be anything other than a jocular word, however. *Galimony*, a similar form though of course more jocular, has been used of *palimony* between lesbians.

palming off; passing off. The two terms are perfectly synonymous ("putting into circulation or dispersing of fraudulently" [*OED*]), both being used with almost equal frequency in the AmE and BrE. *Passing off* is more peculiarly legal. E.g., "Unfair competition is almost universally regarded as a question of whether the defendant is *passing off* his goods or services as those of the plaintiff."/ "*Passing off* may be found only where the defendant subjectively and knowingly intended to confuse buyers." *Palming off* is used additionally in metaphorical lay senses. E.g., "Have you not tried to *palm off* yesterday's pun?"

palpable (lit., "touchable") = tangible; apparent. There is nothing wrong with using this word in figurative senses ⟨palpable weaknesses in the argument⟩, as it has been used since at least the fifteenth century.

pamphlet. This word is pronounced with the *-ph-* as if it were an *-f-*. A great many people incorrectly say /*pam-plĕt*/. Cf. *ophthalmology, amphitheater.*

panacea (= cure-all; nostrum) is sometimes confused with other words. E.g., "To allow the state to raise new matters not brought out in the original appeal or on rehearing would *open up a panacea* [read *bring on a plethora*? or *open up a pandora's box*?] of problems by way of precedent." This is a MALAPROPISM.

pandemic (= [of a disease] prevalent over the whole of a country or continent, or over the whole world). The word is usually adjectival, but may be used as a noun: "The strain was related to the one that was prevalent during the 1918-19 swine flu *pandemic* that was responsible for 20 million deaths worldwide, including the deaths of 500,000 Americans." See **epidemic.**

panel-shopping is analogous to *forum-shopping* in reference to panels usually consisting of three members of a court. E.g., "[The law of the case doctrine] discourages *panel shopping* at the circuit level, for in today's climate it is most likely that a different panel will hear subsequent appeals." *Lehrman v. Gulf Oil Corp.*, 500 F.2d 659, 662 (5th Cir. 1974).

panic, v.i., makes *panicked* and *panicking.* Usually intransitive, *panic* has appeared as a transitive verb, meaning "to affect with panic." E.g., "She did not want to *panic* the audience."

paper has a special legal sense in the phrase *commercial paper* (= negotiable documents and bills of exchange). The plural *papers* often refers to pleadings and other court documents ⟨We filed all the necessary papers⟩. See **negotiable instruments.**

paperwork should be spelled as one word.

parachronism. See **anachronism.**

paradigm. The preferred plural is *paradigms,* as opposed to *paradigmata.*

parajudge has been used to refer to U.S. Magistrates, who have some adjudicative power, but not the extent of power vested in Article III judges: "Under the 'para-judge' rationale, the Magistrates Act comports with Article III [of the U.S. Constitution] because it subjects magistrates' rulings to de novo determination by a federal district judge." *United States v. Saunders,* 641 F.2d 659, 663 (9th Cir. 1980).

paralegaling is a COLLOQUIALISM to name what it is that a paralegal (or *legal assistant*) does. The term is similar to *bailiffing* (see **bailiff**). See NOUNS AS VERBS.

PARALEIPSIS is a rhetorical tactic whereby a speaker or writer mentions something in disclaiming any mention of it. For example, a less than scrupulous cross-examiner would engage in paraleipsis if he stated, "Mr. Smith, I won't bring up your unsavory past as a wife-beater and pimp, but I would like to ask you some questions about your prior business dealings with the plaintiff." To which the fitting response is "Objection!," preferably after *unsavory.*

Following is an example of judicial paraleipsis in which the judge appears to be suggesting a tactic to one of the parties: "I purposely refrain from commenting on the possibility of any relief against Malcolm Dever's attorney, Dalona, which may be available to the defendants, or any title company that may have insured a Radner Heights fee for one of them." *Devers v. Chateau Corp.,* 792 F.2d 1278, 1299 (4th Cir. 1986) (Murnaghan, J., dissenting).

PARALLELISM refers to matching parts, i.e., analogous sentence-parts that must match if the sentence is to make logical sense. The problem of unparallel sentence-parts usually crops up in the use of correlative conjunctions and in lists. Following are a number of examples, with corrections in brackets within quotations or in parentheses following the quotations: "The 1975 rule abolishing sovereign immunity will not take effect until 1976 and will not apply to the case at bar or [to] any pending cases."/ "The essential elements of recklessness are present in this case, viz., proceeding through the intersection on a green light *and* [read *that was*] plainly visible on a broad well-lighted thoroughfare."/ "For federal diversity purposes, a corporation is a 'citizen' *of not only* [read *not only of*] the state in which it is incorporated, *but also of* the state where it has its principal place of business."/ "Marketing quotas *not only embrace* [read *embrace not only*] all that may be sold without penalty, *but also* what may be consumed on the premises" (Jackson, J.)./ "*Its continuance is contingent upon legally recognized rights of tenure, transfer, and of succession* [delete second *of* or insert *of* before *transfer*] in use and occupancy."/ "Defendants object to the request for production of documents on the grounds of relevancy, overbreadth, *burdensome* [read *burdensomeness*], oppression, and confidentiality." (This sentence contains ILLOGIC as well, because each item in the list spells out why the defendants object to it—hence *irrelevancy* should appear where *relevancy* does.)/ "The trial court was correct in excluding both the testimony of V.T.W. and *in excluding* [delete *in excluding* and insert *the*] defendant's exhibits 7 and 11."

Failures of parallelism are especially common in cumulative sentences, as here: "The defendants *admitted* that they published the article; *disavowed* any intention to defame and injure the plaintiff in his good name and reputation; *denied* that the article was maliciously composed, printed, or published; [read *and asserted*] *that* the article appeared simply as a news item and was brought in by one of its news-gatherers."/ "Cars may be seized if they constitute a traffic hazard, are evidence, *or if they are* [read *or are*] subject to forfeiture proceedings." If the writer wished to be more emphatic, whatever the cost of repetition, he could write: "Cars may be seized if they constitute a traffic hazard, if they are evidence, or if they are subject to forfeiture proceedings."

Less troubling is a lack of parallelism where two or more sentence-parts are balanced by *and*; but even this should be avoided: "The boy's operation of the car was unlawful and *negligence* [read *negligent*] per se."/ "Johann was a tall, thin man, dark-haired, near-sighted, not bad-looking, and *a fop* [read *foppish*]." (Here we have a string of adjectives—all implicitly modifying *man,* the antecedent of which is *Johann;* but the writer changes the last in the string to a noun phrase.) See CORRELATIVE CONJUNCTIONS.

paralyze, -lyse. The former spelling is the only one used in AmE; the latter is used in BrE.

parameters. Technical contexts aside, this jargonistic VOGUE WORD is not used by those with a heightened sensitivity to language. To begin with, no one who is not a specialist in mathematics or computing knows precisely what it means: it is a mush word. Second, when it does have a discernible meaning, it is usurping the place of a far simpler and more straightforward term. It abounds in legal writing, but does not occur in the best legal writing. E.g., "Since the parties have become legally obligated through their expression of assent, the *parameters* [read *boundaries?*] of their assent must be established, at least primarily, by their expressions."/ "The terms of its consent to be sued define the *parameters* [read *limits*] of the court's jurisdiction to entertain suit."/ "Within broad *parameters* [read *guidelines*], families are free to choose their method of child-rearing and to pick the values and aspirations transmitted to their offspring."/ "The purpose of pleadings is to put one's opponent on notice as to the *parameters* [read *grounds*] of the forthcoming battle."/ "Although it would have been appropriate to outline the *parameters* [read *elements*] of agency for purposes of the entrapment charge, a reading of the court's instructions satisfies us that the jury was neither misled nor confused."

Rarely is the word used in the singular, but

it does occur: "The dismissal in the instant case falls within the *parameter* of the present rule." *Clifford Ragsdale, Inc. v. Morganti, Inc.,* 356 So. 2d 1321, 1323 (Fla. Dist. Ct. App. 1978).

Sometimes *perimeter*, the meaning of which has influenced the senses of *parameter*, is used ostensibly so that the writer can sidestep any criticisms for the use of *parameter*. E.g., "The plurality held that the immunity extended even to malicious acts that were within the outer *perimeter* of the federal employee's line of duty."/ "All that is left for the district court to decide on is whether specific acts and allegations fall within this *perimeter*." Although this usage makes literal sense, *limit* or *boundary* or *border* would be a simpler term for the same notion.

paramount means "most important," not merely "important."

paramountcy is the nominal form of *paramount*, not often seen but quite proper.

paraphrase is occasionally misrendered *paraphraze*, as in *Eades v. Drake*, 332 S.W.2d 553, 556 (Tex. 1960). See **rephrase.**

parasitic, in reference to damages, does not mean merely "additional." Rather, the term means, in the words of Lord Denning, M. R.,

> that there are some heads of damage which, if they stood alone, would not be recoverable: but, nevertheless, if they can be annexed to some other legitimate claim for damages, may yet be recoverable. They are said to be *parasitic* because, like a parasite, in biology, they cannot exist on their own, but depend on others for their life or nourishment. . . . I do not like the very word *parasite.* A *parasite* is one who is a useless hanger-on sucking out the substance of others. *Parasitic* is the adjective derived from it. It is a term of abuse. It is an opprobrious epithet. The phrase *parasitic damages* conveys to my mind the idea of damages which ought not in justice to be awarded, but which somehow or other have been allowed to get through by hanging on to others. If such be the concept underlying the doctrine, then the sooner it is got rid of the better . . . . I hope it will disappear from [the textbooks] after this case.
> *Spartan Steel & Alloys Ltd. v. Martin & Co.,*
> [1973] Q.B. 27, 34–35.

Parasitic should not be used as a fancy variant of *dependent*, as here: "The legal characteristics of an individual's mental state under *Rees* are *parasitic* [read *dependent*] on the factual conclusions rendered by those testifying on the issue." The quotation from Lord Denning makes plain the metaphorical baggage that *parasitic* carries with it; and unless the metaphor is perfectly apt, the word should not be used.

parcel, n. (= a tract of land), is now primarily a LEGALISM. E.g., "This is a suit for a declaratory judgment to establish a trust in a two-fifths interest in five *parcels* of land devised absolutely to the respondent."

parcel out is a common PHRASAL VERB in the legal idiom. E.g., "It is not our job to decide whether the FSLIC could *parcel out* Old North's assets in this particular manner."

parcener. See **coparcener.**

pardon. See **commute** (B).

parens patriae = the father of a country. In England, the phrase is used of the king or queen; in the U.S., it is used of the state as a sovereign. E.g., "The Attorney General of Georgia was made a party after remand from this court, and, acting as *parens patriae* in all legal matters pertaining to the administration and disposition of charitable trusts in the State of Georgia in which the rights of beneficiaries are involved, he opposed the reversion to the heirs and argued that Baconsfield should be maintained as a park for the citizens of Georgia."/ "The practice has never, as far as we know, been introduced into any court in this country; and, if it exists anywhere here it is in the legislature of the Commonwealth as succeeding to the powers of the king as *parens patriae*."

parentelic method = the scheme of computation used to determine the paternal or maternal collaterals entitled to inherit. E.g., "Some American states have adopted a variety of the *parentelic method* for computing the kinship among collaterals."

PARENTHESES. A. Syntactically. Words contained within parentheses do not affect the syntax of the rest of the sentence. E.g., "We must determine whether each (or both) appellants are entitled to immunity." The writer of that sentence would not have made this error (*each appellants are*) if he had read the sentence omitting the parenthetical phrase. See PUNCTUATION (F).

B. Overuse of. Virtually any punctuation mark is subject to an annoying overuse, but this is especially true of parentheses—and long dashes—which to be effective must be used sparingly. When they appear at all frequently in writing, they tire the reader's eye, add to his burden in decoding, and cloy his interest. The sentence begins to sag with the qualifications here and there. The following is a two-sentence example from an opinion published in 1985:

> Marshall also relies upon his cross-examination of the government investigator (Ms. Sandlin) and of a government witness (Bitner; the Four Seasons manager and the custodian of its records—although he was not called upon by the government to authenticate the Four Seasons lawn-mower records) as showing the unreliability of Ms. Sandlin's opinion that three (or any) lawn mowers were actually missing, as she had testified on the basis of her deductions from the (incomplete) Four Seasons records . . . . However, if the testimony of Marshall's witnesses was to be believed (which was for the jury to determine), Marshall could not have been at the Frederick Street residence at the time Lee (thus mistakenly) believed that he saw him there.

None of these parenthetical interpolations is syntactically or stylistically justified.

C. With Appositives. See APPOSITIVES (B).

pari delicto, in. See **in pari delicto.**

pari materia, in. See **in pari materia.**

pari passu = with equal pace; equally; at the same time. The phrase is frequently used in contracts when several persons are paid at the same level or out of a common fund. E.g., "Hence when this £25 is withdrawn and mixed with £175 in the second account, the charges extend over the whole resulting £200, but only to the extent of £25, and this is divided up *pari passu* amongst the ten." (Eng.)

parol, synonymous with *oral*, is most properly pronounced /*par-ŏl*/. Yet, in the AmE, it is frequently pronounced like *parole*, namely, /pă-**rohl**/. That pronunciation is acceptable. Most commonly, *parol* is used adjectivally as an exact equivalent of *oral*: "When the mother placed the deed in her eldest daughter's name and that of her husband, she was relying on more than a bare *parol* promise made by a grantee to a grantor."/ "As a general rule, a cloud that may be removed by suit to quiet title is not created by a mere *parol* assertion of ownership of an interest in property."

It may, however, act as a noun meaning "word of mouth." E.g., "To permit such subsequent declarations to have such effect would be to convey an estate in land *by parol,* which is expressly prohibited by statute." *By parol* (= by word of mouth) is the commonest construction with the noun *parol,* but *in parol* (= in something said or spoken; in a statement or declaration) is also used: "Such agreements were often *in parol,* and where an unenforceable agreement *in parol* is attended by certain special circumstances, equity resorts to the remedial device of a constructive trust to accomplish justice."/ "Certainly it was not intended to enable anyone to make out of record a title resting solely *in parol.*"

parole (= the conditional release of a prisoner from prison) has long been the standard term in AmE; it existed in British military terminology in a related sense from the seventeenth century, and in this century has become standard in BrE in the American sense. *Ticket-of-leave* and *order of licence* were earlier BrE variants; *release on licence* is still a common equivalent in British legal contexts.

parricide; patricide. *Parricide* is the more usual word meaning (1) "the murder of one's own father"; or (2) "one who murders his own father." It is also used in extended senses, such as "the murder of the ruler of a country" and "the murder of a close relative." These are not examples of SLIPSHOD EXTENSION, however, for even the Latin etymon (*parricida*) was used in these senses.

part. See **portion.**

part, in. See **in pertinent part.**

partake is construed with either *in* or *of* in the sense "to take a part or share in some action or condition; to participate." *In* is the more common preposition in this sense: "As lawyers are *partakers in* a common enterprise,

the honor and reputation of every member should be the cause of all."

Of is common when the sense is "to receive, get, or have a share or portion *of*; to have something *of,* possess a certain amount *of*": "Voting by proxy is altogether unsuited to the performance of duties that *partake of* the nature of the judicial function."/ "The view that the defendant's fault *partakes of* wanton and intentional wrong was questioned."/ "The venture does not come within the purview of a special business arrangement *partaking of* some essentials of partnership."/ "The restrictive view is that the court's interpretation *partakes of* the same quality as the statutory text itself."

part and parcel is an idiomatic DOUBLET that emphasizes the sense of "an essential or integral portion; something essentially belonging to a larger whole." E.g., "We specifically held in *Barksdale* that a revoking clause in a will is a *part and parcel* of the will itself, without independent and immediate life or power, and that it survives or perishes with the will."

partially; partly. Whenever either word could suffice in a given context, *partly* is the better choice. *Partially* occasionally causes AMBIGUITY because of its other sense "in a manner exhibiting favoritism." *AHD* notes that *partly,* which has wider application, "is the choice when stress is laid on the part (in contrast to the whole), when the reference is to physical things, and when the sense is equivalent to *in part, to some extent*" ⟨partly to blame⟩ ⟨a partly finished building⟩. "*Partially* is especially applicable to conditions or states in the sense of *to a certain degree*; as the equivalent of *incomplete,* it indirectly stresses the whole" ⟨partially dependent⟩ ⟨partially contributory⟩ (*AHD*).

partible; partitionable. The latter is a NEEDLESS VARIANT not recorded in the dictionaries. *Partible* = subject to partition; separable ⟨the concurrent estate is partible⟩.

particeps criminis is an unjustified LATINISM in view of our simpler equivalent *accessory.* E.g., "A *particeps criminis* [read *accessory*] in the fraud has been permitted to recover in his own name against one who was no more guilty than he, when the marriage had taken place by reasons of such fraud." (Eng.)

PARTICIPLES, MISCELLANEOUS PROBLEMS WITH. **A.** Misleading as to Subject. E.g., "When purchasers of defective products sustain economic losses, considerations of justice require a court to interest itself in *originating causes* [read *the originating causes of the defect*] and to apply the principle of implied warranty on that basis."

B. Historical Present Participle. When a present participle in *-ing* is used in reference to a past action or event, it may create a vague or even ambiguous time frame. E.g., "Mrs. Marshall was injured in a fall *occurring* [read *that occurred*] on certain business premises located in Massachusetts."

C. Overeager. "If you are suffering from 'cabin fever,' *having* attended four of the last five of these national get-away get-togethers, I can heartily recommend this delightful form of relaxation." (*Having* appears at first to modify *you,* but in fact was meant to modify *I*.) See ANTICIPATORY REFERENCE & MISPLACED MODIFIERS.

D. For related discussions, see DANGLERS, FUSED PARTICIPLES, & PAST-PARTICIPIAL ADJECTIVES.

PARTICLES, UNNECESSARY. Any number of English verbs are regularly given particles in informal or colloquial contexts, and these particles often help to establish the informality or colloquiality of the writing. Thus a Good Samaritan *helps out* another rather than merely *helping* him. Following are a number of other examples. The particles are best avoided in legal prose: *award over (award), continue on (continue), convey away (convey),* and *proceed on (proceed).* Slight DIFFERENTIATION is possible with a number of phrases, such as *die off (die), face up to (face), meet up with (meet), lose out (lose), pay off* or *pay out (pay)* (see **pay** & **pay over**); with these phrases, the particles arguably add a nuance to the verb. One must always be on guard to ask whether the particles in one's writing pull their weight or give, instead, a breezy, slangy quality to one's prose.

PARTICLE VERBS. See PHRASAL VERBS.

particularized for *particular.* "Note that the doctrine of partial performance antedated the general concept of promissory estoppel and has its own *particularized* [read *particular*] rules." The sense here is not "made particular" but "particular"; hence *particularized* is

the wrong word for the context. Cf. **generalized.**

parties hereto is a REDUNDANCY. *Parties* are necessarily *parties hereto.*

partisan; partizan. The former is the preferred spelling in both AmE and BrE. Although the term denotes "one who takes part or sides with another," it has connotations of "a blind, prejudiced, unreasoning, or fanatical adherent" (*OED*).

partition. To a layman this is something that separates, esp. one part of a space from another; to a lawyer, *partition* = a division of real property into severalty. The word is also commonly a verb in legal writing; it means "to divide (land) into severalty" ⟨action for partitioning an inheritance⟩. See **partible.**

partitionable. See **partible.**

partizan. See **partisan.**

partner. See **copartner** & **coparcener.**

party is a LEGALISM that is unjustified when it merely replaces *person.* If used as an elliptical form of *party to the contract* or *party to the lawsuit, party* is quite acceptable as a TERM OF ART. E.g., "Either *party* may enforce the terms of this contract, and in the event that either *party* must use attorneys to effect such enforcements, then such expenses and other fees may be charged against the other *party*." See **party of the first part.**

PARTY APPELLATIONS. Generally, it is best to humanize the parties in a lawsuit by calling them by their names, e.g., "Jones" and "Smith." This principle holds true for briefs as well as for opinions. Otherwise, the reader is forced continually to rethink who is the petitioner and who the respondent; who the appellant and who the appellee; or, worse yet, who was plaintiff below, now appellee (or is it appellant?). It is easier to remember that Jones is the appellant than that the appellant is Jones, for every case has an appellant, but not every case has a Jones.

Problems arise, however, with matters of procedure. "Jones failed to preserve error" is an invidious legal fiction, inasmuch as it was Jones's attorney, not Jones, who failed to preserve error. Judicial opinions should avoid obscuring the responsibility for procedural mistakes. In such contexts, *appellant, appellee, plaintiff,* and other other such appellations are preferable, for they more nearly connote attorney and client jointly. Even phrasing the statement thus, "Counsel for appellant failed to preserve error," would not be inappropriate, although from the lawyer's perspective it is a harsher statement. See **plaintiff.**

party in interest = a natural or juristic person having a legal or economic interest in litigation or arbitration. E.g., "The trouble with appellant's position in this case is that no stipulation was presented to the court signed by all *parties in interest.*"

party litigant. See POSTPOSITIVE ADJECTIVES.

party of the first part, etc. This time-worn expression, formerly common in contracts, is invariably inferior to the name of the party (of whichever part), or *buyer* and *seller,* etc. The phrase is quintessential LEGALESE. See PERSON.

pass. A. Judicial Senses. The phrase *pass on* or *pass upon* has a peculiar meaning in legal writing, namely, "to decide." It is used primarily of questions of law: "Justice Pope has asked his associates to *pass upon* this matter."/ "The question whether the English rule prevails in this state was left undetermined in *Phelps v. Robbins,* and has never been *passed upon* since."

Yet the phrase has been used also in reference to juries, which of course decide questions of fact: "It is not the province of this court to *pass upon* the weight of the evidence; we think there was a fair question for the jury, and they must *pass upon* it uninfluenced by any intimation from us."/"Some courts have nearly gone to the extent of holding that where the language is severe, the jury should *pass upon* the case under proper instructions."

B. Testamentary Senses. In the context of wills and estates, *pass* may be either transitive or intransitive. Ordinarily it is intransitive: "The purpose and will of the makers was that the property of the one first to die *pass* at his or her death as he or she directed by and under that instrument, and that it, by its terms, necessarily cease to operate as to the estate of the survivor."/ "Intestate real property *passes* by descent and intestate personal property *passes* by distribution."

But it may also be transitive: "The instrument is supposed to *pass* property only upon death."/ "The judgment of the county court construing the first paragraph of the will to *pass* all personal property possessed by the testator at his death to his widow is affirmed."

passable; passible. The former means "capable of being passed; open"; the latter means "feeling; susceptible to pain or suffering."

passim is used in citing generally to references, and indicates that the work cited treats the point at hand throughout. Specific references are preferred in legal citations; when a general reference is called for, *see generally* is the signal most frequently used. *Passim* is especially useful in the index of authorities contained in the front matter of a brief.

passing off. See **palming off.**

PASSIVE VOICE. "Avoid the passive," one often hears; yet many do not really understand what voice is in grammar, let alone what the passive voice is. The active voice indicates that the subject does or is something: "John hits the ball." The passive voice represents the subject as something that is acted upon: "The ball is hit by John." The two sentences say essentially the same thing, but the emphasis is changed. The passive is wordier, and problematic inasmuch as one need not name the actor: "The ball is hit." Thus passive voice may lead to vagueness, or lend itself to purposeful obfuscation (see (E) below).

Moreover, although the passive voice has its occasional legitimate uses, when it appears at all frequently the writing becomes much less interesting and readable. Avoiding the passive is good general advice; but one should not make a fetish of it. Following are different types of passive voice with their own peculiar problems, along with suggested remedies.

A. The Otiose Passive. This is the type of passive that results from lazy thinking, as in "The ball is hit by John." This syntax subverts the English-speaking reader's reasonable expectation of a direct subject-verb-object sequence, unless a departure from that sequence is in some way an improvement. Examples of the unjustified passive-verb sequence follow. "Common trust fund legislation *is addressed to* [read *addresses*] a problem appropriate for state action."/ "The fee simple interest could have been conveyed by her to the defendant." [Read *She could have conveyed the fee simple interest to the defendant.*]/ "It is not found that [read *The court does not find that*] defendant did so with the intent and purpose of destroying the value of plaintiff's interest in the promissory note, as the complaint alleges."/ "After both sides had rested, *a conference was had between the trial judge and counsel* [read *the trial judge and counsel conferred* (or *had a conference*)]."/ "It is insisted by Sue [read *Sue insists*] that the power of appointment given George in their mother's will was nonexclusive."

B. Confusion of Active and Passive Constructions. "Assuming Hager drew up the contract, it becomes even more clear that *it was done so without* [read *he did so without*] any approval by us."/ "Either review can be summarized, *as did Judge Rubin*, with the following observations." If the first clause is to be passive in the latter specimen quoted, then the second must also be passive [read *as was done by Judge Rubin*] to make the clauses parallel. But the best version would be to write both clauses in the active voice: "*One can summarize* either review, *as Judge Rubin did*, with the following observations."

Here the combination of active and passive constructions leads to problems of syntax and logic: "In his affidavit in opposition to defendants' motion, plaintiff Nishimura acknowledges *that plaintiffs were never interested in, much less sought* [read *that plaintiffs never had an interest in, nor sought*], rights to produce and distribute the teams' games on an exclusive, metropolitan-wide basis."

C. The Ambiguous Passive. Here an ambiguity is caused by the lack of subjects before the passive verbs: "To avoid dermatitis, skin contact with the epoxy must be minimized, rigorous personal cleanliness encouraged [by the user?], and suitable protective equipment used by the operator." The operator is not the one to encourage personal cleanliness; he must *practice* it. Rather, the manufacturer is encouraging cleanliness.

D. Active Wrongly Used for Passive. With a few verbs, it has become voguish to use the active construction where, according to sense, the passive should appear. Thus the following statement was made to a psychiatric patient: "At the time you *were counseling* [read *receiving counseling* or *being counseled*], were you contemplating suicide?" Cf. the colloquial British usage, "You need your head *examining* [read *examined*]."/ "The video deposition is *now filming* [read *being filmed*]."/ "The cases *divide* [read *can be divided*] into two categories, roughly paralleling the sometimes fuzzy distinction between legislative and interpretative rules." See **owing; owed.**

E. The Dishonest Passive. Sometimes the passive is used (as there!) in a way that is of questionable honesty. In a negligence case in which plaintiffs, a minor and his mother, have accused the retailer defendant of negligence in selling lighter fluid to the minor, this sentence occurs: "The minor plaintiff attempted to fill said lighter and *was caused to* set himself on fire."—*Was caused to* is superfluous and misleading, for one immediately wonders, by whom?

F. The Double Passive. The problem here is using one passive immediately after another. E.g., "This article refers to the portion of the votes *entitled to be cast* by virtue of the articles of incorporation." (Votes are not *entitled to be cast*; rather, persons are *entitled to cast votes*.)/ "Had an absolute liability theory *been intended to have been injected* into the Act, much more suitable models could have been found." Fowler writes that "monstrosities of this kind . . . are as repulsive to the grammarian as to the stylist" (*MEU2* 138).

In legal writing, the problem is especially common where the verb *attempt* appears: "The possibility that such a pleading informality may occur in a proceeding of this nature *has been attempted to be prevented* by our Rule 27(a)."/ "The second ground on which this action *is attempted to be supported* fails also." (Eng.)/ "Explosions were not what *was attempted to be guarded against* by the statute." [Read *The statute did not purport to guard against explosions.*] This construction is likewise common with *seek:* "The defendant against whom the option *was sought to be exercised* was in fact the assignee of the reversion." (Eng.)/ "A distinction *is sought to be drawn* between this case and those cases in which the decedent was an infant and the negligent parent a beneficiary." These are the types of constructions that Fowler called "monstrosities."

Some double passives are defensible, e.g.: "Offerings made in compliance with Regulation D *are not required to be registered* with the SEC under the Securities Act." As Fowler notes, "In legal or quasi-legal language this construction may sometimes be useful and unexceptionable: *Diplomatic privilege applies only to such things as are done or omitted to be done in the course of a person's official duties.*/ *Motion made: that the words proposed to be left out stand part of the Question"* (*MEU2* 139). But these are of a different kind from *are sought to be included* and *are attempted to be refuted,* which can be easily remedied by recasting. "The rule," states the *Oxford Guide* (p. 148), "is that if the subject and the first passive verb can be changed into the active, leaving the passive infinitive intact, the sentence is correctly formed." Here, e.g., a recasting of the first passive verb form into the active voice results in a sentence that makes sense:

Passive/Passive: The prisoners were ordered to be shot.

Active/Passive: He ordered the prisoners to be shot. But in the following example, a recasting of the first passive verb into the active voice does not make sense:

Passive/Passive: The contention has been attempted to be made.

Active/Passive: He attempted the contention to be made (unEnglish). Sense can be restored to this sentence by casting both parts in the active voice:

Active/Active: He attempted to make the contention.

G. Special Active Use with *issue.* In contexts discussing mandamus and other writs, *issue* is used actively where most laymen would make it passive: "At the last term, viz., December term, 1801, William Marbury [et al.] severally moved the court for a rule to James Madison, Secretary of State of the United States, to show cause why a mandamus should not issue [a layman would write *be issued*] commanding him to cause to be delivered [better: *commanding him to deliver*] to them respectively their several commissions as justices of the peace." (Marshall, C.J., in *Marbury v. Madison.*)/ "Mandamus will not *issue* to compel performance of an act that involves exercise of discretion." See **issue.**

pass muster. See **muster.**

pass on; pass upon. See **pass** (A).

past experience is one of our commonest REDUNDANCIES, for experience by its very nature is rooted in the past.

pastime is sometimes misspelled *pasttime.* The misspelling derives from a misunderstanding of the word's origin, *pass* (v.t.) & *time,* not *past* & *time.*

PAST-PARTICIPIAL ADJECTIVES. Some past participles work perfectly well as adjectives, and others do not. There can be a tired or irritated person, but not a disappeared person: "Because of the nonaccess between C.W. and her *disappeared husband* [read *husband who has disappeared*], such a presumption should fail." The reason is that *disappeared* has not been accepted idiomatically as a prepositive adjective, whereas other past participles such as *tired* and *irritated* have been. Some legal phrases can be framed either way, thus (most traditionally) *cases decided* and *cases cited,* or *decided cases* and *cited cases.*

patdown, n. (= frisk), is one word.

patent, n., v.t. & adj. In the adjectival sense of "obvious, apparent," the preferred pronunciation is /**payt**-ŭnt/. In all other senses and uses the pronunciation is /**pat**-ŭnt/.

patentable began as a nineteenth-century Americanism, but is now widely used in BrE as well as AmE.

patent ambiguity. See **ambiguity.**

pathos. See **bathos.**

patricide. See **parricide.**

paucital; multital. These legal terms were used by Hohfeld and other legal philosophers, but are not recorded in the dictionaries and are now generally disused. *Paucital* = in personam; *multital* = in rem. E.g., "If B owes A a thousand dollars, A has an affirmative right in personam, or *paucital* right, that B shall do what is necessary to transfer to A the legal ownership of that amount of money. If, to put a contrasting situation, A already has title to one thousand dollars, his rights against others in relation thereto are *multital* rights, or rights in rem."/ "A *multital* right, or claim (right in rem), is always one of a large class of fundamentally similar yet separate rights, actual and potential, residing in a single person but availing respectively against persons constituting a very large and indefinite class of people."/ "Some of the overspreading classifications consist in the following: relations in personam (*paucital* relations) and relations in rem (*multital* relations)." (Hohfeld) See **in rem** & **in personam.**

paucity means "dearth; fewness." The word indicates a small quantity, not a complete lack of something, as this sentence erroneously suggests: *"There is a complete paucity of evidence as to* [read *There is no evidence on*] whether Malinda's back condition might reasonably be expected to cause any pain or disability."

pauper is no longer used in lay contexts except for historical or humorous purposes. It is still used, however, by straight-faced judges of impecunious parties in litigation. E.g., "I am of the opinion that the defendant should pay the costs of this House to a successful *pauper appellant.*" (Eng.) See **in forma pauperis.**

pawnor; pawnee. The *pawnor* is the owner of an item of goods who transfers it to another (the *pawnee*) as security for a debt. Nonlegal writers and dictionaries use the spelling *pawner.*

pay; pay up. The latter means "to discharge completely (a debt)." The former may refer to partial or total payments. Thus, because of this slight DIFFERENTIATION, *up* is not a needless particle. Cf. **pay over.** See PARTICLES, UNNECESSARY.

payor. The *OED* and *W3* have their main entries under *-er,* but *-or* is more common in American legal writing. E.g., "If the *payor* raises a purchase money resulting trust, the oral agreement is regarded as confirming the presumption of surplusage." Ironically, the spellings are *payor* but *taxpayer.* In BrE the spelling *payer* is common.

pay over. Though appearing to be a REDUNDANCY, this common legal idiom is often justifiable. *Over* signifies in this phrase the perfective aspect of the verb (the payment is completed); *pay* alone is imperfective. This is not to say that *pay over* is justified in all the examples quoted below, but it might well be in the first and fourth: "When sovereigns or banknotes are *paid over* as currency, as far as the payer is concerned, they cease ipso facto to be the subjects of specific title as chattels." (Eng.)/ "During the first three quarters of 1978, appellee failed to *pay over* [read *pay*] to the United States certain withheld income taxes."/ "The fact that the money was *paid over* [read *paid*] to the wife, for her support and the support of the children, certainly does

not conflict with the order of this court."/ "Upon her death, the principal was to be *paid over* by the trustees to such persons as the settlor might appoint by will, or, in default of such appointment, to the settlor's heirs at law and next of kin as in intestacy." See PARTICLES, UNNECESSARY.

peaceable; peaceful. Bill Bryson writes that *"peaceful* means tranquil and serene. *Peaceable* is a disposition towards the state of peacefulness." *A Dictionary of Troublesome Words* 114 (1984). The two words overlap a great deal, although strict DIFFERENTIATION between the words is worth encouraging.

peccavi (lit., "I have sinned") = an acknowledgment or confession of sin. The word is pronounced /pĕ-**kah**-vee/.

pectore, in. See LOAN TRANSLATIONS.

peculation has a more specific meaning than *embezzlement,* namely, "the appropriation of public money or property by one in an official position" (*OED*). In neither of the following quoted sentences is *peculation* quite the right word: "The most one can say for plaintiff's proofs as to the three lots is that a major part of the total down payment, on the home lot proper, by fair inference came from a then recent *peculation* [read *embezzlement*] of $2000 rather than from a sale of the Investors' Mutual stock." / "Here the evidence demonstrated that, had the officers of the defendant company exercised adequate supervision and been less willing to assume that Kershaw was a man of integrity, they could have prevented or discovered Kershaw's *peculations* [read *defalcations*]." See **defalcate.**

pecuniary; pecunious. The suffixes distinguish these words. *Pecunious* = moneyed; wealthy. (Its opposite is *impecunious* [= destitute].) *Pecuniary* = relating to or consisting of money. The adverb is *pecuniarily*: "They were quite unaware of the fact that it was to the plaintiff's advantage, *pecuniarily* or otherwise, to deal with Watson rather than with Ritchie's." (Eng.)

pediatrician; pediatrist. The former is the common, preferred term. The latter has the liability of causing confusion with *podiatrist* (= a foot doctor).

pejorative. So spelled, though sometimes mistakenly spelled *perjorative*, as in Leff, *The Leff Dictionary of Law*, 94 Yale L. J. 1855, 1865 (1985). (Ah, the hazards of being published posthumously!)/ "The majority resorts to *perjoratives* [read *pejoratives*]." *Compagnie des Bauxites de Guinea v. Insurance Co. of North America*, 651 F.2d 877, 889 (3d Cir. 1981) (Gibbons, J., dissenting).

penal; punitive; penological. *Penal* = of or relating to punishment or retribution. *Punitive* = serving to punish; intended to inflict punishment. *Penological* = of or relating to the study of the philosophy and methods of punishment and treatment of persons found guilty of crime. The words thus have distinct senses.

Penological is often used inappropriately for *penal*, perhaps because the usual phrase is *the state's penological interest*, and the state's interest sounds more clinical and dispassionate if *penological* rather than *penal* is used. That is not, however, sound justification for misusing the word. E.g., "The state by this statute imposing a fine has declared its *penological* [read *penal*] interest—deterrence, retribution, and rehabilitation—satisfied by a monetary payment, and disclaimed, as serving any *penological* [read *penal*] purpose in such cases, a term in jail." See EUPHEMISMS.

pend, v.i., (= [of a lawsuit] to be awaiting decision or settlement; to be pending) is a sense unrecorded by the *OED* and *W3*. In this novel AmE legal sense *pend* is really a BACK-FORMATION from the present participial form *pending* ⟨the case has been pending for three years⟩. *Pending* sounds more natural in most contexts in which *pend* appears. E.g., "[W]hile plaintiff's case *pended* [read *was pending*] in the trial court, . . . the defendant had presented itself as a contestant of any right of the plaintiff to obtain a valid judgment." *Car & Concepts, Inc. v. Funston*, 601 S.W.2d 801, 803 (Tex. Civ.App.—Ft. Worth 1980)./ "There is apparently no intimate relationship between the case sub judice and the proceeding that *pends* [read *is pending*] in an alien jurisdiction."

pendant. See **pendent.**

pendency (= the state or condition of being pending or continuing undecided) is largely a legal term. E.g., "The district court erred in awarding appellant interest during the *pendency* of the first appeal." *Pendence* is a

NEEDLESS VARIANT. E.g., "A severance will not be granted for the purpose of making a judgment final which otherwise would be interlocutory because of the continued *pendence* [read *pendency*] of other claims in the case." Dallas Civil Court Rules § 1.4(a) (1981).

pendent; pendant. The first is an adjective literally meaning "hanging; suspended"; the second is a noun meaning "something suspended, as a chain around one's neck."

Pendent, common in the legal phrase *pendent jurisdiction*, is occasionally misspelled *-ant.*

pendente lite. See **lis pendens.**

pendent jurisdiction. See **concurrent jurisdiction.**

penitentiary (= a reformatory or correctional prison) originally referred to an ecclesiastical office (i.e., a person appointed to deal with penitents). The idea of reform is embedded in the root meaning. Although for some time rehabilitation was not a major objective of American prisons, today it is on the rise.

penological. See **penal.**

pensioner. See **annuitant.**

penultimate; antepenultimate. The former means "next to the last," the latter "next to the next to last, or second from the last." *Penultimate* is common among educated writers, lawyers and laymen alike. E.g., "The *penultimate* paragraph of this opinion is deleted and the following is substituted."/ "The *penultimate* paragraph in *Witherspoon* includes a statement that on its face seems almost like a rule."

penumbra. The dictionaries prefer the plural *-ae*, but one could hardly be faulted for anglicizing the term and using *-as*, as Justice Douglas did in the quotation immediately following: "The foregoing cases suggest that specific guarantees in the Bill of Rights have *penumbras*, formed by emanations that help give them life and substance." (Douglas, J.)/ "We see no persuasive reason to extend the right of privacy, based as it is on '*penumbras* and emanations' of other more explicit constitutional rights, to evidentiary matters protecting marital relationships."

penumbral, -brous. The latter is a NEEDLESS VARIANT.

people; persons. The former is general, the latter specific. One refers to *English-speaking people* (or *peoples*) but to *the twelve persons on the jury*. *Persons* should virtually always be used with small, specific numbers.

peoplekind is an unnecessary formation for *mankind* or *humankind*. E.g., "While this solution would make everyone truly equal, it would be undesirable, because there would be no extraordinary individuals to lead *peoplekind* [read *mankind* or *humankind*] to new frontiers or new ideas." See **humankind.**

PER- as a prefix may mean "through" (*perspicuous, impervious*), or it may be an intensive (*perfervid, perforce, perchance*).

per. **A.** In Citations. *Per* is used to indicate the judge who has written a majority opinion. E.g., *In re City of Houston*, 745 F.2d 925 (5th Cir. 1984) (per Reavley, J.). *A Uniform System of Citation* now recommends omitting *per*; it is sometimes useful, however, when a writer cites a case and believes that the authorship of the opinion is in some way noteworthy.

B. For *a*. *Per* may become a necessary substitute for *a* when it is used prepositively in an adjectival phrase. E.g., "Entwistle calculated a *per-winch* profit figure of $3.20."/ "Defendants appeal, contending that the award of $150,000 *per* parent is excessive." See **a** (B).

peradventure is archaic in what used to be its primary sense, "perhaps." In the hackneyed phrase *beyond peradventure*, it means "doubt." E.g., "It is clear *beyond peradventure* that the income tax on wages is constitutional."/ "The meaning of the term in that subdivision is plain *beyond all peradventure.*"

Beyond peradventure of a doubt is a REDUNDANCY: "But it is clear *beyond peradventure of a doubt that* [read *beyond peradventure that*] appellant and Nelda considered these weekends as devoted to recreation and refreshment." Cf. **cavil, beyond.**

per annum is unnecessary for *a year, per year*, or *each year*. Cf. **per diem.**

per capita; per caput. The first is the frequently used plural ("by heads"), the second the rare singular ("a head; by the head").

per capita; per stirpes. The first means "by heads," the second "by stocks." In an in-

testate succession *per capita*, all claimants entitled to intestate shares take equally irrespective of the share to which an ancestor through whom they claim would have been entitled. In succession *per stirpes*, the shares are determined usu. at the first generation of takers, so that if one family stock has skipped a generation because a child has predeceased the decedent, the grandchildren of the decedent would divide among themselves an amount equal to what their deceased parent would have been entitled to.

percent; per-cent; per cent; per cent.; per centum. This sequence illustrates in reverse the evolution of this word, earlier a phrase. Today it is best spelled as a single word. The plural of *percent* is *percent*; adding an *-s-* is not uncommon, but is substandard.

perchance is an ARCHAISM for *perhaps*. "For if your system, *perchance*, lacks absolute utility, it is so much more efficient than that which we have had in our own country as to lead some to look to you for the solution of many of our common problems." (Eng.)

per contra = on the other hand; to the contrary; contrariwise. The phrase is sometimes a useful LATINISM because of its brevity.

per curiam is sometimes used as an elliptical form of *per curiam opinion*. E.g., "In the *per curiam* denying rehearing in *Bennett*, the en banc court for this circuit unanimously agreed on the statement of governing criteria by which a municipality's section 1983 liability is to be determined." See **by the court** & **per incuriam.**

per diem = for or by the day ⟨per diem fee⟩. Generally, it makes more sense to write *a day* ⟨$50 a day⟩ or *daily* ⟨daily fee⟩. See **a** (B). *Per diem*, a LATINISM, has been defended when it is positioned before the noun it modifies, but *daily* is undoubtedly an improvement. In no legal context, one can safely say, is *per diem* the best available phrase.

perempt. See **preempt.**

peremption. See **preemption.**

peremptory, adj., = admitting no contradiction or denial; incontrovertible. "The trial court erred in refusing to give the *peremptory* instruction that asked it to return a verdict of not guilty." *Peremptory* was originally a term from Roman law, meaning "that destroys, puts an end to, or precludes all debate, question, or delay" (*OED*) ⟨peremptory edict⟩.

Peremptory is often used as an elliptical form of *peremptory challenge* or *strike,* which denotes the removal of a venireman without showing cause. E.g., "In contrast to the course in England, where both peremptory challenge and challenge for cause have fallen into disuse, *peremptories* were and are freely used and relied upon in this country. . . ." *Swain v. Alabama,* 380 U.S. 202, 218 (1965)./ "After the *peremptories* were completed, Leslie's counsel moved for a mistrial."

perfect, v.t., = to bring to completion; to complete, finish, consummate; to carry through, accomplish (*OED*). This sense is now largely legal. "Both parties have *perfected* writs of error to this court."/ "A party capable of *perfecting* pro se an appeal from an order denying counsel is likewise capable of so *perfecting* an appeal after judgment on the merits."

perimeter. See **parameters.**

per incuriam is not the opposite of *per curiam* (= by the court); rather, it means "through inadvertence." Today it is used more commonly in G.B. than in the U.S. "Where the mind of the draftsman has never really been applied to the words in a particular clause, and the words are introduced into the will *per incuriam,* without advertence to their significance and effect by mere clerical error on the part of the draftsman or engrosser, the testator is not bound by the mistake unless the introduction of such words was directly brought to his notice." (Eng.) *Inadvertently* is a ready English substitute.

periodic tenancy; tenancy from year to year (or month to month). These phrases are equivalent, although the latter has the convenience of more universal comprehensibility.

period of time is usually unnecessary in place of either *period* or *time.*

PERIPHRASIS = a roundabout way of writing or speaking. Many a legal writer uses "jargon to shirk prose, palming off periphrasis upon us when with a little trouble he could have gone straight to the point." Quiller-Couch, *On the Art of Writing* 108 (1916; repr. 1961). See REDUNDANCY, EUPHEMISM & MALADROIT PROSE.

PERIPHRASTIC COMPARATIVES. See COMPARATIVES AND SUPERLATIVES (B).

perjorative is erroneous for *pejorative,* q.v.

perjure is now used only as a reflexive verb. "The petitioner maintains that he was unable to discover that these witnesses *perjured themselves.*" See **perjury.**

perjured; perjurious. *Perjured* is now the usual adjective corresponding to *perjury.* "The evidence must show beyond the existence of a reasonable doubt that the alleged *perjured* testimony of the person suborned was under oath duly and legally administered."

Perjurous is an obsolete spelling of *perjurious,* which is analogous in formation to *injurious.* E.g., "[A]n affidavit . . . was [allegedly] 'false and *perjurious.*'" *Sprecher v. Graber,* 716 F.2d 968, 970 (2d Cir. 1983)./ "The Supreme Court of Arizona has held that succumbing to a client's demand to elicit obvious *perjurious* testimony amounts to ineffective assistance of counsel." *Sanborn v. State,* 474 So. 2d 309, 313 (Fla. App. 1985).

perjury; false swearing; forswearing. The popular meaning of the first two terms is the same, namely, "swearing to what the witness knows to be untrue." *Forswearing* is a little-used equivalent of *false swearing; forswearing* also means, of course, "repudiating, renouncing." The technical DIFFERENTIATION at common law between *perjury* and *false swearing,* apart from their being separate indictable offenses, is that *perjury* connotes corruption and recalcitrance, whereas *false swearing* connotes mere falsehood without these additional moral judgments.

permanence, -cy. Both forms are used frequently. The two are synonymous in meaning "the quality or state of being permanent," although *permanence* emphasizes durability ⟨the permanence of the snow⟩ and *permanency* emphasizes duration ⟨the permanency of fees tail⟩.

permissive, -sory. The latter is a NEEDLESS VARIANT.

permit. See **allow.**

permit of = to leave room for ⟨the words permit of more than one interpretation⟩. This phrase is common in contexts involving the interpretation of drafted documents, or statutes.

permittee. See -EE.

permute; permutate. The latter is a NEEDLESS VARIANT.

perorate; orate. The former means "to conclude a formal address," although it is infrequently misunderstood as meaning "to declaim rhetorically or emotionally." *Orate*, a BACK-FORMATION, was once widely considered objectionable or merely humorous; yet it is losing this stigma.

Here *peroration* is used without regard for its literal sense: "Indeed, this whole argument strikes us as repetitive of Humpty Dumpty's *peroration* to Alice: 'when I use a word, it means just what I choose it to mean—neither more nor less.'"

perpetuate (= to make last indefinitely; prolong) and *perpetrate* (= to commit or carry out) are surprisingly often confounded. E.g., "Respondent has demonstrated over the years a course of dishonest behavior: charging for services not rendered, performing unnecessary services, engaging in sexually inappropriate touching of patients, and *perpetuating fraud* [read *perpetrating fraud*] upon patients and third-party payers." Here the word is correctly used: "Amassing wealth over an extended period of time may have been attractive to some of the landed gentry of England who sought to *perpetuate* family fortunes in the feudal tradition, unhampered by income or estate taxes."

per procurationem = by proxy. The phrase is abbreviated *p.proc., p.pro.,* or *p.p.*

perquisite; prerequisite. *Perquisite*, often shortened to *perk*, means "a privilege or benefit given in addition to one's salary or regular wages." *Prerequisite* = a previous condition or requirement.

per quod; per se. These terms are differentiated in the law of defamation. E.g., "The law has always made a distinction between false imputations that may be actionable in themselves, *per se*, and those that may be actionable only on allegation and proof of special damage, or *per quod*." Literally, *per quod* = whereby. In actions for torts, *per quod* introduced the allegations giving rise to special damages by a showing of consequences stemming from defendant's acts. *Per se* violations required no such showing. The phrases are still used in defamation cases. See, e.g., *Kurz v. The Evening News Association*, 375 N.W.2d 391, 394 (Mich. App. 1985). See the following entry.

per se (lit., "through [or *in, by, of*] itself") is both adverb and adjective. Formerly used almost always as a POSTPOSITIVE phrase, today it is commonly used prepositively: "The district court submitted the case to the jury on the theory that such a conspiracy, if proved, is *per se* illegal."/ "The case is being closely watched by antitrust specialists, because the decision may revise an old and important antitrust doctrine known as the *per se* rule."/ "Appellant asserts that his back ailment is *per se* disabling."/ "There is no longer a presumption of specific deadly intent when a *per se* deadly weapon is used by the defendant."

The phrase usually takes no punctuation, even though its English equivalent *in itself* or *of itself* is ordinarily set off by commas. When, however, *per se* is used as a direct functional equivalent of one of these phrases, it should be set off: "That the propriety, *per se*, of searches of law offices is an area of some controversy makes it more, not less, imperative that public officials not disregard the strictures of the fourth amendment."

Prepositively, *per se* often means "absolute." E.g., "This inquiry calls for line-drawing, but no fixed *per se* rule can be expressed or applied in any particular case."/ "We are not disposed to fashion a *per se* rule requiring reversal of every conviction following tardy appointment of counsel."

Per se has become a TERM OF ART in antitrust law, referring to an outright violation of the antitrust statutes. The Supreme Court of the United States has defined *per se* antitrust violations as those "which because of their pernicious effect on competition and lack of any redeeming virtue are conclusively presumed to be unreasonable and therefore without elaborate inquiry as to the precise harm they have caused or the business excuse for their use." *Northern Pacific Ry. v. United States*, 356 U.S. 1, 5 (1958). *Per se* is not absolute in American antitrust law: there may be behavior that is a *per se* violation of the statute, yet the violator may still raise defenses, such as impossibility due to market conditions.

The phrase has been extended in antitrust contexts well beyond its usual sense, from *per se illegality* to *per se rules* or *analysis* to *per se language*, e.g.: "*Per se* language expresses a mood of undoubted hostility to a practice." 7 P. Areeda, *Antitrust Law* § 1510, at 417 (1986). See **per quod.**

persecute. See **prosecute.**

persevere is frequently a victim of the intrusive -*r*-, and so mispronounced *perservere.*

PERSON. It is important in any piece of writing, and especially in DRAFTING, not to confuse one's references to persons, as by switching the voice through which the prose is set down. The person through whom the writing speaks should not change the manner in which he refers to himself and others, as by slipping in and out of third person, with first person interspersed.

Here is an example from a will quoted in an opinion: "The party of the first part . . . does hereby remise, release, and forever quitclaim unto the said party of the second part, his heirs and assigns forever, all the real estate of the said Ella F. Sherwood [the party of the first part], wherever situate, to have and to hold the same unto the party of the second part, his heirs, executors, and administrators and assigns forever, and for the same considerations, *I do* hereby sell . . . unto the party of the second part all personal property." Here is another specimen, in which *testator* = party of the first part. "This conveyance and transfer is made upon the condition that the party of the second part, *my husband,* survive *me,* and the same is intended to vest and take effect upon *my decease* and until said time the same shall be subject to revocation upon the part of the *party of the first part.*" In both of these examples, certainly, use of the first person would be preferable throughout. See FIRST PERSON & **party of the first part.**

persona grata. See **persona non grata.**

personalty (= personal property) is contrasted with *realty.*

personam, in. See **in personam.**

persona non grata; persona grata. The plural forms are *personae non gratae* and *personae gratae.*

PERSONIFICATION OF CASES is a mannerism characteristic of hack-writing in law. "*INS v. Lopez-Mendoza,* in declining to apply the exclusionary rule to deportation proceedings, cited approvingly cases finding that the absence of *Miranda* warnings did not render otherwise voluntary statements inadmissible in deportation proceedings." The way to correct the problem, of course, is to write *The court in* INS v. Lopez-Mendoza, etc. See CASE REFERENCES.

personnel may take either a singular or a plural verb, depending upon whether it is intended as a COLLECTIVE NOUN.

persons. See **people.**

perspicuous; perspicacious. *Perspicuous* is to *perspicacious* as *intelligible* is to *intelligent. Perspicuous* may be defined etymologically as "see-through-it-ive-ness"; it means "clear; lucid; seen readily," and is applied to thought and expression. E.g., in the nominal form: "The former term indicates with tolerable *perspicuity* a right available in personam." *Perspicacious* = penetrating in thought; acutely discerning; keen; shrewd ⟨a scholar as perspicacious as Charles Alan Wright⟩.

per stirpes = by family stocks. E.g., "The principal should be distributed to my issue then living *per stirpes.*" See **per capita** & **stirpital.**

persuadable, -ible; persuasible. The preferred form is *persuadable.* See -ABLE (A).

persuade; convince. One *persuades* another *to do* something, but one *convinces* or, archaically, *persuades* another *of* something. Either *persuade* or *convince* may be used with a *that-*phrase object, although *persuade that* occurs seldom outside law. American judges seem addicted to the expression. E.g., "If the statutory language were not enough to *persuade* us *that* the Secretary's interpretation is incorrect, these limitless consequences would certainly give us pause."/ "We are *persuaded that* the indemnity provision clearly encompasses negligence of the indemnitee and losses arising from strict liability." See **convince.**

persuadible; persuasible. See **persuadable.**

pertain. See **appertain.**

pertinence, -cy. The first is now the usual, and the preferred form. E.g., "I concede that a testator cannot prescribe in his will that an act to be performed by him, indifferent in itself and having no *pertinency* [read *pertinence*] except its effect on his testamentary dispositions, shall change such dispositions."/ "To appreciate the *pertinency* [read *pertinence*] of these statements, we may ask ourselves what the duty of counsel would have been had they been true." See **impertinence.**

pertinent part, in. See **in pertinent part.**

peruse means "to read with great care"; thus it should not be used merely as a fancy substitute for *read.* It is pronounced /pĕ-*rooz*/, and the noun *perusal* /pĕ-*rooz-ăl*/.

petitio principii. See **beg the question.**

petitioner. See PARTY APPELLATIONS & **plaintiff.**

petit jury; petty jury. The former is now the accepted spelling; the development is perhaps a favorable one, for laymen are likely to read *petty* in its modern sense even though they are familiar with the phrase. E.g., "It would, of course, be impossible to obtain a *petit jury* that reflects all the distinctive groups in a community."/ "The Supreme Court has stated that the systematic exclusion of persons based upon race from the grand jury pool, the *petit jury* pool, or the *petit jury* through the prosecutor's use of peremptory challenges, violates a defendant's equal protection rights guaranteed by the fourteenth amendment."

petit larceny; petty larceny. The former is now the predominant spelling. E.g., "At the time of the trial he was brought as a witness from the county jail where he was serving a term for *petit larceny.*"

petitory is an adjective used in reference to suits seeking to try title to a vessel independent of possession. E.g., "Former Admiralty Rule 19 dealt with possessory and *petitory* actions."

pettifogger; shyster. Both are contemptuous words for *lawyer*, but there is a difference, as explained here, rather magniloquently:

> The *pettifogger*, as a lawyer, is an unlearned, little, mean character, lacking in ability, sound judgment or good common sense, while the *shyster* may be possessed of much learning, great ability or an abundance of shrewdness and cunning, but he is a trickster and a dishonest schemer; he is a fomenter of litigation, strife and discord in the community; he is a manufacturer of evidence, a fosterer of perjury and a promoter of bribery; he is a cunning thief, who conceals his perfidy and rascality under the cloak of the law; he cunningly abuses the noble profession to which he has been admitted as a weapon of offense in deeds of unjust oppression, scheming knavery and the procurement of confidence and the repose of trust, which he basely abuses, when there is opportunity to profit by so doing.
>
> R. L. Harmon, addressing the Alabama
> Bar Ass'n in 1897 (quoted in G. W.
> Warvelle, *Essays in Legal Ethics* 69 (1902)).

See LAWYER, DEROGATORY NAMES FOR.

petty jury. See **petit jury.**

petty larceny. See **petit larceny.**

phantasy. See **fantasy.**

Philadelphia lawyer. See LAWYER, DEROGATORY NAMES FOR.

PHRASAL VERBS are verbs that comprise more than one word, often a verb and a preposition. When using a phrasal verb, one must be certain to include the entire phrase and not just the primary verb. Thus statutes are *struck down*, not just *struck.* Likewise, contracts are *entered into*, not just *entered.* One *gets up* in the morning; one does not *get* in the morning. *Sue out*, q.v., means something different from *sue.* We must respect, then, the latter part of phrasal verbs as much as the earlier. *Prove up*, *make whole*, *hold over*, *hand down* or *out* (an opinion), *make payment for*, and *work out* (a settlement) are a few of the phrasal verbs common in law. For a full collection of verbs of this kind, see G.W. Davidson, *Chambers Pocket Guide to Phrasal Verbs* (1982).

With DOUBLETS, phrasal verbs may cause ambiguities: "In no case shall a corporation purchase or make payment, directly or indirectly, for its own share when there is reasonable ground for believing that the corporation is insolvent." Does the phrase *directly or indirectly* apply to *purchase*? If so, read *purchase or make payment for, directly or indirectly*. . . .

Generally, writers should not be timid in using phrasal verbs; they are usually not substandard or even colloquial, unless the particle is unnecessary. (See PARTICLES, UNNECESSARY.) In the following specimen, the writer left the phrasal verb incomplete, apparently out of fear of using a needless particle: "*Drawing* [read *Drawing on*] the principle that the acquisition of monopoly power is illegal only if not accomplished by legitimate means such as business acumen or historical accident, appellee observes that appellant's sole theory of exclusionary conduct is unsupported by the record." See **strike**.

PHRASING refers to syntactic structures, their concinnous grace or maladroit clumsiness. The writer should have some sense of how best to order the parts of his sentence, so that it will be logically, and preferably even elegantly, constructed. Many of the specific maladies of construction are discussed throughout this work. Hence this entry can do little more than exemplify some of the general problems and offer remedies. E.g., "The plaintiff having conveyed away by deed, purporting to grant a fee simple interest in the lands in question, and having had them conveyed back to her, is now seized of a fee simple interest." This sentence can be greatly improved by repositioning the subject directly before the verb and by making the participial phrase an introductory one that leads into the main clause. The sentence now reads: *Having purported to convey* [less redundant than *having conveyed away*] *a fee simple interest in the lands in question, and having had them conveyed back to her, the plaintiff is now seised* [the better spelling] *of a fee simple interest.* (See ANFRACTUOSITY.)/ "The jury made a special finding that the defendant, in firing the bomb, exercised reasonable care." (This sounds as if the bomb was fired *in order to pursue such care*! [Read *The jury made a special finding that the defendant exercised reasonable care in firing the bomb.*])/ "Clearly, if the policy was to be preserved some means was needed adapted to the new types of interest made possible by new methods of transforming ownership." [Read *If the policy was to be preserved, what was needed was some means*

adapted to the types of interest made possible by novel methods of conveyancing.]/ "In the case of a vested remainder, there is a person in being ascertained and ready to take, has a present right of future enjoyment." (This is downright ungrammatical. [Read . . . *there is a person in being, ascertained and ready to take, who* . . . .])/ "The Erie had contended that application of the Pennsylvania rule was required, among other things, by section 34 of the Federal Judiciary Act of September 24, 1789 . . ." (Justice Brandeis in *Erie v. Tompkins*). This phrasing suggests that the Pennsylvania rule was not just required, but mandated, demanded, necessitated ("among other things"). [Read *application of the Pennsylvania rule was required by, among other things, section 34* . . . .]

picaresque; picturesque. These words are quite different. *Picaresque* = roguish. *Picturesque* = fit to be the subject of a picture; strikingly graphic.

picnic, v.i., makes *picnicking* and *picnicked.* Cf. **panic** & **mimic**.

picturesque. See **picaresque**.

piercing the corporate veil; lifting the corporate veil. The former is the American, the latter the British phrase meaning "the act of disregarding the veil of incorporation that separates the property of a corporation from the property of its security holders."

Sometimes *pierce* is used in extended, elliptical senses, as here: "Were a corporation to attempt to perpetrate a fraud on the court by improperly creating or destroying diversity jurisdiction, we would not elevate form over substance but would accomplish whatever *piercing* and adjustments were considered necessary to protect the court's jurisdiction." (The *piercing* referred to apparently would entail judicial directives or sanctions against corporate officials—in effect, the court would disregard the veil of incorporation.)

pitiable; pitiful; piteous, pitiless. *Pitiable* = calling for or arousing pity. *Pitiful*, strictly, means "feeling pity," but in modern speech and writing it is almost always used in the sense "contemptible." The word *piteous* "had become misused as a form of *pitiable* as early as Shakespeare's time: for him hearts could be *piteous* in the active sense and corpses in the passive." I. Brown, *I Give You My Word & Say the Word* 235 (1964). Today *piteous* is archaic and poetic—not a word for ordinary uses. *Pitiless* = showing no pity.

PLACE-NAMES AS ADJECTIVES. The practice of using place-names as adjectives is to be resisted, although it is increasingly common. E.g., "A *Marion County, Indiana,* jury [read *A jury in Marion County, Indiana,*] convicted petitioner of theft, a Class D felony, on November 19, 1979."/ "*The Gulfport, Mississippi law firm of Jones & Jones* [read *The law firm of Jones & Jones in Gulfport, Mississippi*] represented appellant's parents before this litigation began." Such constructions contribute to NOUN PLAGUE, lessen readability, and offend sensitive, literate readers.

plain, it is. See **clearly.**

PLAIN ENGLISH. A. General Drafting. See Richard Wydick, *Plain English for Lawyers* (1979); R. Wincor, *Contracts in Plain English* (1976); C. Felsenfeld & A. Siegel, *Writing Contracts in Plain English* (1981); Practising Law Institute, *Drafting Documents in Plain Language* (R. A. Givens, chmn., 1981); Practising Law Institute, *Drafting Documents in Plain Language* (D. A. McDonald, chmn., 1979).

B. Jury Instructions. See Charrow & Charrow, *Making Legal Language Understandable: A Psycholinguistic Study of Jury Instructions,* 79 Colum. L. Rev. 1307 (1979).

plainly. See **clearly.**

plaint = a written statement of a cause of action, used to institute an action in the county courts in England (*CDL*). Following is a nineteenth-century example of this term as still used in England: "The defendant refused to deliver them up, and the plaintiff brought a *plaint* . . . to recover the notes." *Bridges v. Hawkesworth,* (1851) 21 L.J.Q.B. 75, 76. The term is used in the U.S. only in nonlegal senses. E.g., "I already hear the querulous *plaint* that questions dealt with in this opinion have not been raised in the court below or in the briefs on appeal."

plaintiff; complainant; demandant; objectant; exceptor. *Plaintiff* = the party who brings a suit into a court of law (*OED*). This party may have other special names, de-

pending on the jurisdiction and the cause of action asserted. (See, e.g., **pursuer.**) *Complainant* is used in even more general senses of any party who brings a complaint. *Demandant* = one who makes a demand or claim; the *OED* suggests that this term may be used of a plaintiff in a civil action.

The remaining terms are quite distinct from the others. *Objectant* = one who objects. *Exceptor* = one who objects or takes exception. See **exceptor & objectant.**

plaintiff & defendant; petitioner & respondent; appellant & appellee. A. Articles before. It is often useful in legal writing to omit *the, a,* or *an* before *plaintiff* or any other party designations, for excision even of such slight words can lead to leaner, more readable sentences. One need not even be consistent within a piece of writing, where euphony would be served by departing from consistency.

Still, omission of articles can cause problems where two party denominations are proximate: "The motion preserves no error because it fails to specify which plaintiff defendant contends failed to prove a prima facie case." Inserting *the* before *defendant* removes the reader's impediment. See ARTICLES (A).

B. Relative Pronouns with. Though personal relative pronouns (i.e., *who* and *whom*) are normally used with these denominations, where *plaintiff,* etc., is a company, corporation, or entity other than an individual or a set of easily identifiable individuals, then *which* is correct as an example of SYNESIS. See PARTY APPELLATIONS.

plaintiff in error; defendant in error. In some jurisdictions, the first is an equivalent of *appellant* or *petitioner,* the latter an equivalent of *appellee* or *respondent,* when the appeal is by writ of error. E.g., "The railway company and Mercer each filed an application for a writ of error and each application was granted, from which it results that in this court each party is both *plaintiff in error* and *defendant in error.*" See **error** (A).

plaintive was for centuries used interchangeably with *plaintiff* in legal prose. But now the sense "being or pertaining to the plaintiff in a suit" (*OED*) is an ARCHAISM, probably obsolete. The sole current meaning of *plaintive* is as an adjective: "sorrowful; mournful."

playwrighting; playwriting. The second is a corrupt form of the first.

plea; pleading, n. A *plea* is now given only in criminal cases, although at common law a defendant's answer to the plaintiff's complaint was termed a *plea*. In U.S. federal courts today, the only criminal pleas are *guilty, not guilty,* and *nolo contendere*. A *pleading* is the complaint or answer in a civil case, or the criminal indictment and the answer in a criminal case.

plead does not mean, as some laymen think, "to argue in court." Eric Partridge amended his note on *lawyer* in *Usage and Abusage* by quoting a British man-of-law who corrected Partridge's "layman's misusages" as follows: "A barrister does not 'plead' in Court. He argues a case in Court, or—colloquially— *does* a case in Court. Pleadings are the written documents preparatory to a case, e.g., Statement of Claim, Defence in a civil action, Petition or Answer in divorce." *Usage and Abusage* 379 (1973). See **pleaded.**

pleadable = that may be pleaded; that may be legally maintained in a court of law (*OED*). E.g., "This feature would not prevent a like construction if the language, intendment, and history thereof convinced us it was a *pleadable* position."

pleaded; pled; plead. The best course is to treat *plead* as a weak verb, so that the correct past tense, as well as past participle, is *pleaded*. *Pled* and *plead* are alternative past-tense forms to be avoided; they were once chiefly dialectal, but now have some standing in AmE. The spelling *plead* as a past tense (for *pled*) appeared in the eighteenth century, apparently on the analogy of *read 〉 read*. Cf. *lead*. E.g., "The legal proposition *plead* [read *pleaded*] by plaintiff is unpersuasive."/ "Defendant, having *plead* [read *pleaded*] payment of the note, had the burden of proving the fact of payment."

Pled, dating from the sixteenth century, is obsolete in BrE, except as a dialectal word. Nor is it considered quite standard in the AmE, although it is a common variant in legal usage throughout the U.S. E.g., "Defendant *pled* [read *pleaded*] guilty to the lesser offense." *State v. Carlberg*, 375 N.W.2d 275, 277 (Iowa App. 1985)./ "In the second count of their petition, they *pled* [read *pleaded*] their title specially." *Jensen v. Wilkinson*, 133

S.W.2d 982, 983 (Tex. Civ. App.—Galveston 1939)./ "Gerald Eastman *pled* [read *pleaded*] guilty to one count of violation of 18 U.S.C. § 2314, transportation of stolen moneys known to be taken by fraud."/ "Defendant *pled* [read *pleaded*] guilty to two counts of bank robbery."

pleader, -or. Only the former is correct.

pleading. See **plea.**

pleading; prayer. The *pleading* is the document in which a party in a legal action sets out the cause of action or defense. A *pleading* consists of: (1) a commencement; (2) a body (or charging part); (3) a prayer, or demand for judgment; (4) a signature; and, when required, (5) a verification. The *prayer*, which usually appears at the end of the pleading, is the request for relief from the court. E.g., "The court merely held that if there is a requirement that the complainant specifically plead for prejudgment interest, a *prayer* for general relief will not satisfy the requirement if the *pleadings* also contain a specific *prayer* for a different kind of interest." A typical *prayer* might read: "Wherefore, defendant prays that plaintiff take nothing in this action (etc.)." See **prayer.**

plead innocent. It used to be that only newspapermen made the mistake of writing *plead innocent* rather than *plead not guilty*, but now this phrase has made it even into judges' writing: "He refused to take urine, blood, or breath sobriety tests and *pleaded innocent* [read *pleaded not guilty*] to the two charges." Lawyers should avoid the phrase. There is no such thing in criminal law as a plea of innocent.

plea in abatement; plea of abatement. In jurisdictions in which the plea is used, *plea in abatement* is the usual form.

please find enclosed is, like its inverted sibling *enclosed please find*, q.v., an old-fashioned, stilted phrase that lawyers are fond of using in letters. A better, more modern substitute is *I am sending with this letter* or *I have enclosed.*

pled. See **pleaded.**

pledge. See **lien.**

pledg(e)or, -er; pledgee. The preferred spelling is *pledger*, not *pledgeor* or *pledgor*. E.g., "A stipulation in the contract of pledge, intended to defeat the right of redemption, to the effect that upon the *pledgeor's* [read *pledger's*] failure to make prompt payment the title should become absolute in the pledgee, or that the *pledgeor's* [read *pledger's*] equity of redemption should terminate or be forfeited, is invalid." *Black's* lists *pledgor*, which is less logical even than *pledgeor*. See MUTE E.

plenary is a FORMAL WORD for *full*. E.g. ,"A *plenary trial* is hardly necessary to apprise the court that what it saw really happened." Here *full trial* would be better.

plenitude. So spelled; a common misspelling is *plentitude*.

plentiful;ˎ plenteous. No distinction in meaning being possible, writers should prefer the prevalent modern form, *plentiful*. *Plenteous* is archaic and poetic.

plentitude. See **plenitude.**

PLEONASM. See VERBOSITY.

plurality opinion = an appellate opinion without enough judges' votes to constitute a majority, but having received the greatest number of votes of any of the opinions filed. See **majority** (A).

PLURALS. A. Borrowed Words. Words transported into the English language from other languages, especially Greek and Latin, present some of the most troublesome aspects of English plurals. At a certain point borrowed words become thoroughly anglicized and take English plurals. But while Classical words are still new and only questionably naturalized, writers who see the words as primarily foreignisms use the native-language plural. Then again, with certain words, the foreign plurals become so well established that anglicization never takes place.

So many variations on this theme have occurred that it is impossible to make valid generalizations. *Minimum* makes *minima* but *premium* makes *premiums*; *pudendum* makes *pudenda* but *memorandum* makes either *-dums* or *-da*; *colloquium* generally makes *-quia* in BrE, *-quiums* in AmE. The only reliable guide is a certain knowledge of specific words, or

habitual reference to a work of this kind. In words with a choice of endings, one English and the other foreign, we should generally prefer the English plural. It is an affectation for college professors to insist on using *syllabi* rather than *-buses*; the fear of being wrong or sounding unacademic leads some of them to use forms like *auditoria* and *stadia*.

Fowler called the benighted stab at correctness "out of the frying pan into the fire," and many writers who try to be sophisticated are susceptible to writing, e.g., *ignorami* and *octopi*, unaware that neither is a Latin noun in *-us* that, when inflected as a plural, becomes *-i*. The proper plural of the Greek word *octopus* is *octopodes*; the proper English plural is *octopuses*. *Ignoramus* makes only *ignoramuses*, for in Latin the word is a verb, not a noun.

French words also present problems. *Fait accompli* becomes *faits accomplis* and *force majeure* becomes *forces majeures*. But then we have the LAW FRENCH words such as *feme sole*, which becomes *femes sole*, and *feme covert* (or *femme couverte*), which as a plural becomes *femes covert* (or *femmes couvertes*). The best policy is to make a habit of consulting a good dictionary, and to use it discriminatingly.

B. Mass (Noncount) Nouns. A recent trend in the language is to make plurals for mass nouns—general and abstract nouns that cannot be broken down into discrete units, and that therefore should not have plural forms. One example of this phenomenon is the psychologists' and sociologists' term *behaviors*, as if the ways in which one behaves are readily categorizable and therefore countable. Granted, one can have good or bad behavior, but not, properly, *a* good behavior or *a* bad behavior. Following are examples of other words infected by the contagion.

1. *Coverages.* "The policy allowed for separate *coverages* of the three cars."

2. *Discriminations.* "The statute disadvantages those who would benefit from laws barring racial, religious, or ancestral *discriminations* as against those who would bar other *discriminations* or who would otherwise regulate the real estate market in their favor." See **discrimination.**

3. *Inactions.* "The findings of the district court on the actions and *inactions* by the defendants are supported by substantial evidence and are not clearly erroneous."

4. *Languages.* Speaking of different passages in a statute, or of different statutes, a writer states: "The statutory *languages* are not

enough to persuade us that the Secretary's interpretation is incorrect." See **language**.

5. *Litigations.* "Indeed, just as antitrust actions occupied the *attentions* of the litigation bar in the 1960s and class action *litigations* proliferated in the 1970s, insurance-coverage *litigations* are currently engaging the *attentions* of many of the nation's most prominent litigators."/ "Under the circumstances, there need not be two *litigations* when one will suffice." See **litigation**.

6. *Managements.* "If followed, these procedures would have a beneficial effect on the *managements* of brokerage firms and those charged with supervision." (Does *managements* refer to managerial departments, or to methods of management? The plural causes this ambiguity.)

7. *Outputs.* "Interpersonal relations of the justices have been shown to have measurable effects on the court's public *outputs.*"

8. *Participations.* Sometimes this phenomenon occurs through attributive uses, as where *participation* is substituted for *unit of participation*: "The D.C. Circuit has declared that the Glass-Steagall Act does not prohibit banks from marking *participations* in collective investment trusts for I.R.A. assets." The same principle is at work when *proofs* is substituted for *elements of proof.* See **proof** (B).

C. -O(E)S. Fowler laid down a number of guiding principles for words ending in -*o*: first, monosyllables and words used as freely in the plural as in the singular usually have -*oes* (*embargoes, heroes, noes, potatoes, vetoes*); second, alien-looking words, proper names, words that are seldom used as plurals, words in which -*o*- is preceded by a vowel, and shortened words (e.g., *photo*) do not take the -*e*- (*hippos, kilos, embryos, ratios*). Good dictionaries contain the preferred spellings.

D. Attributive Past-Participial Adjectives. These are usually awkward and alien-looking to laymen. E.g., "The firm represented one of the company's *insureds* in an action that had been brought against the insured in county court." See **assured, condemned, insured & deceased**.

E. Compound Nouns. Plurals of compound nouns made up of a noun and a POSTPOSITIVE ADJECTIVE are formed by adding -*s* to the noun: *courts martial, heirs presumptive.* The British and Americans differ on the method of pluralizing *attorney general*, q.v. Those words in which the noun is now disguised add -*s* at the end of the word, as with all compounds ending in -*ful*: *lungfuls, spoonfuls, handfuls.*

ply (= fold) forms the plural *plies. Plys* is incorrect.

p.m. See **a.m.**

poetic justice, nowadays a CLICHÉ, refers to the system exemplified in older fiction in which villains always receive condign punishments, and heroes their fitting rewards.

point, in. See **in point.**

point of fact. See **in point of fact.**

point of view. See **viewpoint.**

point, on. See **in point.**

point out; point to; point up. *Point out* = (1) to observe; (2) to call to others' attention. *Point to* = to direct attention to (as an answer or solution). *Point up* = illustrate. *Point up* is perhaps comparatively more frequent in legal than in nonlegal writing. E.g., "We mention *Lowe* not to intimate any view on the merits of the decision here, but rather because it *points up* how the present case falls so clearly within the first amendment exception for pure commercial speech that is both misleading and tends to promote illegal conduct."/ "Philosophical criticism has *pointed up* a lack of precision in the langauge of the law as a facet of the basic deficiency of all language."

pole star = lodestar, q.v. E.g., "The intention of the testator as expressed in the testamentary instrument is always the *pole star* in the interpretation of a will."

policy; polity. *Policy*, by far the more common of these words, means "a concerted course of action followed to achieve certain ends; a plan." It is more restricted in sense than *polity*, which means (1) "the principle upon which a government is based"; or (2) "the total governmental organization as based on its goals and policies." E.g., in the more usual sense (2): "The ancient doctrine of the common law, founded on the principles of the feudal system, that a private wrong is merged in a felony, is not applicable to the civil *polity* of this country."/ "As to the practicing lawyer, in our *polity* he is potentially law-writer, law teacher, legislator, or judge." (R. Pound)

policyholder. One word.

policy-making should be hyphenated. Cf. **decision-making.**

politic, adj.; **political.** The adverbial forms are *politicly* (= in a politic manner; shrewdly; prudently) and *politically* (= in a political or partisan way or manner).

politic(al)ize. *Politicalize* is inferior to *politicize.*

politick, v.i.; **politicize.** *Politick*, a BACK-FORMATION from *politics*, at one time was not recognized as an acceptable word. Today it is more common in AmE than in BrE, and means "to engage in partisan political activities." *Politicize* has a similar sense "to act the politician," but also the broader sense "to render political" ⟨politicizing judicial races⟩.

politics may be either singular or plural. Today it is more commonly singular than plural ⟨politics is dirty business⟩, although formerly the opposite was true.

polity. See **policy.**

pollicitation is a fancy LEGALISM meaning "a promise." It is primarily a civilian term with the more specific sense "an offer not yet formally accepted, and therefore usually revocable."

polygamy; polyandry; polygyny. The first is the broadest term, referring to a person's being simultaneously married to more than one spouse. *Polyandry* is the practice of having more than one husband; *polygyny* is the practice of having more than one wife. See **bigamy.**

POLYSEMOUS WORDS. See CHAMELEON-HUED WORDS.

pompous ass is a hackneyed phrase that could use a rest among lawyers and, especially, law students (usu. applying it to law professors). There may be a great many fellow practitioners and academics whom we would like to characterize thus, but we should per-haps show more originality than to mouth this shopworn epithet.

pooling; unitization. See **communitization.**

POPULARIZED LEGAL TECHNICALITIES. Fowler observed that when technical terms pass into everyday speech and writing, two things often occur. First, the popular use more often than not misrepresents the original meaning; and second, free indulgence in terms of this sort results in a tawdry style. These observations are no less true with legal technicalities than with those of other kinds. The prime example is *alibi*, which in law refers to the defense in a criminal case of proving that one was elsewhere when the crime was committed. Laymen picked up the term and, through misunderstanding perhaps coupled with SLIPSHOD EXTENSION, came to use it as a synonym for *excuse*, especially a lame excuse. Today even lawyers misuse the term in this way. (See **alibi.**) For other, mostly historical examples from the legal lexicon, see the discussions under **alias, compound, gist, ignoramus, hue and cry** & **pale.**

populous (= thickly populated) for *populist* (= of or relating to a movement claiming to represent the whole of the people) is a startling misusage. E.g., "The advent of the Jacksonian era and its emphasis on democratic *populous* [read *populist*] ideals . . . promoted . . . the notion that . . . judges should be popularly elected." Krirosha, *Acquiring Judges by the Merit Selection Method*, 40 Sw. L.J. 15 (1986).

portend (= to foretell or foreshadow) should not be used as a substitute for *to mean*. "The term 'beneficial shareholders' *portends* [read *means*] something different from 'shareholders.'" The word *portend* necessarily has negative connotations.

portentous. So spelled, although the word is sometimes incorrectly rendered *portentuous* or *portentious.*

portion; part. There are connotative differences. *Portion* = share (as of an estate or of food). It is an entity cut or as if cut away from the whole ⟨his portion of the contract⟩ ⟨her portion of the grain⟩. *Part*, in contrast, merely connotes a constituent part of the whole ⟨part of a house, a country, etc.⟩.

PORTMANTEAU WORDS. Lewis Carroll improvised this term to denote words that are formed by combining the first part of one word with the last part of another. (Linguists use the term *blend* to name an example of this phenomenon.) Thus *insinuendo* was arrived at by combining *insinuation* with *innuendo*; *quasar* is from *quasi* and *stellar*; *aerobicise* derives from *aerobic exercise*. Other recent innovations are *avigation*, q.v., from *aviation* and *navigation*, *pictionary* for *picture-filled dictionary*, and *videbut* for *video debut*. Most portmanteau words are nonce words that do not gain currency; others, like *brunch* (*breakfast* + *lunch*), become standard.

posit (= [1] to set in place, fix; [2] to postulate or lay down as the basis for argument) should not be used for *to present*, as here: "The purpose is not to study procedure for its own sake; the procedural issues are raised and considered primarily as indicia of the overall problems *posited* [read *presented*] by the unique nature of complex litigation."

positive (= having real existence) is a common meaning of the word in law, but little used in nonlegal writing today. E.g., "The wrong was actuated by a *positive* design to injure the third person to whom the duty was due."

positive law. This term is sometimes used with little idea of its precise sense. *Positive law* refers primarily to statutes and regulations, and has been defined as "law laid down within a particular political community by men, as political superiors, to other men, as distinct from moral law or law existing in an ideal community or by virtue of the law of nature or other nonpolitical authority" (*OCL*). This term, associated originally with John Austin's jurisprudence, is frequently used by common-law writers. E.g., "One of the primary rights of the citizen, sanctioned by the *positive law* of the state, is security to life and limb, and indemnity against personal injuries occasioned by the negligence, fraud, or violence of others."/ "The defendant may retain the money with a safe conscience, though by *positive law* he was barred from recovering." (Eng.)

positive mental attitude. See **mental attitude.**

posse, in. See **in esse.**

posse comitatus (lit., "the force of the county") = a body of citizens called together to suppress riots, pursue felons, or act in military defense of the country. The American frontier term *posse* originated as a shortened form of this early common-law term.

possession. See **custody.**

possessive, -sory, -sorial. The terms *possessive* and *possessory* have undergone DIFFERENTIATION. *Possessive* = exhibiting possession or the desire to possess; (2) [in grammar] denoting possession. *Possessory* = (1) of or pertaining to a possessor; (2) arising from possession ⟨possessory interest⟩; or (3) that is a possessor ⟨possessory conservator⟩.

POSSESSIVES. A. Generally. The best practice, advocated by Strunk and White in *The Elements of Style* and by every other authority of superior standing, is to add *-'s* to all singular possessives, hence *witness's*, *Vitex's*, *Jones's*, *Congress's*, *testatrix's*. E.g., "We next considered Jim Walter Homes's contention that there is no evidence to support the jury's findings."/ "Appellants contend that the memoranda, in the handwriting of someone other than the testatrix, together with the *testatrix'* [read *testatrix's*] signatures, are sufficient to effect a revocation by cancellation." So misunderstood is the rule that *witness's* actually gets a *sic* in *Yeager v. Greene*, 502 A.2d 980, 982 (D.C.App. 1985). The one exception to this rule is with Biblical and Classical names, hence *Jesus' suffering*, *Moses' discovery*.

To form the plural possessive, an apostrophe is added to the *-s-* of the plural, e.g. *bosses'*, *Joneses'*, *Sinzes'*, *octopuses'*. The one exception is for plurals not ending in *-s-*, for which *-'s* is added as in the singular possessive: *brethren's*, *children's*, *women's*.

B. Units of Time or Value and the Genitive Adjective. The idiomatic possessive should be used with periods of time and statements of worth. E.g., "The court said the holding was a tenancy from year to year ordinarily requiring *60 days*['] *notice* to terminate, but the special statute was held controlling." (The correct phraseology is *sixty* [or *60*] *days' notice*, just as it is *several years' experience* and *two months' time*.)/ "The initial *six months confinement* [read *six months' confinement*] was to be followed by *eighteen months probation* [read *eighteen months' probation*]."/ "This lawsuit arises out of the alleged misappropriation of a million dollars' worth of equipment." (If the number is not spelled out, the arabic numerals do not take a possessive apostrophe.)

C. Of Inanimate Things. Possessives of nouns denoting inanimate objects are generally unobjectionable. E.g., "The constitutional claim is rooted in the Fifth Amendment's guarantee of due process." But they can be overdone: "Section 922(f)'s unambiguous language regarding the section's applicability requires us to decline the invitation to extend 922(f)'s coverage; the first sentence of 922(f) defines the statute's scope." In fact, it is generally best to avoid use of possessives with statutes: "Relying on *section 1471(a)'s legislative history* [better: *the legislative history of section 1471(a)*], the court found that the regulation was not reasonably adopted."

The practice of using possessives with case names becomes preposterous when later courts interpolate full citations, as here: "Consistent with *Milliken* [*v. Bradley*, 433 U.S. 267, 97 S.Ct. 2749, 53 L.Ed.2d 745 (1977)]'s teachings, a remedial order must be carefully tailored to correct the constitutionally infirm condition." *United States v. Crucial*, 722 F.2d 1182, 1189 (5th Cir. 1983).

D. Incorrect Omission of Apostrophe. It seems that possessive apostrophes are increasingly omitted nowadays. This sloppy habit is to be avoided. E.g., "Brown had hired Jack Rogers, a Lake Charles attorney, to procure *Governor Edwards* [read *Governor Edwards's*] signature." *Brown v. Maggio*, 730 F.2d 293, 294 (5th Cir. 1984). Where two possessives are proximate, writers will often inadvertently omit one: "We have considered the import and admissibility of the Alexanders' expert *witnesses testimony* [read *witnesses' testimony*] touching on the drilling of additional wells." See **attorney's fees.**

E. Attributive Past Participial Adjectives. These can become awkward. With such phrases as *the insured's death* or *the deceased's residence*, it is better to use an *of*-phrase; hence *the death of the insured* and *the residence of the deceased*. (Better yet, one might prefer *decedent* to *deceased*.) See **assured, condemned, insured, & deceased.**

F. Phrasal Possessives. These are to be avoided when possible. Genitives with *of* are only slightly longer; more important, however, they are correct. "The *court of civil appeals' opinion* [read *opinion of the court of civil appeals*] uses substantially the same alter ego test that is stated in the briefs."/ "The plaintiff in error's mother [read *mother of the plaintiff in error*] died before the trial court's decision was appealed."/ "The *court below's error* [read *error of the court below*] was in granting summary judgment."/ "We reject the court of appeal's denial of Mitchell's claim to absolute immunity." [Read *We reject the denial of Mitchell's claim to absolute immunity by the court of appeals.*]/ "The *trier of fact's award* [read *fact-trier's award*] is not to be disturbed unless it is entirely disproportionate to the injury sustained." (See **trier of fact.**)/ "This *appeal of the court below's determination* [read *appeal of the determination by the court below*] of the compensation to be paid appellee is frivolous." The only well-established forms of phrasal possessives are variations on *anybody else's*: "The court's ruling disposed of *no one else's* claim."

G. Followed by Relative Pronouns. A nominal relative pronoun should not follow a possessive noun. "Or there may have been inimical voices raised among the committee, such as Palffy's or Nikilaus Esterhazy's, who just then had had an unpleasant brush with the composer." [Read *Or there may have been raised among the committee inimical voices, such as those of Palffy or Nikilaus Esterhazy, who just then had had an unpleasant brush with the composer.*] See ANTECEDENTS.

H. Of Attributive Possessives. It is common for businesses to be named with a proper single name in possessive form, as *McDonald's* or *Sambo's*. Although possessive in form, these are functionally nouns, as in *Sambo's brings this action*, etc. How, then, does one make a possessive of the noun *Sambo's?* One court did it this way: "On February 26, 1973, *Sambo's* certificate of authority to do business in this state was forfeited . . . ." *Farris v. Sambo's Restaurants, Inc.*, 498 F. Supp. 143, 147 (N.D. Tex. 1980). The judge should have written *Sambo's'*, because *Sambo's certificate* = certificate of Sambo, whereas *Sambo's' certificate* = certificate of Sambo's, the latter being the desired sense. Where *Buddy's Food Store* is shortened to *Buddy's*, one writes of *Buddy's' manager*. Good PHRASING requires *the manager of Buddy's*.

I. With APPOSITIVES. See that entry.

possessor (= one who possesses) has the special legal sense "one who takes, occupies, or holds something without ownership, or as distinguished from the owner" (*OED*). Hence the following specimen in reference to a life estate: "The materials that follow are not intended to cover either the substantive law of waste under which the *possessor* may be liable to the holder of the future interest or the substantive law relating to liability of a *nonpossessor.*"

possessory. See **possessive.**

possible; practicable. The author of the following advice was ill-informed: "Do not use *possible* when you should use *practicable*, as it may make a world of difference whether an act is to be done if *possible* or only if *practicable.*" *Notes on the Art of Drafting Contracts* 11 (Cornell Law School 1934). Rather, *practicable* (= feasible) is virtually a synonym of *possible*; the words to be distinguished are *practical*, q.v., and *practicable.*

POST- for *since* or *after* is a sloppy way of achieving feigned brevity. "*Post-Flanagan* [read *Since Flanagan*], only two circuits have spoken to the precise question."

post. See **ante.**

post facto. See **ex post facto.**

posthaste is archaic in all but its adverbial sense.

post hoc, ergo propter hoc denotes the fallacy of confusing sequence with consequence. Literally, the phrase means "after this, therefore because of this." Two common usages, *since* for *because* (acceptable) and *consequent* for *subsequent* (unacceptable), exemplify the fallacy. The following specimen demonstrates a canny use of the maxim: "Here, as elsewhere in the law, *propter hoc* must be distinguished from *post hoc.*" *Hennigan v. Ouachita Parish School Board*, 749 F.2d 1148, 1152 (5th Cir. 1985) (per Rubin, J.). See **post hoc.**

post hoc (= [of or relating to] the fallacy of assuming causality from temporal sequence) for *ex post facto* or *after the fact* is a common error. E.g., "Petitioners observe correctly that if the lawyer's brief for the ICC had simply announced its clarifying analysis in the form of allegations or new explanations, such would constitute pure *post hoc* [read *after-the-fact*] rationalization not entitled to any consideration by this court. The clarifying

opinion of the commissioner, however, differs sharply from *after-the-fact* rationalizations made by attorneys or by courts." *Public Service Co. of Indiana, Inc. v. I.C.C.*, 749 F.2d 753, 759 (D.C. Cir. 1984)./ "We reach no conclusion on the validity of the 1984 assessment, but remind the district court that, to some extent, the 1984 assessment is a *post hoc* [read *after-the-fact*] rationalization and thus must be viewed critically."/ "In applying these criteria, it is important that the district court resist the understandable temptation to engage in *post hoc* [read *after-the-fact*] reasoning by concluding that, because a plaintiff did not ultimately prevail, his action must have been unreasonable or without foundation." See **post hoc, ergo propter hoc.**

postman. At early common law, this word was equivalent to *lawyer*; more particularly, it referred to a barrister in the Court of Exchequer who had precedence in motions except in Crown business. The *OED* records that "the name was derived from the post, the measure of length in excise cases, beside which he took his stand." Surely this sense of the word was unrelated to another sense recorded by the *OED*: "a hireling writer of libels or scurrilous falsehoods." But see LAWYER, DEROGATORY NAMES FOR. See also **attorney** (A).

postmortem. See **autopsy.**

postnuptial = made, occurring, or existing after marriage. The term refers to the time after the wedding, not after a divorce. E.g., "The trend is toward upholding *postnuptial* agreements, even where obsolete statutes codify the common-law rules on jointure." See **antenuptial.**

POSTPOSITIVE ADJECTIVES follow the nouns they modify, in accordance with Romance rather than Germanic (or English) syntax. They exist in English as a remnant of the Norman French influence during the Middle Ages, and especially in the century following the Norman Conquest. The French influence was most pronounced in the language of law, politics, religion, and heraldry. In law as in these other fields, French phrases were adopted wholesale—syntax and all—and soon passed into the English language unchanged, though in English adjectives almost invariably precede the nouns they modify. Following is a list of frequently used law-related phrases with postpositive adjectives:

accounts payable, accounts receivable, annuity certain, appearance corporal, attorney general, body corporate (Eng.), *body politic, brief amicus curiae, chattels personal, chattels real, condition precedent, condition subsequent, corporation de facto, corporation de jure, court martial, date certain, decree absolute, easement appurtenant, fee simple, fee tail, gap certain, heir apparent, law merchant, letters rogatory* (U.S.), *letters testamentary, notary public, parties defendant, parties litigant, postmaster general, president-elect, queen regent* (or *regnant*), *secretary general, sum total.*

On the troublesome issue of pluralizing the nouns in phrases such as these, see PLURALS (E).

At least two common English nouns, *things* and *matters,* often take postpositive adjectives that are ordinarily prepositive. Thus we say that someone is interested in *things philosophical,* or *matters philological.* Similarly, *alive* may only be postpositive.

Sometimes a writer will attempt to create a prepositive adjectival phrase where properly the phrase would normally and most idiomatically be postpositive. The result is ungainly indeed: "*The complained of summaries* [read *The summaries complained of*] in this case are contained in the government's exhibit."

There is, however, a tendency in modern writing to make prepositive adjectival phrases out of what formerly would have been postpositive. Thus, instead of having *payments past due,* we just as often see *past-due payments:* "The precise issue is whether a bankruptcy court may decline to approve a Chapter 13 plan solely because a debtor proposes to pay off in installments during the term of the plan *past-due payments* on a promissory note."

post-sentencing should be hyphenated for visual reasons.

potence, -cy. Oddly, *potency* is more common in the positive, and *impotence* in the negative. See **impotence, -cy.**

potentiality is jargonistic when used merely for *potential,* n.

pour-over is a term used in estate planning of statutes that allow testamentary assets to be incorporated into living trusts. E.g., "The enactment of *pour-over* statutes may result in decreased reliance on the doctrine of incorporation by reference; but at the same time *pour-over* statutes may induce the courts to be-

come more liberal in applying the doctrine, since the statutes reflect a legislative judgment that the policy to prevent fraud thought to underlie the Wills Acts is of diminished importance in the current estate-planning context."/ "The doctrines of incorporation by reference and nontestamentary acts, both potentially involved in *pour-overs* from wills to living trusts, are considered here with modern statutes designed to permit *pour-overs* without complications produced by the Wills Acts."

power of attorney; letter of attorney.
The former is the usual phrase in both the U.S. and G.B. *Letter of attorney* is a BrE variant, but usually it refers more properly to the *document* giving one authority to act on another's behalf, rather than to the *authority* itself. *Power of attorney,* however, is used both for the document and for the authority given by the document. The plural is *powers of attorney.* See PLURALS (E).

power of termination. See **right of entry for condition broken.**

p.p. is an ambiguous abbreviation, for it may be short for *propria persona* (= in his proper or own person), *per procurationem* (= by proxy), or *pages* (*pp.* or *pp*).

practical; practicable. Though similar, these words should be distinguished in use; in both words, the first syllable is stressed. *Practical* = manifested in practice; capable of being put to good use. Its opposite is *theoretical. Practicable* = capable of being accomplished; feasible; possible. E.g., "As a matter of construction, the court must, irrespective of what is *practicable* by way of financial provision, determine whether grave financial hardship will be caused to the respondent as a result of dissolution." (Eng.)/ "Not only might it be unfair to give general guidance without knowledge of the day-to-day *practicability* of such guidance, but also in depriving itself of such knowledge the court might well deprive itself of the opportunity of giving the best guidance." (Eng.) See **possible.**

practice; practise. In AmE, the former is both the noun and verb; in BrE the former is the noun, the latter the verb. Occasionally *practise* is used by modern American courts, but *practice,* n. & v.t., is the preferred spelling.

One well-known exception to the general rule in the U.S. is the lawyers' organization called the Practising Law Institute.

practitioner; practiser. The former is the term primarily used in the U.S. and G.B. for "one who exercises a profession or occupation." The latter is used almost exclusively in G.B., though not commonly. E.g., "This cause has been carefully instructed with evidence by the *practisers.*" (Eng.) The variant *practicer* sometimes occurs in the U.S.

pr(a)edial /*pree-dee-ăl*/ = consisting of or pertaining to or attached to the land. The spelling *predial* is now predominant. The usual phrase in law is *predial servitude,* which means, in Scots and civil law, "a servitude affecting heritable property; a servitude constituted over one subject or tenement in favor of the proprietor of another subject or tenement" (*OED*). E.g., "A *predial servitude* is a charge on a servient estate for the benefit of a dominant estate." La. Civ. Code art. 646 (West 1980). See **servitude** (A).

pray, in the legal sense "to request earnestly," is a survival from Elizabethan usage, as in Shakespeare's "a conqueror that will *pray* in aid for kindness, where he for grace is kneeled to." *Antony & Cleopatra,* 5.2.27–28. The religious sense of *pray* grew alongside the broader secular sense, and neither it nor *prayer,* q.v., should be viewed as symptomatic of BIBLICAL AFFECTATION. E.g., "Appellants *pray* for an injunction restraining defendant from making the patented device."/ "The wife by her answer cross-*prayed* for a divorce on the ground of desertion." (Eng.)

prayer = a request addressed to the court that appears at the end of a pleading. E.g., "Taking up first the *prayer* for an injunction pendente lite, I cannot find that any case has been made out for enjoining action by the two corporate defendants." See **pray & pleading.**

preachify is a derogatory word for *preach;* the *OED* defines it as "to preach in a factitious or a tedious way." See **argufy & speechify.**

PRE- + noun, used in adverbial senses, is a poor substitute for *before* plus the noun. E.g., "There was no specific requirement *pre-Ruiz* [read *before Ruiz*] that each prison unit maintain a full-service law library."/ "Any number of specific programs effective now were not *pre-Ruiz established* [read *established before Ruiz*]." See POST-.

precatory (= of, relating to, or expressing entreaty or supplication) is a word not much used outside the law. *Precatory words* in a will, or in motions at shareholders' meetings, are words praying or expressing a desire that a thing be done; usually precatory words are not binding. The word is ordinarily opposed to or contrasted with *mandatory.* E.g., "Testators frequently annex *precatory* words to devises or bequests and thus create doubt whether an absolute gift or trust is intended."/ "While the words used in the residuary clause are *precatory,* the intent of the testatrix in the disposition of the residue of her property to the person who should care for her is manifest, and the language is mandatory in effect."/ "I vote to reverse and to dismiss the complaint upon the ground that the words of the will on which plaintiff's cause of action is based are *precatory* but not mandatory."

precautionary; precautious. These terms have been differentiated since they were first used in the eighteenth century. *Precautionary* = (1) suggesting or advising provident caution; or (2) of, relating to, or of the nature of a precaution. *Precautious* = using precaution; displaying previous or provident caution or care (*OED*). See **cautionary.**

precede for *preface* seems to be an anomalous error. E.g., "The publisher *precedes* [read *prefaces*] its collection of documents with an essay about the entire editorial process."

precede; proceed. These words are sometimes confused even by otherwise literate professionals. Both may mean "to go ahead," but in different senses. *Precede* = to go ahead of; to come before. *Proceed* = to go ahead; to continue. On the common misspelling, see **preceed.**

precedence, -cy. Today the latter is a NEEDLESS VARIANT of the former; it was used up through the beginning of the nineteenth century, but today -ce serves more ably for all purposes.

precedence; precedents. Pronunciation of these words is usefully distinguished in the U.S. The former is best pronounced with the second syllable stressed, i.e. /prĕ-*seed*-ĕns/, whereas the latter has the primary accent on the first syllable, i.e. /*pres*-ĕ-dĕns/. *Precedence* is nevertheless acceptably pronounced /*pres*-ĕ-dĕns/ in the U.S., as it is usually sounded in the common phrase *take precedence over.* In G.B., /*pres*-ĕ-dĕns/ is the only known pronunciation.

precedent, adj., is inferior to *prior* or *previous,* except when used as a POSTPOSITIVE ADJECTIVE in a phrase such as *condition precedent.* E.g., "This rule in no respect impinges on the doctrine that one who makes only a loan on such paper, or takes it as collateral security for a *precedent* [read *prior*] debt, may be limited in his recovery to the amount advanced or secured." This adjective is best pronounced /*pri-seed-ĕnt*/, although /*pres*-ĕ-dĕnt/ is acceptable.

Precedent, adj. (= preceding in time or order), should not be used for *precedential* (= of the nature of, constituting, or relating to a precedent): "Under the *precedent* [read *precedential*] theory of this court, one panel may not overrule the decision of another panel of this court squarely on point and in the absence of intervening and overruling Supreme Court decisions."

precedential ordinarily means "furnishing a guide or rule for subsequent cases." (See the preceding entry.) E.g., "The conferees believe the case does not comport with the legislative intent of the statute or with its interpretation from 1927 through 1983; the case should not have any *precedential* effect."

preceding, when used simply for *before,* is best replaced by that word. E.g., "Appellants alleged in their complaint that *preceding* [read *before*] their arrests they were engaged only in peaceful and constitutionally protected protest activities." Cf. **next preceding.**

preceed is a misspelling of *precede* caused by confusion with *proceed.* It occurs in print surprisingly often: see, e.g., *Drennen Land & Timber Co. v. Angell,* 475 So. 2d 1166, 1172 (Ala. 1985). See **precede.**

precipitancy, -ce; precipitation. *Precipitancy* = excessive or unwise haste in action; rashness. *Precipitance* is a NEEDLESS VARIANT. *Precipitation* = (1) haste, hurry; (2) the act of precipitating (the precipitation of the riot is still a mystery); or (3) something precipitated (as rain or snow).

precipitate, adj.; **precipitous.** These words are quite different, though often confused. *Precipitate* = sudden; hasty; rash; showing violent or uncontrollable speed. This word is applied to actions, movements, or demands. *Precipitous* = like a precipice; steep. It is applied to physical things and not to actions.

Precipitous is frequently misused for *precipitate,* as here: "A federal court should await a definitive construction by a state court rather than *precipitously* [read *precipitately*] indulging a facial challenge to the constitutional validity of a state statute."/ "Within weeks the price of yarn began a *precipitous* decline." Perhaps this last usage is excusable, if we picture a graph with a sharp drop, or if we visualize a decline; but if "sudden" is meant, *precipitate* is the word.

Precipitant is a NEEDLESS VARIANT for *precipitate.* E.g., "The stakeholder may have instituted interpleader proceedings *precipitantly* [read *precipitately*] and without any reasonable fear of adverse claims."

precipitation. See **precipitancy.**

precision; precisian, precisionist. *Precision* = accuracy; *precisian* = a person who adheres to rigidly high standards (often with regard to moral conduct); *precisionist* = a person who prizes absolute correctness of expression and performance, esp. in language and ritual.

predacious; predaceous; predative, -tory, -torial. *Predatory* = preying on other animals. The word is applied figuratively in the phrase from antitrust law, *predatory pricing.* The forms *predaceous, predatorial,* and *predative* are NEEDLESS VARIANTS. The spelling *predacious* has undergone DIFFERENTIATION and means "devouring; rapacious."

predate. See **antedate.**

predative, -tory, -torial. See **predacious.**

predial. See **pr(a)edial.**

predicable; predicative, -tory. The first means "that may be predicated or affirmed." The second means "having the quality of predicating, affirming, or asserting." The third means "of or pertaining to a preacher."

predicate, v.t. (= to affirm a statement or proposition), is usually construed with *on* in modern writing. E.g., "Even without *Leavell,* we would decline to *predicate* a broad immunity *on* the basis of the narrow holding of *Miller.*"

PREDICATE NOMINATIVES are nouns or pronouns in the nominative or subjective case that appear after copulative verbs—usually *be*-verbs. "It is *I*," one writes, for instance, or "It seems to be *she*," "You appeared to be *I*," and so on. In formal contexts these constructions are not affectations; they are obligatory. For example, the following error occurred merely because of an imperfect knowledge of grammar, together with aspirations to correctness: "The description 'plaintiff-appellee' or 'respondent below' forces us to keep looking at the title block on the opinion's first page to keep track of who is *whom* [read *who*]."

Nevertheless, in informal contexts and primarily in speech, it is quite acceptable today to say "It's me." On formal occasions, or if one is particularly fastidious in language, one should feel perfectly comfortable saying "It is I" under any circumstances (in which the statement is apt). See NOMINATIVE AND OBJECTIVE CASES.

predominate, adj., is a NEEDLESS VARIANT for *predominant.* In good usage, *predominate* is the verb, *predominant* the adjective. Readers may be confused when *predominate* is used adjectivally: "These facts were *predominate* [read *predominant*] in the court's decision to pierce the corporate veil."/ "The *Roth* opinion referred to the Model Penal Code definition of obscenity—material whose *predominate* [read *predominant*] appeal is to 'a shameful or morbid interest in nudity, sex, or excretion.'" Cf. **preponderant.**

preempt; perempt. These words are to be distinguished. *Preempt* (now generally spelled as one word without a hyphen) is a BACK-FORMATION from its noun, *preemption.* To *preempt* is to acquire or appropriate beforehand, usu. to the exclusion of others. To *perempt*, in contrast, is to quash, do away with, or extinguish. The *OED* and *W3* record *perempt* as an obsolete or archaic term, but it is current at least in Louisiana in intransitive uses: "The privilege contained in article 3237 *perempts* or dies at the end of six months."

preemption; peremption. *Peremption* is a rare legal term meaning "the act or process of quashing" (*W3*), "a nonsuit." It is rare everywhere, apparently, but in Louisiana. "[*P*]*eremption* is but a form of prescription, a species thereof, but with the characteristic that it does not admit of interruption or suspension." *Flowers, Inc. v. Rausch*, 364 So. 2d 928, 931 (La. 1978)./ "Actually, *peremption* is a common-law term which has crept into our [civil] jurisprudence. Its counterpart in the civil law is really *forfeiture.*" (*Id.* at 931 n.1). *Peremption* and its derivatives are used throughout *Equilease Corp. v. M/V Sampson*, 756 F.2d 357 (5th Cir. 1985).

Preemption, by far the more common word, means: (1) "the right to buy before others"; (2) "the purchase of a thing under this right"; or (3) "a prior seizure or appropriation" (*W9*). *Preemption* has one other legal meaning: "the occupation of (public land) so as to establish a preemptive title" (*OED*). See **preempt.**

preemption, federal; exclusive federal jurisdiction. "*Federal preemption* ... should be distinguished from *exclusive federal jurisdiction*. In the former, federal substantive law supplants state law, but, absent other provisions, both state and federal courts have concurrent jurisdiction of actions arising under that law; in the latter, only the specified federal instrumentalities have jurisdiction of the matter, irrespective of the law to be applied." 1A *Moore's Federal Practice*, ¶ 0.160 at 189 (2d ed. 1981).

preemptioner; preemptor. These words should be differentiated. A *preemptioner* holds the right to purchase public land by preemption. A *preemptor* actually acquires land by using this right. Of course, *preemptor* serves also as the general agent noun corresponding to the verb to *preempt.*

preemptive, -tory; peremptive, -tory. The adjectives most commonly used and distinguished are *preemptive* (= relating to or of the nature of preemption) and *peremptory*, q.v. The two other forms have bona fide existences, however. *Preemptory* = of or relating to a preemptor. (See **preemptioner.**) *Peremptive* = of or relating to peremption. E.g., "Authority exists in Louisiana cases to support the proposition that a prescriptive period defined in a statute conferring a right is actually a *peremptive* period." See **preemption.**

PREEMPTIVE PHRASES. See ANTICIPATORY REFERENCE.

preemptor. See **preemptioner.**

preemptory for *peremptory* is a fairly common misspelling. Properly, the former means "of or relating to a preemptor." See **preemptioner** & **preemptive.**

pre-established must either be hyphenated or have a diaeresis. Hyphenation is more natural in AmE.

prefatory, -torial; prefatial. The last two terms are NEEDLESS VARIANTS of the first.

prefer, which generally means "to like better," survives in a number of older senses in legal writing. For example, the *OED* records the sense "to advance oneself or one's interests," exemplified in this quotation: "People can properly *prefer* their own self-interests." Additionally, *prefer* has the sense "to lay (a matter) before anyone formally for consideration, approval, or sanction; to bring forward (as an indictment)" ⟨to prefer charges⟩. Hence: "A state's attorney is under a moral duty to enter a nolle prosequi whenever he is satisfied that a prisoner is innocent of the charge *preferred* against him."/ "Informations were also *preferred* against the first defendant that he did aid and abet each of the other defendants to engage in retail trading on Sunday by providing them with a stall and pitch for the sale of their goods." (Eng.)

preferable is inherently a comparative adjective; therefore it should not be used with it the periphrastic comparative *more.* E.g., "Unsatisfied with the steps toward first use protection that have thus far occurred under the Federal Trademark Act of 1946, he suggests a more flexible interpretative approach by the courts and administrative agencies *or, more preferably* [read *or, preferably*], congressional amendment." See COMPARATIVES AND SUPERLATIVES & ADJECTIVES (A).

Preferable is accented on the first, not on the second, syllable.

prejudge. See **forejudge.**

prejudice, v.t., is a LEGALISM for *to harm*; in ordinary discourse, it is a lawyer's pomposity. E.g., "I doubt that he will *prejudice* [read *hurt* or *harm*] her chances of getting a job by advancing too quickly." Following are two typical specimens in which the reference is to legal harm: "The critical inquiry is whether, for whatever reason, counsel's performance was deficient and whether that deficiency *prejudiced* the defendant."/ "A stay of the plaintiff's action here will not *prejudice* him." (Eng.)

prejudice, with(out). These terms are used in reference to dismissed legal actions to signify whether the determination or adjudication was on the merits of the case and hence a bar to future action. A *dismissal with prejudice* is an adjudication on the merits, whereas a *dismissal without prejudice* is not, and no right or remedy is foreclosed to the parties.

prejudicial; prejudiced. *Prejudicial* applies to things and events; *prejudiced*, to people. The former is potential; the latter describes a present fact. The meaning of a sentence can frequently be made clearer by using *harmful* in place of *prejudicial.*

prejudicial; pre-judicial. The hyphen makes an important difference. *Pre-judicial* was used in Roman law in reference to a class of preliminary actions in which questions of right of fact, usually as relating to status, were determined. Today the hyphenated form is used somewhat differently: "Professor Schwartz opens his book with a brief chapter on Warren's *pre-judicial* career."

The more usual term is *prejudicial*, discussed in the previous entry. E.g., "The allegedly *prejudicial* remarks pointed to by appellee were clearly made in the context of a hypothetical involving a worker who becomes disabled after a second accident."/ "The trial judge should have made a determination of the relative probative value of the twenty-three-year-old conviction as against the *prejudicial* effect on the jury."

preliminary to for *before* is a silly pomposity. E.g., "*Preliminary to* [read *Before*] the date set for trial a pretrial hearing was held by the state court." Cf. **prior to** & **antecedent to.**

premier(e). Two observations are in order for these words. First, *premier*, the adjective, is often pretentious in place of *first* or *foremost.* Second, *premiere*, the noun, is not in good use as a verb.

premise; premiss. In the sense "a previous statement or proposition from which another is inferred as a conclusion," the first is the AmE, the second the BrE spelling.

premises (= a house or building) has a curious history in legal usage. Originally, in the sense of things mentioned previously, it denoted in law "that part in the beginning of a deed or conveyance that sets forth the names of the grantor, grantee, and things granted, together with the consideration or reason of the grant" (*OED*). Then, through HYPALLAGE, it was extended to refer to "the subject of a conveyance or bequest, specified in the premises of the deed." Finally, it was extended to "a house or building with its grounds or other appurtenances" (*OED*).

The term always takes a plural verb, e.g., "The *premises* were put under surveillance."

premiss. See **premise.**

premium. Pl. *-iums.* See PLURALS (A).

premortal; premortem. See **antemortem.**

prenuptial. See **antenuptial.**

preparatory, -tive. As an adjective, *preparative* is a NEEDLESS VARIANT of *preparatory.* It is a legitimate noun, however, meaning "something that prepares the way for something else."

preparatory to, used in the sense "in order to prepare for," is legalistic. E.g., "A recovery for breach of promise of marriage included recompense for various efforts and expenditure by the plaintiff *preparatory to* [read *to prepare for* or *in preparation for*] the promised wedding."/ "Plaintiff and her husband went out of the station *preparatory to* [read *to prepare for*] boarding the train."

The phrase is likewise pretentious in place of *before*: "The defendant told the judge during his interrogation *preparatory to* [read *before*] accepting the guilty plea that no law enforcement officer had abused him." Cf. **preliminary to, prior to** & **antecedent to.**

prepense. The phrase *malice prepense* is obsolete for *malice aforethought.* See **aforethought** & **malice aforethought.**

preplanned is illogical for *planned.* One can plan something beforehand only.

preponderant; preponderate, adj. The latter is a NEEDLESS VARIANT. E.g., "We believe that the court's rejection of the claim was not *preponderately* [read *preponderantly*] reasonable." *Preponderate* should be used only as a verb. Cf. **predominate.**

PREPOSITIONS. A. Redundancy of. Writers often unnecessarily repeat prepositions when there are intervening phrases or clauses. E.g., "The Massachusetts court argued that promoters stand *in* as much *in* [omit the first *in*] a fiduciary position to the corporation when uninformed shareholders are expected to be brought in after the wrong has been perpetrated as when there are current shareholders to whom no disclosure is made." Cf. **so as + infinitive.**

B. Wrongly Elided. Just as often, however, necessary prepositions are wrongly omitted, usually because of the proximity of the same preposition performing a different function. The corrections in brackets should be self-explanatory: "An acceptance that requests a change [*of*] or addition to terms *of* the offer is not thereby invalidated unless the acceptance is made to depend on assent to the changed or added terms."/ "Maxi Corporation is a Texas corporation [*of*] which Smith owns sixty percent *of* the stock."/ "Forty years of subsequent experience has shown that such a hope was *in* large part, but not altogether, [*in*] vain."

Occasionally prepositions are omitted for fear of ending a sentence with one: "There are no unasserted claims and assessments of any nature that we are aware [*of*]."/ "The courts recognize that the seller and buyer are not the only persons interested in this transaction and have imposed duties on the selling shareholder with respect to whom he sells [*to*]." The writers should not have feared writing *aware of* and *sells to.* See (c) below.

There is at least one other type of problem caused by prepositions wrongly omitted. *Attorney Solicitation* is the title of a law review article; yet from the title, one does not know whether the article refers to the solicitation of, or solicitation by, attorneys. That anyone with legal knowledge would presume the latter does not vindicate the writer's vagueness. See NOUN PLAGUE.

C. Ending Sentences with. The spurious rule about not ending sentences with prepositions is a remnant of Latin grammar, which cannot properly straitjacket English grammar. Insofar as it may be called a "rule," it is a rule of rhetoric and not of grammar, the idea being that one should end sentences with strong words that drive home one's point. That principle is, of course, sound, but not to the extent of meriting lockstep adherence.

Churchill's witticism about the preposterousness of the "rule" should have laid to rest this bugaboo. When someone once upbraided him for ending a sentence with a preposition, he rejoined, "This is the type of arrant pedantry up with which I shall not put." Avoidance of ending sentences with prepositions can lead to preposterous monstrosities.

Perfectly natural-sounding sentences end with prepositions: "The act must have some causal connection with the injury complained *of.*" When one varies such formal constructions, sometimes downright stilted, as *of which, on which,* and *for which,* with the relative *that,* the preposition is necessarily sent to the end of the sentence. "I must respectfully dissent, for this is a point on which I must insist" becomes far more natural as, "I must respectfully dissent, for this is a point that I must insist on." See **which & that.**

D. Correctly Matching with Verbs. A useful rule of thumb—by no means to be taken as an absolute rule—in determining what preposition to use with a given verb is to follow the prefix of that verb. Hence *inhere in, comport with, attribute to,* and so on. There are many exceptions, however. *Impute* takes *on, oblivious* takes *of,* and *in respect* can take either *of* or *to,* though *with respect* takes only *to.* Many other verbs are treated throughout this work. Readers with an interest in a more detailed, comprehensive treatment of this subject may benefit from the following works: M. Benson, E. Benson, & R. Ilson, *The BBI Combinatory Dictionary of English: A Guide to Word Combinations* (1986); F. T. Wood, *English Prepositional Idioms* (1967); and A. P. Cowie & R. Mackin, *The Oxford Dictionary of Current Idiomatic English* (1975).

E. Repetition of after Conjunctions. Often it is useful in avoiding AMBIGUITY to repeat the preposition governing the noun after *or* or *and.* E.g., "Is it a question *of* law or *of* fact?"

F. Getting It Wrong. In the following examples, the incorrect preposition is used:

1. *About* for *at*: "To get upset about Begelman in Hollywood is to get upset *about* [read *at*] a cannibal for chewing his own cuticles."

2. *To* for *for*: "In sum, the common-law widow's election has no tax consequences *to* [read *for*] the surviving spouse."

3. See **as to.**

prerequisite; requisite. "Properly, a *prerequisite* has to be obtained or fulfilled before a *requisite* can be attended to. In short, *prerequisite* is rarely permissible." Vigilans, *Chamber of Horrors* 114 (1952).

prescribe, v.i. In lay writing, *prescribe* is transitive only: doctors prescribe drugs and moralists prescribe ethics. In Louisiana and Scots law, *prescribe* has a special intransitive sense: "[of an action] to suffer prescription; to lapse, to become invalid or void by passage of time; to be no longer capable of prosecution" (*OED*). Hence: "We need not unravel this jurisprudence to determine whether any of his trespass claims for damages for the actual taking of his property have *prescribed* [i.e., *become void by passage of time*]."/ "Appellee's right to claim just compensation for this interest does not *prescribe* [i.e., *cease to be capable of prosecution*] until two years from the date of the judgment of the district court."/ "The district court correctly held, therefore, that appellee's claims for damages incident to the taking of his property for use as a gas storage reservoir had *prescribed* [i.e. *lapsed*]."

Prescribe has been used transitively (and therefore passively) in this sense: "It was shown that the property involved was the same property as that in a suit brought in the Louisiana court a few years earlier where the same restrictive covenant was held *to have been prescribed* by two years' continued violation." *Warner v. Walsdorf,* 277 F.2d 679, 680 (5th Cir. 1960). The *OED* does not list this transitive sense of the word. See **proscribe.**

prescription. See **proscription.**

present. Phrases such as *the present testator* and *the present trust* have become common spin-offs of *the present case* and *the present writer.* Rarely, however, does *present* serve any purpose. See **instant case.**

presenter, -or. The preferred spelling is *-er.*

presentiment. See **presentment.**

presently contains an ambiguity. In the days of Shakespeare, it meant "immediately." Soon its meaning evolved into "after a short time" (perhaps because people exaggerated about their promptitude); this sense is still current. Then, chiefly in the AmE, it took on the sense "at present; currently." This last sense has been deprecated by some writers, but the *Oxford Guide* states that it is "widely used and often sounds more natural than *at present.*" It certainly appears in formal legal prose in this sense, especially in the U.S.: "Enough instances of self-enrichment *presently* occur, even in the case of managers of public corporations, to suggest that the market cannot fully control this phenomenon."/ "*Presently* pending before this court is an appeal from the decision of the district court that denied appellants' application to present a next-friend petition for a writ of habeas corpus on behalf of their son, a death-sentenced prisoner." For another example, see the quotation of Leff under **adulterine bastard**. Cf. **momentarily.**

presentment; presentiment. The first means "the act of presenting or laying before a court or person in authority a formal statement of some matter to be legally dealt with" (*OED*). (For the special sense of *presentment* in criminal law, see **indictment.**) The second means "a vague mental impression or feeling of a future event."

presents, know all men by these = take notice. In this phrase, *these presents* = this legal document. E.g., "Vendor does by *these presents* grant the following property to the purchaser." The phrase is now almost always unnecessarily legalistic.

present writer is today generally considered inferior to *I* or *me*. See FIRST PERSON (B).

preservation; preserval. The latter is a NEEDLESS VARIANT.

presidence, -cy. The former means "the action or fact of presiding"; the latter means "the office or function of president."

presiding judge. See **chief judge.**

presiding juror. See **foreman** & SEXISM (B).

presume. See **assume.**

presumption = a judicially applied prediction of factual or legal probability. E.g., "After adjudication of insanity, a *presumption*

of insanity continues, but a subsequent adjudication of restoration to sanity by competent authority restores the previous *presumption* of sanity until the contrary is made to appear."/ "By the provisions of the Restatement of the Law of Contracts it is expressly provided that there is a *presumption* that the offer is to enter into a bilateral contract."

A *presumption of law* is a rule of law by which the finding of a basic fact gives rise to a presumed fact capable of being rebutted. A *presumption of fact* is simply an argument; it is an inference that may be drawn from the establishment of a basic fact, but need not be drawn as a matter of law. *Black's* notes that this distinction is increasingly rejected.

presumptive; presumptuous. *Presumptive* = (1) giving reasonable grounds for presumption or belief; warranting inferences; or (2) based on presumption or inference. E.g., in sense (2): "The interest limited in that case was a remainder and the settlor's intent to revoke the instrument was ineffective since *presumptive* remaindermen were not parties to the revocation." (See **heir presumptive.**) *Presumptuous* = arrogant, presuming, bold, forward, impudent.

presumptively; presumably. These words are often used synonymously in English prose, but in legal writing are commonly differentiated. *Presumptively* = by legal presumption. E.g., "The literal words of the statute are *presumptively* conclusive of legislative intent, but that presumption may be defeated by contrary indications of intent also evident on the face of the statute." *Presumably* = as one may presume or reasonably suppose; by presumption or supposition.

presumptuous. See **presumptive.**

pretence. See **pretense.**

pretend as though for *pretend that* (by analogy of *act as though*) is unidiomatic.

pretense, -ce. The AmE spelling is *-se*, the BrE spelling *-ce*.

pretentious (= making claim to great merit or importance) for *pedantic* (= overrating or parading book-learning or technical knowledge) is an unthinking blunder: "The line between owner and repairman is dull and elusive at best; fortunately, Congress has for future cases ended this sometimes *pretentious* [read *pedantic*] distinction."

pretermit   generally connotes "to overlook or ignore purposely," as here: "Our deliberate choice, however, is to dispose finally of the appeal on its merits and *pretermit* a difficult jurisdictional issue."/ "*Pretermitting* other problems with appellant's claim, we find based on these facts that appellant's failure to present evidence of the existence of the vodka bottles was due to his own lack of diligence and that of his counsel."/ "We *pretermit* the question whether the PKPA would allow Louisiana, as the child's home state, to make temporary emergency orders regarding visitation for such protection; we are not presented with such an emergency situation in this *case.*"

Yet in legal phrase *pretermitted child statutes, pretermitted* means "neglected or overlooked accidentally." E.g., "*Pretermitted* heir statutes are designed to prevent inadvertent disinheritance of a child or other descendant by the testator; the statutes are not intended to prevent the testator from disinheriting a child if he desires to do so." This sense derives from Roman law, which had the special term *preterition* for the omission by a testator to mention in his will one of his children or natural heirs.

Pretermit means "to omit, whether purposely or by oversight." It does not properly mean "to prevent or preclude," the most common error with this word. E.g., "We do not read *Weeks* as mandating remand in all cases where a removal petition is untimely; we are unwilling to allow a model defect to *pretermit* [read *prevent*] our substantive inquiry."/ "It is incorrect to read the 'subject only to' language as *pretermitting* [read *precluding*] a reading of the contract as a whole to flesh out the extent of Global Marine's obligation under this provision."/ "We note that a finding that a claimant is disabled or not disabled at any point in the review *pretermits* [read *precludes*] further review."

pretextual   (= constituting a pretext) is not recognized in the *OED,* the *OED Supp.,* *W9,* or *W3.* The term is common in American legal writing, however. E.g., "There is no evidence to support a contention that the arrest for the traffic violation was *pretextual.*" State v. Moody, 443 S.W.2d 802, 804 (Mo. 1969)./ "Beckendorf's explanation for hiring Roberson was purely *pretextual,* and the trial court was

clearly erroneous in failing to recognize this." See **nonpretextual.**

pretrial   should not be hyphenated.

pretty,   used as an adverb, is still considered informal or colloquial. E.g., "Handicapped as counsel was by a defendant under present confinement and with a rich history of earlier state convictions, it was *pretty* clear that counsel could not run the risk of putting the defendant on the stand." *Pretty* adds nothing to the sentence.

prevalent   is accented on the first, not the second, syllable: /**prev**-ă-lĕnt/.

prevent   nowadays ordinarily takes *from,* although archaically it is used with a direct object and a gerund. E.g., "There are various matters that interfere with this normal course and *prevent* the action proceeding to final judgment." In BrE this usage is informal.

Prevent there causes ugly and ungrammatical constructions. "Their action *prevented there from being* a quorum." [Read *Their action prevented a quorum from being reached.*]

prevent(at)ive.   The correct form is *preventive,* although the corrupt, epenthetical form *preventative* is unfortunately not uncommon. E.g., "In Blackstone, one of the two named species of the genus '*preventative* [read *preventive*] criminal procedure' was the magistrate-required recognizance (or bond) with sureties to keep the peace." Leff, *The Leff Dictionary of Law,* 94 Yale L.J. 1855, 1861 (1985)./ "It is in no sense a *preventative* [read *preventive*] remedy, but is prospective merely." 52 Am. Jur. 2d *Mandamus* § 9 (1970).

previously   for *before,* adv. In the entry following this one, it is stated that *previous to* is much inferior to *before* as a preposition. Just the opposite holds true for the adverbs, where *previously* is better than *before,* at least when the adverb is prepositive: "M. S. was then operating the filling station on lot three as *before* [read *previously*] mentioned."

previous to   for *before* is unnecessarily highfalutin. (Cf. **anterior to** & **antecedent to.**) One sometimes even finds *previously to*: "Judge Critz was a member of the three-judge court, as well as having been a commissioner *previously to* [read *before*] becoming a judge." (A more drastic rewriting will greatly improve this sentence: *Judge Critz was a member of a three-judge court after having been a commissioner.*)/ "Throughout 1938 and for many years *previously and subsequently* [read *before and after*], defendants carried on their business in Newark."/ "*Previously to* [read *Before*] December 1950, appellants carried on business at Liverpool." (Eng.) See **prior to.**

prevision (= foresight) is not to be confused with the ordinary term, *provision.* E.g., "Life will have to be made over, and human nature transformed before *prevision* so extravagant can be accepted as the norm of conduct, the customary standard to which behavior must conform." (Cardozo, J., in *Palsgraf*).

prideful. See **proud.**

prima facie (= at first sight) is two words. The phrase, which may be either adverbial or adjectival, should not be hyphenated. Here it acts as an adverb: "Publication of this language *prima facie* constitutes a cause of action and *prima facie* constitutes a wrong without any allegation or evidence of damage other than what is implied or presumed from the fact of publication."/ "They hold that if he and the attesters are in the same room all are *prima facie* in each other's presence, but if the attesting signatures are written in another room, then *prima facie* the statutory requirement was violated."

Adjectival uses are perhaps even more common today: "The cases at most attributed but *prima facie* meaning to such words, and a competent draftsman would not deliberately pick a word that instead of controlling the context is easily colored by it."

Sometimes the phrase appears to have been misused for *per se*, as here: "There are certain exceptional cases where a communication is privileged, though *prima facie* libelous." See **at first blush.**

prima facie case = (1) the establishment of a legally required presumption that may be rebutted; or (2) the plaintiff's burden of producing enough evidence to permit the fact-trier to infer the fact at issue. *Texas Department of Community Affairs v. Burdine*, 450 U.S. 248, 254 n. 7 (1981). The *CDL* defines *prima facie case* as "a case that has been supported by sufficient evidence for it to be taken as proved in the absence of adequate evidence to the contrary." E.g., "Until he has proved that the defendant will in that case profit at his expense,

he has not made out a *prima facie case* to be paid anything, and until he has proved how much that profit will be, his *prima facie case* is not complete."

primary jurisdiction. See **original jurisdiction.**

prime (= to take priority over) is a usage unknown to lay writing. E.g., "It is undisputed that the 1977 and 1979 mortgages were preferred mortgages that *primed* Belcher's lien."/ "The letter states only that the rights of Rivercity under the option agreement will *prime* the rights of Whitney under the Act of Collateral Mortgage."

primer, in the sense of "an introductory or refresher book," is always /**prim**-ĕr/. The undercoat to paint is pronounced /**prī**-mĕr/.

primogenitor; primogeniture. The former denotes "the first parent; earliest ancestor." (Loosely, it is used for *progenitor* [= forefather, ancestor].) The latter means (1) "the fact or condition of being the first-born of the children of the same parents"; or (2) (at common law) "the right of succession or inheritance belonging to the first-born." See **progenitor.**

principal. See **corpus.**

principal, n. & adj.; **principle,** n. In lay usage, it is usually enough to remember that *principal* (= chief, primary, most important) is almost always an adjective, and *principle* (= a truth, law, doctrine, or course of action) is virtually always a noun. Although *principle* is not a verb, we have *principled* as an adjective. (See the next entry.)

In legal language, *principal* is often a noun, an elliptical form of *principal person*, primarily in the law of agency. *Principal* also acts as a shortened form of *principal investment* in the context of investments, banking, and trusts. See **corpus & res.**

principled, as often used of decisions and judgments, means "resting on reasons that in their generality and neutrality transcend the immediate result involved." Wechsler, *Toward Neutral Principles of Constitutional Law,* 73 Harv. L. Rev. 1, 19 (1959). When used of persons, *principled* = having principles or scruples.

prior; previous. The adjective *prior* or *previous* for *earlier* is within the stylist's license; *prior to* and *previous to* in place of *before* are not. See **previous to** & **prior to.**

prioritize is a cant word to be avoided. See -IZE.

prior restraint = censorship before publication. E.g., "The photo processor thus becomes the censor of the nation's photographers; worse yet, his actions become a particularly obnoxious form of *prior restraint*: he condemns the photo before anyone, including the photographer or a neutral magistrate, has had an opportunity to see the final print."

prior to is a terribly overworked lawyerism. Only in rare contexts is it not much inferior to *before*. Even the U.S. Supreme Court has suggested that the phrase is "clumsy," noting that "[l]egislative drafting books are filled with suggestions that *prior to* be replaced with the word *before*." *United States v. Locke,* 471 U.S. 84, 96 n.11 (1985). Nevertheless, examples abound in virtually any piece of legal writing: "*Prior to* [read *Before*] hearing in the Appellate Division, we certified the cause on our own motion."/ "*Up to December 24, 1936, and for many years prior thereto* [read *For many years up to December 24. 1936*], petitioner and his wife were domiciled in the State of Oklahoma."/ "There is no evidence that *prior to* [read *before*] being made a party to this suit the Tennessee Higher Education Authority ever used its authority in any way to facilitate desegregation in these institutions."

As Bernstein has pointed out, one should feel free to use *prior to* instead of *before* if one is accustomed to using *posterior to* for *after*. T. M. Bernstein, *The Careful Writer* 347 (1979). Cf. **previous to** & **subsequent to.**

prise. See **prize.**

privation. See **deprivation.**

privileges and immunities; privileges or immunities. The former phrase appears in Article 4, Section 2 of the U.S. Constitution; the latter in the fourteenth amendment to the Constitution.

privity; privy. To laymen, a *privity* is something that is kept secret. To a lawyer, it is a relationship between two parties that is rec-

ognized by law, usually a mutual interest in a transaction or thing ⟨in privity of contract⟩.

Privy likewise has different associations for layman and lawyer. To the former it is an adjective meaning "secret, private," or a plural noun meaning "outhouse; toilet." Lawyers mean no harm in calling other people *privies*; a *privy* in law is one who is a partaker or has any part or interest in any action, matter, or thing. E.g., "Respondents cite the portion of *Stiller* in which the New York court (the new forum) acknowledged that the Ohio court (the original forum that issued the injunction) lacked jurisdiction over the New York respondents who were *privies* with the enjoined party."

The word is also used adjectivally in this legal sense: "Admissions may be made on behalf of the real party to any proceeding by any party who is *privy* in law, in blood, or in estate to any party to the proceeding on behalf of that party." (Eng.) Still, *privy* is used in its lay senses in legal writing, and the legal reader must be adept at discerning which sense is intended: "The jury was not *privy* to the parties' settlement negotiations."

prize; prise. The second is the better spelling in the sense "to pry or force open," although in AmE *prize* often appears in this sense. The DIFFERENTIATION is worth promoting, however. *Prize* is the spelling for all other senses.

pro and con; pro et con(tra). The English rendering is preferred. The phrase may be used nominally: "We are satisfied that the Commission adequately considered the *pros and cons* of the new grants of authority with a view toward the industry's economic well-being." Or it may be adverbial: "A number of affidavits are filed *pro and con*, which it is not necessary to consider." Or, again, it may be adjectival: "A number of *pro and con* briefs have been filed." One should not depart from the SET PHRASE: "Now we are obliged to advert to those elements of proof and legal concepts *pro and contra* [read *pro and con*] bearing on the validity of the instrument in question." *In re Powers's Estate,* 134 N.W.2d 148, 151 (Mich. 1965).

Pro and con has also been used as a verb phrase ⟨to pro-and-con the issue⟩, and although today this use sounds somewhat odd, it has the sanction of long standing. The *OED Supp.* and *W3* record another use not here recommended: the phrase has been used prepositionally ⟨arguments pro and con the pro-posal⟩, but here *for and against* would be better.

probate, n., originally was the process of proving a will—it has developed, however, into a broad area of the law relating to dece-dents' estates and guardianships. Today the word is frequently an adjective: "Since the main burden of taxes, debts, and other admin-istration expenses falls on the *probate* estate, there may in larger estates be heavy demands for cash." See **probatum** & **proof** (A).

probate, v.t., is an Americanism. The word means "to admit (a will) to proof"; recently, however, it has acquired the sense "to grant probation to (a criminal), to reduce (a sen-tence) by means of probation." For examples of sense (2), see *Wood v. State,* 68 Ga. App. 43, 47, 21 S.E.2d 915, 918 (1942) ("a suspended sentence shall have the effect of *probating* the defendant"), and *United States v. Francischine,* 512 F.2d 827, 828 (5th Cir. 1975) ("the conviction['s] . . . validity plays no necessary part in the consideration of whether a *pro-bated* prison term should be continued").

probationary, -al. The latter spelling is a NEEDLESS VARIANT.

probationer; parolee. *Probationer* = one on probation. *Parolee* = one released on pa-role, q.v.

probative, -tory. *Probatory* is a NEEDLESS VARIANT of *probative* (= [1] tending or serving to prove; or [2] exploratory; serving to test). In the law of evidence, the first meaning of *probative* is invariably the one intended, though it is of more recent origin. E.g., "In this circuit, we have found *probative* the fact that a hospital district was financed through levies that were separate from other county or state taxes and through bonds sold upon the full faith and credit of the district." See **probity.**

probatum = something proved or conclu-sively established. (Cf. **ipse dixit.**) The term has nothing in common with *probate,* except etymology.

probity means "honesty; integrity." Here it is used correctly: "It is beyond either human capacity or the demands of justice that the trial judge decide correctly every issue arising

in the trial; what is required is not a perfect score, but fairness, *probity,* and the avoidance of substantial prejudice."

Unfortunately, *probativeness,* which means "the quality of tending to prove something," and its adjective, *probative,* are frequently con-fused with *probity.* E.g., "The majority ad-dresses the trial court's ruling admitting can-cer evidence; relevance, *probity* [read *probativeness*], and prejudice are dealt with sep-arately."/ "Proof that the inhalation of asbes-tos fibers can cause cancer is not the sine qua non of plaintiff's case; it has only incremental *probity* [read *probativeness*]."/ "The *probative* value of the extrinsic offense correlates posi-tively with its likeness to the offense charged; we cannot say that the district court abused its discretion in determining that the *probity* [read *probativeness*] of this proof outweighed its prejudice." (This is an attempt at what is here termed INELEGANT VARIATION.)

Probity is also occasionally misused for *pro-priety:* "Although the *probity* [read *propriety*] of using affidavits to resolve fact issues is per-haps open to question, reliance upon the prosecutor's affidavits in this case is appropriate."

problematic(al). Both forms appear in modern writing. E.g., "It is highly *problematic* whether the Supreme Court would today grant officials manning such checkpoints un-bridled discretion to search any person and any vehicle for contraband without any of the constraints normally imposed upon federal of-ficers by this country's Constitution."/ "Evi-dence of the loss of earnings of a minor child is *problematical* and speculative." Euphony should govern the choice of form.

problem-solving is a VOGUE WORD among lawyers and social scientists. It is best avoided when possible. E.g., "The emphasis is on the method or technique of *problem-solving* [read *solving problems*]."

proceed. See **precede.**

process has the special legal senses (1) "the proceedings in any action or prosecution" ⟨due process⟩ and (2) "the summons by which a person is cited to appear in court" ⟨service of process⟩. Sense (2) is especially baf-fling to laymen not familiar with legal pro-cedures. E.g., "An execution is a *process* of the court issued to enforce the judgment of that court."

prochein ami. This is the preferred spelling. *Prochein amy* (used by Blackstone) and *prochain amy* are variant spellings to be avoided. See **next friend** & LOAN TRANSLATIONS.

prochronism. See **anachronism.**

proconsulate; proconsulship. The latter is a NEEDLESS VARIANT.

procreative, -tional. "The hysterectomy, involving complete removal of her *procreative* organs, rendered her perfectly sterile." *Procreational* is a NEEDLESS VARIANT.

procuration; procurement; procurance; procuracy. Traditionally, *procuration* has meant "the act of appointing another as one's attorney-in-fact or agent." By transference it has referred also to the authority vested in a person so appointed. E.g., "If a bill be drawn by *procuration*, no acceptor of the bill is permitted to deny the authority of the agent, by whom it purports to be drawn, to draw in the name of the principal." (Eng.) Finally, it has been used as the generic noun for *procure*; yet this broad sense is generally reserved for *procurement*. E.g., "Jureczki argues that White's improprieties in the *procurement* of the arrest warrant, as opposed to mere reliance on an existing order, places the defendants outside the immunity of *Baker v. McCollan.*"/ "As the evidence of contestant failed to show any activity on the part of Mrs. Logan in the *procurement* of the will of decedent, it was inadequate to prove undue influence on her part in the execution of the will."/ "Appellee filed the motion to remand the contractual indemnity claim to permit *procurement* of documentary evidence."

Yet *procurement* has had another, more restricted sense in legal contexts: "persuading or inviting a woman to have sexual intercourse" (*CDL*). E.g., "Appellee maliciously procured her to make a charge of bastardy, in that, by the *procurement* of appellant, she did make complaint under oath before a justice of the peace, charging appellant with having begotten the child."

Even though *W9* wrongly suggests that *procurance* is preferred over *procurement*, *procurance* remains a NEEDLESS VARIANT of *procurement*. Finally, *procuracy* = a letter of agency; the document empowering an attorney-in-fact to act."

procurator. See **attorney** (A).

procure is a FORMAL WORD for *get*. E.g., "It is urged that under Article 17 of the government contract, the overall company could have *procured* an extension of time for its performance had it applied to the government."

procurement. See **procuration.**

procuring breach of contract. See **tortious interference with contractual relations.**

prodigality; profligacy. The former means "lavishness; extravagance." The latter means primarily "salaciousness; licentiousness," but it also shares the sense of the former.

prodigious for *prestigious* is a MALAPROPISM. E.g., "The American Law Institute is one of the most select and *prodigious* [read *prestigious*] legal organizations in this country."

producible. So spelled; *producable* is an infrequent misspelling.

producing cause. See CAUSATION (C).

product(s) liability. The general area of law is known as *products liability*. Occasionally one sees the singular form *product liability*, usually in reference to a particular product of a particular manufacturer. When the phrase is used adjectivally, it should be hyphenated ⟨products-liability case⟩. See ADJECTIVES (C).

pro et con. See **pro and con.**

profane; profanatory. That which is *profane* is irreverent or blasphemous; that which is *profanatory* tends to make profane.

profession. This word has been much debased of late, primarily at the hands of egalitarians who call any occupation a profession. In any American city today, if one wants a job as a barber, manicurist, or manager of a fast-food store, one turns in the classified advertisements to the section "Professions." If one is a lawyer looking for a change in jobs, one turns to "Advanced Degree Required," a section of its own rather than a subsection of "Professions."

Traditionally there have been but three professions: theology, law, and medicine. These were known either as *the three professions* or as *the learned professions*. The term was ultimately extended to mean "one's principal vocation," which embraces prostitution as well as medicine. (*The oldest profession* originally had an irony much stronger than it has today.)

The restricted sense of *profession* no doubt strikes many people as snobbish and anachronistic. What about university professors, atomic physicists, and engineers? Perhaps three professions are not enough: but we ought at least to use *some* discrimination, with emphasis on "prolonged specialized training in a body of abstract knowledge." Goode, *Encroachment, Charlatanism, and the Emerging Profession*, 25 Am. Soc. Rev. 902, 903 (1960). Professional training "must lead to some order of mastery of a generalized cultural tradition, and do so in a manner giving prominence to an *intellectual* component." Parsons, *Professions*, 12 Int'l Encycl. Soc. Sci. 536, 536 (1968).

Notably, the traditional, artificially restricted view of the term has long been considered archaic. Holmes wrote in 1896: "It is not likely . . . that anybody will be prejudiced against business or will take formal views of the dignity of callings such as a hundred years ago put the ministry first, law and medicine next, and below them all other pursuits." Holmes, *The Bar as a Profession*, in *Collected Legal Papers* 153, 153 (1952).

proffer is chiefly a literary and legal term; it is equivalent to *offer*, and like that word, may be both noun and verb. Here is the nominal use: "Because of Delaware's absolute rule, its courts did not have occasion to consider the *proffer* put forward by petitioner Franks."/ "Because the expert testified during the *proffer* of proof that he was not aware of the agreement, the district court's exclusion of the evidence was not an abuse of discretion." Just as frequently it acts as a verb, as here: "The daughter *proffered* her own testimony to show, among other things, that the parents intended the conveyance to be an absolute gift and not an advancement."/ "We reject the *proffered* [i.e., suggested] distinctions."

profferer. So spelled. "This state of affairs is said to arise because of inequality of bargaining power between the *profferor* [read *profferer*] of the contract and the 'weaker' party." Leff, *The Leff Dictionary of Law*, 94 Yale L.J. 1855, 1931 (1985).

profits à prendre, known also as *right of common*, denotes the right exercised by one person in another's soil, along with a share in the profits of the other's soil. *Profits à prendre* is a LAW FRENCH survival still commonly used. E.g., "For example, trust property may consist of a life estate in land, a *profit à prendre* to remove minerals, an undivided interest in land as a tenant in common, or an absolute interest in a specific bond or share of stock."

Profit à prendre has been rendered *profit a' prendre* by some for whom the grave accent apparently was not typographically possible. See, e.g., *McDonald v. Board of Mississippi Levee Commissioners*, 646 F. Supp. 449, 469 (N.D. Miss. 1986). Omitting the accent completely from this phrase is preferable, however, to using an apostrophe in its stead.

profligacy. See **prodigality.**

pro forma (= as a matter of form; for the sake of form) usu. has a slightly depreciative tone in modern usage. The term need not be hyphenated as an adjectival phrase. See ADJECTIVES (C).

progenitor. A *progenitor* is one that yields *progeny*, q.v. E.g., "The *progenitor* of the *Blackledge* decision, *North Carolina v. Pearce* forbids increasing a sentence upon retrial after the defendant has successfully appealed, absent new facts unrelated to the appeal, affecting sentence." See **primogenitor.**

progeny is usually plural in sense, and thus takes a plural verb. E.g., "The *progeny* of *Williamson v. United States indicates* [read *indicate*] that *Williamson* requires reversal only when the specific defendant was picked out for the informer's effort by a government agent." Another word is required when the sense is singular, as in the following sentence: "In a *Blanchard* progeny [read *In a case that follows the rule in Blanchard*], *Chavers v. Exxon Corp.*, we quoted from and explained *Blanchard's* holding."

prognosis; prognostication; prognostic, n. *Prognosis* is usually used in medicine to mean "a forecast of the probable course and termination of an illness." (See **diagnosis.**) *Prognostication* is more general, denoting "a prediction or prophecy" or "a conjecture of some future event formed upon some supposed sign." E.g., "Some kinds of *prognostications* simply are not possible: it is foreseeable that a thirsty man will drink, but it may not be possible to foretell his choice of beverage."/ "A picture of the future size of this accumulation can be painted with gigantic lines; such a *prognostication* is not without precedent." *Prognostic* = an advance indication or omen.

program(m)atic. The word is spelled *-mm-* in both BrE and AmE.

program(me). *Program* is the AmE, *programme* the BrE spelling. The ending *-am* is used in G.B., however, in reference to computer programs.

program(m)er, -ing. The best spellings are in *-mm-* whether in AmE or in BrE. The double *-m-* in AmE appears to be descended from *programme*, the BrE spelling. A few American dictionaries give priority to *programer* and *programing*, but these forms are rare in practice. See DOUBLING OF FINAL CONSONANTS.

pro hac vice (= for this occasion or particular purpose) is a LATINISM not easily replaced in much legal writing. Often it is used adjectivally, e.g.: "The question narrows therefore to whether Litton was the owner *pro hac vice* of the vessel."/ "Plaintiff alleges that defendant was the *pro hac vice* owner of the barges involved." The phrase is also used adverbially, when, e.g., a lawyer appears in a court proceeding in a jurisdiction in which he has not been admitted to practice: "Butler entered an appearance *pro hac vice* for respondent on January 26, 1981; his partner Allis was admitted *pro hac vice* on October 19, 1982." Cf. **ad hoc.**

prohibit takes the preposition *from*; formerly, *prohibit* could take *to* ⟨the law prohibits persons to litter⟩, but now this construction is an ARCHAISM.

prohibition; proscription. The latter implies a prohibition in writing, whereas the former does not have this connotation. See **proscription.**

prohibitive, -tory. These terms have undergone a latent DIFFERENTIATION that needs to be further encouraged. *Prohibitive* may mean generally "having the quality of prohibiting," but more and more in modern prose it has the sense "tending to preclude consumption or purchase because of expense" ⟨the costs are prohibitive⟩.

Frequently used in the phrase *prohibitory in-*

junction, prohibitory has carved out a niche in the law in the sense "expressing a prohibition or restraint." E.g., "It is established in New York that violation of a *prohibitory* statute gives rise to tort liability."/ "Appellee seeks a *prohibitory* injunction restraining appellant from operating the sign and a mandatory injunction requiring appellant to remove the sign."/ "One of the tests for determining whether a statute is directory or mandatory is the presence of negative or *prohibitory* words plainly importing that the act should be done in a particular manner or at a particular time, and not otherwise."/ "The publication complained of accused plaintiff of having repudiated an honest indebtedness for liquor sold, by availing himself of the provisions of the *prohibitory* liquor law."

prohibitory injunction. See **mandatory injunction.**

prolificness is inferior to *prolificacy* as the noun corresponding to *prolific.* E.g., "Judge Posner's *prolificness* [read *prolificacy*] is no surprise to anyone familiar with his academic output: eleven books and more than 100 articles." Cf. **generic(al)ness.**

PROLIXITY. See VERBOSITY.

promise. See **offer.**

promisor, -er. The usual legal spelling is *-or* (as the correlative to *promisee*), but *-er* is equally good. E.g., "To allow him to keep such a payment or other consideration would be giving the *promisor* something for nothing." Cf. **purchaser, -or.**

promis(s)ee. The preferred spelling is *promisee*; the *-ss-* spelling is common but inferior.

promotive = tending to promote. E.g., "It is claimed that the two yearly payments to be made to the children just before Christmas and Easter produce a 'desirable social effect' and are *promotive* of public convenience and needs, and happiness and contentment." See BE-VERBS (B).

promulgate, a perhaps too well-liked lawyer's word, means (1) "to make known by public declaration"; or (2) "to disseminate (some creed or belief), or to proclaim (some law, decree, or things)" (*OED*). E.g., in sense (2): "It is my desire that any disbursements made under this paragraph shall be made to persons who believe in the fundamental principles of the Christian religion and in the Bible and who are endeavoring to *promulgate* the same."

PRONOMINAL   INDEFINITE   ADJECTIVES (e.g., *each, any, every, all, no, some*) should be used only when they serve some demonstrable purpose. When a subject is plural, such an adjective is usually unnecessary; e.g., *All corporate officers shall* . . . should read *Corporate officers shall* . . . .

A few conventions with these words are quite useful in the realm of DRAFTING. First, if a right, privilege, or power is extended, the drafter should use *each* ⟨each director may⟩. Second, if a duty is imposed, he should use *each* ⟨each director shall⟩. And third, if a proscription is set out, the word called for is *no* ⟨no director may⟩. See STATUTE DRAFTING.

PRONOUNS, PREEMPTIVE. See ANTICIPATORY REFERENCE (C).

PRONUNCIATION.   A. General Principles. The best advice to be given on this topic is to follow the pronunciation current among educated speakers in one's region. *Voir dire* is pronounced differently in Texas, New York, and London. A few words have universally accepted pronunciations and rejected mispronunciations; where prescriptions on pronunciation appear in this book, the preferred pronunciation is generally universally preferred.

Fowler's advice still speaks to us with clarion wisdom: "The ambition to do better than our neighbours is in many departments of life a virtue; in pronunciation it is a vice; there the only right ambition is to do as our neighbours" (*MEU1* 466).

When it comes to words that are not frequently pronounced by English-speaking people—as with any learned word, such as those from the law—the advice to conform with our neighbors' pronunciation becomes problematic. For here we find diversity, not uniformity, the result of the infrequency of occasions on which the words are pronounced. "Where there is a diversity of opinion and practice among reasonable [and educated] people, there must be also an equally broad charity in judgment. Could anything be more absurd than to stigmatize as incorrect a pronunciation which is actually in general

use . . .?" G. P. Krapp, *The Pronunciation of Standard English in America* iv (1919).

B. Commonly   Mispronounced   Lawyers' Words. Many words that prove troublesome to lawyers are listed throughout this work, with the correct pronunciation noted. Among the most frequently mispronounced words in the law are *substantive, lien,* and *cestui.*

C. Of Latin Terms. Pronunciation of Latin terms that survive in the language of the law is always troublesome for lawyers, since so few are trained in Latin and all are compelled to use such terms in the course of practice. The difficulty is, depending on one's point of view, exacerbated or ameliorated by the existence of three distinct—and equally acceptable—methods of Latin pronunciation. As an example, *sub judice*, q.v., is pronounced in two quite different ways, with minor variations on each. Further, a number of legal LATINISMS are primarily read and not spoken (e.g., *inclusio unius est exclusio alterius*). Most of the common Latinisms, such as *de minimis, de facto,* and *ipso facto* have readily apparent pronunciations. One should attempt to cultivate a sensitivity to the way in which Latin terms are pronounced within the professional community of one's geographic area, and stay within the mainstream in one's own speech community. Of course, drawing on one's own training in Latin or recourse to dictionaries is always helpful.

proof A. For *probate. Proof* has the general legal sense "evidence such as determines the judgment of a court," and more specifically often means "a written document or documents so attested as to form legal evidence" (*OED*). In practice this latter sense translates into the idiomatic equivalent of *probate:* "Bearing these opposing considerations in mind, the court is of the opinion that the will should be admitted to *proof.*" *Eaton v. Brown,* 193 U.S. 411, 414 (1904) (per Holmes, J.). *Proving a will* = obtaining probate of a will. See **probate, n.**

B. For *element of proof.* Generally, of course, *proof* is a mass noun. But when *proof* is used as an ellipsis for *element of proof* (as a type or a piece of evidence), it often takes the plural form *proofs*, as here: "The trial court placed extreme if not wholly unreasonable requirements on the government respecting particularized *proofs* of the underlying complaint."/ "A case is made for the jury whenever the *proofs* justify with reason the inference desired." See COUNT AND MASS NOUNS & PLURALS (B)

propaganda, a singular noun, makes the plural *-das.* It is sometimes mistaken to be a plural in the class of *data* and *strata.*

propelment. See **propulsion.**

properly. Placement of this word in relation to a BE-VERB or copula may affect meaning in significant ways: *be properly* means something different from *properly be.* The latter phrase means that the thing in question (the subject) is proper, or that it is proper for the thing to be done ⟨this question may properly be raised on appeal⟩, whereas the former means that the thing should be done in a proper way ⟨briefs should be properly submitted⟩.

pro persona (= for his own person, on his own behalf) is a LATINISM used in some jurisdictions as an equivalent of *pro se* and *in propria persona,* qq.v. E.g., "Defendant has raised a number of other issues in a *pro persona* brief." *State v. Kreps,* 706 P.2d 1213, 1218 (Ariz. 1985).

property. **A.** Legal Meaning. W. N. Hohfeld elucidated what was traditionally viewed to be the correct and incorrect uses of this word. The traditionally proper meaning of the term is "a right over a determinate thing, either a tract of land or a chattel." The transferred (and arguably loose) sense sometimes attached to this term is "any external thing over which the rights of possession, use, and enjoyment are exercised." See W. N. Hohfeld, *Fundamental Legal Conceptions* 28–29 (1919; repr. 1946). Thus the correct emphasis was seen as being on the rights over a thing, and not on the thing itself. Today, however, even in legal writing *property* generally carries the nontechnical sense Hohfeld disapproved of.

B. As a COUNT NOUN. Generally, *property* used as a count noun is realtors' cant in AmE. E.g., "It was the second marriage for the bridegroom, a real estate lawyer with *properties* [read *property*] in Mexico, Italy, and Palm Beach."/ "People won't realize the effect of this act until they try to buy *a property* [omit *a*]."/ "That word is exceedingly comprehensive and covers *every property* [read *all the property*] that the decedent might have had."/

"Because only *one adjacent property* [read *one adjacent piece of property*] was flooded, the court properly concluded that the damage resulted from a condition solely related to appellant's premises and within appellant's control." See COUNT & MASS NOUNS.

prophesy; prophecy. *Prophesy* is the verb meaning "to predict or foretell," *prophecy* the noun meaning "a prediction or foretelling." The words are pronounced differently. The last syllable in *prophesy* is pronounced "sigh," whereas the last syllable in *prophecy* is pronounced "see."

prophylactic, n. To an educated layman, this word is synonymous with *condom.* Doctors use the term for anything that prevents disease. To lawyers, it means "anything that is designed to prevent (something undesirable)." E.g., "The Supreme Court recognized that the predeprivation notice and hearing were necessary *prophylactics* against a wrongful discharge." The example quoted does not demonstrate the keenest linguistic sensitivity: in view of the layman's understanding, it is perhaps unwise to use *prophylactic* in the same sentence with *discharge.* (See VERBAL AWARENESS.) *Prophylactic* is also frequently an adjective in legal writing ⟨a prophylactic rule⟩.

proponent; propounder. Both mean "one seeking to have a will admitted to probate." The usual term is *proponent*: "The evidence of the *proponent,* having established that the decedent made a will and persisted in statements of satisfaction with its contents up to the day of his death, is sufficient to sustain the finding of the trial court that the presumption of destruction was overcome."/ "The *proponent* may be able to produce witnesses who can shed some light upon the execution of the will or identify particular pages, but this will be unusual since holographic wills are usually prepared in private."

Propounder is a NEEDLESS VARIANT. E.g., "The *propounder* [read *proponent*] admits that the instrument dated August 14 (the second will) is a part of the maker's testamentary disposition, but insists that it does not affect the validity of the instrument dated July 31 (the first will)." See **protagonist.**

proportion should not be used when *part* or *portion* is intended. See **portion.**

proportion, v.t.; proportionalize; proportionate, v.t. The second and third are NEEDLESS VARIANTS.

proportionate, -al, -able. The distinction to be observed is between *proportional* and *proportionate*; admittedly, at times the distinction is foiled by the frequent interchangeability of the terms. Nevertheless, it is possible to formulate the nuance that *proportional* = (1) of or relating to proportion; (2) in due proportion; whereas *proportionate* = proportioned, adjusted in proportion. As a Latinate perfect passive participle, *proportionate* suggests the conscious proportioning of an agent.

Apart from this nice distinction, it is worth observing that *proportionate* seems to be used more commonly in legal writing than *proportional*. E.g., "The court rejected appellant's contention that appellee's claim for compensation had also prescribed and awarded appellee his *proportionate* share of the value of the recoverable reserves."/ "Defense fees and costs incurred in defending personal injury actions are assessable as an element of damages in *proportionate*-fault collision cases." Especially is this so in the negative form of the word: "If the provision made for the prospective bride is unreasonably *disproportionate* to that which she would receive out of her husband's estate but for the agreement, it will be presumed that the prospective bride was not sufficiently informed about the extent, nature, and value of her husband's property."

Proportionable is an ARCHAISM that still sometimes occurs in legal writing. E.g., "The note for additional interest shall be *proportionably* [read *proportionately*] reduced." It has no place. Cf. **commensurate.**

propound (= [1] to put forth for consideration or discussion; or [2] to make a proposal, to propose) is easily used correctly, as the examples following demonstrate. Yet it is also frequently misused (see **expound**). E.g., "The jury initially gave inconsistent answers to special interrogatories *propounded* to it by the court."/ "Where one party opposes summary judgment by *propounding* a reasonable interpretation of a disputed matter, it may be sufficient to defeat the motion."/ "Petitioner married the decedent on February 10, 1951; the *propounded* instrument was executed on May 18, 1951 and the decedent died on July 1, 1951."/ "The privilege of cross-examination does not carry with it the right to indulge in irrelevant investigations of the private life of the witness, or to *propound* questions intended only to degrade and humiliate him before the jury."

propounder. See **proponent.**

proprietary, -tory The latter is an erroneous form. The adjectival form corresponding to the noun *proprietor* is either *proprietary* or *proprietorial*. *Proprietary* also means "of, relating to, or holding as property."

propulsion; propelment. The latter is a NEEDLESS VARIANT.

propulsive, -sory. The latter is a NEEDLESS VARIANT.

pro rata should be spelled as two words. E.g., "Appellant argues that the will shows that the testator intended his debts and estate costs to be paid *pro rata.*" *Proportionate(ly)* will sometimes serve in place of *pro rata.*

prorate (= to divide or assess proportionately) is an Americanism, although the British have now adopted the nominal form *proration*. Instead of the AmE *prorating*, common in the law of oil and gas, the British use *prorationing.*

prorogue; prorogate. *Prorogue* = (1) to postpone; (2) to discontinue the meetings of (a legislative assembly, usually Parliament) for a definite or indefinite time without dissolving it; or (3) to discontinue meeting until the next session. *Prorogate* is a NEEDLESS VARIANT except in Scots and civil law, in which the term means "to extend by consent (the jurisdiction of a judge or court) to a cause in which it would otherwise be incompetent."

proscribe; prescribe. The former means to prohibit, the latter to impose authoritatively. See **prescribe.**

proscription; prescription. As with the verbs, discussed in the entry immediately preceding, the nouns are sometimes confused. Sometimes it is difficult to determine whether the use is proper or improper, as here: "The thrust of her argument is that she could not have been constitutionally arrested under the disorderly conduct statute because her conduct did not fit the *proscriptions* [read *prescriptions*?] of that statute." If the writer meant to say her conduct did not match the types of conduct prohibited by the statute, *proscription* was the correct word; but if he meant to say that her conduct did not fall within the definitions of disorderly conduct laid down by the statute, *prescription* would have been the correct word. See **prohibition**.

pro se = on his own behalf. The phrase is two words, and should not be hyphenated. Functionally, the phrase may be either adjectival or adverbial. Here it is the former: "In this *pro se* action, plaintiff contends that defendant absconded with personal property and household goods belonging to him, in violation of a temporary restraining order." Just as frequently it is adverbial, as here: "The taxpayer-petitioner appeals *pro se* from an order and decision of the United States Tax Court." See **in propria persona** & **pro persona**.

PROSE, THE SOUND OF. See SOUND OF PROSE, THE.

prosecute; persecute. Heaven forbid that one with legal training should confuse these terms. *Prosecute* = to begin a case at law for punishment of a crime or of a legal violation. *Persecute* = to oppress, coerce, treat unfairly, often out of religious hatred.

Today *prosecute* is largely confined to criminal contexts (= to institute legal proceedings against [a person] for some offense), but the word survives as an ARCHAISM in civil contexts in the sense "to carry out or engage in a legal action; to follow up on a legal claim." E.g., "A statute of Illinois provided that no action should be brought or *prosecuted* in that state for damages occasioned by death occurring in another state in consequence of wrongful conduct." (Holmes, J.)/ "Appellants have *prosecuted* an appeal to this court."/ "There was a jury trial, resulting in a verdict and judgment in behalf of appellee, from which this appeal is *prosecuted*."/ "Plaintiff *prosecutes* this appeal from a judgment of dismissal entered after sustaining of defendants' general demurrer."

When used in reference to something other than legal business, *prosecute* generally means "to carry on." In this sense, the term is a LEGALISM and an ARCHAISM ⟨he continued to prosecute his business⟩. E.g., "All unexpended balances of appropriations prior to May 15, 1928, made for *prosecuting* work of

flood control on the Mississippi River, are made available under this title."

prosecution meant originally (fr. 16th c.) "the following up, continuing, or carrying out of any action, scheme, or purpose, with a view to its accomplishment or attainment." Then it came to be associated with criminal law in the eighteenth century, and took on the meaning "a proceeding either by way of indictment or information in the criminal courts, in order to put an offender upon his trial" (*OED*). Today, both in AmE and in BrE, it is used for *prosecutor*, the process of HYPALLAGE having done its usual work. E.g., "The *prosecution* made improper arguments."/ "The *prosecution* marshaled evidence tending to link appellant with these practices."

prosecutional, -tive. See **prosecutorial**.

prosecutor. See **prosecution**.

prosecutorial, -tory, -tive, -tional. The most common term in criminal-law texts is *prosecutorial*; but this variant is not included in *W3*. *Prosecutory* and *prosecutive*, less common in legal writing, are defined as "of or pertaining to prosecution." A distinction might obtain if we restricted *prosecutorial* to be the adjective for *prosecutor*, already its primary function. E.g., "The *prosecutorial* decision not to prosecute has a deterrent effect on police misconduct." See, e.g., B. Gershman, *Prosecutorial Misconduct* (1985); J. Lawless, *Prosecutorial Misconduct* (1985).

But sometimes it appears where *prosecutory* might be more appropriate (*prosecutive* being a NEEDLESS VARIANT): "*Miranda* does not interfere with the *prosecutorial* [read *prosecutory*] function."/ "The bar committees are composed of private 'competitors' and perform both *prosecutorial* [read *prosecutory*] and adjudicative functions in enforcing a self-regulatory disciplinary process."/ "Todaro contends that this case presents such circumstances and invites us to ignore the government's asserted *prosecutorial* [read *prosecutory*] interest in the witnesses."/ "This case concerns the doctrines of judicial and *prosecutorial* [read *prosecutory*] immunity."

Prosecutional is but a NEEDLESS VARIANT not countenanced by the dictionaries.

prosecutrix /pro-sĕ-*kyoo*-trĭks/, a word traditionally used in reference to a female who prefers criminal charges against a sexual assailant, has been objected to on grounds that it is sexist and obscurantist. See *Allen v. State*, 700 S.W.2d 924, 935–36 (Tex. Crim. App. 1985) (Miller, J., concurring). Judge Miller offers *victim* as a clearer, more sympathetic term. But *victim* would surely be prejudicial and ineffective if, for example, it has not been established that a rape actually took place or who the rapist was. Judge Miller observes that, "if *prosecutrix* is used to refer to the female victim of a sexual assault, would not the term *prosecutor* be appropriate for a male victim of a sexual assault?" *Id.* at 936 n. 3. Of course, *prosecutor* is not used in that sense, and it is that lack of equivalency that lends some credence to the charge that the word evinces a discriminatory bias in the language. See SEXISM (C). More likely, however, the language of the law has not needed a word for the male victim of a sex crime.

proselytize; proselyte, v.t. The former is preferred. "Nothing in the record indicates that shared-time instructors have attempted to *proselytize* their students." (O'Connor, J.)

prospective heir. See **heir** (B).

prospectus for *perspective* is a MALAPROPISM. E.g., "The players were able to keep everything in *prospectus* [read *perspective*]." Properly, of course, *prospectus* = a printed document describing the chief features of a school, commercial enterprise, forthcoming book, or the like. See **conspectus.**

prostitution, meaning in one sense "the act of debasing," is connotatively charged with its other sense of harlotry. E.g., "Solicitation of clients by following accidents and soliciting retainers from the injured is a vile *prostitution* of the advocate's calling." Where the tone is intentionally provocative or connotatively charged, it may be the right word. *Prostitution* should not be used, however, wherever *debasement* might adequately be used.

protagonist. Literally, *protagonist* = the chief character in a drama; derivatively, it means "a champion of a cause." It should not be used loosely of any upholder or supporter of a cause; it should refer to a prominent and active supporter. E.g., "The complexity of the community property system is not offset by those values claimed for the system by its most ardent *protagonists* [read *supporters*]."

Protagonist is all too frequently confused with *antagonist*. E.g., "On this point there was an internecine struggle in the Second Circuit, with Judges Clark and Friendly as the *protagonists* [read *antagonists*]." (Note that *internecine* means "mutually deadly," and that is hardly the intended meaning here.)/ "On this promising note the two *protagonists* [i.e., now angry litigants] parted." (This sentence contains an example of the rhetorical figure prolepsis—the representation of a future fact as presently existing; that is, when the two persons parted on a promising note, they were not antagonists or opponents; only in retrospect or from a current perspective may they been seen as angry litigants.)

In the following sentence, the writer attempted to use *protagonist* figuratively in its dramatic sense, but failed in the metaphor, because a drama has only one protagonist: "Slugs, larvae, nematodes, and rodents form the supporting cast in this trademark drama; the *protagonists* [read *principal characters*] are the terms *Larvacide* and *larvicide*." *Soweco, Inc. v. Shell Oil Co.*, 617 F.2d 1178, 1181 (5th Cir. 1980).

Perhaps the most objectionable watering-down of the meaning of *protagonist* occurs when it is used as an equivalent of *proponent*: "*Protagonists* [read *Proponents*] of a more active role and greater freedom of technique for courts in private law reform have sometimes failed to recognize the need to revise, too, prevailing attitudes about the role and technique of legislatures."

pro tanto (= to that extent; as far as it goes) is a defensible LATINISM commonly used in law. No other word quite works without substantial rewording. It may be used adjectivally: "There may be a *pro tanto* ademption by satisfaction if the evidence indicated that the testator so intended the inter vivos gift to work such an ademption."/ "It would be a matter of pure speculation whether—whatever the change of conditions since her death—she would not want part of the corpus of the trust turned over to the petitioner, involving, as it would, the *pro tanto* depletion of the fund from which the income was to be derived."/ "It was an offer capable of being accepted and turned into a contract *pro tanto* on the occasion of each discount." (Eng.)

Or it may be used adverbially: "The bequest would be deemed *pro tanto* void if the testator had deliberately used unmeaning words." (Eng.)/ "We deal of course with a later Congress and an Act that sets aside by section 208(b) *pro tanto* the earlier Act."/ "If defendant received less than the value of plaintiff's work, as defendant seems to contend, then plaintiff should recover *pro tanto*."

protectible, -able. The former is preferred. Inconsistencies often arise even within one piece of writing. See, e.g., headnotes 1 and 5 of *Velo-Bind, Inc. v. Scheck*, 485 F. Supp. 102 (S.D.N.Y. 1979). See -ABLE (A).

protective, -tory. As an adjective, the latter is a NEEDLESS VARIANT.

pro tem. is the abbreviation for *pro tempore* (= for the time being). This fairly common LATINISM is used as a POSTPOSITIVE ADJECTIVE in phrases such as *mayor pro tem.*

protest, n.; protestation. The difference is that *protest*, the ordinary word, usually refers to a formal statement or action of dissent or disapproval, whereas *protestation*, a learned word, generally denotes a solemn affirmation.

protest (vb.) is transitive or intransitive in AmE, but solely intransitive in most BrE writing. In G.B., one writes, "They *protested against* discrimination," but not, "They *protested* discrimination." Partridge considered the latter, AmE usage incorrect (and quoted an American writer as an offender against idiom), although he was writing solely on British usage. See E. Partridge, *Usage and Abusage* 248 (1973). The phrase *protest against* is common also in the U.S. E.g., "Appellants were *protesting against* American policy in Vietnam." In legal writing in the U.S., however, *against* is regularly omitted. An exception to the general British legal idiom is the phrase *protest a bill of exchange* (Horwill).

protestant /*prot-ĕ-stănt*/ (= a protesting person) is often used in law to mean "one who protests an administrative decision." E.g., "In arguing that the ICC's method of evaluating any *protestant*'s proof of inconsistency with public convenience and necessity violates the national transportation policy, Steere insists that under current Commission policy it is impossible for a *protestant* to dem-

onstrate that inconsistency."/ "Once a petitioner makes out a prima facie case, a presumption is created that the new authority will be consistent with the public convenience and necessity, and the burden of proof is shifted to the *protestant* that it will not." Cf. **caveator, contestant & objectant.**

prot(h)onotary means generally "the chief clerk of a court of law." The spelling with the -h- is prevalent in the U.S.; the spelling without it predominates in G.B., where the institution denoted by the word is obsolete. Following are two American quotations: "A judgment lien arises upon entry by the *prothonotary* and ceases to be enforceable five years from that date."/ "Ordinarily, the judgment is to be entered by the *prothonotary* in the appearance docket, if it is obtained in an action, and in the D.S.B. docket if it is by confession." The word is obsolescent in the U.S. It is pronounced /*proh-thon-ŏ-tar-ee*/ or /*proh-thŏ-nod-ă-ree*/.

prototype. See **archetype.**

prototyp(ic)al. The usual and preferred form is *prototypical*. See **archetypical.**

protuberate is frequently misspelled and mispronounced as if it were *protruberate.*

proud; prideful. The connotative distinction to bear in mind is that *prideful* suggests excessive pride, haughtiness, and disdain.

prove; prove up. Generally, it is sufficient to use *prove* transitively, and hence to write, "He attempted to *prove* his title to the land." A common Americanism in law, however, is the phrasal verb *prove up* (= to adduce or complete the proof of right to (something); to show that one has fulfilled the legal conditions). E.g., "He attempted to *prove up* his title to the land." The *OED Supp.* indicates that this usage has spread to Canada. See PHRASAL VERBS & PARTICLES, UNNECESSARY.

proved; proven. *Proved* is the universally preferred past participle of *prove; proven*, like *stricken*, properly exists only as an adjective. E.g., "Evidence may be offered, not to show its already *proven* existence, but . . . ."/ "In judging human conduct, intent, motive, and purpose are elusive subjective concepts, and their existence usually can be inferred only from *proven* facts."/ "Difficulty of ascertainment is no longer confused with the right of recovery for a *proven* invasion of the plaintiff's rights."

Proven has survived as a past participle in legal usage in the verdict *Not proven*, but that jury answer is no longer widely used except in Scots law. One writer has defined this verdict as meaning, "Not guilty, but don't do it again." Roughead, *The Art of Murder* 131 (1943) (quoted in Simon, *English Idioms from the Law*, 76 Law Q. Rev. 429, 443 (1960)).

Often, however, *proven* is wrongly used as a past participle. E.g., "In *Beaumont v. Feld*, a bequest to 'Catharine Earnley' was *proven* [read *proved*] to have been intended for Gertrude Yardley, and was given to the latter."/ "Since the serious bodily injury suffered by complainant at the hands of appellant was *proven* [read *proved*] beyond a reasonable doubt, the error, if any, was harmless."

provenance; provenience. Both are FORMAL WORDS for *origin* or *source*. *Provenience* is chiefly American, whereas *provenance* is more common elsewhere in the English-speaking world. But it too is used in AmE.

proves the rule, the exception. See **exception proves the rule, the**.

prove too much = to make an overbroad argument; (of an argument) to be overbroad. E.g., "It is further argued that it is unlikely that an elderly lady in poor health would be capable of understanding a trust agreement several pages long, couched in precise and formal legal phraseology; the argument *proves too much*, for if such a contention had merit, very few modern legal instruments could withstand attacks of this kind."/ "The court is quite right in stating that the 'outcome-determinative' test of *Guaranty Trust Co. v. New York*, if taken literally, *proves too much*, for any rule, no matter how clearly 'procedural,' can affect the outcome of litigation if it is not obeyed."

prove up. See **prove**.

provided that; providing that. In the conjunctive sense ("only if"), the former is the preferred phrasing. In DRAFTING, this phrase is best used to create exceptions in provisos, and not conditions. Thus, a statute might lay out the general provisions of its applicability, fol-

lowed by a proviso creating an exception and beginning *provided that*. It is considered poor legislative DRAFTING, however, to create a condition with this phrase, as in the following: "*Provided that* an order under this section is approved, it shall be binding upon all persons concerned." [Read *An order approved under this section shall be binding upon all persons concerned.*] See A. Russell, *Legislative Drafting and Forms* 103–04 (1938).

Even provisos introduced by *provided that* are often wholly unnecessary, when the matter contained in the proviso is easily integrated into a subordinate clause. E.g., "No person who has not attained the age of twelve years shall be competent to testify, *provided that*, if the court finds that any such person understands the nature and obligation of the oath, such person shall be competent to testify." This statute is best rephrased: "Persons over the age of twelve years shall be competent to testify, but a person under that age shall also be competent if the court finds that the person understands the nature and obligation of the oath." (Ex. fr. Younger, *Symptoms of Bad Writing*, 72 A.B.A. J. 113 (1986).)

province, the peculiar is a legal CLICHÉ throughout common-law countries. E.g., "It is, of course, within the peculiar *province* of the Queen's Proctor to know all that bears on his office, and he does." (Eng.)

provincial, in a country without provinces, has been narrowed primarily to its extended meaning, "parochial, narrow." Yet it still carries its primary sense, "of or relating to a province." Hence, "As the preparations for the *provincial* tour progressed, William became morose."

proving a will. See **proof** (A).

provision See **prevision** & **proviso**.

provision of law is usually unnecessary for *law* or *provision*.

proviso generally has a narrower sense than *provision*. In DRAFTING, a *proviso* is a clause inserted in a legal or formal document that makes some condition, stipulation, exception, or limitation, or upon the observance of which the operation or validity of the instrument depends. E.g., "When there is no accuracy or promptitude, the company should answer for all injury resulting, subject to the *proviso* that the injury must be the natural and direct consequence of the negligent act."

provocative, -tory. The latter is a NEEDLESS VARIANT.

prox. See **ult.**

proximate, -mal. Both mean "lying very near or close." Yet *proximal* is primarily a technical, scientific term, whereas *proximate* is the ordinary term with the additional senses (1) "soon forthcoming; imminent"; (2) "next preceding" ⟨proximate cause⟩; and (3) "nearly accurate; approximate." See **approximate.**

proximate cause, an anglicization of the Latin phrase *causa proxima*, is a TERM OF ART having little to do with physical causation, but emphasizing instead the continuity of the sequence that produces an event. (See CAUSATION (A).) The phrase is basic to tort law in the U.S., and is used, albeit much less frequently, in G.B. Mellinkoff rather uncharitably terms *proximate cause* "concise gibberish." D. Mellinkoff, *The Language of the Law* 401 (1963). See CAUSATION (A).

prudent(ial). *Prudent* = exhibiting prudence. *Prudential* = pertaining to, considered from the point of view of, or dictated by, prudence. E.g., "This limitation is not constitutionally mandated but a rule of self-restraint justified by a *prudential* concern that courts should not adjudicate constitutional rights unnecessarily."/ "*Prudential* guidelines govern the administration of this rule."

"To call an act *prudent*," wrote Fowler, "is normally to commend it; to call it *-ial* is more often than not to disparage it. A prisoner's refusal to go into the witness-box is prudential but not prudent if he refuses for fear of giving himself away but actually creates prejudice against himself, prudent but not prudential if it deprives the prosecution of a necessary link in the evidence but is dictated merely by bravado, and both or neither in conditions as easy to invent" (*MEU1* 473).

prurience, -cy. The latter is a NEEDLESS VARIANT.

pseudonym = a fictitious name. In law, common pseudonyms for persons involved in suits are *John Doe*, *Jane Doe*, and *Richard Roe*.

Here the word is wrongly used for *euphemism*: "Graglia implies that affirmative action is a *pseudonym* [read *euphemism*] for preferring blacks and browns over whites." See EUPHEMISMS. See also **anonym(e).**

PSITTACISM is parrotlike speech. If there is a malady endemic in legal writing, it is the practice or habit of mechanically repeating previously received ideas or images that reflect neither true reasoning nor feeling, the parrot-like repetition of words. Many legal opinions and law review articles seem little more than ready-made legal phrases strung end on end to justify a given proposition. The CLICHÉS give themselves away with the first couple of words in the line, so that the adept reader knows what the psittacistic writer will say before reading the end of the line. *In derogation of* is rarely followed by anything other than *the common law;* and so endemic are such phrases as *case of first impression, it is well-established that,* and *notwithstanding anything herein to the contrary* that they finally numb the intellect of both reader and writer. For more examples, see CLICHÉS. The best legal writers attempt to formulate their thoughts anew; their writing is fresh and original. And it is rare.

psychal. See **psych(ic)(al).**

psychedelic; psychodelic. The latter is a misspelling.

psych(ic)(al); psychological. *Psychical* (= of or relating to the mind) is contrasted with *physical. Psychal* is a NEEDLESS VARIANT. *Psychic* = (1) of or relating to the psyche; (2) spiritual; (3) paranormal. *Psychological* = (1) of, pertaining to, or of the nature of psychology; dealing with psychology; (2) of or pertaining to the objects of psychological study; of or pertaining to the mind, mental (*OED*). The *OED* states that sense (2) of *psychological* is a loose usage, but it is now firmly established.

psychodelic. See **psychedelic.**

psychodynamics is a trendy term that rarely signifies anything not conveyed equally well by *psychology.* E.g., "Sanford N. Kantz, a family-law specialist, says that lawyers 'don't understand the *psychodynamics* of adoption. They should deal only with the legal issues.'" Nat'l Law J., Aug. 20, 1984, at 10.

psychological. See **psych(ic)(al).**

pubes has two syllables /*pyoo-beez*/.

public, a COLLECTIVE NOUN, usually takes a singular verb in AmE ⟨public is⟩ and a plural verb in BrE ⟨public are⟩.

publication = (1) (in the law of defamation) the communication of defamatory words to a person or persons other than the one defamed (*CDL*); (2) (in the law of wills) the formal declaration made by a testator at the time of signing his will that it is his will. Following are examples of sense (2), in which the word is a TERM OF ART: "When a codicil is executed to a will, the act is said to be a '*re-publication*' and '*revalidation*' of the will as of the date upon which the codicil was executed."/ "Some states require the testator to indicate to the attesting witnesses that the document executed or to be executed by him is a will; this action is called *publication.*"
In sense (1) as in sense (2), the verb corresponding to *publication* is *to publish.* In the law of defamation, to *publish* is to make public. E.g., "The libel was *published* by the attorney to persons having no relationship to the pending judicial proceeding." Spoken as well as written defamation is said to be *published.*

publicist (= one who is learned in public or international law; a writer on the law of nations [*OED*]) ordinarily means "publicity agent" to laymen. Hence the legal use of the term generally requires explanation if the audience is a broad one.

public policy. Today this term, when used nominally, is not preceded by an article. E.g., "Generally, the duty of a husband to support his wife and children is grounded *on the public policy* [read *on public policy*]."

publish. See **publication.**

pudenda is the plural of *pudendum.*

puffing = the action of praising or extolling in inflated language for a purpose, esp. by way of advertisement (*OED*). The term is perfectly appropriate in formal contexts; it is not a colloquialism. E.g., "General commendations, commonly known as dealer's talk, seller's statements, or *puffing*, do not amount to actionable misrepresentations where the parties deal at arm's length and have equal means of information and are equally well qualified to judge the facts." 41 Tex. Jur. 3d *Fraud & Deceit* § 28 (1985).

puisne (= younger or of lower rank), sometimes used in reference to judges, is pronounced like *puny.* Etymologically, *puisne* is *puis-né* "later-born." The term has been extended in British legal usage to apply to mortgages and other incumbrancers; it is also used in BrE as an attributive adjective in the sense "a puisne judge" ⟨five puisnes upheld the plea⟩.

PUNCTUATION. Judges and jurists have written more nonsense about punctuation than about any other facet of the language. The well-known dictum that "punctuation is not a part of the statute" has given rise to even more surreal pronouncements: "[P]unctuation at any rate is not a part of the English language." *Kansas City Life Insurance Co. v. Wells,* 133 F.2d 224, 227 (8th Cir. 1943). The effect of punctuation on writing has long been minified by legal authors. E.g., "[P]unctuation or the absence of punctuation will not of itself create an ambiguity." *Anderson v. Kerr Drilling Co. v. Bruhlmeyer,* 136 S.W.2d 800, 803 (Tex. 1940).
The fallacies underlying these quoted statements are too obvious to require extensive explanation. Mellinkoff has explained at length the history of the canard that punctuation is irrelevant to meaning. He writes that the

> principle was born of error: the law does not concern itself with punctuation *because* (it was said) from antiquity the statutes and other legal documents were not punctuated. The practical result for later generations of lawyers and legal scriveners was an indifference to punctuation and an addiction to the long sentence. [See ANFRACTUOSITY.] The long sentence was not a matter of carelessness but of principle. That was the way it had always been done and that was the way to do it. Since the original basis—the oral basis—of punctuation was either not known or forgotten, the long sentence continued in the law despite a change outside the law to 'grammatical' or 'logical' theories of punctuation.
> D. Mellinkoff, *The Language of the Law* 164 (1963).

What follows are some of the principles drawn from "grammatical" or "logical" theories of punctuation, taken (with minor adaptations and additions) from the *Oxford Guide*, pp. 193–197.

A. The Apostrophe [']. This punctuation mark is used in English for either of two purposes: (1) to indicate the possessive case, e.g., "Lord Mansfield[']s speech"; "Mother Jones[']s recipe"; and (2) to mark the omission of one or more elements and the contracting of the remaining elements into a meaningful expression, e.g., "ever" into "e[']er"; "we will" into "we[']ll"; "1969" into "[']69." See POSSESSIVES.

B. The Colon [:]. This mark may link two grammatically complete clauses by indicating a step forward from the first to the second: the step may be from an introduction to a main theme, from a cause to an effect, from a general statement to a particular instance, or from a premise to a conclusion. E.g., "The remedy is simple[:] enact legislation that discourages American employers from hiring illegal aliens." The colon is also used, and perhaps more commonly, to introduce a list of items, often after expressions such as "for example"; "namely"; "the following"; "as follows"; and "including." E.g., "The *following* officers were present[:] J. Smith, J. Brown, P. Thompson, and M. Griffin."

C. The Comma [,]. This is the least emphatic mark of punctuation, and the one used in the greatest variety of circumstances:

1. To separate adjectives that each qualify a noun in the same way, e.g., "a cautious[,] reserved person." But when adjectives qualify the noun in different ways, or when one adjective qualifies another, no comma is used, e.g., "a distinguished [no comma] foreign journalist"; "a bright [no comma] red tie.

2. To separate items (including the last from the penultimate) in a list of more than two, e.g., "the defendants, the third-party defendants[,] and the counterdefendants." The question whether to include the final comma in an enumerative series has sparked many arguments in law offices and judges' chambers. It is easily answered in favor of including the final comma, for its omission may cause ambiguities, whereas its inclusion never will. One example will suffice: "A and B, C and D, E and F[,] and G and H." When the members are compound, calling for *and* within themselves, clarity demands the final comma. See ENUMERATIONS (B).

3. To separate coordinated main clauses, e.g., "Cars will turn here[,] and coaches will

go straight." The exception occurs when the main clauses are closely linked: "Do as I tell you [no comma] and you will not regret it."

4. To mark the beginning and ending of a parenthetical word or phrase, e.g., "I am sure [,] however[,] that it will not happen." / "Fred[,] who is bald[,] complained of the cold." (N.B.: With RESTRICTIVE CLAUSES [i.e., those that are necessary to define the antecedent or to limit it] *no* commas are used. E.g., "Men [no comma] who are bald [no comma] should wear hats."/ "Facts [no comma] not unlike those found in this record [no comma] were considered in that case.")

5. To separate a participial or verbless clause, a salutation, or a vocative, e.g., "Having had breakfast[,] I went for a walk."/ "The sermon *over* [or *being over*], the congregation filed out."/ "Fellow lawyers[,] the bar must unite in seeking reform of the system of electing judges." (N.B.: Not "The sermon[,] being over[,] . . ."; and no comma with restrictive expressions like "My friend Judge Smith" or "my son John.")

6. To separate a phrase or subordinate clause from the main clause so as to avoid misunderstanding. E.g., "In the valley below[,] the villages looked very small."/ "In 1982[,] 1918 seemed like the distant past." (N.B.: A comma should not be used to separate a phrasal subject from its predicate, or a verb from an object that is a clause. E.g., "A car with such a high-powered *engine, should* [read *engine should*] not fail on that hill." / "They *believed, that* [read *believed that*] nothing could go wrong.")

7. To distinguish indirect from direct speech. E.g., "They answered[,] 'Here we are.'"

8. To mark the end of the salutation, e.g., "Dear Mr. Crosthwaite[,]"; "Dear Rebecca[,]", etc. and the complimentary close, e.g., "Very truly yours[,]"; "Yours sincerely[,]; etc. In formal letters, the salutation is separated from the body by a colon "Dear Sir[:]"; "Dear Madame[:]"; etc. (N.B.: No comma is needed between the month and year in dates written "December 1984" or "18 December 1984"; a comma is required when the date is written "December 18, 1984.") See DATES.

Writers cause needless confusion or distraction for their readers when they insert commas erroneously:

1. The Archaic Comma Preceding a Verb. Formerly, it was common for writers to insert a comma in the main clause before the verb,

but this practice has been out of fashion since the mid-nineteenth century. Today it is considered incorrect. E.g., "Whether or not a contract has been modified, [omit the comma] is a question of fact for the jury."/ "Only if this were true, [omit the comma] could it be said that plaintiffs received their bargained-for equivalent of the $30,000 payments."

2. Misplaced Emphasis. "I, *accordingly,* [read *accordingly* without the embracing commas] dissent."/ "We, *therefore,* [read *therefore* without the embracing commas] conclude that the ancient doctrine of sovereign immunity has lost its underpinnings." (N.B.: If the emphasis in the preceding sentence is to fall on *We*—as clearly separated from some other group and its thinking—the commas should stand; but, if the emphasis is to fall on the *therefore* as a simple consequence of our reasoning from the evidence, then the commas should be omitted. See **therefore**.)

The omission of commas can often blur the sense of a sentence, as in the following examples: "Substantial performance cannot occur where the breach is intentional [insert a comma] as it is the antithesis of material breach."/ "Because, prior to their filing [insert a comma] consignor's claims will be subordinate to those of lien creditors, in practice the consignee's creditors will have effective claims to the consigned goods."/ "Something may be said for it, since it furnishes a simple, if arbitrary [insert comma] test."

D. The Dash [—; –]. There are two kinds of dashes, which printers are able to distinguish by their length.

1. The *em-dash,* which is as wide as the square of the type size, is used to mark an interruption in the structure of a sentence. In typewriting, it is commonly represented by two hyphens, often with a space at either end of the pair (--). A pair of em-dashes can be used to enclose a parenthetical remark or to mark the ending and the resumption of a statement by an interlocutor. E.g., "He was not[—]you may disagree with me, Henry[—]much of an artist."/ "I didn't[—] 'Speak up, boy!'[—]hear anything." The em-dash can also be used informally to replace the colon.

2. The *en-dash,* which is half as wide as an *em-dash,* is distinct (in print) from the *hyphen* and is used to join pairs or groups of words wherever movement or tension, rather than cooperation or unity, is felt: it is often equivalent to *to* or *versus.* In typewriting, it is com-

monly represented by one hyphen, often with a space at either end (-). E.g., "The 1914[–]1918 war"; "current[–]voltage characteristic"; "the London[–]Horsham[–]Brighton route"; "the Fischer[–]Spassky match"; "the Marxist[–]Trotskyite split." (N.B.: Phrases such as "the Marxist-Leninist position" and "the Franco-Prussian war" are formed with hyphens.) The en-dash is also used for joint authors, e.g., "the Prosser[–] Keeton hornbook" (two men); but not for one person with a double-barreled name: "the Lloyd-Jones hypothesis."

E. The Exclamation Mark [!]. This mark is used after an exclamatory word, phrase, or sentence. It usually counts as the concluding full stop, but need not. E.g., "Hail, Source of Being! Universal Soul!" It may also be used within square brackets, after or in the midst of a quotation, to express the editor's amusement, dissent, or surprise. Rarely is the exclamation mark called for in legal writing.

F. Parentheses [(. . .)]. These marks enclose words, phrases, and even whole sentences (but usually not more than a whole paragraph). If what is enclosed is a full sentence, the closing parenthesis includes the end punctuation; if not, the end punctuation is swept outside, as in the previous sentence here. More specifically, parentheses are used as follows:

1. To indicate interpolations and remarks by the writer of the text, e.g., "Mrs. X *(as I shall call her)* now spoke."

2. To specify, in one's own running text, an authority, definition, explanation, reference, or translation.

3. To indicate, in the report of a speech, interruptions by the audience.

4. To separate reference letters or figures that do not need a full stop, e.g., *(1) (a).*

G. The Period [.]. This mark is used:

1. To end all sentences that are not questions or exclamations. The next word should normally begin with a capital letter.

2. To indicate abbreviations (see ACRONYMS & INITIALISMS). If a point marking an abbreviation comes at the end of a sentence, it also serves as the closing full stop. E.g., "She also kept dogs, cats, birds, etc[.]" But where a closing parenthesis or bracket intervenes, a period is required: "She also kept pets (dogs, cats, birds, etc[.).]" When a sentence concludes with a quotation that ends with a period (i.e., a full stop), question mark, or exclamation mark, no further period is needed.

E.g., "He cried, 'Be off!' [no period] But the child would not move."

H. The Question Mark [?]. A question mark follows every question that expects a separate answer; the next word should begin with a capital letter. "He asked me, 'Why are you here?' A foolish question." (N.B.: A question mark is not used after indirect questions, e.g., "He asked me why I was there.") A question mark may be placed after a word, etc., whose accuracy is doubted, e.g., "Sangad Anurugsa[?]"

I. Quotation Marks. In using quotation marks (or "inverted commas" as the British call them), writers and editors of AmE and BrE have developed conventions that are markedly different.

1. In AmE, double quotation marks are used for a first quotation; single marks for a quotation within a quotation; double again for a further quotation inside that, etc. In BrE, the practice is exactly the reverse at each step.

2. With a closing quotation mark, practices vary. In AmE, it is usual to place a period or comma within the closing quotation mark, whether or not the punctuation so placed is actually a part of the quoted matter. E.g., "Joan pointedly said, 'We do not intend to see "Les Miserables."'" In BrE, by contrast, the closing quotation mark comes before all punctuation marks, unless these marks form a part of the quotation itself (or what is quoted is *less* than a full sentence in its own right). E.g., 'Joan pointedly said, "We do not intend to see 'Les Miserables'."' / 'She looked back on her school years as being "unredeemably miserable".' (N.B.: In both of these specimens the outermost quotation marks indicate our quoting of a printed source directly.)

When question and exclamation marks are involved, AmE and BrE practice is the same. E.g. (AmE), "Did Nelson really say 'Kiss me, Hardy'?"; (BrE) 'Did Nelson really say "Kiss me, Hardy"?' But, when the question or exclamation mark is an integral part of what is being quoted, it is swept inside of all quotation marks (i.e. inverted commas): (AmE) "Banging her fist on the table, she exclaimed, 'And that's *that!*'"; (BrE) 'Banging her fist on the table, she exclaimed, "And that's *that!*"' (N.B.: When the ending of an interrogatory or an exclamatory sentence coincides with the ending of another sentence that embraces it, the stronger mark of punctuation is sufficient to terminate *both* sentences; i.e., a period [i.e., a full stop] need not also be included.)

As to quotations that are interrupted to indicate a speaker, AmE and BrE again show different preferences. In AmE, the first comma is swept within the quotation mark, e.g., "Sally," he said, "is looking radiant today"; in BrE, the first comma (usually) remains outside the inverted comma, just as though the attribution could be lifted neatly out of the speaker's actual words, e.g., 'Sally', he said, 'is looking radiant today.' See QUOTATIONS (B).

3. In nonlegal citations, quotation marks (and roman type) are often used when citing titles of articles in magazines, chapters in books, poems not published separately, and songs. (Titles of books and magazines are usually printed in italic in nonlegal citations.) See CITATION OF CASES.

J. Semicolon [;]. This mark separates those parts of a sentence between which there is a more distinct break than would call for a comma can signal, but which are too closely connected to be made into separate sentences. Typically these will be clauses of similar importance and grammatical construction. E.g., "To err is human; to forgive, divine." (N.B.: The comma here flags the dropping of a word: "is.")

K. Square Brackets. These enclose comments, corrections, explanations, interpolations, notes, or translations that were not in the original text but have been added to it by subsequent authors, editors, or others. E.g., "My right honorable friend [John Smith] is mistaken."

In legal writing, brackets are customarily used for adjustments in quoted matter, such as making lowercase a letter that was uppercase in the source of the quotation ("The court stated that '[a]nother problem in determining the existence of apparent authority relates to the extent of the knowledge of the person invoking the doctrine.'") or signifying an omission of an inflection in a word ("If the trustees 'fail[ ] to re-elect or re-employ the superintendent' without giving notice, his contract is automatically reviewable.").

The following works are useful for further inquiry: G. V. Carey, *Mind the Stop* (1977 ed.); K. E. Gordon, *The Well-Tempered Sentence: A Punctuation Handbook for the Innocent, the Eager, and the Doomed* (1983); E. Partridge, *You Have a Point There: A Guide to Punctuation and Its Allies* (1953); H. Shaw, *Punctuate It Right!* (1963).

punitive, -tory. *Punitory* is a NEEDLESS VARIANT of *punitive*, which is much more common in legal than in nonlegal texts. These two forms are commonly used by those who practice INELEGANT VARIATION. E.g., "Florida cases follow the orthodox theory that *punitive damages* are *punitory* [read *punitive*] and deterrent." Even worse: "The law with respect to *punitive damages* is that in order to justify the *infliction* [read *imposition?*] of *punitory damages* [read *punitive damages*] for the commission of a tort, the act complained of must have been done wantonly or maliciously." *Stenson v. Laclede Gas Co.*, 553 S.W.2d 309, 315 (Mo. App. 1977).

punitive damages; exemplary damages; vindictive damages; aggravated damages; retributory damages. The first two terms are by far the most common in both AmE and BrE. Each one tells only half the story, for the two-pronged rationale for awarding such damages in civil cases is (1) to punish the defendant, and (2) to make an example of the defendant so as to deter others. *Exemplary damages* appears to be the more usual phrase in G.B. (although the *CDL* and the *OCL* mention only punishment as the basis), whereas in the U.S. the term *punitive damages* is slightly more frequent. These terms should be allowed to co-exist, inasmuch as neither is completely adequate to convey the intended sense. The other forms, sometimes used in strings (as in the following example), should be avoided as NEEDLESS VARIANTS. "Much has been written by the courts and by text writers upon the question whether *punitive, vindictive, exemplary, aggravated*, or *retributory damages* should be allowed in any case without reaching a generally accepted conclusion."/ "The question distinctly arises whether the plaintiff is entitled to recover *punitive* or *vindictive damages* against the defendants." See **parasitic.**

PUNS. Puns (or paronomasia) can add zest to writing if artfully used. Fowler and Bernstein have dispelled the notion that puns are the lowest form of wit. Bad puns, of course, create a bad impression in either speech or writing. But the well wrought pun often serves to reinforce the point one is making. The good pun should give the sentence added meaning in both (or all) its senses, and it should not be too obvious.

Puns seem increasingly popular in American legal prose. Some are good and some are not. The title of a recent law-review article by Mosteller, *Simplifying Subpoena Law: Taking the Fifth Amendment Seriously*, 73 Va. L. Rev. 1 (1987), plays effectively on two English idioms, *to take the Fifth Amendment* and *to take (something) seriously*. Both senses fit the purpose of the article, hence the aptness of the pun. A more strained but nevertheless clever pun occurred to the federal appellate judge who wrote: "*Ticonic's* cloth cannot be cut to fit Interfirst's *suit*." *Interfirst Bank–Abilene v. F.D.I.C.*, 777 F.2d 1092, 1097 (5th Cir. 1985) (discussing *Ticonic National Bank v. Sprague*, 303 U.S. 406 (1938)). Here *suit* carries the double sense, on the one hand, of completing the tailoring metaphor (cutting cloth for a suit) and, on the other hand, of denoting the lawsuit at issue. Yet another aesthetically pleasing pun is this subtle one from the pen of Justice Frankfurter: "The liability rests on the *inroad* that the automobile has made on the decision of *Pennoyer v. Neff*, as it has on so many aspects of our social scene." *Olberding v. Illinois Central R.R.*, 346 U.S. 338, 341 (1953). Ordinarily, of course, *inroad* is an abstract word, but Justice Frankfurter's placement of *automobile* next to it gives the word a new and unexpected concrete sense; again, the pun is felicitous.

But probably half the puns one sees in modern legal writing are the empty kind of wordplay in which one of the senses is inapposite or, at worst, gibberish. E.g., "The bells do not *toll* the statute of limitations while one ferrets out the facts." The pun here is *toll*, which on the obvious level (*bells . . . toll*) means, nonsensically, "to ring"; the legal sense of *toll*, the one that gives meaning to the sentence, is "to abate." The pun in no way contributes to the sense; in fact, it is more likely to confuse than to enlighten. Here is another ill-wrought specimen: "The official cannot hide behind a claim that the particular factual predicate in question has never appeared *in haec verba* in a reported opinion; if the application of settled principles to this factual tableau would inexorably lead to a conclusion of unconstitutionality, a prison official may not take solace in *ostrachism*." *Ostrachism* here apparently means "the practice of hiding one's head in the sand" (foreshadowed earlier in the sentence in the phrase *hide behind a claim*). The pun is on *ostracism* (= exclusion from association with another or others), but this nearhomophone has nothing to do with the meaning of the sentence. Hence the writer has gone out of his way to create a punning

NEOLOGISM whose suggestiveness bewilders, rather than charms, the reader.

purchase = to acquire real property other than by descent. Thus, in very technical legal parlance, gifts are *purchased* by those who receive them. *Purchase*, in legal writing, also commonly has the more general sense "to buy." (When used in this lay sense, *purchase* is a FORMAL WORD.) The following sentence conveys the special legal sense of the word (here as a noun): "Every legal mode of acquisition of real property except by descent is denominated in law a *purchase*, and the person who thus acquires it is a *purchaser*." This legal technicality appears also in the phrases *words of purchase* and *take by purchase*.

The verb *purchase* may take *from* or *of*, though the latter form is an ARCHAISM. E.g., "Bunguss *purchased of* Blades the tract of land in controversy." See **words of purchase**. See also **buy** & **descent** (A).

purchaser, -or. The former is the only correct spelling.

PURPLE PROSE, or ostentatious writing, has a certain fascination for some legal writers, as it does for any number of aspiring novelists.

> There has apparently grown up of late a wide-spread passion for 'fine-writing,' but in this tendency there lurks great evil, for, unless the pen be guided by the hand of genius, there is apt to result a sacrifice of legal sense to purely artificial verbiage. Form should fit substance, like clothes the well-dressed man which, when appropriate, never attract attention on their own account. An ornate, pretentious, grandiose style, replete with superfluous frills and rhetorical extravagances, can act only as an undesirable distraction. Nor is a judicial opinion [or virtually any other legal writing] a proper vehicle for the exploitation of pedantic learning or extraneous disquisitions.
>
> H. Stern, *The Writing of Judicial Opinions,* 18 Pa. Bar Ass'n Q. 40, 41–42 (1947).

Similes are especially likely to turn purple. Whereas METAPHORS are quite acceptable in legal writing, similes tend to signal overwriting: "Eliciting the value and whereabouts of assets from the plaintiff was akin to trying to pull molasses outdoors in Green Bay in the month of January" (quoted in R. Goldfarb & J. Raymond, *Clear Understandings* 86 (1982)).

Rarely can a short sentence turn purple, but this one comes as close as any: "A miniscule [sic] error must coalesce with gargantuan guilt, even where the accused displays an imagination of Pantagruelian dimensions." *Chapman v. United States,* 547 F.2d 1240, 1250 (5th Cir. 1977).

Purple prose is seductive: it may skew the literary sensibilities especially of those who purport to be stylists, and is commonest among those who fancy themselves masterly writers. To name three guilty parties, Norman Brand and John O. White, in their otherwise solid book *Legal Writing: The Strategy of Persuasion* 111–12 (1976), offer up as an example of a "well-written decision" this, by Justice Carlin of New York:

> This case presents the ordinary man—that problem child of the law—in a most bizarre setting. As a lowly chauffeur in defendant's employ he became in a trice the protagonist in a breath-bating drama with a denouement almost tragic. It appears that a man, whose identity it would be indelicate to divulge, was feloniously relieved of his portable goods by two nondescript highwaymen in an alley near 26th Street and Third Avenue, Manhattan; they induced him to relinquish his possessions by a strong argument *ad hominem* couched in the convincing cant of the criminal and pressed at the point of a most persuasive pistol. Laden with their loot, but not thereby impeded, they took an abrupt departure and he, shuffling off the coil of that discretion which enmeshed him in the alley, quickly gave chase through 26th Street toward 2d Avenue, whither they were resorting "with expedition swift as thought" for most obvious reasons. Somewhere on that thoroughfare of escape they indulged the stratagem of separation ostensibly to disconcert their pursuer and allay the ardor of his pursuit. He then centered on for capture the man with the pistol, whom he saw board the defendant's taxicab, which quickly veered south toward 25th Street on 2d Avenue, where he saw the chauffeur jump out while the cab, still in motion, continued toward 24th Street; after the chauffeur relieved himself of the cumbersome burden of his fare the latter also is said to have similarly departed from the cab before it reached 24th Street. . . .
>
> The chauffeur—the ordinary man in this case—acted in a split second in a most harrowing experience. To call him negligent would be to brand him a coward; the court

does not do so in spite of what those swaggering heroes, "whose valor plucks dead lions by the beard," may bluster to the contrary. The court is loathe [q.v.] to see the plaintiffs go without recovery even though their damages were slight, but cannot hold the defendant liable upon the facts adduced at the trial. Motions, upon which decision was reserved, to dismiss the complaint are granted, with exceptions to plaintiffs. Judgment for defendant against plaintiffs dismissing their complaint upon the merits.
Cordas v. Peerless Transportation Co., 27 N.Y.S.2d 198,199, 202 (N.Y. City Ct. 1941).

This very opinion has been justly criticized for its purplishness in R. Goldfarb & J. Raymond, *Clear Understandings* 142–43 (1982).

purport, n., = that which is conveyed or expressed, esp. by a formal document. As a noun, this term is now primarily a legal word (the verb *to purport* being common). E.g., "The circumstances of the publication must be such that either from the plain *purport* of what is published, or from the circumstances of the publication itself, the presumption of malice and injury is raised."/ "Other early decisions . . . are difficult to reconcile with the clear *purport* of Rule 12." (Charles Alan Wright) The verb, of course, is much more common, e.g.: "Hobart L. Arnold died leaving what *purported* to be a holographic will."/ "The result in this case ought to be intolerable in any society that *purports* to call itself an organized society."

purported, adj. = reputed, rumored. It does not mean "alleged," as here erroneously used: "There were many *purported* [read *alleged*] violations of the defendant's rights."

purpose, v.t., = to set as a goal for oneself; to intend; to resolve. This FORMAL WORD is little used now in ordinary lay contexts. "The giving of these instructions was a reasonable means to the end *purposed* and they were adopted in good faith."

purposeful. See **purposive.**

purposely; purposefully. The former means "on purpose; intentionally"; the latter means "with a specific purpose in mind; with the idea of accomplishing a certain result."

purposive; purposeful. Fowler and the *OED* editors objected to *purposive* as an ill-formed hybrid. Today, however, it is usefully distinguished in one sense from *purposeful* (= [1] having a purpose; or [2] full of determination). *W9* records under *purposive* the sense "serving or effecting a useful function though not as a result of planning or design." In other senses it is a NEEDLESS VARIANT of *purposeful.* Following are two specimens in which *purposive* is used pointlessly: "References to 'the *purposive* [read *purposeful*] use of ambiguity' are usually directed to the *purposive* [read *purposeful*] use of vagueness or generality."/ "There is ample evidence in this case of the correlation between municipal service disparities and racially tainted *purposiveness* [read *purposefulness*] to mandate a finding of discriminatory intent."

pursuant to (= in carrying out) is sometimes a useful LEGALISM. Partridge was wrong to call this phrase "OFFICIALESE for *after." Usage and Abusage* 257 (1973). It may be officialese, but it does not, ordinarily, mean "after." Following are typical uses: "Appellant is a state prisoner incarcerated in the Louisiana State Penitentiary in Angola, Louisiana, *pursuant to* a 1964 aggravated rape conviction."/ "*Pursuant to* the mandate of the Supreme Court in *Escondido,* the decision of the Federal Energy Regulatory Commission to grant a license in these proceedings is reversed."

British legal writers often use *in pursuance of,* e.g.: "Notice was therefore given to the plaintiffs that after May 2, 1972, the council would, under and *in pursuance of* section 15 of the Act of 1936, by their contractor proceed to construct the sewer." (Eng.) This usage was formerly common in the U.S.

pursuer, defender. These are the names equivalent to *plaintiff* and *defendant* in Scots and canon law. E.g., "My Lords, the *pursuers* supply to local authorities litter bins which are placed in the streets. The *defender* carried on a garage in Clydebank and in 1954 he made an agreement with the pursuers . . . ." (Scot.)

put is often used as a noun in securities law in the sense "an option to sell securities." E.g.,"'*Puts*' and automatic buybacks at the same price should be avoided."/ "Although the uncertainty in Murchison's engagement to develop a potentially more lucrative *put* option may evidence an intent not to contract, we cannot say that the agreement lacks sufficient definiteness on that ground alone." *Put* is usually contrasted in such contexts with *call* (= an option to buy securities).

put another way. See **to put it another way.**

putative = supposed, believed, reputed. E.g., "The facts of causation were in the control of the *putative* defendant but unavailable to the plaintiff or at least very difficult to obtain." *Putative marriage,* a term originally from canon law, denotes a marriage that, though legally invalid, was contracted in good faith by at least one of the parties. E.g., "The court of civil appeals held that the *putative* wife's knowledge of pending divorce involving husband terminated the *putative* marriage."/ "A *putative* marriage is one into which one or both spouses enter in good faith but which is invalid because of an existing impediment."

put option. See **put.**

putrefy; putrify. The latter is a misspelling.

Q

Q.B.D. = Queen's Bench Division.

Q.C. = Queen's Counsel.

Q.E.D. is the abbreviation for *quod erat demonstrandum* (= which was to be proved or demonstrated).

Q.E.F. is the abbreviation for *quod erat faciendum* (= which was to be done).

qua = in the capacity of; as; in the role of. The word is often misused and little needed in English. "The real occasion for the use of *qua,*" wrote Fowler, "occurs when a person or thing spoken of can be regarded from more than one point of view or as the holder of various coexistent functions, and a statement about him (or it) is to be limited to him in one of these aspects" (*MEU1* 477). Fowler's example of a justifiable use of the term is this: "*Qua* lover he must be condemned for doing what *qua* citizen he would be condemned for not doing." Alas, this proper use of the term is rarely if ever seen today.

One is hard-pressed to divine any purpose but rhetorical emphasis in the examples following: "We seek simply to keep the government, *qua* government, neutral with respect to any religious controversy."/ "The question of res, *qua* res, causes us no difficulty."/ "The only immunities in an official-capacity action are forms of sovereign immunity that the entity, *qua* entity, may possess."

Nor are the unemphatic modern uses of a nature that would justify the choice of *qua* over *as.* Indeed, these are the very types of uses that Fowler rightly objected to: "Hudspeth can challenge the FSLIC's behavior *qua* [read *as*] receiver before the FHLBB and, if unsatisfied, can seek judicial review under the APA."/ "*Qua* [read *To test its claim as a*] patent, we should at least have to decide, as tabula rasa, whether the design or machine was a new and required invention."/ "The right of fair comment, though shared by the public, is the right of every individual who asserts it, and is, *qua* [read *as claimed by*] him, an individual right whatever name it be called by, and comment by him which is coloured by malice cannot from his standpoint be deemed fair." (Eng.)

quadrennial; quadriennial. The latter is a NEEDLESS VARIANT.

quaere; query. *Quaere* is the Latin word meaning "question," sometimes appended or prefixed to doubtful statements. E.g., "Whether a plea in abatement is not the proper mode of defense when the facts relied on do not appear of record, *quaere.*" *Engelke & Feiner Milling Co. v. Grunthal,* 46 Fla. 349, 35 So. 17, 18 (1903). The term is used occasionally in modern pedagogical writing: "One can affix one's signature to a document by writing thereon, and one can affix one sheet of paper to another with a staple or sticky tape; but *quaere* as to a paper clip." Leff, *The Leff Dictionary of Law,* 94 Yale L.J. 1855, 1969 (1985). The original form of *query, quaere* is now but a NEEDLESS VARIANT in other than this technical use.

quai. See **quay.**

qualifiedly = in a qualified fashion. Often the adjective works better than the adverb. "*Although the sheriff is not qualifiedly privileged,* [read *Although the sheriff has no qualified privilege*], the summary judgment was entered in favor of the parish and not the sheriff." Unfortunately, adverbs in *-edly* are unqualifiedly fashionable in modern legal writing. See -EDLY.

QUALIFIERS, PREEMPTIVE. See ANTICIPIATORY REFERENCE.

qualit(at)ive. The longer form is preferred. The adjective corresponds to *quality* in the sense of character or nature, not in the sense of merit or excellence. See the following entry.

quality, adj., (= of high quality) is a VOGUE WORD and a casualism ⟨a *quality* law firm⟩. One is better advised to use *good* or *fine* or some other mundane adjective that is not branded as a cant term.

quandary is a word naming a mental state of perplexity or confusion. It is, most emphatically, descriptive of a state of mind, and should not be detached from mental processes, as here: "Conflicting state interests may make the use of either state's law inappropriate; the asbestos cases present this precise *quandary* [read *dilemma, enigma,* or *problem*]."

quanta. See **quantum.**

quantificational. See **quanti(ta)tive.**

quantify; quantitate. The latter is a NEEDLESS VARIANT newly popular with social scientists, whose choice of terms has never been a strong recommendation for the use of those terms.

quanti(ta)tive. The preferred form is *quantitative,* not *quantitive.* Variants such as *quantificational* should be avoided. Cf. **qualit(at)ive.**

quantity (usu. "portion, amount") has been used by legal theorists in a sense borrowed from logic, "the extent in which a term in a given logical proposition is to be taken" (*W3*). E.g., "While, no doubt, in the great majority of cases no harm results from the use of such expressions, yet these forms of statement seem to represent a blending of nonlegal and legal *quantities* which, in any problem requiring careful reasoning, should

preferably be kept distinct."/ "If, however, the problem is analyzed, it will be seen that as of primary importance, the grantor has two legal *quantities*: the privilege of entering and the power, by means of such entry, to divest the estate of the grantee."

The *OED* notes that *quantity* in the sense "length or duration of time" exists now only in the legal phrase *quantity of estate* ⟨the quantity of estate is 99 years⟩.

quantum, a favorite word of lawyers and judges, means "amount; share, portion; the required, desired, or allowed amount." The term should not be used for *degree,* as here: "The injury suffered by Lyons was several *quanta* [read *degrees*] greater than Raley's."/ "The scope of intrusiveness of a particular search, and thus the corresponding *quantum* [read *degree*] of suspicion, is determined in the light of three factors."

Ordinarily in legal writing it appears as a synonym of *amount,* for which it would not be audacious to term *quantum* a NEEDLESS VARIANT. Following are a number of representative examples: "The agent had been given that *quantum* [read *amount*] of reliable information necessary to application of the collective knowledge doctrine."/ "Although incarceration immediately following conviction is disadvantageous, it does not change the *quantum* [read *amount*] of punishment attached to the offense."/ "The only question remaining, then, is the *quantum* [read *amount*] and value of the commercially recoverable reserves."/ "My Lords, it is well established that in considering questions as to the *quantum* [read *amount*] of damages that have been awarded, the approach of an appellate court must differ according to whether the assessment has been by a judge or by a jury." (Eng.)

Assuming the writer still wants to use *quantum,* he should beware of using it redundantly with *amount*: "The consequences of that failure will *amount to* [read *determine*] the *quantum* of the compensation he will have to pay."

The only accepted plural of this word is *quanta.* The erroneous form *quantums* is occasionally seen. E.g., "Without regard to the number of rungs that appellant may climb on an appellate ladder, if minimum evidentiary *quantums* [read *quanta*] have been satisfied, the American tradition generally does not permit a reviewing court to disturb findings of facts." This foreign plural is one of the exceptions to the general rule enunciated in the entry PLU-

RALS (A). Following are examples of the correct plural: "There is a difference in the *quanta* and modes of proof required to establish guilt and probable cause."/ "Absent hard data, I would rather err on the side of receiving little additional benefit from imposing additional *quanta* of liability than err by adhering to *Robins's* inequitable rule."

quantum meruit; quantum valeba(n)t. These counts were used at common law by pleaders in suits in assumpsit, and are still used today. *Quantum meruit* = the reasonable value of services; *quantum valebant* = the reasonable values of goods and materials. *Quantum meruit* means literally "as much as he deserved," and shows no signs of waning in legal use. The term, however, "is ambiguous; it may mean (1) that there is a contract 'implied in fact' to pay the reasonable value of the services, or (2) that, to prevent unjust enrichment, the claimant may recover on a quasi contract (an 'as if' contract) for that reasonable value." *Martin v. Campanaro*, 156 F.2d 127, 130 n. 5 (2d Cir. 1946).

The distinction between *quantum meruit* and *quantum valeba(n)t* is that the former (often termed *quasi-contract*) is used of an action to recover for services performed, and the latter is used to recover for the value of goods sold without a price having been set. E.g., "Although such fees are recoverable in an action based on *quantum meruit* or *valebant*, no attorneys' fees are recoverable if the *quantum meruit* or *valebant* claim is an insignificant part of the relief sought by a party."

Quantum valebant and *quantum valebat* both appear in the cases; and both are correct Latin: *quantum valebant* means "as much as they were worth," whereas *quantum valebat* means "as much as it was worth." Hence the choice is between using the singular or plural Latin construction. As a matter of usage, *valebant* predominates among American legal writers generally, and *valebat* among British legal writers. But gradually the phrase is falling into disuse.

quare clausum fregit. See **trespass.**

quartile is unnecessarily technical for *quarter* in any context not involving complex mathematical calculations. E.g.,"Restricting admission to teacher-training institutions to students ranked in the upper *quartile* [read *quarter*] of their graduating classes should be a requirement common to all plans for bettering the quality of entering teachers."

quash = (1) to suppress or subdue; to crush out, beat into pieces; (2) to annul; to make void (as a writ or indictment); to put an end to (as legal proceedings). Sense (2) is the more frequent legal meaning: "Their petition for writ of certiorari was granted on December 11, 1980, but was subsequently *quashed* for lack of prosecution."

quashal, the American noun corresponding to the verb *to quash*, is recorded in no major English dictionary. Yet it is fairly common in legal writing in the U.S. ⟨quashal of the writ⟩, and it is useful. Indeed, the word seems to have been coined by a judge on the Florida Supreme Court: "When the appellate proceeding is irregular, . . . the policy of our statutes as to a regular hearing on the merits in due course of procedure is not contravened by a *quashal* or summary disposition." *Holland v. Webster*, 43 Fla. 85, 29 So. 625, 630 (1901) (Mabry, J., dissenting)./ "[T]he court, upon the *quashal* of the first venire, directed the sheriff to summon 18 persons to serve as a grand jury." *Ford v. State*, 44 Fla. 421, 33 So. 301, 302 (1902) (per Mabry, J.). Justice Mabry's colleagues on the court soon adopted the word: "The discharge of the former grand jury amounted, in law, to a *quashal* of such jury." *Davis v. State*, 46 Fla. 137, 35 So. 76, 77 (1903) (per Cockrell, J.). Since these early uses of the word, of course, it has come to be used occasionally in most American jurisdictions. E.g., "Like the *quashal* of the subpoena, this injunctive relief was related to the central purpose of a proceeding that is essentially criminal in nature." *Lee v. Johnson*, 799 F.2d 31, 42 (3d Cir. 1986) (Becker, J., dissenting). Fowler might find fault with its formation in *-al*, but the etymon is appropriately Latin and there appears to be no serviceable alternative. Even if there were, *quashal* has taken hold.

quasi = seeming or seemingly; in the nature of; nearly. Corbin wrote sensibly of *quasi*: "The term *quasi* is introduced as a WEASEL WORD that sucks all the meaning *of* [read *from*] the word that follows it; but this is a fact the reader seldom realizes." *Corbin on Contracts* 27 (1st ed. 1952). In legal writing, *quasi* may stand alone as a word, and need not always be hyphenated as a prefix; it is a separable prefix. E.g., "Damages being insufficient, *quasi* specific performance should be awarded in order to remedy the wrong."/ "The usual remedy is a constructive trust upon property passing from the testator in violation of his agreement for the benefit of the injured party, commonly described as *quasi* specific performance." / "We can hardly fail to recognize that for this purpose, and as between them, the news must be regarded as *quasi* property, irrespective of the rights of either as against the other."/ "In such cases the communication is classified as privileged or *quasi* privileged in the law."

quasi contract; contract implied in law. The terms are now regarded as synonymous. See *United States v. Neidorf*, 522 F.2d 916, 919 (9th Cir. 1975), *cert. denied*, 423 U.S. 1087 (1976). See **implied contract.** *Quasi contract* was earlier termed *indebitatus assumpsit*. See **assumpsit.**

quasi ex contractu = in the nature of quasi contract. E.g., "Surely, if a man is bona fide obliged to refund whatever money he has unlawfully received, an implied question is thereby raised, *quasi ex contractu.*" See **ex contractu** & **quasi contract.**

quay; quai. The first spelling is preferred.

queen regnant; queen regent. There is a distinction. The first is a queen who rules in her own right; the second is a queen who rules either in her own right or in behalf of another. The plural forms are *queens regnant* and *queens regent.*

querist. See **questioner.**

querulous (= apt to complain; whining) is a MALAPROPISM when used for *query-like*. E.g., "His statement was *querulous*; that is, it was framed as a question." [Read *His statement was framed as a question.*]

query. See **quaere.**

questionary. See **questionnaire.**

question as to whether; question of whether. Both are common prolixities for *question whether*. Examples of *question as to whether* are legion in the prose of lawyers and judges. E.g., "The question sometimes *arises as to whether* [read *arises whether*] today a man

may by a conveyance to himself and his wife create a tenancy by the entirety."/ "The *question as to whether* [read *question whether*] the equitable defense of unclean hands applies as a defense to a legal action appears to be one of first impression." Even where *question* = doubt, the preferred form is *question whether*: "There is some *question as to whether* [read *question whether*] the defendant could be held personally liable." See **issue** (B).

The only context in which *question as to whether* might be justified is where an intervening phrase might cause an ambiguity or awkwardness: "There may be a *question* of statutory interpretation *as to whether* this 'consent' comprehends only those actions done within the state or is broad enough to cover all personal actions."

The other common prolixity is *question of whether*. E.g., "The answer to the *question of whether* [read *question whether*] the state courts of Ohio are open to a proceeding in personam rests entirely upon the law of Ohio."/ "Without mentioning the *question of whether* [read *question whether*] an adequate remedy at law was available, we have held that rights similar to those of the plaintiff in this case may be enforced by actions in the nature of specific performance." Yet *question of whether* is preferred when one uses the idiom *it is a question of . . .* , as in: "a question of ethics," "a question of materiality." Here the phrases are combined: "It is a *question of whether* the defendant is passing off his goods as those of the plaintiff."

question-begging is the adjectival form of the phrase *begging the question*, q.v. E.g., "The cases simply state the rule without explaining its origin; it certainly could not rest upon the *question-begging* maxim that 'equity will not determine legal rights,' for quite often equity would determine controversies involving the construction of purely legal rights and questions of fact."

questioner; querist. The former is the ordinary, more natural term.

questionnaire; questionary. The latter is a NEEDLESS VARIANT.

question of whether. See **question as to whether.**

quick originally meant "alive," as in the surviving phrase *the quick and the dead*, used by one judge to turn a nice phrase: "There are only two conduits, the statute of wills and intestate succession, by which the transmission of property and estate to the *quick* from the dead may be effected."

Up to the nineteenth century, *quick* was used as an equivalent of *live* or *alive* in general contexts. Here is a specimen from 1865: "The defendant then proved that Dygert was arrested January 2, 1862, and held to bail upon a criminal warrant charging him with the criminal offense of assisting in procuring an abortion of a *quick* child upon the person of the plaintiff, at Ilion, July 5, 1861." Today this usage would be an affected ARCHAISM.

quid pro quo (= this for that; tit for tat) is a useful LATINISM, for the only English equivalent of this LATINISM is *tit for tat*, which is unsuitable in formal contexts. "The settlor seeking to revoke or modify the trust may supplement his appeal to equity with a *quid pro quo* offered to the heirs for their consent."/ "Assumpsit would lie in any case in which there was a promise to pay a sum certain upon receipt of a benefit (the *quid pro quo*)."

The phrase is here wrongly used: "The employer's liability under the act is made exclusive to counterbalance the imposition of absolute liability; there is *no comparable quid pro quo* [read *no comparable balancing*] in the relationship between the employer and third persons."

The best plural is *quid pro quos*; *quids pro quos* is a pedantic alternative. *Quids pro quo* is in incorrect attempt at hypercorrectness.

quiescence, -cy. *Quiesence* is a fairly common misspelling. See, e.g., 61 Texas L. Rev. 866 (1983). The *-ce* form is standard.

quiet, v.t.; **quieten.** The preferred verb form is *quiet*, as in the phrase *to quiet title*. E.g., "The same issue may be presented in other types of litigation such as a suit to *quiet title*."/ "The assignee of an automobile conditional sales contract sued to *quiet title*."/ "That was an action to recover possession of land, and to *quiet title*." Chiefly a Britishism, *quieten* was considered a superfluous word by the great British writer on usage, H. W. Fowler; it is to be avoided.

Adjectivally, the phrase *quiet title* is hyphenated: "The original *quiet-title* suit in equity arose as a bill of peace to forestall repeated ejectment actions at law."

quietus forms the plural *quietuses*.

quiritary, -tarian. The latter is a NEEDLESS VARIANT of the former term, which means "in accordance with Roman civil law; legal, as opposed to equitable."

quit = (1) to stop; or (2) to leave. For sense (1), the past tense is *quit* ⟨the defendant then quit making the harassing phone calls⟩. For sense (2), the past tense is *quitted*. E.g., "It must now be considered clear law that a person who wrongfully or maliciously interrupts the relation subsisting between master and servant by harbouring and keeping him as servant after he has *quitted* it and during the time stipulated for as the period of service, commits a wrongful act for which he is responsible at law." (Eng.)/ "These authorities and practices were to the effect that alimony decreed to a wife would be enforced by a writ of ne exeat, but only to the extent of arrears actually due, against a husband before he *quitted* the realm."

quitclaim was formerly two words, then hyphenated, and now is one word. The word may be noun, adjective, and verb. The use of the term as a verb, illustrated in the examples following, dates from the fourteenth century: "He and his wife executed, about three months after his mother's death, an instrument releasing, *quitclaiming*, and conveying unto his two brothers all interest and right of every kind that he had or might have in his mother's estate."/ "This tract of land was *quit-claimed* by R. E. Jones to R. E. Jones Gravel Co."

quittance = (1) the discharge from a debt or obligation; or (2) the document serving as evidence of the discharge. Cf. *acquittance*, treated under **acquittal.**

quitter, -or. For "one who quits," the former is preferred. *Quittor* = an inflammation of the feet usu. in horses.

quoad (= as regards; with regard to) is a LATINISM that is easily Englished. E.g., "It seems to me that, if anything, this was a case of wilful refusal; invincible repugnance is a lack of capacity *quoad* this man." (Eng.) The term often appears in the phrase *quoad hoc* (= with regard to this). E.g., "When a justice undertakes the issuing of a warrant of arrest which commands and secures the arrest, and possibly the imprisonment, of the person charged, he *quoad hoc* acts ministerially [omit *quoad hoc*, which is superfluous]."

quo animo (lit., "with what intention or motive") is used by some legal writers as an arcane LATINISM in place and as an equivalent of *animus*, q.v. "Such acts are against the express declarations of the *quo animo.*" Those legal writers are, happily, becoming rarer.

quod erat demonstrandum.   See **Q.E.D.**

quod erat faciendum.   See **Q.E.F.**

quod vide = which see. The abbreviation *q.v.* (pl. *qq.v.*) is used throughout this work.

quondam (= former) is an ARCHAISM.

quorum.   Pl. *quorums.* See PLURALS (A).

QUOTATIONS.   A. Use of Quoted Material. The deft and incidental use of quotations is a rare art. Legal writers—especially the bad ones—are apt to quote paragraph after paragraph in block quotations. This practice is an abrogation of the writer's duty, namely, *to write.* Readers tend to skip over such single-spaced mountains of prose, knowing how unlikely it is that so much of a previous writer's material is apposite in the context at hand. Especially to be avoided is quotation of another writer at the end of a paragraph or section, a habit infused with laziness. The skillful quoter subordinates the quoted material to his own prose, and uses only the most clearly applicable parts of the previous writing. And even then, he weaves it into his own narrative or explication, not allowing the quoted to overpower the quoter.

   B. American and British Systems. In AmE, quotations that are short enough to be run into the text (usu. fewer than 50 words) are set off by pairs of *double* quotation marks (". . ."). In BrE, quoted text that is not long enough to be a block quotation is set off by *single* quotation marks ('. . .'). See PUNCTUATION (I).

quote (properly a verb) for *quotation* is a casualism. The same is true of the negative form, e.g.: "The good brief-writer does not belabor *misquotes* [read *misquotations*] in his opponent's brief." See **cite** (B).

q.v.   See **quod vide.**

R

racial   discrimination;   race   discrimination.   The former phrase is slightly better, because, other things being equal, the functional adjective (*racial* or *race*) should have the form as well as the function of an adjective (hence *racial*). But cf. **sex.**

rack.   See **wrack.**

racketeer, n. & v.i. The noun *racketeering* = the business of racketeers; a system of organized crime traditionally involving the extortion of money from business firms by intimidation, violence, or other illegal methods. Oddly, the verbal noun *racketeering* and the verb *racketeer* are characterized by the *OED Supp.* as Americanisms, whereas the adjective *racketeering* is exemplified in that dictionary only by British quotations. If the verb and its derivative forms began as Americanisms, they will inevitably spread to G.B., given the inroads already made. The U.S. Congress recently passed the Racketeer-Influenced Corrupt Organizations Act (RICO), 18 U.S.C. §§ 1961–68 (1982), which has led to a resurgence of the word in the U.S. Today *racketeering* often has the broad sense "the practice of engaging in a fraudulent scheme or enterprise."

radiocast.   See **broadcast.**

railroad; railway.   As nouns these words are virtually equivalent. *W2* makes the following distinction: "*Railroad* . . . is usually limited to roads [with lines or rails fixed to ties] for heavy steam transportation and also to steam roads partially or wholly electrified or roads for heavy traffic designed originally for electric traction. The lighter electric street-car lines and the like are usually termed *railways.* In Great Britain and the British colonies, except Canada, all such roads, whether for heavy or light traffic, are usually called *railways.*"

   The abbreviations for the two words are *R.R.* and *Ry. Railroad* is used universally as a verb ⟨passenger railroading⟩, but originally only in the U.S. had the figurative sense "to accomplish (an action) with great speed; to rush through a process," as here: "An attempt is being made, while wartime psychology for national security is high, to *railroad* through Congress a bill providing for compulsory military training for one year of all young men between the ages of 18 and 22." This sense is now used in G.B. as well as in the U.S.

raise; rear. The old rule, still to be observed in formal contexts, is that crops and livestock are *raised* and children are *reared.*

rape. See **ravish.**

rarefy is often misspelled *-ify.* Cf. the misspelling *stupify* for the correct *stupefy.*

rarely ever is incorrect for *rarely* or *rarely if ever.*

rat(e)able. In AmE, the spelling *ratable* is preferred, whereas in BrE *rateable* is more common. *Ratably* is frequently used in legal writing in the sense "pro rata, proportionately" (they will share ratably in the assets). E.g., *"Nolte v. Nolte* holds that specifically devised realty and specifically bequeathed personalty should abate *ratably."* See MUTE E.

rate(-)making is best hyphenated.

rather. See **but rather.**

rather unique. See ADJECTIVES (A).

ratification. See **adoption.**

ratiocination; rationalization. *Ratiocination* /rat-i-os-i-*nay*-shŏn/ = the process or an act of reasoning. *Rationalization* = (1) an act or instance of explaining (away) by bringing into conformity with reason; or (2) (colloq.) the finding of "reasons" for irrational or unworthy behavior. Sense (2) is responsible for the negative connotations of *rationalization* among laymen.

ratiocinative, -tory. The latter is a NEEDLESS VARIANT.

ratio decidendi /raht-i-oh-dĕs-i-*dĕn*-dee/ (lit., "the reason for deciding") = the principle or principles of law on which a court reaches its decision (*CDL*). This term is basic to the common-law system of precedents. E.g., "Lower courts read the opinions of this Court with a not unnatural alertness to catch intimations beyond the precise *ratio decidendi." Johnson v. United States,* 333 U.S. 46, 56 (1948) (Frankfurter, J., dissenting)./ "The words of an opin-

ion are not scriptural admonitions or statutory mandates; we are bound by the rationale of a decision, its *ratio decidendi,* not its explanatory language."/ "The observations of Lindley L.J. are less to the purpose, but indicate no dissent from the views of his brethren, which as part of our *ratio decidendi* cannot in our opinion be dismissed as merely obiter [q.v.]." (Eng.)/ "The actual point in this case did not arise in *Ringrose v. Bramham,* but still the *ratio decidendi* clearly applies." (Eng.)

The *OCL* states that *"ratio decidendi* is unsatisfactorily translated as 'the reason for the decision' because the reason may in fact be something other, such as the judge's dislike of the defendant. Nor is the *ratio* the decision itself, for this binds only the parties whereas the *ratio* is the principle which is of application to subsequent cases and states the law for all parties." When discussing the *ratio* of this or that decision, one must remember that the plural form is *rationes; rationale* is usually a serviceable English substitute. See **stare decisis.** Cf. **dictum** (A) & **obiter.**

rational. See **reasonable.**

rationale (= a reasoned exposition of principles; an explanation or statement of reasons) is not to be confused with *rationalization* (see **ratiocination**). *Rationale* is regularly three syllables, although Fowler believed that it should be four syllables based on etymology (*-ale* being two syllables). Today the final syllable is pronounced like that in *morale* or *chorale,* the pronunciation disapproved by Fowler. His preferred pronunciation would be considered terribly pedantic in most company. See **ratio decidendi.**

rationalization. See **ratiocination.**

rationalize for *analogize* or *harmonize* is an unlikely error. E.g., "Since the argument in this case, appellants have called our attention to the recent Supreme Court case of *Indian Towing Co. v. United States,* but it is difficult to *rationalize* [read, depending on the sense, *analogize* or *harmonize*] that case with the one at bar."

ration allotment is a REDUNDANCY. E.g., "Many people came up at night and asked, even demanded, a drink of water beyond their *ration allotment."* Either word would be sufficient.

ravish (= to rape) is now more literary or archaic than is appropriate for modern legal contexts. E.g., "When a man is presented for rape or an attempt to *ravish* [read *rape*], it may be shown that the woman against whom the offence was committed was of a generally immoral character, although she is not cross-examined on the subject." (Eng.) One problem with *ravish* is that it has romantic connotations: it means not only "to commit rape upon a woman," but also "to fill with ecstasy or delight" (*OED*). The latter sense renders the word unfit for acting as a technical or legal equivalent of *rape*. The term describing the act should evoke outrage; it should not be a romantic abstraction, as *ravish* is.

-RE & -ER. See -ER & -RE.

RE- PAIRS. Any number of English words beginning with the prefix *re-* take on certain meanings when the prefix is hyphenated that are different from the meanings when the prefix is flush. Some of these words, whose two different senses with and without the hyphen should be self-explanatory, are: *re(-)bound, re(-)claim, re(-)collect, re(-)count, re(-)cover, re(-)create, re(-)form, re(-)lay, re(-)lease, re(-)mark, re(-)move, re(-)place, re(-)search, re(-)sign, re(-)sound, re(-)store, re(-)treat.*

re. See **in re.**

reaction. A. For *response.* A number of usage critics have objected to this use of the term, as in "What was the judge's *reaction* to this argument?," on grounds that *reaction* is primarily a scientific term that in any event is not applicable to people. The objection is well taken, although we need not make a fetish of it.
   B. For *effect.* Justice Holmes once nodded and made this mistake: "The question then is narrowed to whether the exercise of its otherwise constitutional power by Congress can be pronounced unconstitutional because of its possible *reaction* [read *effect*] upon the conduct of the States in a matter upon which I have admitted that they are free from direct control." *Hammer v. Dagenhart*, 247 U.S. 251, 278 (1918) (Holmes, J., dissenting).

reactionary; reactionist; reactionarist. The second and third are NEEDLESS VARIANTS.

real is dialectal when used for *very.*

real estate agent. See **realtor.**

real facts. See **fact & actual fact, in.**

realtor (= a real estate agent or broker) has two syllables, not three. This Americanism is a MORPHOLOGICAL DEFORMITY, inasmuch as the *-or* suffix in Latin is appended only to verb elements, and *realt-* is not a verb element, but the term is too well established in AmE to quibble with its makeup. The shortness of the word commends it.
   Some authorities suggest that it should be capitalized and used only in its proprietary trademark sense, that is, "a member of the National Association of Realtors"; the organization invented and registered the trademark in 1916. Seemingly few people know about the trademark, and consequently in the U.S. the term is used indiscriminately of real estate agents generally. In G.B., *real estate agents* are known as *estate agents; realtor* is virtually unknown there, and *real estate* is only a little better known to British laymen.

realty. The only current sense of this term is the legal one, "real property." Formerly, the term denoted "royalty" and "a reality" as well.

rear. See **raise.**

reasonability. See **reasonableness.**

reasonable; rational. Generally, *reasonable* = according to reason; *rational* = having reason. Yet *reasonable* is often used in reference to persons in the sense "having the faculty of reason" ⟨reasonable man⟩. When applied to things, the two words are perhaps more clearly differentiated: "In application to things *reasonable* and *rational* both signify according to *reason*; but the former is used in reference to the business of life, as a *reasonable* proposal, wish, etc.; *rational* to abstract matters, as *rational* motives, grounds, questions, etc." G. Crabb, *Crabb's English Synonymes* 589 (2d ed. rev. J. H. Finley 1917).

reasonable-minded is prolix for *reasonable.* E.g., "If any objective event or combination of events in the proceedings should indicate to a *reasonable-minded defendant* [read *reasonable defendant*] that the prosecutor's decision to increase the severity of charges was motivated by some purpose other than vindictiveness, no presumption of vindictiveness is created."

reasonableness; reasonability. The latter is a NEEDLESS VARIANT of the former.

reason is because. This construction is incorrect. After a *be*-verb or other copula, there should be a noun phrase, or a clause introduced by *that*. E.g., "The *reason* such matters are not material and need not be disclosed *is because* [read *is that*] public disclosure of tentative, indefinite, and contingent facts would itself be misleading."

Variations on the phrase, such as *reason is due to,* and *reason is based on,* are no better. E.g., "Two prosecutors stated in affidavits that the *reason* the state moved to dismiss the enhancement counts *was due to* [omit *due to*] difficulty of proof."/ "The *reason* for the requirement of delivery, as provided for in the statute, is *based upon* public policy." [Read *The requirement of delivery, as provided for in the statute, is based on public policy.*]

reason of for *rationale for* is an ARCHAISM. "Clearly, the *reason of* [read *rationale for*] section 2-202 is sensible and should be applied by analogy to article eight."

reason why; reason that. Both forms are correct. "The district court found that there was no *reason that* [or *why*] Hauser could not have joined in her husband's earlier action."

rebellion See **insurrection.**

rebound; re-bound. See RE- PAIRS.

rebus, in. See **in rem.**

rebut; refute. *Rebut* means "to attempt to refute." *Refute* means "to defeat (countervailing arguments)." Thus one who *rebuts* certainly hopes to *refute;* it is immodest to assume, however, that one has *refuted* another's arguments. *Rebut* is sometimes wrongly written *rebutt.* See **refute.**

rebuttable presumption (= a legal presumption subject to valid rebuttal) becomes illogical when turned into a adverb and verb. E.g., "Texas courts *rebuttably presume* such warnings will be read and heeded." This suggests that the courts *presume in a rebuttable*

manner, which is not the sense; a better way of phrasing the thought is to write: "Texas courts *adopt the rebuttable presumption* that such warnings will be read and heeded."

rebuttal; surrebuttal. *Rebuttal* = the act of rebutting. The term is used especially in legal sense, and is much broader than *rebutter,* q.v., which is the name of the pleading intended to rebut. *Surrebuttal* is not an answer to a rebuttal, but is a variant name for the pleading called *surrebutter,* q.v., and is a NEEDLESS VARIANT of that term.

rebutter = (1) (formerly) a defendant's answer to a plaintiff's surrejoinder; the pleading that followed the rejoinder and surrejoinder, and that might in turn be answered by the surrebutter; (2) one who rebuts. Sense (1) is the only strictly legal sense of the term.

receipt, as a verb, began as an Americanism in the eighteenth century and has now spread to G.B. It is COMMERCIALESE, but there is no grammatical problem in writing, "The bill must be *receipted,*" or "The sale was *receipted.*" *Receipt* is ordinarily used in the PASSIVE VOICE: "The preceding sentence shall not be construed [see STATUTE DRAFTING (A)] to mean that new receipts are to be obtained each year from continuing employees who have previously been *receipted* for copies of identical provisions." Still, the PHRASAL VERB *to be receipted for* is a REDUNDANCY, as well as a graceless phrase. "Each certificate issued by the corporation shall *be receipted for* by the person receiving it or by his duly authorized agent." [Read *The person, who receives a certificate issued by the organization, or his duly authorized agent, shall execute a receipt for it.*]

receipt of, be in. This insipid phrase, which usually occurs in letters, is to be avoided as OFFICIALESE or commercialese or LEGALESE.

receiptor (= a person who receipts property attached by a sheriff; a bailee) is noted as being an Americanism by the *OED.* It dates from the early nineteenth century. The *-or* spelling is preferred to *-er.*

receivables (= debts owed to a business and regarded as assets) began in the mid-nineteenth century as an Americanism but is now current in BrE as well. It is the antonym of *payables*. See ADJECTIVES (B).

receiver is used in both the U.S. and G.B. in the specific legal sense of "a person appointed by a court, or by a corporation or other person, for the protection or collection of property." Usually the *receiver* administers the property of a bankrupt, or property that is the subject of litigation, pending the outcome of lawsuit.

recense. See **revise.**

recension (= the revision of a text) is not to be confused with *rescission*, q.v.

receptioning (= to do the job of a receptionist) is American law-firm cant that illustrates the same tendency in modern usage as *paralegaling* and *bailiffing*, qq.v.

recidivate (= to fall back, relapse), a word used now usu. of criminals, has regained currency after several centuries of disuse.

recidivous; recidivist. The former is the preferred adjective. The latter is the noun meaning "one who habitually relapses into crime" (*OED*).

recision. See **rescission.**

recital; recitation. These words overlap, but are distinguishable. The term from DRAFTING is *recital*, meaning "the formal statement, or setting forth, of some related matter of fact in any deed or writing, as to explain the reasons for a transaction, to evidence the existence of facts, or, in pleading, to introduce a positive allegation" (*W2*). E.g., "This version of the parties' proposed consent decree contains no *recital*, finding, or adjudication of any illegality."/ "*Recitations* [read *recitals*] of consideration and use in a recorded deed are not binding upon a complainant who seeks a purchase money resulting trust." More generally, *recital* may mean "a rehearsal, account, or description of some thing, fact, or incident." E.g., "The facts are sordid, but a brief *recital* of them must be made."

Recitation often connotes an oral delivery before an audience, whether in the classroom or on stage. Yet it is oftener the general noun meaning "the act of reciting": "The interrogator's *recitation* of the suspect's rights was suf-

ficient."/ "The carnage caused by drunk driving is well documented and needs no detailed *recitation* here."/ "This court's *recitation* of the history of the case is replete with examples of the district court's having placed extreme requirements of particularized proof upon the government."

reckon (= to count or compute) is probably an ARCHAISM. E.g., "The law *reckons* in days, not commonly in fractions of days, and an agreement made at six o'clock in the morning stands on the same footing with one made at eleven o'clock in the evening." The word is dialectal in the sense "to suppose, think" ⟨I reckon the judges will affirm⟩.

reclaim; re-claim. See RE- PAIRS.

recognizance; reconnaissance; reconnoisance. *Recognizance* = a bond or obligation, entered into and recorded before a court or magistrate, by which a person engages himself to perform some act or observe some condition (as to appear when called on, to pay a debt, or to keep the peace)" (*OED*). E.g., "The suspect was released on his own *recognizance*." *Reconnaisance* = a preliminary survey; a military or intelligence-gathering examination of a region. *Reconnoisance* is an older spelling of *reconnaissance*; it is also a NEEDLESS VARIANT of *recognizance* and of *recognition*. The verb corresponding to *reconnaisance* is *reconnoiter, -re*, q.v. See **cognizance.**

recollect; re-collect. See RE- PAIRS.

recommend against. *Recommend* is a word with positive connotations; in all the examples in the *OED*, it is construed with *to*. The antonym of *recommend* is *discommend*, which should appear in place of *recommend against* in the following sentence: "Shortly thereafter, 45 college hours were required for applicants, even though civil-service officials *recommended against* [read *discommended*] this increase in the number of required hours." See **discommend.**

recompensable is a NEEDLESS VARIANT of *compensable*, q.v.

recompense is both a transitive verb ("to repay, compensate") and a noun ("payment in return for something"); the word is more learned than *compensate* or *compensation*. In

G.B. the noun is sometimes spelled *-ce*. The nominal use is more frequent than the use as a verb: "Although foreseeability may be a proper test for determining damages for unintentional tort violations of civil rights, it is not a proper prerequisite to obtaining *recompense* for intentional violations."/ "The statute does not assure the prevailing party munificent *recompense*, for it remains for the district court to determine what fee is reasonable."/ "Punitive damages are not only a *recompense* to the sufferer but a punishment to the offender and an example to the community." See **compensate** (B).

recompensive (= compensatory) is a rare term whose use in modern prose strikes the reader as a straining for the recherché term.

reconnaissance;   reconnoisance. See **recognizance.**

reconnoiter, -re. The verb form corresponding to the noun *reconnaissance* is preferably spelled *-er* in AmE, and *-re* in BrE. See **recognizance.**

record frequently occurs in law in the phrases *in the record* and *of record* ⟨attorney of record⟩. Usually *record* refers to the official report of the proceedings in any case coming before a court, together with the judgment given in the case, taken down by a court reporter. The *record* is read on appeal by the judges who review it for reversible errors. In administrative law, *record* refers to all considerations actually taken into account in deciding an issue.

Record has come to be used adjectivally as shorthand for *in the record.* E.g., "We find no *record support* [i.e. support in the record] for this contention." It is preferable not to collapse the prepositions into a nominal adjective in this way. [Read *We find no support in the record for this contention.*]

recordation; recordal. The latter is not a proper word, though it has erroneously appeared in such phrases as "*recordal* of a trademark with the Treasury Department." *Recordation* is the word. E.g., "The supplemental complaint requests that both the Customs Service and Art's Way remove the *recordal* [read *recordation*] of the DION registration to permit unimpeded entry of the machinery into the United States." *B. & R. Choiniere Ltd.*

v. Art's-Way Manufacturing Co., 207 U.S.P.Q. (BNA) 969, 971 (N.D.N.Y. 1979).

recount; re-count. See RE- PAIRS.

recourse; resort. *Recourse* (= application) is used in the idiomatic phrases *without recourse* and *have recourse to.* The former is the peculiarly legal phrase, which, when added to the endorsement of commercial paper, protects the endorser from liability to the indorsee and later holders. "When an inter partes proceeding has been conducted the only *recourse* is an appeal from the decision of the court." *Resort* = that which one turns to for refuge or aid.

recover, in legal ARGOT, is an elliptical form of *recover damages*. E.g., "The United States filed suit against Central Gulf to *recover* for the missing soybean oil."

recover; re-cover. See RE-PAIRS.

recover (= to secure by legal process) takes *from* or *against* in modern usage. The collocation *recover of* is an ARCHAISM for *recover from.* E.g., "It is equally well settled that the reasonable expenses incurred by an indemnitee in defending a claim against him may be *recovered of* [read *recover from*] his indemnitor."/ "This is an action of tort to *recover of* [read *recover from*] the defendant damages for a malicious abuse of process." Cf. **purchase of & of** (D).

recoverable = compensable, q.v. The term originally meant "capable of being recovered or regained," but was extended in legal usage, because of the nature of damages, to "capable of being legally obtained." E.g., "The rule is that special damages for breach of contract are not *recoverable* unless they can fairly and reasonably be considered as arising naturally from the breach." Strictly speaking the special damages are not to be *recovered,* for they are being awarded for the first time to the complainant; but this usage is quite permissible in the legal idiom.

recover back might appear to be a legal RE-DUNDANCY. E.g., "Generally, a co-owner who pays a disproportionate share of the necessary expenses of the property may *recover back* the excess in an action for contribution, accounting, or partition." But in common-law terminology a distinction exists between *to recover* (= to obtain, as in recovering damages) and *to recover back* (= to secure the return of, as in recovering back money paid by mistake).

recover of. See **recover.**

recreate; re-create. The former means either (of a pastime or relaxation) "to refresh or agreeably occupy" or "to amuse oneself, indulge in recreation" (*COD*); the latter means "to create anew." The hyphen makes a great difference: "The words of the witness cannot 'give' or *recreate* [read *re-create*] the 'facts,' that is, the objective situations or happenings about which the witness is testifying."/ "The company's termination of the positions was a pretext for unfair labor practices, which demonstrates that these positions must now be *re-created* to provide an efficacious remedy." See RE- PAIRS.

recreational; recreative. The former is the preferred adjective corresponding to the noun *recreation*. E.g., "In the first few months of army training, the emphasis was on athletic activities for their *recreative* [read *recreational*] value, but soon the need for exercise as physical training became evident."

recriminatory, -tive. The latter is a NEEDLESS VARIANT.

rectal; rictal. Both words relate to orifices, but there the similarities end. *Rectal* = of or relating to the rectum. *Rictal* = of or relating to the mouth, or to a gaping grin.

recur. See **reoccur.**

recurrence, -cy; reoccurrence. *Recurrence* is the preferred form, *reoccurrence* being a secondary variant meriting only careful avoidance. *Recurrency* is likewise a NEEDLESS VARIANT.

recusal; recusation; recusement; recusancy, -ce. The preferred nominal form of the verb *recuse* (= to remove [oneself] as a judge considering a case) is *recusal*, though its earliest known use is only 1958 (*OED Supp.*). The word appeared in the *Manchester Guardian* in August 1958 (see *OED Supp.*), and in the same year in a reported opinion from Alabama: "[T]he statute on *recusal* rests on kinship or pecuniary interest . . . ." *Wiggins v. State*, 104 So. 2d 560, 564 (Ala. App. 1958).

Recusement (not listed in the *OED*) and *recusation*, though once common, are now to be termed NEEDLESS VARIANTS in common-law contexts. *Recusation* appears not uncommonly, and esp. in civil-law writing. See, e.g., *State v. DeMaio*, 58 A. 173 (N.J. 1904); *Stewart v. Reid*, 38 So. 70 (La. 1905). Although *recusation* is common in Louisiana, it persists, oddly, in other jurisdictions. E.g., "[T]he plaintiff asserts the 'essence' of his motion for *recusation* [read *recusal*] is what the trial justice 'himself said and how he has ruled.'" *Barber v. Town of Fairfield*, 486 A.2d 150, 152 (Me. 1985)./ "The trial judge admitted making these remarks upon defendant's motion for continuance and *recusation* [read *recusal*]." *State v. Majors*, 325 S.E.2d 689, 690 (N.C. App. 1985)./ "[O]nce a prosecutor recuses himself, the *recusation* [read *recusal*] applies to all aspects of the case." *Daugherty v. State*, 466 N.E.2d 46, 49 (Ind. App. 1984)./ "Canon 3C(1)(a) is basically a broad standard by which a judge should sua sponte [q.v.] determine the matter of *self-recusation* [read *recusal*]." *State v. Smith*, 242 N.W.2d 320, 323 (Iowa 1976). For an example of INELEGANT VARIATION with *recusal* and *recusation*, see *Reilly by Reilly v. Southeastern Pennsylvania Transportation Authority*, 489 A.2d 1291, 1297–98 (Pa. 1985).

Recusement appears far less commonly, e.g.: "[P]laintiff filed a challenge for Mr. Booker's *recusement* [read *recusal*] upon the ground that he had prejudged the case." *Cobble Close Farm v. Board of Adjustment*, 10 N.J. 442, 92 A.2d 4, 10 (N.J. Sup. Ct. 1952)./ "[I]t presents no adequate or sufficient basis for a *recusement* [read *recusal*] of the undersigned in the present case." *Shotkin v. Rowe*, 100 So. 2d 429, 431 (Fla. Dist. Ct. App. 1958)./ "Following our opinion . . . , the Honorable Paul M. Marko . . . entered an order of *recusement* [read *recusal*] in the fall of 1982." *Irwin v. Irwin*, 455 So. 2d 1118, 1119 (Fla. Dist. Ct. App. 1984).

Recusancy is a different word, meaning "obstinate refusal to comply." *Recusance* is a NEEDLESS VARIANT of *recusancy*.

redact. See **revise.**

redeemable; redemptible. Writers should eschew the latter; it is pedantic, unnecessary, and irredeemable.

redemptive, -tory, -tional. *Redemptive* = tending to redeem, redeeming. *Redemptional* = of or pertaining to redemption. *Redemptory* is a NEEDLESS VARIANT of *redemptive*.

redhibition is a civil-law term used in the U.S. only in Louisiana. It denotes the voidance of a sale as the result of an action brought on account of some defect in something sold, on grounds that the defect renders the thing sold either useless or so imperfect that the buyer would not have purchased it if he had known of the defect. *Redhibitory* is the usual adjectival form.

redintegration. See **reintegration.**

redound, now used most commonly in the CLICHÉ *to redound to the benefit of* (which is verbose for *to benefit*), may be used also in negative senses ⟨to redound against or to the shame of⟩.

redressable, -ible. The former spelling is standard.

reduce should not be used as a reflexive verb. E.g., "The question *reduces itself* [read *is reducible* or *may be reduced*] to one of statutory interpretation."/ "The government's case *reduces itself* [read *is reducible*] to this: the defendant was in a public restaurant at a time when someone said that a drug deal might be going on."

REDUNDANCY. Washington Irving wrote that "redundancy of language is never found with deep reflection. Verbiage may indicate observation, but not thinking. He who thinks much says but little in proportion to his thoughts." Lawyers should think much about those words, and begin to write less. (See CUTTING OUT THE CHAFF.) Following are some of the typical manifestations of redundancy in legal writing.
    A. General Redundancy. This linguistic pitfall is best exemplified, rather than discoursed on; comments follow the less obvious redundancies here listed. "No one need fight city hall unnecessarily." [Read *One need not fight city hall.* Or: *It is unnecessary to fight city hall.*]/ "This type of obligation imposes an undue restriction on alienation or an *onerous burden* in perpetuity." (Onus = *burden,* hence *onerous burden* is redundant.)/ "National is discharged from all its *obligations as obligor.*" [Read *National is discharged as obligor.* Or: *National is discharged from all its obligations.*]/ "By allowing representatives of the tenants, who obviously *shared a common interest* [read *shared an interest* or *had an interest in common*], to

maintain a single action, the equity court eliminated the necessity of trying the common questions repetitively in separate actions." / "These two paragraphs are the least legible and the most difficult to read [omit *and the most difficult to read*] in the instrument, but they are most important in the evaluation of the rights of the contesting parties." / "The mere fact that the association acquired its knowledge *later in point of time* [omit *in point of time*] gave the appellant no superior legal position over the association." / "The purpose of the statute is to ensure a high standard of education for Texas citizens *while at the same time* lessening the incentive for aliens to enter the United States illegally." (See **while at the same time.**)
    B. Awkward Repetitions. Samuel Johnson once advised his readers to "avoid ponderous ponderosity." The repetition of roots was purposeful, of course. Many legal writers, however, engage in such repetitions with no sense of irony, as in the phrases *build a building, refer to a reference, point out points, an individualistic individual.* As great a writer as he was, Chief Justice Marshall seems not to have had a stylistic design in the repetition here: "The question is, *in truth, a question of supremacy* [read *is, in truth, one of supremacy*]." *McCulloch v. Maryland,* 4 U.S. (4 Wheat.) 316, 433 (1819). Then again, Justice Marshall may have been striving for a rhetorical effect; in the sentences that follow, however, the repetitions are mere thoughtless errors: "Said *use of the trademark* [read *The trademark*] has been *used* in foreign commerce and interstate commerce in the United States continuously since 1926." The *use* has not been used, but rather the *trademark.* This sentence exemplifies one strain of ILLOGIC./ "The plaintiffs' number was number 37." [Read *The plaintiffs' number was 37.*]/ "This *judicially required warrant requirement* [read *This judicial requirement of a warrant*] has been described as a 'narrow one.'" / "Notice was mailed by registered mail." [Read *Notice was sent by registered mail.*]/ "But the basis of his liability here was based [read *His liability was based*] on a legal relationship only, not his primary negligence." / "The subdivided lots were sold as individual lots *with deed restrictions restricting development to single-family homes* [read *with deeds restricting development to single-family homes*]."/ "The resolution of the board of directors accepting property for shares must *specify the specific* [omit *specific*] property involved." / "By cheating, he avoids pursuing *knowledge* that he, according to his transcript,

should *know* [read *have*]." (One does not know knowledge; one has it.) See **injunction enjoining.**

C. Common Redundancies. Many of these are treated in separate entries. It is useful to be aware that phrases such as the following are redundant: *named nominee, adult parent* (but maybe this is no longer redundant), *to plead a plea, cost-expensive, active agent, end result, integral part, past history* (arguably established), *connect up or together, future forecast, merge together, mingle together, join together* (arguably acceptable), *mix together.* For idiomatic redundancies in the form of coupled synonyms, see DOUBLETS AND TRIPLETS OF LEGAL IDIOM.

reek; wreak. These homophones are occasionally confused. *Reek* = to give off an odor or vapor. As a noun, *reek* = an odorous vapor. *Wreak* = to inflict ⟨to wreak havoc⟩.

re-emerge is best hyphenated. See the next entry.

re-enactment, like most words in which the vowel ending the prefix is also the first letter of the word proper, should be hyphenated.

re-enforce. See **reinforce.**

re-enter; re-entry. Both terms are best hyphenated.

re-establish should be so hyphenated.

re-examination, primarily a BrE term, is equivalent to the AmE term *redirect examination.* Following are examples of the corresponding verb: "Witnesses examined in open court must be first examined in chief, then cross-examined, and then *re-examined.*" (Eng.)/ "After the cross-examination is concluded, the party who called the witness has a right to *re-examine* him." (Eng.) See **direct examination.**

referable. See **refer(r)able.**

refer back is a common REDUNDANCY, *refer* alone almost always being sufficient. E.g., "As to the use of memoranda, *refer back to* [read *refer to*] *Ward v. Morr Transfer & Storage Co.*, at page 446 *supra*."/ "Section 72411.5 simply *refers us back to* [read *refers us to*] the contract." Cf. **relate back.** *Refer back* may be justified in those rare instances in which it

means "to send back to one who or that which has previously been involved," as here: "The case is simply *referred back* to the arbitrator for a rewording of his opinion."

reference, as a verb meaning "to provide with references," is defensible. E.g., "The cross-*referenced* statute contains two subsections." It should not, however, be used for *refer*, as here: "He stated that, without *referencing* [read *referring* to] that file, he could not answer the question."

reference, n. See **allude & referral.**

referendary, -al. The latter is a NEEDLESS VARIANT for the term meaning "of or relating to a referendum."

referendum. Pl. *-da.* The English plural *-dums* is a secondary variant. See PLURALS (A).

refer(r)able, -ible. The preferred form is *referable*, which is accented on the first syllable; otherwise the final *-r-* would be doubled. The sense is "capable of being referred to." E.g., "The maxim of clean hands will not be invoked unless the inequitable conduct sought to be attributed to plaintiff is *referable* to the very transaction that is the source of the instant controversy."

Referrable often mistakenly appears; the form is old, but has long been held inferior to *referable*. E.g., "The only other causes of action pleaded by plaintiff *referrable* [read *referable*] to reimbursement are those of constructive fraud arising out of Tony's alleged operation of the corporation as his alter ego."/ "After review of the procedure followed, that board decided that the dispute was not *referrable* [read *referable*] to a public law board for reconsideration on the merits."

referral; reference. Both mean "the act of referring." *Reference* is the broader, general term. *Referral*, which began as an Americanism in the early twentieth century but now is used commonly in BrE as well, means specifically "the referring to a third party of personal information concerning another" or "the referring of a person to an expert or specialist for advice."

reflection; reflexion. The former spelling is preferred in both AmE and BrE. *Reflexion* was formerly common in British writing. Fowler recommended *-ction* in all senses.

reform; re-form. See RE- PAIRS.

refoulement /ri-*fowl-měnt*/ is a French term meaning "return of a person to his country of origin; the turning back of an immigrant." It originally appeared as a title for Article 33 of the 1951 Geneva Convention Relating to the Status of Refugees, which reads: "No contracting state shall expel or return (*'refouler'*) a refugee in any manner whatsoever to the frontiers of territories where his life or freedom would be threatened." (See *Lin v. Rinaldi*, 361 F. Supp. 177, 183 (D.N.J. 1973).) The title of that article of the Convention, *Refoulement*, is enclosed in quotation marks, no doubt signifying that in 1951 it was taken as a foreign word.

Its earliest known use as an English term is in the negative, and appears in *Chun v. Sava*, 708 F.2d 869, 877 n.25 (2d Cir. 1983): "[T]he United States appears to recognize a liberty interest, the right of *nonrefoulement* for a refugee." See also *Ramirez-Osorio v. Immigration & Naturalization Serv.*, 745 F.2d 937, 944 (5th Cir. 1984) ("there is a sufficiently secured right of *nonrefoulement* . . . to give rise to a protectible liberty interest"). The word is yet to be recorded in an English dictionary.

refractory, -tive. These terms have undergone DIFFERENTIATION. *Refractory* = stubborn, unmanageable, rebellious. E.g., "Under such circumstances the disappointed legatee may in a court of equity compel the sequestration of the legacy to the *refractory* legatee for the purpose of diminishing the amount of his disappointment." *Refractive* = that refracts light.

refrain; restrain. Both mean generally "to put restraints upon," but *refrain* is used of oneself in the sense "to abstain" ⟨he refrained from exchanging scurrilities with his accuser⟩, whereas *restrain* is used of another ⟨the police illegally restrained the complainant from going into the stadium⟩.

refus(e)nik = a Jew in the Soviet Union who has been refused permission to emigrate. The spelling *refusenik* is coming to be the standard spelling for this decade-old word.

refutation; refutal. The latter is an unnecessary and ill-formed variant of *refutation*. See NEEDLESS VARIANTS.

refutative, -tory. The latter is a NEEDLESS VARIANT.

refute is not synonymous with *rebut*. It does not mean merely "to counter an argument," but "to disprove beyond doubt; to prove a statement false." Yet the word is commonly misused for *rebut*, as here: "The findings of the Commissioner carry a presumption of correctness and the taxpayer has the burden of *refuting* [read *rebutting*] them."/ "Appellant was allowed to put on witnesses to *refute* [read *rebut*] the sexual harassment charges, and he or his lawyer, or both, were present to cross-examine all the university's witnesses." See **rebut.**

regard. This word is correctly used in the phrases *with regard to* and *in regard to*. The forms *with regards to* and *in regards to* are, to put it charitably, poor usages. The acceptable forms are best used as introductory phrases. Usually, however, they may advantageously be replaced by some simpler phrase such as *concerning, regarding, considering*, or even the simple prepositions *in, about*, or *for*.

The plural form, *regards*, is acceptable only in the phrase *as regards*. "With regards to [read *With regard to*] the 1962 adoption of the at-large election scheme, plaintiffs argue with some merit that more should have been said about this event." See **as regards & in regards to.**

regardless (= without regard to) should not be used for *despite* (= in spite of). E.g., "The appellants voted to reject the plan, reiterating the grounds for their suit against Martin; *regardless of* [read *despite*] the appellants' vote, the plan was approved with two-thirds of the creditors voting for the plan." See **irregardless.**

regardless whether is incorrect for *regardless of whether*. E.g., "Regardless whether [read *Regardless of whether*] COGSA or Texas state law controls, appellee is not liable for any damages caused by the delay that was not its fault." See **whether.**

regards. See **regard & as regards.**

regard to, in or *with*. See **in regards to & regard.**

regist(e)rable. The preferred form is *registrable* ⟨a registrable trademark⟩.

registrant /rej-ĭ-stränt/ does not rhyme, in the final syllable, with *restaurant*.

regress. See **egress.**

regretful; regrettable. Errors made are *regrettable*; the persons who have committed them, assuming a normal level of contrition, are *regretful*. Here the wrong word appears: "Many of the grievances appear justified; yet, *regretfully* [read *regrettably*], as the Supreme Court stated in *Radovich*, we are not here writing on a clean slate."

regulable = able to be regulated; susceptible to regulation. *Regulatable* is incorrect. See -ATABLE.

regulatory, -tive. The two forms of the adjective are used about equally often. *Regulatory* is accented in AmE on the first syllable, in BrE often on the third.

reify (= to make material, or convert mentally into a thing) is transitive only. Here it is misused as an intransitive verb: "As soon as Schultz's objective *reifies* [read *materializes*], critics will have a more solid basis on which to evaluate his policies."

reinforce (= to strengthen) is the universal form, though the noun is *enforce*, not *inforce*. (Likewise with *reinstate*.) Rather than hyphenate or use a diaeresis and retain the -*e*- in such words (e.g., re-enforce, re-enstate), the -*e*- in each word is changed to -*i*- when the prefix is added. *Re-enforce* (= to enforce again) is sometimes seen in AmE.

rein in, not *reign in*, is the correct form of the phrase meaning "to check, restrain." The metaphorical image is of the rider pulling on the reins of his horse to slow down (i.e., "hold his horses"). E.g., "Even when we make law judicially, we can tighten up the product dramatically if we *reign in* [read *rein in*] the staff attorneys and law clerks." Moreover, we can tighten up the product if we use idioms correctly.

reintegration; redintegration. *Reintegration* is the usual form of the word in the sense "the act of restoring to a state of wholeness; renewal; reconstruction." *Redintegration* was formerly more common in this sense; it is still used in scientific and other technical contexts.

reiterate; iterate. It is perhaps not too literalistic to use *iterate* in the sense "to repeat," and *reiterate* in the sense "to repeat a second time [i.e. to state a third time]." The distinction is observed only by the most punctilious writers, *reiterate* being the usual term in either sense.

rejoinder; surrejoinder. A *rejoinder*, in British practice, is the pleading served by a defendant in answer to the plaintiff's reply (the pleading in answer to the defense). In older practice, a *surrejoinder* is a plaintiff's pleading in reply to a defendant's rejoinder. The *CDL* notes that these pleadings are very rare in modern practice, and can be served only with leave of court.

reknowned. See **renowned.**

relate back is not a REDUNDANCY in law. It is the verbal invocation of the doctrine of *relation back*, q.v. "Whenever the claim or defense asserted in the amended pleading arose out of the conduct, transaction, or occurrence set forth or attempted to be set forth in the original pleading, the amendment *relates back* to the date of the original pleading." Fed.R.Civ.P. 15(c)./ "Because the 1982 mortgages are between different parties from the 1977 mortgages, their priority does not *relate back*."

relatedly is an adverb inferior even to *reportedly*, q.v. E.g., "*Relatedly*, Idaho also adheres to the tenets of concurrent causation." Some better connective such as *moreover* or *furthermore* should be used.

relate to ⟨the jury can relate to that experience⟩, when used as in the example just given, is a voguish expression characteristic of popular American cant in the 1970s and 1980s. It is unlikely to lose that stigma.

relater, -or. The former is the preferred spelling in the sense "narrator, one who relates." *Relator* is the legal term meaning "a private person at whose relation or in whose behalf an application for a quo warranto or mandamus is filed." E.g., "Members of the charitable organization can bring suit as *relators* in the name of the attorney general, but this is not always a practical remedy; not only do the *relators* bear the cost of the suit, but also the conduct of the litigation is controlled by the attorney general."

relation. **A.** And *relative.* These terms are interchangeable in the sense "a kinsman," although currently *relative* is slightly more usual.

B. And *relationship. Relation* is the broader term in this pair, inasmuch as *relationship* refers either to kinship or to the fact of being related by some bond. The phrase *in relationship with* is almost always incorrect for *in relation to.* To be correct, the phrase would almost have to be *in his* (or *its*) *relationship with,* etc.

C. Legal Sense. Some legal scholars, most notably Professor Leon Green, have used *relation* as "the best term available to express the value of one human being to another. . . . Relations may be classified as family relations, trade relations, professional and political relations, labor relations, and general social relations." L. Green, *Cases on Injuries to Relations* 1 (1940).

relation back, in legal ARGOT, refers to the doctrine that an act done at a later time is considered in the eyes of the law to have occurred at a prior time. E.g., "To the extent that a power of appointment has been thought of as a mere authority to act for the donor in the completion of a disposition initiated by the donor, the agency factor has dominated and the doctrine of *relation back* has been applied."/ "How a magistrate who has acted within his jurisdiction up to the point at which the missing evidence should have been, but was not, given, can thereafter be said, by a kind of *relation back,* to have had no jurisdiction over the charge at all, it is hard to see." (Eng.) See **relate back.**

relational = of or relating to relations between persons. E.g., "Out of the mass of decisions and scholarly writings it is now possible to chart a course of study for the lawyer whose professional activities will more and more be concerned with the protection of the *relational* interests of his clients" (i.e., interests in other human beings). The term is thus distinct from the adjective *relative.* See **relation** (C).

relationship. See **relation** (B).

relative, n.; relation. See **relation** (A).

relative(ly) to. *Relative to* is a variant of *in relation to* or *in comparison with;* usually one of these longer phrases adds clarity. Partridge called *relative to* GOBBLEDYGOOK. In no event is *relatively to* proper. "*Relatively to* [read *In relation to*] her, his act was not negligent."

The phrase is also an awkward substitute for *concerning* or *regarding*: "The latter part of the paragraph contains language similar to that of paragraph (a) *relative to* [read *concerning*] the discharge of the corporation's liability if an agreement is signed by the parties."

relator. See **relater, -or.**

relatrix. See SEXISM (C).

relay; re-lay. See RE- PAIRS.

release; re-lease. See RE- PAIRS.

release on licence. See **parole.**

relegate; delegate. To *relegate* is to consign to an inferior position or to transfer for decision or execution. E.g., "The administratrix of the prisoner's estate was not *relegated* exclusively to an FTCA remedy." To *delegate* is to commit (as powers) to an agent or representative or to depute (someone).

relevance, -cy. The former is preferred in both AmE and BrE. *Relevancy* was the predominant form in American and British writings on evidence of the nineteenth century, but now *relevance* is more common except in Scotland. See **irrelevance.**

relevant is often misused for *applicable* or *appropriate.* E.g., "The board of directors might then allocate such amounts among the several outstanding series of stock on the basis of any criteria it deems *relevant* [read *applicable* or *appropriate*]." See **material.**

relevant part, in. See **in pertinent part.**

relic; relict; relique. *Relic* = a surviving trace or memorial; something interesting because of its age. E.g., "The Rule in Shelley's Case is a *relic,* not of the horse-and-buggy days, but of the preceding stone-cart-and-oxen days." *Relique* is an archaic spelling of the word.

Relict = widow; survivor. Inasmuch as *relict* is used only in legal writing, is unknown to laymen, is sometimes mistaken for *relic,* and invariably means merely "widow" or "widower," we might justifiably seek to conform to general English usage and write *widow(er)*. Some legal writers have resorted to the tautologous DOUBLET *widow and relict*: "After the husband's death, the wife obtained probate of his will in common form in which she is described as '*widow and relict* of the deceased.'" (Eng.) Widows unfamiliar with the term will not take kindly to being called *relicts*.

relief. See **remedy.**

relief over. See **over.**

relique. See **relic.**

relitigate (= to litigate again) is not recorded in the dictionaries, but is an implied form that is unquestionably useful. E.g., "The mere fact that the en banc court affirmed the district court's vacation of the consent decree and has remanded for further proceedings fails to establish any reason to *relitigate* the grant of limited intervenor status."

remainder. See **rest, residue, and remainder** & DOUBLETS.

remainder; reversion. These terms are to be distinguished. "A *remainder* is defined as 'what is left' of an entire grant of lands or tenements after a preceding part of the same grant or estate has been disposed of in possession, whose regular expiration the remainder must await. . . . A *reversion* is the remnant of an estate continuing in the grantor, undisposed of, after the grant of a part of his interest. It differs from a *remainder* in that it arises by act of law, whereas a *remainder* is by act of the parties. A *reversion*, moreover, is the remnant left in the grantor, whilst a *remainder* is the remnant of the whole estate disposed of, after a preceding part of the same has ɔeen given away." 1 J.B. Minor, *Law of Real Property* 916, 1005 (2d ed. 1910). See **reversion.**

remainderman (= the person to whom a remainder is devised) was formerly two words, but is now regularly spelled as a single word. E.g., "A court may find, for example, that the donees take the property as joint tenants, as tenants in common, or that one donee takes as life tenant and the others as *remaindermen*." See SEXISM (B).

remainder over. See **over.**

remand, n.; **remandment.** The latter is a NEEDLESS VARIANT, as is *remission*, q.v.

remand, v.t. **A.** Objects. People as well as causes may be *remanded* (or "sent back"). E.g., "Fagan, who pleaded not guilty to the charge, was *remanded* to Brixton Prison for psychiatric and medical reports." (Eng.)

B. *Remand back* is a REDUNDANCY. "*Maine v. Thornton* has been *remanded back* [omit *back*] to the Maine Supreme Judicial Court for action not inconsistent with the Supreme Court's decision."/ "The court *remanded* the case *back* [omit *back*] to the circuit court for a new hearing." See **send back.**

C. Pronunciation. *Remand* is pronounced /ri-**mand**/ both as noun and as verb.

remanent. See **remnant.**

remark; re-mark. See RE- PAIRS.

remediable; remedial. *Remedial* (= providing a remedy; corrective; curative) is frequently pejorative in lay language ⟨remedial learning⟩. In law, however, it usually acts as the adjective for *legal remedy*: "The constructive trust is a *remedial* device imposed to prevent a person from retaining title to property if the retention would unjustly enrich him at the expense of another."

Remediable = capable of being remedied. E.g., "A refusal to enforce that stems from a conflict of interest, that is the result of a bribe, vindictiveness, or retaliation, or that traces to personal or other corrupt motives ought to be judicially *remediable*."

remediless; remedyless. The former form is correct (by analogy with *merciless* or *penniless*). The term is equivalent to *irremediable*.

remise = to give up, surrender, make over to another, release (any right, property, etc.) (*OED*). The term is fast becoming a legal ARCHAISM, for a number of words are more specific and more widely understood.

remission. As a noun meaning "the act of remanding," *remission* is a NEEDLESS VARIANT of *remand*, n., q.v. Here is an example suggesting the writer's indulgence in INELEGANT VARIATION: "[A]n appellate court 'may *remand* the cause. . . .' The procedure for *remission* [read *remand*] of the cause to the lower court . . . is further regulated and controlled generally by the rules of the appellate courts." 14A S. Flanagan, *Cyclopedia of Federal Procedure* § 69.01 at 65 (1984). See **remittance &** **renvoi.**

remit = (1) to pardon; (2) to abate, slacken; mitigate; (3) to refer (a matter for decision) to some authority, send back (a case) to a lower court; (4) to send or put back; or (5) to transmit (as money). Senses (1) and (2) are uncommon today. Sense (4) is frequent in legal writing: "[T]he breach by the landlord of his covenant does not justify the refusal of the tenant to perform his covenant to pay rent. . . . The tenant is *remitted* to the right to recoup himself in the damages resulting from the landlord's breach of his covenant to repair." *Mitchell v. Weiss*, 26 S.W.2d 699, 700-01 (Tex. Civ. App.—El Paso 1930)./ "In *remitting* the members of this class to a solution at the ballot box, rather than dangling the carrot of reform by judicial injunction before them, the district court followed the course of wisdom and practicality."

Sense (3) was formerly common in legal prose. *Remit* is here used synonymously with *remand*: "The order should be reversed, with costs to the appellant payable out of the estate, and the proceedings *remitted* to the surrogate for entry of a decree in accordance with this opinion."/ "Nolan, Presiding Justice, dissents and votes to reverse and to *remit* the proceeding to Surrogate's Court for the entry of a decree as prayed for in the objections interposed by appellants."/ "The case is *remitted* to the Superior Court for the entry of a judgment on the verdict as directed." Sense (5) is also quite common (upon receiving the demand letter, she promptly remitted the amount due).

remittance; remittal; remission; remitment. *Remission* is the noun corresponding to senses (1) through (4) of *remit, q.v.*; it means either "forgiveness" or "diminution of force, effect, degree, or violence." *Remittal* is a NEEDLESS VARIANT. *Remittance* corresponds to sense (5) of *remit*, and means "money sent to a person, or the sending of money to a person." E.g., "On the other hand is the innocent shipper who paid the full amount of the charges to such defaulting party for *remittance* to the agent." *Remitment* is a NEEDLESS VARIANT.

remitter, -or; remittitur. A *remitter* is one who sends a remittance. (See the previous entry.) The *-or* spelling is inferior. Formerly it was used as a technical term for the relation back of a later defective title to an earlier valid title to an estate. A *remittitur* is the process by which the court reduces the damages awarded in a jury verdict.

Remittitur of record is entirely distinct; it refers to the return of the trial record by a court of appeal to the trial court.

remittitur. See **remitter.**

remittitur of record. See **remitter.**

remittor. See **remitter.**

remnant; remanent. The latter is an archaic spelling to be avoided.

remonstrate. The second syllable is accented /ri-**mon**-strayt/ in AmE, the first syllable /**rem**-ŏn-strayt/ in BrE.

remote has a special legal meaning in contexts involving the Rule against Perpetuities: "beyond the 21 years after some life in being by which a devise must vest." E.g., "In *Leake v. Robinson*, there actually were afterborn children with respect to whom the remainder might have vested *remotely*."

removable. See **remov(e)able.**

remove, re-move. See RE- PAIRS.

remove, -al. These terms have procedural senses in law that are generally unknown to laymen. *Removal* = the transfer of an action from a court on one jurisdictional level to a court on another level. Thus, in the U.S., some state-court actions may be *removed* to federal court if the proper statutory basis exists. (The correlative term for transferring the action back to state court is *remand, q.v.*) In G.B., *removal* is the transfer of a High Court action from a district registry to London (or vice versa) or of a county court action to the High court (or vice versa) (CDL).

remov(e)able. The preferred spelling is *removable*. See MUTE E.

remuneration. So spelled; *renumeration* is an all-too-common misspelling and mispronunciation.

renant. See ren(i)ant.

rencontre; rencounter. Very little is certain about these words. *W9* lists the main entry for this word under *rencontre;* the *COD* lists the main entry under *rencounter,* as did *W2.* The *COD* labels both archaic, although the Merriam-Webster dictionaries list *rencontre* as a current word in the senses (1) "a hostile meeting or contest between forces or individuals; combat"; and (2) "a casual meeting." The *OED Supp.* adds the sense "an organized but informal meeting of scientists" under *rencontre,* dating from 1975 in BrE.

rend. See heart-rending.

render = (1) to make, cause to be; or (2) to give. *Render* is a FORMAL WORD worthy of describing judicial actions, although generally it is used in this context primarily in the U.S. For example, with regard to sense (2), judicial decisions are *rendered.* Nonjudicial responses are *given,* not *rendered:* "The majority seizes upon the petitioner's seven-word response, 'Uh, yeah, I'd like to do that,' *rendered* [read *uttered*] during a colloquy that could not have taken five minutes." Such an inarticulate statement from a habeas corpus petitioner should hardly be said to have been *rendered.* See heart-rending.

In AmE, the usual expression is that judgment is *rendered;* in BrE it is commonly written that judgment is *given.* E.g., "Judgment accordingly was *given* for the plaintiffs for the balance of the claim." (Aus.)

rendezvous, v.t. & v.i., is inflected *rendezvouses* in the present tense and *rendezvoused* in the past tense. The present participle is *rendezvousing.* The plural of the noun *rendezvous* is *rendezvous,* not *-vouses* ⟨several rendezvous⟩.

rendition (= the action of rendering, giving out or forth) is labeled an Americanism in the *OED,* but the *OED Supp.* notes that this sense of the term has now spread throughout G.B.

rendition of judgment; entry of judgment. Courts have traditionally distinguished between *rendition of judgment* (= the oral or written ruling containing the judgment entered) and *entry of judgment* (= the formal recordation of a judgment by the court). It has been said that *rendition* is the ul-timate judicial act, whereas *entry* is merely ministerial in nature and evidentiary in purpose.

This distinction at one time posed problems in some cases in which no terminal judicial intervention was required, as with a jury's general verdict. In current American practice (Fed. R. Civ. P. 58), the verdict *rendered* by a jury or a decision *rendered* by the judge is converted into an 'inchoate' judgment, effective upon *entry.*

renege; renegue; renig. The first is the preferred form in AmE, the second the standard spelling in BrE, although the first is making inroads. *Renig* is a variant spelling in AmE.

renewal of judgment; revival of judgment. "[G]enerally speaking there exists an important distinction between *revival* and *renewal* of judgments. *Revival,* by judicial decree on scire facias, removes dormancy and authorizes belated issuance of a writ of execution. Conversely, *renewal,* by civil action on the judgment, consists [in] a new money judgment endowed with its own actionability, executability, and creation of a lien." S. Riesenfeld, *Creditors' Remedies and Debtors' Protection* 101 (West 1979).

ren(i)ant. This obsolete term from early common law (meaning "denying") was more commonly spelled *renant.*

renig. See renege.

renowned. So spelled; *reknowned* is wrong but fairly common for *renowned.* The noun is *renown;* there is no verb, though the past participial adjective exists.

rent, n.; rental, n. Generally, one should not use *rental* where *rent* will suffice. *Rental* denotes the amount paid as rent, or the income received from rent. "The lessee agrees to pay said *rental.*" If the writer had merely meant that the lessee must pay the rent (as opposed to a specific sum due periodically, e.g., monthly), then *rent* would have been the better term.

rent, v.t., is ambiguous insofar as it may refer to the action taken by either the lessor or the lessee; the word has had this doubleness of sense from at least the sixteenth century. Both the lessee and the lessor are *renters*, so to speak, though usually this term is reserved for tenants. Cf. **lease from; lease to.**

rental, n. See **rent,** n.

rent(-)charge. Hyphenated in the *OED*, this word is now one word in BrE (as in the Rentcharges Act of 1977), and two words in AmE.

renvoi /rĕn-*voi*/ (F. "sending back") = the problem arising in private international law when one country's rule on conflict of laws refers a case to the law of a foreign country, and the law of that country refers the case either back to the law of the first country (*remission*) or to the law of a third country (*transmission*) (*CDL*).

reoccur is a NEEDLESS VARIANT of the much preferable *recur*. See **recurrence.**

reparable; repairable. Of these two terms, the former term has acquired a broader meaning. Used of damages, losses, or injuries, *reparable* means "capable of being set right again." Used of things, *repairable* means "capable of being repaired." The antonyms of these words are *irreparable* and *unrepairable*.

reparative, -tory. The latter is a NEEDLESS VARIANT.

repay back is a REDUNDANCY.

repealer = (1) one who repeals; or (2) a legislative act abrogating an earlier act. Sense (2) is of recent origin. E.g., "Another method of reviving the judgment lien was docketing and indexing a writ of execution, now subject to special *repealer*."

repeat again; repeat back. Both are REDUNDANCIES.

repel; repulse. *Repulse* is primarily physical ⟨after repeated warnings, he was repulsed from the premises⟩, *repel* primarily figurative—hence *repel* is the verb corresponding most closely in meaning to the adjective *repulsive*. A person who experiences *repulsion* is *repelled*.

In each of the following sentences, *repel* is acceptably used as a near-synonym of *rebut*: "In such cases the burden of proof rests upon the party claiming the benefit under the

transaction to *repel* the presumption thus created by law by showing a severance of the relation."/ "The circumstances *repel* any thought of fraud and speak cogently of the integrity of the instrument under review."/ "Where there was evidence both that the will existed and that it was surreptitiously withdrawn from the possession of the testatrix, the presumption of revocation might have been *repelled*."

repellent; repulsive. Both mean, lit., "causing to turn away." *Repulsive* is the stronger word; it applies to whatever disgusts or offends in the extreme. *Repellant*, a variant spelling of *repellent*, is to be eschewed. See **repel.**

repetitive; repetitious. A certain DIFFERENTIATION is emerging between these terms. *Repetitive* generally means "repeating, containing repetition." It is a largely colorless term. *Repetitious*, which has taken on pejorative connotations, means "tediously repeating." E.g., "The court's holding today has the effect of requiring precisely this kind of *repetitious* appellate review."/ "None of the discovery sought, which in some instances is *repetitious*, cumulative, and peripheral, is relevant as far as the teams are concerned."

rephrase for *paraphrase*. One cannot use these two words interchangeably. One may *paraphrase* either statements or persons, but one may *rephrase* only statements. The writer of this sentence incorrectly used *rephrase* for *paraphrase*: "To *rephrase* [read *paraphrase*] Justice Frankfurter, newspapers are inherently available to all as a mode of expression."

replace; re-place. Here *replace* is used for *re-place*: "Where land or chattels have been wrongfully taken from a person, he can be *replaced* [read *re-placed*] substantially in the position which he formerly occupied by restoring to him in specie that which was taken from him." See RE- PAIRS.

replenish makes the noun *replenishment*, not *repletion* (= a surfeit, plethora).

replete means not "complete," but "abundantly supplied with; full to overflowing." *Repleat* is an infrequent misspelling committed, e.g., by the court in *Commonwealth v. Belmonte*, 502 A.2d 1241, 1252 (Pa. Super. 1985).

repleviable; replevisable. Blackstone was ahead of his time in using *repleviable* rather than *replevisable*. The *OED* contains its main entry under the latter term, whereas *W2* and *W3* state that *replevisable* is now rare and define the term at *repleviable*. Another BrE dictionary, *Lloyd's Encyclopaedic Dictionary* (1895), concurs with the Merriam-Webster dictionaries in their preference for *repleviable*.

replevin; replevy. The latter is an archaic variant of *replevin* as a noun, although it still appears: "A plaintiff who sought to recover a firearm allegedly illegally seized by a treasury agent was precluded from *replevy* [read *replevin*] of the weapon by a statute providing that all property taken under any revenue law of the United States shall not be *repleviable*."/ "The statute was designed to aid the collection of federal taxes by preventing a *replevy* [read *replevin*] under a state law of property seized by the collector." *Replevin* is the name of both the writ and the cause of action. See **detinue.**

replevin, v.t., is an obsolete variant of the verb *replevy*, q.v.

replevisable. See **repleviable.**

replevy, v.t., = to recover possession of (as goods wrongfully seized) upon giving security to try the right to them in court, and to return them if the suit fails. E.g., "The difficulty that arises in an attempt to *replevy* money is to describe it with that degree of accuracy which is required in replevin." For the noun, see **replevin.**

reportedly. "Newspapermen and broadcasters live on a steady diet of this adverb," wrote Wilson Follett. "It is so lacking in the characteristics of a respectable adverb that one would like to see its use confined to cable messages, where it saves money and can await translation into English." *Modern American Usage* 279 (1966). E.g., "Such convictions are extremely rare, and *reportedly there had been only four previous ones* [read, according to Follett, *only four previous ones had been reported*] since the law was passed."

To be sure, adverbs in *-edly* are often cumbersome and opaque (at first). *Reportedly* is not nearly as common in legal writing as *allegedly*, *confessedly*, and *assertedly*. All such forms ought to be avoided unless there is virtually no

other way of conveniently saying what needs to be said with comparable conciseness. If that test is met, as it often is, we should use *reportedly* or any of the other terms without apology. See -EDLY, **allegedly & confessedly.**

repose is not "indefinite dormancy," but rather suggests temporary rest, after which there will again be activity. Hence the court in this pronouncement was not aspersing the doctrine in question as strongly as it might have thought: "As to sovereign immunity, that doctrine, insofar as it has been created by courts, seems headed for a deserved *repose*." This is slovenly writing that makes little sense—why "insofar as it has been created by the courts," which is ambiguous? The judge might better have written, "Sovereign immunity as created by the courts seems to be moribund." This says the same thing in almost half the words. See CUTTING OUT THE CHAFF.

Statute of repose is a curious AmE legal usage for a statute that sets up a legal defense, usu. by the passage of time: "[Article 5536a] is the ultimate statute of *repose* for architects, engineers, and builders. . . . [I.e., it] provides an absolute defense to a registered or licensed architect or engineer once more than ten years have passed since the substantial completion of any allegedly defective improvement to real property." *Brown v. M.W. Kellogg Co.*, 743 F.2d 265, 267 (5th Cir. 1984)./ "[W]here injury or death is alleged to have resulted from disease, the six-year statute of *repose* is inapplicable." *Guy v. E. I. DuPont de Nemours & Co.*, 792 F.2d 457, 460 (4th Cir. 1986).

repository, -tary. The former spelling is standard. E.g., "No court has yet suggested that Congress may insulate a compelled disclosure statute from Fifth Amendment attack by the tactic of creating a nongovernmental *repository* for the disclosures."/ "The petitions sought review of the Secretary's designation of two sites in Texas as potentially acceptable for development as nuclear waste *repositories* under the Nuclear Waste Policy Act." Cf. **depositary, -tory.**

represent; re-present. See RE- PAIRS.

representation; misrepresentation. One should be careful in using these two terms; if by *fraudulent representation* one really means *fraudulent misrepresentation*, then the latter phrase ought to be used.

reprise; reprisal. *Reprise* = (1) an annual deduction, duty, or payment out of a manor or estate, as an annuity or the like; or (2) (in music) a repetition. *Reprisal* = an act of retaliation, usu. of one nation against another but short of war.

reprobate (= to reject [as an instrument or deed] as not binding on one) is the antonym in Scots law of *approbate*, q.v.

repugn. See **impugn.**

repugnant, in law, is frequently used in its oldest sense, "contrary or contradictory to," used esp. of two things in relation to each other. E.g., "The annexing of such incident to such contract would be *repugnant* to the express terms of the contract." (Eng.)/ "The validity of the state statute was drawn into question on grounds that it was *repugnant* to the United States Constitution." In lay usage, *repugnant* today denotes "exciting distaste or aversion."

repulse. See **repel.**

repulsive. See **repellent.**

reputation. See **character.**

reputational (= of or pertaining to reputation) is not recorded in *W3*, but dates from 1921 in the *OED Supp.* The term is useful in law: "Nor is any liberty or *reputational* interest implicated." *Findeisen v. North East Independent School District*, 749 F.2d 234, 240 (5th Cir. 1984) (Garwood, J., dissenting)./ "Management may well value more highly the time that would be expended in litigation and any *reputational* effects of a loss, whereas plaintiffs might well assign a high value to the potentially recoverable damages."

requiescat in pace. See R.I.P.

require. See **necessitate.**

requisite. See **prerequisite.**

res; re; rem. *Res* (= thing) is used in a number of different ways in legal contexts. Most often it is a synonym of *principal* or *corpus* in reference to funds. E.g., "When the *res* of a gratuitous private express trust is excessive for the purpose specified by the settlor, a resulting trust of the excess is presumed for the benefit of the settlor or his successors in interest."/ "The difficulties of applying the common-law concept of joint tenancy to a fluctuating *res* prevent the traditional joint tenancy estate from providing a logical solution."/ "In the charitable trust situation, cy pres operates to prevent failure of most charitable trusts and to dispose of any excess income or surplus trust *res*." See **corpus.**

Yet it is often used in its literal sense "thing," in reference to a particular thing, known or unknown. E.g., "We found, as a matter of trademark law, that the *res* in the case, the registered trademark of the Cuban corporation, was located in the United States."/ "The courts have consistently emphasized the need for circumspection in undertaking any action that might result in the interference with a *res* in the custody of another court and thereby might violate the autonomy of the state and federal judicial systems."/ "Defendants argue that the superior court is without jurisdiction of the cause of action pleaded because the court does not have jurisdiction of the *res*—the realty in Illinois."

Res has even been used as a EUPHEMISM for "sexual organ" in legal writing: "[T]he weight of authority, both English and American, is that although [for rape to be proved] some penetration must be shown beyond a reasonable doubt, it need not be full penetration; nothing more than *res in re* being requisite." 44 Am. Jur. *Rape* § 3 (1942).

Rem is the accusative case of the noun, and *re* is the ablative case. See **jus in re(m) & in personam** (B).

res adjudicata. See **res judicata.**

res administrata is a NEOLOGISM meaning "res judicata as applied to administrative decisions." E.g., "Principles of res judicata— perhaps better dubbed *res administrata*—can apply to successive proceedings before a single agency." 18 Wright, Miller & Cooper, *Federal Practice and Procedure* § 4475 (1981).

rescindable; rescissible. The first form is better because of its more recognizable relation to the verb. It is the only form listed in the *OED*; *W3* contains both forms.

rescindment is a NEEDLESS VARIANT of *rescission*, q.v.

rescission; recision; recission. In the sense "an act of rescinding, annulling, vacating, or canceling," the first form is the best. *Recision* is from the Latin verb *recisio*, meaning "to cut back, lop off." Through the process known as folk etymology, this word became the altered form of *rescission*, the true Latin (fr. the accusative *rescissionem*) and English form. *Rescission* is preferable also because of the consistency of spelling between verb and noun (*rescind/rescission*). *Recission* and *recision*, common misspellings resulting from combinations of *recision* and *rescission*, are not accepted spellings. The misspelling *recission* is used, e.g., in *Malone v. Safety-Guard Mfg. Co.*, 748 F.2d 312, 314-15 (5th Cir. 1984); and the inferior spelling *recision* is used here: "[T]he customary legal incidence of voidance would follow, including the availability of a suit for *recision* [read *rescission*] or for an injunction against continued operation of the contract." *Transamerica Mortgage Advisors, Inc. v. Lewis*, 444 U.S. 11, 19 (1979). See **recension**.

The sound of the *-ss-* in *rescission* is like that in *precision*, not that in *permission*. This is one of very few words in the English language in which the *-ss-* has the sound /zh/ instead of /sh/. Two others are *fission* (in AmE) and *abscission*. Cf. *-mission* (with /sh/) in its many forms.

rescissory is the adjective corresponding to the noun *rescission* and the verb *to rescind*. Cf. **rescindable**.

research; re-search. See RE- PAIRS.

res gestae (lit., "things done") has, it seems, irrevocably ensconced itself in the terminology of the law of evidence, although Wigmore considered it "not only entirely useless, but even positively harmful." 6 J.H. Wigmore, *Evidence in Trials at Common Law* § 1767 at 255 (4th ed. rev. Chadbourn 1976). The *CDL* defines it as "the events with which the court is concerned or others contemporaneous with them." In the law of evidence, *res gestae* may be either a rule of relevance that makes testimony about the events forming part of the *res gestae* admissible, or an exception to the hearsay rule allowing for the admissibility of *res gestae* (e.g., if they accompany or explain a declarant's contempora-

neous state of mind or physical sensations). See TERMS OF ART.

residence, -cy. Although both are used in the sense "domicile," only *residence* is used as a FORMAL WORD for "house" ⟨a three-story residence⟩. It would be useful to restrict *residence* to this sense, and to use *residency* in the sense "domicile," but there is little consistency in today's usage. Following are some typical uses, with suggested revisions in brackets for the first two specimens: "Both those favoring lengthy *residence* [read *residency*] requirements and those opposing all requirements pleaded their cases during the congressional hearings on the Social Security Act."/ "Thirty-three states required at least one year of *residence* [read *residency*] in a particular town or county."/ "Unlike those states which condition veterans' preferences on either *residency* at the time of service or length of *residency* in the state, New Mexico requires only that a veteran establish *residency* sometime before a cut-off date, and that he currently qualify as a state resident." See **citizenship**.

resident. See **citizen** (A).

residuary; residual; residuous. In the context of residues of estates and trusts, *residuary* is the preferred adjective. E.g., "The instrument is signed by the testatrix and properly attested; the *residuary* dispositions are therefore revoked."/ "The codicil contained a bequest of his *residuary* estate to charity, but the bequest was not effective because the testator died within thirty days after the codicil was executed."

Yet there are many examples of *residual* used in such contexts. E.g., "We have before us taxpayers who have inherited what is effectively a *residual* [read *residuary*] estate."/ "On May 5, 1949, decedent executed a codicil partially revamping his testamentary scheme by establishing, in lieu of the outright *residual* [read *residuary*] gift, a trust for the benefit of his son Joseph." *Residual* and *residuary* are susceptible to INELEGANT VARIATION: "In 1965 the testatrix executed a holographic instrument distributing all the assets she controlled, the *residual* [read *residuary*] disposition omitting Mariana Erback, who was one of the *residuary* distributees in the 1945 will."

When one writes of a person's capabilities and functions remaining after an injury, *residual* is the correct term: "She retained a *residual* function to perform her relevant past work as a nurse's aid."/ "Dr. Barrio's final report stated that claimant's *residual* functional disability will interfere with her normal activities at work, which require significant physical effort as a sewing machine operator." *Residuous* is a NEEDLESS VARIANT of the other two words.

residue; residuum; residual, n.; residuary, n. Both *residue* and *residuum* (pl. -*dua*) mean "that which remains." *Residue* is the usual and preferred term for contexts involving decedents' estates. It means "the property comprising a deceased person's estate after payment of his debts, funeral expenses, costs of administration, and all specific and demonstrative bequests" (*CDL*). E.g., "I give, bequeath, and devise the rest, *residue*, and remainder of my estate of every description, of which I shall die seised and possessed, to my son X."/ "The unmistakable intention of the testatrix, apparent upon the fact of the will, was that the *residue* of her estate should go to the person who should have given her the best care in her declining years." Although Blackstone wrote that "the surplus or *residuum* must be paid to the residuary legatee," *residuum* is now to be avoided in such contexts: "The court ordered the executor to divide the *residuum* [read *residue*] among the residuary legatees."

Residuum is a technical term used correctly in chemical contexts. E.g., "There is testimony that a blend of *residuum* and diesel fuel or kerosene would satisfy the definition of crude oil."

Residue and *residuum* often tempt those who fancy INELEGANT VARIATION. In the phrase *residue of a residue*, there is nothing wrong with repeating the word *residue*. Varying the form of the word is an affectation: "Some courts have held that the gift passes by intestacy on the theory that there can be no *residue of a residuum* [read *residue of a residue*]."

Residual, n., = a remainder; an amount still remaining after the main part is subtracted or accounted for (*OED*). E.g., "Some *residual* of the old civic duty to 'cry out' remains."

Residuary, when used elliptically as a noun for such full phrases as *residuary estate* (= *residue*) is uncommon and possibly confusing. It should be avoided. E.g., "He received the *residuary* [read *residue*] of his parents' estate long after his mother's death.

resign; re-sign. See RE- PAIRS.

resign is almost always intransitive in the U.S. ⟨resign from office⟩, but is often transitive in England ⟨resign the office⟩.

res integra; res nova. These terms are fairly common in legal writing. Both terms mean "an undecided question; a case of first impression"; *res nova* is used primarily in the U.S. and *res integra* in G.B. Following are examples of the latter: "If the matter were *res integra* in this jurisdiction I should, for my part, have felt very much tempted to follow the views expressed by the majority of the court in *Skelton v. Collins*." (Eng.)/ "If the matter were *res integra* it might not, to my mind, be a hopeless argument, but in the light of the long-standing law it is today an argument that must be rejected." (Eng.)/ "The court added that if it were *res integra* it would hold that calling a man a rogue or a woman a whore in public company is actionable."

American legal writers use *res nova* far more often than *res integra*. E.g., "Never cite a lower court decision to a higher court; however, if you have found a point that is *res nova* in the higher court but which is found among the decisions of a lower court, cite it with a suggestion of apology."/ "The case involves many issues that are *res nova*, and appellant feels that oral argument would be of great benefit to the court and to both parties." See **first impression, case of.**

res ipsa loquitur (= the thing speaks for itself) is known in G.B. but is far more common in the U.S., where it has become familiar enough that *res ipsa case* and even *resipsy* have become lawyers' elliptical colloquialisms. *Res ipsa loquitur* is one of those LATINISMS that have become so common in lawyers' ARGOT, or more specifically as a TERM OF ART, that their usefulness is unquestioned. The last syllable is sometimes misspelled -*or* or -*er*.

The tendency toward the elliptical dropping of the final word in the phrase is illustrated in this specimen: "The doctrine of *res ipsa* does not relieve the plaintiff of the burden of proving negligence." Kramer, *The Rules of Evidence in Negligence Cases* 35 (3d ed. 1963).

resistible, -able. The former spelling is preferred. See -ABLE (A).

resister, -or. The former is the term meaning "one who resists." The latter is a technical electrical term.

res judicata; res adjudicata. For distinctions between this and related terms, see **collateral estoppel.** The phrase meaning literally "a thing adjudicated" is now universally spelled *res judicata.* The other form, *res adjudicata*, ought to be rejected as a NEEDLESS VARIANT. *Adjudicata* was formerly common, e.g.: "The court held that the final judgment in the original probate proceedings was not binding on the afterborn grandchildren; hence the defense of *res adjudicata* was without merit." It is almost never seen in contemporary legal writing.

Res judicata takes *of* or *to.* E.g., "[A]n acquittal on one [indictment] could not be pleaded as *res judicata* of the other." *Dunn v. United States*, 284 U.S. 390, 393 (1932) (per Holmes, J.)/ "If Stewart had been separately indicted and tried for armed robbery and a hung jury resulted in a mistrial, that could not be pleaded as *res judicata* to a subsequent separate indictment for attempted second degree murder." *Stewart v. Blackburn*, 746 F.2d 262, 264 (5th Cir. 1984). The plural, rarely if ever used, is *res judicatae.*

In American legal writing the phrase is frequently used as a kind of predicate adjective, as here: "A judgment is not *res judicata* as to, or legally enforceable against, a nonparty." See **res administrata** & **chose jugée.**

res nova. See **res integra.**

resolvable, -ible; resoluble. The first is far more common than the others in meaning "able to be resolved." E.g., "We held that the pilot base dispute was a 'major' dispute subject to the court's jurisdiction and not a 'minor' dispute *resolvable* by the Railway Labor Act's adjustment mechanism." *Resoluble* has the liability of meaning also "capable of being dissolved again." The variant spelling *resolvible* is to be avoided.

resort. See **recourse.**

resound; re-sound. See RE- PAIRS.

respect. The phrases *in respect of* and *with respect to* are usually best replaced by simpler expressions, such as single prepositions. See **regard** & **as regards.**

respectfully. The term is greatly overworked in lawyers' writing directed at judges. E.g., "If this court were to allow recovery based on such speculative evidence, then we would *respectfully* wonder where this might lead us." See **respective.**

respective; respectively. Both of these terms are overused in legal prose. Often they add absolutely nothing, as here: "Appellee's and appellant's *respective* citizenships of France and Georgia therefore supported diversity jurisdiction." As Fowler wrote, "Delight in these words is a widespread but depraved taste; like soldiers and policeman, they have work to do, but, when the work is not there, the less we see of them the better; of ten sentences in which they occur, nine would be improved by their removal" (*MEU1* 500).

A well-known form book contains a petition for recovery of unpaid rent with the closing, just before the line for the lawyer's signature, "Respectively submitted." One might have thought that everyone knows the difference between *respective* and *respectful*, q.v.

responsibility, when used in the sense "liability," is a LEGALISM not generally understood by laymen, although its sense is sometimes deducible. E.g., "The mayor's freedom from monetary *responsibility* stems from his sovereign immunity." See **vicarious responsibility.**

-ress. See SEXISM (C).

restaters = authors of the Restatements.

restaurateur. So spelled; *restauranteur* is incorrect, although the Merriam-Webster dictionaries list it as a variant.

rest in peace. See R.I.P.

restitutive, -tory; restitutional, -ary. *Restitutional* and *restitutionary* are not recognized adjectives; the correct adjectival forms of *restitution* are *restitutive* and *-ory*, the former being preferred. Nevertheless, the unrecognized forms are used frequently in the law of damages, though they add nothing to our already existing terms. E.g., "A great deal of *restitutional* [read *restitutive*] law developed under the wing of indebitatis assumpsit."/ "The *restitutionary* [read *restitutive*], remedial goal in contracts cases, the return of the parties to a broken contract to their original positions, is the antithesis of the usual aim of fulfilling the plaintiff's expectancy."/ "While the United States has yielded sovereign immunity with respect to liability on its actual contracts and its torts, it has not yet done so with regard to suits of a *restitutionary* [read *restitutive*] nature."/ "In certain other cases a plaintiff is merely seeking protection of his *restitutionary* [read *restitutive*] interest."

restive, despite its misleading appearance, does not mean "restful." Formerly it meant "stubborn, refusing to budge," but now has become synonymous with *restless*, a development that some language critics lament.

restoration; restoral. The latter is a NEEDLESS VARIANT.

restore; re-store. See RE- PAIRS.

restrain. See **refrain.**

rest, residue, and remainder is a collocation beloved by draftsmen of wills. Mellinkoff recommends *all other property* in its stead. D. Mellinkoff, *The Language of the Law* 362 (1963). The advice is well taken; but the triplet is unlikely to be misunderstood or misconstrued. See DOUBLETS AND TRIPLETS OF LEGAL IDIOM. See also **residue.**

RESTRICTIVE AND NONRESTRICTIVE CLAUSES. Restrictive (or defining) clauses are essential to the grammatical and logical completeness of a sentence. Nonrestrictive (or nondefining) clauses, in contrast, are so loosely connected with the essential meaning of the sentence that they might be omitted without changing the essential meaning. Restrictive clauses, which usually begin with *that*, are not set off by commas, whereas nonrestrictive clauses, which usually begin with *which*, are set off by commas.

It is wrong to think that the distinction between *that* and *which* is tonal as opposed to syntactic. "A supposed and misleading distinction," wrote Fowler,

is that *that* is the colloquial and *which* the literary relative. That is a false inference from an actual but misinterpreted fact; it is a fact that the proportion of *that*s to *which*s is far higher in speech than in writing; but the reason is not that the spoken *that*s are properly converted into written *which*s, but that the kind of clause properly begun with *which* is rare in speech with its short detached sentences, but very common in the more complex and continuous structure of writing, while the kind properly begun with *that* is equally necessary in both. This false inference, however, tends to verify itself by persuading the writers who follow rules of thumb actually to change the original *that* of their thoughts into a *which* for presentation in print.

MEU1 635.

The distinction between the words, esp. important in formal prose, is properly viewed as syntactic: *that* introduces restrictive clauses, and *which* best introduces nonrestrictive clauses.

Yet that explanation has confused perhaps more educated writers than it has helped. The differentiation between restrictive (or defining) and nonrestrictive (or nondefining) clauses has eluded a number of otherwise fastidious writers. The simplest test for determining the type of relative clause is this: if the clause can be inserted in parentheses and the sentence still have the same kernel sense, the clause is nonrestrictive (properly a *which*-phrase). If the sentence is rendered nonsensical in context when the clause is put in parentheses, or gives the sentence an entirely different sense, then it is restrictive (properly a *that*-phrase). Hence,

"The court that overturned the case is now defunct."
"The court, which overturned the case, is now defunct."

In the first sentence, the court is defined or identified by the fact that it overturned a certain case; it has not been previously discussed with any particularity. In the second sentence, the court perforce is already known, and the fact that it overturned a certain case is merely thrown in as incidental information. The purpose of a restrictive clause is "the more sharply to define or to limit the antecedent, which without the ensuing relative clause would either make no sense or convey a sense different from the intended one." E. Partridge, *Usage and Abusage* 364 (1973). The purpose of a nonrestrictive clause is "the more fully to give information about something (the antecedent) that is already defined sufficiently to make sense." (*Id.*) Some of the common errors that occur with the two types of relative clauses are discussed in the sections below.

A. *Which* for *that.* Using the nonrestrictive relative pronoun (*which*) where the restrictive relative pronoun (*that*) is called for is perhaps the commonest blunder with these words. In none of the sentences that follow could the phrase introduced by *which*, and changed to *that* in brackets, be set off in parentheses without a nonsensical result or one with a drastically different sense. E.g., "A lawyer should ensure that the information *which* [read *that*] the lawyer publishes would facilitate the prospective client's ability to judge reasonably."/ "It seems quite clear to me that there is nothing in the Due Process Clause *which* [read *that*] denies Florida the right to determine whether Mrs. Donner's appointment was valid." (Black, J.)/ "We understand that every right *which* [read *that*] beneficiaries would otherwise have against the trust company is sealed and wholly terminated by the decree." (In the three sentences just quoted, the first *that* made the writers want to vary the word in the second phrase, but they should not have succumbed to this misplaced desire.)/ "In a shareholder's derivative suit, the cause of action *which* [read *that*] such a plaintiff brings before the court is not his own but the corporation's."/ "It is precisely the significance or lack of significance of these contacts *which* [read *that*] troubles us."/ "The injunction runs against only one of the parties of the dispute, a dispute *which* [read *that*] is of the kind *which* [read *that*] led to the passage of PKPA."/ "In such a case he would not be exercising his legal right, or doing an act *which* [read *that*] can be judged separately from the motive *which* [read *that*] actuated him."/ "For us to allow the judgment to stand as it is would risk an affirmance of a decision *which* [read *that*] might have been decided differently had the court below felt unconstrained."

B. Restrictive Clause Wrongly Made Nonrestrictive. This error is not at all uncommon. The relative clauses illogically set off by commas are necessary to the meaning of the sentence; one could not drop those phrases out of the sentences and retain the intended kernel meanings. E.g., "A state will not exercise judicial *jurisdiction, which* [read *jurisdiction that*] has been obtained by fraud or unlawful force, over a defendant or his property."/ "The jury could find that a *woman, who* [read *woman who*] believed she had a special relationship with God and was the chosen one to survive the end of the world, could believe that God would take over the direction of her life to the extent of driving her car."

C. Series. There is a tendency to substitute *and who* or *and which* in place of *and that* for the last in a series of relative clauses beginning with a *that*-phrase, perhaps because the relative *that* may be confused with the demonstrative *that*, whereas *which* and *who* are consistently relatives. Parallelism is nevertheless better: "A corporation *that* has failed to pay its franchise taxes, *that* has persisted in its delinquency for more than one year, and *which* [read *that*] has had its charter revoked can no longer operate as a business within the state."

resurface, like *surface,* is both v.i. & v.t. *Resurface* = (1) to come to the top again; or (2) to put a new surface on.

retaliatory, -tive. The two forms have undergone DIFFERENTIATION. The former means "of, relating to, or of the nature of retaliation" ⟨retaliatory eviction⟩, whereas the latter means "vindictive, tending to retaliation" ⟨a retaliative landlord⟩.

reticence, -cy. The latter is a NEEDLESS VARIANT.

reticent (= reserved, disinclined to speak freely; taciturn) is frequently misunderstood as being synonymous with *reluctant*. E.g., "Contemporary courts have been more *reticent* [read *reluctant*] to discard the privity requirement and to permit recovery in warranty by a remote consumer for purely economic losses."/ "It is probable that in such a case a court would be *reticent* [read *reluctant*] to raise a constructive trust since normally the constructive trust would be declared for the estate and the child in this case is the heir."/ "In contrast to Park, his fellow realtors were not so *reticent* [read *reluctant*] about bringing ethics complaints."

retract. See **revoke.**

retractable, -ible. The former spelling is correct. See -ABLE (A).

retract(at)ion. In the figurative sense "the act of recanting" or "a statement in recantation," *retraction* is usual in AmE, *retractation* in BrE. The British use *retraction* as the noun corresponding to *retract* in literal senses ("to draw back," etc.).

retreat; re-treat. See RE- PAIRS.

retributive, -tory, -tional. *Retributive* = characterized by, of the nature of, retribution (*OED*). E.g., "Some courts have treated punitive damages as *retributive*." *Retributory* = involving, producing, or characterized by retribution or recompense (*OED*). The only sense that *-tory* has that is lacking in *-tive* is that of causing or producing retribution; but euphony often governs the choice of term. *Retributional* is a NEEDLESS VARIANT not contained in the major English dictionaries.

retributory damages. See **punitive damages.**

retroactive; retrospective; retrogressive. In law, the first two terms are used synonymously in reference to statutes that extend in scope or effect to matters that have occurred in the past. E.g., "It is a general rule that a constitution should not be construed to have a *retroactive* effect."/ "There is a general rule concerning the question whether statutes in general should be given *retrospective* effect."/ "Though the amendment is remedial insofar as it establishes a prescriptive period to be applied prospectively, if interpreted as applying *retrospectively* it would destroy a substantive right." The one advantage of *retrospective* is that it corresponds etymologically to its antonym *prospective*.

Retrogressive = retrograde; tending to return to an inferior state; going back to a worse condition (*OED*). E.g., "The court nevertheless upheld the procedures because they were not *retrogressive*—they would not exacerbate vote dilution in Lockhart."

retrofit, n., is a HYBRID meaning "a modification of equipment or an airplane to include changes made in later production models" (*W3*). The term has now been extended to use as a verb by less than cautious writers: "Austin's Sheraton Crest Inn claims that the recent installation of a $200,000 fire-safety system makes the hotel the first high-rise structure to be *retrofitted* to meet the city's revised safety codes."

retrogressive. See **retroactive.**

retrospective. See **retroactive.**

return back is a fairly common REDUNDANCY.

returnee. See -EE.

re-urge should be hyphenated.

reus; rea. These are the forms of the term used in Roman, civil, and canon law to denote "a defendant." The plural forms are *rei* and *reae*. *Reus* is the more commonly encountered form.

re(-)use. Generally this word is not hyphenated: *reuse.*

revalidate; revive. These words, used in reference to re-establishing the validity of revoked wills, are distinguished in use. *Revalidation* consists in repetition of the formalities of execution of the will previously revoked. *Revival* consists in revocation of the superseding or revoking will (i.e., the will that displaced or invalidated the original will).

revenge. See **avenge.**

reverence, v.t.; revere. The former is a FORMAL WORD equivalent to the latter. "No person more than the present writer *reverences* this internal mentor we call conscience, but the experience of the ages teaches us that it is a most fallible guide." See **lapsus calami.**

reverie; revery. The former spelling is preferred.

reversible, -able. The former spelling is preferred. See -ABLE (A).

reversal; reversion; reverter. The first is the noun corresponding to the verb *to reverse*. The second and third are nouns corresponding to the verb *to revert*. Fowler quotes the following misuse of *reversion* for *reversal*: "The *reversion* [read *reversal*] of our free trade policy would, we are convinced, be a great detriment to the working class." For the distinction between *reversion* and *reverter*, see the entry under the former.

reverse. See **converse.**

reversion; reverter. Both are reversionary interests in property having been conveyed. A *reversion* is an interest in land arising by operation of law whenever the owner of an estate grants to another a particular estate, e.g., a life estate or a term of years, but does not dispose of the whole of his interest (*OCL*). A *reverter* is a possibility of reversion of an estate in land; it occurs when a grant is limited so that it might terminate. A *reversion* occurs automatically upon termination of the prior estate (as when a life tenant dies), whereas a *reverter*—usually termed a *possibility of reverter*—under orthodox theory, does not occur automatically, but is subject to a return to the grantor when a condition is breached (as upon the lapse of a conditional fee).

Reverter and *reversion* are susceptible to INELEGANT VARIATION. Justice Brennan, in his dissent in *Evans v. Abney*, 396 U.S. 435, 450 (1970), switches back and forth between the terms in describing the single interest that heirs had in a fee simple subject to condition subsequent. The correct term to describe such an estate is *possibility of reverter*. See **remainder** & **reversal**.

reversionary, -al. The latter is a NEEDLESS VARIANT. "We are again asked to determine whether a limitation over to the heirs of the grantor in an inter vivos conveyance created a remainder in the heirs or left a *reversionary* interest in the grantor."/ "Often the settlor is willing to part with all remnants of control during this period, but wishes to retain a *reversionary* interest in the principal."

reversioner = the grantor; one who possesses the reversion to an estate; an heir in reversion. E.g., "Under the doctrine of destructibility the holder of the life estate could defeat the contingent remaindermen by a tortious feoffment or by effecting a merger with the *reversioner*."/ "A statement made by a declarant holding a limited interest in any property and opposed to such interest is deemed to be relevant only as against those who claim under him, and not as against the *reversioner*." See **reversion** & **remainder**.

revert = (1) (of property) to return by reversion; (2) to return to a former state; (3) to go back to (as a former state or condition); (4) or to turn (eyes or steps) back.

A. *Revert* for *refer*. This is a curious mistake: "By *reverting* [read *referring*] to the language of the contestant's petition, we can see that the contestant admits that the document under consideration actually bears the testator's and attesters' signatures." Even if the writer intended in this sentence to say that he was "going back" to focus on particular words, his use of *revert* was ill-advised, for sense (3) subsumes the connotations of sense (2) or returning to a former state or condition.

B. *Revert back.* This is a REDUNDANCY. E.g, "If Nathaniel T. Braswell should die leaving no lawful heir from his body, then the land herein conveyed shall *revert back to the said James J. Braswell* [read *revert to James J. Braswell*] or to his lawful heirs."

reverter. See **reversion**.

revery. See **reverie**.

review, n.; reviewal. The latter is a NEEDLESS VARIANT.

revisal. See **revision**.

revise; recense; redact. The first is the ordinary word that serves in most senses. The second and third terms are used especially of revising texts with close scrutiny. *Redact* = (1) to make a draft of; (2) to edit. In American legal writing it is often used in the sense "to edit out or mask the impertinent or objectionable matter in a document." *Recense* is more of a literary term in modern usage; it relates to scholarly editing of ancient texts, etc.

reviser, -or. Both forms appear in modern legal prose. The *-er* form is preferred. E.g., "The *revisors* [read *revisers*] of the Code of 1919 had adopted some of the suggestions contained in the address but recommended no time limitation on probate."/ "As to the content of what constitutes revocation by implication of law, the *Reviser's* Note makes plain that the revision was merely an acceptance of *Pascucci*, which in turn merely accepted revocation by implication from a subsequent marriage and children as a common-law rule that had emerged before our Revolution."

revision; revisal. The latter is a NEEDLESS VARIANT. E.g., "Before the general *revisal* [read *revision*] of laws in this state in 1849, it was generally held that the destruction of a will containing a revocatory clause revived a preserved uncanceled will with no proof to the contrary being allowed."

revisionary, -al; revisory. *Revisionary* = of, pertaining to, or made up of revision ⟨revisionary methods⟩. *Revisional* is a NEEDLESS

VARIANT. *Revisory* = having power to revise; engaged in revision ⟨a revisory board⟩.

revisor. See **reviser.**

revitalize has become a VOGUE WORD among politicians and businessmen ⟨to revitalize the inner city⟩.

revival. See **renewal.**

revive. See **revalidate.**

reviver, -or. The two forms mean different things. *Reviver* = one who or that which revives. *Revivor* is a primarily BrE legal term denoting a proceeding for the revival of a suit or action abated by the death of one of the parties, or by some other circumstance (*OED*). E.g., "A number of jurisdictions extend the process of *revivor* to judgment liens."

revocability is pronounced /rev-o-ka-**bil**-i-tee/.

revocable; revokable. The first form is preferred; the word is pronounced /**rev**-ŏ-kă-bĕl/. *Revokable* and *revokeable* are NEEDLESS VARIANTS. See **irrevocable.**

revocatory, -tive. The former is preferred. E.g., "Although the language of the applicable wills act must be consulted when an issue of revocation by physical act is presented, certain *revocatory* acts appear in the statutes with some frequency."/ "It is true that in the absence of reservation of *revocatory* powers, a voluntary trust may generally be set aside only upon a showing that it was induced by fraud, duress, undue influence, or mistake."

revoke; retract. An offer is revoked; an anticipatory repudiation of a contract is retracted.

rewrite is both noun and verb, although *write* itself cannot be a noun. E.g., "The Reagan administration's Treasury Department says that its proposed *rewrite* of the Internal Revenue Code will make taxes simpler and fairer."

rhadamant(h)in(e) /răd-ă-**măn**-thĭn/. This term, meaning "of or relating to a rigorous or inflexible judge," is best spelled *rhadamanthine*. The word is a type of LITERARY ALLUSION (see (D)), Rhadamanthus being, in Greek my-thology, a son of Zeus and Europa who served as one of the judges in the lower world.

RHETORICAL QUESTIONS (those posed without the hope or expectation of an answer, often because the answer is obvious), especially when not unusually long, should end with a question mark. E.g., "Who would deny that the victim of a nuisance may have it abated regardless of the intent of the offending party?" Note that they quickly become tiresome if overused.

rhodomontade. See **rodomontade.**

rhyme or reason. This CLICHÉ should be avoided. E.g., "Nor do we find that the jury's verdict was *without rhyme or reason* [read *without reason*]."

rictal. See **rectal.**

rid ⟩ rid ⟩ rid. The preterite and past participial form *ridded* is now obsolete.

ridden. See **laden** (B).

ridiculous has moved a long way from its etymological suggestion of "causing laughter," so that writers nowadays often term *ridiculous* what causes them anger, frustration, distress, or (even) sadness. In other words, it is frequently used when people are far from laughing. It is unreasonable and unrealistic today to insist on etymological rigor with this word.

right; righteous; rightful. *Right* = correct, proper, just. *Righteous* = morally upright, virtuous, or law-abiding. This term has strong religious connotations, often of unctuousness. *Rightful* = (1) (of an action) equitable, fair; (2) (of a person) legitimately entitled to a position ⟨the rightful heir⟩; or (3) (of an office or piece of property) that one is entitled to ⟨his rightful inheritance⟩.

These terms are sometimes confused. In the specimen that follows, *rightfully* is misused for *rightly*: "The jury *rightfully* [read *rightly*] could reason that Marvin knew the conditions through which he had to fly."

right of action. See **cause of action** & **ground of action.**

right of common. See **profits à prendre.**

right of entry; right of re-entry. The former is the standard phrase, to which the latter adds nothing.

right of entry for condition broken; power of termination. Both terms refer to the rights of the grantor and his successors after conveyance of a fee simple conditional, which creates a possibility of reverter. See **reversion.**

right of re-entry. See **right of entry.**

right of way. In England, *right of way* is a legal term meaning "the legal right, established by usage, of a person or persons to pass through grounds or property owned by another." In the U.S., it is also a railway term ("the right to build and operate a railway line on land belonging to another, or the land so used"). In addition, *right of way* means "the right to take precedence in traffic" in both AmE and BrE. The plural is *rights of way.* See **easement.**

right reason. "We conclude that, although the award as remitted by the trial judge was generous, it was not so gross as to be contrary to *right reason.*" The *OED* states that this phrase is now rare (at *reason* (10)(b)); yet it remains common in much legal writing. It ought to be rare, since *reason* alone suffices.

rigorous (= extremely strict, austere) should not be misused for *rigid,* as here: "The *rigorous* [read *rigid*], inflexible view of the majority rejects the improvements to be gained by changing the old rule."

R.I.P.; requiescat in pace; rest in peace. The phrase *requiescat in pace* means "may he (or she) rest in peace." The abbreviated form, though commonly taken to be a shortened form of the English phrase, stands for the Latin phrase.

rob; steal; burglarize. Persons are *robbed;* things are *stolen;* and places are *burglarized.* See **burglary.**

robbery. See **burglary.**

rodomontade; rhodomontade. Pronounced /rod-ŏ-măn-**tayd**/, the word is preferably spelled *rodomontade.*

rogatory letter. See **letter rogatory.**

Romanist = one who is versed in or practices Roman law; a lawyer of the Roman school. The term, generally capitalized, has also been a pejorative epithet for Roman Catholics.

round. See **around.**

routinize is an -IZE neologism best avoided as GOBBLEDYGOOK. E.g., "Administration is a means of *routinizing coercion* [read *making coercion routine*]."

royalty. See **nonparticipating royalty.**

ruin, n.; ruination. The former is the ordinary term; the latter is humorous and colloquial. E.g, "The failure of Congress to do so explicitly shows that such a suit may not be entertained merely because collection would cause an irreparable injury, such as the *ruination* [read *ruin*] of the taxpayer's enterprise."

rule absolute. See **decree absolute.**

rule against opinions. See **opinions, rule against.**

Rule against Perpetuities; rule against perpetuities; Rule Against Perpetuities. "In Gray's book [John Chipman Gray, *The Rule against Perpetuities* (1886)] the Rule is capitalized *Rule against Perpetuities,* a style followed by the Blue Book until 1955. In that year, for mysterious reasons—perhaps merely a new font fetish—the Blue Book decreed that the Rule should be capitalized *Rule Against Perpetuities.*" J. Dukeminier & S. Johanson, *Family Wealth Transactions* 970 n. 1 (1978).

Professor Dukeminier has identified three styles of capitalizing the phrase: the classic style (*Rule against Perpetuities*); the modern style (*rule against perpetuities*); and the Blue Book Style (*Rule Against Perpetuities*), sanctioned by the Blue Book in the ninth edition of 1955. See Dukeminier, *Perpetuities: Contagious Capitalization,* 20 J. Legal Educ. 341 (1968). Dukeminier's research turned up no historical justification for the Blue Book Style (no longer included in the Blue Book), but long-sanctioned use of both the classic and modern styles (the only ones known in BrE). Dukeminier himself prefers the classic style, perhaps as a nod of respect to Gray; his preference should be ours. See CAPITALIZATION (A).

rulemaking is best an adjective ⟨rulemaking authority⟩ or an abstract noun ⟨rulemaking in administrative law⟩. It has become a COUNT NOUN in administrative law, in which it means "an administrative adjudication." E.g.,: "When the agency used statistics derived from this survey in a formal *rulemaking* to set minimum wages for government contractors in the industry, it made available for cross-examination the statistician who had tabulated the figures from the questionnaires." This usage smacks of jargon, but it may well become accepted as standard AmE legal terminology. See PLURALS (B).

rule nisi; order nisi. See **nisi & decree absolute.**

rule of law; rule of construction. A *rule of law* is a rule followed by a court that determines the substantive position of the parties; a *rule of construction* is a guide to the court in interpreting a statute or legal instrument. E.g., "Before its abolition in England, the Rule in Shelley's Case seems to have been a *rule of law* rather than a *rule of construction.*"

ruling means "decision," q.v., not "opinion," q.v., as here wrongly suggested: "The action by Mesa Partners II 'strongly suggests a studied effort by Mesa to conceal its true intent,' the judge wrote in a 33-page *ruling* [read *opinion*]." See JUDGMENTS, APPELLATE-COURT.

run. **A.** Statutes of Limitation. In the U.S., statutes of limitation are said to have *run* when the time limit has passed. In G.B., the usual phraseology is that the period set by the statute of limitation has *expired.* Hence, "In January 1971 the architect's solicitors suggested that the preliminary points of law should be tried, primarily on the question of the architect's duty in the circumstances and whether the claims were barred under the Limitation Acts, though the writ had been issued before the six-year period of limitation in respect of a tort had *expired.*" (Eng.)

B. *Running with the land.* Covenants are said to *run with the land* when the liability to perform the covenant or the right to take advantage of it passes to the assignee of that land (*Black's*). Cf. **in gross.**

C. Meaning "to apply." This is an idiom properly classed as a LEGALISM: "The injunction *runs* only against one of the parties in the dispute."

RUN-ON SENTENCES do not stop where they should. Most of us will recognize the term from the days when schoolteachers scrawled "run on" in the margins of our papers. The problem usually occurs when the writer is uncertain about how to handle marks of PUNCTUATION, and such adverbs as *however* and *otherwise*, which are often mistakenly treated as conjunctions. Following are some specimens, with suggested remedies in brackets.

The volume of examples should illustrate the frequency of this syntactic blunder in modern legal writing: "In the final analysis, it fastens liability on the master where his servant is *negligent, otherwise* [read *negligent; otherwise*] there is no liability."/ "The competitors got together, that [read *as*, or drop comma and put an em-dash between *together* and *that*] happens in business, politics, and the theater."/ "State sovereignty is not a proper basis on which to rest *jurisdiction, instead* [read *jurisdiction; instead*] the focus is on whether the defendant's due process rights are infringed by the court's assertion of jurisdiction."/ "There are two levels of qualification prescribed by the *NASD, one* [read *NASD: one*] is for principals and the other is for registered representatives."/ "We do not now decide whether the INS has complied fully with its own *regulations, rather* [read *regulations; rather*] we decide that it must in the first instance address petitioner's specific factual claims that it failed to do so."/ "It is true that defendants' right to the insurance payment was a contract right embodied in the policies of *insurance, nevertheless* [read *insurance; nevertheless*] the indemnity payment was based in part on a claim of loss that did not exist."/ "But the court has no power to do by indirection what it is doing *directly, particularly* [read *directly; particularly*] is that true in an action for specific performance in which a decree is given as a matter of grace and discretion."/ "The defendants were not the agents or servants of the *plaintiff, they* [read *plaintiff; they*] were independent contractors."/ "The generator's analysis may be used to justify a less-than-complete waste analysis by the site *operator, thus* [read *operator; thus*] incompatible wastes may be buried in the same subcells, or restricted wastes may be entering the landfill."/ "The operation of hauling gasoline is an inherently dangerous *activity, therefore, the* [read *activity; therefore, the*] standard of strict liability must be imposed."

run the gantlet. See **gantlet.**

S

sacrilegious. So spelled; *sacreligious* is a common misspelling. E.g., "Surely moral merit is at least as elusive as other terms the Court has declared infirm, such as 'gangsters,' '*sacreligious* [read *sacrilegious*],' 'humane,' and 'credible and reliable.'" Rhode, *Moral Character as a Professional Credential*, 94 Yale L. J. 491, 571 (1985). The correct spelling can be remembered easily if one recalls the noun: *sacrilege.*

said.   A. Generally. *Said* should be rigorously eschewed in place of *the, that, this,* or any other DEICTIC or "pointing" word. Used in place of such a word, *said* typifies LEGALESE and is often parodied by laymen; it is sometimes unconsciously parodied even by lawyers, e.g.:

> A considerable number of persons were attracted to *said* square by *said* meeting, and *said* bombs and other fireworks which were being exploded there. A portion of the center of the square about 40 to 60 feet was roped off by the police of *said* Chelsea, and *said* bombs or shells were fired off within the space so inclosed, and no spectators were allowed to be within *said* inclosure. The plaintiffs were lawfully in *said* highway at the time of the explosion of *said* mortar, and near *said* ropes, and were in the exercise of due care. (Eng.)

The cancer has a tendency to metastasize dangerously in wills; here is an example of nine growths in a single sentence:

> If the *said* Grant R. Shelley shall die, and leave surviving him children, it is my desire that, if my wife be then dead, or upon the death of my wife if she would survive my *said* son, my trustee shall continue *said* trust for the benefit of *said* children of my son, Grant R. Shelley, and shall make periodic payments for their benefit at intervals of not less than

three months apart, and shall hold *said* estate in trust to and until the youngest child of Grant R. Shelley shall attain the age of twenty-one years; thereupon, *said* trust shall terminate, and *said* estate shall be distributed to the children of my son, share and share alike; if any of *said* children die before the youngest attains the age of twenty-one years, *said* distributable estate shall be distributed to the surviving children, share and share alike.
> Quoted in *Shelley v. Shelley*, 223 Or. 328, 354 P.2d 282, 284 (1960).

This usage may have had its origins in LOAN TRANSLATION. Mellinkoff quotes this Latin phrase, from a general demurrer of the seventeenth century: *tam contra pacem dicti nuper Regis*, translated *against the peace of the said late King* [*dicti* = said]. D. Mellinkoff, *The Language of the Law* 184 (1963).

B. *The said.* As used in legal writing, the word *said* is a Middle-English sibling of *aforesaid,* and has the sense "above-stated." Originally legal writers would write *the said defendant,* just as they would write *the aforesaid defendant* or *the above-stated defendant.* Gradually, however, the usage became so common that *the* was dropped before *said,* which has come to act almost as an article. Hence *the said* seems redundant today, though it was well established at one time. It still occasionally appears in cases both English and American: "J.W.T. had induced his wife to furnish him money with which to acquire *the said* [omit *said*] property."/ "The transaction resulted in an exorbitant profit to *the said* [omit *said*] defendant." (Eng.)/ "The case for the appellants was that *the said* [omit *said*] libel consisted partly in the repetition of alleged rumours and partly of defamatory statements." (Eng.)

One writer has stated that "*the said person* is better than *said person.*" E. A. Dreidger, *The Composition of Legislation* 87 (1957). From a stylistic point of view, however, both are so ghastly that it is inconsequential which is "better"; the question is better framed, "Which is less bad?"

C. *His said,* etc. This collocation is similar to *the said;* both *saids* are quite superfluous here: "He wrongfully, knowingly, intentionally, and maliciously induced *said* [omit *said*] McClure to violate, repudiate, and break *his said* [omit *said*] agreement with the plaintiff."

D. In Pleadings. *Said* appears at the beginning of pleadings in the SET PHRASE, *To the honorable judge of said court, said* referring to the name of the court in the caption of the case.

If one is particularly conservative or traditional, one might allow this use of *said* and no other. *To the honorable court*, however, is a simpler, more serviceable substitute.

E. As Referring to Preceding Matter. When *said* is used in the way here disapproved, as we must grudgingly accept that it will be, it should refer to something above ("already said"), not to what is about to be said: "Any person who does any of the acts hereinafter enumerated thereby submits himself to the jurisdiction of the courts of this State regarding any cause of action arising from any of *said acts* [read *these acts*]: [an enumeration follows]."

F. As a Noun. As suggested above, *said* is merely a DEICTIC TERM. Thus it cannot stand on its own as a noun. In this sentence, the writer has misused *said* for *same*: "Defendants exercised control over Mobay's ownership interest in that property, and thereby converted *said* [read *same*]." See **same**.

G. Modifying Proper Names. *Said* is especially ludicrous when used to modify a proper name, where no confusion could result from use of the name alone: "The first count of the indictment alleged, in substance, that George Smith was an idiot, and under the care, custody, and control of the respondents; that the respondents assaulted *said George* [read *George*]. . . ." (Cf. *said Chelsea* in the first passage quoted in this entry.)

sailor's will. See **oral will.**

sal(e)able; sellable. The preferred spellings are *salable* in AmE (*W9 & W3*), and *saleable* in BrE (*OED & COD*). *Sellable*, arguably a more logical form, was formerly used by some writers, but never gained widespread currency.

salience, -cy. The latter is a NEEDLESS VARIANT.

salutary, -tiferous; salubrious. *Salutary* = beneficial; wholesome. *Salutory* is a common misspelling. E.g., "The court must be careful to implement this sanction in a way that advances its *salutory* [read *salutary*] purpose while avoiding its potential danger." Kilgarlin & Jackson, *Sanctions for Discovery Abuse Under New Rule 215*, 15 St. Mary's L.J. 767, 791 (1984)./ "It is a corollary to the necessary and *salutory* [read *salutary*] presumption that a child born during the pendency of a legal marriage is the legitimate offspring of the husband and wife."/ "Legal realism has probably, on the whole, had a *salutary* effect on the system." *Salutiferous* is a NEEDLESS VARIANT of *salutary*. *Salubrious*, a close synonym of *salutary*, means "healthful; promoting health or well-being."

salvable. See **savable.**

salvage, n.; selvage. *Salvage* = the rescue of property (as at sea or from fire). *Selvage* = the edging of cloth.

salvageable. See **savable.**

salvag(e)(o)r. *Salvager* is the preferred spelling. *Salvor* is a variant term.

same. A. As a Pronoun. This usage, well exemplified in the common phrase *acknowledging same*, is symptomatic of LEGALESE; Fowler termed the usage an illiteracy. One should substitute *it*, *them*, or the noun for which *same* is intended to stand. "The informer told the officer that a white male would usually load the buyer's car with marijuana at a residence and then deliver *same* [read *it*] to buyer." Similar examples abound in legal writing: "Even though such a witness discloses a new lead, one is best advised to make note of *same* [read *it*], but not to depart from the original objective until its possibilities have been extended."/ "Tucker received said envelope and its said contents in due course the following day and he opened same and has refused to file same." [Read *Tucker received the envelope and its contents in due course the following day. He opened the envelope and refused to file its contents.*]/ "He grabbed the will and destroyed the same [read *it*]."/ "We should not write until the court below shows that it considered all the evidence by *discussing the same* [read *discussing it*] in full."

B. *Same . . . as are. Are* is often superfluously inserted in comparisons of similarity: "The government here does not suggest that appellee is not entitled to the *same* Fourth Amendment protection as *are* [omit *are*] citizens."/ "Every member of the proposed class is in the *same* position with respect to that question *as are* [read *as the*] plaintiffs." See **as . . . as** (B).

C. *Same difference* is an illogical AmE casualism that is to be avoided not only in writing but in speech as well. "It's all the *same*," "It's the *same* thing," etc. are better.

sanat(at)ive, -tory. See **sanitary.**

sanatorium. See **sanitarium.**

sanction = (1) to approve; or (2) to penalize. Laymen usually understand *sanction* in sense (1); thus lawyers, who use it primarily in sense (2), are liable to be misunderstood. Yet sense (1) also appears in legal writing, as here: "The courts will not *sanction* a trust disposition if it is inimical to public policy."

As a noun, *sanction* is burdened by the same ambiguity, meaning either "approval" or "penalty." Here it carries the latter meaning: "There is no statutory provision stating a *sanction* for violation of the act." In phrases such as *give sanction to*, it means "approval." The terms used above in defining the senses of *sanction* may serve as substitutes that avoid ambiguities.

sanitary; sanatory, -tive. *Sanitary* = of or relating to health or, more usu., cleanliness. *Sanative* = health-producing; healthful. *Sanatory* is a NEEDLESS VARIANT.

sans is an archaic literary GALLICISM to be avoided, unless a tongue-in-cheek or archaic effect is intended. *Without* should always be favored over *sans* (as long as one is using the English language). E.g., "Arrogation to an appointed official of the denial of the right to hear and see a controversial play cannot be accomplished *sans* [read *without*] standards."/ "Has Findeisen alleged a deprivation under color of state law of a federally protected property right, *sans* [read *without*] due process?"

sans recours. See **without recourse.**

satisfaction. See **accord.**

savable; salvable; salvageable. *Savable* = capable of being saved. Originally this word was used in theological senses, and it still carries religious connotations. *Salvable*, too, has the theological sense ("admitting of salvation"), as well as the sense (used of ships) "that can be saved or salvaged." *Salvageable*, dated from 1976 in the *OED Supp.* but doubtless older in the U.S., has become common in the sense "that can be salvaged." E.g., "Defendant's publication costs may not be reduced by the full cost of printing plates to the extent that such plates are *salvageable.*"

save is an ARCHAISM when used for *except*. It should be eschewed, although, as the examples following illustrate, it is still common in legal prose. E.g., "The law-of-the-circuit rule forbids one panel to overrule another *save* [read *except*] when a later statute or Supreme Court decision has changed the applicable law."/ "The district court granted summary judgment in favor of the defendants on all of appellant's due process claims *save* [read *except for*] those alleging bias, which were tried to the court."/ "As long as the law requires disclosure, the scales come down decisively, in my opinion, in favour of a renewed inquiry on or very shortly before the day of the hearing, *save* [read *except*] in very exceptional circumstances." (Eng.)

saving(s) clause; saving to suitors clause. *Saving clause* is the preferred form of this phrase generally, and particularly in admiralty law. The U.S. Constitution grants federal courts jurisdiction over "all Cases of admiralty and maritime Jurisdiction." U.S. Const. art. III, § 2. The statutory grant of this admiralty jurisdiction negated exclusive jurisdiction by "saving to suitors, in all cases, the right of a common[-]law remedy where the common law is competent to give it." 28 U.S.C. § 1331(1) (1982). This language is known as the *saving clause*, which allows a plaintiff to bring an action in any forum that will take jurisdiction of the case.

Savings clause is not an uncommon variant, but it is not as good, for it (1) suggests financial savings, and (2) makes *saving* a nominal rather than a participial adjective when the latter is more specific. E.g., "The note also contained a *savings clause* [read *saving clause*] providing that any charge that caused or was interpreted to cause the interest to exceed the maximum lawful rate was to be reduced to the extent necessary to eliminate the usurious violation."/ "The applicable statute provided that, no such party appearing within that time, the probate shall be forever binding with a *saving clause* for nonresidents and persons under disabilities."

scarify; scorify. *Scarify* means (1) "to make superficial incisions in, cut off skin from"; (2) "to pain by severe criticism"; or (3) "to loosen soil by means of an agricultural machine [a scarifier] with prongs for spiked road-breaking." *Scorify* means "to reduce to dross or slag."

scatter-gun. See **blunderbuss.**

sceptic(al). See **skeptic(al).**

schism (= division, separation) is pronounced /*siz-ĕm*/. The term is now usually used figuratively. E.g., "The dispute in this case grows out of the *schism* between 'professional' and 'commercial' optometrists in Texas."

scienter (= prior knowledge) is a noun in Anglo-American jurisprudence, although the Latin word *scienter* is an adverb meaning *knowingly*. The term has been common in legal writing since the nineteenth century. Often meaning "guilty knowledge," the term is used most commonly in contexts of fraud, and as a standard for criminal intent. E.g., "[T]he account executive's *scienter*, defined as intent to defraud or reckless disregard, must be established." *Shad v. Dean Witter Reynolds, Inc.,* 799 F.2d 525, 530 (9th Cir. 1986).

scilicet (= that is to say) is usually abbreviated *sc.* It is much rarer than *viz.*, q.v., which has essentially the same meaning.

scintilla (= a spark or minute particle) is often applied to law in the phrase *scintilla of evidence.* Pl. *-las.* The phrase *mere scintilla* has become a legal CLICHÉ.

scire facias, literally "you should cause to know," is the LATINISM that has given its name to the judicial writ founded upon a matter of record requiring the person against whom it is issued to show cause why the record should not be annulled or vacated. E.g., "*Scire facias* to revive a judgment being a continuation of the suit, jurisdiction thereon is in the court where the judgment was rendered, regardless of the residency of the parties." The phrase is abbreviated *sci. fa.*

scofflaw (= one who treats the law with contempt) is a twentieth-century AMERICANISM. Oddly enough, the word was coined by two entrants in a competition held in 1924 to characterize the "lawless drinker" of liquor illegally made or obtained. *Scofflaw* was chosen from more than 25,000 words, and since that time, of course, it has been extended beyond its original meaning, which lost its pungency with the repeal of Prohibition. Now *scofflaw* refers esp. to a person who avoids various kinds of not easily enforceable laws (*OED Supp.*).

score = twenty, though various other numbers are often mistakenly attached to the word.

scorify. See **scarify.**

Scotch law; Scottish law; Scots law. F. T. Wood, an Englishman, writes: "The Scots (or Scotch?) themselves are less particular than the English in the matter of these three words [*Scotch, Scottish,* and *Scots*]." *Current English Usage* 207 (1962). He recommends *Scots* for the noun denoting the people; and *Scottish* when referring to characteristics of the country.

Boswell, a Scottish lawyer, uses *Scotch law* throughout his *Life of Johnson,* and occasionally *Scottish law* as well. Even modern British writers do not use the terms consistently. E.g., "It follows that, if the proper law of the arbitration is to be held to be *Scots* law, this conclusion must come about by some inference . . . from the contract. . . . There is absolutely nothing in this contract from which it could be said to be governed by *Scottish* law." *James Miller & Partners v. Whitworth Street Estates,* 1970 A.C. 583, 599 (H.L.).

One might defensibly say that the preferred forms are *Scots law,* but *Scottish procedure, Scottish arbitration, Scottish legal forms.* (*Black's* uses *Scotch law* in references throughout.) *Scotch,* recorded in the *OED* as a "contracted variant of *Scottish,*" is best avoided by those in doubt. E.g., "When I look at the report, I find that Lord Cottenham abstains from laying down a rule in that case, but expresses a hope that the *Scotch judges* [*Scottish judges* might be better] would take care to exercise the jurisdiction of the court with discretion and consistency." (Eng.)/ "Crawford sought to depose two principals of Hydrasum (Aberdeen) Ltd., a *Scottish* corporation."

It is sometimes said that *Scotch* should be used of material objects, as *Scotch tartans, Scotch whiskey,* and *Scotch thistle.*

scot-free is a predicative adjective meaning "exempt from injury or punishment." E.g., "It would be contrary to the decided weight of authority to hold that since plaintiff has a cause of action against the company for breach of contract, Sander should go *scot-free.*" (Eng.) The phrase derives from the early

English "scot" or contribution or payment into a common fund.

Scottish; Scots. See **Scotch law.**

scrivener, -or; scribe. The spelling *scrivener* is preferred. E.g., "Attorney David Smith [see TITULAR TOMFOOLERY], a witness and scrivenor [read *scrivener*] of the 1965 will, testified that the original will was executed near the vault in the Montellow State Bank."/ "The testator thought the attorney was trying to place him in a mental hospital and had another *scrivener* draft a will in which he left the attorney nothing."

Scrivener, as illustrated in the two sentences just quoted, and *scribe*, as evidenced in the name of the American lawyers' organization devoted to improved legal writing (the *Scribes*), either are frequently taken by lawyers to be terms of praise for the person named, or are unusual lawyers' attempts at self-effacement. Technically, a *scrivener* is merely a copyist or amanuensis, not a draftsman. The same is true of *scribe* in all but historical senses; the *OED* notes that it is additionally "applied to a political pamphleteer or journalist; chiefly with contemptuous notion, a party hack."

sculpture(r); sculpt(or). The preferred verb is *sculpture* ⟨to sculpture a bust⟩, although *sculpt*, a BACK-FORMATION from *sculptor*, is commonly seen in the U.S. *Sculptor* is the preferred agent noun.

Scylla and Charybdis, between. As described by Homer, *Scylla* was a sea monster who had six heads (each with a triple row of teeth) and twelve feet. Though primarily a fish-eater, she was capable of snatching and devouring (in one swoop) six sailors if their ship ventured too near her cave in the Straits of Messina. (In the accounts of later writers, she is rationalized into a rocky promontory.) Toward the opposite shore, not far from Scylla's lair, was *Charybdis*, a whirlpool strong enough thrice daily to suck into its vortex whole ships if they came too close. (See N.G.L. Hammond & H.H. Scullard, *The Oxford Classical Dictionary* (2d ed. 1970).)

Thus, to say that one is "between Scylla and Charybdis" is the literary man's way of saying "between a rock and a hard place." E.g., "To hold otherwise, the court noted, would be to place the hapless plaintiff between the *Scylla* of intentionally flouting state

law and the *Charybdis* of forgoing what he believes to be constitutionally protected activity to avoid become enmeshed in a criminal proceeding." The term has become a CLICHÉ. See LITERARY ALLUSION (A) (4).

sea lawyer is a nautical term of contempt meaning "a carping or captious person." E.g., "So long as the teacher acts reasonably the Constitution does not require him to work in an atmosphere of litigious contest with any juvenile *sea-lawyer* who may appear in his class." *Meyers v. Arcata High School Dist.*, 75 Cal. Rptr. 68, 76 (Cal. App. 1969) (Christian, J., dissenting). See LAWYER, DEROGATORY NAMES FOR.

seasonable. A. And *seasonal*. *Seasonable* = (1) occurring at the right season; opportune; or (2) (of weather) suitable to the time of year (*OED*). *Seasonal* = (1) pertaining to or characteristic of the seasons of the year, or some one of them; or (2) dependent on the seasons, as certain trades (*OED*).

B. And *timely*. In legal contexts, *seasonable* is often used to mean "timely," whereas in lay contexts it ordinarily means "in season." One writer has insisted that "these terms [*seasonable* and *timely*] are not synonymous. That which is *seasonable* is in harmony or keeping with the season or occasion; that which is *timely* is in good time. A thing may be *timely* in appearance that is not *seasonable*." F. Vizetelly, *A Desk-Book of Errors in English* 194 (1909). Yet in American legal writing, the word is regularly used as a synonym of *timely*, whether advisedly or not. E.g., "If the dominant party receives the benefit or donation during the existence of the confidential relation, the party reposing the confidence, on *seasonable* application to a court of equity, may obtain relief from the burdens and duties imposed simply by showing the transaction and the confidential relation."

seasonal, n., is used in AmE as an elliptical form of *seasonal worker*. E.g., "The policy that Congress adopted the adverse action protection to serve thus does not favor application of those protections to *seasonals*' layoffs."

seaward(s). See **-ward(s).**

secede. See **cede.**

secern is a little-used word that would be a happy addition to the legal vocabulary. It means, basically, "to distinguish or discriminate in thought," and has the advantages of shortness and euphony, if not of universal lucidity.

2d; 2nd. The former is preferred in legal citations.

secondhand evidence. See **hearsay evidence.**

secretaryship, -iship. The former spelling is standard.

secrete = (1) to hide; or (2) to exude or ooze through pores or glands; to produce by secretion. *Secrete away* is redundant. Sense (1) is becoming increasingly learned or literary, but it is frequently used in legal writing, e.g.: "The plaintiffs also suffer a heavy burden in having to commence actions wherever the enjoined party and his agents choose to *secrete* the funds."

secretive, -tory. The first is the adjective ("inclined to secrecy, uncommunicative") corresponding to sense (1) of *secrete*; the second is the adjective ("having the function of secreting") corresponding to sense (2) of *secrete*. *Secretive* is best pronounced /si-**kree**-tiv/, and *secretory* /si-**kree**-tŏ-ree/.

sectionalize (= to divide into sections) has become commonplace in lawyers' cant. E.g., "The firm is *sectionalized*, so that each associate will know to whom he or she may turn for consultation and advice. *Sectionalization* facilitates orderly distribution of work and the opportunity for concentration." See -IZE.

secular, like *lay*, has been extended beyond the religious meaning, namely, "outside the ecclesiastical calling," and now can refer to persons and things outside a profession, most commonly the law. Cf. **temporal.**

seduction; seducement. Although the latter is sometimes used for the former, the two are best kept separate. *Seduction* = the action or an act of seducing (a person, esp. a woman) to err in conduct or belief, esp. of enticing a woman to engage in illicit sexual intercourse. *Seducement* = something that seduces or serves as a means of seduction; an insidious temptation (*OED*).

seem (to be) + **noun phrase.** In formal writing it is best to include the infinitive *to be.*

E.g., "There certainly *seemed no enlightening purpose* [read *seemed to be no enlightening purpose*] served by giving some slick operator from the K.K.K. a nationwide forum on which to spread his rancid twaddle."

segment, v.t.; **segment(al)ize.** The latter forms are NEEDLESS VARIANTS. Cf. **sectionalize.** See -IZE.

segregate out. See **out.**

segregative = having the power or property of separating. In American legal writing, the term is used almost exclusively of racial segregation. E.g., "Confronted with *segregative* assignment of faculty and administrators, *segregative* bus transportation of students and other *segregative* post-*Brown* decisions of the Ector County I.S.D, the district court held that the Ector County School District not only continued to fail to meet its duty to dismantle its dual school system, but actually increased the segregation in its schools." See **separate.**

seise; seize. The two identically pronounced words are related, but may fairly be said to have undergone DIFFERENTIATION. In the legal sense "to put in possession, invest with the fee simple of," the spelling *seise* is preferred in both AmE and BrE. E.g., "Historically, the doctrine of seisin required that a taker by descent had to be an heir of the person last *seised*."/ "Inheritances shall lineally descend to the issue of the person who last died actually *seised*, in infinitum; but shall never lineally descend." (Blackstone)

Seize is principally a nontechnical lay word meaning: (1) "to take hold of (a thing or person) forcibly or suddenly or eagerly"; (2) "to take possession of (a thing) by legal right" ⟨to seize contraband⟩; or (3) "to have a sudden overwhelming effect on" ⟨to be seized by fear⟩ (*OAD*). *Seize* should be confined to these senses; thus in the following examples, *seise* would have been the better spelling: "At common law, the widow was entitled to one-third of all the property in which her husband was *seized* [read *seised*] in fee at any time during the marriage."/ "Neither of them could have died intestate *seized* [read *seised*] and possessed of the property."/ "This is a suit to enjoin the sale of real estate at sheriff's sale under an execution issued on a judgment against an heir of an intestate who died *seized* [read *seised*] of the land, although the heir had filed a renunciation of all interest in the estate." The spelling *seize* would make sense if the noun were predominantly spelled *seizin*; but it is not. See **seisin**.

Seize is not infrequently used in the lay sense (1) in legal writing, a fact that provides still greater impetus for strict DIFFERENTIATION between the spellings: "Equity *seizes* the property on its way from the donor to the appointee, and applies it to the satisfaction of the obligations of the appointor."

seisin /*seez-ĭn*/ originally meant "possession," then grew into a TERM OF ART in land law up to the nineteenth century, much of which is now defunct. E.g., "Someone must always be *seised* of each tract of land; *seisin* can never be in abeyance." The term *seisin* has persisted, however, the spoor of a complicated history. Today it generally means "possession of a freehold estate in land." Yet "there can be no definition of *seisin* which both preserves its historical flavor and gives guidance in an age that talks of *ownership* and stakes its existence on record *title* divorced from physical contact with the land. The tortured language that attempts still to make use of *seisin* meanders through redundancy and illogic, inaccuracy and chaos." D. Mellinkoff, *The Language of the Law* 343 (1963).

The best advice is to study seisin as a historical concept, and to use the word *seisin* in historical contexts in which the sense is well-defined. If *possession* or *ownership* is all that one means by *seisin*, one should write in its place *possession* or *ownership*.

The word is sometimes spelled *seizin*, as in 2 B.W. Pope, *Legal Definitions* 1453 (1920). This was more common formerly than it is today, but -*zin* still appears, usu. in quotations of old authorities. E.g., "The covenants of *seizin*, and of right to convey, and against incumbrances are personal covenants. . . ." *Profitt v. Isley*, 683 S.W.2d 243, 244 (Ark. App. 1985) (quoting *Logan v. Moulder*, 1 Ark. 313, 320 (1839)).

seize. See **seise**.

select, adj.; **selected.** The former is the adjective meaning "choice; esp. excellent." Here the past participial form of the verb (*selected*) is used inappropriately for the adjective: "These students are all educated young men, and—since the law school's standards are known to be high, and the work is notoriously difficult—it may reasonably be sup-

posed that they are a *selected* [read *select*] group." (Prosser)

selectee. See -EE.

selectman is an Americanism dating from 1635 and meaning "one of a board of officers elected annually to manage various local concerns in a 'town' or 'township' in New England." No doubt today there is a tendency to change the word to *selectperson*, which is not necessarily a happy development. See SEXISM (B).

self-actualization is a phrase from pop psychology, which, like others with that association, should generally be eschewed. Rough equivalents that do not smack of voguishness are *achievement* and *success* or *happiness*.

self-complacent is redundant; *complacent* itself is sufficient.

self-crimination. See **criminate** & **incriminate**.

self-dealing (= financial dealing that is not at arm's length; borrowing from or lending to a company by a controlling individual primarily to his own advantage [*W9*]) is an Americanism that originated in the mid-twentieth century. E.g., "The conferred right to exercise all these plenary powers of ownership necessarily modified or displaced the otherwise absolute limitation against *self-dealing*."

self-deprec(i)ating. See **deprecate**.

self-proving, not included in any of the major dictionaries, is a phrase used of affidavits appended to modern wills. *Self-proving affidavits* are signed by the witnesses to the will, and state that the testator was under no compulsion and had a sound mind when executing his will.

sellable. See **sal(e)able**.

selvage. See **salvage**.

SEMANTICS. For solid treatment of general semantics as applied to law, see W. Probert, *Law, Language and Communication* (1972); G. Williams, *Language and the Law*, 61 L.Q. Rev. 387-406 (1946); and F.A. Philbrick, *Language and the Law* (1949).

semble (= it seems) is used in law reports as a technical expression of uncertainty, usu. in introducing an obiter dictum. In the first two examples, the brackets are those of the original authors of the sentences: "This judgment is not conclusive in an action by the owner of ship A, for the damage done to ship B. [*Semble*, it is deemed to be irrelevant.]" (Eng.)/ "It is the duty of all judges to take judicial notice of the accession and [*semble*] the sign manual of her Majesty and her successors."/ "A bequest to X and/or Y, where both survived, was held to create a joint tenancy; *semble*, if either predeceased, the survivor would take the whole."

semi-. See **bi-.**

semiannual (U.S.); **half-yearly** (Br.). See **biannual.**

send back is occasionally used in place of *remand*, q.v., the more formal legal term. E.g., "This was clearly error, and of such vital importance that the case must be reversed and *sent back* for a new trial." Cf. **return back.**

sensitize; sensitivize. Although Fowler championed the latter, the former is now usual in AmE and BrE.

sensory; sensatory; sensorial. *Sensory* = of sensation or the senses. *Sensatory* is a NEEDLESS VARIANT. *Sensorial* = primarily responsive to sensations. This word may also be a NEEDLESS VARIANT of *sensory*, however.

sensuous; sensual. These words derive from the same root, meaning "appeal to the senses," but the precise meanings have undergone DIFFERENTIATION. *Sensuous* = of or relating to the five senses; arousing any of the five senses. The word properly has no risqué connotations, though it is gravely distorted by hack novelists. *Sensual* = sexual; salacious; voluptuous ⟨sensual desires⟩. *This* is the word intended by the hack novelists who erroneously believe that *sensuous* carries sexy overtones.

sentence. In most jurisdictions, criminal *sentences* are imposed by judges and not by juries. E.g., "The Supreme Court of Alabama agrees that 'the jury is not the sentencing authority in Alabama,' and has described the sentencing judge not as a reviewer of the jury's sentence, but as *the* sentencer." *Baldwin v. Alabama*, 472 U.S. 372, 384 (1985).

SENTENCE ADVERBS are adverbs conveying the speaker's comment on the statement being made rather than qualifying a single word in the sentence. A sentence adverb does not resolve itself into the form *in a ⸺ manner*, as most adverbs do. Thus, in *Happily, the bill did not go beyond the committee*, the introductory adverb *happily* conveys the writer's opinion on the message he imparts. Similar adverbs are *fortunately, sadly, ironically, curiously, regrettably, strangely, oddly, interestingly, importantly, accordingly, consequently, admittedly,* and *concededly.*

These and a few other words are the conventional sentence adverbs in *-ly.* Improvising sentence adverbs from traditional adverbs like *hopefully* (= in a hopeful manner) and *thankfully* (= in a thankful manner), qq.v., is objectionable to many stylists, but seems to be on the rise. E.g., "*Explanatorily* [read *By way of explanation*], these consolidated causes were positioned as the ordinary and uncomplicated condemnation case." *O'Neil Corp. v. Perry Gas Transmission, Inc.*, 648 S.W.2d 335, 341 (Tex. App.—Amarillo 1983). (See **corollarily** for an example of that form in place of *as a corollary.*) Newfangled sentence adverbs of this kind are to be discouraged. In formal prose, even those like *hopefully* and *thankfully*, with a short, beleaguered history but increasingly common, should be eschewed.

Because sentence adverbs contain the writer's own thoughts and reveal his biases, lawyers often overuse them in argumentation; the danger here lurks in words like *clearly, undoubtedly,* and *indisputably.* See **clearly** & OVERSTATEMENT.

separate means "to segregate" in the legal phrase *to separate the jury.* The *OED* suggests that this use of the word is "chiefly in Biblical language," and does not mention the legal use. See BIBLICAL AFFECTATION.

separate out. See **out.**

sepulcher, -re; sepulture. The preferred spelling of the first term is *sepulcher* in AmE, *-re* in BrE. The word means "burial place; tomb," and is pronounced /sĕp-ĕl-kĕr/. *Sepulture*, sometimes a NEEDLESS VARIANT of *sepulcher*, justifies its separate form in the sense "burial." These words are very formal, even literary. They should be used cautiously.

SEQUENCE OF TENSES. This term refers to the relationship of tenses in subordinate clauses to those in principal clauses; the former follow from the latter. In correct writing there is a logical and grammatical agreement of tenses. The basic rules of tense-sequence are easily stated, although the plethora of examples that follow belie their ostensible simplicity in practice. When the principal or governing clause has a verb in the present (*he says*), present perfect (*he has said*), or future (*he will say*), the subordinate clause has a present-tense verb. This is called by grammarians the primary sequence. The secondary sequence involves governing clauses in past (*he said, he was saying*), or pluperfect or past perfect (*he had said*), and subordinate clauses in the past tense.

The primary sequence has proved to be a little less troublesome than the secondary sequence. Examples may be readily found, however: "It *was* [read *is*] as a professor of law—teaching torts especially—that Leon Green *will be* remembered."

Following are examples involving errors in the secondary sequence: "The majority opinion *did not go* [read *does not go*] so far, Justice Marshall said, and he would have dissented if it did." Or "The majority opinion *did not go* so far, Justice Marshall said, and he would have dissented *if it did* [read *if it had*]."/ "Unless there *was* a formed writ that exactly or nearly fitted the applicant's case, he generally *must* [read *had to*] take such inadequate relief as the inferior local courts offered."

Continuous tenses cause problems when the action described in the subordinate clause is supposed to have preceded the action that is stated in the past tense in the governing clause. E.g., "A jury being waived, the case was tried. . . ." [Read *A jury having been waived, the case was tried.* . . ."]/ "Fossils have been collected from the area on several occasions, the largest collection being [read *having been*] made by L. Kohl-Larsen in 1938-39."/ "Plaintiff sued in an Illinois District Court for damages he suffered in an accident occurring [read *that occurred* or *having occurred*] in Indiana." Or, better still, end the sentence as follows: *suffered in an accident in Indiana*, but not *suffered in an Indiana accident.*

A related problem occurs with (tenseless) infinitives, which, when put after a past-tense verb, are often wrongly made perfect infinitives, as here: "Accordingly, the trial judge was required *to have recused himself* [read *to recuse himself*] pursuant to the unambiguous dictates of the statute."/ "Although all but M. had served the number of years required for

their pension benefits *to have accrued* [read *to accrue*], all were still on active duty when their marriages were dissolved."/ "Today we witness another startling valid legal reason why this court *should have aborted, rather than to have given birth to,* [read *should have aborted, rather than given birth to,*] the monster child now known in our legal circles as '*Almanza* the Terrible.'"/ "When this happened (and without any negligence on the part of the bus driver) there did not remain sufficient time and distance for the bus driver *to have done* [read *to do*] anything to avoid the collision."/ "To have been fortunate enough *to have grown up* [read *to grow up*] with this fascinating book at hand . . . we count among such blessings as to be healthy (which we are), wealthy (which we aren't), and wise (which we may yet become)."/ "Certainly, it *would have been* desirable for the court *to have instructed* [read *to instruct*] the jury as to the proper standard for judging unreasonableness."

Still another bugbear is the incomplete verb phrase by which the writer attempts to give two tenses, but only one tense is actually completed: "This mischaracterization of pension rights *has, and unless overturned, will continue to result* [read *has resulted and, unless overturned, will continue to result*] in inequitable division of community assets."/ "This diversity case is one of a multitude of asbestos cases, presently filed and reasonably anticipated, in which injured plaintiffs or their survivors *have or will seek damages* [read *have sought or will seek damages*] for injuries associated with exposure to asbestos." See VERB PHRASES, INCOMPLETE.

As Partridge has pointed out, not sequence but mood is involved in the correct use of SUBJUNCTIVES, but the mistakes are common enough and closely enough related to merit treatment here: "This would have been a funny story if the headhunter *were* [read *had been*] joking, but he wasn't."/ "William put his arm around Ann and she could not thrust him away for fear he *fell out of the door* [read *would fall out the door*]." (Eng.)/ "If the title *were acquired* [read *was acquired*; see SUBJUNCTIVES] by purchase, the disseisee's entry was not barred." See STATUTE DRAFTING (B).

sequential; sequacious. *Sequential* means "forming a sequence or consequence." *Sequacious* means "intellectually servile."

sequential order is a REDUNDANCY. E.g., "The computer placed the checks *in sequential* *order* [read *in order* or *in sequence*] by account number."

sequester; sequestrate. *Sequestrate* means nothing that *sequester*, the more common term, does not also mean. Both terms are old: *sequester* dates from the fourteenth century, *sequestrate* from the early sixteenth century. In law, *sequester* = to remove (as property) from the possession of the owner temporarily; to seize and hold the effects of a debtor until the claims of creditors are satisfied (*OED*). The lay meaning of the term, of course, is "to set aside, separate," as *to sequester* (or *separate*) the jury. See **separate**.

Sequestrate is given two slightly different senses by the *OED*, in addition to the overlapping senses: (1) "to divert the income of an estate or benefice, temporarily or permanently, from its owner into other hands"; and (2) (in Scots law) "to place (lands belonging to a bankrupt, or of disputed ownership) in the hands of a judicial factor or trustee, for the prevention of waste." These two senses are rare, however, and the advice here is to avoid *sequestrate* as a NEEDLESS VARIANT unless a nuance conveyed by one of these specialized senses is intended. The sole weakness of this advice is illustrated in the next entry— namely, that the agent noun is *sequestrator* and not, ordinarily, *sequesterer.*

In the following examples, no such nuance was intended, and *sequester* would have been the better word: "It is difficult to see why a plaintiff in any action for a personal judgment in tort or contract may not also apply to the chancellor for a so-called injunction *sequestrating* [read *sequestering*] his opponent's assets pending recovery and satisfaction of a judgment in such a law action."/ "The practice of *sequestrating* [read *sequestering*] the property of the defendant to coerce his obedience to the decree was soon developed."

sequestrator = one who sequesters property. E.g., "The court appointed *sequestrators* to take possession of defendant's chattels." See the preceding entry.

Serbonian bog. See LITERARY ALLUSION (A) (4).

serendipity forms the adjective *serendipitous,* a useful term of recent vintage (c. 1943).

sergeant; serjeant. In medieval times this word (ultimately deriving fr. L. *servient* "serving") came to mean someone performing a specific function in the household or jurisdiction of a king, lord, or deliberative assembly and reporting directly to the top authority under which that person served. Of the more than fifty variant spellings of the term over the centuries, the preferred spelling in AmE today is *sergeant.* In BrE, there is some DIFFERENTIATION between the spelling: *sergeant* is largely military (*sergeant-major*) and *serjeant* largely legal (*serjeant of the coif, serjeant-at-law, serjeant-at-arms*). *Sargeant* is a common misspelling stemming perhaps from the casualism *sarge.*

sergeanty (or *serjeanty*) is the term for a form of feudal tenure under which a specified personal service was rendered to the king. The spelling *sergeantry* is incorrect. See the previous entry.

seriatim = in turn; serially; one after another; in sequence; successively. Though not uncommon, the word is a LATINISM to be eschewed in favor of its anglicized siblings *serially* and *in series.* E.g., "After presenting the factual and procedural setting, we dispose of the issues *seriatim* [read *serially*]."/ "One court refused to sever the civil-rights claims or to dismiss the state law ones, electing to submit all claims *serially* to the same jury."

series is ordinarily used in the singular, though it serves as a plural where more than one series is intended. Here the verb is incorrectly plural: "There *have* [read *has*] been a series of efforts made by the central P.L.O. but also splinter groups to move through Jordan into the West Bank."

Boswell quoted Samuel Johnson as using the now-obsolete plural *serieses* in a legal context: "Entails are good, because it is good to preserve in a country, *serieses* of men, to whom people are accustomed to look up as leaders." 2 Boswell, *Life of Johnson* 428 (1791).

serjeant. See **sergeant.**

servant. See **master & employer and employee.**

serve (= to make legal delivery of process or a writ) as a legal term dates back to the fifteenth century. In the legal idiom, one who serves process may either *serve* a writ *on* or *upon* another, or *serve* another *with* a writ.

service was once only a noun, but since the late nineteenth century has been used as a transitive verb as well. It may mean "to provide service for" ⟨the mechanic serviced the copying machine⟩, "to pay interest on" ⟨to service a debt⟩, or generally "to perform services for." Ordinarily, the verb *to serve* ought to be used in broad senses; *service*, v.t., should be used only where the writer believes that *serve* would not be suitable in idiom or sense.

service mark. See **trademark.**

servient. See **dominant.**

servitude. A. And *easement. Servitude* is primarily a civil-law term, deriving from L. *servitus* (= easement), and equivalent to the term *easement* in common law. But even in the common law, *servitude* has a restricted currency in referring to a servient tenement (i.e., land subject to an easement). Hence the DIFFERENTIATION usually observed in common-law countries is that *easement* refers to the personal enjoyment of the burdened property, and *servitude* to the burdened property itself.

An extension of *servitude* in this sense is its acceptation in international law: "an international agreement impressing on a territory a permanent status, such as one demilitarizing or neutralizing a state, or creating rights over water" (adapted fr. *OCL*).

B. And *slavery.* "[The] word *servitude* is of larger meaning than *slavery*, as the latter is popularly understood in this country, and the obvious purpose [of the thirteenth amendment] was to forbid all shades and conditions of African slavery." *Slaughter-House Cases*, 83 U.S. (16 Wall.) 36, 69 (1872). Both terms, in addition to denoting "the condition of being a slave or serf, or of being the property of another person," carry the notion of subjection to excessive labor.

session. See **cession.**

sessional, -ary. The latter is a NEEDLESS VARIANT of the adjective corresponding to the noun *session.*

set aside is often misunderstood by laymen. The courts use it, of course, to mean "to vacate." One lay writer on legal language misinterpreted the phrase as meaning "to lay to the side temporarily, as for review" (as "to take under advisement"). See LeClercq, *Jargon 2: Just When You Thought It Was Safe . . .* , 48

Tex. B. J. 852, 852 (1985). Such are the pitfalls awaiting those uninitiated into legal ARGOT. Rather, "[t]o *set aside* is to annul, to make void." *Migdol v. United States*, 298 F.2d 513, 516 (9th Cir. 1961). E.g., "The court held that a state has no power to retry an accused for murder after an earlier guilty verdict on the lesser included offense of voluntary manslaughter had been *set aside* because of a trial error."/ "The rule has long been established that where the grantor has not reserved a power to revoke, a voluntary trust may be *set aside* only upon a showing that it was induced by fraud, duress, undue influence, or mistake." See **overrule.**

set-off, n., is older than *offset*, and is considered more correct by purists. E.g., "That payment had been made only in respect of the plaintiff's claim and not in respect of the claim less the equitable *set-off*." (Aus.) The *OCL* includes *set-off*, which is usual in BrE, but not *offset*. See **offset.**

set of facts is more elegant, dignified, and descriptive than either *factual situation* or *fact situation.*, q.v.

set over = to alienate; convey. E.g., "Vendor does by these presents grant, bargain, sell, assign, convey, transfer, *set over*, and deliver to the purchaser the following described property."

SET PHRASES. Fossilized language should not be consciously de-fossilized—which is to say that one should not try to vary what has been set in stone. Thus *set in stone* should never become *set in shale*, or whatever variation one might lamely invent. One should not change *madding crowd* to *maddening crowd*, for instance. Cf. INELEGANT VARIATION. Set phrases are sometimes changed out of a sense of cleverness, sometimes out of ignorance. A maladroit example appears in the following sentence: "Time is the essence of this subcontract." [Read *Time is of the essence in this subcontract*.] Indeed, so well entrenched in the language are many expressions that the slightest change will make them unEnglish. E.g., we have the phrase *out from under*, ruined by a metamorphosis in this sentence: "Plaintiff was injured when the back of the teller stool on which she was sitting fell off and the chair rolled *out from underneath her* [read *out from under her*]."

Follett called set phrases "inviolable" (if

not quite inviolate): "the attempt to liven up old clichés by inserting modifiers into the set phrase is a mistake: the distended phrase is neither original, nor unobtrusive, nor brief, and sometimes it has ceased to be immediately clear, as in *They have been reticent to a tactical fault." Modern American Usage* 303 (1966). In addition to the fault of inserting modifiers into set phrases, three other faults commonly occur. First, it is wrong to wrench a set phrase into ungrammatical contexts, as here: "This was reported to *we the people.*" The phrase *we the people*, of course, derives from the U.S. Constitution; but the sentence calls for the objective *us.* Second, it is bad style to substitute an alien word for the familiar one in a well-known phrase. E.g., changing *in large part* or *in large measure* to *in large degree* does not work: "The prejudice to appellant is attributable *in large degree* [read *in large part*] to appellant's own conduct." Third, it is poor to aim at novelty by reversing the usual order of a phrase: "Many persons must rely upon Medicaid for their well-being and health." (The standard phrase is *health and well-being.*)

settled. See **well-settled.**

settlement. See **compromise & accord and satisfaction.**

settler, -or. The two forms usually convey different senses. *Settler* = (1) one who settles; or (2) a homesteader. *Settlor* = the creator of a trust; a party to an instrument. *Settlor* has also been used, however, of one who settles a case: "The *settlors* [read *settlers*] have agreed between themselves that the worker shall retain the face value of the settlement and that the third party shall be responsible for satisfaction of the compensation lien."

settlor; trustor; donor; creator. These four terms are used to name the person who establishes a trust. The first is the commonest. It should be spelled with the *-or* suffix to differentiate it from the quite different word *settler*, q.v. See **creator.**

several for *separate* is an ARCHAISM of Shakespearean vintage that has survived only in legal language. The usage survives primarily in the phrase *joint and several liability*, but thrives in other contexts as well: "It was early established that the inheriting daughters did not hold as joint tenants; they were not subject to procedural rules which governed joint tenancy, and each had a *several* interest."/ "The share of each tenant in common is, unlike that of a joint tenant, *several* and distinct from the shares of his cotenants."/ "The constitutional rule requiring bills to be read on three *several* days in each house is hereby suspended."/ "The dispute does not cease to be a priori because it is a matter of the cumulative effect of *severally* inconclusive premises." (Eng.) See **joint and several.**

severalty = the condition of being separate or distinct. The legal phrase *in severalty* is used in law in reference to land, and means "held in a person's own right without being joined in interest with another" (*OED*). E.g., "The whole transaction required the cooperation of all for its success; the division of the shares among them was as much a part of it as any other; they selected each other as owners in *severalty*; and they should be held liable for any defaults of those whom they chose, although their liability is secondary."

sewage; sewerage. *Sewage* is the refuse conveyed through sewers, and *sewerage* means either the removal of sewage or the system of removal.

sex, adj.; **sexual.** Both *sex discrimination* and *sexual discrimination* appear in law reports. The former is perhaps better, inasmuch as *sexual* has come to refer more to sexual intercourse and things pertaining to it than to gender. See **gender.**

SEXISM. Many who at first shrugged off the claims of feminists that the English language can be detrimentally sexist have come to shrug off only the wilder and more militant claims; that is to say, many of the contentions are valid. The best advice that can be given is to minimize in our writing whatever might be deemed sexist by sensitive persons, while not resorting to ugly or awkward linguistic artifices to achieve that effect. The balance is a delicate one, and it is impossible at this point to offer ironclad rules.

 A. The Pronominal Problem. English has a number of common-sex general words, such as *person, anyone, everyone,* and *no one,* but no common-sex singular personal pronouns. Instead, we have *he, she,* and *it,* the first denoting a male; the second denoting a female; and the third denoting a nonhuman object or being (albeit occasionally babies). In general literary and legal usage, the traditional course has been to use the masculine pronouns *he* and *him* to cover all persons, male and female alike. That this practice has come under increasing attack has caused the single most difficult problem in the realm of sexist language. Other snarls are far more readily solvable.

The inadequacy of the English language in this respect becomes apparent when one reads, for example, in an opinion addressing medical malpractice in the performance of a hysterectomy: "The objective of the doctrine of informed consent is to ensure that the patient's right to self-determination by requiring that *he* have access to all [the] knowledge necessary for *him* to give an intelligent and informed consent." Then again, at times, although the context may not render the masculine ludicrous, one feels bludgeoned by its use at every turn: "The vital principle is that *he* who by *his* language or conduct leads another to do what *he* would not otherwise have done, shall not subject such person to loss or injury by disappointing the expectations upon which *he* acted." The sentence is hardly outrageous, but one who writes this way today shows little sensitivity in the gratuitous introduction of the masculine personal pronoun.

"There are," Fowler notes, with contributions from Gowers,

> three makeshifts: first, *as anybody can see for himself or herself*; second, *as anybody can see for themselves*; and third, *as anybody can see for himself.* No one who can help it chooses the first; it is correct, and is sometimes necessary, but it is so clumsy as to be ridiculous except when explicitness is urgent, and it usually sounds like a bit of pedantic humour. The second is the popular solution; it sets the literary man's teeth on edge, and he exerts himself to give the same meaning in some entirely different way if he is not prepared to risk the third, which is here recommended. It involves the convention (statutory in the interpretation of documents) that where the matter of sex is not conspicuous or important the masculine form shall be allowed to represent a person instead of a man, or say a man (*homo*) instead of a man (*vir*).
>
> *MEU2* 404 (1965).

A fourth makeshift is now available, and it is commonly used by American legal writers: *as anybody can see for herself.* Such phrases are often alternated with those containing masculine pronouns, or, in the writing of women, are often uniformly used. Whether this phra-

seology will cease to sound strange to us only time will tell. This is the one possibility, however, of: (1) maintaining a grammatical construction; (2) avoiding the awkwardness of alternatives like *himself or herself*; and (3) satisfying the feminists, who are bound to prevail in some way in the end. The risk in this method, however, is that unintended connotations may invade the writing. A recent novel was published in two versions, one using masculine generic pronouns, and the other using feminine generic pronouns; the effects on readers of the two versions were reported to have been startlingly different in ways far too complex for discussion here.

Typographical gimmickry may once have served a political purpose, but it should be avoided as an answer to the problem. It is trendy, ugly, distracting, and usually unpronounceable. E.g., "A district judge who, on reflection, concludes that *s/he* erred may rectify that error when ruling on post-trial motions." *United States v. Miller*, 753 F.2d 19, 23 (3d Cir. 1985). Variants are *he/she* and *she/he.* If we must have alternatives, *he or she* is the furthest we should go. See **he or she.**

The likelihood is, however, that the masculine singular personal pronoun will survive indefinitely as the generic term. Among the more militant claims of the feminists is that "[e]veryone who defends this system of using male terms to include women helps to cheat women." Ritchie, *The Language of Oppression—Alice Talks Back*, 23 McGill L.J. 535, 536 (1977). To paraphrase Fowler, though, whether the convention of using the masculine singular to include both sexes is an arrogant demand by males of the English-speaking world, everyone must decide for himself (or for himself or herself, or for herself, or for themselves).

B. Words in *man-* and *-man.* "The Supreme Court is struggling *manfully*, but with questionable success, to establish a formula for delimiting who may sue that stops short of 'anybody who might be significantly affected by the situation [q.v.] he seeks to litigate.'"/ "For the lawyer more than for most *men*, it is true that *he* who knows but cannot express what *he* knows might as well be ignorant." The second sentence quoted begins Henry Weihofen's *Legal Writing Style* (2d ed. 1980); were he writing today, no doubt Weihofen would express himself in neutral language.

In September 1984, the Commonwealth Attorney-General's Department in Canberra,

Australia, issued a press release entitled "Moves to Modify Language Sex Bias in Legislation." The release states that "[t]he Government accepts that drafting in 'masculine' language may contribute to some extent to the perpetuation of a society in which men and women see women as lesser beings." The press release recommends, "[w]here possible and appropriate, avoidance of the use of words ending in *man*, such as *chairman, serviceman, seaman*, and so on." See Note, *The De-Masculinisation of Language in Federal Legislation*, 58 Aus. L.J. 685, 685–86 (1984). Similarly, on March 2, 1987, the U.S. Supreme Court announced its adoption of changes to the Federal Rules of Civil Procedure that weed out references to gender; thus Rule 4(b) has been changed so that *him* and *his* now read *the defendant* and *the defendant's*. See 55 U.S.L.W. 1138, 4265–90 (March 10, 1987).

The process is at work elsewhere. The Longshoremen's and Harbor Workers' Compensation Act, 33 U.S.C. § 901 (1927), was amended by the Longshore and Harbor Workers' Compensation Act (1984). Similarly, American courts have begun to write opinions in more neutral language, sometimes obtrusively neutral. E.g., "The affreightment contracts are commercial undertakings entered into by sophisticated *businesspersons*."/ "This diversity case involves a breach of a personal service contract between Gaylord, the owner of a New Orleans television station, and Lynn Gansar, one of Gaylord's former news *anchorpersons*." Some of the extremes to which the trend has been taken seem absurd, e.g., "This case presents another example of the waste of time, energy, legal and judicial *personpower* and consequent waste of money occasioned by the existence of the Family Court as a separate court of limited jurisdiction." *In re Anthony T.*, 389 N.Y.S.2d 86, 87 (N.Y. Fam. Ct. 1976).

The traditional language of the law abounds in *-man* words: *remainderman, venireman* (q.v.), *warehouseman, materialman, foreman* (q.v.), *landman, bondsman*, and *juryman*. The last of these is virtually obsolete alongside *juror*; it was in common use, however, up to a quarter-century ago. Courts have experimented with replacements for *foreman*, e.g.: "[W]e are unable to conclude that the state trial judge erred in deciding that the *foreperson's* statement that the jury was unable to agree was more than an expression of present inability to agree." *Fay v. McCotter*, 765 F.2d 475, 478 (5th Cir. 1985). Stylists generally acknowledge that the *-person* words are ugly and ineffective, although *chairperson* lingers on. (See **chairman.**) With *foreman*, a happier nonsexist expression is *presiding juror*.

Venireman is gradually undergoing transmutation, or, more accurately, emasculation: "It was not error for the court to refuse to ask *venirepersons* whether the testimony of the government investigator was entitled to more weight than the testimony of any other witness."/ "I respectfully dissent from the holding that this case should be remanded for inquiry into the prosecution's reasons for exercising its peremptory challenges against black *venirepersons*." Justice Rehnquist has used both *venireman* and *veniremember* in a single opinion. See *Wainwright v. Witt*, 469 U.S. 412, 418-19 (1985). (See INELEGANT VARIATION.) In that opinion, one use of *venireman* was specifically in reference to a woman, a Mrs. Colby. (See *id.*) Justice Rehnquist is right, however, to avoid the *-person* form. If we must have a neutral term, *veniremember* seems to be the better option.

Remainderman, warehouseman, and *longshoreman* are less easily neutralized. Legal writers have experimented with *remainderperson, remainderer, -or*, and *remainor*. None is quite satisfactory. The *-er* suffix does show promise, though: *warehouser* is listed in *W3*; it would certainly take some getting used to, like all linguistic changes. Yet *longshorer* and *remainderer* are more difficult to pronounce distinctly with the *-er*. Perhaps we can satisfy ourselves, however, that, in having reached these words in our analysis of sexist terminology, we have gone to the very outskirts of the language.

But it would be inappropriate to end our discussion here. Many of us, males and females alike, view language from a historical perspective, and do not consider *-man* any more sexist than *-or* (the masculine agent-noun suffix for Latinate words). We see nothing incongruous in a female chairman or remainderman. Are we to be stereotyped as perpetrators of evil upon women, as relegating them to the status of lesser beings than men? Perhaps so, in these days, no matter how benighted or unjust that stereotype is. As the English language lumbers toward solution of these problems, there is no resting easy: we run the risk of being called Neanderthal if we stick with traditional terms, or Trendy Fop if we snap up the first suggested alternative (no matter how preposterous). For the time being, a middle ground of "nothing overmuch" is hard to find.

C. Feminine Forms in *-ess* and *-trix*. Legal prose is perhaps the last bastion of these feminine forms. We have *prosecutrix; testatrix; tutrix; relatrix; conciliatrix, -tress; heritrix, -tress; inheritrix, -tress,* and even such rarely seen oddities as *dictatrix, -tress; victrix, -ess;* and *aviatrix, -ess.* Most of these are moribund, and the advice here given is to speed them to their graves. For most legal writers, it is far less bothersome to read of a *woman testator* than it is to read of a *lady booksalesman.* The Latinate agent nouns in *-or* are almost universally perceived as being common-sex terms. We have never, for example, thought it odd that women may be termed *litigators*—and we have gotten along fine without *litigatrix.* With the loss of terms in *-ess* and *-trix* we lose a nuance in the language, but the nuance is hardly worth preserving.

shadow of a doubt, beyond the. This phrase is a CLICHÉ to be avoided. E.g., "It is clear *beyond the shadow of a doubt* [read *beyond doubt*] that no TVA employee with proper authority had either ordered or accepted this microfilm."

shall. A. In Legislation. This overworked auxiliary verb invariably denotes an imperative rather than futurity when it appears in DRAFTING. Pitfalls await especially the statute-drafter who is not familiar with some of the niceties of this word, however. See STATUTE DRAFTING (B).

1. And *may.* The word *shall* ordinarily connotes language of command. *Anderson v. Yungkau,* 329 U.S. 482, 485 (1947); *Ballou v. Kemp,* 92 F.2d 556, 558 (D.C. Cir. 1937). *May* is permissive; it merely states what is allowed.

2. Rights Stated as Duties. Especially in statutes, drafters should not state a right as a duty to enjoy the right. E.g., "He shall receive a salary of $80,000 a year." [Read *His salary will be $80,000 a year,* or *He is entitled to a salary of $80,000 a year.*]

3. Negative Subject with Mandatory Verb. Statute-drafters should also avoid use of a negative subject with the verb *shall.* "No person shall" is weaker than "No person may," for the former, rather than proscribing an act, says literally that no one is required to act. *No person may* not only negates all obligation but denies all permission as well. See STATUTE DRAFTING (A).

B. And *will.* Grammarians formerly relied on the following paradigm, which remains helpful in formal prose:

SIMPLE FUTURITY

	Singular	Plural
First Person	I shall	we shall
Second Person	you will	you will
Third Person	he will	they will

DETERMINATION, PROMISE, OR COMMAND

	Singular	Plural
First Person	I will	we will
Second Person	you shall	you shall
Third Person	he shall	they shall

Legally, of course, it usually makes no difference whether *will* or *shall* is used, as long as the writer is consistent. One pitfall of unconscious inconsistency, esp. in DRAFTING, is that *shall* is seen as being stronger than *will,* so that switching from one to the other may suggest to a court interpreting the writing that some duties or obligations are stronger than others.

sham plea. See **false plea.**

shave ⟩ shaved ⟩ shaved. *Shaven* exists only as a past participial adjective ⟨clean-shaven face⟩. Cf. **proved.**

s/he. See SEXISM (A).

sheaves is the plural both of *sheaf* (= a bundle) and of *sheave* (= a pulley). *Sheaves* is also, as a verb, the second-person singular of the verb *to sheave* (= to bind into a sheaf).

Shelley's Case, the Rule in. See CAPITALIZATION (A).

shepardize is a mid-twentieth-century -IZE NEOLOGISM derived from *Shepard's Citators.* Originally, the word was capitalized as a word derived from a proper name: "If you have before you a recent case in a nisi prius court or in an intermediate court of appeal, do not rest content with *Shepardizing* it." Blair, *Appellate Briefs and Advocacy,* 18 Fordham L. Rev. 30, 40 (1949). Today, however, the word has lost the initial capital deriving from the source-word. E.g., "Apparently failing to properly *shepardize* that case, neither plaintiff's nor defendant's counsel cited to this Court a Florida case . . . which specifically rejects *Touissaint.*" *Caster v. Hennessey,* 727 F.2d 1075, 1077 (11th Cir. 1984).

In G.B., the equivalent volumes are termed *noter-ups*, and one *notes up* one's cases. See **note up.**

sheriffalty; shrievalty. Both terms date from the early sixteenth century and refer to a *sheriff*: to his jurisdiction, to his term of office, to his reponsibilities in office, or to all three. In English antiquity, the *sheriff* represented the royal authority in a district (i.e., a *shire*) and presided at the *shire-moot*, the judicial assembly of the shire. Today the position of *high sheriff* of a county (i.e., of a *shire*, a term no longer used officially, though it continues to have historic and literary meaning) is an honorary one, largely nominal and ceremonial.

W3 and the *OED* suggest that *shrievalty* is the more widely used term and that *sheriffalty* is a NEEDLESS VARIANT, even though *shrieve* is an obsolete variant of *sheriff*. Nevertheless, *sheriffalty* is surely more widely comprehensible.

sheriff. See **sheriffalty.**

sheriffdom; sheriffwick. See **bailiwick.**

shew is an obsolete spelling of *show* that occurred in AmE and BrE writing, legal as well as nonlegal, up to the early nineteenth century.

shifting use. See **springing use.**

shire. See **sheriffalty.**

shoe-in is incorrect for *shoo-in*, q.v.

shone; shined. The former is the past tense of the intransitive *shine* ⟨the sun shone⟩, the latter the past tense of the transitive *shine* ⟨he shined his shoes⟩.

shoo-in. The colloquialism is so spelled.

should. See **ought to** & **shall.**

should/could is the type of monstrosity that would-be profound writers, or terminally wishy-washy ones, are fond of. E.g., "*Should/could* states impose additional requirements that must be met in order to obtain a hearing?" Typographical gimmickry of this sort ought to be avoided; surely the perpetrator does not actually believe he conveys otherwise overlooked nuances. See **and/or** & SEXISM (A).

show + (to be) (as). The infinitive *to be* is generally preferable to *as* after this verb. E.g., "It is incumbent upon the district court to weigh that claim in light of the facts at hand and in light of any alternatives that may be *shown as* [read *shown to be*] feasible and more promising in their effectiveness."

show cause (= to give a reason) is common lawyer's ARGOT. E.g., "The district court issued an order to *show cause* why the union should not be required to appear before the Secretary of Labor and produce the papers specified in the subpoena."

This verb phrase has of late given rise to a corresponding compound adjective: "The *Ruiz* court may issue a *show-cause* order for criminal or civil contempt."/ "At the *show-cause* hearing, appellant testified that because no one had called to schedule his testimony, he assumed that the case had been settled or continued." See ADJECTIVES (C).

shrievalty. See **sheriffalty.**

shyster = a rascally lawyer; one that is shrewdly dishonest. See **pettifogger** & LAWYER, DEROGATORY NAMES FOR.

sic (= thus, so) is used to indicate that a word preceding this bracketed editor's mark in a quoted passage is reproduced as it appeared in the original document. *Sic* at its best is intended to aid the reader (or a typesetter following copy), who may be confused by whether it was the quoter or the writer quoted who is responsible for the spelling or grammatical anomaly.

Some writers, however, use *sic* meanly and with a false sense of superiority. Its use may frequently reveal more about the quoter than about the author of the quoted material. For example, a recent book review of an English legal text contained a *sic* in its first sentence after the verb *analyse*, which appeared thus on the book's dust-jacket. In AmE, of course, the preferred spelling is *analyze*; in BrE, however, the spelling *analyse* is not uncommon and certainly does not deserve a *sic*. In fact, all the quoter demonstrated was his own ignorance of British usage.

Another irksome use of *sic* occurs when writers insert it in others' citations, as if to belittle the person quoted for his ignorance of correct citation form. For example, a federal appeals court judge had the audacity to *sic* the

Supreme Court's citation of one of its own cases: "We strike the balance in favor of institutional security, which we have noted is 'central to all other corrections goals,' *Pell v. Procunier*, 417 U.S., [*sic*] at 823, 94 S. Ct., [*sic*] at 2804." *Thorne v. Jones*, 765 F.2d 1270, 1275 (5th Cir. 1985). The better course would be to leave the citations as they are without comment, or to give one's own "correct" version in brackets without comment.

sic transit. "With our decision today, all I can say is *sic transit United Beef Producers, Inc.* and Rule 320, Tex. R. Civ. P." A fairly common Latin maxim from Classical literature is *Sic transit gloria mundi*, "so passes away the glory of the world." Some legal writers have adapted the first two words of the phrase to denote the lamentable passing of a convention or doctrine, as in the sentence initially quoted in this entry.

sic utere. The *sic utere* doctrine embodies the Latin maxim *sic utere tuo, ut alienum non laedas*, which means "use your own property in such a manner as not to injure that of another." E.g., "These sections of the Louisiana Civil Code owe an expression of the *sic utere* doctrine that limits the rights of proprietors in the use of their property." Holmes called this Latin maxim an "empty general proposition" that leads to "hollow deductions." O.W. Holmes, *Privilege, Malice, and Intent*, in *Collected Legal Papers* 120 (1920).

sidebar, n., is an ellipsis in the U.S. for *sidebar conference* (= a discussion among the lawyers involved in a case and the judge outside the hearing of the jury). E.g., "Counsel then requested a *sidebar*."

The term *sidebar* derives from a bar or partition formerly within Westminster Hall. Each morning in term, attorneys argued motions to the judges *ex parte* from within the sidebar.

sideswipe; sidewipe. *Sideswipe* (= to strike a glancing blow), dating from the early automotive age (1926), is the term to use. *Sidewipe*, an artificial form, has no valid standing.

sight unseen. From a strictly logical point of view, the phrase makes little sense. In practice, however, it has an accepted and useful meaning: an item is bought *sight unseen* when it has not been inspected before the purchase.

signatary, adj. See **signatory**, adj.

signatary, n.; **-tory; signator.** Fowler and Krapp both recommended in 1927 that *signatary* be adopted as the preferred noun. See Fowler, *MEU1* 534; Krapp, *A Comprehensive Guide to Good English* 540 (1927). Today, however, *signatary* is virtually never used; the *COD* and *W9* contain *signatory* only. E.g., "International commercial litigation involving nationals of *signatories* to the Hague Convention is not at all infrequent." *Signatory* may be an adjective as well as a noun (Krapp considered it the only adjectival form), often a POSTPOSITIVE ADJECTIVE, e.g.: "It has been finally executed by the parties *signatory*, and is, in and of itself, supposed to pass property only upon death." See the following entry.

Signator, modeled on Latinate agent nouns, is a NEEDLESS VARIANT of *signatory*, n. E.g., "Liability under section 11 is limited to *signators* [read *signatories*] of the registration statement, directors or partners of the issuer, experts named as preparing or certifying a portion of the registration statement, or underwriters with respect to the issue."

signatory, adj.; **signatural.** *Signatory* = forming one of those (persons or governments) whose signatures are attached to a document (*OED*). See **signatary.** *Signatural* = of or pertaining to signatures.

signature. See **countersignature.**

significance; signification. These should be distinguished. *Significance* = (1) a subtly or indirectly conveyed meaning; suggestiveness; the quality of implying; or (2) the quality of being important or significant. *Signification* = (1) the act of signifying, as by symbols; or (2) the purport or sense intended to be conveyed by a word or other symbol.

silk; silk gown. These terms are metonymous for "jurist." In England, a Queen's Counsel wears a silk gown; hence to *obtain, receive*, or *take silk*, means to become a Queen's Counsel, and *silk* and *silk gown* have come to denote a person who has achieved this rank.

SIMILES, very simply, are comparisons constructed with *like* or *as*. They are unlike METAPHORS inasmuch as comparisons through metaphor are implicit (e.g., "this case *is* a real bear") and comparisons through simile are explicit (e.g., "trying this case *is like* wrestling with a grizzly bear"). Today similes have largely fallen out of favor with nonfiction stylists, and especially with legal stylists, for they are essentially irrelevant and usually unpersuasive. E.g., in an appellate brief, the following similes pose if anything setbacks to the advocate; both sentences actually appeared in American lawyers' briefs: "Not reversing this case would be *like the United States's failing to challenge the pernicious crimes of Hitler in the Second World War*; the United States did so, and this honorable Court should likewise reverse."/ "To allow what was done in the instant case would be not only to expand Rule 35 to a point where it is no longer frozen *as a mastodon in a glacier* but to allow resentencing under Rule 35 to be *as molten lava cascading down a mountain* and destroying the remainder of the double jeopardy protection afforded by the Constitution." (In the second example, of course, the word of comparison should be *like*, not *as*.) See PURPLE PROSE.

Not all similes are quite so insipid; nor have they always been so disfavored. Chief Justice Marshall, who was by no means inclined to this figure of speech, found simile useful on occasion: "To waste time and argument in proving that without [the authority to make necessary and proper laws] Congress might carry its powers into execution, would be *not much less idle than to hold a lighted taper to the sun.*" *McCulloch v. Maryland*, 4 U.S. (4 Wheat.) 316, 419 (1819). Judges, of course, are allowed more leeway than advocates in waxing poetic.

simony. See **barratry.**

simpliciter (= simply, summarily, taken alone) can usually be said more simpliciter. E.g., "I concur heartily in the court's judgment that a grand jury subpoena *simpliciter* [read *simply* or, depending on the sense, *taken alone*] does not satisfy the more rigorous requirements." *Doe v. DiGenova*, 779 F.2d 74, 92 (D.C. Cir. 1985) (Starr, J., concurring)./ "If I were satisfied that these remarks could be read as intending *to include racial 'differentiation' simpliciter* [read *simply to include racial 'differentiation'*], I would be happy to regard the whole question as concluded by authority." (Rhod.) The LATINISM adds only obscurity. See FORBIDDEN WORDS.

simplistic is a pejorative adjective meaning "oversimple; facile." E.g., "I do not mean to endorse the *simplistic* view that the words printed in the United States Code can answer all questions regarding the meaning of stat-

utes." It is not a synonym for *simple*, though apparently used thus in this sentence: "The *simplistic* [read *simple?*] notion that parties exercise their volition by committing themselves to future action (or inaction), and that the law provides their circle of assent with the status of private law, is fundamental to any discussion of contracts."

since. See **as** (A).

since ... then is catachrestic as a causal construction. E.g., "*Since* plaintiff purchased the pool after defendant had built it for the previous owner, *then* the express warranty is void according to the terms of the contract." The problem is remedied by leaving out *then*.

sine damno (= without damage) is an unnecessary LATINISM. E.g., "If the act be *sine damno* [read *without damage*], no action on the case will lie." (Eng.) See **damnum.**

sine die (= without a day) is used to indicate that no date has been set for resumption (meeting adjourned sine die). It is OFFICIALESE for "indefinitely." E.g., "The court adjourned *sine die.*" 2 U.S. (2 Dall.) 400 (1790). A related phrase, *go hence without day*, is a LOAN TRANSLATION of the LAW FRENCH *aller sans jour*; the phrase is used exclusively in reference to adjournment taken with no date set for resumption of the proceedings or meeting.

sine qua non (L. "without which not") = an indispensable condition or thing. This LATINISM is common in both lay and legal writing, and should remain unmolested by plain-English reform. E.g., "In my view the temporary injunction is not supported by an adequate showing of irreparable injury, the recognized *sine qua non* of such relief in this character of case."/ "*Goldfarb* is not properly read as making compulsion a *sine qua non* to state-action immunity."/ "We are mindful that *sine qua non* [read *the sine qua non*] in a prosecutorial vindictiveness claim is that the second charge is in fact harsher than the first." Cf. **but for.**

singlehanded(ly). The preferred adverb is *singlehanded*; *-ly* is an unnecessary adverbial form.

single out. It would be simplistically literal to insist that this phrase cannot refer to more than one thing. E.g., "These two men have been *singled out* for their bravery in the face of disappointment and hardship."

sister, as an adj. ⟨sister state⟩, is rather quaintly used in a number of expressions, perhaps more commonly today in legal than in lay contexts. Like *she* in reference to states or ships, *sister* may be obsolescent because of whatever latent SEXISM may be dredged up by feminists who seek to eliminate every vestige of male-female differentiation in the language.

Some typical examples of *sister* as traditionally used follow: "Our holding is therefore that, as a matter of comity, we will enforce the equitable decrees of a *sister state* affecting Texas land as long as such enforcement does not contravene an established public policy in this State."/ "It is a general rule that, upon a sufficient showing of facts, a court of equity in any state may enjoin a citizen of that state from prosecuting a suit against another citizen thereof, in the courts of a *sister state.*"

Not only does a state have 49 *sister states* in the U.S., but also the federal judicial circuits, by analogy, have *sister circuits.* E.g., "Four of our sister circuits have held that the time expended by an attorney litigating the fee claim is justifiably included in the court's fee award."

sistren is the archaic and dialectal equivalent of *brethren,* q.v. Karl Llewellyn once began a speech with the jocular remark, "Well, Brethren and *Sistren,* I find myself in a completely impossible position." Llewellyn, *A Lecture on Appellate Advocacy,* 29 U. Chi. L. Rev. 627, 627 (1962).

site, v.t., (= to locate, place, or provide with a site) is to be distinguished from *cite,* q.v. E.g., "The state law of Texas defines whether the taxpayer has a property right in the Texas-*sited* realty; if he does, it is subject to the government tax lien."

site, n. See **situs.**

situate, p.pl.; **situated.** The language of the law abounds in needless ARCHAISMS, and *situate* used as a past participle is one of them. Historically, it is one of a great many English participial adjectives formed from Latin perfect passive participles—e.g., *corrupt* (from the Latin *corruptus,* "having been spoiled"), *select, compact, effeminate, legitimate,* and *adequate.* In the Renaissance, many more such participial

adjectives existed than do today. Those that have not survived in the Latinate *t*-form (ending in *-t* or *-te*) have been thoroughly anglicized, taking on the English past participial suffix *-ed.* The verb *to situate* is among these.

Many wills contain phrases such as the following: "All the rest, residue, and remainder of my estate, real as well as personal and wheresoever *situate* [read *situated*], of which I die seised and possessed, I direct my executor to distribute as he considers it will be most effective in the advancement of Christ's Kingdom on Earth."/ "I give, devise, and bequeath all my property and estate of whatsoever nature whether real, personal, or mixed, and wheresoever *situate* [read *situated*], unto my two beloved children."

The usage appears even in judicial opinions and statutes. E.g., "The land in question, *situate* [read *situated*] in Multnomah County, was bought by the defendant Pennoyer at a sale upon the judgment of such suit."/ "Such a decree may perhaps be attacked on the ground that its enforcement would violate some fundamental policy of the laws of the state where the land is *situate* [read *situated*]."/ "[T]he county court of the district in which the registered office of the company is *situate* [read *situated*] shall . . . have concurrent jurisdiction with the High Court. . . . " Companies Act 1948 § 218(3).

Shakespeare, in *Love's Labour's Lost,* had one of his pompous comic characters say, "I know where it is *situate.*" Some lawyers continue to use the word similarly, probably unaware of the comic pomposity of the word. It is time they came into the twentieth century and wrote *situated.*

One other point about this word merits attention. *Situate* is often superfluous, as in "Appellee's car was *situated* about three feet from the south curb of Jackson Street." The word could be dropped from the sentence with no change in meaning, and with enhanced concision.

situation has, in one of its senses, become a VOGUE WORD, and is often used superfluously, as here: "The instructor told his class that there had been many instances *of starvation situations, where* [read *of starvation, when*] people simply could not eat monkey, snake, horse, or rodent meat, and died because of it."

It is also often used illogically: "He might be significantly affected by the *situation* he seeks to litigate." One does not litigate a situation. *Dispute, issue,* and *claim* are all more specific examples of what can be litigated. See **litigate.**

situs is a legal word not quite equivalent to *site. Situs* (pl. *situs*) = the location or position of (something) for legal purposes. E.g., "Historically, federal courts used a *situs* or locality test to determine whether a tort action was within admiralty jurisdiction."/ "The validity of a will of land is determined by the *situs* of the land."

Sometimes *situs* is misleading: "If the will contains a devise of land, the will must be probated *at the situs of the land* [read *in the jurisdiction in which the land is located*] in order to establish title." (It is not necessary that probate be obtained at the very site where the land is; rather, the will must be probated by a court having territorial jurisdiction over the land.) See **locus.**

six of one, half a dozen of the other is one of our most shopworn CLICHÉS.

siz(e)able. The preferred spelling is *sizable* in AmE, *sizeable* in BrE. See MUTE E.

skeptic(al); sceptic(al). The former is the AmE, the latter the BrE spelling.

skid is incorrect as a preterite; *skidded* is the correct form. "He *skid* [read *skidded*] down the slope."

skil(l)ful. In AmE the term is written *skillful*; in BrE, *skilful.* Cf. **wil(l)ful.**

skul(l)duggery; scul(l)duggery. *Skullduggery* is a misspelling of *skulduggery* (= trickery; unscrupulous behavior), the spelling preferred over the forms beginning *sc-*.

skyjack; hijack. Today airline hijackings are still sometimes termed *skyjackings* by journalists. *Skyjacking* is a PORTMANTEAU WORD. *Hijacking* remains the more common word, however. See **hijack.**

skyrocket, v.i., is a favorite CLICHÉ of hyperbolists; in the following sentence, however, it may be accurate: "Most close corporations simply do not have the capital to afford the *skyrocketing* costs of products liability insurance."

slander. See **libel & defamation.**

slip opinion; advance sheet. In the U.S., reported opinions appear first individually in *slip opinions,* and are then collected in softcover *advance sheets,* before appearing in the hard-cover reporters.

SLIPSHOD EXTENSION is the extension of a word beyond its accepted denotation or connotations, because of a misunderstanding of its true sense. Several individual entries in this dictionary refer to this heading. "Slipshod extension is especially likely to occur," explained Fowler, "when some accident gives currency among the uneducated to words of learned origin, and the more if they are isolated or have few relatives in the vernacular" (*MEU1* 540). Today one might rightly accuse not only the uneducated, but the educated as well, of the linguistic distortion of *a priori* and *protagonist,* qq.v., to name but two of any number of possible examples. For other examples, see **ad hoc, alibi, alias, calculus, compound, dilemma, duplicity, egoism, enjoinder, factor, hopefully, literally, material, medicine, veracity, verbal, viable, & vitiate.** See also POPULARIZED LEGAL TECHNICALITIES.

slow has long been treated as an immediate adverb, i.e., one not requiring the *-ly* suffix. It is ill-informed pedantry to insist that *slow* cannot be an adverb; though *slowly* is more common, and is certainly correct, *slow* is often just as good in the adverbial sense. Euphony should govern the choice between *slow* and *slowly.* E.g., Coleridge wrote, in "The Complaint of a Forsaken Indian Woman": "I'll follow you across the snow,/ You travel heavily and *slow.*" The usage is common in legal contexts: "One should go *slow* about relying on decisions of the Supreme Court of the United States in any but the federal field."

smellfungus (= a faultfinder, grumbler) is too valuable a word, especially for lawyers in ad hominem reference to other lawyers, to be as neglected as it is.

snuck is a nonstandard preterite of *sneak* common in American dialectal and informal English. The past tense to be used in formal writing is *sneaked.*

so. A. Omission of. This error is not uncommon. E.g., "The court of appeals concluded, although it was the first *court to* [read *court so to*] hold, that the nineteenth-century joinder cases in this court created a federal, common-law, substantive right in a certain class of persons to be joined in the corresponding lawsuits."

B. For *very.* The casualism of substituting *so* for *very* should be avoided in formal writing. E.g., "He cannot reason *so well* [read *very well*]."

so as + infinitive. This construction is a common and a useful one in legal writing, but it often leads to problems. Most common among these is the unnecessary repetition of *so*: "Was the omission by Jacobs *so* trivial and innocent *so as* [read *as*] not to be a breach of the condition?"/ "A change will not be tolerated if it is *so* dominant and pervasive *so as* [read *as*] to frustrate the purpose of the contract."/ "If you define it *so* broadly *so as* [read *as*] to exclude nothing, then you have done nothing."/ "The issue is whether the company *so* clothed H. with the mantel of authority *so as* [read *as*] to cause X. to rely upon his words."

In the following sentences, *as* has been suppressed, leaving the syntax incomplete: "We do not believe that the acceptance in the case at bar diverged *so* radically from the terms of the offer *to warrant* [read *as to* warrant] this result."/ "If a defendant's activities are not *so pervasive to subject* [read *so pervasive as to subject*] it to general jurisdiction, this court makes an evaluation in determining whether there is limited jurisdiction."

Here, the phrase is simply misused for *to* or *in order to*: "Res ipsa loquitur is invoked *here so as to avoid* [read *here to avoid*] having to name a particular defendant out of several possible defendants." The meaning of this sentence calls for "in order to," not "in such a way as to," so *to* can stand alone. (Note the ugly use of the PASSIVE VOICE, which deprives the verb *avoid* of an acting subject. For an active construction, read *By invoking res ipsa loquitur here, counsel avoids having to name one particular defendant out of several possible defendants.*)

Not infrequently, and especially in long sentences, *so as to* and *such as to* are improperly mixed, as here: "The necessity that the plaintiffs should join this association is not *so great*, nor is the association's relation to the rights of the defendants, as compared with the right of the plaintiffs to be free from molestation, *such as to* [read *as to*] bring the acts of the defendants under the shelter of the principles of trade competition." See **such** (c) & **sufficiently . . . as to.**

social; societal, -tary. These words overlap to some degree, but may be validly distinguished. *Social* = (1) living in companies or organized communities ⟨man is a social animal⟩; (2) concerned with the mutual relations of (classes of) human beings ⟨the social compact⟩; or (3) of or in or toward society ⟨social intercourse⟩ (*COD*). *Societal* has replaced *societary* (now merely a NEEDLESS VARIANT) in the sense "of, pertaining to, concerned or dealing with, society or social conditions" (*OED*). E.g., "Certainly the defendant will accept the *societal* postulate that parents have the obligation to support their children."

society, in torts and family law, often means "consortium; sexual and other intimate companionship." E.g., "The spouse of an injured crew member who survives his injury may recover her loss of *society* in an action for unseaworthiness."/ "The jury could take into consideration only the bruises that the plaintiff sustained, and the loss of his wife's *society.*"/ "The right of consortium is a right growing out of the marital relation, which the husband and wife have, to enjoy the *society* and companionship and affection of each other in their life together." See **consortium.**

socius criminis = a partner in crime; an accessory. This LATINISM, which appears primarily in BrE, is invariably unnecessary for *accessory.* E.g., "In *Mapolisa v. The Queen*, the board held that the relevant provision in the Law and Order (Maintenance) Act of 1960 applied to *a socius criminis* [read *an accessory*] and that a participant in a crime under that section was subject to the same mandatory penalty as the principal offender." (Eng.)

Socius is sometimes used as an elliptical form of *socius criminis.* E.g., "To establish the degree of proximity of the appellant to the crime, the evidence must establish that he had exact knowledge of the crime and of the identity of the principal; the appellant can be *a socius* [read *an accessory*] only on establishing his own mens rea." (Eng.) See **accessory.**

sodomist; sodomite. The latter is an example of BIBLICAL AFFECTATION.

so far as. See **as . . . as** & **insofar as.**

soi disant = self-proclaimed. This French affectation is inferior both to the translation just given and to *self-styled.*

sole (= the one and only, single) should not be used with a plural noun, as in *the sole criteria* [read *the only criteria*]. See **fem(m)e sole.**

solecism. Generally, *solecism* means "a grammatical or syntactic error." Here it is close to the literal sense: "It is no more a *solecism* to say 'immovable personal property' than it is to say 'removable fixtures,' nor more contradicting than in the division of actions to use the term 'in rem,' when, under the particular state of facts, the action is primarily 'in personam.'"

The word has been extended to figurative senses, however: "The common law recognized no such *solecism* as a right in the wife to the estate, and a right in someone else to use it as he pleased, and to enjoy all the advantages of its use."/ "The plaintiff asks for protection only during the season, and needs no more, for the designs are all ephemeral; it seeks in this way to persuade us that, if we interfere only a little, the *solecism*, if there be one, may be pardonable."

solely. The placement of this word sometimes causes trouble. E.g., "The responding document states a condition *solely advantageous* [read *advantageous solely*] to the party proposing it." See **only.**

solicit for *elicit* is a MALAPROPISM. E.g., "As noted by the Texas Court of Criminal Appeals, the question that came closest to *soliciting* [read *eliciting*] the information in question was a two-part question asked by the prosecutor." (Note also the awkward repetition of *question.*)

solicitor. In G.B., and many of the former Commonwealth countries, this term refers to a member of one of the two branches into which the legal profession is divided, handling usu. general legal and business advice, conveyancing, and instruction of and preparation of cases for counsel (barristers). In the U.S., the term refers to an advertiser or to one who solicits business—and is frequently used disparagingly. See **attorney** (A).

solicitude has two important senses that may render the word ambiguous: (1) "anxiety"; and (2) "protectiveness."

solidary liability. See **joint and several.**

solon, journalese for *legislator*, is derived from the name of Solon, an Athenian statesman, merchant, and poet (ca. 640–560 B.C.). In the early sixth century, Solon achieved important political, commercial, and judicial reforms that greatly improved life in the city-state of Athens. He reversed the trend to convert impoverished Athenians into serfs at home or to sell them abroad as slaves. He also standardized Athenian coinage and its system of weights and measures, granted citizenship to immigrant craftsmen, and enhanced the prosperity and independence of Athenian farmers. In modern times, his name has been used to denote either a "sage" or a "wiseacre" (OED). Today, the term "may be inescapable, and thus grudgingly admissible, in headlines, where *legislator*, *senator*, or *representative* will not fit, but in text it is to be avoided." R. Copperud, *Webster's Dictionary of Usage and Style* 368–69 (1964).

so long as. See **as long as** & **as . . . as.**

soluble; solvable. *Soluble* is usually applied to substances in solvents, whereas *solvable* is usually applied to problems. *Soluble* is often used in reference to problems, however; this usage is acceptable, though not preferred. Cf. **resolvable.**

solution may take either *to* or *of* as its preposition.

solvabilité, in French civil law, means "solvency," not "solvability" or "solubility."

solvable. See **soluble.**

some . . . as for *such . . . as* or *some . . . that.* E.g., "The two-year statute of limitations applicable to an action based on fraudulent inducement to execute a contract begins to run when plaintiff learns of the alleged wrongdoing or knows of facts sufficient to excite *some inquiry as* [read *such inquiry as* or *some inquiry that*] would have been made in the exercise of reasonable diligence."

somebody; someone. The words are equally good; euphony should govern the choice of term. *Someone* is often better by that standard. Each is a singular noun that, for purposes of CONCORD, is the antecedent of a singular pronoun. *Some one* as two words is an obsolete spelling, though Cardozo used this spelling as recently as 1928.

someplace is informal for *somewhere*; it is out of place in formal prose, although it is acceptable in speech.

sometime; some time. *Sometime* = at a time in the future; *some time* = quite a while. The difference may be illustrated by contrasting the senses of these two sentences: "It was not until *sometime* later that he quit."/ "It was not until *some time* later that he quit."

Sometime, in a slightly archaic sense, means "former." In such phrases as *my sometime friend*, it does not properly signify "on-again-off-again" or "on occasion."

somewhat should be avoided as a filler or buzzword. "In approaching solution to this problem we must look *somewhat* [omit *somewhat*] beyond the immediate consequences of the decision in this case." See FLOTSAM PHRASES & FUSTIAN.

The placement of *a* in relation to *somewhat* occasionally causes trouble, as when writers lapse into *somewhat of a*: "The 1,611 footnotes may make Dean Cloper *somewhat of an infamous figure* [read *a somewhat infamous figure*]."

sonorous is accented on the second syllable /sŏ-*nohr*-ŭs/ in AmE, and on the first syllable /*sohn*-ŏr-ŭs/ in BrE. The latter pronunciation is a secondary variant in AmE.

sophic(al). See **sophistic(al).**

sophist(er). *Sophister* is, except in historical contexts denoting a certain rank of student, a NEEDLESS VARIANT of *sophist*, which today has primarily negative connotations in the sense "one who makes use of fallacious arguments; a specious reasoner." Formerly it was a respectable word meaning "one who is distinguished for learning; a wise or learned man" (*OED*).

sophistic(al); sophic(al). These words have opposite connotations. The former (usu. *sophistical*) means "quibbling, specious, or captious in reasoning." The latter (usu. *sophic*) means "learned; intellectual."

The disparaging term is more common: "The hospital makes the *sophistic* [read *sophistical*] argument that its admission requirement does not turn on the physician's academic medical degree, but on the nature of the institution at which he received his post-doctoral training."/ "Thence 'special pleader' came in time to be used for any disingenuous or *sophistical* disputant." (Eng.)

sorb. See **adsorb.**

sort of, adv., is a dialectal casualism to be avoided in writing. E.g., "The prosecutor *sort of* agreed that . . . ." It is also a FUDGE-WORD.

so . . . so as. See **so . . . as + infinitive.**

sought for. The preposition is unnecessary. E.g., "As the relief *sought* is the appointment of a trustee, and the necessity for such appointment requires the construction of the will as an incident to the relief *sought for* [read merely *sought*], the complainant is properly here."

sound, v.i. This verb has a special legal sense, "to be actionable (in)." E.g., "As for the claims *sounding* in malicious prosecution, however, neither Smith nor any of the other authorities advanced by appellees controls them."/ "In determining whether a cause of action *sounds* in tort, it makes no difference that liability may be imposed by statute."/ "There is no doubt that an easement may be created by words *sounding* in covenant."

The *OED* refers to the expression *sound in damages* (= to be concerned only with damages), e.g., "This covenant did not create a specifically ascertained debt, but only a claim which *sounded* in damages" (quoted in *OED*). Today the sense has been carried beyond "to be concerned only with," to the meaning set forth at the outset of this entry.

SOUND OF PROSE, THE. We all are occasionally guilty of having a tin ear. One must train oneself not to write in a way that distracts by undue alliteration, unconscious puns, or unseemly images, for these may irritate or distract the reader. The writers of the following sentences would have benefited from reading their prose aloud.

A. Undue Alliteration or Rhyme. Cardozo, a masterly stylist, wrote in one of his classic opinions: "Nothing in this situation gave notice that the fallen *package* had in it the *potency* of *peril* to *persons* thus removed." *Palsgraf v. Long Island R. Co.*, 248 N.Y. 339, 162 N.E. 99, 99 (App. Div. 1928). This type of wordplay should be undertaken cautiously, for it declares that one's purpose is to be wry or coy.

Intentional but ineffective alliteration is one thing; thoughtless alliteration is quite another: "The unauthorized *publication* of *personal* letters is a *piracy* of a *portion* of the sender's *personality.*"/ "Such a claim makes little *sense since* the plaintiff in no way relied on the fact that he was trading with an insider."/ "The change in the *complexion* of *complex* litigation necessitates a more concentrated and prolonged inquiry into this area."/ "Such taxes merely apportion the cost of state services among all beneficiaries, and imports must *bear their fair share.*"/ "She was, at the time of the ceremony of marriage, and has been ever *since,* incapable of consummating the marriage with her husband in that she *evinced* an *invincible* repugnance to him." (Eng.) See ALLITERATION, UNDUE.

B. Unwieldy or Illogical Imagery. "That case held that quasi in rem jurisdiction over a defendant could not be exercised unless the defendant had such 'minimum contacts' with the forum state that in personam jurisdiction could be exercised over him under *International Shoe.*" (Prepositional clash: *over . . . under;* image: *under . . . shoe.*)/ "The accounting problem has already *come to a head at the SEC* in connection with initial public offerings." (Two idioms collide in the reader's mind: *come to a head* and *head of an organization or department.*)

C. Unnecessary or Awkward Repetition. "The decision in *Klaxon v. Stentor* would have suggested that Illinois conflict of laws should be looked *to to* determine whether Illinois or Indiana law on physical examination orders is to be observed." (Substitute *followed* for *looked to;* or, if this seems to change the meaning, insert *in order* before the second *to.*) See REDUNDANCY (B).

Proximity of roots may be especially distracting. Legal writers often use in succession two different forms of the same root, as an agent noun and a verb. E.g., "In *conference* the *conferees* largely acceded to the Senate's approach to Indian regulatory authority."/ "By the first clause the *covenantor covenanted* as follows." (Eng.) Thoughtful writers vary one of these words, usually the verb: "By the first clause the covenantor agreed [or *bound himself*] as follows." This type of variation is unobjectionable, its purpose being to avoid obtrusiveness; hence it is entirely distinct from INELEGANT VARIATION.

Here a root is used in two words with now rather remote senses: "From what has been said we are convinced that appellant's profits in question were not *impressed* with a trust when they first came into existence; the board *was obviously of the impression* [read *obviously thought*] that the trust first attached when appellant credited them to the beneficiaries on his books of account."

D. Arrhythmic Plodding. "Nevertheless, the lengthy process of securing a final state-court judgment that reviews the Board's denial—which envisions state district court trial, intermediate state court appeal, and state supreme court certiorari review—augurs much-belated and possibly ineffective relief to a recent law-school graduate ultimately held to have been improperly denied a certificate of fitness that would have made him eligible to take a bar examination soon after he had completed his legal studies and received his law degree." This sentence can hardly be meaningfully read aloud on first or second try; it should be split into smaller clauses in which the emphasis, the author's implied intonation is clearer.

E. Jarring Contrasts. "That such tenancy found its existence in the lease of July 14 is admittedly true, for plaintiff contends that defendant is holding *over under* it, and defendant contends that he is holding *under* it."/ "There is *here* no claimed invasion of any substantive constitutional right."

F. Misleading Parts of Speech. In the following sentence, *will* (futurity) sounds like *will* (testament): "Although the courts have been more liberal in admitting extrinsic evidence for the purpose of integrating holographs than they have for the purpose of integrating attested *wills,* it is likely that the proponent *will* have to rely upon evidence appearing in the various pages because sufficient extrinsic evidence may be impossible to obtain." See MINGLE-MANGLE, ANFRACTUOSITY, & ACRONYMS AND INITIALISMS.

source, though it has a respectable history as a verb in certain contexts, has recently been adopted by jargonmongers as a VOGUE WORD. Like other such words, it should be avoided. Examples of its objectionable uses follow: "This information is not *sourced,* [i.e., its sources are not cited (intelligence jargon)]."/ "In making concessions on such questions as *sourcing*—where parts should be made—GM tacitly conceded Toyota's superiority in small-car design and manufacture."

sour grapes is one of the most commonly misused idiomatic metaphors. It is not a mere synonym of *envy* or *jealousy*; rather, as in Aesop's fable of the fox who wanted the grapes he could not reach, *sour grapes* denotes the human tendency to disparage as undesirable what one really wants but cannot attain (or has not attained). Following is a typical journalistic misuse: "Great Britain's reaction [in the Falklands war] was more a case of *sour grapes* and wounded pride than any genuine desire to right a terrible wrong."

sovereign(ty); sovran(ty). The former spellings are preferred.

spatial; spacial. The former spelling is preferred both in AmE and in BrE.

spawn litigation is a legal CLICHÉ.

special. See **especial** & **write specially.**

special appearance. See **de bene esse.**

special(i)ty. The legal term for a contract under seal is spelled *specialty* in both AmE and BrE. In the general lay sense "a special thing," the word is *specialty* in AmE, *speciality* in BrE.

specie; species. *Specie* means "coined money"; it has no plural, unless one means to refer to different types of coined money. *Species* is both singular and plural and means "a group of similar plants and animals that can breed with each other but not with others." From that sense have grown natural extensions of the meaning of the word. Sometimes *species* is correctly used as an equivalent of *type*, as here: "Loss of services was the gist of this *species* of action." The writer of the following sentence was erroneously attempting to make *specie* a singular of *species*: "Penalties are a *specie* [read *species*] of punishment for wrongdoing and are not looked upon with favor." The same blunder appears in the title of an article: Bloomenthal, *Shareholder Derivative Actions under the Securities Laws—Phoenix or Endangered* Specie [read Species]?, 26 Ariz. L. Rev. 767 (1984).

In specie (= in kind; specifically; without any kind of substitution) is a LATINISM that is sometimes justified in providing a valuable nuance to legal writing. E.g., "The beneficiary must account to the trustee for the prop-

erty remaining in his hands *in specie* before a surcharge is ordered."/ "It is presumed that the testator intended the transferee for life to receive the income arising from investing the proceeds realized on selling the consumables, rather than to enjoy the consumables *in specie.*"

In specie has given rise to the elliptical adjectival form *specie*: "The executor will permit beneficiaries of any and all trusts hereunder to enjoy the *specie* use or benefit of any household goods, chattels, or other tangible personal property."

specious; spurious. *Spurious* is used of things, and *specious* of arguments or reasoning. *Spurious* = not genuine. *Specious* = having superficial appeal but false. E.g., "Many *specious* reasons for practices revolting to our ideas of justice may be found in old books."

spectate. See BACK-FORMATIONS.

specter, -re. This favorite word of legal writers is preferably spelled *-er* in AmE, *-re* in BrE. Curiously, however, many Americans cling to the British spelling. A California court writes: "We were not halted by the *spectre* [read *specter*] of an inability to prejudge every future case."/ "Neither one objected below or raised on appeal the *spectre* [read *specter*] of an inadequate hearing." In American writing, the usual spelling of many words such as *theater* is *-er*. See -ER, -RE.

Specter is sometimes misspelled *spector*, as in *Ingalls Shipbuilding Division, Litton Systems, Inc. v. White,* 681 F.2d 275, 279 (5th Cir. 1982).

spectrum. Pl. *spectra.* See PLURALS (A).

speechify = to deliver a speech. The word is used in a mocking or derogatory way. Cf. **argufy.**

speed, all deliberate. See **with all deliberate speed.**

speeded; sped. The best preterite and past participial form of the verb *to speed* is *sped*, except in the phrase *to speed up* (= to accelerate) ⟨she speeded up to 80 m.p.h.⟩.

spiritual(istic); spirituous; spiritous; spirituel(le); spirited. *Spiritual* is the broadest of these terms, meaning "of the spirit as opposed to matter; of the soul esp. as acted on by God; concerned with sacred or religious things" (*COD*). *Spiritualistic* = of or relating to spiritualism, i.e., the belief that departed spirits communicate with and show themselves to the living, esp. through mediums. *Spirituous* = alcoholic. E.g., "The indictment charges the unlawful sale of *spirituous* liquors within two miles of Bethel Methodist Church in Macon County." *Spiritous* is an ARCHAISM in the sense of "highly refined or dematerialized," and is also a NEEDLESS VARIANT of *spirituous*. *Spirituel* (masculine) or *spirituelle* (feminine) means "witty" or "of a highly refined character or nature, esp. in conjunction with liveliness or quickness of mind" (*OED*).

spite of, in. See **despite**.

splendiferous is a usually comic or colloquial word for *splendid*.

split between (or in) the circuits. This phrase is used in American legal writing to denote the fact that federal courts of appeals have arrived at contrary holdings on the same point of law. E.g., "Recognizing that the *split in the circuits* exists, we find that *Bailey* and not *Collins* provides the appropriate analysis, which we now follow." Only the U.S. Supreme Court or Congress is capable of remedying splits between the circuits, by laying down an explicit rule of law that the circuit courts must henceforth follow.

SPLIT INFINITIVES abound in legal writing, often needlessly. The English language gives us "the inestimable advantage of being able to put adverbs where they will be most effective, coloring the verbs to which they apply and becoming practically part of them. . . . If you think a verb cannot be split in two, just call the adverb a part of the verb and the difficulty will be solved." Lee, *A Defense of the Split Infinitive*, 37 Mass. L.Q. 65, 66 (1952).

Fowler divided the English-speaking world into five classes: (1) those who neither know nor care what a split infinitive is; (2) those who do not know, but care very much; (3) those who know and condemn; (4) those who know and approve; (5) those who know and distinguish. It is this last class to which we should aspire; the following discussion is proffered to help the reader attain that goal. An infinitive, of course, is the tenseless form of a verb preceded by *to*, such as *to reverse* or *to modify*. Splitting the infinitive is placing one or

more words between *to* and the verb, such as *to summarily reverse* or *to unwisely modify*.

A. Splits to be Avoided. "It is not necessary *to here enlarge* upon them." This is an excellent example of the capricious split infinitive, which serves no purpose, unless that purpose is to jar the reader. "This issue is confusing the court, and *we would like to all clear it up* [read *we would all like to clear it up*]."/ "The equal protection clause will continue *to almost automatically invalidate* [read *to invalidate almost automatically*] classifications that are unmistakably racial on their face. . . ."/ "This statement appears to be an objection to the trial court's failure *to more clearly explain* [read *to explain more clearly*] Harper's defensive theory."/ "*In order for someone to voluntarily take a risk* [read *For someone to take a risk voluntarily*], he must know the dangers involved, and decide to take the chance anyway." Wide splits are to be avoided. E.g., "We encourage counsel on both sides to utilize the best efforts *to understandingly, sympathetically, and professionally arrive at* [read *to arrive understandingly, sympathetically, and professionally at*] a settlement regarding attorneys' fees."

With CORRELATIVE CONJUNCTIONS, q.v., a split infinitive simply displays carelessness, "White was *to either make or obtain* a loan." [Read *White was either to make or to obtain a loan.*] See PARALLELISM.

B. Justified Splits. A number of infinitives coupled with adverbs do not look or sound correct when the infinitive remains unsplit. E.g., "The confidentiality of a marketing concept does not create a continuing competitive advantage because, once it is implemented, it is exposed for the world to see and for competitors *to legally imitate*." (Changing placement of the adverb here would change the sense.)/ "The statute denies to respondent the right *to reasonably manage* or control its own business."/ "The majority improperly places the burden of proof on the appellees *to affirmatively establish* the existence of a statutory exemption."/ "He asserted self-defense in order *to affirmatively avoid* appellant's cause of action."/ "The statute prohibits supplying others with the necessary information and documents *to falsely claim* their income as tax exempt."/ "Appellants failed *to timely file* their notice of appeal."/ "Inability *to directly attain* the remedial goal of prevention of harm in tort cases is a major deficiency of the common-law system of substitutional money damages." Distinguishing these examples from those under (A) may not be easy for all readers. As John Simon has written, "infinitives begging to be split are relatively rare; a sensitive ear, a good eye for shades of meaning will alert you whenever the need to split arises; without that ear and eye, you had better stick to the rules." *Paradigms Lost* 213 (1980).

C. Awkwardness Caused by Avoiding Splits. Occasionally, sticking to the rules, as Simon advocates in the passage just quoted, leads to awkward constructions. The following sentences illustrate maladroit attempts to avoid splitting the infinitive. In the first two examples, the adverb may be placed more naturally than it is without splitting the infinitive; in the third and fourth examples, a split is called for: "Now to legitimize L's breach of the contract by the retroactive application of the October 1982 amendments would be *unjustly to enrich L* [read *to enrich L unjustly*] while unjustly penalizing U."/ "We should not permit Congress *to continue inadequately to compensate judges* [read *to continue to compensate judges inadequately*]."/ "The court does not have the resources necessary *effectively to superintend* [read *to effectively superintend*] the day-to-day details of the execution of the program to be set out in the decree."/ "We are not impressed with the soundness of the doctrine, which, in the case at bar, would be an attempt *judicially to interpret* [read *to judicially interpret*] the language of the donor provisions contrary to his actual intent as expressed."

spoil(s). Although the word is plural in the phrase *spoils of war*, it is traditionally singular in the sense "goods, esp. such as are valuable, seized by force or confiscated." E.g., "No right to the *spoil* is vested in the piratical captor."

spoonfuls; spoonsful. The former is preferred. See PLURALS (E).

spotted pony case. See **whitehorse case.**

spousal, adj. The *OED* defines this term as (1) "of, pertaining or relating to, espousal or marriage; nuptial; matrimonial"; or (2) "(of a hymn, poem, etc.) celebrating or commemorating an espousal or marriage." *W3* contains like definitions. In modern American law, however, *spousal* = of, relating to, or by a spouse or spouses. E.g., "Pragmatically, *spousal* support now serves to deliver economic justice based on the financial needs of the specific parties involved in a dissolution proceeding." See **interspousal.**

spread, v.t. The figurative parliamentary idiom *to spread upon the minutes* has been extended in legal usage to other printed matter, and, as in the second example, even to unprinted matter. E.g., "The court's findings that lesser sanctions would be inadequate must be *spread* upon the record."/ "Appellee has had this picture of its indifference, or at least ineptness, *spread* before a jury and now upon the pages of this reporter."

springing use; shifting use. A *springing use* is one that arises on the occurrence of a future event, whereas a *shifting use* is one that operates to terminate a preceding use. A *springing use* arises, e.g., when property is given to X to the use of A when A marries; A has a springing use that vests in him when he marries. A *shifting use*, by contrast, might arise when property is given to X to the use of A, but then to B when C pays $1000 to D; B has a shifting use that arises when C makes the specified payment. (With acknowledgments to *CDL.*) In G.B., *secondary use* is a variant of *shifting use*, although all these terms are of historical interest only there. See **use.**

spurious. See **specious.**

ss. is an abbreviation that often appears on the top of the first page of an affidavit. The abbreviation is commonly understood to signify *scilicet* (= namely, to wit), but the better abbreviation for that term is *sc.* or *scil.* Despite the myth to the contrary, *ss* is not necessary in affidavits. There are no judicious uses of this LEGALISM: "Lawyers have been using *ss* for nine hundred years and still are not sure what it means." D. Mellinkoff, *The Language of the Law* 296 (1963).

stabilize; stabilify; stabilitate. The second and third are NEEDLESS VARIANTS.

stakeholder; stockholder. These terms are not to be confused. *Stakeholder*, not listed in the *OED* but included in *W2* and *W3*, originally meant "the holder of a stake or wager," a meaning it still carries. But in modern American legal writing it usually denotes one who holds property, the right or possession of which is disputed between two other parties, (as in an interpleader action).

Stockholder = (1) a shareholder in a corporation; or (2) one who is a proprietor of stock in the public funds or the funds of a joint-stock company (*OED*). Sense (1) is labeled an Americanism in the *OED*, although the *COD* definition suggests that this sense is now current in BrE. Sense (2) is largely confined to BrE.

stanch. See **staunch.**

stand; witness-box. The former is American, the latter British. See **witness-box.**

standee. See -EE.

standing; locus standi. These synonymous TERMS OF ART mean "a position from which one may validly make a legal claim or seek to enforce a right or duty." The first is primarily American, and the second (a LATINISM) is commonly used in G.B. and former Commonwealth countries. One is said to have *standing* when one's arguments on the merits of a case are able to be heard by an adjudicator. E.g., "They . . . argue that no individual blind vendor or state agency would have *standing* because none has alleged a 'concrete, perceptible harm of a real, nonspeculative nature.'" *Randolph-Sheppard Vendors v. Weinberger*, 795 F.2d 90, 99 (D.C.Cir. 1986)./ "Hill's *standing* to litigate the constitutionality of the ordinance must not be confused with the apparent merit or lack of merit in his challenge." See **locus standi.**

standpoint. See **viewpoint.**

stare decisis (L. "to stand by things decided") = the doctrine of precedent, under which it is necessary to abide by former judicial decisions when the same points arise again in litigation. Though a verb phrase in Latin, the phrase is used as a noun phrase in English, and in the U.S. has even come to be used commonly as an adjectival phrase, e.g.: "The *stare decisis effect* [read *precedential effect*] of the judgment obtained by the plaintiff established as a matter of law the right of a discernible class of persons to collect upon similar claims."

start. See **begin** (B) & **commence.**

stated otherwise is a pompous version of *in other words.* E.g., "*Stated otherwise* [read *In other words*], the deduction will invariably affect the taxpayer's liability."

state-of-the-art, adj.; **state of the art,** n. These VOGUE WORDS illustrate the interests of a fast-changing society with rapidly effected technological innovations ⟨state-of-the-art products⟩. For the moment, they are tainted by association with salesmen's cant.

stationary; stationery. The former is the adjective ("remaining in one place"), the latter the noun ("materials for writing on or with").

statistic (= a single term or datum in a statistical compilation) is a BACK-FORMATION from *statistics* dating from the late nineteenth century. Today its correctness is beyond challenge. E.g., "When this *statistic* is considered with the massive discovery involved, and with the fact that few of the large class-action cases are ever tried, the real impact of complex litigation is seen."

statu quo, in. See **in statu quo.**

status quo; status quo ante; status in quo. *Status quo* means "the state of affairs at present"; hence *current status quo* is a REDUNDANCY. (See **in statu quo.**) *Status quo ante* (= the state of affairs at a previous time) is a common and useful LATINISM in contexts involving torts and contracts. E.g., "There is an understandable tendency to consider restitution, in the form of restoration of the *status quo ante*, a tort or contract remedy."/ "A court of equity may exercise the full range of its inherent powers to accomplish complete justice between the parties, restoring if necessary the *status quo ante* as nearly as may be achieved."

Status quo in the sense "the original condition" (as opposed to "the present condition") is a LEGALISM to be avoided, for lawyers as well as laymen are likely to misunderstand the import. *Status in quo* is an archaic variant of *status quo.*

statutable; statutory. These words overlap to a small degree; they are generally quite discrete, however. *Statutory* (= pertaining to or consisting in statutes; enacted, appointed, or created by statute; conformable to the provisions of a statute) is the far more usual word in modern law. *Statutable* = (1) prescribed, authorized, or permitted by statute; (2) conformed to the requirements of the statutes as to quality, size, or amount; (3) (of an offense) legally punishable (*OED*). In the early nineteenth-century specimen that follows, *statutable* is used in a context in which *statutory* would surely appear today: "But there are express *statutable* provisions, which directly apply to the present case." *Gelston v. Hoyt*, 16 U.S. (3 Wheat.) 246, 310 (1818).

STATUTE DRAFTING. An important early work on the writing of statutes is *Coode on Legislative Expression* (1842). Though the work is old and well-known, and most of its recommendations have been repeated in more recent works, much of the advice is neglected by modern drafters of statutes.

The fundamental mode of expression in statutes, as worked out by Coode, is to recite facts concurrent with the statute's operation as if they were present facts, and facts precedent to the statute's operation as if they were past facts. This statement is deceptively simple.

A. *Shall & may* in Proscriptions. Coode recognized that much of the trouble in statute drafting originates in the use of *shall*. Proscriptions that begin "No person *shall*..." are inferior to those that begin "No person *may*..." because *shall* can be understood in two senses: simple futurity (i.e., *will*) and obligation (i.e., *must*). See **shall**.

B. Tenses Generally. What follows is a modernization of Coode's precepts on the use of tenses in statutes, and esp. the use of *shall* and *may*. (This adaptation paraphrases Coode as quoted in E.A. Dreidger's *The Composition of Legislation*, 225–228 [1957]. For a general discussion of draftsmanship, see DRAFTING.)

The drafter should not attempt to render every action referred to in a statute in a future tense. Some drafters erroneously assume that the words *shall* and *shall not* put the enacting verb into a future tense. Yet, in commanding, as in a statute that mandates a certain action, *shall* is modal rather than temporal. Thus it denotes compulsion, the obligation to act, not a prophecy that the person will or will not at some future time do the act. "Thou shalt not murder" is not a prediction; it is obligatory in the present tense, continuously through all the time of the law's operation.

Likewise, when the verb *may* is used, the expression is not of future possibility; instead, it is of permission and authority. "The chairman *may canvass* committee members" means "The chairman *is authorized to canvass* the committee members."

Yet, because the legal action referred to in a statute is sometimes—when *shall* is used—supposed to be in the future tense, drafters often attempt (for the sake of consistency) to express the circumstances that are required to precede the operation of the statute (i.e., the case or condition) in the future or future perfect tenses. Thus, in poor drafting language, one frequently finds the following expressions:

1. If any person *shall give* [read *gives*] notice, he *may* appeal . . . .

2. If the commissioners *shall instruct* [read *instruct*] by any order . . . .

3. All elections *shall* [read *are*] hereafter, so far as the commissioners *shall direct* [read *direct*] . . . .

4. In case any person *shall willfully neglect or disobey* [read *willfully neglects or disobeys*] . . . .

5. When such notice *shall have been published* [read *is published*] . . . .

6. If any balance *shall have been found* [read *is found*] to be due . . . .

The fear that gives rise to this use of *shall* is that, if the case or condition for operation of the statute were expressed in the present tense ⟨when any person is aggrieved⟩, the law would be contemporaneous, and would operate *only* on cases existing at the moment of the enactment of the statute. Likewise, it is erroneously assumed that if a statute were expressed in the past tense ⟨when any person has been convicted⟩ the law would be retrospective, and would apply *only* to convictions that took place before the act was passed.

This apprehension is founded on a mistake. An elementary rule of statutory construction is that past tenses never give retrospective effect to a statute, unless the intention for retrospectivity is clearly and distinctly framed in words to that effect. Any number of statutes are written in the present or present perfect tense but still are given prospective application only.

If a law is regarded, while it remains in force, as *constantly speaking*, then a simple two-part rule will serve to guide legislators and their staffs in drafting statutes:

1. Use the *present tense* to express all facts and conditions required to be concurrent with the operation of the legal action. E.g., "Where by reason of the largeness of parishes the inhabitants *cannot* reap the benefits of this Act, two or more overseers *shall be chosen*." (The first clause in this conditional sentence is in the present tense; the main clause that follows contains obligatory language still in

the present [not the future] tense.) See **shall** (A).

2. Use the *present perfect tense* to express all facts and conditions required as precedents to the legal action. E.g., "When the justices of the peace of any county *assembled* at quarter sessions *have agreed* that the ordinary officers appointed for the preservation of the peace *are* not sufficient for the preservation of the peace, the justices *may* appoint a chief constable." (The left-branching dependent clauses contain verbs in the past perfect [*assembled, have agreed, appointed*] to indicate necessary precedent conditions that now exist [*are*] and thus make legal action possible; the main clause is in the present [permissive] tense to indicate the specific legal action that is open to the justices of the peace.)

D. Diction. The simplest, most concise English is the best for legislation: "The draftsman should bear in mind that his Act is supposed to be read by the plain man. In any case he may be sure that if he finds he can express his meaning in simple words all is going well with his draft, while if he finds himself driven to complicated expressions composed of long words it is a sign that he is getting lost and he should reconsider the form of the section." A. Russell, *Legislative Drafting and Forms* 12 (4th ed. 1938).

E. *Each, any, all, no* (etc.). See PRONOMINAL INDEFINITE ADJECTIVES.

statute law. See **statutory law.**

statute of limitation(s). Either *statute of limitations* or *statutes of limitation* is idiomatic and correct. *Statute of limitations* is often made into the elliptical form *limitations*: "The court ruled that *limitations* were tolled for all 809 workers during the time that elapsed between the date suit was filed and the date the trial court denied class certification." (Cf. the English quotation under **run.**) See **laches** (B).

statute of repose. See **repose.**

statutory, -torial. The latter is a NEEDLESS VARIANT not recognized in the dictionaries. The adverb *statutorily* is not infrequently rendered, by mistake, *statutorially*. For the sense of *statutory*, see **statutable.**

statutory charge. Copperud has observed that in lay parlance *statutory rape*, a precise term, has been stretched into phrases such as *statutory charge* or *statutory offense*. See R. Copperud, *American Usage and Style* 363 (1980). These phrases are illogical, inasmuch as criminal offenses or charges are invariably statutorily defined or codified.

statutory enactment is a REDUNDANCY for *statute*. The word *enactment*, q.v., is misused in this phrase. E.g., "This article is designed to cover general principles relating to *statutory enactments* [read *statutes*]."

statutory law; statute law. Both forms appear in the U.S., but the former is the more common. In G.B., *statute law* is the predominant form. The *OCL* defines *statute law* as "the body of principles and rules of law laid down in statutes and statutory instruments as distinct from the common law, or the body of principles and rules of law developed and stated by judges in their opinions . . . , or derived inductively from examination of various opinions in various relevant cases."

staunch; stanch. *Staunch* is preferable as the adjective ("trustworthy, loyal"), *stanch* as the verb ("to restrain the flow of [usu. blood]").

stay, n. & v.t. In law, *stay* = (1) to postpone ⟨to stay the mandate⟩; or (2) to halt ⟨to stay waste⟩. As a noun, it means "postponement" ⟨stay of the mandate⟩. Although the verb *to stay* is usually intransitive in lay contexts ⟨he stayed awhile⟩, it is transitive in its legal sense: "An injunction to *stay* waste may be granted in favor of one who is entitled to a contingent or executory estate of inheritance."/ "Filing of the petition under Chapter 11 automatically *stayed* the proposed sale to enforce the maritime lien." See **continue.**

ste(a)dfast. The preferred spelling is *steadfast.*

steal. See **rob.**

steamroll(er), v.t. The longer form of this verb is the preferred, except (oddly) in the *-ing* participle. E.g., "Theoretically, the inquisition model will produce more information than one premised upon heavy incentives to advance one's position and can prevent a wealthier opponent from *steamrolling* his adversary."

stedfast. See ste(a)dfast.

stereotypic(al). The longer form is preferred in figurative senses. E.g., "In *City of Thomas*, the Ninth Circuit recognized that constitutional concerns are heightened by any classification scheme singling out former mental patients for differential treatment because of the possibility that the scheme will implement inaccurate stereotypic [read *stereotypical*] fears about former mental patients." *Stereotypic* is the better form for the narrow sense "of or produced by stereotypy (the process of printing from stereotype plates)."

stigma. Pl. *-mas, -mata.* As with many other such words, the English plural (*-mas*) is preferable. See PLURALS (A).

stimulus. Pl. *-li.* Unlike the preceding headword, this word does not make a native-English plural. See PLURALS (A).

stipital. See **stirpital.**

stipulate = (1) (of an agreement) to specify (something) as an essential part of the contract; (2) (of a party to an agreement) to require or insist upon (something) as an essential condition; or (3) to make express demand *for* something as a condition of an agreement.

This verb belongs to the language of contracts, and is not felicitously transported into contexts involving statutes, where it becomes a substitute for *provide*. E.g., "The statute *stipulates* [read *provides*] that any cause of action under this subsection must be brought before the court within two years."

Nor has the verb traditionally meant "(of counsel) to reach an agreement about business before a court," although this extension of sense is not uncommon in American trial practice: "The relevant facts *are stipulated*." *United States v. National Bank of Commerce*, 472 U.S. 713, 715 (1985)./ "The district court adopted a plan, *stipulated to* by the Ector County school district and by the United States but forcefully objected to by the plaintiff-intervenors."/ "This organization appeals the district court's adoption of the *stipulated* plan."

Stirpes. See **stirps.**

stirpital; stipital. The preferred adjectival form of *stirps* (= branch of a family), used in reference to a per stirpes distribution, is *stirpital*. *Black's* (4th & 5th eds.) lists only *stipital* as the correct form. *W3* defines *stipital* as "of or relating to the stipes," *stipes* being a botanical or zoological term meaning "peduncle" or, less commonly, "stirps." *W3* does not, however, include *stirpital*. And *Words and Phrases* contains *stirpital* but not *stipital*.

The *OED* records *stirpital*, noting that it is ill-formed and should be *stirpal* if properly Latinized, and dates it from 1886 with the following quotation: "A division of the proceeds of sale per stirpes is more in accordance than a division per capita with the original *stirpital* division of the income." The *OED* does not contain *stipital*.

Following are examples of the words as used in legal writing. *Stirpital* is far more common: "Counsel for the defendant Nolan, as an alternative claim, suggest the application of the doctrine of *stirpital* survivorship." *State Bank & Trust Co. v. Nolan*, 130 A. 483, 489 (Conn. 1925)./ "Some courts, on the other hand, take a position contrary, or at least in opposition, to the foregoing . . . *stirpital* distribution." 57 Am. Jur. *Wills* § 1292 (1948)./ Though it has the approval of some dictionaries, *stipital* is rarely encountered. E.g., "Considering the circumstances it may be inferred that it would have been impracticable for the testator to have designated his half brothers as *stipital* progenitors." *Theopold v. Sears*, 357 Mass. 460, 258 N.E.2d 559, 561 (Mass. 1970).

With all due respect to *Black's* and *W3*, *stirpital* must be deemed better than *stipital* as the adjective of *per stirpes*. Most lawyers know the term *per stirpes* and understand *stirpital* if they hear or read it; *stipital* is another matter. And if a legal term is obscure to lawyers, what hope is there for the layman?

Then again, in most contexts the phrase *per stirpes* might be used where an adjective is called for ⟨per stirpes distribution⟩. The phrase *per stirpital*, however, is a needless hybrid: In *Mercantile Trust Co. v. Davis*, 522 S.W.2d 798 (Mo. 1975) (en banc), the court quotes a lower court as having used *per stirpital* and attaches *sic* to the phrase (at 803), and then uses the phrase itself (at 805): "[T]his court reversed and ordered a *per stirpital* [read *per stirpes*] distribution to be made."/ "The Uniform Probate Code § 2-106 requires per capita distribution among surviving heirs in the nearest degree with *per stirpital* [read *per stirpes*] distribution among those entitled to take but who are in a more remote degree."

stirps. Pl. *stirpes.*

stochastic. See **aleatory.**

stockholder. See **stakeholder.**

straightjacket is a common error for *straitjacket*. E.g., "Litigation is not a game of chess, nor, this court finds, should a nonresident defendant be *straightjacketed* [read *straitjacketed*] or deprived of its legitimate entitlement to removal by a plaintiff's artful maneuvering."

straight-laced is incorrect for *strait-laced.*

stratum. Pl. *strata.* See PLURALS (A).

stray. See **estray** & **waifs and (e)strays.**

stricken, though common as a past participle in much legal writing, is considered by the better authorities to be inferior to *struck*. It is an ARCHAISM in all but the adjectival sense (a stricken community). Following are typical sentences with recommended improvements: "Had George been suddenly *stricken* [read *struck*] blind instead of having become afflicted with an abdominal illness, the circumstances determining whether the attestation took place in his presence would have been no different."/ "Appellant also argues that the special term of parole authorized by 21 U.S.C. § 841(b)(1)(A) is unconstitutional, and should be *stricken* [read *struck*] from his sentence."/ "Lora T. Bott's name was also *stricken* [read *struck*] as conditional legatee of shares given to two other friends and as co-executrix."/ "The government had not produced the criminal record of this witness, and Jennings therefore moved that the witness's testimony be *stricken* [read *struck*] and the jury instructed to disregard the testimony of the witness for failure to comply with the court's order."

The participial usage has given rise to the mistaken use of *stricken* for *strike* as a present-tense verb. E.g., "The law does not provide a remedy for every ill that may *stricken* [read *strike*] a community."/ "When such a tragedy *strickens* [read *strikes*] a community, the people must rely upon each other to a degree otherwise never realized."

Stricken is sometimes used as a preterite in the guise of an adjective. E.g., "He has not shown that the striking was in fact premised on a determination of the merits of the allegation [that was] *stricken* [read *struck*]." See **strike.**

strictest sense of the word, in the. See WORD-PATRONAGE.

stricti juris; strictissimi juris. These words mean, respectively, "of the strict right of law" and "of the strictest right of law." The LATINISM, as infrequently used in modern contexts, is not easily simplified. E.g., "The lien created by Article 3237 is *stricti juris*; it cannot be extended by implication or analogy." The nuance provided by the differing forms is probably illusory.

strict liability; absolute liability; liability without fault. *Strict liability* is the commonest term in both the U.S. and G.B. The second and third phrases were formerly common, and are still occasionally used.

stricto sensu (= in the strict sense) is an unjustifiable LATINISM. "There are aspects of a so-called compulsory sale that clearly distinguish it from a sale *stricto sensu* [read *in the strict sense*]." The phrase is often Englished: "As long as the principles of equity were administered by separate courts, questions of equity jurisdiction were often considered, *in the strict sense*, jurisdictional."

strike for *strike down*. When a court invalidates a statute, it is best to write that the court *strikes it down*. E.g., "While the Rule against Perpetuities normally operates to *strike down* only the remote contingent interest, this interest may be so integral a part of the plan of distribution that the settlor or testator would have preferred a complete failure of the entire transfer."

Strike as a lone verb has so many other meanings that making it more precise in this context is desirable. "The Court *strikes* [read *strikes down*] Alaska's distribution scheme, purporting to rely solely upon the Equal Protection Clause of the Fourteenth Amendment."

Strike yields *struck* for both its past tense and its past participle. *Stricken* is archaic as a past participle, and should be reserved only for adjectival uses ⟨a stricken man; stricken with polio⟩. See **stricken.**

stultify (now "to make stupid or cause to appear foolish") formerly meant "to attempt to prove one's own mental incapacity." E.g., "Dr. Johnson seemed much surprized [sic] that such a suit was admitted by Scottish law, and observed that in England no man is allowed to *stultify* himself." (Eng.) The term is now used in British legal writing of a witness who, e.g., casts doubt on his own account of a remark alleged to have been overheard by him by admitting that he was too far away to hear it. See *Phipson on Evidence* 394 (8th ed. 1959).

The word is sometimes misunderstood as being synonymous with *disgrace* or *dishonor.* Nor does it mean "to retard" or "to emasculate": "To hold that the Commission had no alternative in this proceeding but to approve the proposed transaction would be to *stultify* [read *emasculate?*] the administrative process."

stupefy. So spelled; *stupify* is a fairly common misspelling. Cf. **rarefy.**

stupid. See **ignorant.**

style = case name. E.g., "The *style* of the case in which this certificate is made is Joseph Boardman and Henry Boardman, plaintiffs/appellees v. United Services Automobile Association, defendant/appellant." In G.B., *style* also means "the name or title of a person" ⟨royal style and titles⟩, and in Scotland, "a model form or precedent of a deed or pleading" (*OCL*).

STYLE. See LEGAL WRITING STYLE.

stylish; stylistic. *Stylish* = in style (sometimes pejorative). *Stylistic* = having to do with style (of general application); in the appropriate style (of music).

stymie; stymy. This term, originally from golf, is best spelled *-ie.* E.g., "Commentators had argued that greater attention should be paid to this potential solution to a joinder *stymie.*"

suability. The adjective *suable* has existed from the early seventeenth century; the noun *suability* began as an Americanism (first used,

as far as documentation reveals, by Chief Justice John Jay in 1798) and has remained so. The words written about these words in 1798 remain valid today: "*Suability* and *suable* are words not in common use, but they concisely and correctly convey the idea annexed to them" (quoted in *OED*). E.g., Kelly, *Workmen's Compensation and Employer Suability,* 5 St. Mary's L.J. 818 (1974)./ "The principal contracts known to the common law and *suable* in the King's Courts, a century after the Conquest, were suretyship and debt." O. W. Holmes, *The Common Law* 289 (1881; repr. 1963).

sua sponte = on its own motion; without prompting. The phrase is ordinarily used of courts. *Sua sponte* is a LATINISM that is often not easily Englished. E.g., "It is the duty of a court to take notice of a lack of jurisdiction *sua sponte* even though the question is not raised by the contending parties." *On its own motion,* if inserted in place of the Latin phrase, incorrectly and rather unidiomatically suggests that the court can make a motion.

In the sentence that follows, the phrase is used illogically: "The court, *sua sponte,* granted defendant's motion for summary judgment." If there was a motion by the defendant before the court, then the court could not have granted it *sua sponte.*

The Latin, it must be remembered, means literally "on his or its own motion." Thus it is probably wrong for the courts to use this phrase in reference to their own actions, as here: "*Sua sponte* we note that the same problem exists in this case as existed in *Reyes.*" *State v. White,* 706 P.2d 1331, 1333 (Haw. App. 1985). The phrase should have been entirely omitted in that sentence. The phrase may acceptably be used with a plural noun. E.g., "*Courts* should not, *sua sponte,* take up waivable rights not asserted by the parties."

sub-. Legal writers are fond of *sub-* words. This fondness often manifests itself in fussy distinctions drawn as analogues to *subheading* (e.g. *subcategory, subissue, subaspect*). The only adequate description of such forms is substandard. E.g., "There are several distinct *subaspects* of the doctrine."/ "These cases on waiver present two distinct *subissues.*" Surely there is a better way of saying that there are two issues within a broad issue, or more than one aspect within a broad aspect; words like *issue* and *aspect* are abstract enough without allowing them to become more so with prefixed forms. See ABSTRACTITIS.

The apotheosis of the fetish for this prefix consists in *subsub-*, as here used in an analogue to *subcontract*: "The charterparty was executed in the United States between the *subsubcharterer*, an American corporation, and the subcharterer, a Liberian corporation." The device saves a little space, but is inelegant and really fails to save the reader mental effort.

subaspect. See **sub-**.

sub-bidder should be spelled thus, with the hyphen.

subcontractor is not hyphenated.

subissue. See **sub-**.

subject, n. See **citizen** (B).

subjectability. "It would appear that the manufacturer and the importer, whose *subjectability* to Oklahoma [read *Oklahoma's*] jurisdiction is not challenged before this Court, ought not to be judgment-proof." (Blackmun, J.) The word is listed in neither *W2* nor *W3*, and is included in *OED* merely with the notation "in recent dictionaries." The word is arguably useful, if somewhat inaesthetic.

subject-matter is best hyphenated as an adjectival phrase ⟨subject-matter jurisdiction⟩ in both AmE and BrE. Only in BrE is the phrase hyphenated as a noun.

subject-matter jurisdiction; jurisdiction of the subject matter. The phrase is rendered both ways in modern legal writing. E.g., "The district court dismissed petitioner's complaint for want of *jurisdiction of the subject matter*." *Subject-matter jurisdiction* is more common and usually less cumbersome.

subject matter of the trust. See **corpus**.

SUBJECT-VERB AGREEMENT. A. False Attraction to Noun Intervening Between Subject and Verb. The simple rule is that plural subjects take plural verbs, and singular subjects take singular verbs. This subheading denotes a mistake in number in the use of a verb that usually results when a plural noun intervenes between a singular subject and the verb. The writer's eye is thrown off course by the plural noun that appears nearest the verb. E.g., "The first group of cases *discuss* [read *discusses*] the applicability of the doctrine of collateral estoppel to administrative-agency decisions and the second group *discuss* [*discusses*] the *Noerr-Pennington* doctrine and the sham exception."/ "This problem is also declining in importance as the language of statutes *are* [read *is*] modernized."/ "Since the corporation rate is generally lower and only mildly progressive, accumulating earnings in a corporation generally increases in attractiveness as outside income of the shareholders *increase* [read *increases*]."/ "Concededly, the *length* of opinions *vary* [read *varies*] from case to case and from writer to writer."/ "At first, the *difference* between McCormick and Wigmore—or between McCormick and any of the other writers mentioned here—*are* [read *is*] a bit startling." Sometimes the reverse error, plural to singular, occurs: "The interests of the class representative, Mr. Sampson, *is* [read *are*] not the same as those of the absent parties."/ "Gradual losses by erosion *causes* [read *cause*] shrinkage of the land owned by O." See SYNESIS.

B. False Attraction to Predicate Noun. Occasionally a writer incorrectly looks to the predicate rather than to the subject for the noun that will govern the verb. E.g., "The appellate judge's immediate audience *are* [read *is*] his colleagues who sat with him when an appeal was argued."

C. Reverse False Attraction. This occurs when the writer ignores the true and proximate subject by wrongly searching for a more remote subject earlier in the sentence. E.g., "The character of the punitive damages depends on the function such damages *serves* [read *serve*]." (The writer apparently thought *function* to be the subject.)

D. Compound Subjects Joined Conjunctively. "But recent *research and commentary has* [read *have*; research and commentary are two different things] suggested that the emphasis upon eyewitness identification may lead to questionable results." Sometimes the two nouns joined by *and* arguably express a single idea, and hence should take a singular verb: "The *confusion and uncertainty is* [*confusion and uncertainty* really describing a single mental state] compounded by doubt regarding the question whether the complete liquidation and reorganization provisions can have concurrent application."/ "Published *criticism and vituperation is* not necessarily libelous."

One must be careful of the compound noun phrase followed by a singular noun that properly is the singular subject: "First, we must decide whether the claim presented and the relief sought are of the type that *admit* [read *admits*, for the subject of the verb is *type*] of judicial resolution."

E. *What* as Subject. As subject, *what* generally takes a singular verb, whether the complementary noun that follows is singular or plural. E.g., "What we need is more good students." See **what** (A).

F. Alternatives. The last element in a disjunctive series determines the number of the verb. Thus: "Consent to contract may be vitiated if fraud, error, violence, or threats *induce* the consent." Where two singular subjects appear in the alternative, the verb should be singular: "But the jury or the court *are* [read *is*] not bound to accept the statement of a witness as true because it is not directly or expressly contradicted or impeached by other witnesses."/ "Bailments are frequently classified according to which of the parties [i.e., the bailor or the bailee] *derive* [read *derives*] the most benefit."/ "The decree undoubtedly contemplates that the government would be able to object where, as here, the process of combatting discrimination depends not merely on the development of particular lists, but on *which* of two alternative lists *are* [read *is*] used." See **either** (c).

G. Plural Words Referred to as Words. These take a singular verb. "Neither 'per stirpes' nor 'descendants' *were* [read *was*] used in reference to the part of the estate Sue would get had George died intestate."/ "But 'per stirpes' *were* [read *was*] not used in the phrase granting power of appointment; *they were used* [read *it* (i.e., the phrase) *was used*] only in disposing of the property if George died intestate."

H. Misleading Connectives. The phrases *as well as, added to, coupled with,* and *together with* do not affect the grammatical number of the nouns preceding or following them. When such a phrase joins two singular nouns, the singular verb is called for. E.g., "Logic, *as well as* equity, *dictate* [read *dictates*] this result." *Affiliated Capital Corp. v. City of Houston,* 793 F.2d 706, 709 (5th Cir. 1986) (en banc)./ "The pro-

vision for the payment of interest on the fund held by appellee, *together with* the fact that there was no designation or segregation of any particular fund from which payment was to be made, *are* [read *is*] of interest in determining the settlor's intent." See **together with.**

I. COLLECTIVE NOUNS Denoting Amounts. In AmE, collective nouns generally take singular verbs. E.g., "The majority *regard* [read *regards*] as immaterial the question whether the license was valid." In BrE, it would be more usual to write *the majority regard . . . .* See COLLECTIVE NOUNS.

J. The False Singular. "The situation of the employer and the employee in today's society is equivalent." [Read *The situation of the employer and that of the employee in today's society are equivalent.*] It is the situations of the employer and the employee, not the persons themselves, that are being compared. See COMPARISONS, FALSE.

K. Inversion. In the sentence that follows, the two *that*-clauses, dual subjects, demand a plural verb, although the writer was misled by the INVERSION into thinking a singular was needed: "*That this court has jurisdiction* to enforce a covenant between the owner of the land and his neighbor purchasing a part of it, *and that the latter shall either use or abstain* from using the land purchased in a particular way, *is* [read *are*] what I never knew to be disputed." See **there is.**

L. Other False Plurals. E.g., "Exception after exception *have* [read *has*] whittled away the rule." See CONCORD. Cf. **media.**

subjoin = to annex, append. This word was formerly extremely common in LEGALESE. E.g., "Other statements of the rule will be found in the *subjoined* footnote." Today the term is falling into disuse, *subjoined footnote* conveying nothing that *footnote* does not equally clearly convey. Where the word is not, as above, completely superfluous, *join* or *attach* will often suffice in place of this pomposity: "The next verbal repetition, 'consigned pianos,' is *subjoined* [read *attached*] to the stipulation for the dealer to make monthly stock reports."

sub judice is an unnecessary phrase in almost every context in which it appears. The phrase means merely "before the court." Structurally an adverbial of place, the phrase functions as a POSTPOSITIVE ADJECTIVE. *Case sub* *judice* is readily made into the English phrase *case at bar*. Better yet, one might write *this case*: "In the case *sub judice* [read *In this case*], extensive controversy was present in the medical opinions."/ "Appellees argue that *the case sub judice* [read *this case* or *the present case*] does not fall within any of the three categories enumerated in *Blagge*."/ "As in *Crouch*, *the case sub judice* [read *the present case*] involves none of the concerns upon which the domestic-relations exception exists."/ "The case *sub judice* [read *The present case*] is clearly distinguishable on its facts from those two cases." See **case at bar, present** & **instant case.**

The phrase is best pronounced either /sub-**yood**-ĭ-kay/ or /sub-**jood**-ĭ-see/.

subjugate (= [1] to conquer or bring under control; or [2] to subdue) should not be used for *subordinate*. E.g., "We decline to require them to name their remedy when to do so would be to *subjugate* [read *subordinate*] fairness and common sense to technical nicety."

SUBJUNCTIVES are concededly obsolete for the most part in English. They still survive in such constructions as "If I were," "If he were," etc. Legal writers frequently omit the subjunctive mood of the verb when they should use it—usually when the situation postulated is hypothetical or contrary to fact. E.g., "Would your answer be different [hypothetical] if the basis of judicial jurisdiction *was* [read *were*] an attachment of real estate, the value of which would not be known until it was sold to satisfy judgment?"/ "Suppose now that the foreign corporation in question *was* [read *were* or *had been*] doing business within the state."/ "The claims of workmen who were employed in such a factory, and cannot continue to work there because of fire, represent only a small fraction of the claims which would arise if recovery *is* [read *were*, because the *if* is hypothetical] allowed in this class of cases."/ "If there were no state statutes, then of course the federal courts *did* [read *would*] not have to refer to state law at all, unless the action were local."/ "This section of the Act was designed to ensure *that the government was not prevented* [read *that the government not be prevented*] from exercising its leadership and planning functions."

It is ironic, in view of the sentences just quoted, that legal writers still often cling to basically outmoded subjunctives. Krapp labeled the usage *If I be* an "archaic survival" in

1927. See G. Krapp, *A Comprehensive Guide to Good English* 651-52 (1927). Following are similar archaic examples from legal prose: "If one partner *go* [read *goes* or *went*] to a third person to buy an article on time for the partnership, the other partner *cannot* [read as is if *goes* is in the first clause, or *could not* if *went* is in the first clause] prevent it by writing to the third person not to sell to him on time."/ "If the nonresident *have* [read *has*] no property in the state, there is nothing for the tribunals to adjudicate."/ "In the interpretation of contracts, whether they *be* [read *are*] ambiguous in the sense that that term is here defined or simply contain language of doubtful meaning, the primary concern of the courts is to ascertain and to give effect to the true intention of the parties."/ "In any event, whether or not *it be true* [read *it is true*] that the modern decisional law has minimized past confusing distinctions among different kinds of torts, there should be much less confusion under CPLR."

When one relates an indirect question asking about past condition, and no hypothetical or contrariety to truth is implied, the simple past should be employed, and not the subjunctive. Confusion on this point is the most common among those who profess to know how to handle subjunctives. E.g., "One inquired whether the money *were* [read *was*] lost property, and the other inquired whether the money *was* [read *had been*] mislaid."/ "In *Wagner*, the court rejected the defendant's theory that it would be liable to a rescuer only if the rescue *were* [read *was*] 'instinctive'."/ "In the instant case, there was sufficient reason to allow the questioned demonstration; however, even if it *were* [read *was*] error, it was harmless error."/ "It was not that these scriveners did not know how to punctuate; they were simply operating under the old rules; if there *were* [read *was*] a compelling oral reason for punctuation, punctuation would be supplied."

The three following sentences contain constructions in which the subjunctive is called for. In the first two examples, a demand or intention is expressed (this is one of the few exceptions to the obsolescence of subjunctives; the third sentence describes a condition that is contrary to fact: "These prisoners demanded that they all *engaged* [read *engage*] in sex and, although the complainant was frightened, he refused and climbed back into bed."/ "Parties may intend that a certain document *is* [read *be*] the final expression of agreement as to matters dealt with in that writing."/ "Some courts have construed wills acts patterned upon the Statute of Frauds as if the signature rather than the will *was* [read *were*] the thing to be acknowledged by the testator."

In the three following sentences, the use of the subjunctive is vestigial and moribund, and should be changed to the indicative: "What has been said, however, does not mean that the taxpayer had no right to carry out his declaration after the subject matter had come into existence, even though there *were* [read *was*] no consideration."/ "In Iowa, and generally elsewhere, the title to a decedent's real estate, whether he *die* [read *dies*] intestate or testate, including the right of dower, vests in the heir, devisee, or spouse instantly upon the death of the decedent, subject, of course, to the payment of his debts, and costs of administration."/ "In England, fair comment includes the inference of motives, if there *be* [read, in modern prose, *is*] foundation for the inference."

After such a plethora of examples of misusages, it is best to end this article propitiously with a correct use of the subjunctive in its most common setting: "Where an attesting witness has denied all knowledge of the matter, the case stands *as if there were* no attesting witness." (Eng.)

sublease, n.; **subtenancy; underlease.** The first is the usual term in AmE and BrE. The other two are primarily BrE variants.

sublease, v.t. See **let** & **underlease.**

sublessor (AmE & BrE); **underlessor** (BrE). See **sublease.**

sublet. See **let.**

submersible; submergible. Though the latter seems simpler (cf. *persuadable* and *persuasible*), the former is more common in both AmE and BrE. E.g., "That case involved claims for property damage arising from a blowout of a high-pressure gas well that occurred during workover operations on the well aboard a *submersible* drilling barge."

submittal (= the act of submitting), though not uncommon in American legal writing, is a NEEDLESS VARIANT of *submission*.

E.g., "Counsel made his *submittal* [read *submission*] to the court *outside* [or *off*] the record."/ "[T]he public may obtain information, [or] make *submittals* [read *submissions*] or requests." Administrative Procedure Act, 5 U.S.C. § 552(a)(1)(A) (1982).

sub modo (= under a qualification; subject to a restriction or condition) is a recherché LATINISM. "But whether a creditor or a grantee of the plaintiff in this case would be entitled to the immediate possession of the property, *or would only take the plaintiff's title sub modo* [read *or would take title subject to the restrictions on plaintiff's title*], need not be decided."

sub nom. (fr. L. *sub nomine*) = under the name. This abbreviation is commonly used, and justifiably so, in citations to note that a certain case may have involved different parties at an earlier or later procedural stage.

subornation of perjury. Although *subornation* may have the general sense "the act of inducing or procuring a person to commit an evil action, by bribery, corruption, or the like" (*OED*), in practice today it almost invariably means "the act of procuring a person to commit perjury." Hence *subornation of perjury* is a virtual REDUNDANCY, albeit an established and therefore a pardonable one.

The verb corresponding to this noun is *suborn* (= to procure [another] to commit perjury) and the agent noun is *suborner*.

subornee = one who is suborned. See -EE.

suborner is the only form of the word. See -ER, -OR.

subpart. See **sub-.**

subp(o)ena. *Subpena*, which the *Government Printing Office Manual* (1973) recommends, appears in any number of American federal statutes, e.g., in the Administrative Procedure Act and in 28 U.S.C. § 636(e)(4) (1982). *Subpoena* is, however, by far the more common spelling and for that reason alone is to be preferred.

The inflected forms of the verb *subpoena* are *subpoenaed* and *subpoenaing*. *Subpoenaed* is sometimes miscast *subpoened*. The preferred plural of the noun is *subpoenas*: "The *subpoenae* [read *subpoenas*] specifically called for, once again, interview memoranda. On June 6,

1984, the Government filed a motion to quash the *subpoenae* [read *subpoenas*]." *United States v. Omni International Corp.*, 634 F. Supp. 1414, 1427 (D.Md. 1986). The word is pronounced /sŭ-*pee*-nă/ as both noun and verb.

W3 lists *subpoena* as an adverb meaning "under penalty." This, of course, is its etymological sense. It virtually never appears in modern legal writing with this meaning, and should be considered obsolete in that use. See the following entry.

subpoenal (= required or done under penalty [*W2*]) is listed in *W2*, but not in the *OED* or in *W3*. It may occasionally be useful as the adjective corresponding to the noun in the sense "required or done in compliance with a subpoena."

subrogate = to put (a person) in the place of, or substitute (him) for, another in respect of a right or claim; to cause to succeed to the rights of another (*OED*). It was once a general English word, rather more literary than vernacular; today it is generally confined to legal contexts.

subrogee; subrogatee. The latter is an erroneous form of *subrogee* (= a person put in the place or substituted for another in upholding a right or claim). E.g., "A drawee bank under current Texas law will not be deemed the equitable *subrogatee* [read *subrogee*] of the maker on the ground that the maker has a valid defense to the debt evidenced by the check." *Subrogee* is pronounced /sŭb-rŏ-*jee*/. Cf. **obligee.** See -EE.

subrogor (= one who allows another to be substituted for oneself as creditor, with a transfer of rights and duties) is a twentieth-century legal NEOLOGISM created to correspond to *subrogee*, q.v. It is listed in *W3*, but not in the *OED* or in *W2*. As a term corresponding to *subrogee*, *subrogor* is quite acceptable. The word is pronounced /sŭb-rŏ-*gohr*/.

subscribe lit. means "to write (one's name or mark) on, orig. at the bottom of, a document, esp. as a witness or consenting party" (*OED*). In this sense the word is now purely a LEGALISM. Arguably it has its uses, although *sign* will almost always suffice more comprehensibly. E.g., "The summons is the mandate of the court and is *subscribed* [read *signed*] by an attorney who is an officer of the court."

subsequent to is a lawyer's pomposity for *after*. E.g., "The controversy in *Kulko* involved an attempted modification of child custody and support several years *subsequent to* [read *after*] the divorce of the parents."/ "*Subsequent to* [read *After*] drawing the will in Detroit, the decedent became a resident of Webberville."/ "The petitioner may, of course, *subsequent to* [read *after*] the execution of the trust agreement, have issue, but until such issue come into being, they cannot be said to have the status of existing beneficiaries."

Subsequent, used adjectivally, is perfectly acceptable in phrases such as *condition subsequent* and *subsequent history* (of a case). See **consequent(ial).**

subserve is an ARCHAISM for *serve*. E.g., "In that way the ends of justice and the best interests of the public will be *subserved* [read *served*]."/ "The interests of the people are best *subserved* [read *served*] by sustaining the statute quoted as it is written."/ "The beneficial ends to be *subserved* [read *served*] by public discussion would in large measure be defeated if honesty must be handled with delicacy."

subsidence is pronounced /sŭb-*sId*-ĕns/ or /*sŭb*-sĭd-ĕns/.

sub silentio is an unnecessary LATINISM for *silently, under silence,* or *in silence.* E.g., "The district court may have accepted, *sub silentio* [read *in silence*], the appellees' contention that appellant waived all claims in his pleadings except the claim for denial of procedural due process."/ "It does not make sense that Congress intended *sub silentio* [read *under silence*] to broaden the required exemption to preclude pro rata reductions."/ "In the discussion it has been assumed, *sub silentio of course* [read *silently of course*], that an injury to a contract right is an injury to a property interest."

subsist. This verb was formerly used regularly in the sense "to exist." This usage is now a legalistic ARCHAISM. E.g., "Such laws must be invariably obeyed, as long as the creature itself *subsists*, for its existence depends on that obedience." (Blackstone) The more common word *exist* should now be preferred, especially inasmuch as the usual meaning of *subsist* today is "to survive with a bare minimum of sustenance, to continue to exist; to keep oneself alive."

In the following sentences, *subsist* is used in

its archaic sense: "Joint tenancy is a relationship *subsisting* [read *existing*] between two or more persons in respect to an interest in land."/ "It did not appear in the declaration that the relation of master and servant ever *subsisted* [read *existed*] between the plaintiff and Miss Wagner." (Eng.)/ "The respondent by his amended answer has alleged that, at the time of the ceremony of marriage which he went through with the petitioner, there was already *a subsisting* [read *an existing*] marriage which had previously taken place between him and another lady in Pakistan." (Eng.)

The general lay sense also appears in legal writing, a fact that may lead to AMBIGUITY if the archaic sense is retained: "On the basis of this sole difference the first class is granted and the second class is denied welfare aid upon which may depend the ability of the families to obtain the very means to *subsist*—food, shelter, and other necessities of life."

substantive, one of the words most commonly mispronounced by lawyers, has three, not four syllables /*sub-stăn-tiv*/. The common error in the U.S. is to insert what is known as an epenthetical -e- after the second syllable /*sub-stă-nĕ-tiv*/. Still another blunder is to accent the second syllable /*sŭb-stan-tiv*/.

substantuate is solecistic for *substantiate.*

substitutional, -ary. The latter is a NEEDLESS VARIANT, although it appears almost as frequently as -*al* in the law of wills. It should, like all of its ilk, be uprooted. E.g., "If the word 'and' is read 'or,' the language creates a *substitutionary* [read *substitutional*] gift in favor of the heirs and assigns of George's sisters, who would take as purchasers."/ "In equity, such *substitutionary* [read *substitutional*] relief is afforded by the constructive trust, equitable lien, and the doctrine of subrogation."

Substitutional is plainly the more common term: "Having demonstrated her ability to create *substitutional* gifts of the residue, the testatrix probably did not intend other than that, in devising real estate to a number of infant co-owners, it would be inalienable except by order of the court."/ "The questions are whether certain legacies given in the codicil are cumulative or *substitutional* in respect of legacies given in the will to the same persons."/ "Refinement of this elementary classification leads to certain concepts of the judicial system operating in terms of the person

(in personam) or his things (in rem), as well as concepts of 'specific' as distinguished from 'substitutional' relief."

subtenancy is a chiefly BrE variant of *sublease*, q.v.

subterfuge is pronounced /*sub-tĕr-fyooj*/, not /*fyoozh*/.

subsub-. See **sub-.**

subsumed takes *under* or *in.*

subtle; subtile. The latter is an archaic and NEEDLESS VARIANT. E.g., "It is enough for the present case that the law should at least be prompt to recognize the injuries that may arise from an unauthorized use in connection with other facts, even if more *subtilty* [read *subtlety*] is needed to state the wrong than is needed here."

succedent. See **successive.**

succeeding for *after* or *following* is unnecessarily stuffy in most contexts. E.g., "The year *succeeding* [read *after*] the sale the company sold its real estate holdings."

succession in law refers primarily to the taking of an intestate share of an estate. E.g., "If a decedent died intestate, property passes by *intestate succession* to his heirs."/ "The daughter transferred the property to her mother upon an oral agreement to hold in trust for the daughter and to be returned to the daughter by *intestate succession*." (See **descent** (B).) The adjectival form of *succession* in this sense is *successional*. (See **successive.**)

LIKE *success*, *succession* is pronounced with the first -*c*- as if it were a -*k*-. Otherwise it is easily confused with *secession*. Cf. **accession & accessory.**

successive; successional; succedent. *Successive* = consecutive; following one after another, in uninterrupted succession. *Successional* = proceeding or passing by succession or descent. (See the preceding entry.) *Succedent to* is a pompous phrase meaning "following; after; subsequent to."

succinct. The first -*c*- is hard in this word. Cf. **succession, accession, & accessory.**

such. A. As a Demonstrative Adjective. *Such* is properly used as an adjective when reference has previously been made to a category of persons or things: thus *such* = of this kind, not *this*, *these*, or *those*. With this word two points should be kept in mind. First, when used as a demonstrative adjective to modify a singular noun, *such* typifies LEGALESE as much as *aforesaid* and *same*, n. Contrary to what some think, *such* is no more precise than *the*, *that*, or *those*. Second, *such* is a DEICTIC TERM that must refer to a clear antecedent. In the following sentence, *such* is used once vaguely (without an antecedent), once clearly: "The Association agreed to compile data on all conventions that will occur in cities where there are interested Gray Line members and to forward *such* report to *such* members." The first *such* would best have been omitted; no reports have been referred to—only the compilation of data, which is not necessarily the same as a report. The second *such*, less objectionable because the noun following it is plural, would read better as *those*.

Fowler calls the use of *such* in place of *the* or *that* "the illiterate *such*." E.g., "We adopt the opinion of the Court of Appeal. *Such* [read *The*] opinion is as follows."/ "*Such* cause of action, if any such there was, survived her death." [Read *The cause of action, if there was any, survived her death*.]/ "The general rule is that objection to a juror because of his disqualification is waived by failure to object to *such* [read *that*] juror until after the verdict." Cf. **said** & **same**.

B. As a Noun ⟨she has no dealings with such⟩. This use of the word is a legal barbarism. E.g., "I must dissent from the majority's holding that appellant's detention and ensuing search and seizure were lawful; *such* [read *that holding*] is pure dictum."

C. *Such . . . as to*. This generally unobjectionable construction should not be split by more than a few words: "Nothing in the letters was *such* an outrage *as to* inflame the passions of the jury." See **so as + infinitive.**

sue out. *Sue* is best known to lawyers and laymen alike in the sense "to institute legal proceedings against." Historically it has also been used in the PHRASAL VERBS *sue out* and *sue forth*, more commonly the former, in the sense "to make application before a court for the grant of (a writ or other legal process), often with implication of further proceedings being taken upon the writ" (*OED*). E.g., "This is the state in which the attachment was *sued out*."/ "The lien thus acquired was a legal

lien, and remained so as long as the capacity to *sue out* an elegit continued, whether the writ was *sued out* or not."/ "If no execution was *sued out* within a year and a day, the judgment became dormant."/ "'Defendant in error' is the distinctive term appropriate to the party against whom a writ of error is *sued out*." The phrase *sue out*, then, is not one of the phrases in which a preposition (here *out*) is merely an unnecessary particle. See **out** & PARTICLES, UNNECESSARY.

sufferance. So spelled; *suffrance* is a common mistaken spelling.

suffice it to say is the SUBJUNCTIVE form of *it suffices to say*. E.g., "*Suffice it to say* that those cases were decided under facts dissimilar to those existing in the present case." The phrase is sometimes wrongly metamorphosed into either *suffice to say* or *sufficient to say*. E.g., "*Suffice to say* [read *Suffice it to say*] that, as things stood in 1973, common-law rules of allowable pleading of matters in several counts of a single indictment, and the permissible consequences of so pleading, had been melded with predecessor articles before the 1965 changes in article 21.24."/ "Congress had no authority to ratify the sale of the lien lands; *sufficient to say* [read *suffice it to say*] that the law is complete on the subject."

sufficiency, -ce. The latter is a NEEDLESS VARIANT.

sufficient. See **adequate.**

sufficient number of is verbose for *enough*.

sufficiently . . . as to for *sufficiently . . . to* results from confusion with *so . . . as to*. E.g., "These anomalies appear *sufficiently* [read *so*] enmeshed in the current tangled web of the jurisprudence on this subject *as to* be beyond attempted amelioration by a panel of this circuit."/ "If the machine was in fact *sufficiently defective as to* [read *so defective as to*] create liability merely for marketing it, the failure to test adequately adds nothing." [Or read: *If the machine was in fact sufficiently defective to create liability . . . .*] See **so as + infinitive.**

suffrance. See **sufferance.**

suggestible, -able. The former spelling is preferred. See -ABLE (A).

suggestio falsi; suppressio veri. *Suggestio falsi* (lit., "suggestion of an untruth") = misrepresentation without direct falsehood. *Suppressio veri* (lit., "suppression of the truth") = a tacit misrepresentation; a silent lie. These LATINISMS may be useful (with, of course, an accompanying explanation), for there are no comparably short English phrases that convey the same notions.

suicide victim is almost an OXYMORON.

sui juris; sui generis. *Sui juris* = of full age and capacity. E.g., "Since in the present case all the beneficiaries are not in being and *sui juris*, revocation by consent is impossible."/ "If the beneficiary is *sui juris*, the promisee, at his election, may maintain an action for breach of contract."/ "Resignation is effective only when approved by the proper court, unless the trust terms provide otherwise, or by consent of all the beneficiaries if they are *sui juris*." Often this LATINISM is easily translated into ordinary English; when that is so, it should be.

Sui generis (= individual; like only to itself; one-of-a-kind) is an acceptable LATINISM because of its familiarity. The phrase is singular only, and should not be used with plural nouns. E.g., "That case has always been considered *sui generis*, and inconsistent with the fundamental principle of the action."/ "Garnishment is an anomaly, a statutory invention *sui generis*, with no affinity to any action known to the common law."/ "The strictly fundamental legal relations are, after all, *sui generis*; and thus it is that attempts at formal definition are always unsatisfactory, if not altogether useless."

The terms are sometimes confused. Here *sui juris* is wrongly made *sui generis*: "It is elementary that neither a guardian ad litem nor a next friend can maintain a suit in court on behalf of persons not *sui generis* [read *sui juris*], unless the court has jurisdiction of the subject matter."

suit; bill. At common law, one brought a *suit* in law and a *bill* in equity.

suit, v.t. (= to sue), is obsolete in legal English, although the negative form *nonsuit*, q.v., is still used as a verb.

suitability, in the sense "liability to suit" ⟨the suitability of the states of the union⟩, is

recorded in none of the major dictionaries. This sense is obfuscatory at best for lawyer-readers as well as for laymen; it should be avoided.

suit at law is an esp. formal way of saying *lawsuit*, the usual term today.

suitor has quite opposite meanings in lay and legal language. The lay *suitor* seeks matrimony, whereas the legal *suitor* seeks legal redress. *Suitor* is properly used only of a *complainant* or *plaintiff* in a suit, as opposed to a *defendant*. E.g., "[A] *suitor's* conduct in relation to the matter at hand may disentitle him to the relief he seeks." *Sanders v. United States*, 373 U.S. 1, 17 (1963)./ "Every *suitor* who resorts to chancery for any sort of relief by injunction may, on a mere statement of belief that the defendant can easily make away with or transport his money or goods, impose an injunction on him."/ "In an era when the greatest effort in history is being made to neutralize financial disparity in litigation, there is little reason why a *suitor* should have permitted his limited means to influence too late a start."

suit over. See **over.**

suitwrong. This recent legal NEOLOGISM, unrecorded in the dictionaries, is hardly a model of lucidity. E.g., "The filing of the action against a *suitwrong* [read *an inappropriate*] corporate defendant did not toll the statute of limitations as to the correct defendant."

summing-up is the British phrase meaning "the judge's summary for the jury of the main points in evidence, together with his guidance on the form of the verdict to be given." E.g., "Their Lordships would repeat, it is the effect of the *summing-up* as a whole that matters and not any stated verbal formula used in the course of it." (Eng.)

summer associate. See **clerk.**

summons, v.t., = to cite before a court or a judge or magistrate; to take out a summons against (*OED*). The verb is properly inflected *summonsed* in the past tense, *summonses* in the third-person singular. Generally, *persons* are *summonsed* to give information; in modern legal usage, however, by HYPALLAGE has arisen the idiom that *information* may be *sum-*

monsed. E.g., "We view the requirement in this Circuit to be that the taxpayer must show that the government actually possesses the information *summonsed,* such that enforcement of a summons is 'unnecessary.'" *United States v. Texas Heart Institute,* 755 F.2d 469, 476 (5th Cir. 1985)./ "We conclude that the IRS is not already in possession of the *summonsed* information in the instant appeal."

summonses is the correct plural form of *summons,* n. E.g., "Mr. Winn does not ask us to send back the other *summonses* that are consequential *summonses.*" (Eng.)/ "Before us are two appeals from separate orders of the district court enforcing two sets of Internal Revenue Service *summonses.*"

sumptuous, -tuary. These words have almost opposite senses. *Sumptuous* = excessively luxurious; made or produced at great cost. *Sumptuary* = pertaining to or regulating expenditure (*OED*).

sundry (= various) is, in AmE., a quaint term with literary associations. The clichéd DOUBLET *various and sundry* is generally best avoided even in the most casual contexts, for it smacks of glibness.

superadd (= to add over and above) is rarely used in lay, and infrequently in legal, contexts. It is usually pompous in place of *add.* E.g., "It is, of course, equally clear that even though all such facts be present as last supposed, the *superadded* fact of malice will, in cases of so-called 'conditional privilege,' negative the privilege that otherwise would exist."

supercede. See **supersede.**

supererogatory has two almost opposite sets of connotations, some positive and others negative. The core sense is "going beyond what is required." On the one hand, the word may connote "superfluous," and is often used in this way. On the other hand, it may mean "performing more than duty or circumstances require; doing more than is minimally needed."

SUPERFLUITIES of various kinds may be found in most legal writing. This entry contains a few common examples of unnecessary words. E.g., "A foreign mining corporation may carry on such functional intrastate operations as *those of* [omit *those of*] mining or refining." Verbs are often unnecessarily repeated in comparisons, as here: "Of the many possible forms of human capital, none has received more attention over the past two decades than *has* [omit *has*] the economics of education." Superfluous commas abound in many of the older judicial opinions, but in modern ones as well. "The witness who proved this, [omit comma] said . . . . " (1809)/ "The declaration stated, [omit comma] that the plaintiff . . . ." (1842). These might easily have been written today. The best contemporary writing is free from even this minor refuse; the fewer impediments we put in the reader's way, the more likely he is to follow us. See CUTTING OUT THE CHAFF & VERBOSITY.

superimpose; superpose. Both forms are used in legal writing, the older form, *superimpose* (1794), being more familiar to most readers. E.g., "*Superimposed* upon this uniform system is the maximum grant regulation, the operative effect of which is to create two classes of needy children and two classes of families." *Superpose,* today rightly counted among NEEDLESS VARIANTS, is recorded from 1823.

superior. See **inferior.**

superlegislature. This is a tendentious term used to describe a court that usurps the power of the legislative branch of government. E.g., "Rights such as these are in principle indistinguishable from those involved here, and to extend the 'compelling interest' rule to all cases in which such rights are affected would go far toward making this Court a 'superlegislature.'" *Shapiro v. Thompson,* 394 U.S. 618, 661 (1969) (Harlan, J., dissenting).

superpose. See **superimpose.**

supersede, not *supercede,* is the correct spelling. Writers who misapprehend the Latin root from which the word is composed (*-sed* "to sit," not *-ced* "to move") distort it to reflect their misconception. Correct spelling of this word is one of the hallmarks of a punctilious writer. The misspelling occurs in some rather surprising places, as in Leff, *The Leff Dictionary of Law,* 94 Yale L.J. 1855, 1867 (1985), under "Abortion Act." And here: "[W]e can see no functional reason for remanding to the district court to order it to vacate the already *superceded* [read *superseded*] . . . orders relating to pretrial detention and bail." *United States v. O'Shaughnessy,* 772 F.2d 112, 113 (5th Cir. 1985).

In law, *supersede* sometimes carries the specialized sense "to invoke or make applicable the right of supersedeas against [an award of damages]", a sense unknown to laymen, for whom the term means "to replace, supplant." Following are examples of the special legal use: "It is clear that, if the relator was entitled to *supersede* the judgment against him [i.e. post a supersedeas bond], the court of appeals has the power to enter any order necessary for that purpose."/ "In *Aetna Club v. Jackson,* the court of civil appeals had before it an original application for a writ of mandamus to require the trial judge to fix the amount of the bond necessary to *supersede* a final judgment granting an injunction."

Note that *supersession* is the nominal form, meaning either "the act of superseding" or "the state of being superseded." *Supersedure* is a NEEDLESS VARIANT in all but beekeeping contexts.

supersedeas, when used elliptically as an attributive noun for *supersedeas bond* or *writ,* forms the plural in *-es.* E.g., "It also prescribed the conditions upon which such appeals or writs of error should operate as *supersedeases.*" *Holland v. Webster,* 29 So. 625, 630 (Fla. 1901) (Mabry, J., dissenting).

superseding cause.   See CAUSATION (E).

supervene (= to come on or occur as something additional or extraneous; to come directly or shortly after something else, either as a consequence of it or in contrast with it) is rarely seen outside the law. E.g., "The attachment of a judgment lien will not sever the joint tenancy, thus leaving the judgment creditor exposed to the destruction of the lien by a *supervening* death of the judgment debtor."

supervening cause.   See CAUSATION (D) & (E).

supplementary, -al; suppletory. *Supplementary* is the ordinary word. The other forms have the same meaning, namely, "of the nature of, forming, or serving as, a remedy to

the deficiencies of something." One might jump to brand the other forms as NEEDLESS VARIANTS, yet the law has found niches for them in special phrases. In the U.S., we refer usually to *supplemental pleadings,* not *supplementary.* And in older Anglo-American law, a *suppletory oath* was "an oath (given by a party in his own favor) admitted to supply a deficiency in legal evidence." These variant forms should be confined to these particular uses.

suppliant; supplicant. The latter is a NEEDLESS VARIANT of the former, an ARCHAISM meaning "one who supplicates; a humble petitioner." E.g., "Consequently, *suppliants* began to address their prayers to the Chancellor instead of to the King or Council."/ "In any petition the *suppliants* put forward an alternative ground for their claim." (Eng.)

supply an omission. In the modern idiom, we *make up for* or *remedy* or *compensate for* an omission rather than *supplying* it. E.g., "The class action rule does not suggest that the zeal or talent of the representative plaintiffs' attorney can *supply* [read *make up for*] the omission of the requirement that claims of the representative parties be typical of the class." Nothing can *supply* an omission. One can *supply* (= to make up a deficiency in [*OED*]) in an obsolete sense of the word. But today *supply* is so closely connected with the sense "to provide" that it seems almost contradictory to write of *supplying (providing) an omission.*

supposable; supposit(it)ious; suppositional; suppositive. *Supposable* = capable of being supposed; presumable. *Suppositious* and *supposititious* sometimes cause confusion. Although some modern dictionaries list these as variants, some DIFFERENTIATION is both possible and desirable. *Suppositious* should be used to mean "hypothetical; theoretical; assumed." *Supposititious* should be confined to its usual sense, "illegitimate; spurious; counterfeit." In legal contexts, *supposititious* when applied to a child means "falsely presented as a genuine heir" (*W9*). E.g., "The main question in dispute was whether one calling himself 'Archibald Douglas' was the legitimate child of Lady Jane Douglas or was *supposititious.*" (Eng.) The phrase *supposititious will* = a fake or falsified will.

Suppositional = conjectural, hypothetical. It has much the same sense as *suppositious,* and is perhaps generally the clearer word. *Suppositive* (= characterized by supposition; supposed) is a NEEDLESS VARIANT of *supposititious* and *suppositional.*

supposing   is inferior as an opening imperative to *suppose.* E.g., "*Supposing* [read *Suppose*] that car A collides with car B at this intersection."

supposition; supposal; suppose, n.   In legal contexts, as in most contexts, *supposition* is the ordinary word, and the others are probably NEEDLESS VARIANTS. *Supposal* is sometimes used by logicians.

supposit(it)ious; suppositional; suppositive.   See **supposable.**

suppressible, -able.   The former spelling is standard. See -ABLE (A).

suppressio veri.   See **suggestio falsi.**

supra.   This citational signal is disfavored in modern legal writing, inasmuch as short-form citations are more convenient for the reader. An archaic variant of *supra* is *ubi supra* (= as above). E.g., "In *Inches v. Hill, ubi supra* [read *698 F.2d at 344,* e.g., if the case has previously been cited in full], the same person had become owner of the equitable life estate and of the equitable remainder, and, no reason appearing to the contrary, the court decreed a conveyance by the trustees to the owner." See **ante.**

supreme court,   in most American jurisdictions, denotes the highest court of appeal. New York, however, is an exception; *The New York Times* has editorialized about the names of the New York courts and their judges: "The trial court is misnamed the Supreme Court, which is what most people expect to find at the top. A system that uses the term Supreme Court justice for judges of original jurisdiction is a system that resists modernization and invites cynicism." N.Y. Times, Jan. 3, 1985, at Y18, col. 2.

sur   appears in various LAW FRENCH phrases. It means merely "on"; the English word should supplant it wherever possible. E.g., "About 18 months thereafter the plaintiff caused to be issued an attachment *sur judgment* [read *on the judgment*] in which the City

of Philadelphia Police Beneficiary Association was summoned as garnishee." *Mamlin v. Tener,* 23 A.2d 90, 91 (Pa. Super. 1941).

surcease   = a cessation; a temporary respite. To confuse this word with *solace* (= that which gives comfort in disappointment, stress, or grief) is a MALAPROPISM. "Having failed to offer the challenged testimony in an acceptable manner, appellant may not draw *surcease* [read *solace*] from *Chambers,* which is inapplicable."/ "Knighton sought a stay of execution and other habeas *surcease* [read *solace*] in a petition filed in district court." See **death.**

surety, n., in law, usu. means either "a guarantor" or "a formal engagement entered into, a pledge, bond, guarantee, or security given for the fulfillment of an undertaking" (*OED*). The latter sense applies in this sentence: "One nominated as trustee is not required to take an oath that he will faithfully discharge his duties as trustee, or to execute a bond with satisfactory *sureties* conditioned upon the faithful performance of his duties." The word has three syllables /*shoor-ĕ-tee*/. The archaic lay sense "certainty" is rarely encountered today.

suretyship; suretiship.   The former spelling is preferred.

surplus   is the tendentiously humorous group term for lawyers; it was the invention of Eric Partridge, in *Usage and Abusage,* s.v. "Sports Technicalities." Hence we have a gaggle of geese, a bevy of quail, a flock of sheep, and a surplus of lawyers.

surplusage; surplus.   The distinction is slight. *Surplus,* the fundamental term, means "what remains over, what is not required for the purpose at hand, esp. excess of public revenue over expenditure for the financial year" (*COD*). *Surplusage* is a NEEDLESS VARIANT in all senses but the primarily legal one: "an excess or superabundance of words; a word, clause, or statement in an indictment, plea, or legal instrument that is not necessary to its adequacy, or in a statute that is merely redundant and insignificant." *Surplusage,* like *surplus,* is stressed on the first syllable.

surrebuttal.   See **rebuttal.**

surrender (= the termination of a lease, which occurs when a tenant gives up his interest to his landlord [*CDL*]) is a TERM OF ART.

surrogacy; surrogateship. Both may mean "the office of a surrogate (q.v.)." *Surrogacy* is more usual. *W3* even omits *surrogateship*, which at best is a NEEDLESS VARIANT. *Surrogacy* is the only form used in the sense "the fact or state of being a surrogate (as a surrogate mother)." E.g., "The British bill permits a surrogate mother to be paid for her services, which is reasonable, but then would throw the criminal law at any intermediary who might be involved, or at any service that advertises *surrogacy*." (Eng.)

surrogate, n., = (1) (in some states of the U.S.) a judge with probate jurisdiction; (2) (in G.B.) the deputy of an ecclesiastical judge, of a bishop or bishop's chancellor, esp. one who grants licences to marry without banns (*OED*). Sense (1) is common esp. in New York and other jurisdictions in the eastern U.S. E.g., "In rejecting this contention, *Surrogate* Thomas stated, 'In no case that has been brought to my notice has a will been refused probate on proof extraneous to the document of a mistake by the testator as to a fact that might possibly have led him to do something different from what he has done.'"

surveil is a relatively new, and decidedly useful, verb corresponding to the noun *surveillance*. It is, in fact, a BACK-FORMATION from the noun. The participial and preterite forms are *surveilling* and *surveilled*. E.g., "The chief of police directed several police officers to *surveil* different locations in town."/ "The simple fact of a meeting at a restaurant takes on a much greater meaning based upon the information that the *surveilling* agents had obtained from the informants." The *OED* gives the year 1960 as the date of its first recorded use, by an American Court at that: "The plaintiff also stresses that the store as a whole, and the customer exits especially, were closely *surveilled*." *Alexandre of London v. Indemnity Insurance Co.,* 182 F. Supp. 748, 750 (D.D.C. 1960).

surveillance, place under, is an established phrase that was necessary before *surveil,* q.v., was developed as a verb. The metaphor of *placing under surveillance* does not work

in all contexts, however. *Surveillance* can be had of both persons and places, but only persons can be "placed under surveillance," because the metaphor of "placing" will not work for real property (which, as an immovable, cannot conceivably be "placed"). E.g., *"The parking lot was placed under surveillance, and the watching officers* [read *The officers conducted surveillance of the parking lot and*] observed Miller drive up in a 1979 Lincoln Continental at 8:00 p.m."

survivance is not a mere NEEDLESS VARIANT of *survival,* although it is increasingly rare. *Survivance* is used solely in G.B. and means "the succession to an estate, office, etc. of a survivor nominated before the death of the existing occupier or holder; the right of such succession in case of survival" (*OED*). E.g., "The right exists by virtue of *survivance* and cannot be excluded by will or otherwise, nor can it be apportioned unequally among the children." (Scot.)/ "He would have to exercise on *survivance* the rights, and come under the obligations, stipulated in regard to the surviving partner by the articles of association." (Eng.)

susceptible (of) (to) (for). The only prepositions with which this verb may properly be construed are *of* and *to.* Usage has differentiated *susceptible of* from *susceptible to,* the latter now being more common in ordinary lay contexts. *Susceptible to* = capable of receiving and being affected by (external impressions, influences, etc., esp. something injurious); sensitive to; liable or open to (attack, injury, etc.). *Susceptible of* was formerly used in this sense, but is now confined to the senses, common in law, of (1) "capable of undergoing, admitting of (some action or process such as interpretation)"; (2) "capable of taking or admitting (a form, meaning, or other attribute)"; or (3) "capable of receiving into the mind, conceiving, or being inwardly affected by (a thought, feeling, or emotion)."

Sense (1) of *susceptible of* is quite common in legal writing. E.g., "These damages are not *susceptible of* exact proof and the amount is left largely to the sound discretion and common sense of the jury."/ "The timberland was theoretically *susceptible of* such use."/ "Admittedly, this language is *susceptible of* the interpretation placed upon it by the district court." Sense (2) also frequently appears in modern legal prose: "A latent ambiguity exists where the language of the will, though clear on its face, is *susceptible of* more than one meaning, when applied to the extrinsic facts to which it refers."/ "News matter, however little *susceptible of* ownership or dominion in the absolute sense, is stock in trade to both parties alike."

In the following sentences, *to* wrongly appears where *of* should in sense (2): "The phrase is susceptible *to* [read *of*] more than one interpretation."/ "The rule that statutes in derogation of the common law should be strictly construed does not mean that the statute should be given the narrowest meaning *to* [read *of*] which it is susceptible."

Susceptible to is here properly used: "We conclude that details of identification, particularly such matters as middle initials, street addresses, and the like, which are highly *susceptible to* mistake, particularly in metropolitan areas, should not be accorded such sanctity as to frustrate an otherwise clearly demonstrable intent."/ "Some courts have not required that the contestant produce evidence to indicate that the testator is *susceptible to* undue influence."

Rarely is *susceptible of* misused for *susceptible to*, but here is an example: "The selection procedure is *susceptible of* [read *to*] abuse and is not racially neutral."/ "Appellant argues that that complaint, labeled conversion, does not state a cause of action because the subject matter is money, and mere money is not *susceptible of* [read *to*] conversion."

Susceptible for is merely incorrect: "We remanded for factual findings concerning whether the timberland at issue was *susceptible for* [read *of*] use to produce interest, dividends, rents, or royalties."

Susceptible is sometimes pronounced, even by educated speakers, /sŭk-**sep**-tĭ-bĕl/ rather than /sŭ-**sep**-tĭ-bĕl/.

suspect, adj.; **suspicious.** The DIFFERENTIATION between these words is that the former denotes a fully formulated impression, whereas the latter denotes only an incipient impression. *Suspect* = regarded with suspicion or distrust; suspected. *Suspicious* = (1) open to, deserving of, or exciting suspicion; (2) full of, inclined to, or feeling suspicion.

suspendible, -able. The former is the only one listed in the *OED* and *W3*. See -ABLE (A).

suspicious. See **suspect.**

sustain is a CHAMELEON-HUED WORD if ever there was one. Idiomatically, we speak of *sustaining damage,* of *sustaining motions,* and of *sustaining a population.* Other variations with slight nuances are possible, and all are permissible because of historical usage. *Sustain* may mean "to undergo, experience, have to submit to (evil, hardship or damage)" (*OED*). E.g.: "The testatrix died from injuries she *sustained* in the automobile accident."/ "Various train cars *sustained* damage totaling over a million dollars." Or it may mean "to uphold the validity of." E.g.: "The important question is whether the statute can be *sustained.*"

The sense "to nourish or support life in" is one of the general lay senses of the word. Additionally, *sustain* may mean "to keep up or keep going"; e.g.: "Green's medical records indicate that he has *sustained* [better *experienced*] remarkably good health during his confinement in the prison."

Given these multifarious senses, few uses of the word seem to be objectionable; in the following sentence, however, it appears to have been used as a turgid substitute for *have*: "Neither the defendant nor the man who made the patterns *sustained* [read *had*] any relation by contract with the plaintiff."

SWAPPING HORSES while crossing the stream is Fowler's term for "changing a word's sense in the middle of a sentence, by vacillating between two constructions either of which might follow a word legitimately enough, by starting off with a subject that fits one verb but must have something tacitly substituted for it to fit another, and by other such performance." (*MEU1* 589). E.g., "The subject of this paper, however, is the evidentiary rule and concerns those situations where evidence is sought from the lawyer through compulsion of law." The writer has switched gears mentally from "subject . . . is" to "paper . . . concerns." [Read *The subject of this paper, however, is the evidentiary rule and those situations in which . . .* , or *This paper, however, concerns the evidentiary rule and those situations in which. . . .*]

swear, v.t., in law often takes phrasal objects, whereas in nonlegal contexts its objects are almost uniformly clauses beginning with the relative pronoun *that.* Specimens of the legal usage follow: "I might add that the reference to *swearing* a petition and an affidavit in support is to a practice no longer in use." (Eng.)/ "In correct legal phraseology, the deponent *swears* an affidavit and the judge takes it."/ "*Swear* the witness."

sweat ⟩ sweat ⟩ sweat. So declined.

syllabus. Pl. *-buses, -bi.* American college professors are fond, perhaps overfond, of the Latin plural. See PLURALS (A).

SYLLEPSIS is a rhetorical figure that makes one word refer to two terms incongruously. It is not, however, like zeugma (see JANUS-FACED TERMS), grammatically incorrect. E.g., "The jury sentenced the defendant *to ten years* in prison and *to right a wrong.*" See ZEUGMA.

sympathy. See **empathy.**

symposium. Pl. *-siums. Symposia* is a pedantry. See PLURALS (A).

sync, short for *synchronism* or *synchrony,* is preferred to *synch.* E.g., "Section 7 is simply out of *sync* with a changing jurisprudence."

synchronous, -ic, -al. The second and third are NEEDLESS VARIANTS.

SYNESIS is a grammatical principle whereby in certain contexts meaning, rather than the requirements of grammar or syntax, controls SUBJECT-VERB AGREEMENT. The English grammarian Sweet called these triumphs of logic over grammar "antigrammatical constructions." (Expressions in which grammar triumphs over logic are termed "antilogical.") As an example of an antigrammatical construction, *a number of* (= several; many) is routinely followed by a plural verb, even though technically the singular noun *number* is the subject: "There *are* a *number* of special problems confronting the courts in determining whether an injunction should or should not be granted under the Securities Act." See **number of, there are a.**

For example, where *a variety of* = many, it would be incorrect to write: "An endless variety of techniques *was* [read *were*] employed."/ "*There is* [read *There are*] now a variety of antidepressant drugs that can help lift these people out of their black moods." Likewise, where *handful* = several, it is wrong to

write: "Few younger lawyers have escaped his influence, but only a *handful* of them *possesses* read [read *possess*] his creative zest or renovating energy."

Note, however, that this principle does not govern where an intervening adjective reinforces the noncountability of the noun: "There *are* [read *is*] an ever-increasing number of meetings around the land about ethnicity." The number (an amount) is ever increasing—hence the sentence calls for a singular verb. (Cf. "An *increasing number* of American law schools *are* [not *is*] offering courses rather consistently labeled Comparative Law.")

SYNONYMIA. The myth is that no two words in the language can have precisely the same meaning, as stated here: "Strictly speaking, no two words have the same meaning. There are connotations that attach to language and even two synonyms will suggest slightly different meanings to a reader." N. Brand & J. O. White, *Legal Writing: The Strategy of Persuasion* 114 (1976). This belief may explain the inclination of lawyers to use DOUBLETS AND TRIPLETS. E.g., "The indictment alleged that respondents unlawfully *kept, confined, and imprisoned* George in a *dark, cold, and unwholesome* room."/ "Vendor does *grant, bargain, sell, assign, convey, transfer, set over, and deliver* the land to the purchaser." Instead of using these verbal strings, the writer should determine which of the words can be subsumed under (and therefore omitted because of the presence of) broader terms. In the first sentence quoted above, *imprison* certainly encompasses *confine* and *keep;* in the second, *grant* or *convey* would easily suffice. Lawyers generally seek to cover every contingency, esp. in DRAFTING; we should do so, however, discriminatingly rather than in blunderbuss fashion.

synonym(it)y. *Synonymy* is the preferred form. See **synonymous.**

synonymous (in the sense "coextensive") is a LEGALISM not found in general lay writing. E.g., "Nor do we subscribe to the argument that Merrill's powers of control over partnership property as a general partner of a limited partnership are per se *synonymous* with the partnership's."/ "Given the *synonymy* between the limits of the Louisiana long-arm statute and those of due process, it becomes necessary to consider only whether the exercise of jurisdiction over a nonresident defendant comports with due process."

syphon. See **siphon.**

system(at)ize. *Systemize* is a NEEDLESS VARIANT of *systematize.*

systemic; systematic. *Systemic* should be *systematic* unless the reference is systems of the body, as in *systemic disorders.* E.g., "The plaintiffs alleged *systemic* [read *systematic*] disparate treatment of minority groups."/ "The complaint alleged across-the-board, *systemic* [read *systematic*] discrimination against black employees."

T

taboo; tabu. The former spelling is standard. For the verb *to taboo* (= to exclude or prohibit by authority or social influence [*COD*]), the preterite and past participle is formed *tabooed* rather than *taboo'd.* E.g., "A copyrighted work is not *tabooed* to subsequent workers in the same field."

tabula rasa (= a blank tablet ready for writing; a clean slate) has been an esp. common metaphor in legal writing. It has grown into a CLICHÉ.

tactile; tactual. The latter has become merely a NEEDLESS VARIANT. *Tactile* is the usual word meaning either "of or relating to touch" or "touchable; tangible."

tail, in the legal sense denoting a type of limited freehold estate, is a LAW FRENCH term, deriving ultimately from the Old French verb *taillier* "to cut, shape, hence to fix the precise form of, to limit." Formerly it was spelled *taille.* It commonly appears in the phrase *in tail.* E.g., "It has been repeatedly determined that if there be tenant for life, remainder to his first son *in tail,* remainder over, and he is brought before the court before he has issue, the contingent remaindermen are barred." Sometimes the word is used without *in,* as in the phrases *fee tail,* q.v., and *estate-tail,* as here: "Under the first rule, if A devises his lands to B and to B's children or issue, and B has not any issue at the time of the devise, the same is an *estate-tail.*"

Tail may be a noun taking POSTPOSITIVE ADJECTIVES (*tail female, tail special*) or may itself be a postpositive adjective (*fee tail*). See **entail** & **disentail.**

taint. See **attaint.**

take (= to receive by inheritance) is peculiar to the legal idiom. E.g., "The will itself indicates the proportions according to which the beneficiaries shall *take.*" See **taker.** See also **bring.**

take exception. This phrase means "to object" in general lay contexts, but is used in legal writing in the sense "to posit an error on appeal." E.g., "The defendants *took* five *exceptions*; the questions raised by *exceptions* as we have shown are four."

taken. Appeals to higher courts are said, in the legal idiom, to be *taken.* E.g., "We do not discuss various objections to the plan of merger filed after this *appeal* was *taken.*"

taken back, to be is an illiteracy when used for *take(n) aback.*

take-nothing judgment (= a judgment for the defendant providing that the plaintiff recover nothing) should be hyphenated thus.

take precedence. See **precedence.**

taker = one who receives property by inheritance. E.g., "With respect to real estate, such a gift over, in the event of the indefinite failure of the issue of the *first taker,* was construed to cut down and limit the interest of the *first taker* to an estate tail."/ "The fact that the trust agreement reserved a power of appointment is evidence that the settlor believed she had created an interest in the property on the part of others and reserved the power in order to defeat that interest or to postpone until a later date the naming of specific *takers.*" See **take.**

take silk is a BrE phrase meaning "to become a Queen's Counsel [Q.C.] or King's Counsel [K.C.]." See **silk.**

take under advisement. See **advisement.**

tales /*tay-leez*/. The *OED* states:

Originally, in plural, Persons taken from among those present in court or standing by, to serve on a jury in a case where the original panel has become deficient in number by challenge or other cause, these persons being *such* as those originally summoned; loosely applied in Eng. as a singular (*a tales*) to the supply of men (or even one man) so provided. Also contextually applied to the order or act of supplying such substitutes, as *to pray, grant, award a tales*. In English use [till 1971] restricted to such summoning of common jurors to serve on a special jury; orig. and still in U.S. in general use (including criminal jurisdiction).

In the U.S. may be found examples of what is termed a "loose" usage in England (a number of jurors added to make up for a deficiency in a panel), but probably not in reference to a single juror. *Talesman*, q.v., is used in this latter sense in both the U.S. and G.B.

talesman; tales-juror. The usual form has been *talesman*, *tales-juror* being a variant. Both terms are coming to be ARCHAISMS, as methods of selecting veniremen become more sophisticated. E.g., "While it is still proper in some places to select additional jurors from bystanders, the modern practice to supply a deficiency in the jury panel is a drawing from the jury wheel or box and the issuance of a special venire, the object of which is to get a body of men less liable to causes of challenge than would be *tales-jurors* picked up in the courtroom."

talisman (= a charm, amulet, or other thing supposed to be capable of working wonders), a favorite word of judges, is not to be confused with *talesman*, q.v. E.g., "The law has outgrown its primitive stage of formation when the precise word was the sovereign *talisman*, and every slip was fatal." (Cardozo)/ "Freedom of choice is not a sacred *talisman*; it is only a means to a constitutionally required end—the abolition of the system of segregation and its effects." The plural form is *talismans*, not *talismen*.

The adjective is *talismanic*. E.g., "Ritual and *talismanic* recitations of boilerplate affidavits are a thing of the past."/ "Libel law can claim no *talismanic* immunity from constitutional limitations and must be measured by standards that satisfy the First Amendment."

talk to; talk with. The former suggests a conversation in which the remarks strongly preponderate from one side, as between a superior and an inferior. The latter suggests a conversation between equals, with equal participation.

tantalize (= to torment or test [a person] by sight or promise of a desired thing withheld or kept just out of reach [*COD*]) is not infrequently confused with *titillate* (= to excite pleasantly or tickle).

The verb *tantalize* is derived from the Greek myth about Tantalus, king of Sipylos, born of the union of Zeus and the nymph Pluto. Tantalus offended the gods by stealing some of their food and giving it to mortals. Because the father of Tantalus was divine, Tantalus was himself immortal (though not a god) and thus could not be executed for his crime. Instead, as an eternal punishment, he was placed in a pool of fresh water up to his chin, while overhead boughs of edible fruit hung temptingly near. Whenever he dipped to drink, the water receded; whenever he stretched to eat, a wind blew the laden boughs out of reach.

tantamount used as a verb is incorrect; it is an adjective only, meaning "equivalent." This lapse is probably rare: "The legal effect of the judgment in the class action *tantamounts* [read *is tantamount*], we think, to removing Humphrey from the representative class."

tape-record, v.t. This verb is always hyphenated.

tautologous; tautological. The latter, though older, has become a NEEDLESS VARIANT of the former. E.g., "It is not enough to say that the legislature sought to prefer one class of litigants over another and succeeded in doing so, for that is a mere *tautological* [read *tautologous*] recognition of the fact that the legislature did what it intended to do."

TAUTOLOGY. "What's the first excellence in a lawyer? Tautology. What the second? Tautology. What the third? Tautology." R. Steele, *The Funeral* I (1701). It is worth pointing out, lest the irony escape those who have used this book at all and still are fond of LEGALESE, that the words quoted are derisive, not serious. Yet tautologies continue to proliferate: "Wide public participation in rulemaking *obviates* the problem of *singling out a* *single defendant* among a group of competitors for initial imposition of a new and inevitably costly legal obligation." See REDUNDANCY (B).

taxable = (1) subject to taxation ⟨taxable income⟩; or (2) (of legal costs or fees) assessable ⟨taxable expenses⟩. Sense (2) is illustrated in this sentence: "Expert-witness fees are not *taxable* as costs of court."

taxpayer. See ARTICLES (A) & **payor.**

teachings = holdings and dicta. E.g., "The threshold question is whether appellant has stated a procedural due process claim under section 1983, particularly in light of the Supreme Court's *teachings* in *Parratt v. Taylor*."/ "The failure of the interrogating officers to avoid asking more questions violated the *teachings* of *Miranda* and *Edwards v. Arizona*, thereby tainting his confession." See **hold** & **dictum.**

tear gas, n.; **teargas,** v.t. This term is spelled as two words for the noun, as one for the verb.

technic. See **technique.**

technical; technological. The distinction is sometimes a fine one. *Technical* = of or in a particular science, art, or handicraft; of or in vocational training. *Technological* = pertaining to the science of practical or industrial arts. *Technological* connotes recent experimental methods and development, whereas *technical* has no such connotation.

technique; technic. The latter, a variant spelling, is to be avoided.

technological. See **technical.**

technologies for *technological methods* is a VOGUE WORD. See PLURALS (B).

telecast. See **broadcast.**

teleconferencing. See **conferencing.**

telephonee. See -EE.

telephonic is a highfalutin adjectival form of *telephone*, which ordinarily serves as its own adjective. "*Ross* makes no reference to *telephonic warrants* nor have any cases been found

following *Ross* that involve *telephonic warrants* [read, in both instances, *warrants issued over the telephone*]."/ "On request, the clerk will notify counsel who desire immediate collect *telephonic* notification when the decision is rendered." [Read *The clerk will call counsel collect, if they so desire, when the decision is rendered.*]

tell for *say. Tell* is a transitive verb that demands an indirect as well as a direct object. E.g., "One of the industry's major producers *told* [read *said*] recently that a large studio receives 20,000 stories or ideas per year, of which but twenty are made into motion pictures."

temperature is pronounced /tem-pĕ-ră-chŭr/, not /tem-pĕ-ră-tyŭr/, which is precious, or /tem-pă-chŭr/, which is slovenly. A combination of the precious and the slovenly, /tem-pă-tyŭr/ is humorously affected.

temporal = (1) of relating to time; (2) worldly; (3) nonecclesiastical; (4) transitory; (5) pertaining to the temple (part of one's head); or (6) pertaining to bones in the vertebrae. In other words, this is a classic CHAMELEON-HUED WORD. Usually, *temporal* refers to time (sense 1) in legal writing, e.g.: "Although not *temporally* clear from the record, it appears that while the attorneys and the trial judge were in chambers, the court coordinator and the bailiff conducted a shuffle of the panel."

Temporal was a favorite word of Justice Holmes, who used it in the special legal sense, a variation on sense (3) given above, "civil or common as opposed to criminal or ecclesiastical." E.g., "In numberless instances the law warrants the intentional infliction of *temporal* damage because it regards it as justified." (Holmes, J.)/ "Actions of tort are brought for *temporal* damage; the law recognizes *temporal* damage as an evil which its object is to prevent or to address." (Holmes, J.)/ "The *temporal* rights of the complainant were prejudiced."

Sense (2) is also common: "The reason behind the exception is a simple one of human relationships, implicit in the principle that human laws, and other *temporal* things, are for the living."

temporal limit is unidiomatic and stuffy in place of *time limit*, which is well-established. E.g., "The Supreme Court has yet to decide how long an auto search may be delayed before a warrant must be obtained, or indeed whether there is a *temporal limit* [read *time limit*]."

TEMPORAL SEQUENCES. See SEQUENCE OF TENSES.

temporize has three important senses: (1) "to act so as to gain time" ⟨defendant temporized by filing dilatory pleas⟩; (2) "to comply with the requirements of the occasion" ⟨politicians are adept at temporizing⟩; (3) "to negotiate or discuss terms of a compromise" ⟨defendant attempted to temporize with plaintiff rather than go to trial⟩.

tenancy; tenantship; tenantry. The first is, of course, the usual term, meaning (1) "a holding or possession of lands or tenements, by any title of ownership"; (2) "occupancy of lands or tenements under a lease"; or (3) "that which is held by a tenant." *Tenantship* is a NEEDLESS VARIANT. To the extent that *tenantry* overlaps with any of the senses outlined above, it too is a NEEDLESS VARIANT; yet *tenantry* may stand on its own in the senses (1) "property leased to tenants" (i.e., from the point of view of the lessor) ⟨his tenantry, an apartment complex, proved to be a sound investment⟩; and (2) "the body of tenants" ⟨the tenantry is dissatisfied with the proposed improvements⟩.

tenancy by the entireties, -ty. The plural is slightly more common in both the U.S. and G.B., although *Black's* (4th ed.) contains its definition under *tenancy by the entirety*, which is also widespread. E.g., "But a conveyance by one *tenant by the entirety* does not defeat the survivorship rights of the other."

tenancy in common. See **joint tenancy.**

tenancy per la verge; tenancy by the verge; tenancy by the rod. These equivalent phrases denote "a copyhold." The first is LAW FRENCH, the second somewhat anglicized LAW FRENCH, and the third an anglicized LOAN TRANSLATION of the first phrase. The terms are little used but in historical contexts (the rod having been delivered for purposes of conveying seisin). Any of the phrases would require explanation by the user.

tenant; tenanter. The latter is a NEEDLESS VARIANT.

tenant at sufferance; tenant by sufferance. The former is the traditional idiomatic phrase. See **sufferance.**

tenant by the entirety. See **tenancy by the entirety.**

tenanter. See **tenant.**

tenantry. See **tenancy.**

tenantship. See **tenancy.**

tendentious means "biased (usu. in favor of something); prejudiced." Its meaning is often misapprehended, as in this specimen, in which the writer apparently thought the word means "frivolous": "Even though Texas did not move to dismiss the appeal as frivolous, the fact is that it patently has no merit. The removal petition does not even colorably fall within the strict tests set out in *Johnson*. We believe the appellant had ample reason to know that his appeal lacked merit and that it was *merely tendentious*." The phrase *merely tendentious* gives away the writer's ignorance of the meaning of the word *tendentious*.

Tendencious is a variant spelling to be eschewed.

tender, n. See **bid.**

tender, v.t., is a FORMAL WORD for *make* or *give*.

tendinitis; tendonitis. *Tendinitis* = inflammation of a tendon. *Tendonitis* is incorrectly arrived at by association with the spelling of the noun *tendon*.

tenement (= [in law] an estate in land) usu. denotes in lay contexts "a building or house."

TENSES. See SEQUENCE OF TENSES.

tentative trust. See **Totten trust.**

tenurial is the adjective corresponding to *tenure*; it is almost exclusively a legal term. E.g., "The importance of a lease to such a tenant today is not to create a *tenurial* relationship but to arrange for a habitable dwelling."

term, n. (= a limit in space or duration), has the special legal senses "an estate or interest in land for a certain period" (term of years) and, as a plural (terms), "conditions or stipulations limiting what is proposed to be granted or done" (OED). See **terms.**

term for years. See **term of years &** **termor.**

terminus; terminal, n. Terminus = the city at the end of a railroad or bus line. Pl. termini. Terminal = the station of a transportation line.

terminus a quo; terminus ad quem. The former means "departure point"; the latter, "destination." Figuratively, the words are used of the beginning and ending points of an argument. Both figuratively and literally, the phrases are pomposities.

term of years; term for years. The CDL contains its entry under term of years (BrE), whereas W2 and Black's list term for years (AmE).

termor = one who holds lands or tenements for a term of years, or for life (OED). Generally, however, the word is not used of those with life estates. E.g., "But when today we speak of someone taking on 'a new lease on life,' we do not think of him as a termor."

terms has increasingly been used as an elliptical form of terms of the contract or terms of payment. See **term.**

TERMS OF ART are words having specific, precise significations in a given specialty. The phrase is common in law, because the legal field abounds in terms of art, as well as in ARGOT constituting would-be terms of art. With regard to these latter, "the unnecessary or inartistic employment of more or less technical terms in the drafting of legal documents is by no means rare." Lancaster Malleable Castings Co. v. Dunie, 73 A.2d 417, 418 (1950). On the other hand, "Not to use a technical word, even if it is a long one, in its proper place, would be an affectation as noticeable as the overfrequent use of such words where they are not needed." E. L. Piesse, The Elements of Drafting 46 (7th ed. rev. Aitken 1987).

One secret to good legal writing is distinguishing terms of art from mere jargon. It is

elementary to know that and the heirs of his body, and his heirs, and elegit have historically been terms of art; yet only the first is a living term of art, the second and third having become archaic (and therefore useful primarily in historical contexts). Is res gestae, q.v., a term of art? Or scire facias and fieri facias? Many such questions are debatable: but the debate is important, for we must attempt to winnow the useful law words from the verbal baggage amid which so many of them are buried.

terre-tenant; tertenant. The latter, a Middle English anglicized version of the former, a LAW FRENCH term, has never displaced the older term. In the OED's only listed sense, "one who has the actual possession of land; the occupant of land," the word hardly seems justified. But W3 adds the following definition, probably purely AmE: "one other than a judgment debtor owning an interest in the debtor's land after the lien of the judgment creditor attached thereto," a sense that Black's (4th ed.) limits to Pennsylvania. Terre-tenant should not be used unless the writer understands and makes clear the precise sense in which he uses it, and has a reason for doing so.

territory; dependency; commonwealth. The distinctions in AmE usage are as follows. A territory = a part of the U.S. not included within any state but organized with a separate legislature (W9). Guam and the U.S. Virgin Islands are territories of the United States; Alaska and Hawaii were formerly territories. Dependency = a land or territory geographically distinct from the country governing it, but belonging to it and governed by its laws. The Phillippines was once a dependency of the U.S. Commonwealth = a political unit having local autonomy but voluntarily united with the U.S. Puerto Rico and the Northern Mariana Islands are commonwealths. Puerto Rico is sometimes referred to as a dependency, but its proper designation is commonwealth.

tertenant. See **terre-tenant.**

tertius gaudens = a third party who profits when two others dispute. Literally, the term means "a rejoicing third." It is good to have a word for this concept, which is not uncommon in law, but it is unfortunate that the word is so abstruse.

testacy; intestacy. *Testacy* = the condition of leaving a valid will at death. *Intestacy* is its antonym. See **intestate.**

testament is not, as is sometimes supposed, obsolete outside the phrase *last will and testament,* q.v. In legal prose, it is still sometimes contrasted with *devise,* for in the legal idiom *testament* has come generally to signify a will disposing of personal property, whereas *devise* is traditionally the word for a will disposing of land. E.g., "The Wills Acts of 1837 eliminated substantive distinctions between devises and *testaments.*"

Usually, however, the word is used not for reasons of fastidiousness, but for less good reasons. Here it is an archaic pomposity, to which *will* is preferred: "A valid *testament* [read *will*] includes two essential elements: there must be a sufficient designation of the beneficiary and of the property given to him."/ "In *In re Bluestein's Will,* both the language of the *testament* [read *will*] and the attendant circumstances were said to support the conclusion that, in context, the testator's 'request' bespoke a direction, imposing an obligation upon the legatee." See **will.**

testamentary. A. And *testorial.* The latter, a NEEDLESS VARIANT without foundation, does not appear in the *OED, W3,* or *Black's.* But it has occurred in American legal writing: "[I]t is enough if the circumstances, taken together, leave no doubt as to the *testorial* [read *testamentary*] intention, and in some cases it is said that the implication may be drawn from a slight circumstance appearing in the will." 57 Am. Jur. *Wills* § 1192 (1948). See also *id.* § 1191.

Testamentary (= of or relating to a will) is not ordinarily confined to contexts involving testaments of personal property (as opposed to devises of real property). E.g., "It is everywhere recognized that the purpose of the law of wills to give effect to the last valid *testamentary* act of the testator."/ "This court points out that a man's last will may consist of several *testamentary* papers of different dates and that it is not indispensable that they should be probated at the same time." *Testamental,* a variant of *testamentary,* is not used in legal contexts.

B. For *testimonial.* Surprisingly, this error has appeared in reported opinions: "Appellee filed a motion to remand the contractual indemnity claim to allow procurement of documentary and *testamentary* [read *testimonial*] evidence." Here the distinction is made clear: "Lay witnesses, before they express a *testimonial* opinion as to *testamentary* capacity must first testify to facts inconsistent with sanity." *In re Powers's Estate,* 134 N.W.2d 148, 161 (Mich. 1965).

testate (= a testate person), though corresponding in form to *intestate,* n., is generally a NEEDLESS VARIANT of *testator. Testatus* is the civil-law term. See **intestate.**

testation = the disposal of property by will ⟨power of testation⟩. E.g., "The loss of charitable trusts such as Baconsfield is part of the price we pay for permitting deceased persons to exercise a continuing control over assets owned by them at death; this aspect of freedom of *testation,* like most things, has its advantages and disadvantages."

testator; devisor. Because *testament* historically came to be more or less confined to dispositions of personal property, and *devise* to those of real property, it has been thought that *testator* was at one time confined to a person who left personal, as opposed to real, property. See, e.g., M. S. Freeman, *A Treasury for Word Lovers* 173 (1983). No such crabbed meaning ever attached to the word, however; Blackstone wrote, in 1766, "that all devises of lands and tenements shall not only be in writing, but signed by the *testator*" (quoted in *OED*). See **testate & deviser.**

testatrix. See SEXISM (c).

testatus. See **testate.**

teste is the name in DRAFTING of the clause that states the name of a witness and evidences the act of witnessing. E.g., "Judgments did not bind chattels, but at early common law a writ of *fieri facias* bound chattels from the date of the *teste,* i.e., the date of the issuance, thereby invalidating all subsequent alienations." In older instruments *teste* was used in much the same way as some legal writers use *witnesseth,* q.v., today. Cf. **testimonium.**

testification is an unnecessary word for *testimony* or *testifying.*

testifier. See **witness.**

testimonial, not *testamentary*, q.v., is the adjective corresponding to *testimony*. E.g., "Appellants have not been given immunity from the *testimonial* self-incrimination arising from their admissions." See **testamentary** (B).

testimonium = the phrase *In witness whereof*, which commonly concludes legal instruments and pleadings. The plural of this term is either *-iums* or *-ia*, the former being preferable. See **attestation clause.** Cf. **teste.**

testimony is sometimes loosely used as a COUNT NOUN. E.g., "This court has no way of actually knowing *which testimonies or parts of testimonies* [read *which testimony*] the jury accepted as the most credible."/ "Even if the *testimonies* [read *testimony*] of the various witnesses *are* [read *is*] looked upon in the light most favorable to the appellees, the verdict returned by the jury is not supported by *those testimonies* [read *that testimony*]." See **evidence** (B).

testis [L.] = (1) a witness; or (2) a testicle. Modern witnesses are not likely to take kindly to being called *testes*. See **witness.**

testorial. See **testamentary** (A).

text as an adjective is inferior to *textual*: "This is made clear by quotations from recognized *text* [read *textual*] authorities." See **textual.**

textual, -tuary. As an adjective, the latter is a NEEDLESS VARIANT.

thankfully = gratefully; in a manner expressing thanks. The word should not be misused in the way that *hopefully*, q.v., is misused, namely, in the sense "thank goodness; I am (or we are) thankful that." Following is an example of the all-too-common fall from stylistic grace: "The brutal racial violence that struck such places as Cornell, Harvard, and Texas Southern in the 1960's seems, *thankfully*, to be a thing of the past." See **hopefully** & SENTENCE ADVERBS.

than.   A. Verb Not Repeated After. Usually it is unnecessary to repeat *be*-verbs after *than*. E.g., "The controlling issue is whether the decision-makers who *are* in a better position

than is the judiciary* [read *than the judiciary*] to decide whether the public interest would be served have created a scheme with which the remedy would interfere."

B. *Than what*. This collocation usually signals a poor construction. E.g., "The jurisdictional reach of courts became substantially broader *than what* [omit *what*] it had been under the strict territorial guidelines of the *Pennoyer* case."

C. For *then*. This error is so elementary that one might fairly wonder whether it is merely a lapse in proofreading; but it occurs with some frequency. E.g., "If Blom-Cooper's judgment is correct, *than* [read *then*] the failure is in Lord MacNaghten's style, not in his subject-matter." (Eng.)

that.   A. Relative Pronoun. 1. Wrongly Suppressed *that*. Although in any number of constructions it is perfectly permissible, and even preferred, to omit *that* by ellipsis (e.g., *The dog you gave me* rather than *The dog that you gave me*), in formal writing *that* is often ill-advisedly omitted where it creates an ambiguity, even if only momentarily. E.g., "I noticed those who left the city attorney's office* [read *I noticed that those who left the city attorney's office*] early in their careers were unhappy also in private practice." (The sentence at first leads the reader to believe that the writer refers to the persons who have left, not to their unhappiness.)/ "In *Eleason, we held the driver, an epileptic,* [read *we held that the driver, an epileptic,*] possessed knowledge that he was likely to have a seizure."/ "There are authorities *which* [read *that*] *generally hold insanity is not* [read *generally hold that insanity is not*] a defense in tort cases except for intentional torts."/ "She thought Batman was good [read *thought that Batman was good*] and was trying to help save the world and her husband [read *that her husband*] was possessed of the devil." (Without the relative pronoun, it sounds as if the writer is stating a fact—that her husband was possessed by the devil)./ "Carbide International *prays we reverse* [read *prays that we reverse*] an adverse trial court judgment."

2. Unnecessarily Repeated. One must be careful not to repeat the relative pronoun after an intervening phrase; either suspend it till just before the verb, or use it early in the sentence and omit it before the verb. E.g., "The officers told Mr. P. *that*, if he would waive his right to receive any benefits from

A.I. under the deferred compensation portion of his employment contract, *that* [omit *that*] they would take care of him."/ "Rule 10b-10(a) requires *that* prior to the completion of a transaction *that* [omit *that*] a written statement be sent or given to a customer setting forth prescribed information relating to the transaction."/ "Appellant argues *that* since Lent, Inc. was the principal in the indemnity agreement, *that* [omit *that*] it cannot also be an indemnitor in the same agreement."

B. The Biblical *that*. In lieu of *so that* or *in order that*, *that* often smacks of the Biblical, as in: "A lawyer may never give unsolicited advice to a layman *that* [read *in order that*] he retain a client."/ "We must preserve the work of art *that* [read *so that*] it may continue to convey to the sympathetic spectator the creative ecstasy that went into its making." See BIBLICAL AFFECTATION.

C. As an Ellipsis for *the fact that*. This construction is often useful; here, however, the phrase is badly used, because the subject and verb are too far removed: "*That* the district court's order authorizing the sale of the Charles House property and judgment confirming the sale and passage of title to Southmark operated as a final judgment on the merits is evident." [Read *It is evident that. . . .*] See **the fact that.**

D. Relative Adverb. E.g., "Many charities fail by change of circumstances and [by] the happening of contingencies that no human foresight can provide against." (See PREPOSITIONS (E).) Some lightweight authorities do not understand that the construction in the sentence just quoted is perfectly acceptable. One such manual for legal writers recommends, "The case *on which* the lawyer was working never went to trial," instead of, "The case *that* the lawyer *was* working *on* never went to trial," and labels the latter incorrect. See *Texas Law Review Manual on Style* 28–29 (4th ed. 1979). Actually, both constructions are correct—and the construction with *that* is far more natural-sounding.

E. For *so* or *very*: "This case is not *that* important." This usage is informal and colloquial and, though it hardly merits condemnation in speech, it should be avoided in writing: "This case is not *so* [or *very*] important."

F. *That of.* This phrase is often used unnecessarily. E.g., "In another comparative study, *that of* [omit *that of*] anthropology, they also

find much to make them question current ethics."

G. And *which*. See RESTRICTIVE AND NONRESTRICTIVE CLAUSES.

H. And *who*. See **who.**

I. The Demonstrative *that*. See DEICTIC TERMS.

that is to say, a common explanatory phrase, should not begin a sentence. It may follow a comma or a semicolon; but as an initial phrase it invariably creates an incomplete sentence. Cf. **viz.** & **namely.**

that which; those which; those that. When a noun introduced by *that*, as a DEICTIC TERM, is followed by defining matter, that matter is introduced by *which*. E.g.: "The commission merchant must exercise *that* degree of care *which* a prudent person would exercise in the conduct of his own affairs." Sometimes the construction is wrongly made *that . . . that*, as in: "We must distinguish between a belief in the literal truth and falsity of a statement and *that* type of belief in falsity *that* [read *which*] underlies the fraudulent misrepresentation."

When *that* becomes, in plural, *those*, it is permissible for the second member of this construction to be either *which* or *that*. E.g.: "Deductible distributions are usually *those that* [or *those which*] are made to the residuary beneficiaries."/ "*Those issuers that* [or *Those issuers which* (or *who*)] have already issued stock under such plans will have to fight hard to obtain some sort of grandfathering relief."

the. See ARTICLES.

theater, -re. See -ER, -RE.

the case of. This FLOTSAM PHRASE is always best omitted. See **case** (A).

the fact that. At the beginning of a sentence, the best approach is merely to begin with *that*, as in: "*That* the police officer was engaged in the performance of his duties did not relieve him of the duty of care at intersections or absolve the city of liability for his negligence in the course of duty." See **that** (C). But *the fact that* is sometimes useful, as here: "There is probably no getting around *the fact that* more successful lawyers will be able to use these rules to their advantage more often than their less successful counterparts."

theft. See **burglary.**

theirself. See **ourself.**

themself, sometimes used in reference to a corporation, is an illiteracy.

then. **A.** Adjective. *Then* should not be hyphenated when used in the sense "that existed or was so at that time." E.g., "In *Griggs* the Supreme Court noted that *the then-guidelines* [read *the then guidelines*] issued by the Equal Opportunity Commission were to be accorded 'great deference' by the courts."/ "The 1969 and 1962 convictions were proved for enhancement, and Carter received *the then-mandatory* [read *the then mandatory*; here the word is adverbial] life sentence."/ "At the time of the events critical to the determination of this case, three of the board members had been appointed by *the then* mayor."/ "In a trial presided over by *the then* magistrate, now district judge Marcel Livandais, the jury returned a verdict in favor of each parent."

B. For *than*. This is a distressingly common error, esp. in newsprint: "'I could not be any more excited *then* [read *than*] I am right now,' said C.B., a supporter of the measure."/ "Under section 183, if dependency is the basis of recovery, the measure of damages is very much greater *then* [read *than*] it would be under section 184." For the reverse error, see **than** (C).

thence; whence; hence. *Thence* = from that place or source; for that reason. *Whence* = from there. *Hence* = (1) from here; or (2) therefore. These are literaryisms as well as LEGALISMS, acceptable perhaps in the more literary style of legal prose, despite carping by those who advocate "consumer English."

thenceforth; thenceforward. The latter is a NEEDLESS VARIANT.

theoretic(al)(ly). The best, most usual form of the adjective is *theoretical*, not *-tic*. Walter Wheeler Cook makes an apt observation about a common use of *theoretical*: "Theory which will not work in practice is not sound theory. 'It is *theoretically* correct but will not

work in practice' is a common but erroneous statement. If a theory is '*theoretically* correct' it will work; if it will not work, it is '*theoretically* incorrect.'" Introduction to Hohfeld's *Fundamental Legal Conceptions* 21 (1919). Holmes likewise observed, "I know no reason why theory should disagree with the facts." *The Theory of Legal Interpretation*, 12 Harv. L. Rev. 417, 417 (1899).

therap(eut)ist. The standard term is *therapist.*

thereabout(s). The form *thereabout* is preferred.

there are. See **there is** & EXPLETIVES.

thereat (= there; at it). Even at the turn of the century, when the *OED* was being compiled, this word was considered "formal [= pompous] and archaic." Today it is more so. E.g., "He was astonished *thereat* [read *at it*]."/ "The purpose of the bill as stated in the prayers for relief was to enjoin the defendants from combining and conspiring to interfere with the complainants in the practice of their trade and occupation, or to prevent them from obtaining further employment *thereat* [read *in their trade*]." The word is not a locative. Cf. **whereat.** See HERE- AND THERE- WORDS.

thereby cannot rightly be considered a FORBIDDEN WORD, but see HERE- AND THERE- WORDS.

therefore; therefor. The former means "for that reason," "consequently," or "ergo"—this is the word known to laymen; the latter means "for that" or "for it."

A. Proper Uses of *therefor*. The proper use of *therefore*, which always states a conclusion, needs no illustration; following are correct uses of *therefor*: "Mrs. W. bought 275 acres of land soon after the death of her second husband, paying *therefor* [i.e., "for it"] $2,000." (The more common word-order would be *paying $2,000 therefor.*)/ "We are not unmindful of the sound and salutary rule, and of the obvious reasons *therefor*."/ "Recovery should be limited, in any event, to the reasonable value of the necessaries furnished rather than the contract price *therefor*."/ "What we have said does not foreclose a true corporate agent or trustee from handling the property and income of its owner-principle without being taxable *therefor.*"/ "The plaintiff discharged union cutters and shop foremen without just cause *therefor.*"

B. *Therefore* for *therefor.* In the sentences that follow, *therefore* is wrongly used for *therefor,* a surprising lapse: "This memorandum is solely for the use of the person named below and may not be reproduced or used for any other purpose; any action to the contrary may place the persons responsible *therefore* [read *therefor*] in violation of state and federal securities laws."/ "Dividends on the stock may be declared and paid by the board of directors of the company only out of the funds legally available *therefore* [read *therefor*]."/ "To confiscate private property of its citizens, the government must not only show actual notice of its intention, but lawful grounds *therefore* [read *therefor*]."

C. *Therefor* for *therefore.* This is the more usual error with these homophones. In the first example, the misuse occurs twice in two sentences: "The point is that the Delaware statute contains no such limiting language and *therefor* [read *therefore*] must be construed to authorize any reasonable corporate gift of a charitable or educational nature. Significantly, the corporation was incorporated in Delaware in 1958, before 8 Del. C. § 122(9) was cast in its present form; *therefor* [read *therefore*], no constitutional problem arises."/ "These were not the acts of a competent master; they *therefor* [read *therefore*] rendered the vessels unseaworthy to a gross degree."/ "The Supreme Court (per Vinson, C.J.) *therefor* [read *therefore*] shifted from constitutional to other grounds."

D. Punctuation around *therefore.* One must take care in the punctuation of *therefore.* In short sentences it need not, indeed should not, be set off by commas. Punctuating around it in short sentences creates great awkwardness: "We, *therefore,* dismiss the appeal." (The commas destroy the rhythm and emphasize *we,* as opposed to *dismiss.*)/ "It, *therefore,* becomes our duty to review these findings and to determine for ourselves whether they are sustained by the weight of the evidence." (Again, omit the commas around *therefore.* Whenever a single word like *it* precedes *therefore,* the latter should not be preceded by commas unless that initial word is to receive stress.)/ "The court, *therefore,* remanded the action to the Secretary with instructions that he furnish the court with the

basis of his final determination." (Who else would remand the action? Omit the commas around *therefore.*)

E. RUN-ON SENTENCES with *therefore.* One should take care not to create run-on sentences in this common way: "These works might be of paramount public *interest, therefore* [read *interest; therefore*] the rights of their compilers are accordingly [omit *accordingly,* which is here redundant] in the public interest." See HERE- AND THERE- WORDS.

therefrom (= from that or it) for *therefor* (= for that or it) is an odd blunder. E.g., "Petitioner has not presented any valid reason for allowing costs in this particular case and, there being no indication that defendant's removal petition was not made in good faith, the court denies petitioner's request *therefrom* [read *therefor*—i.e., for costs]."

Here the term is used correctly: "We note that the trial counsel referred to the testimony about the upcoming marriage of the prosecutrix and her decision to leave town in his argument and deduced *therefrom* why she would not claim she did not consent."

therein. See HERE- AND THERE- WORDS.

there is; there are. The number of the verb is controlled by whether the subject that follows the inverted verb is singular or plural. Mistakes are common, e.g.: "It has also been held (although dealing with exclusions from public places where *there are* [read *there is*] discrimination on the basis of race or color) that preventive relief is available where a public agency operates the public place." See EXPLETIVES & SUBJECT-VERB AGREEMENT (K).

thereon. See HERE- AND THERE- WORDS.

thereout is an ARCHAISM for *therefrom,* q.v. E.g., "[T]he Arbitration Act rendered a written provision in a contract by the parties to such a transaction, to arbitrate controversies arising *thereout* [read *therefrom*], specifically enforceable," *Barge "Anaconda" v. American Sugar Refining Co.,* 322 U.S. 42, 44 (1944).

thereto. **A.** Superfluously Used. E.g., "Five of the children were born before the execution of the deed. The others were born subsequently *thereto* [omit *thereto*]." See HERE- AND THERE- WORDS & CUTTING OUT THE CHAFF.

B. For *thereon:* "It comes as a surprise that

the 1972 Code amendments and official comments *thereto* [read *thereon*] refer to the 'requirement' of filing." (One *comments on*, not *to*, a statute.)

theretofore. See **hitherto.**

thereupon, adv., usefully pinpoints the ordinarily time of an action. The word should ordinarily not be used, however, to begin sentences. See **thereon,** HERE- AND THERE- WORDS & **whereupon.**

the said. See **said.**

thesaurus. Pl. *-ri.* See PLURALS (A).

these. See DEICTIC TERMS.

these kind of is an illogical form that, in a bolder day, would have been termed an illiteracy. Today it merely brands the speaker or writer as being slovenly.

thing. Users of this word are often chastised by ill-informed amateurs of usage. Though frequently derided, *thing* can be very useful in contexts in which no more specific or pseudospecific term is needed. Still, the word is easily overused.

3d; 3rd. In legal writing, and esp. in citations, the first of these abbreviations is preferred. See **2d.**

third(-)party is spelled as two words as a noun, and hyphenated as an adjective and verb.

third-party, v.t., = to bring into litigation as a third-party defendant. E.g., "The defendant hospital did not *third-party* Travenol." *Richard v. Southwest Louisiana Hospital Association,* 383 So. 2d 83, 90 (La. App. 1980). This usage is informal at best, although it is increasingly common in the U.S. See NOUNS AS VERBS.

third-party plaintiff. Pl. *third-party plaintiffs.* E.g., "The settlement did not subrogate *third-parties plaintiff* [read *third-party plaintiffs*] to plaintiff's rights against Ford."

third person should be pluralized *third persons,* never *third people.*

this. See DEICTIC TERMS & ANTECEDENTS.

thither = there; to that place. See **hither** & **whither.**

thitherto. See **hitherto.**

thorough-going = thorough, but connotes zeal or ardor. It is not, therefore, merely a NEEDLESS VARIANT. E.g., "The conflicts on the applicable interest rates alone—which we do not think can be labeled 'false conflicts' without a more *thorough-going* treatment than was accorded them by the Supreme Court of Kansas—certainly amounted to millions of dollars in liability."

those. See DEICTIC TERMS.

those kind of. See **these kind of.**

those which; those that. See **that which.**

though. See **although.**

though . . . yet. See **although . . . yet** & CORRELATIVE CONJUNCTIONS.

threshold. So spelled; *threshhold* is a common misspelling (see, e.g., *Zweygardt v. Colorado National Bank,* 52 Bankr. 229, 231 (Bankr. D. Colo. 1985)). But cf. *withhold.*

thrice is a literary ARCHAISM, and sometimes a useful one, meaning "three times." E.g., "The words are *thrice* repeated in the statute." (A literalist would read this sentence as meaning that the words appear four times in the statute—once perhaps at the beginning and three times *repeated.*) / "Before the instant conviction Avery, albeit a relatively young man, had at least *thrice* been convicted of felony charges."

thrift institution is the current jargon for *savings and loan association.*

thrive 〉 throve 〉 thriven. *Throve,* not *thrived,* is the better past tense. E.g., "Infantile sexuality lived and *throve*—in child and adult—before Freud brought it to scientific attention."

thru, an aborted variant spelling of *through,* should be shunned.

thus. A. General Senses. *Thus* has four meanings: (1) in this or that manner 〈One does it thus.); (2) so (thus far); (3) hence, consequently; and (4) as an example. Here *thus* is given none of these meanings: "The factors that determine whether Article 2 applies are thus: (i) the type of transaction (sale); and (ii) the subject matter of the transaction (goods)." The best approach to remedying the problem in this sentence would be to remove *thus* and to place the colon after *are*.

B. Thusly. *Thus* itself being an adverb, it needs no *-ly*. Formerly, one might have labeled the use of *thusly* illiterate; yet it has appeared in otherwise respectable legal writing. It remains, however, a grave lapse. E.g., "*Grubbs* is hardly a surprising decision when it is *thusly interpreted* [read *interpreted thus*]." *Paxton v. Weaver*, 553 F.2d 936, 942 (5th Cir. 1977)./ "The major issue in this appeal may be framed *thusly* [read *thus*]: Does a Louisiana capital defendant have a constitutionally protected right to have the Louisiana Supreme Court review and dispose of his death sentence without expressly relying on intensely prejudicial information that has not been brought within the realm of the penalty jury's consideration." Cf. **overly** & **muchly.**

ticket-of-leave. See **parole.**

tidings is an ARCHAISM in AmE, although it persists in BrE literary usage. "A sues B on a policy of insurance, and shows that the vessel insured went to sea, and that after a reasonable time no *tidings* of her have been received, but that her loss has been rumoured; the burden of proving that she has not foundered is on B." (Eng.)

tie makes *tying*. *Tieing* is incorrect. E.g., "The court's determination that the surplus income is intestate, effectively avoiding, as it does, *tieing up* [read *tying up*] and so depriving Olive and her children of the enjoyment of it for what might prove to be a long term of years, is a result that fortifies this conclusion."

till; until. *Till* is, like *until*, a bona fide preposition and conjunction. Though less formal than *until*, *till* is neither colloquial nor substandard. The form *'til* is incorrect.

time-bar, in AmE legal usage, means "a bar to a legal claim arising from a statute of limitations." E.g., "The government bases its *time-bar* claim upon an earlier letter." Hence

time-barred = barred by the statute of limitations. The phrase is useful shorthand, if somewhat inelegant. E.g., "A unanimous court held the enforcement action to be *time-barred*; the limitations period had begun to run at the time of the violation and had run out before the government filed its enforcement complaint."/ "The result may indeed differ, depending upon what body of law governs the availability of a third-party claim in this case, when the cause of action accrues, and when it becomes *time-barred*."/ "In each case, plaintiffs appeal the grant of an adverse summary judgment dismissing their claims as *time-barred* by article 5536a, the Texas architectural/engineer statute of ultimate repose."/ "The evidence presented an issue of fact on whether any claim for breach of the software sale contract was *time-barred*."

timbre; timber. These are different words in BrE and AmE alike. *Timbre* is primarily a musical term meaning "tone quality." *Timber* is the correct form in all other senses.

timely, adj. & adv. Because *timely* may be an adverb as well as an adjective in AmE, phrases such as *in a timely fashion* and *in a timely manner* are wordy and should be shortened. E.g., "*Unless he renounces his power in timely fashion* [read *unless he timely renounces his power*], the trust corpus will be handled as part of his gross estate for tax purposes."/ "Here, Orpiano *filed his objections in a timely fashion* [read *timely filed his objections*], but the district court felt that a de novo determination of the portions Orpiano objected to was unnecessary."

Timely is archaic as an adverb in BrE. The rare adverbial form *timelily* is to be avoided. In British law reports, *timeous* (= coming in due time) and *timeously* (= in a *timeous* manner) are common. These never occur in the U.S.

tippee = one who receives a tip (i.e., a critical bit of information); one who is illicitly tipped off. E.g., "Absent other culpable actions by a *tippee* that can fairly be said to outweigh these violations by insiders and broker-dealers, we do not believe that the *tippee* properly can be characterized as being of substantially equal culpability as his *tippers*." *Bateman Eichler, Hill Richards, Inc. v. Berner*, 472 U.S. 299, 314 (1985)./ "The scope of that implied right of action for investors is yet again before the Supreme Court—this time in the context of several defrauded and defrauding *tippees* of inside information seeking to recover against their also defrauding *tipper.*"

The word is recorded in the *OED* from 1897 in a rather different sense: "the receiver of a 'tip' or gratuity."

tipper; tipster. Both mean "a person who gives tips (= critical pieces of information)." *Tipster* often refers to one who gives tips to police in criminal investigations, or sells tips relating to speculative or gambling subjects. Here the former sense applies: "An anonymous *tipster*, whose information was relayed to police by a private investigator, implicated appellant."

Tipper shares the meaning with *tipster* of an informer who tips off police on illegal activities; more commonly in legal AmE, it signifies "one who gives or sells tips to securities and other investors." See **tippee.**

tiro. See **tyro.**

title-deed. This term conveys nothing not included in the simple word *deed. Title-deed =* the deed or one of the deeds constituting the muniments or evidences of a person's legal ownership (*W3*). A *deed* likewise ordinarily serves as such evidence. Following are examples of uses of the term in practice: "No witness who is a party to a suit can be compelled to produce his *title-deeds* to any property." (Eng.)/ "Those scholars regard the statements contained in the *title-deeds* as written statements made by persons not called as witnesses."

TITULAR TOMFOOLERY, primarily an outgrowth of weekly news- and viewspapers in the U.S., consists in the creation of false titles for people. Instead of *Ches Williams, the policeman,* it is today commonplace in less-well-edited journals to read of *policeman Ches Williams,* or, worse yet, *Policeman Ches Williams.* Officer, granted, is a title to be prefixed to a person's name; *policeman* is not.

This informal verbal contagion has spread into the law. E.g., "*Venireman Hal Ray* [read *The venireman Hal Ray* or *A venireman named Hal Ray*] was excluded properly because he was unable to follow the law."/ "Counsel asked *Juror Franklin* whether he had any personal knowledge of the case." (In this sentence, if we already know Franklin is on the jury, omit *Juror;* if not, read *asked Franklin, one*

of the jurors, whether. . . . Moreover, the term *juror* may be inappropriate here; for, if the question were posed at voir dire, the proper term would be *venireman.*)/ "According to Attorney John Smith, [read *According to John Smith, an* (or *the*) *attorney,*] the notice was not served properly."/ "The district judge then went into the chambers and called for *juror Graham* [read *the juror Graham*]."/ "Early in 1979, Brown, with the help of *attorney Rogers* [read *his attorney, Rogers*], took steps to obtain credit for the time he served between arrest and conviction."/ "Marion Smith, *widow* [read *the widow*] of George P. Smith, and her six children appeal the dismissal of this diversity action under Fed. R. Civ. P. 12(b)(6)."

TMESIS, the practice of separating parts of a compound word by inserting another word between those parts, occurs much more frequently in legal than in lay writing. A classic colloquial example—some would say dialectal example—is the phrase *a whole 'nother,* which, surprisingly, has actually appeared in legal contexts: "The plaintiff must have *a complete 'nother* trial." (See SET PHRASES.)

The traditional form of tmesis in legal prose, however, occurs with formal legal words ending in *-soever.* E.g., "Recusal is an act, of *what nature soever* it may be, by which a strange heir, by deeds or words, declares he will not be an heir."/ "A man is also prohibited on the ground of affinity from intermarrying with the wife of his father or father's father, *how high soever.*"/ "This presents *a whole nother* question." The modern tendency, which we should heartily encourage, is to avoid such stuffiness by writing, e.g., *of whatever nature* and *however high.*

to for *until* or *up to* is a casualism. "*To* [read *Up to*] September 1964, no Negro pupil had applied for admission to the New Kent school under this statute."

to all intents and purposes. See **for all intents and purposes.**

together appears in a number of REDUNDANCIES, such as *merge together, connect together, consolidate together, couple together,* and *join together,* q.v. These phrases should be avoided.

together with; coupled with; as well as; added to. These expressions do not affect the number of the terms that precede or follow them. See SUBJECT-VERB AGREEMENT (H).

tolerance; toleration. The former is the quality, the latter the act or practice.

toll has a special legal meaning in the context of statutes of limitation. It means "to abate," or "to stop the running of (the statutory period)." E.g, "There are various ways in which the statute of limitations may be *tolled*, such as by the absence of the defendant from the state."/ "Plaintiff's delays after being required to perfect service could not *toll* the limitation period."

tome refers not to any book, but to one that is imposingly or forbiddingly large.

too. A. Beginning Sentences with. *Too* should not begin sentences, although there is a tendency in facile journalism today to use the word in this position. E.g., "*Too*, not only are existing laws read into contracts in order to fix obligations between the parties, but the reservation of essential attributes of sovereign power is also read into contracts as a postulate of the legal order." *Also* may unobjectionably appear at the beginning of a sentence. Also, words such as *moreover, further,* and *furthermore* serve ably in this position.
B. For *very.* This informal use of *too* occurs almost always in negative constructions, e.g., *not too common.*

toothless (= ineffectual; lacking the means of enforcement) is a snarl-word used, in legal discourse, against a statute or court decision that the writer or speaker opposes. E.g., "Even if something less than complete separability were required, the court's *toothless* standard disserves the important purposes underlying the separability requirement."

to put it another way; put another way. Either is acceptable, although the former is somewhat better from a literary point of view. Here the two idioms are confused: "*Or, put it another way* [read *Or, to put it another way*], they are estopped from denying that they were exercising the right they had under the original mortgage."

tornadic (= of or relating to a tornado or tornadoes) is a pomposity ⟨tornadic activity⟩ akin to *telephonic*, q.v.

torpid. See **turbid.**

tort = the breach of a duty that the law imposes on everyone. The word derives from LAW FRENCH, meaning lit. "wrong, injustice." For the adjectival form, see **tortious.**

tortfeasor was once spelled as two words (as late as 1927 in the U.S. Supreme Court), then was hyphenated, and now has been fused into a single word.

tortious. A. Two Senses. *Tortious* = (1) of or relating to tort ⟨tortious causes of action⟩; (2) constituting a tort ⟨tortious acts that are also criminally punishable⟩. Sense (2) is now more common than sense (1), which is exemplified in this sentence: "In tort, the duty is imposed by law; the person under that *tortious* duty has no choice about whether he will shoulder it or not." See **delict(u)al.**
B. And *tortuous, torturous.* Cardozo's famous opinion in *Palsgraf* demonstrated that a *tortious* act could result from a *tortuous* chain of events with *torturous* consequences. *Tortuous* = full of twists and turns. *Torturous* = of, characterized by, pertaining to torture. The word aptly appears in the phrase *the conscienceless or pitiless crime which is unnecessarily torturous to the victim,* used in *State v. Dixon,* 283 So. 2d 1, 9 (Fla. 1973).
Tortuous is here misused for *tortious*: "Loss of anticipated profits occasioned by *tortuous* [read *tortious*] interruption of an established business is recoverable as damages." Here *tortuous* is correctly used: "The litigation has followed a *tortuous* path through the federal and state courts."

tortious interference with contractual relations; procuring (or inducing) breach of contract; interference with a subsisting contract. The first is the American phrase; the latter two are primarily British. Each one means "the tort of intentionally persuading or inducing someone to break a contract made by him with a third party" (*CDL*).

totality of the circumstances is a common legal catch-phrase, esp. in AmE. E.g., "Our recent cases have thoroughly rejected the *Palko* notion that basic constitutional rights can be denied by the states as long as the *totality of the circumstances* do not disclose a denial of fundamental fairness."

total(l)ed. See DOUBLING OF FINAL CONSONANTS.

to the effect that is often verbose for *that.*

Totten trust; tentative trust. These phrases, which are equivalent, denote "a revocable trust created by one's deposit of money in one's own name as a trustee for another." E.g., "It seems well settled that the creditor of one who deposits money in a savings account in the name of the depositor as trustee for another, in a jurisdiction in which this transaction creates a so-called *tentative* or *Totten trust*, can reach the deposit in satisfaction of his claims." The name *Totten trust*, which is perhaps slightly more common, derives from the case *In re Totten*, 71 N.E. 748 (N.Y. App. 1904). See CASE REFERENCES (C).

touching (= concerning; about; bearing on) is today virtually peculiar to the legal idiom. E.g., "Such evidence as was adduced *touching* the affidavit for the search warrant showed that it was issued on information and belief without stating the grounds of belief."/ "*Touching* the guilt of the appellant, the evidence was conflicting." The *OED* labels this use of the word "somewhat archaic"; today it is rightly considered an ARCHAISM.

toward for *to.* "One has an affirmative responsibility *toward* [read *to*] others when one has taken active part in directing the manner in which those others perform their work."/ "There is no legal objection *toward* [read *to*] constituting such a trustee in favor of one who was not in esse [q.v.] when the fraud was perpetrated."

toward(s). In AmE, the preferred form is *toward; towards* is prevalent in BrE.

to(-)wit. The ordinary progression in such common phrases is from two words, to a hyphenated form, to a single word. Mellinkoff spelled this as a single word throughout *The Language of the Law* (1963), and the hyphenated form was once common: "Appellant contends that the trial court erred in finding that appellant used a deadly weapon, *to-wit*, a crowbar." Today, however, it seems that *to wit* is destined to remain two words, if indeed its destiny is not oblivion. *To wit* is a legal ARCHAISM in the place of which *namely* is almost always an improvement. Cf. **viz.**

toxic for *toxin. Toxic* (= poisonous) is the adjective, and *toxin* (= poison) the noun. "Solvents can increase the mobility of certain *toxics* [read *toxins*] in the soil."

toxicology (= the science of poisons). So spelled, though a mistaken form *toxology* is infrequently heard. See M. Ottoboni, *The Dose Makes the Poison: A Plain-Language Guide to Toxicology* (1984).

track is sometimes misused for *tract* (= a parcel of land) in the phrase *tract of land; track of land* is incorrect. *Tract* should be distinguished in pronunciation from *track.* See **treatise.**

trade(-)mark; trade(-)name. The unhyphenated, one-word spellings are preferred. Formerly, in the U.S., these terms were distinguished: A *trademark* was an arbitrary, fanciful, or suggestive name of, or symbol for, a product or service that was protectible under trademark laws. A *tradename*, by contrast, was a descriptive, personal, or geographical name or symbol protectible under the law of unfair competition. With the enactment of the Lanham Act in 1946, this distinction became defunct. Today in the U.S., the term *trademark* embraces all the types of names or symbols just mentioned. *Tradename* continues only in the sense "a symbol used to distinguish a company, partnership, or business (as opposed to a product or service)." See 1 J. McCarthy, *Trademarks and Unfair Competition* § 4.2-4.5 (1984); 3 Callmann, *Unfair Competition, Trademarks, and Monopolies* § 17.05 (4th ed. L. Altman 1983).

traduce is a literary word meaning "to slander; calumniate." It has never been a law word per se, although occasionally it is used in legal contexts. E.g., "Libelous statements tend to excite the wrath of the person so *traduced* or to deprive him of public confidence."

traffic, v.i., forms *trafficking* and *trafficked,* but *trafficable* and *trafficator.*

transcendent(al). *Transcendent* = surpassing or excelling others of its kind; preeminent. It is loosely used by some writers in the sense "excellent." *Transcendental* = supernatural; mystical; metaphysical; superhuman. The adverbial forms are *transcendently* and *transcendentally.*

transcript; transcription. The former is the written copy, the latter the process of producing it.

transfer, v.t., is accented on the second syllable, hence the preterit spelling *transferred*, not *transfered*. *Transferor* but *transferral*; *transferred, -ferring*, but *transferability, -ferable.*

transfer, n.; **transference; transfer(r)al.** Of these three, *transfer* is the all-purpose noun. E.g., "As far as the question has been considered, this court is committed to the doctrine that a *transfer* of shares on the books of the corporation passes the legal title to the person named in the stock certificate." *Transfer* commonly appears in the legal phrase *transfer of venue*. *Transferral* (the spelling included in the *OED*) is a NEEDLESS VARIANT of *transfer*. For those who care about the spelling of words to be consigned to oblivion, *W3* contains its entry under *transferal*.
Transference justifies its separate existence primarily in psychological contexts, in the sense "the redirection of feelings or desires." E.g., "Appellant also contends that the probability of *transference* of guilt was heightened because the two defendants were brothers."

transferable, -ferrible. The former spelling is preferred. See -ABLE (A).

transferor. So spelled in legal contexts. E.g., "The advantage of the statutory trust concept is that it avoids probing into subjective matters of intent and minimizes inquiry into the degree of control retained by the *transferor*." *W3* lists *transferor* as a variant spelling of *transferrer*, but notes under the legal definition "usu. *transferor*." For *transferee*, see -EE.

transferral. See **transfer,** n.

transferrible. See **transferable.**

transfusible, -able. The former spelling is preferred. See -ABLE (A).

transience, -cy. The latter is a NEEDLESS VARIANT.

transient; transitory, -tive. *Transient* = impermanent; quickly passing. The word is used in the phrase *transient jurisdiction*. *Transitory*, which has virtually the same meaning, is used in the legal phrase *transitory action* (Eng.) = an action in which the venue might be laid in any county (*OED*). *Transitive* is a grammatical term denoting a verb that takes a direct object.

transmissible; transmittable. The former is preferred; the latter is a NEEDLESS VARIANT. E.g., "This discussion leads to the principal question of the case: whether the testator intended that Mary Silva must survive the trust beneficiary before her interest could be *transmissible* to her heirs."

transmittal, -ance; transmission. *Transmittal* is more physical than *transmission*, just as *admittance* is more physical than *admission*, q.v. *Transmittal*, though labeled rare in the *OED*, is common in AmE legal writing, esp. in the phrase *transmittal letter* (= a cover letter accompanying documents or other things being conveyed to another). E.g., "The taxpayers contend that the corporation's *transmittal* of the loan proceeds to the partnership satisfies this criterion."/ "The company will send a check for the amount due directly to the beneficiary and will send the executor a copy of its letter of *transmittal* for his records."/ "Both the preparation of the report and its *transmittal* to Jaworski occurred several months before any negotiations for the sale of the subsidiary." *Transmittance* is a NEEDLESS VARIANT.

transmutation is used in some legal contexts for "transfer," but conveys nothing that the latter word does not, e.g., in phrases such as *transmutation of possession*. In American community-property states it means something rather different from "transfer," as here illustrated: "The problem is further complicated by the ability of the husband and wife to change property of one kind into the other by agreement or transfer, a process sometimes called *transmutation*."

transnational. So spelled.

transpire. Though the traditionally correct meaning of this word (i.e., "to come to light; to become known by degrees") is, alas, beyond redemption, lawyers and judges should be aware of the ambiguity created by the coexistence of the popular meaning, "to happen, occur." *Transpire* is a mere pomposity for *happen*. The word is badly needed in its true sense. E.g., "Many changes have *transpired* [read *occurred*] with regard to state-authorized administrative agencies."/ "A discussion then *transpired* [read *took place*] between the trial judge and counsel regarding the pleadings and damages, followed by the return of the jury and closing arguments."

Another loose usage occurs (not *transpires*) when *transpire* is used for *pass* or *elapse*, as here: "Only ten days *transpired* [read *passed*] between filing of the joint motion for entry of consent decrees and the time that plaintiffs first gave notice of appeal."

transportation; transportal; transport-ment. The second and third forms are NEEDLESS VARIANTS.

trauma, in pathology, means "a wound, or external bodily injury in general," although in popular contexts it has been almost confined to figurative (emotional) senses.

traverse, v.t. & n. As a verb, *traverse* means "to deny an allegation of fact made in the pleading of the opposite party" (*CDL*). E.g., "The declaration states that the ass was lawfully on the highway, and the defendant has not *traversed* that allegation."/ "In some jurisdictions, it has been held that each fact perjuriously sworn to should be stated in distinct and separate assignments, and each *traversed*, so that if any assignment is proved, the indictment may be sustained."

As a noun, *traverse* = a denial of an allegation of fact made in the pleading of an opposite party. E.g., "Brown filed a *traverse* to the state's response, asserting that he failed to seek relief earlier because he was not aware of his right to file on his guilty plea."/ "At common law the respondent . . . was required to plead specially by distinct *traverse* of the allegations of the writ." *Sansom v. Mercer,* 5 S.W. 62, 65 (Tex. 1887).

tread. See **trodden.**

treasonable; treasonous. The latter is a NEEDLESS VARIANT.

treasure trove, lit. "treasure found," is a remnant of LAW FRENCH. In Anglo-American law, it means "treasure (usu. gold or silver) found hidden in the ground or other place, the owner of which is unknown."

treble; triple. These words are distinguishable though sometimes interchangeable. *Treble* is more usual as the verb, especially in legal contexts: "Before enactment in the 1979 amendments to the Deceptive Trade Practices Act, *trebling* of any damages was mandatory." As an adjective, *treble* usually means "three times as much or as many" 〈treble damages〉, whereas *triple* means "having three parts" 〈a triple bookshelf〉 〈triple bypass surgery〉.

trespass. At common law, the action of trespass took on a variety of forms, among which it is useful to distinguish. *Trespass vi et armis* = an action for intentional injuries to the person. *Trespass de bonis asportatis* = an action for taking personal property. *Trespass quare clausum fregit* = an action for invasion of possession of realty. *Trespass on the case* = an action for myriad injuries, from negligence to nuisance to business torts. (See the next entry.)

trespass on the case is a form of action that, at common law, provided compensation for a wide spectrum of injuries, from personal injuries caused by negligence to business torts and nuisances.

Case is often used as an elliptical form of the phrase *trespass on the case.* E.g., "While the actions of trespass and trover, and even *case*, are described above in the past tense, it is erroneous to assume that these legal labels have altogether dropped out of current usage."/ "The rule for ascertaining what damages a plaintiff could recover did not depend on whether his action was framed in *case* or assumpsit: the principles laid down in *Hadley v. Baxendale* applied in either case." (Eng.) See **action on the case.**

trespassory, dating from 1888, is the adjective corresponding to the noun *trespass.* Included in *W2,* it is, oddly, missing from *W3.*

-tress. See SEXISM (C).

triable = capable of being tried in a court of law; liable to judicial trial (*OED*). This term is used of persons as well as of issues and offenses, but primarily of the latter: "Whether a given offense is to be classed as a crime so as to require a jury trial or as a petty offense *triable* summarily without a jury depends primarily upon the nature of the offense."/ "Appellant failed to carry his burden of raising a *triable* issue of fact on the question of voluntariness."/ "The affidavits filed by Kress did not foreclose a *triable* issue of fact."

trial lawyer, in AmE, has come to have connotations somewhat different from *litigator*. In journalistic and even in some legal writing, *trial lawyer* often suggests one who represents primarily plaintiffs, esp. in tort actions. E.g., "Aside from the *trial lawyers* themselves, no group has lobbied as hard to expand the scope of liability as the consumer movement." Olson, *A Naderite Backflip on Liability*, Wall St. J., March 11, 1986, at 30, col. 3. The American Trial Lawyers' Association is composed primarily of the plaintiffs' bar, as opposed to defense counsel.

trial to the bench. See **bench trial.**

trier of fact; fact-trier. These terms refer to the finder of fact in a judicial proceeding, i.e. the jury or, in a bench trial, the judge. *Trier of fact* is the older phrase, *fact-trier* a form that has recently come into use in American legal writing, and that reduces the awkwardness of *trier of fact* when a possessive is called for ⟨the fact-trier's impartiality⟩. See POSSESSIVES (F).

trilemma is a MORPHOLOGICAL DEFORMITY to be avoided; it is just as bad as *triphibian*, objected to by Fowler. See **dilemma.**

trillion, in the U.S. and France, means "a million millions," and traditionally in G.B., "a million million millions." The difference is more than substantial. Today many British writers follow the American usage, however. Cf. **billion.**

trip (= appeal) is judges' ARGOT in the U.S. "In Milton's first habeas *trip*, we set out the procedural history of his case."

triple. See **treble.**

TRIPLETS. See DOUBLETS AND TRIPLETS OF LEGAL IDIOM.

triumphant, -al. Persons are *triumphant* (= celebrating a triumph), and things are *triumphal* (= of, pertaining to, or of the nature of a triumph).

-trix. See SEXISM (C).

TRO = temporary restraining order. The letters in this abbreviation are usually capi-

talized in the U.S., and are usually not followed by periods. See ACRONYMS AND INITIALISMS.

trodden is preferred over *trod* the past participle of *tread*. Ironically, however, *untrod* is preferred to *untrodden* as the adjectival form.

troops for *soldiers.* Properly, *troop* refers to a company of soldiers, not to individual soldiers. "There are now some 10,000 Argentine *troops* [read *soldiers*] on the Falkland Islands."

trove = accumulation, hoard. Hence *treasure trove*, q.v.

trover. See **detinue.**

true bill = an indictment. E.g., "A second grand jury impaneled in Potter County returned a *true bill* indicting Miracle for aggravated robbery, a first degree felony, with two felony convictions alleged for enhancement."

true bill, v.t. = to indict. See the quotation under NOUNS AS VERBS.

true facts. See **fact** & **actual fact, in.**

trust = the confidence reposed in a person in whom the legal ownership of property is vested to hold or use for the benefit of another; hence, an estate committed to the charge of trustees (*OED*). This definition makes plain how the sense of the word developed into its current meaning. The word commonly appears in the phrase *in trust*: in a formal express trust, it is usual to designate the trustee as such and to state that the transfer is *in trust.*

trust agreement. See **declaration of trust.**

trust deed. See **deed of trust** & **declaration of trust.**

trustee; trusty. *Trustee* = a person having a nominal title to property that he holds for the benefit of one or more others, the beneficiaries (*CDL*). *Trusty*, only an adjective in BrE (archaic, meaning "trustworthy"), is a noun in AmE meaning "a (trusted) convict or prisoner." E.g., "A *trusty* who had accompanied the officers crawled under the house and retrieved a lady's girdle from inside one of the vents underneath the house, along with several rectal syringes." *In re Wright,* 282 F. Supp. 999, 1005 (W.D. Ark. 1968).

trustee, v.t., dates from the early 19th century, though it looks like a newfangled verbalization of a noun. The term has three senses: (1) "to place (a person or his property) in the hands of a trustee or trustees"; (2) (AmE) "to appoint (a person) trustee, often of a bankrupt's estate in order to restrain the debtor from collecting moneys due him"; and (3) (AmE) "to attach (the effects of a debtor) in the hands of a third person." E.g., "He *trusteed* his publications" (Horwill)./ "The defendant in this case . . . is a jointly *trusteed* employee health and welfare benefit plan." *Powers v. South Central United Food & Commercial Workers Unions,* 719 F.2d 760, 761 (5th Cir. 1983). The first quotation illustrates sense (1), the use common in BrE; the second illustrates sense (2), which is predominant in AmE.

trustor. See **settlor.**

trust property. See **corpus.**

trusty. See **trustee.**

try. In G.B., only judges and juries *try* cases; but in the U.S., lawyers are said to *try* cases, as well as judges and juries. E.g., "The court would say unequivocally that this case has been well *tried* by excellent attorneys." See **litigate.**

try and is a casualism for *try to.*

tu quoque (lit., "you're another") = a retort in kind.

turbid; turpid; torpid. *Turbid* = (of water) muddy, thick; (fig.) disordered. *Turpid* is a rare word meaning "filthy, worthless." *Torpid* = dormant, sluggish, apathetic.

turn state's evidence (U.S.) = *turn King's* (or *Queen's*) *evidence* (G.B.).

turpid. See **turbid.**

tutrix = a female guardian. E.g., "She brought this action individually and as natural *tutrix* of her minor son."/ "On June 14, 1967, Fisher's widow as natural *tutrix* of her minor children instituted this suit." Male guardians are never, apparently, called *natural tutors.* See SEXISM (C).

twofold, threefold, fourfold, etc., should be spelled as one word.

type of is often used unnecessarily and inelegantly. E.g., "*In this type of case* [read *In a case of this kind*] it is not the function of the board to reconsider the evidence but only to consider whether there was evidence that, if reasonably considered by the trial court, would justify its view as to the appellant's guilt." (Eng.)

Of is merely elided in the following examples, which are typical of the modern American colloquial trend: "Under *Almanza v. State, this egregious type error* [read an *egregious error of this type*] does not deprive a defendant of due process."/ "In a 'manifested and proved' *type* [omit *type*] jurisdiction, when the owner of an interest in land transfers it inter vivos to another person in trust, a writing properly evidencing the trust will satisfy the statute if it is signed by the transferor prior to, or at the time of, the transfer."/ "*That is a legislative-type choice* [read *That is a choice of a legislative nature*], one that is designed to put all parties on notice that henceforth, in cases of divorce, all outstanding wills are revoked and new testaments are required." (With regard to *will . . . testament* in that sentence, see INELEGANT VARIATION).

tyrannical; tyrannous. Although the senses often seem to merge, it is useful to remember that the former corresponds to *tyrant,* the latter to *tyranny.* "In all *tyrannical* governments the supreme magistracy, or the right of making and enforcing the laws, is vested in one and the same man, or one and the same body of men." (Blackstone)/ "They will act considerately and cautiously, mindful at all times of the dignity of the bar and of the resentment certain to be engendered by any *tyrannous* intervention." (Cardozo)

tyro; tiro. The former spelling is standard in AmE, the latter in BrE.

U

uberrima fides (uberrimae fidei). This phrase, meaning lit. "the utmost good faith," describes a class of contracts in which one party has a preliminary duty to disclose to the other material facts relevant to the subject matter. In the U.S., the nominative *uberrima fides* (as defined above) is more common, whereas in G.B. the genitive *uberrimae fidei* (= of the utmost good faith) is prevalent (see *CDL*).

ubi supra. See **ante** & **supra.**

ukase, orig. a Russian term, meant lit. "a decree or edict, having the force of law, issued by the Russian emperor or government" (*OED*). By extension it has come to mean "any proclamation or decree, esp. of a final or arbitrary nature." E.g., "If the revolution in sexual mores that appellant proclaims is in fact ever to arrive, we think it must arrive through the moral choices of the people and their elected representatives, not through the *ukase* of this court."

ult. (*[ultimo]* = of last month); *prox.* (*[proximo]* = of next month); *inst.* (*[instant]* = of this month). These abbreviations, primarily from commercialese, are to be avoided in preference for straightforward terms such as *March 12*, or *next month*, or *last month*. See **inst.**

ultima ratio = the final argument; a last resort (often force).

ultimate destination is not necessarily a REDUNDANCY, as is often assumed. Where a shipment has a series of stops or transfers—i.e., a series of 'immediate destinations'—it may be appropriate to use the phrase *final* or *ultimate destination*. One may be on one's way to Bangkok, with a stopover in Tokyo. If, on that flight to Tokyo someone asks about one's destination, it would not be inappropriate to characterize Tokyo as the *immediate destination* (i.e., the destination of that particular flight) and Bangkok as the *ultimate destination* (the destination of the entire trip).

Yet the phrase *final destination* or *ultimate destination* should not be used (as it commonly is) in contexts in which such specificity is not called for. Cf. **final wrap-up.**

ultimately = (1) in the end ⟨she ultimately reached her destination⟩; or (2) at the beginning ⟨the two doctrines are ultimately related⟩.

ultimatum. Pl. *-ums.* See PLURALS (A).

ultimo. See **ult.**

ultra (= [1] beyond due limit; extreme; or [2] extremist; fanatical), when used for *beyond*, is erroneous. E.g., "Exemplary damages are therefore damages *ultra* [read *beyond*] compensation."

ultra vires = unauthorized; beyond one's power. The word is classically used as an adverb, as here: "Petitioner maintains that the commission acted *ultra vires* when it applied its new interpretation of its suspension powers to him." See **intra vires.**

It is now perhaps more frequently used adjectively: "Section 60 of the Constitution did not enable the court to declare an enactment imposing a punishment to be *ultra vires* on the ground that the court considered it inappropriate or excessive for the particular offence." (Eng.)/ "Since the fictitious contract that was to be imputed to the corporate defendant was an *ultra vires* one, the action for money had and received could not stand."/ "The liability of municipal governments for restitution for benefits received under unauthorized, *ultra vires*, or illegal contracts will be further treated later in the book."

unalienable. See **inalienable.**

unavailing = of no avail. E.g., "If Johnson lacks sufficient assets, reversing the district court on this issue as a part of this judgment would be *unavailing*." See **avail.**

unbeknown(st). Krapp suggested that both forms are humorous, colloquial, and dialectal. G. P. Krapp, *A Comprehensive Guide to Good English* 602 (1927). The *COD* likewise suggests that both are colloquial. Eric Partridge and John Simon have written, in conformity with the *OED*, that *unbeknown* is the preferred form in the phrase *unbeknown to*, and that *unbeknownst* is dialectal.

These inconsistent pronouncements serve as confusing guides. We can perhaps accept as British orthodoxy the pronouncement of the *COD* that in BrE the forms are colloquial (for *unknown*). In AmE, neither can really be called dialectal or colloquial, for the word is essentially literary. In current AmE usage, *unbeknownst* far outranges *unbeknown* in frequency of use, and it must therefore be considered at least acceptable. I have always preferred *unbeknown*, however, for the *-st* forms (e.g. *whilst, amidst*) uniformly come less naturally to AmE. Following are examples of typical uses: "*Unbeknown* to appellant, appellee Horn sent a plane ticket to her son."/ "The court upheld the admissibility of a statement given by a defendant in the absence of counsel after his lawyer, *unbeknownst* [read *unbeknown*] to the defendant, had called the police station."/ "The fact that, *unbeknownst* [read *unbeknown*] to Towers and Parks, undercover government involvement made any actual export impossible does not alter the jury's finding." *Unknown*, q.v., would be equally good if not better in the sentences quoted.

unbelief. See **disbelief.**

unclean hands. See **clean hands.**

unconscionable = (1) (of persons) having no conscience; or (2) (of actions) showing no regard for conscience; not in accordance with what is right or reasonable. Lawyers use the word a great deal, often without fastidiously observing its meaning. See **conscionable.**

unconstitutional. See **nonconstitutional.**

uncontrovertible should be *incontrovertible.*

UNCOUNTABLES. See COUNT & MASS (NON-COUNT) NOUNS.

uncovered is inherently ambiguous; it may mean (1) "not covered," or (2) "having had the cover removed."

unctious is a not uncommon misspelling of *unctuous.*

undeniably. See **clearly.**

under advisement. See **advisement.**

under appeal. See **appeal.** (A).

underhand(ed). The shorter form is much older. E.g., "And what shall we say to the *underhand* manner in which the incompetence of the worker, and hence his lack of right to a share of the world's goods, are suggested in these verses."/ "'Pettifogger' was also shortened as the sixteenth-century 'fogger,' applied mostly to lawyers, but also to others given to *underhand* practice for gain." *Underhanded* is also perfectly acceptable, however.

under law; in law; at law; by law. These idioms have long been common in Anglo-American legal writing. They cannot be dif-

ferentiated so much by meaning as by the particular context in which they appear. A few examples suggest the broad range of these phrases: "We believe the proper focus concerns whether the state has exercised coercive power or has provided such significant encouragement, either overt or covert, that the choice must *in law* be deemed to be that of the state."/ "*By law* all owners of firearms must have a permit."/ "Every person has a right *under law* as between him and his fellow-subjects to full freedom in disposing of his own labour or his own capital according to his own will." (Eng.)

underlease is a BrE variant of *sublease*, q.v., the usual term in both AmE and BrE.

underlessor. See **sublessor.**

under-mentioned. See **below-mentioned.**

undermine. See **circumvent.**

under my signature. This expression should not be taken too literally. It means "under my authorization," and has nothing necessarily to do with the physical placement of one's signature.

undersigned is little used outside of legal contexts. Usually it is an attributive noun ⟨the undersigned agrees to forbear from execution⟩.

UNDERSTOOD WORDS are common in English, and usually are not very troublesome if we are able to mentally supply them. Often they occur at the outset of sentences. *More important* is short for *What is more important; as pointed out earlier* is an ellipsis of *as was pointed out earlier.* Objects, too, are often elided with the understanding that the reader will know and mentally supply the missing term, e.g.: "Not mentioned was the fact that the standard auto liability also obligates the insurer to *defend.*" (After *defend*, the object *suit* is understood.) On verbs supposedly "understood" whose absence detracts from clarity, see BE-VERBS (A). See also JUDGMENTS, APPELLATE-COURT (ex.8).

under submission = being considered by the court; under advisement. E.g., "*Norton v. National Bank of Commerce* remained *under submission* for nine months."

undertaking (= a promise, pledge, or engagement) is peculiar to legal ARGOT, and is perhaps more common today in BrE than in AmE.

under the circumstances. See **circumstances**.

under (the) law. See **under law**.

under way; underway. This term is two words adverbially, one word as a prepositive adjective ⟨underway refueling⟩. In the phrases *get under way* (= to get into motion) and *be under way* (= to be in progress), the term is two words. It is often wrongly made one word in these adverbial senses, e.g.: "While the search was *underway* [read *under way*], the defendant surrendered to the authorities and, as a result of an illegal interrogation, directed the police to the child's body."/ "This responsibility includes making emergency repairs to the propulsion plant that must be made while the vessel is *underway* [read *under way*]." / "The principal purpose of the Limitation Act is to afford protection to the remote owner who, after the ship is *underway* [read *under way*], has no effective control over the vessel."/ "A legislative reform drive was *underway* [read *under way*], its urgency underscored by angry street demonstrations."

undocumented alien; undocumented (migratory) worker; illegal alien. The usual and preferable term in AmE is *illegal alien*. The other forms have arisen as needless euphemisms, and should be avoided as near-GOBBLEDYGOOK. The problem with *undocumented* is that it is intended to mean, by those who use it in this phrase, "not having the requisite documents to enter or stay in a country legally." But the word strongly suggests "unaccounted for" to those unfamiliar with this quasi-legal jargon, and it may therefore obscure the meaning.

More than one writer has argued in favor of *undocumented alien*. E.g.: "An alien's unauthorized presence in the United States is not a crime under the Immigration and Naturalization Act of 1952, ch. 477, 66 Stat. 163 (currently codified in 8 U.S.C. §§ 1101-57 (1982)). . . . Thus many people find the term *undocumented alien* preferable to *illegal alien*, since the former avoids the implication that one's unauthorized presence in the country is a crime." Hull, *Undocumented Aliens and the*

Equal Protection Clause, 48 Brooklyn L. Rev. 43, 43 n. 2 (1981). This statement is only equivocally correct, however: although illegal aliens' presence in the country is no crime, their *entry* into the country is. As Justice Brennan wrote in *Plyler v. Doe*, 457 U.S. 202, 205 (1982): "Unsanctioned entry into the United States is a crime, 8 U.S.C. § 1325." Moreover, it is wrong to equate illegality with criminality, inasmuch as many illegal acts are not criminal. *Illegal alien* is not an opprobrious epithet: it describes one present in a country in violation of the immigration laws (hence "illegal").

Those who enter the U.K. illegally are termed by statute *illegal entrants*.

undoubtably is an obsolete equivalent of *undoubtedly* and *indubitably*. Cf. **supposably**. See **doubtless**.

undoubtedly. See **doubtless & clearly**.

uneconomic(al). See **economic**.

unenforceable; nonenforceable. The former is preferred. E.g., "The defense is that the alleged promise on which the action is based is without legal consideration and is therefore *nonenforceable* [read *unenforceable*]." See **non-**.

unequivocal; unequivocable. The latter is erroneous, yet the error is surprisingly common. The dictionaries contain only the former, though undaunted lawyers and judges have written, e.g.: "The court *unequivocably* [read *unequivocally*] stated that it rejected its previous premise."/ "The judgment states *unequivocably* [read *unequivocally*] that respondent is to pay petitioner $375 per month until the minor turns eighteen."/ "The court would say *unequivocably* [read *unequivocally*] that this case has been well tried by excellent attorneys."

unexceptionable; unexceptional. See **exceptionable**.

unfeasible. See **infeasible**.

unfind (= to undo a judicial finding) is a NEOLOGISM of arguable utility. E.g., "Other reasons and other names would require this Court to 'unfind' the factual determination heretofore decided." *Longoria v. Robertson*, 669 S.W.2d 870, 872 (Tex. App.—Corpus Christi 1984) (Nye, C. J., concurring).

unilateral. See **bilateral.**

uninheritable. See **heritable.**

unintentional; involuntary. There is an important distinction between these two words, for one may commit a voluntary act that has unintentional consequences. *Voluntariness* therefore generally refers to the cause, and *intentionality* to the effect. See **intentional.**

uninterest(ed). See **disinterest(ed).**

unique. A. Broad Definition in Contracts. In law, *unique* carries the sense "practically unique"; absolute uniqueness is usually too stringent a definition. E.g., "Is the new automobile *unique* or peculiar to the buyer, so as not to be measurable in money damages?"

B. For *unusual.* See ADJECTIVES (A).

unitize. See **communitize.**

unjust enrichment; unjust benefit. The former began as an American legal term but is now used on both sides of the Atlantic; the latter is a primarily British variant. Denoting the principle that provides the basis for most quasi-contracts, *unjust enrichment* = a benefit obtained from another, not intended as a gift and not legally justifiable, for which the beneficiary must make restitution or recompense. See **impoverishment.**

unknown is perfectly acceptable where *unbeknown* would usually appear. "*Unknown* to the parties, there were two ships called 'Peerless,' each of which was carrying cotton from Bombay to Liverpool." See **unbeknown(st).**

unlaw = (1) a violation of law; (2) lawlessness; or (3) a fine. The term is rare; Pollock and Maitland used it in sense (2): "Times of *unlaw* alternate with times of law" (quoted in *W2*).

unlawful. See **illegal.**

unlike. A. For *despite what.* This is a solecism. E.g., "*Unlike some believe* [read *Despite what some believe*], that the name of 'Christ' came from 'Krishna,' which means 'the black one,' many scholars note that 'Christ' comes from the Greek 'Christos.'"

B. For *unlike in.* This misuse leads to faulty comparisons. E.g., "*Unlike* Bayou Bottling, *in which* [read *Unlike in* Bayou Bottling, *in which*], a full-line competitor would not have been unfairly threatened by the uniform decrease in price of a single product in its line, in this case appellant has produced evidence sufficient to support the possibility that appellee's product was predatory as to *appellant,* the sole victim of the lower prices."/ "Thus, *unlike the present case* [read *unlike in the present case*], allowing recovery in that suit would have been tantamount to having the court enforce the precise conduct that the antitrust laws forbid."/ "*Unlike the instant case* [read *Unlike in the instant case*], the original party that induced Hudson's breach of contract was a plaintiff in the action for an injunction, and thus sought to benefit from its own wrongdoing." (The original party is not being compared to the instant case, as the syntax suggests.) See COMPARISONS, FALSE.

unlimitedly, though an ugly word, has become common in the phrase *unlimitedly liable,* perhaps no longer an exaggeration given the proclivities of American juries. See -EDLY.

unmoral. See **immoral.**

unobjected to is a common idiom in the law of evidence. E.g., "The cross-examination complained to be prosecutorial misconduct was also *unobjected to.*" When the phrase is placed before the noun, it is hyphenated: "Clearly, the district court's *unobjected-to* comments, when reviewed in context, do not amount to fundamental error resulting in a miscarriage of justice."

unorganized. See **disorganized.**

unpaid, adj. One should not write "the unpaid automobile," because one does not pay an automobile—rather, one pays *for* it. Yet *unpaid-for automobile* is unpalatable because awkward. *Unpaid debt on the auto* is better; the loss in brevity is outweighed by the gain in clarity and euphony.

unpractical. See **impractical.**

unproportionate, -al. See **disproportionate, -al.**

unqualified. See **disqualified.**

unqualifiedly. See **qualifiedly.**

unreadable. See **illegible.**

unreason; unreasonableness; unreasonability. *Unreason* = absence of reason; indisposition or inability to act or think rationally or reasonably (*OED*). *Unreasonableness* = (1) an act not in accordance with reason or good sense; or (2) the fact of going beyond what is reasonable or equitable. *Unreasonability* is a NEEDLESS VARIANT of *unreasonableness*. Cf. **reasonableness**.

unreasonable. See **arbitrary**.

unresponsive; irresponsive. The former is more usual.

unrevokable. See **irrevocable**.

unsatisfied. See **dissatisfied**.

unsolvable. See **insoluble**.

unsuitable, unsuitableness. See **nonsuitability**.

untenable; untenantable. The former means "indefensible" (figuratively) as well as "unable to be occupied." The latter means "not capable of being occupied or lived in."

until. See **till**.

until such time as is verbose for *until*.

unto is an ARCHAISM for *to*. It is quite common in legal prose, and is easily overdone: "To have and to hold the same *unto* [read *to*] the said Martha Florence and *unto* [read *to*] her bodily heirs and assigns forever, with all the appurtenances *thereunto belonging* [read *belonging thereto*]."/ "Plaintiff assigned all claims arising out of the accident *unto* [read *to*] the intervenor-appellant."/ "Comes now the plaintiff . . . and will show *unto* [omit *unto*] the court the following."/ "There were many alleged violations of *appellant's rights guaranteed unto him by the Constitution* [read *appellant's constitutional rights*]."/ "It seems *nigh unto* [read *almost*] superfluous to remind that section 1983 provides a federal civil remedy in federal court for violations, under color of state law, of the rights, privileges, and immunities secured by the Constitution and laws of the United States."

Margaret M. Bryant prematurely pronounced this usage obsolete in 1930, stating: "Ordinarily [in general English contexts] *unto* denotes 'until.' If Mr. Brown says, '*Unto* this day, John has not taken a drink,' he means until this day. Its obsolete meaning is 'to.' Many illustrations of this meaning are found in the Bible, such as 'Give *unto* the Lord,' signifying 'to the Lord.'" M. M. Bryant, *English in the Law Courts* 180 (1930).

untrod(den). See **trodden**.

untypical. See **atypical**.

unwisdom = lack or absence of wisdom; ignorance, folly, stupidity. This term was common through the Middle Ages, fell into disuse in the seventeenth century, but was revived in the nineteenth century, much to the delight of common-law judges, who enjoy writing about it. E.g., "When an interest postponed as to possession or control is coupled with a gift of the economic benefits produced meanwhile by the thing, the conveyor thereby indicates an intent to have the postponement operate solely as a protection of the taker against his possible intermediate *unwisdom*, rather than as a condition precedent of his interest."/ "His losses would not be attributable to the defendant's breach, but to the *unwisdom* of the bargain."

upon is a FORMAL WORD that is often unnecessary in place of *on*. It is permissible in some phrases, such as, "*Upon* a showing of illegal discrimination, plaintiff is entitled to relief." Or: "In support of his motion, Donovan asserted that plaintiff had perpetrated a fraud *upon* the court by claiming that he was a resident of Florida, rather than Massachusetts, to avail himself of diversity jurisdiction."

Upon is quite justifiable when the sense is *upon the occasion of*, or *when* (something) *occurs*, e.g.: "*Upon* a proper showing, a permanent or temporary injunction, decree, or restraining order shall be granted without bond."/ "*Upon* plaintiff's refusal to amend, his action was dismissed and he appealed." The sense "with little or no interval after" is often an important nuance. E.g., "The order of the commission was made *upon* petition and *upon* hearing after due notice to plaintiff in error."

Upon is inferior, however, when a shorter, simpler, and more direct word will suffice, as in any of the three following types of examples:

A. For *on*. "My Lords, if these conclusions are applied to the present case, it is not difficult to arrive at a decision *upon* [read *on*] this appeal." (Eng.)/ "As the plaintiff had placed the perfected pump *upon* [read *on*] the market without obtaining the protection of the patent laws, he thereby published that invention to the world and no longer had any exclusive property therein." See **on.**

B. For *to.* "Threat *upon* [read *to*] the victim is an element of the crime of aggravated robbery."

C. For *in.* This is a legalistic ARCHAISM: "At the time they were served, they were subject to a compulsory attendance *upon the* [read *in*] court."

upon the trial. See **at (the) trial.**

upper court. See **higher court.**

upset (= to set aside; overturn) is legal ARGOT. E.g., "The court is loath to *upset* these restrictive covenants that have run with the land."

up-to-date should be hyphenated as an adjective, unhyphenated as an adverb. Hence, "Once the log is brought *up to date,* we will have an *up-to-date* log."

upward(s). See **-ward(s).**

urge (in law) = (1) to argue in favor of; or (2) to argue. Sense (1) is here illustrated: "Appellee *urges* affirmance of the order."/ "Appellant *urges* the first solution; appellee the second, adopted by the trial court, and by us." When *urge* in sense (2) is followed by a clause, it should be followed by *that*: "The plaintiff *urged payment* [read *urged that payment*] by the owner was a condition precedent to its duty to pay the subcontractors."/ "She *urges that* the district court abused its discretion by denying her request to amend her complaint." Following is an example of sense (2) with a simple phrase: "Since the causes of action, as well as the facts and legal theories necessary to *urge* such causes of action, are very different in the two suits, a judgment on the merits in either one will not bar proceedings in the other."

usable. So spelled; *useable* is incorrect.

usage, in law, usu. means "a customary practice." E.g., "These fundamental principles are traceable to ancient customs and *usages* and are fixed by tradition and evidenced by the decisions of the courts."/ "While both the conception and the term

'privilege' find conspicuous exemplification under the law of libel and the law of evidence, they nevertheless have a much wider significance and utility as a matter of judicial *usage.*"/ "Both parties had adopted the practice in accordance with common business *usage.*"

Usage should refer to the established custom of a number of persons. In the following specimen, *usage* is ill-advisedly used in the sense "personal habit":

> Sometimes when the described legatee might be an object of the testator's bounty, some unusual personal *usage* can be shown. In *Moseley v. Goodman*, the testator bequeathed $20,000 to "Mrs. Moseley," and a Mrs. Moseley whose husband knew the testator claimed the legacy. The court admitted evidence to show that the testator habitually referred to a Mrs. Trimble as "Mrs. Moseley" and that Mrs. Trimble had cared for the testator while she was ill.

See **custom and usage** & **use.**

Usage also means "an idiom or form of speech," or forms of speech in general. E.g., "That the word has a wider signification even in ordinary nontechnical *usage* is sufficiently indicated, however, by the fact that the term 'special privileges' is so often used to indicate a contrast to ordinary or general privileges."

Here the *use* [not *usage*] of the word is poor: "But *bad language usage* [read *the bad use of language* or *bad usage*] can hurt good law; *good language usage* [read *the good use of language* or *good usage*] can promote respect for good law." Where *use* is possible, it should be used. *Usage* for *use,* however, is not an uncommon error. E.g., "Unless their impact on land *usage* [read *use*] denies the owner the 'justice and fairness' guaranteed by the constitution, they should be upheld."/ "Holmes's position is an endorsement of the 'pretext' *usage* [read *use*] of the power."/ "I want to emphasize that this decision should not be read as an endorsement of a more generalized *usage* [read *use*] of the harmless error rule."/ "Defendant's expert testified that recent or excessive marijuana *usage* [read *use*] has a negative effect on police work."

usance is unjustified in all senses but this, from mercantile law: "the time or period (varying in respect of different countries) allowed by commercial usage or law for the payment of a bill of exchange, etc., esp. as drawn in a foreign or distant land" (*OED*).

use = a passive trust. E.g., "The will, therefore, creates a *use*, or, in more modern phraseology, a 'dry,' 'passive,' or 'naked' trust, and as such it is executed by force of the statute of uses, a statute that has been regarded as in effect in this jurisdiction from the earliest times." See **trust** & **springing use**.

use; utilization. *Use* is the general all-purpose noun and verb, ordinarily to be preferred over *utilize* and *utilization*, except in certain formal contexts in which the longer forms are more natural. *Utilize* is both more abstract and more favorable connotatively than *use*.

Where the connotative nuance of using something to its best advantage is missing, *utilization* should not appear. Here it is defensible: "The section on efficient *utilization* of information concerns one of the most rapidly developing areas of law." Here it is not: "Plaintiff's prompt *utilization* [read *use*] of the charge embraced in the criminal prosecution as the basis for a civil action was likewise voluntary."

user-friendly. See COMPUTERESE.

usufruct is a civil-law term meaning "the right of temporary possession, use, or enjoyment of the advantages of property belonging to another, [as] far as may be had without causing damage or prejudice to him" (*OED*). E.g., "In 1961, Samuel Zemurray bequeathed the naked ownership of his one-half interest in the land to plaintiff and bequeathed to his wife Sarah the *usufruct*." (La.)

usufructuary, n. & adj., = (adj.) of, relating to, or of the nature of, a usufruct; (n) one having the usufruct of property. E.g., "The English lawyer treats the *usufructuary* as a limited owner—the nearest equivalent seems to be a life tenant." (Eng.)

usurpation; usurpature. The latter is a NEEDLESS VARIANT. E.g., "The Supreme Court has stated that only exceptional circumstances amounting to a judicial *usurpation* of power will justify the invocation of the extraordinary remedy of a mandamus directed to a district judge."

usury = the lending of money at an excessive interest rate. Formerly, it meant "the lending of money for interest [i.e., any interest at all, this being proscribed]." The adjective corresponding to this noun is *usurious*.

As for the pronunciation of *usury* and *usurious*, the first syllable of these words is pronounced "you." Because the words begin with a consonant sound, -*y*-, they should be preceded by *a* and not *an* where an indefinite article is called for: "In its counterclaim, N.T. contended that M.'s prayer for interest amounted to *an usurious* [read *a usurious*] charge of interest in violation of the statute." See **a** (A).

uterine. See **consanguineous**.

utilization. See **use**.

utilize = to put to useful purpose. It is not an exact synonym of *use*, q.v.

ut infra = as below. See **ante**.

ut supra = as above. See **ante** & **supra**.

utter is a LEGALISM used in reference to written instruments to mean "to put or send into circulation." Hence, to *utter* a forged instrument is to present it to another with knowledge that it is a forgery. E.g., "On October 3, 1960, an indictment was filed in the United States District Court for the District of Columbia charging the applicant in four counts with forgery and four counts with *uttering* a fake check."

utter bar. See **outer bar**.

ux., an abbreviation of *uxor* (= wife), was formerly commonly used in the phrase *et ux.* to indicate that a wife is joined with her husband in a legal action. Today the wife is usually accorded the dignity of being named, or at least she should be. If her name does appear, there is certainly no reason for *et ux.*, as some real estate brokers seem mistakenly to believe. See SEXISM.

uxorial; uxorious. The first is neutral, the second pejorative. *Uxorial* = of or relating to a wife; *uxorious* = submissive to or excessively fond of one's wife.

V

v.; vs. Both are acceptable abbreviations of *versus*. In case names, *v.* is the accepted abbreviation. *Vs.* is more common among laymen.

In pronouncing case names, one should be careful to say *versus* or *against*, not "vee."

vacate. See **overrule** & **set aside.**

vacation, n., in law may mean: (1) the period during which court is not in term; or (2) the act of vacating. The following specimen illustrates sense (1): "Under a statute authorizing a judge either before or during the term to order additional jurors, an order directing the additional jurors, made in *vacation*, is within the court's discretion." More commonly, sense (2) applies. "The remedy provided by the National Prohibition Act and the Espionage Act for *vacation* of a warrant improperly issued and for return of property was not applicable."

VAGUENESS. See AMBIGUITY.

variable; variant; variational; variative. *Variable* = subject to variation; characterized by variations. *Variant* = differing in form or in details from the one named or considered, differing thus among themselves (*COD*). *Variational* = of, pertaining to, or marked or characterized by variation. *Variative* shares the senses of *variational*, and, being the rarer word, might be considered a NEEDLESS VARIANT; the courts have found uses for it, however; e.g.: "The *variative* approach to intrastate branching was nicely illustrated at the time by the structure in New York." *Northeast Bancorp, Inc. v. Federal Reserve System,* 472 U.S. 159, 172 (1985).

variance; variation; variant, n. *Variance* is common in legal writing in the sense "a difference or discrepancy between two statements or documents," esp. in criminal contexts. E.g., it is used of charging instruments: "The second conviction was tainted by a *variance* between what was alleged in the indictment as the cause number and the proof."

At variance = (of persons) in a state of discord; (of things) conflicting; in a state of disagreement or difference. E.g., "In *Boxsius v. Goblet Freres,* Lord Esher expressed views quite *at variance* with his utterance in *Pullman v. Hill.*" (Eng.)/ "This exact question has not been decided by this court, and the decisions of the courts of other jurisdictions are somewhat *at variance.*"/ "Such a result is plainly *at variance* with the policy of the legislation as a whole."

Variation = a departure from a former or normal condition or action or amount, or from a standard or type, or the extent of this departure. The terms *variance* and *variation* are especially susceptible to INELEGANT VARIATION. E.g., "The plaintiffs as a matter of law do not have a cause of action for the allegedly arbitrary and discriminatory denial of their request for a zoning *variance*; in any event the denial of a zoning *variation* [read *variance*] is not a deprivation of property."

Variant = a form or modification differing in some respect from other forms of the same thing (*OED*). E.g., "Some jurisdictions having modern *variants* of the rule would approach the problem differently."

vehicle. The *-h-* is not pronounced. Hence /**vee**-i-kĕl/.

vehicular. **A.** *Vehicular homicide. Vehicular* is not objectionable per se. Several states in the U.S. have *Vehicular Homicide Statutes,* for which there is no ready substitute for *vehicular.* E.g., "A conviction of *vehicular homicide* requires, as a matter of law, a finding that the defendant has either driven recklessly or driven while under the influence of alcohol."

B. *Vehicular accident* is pompous LEGALESE and OFFICIALESE for *traffic accident, car accident,* or *motoring accident.*

C. *Vehicular unit* is especially absurd for *car:* "The declaration sheet seeks to provide separate coverages for uninsured motorists on three *vehicular units.*" If *car* or *automobile* were too specific, then *vehicle* would suffice.

vel non (lit., "or not") is almost always superfluous; it is *always* vexatious. *W3* defines the phrase as "whether or not," but these words could hardly be plugged into the following sentences. A more accurate definition of the phrase as frequently used in American legal writing is "or the lack thereof." E.g., "We come finally to the merits *vel non* of this appeal."/ "We need address only the propriety of the ultimate finding of discrimination *vel non.*"/ "Yet another barometer of the descriptiveness *vel non* of a particular name is the extent to which it has been used in the tradenames of others offering a similar service or product."

Usually the phrase is completely superfluous, as in the sentences just quoted, and in these: "The ultimate issue, that of discrimination *vel non,* is to be treated by the district and appellate courts in the same manner as any other issue of fact."/ "Clearly, the argument bears solely on the nature of the violation, not on the existence of a violation *vel non*."/ "The vice in the decree lies in the fact that it enjoins, not specific acts or omissions, but results, evidence of the existence *vel non* of which must be determined by the opinions of witnesses." See **devastavit**.

venal; venial. These words are frequently mistaken. *Venal* = (1) purchasable; for sale; or (2) highly mercenary; amenable to bribes; corruptible. E.g., in sense (2): "Child labor laws protect children against themselves, but also from the prospect of exploitation by *venal* parents."/ "Even though we admit that the advocate is ready to undertake either side of a cause for hire, it does not thereby follow that he is *venal* or that his attitude contravenes the principles of a sound morality."/ "That *venality* exists among certain members of the bar it would be idle to deny."

Venial = slight (used of sins); pardonable; excusable; trivial. E.g., "There will be no assumption of a purpose to visit *venial* faults with oppressive retribution." (Cardozo, J.)

vend is now usu. commercialese for *sell*, though it has been established since the seventeenth century.

vendable. See **vendible**.

vendee, an unnecessary LEGALISM for *buyer* or *purchaser*, is most commonly used in real estate transactions. Arguably it is useful in some contexts as a correlative of *vendor*, q.v. "A sale contract was then drawn, naming the Millers individually as vendors, and the lessee's sister as *vendee*." Cf. **breachee**. See -EE.

vendible, -able. The former spelling is preferred. See -ABLE (A).

vendor. *Seller* is generally a better word, along with the corresponding *buyer* rather than *vendee*, q.v. Use of the better-known words increases readability and reduces the possibilities of typographical error.

venerable is a CLICHÉ when used inaccurately for *old*. E.g., "This firmly rooted principle was first established *in the venerable case of* [read, e.g., *more than a century ago in*] *Strawbridge v. Curtiss*." Properly, *venerable* = (of persons) worthy of being venerated, revered, or highly respected and esteemed, on account of character or position; commanding respect by

reason of age combined with high personal character and dignity of appearance; (of things) worthy of veneration or deep respect.

venial. See **venal**.

venire, /vĭ-*nI*-ree/ or /vĭ-*neer*/, was originally an elliptical form of *venire facias* (lit., "that you cause to come"), the name of the writ directed to a sheriff requiring him to summon a jury to try a case or cases at issue between parties. Today *venire* is used in the sense "a panel of persons selected for jury duty and from which the jurors are to be chosen." *Jury venire* is a fairly common REDUNDANCY, e.g.: "In *Witherspoon v. Illinois*, the Supreme Court held that those individuals *in the jury venire* [read *in the venire*] who indicate that they could never vote to impose the death penalty, or that they would refuse even to consider its imposition in the case before them, may be excluded from juries in the trial of the penalty phase in capital cases."

venireman, -person, -member. The terms all mean "a prospective juror." E.g., "One issue has remained common and critical in virtually every capital trial in the nation: whether *veniremen* opposed to capital punishment may serve on the jury." For those seeking a nonsexist equivalent, *veniremember* is better than *-person*. E.g.,"I respectfully dissent from the holding that this case should be remanded for inquiry into the prosecution's reasons for exercising its peremptory challenges against black *venirepersons* [read *veniremembers*]."/ "It was not error for the court to refuse to ask *venirepersons* [read *veniremembers*] whether the testimony of the government investigator was entitled to more weight than the testimony of any other witness." Though today common in legal writing, neither *venireperson* nor *veniremember* is included in the standard unabridged dictionaries. See SEXISM (B).

venue. See **jurisdiction** (A).

veracity = (1) truthfulness; observance of the truth; or (2) truth; accuracy. Sense (1), denoting a quality that persons have, is the traditionally correct use. Sense (2) began as a SLIPSHOD EXTENSION in the eighteenth century, and still might be so considered; it is not, however, uncommon in legal prose: "The controversy over the *veracity* [read *accuracy*] of the search-warrant affidavit arose in connection with petitioner's state conviction for rape, kidnapping, and burglary."/ "The fact that there are clerks or carriers at the Greenville Post Office with seniority dates between September 1979 and April 1979 does nothing to call into question the *veracity* [read *accuracy*] of Smith's affidavit."/ "Control Data disputes the *veracity* [read *accuracy*] of each point, but the resolution of these factual issues is for another place and another time."

Veracity is not to be confused with *voracity* (= greediness in eating). See MALAPROPISMS.

verbal is, unfortunately, "[a] term often used as meaning oral, parol, or unwritten." 92 C.J.S. at 995 (1955). It should not be so used. *Verbal* means "of or relating to words," as here: "The transposition of the words 'the court' and the addition of the word 'and' at the beginning of the first sentence [of the Rule] are merely *verbal* changes." Fed. R. Civ. P. 60(b) advisory committee note. The movie producer Sam Goldwyn's supposedly ironic remark, "A *verbal* contract isn't worth the paper it's written on," was not ironic at all given the proper sense of the word *verbal*, because a written contract *is* verbal. The phrase requires *oral*, which is restricted to what is spoken. For those senses cited in *Corpus Juris Secundum* and quoted at the outset of this entry, *oral*, *parol*, or *unwritten* should be used.

The error is especially acute when *verbal* is opposed to *written*, as in a statute quoted in *Franklin v. South Carolina*, 218 U.S. 161, 163 (1910): "Any laborer working on shares of crop or for wages in money or other valuable consideration, under a *verbal* [read *oral*] or written contract to labor on farm lands, who shall receive advances . . . and thereafter wilfully . . . fail to perform the reasonable service required of him . . . shall be liable to prosecution for a misdemeanor." Or here: "*Verbal* [read *Oral*] or written threats may become intimidating or coercive."

The misuse of *verbal* for *oral* is common, but we should not let the distinction between these words be blurred in legal prose: "I find the value of said aerolite to be one-hundred and one dollars as *verbally* [read *orally*] stipulated in open court by the parties to this action." (One cannot stipulate other than by words.)/ "In 1909 Congress was concerned with *verbal* [read *oral*] orders to depart."/ "Note that even though an offer is for the bilateral contract and can be accepted only by a promise, the promise need not be *verbal* [read *oral*]."

Because *verbal* is always used in reference to words, *verbal definition* is redundant, as there can be no definition without words: "Neither scientists nor philosophers have been more successful than judges in providing a *verbal definition* [omit *verbal*] for the concept of causality."/ Similarly, *verbal* is redundant in such phrases as *verbal promise*, *verbal denial*, *verbal affirmation*, and *verbal criticism*, as these activities usually cannot occur without words.

VERBAL AWARENESS. Lest writers commit unconscious puns, they must be aware of all the meanings of a given word, where one particular meaning is intended but other potential meanings may confuse or seem odd. E.g., "The language of the press may carry 'All the news that's fit to print'; the language of the law expresses the fit and the unfit, the *fleeting* and what *passes* for permanent." Mellinkoff, *The Language of the Law* 33 (1963). (In that sentence, *passes* should not be used alongside *permanent* (esp. just after *fleeting*), because what passes is impermanent.)/ "At stake was no mere matter of taste; ammonium nitrate cakes when wet and is difficult to spread on fields as fertilizer." The proximity of *taste* and *cakes*, which may not at first be recognized as a verb, and the immediate proximity of *ammonium nitrate*, which must be torturous to the palate, do not make for pleasant reading. A less gustatory version would read: "At stake was no mere matter of personal preference; for ammonium nitrate, when wet, cakes and becomes difficult to spread on fields."

A heightening of verbal awareness would prevent writers from rending sentences with seeming contradictions: "After the *work stoppage started* [better: *workers walked off the job*], he was assigned to answer telephone complaints about company service." Cf. ETYMOLOGICAL AWARENESS.

verbals (Eng.) = any remarks that an accused person has made in the presence of the police (*CDL*). The term appears to be an elliptical form of *verbal statements*, itself incorrect for *oral statements*. But *verbals* appears to be ensconced in BrE legal ARGOT. See **verbal.**

verbatim; ipsissima verba; literatim. These near-synonyms carry slight nuances. *Verbatim* = word for word. *Literatim* = letter for letter. Sometimes the phrase *verbatim et literatim* is seen. *Ipsissima verba* (lit., "the selfsame words") = the exact language used by someone quoted (*W9*). E.g., "Had the application for costs against the solicitors personally been pursued in this case, it would have been a weighty factor in favor of the solicitors; moreover, the *ipsissima verba* of a judgment can be of help." (Eng.) See **in haec verba.**

verbiage was formerly unerringly pejorative. It referred to prolix language and redundancies. More recently, it has come to signify, esp. to American lawyers, "wording, diction," in a neutral sense. Perhaps it is neutral because lawyers have become inured to their prolixities and inelegancies: "Mr. Smithson was preparing the *verbiage* for the agreement." Strictly, the word should maintain the negative connotations it has always had; *verbiage* describes a vice of language. Note that in the sentence just quoted, the writer might have CUT OUT THE CHAFF by writing, "Mr. Smithson was preparing the agreement." A somewhat different error is illustrated in this specimen: "It is well settled that the exact *verbiage* [read *wording*] of the statute need not be alleged in an indictment when there is no material difference between the language of the *statute* and the allegations employed."

Verbage for *verbiage* is a common error.

VERBOSITY. Samuel Johnson once said, "It is unjust, sir, to censure lawyers for multiplying words when they argue; it is often necessary for them to multiply words" (quoted in *Boswell's Life of Johnson* (1781)). Perhaps so. But lawyers must at least attempt to distinguish between those occasions when it is necessary, and those when it is not.

For example, verbosity is virtually never appropriate (much less necessary) in statutes. Yet it is especially common in STATUTE DRAFTING. The following statute says nothing more than that the industrial commission is to lay down rules to ensure safety in the handling of liquefied petroleum gases:

> The industrial commission shall ascertain, fix, and order such reasonable standards, rules, or regulations for the design, construction, location, installation, operation, repair, and maintenance of equipment for storage, handling, use, and transportation by tank truck or tank trailer, of liquefied petroleum gases for fuel purposes, and for the odorization of said gases used therewith, as shall render such equipment safe.
>
> Wis. Stat. §§ 101.105(2) (1963) (quoted in Friedman, *Law and Its Language,* 33 Geo. Wash. L. Rev. 563, 575 (1964)).

Certain verbose phrases recur in statutes, e.g.:

Verbose Expression	Kernel Expression
at the time of his death	when he dies
have need of	need
have knowledge of	know
give consideration to	consider
give recognition to	recognize
make application	apply
make payment	pay
make provision for	provide for

Judicial writing is also a sanctuary for verbosity. Following are some typical specimens, with recommended ways of CUTTING OUT THE CHAFF: "He contends that while assisting in hooking cables to the cover of said barge, while assisting in the offloading of it, he was injured when the cover of said barge was moved, causing him to sustain a downward fall." [This sentence appears to have been dictated and unedited. Read *While offloading the barge and, in particular, assisting in hooking cables to its cover, he fell when the cover was moved.*]/ "Upon *the filing of the petition* [read *Upon filing the petition*], appellant was appointed special guardian and attorney for all persons known or unknown who had any interest in the income of the common trust fund."/ "The court should not attempt to enforce any variation of the relations between insured and insurer while the insurance contract is *in process of performance* [read *being performed, in effect,* or *under way*]."/ "With the benefit of *hindsight and its unerring superb visual acuity*, one might suggest that the trial strategy chosen by Austin's appointed counsel left much to be desired." (Omit that desultory amplification of hindsight, the qualities of which people know well enough.)/ "The testator devised 'all my real estate now had by me wheresoever the same may be located' to his four sons." [Read *The testator devised all his real estate to his four sons.*]/ "A *venture*, to constitute a joint *adventure*, must be for *profit in a financial or commercial sense* [read *financial profit*]." (On the variation of *venture/adventure*, see INELEGANT VARIATION.)/ "The existing partners and incoming partners desire by this amendatory agreement to admit the incoming partners as partners in the partnership." (This bit of verbosity needs no comment.) See SUPERFLUITIES & FLOTSAM PHRASES. See also BE-VERBS (B), REDUNDANCY, DOUBLETS AND TRIPLETS OF LEGAL IDIOM, & SYNONYMIA.

VERB PHRASES, INCOMPLETE, or the Problem of Nontransferable Auxiliaries. This problem plagues a great deal of legal writing, primarily because lawyers frequently attempt to express themselves alternatively, or with elaboration. E.g., "They were not liable at law for the continued suffering of the man who fell among thieves, *which they might, and morally ought to have, prevented* [read *which they might have, and morally ought to have, prevented*]. "/ "But many of these holdings *have or will be overruled* [read *have been, or will be, overruled*]. "/ "Plaintiff claims that he *has and will continue to receive* [read *has received and will continue to receive*] fewer benefits from the trust than he should." See SEQUENCE OF TENSES.

verdict. A. Juries, not judges, hand down verdicts (both civil and criminal). Strictly, verdicts are *returned* by juries, although we have the lay colloquialisms *to pass a verdict on* and *to give a verdict on.* Cf. **sentence.**

B. *Verdict* for *vote.* The jury collectively renders a *verdict*; individual jurors tender *votes*, not *verdicts.* E.g., "A prejudice against the defense of insanity will not disqualify one from sitting as juror where the nature of the prejudice is such that the court is satisfied that it will not influence the juror's *verdict* [read *vote*]."

Voir dire, q.v., is etymologically equivalent to *verdict*, having passed into English through French. *Verdict* came through Anglo-Norman (*verdit*) but was refashioned after the medieval Latin *verdictum*, itself based on the Anglo-Norman *verdit.*

verily (= in truth) is an affected ARCHAISM in modern contexts.

versus for *as against*, q.v., is quite acceptable. E.g., "The FCC's decision is consistent with respect to the use of long- *versus* short-form procedures." This word need not be italicized as a foreign word. See **v.**

very. A. As a WEASEL WORD. Often this intensive actually has the effect of weakening a statement rather than strengthening it. E.g., "We are *very* reluctant to substitute our views on damages for those of the jury." Here the word *very* weakens the adjective that follows. Indeed, *very* has been used irresponsibly for so long that its actual effect is often just the op-

posite of its intended effect. A simple statement is usually more forceful.

B. *Very disappointed*, etc. *Very* modifies adjectives (*sorry, sick,* etc.), and not, properly, past participles (*disappointed, uninterested,* etc.). Follett wrote that "finer ears are offended by past participles modified by *very* without the intervention of the quantitative *much*, which respects the verbal sense of an action undergone. Such writers require *very much disappointed, very much pleased, very much engrossed, very well satisfied*, etc. Only a few adjectives from verbs—*tired, drunk,* and possibly *depressed*—have shed enough of their verbal quality to stand an immediately preceding *very.*" W. Follett, *Modern American Usage* 343 (1966). *Very interested* is another acceptable idiom, although *very much interested* seems preferable in formal contexts. When a past participle has become thoroughly established as an adjective (e.g. *drunk*), it takes *very* rather than *very much.*

vest, v.t. & v.i., is used in a number of legal and lay idioms, particularly *to vest in* and *to vest with.* E.g., "The parties' clear and unambiguous expression of consent is required to *vest* a United States Magistrate *with* plenary civil jurisdiction." At common law, in the ceremony known as investiture, the lord handed over to his vassal some object representing the land: "The vassal was thus *vested with* the fief and the fief was *vested in* him: from these terms developed the modern meanings of *to vest*, as first, to place or secure something in the possession of a person; secondly, to place or establish a person in possession or occupation of something; and, thirdly, to pass into possession—the senses, in other words, which are represented in the current idioms *vest in* or *be vested in* and *vest with* or *be vested with.*" Simon, *English Idioms from the Law*, 78 Law Q. Rev. 245, 249 (1962). See **invest.**

vested interest subject to divestment; vested interest liable to be divested. The first is AmE, the second BrE.

vestigial. So spelled; *vestigal* is a not uncommon misspelling.

via = (1) by way of (a place); passing through ⟨they flew to Amarillo via Dallas⟩; (2) by means of, through the agency of ⟨we booked our flight via Qantas⟩. Sense (2) is considered "certainly acceptable in informal use" by the *Oxford Guide*, to which I would add that it is certainly unacceptable in formal prose. Gowers called it a vulgarism in the revised edition of Fowler's *Modern English Usage,* and Follett (*Modern American Usage*) and Bernstein (*The Careful Writer*) concur. The following sentences illustrate the objectionable sense, an example of SLIPSHOD EXTENSION: "Finally, she argues that the tax lien, if it exists, is subordinate to her interest in the property because it was not filed until she 'purchased' it *via* [read *through*] the divorce proceedings."/ "Once they arrived at the Army's criminal investigations headquarters, the FBI agents showed appellant their badges and gave him his *Miranda* warnings *via* [read *off* or *by reading aloud*] an advice-of-rights form."/ "When a party fails to secure a witness's voluntary cooperation by notice or commission procedure, it may seek discovery *via* [read *through*] a letter rogatory."

Here is an acceptable figurative use of sense (1): "Whereas the appellant in *Shelley v. Kramer* arrived *via* a state court, thereby permitting of disposition on fourteenth-amendment grounds, the *Hurd* case arose in the District of Columbia."

viable originally meant "capable of living; able to maintain a separate existence," a sense that still applies in many phrases, such as *a viable fetus.* By acceptable extension it has come to be used figuratively of immaterial things or concepts, as here: "Ancillary jurisdiction presupposes the existence of an action that a federal court can adjudicate and should not be used to breathe life into a lawsuit that is not otherwise *viable.*"/ "We conclude that Powell's claim for back salary remains *viable* even though he has been seated in the 91st Congress and thus find it unnecessary to determine whether the other issues have become moot."

The word has lately been the victim of SLIPSHOD EXTENSION, when used in the sense "feasible, practicable" ⟨a viable plan⟩. This sense is objectionable not alone in being slovenly, but also in its current status as a VOGUE WORD. One writer has noted that "dictionaries now give [as definitions for *viable*] *real, workable, vivid, practicable, important,* newer definitions that seem only to confirm the critics' complaints that the word has had the edge hopelessly ground off it." R. Copperud, *American Usage and Style* 405 (1980). Thus such uses as the following are to be avoided; it is hard even to know what the writer of this sentence

meant: "She intended to transport the aliens to the nearest *viable* [read *practical?*] Immigration and Naturalization Service office for the purpose of allowing them to file applications for asylum."

vicarious liability; vicarious responsibility. The former is the usual term in both AmE and BrE; the latter is a BrE variant. See **responsibility.**

vice versa (= the other way around; just the opposite) should have mirror-image referents, even if only implied. E.g., "It is unlikely that any of the participants in the debates about constitutional theory are going to have their minds changed by reading a polemic by a person of another sect, any more than Baptist theologians are likely to convert to Catholicism *or vice versa* [read *or Catholic theologians are likely to convert to Baptism*] when presented with a 'refutation' of [their] position." (The uncorrected sentence denotes, through *vice versa,* "or Catholicism is likely to convert to Baptist theologians.")

Vice versa does not work here: "A mother may inherit from an illegitimate child whom she has acknowledged and *vice versa.*" If we reverse the equation, we get this: "An illegitimate child may inherit from a mother whom she has acknowledged." An illegitimate child does not acknowledge her parent.

Nor does *vice versa* work with a verb like *distribute.* E.g., "The testatrix intended to give the trustees a broader and more discretionary power that would permit them, to some extent, to distribute as income what would otherwise go as principal and *vice versa.*" The writer did not intend to say, by *vice versa,* that the trustees had the power *to distribute as principal what would otherwise go as income.* The phraseology would work if the verb had been *to treat as.*

vicinity; vicinage. Though *vicinage* (= neighborhood; the relation of neighbors) is the older term in English, dating from the fourteenth century, it is (in AmE) a legalistic variant of *vicinity,* which dates from 1560. *Vicinity,* however, has far outranged *vicinage* in its usefulness. "Changes of venue or continuances may subject the parties and courts to inconvenience and expense and may even violate the defendant's right to speedy trial in the *vicinage.*" This *vicinage* is a legalistic affectation for *venue,* as may be seen from this quotation from Blackstone: "[T]he court will direct a change of the *venue* or *visne*, (that is, the *vicinia* or neighborhood in which the injury is declared to be done)." 4 W. Blackstone, *Commentaries* *294. Fowler wrote that "*vicinage* is now, compared with *neighborhood*, a FORMAL WORD, and, compared with *vicinity*, a dying one" (*MEU1* 693).

victor. See **victress.**

victory. The phrase *win a victory* is a common REDUNDANCY, albeit a venial one.

victress; victrix. *Victor* applies to women as well as to men; the other forms are unnecessary. See SEXISM (C).

victuals, spelled for colloquial uses *vittles*, is pronounced /*vit-ălz*/. It forms *victualer* (= one who provides food and drink for payment), *victualed,* and *victualing* in AmE; these three inflected forms double the *-l-* in BrE. See DOUBLING OF FINAL CONSONANTS.

videlicet. See **viz.**

vi et armis (= by or with force and arms) is a LEGALISM formerly common, but today moribund. It was a necessary part of the allegation in medieval pleading that a trespass had been committed with force and therefore was a matter for the King's Court because it involved a breach of the peace. In England, the term survived as a formal requirement of pleading until 1852 (*CDL*). See **trespass** & LOAN TRANSLATIONS.

viewpoint; point of view; standpoint. The first is not as good, in formal writing, as the second or third. Apart from the fact that *viewpoint* should now be stigmatized as a VOGUE WORD, it has been "considered inferior to *point of view* by some writers and grammarians" (*AHD*). Eric Partridge wrote that the term "has been deprecated by purists; not being a purist, I occasionally use it, although I perceive that it is unnecessary." *Usage and Abusage* 307 (1973).

vindicable. See **-ATABLE.**

vindicate = (1) to clear from censure, criticism, suspicion, or doubt, by means of demonstration; or (2) to assert, maintain, make good, by means of action, esp. in one's own interest; to defend against encroachment or interference (*OED*). Sense (1) is the usual lay sense, sense (2), the legal sense. E.g., "An arrest is the initial stage of a criminal prosecution; it is intended to *vindicate* society's interest in having its laws obeyed."/ "We do not pass upon other claims that may be available to him to *vindicate* his rights." The word implies success in justifying something. This sentence is therefore redundant: "Plaintiffs contend that a class action procedure is the only means of ensuring that the potential claimants will be able *to successfully vindicate* [read *to vindicate*] their rights."

vindicatory, -tive; vindictive. *Vindicatory* = (1) providing vindication; or (2) punitive, retributive. *Vindicative* is a NEEDLESS VARIANT that, if ever used, would be liable to confusion with *vindictive*, a common word meaning "given to or characterized by revenge or retribution." E.g., "We note the interest of the public in shielding responsible federal government officials against the harassment and inevitable hazards of *vindictive* or ill-founded damage suits."

vindictive damages. See **punitive damages.**

violate; contravene; abridge; breach; flout. These verbs are common in legal contexts, and in some contexts have virtually the same senses. *Violate* and *flout* are commonly used of the law ⟨to flout the law⟩. (See **flaunt.**) *Contravene* is also so used, but more commonly is used of something less well defined, such as public policy ⟨the rule contravenes public policy⟩. *Violate* and *abridge* are frequently used of constitutional or statutory rights. (See **abridge.**) And *violate* and *breach* are often used of contractual provisions.

violative. The phrase *to be violative of* is verbose for *to violate.* E.g., "Even if residency requirements would be a permissible exercise of the commerce power, they are so unjustifiable as *to be violative of* [read *to violate*] due process." See BE-VERBS (B).

vires is an unnecessary LATINISM for *power* or *authority.* E.g., "Right from the beginning he never had *vires* [read *the power*] to deal with the matters other than by reference to the Act." (Eng.) See **ultra vires** & **intra vires.**

virile (lit. "masculine, manly") has an odd sense in Louisiana civil law, namely "that can be rightly attributed to or assessed against (a person)." E.g., "The right to enforce contribution does not mature until there has been payment of the common obligation, or at least payment of more than the *virile* share."/ "Among solidary obligors, each is liable for his *virile* portion."

virtue of, in & by. By *virtue of*, not *in virtue of*, is currently the idiomatic phrase; the latter is an ARCHAISM that remains fairly common in legal writing, however: "[*I*]*n virtue of* the State's jurisdiction over the property of the nonresident situated within its limits, [the state courts] can inquire into that nonresident's obligations to its own citizens . . . to the extent necessary to control the disposition of the property." *Pennoyer v. Neff*, 95 U.S. 714, 723 (1877)./ "It merely recognizes a right of action that existed in a living person, whether at common law or *in virtue of* some statute."

vis-à-vis is a CHAMELEON-HUED preposition and adverb in place of which it is usually desirable to use a more precise term. The traditional sense is adverbial, "in a position facing each other." Arguably, the following sentence contains an acceptable figurative use of this sense: "The practical possibility is present in all intrafamilial legal relationships, particularly parent *vis-à-vis* child."
As a preposition, *vis-à-vis* has been extended to the senses "opposite to; in relation to; as compared with." Usually simpler, more precise prepositions are better. E.g., "The advantage of equitable remedies for the misappropriation of money lies in establishing a preferred position *vis-à-vis* [read *over*] others having claims against the wrongdoer, by way of an equitable lien or through equitable subrogation."/ "It is harsh enough when, *vis-à-vis* [read *as between*] the carrier and the shipper, the law commands a shipper to pay the carrier twice the cargo if the latter has not in fact received the money."

viscera (= internal organs) is the plural of *viscus*. See PLURALS (A).

visit, n.; **visitation.** *Visit*, the ordinary word, means "a call on a person or at a place; temporary residence with a person or at a place" (*COD*). *Visitation* denotes a visit by an official, an unduly long visit, or the divine dis-

pensation of punishment or reward. In family law, *visitation* is used in the phrases *visitation rights* (= provisions for spending time with one's children living with another, usu. the divorced spouse). E.g., "This case involves court orders regarding child-support obligations and *visitation* rights under a divorce decree."

visit upon = to inflict punishment for, to avenge. E.g., "The drastic remedy of an involuntary dismissal with prejudice may not under our jurisprudence be *visited upon* a client because of his attorney's deficiencies in professional courtesy."

vis major; force majeure; act of God. The first is a LATINISM, the second a French equivalent, and the third a common English phrase. All are used in legal writing, and the first two appear almost exclusively in legal writing. All three phrases have undergone HYPALLAGE, so that the reference is now usually to the destruction caused by forces of nature, rather than to the forces of nature themselves. See **force majeure.**

visualize does not mean "to see," but "to see in the mind's eye." The word is figurative, not literal. Here the word is wrongly used in a literal sense: "On May 10, 1973, the neurosurgeon performed the surgery. After opening her back, the defendant *visualized* [read *saw*] a slightly bulging annulus on the left at L5-S1."

vitiate = (1) to impair by the addition of (something); (2) to render corrupt in morals; (3) to corrupt or spoil in respect of substance; or (4) to render of no effect; to invalidate either completely or in part; to destroy or impair the legal effect or force of (a deed, etc.) (*OED*). Sense (1) is the most widely used. E.g., "The real complaint in this case, however, is that by treating reasonable retaliation as a separate and distinct element, the judge may have misled jury and *vitiated* the effect of the proper direction which he had previously given."/ "Consent to contract may be *vitiated* if fraud, error, violence, or threats induce the consent [i.e., if one of these elements is added]."
Here *vitiate* is used in the sense "to impair by the subtraction or omission of something," an unexceptionable use: "Excising the racial indicia from Exhibit Z would have

vitiated its relevance in rebutting the claim of discrimination."/ "The omission to refer to the lease did not *vitiate* the memorandum." (Eng.)

Sense (4) is the legal sense. E.g., "Where the object contemplated by one or both of the parties to a contract is unlawful or immoral, though it may not be directly punishable, the contract is *vitiated*."/ "The fact that Hartford Insurance paid compensation to Blanks does not *vitiate* the statutory employment relationship between Blanks and ANR."/ "The Perrys assert that the merger doctrine is inoperative; to *vitiate* the merger doctrine on the basis of mutual mistake, the party seeking to avoid the doctrine must show that both parties had the same misunderstanding about the same material fact." It is perhaps a SLIPSHOD EXTENSION to stretch this sense into "to strike down": "The court *vitiated* [read *invalidated*] the statute on grounds that it conflicted with constitutional provisions."

A frequently misunderstood word, *vitiate* does not mean "to weaken or lessen," as used in the following sentence. "It is conceded that anger can be *vitiated* [read *reduced*] by a change in physical surroundings." Nor does it mean "to belie": "Plaintiff's assertion is *vitiated* [read *belied*] by the plain language of the agreement." Nor "to correct": "[T]he court's later instruction . . . cannot be deemed to have *vitiated* [read *cured* or *corrected*] the prejudice caused by the court's earlier apparent endorsement of the improper questioning." *People v. Wood*, 497 N.Y.S.2d 340, 344 (N.Y. App. 1985). The word is also sometimes misused for *obviate*, q.v.

vittles is not the literary spelling; *victuals*, q.v., is.

vituperative; vituperous. The former is the preferred adjectival form of *vituperation*. *Vituperous* is a NEEDLESS VARIANT.

viz. is an abbreviation of the Latin word *videlicet* (fr. *vidēre* = to see; *licet* = it is permissible). The English equivalents are *namely* or *that is to say*, either of which is preferable to this LATINISM. Like its English counterparts, the term signifies that what follows particularizes a general statement, without contradicting what precedes, or that what follows explains certain obscurities that the writer acknowledges to be lurking in what has just been said. E.g., "[If a testator has] devised certain real estate to his widow, 'her heirs, *viz.*,

her children and grandchildren and assigns,' the words following the *videlicet* have been held not to be repugnant to, but explanatory and restrictive of, the word 'heirs,' and to operate to limit the widow's estate to an estate for life." 57 Am. Jur. *Wills* § 1156 (1948)./ "In its second opinion, the district court certified the main issue, *viz.*, the executive officers' liability under section 23:1032."

The abbreviation is odd, considering the form of the full word. That is because "the *z* in *viz*. is an emaciated version of an ornate court hand Middle English *z*, which—like *t*—was sometimes used as an arbitrary abbreviation of a final *et*." D. Mellinkoff, *The Language of the Law* 87 (1963).

When the abbreviation is used, it is customarily set off from the rest of the sentence by a pair of commas. (Or, when given as the first word within a parenthetical expression, it is set off by one comma.) The same holds true for its companion Latinisms as *i.e.*, and *e.g.*, qq.v.

Scilicet, q.v., = that is to say. It is usually abbreviated *sc.*

vocation. See *avocation*.

vociferous, -ferant. The latter is a NEEDLESS VARIANT. E.g., "We should not penalize litigants for dignified rather than *vociferous* protests of what they consider to be unwarranted treatment."

VOGUE WORDS are those faddish, trendy, ubiquitous words that have something new about them. They may be NEOLOGISMS or they may be old words in novel uses or senses. Often they quickly become CLICHÉS or standard idioms, and sometimes they pass into obscurity after a period of feverish popularity. For whatever reason, they have such a grip on the popular mind that they come to be used in contexts in which they serve no real purpose. "As their popularity and frequency increases," says the *Oxford Guide*, "so their real denotative value drains away, a process that closely resembles monetary inflation. . . . One should carefully guard against using them either because they sound more learned and up to date than the more commonplace words in one's vocabulary, or as a short cut in communicating ideas that would be better set out in simple, clear, basic vocabulary" (198).

The following list is a representative rather than an exhaustive collection of modish diction.

constructive
cost-effective
definitely
dialogue
environment
escalate (= to intensify)
eventuate
exposure (= liability)
federalism (AmE)
framework
impact, v.i. & v.t.
interface
-IZE words
lifestyle
matrix
meaningful
-oriented (e.g., law-oriented)
overly
parameters
scenario
state-of-the-art
user-friendly (see COMPUTERESE)
viable

void; voidable. "It is regrettable that the courts have used the term 'voidable' in the sense of both 'voidable' and 'void.'" Note, *Infants—Contract of Suretyship,* 3 Texas L. Rev. 329 (1925). The DIFFERENTIATION should be evident. *Void* = absolutely null. *Voidable* = capable of being voided or confirmed. Yet confusion seems to abound, as *Corpus Juris Secundum* points out: "There is great looseness and no little confusion in the books in the use of the words *void* and *voidable,* growing, perhaps, in some degree, out of the imperfection of the language, since there are several kinds of defects which are included under the expressions *void* and *voidable,* while there are but two terms to express them all." 92 C.J.S. at 1020–23 (1955).

The phrases *totally void* and *completely void* are REDUNDANCIES. (See ADJECTIVES (A)). *Null and void,* q.v., is questionable as a DOUBLET, *void* itself being perfectly strong: "The natural tendency of the condition contained in the will is to restrain all marriage and for that reason it is *void.*"

voidance. See **avoid.**

void and of no(ne) effect. This DOUBLET is quite redundant. If the phrase must be used, modern idiom requires *void and of no effect.*

voir(e) dire, n., meaning literally "to speak the truth," is a LAW FRENCH equivalent of the Latinate *verdict.* But the two words have come to denote two distinct aspects of jury trials. The preferred spelling is *voir dire.* It is pronounced /vwah-**deer**/, or, in the Southern U.S., /vohr-**dIr**/. See **verdict.**

voir dire, v.t., is colloquial at best. E.g., "The court collectively *voir dired* the panel from which the jury was selected."/ "Some lawyers take voluminous notes as the panel is *voir dired* and pore over them intently as they strike their lists." None of the general English dictionaries list *voir dire* as a verb. See NOUNS AS VERBS. Good substitutes are the verbs *to examine* and *to question (on voir dire).*

volitional; volitive. *Volitional* = of or belonging to volition (i.e., an act of willing or resolving); pertaining to the action of willing. E.g., "A change in a given relation may result from some superadded fact or group of facts not under the *volitional* control of a human being." *Volitive* is a NEEDLESS VARIANT.

voracity. See MALAPROPISMS.

votary; votarist. The latter is a NEEDLESS VARIANT.

vouch, in modern lay contexts, almost invariably means "to answer *for,* be surety *for*" ⟨she vouched for him⟩ ⟨vouched for his honesty⟩. Archaically, *vouch* = to cite as authority; to confirm by evidence or assertion. E.g., "Jhering, emphasizing the effect of trade and commerce in liberalizing the strict law, *vouched* the introducing of Greek mercantile custom into the law of the old city of Rome." (R. Pound) This sense appears to be an extension of the obsolete legal phrase *to vouch to warrant,* meaning "to cite, call, or summon (a person) into court to give warranty of title" (*OED*).

vouchsafe is not equivalent to *grant* or *provide,* as suggested here: "A person is entitled to the actual and continued enjoyment of his civil rights as *vouchsafed* by the statute and these cannot be permanently thwarted by some other avenue of escape." Rather, today it ordinarily denotes "to grant something in a condescending way," or, more neutrally, "to grant something as a special favor." E.g., "[T]he Court does not *vouchsafe* the lower courts . . . guidelines for formulating specific, definite, wholly unprecedented remedies." *Baker v. Carr*, 369 U.S. 186, 268 (1962) (Frankfurter, J., dissenting).

VOWEL CLUSTERS are not indigenous to the English language, although one finds them in our imported vocabulary, in words such as *onomatopoeia* (= the use of imitative or echoic words, such as *fizz* and *buzz*), *maieutic* (= Socratic), and *giaour* (= one outside the Muslim faith). In forming NEOLOGISMS, esp. by agglutination, one should be wary of clumping vowels together in a way that would strike readers as unEnglish. Even three consecutive vowels may have this effect, as in *antiaircraft*, which appears far more natural as *anti-aircraft*.

vs. See **v.** & **versus.**

W

waifs and (c)strays. This legal phrase has passed into common parlance in the sense "abandoned or neglected children," which is an extension of the original sense "unclaimed property; wandering animals." In lay usage, the second element is usually *strays*. Technically in law, *waifs* came to mean, at common law, things stolen and thrown away by the thief in flight, but not things left behind or hidden; they belonged to the Crown by prerogative right if they had been seized on its behalf (*OCL*). *Estrays*, q.v., = valuable tame animals, found wandering and ownerless; at common law, they belonged to the Crown or, by virtue of grant or prescriptive right, to the lord of the manor (*id.*).

wait. See **await.**

wake; awake; awaken; wake up; woke; waked; waked up; woke up; awakened; awaked; awoke. The preterit and participial forms of *wake* and its various siblings are perhaps the most vexing in the language. Following are the preferred declensions:

wake ⟩ woke ⟩ waked (or woken)
awake ⟩ awoke ⟩ awaked (or awoken)
awaken ⟩ awakened ⟩ awakened
wake up ⟩ woke up ⟩ waked up

wane; wax. *Wane* = to decrease in strength or importance. E.g., "The aspect of *Lochner* that curtailed economic regulation has clearly *waned* since the 1930s."/ "The imperative of a predeprivation hearing *wanes* when impractical, as in a negligent tort situation." *Wax* (= [1] to increase in strength or importance, or [2] to become) is used primarily (in sense (2)) in CLICHÉS such as *to wax poetic, eloquent*, etc., or (in sense (1)) as a correlative of *wane* ⟨the doctrine waxed and waned⟩.

want, n., (= lack) is an especially FORMAL WORD, sometimes used in literary contexts but frequently in legal writing ⟨want of prosecution⟩. E.g., "The district court dismissed the action for *want* of jurisdiction, and this court reversed."/ "*Want* of probable cause and malice are seldom established by direct evidence of an ulterior motive." The participial *wanting* (= lacking) also appears often in legal prose: "We first consider the appellee's contention that federal jurisdiction is *wanting*."/ "Authority on these points is *wanting*." (Eng.)

-ward(s). In AmE, the preferred practice is to use the *-ward* form of DIRECTIONAL WORDS, as in *toward, forward, backward, westward*. Words in *-ward* may be either adjectives or adverbs, whereas words in *-wards*, common in BrE, may be adverbs only. See **toward(s).**

warehousemen. See SEXISM (B).

warning of caveat (= a notice given to a person who has entered a caveat [q.v.] warning him to appear and state what his interest is) is a curious but established REDUNDANCY.

warrant, v.t. In the modern idiom, it sounds natural that objects or actions are warranted, but not that people are warranted. Therefore, "Such a conclusion warrants federal judges in substituting their views for those of state legislators," reads more naturally, *Such a conclusion warrants federal judges' substituting their views for those of state legislators.* To illustrate this point, we might say that acts or beliefs are *warranted* or *unwarranted*, but not that actors or believers are *warranted* or *unwarranted.*

Nevertheless, the *OED* contains examples of *warrant* used with personal objects from the seventeenth century, and the usage remains common in law, if not elsewhere. E.g., "The facts and circumstances must have been sufficient in themselves to *warrant* a man of reasonable caution in the belief that an offense has been or is being committed."

warrantable (= that may be authorized or permitted; justifiable) should not be used in the sense "capable of or justifying having a judicial warrant issue."

warranted (= authorized by a search warrant) is common in American legal writing. *Warranted* has had the sense "furnished with a legal or official warrant" (*OED*) since the mid-eighteenth century. E.g., "The United States appeals the suppression of evidence obtained during a *warranted* search." The antonym of *warranted* in this sense is *warrantless*, q.v., not *unwarranted* (= unjustified).

warrantee is incorrect for *warranty*. The *OED Supp.* cites two examples for the existence of this misusage. See **guarantee** (A).

warranter. See **warrantor.**

warrantless = (1) without a warrant ⟨a *warrantless* entry of police upon defendant's premises⟩; or (2) unjustified ⟨completely warrantless accusations⟩.

warrantor, -er. The former spelling is preferred.

warranty; guaranty. See **guarantee** (A).

wastage, as Gowers has noted, "is properly used of loss caused by wastefulness, decay, leakage, etc., or, in a staff, by death or resignation. It would be well if it were confined to this meaning instead of being used, as it habitually is, as a long variant of *waste*" (*MEU2* 688).

waste, as a legal TERM OF ART, carries the sense "spoil, destruction, or injury done to an estate by a tenant (for life or for years) to the prejudice of the heir, or of the reversioner or remainderman." Following is a typical specimen: "Such injunctions include those against *waste* where a person having only a limited interest in an estate in his occupation, threatens to wastefully cut down timber, or otherwise injure the freehold" (quoted in *OED*). The usual legal phrase is *to commit waste.*

wax. See **wane.**

way of necessity. See **easement.**

way which, unseparated by a comma, is erroneous for *way in which.* E.g., "One of the *ways which* [read *ways in which*] the consignor may protect his interests is by filing under Article 9 pursuant to section 2-326(3)(c)."

weald. See **wield.**

we are persuaded that is often just so much verbal baggage in judicial opinions. E.g., "*We are persuaded that* the principles announced in *Tabacalera* and *Maltina* are dispositive here" becomes much more forceful thus: "The principles announced in *Tabacalera* and *Maltina* are dispositive here." See **persuade** & FLOTSAM PHRASES.

WEASEL WORDS. Theodore Roosevelt said, in a speech in St. Louis, May 31, 1916: "One of our defects as a nation is a tendency to use what have been called weasel words. When a weasel sucks eggs it sucks the meat out of the egg and leaves it an empty shell. If you use a weasel word after another there is nothing left of the other." Some writers have incorrectly assumed that the metaphor suggested itself because of the wriggling, evasive character of the weasel. In any event, sensitive writers are aware of how supposed intensives (for example *very*, q.v.) actually have the effect of weakening a statement. Many other words merely have the effect of rendering uncertain or toothless the statements in which they appear. Among these are *significantly, substantially, reasonable, meaningful, compelling, undue, clearly, obviously, manifestly, if practicable, with all deliberate speed* (orig. a weasel phrase, now with a history), *all reasonable means, or as soon thereafter as may be, rather, somewhat,* and *quite.* See **clearly.** Cf. FUDGE-WORDS.

wed is often used metaphorically in American legal prose for *adopt* or *endorse.* E.g., "But, though our Supreme Court has not yet *wedded* this new doctrine, it has certainly at least paid ardent courtship."

wedded is the past participial form, but in the negative the proper form is *unwed. Wed* is a variant past participle to be avoided.

welcher. See **welsher.**

well, when forming an adjective with a past participial verb, is hyphenated when placed before the noun (e.g., *a well-known person, a well-written book*), but is not hyphenated when the phrase is placed predicatively (e.g., *a person who is well known, a book that is well written*). See ADJECTIVES (C).

well-being is hyphenated, not spelled as one word.

well-settled is usually inferior to *settled* in reference to points of law, because, unfortunately, most legal writers use the one for the other undiscriminatingly. See WEASEL WORDS.

welsher; welcher. The former is usual; the term means "one who shirks his responsibility in a joint undertaking."

westerly boundary. To denote something stationary, the term should be *west boundary*; to denote something moving, *westerly direction*. See DIRECTIONAL WORDS.

wet ⟩ wetted ⟩ wetted.

we the people. See SET PHRASES.

wharf. Pl. *wharves*.

what.   A. As Subject. When acting as a subject, a *what*-clause generally takes the singular verb, whether the noun that follows is singular or plural. This is so even if *what* turns out to be an appositive or substitute for a plural noun that appears later in the sentence. "What the courts wrongly ignore *are* [read *is*] their decisions' effects on incentives to produce information that is still unknown." (The sentence is illogical in several ways, for *effect* [the singular] would probably suffice, because the decisions referred to would almost certainly either encourage or hamper the production of information—hence there would be only one *effect*. Moreover, information does not exist in a vacuum—there is no "unknown information," for, ipso facto, it is not information until it is known.)

The general rule that *what* takes a singular verb should be ignored only when observance of it would lead to preposterous results, such as, "What once was great houses is now petty offices." Hence, *What once were great houses are now petty offices* (*Oxford Guide* 185). See SUBJECT-VERB AGREEMENT (E).

whatever; whatsoever. The latter is legalistic; modern stylists prefer *whatever* uni-

formly. E.g., "We now consider whether plaintiff was entitled to recover any damages *whatever* for the death of his wife." *Whatever* often acts as an intensive: "In such cases there are no circumstances *whatever* that would give the court jurisdiction."/"The basis for the denial was their lack of standing to obtain any injunctive relief *whatsoever* [read *whatever*]."/ "In short, the regulation represents no less than the refusal of the state to give any aid *whatsoever* [read *whatever*] for the support of certain dependent children who meet the standards of need which the state itself has established." See TMESIS.

what it is, is. "*What* this case really *is, is* a contest of equities, not between the carrier and a shipper, but between a subrogee of a carrier and that shipper."/ "*What it is*, and as such acknowledged by fame, *is* one of humanity's stablest and strongest artistic treasures." This stylistically poor construction, common in sloppy speech, has now made its way into sloppy writing. Instead of using a *what*-clause, one should state the sense more directly: *This case is really a contest of equities . . .* ; *It is, and is acknowledged to be, one of humanity's strongest artistic treasures.*

whatsoever. See **whatever.**

when and as. See **as and when** & **if and when.**

whence   = from where; from which. Thus *from whence* is a REDUNDANCY, although the locution is seen in some older writers. E.g., "It could scarcely be said that the defendant would be justified in casting the body into the *water from whence* [read *water whence*] it could not be reclaimed." *From which* or *whence* alone should be preferred today to *from whence*. E.g., "If his method is to work at all, it must at least work in the sorts of economic cases *whence* it sprang." See **from hence** & **thence.**

where.   A. For *in which*. In formal prose, *where* should not be used as a relative pronoun instead of as a locative. E.g., "Understanding the operation of equal protection in both of these situations, however, will facilitate an understanding of the equal protection clause in the very different situations *where* [read *in which*] it was meant to apply."/ "We agree that it is a situation *where* [read *in which*] the decedent's trustee would have an impossible burden of explaining how the accident happened if defendant himself could not explain it."/ "There are many cases *where* [read *in which*] as an incident to a judgment creditor's action the defendant has been required to convey to a representative of the court property outside the court's jurisdiction."/ "The power of a factor is regulated, in a great degree, by the usages and customs of the trade *where* [read *in which*] the business is transacted." See **case where** & CASE REFERENCES (B).

B. Wrongly Used in Defining. Those who are unfamiliar with the art of defining terms often use *where* to create maladroit and ambiguous definitions. E.g., "A breach is *where* one party does not fulfill his obligation." [Read *A breach is a party's failure to fulfill his obligation.*]/ "Substantial performance is defined as *where* the performance meets the essential purpose of the contract." [Read *Substantial performance is defined as performance that meets the essential purpose of the contract.*]

whereabout(s). *Whereabouts* is the preferred form. (See **thereabout(s).**) This word may take a singular or a plural verb. E.g., "The *whereabouts* of these persons *are* [or *is*] unknown."

whereas, the archetypal LEGALISM, used to be every lawyer's idea of how to begin a contract. *Whereas* = (1) given the fact that; or (2) although; on the contrary; but by contrast. Sense (1) is legalistic, sense (2) literary. When sense (1) applies, *whereas* frequently begins the sentence, a placement not to be recommended except in formulaic proclamations (*Whereas . . . ; and Whereas . . . ; Now, Therefore, Be It Resolved That . . .*). *Whereas* in sense (1) can be trouble, despite its innocuous appearance. The reader as well as the writer needs to be especially careful about whatever follows it.

One popular writer on usage has stated: "*Whereas* sounds stuffy. In spite of the objections of some grammarians, the common word is now *while*." R. Flesch, *The ABC of Style* 294 (1964). Yet *whereas*, in sense (2), is ordinarily better than *while* in formal writing, for the latter is sometimes thought to have inherent temporal associations. But see **while.**

whereat is an old-fashioned word dating back to the thirteenth century. Still, it is best not used in the twentieth century, for *where*, a locative, includes the concept of "at." E.g.,

"The L.C.R.A. is correct in its brief at page 30, *whereat* [read *where*] it states that the quoted sections of *Galveston City Co.* are from appellants' brief." Cf. **thereat.**

whereby can be a useful word, but lawyers have a tendency to overwork it. It means "by means of or by the agency of which; from which (as a source of information); according to which, in the matter of which" (*OED*). E.g., "There is a competing thought in the trust provision that permits the invasion of the trust corpus in case of an emergency *whereby* unusual and extraordinary expenditures are necessary for the support of the beneficiary's children."/ "The United States has brought suit for breach of a contract *whereby* defendants, it is said, agreed to buy from it 9599 twenty-five-pound boxes of raisins unfit for human consumption which could be converted to alcohol."

wherefor(e) = (1) for what; (2) for which; (3) on account of which; or (4) therefore. Sense (3) is the only useful one in modern writing; all the other senses have simpler equivalents. Here are typical examples of sense (3): "The children alleged that when the father changed his will he was incompetent, *wherefore* it was alleged that the change of beneficiaries was null and void."/ "Defendant breached the contract, *wherefore* plaintiff suffered severe damages."

whereof (= of what; of which) is a FORMAL WORD, perhaps an ARCHAISM ⟨he knows not whereof he speaks⟩. It is best to avoid such words if one does not know precisely how they are to be used. Here is an example of ignorant use of the word: "Is this company one of the directors *whereof* have a controlling interest therein?" What does that mean?

wheresoever is an unnecessary and archaic LEGALISM for *wherever*. See **whatever.**

whereupon. There is nothing wrong with beginning a sentence with this word, as long as it is done sparingly. E.g., "The guardians ad litem for the unborn contingent remaindermen testified that in their opinion the compromise was fair and equitable, and recommended its approval. *Whereupon* the court approved the compromise, and ordered the modification of the trust in the particulars named."/ "Willis replied over the phone that he had not received the acceptance. *Where-upon* Morrow said he was very glad of it, and would then withdraw his acceptance, to which Willis assented." Cf. **but** & **and.**

wherewithal = means, esp. pecuniary means. Hence *financial wherewithal* is redundant. E.g., "After being convinced of Dolphin's intentions and *financial wherewithal* [read *wherewithal*], B & G continued to lease its cranes and mats."

whether usually directly follows the noun whose dilemma it denotes: *decision whether, issue whether, question whether.* (See **question as to whether.**) E.g., "Under Kansas law, the liability of a principal for the negligent acts of his agent is controlled by a *determination as to whether* [read *determination whether*], at the time in question, the agent was engaged in the furtherance of the principal's business."/ "This test was not very helpful since the *determination of whether* [read *determination whether*] the agreement was 'collateral' was also the conclusion sought to be shown." *Regardless,* an adverb, makes *regardless of whether.* See **regardless whether.**

A. *As to whether,* which is rarely justified (see **question as to whether**), is here justified: "We are of the opinion that reasonable men might well reach different conclusions *as to whether* [i.e., on the question whether] the servant was within the area of probable deviation, and therefore within his employment, when the accident occurred."

B. *Issue of whether,* which is also generally better made *issue whether,* has certain justified uses in which *of* is obligatory, usu. when *issue* is modified by an adjective. E.g., "A host of public-policy considerations must be weighed in resolving the threshold *issue of whether* such a remedy should be an addition to or a substitute for the liability imposed by our civil damages suit." See **issue** (B).

C. *Whether or not.* The *or not* is usually superfluous. E.g., "*Whether or not* [read *whether*] the special litigation committee determines that the derivative suit should have been brought remains to be seen."

D. And *if.* See **if** (A).

which. A. *Which* + *noun.* This construction is somewhat outmoded and strikes the general reader as being stilted, though occasionally it is useful to avoid an ambiguity. In these examples it is unnecessary: "The resolution was to award the contract to Ivey subject to the approval of the Public Housing Administration, *which agency* [read *which*] subsequently approved the acceptance."/ "S.I. enclosed a $20,000 check along with its acceptance, which check was deposited." [Read *Along with its acceptance, S.I. enclosed a $20,000 check, which was deposited.*]/ "The facts showed unconscionable delays in the treatment of appellant for his gunshot wounds, which delays amounted to an unconscionable denial of medical treatment. [Better: *In the treatment of appellant for his gunshot wounds, the facts showed unconscionable delays, which amounted to an unconscionable denial of medical treatment.*]

The *which* + noun construction is defensible only if *which* is separated from its antecedent by a phrase, as in the last quoted example of the previous paragraph. But *which* + noun should never, as in the following sentence, directly follow its antecedent: "SEC sanctions can be imposed only after affording the respondent a notice of and an opportunity for a hearing, which hearing must comply with the hearing provisions of the Administrative Procedure Act." [Read *Only after the respondent is afforded a notice of and an opportunity for a hearing, which must comply with the hearing provisions of the Administrative Procedure Act, can SEC sanctions be imposed.*

B. The Overeager *which.* One must be certain, before introducing a subordinate clause with *which,* that this word has a clear antecedent. Often writers actually put the *which*-clause *before* the antecedent. E.g., "Once again, this Court is called upon to apply the law of New York to the issue of damages if it finds (which appellant vigorously urges would be an incorrect finding) that appellant is liable for breach of contract." [Read *Once again, this Court is called upon to apply the law of New York to the issue of damages if it finds that appellant is liable for breach of contract, a finding that appellant vigorously urges would be incorrect.*] See ANTICIPATORY REFERENCE.

C. *And which, or which,* and *but which.* These constructions often signal trouble, for there is only one quite limited context in which any of them can be proper. Each of these phrases must follow a primary *which*-clause, with which it is parallel, not left floating at the end of a sentence without a shore in sight, as in the following sentence:

The offer and sale of the certificates of deposit pursuant to the program shall be conducted in such a manner as to be a separate, distinct offering not integrated with any related offer and sale of similar instruments pursuant to any subsequent pool or program and the organizers shall not otherwise enter into subsequent transactions within a time period, *or which* otherwise satisfy the factual criteria set forth above, with the result that they might be integrated with offerings made pursuant to the program.

One possible decoding and restructuring of this sentence into two sentences, neither of which has an overeager *which*, is as follows:

The offer and sale of the certificates of deposit pursuant to the program shall be conducted in such a manner as to be a separate, distinct offering that shall not be integrated with any related offer and sale of similar instruments pursuant to any subsequent pool or program. In addition, the organizers shall not, within a given period, enter into subsequent transactions that otherwise satisfy the factual criteria set forth above or integrate the present offerings made pursuant to the program with subsequent offerings made pursuant to the same program.

D. Without a Proper Antecedent. Grammarians have termed the mistake here described "broad reference"; *which* refers to a general idea or an entire statement rather than to a specific antecedent. This fault should be carefully avoided. E.g., "Plaintiff is compelled to call the police department, after *which* the keys are returned." [Read *Plaintiff is compelled to call the police, and only then are the keys returned.*]

E. Wrongly Elided. E.g., "This is to advise you that as long as you continue to use the premises for the purposes [insert *for which*] you are now using them, namely, for sawmill and lumber yard purposes, and pay the rentals, your possession will not be disturbed."

F. In Rhetorical Disclaimers for *and.* E.g., "If surrogate motherhood is to be considered legally acceptable in this country (*which* [read *and*] I think it should not be), then state legislatures must act to legalize the contracts drawn up for these arrangements."/ "Even if it could be considered error, *which* [read *and*] this court does not consider it so, it would be harmless error."

G. And *that.* See RESTRICTIVE AND NONRESTRICTIVE CLAUSES.

while for *although* or *whereas* is permissible, despite what purists say about the word's in-

herent temporality. *While* is, however, the more relaxed and conversational term, and therefore is somewhat out of place in formal legal writing. E.g., "*While* [read *Although*] it is true that appellant had been the appliance-parts distributor for eight years, the contract under which the distributorship was carried out was an annual contract, terminable by either party with adequate notice."/ "Appellant argues that the court erred in refusing his request for standby counsel after dismissal of Gravel; *while* [read *although*] this is the preferred practice, it is not mandatory." See **whereas.**

The writer who uses *while* for *although* should be on guard for ambiguities. For instance, does it denote time or concession in this sentence: "*While* the police were waiting beside the house, they did not hear the burglars enter"?

While should not be used merely for *and.* "He is a lawyer while she is a doctor." [Read *He is a lawyer and she is a doctor.*]

while at the same time is a common REDUNDANCY. E.g., "*While* the husband was creating joint tenancies for the benefit of his daughters, he was *at the same time* [omit *at the same time*] building up the value of the farm chattels."

whilst, though a correct form, is virtually obsolete in AmE and reeks of pretension in a modern American writer. *Whilst* is still common in BrE, however. E.g., "Defendant, knowing the premises, maliciously intended to injure plaintiff as lessee and manager of the theatre *whilst* the agreement with Wagner was in force." (Eng.)/ "The plaintiffs' loss would have been only £5 plus a further £11 as his estimated loss through two months' deprivation of a vehicle *whilst* it was being repaired and a purchaser found." (Aus.)

Like its sibling *while*, it may be used for *although* or *whereas*, although this is not the best usage in formal writing and certainly not in AmE. E.g., "The jurisprudence of this state is to the effect that *whilst* [read *while*] it is the rule that costs in a suit follow the judgment before execution, it is likewise the rule that after execution has taken place the question of costs comes before the appellate court as an independent issue."/ "*Whilst* [read *While*], therefore, the end of the writing in point of space may be taken as the end of the disposition, it does not follow that in all cases the signature must, of necessity, be there written."

Whiteacre is the mythical tract of land contrasted with *Blackacre*, q.v., in hypothetical legal problems. E.g., "Let it be assumed, further, that, in consideration of $100 actually paid by A to B, the latter agrees with A never to enter on X's land, *Whiteacre*." (Hohfeld)

whitehorse case; horse case; gray mule case; goose case; spotted pony case; pony case. These are terms meaning "a reported case with virtually identical facts, the disposition of which should determine the outcome of the instant case." The terms are now less commonly used in the law schools than formerly; but they are useful terms.

Goose case is common in the Southern U.S., and esp. in Louisiana. Cf. **on all fours.**

whither is an ARCHAISM meaning (1) "to what place or position" ⟨Whither shall we go?⟩; or (2) "to which" ⟨at Chelsea Square, whither we had gone⟩. It has virtually no place in modern writing. Cf. **hither &** **thither.**

whoever. See **who(so)ever.**

whole. See **in whole.**

who(m). **A.** *Who & whom.* The distinction to keep in mind is that *who* acts as the subject of a verb, whereas *whom* acts as the object of a verb or preposition. Though not commonly observed in informal speech, the distinction is one to be strictly followed in formal legal prose. Some lapses are so flagrant that one can hardly fathom how they could have been committed. E.g., "The three top finishers on the bar exam were Michelle Hirschman, Karen Monse, and Ken Kern, *all of who* [read *all of whom*] took our bar review course!" Others are more forgivable, because the correct use is less obvious: "He orders all exits to the store closed; this has the effect of confining the plaintiff, *who* [read *whom*] the detective does not even know to be in the store."

Many writers have announced the demise of *whom*, but it persists. *Who* would be impossible, for example, in this sentence: "If the person on *whom* the duty of electing rests elects to take in conformity with the will or other instrument of donation, he thereby re-

linquishes his own property, and must release or convey it to the donee upon *whom* the instrument had assumed to confer it." Some legal writers are curiously inconsistent in their use of *who* and *whom*: "The statute does not say *who* [read *whom*] a consumer may sue. With respect to *whom* a consumer may sue, section 17.50(a)(1) expressly states that a consumer may bring suit if he has been adversely affected by the use or employment by any person of an act or practice declared to be unlawful under Section 17.46."

Following are examples of the correct use of *whom*: "Proprietors of private enterprises, such as places of amusement and resort, were under no such obligation, enjoying an absolute power to serve *whom* they pleased."/ "While the rule as declared by the majority opinion would perhaps be consistent with public policy in such a case, it will not much affect the type of case that it is supposed to affect, or restrain the person *whom* it purports to restrain, namely, the litigious troublemaker."/ "A fundamental principle of our representative democracy is, in Hamilton's words, 'that the people should choose *whom* they please to govern them.'"

Here are some rather tricky, but correct, uses of *who*: "If the servant, without authority, entrusts the instrumentality to one *who*, on account of his age, inexperience, or recklessness, he has reason to believe is likely to harm others, the master would be liable." (*Who* is the subject of *is*.)/ "It may, for instance, be negligent on the part of the employer to hire an employee *who* the employer should realize is unfit and poses a risk to others." (*Who* is the subject of *is*.)/ "An 'apparent agent' is one *who* the principal, either intentionally or else by lack of ordinary care, induces third persons to believe *is* his agent, even though no actual authority, either express or implied, has been granted to such agent." (Again, *who* is the subject of *is*, but the sentence, though correct in this respect is badly phrased.) See PHRASING.

B. *Placement of. Who* should directly follow the name it refers to, or be interrupted only by a parenthesis properly set off. E.g., "The largest collection of fossils was made by L. Kohl-Larson in 1938-1939, who also found a small fragment of hominid maxilla." [Read *The largest collection of fossils was made in 1938-1939 by L. Kohl-Larson, who also found a small fragment of hominid maxilla.*]

C. Improperly Used of Nonpersonal Entities (*who* for *that*). E.g., "In this diversity action, we are called upon to decide whether a drawee bank *who* [read *that*] has missed the midnight deadline is accountable to the payee under a special set of circumstances."/ "The Comptroller of Public Accounts is required to give notice to foreign corporations *who* [read *that*] have failed to file the required reports."

D. *Which* for *who.* E.g., "There are twenty-one shareholders in the corporation, two of *which* [read *whom*] are vying for the chairmanship." (The correction assumes, as the context bears out, that the shareholders referred to in the sentence are persons, as opposed to corporations.)/ "Exhibit 9 names the client *which* [read *who* or *that*] Kroeneke served."

whom(so)ever. See **who(so)ever.**

whoredom = (1) prostitution; or (2) idolatry.

who's; whose. The former is the contraction of *who is;* the latter is the possessive form of *who.* The two forms are frequently confused. E.g., "Imagine telling a prosecutor, *who's* [read *whose*] job it is to remove antisocial elements from society, that his work is not in the public interest."

whose, used of nonpersons, should generally be eschewed, though sometimes it is an inescapable way of avoiding clumsiness. *Which,* unfortunately, has no other possessive form, apart from *of which.*

Whose for *of which* can lead to such problems as this: "One of those dealers was J & S Government Securities, Inc., *whose* home office was in New York, but *who* also had offices in Houston." See ANTHROPOMORPHISM. The sentence could be recast in myriad ways, e.g., "which had its home office in New York, but offices in Houston as well." (In this corrected sentence, *offices* is a plural noun, not a verb. See **office.**)/ "What is commonly termed ownership is in fact tenancy, *whose continuance* [read *the continuance of which*] is contingent upon legally recognized rights of tenure, with corresponding duties."

who(so)ever, whom(so)ever; whoso(ever), whomso(ever). A. Choice of Term. The forms *whoever* and *whomever* are preferred in modern writing. Users of *whosoever* and *whomsoever,* as well as *who(m)so,* are liable to criticism on grounds of LEGALESE, ARCHAISM,

and BIBLICAL AFFECTATION. Often these terms are completely superfluous, as here: "This is a right that avails against all persons *whomsoever* [omit *whomsoever*], and is distinguished from a right that avails against a particular individual or a determinate class of persons."

B. Case. The problem of proper case arises with these words, just as it does with *who* and *whom.* E.g., "*Whomever* is [read *Whoever* is] responsible for implementing the program is responsible for its faults." The *Oxford Guide* contains this rather poor advice: "use *whoever* for the objective case as well as the subjective, rather than *whomever,* which is rather stilted" (135). Stilted, perhaps, but correct; and really not very stilted in formal prose. See NOMINATIVE & OBJECTIVE CASES.

C. Possessives. *Whoever's* (colloquial) is incorrect (in formal prose) for *whosever.* Justice Holmes sometimes used *whosesoever,* a correct form made unnecessary by the modern preference of *who(s)ever* over *who(se)soever.*

wide; broad. The former, when used in contexts in which idiomatic English would require the latter, is a LEGALISM. E.g., "A public body has *wide* discretion in soliciting and accepting bids for public improvements." *Baxter's Asphalt & Concrete, Inc., v. Department of Transportation,* 475 So. 2d 1284, 1287 (Fla. App. 1985)./ "The district court did not abuse its *wide* discretion." *Wide* is used more commonly in BrE in this sense. E.g.: "The terms of the order are too *wide.*" (Eng.)

widespread was until the early part of this century spelled as two words, but now it should always appear as one.

widespreadedly is a bastard formation. *W3* records no adverbial form of the adjective *widespread,* although if there were one it would be *widespreadly.* The form *widespreadedly,* malformed perhaps on the spurious analogy of *allegedly* and *reportedly,* wrongly assumes the existence of a past tense form *spreaded.* E.g., "[T]he area of public interest to which [the publications] relate—conditions allegedly capable of *wide-spreadedly* affecting public health—would seem to be one of such inherent public concern and stake that there could be no possible question as to the applicability of the *New York Times* standard for any defeasance." *United Medical Laboratories, Inc. v. Columbia Broadcasting System, Inc.,* 404 F.2d 706, 711 (9th Cir. 1968). See -EDLY.

widow, n. Mellinkoff has rightly pointed out the REDUNDANCY in the Supreme Court's phrase *surviving widows who administer estates.* See *Reed v. Reed,* 404 U.S. 71, 75 (1971) (paraphrased). Mellinkoff, *The Myth of Precision and the Law Dictionary,* 31 U.C.L.A. L. Rev. 423, 440 (1983).

widow, v.t., may apply to a spouse of either sex. Thus *widowed man* is unobjectionable, although to many it may seem at first unnatural.

widow(er). Is one still a widow(er) when one remarries? No.

wield; weald. The former is the verb meaning "to control; handle; hold and use" ⟨he wields his power with good judgment⟩. The latter is the noun meaning "a forest" or "an uncultivated upland region."

will. See **shall** (B).

will; testament. A common belief among lawyers is that, in the Middle Ages, a *will* disposed of real property and a *testament* of personal property. This belief is, strictly speaking, erroneous, although from the eighteenth century such a distinction in usage (unfounded in the substantive law) began to emerge. The distinction is now obsolete, however, so that in modern legal usage the words are interchangeable, although *will* remains the usual term.

The archaic distinction between the words is said to have grown out of the historical development of property dispositions. Ecclesiastical courts had jurisdiction of cases involving the distribution and use of personal property; appeals from these courts were to Rome, under the Catholic hierarchy, until 1533. The common-law courts of England, meanwhile, decided cases involving the use and disposition of real property. The two court systems developed distinct terms for decedents' estates. E.g., "The common-law courts took the position that a *will* was ambulatory in its revocatory effect; the ecclesiastical courts held that a *testament* was revoked at the time the revoking instrument was executed." As a result of the bifurcated judicial system, the myth goes, the terminology for real property dispositions was Anglo-Saxon (*will*), and that for personal property

dispositions Latinate (*testament*), the latter terms having derived from Roman law.

History, especially linguistic history, never comes so neatly packaged, however. It is not surprising, then, to discover that medieval writers are recorded as having used *will* in reference to personal property, and *testament* in reference to land. Even so, the myth concerning these terms may be valid insofar as it explains the tendencies in usage that would later give rise to an idiomatic DIFFERENTIATION. It is at least possible that the DOUBLET *last will and testament,* q.v., had in its origins a purpose for the inclusion of both real and personal property. In any event, *will* now denotes the entire testamentary instrument, a place formerly said to be occupied by *devise,* q.v. See also **codicil** & **testament.**

will, as a verb meaning to dispose of by will, is always transitive. E.g., "In Louisiana a testator can *will* no more than one-tenth of his estate to a woman with whom he has lived in open concubinage."/ "Aliens could, at common law, *will* personalty and devise land, but the state could seize the land in the hands of his devisees."/ "I *will* and bequeath all my effects to my brothers and sisters, to be divided equally among them." See **devise,** v.t.

willable = transferable by will. E.g., "Land became *willable* with the Statute of Wills." The *OED* traces this sense back only to 1880.

wil(l)ful. *Wilful* is the preferred spelling in BrE, *willful* in AmE. *Willfull,* a misspelling, occasionally appears in the U.S.

wil(l)fulness; malice aforethought. These terms are sometimes confused in criminal contexts. *Willfulness* is the broader term. "An act is done *willfully* if done voluntarily and intentionally, and with the specific intent to do something the law forbids. 1 E. Devitt & C. Blackmar, *Federal Jury Practice and Instructions* 384 (1977).

Malice aforethought, q.v., is used in the context of homicide: "*Malice aforethought* means an intent, at the time of a killing, wilfully to take the life of a human being, or an intent wilfully to act in callous or wanton disregard of the consequences to human life; but *malice aforethought* does not necessarily imply any ill will, spite, or hatred toward the individual killed." 2 E. Devitt & C. Blackmar, *Federal Jury Practice and Instructions* 215 (1977).

willy-nilly is an English equivalent of the LATINISM *nolens volens*, q.v. E.g., "If a federal court is to do it, it must act in its traditional manner, not as a military commander ordering people to work *willy-nilly*, nor as the President's Administrative Assistant." (Douglas, J.) It is sometimes, as the *OED* remarks, erroneously used for "undecided, shilly-shally" ⟨a willy-nilly disposition⟩.

win a victory, to. See **victory.**

-WISE. Phrases arrived at with this combining form are generally to be discouraged, for they often displace a more direct wording, and they are invariably graceless and inelegant. E.g., "[W]e must . . . respond to [the] claims . . . that even if acceptable *population-wise* [read *as applied to the population as a whole*], the . . . plan was invidiously discriminatory because a 'political fairness principle' was followed." *Gaffney v. Cummings*, 412 U.S. 735, 751-52 (1973)./ "Whether accumulation of earnings in the corporation is *cheaper tax-wise* [read *cheaper from the standpoint of taxes*] than accumulation in the partnership depends on a comparison of the corporate tax rate and the applicable rate to the individuals involved."/ "There are several other *advantages tax-wise* [read *tax advantages*] but these illustrate the tax inducements for making inter vivos transfers."/ "To continue this litigation, even though the parents should ultimately prevail, may well be, *at least money-wise* [read *at least financially*], like digging a hole to get the dirt to fill another hole."/ "A notice, signed by the commissioners, was file-stamped on the day of the hearing; *content-wise* [omit *content-wise* altogether] this notice met the statutory requirements."

wise (= manner, fashion, way) is an ARCHAISM that still appears infrequently in legal writing. E.g., "The testamentary revocation may be express, in order that the testator may do his new testamentary work without being *in any wise* [read *in any way*] fettered by the contents of his former will."/ "The judgment commands the defendant to refrain from *in any wise interfering* [read *interfering in any way*] with plaintiffs in the conduct of the business of their stable." See **nowise.**

wit, to. See **to wit.**

withal is an ARCHAISM for *besides, nevertheless, with,* or *therewith.* E.g., "The documentation and literature of this case is of truly gargantuan proportions; yet *withal* [omit *withal*] there has been a strange dearth of real issues of fact or of law."

with all deliberate speed calls to mind the Latin phrase *festina lente* (= make haste slowly). The phrase was made famous in *Brown v. Board of Education*, 349 U.S. 294, 301 (1955), and has been characterized as "[a] marvelously flexible phrase . . . added to the constitutional vocabulary, fetched up from another century [the nineteenth] to douse a sizzling bomb." D. Mellinkoff, *The Language of the Law* 450 (1963). See OXYMORONS & WEASEL WORDS.

withhold is sometimes used incorrectly for *deprive of* or *deny.* E.g., "Petitioner filed suit under 42 U.S.C. § 1983 seeking monetary damages and injunctive relief for being forced to work beyond his physical capabilities and for being *withheld* [read *denied* or *deprived of*] necessary medical treatment."

within, adj. "The legal tone is still too strong for common use in *the within letter.*" W. Follett, *Modern American Usage* 45 (1966). Indeed, it is perhaps too strong even for use by legal writers, for *enclosed* is far more common and more natural. E.g., "The *within* property shall not be sold or encumbered without the express written consent of the *within* mortgagees." (This use is apparently elliptical for *within-named*; the writer should have omitted the word or phrase completely, for it adds nothing.)/ "Opposing counsel are being furnished with a copy of the *within* [read *enclosed*] response."

within-named. See the preceding entry.

without for *outside.* Usually, *without* is contrasted to *with*; but in law it is frequently an opposite of *within.* Though somewhat archaic, in formal legal prose this usage should be considered unexceptionable. E.g., "Grants or devises are construed to bring them *within* or *without* the operation of the Rule in Shelley's Case."/ "The plaintiff put himself *without* the pale of the comparative negligence rule, since he was wholly at fault when he received his injury.''

without day. See **sine die** & LOAN TRANSLATIONS.

without prejudice (= without loss of any rights) is peculiar to legal ARGOT.

without recourse; sans recours. The English phrase *without recourse* is preferred over the Gallicism *sans recours* for the stipulation that the drawer or indorser of a bill of exchange may add to his signature, repudiating his liability to the holder.

with the object of —ing is verbose for a simple infinitive, e.g., *with the object of preventing* in place of *to prevent.*

witness; testifier; testis. The second form is rarely if ever justified in practice; the third never is. See **testis.**

witness, v.t. = to attest or act as a witness ⟨to witness a will⟩ is a LEGALISM that is fairly familiar in the lay idiom.

witness-box; witness stand. The former is BrE, the latter AmE. E.g., ''Nor do I agree with the suggestion that the question be asked by the court when the client is in the *witness-box* or by requiring him to sign some pro forma document on the day of the hearing.'' (Eng.) A British philologist writes that ''in the middle 'fifties, a British judge vehemently rebuked the American defendant's use in 'his' court of the expression *witness-stand* and insisted with some heat on having *witness-box.*'' B. Foster, *The Changing English Language* 61–62 (1968). Before the end of the decade, however, *witness stand* had found its way onto B.B.C. airwaves. *Id.* at 62. See **stand.**

witness whereof, in. See **in witness whereof.**

witnesseth is commonly used to introduce clauses in contracts and affidavits. E.g., ''*Witnesseth:* That whereas first and second parties have certain litigations pending in the Mercer Circuit Court . . . it is agreed between all of the parties that all said suits are to be dismissed.'' Says one writer: *Witnesseth that* is a

phrase ''admittedly archaic but so firmly entrenched in the draftsman's vocabulary as to allow of few, if any, substitutes.'' S. F. Parham, *The Fundamentals of Legal Writing* 23 (1976). Actually, the whole mess is easily dispensed with; draftsmen should get right to the point, without *whereas,* q.v., preceding the recital, and without *witnesseth* to introduce the *whereas*-clauses.

woefully is a CLICHÉ, esp. when coupled with adjectives like *inadequate* or *insufficient.* E.g., ''The meager record before us is lacking and *woefully insufficient* to establish that the covenant 'touches and concerns' the land.''/ ''As evidence of the proposition that the government pays a disproportionate share of the cost of hospital malpractice insurance, the Westat Study is *woefully inadequate.*''

womankind. See **humankind** & SEXISM (B).

WOOLLINESS is the quality in expression of being confused and hazy, indefinite and indistinct. Excessive use of cross-references in writing, as in the Internal Revenue Code, is perhaps the apotheosis of woolliness. E.g., ''For purposes of paragraph (3), an organization described in paragraph (2) shall be deemed to include an organization described in section 501(c)(4), (5), or (6) which would be described in paragraph (2) if it were an organization described in section 501(c)(3).'' I.R.C. § 509(a) (1984). See OBSCURITY.

woolsack in G.B. refers to the sack of wool used as the Lord Chancellor's seat when he presides over the House of Lords. E.g., ''I entirely agree with my right honorable and learned friend upon the *woolsack.*'' (Eng.) By extension *woolsack* is sometimes used in the general sense ''a seat of justice.'' Cf. **ermine.**

WORD-PATRONAGE is ''the tendency to take out one's words and look at them, to apologize for expressions that either need no apology or should be quietly refrained from'' (*MEU1* 733). E.g., ''Hopefully—to use an ugly word—the dilemma will be solved by the proposed legislation.'' In his preface to the second edition of *Modern English Usage,* Gowers indulged mildly in word-patronage when he wrote: ''This was indeed an epoch-making book in the strict sense of that overworked phrase."

A variation of this mannerism occurs when one defends one's choice of words in anticipation of the reader's distaste: "[T]he bank may and should be held liable for gratuitously, officiously, and affirmatively—a surfeit of adverbs never hurt anyone—telling the government how to place its grasp upon its customer's funds." *Schuster v. Banco de Iberoamerica, S.A.*, 476 So. 2d 253, 255 (Fla. App. 1985) (Schwartz, J., dissenting).

word processing, n., should be two words thus.

WORDS OF ART. See TERMS OF ART.

words of purchase; words of limitation. In a grant or conveyance of a freehold estate, *words of purchase* designate the persons who are to receive the grant, and *words of limitation* describe the extent or quality of the estate. E.g., "The word 'children' in its primary and natural sense is always a *word of purchase* and not *of limitation,* as the word 'issue' is."/ "What is decided now is, that the words 'lawful issue,' as they stand in this deed, are *words of purchase,* and not *of limitation.*" See **purchase.**

wordy does not mean "sesquipedalian," as many seem to suppose; it means, rather, "verbose; prolix."

workaholic. See **-aholic, -aholism** & MORPHOLOGICAL DEFORMITIES.

work an ademption is a legal idiom akin to the lay idiom *work a hardship* (on someone). E.g., "A change in the form of a security bequeathed does not necessarily *work an ademption.*" See **adeem** & **ademption.**

workman; workingman. Because of the growing awareness of SEXISM, it may be well to use *worker* rather than either of these words.

workmanlike (= characteristic of or resembling [that of] a good workman; businesslike) is a useful word that should not be lost to opponents of SEXISM. We have no neutral word like *workerlike* to take its place. E.g., "Because attorneys' fees in this case are a component of foreseeable damages recovera-

ble for breach of implied warranties of *workmanlike* performance, we find that the district court erred in excluding Todd's liability for attorneys' fees from coverage of the red-letter clause."

workplace. One word. See **worksite.**

workproduct is increasingly spelled as one word. The dictionaries still record the term as two words. But in legal contexts the trend, which is wholly salutary, is to hyphenate it or make it one word. E.g., "To what extent is the Court's equal protection *workproduct* based on a determinate political-moral principle?" Cf. **decision-making** & **policy-making.**

workers' compensation; workmen's compensation. These words contain a plural possessive, hence *workers'* and *workmen's,* not *worker's* and *workman's.* The former phrase is becoming more and more common, doubtless because of a sensitivity to the SEXISM of the other.

worksite. One word. Cf. **job site.**

worship(p)ed, -ing, -er. The *-p-* spellings are the preferred forms in AmE; the *-pp-* forms appear in BrE. See DOUBLING OF FINAL CONSONANTS.

worth. When this word is used with amounts, the preceding term denoting the amount should be possessive. E.g., "This claim is not for a few dollars' worth of hobby goods that were negligently lost." See POSSESSIVES (B).

would is often used as a hedge-word, qualifying the absoluteness of the verb following it. E.g., a federal court states, "*This court would agree* with the Texas Supreme Court's statement of the measure of damages." (If the writer intended to question the applicability of the Texas Supreme Court's statement in certain circumstances, the sentence as written is perhaps right; but it would be better to say *This court agrees* if a direct statement is intended.)

wrack; rack. *Wrack* = to destroy utterly; to wreck. *Rack* = to torture or oppress. *Wrack* is also, and primarily, a noun meaning (1) "wreckage"; or (2) "utter destruction."

wraparound mortgage is current American legal ARGOT meaning "a deed of trust whereby a purchaser incorporates into agreed payments to a grantor or third-party the grantor's obligation in the initial mortgage." A court recently defined it as "a junior mortgage that secures a promissory note with a face amount equal to the sum of the principal balance of an existing mortgage note plus any additional funds advanced by the second lender." *Mitchell v. Trustees*, 375 N.W.2d 424, 428 (Mich. App. 1985) (with minor differences in wording).

wreak. See **reek.**

wreath(e). *Wreath* is the noun, *wreathe* the verb.

writ, n., = a legal document to be submitted to or issuing from a court. The *OED* records the verbal sense of *writ* "to serve (a person) with a writ or summons" (he was writted), and notes that it is Anglo-Irish. *Writ* is an ARCHAISM as a past participle of *write*, except in the CLICHÉ *writ large*. E.g., "If article 9 were *writ large* it would set out that a director is not to be removed against his will." (Eng.)

writ(e)able. The preferred spelling is *writable*. See MUTE E.

writer is an obsolescent Scottishism in the sense "an attorney or law-agent; an ordinary legal practitioner in country towns; a law-clerk" (*OED*).

writer, the present. See FIRST PERSON (B).

write specially = to concur in a separate opinion. E.g., "I fully concur in the opinion written by Judge Politz; however, I *write specially* to say that I believe the Secretary of Health and Human Services is right on track."/ "The three justices who voted for rehearing when the case was before them on appeal voted to deny the writ; these justices *specially* stated that, although each of them voted for a rehearing on the question of appellate review of the proportionality of the sentence, that issue was presented to the Court in a writ application and that application was denied."

wrong; wrongful. The distinction is an important one in law. *Wrong* = (1) out of order;

(2) contrary to law or morality; wicked; or (3) other than the right or suitable or the more or most desirable (*COD*). *Wrongful* = characterized by unfairness or injustice; contrary to law; (of a person) not entitled to the position occupied (the wrongful possessor). Occasionally the words happen to be coextensive, e.g.: "It is a malicious act, which is in law and in fact a *wrong* act, and therefore a *wrongful* act, and therefore an actionable act if injury ensues from it." (Eng.). Cf. **wrongous.**

wrongdoer = one who violates the law. The term is used of tortfeasors as well as of criminals. E.g., "But the circumstance that the wife of one of the *wrongdoers* benefited by the imposition does not afford opportunity for relief of that character."/ "The policy of preventing the *wrongdoer* from escaping the penalties for his wrong, in this case punitive damages, is inapplicable."

wrongful. See **wrong.**

wrongful death. See **death case.**

wrongful discharge (AmE) = *wrongful dismissal* (BrE). E.g., "The only other damages the plaintiff could claim if he had been *wrongfully dismissed* would have been purely nominal." (Aus.) *Wrongful termination* is sometimes used in the U.S.

wrong(ly). Both forms are proper adverbs; *wrongly*, which is less common, appears before the verb modified (the suspects were wrongly detained), whereas *wrong* should be used if the adverb follows the noun (he answered the question wrong).

wrongous, in Scots law, means "wrongful, illegal, unjust." It should be avoided by other than Scottish lawyers.

X

xerox is a registered trademark that is nevertheless used as a noun (he made a xerox of the document), adjective (a xerox copy), and verb (to xerox a will). Careful speakers use *photocopy* or some other similar word. *Zerox* is a common misspelling.

X-ray; x-ray. Either form is correct, although the former is perhaps more common. *W9* suggests that the term is hyphenated as an adjective and verb (*X-ray*), and not hyphenated as a noun (*X ray*). The *COD* hyphenates the term in all parts of speech.

Y

ye. See **hear ye.**

year of our Lord. See A.D.

yellow dog contract (= an employment contract in which a worker disavows membership in and agrees not to join a labor union during the period of his employment [*W9*]) has become a part of American legal ARGOT. The term dates from 1920.

yes-or-no question. See **leading question.**

yet. See **as yet** & **but yet.**

your petitioner and like phrases are quaint ARCHAISMS to be avoided. E.g., "*Your petitioner* [read *The petitioner*] has reliable information and believes that the defendant intends to leave the jurisdiction before April 19, 1985."/ "*Your relator* [read *The relator*], George W. Strake, Jr., Chairman of the State Republican Executive Committee, requests temporary relief."

Z

zetetic(k). The adjective meaning "proceeding by inquiry or investigation" is preferably spelled *zetetic* (*OED* & *W3*), although *Black's* spells it *zetetick.*

ZEUGMA = a figure of speech by which a single word is made to refer to two or more words in the sentence, esp. when properly applying in sense to only one of them, or applying to them in different senses. E.g., "If one party represents that he *has* (or *will*) *put* an oral agreement in writing, and the other party relies on this to his substantial detriment, the first party may be estopped to set up the Statute of Frauds as a defense." (*Put* is made to be both preterit and present.) Fowler gives this example: "Sir Charles Wilson, the newly elected member for Central Leeds, *took* the *oath* and his *seat.*" (*Take* is here given two different senses.) See JANUS-FACED TERMS. Cf. SYLLEPSIS.

zonal; zonary. The adjective corresponding to *zone* is *zonal* in all but medical (obstetric) senses.

zonate(d). The term meaning "arranged in zones" is best made *zonate* rather than *zonated.*

SELECT BIBLIOGRAPHY

I English Dictionaries

The American Heritage Dictionary of the English Language. New York: American Heritage, 1975.
Chambers Twentieth Century Dictionary. Cambridge: Cambridge University Press, 1983.
The Concise Oxford Dictionary. 7th ed. Oxford: Clarendon Press, 1982.
Oxford American Dictionary. New York: Oxford University Press, 1980.
The Oxford English Dictionary. 13 vols. Oxford: Clarendon Press, 1933.
The Oxford English Dictionary Supplements. 4 vols. Oxford: Clarendon Press, 1972–86.
Webster's New International Dictionary of the English Language. 2d ed. Springfield, Mass.: Merriam, 1959.
Webster's Ninth New Collegiate Dictionary. Springfield, Mass.: Merriam-Webster, 1983.
Webster's Third New International Dictionary of the English Language. Springfield, Mass.: Merriam, 1961.

II Law Dictionaries and Wordbooks

Ballentine, James A. *Law Dictionary with Pronunciations.* 3d ed. Rochester, N.Y.: Lawyers Cooperative Publishing, 1969.
Black, Henry Campbell. *Black's Law Dictionary.* 5th ed. St. Paul: West, 1979.
Bouvier, John. *Bouvier's Law Dictionary.* 1839. Rev. William E. Baldwin. New York: Clark Boardman, 1926.
Burrows, R. *Words and Phrases Judicially Defined.* 5 vols. London: Butterworth, 1943–46.
A Consice Dictionary of Law. Oxford: Oxford University Press, 1983.
Jowitt, W. A. *The Dictionary of English Law.* 2 vols. Ed. Clifford Walsh. London: Sweet & Maxwell, 1959.
Mozley, Herbert; and Whiteley, George. *Law Dictionary.* 7th ed. London: Butterworth, 1962.
Stroud, Frederick. *Stroud's Judicial Dictionary.* 4th ed. 5 vols. London: Sweet & Maxwell, 1971–74.
Walker, David M. *The Oxford Companion to Law.* Oxford: Clarendon Press, 1980.
Wharton's Law Lexicon. 14th ed. Rev. A. S. Oppé. London: Sweet & Maxwell, 1938.
Burton, William C. *Legal Thesaurus.* New York: Macmillan, 1980.
Words & Phrases. 90 vols. St. Paul: West, 1940–86.

III Usage

Benson, Morton; Benson, Evelyn; and Ilson, Robert. *The BBI Combinatory Dictionary of English: A Guide to Word Combinations.* Philadelphia: Benjamins, 1986.
Bernstein, Theodore M. *The Careful Writer.* New York: Atheneum, 1979.
―――. *Dos, Don'ts & Maybes of English Usage.* New York: New York Times Books, 1977.
―――. *Miss Thistlebottom's Hobgoblins: The Careful Writer's Guide to the Taboos, Bugbears, and Outmoded Rules of English Usage.* New York: Simon & Schuster, 1971.
Bryson, Bill. *The Penguin Dictionary of Troublesome Words.* Harmondsworth: Penguin Books, 1984.
Copperud, R. H. *American Usage & Style: The Consensus.* New York: Van Nostrand Reinhold, 1980.
Evans, Bergen. *Comfortable Words.* New York: Random House, 1959.

————; and Evans, Cordelia. *A Dictionary of Contemporary American Usage.* New York: Random House, 1957.

Follett, Wilson. *Modern American Usage.* New York: Hill & Wang, 1966.

Fowler, H. W. *A Dictionary of Modern English Usage.* Oxford: Clarendon Press, 1927.

————. *A Dictionary of Modern English Usage.* 2d ed. Rev. E. Gowers. New York: Oxford University Press, 1965.

————; and Fowler, F. G. *The King's English.* Oxford: Clarendon Press, 1906. Repr. Oxford University Press, 1973.

Gowers, Ernest. *The Complete Plain Words.* 1954. Repr. Harmondsworth: Penguin Books, 1980.

Krapp, George Philip. *A Comprehensive Guide to Good English.* 1927. Repr. (2 vols.) New York: Ungar, 1962.

Johnson, Edward D. *The Handbook of Good English.* New York: Facts on File Publications, 1982.

Nicholson, Margaret. *A Dictionary of American-English Usage, based on Fowler's Modern English Usage.* New York: Oxford University Press, 1957.

Partridge, Eric. *Usage and Abusage.* 1947. 5th ed. Harmondsworth: Penguin Books, 1981.

Weiner, E. S. C. *The Oxford Guide to English Usage.* Oxford: Clarendon Press, 1983.

Wood, Frederick T. *Current English Usage.* 2d ed. Rev. R. H. Flavell and L. M. Flavell. London: Macmillan, 1981.

IV Grammar

Curme, George O. *English Grammar.* New York: Barnes & Noble Books, 1947.

Hoenshell, E. J. *Hoenshell's Advanced Grammar.* New York: American Book, 1899.

Jespersen, Otto. *Essentials of English Grammar.* New York: Holt, 1933.

Kittredge, George Lyman; and Farley, Frank Edgar. *An Advanced English Grammar.* Boston: Ginn, 1913.

Morsberger, Robert E. *Commonsense Grammar and Style.* 2d ed. New York: Crowell, 1975.

Opdycke, John B. *Harper's English Grammar.* Rev. ed. Stewart Benedict. New York: Harper & Row, 1965.

Quirk, Randolph; Greenbaum, Sidney; Leech, Geoffrey; and Svartvik, Jan. *A Grammar of Contemporary English.* London: Longmans, 1972.

Sledd, James. *A Short Introduction of English Grammar.* Chicago: Scott, Foresman, 1959.

Zandvoort, R. W. *A Handbook of English Grammar.* 3d ed. Englewood Cliffs, N.J.: Prentice-Hall, 1966.

V Legal Language and Writing*

Dickerson, Reed. *The Fundamentals of Legal Drafting.* 2d ed. Boston: Little, Brown, 1986.

Garner, Bryan A. *The Elements of Legal Style.* New York & Oxford: Oxford University Press, 1991.

Goldfarb, Ronald L.; and Raymond, James C. *Clear Understandings.* New York: Random House, 1982.

Mellinkoff, David. *The Language of the Law.* Boston: Little, Brown, 1963.

————. *Legal Writing: Sense & Nonsense.* St. Paul: West, 1982.

Piesse, E. L. *The Elements of Drafting.* 7th ed. Rev. J. K. Aitken, Sydney: Law Book, 1987.

A Uniform System of Citation. 14th ed. Cambridge: Harvard Law Review, 1986.

Weihofen, Henry. *Legal Writing Style.* 2d ed. St. Paul: West, 1980.

Weisberg, Richard H. *When Lawyers Write.* Boston: Little, Brown, 1987.

Wydick, Richard C. *Plain English for Lawyers.* Durham, N.C.: Carolina Academic Press, 1979.

VI Style

Baker, Sheridan. *The Practical Stylist.* 5th ed. New York: Harper & Row, 1982.

Barzun, Jacques. *Simple and Direct.* Rev. ed. New York: Harper & Row, 1985.

*For additional references, see the dictionary entries BRIEF WRITING, LEGAL WRITING STYLE, and PLAIN ENGLISH.

Graves, Robert, and Hodge, Alan. *The Reader Over Your Shoulder: A Handbook for Writers of English Prose.* 2d ed. New York: Vintage Books, 1979.

Lanham, Richard A. *Revising Prose.* 2d ed. New York: Macmillan, 1987.

Pater, Walter H. *Appreciations.* 1889. Repr. Folcroft, Pa.: Folcroft Library Editions, 1978.

The Problem of Style. Ed. J. V. Cunningham. New York: Fawcett, 1966.

Quiller-Couch, Arthur. *On the Art of Writing.* 1916. Repr. Folcroft, Pa.: Folcroft Library Editions, 1978.

Read, Herbert. *English Prose Style.* 1952. Boston: Beacon Press, 1966.

Reader and Writer. Ed. Harrison Hayford and Howard P. Vincent. 2d ed. Cambridge, Mass.: Riverside Press, 1959.

Simon, John. *Paradigms Lost: Reflections on Literacy and Its Decline.* New York: Potter, 1980.

Strunk, William; and White, E. B. *The Elements of Style.* 3d ed. New York: Macmillan, 1979.

Zinsser, William. *On Writing Well: An Informal Guide to Writing Nonfiction.* 3d ed. New York: Harper & Row, 1985.

VII Etymology

The Concise Oxford Dictionary of English Etymology. Ed. T. F. Hoad, Oxford: Clarendon Press, 1986.

The Oxford Dictionary of English Etymology. Ed. C. T. Onions, with the assistance of G. W. S. Friedrichsen and R. W. Burchfield. Oxford: Clarendon Press, 1966.

Partridge, Eric. *Origins: A Short Etymological Dictionary of Modern English.* 4th ed. London: Routledge & Paul, 1966.

Skeat, Walter W. *An Etymological Dictionary of the English Language.* 4th ed. Oxford: Clarendon Press, 1910.

Weekley, Ernest. *Etymological Dictionary of Modern English.* London: Murray; New York: Dutton, 1921. Repr. (2 vols.) New York: Dover, 1967.

VIII Pronunciation

Kenyon, John S.; and Knott, Thomas A. *A Pronouncing Dictionary of American English.* Springfield, Mass.: Merriam, 1953.

Krapp, George Philip. *The Pronunciation of Standard English in America.* New York: Oxford University Press, 1919.

Lass, Abraham; and Lass, Betty. *Dictionary of Pronunciation.* New York: New York Times Book, 1976.

Lewis, Norman. *Dictionary of Modern Pronunciation.* New York: Harper & Row, 1963.